A Grammar of American Politics

A Grammar of
American Politics

The National Government

BY

WILFRED E. BINKLEY

Ohio Northern University

AND

MALCOLM C. MOOS

The Johns Hopkins University

✳ THIRD EDITION, REVISED ✳

New York ALFRED A. KNOPF *1958*

L. C. catalog card number: 58–5009

© Alfred A. Knopf, Inc., 1958

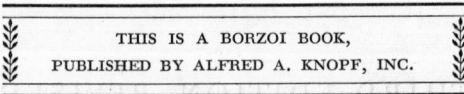

THIS IS A BORZOI BOOK,
PUBLISHED BY ALFRED A. KNOPF, INC.

PUBLISHED 1949. REPRINTED THREE TIMES

SECOND EDITION, REVISED AND ENLARGED, 1952

THIRD EDITION, REVISED AND ENLARGED, 1958

To

DORA *and* TRACY

PREFACE TO THE THIRD EDITION

A GRAMMAR OF AMERICAN POLITICS is by no means an encyclopedic compendium of facts about American government and politics. It is rather an interpretation of and commentary on government and politics in the United States. It aims to provide insights into the nature and functioning of "the great society," the body politic consisting of the citizens of the United States. We hope it will serve as a handbook that will help citizens to function as intelligent members of that society. The information provided herein is, of course, not the end but rather the means to reach that understanding of our government which is the *sine qua non* of a competent citizenry.

The opening chapter, "Social Forces in American Government," sets the pattern of treatment of the book. It is loaded with concrete illustrations of the dynamics of American politics. The basic concept throughout the *Grammar of American Politics* has been succinctly expressed by Sir Ivor Jennings in *The British Constitution:* "Government is not just a matter of giving orders and enforcing obedience. It requires the willing cooperation of all sections of the people." These "sections," it should be noted, are, by and large, organized and articulate groups conscious of their ability to play a part in the formulation and administration of public policies. Such an approach to the interpretation of our government permits a reduction of sheer legalism to an irreducible minimum.

The accelerated dynamism of American political society today would almost call for a loose-leaf system to keep a treatise such as this abreast of the evolution of American political institutions. The ever increasing influence of organized groups on the organs of American government, the current revolution in the nature of our major political parties, the vaulting of our hitherto somewhat isolated nation into leadership of the free world, along with the kaleidoscopic changes in our foreign relations, are but examples of matters requiring reassessment in a new edition.

This third edition is entirely our own work. The three chapters that were contributed by others to previous editions and that dealt with federal finance and government relations to business and agriculture have been replaced by four chapters written by the authors themselves. It is believed that this results in a more integrated treatment of the subject matter of the book and in a somewhat more consistent literary style.

It is hoped that the summary appended to each chapter of this edition will prove useful. V. O. Key's reading and criticism of the manuscript of each edition continues to prove invaluable to the authors. The chapters on Congress were revised in accordance with suggestions of Curtis Johnson, whose contacts with Congress in various capacities give him expert knowledge of that branch of the government. Miss Barbara Johnson and Mr. Donald Rothschild made substantial contributions to the revision of several chapters. The authors are grateful, too, to Dr. Robert Tucker for his suggestions and assistance in recasting and rewriting the chapters dealing with American foreign policy. Invaluable aid in revising the chapter, "Agriculture and Conservation," was provided by members of the staff of the department of agricultural economics of the Ohio State University, Miss Margaret McDonald, librarian, Mr. Riley Dougan, extension economist, and Mr. Wallace Barr.

Finally, a special word of appreciation goes to Joan Tucker for typing a manuscript punctuated by many annoying changes, to Molly Wiberg for a wary eye in proofreading, and to Mrs. Betty Boyer for typing most of the chapters that were entirely rewritten.

WILFRED E. BINKLEY
MALCOLM C. MOOS

September, 1957

CONTENTS

CONTENTS

PART IV. THE PRESIDENCY

PART V. THE FEDERAL ADMINISTRATION

PART VI. THE NATIONAL LEGISLATURE

A Grammar of American Politics

CHAPTER I

SOCIAL FORCES IN AMERICAN POLITICS

W HEN Paul Appleby remarked that "Noses count in politics but noises do too. Big noises count extra," he provided a wholesome corrective to the prevailing assumption that the ballot box is the sovereign organ of public policy in the United States. Let it be understood at once that "politics" as it appears in the title of this chapter as well as in Appleby's comment signifies the determination and administration of public policies rather than the functioning of political parties. It was the philosopher Emerson with his penetrating insight into political processes and his well-nigh clairvoyant perception that government never functions in a social vacuum who observed: "If the government is cruel, the governor's life is not safe. If you tax too high, the revenue will yield nothing. If you make the criminal code too sanguinary, juries will not convict."

What the Competent Citizen Needs to Know

Emerson's observation provides the hint. Of course the citizen ought to know the structure of his government and how it operates, but such knowledge can in itself be superficial and meaningless. No competent citizen can be satisfied with the mere knowledge that legislatures determine public policies and enact them into law, that executives see to the execution of the law, and that the judiciary sits in judgment upon cases and controversies growing out of the law. No matter how detailed and accurate knowledge of these matters may be, the citizen will remain naïve indeed if he has developed no insight into the motivation of private individuals and public officials in performing their civic duties. Consequently the competent citizen will seek to discover what impels the legislator to enact some kinds of legislation and fail to enact others; why executives, whether president, governor, or mayor, enforce some laws vigorously, others indifferently, and treat still others as dead letters; why the courts, even the Supreme Court, sometimes hold Congress to the strictest letter of the Constitution and at other times permit so broad an interpretation of a power of Congress to regulate interstate commerce that Congress is enabled to regulate the relations of employers to employees in a little manufacturing plant deep within a state; and why citizens themselves behave so differently at different times. Why for example do they vote for a presidential candidate who they do not think can be elected? If we knew the reasons for happenings like these we would discover some of the mainsprings of government—the social forces that determine the conduct of private citizens as well as public officials. Such knowledge would be the beginning of the wisdom that would equip the citizen to perform better the great functions of his membership in the body politic.

One of the first things the citizen must learn is that just voting on election day is not enough. The late William A. White had no doubt of it that "men and women who touch practical politics . . . know that men and women now may have as many votes in government as they have interests for which they are willing to sacrifice thought and money. If he is content with one vote at the ballot box or a vote and a half as a member of his party he is a pretty poor stick as a citizen. It is all right to stand proudly on his constitutional rights and decry the invisible government. But it is real government. The ruling classes are those who use their craft societies, medical associations, farm bureaus, labor unions, bankers' associations, women's leagues and the like to influence government. Of course it takes time and intelligence and a little money but not much. For fifty dollars (membership dues) the average family ought to be able to buy half a dozen powerful votes in government each vote ten times as powerful as the vote guaranteed by the Constitution." [1]

The State

By the term "state" is meant the political society whose personnel or membership consists of its citizens. The citizens of a state include all those persons who owe the state allegiance and have the rights and privileges of citizenship. So important is the state that it has been called "The Great Society." Aristotle declared it to be "a common life for a noble end." We know now that the state was not originally a deliberate creation but emerged naturally out of men's social needs and is therefore a product of social experience. Its point of origin appears to have been the primitive family and tribe. Vestigial relics of the primitive patriarchal system persist in our speech today in such terms as the "elders," "city fathers," "seniority," and "the Senate"—literally, the old men.[2] At any rate, the family is where the child first encounters law and government—that of his parents.

[1] *Politics, the Citizen's Business* (New York, 1924), pp. 15, 16.
[2] R. M. MacIver: *The Web of Government* (New York, 1946), p. 34.

The state is, of course, but one of the several forms of social control by which human beings prevent confusion and maintain orderly social life. But so accustomed are we to the state that we take it for granted and sometimes assign to it a mystical existence. So accustomed have we become to the legalistic and consequently artificial conception of the state that we fail to see that, as in the case of all human institutions, it consists of patterns of attitudes and behavior of its citizens. These patterns of collective behavior serve to protect the citizens from external foes and from internal disorder, and to furnish the means for providing such services, among many others, as schools and highways. In brief, the way of life that constitutes the state provides for achieving collectively either what could not be done so well or could not be done at all by the individual. With the insight of the sociologist, the late Franklin H. Giddings devised the term "stateways" to designate the rules of conduct that are legally enforced. However it would be erroneous to assume that coercion constitutes the main activity of the state. It may seem so to law-breakers upon whom the state has "cracked down," but their experience is exceptional among the great body of citizens. Most citizens habitually observe the "stateways." By and large the state as an institution consists of habitual ways the citizens act under a particular form of social control. The state, then, is one of several ways of life that serve to maintain an orderly society where confusion would otherwise prevail.

The Apparatus of the State

Government consists of the apparatus, offices, or agencies by means of which the state accomplishes its purposes. Without organized agencies the body of citizens constituting the state would be incapable of getting performed the functions for which the state exists. Since public policies first have to be determined, a major department, branch, or organ of government has to be established. In nations with Western European culture the typical organ for the determination of public policies is a legislature usually consisting of two houses, at least one of which is directly elected by the voters. The legislature is usually presumed to be the fundamental organ of the state or "the depository of the supreme will of society," as a framer of the Constitution in the Philadelphia Convention expressed it. A law as a legislative enactment has been defined as a "command directed toward an indefinite number of instances."[3] A second major branch of governmental organization is the executive, which consists of an elaborate system of agencies and officials. On this branch falls the responsibility of seeing to the execution of the will of the state as expressed by enactments of the legislature. An executive act, in contrast with a legislative act, consists of a "command directed toward one particular instance." While the chief execu-

[3] C. J. Friedrich: "The Separation of Powers," *Encyclopaedia of the Social Sciences,* Vol. III, p. 663.

tive in the American system is vested with the duty of seeing that the laws are faithfully executed, the detailed performance of this function falls under the direct supervision of officials and agencies established for that purpose. This latter function is known as administration, which has been defined as "the management of men and materials in accomplishing the purpose of the state." A third major function of the state is performed by the judicial branch consisting of a system of courts which determines whether a given situation falls within the general command of the legislature or the particular command of the executive.

How Is the "Political Animal" Motivated?

Citizenship as a function could be improved markedly by the development of the citizen's insight into social situations and forces as they affect the determination and administration of public policies. The study of government ought to include an increasingly active inquiry into the mainsprings of the civic conduct of citizens and officials. There should be a wider dissemination of the accumulating knowledge of the motives for man's behavior as a political animal. Why does he fail to vote in so many instances? How does he reach his judgments as a voter? Why is he often so inadequately informed on public affairs? Why is he not a more consistent aid in making public opinion a guide to public officials? Why does he so often act contrary to his own and the public's interest? It ought to be more generally understood that man is a rationalizing rather than a rational animal. It has been said that he customarily "thinks below the neck," but when judgments are thus irrationally arrived at, he uses ex-post-facto reasoning to justify these judgments. In most instances the citizen's attitude on public affairs is due to the climate of opinion in which he lives. Most men tend to think as their associates think. In three out of four cases party affiliation has been determined by the conversations and attitudes of the parents. The atmosphere of the club, of the fraternal order, of the labor union, and of the church, colors, when it does not actually set, the pattern of the citizen's social philosophy and civic concepts. Whoever would avoid abject submission to the propagandist must guard against popular formulas, catch phrases, dogmas, and labels—against the stereotypes that pass for logic and reason in many political discussions. Of concrete aid to this end are some of the more intelligent news columnists who endeavor to keep the public informed on behind-the-scenes forces that account for political and governmental action.

The Political Power of Organized Interests

It is one of the anomalies of civic education that the significance of groups in the democratic process was so long neglected. It is all the more astonishing when, as Harvey Fergusson points out, "the solid reality of democracy is the slow growth everywhere in industrial society of the proportion of the population which is sufficiently articulate and aware to claim some share of control over its own destiny." [4] "Articulate" here reminds us of the "big noises that count extra" in politics. Fergusson further observes that, "A history of democracy as an organized force would be a history of the organizations which men spontaneously form to serve their shared necessities." [5] It can be said that, with rare exceptions, political power is organization. Politicians are agents of this power. The citizen who prides himself on being "independent" is by no means independent of the power that inheres in organized interests but is at the mercy of them. "Almost every element in his daily life, from the motion pictures he is allowed to see to the income tax he pays is determined by organized pressures. He has some genuine control over his political and economic destiny only if he has some share in organized power. . . . In such a world the typical citizen who stands alone is a pigmy in a battle of giants so tall that often he cannot see what they are doing." [6]

The Pluralistic State

The basic concept needed for an understanding of the dynamics of government is that of the multi-group nature of society or the modern state. The feudal society of Western Europe was characterized by a cultural homogeneity whose disintegration marked the dawn of modern times. Contributing to the breakup of the medieval social structure was the religious strife following the Protestant Revolt and the formation of new economic groups as the industrial revolution, accompanied by technological changes, proceeded. The framers of the American Constitution understood the multi-group structure of society, and Madison gave classic expression to their conception in the tenth article of the *Federalist*. The late Charles A. Beard gave a modern version of Madison's interpretation in the following apt paraphrase: "A landed interest, a transport interest, a railway interest, a shipping interest, an engineering interest, a manufacturing interest, with many lesser interests, grow up of necessity in all great societies and divide them into different classes actuated by different sentiments and views. The regulation of these various and interfering interests . . . constitutes the principal task of modern statesmen and involves the spirit of party in the necessary and ordinary operation of the government." [7]

Nor should it be assumed that only economic interests control. The entire complex of social forces governs politics. It is organized groups of all kinds that compete for control. And classes that seem irreconcilable in one set of circumstances march together in another. "No one form of social power is absolute," writes R. M. MacIver and continues, "The

---

[4] *People and Power* (New York, 1957), p. 117.
[5] *Ibid.*, p. 124.
[6] *Ibid.*, pp. 102, 103.
[7] Charles A. Beard: *The Economic Basis of Politics* (New York, 1922), p. 99.

Emperor goes to Canossa but the Pope suffers the Babylonian exile of Avignon. The state dissolves the economic corporation, but the economic corporation finds a way to control the state. Government at one time forbids labor to organize, at another time organized labor dictates to the government. The church is subservient to the money interest—and the money changers are whipped out of the temple." [8]

Public Opinion as a Resultant of Group Pressures

Democratic government is presumed to be controlled only by public opinion. In a democratic system public policy slowly and hesitatingly emerges from innumerable planned conferences and unplanned conversations. Pressure groups, the press, radio and television commentators, and all other agencies of communication utilized by a free people contribute to the formulation of public opinion. In a multi-group society public opinion tends to become a resultant of the competing influences of the various groups. With respect to a specific issue one might conceive of progressive interests pushing forward, conservatives thrusting to the right, and radicals to the left, and reactionary groups shoving back. The resultant movement of public opinion depends upon the relative strength of the several forces. Sometimes one, sometimes another, is strongest. Professor H. L. Childs conceives the process to be analogous to the play of mechanical forces: "Were it possible to plot pressure groups objectively as parallelograms of forces and compute the resultant, significant predictions might be made not only as to what party platforms are likely to be, which parties will win, but also as to significant trends in public policy." [9]

Democracy often provides the opportunity for competing groups to coordinate their aims in programs they can all support. This is done through institutional means for discovering common ground, as through legislatures, the chief organ for giving formal or legal expression to ultimate agreement. The policies thus declared "tend to become a series of compromises along lines of least resistance." [10] Over a century ago one of the keenest of American philosophers observed that "what is called public opinion, instead of being the united opinion of the whole community is usually nothing more than the voice of the strongest interest or combination of interests; and not infrequently of a small but energetic and active portion of the people." [11] Certainly that part of the public which ignores public affairs, or keeps its opinions concerning them to itself, or expresses them feebly, makes no contribution to the formation of public opinion. As John Dickinson expressed it: "The larger number of members of any political society have no will on nearly all

[8] R. M. MacIver, *The Web of Government* (New York, 1947), p. 93.

[9] H. L. Childs: "Pressure Groups and Propagands," in *The American Political Scene*, edited by E. B. Logan (New York, 1936), p. 225.

[10] R. M. MacIver: *The Web of Government* (New York, 1946), p. 298.

[11] John C. Calhoun: "A Disquisition on Government," in Benjamin F. Wright: *Source Book of American Political Theory* (New York, 1929), p. 537.

matters on which government acts. The only opinion, the only will which exists is the opinion, the will of special groups." [12]

The Pragmatic Test of the Public Interest

It was long customary to assume that concepts of the public interest were determined logically by the reasoning of "right thinking" persons. The fundamental error in that idea is that no human being is free enough from bias and prejudice to know certainly what the public interest is. For the businessman the loftiest view of the public interest is likely to be epitomized in the maxim: "What is good for business is good for the country." The laborer is certain too that the welfare of the worker is the fundamental public interest. The farmer will insist that the public welfare is based incontestably upon agriculture and the prosperity of the farmer. In our multi-group society, functioning as a democracy, there seems to be no way for the public interest to be determined and established other than through the free competition of interest groups. The necessary composing or compromising of their differences is the practical test of what constitutes the public interest. This can be illustrated by the statement of Harold W. Stoke: "Every tariff is a diagram of opposing forces. A conservation policy grows out of the conflict between those who have interests in the immediate exploitation of forest, water, oil, or coal and those whose interests are equally real but in point of time are more remote." [13]

"Interests should have free access to the state" writes Francis G. Wilson, "in order that their representatives may write boldly across the face of the statute book. The competition and compromise of interests give the pragmatic test of the public interest. . . ." [14] Harold Stoke concluded that "by giving to every group its rightful claim to consideration the representative system provides the best means of determining the interests which are common to all by neutralizing of the interests peculiar to each. The national interest in actual practice is that which remains after the mutual cancellation by opposing groups of interests too narrow and particular to be acceptable to a majority of representatives." [15] This, Stoke hopes, "will constitute the general welfare."

During the competition of groups a concept of public interest seldom becomes firmly established as public policy until several private interests coincide with that particular concept. For example, in the early years of radio, station owners regarded proposals of governmental regulation as interference with free enterprise. But before long privately determined wave lengths, power volume, and scheduling of programs

[12] John Dickinson: "Democratic Realities and Democratic Dogmas." *American Political Science Review* (1930), 24:29.

[13] Harold W. Stoke: "The Paradox of Government," in *Essays in Political Science,* edited by J. M. Mathew and James Hart (New York, 1937), p. 82.

[14] "The Pragmatic Electorate," *American Political Science Review,* Vol. XXIV, (Feb. 1930), p. 33.

[15] *Op. cit.,* p. 82.

resulted in confusion. As a consequence, owners of radios were exasperated, manufacturers of radios found their sales threatened, and the station operators were frustrated in their efforts to sell radio time. Eventually radio broadcasters, manufacturers, and listeners joined in demanding governmental regulation in what all had come to recognize as their own and the public interest.[16] Patterns of the public interest are almost never projected deliberately on a grand scale but rather take shape gradually as pressing problems are dealt with. Thus the unemployed are provided jobs and manufacturers get tariff adjustments. As the manifold special interests demanding attention of the government are evaluated and reconciled the configuration of the public interest emerges.[17]

The general recognition of the need of railroad regulation seventy years ago illustrates how the empirical discovery of a concept of the public interest was given legal expression, in this case, in the Interstate Commerce Act of 1887. Shippers who used the railroads, such as manufacturers, mine operators, farmers, and merchants, were suffering, along with the consumers, from the confusion of rates, the evils of rebates to favored communities and shippers, and other discriminations. Cutthroat competition in rates had hurt owners of railroad stock. The consequence was a sudden consensus as to the public interest and the passage of the Act of 1887. Half a century later E. P. Herring observed: "Under the sheltering arm of the Interstate Commerce Commission, the railroads and the shippers have found protection against the harsh impact of *laissez faire*. . . . The railroads have come to identify a high degree of regulation in the public interest with their own best interests." [18]

The Translation of Social Pressures into Law

The high function of the legislator is to translate social ideas, influences, and pressures into public policies if he is to be, in the truest sense, a representative. With keen insight into the realities of this process John Dickinson has said: "Every representative is a potential mediator for the interest which has the strongest control over him in the face of other interests; and in this way opportunity is given for bringing interests into touch and convincing each of the advantage of accommodating itself to the others with which it has to live. These are the substantive merits of representative democracy—these and not the realization of a supposed 'popular' will." [19] Minor matters of legislation may be settled without controversy and indeed many such measures are enacted by unanimous consent. It is in the considerations of such controversial legislation as that dealing with labor relations that there is a

[16] E. P. Herring: *Public Administration and the Public Interest* (New York, 1936), p. 159.

[17] E. P. Herring, *The Politics of Democracy* (New York, 1940), p. 328.

[18] *Public Administration and the Public Interest* (New York, 1936), p. 210.

[19] John Dickinson: "Democratic Realities and Democratic Dogmas." *American Political Science Review* (1930), 24:29.

play of competing pressures on the legislators. Theoretically, legislation represents the will of the majority, but actually, as Judge Learned Hand observes: "Most legislation is not of that kind; it represents the insistence of a compact and formidable minority. Nor are we to complain of that, for while we may be right to say that the problem of democracy lies in minorities, we are not to suppose that the bulk of government can go on on any other terms. . . . So far as we can forecast the future, it is more likely to see an increase of minority rule. The truth appears to be that what we mean by common will is that there shall be an available peaceful way by which law may be changed when it becomes irksome to enough powerful people who can make their will effective. We may say if we like that meanwhile everybody has consented but this is a fiction. They have not. They are merely too inert or too weak to do anything about it." [20]

Competing Interests on the St. Lawrence Seaway Project

The play of competing interests upon a legislative body can be illustrated by the pressures brought to bear upon Congress with respect to the issue of the St. Lawrence waterway, which will give ocean shipping passage to the Great Lakes. Heading the opposition to the canal was a coalition of 264 organizations in 39 states with the rather misleading designation of the National St. Lawrence Project Conference. Opposite this gigantic organization was the National St. Lawrence Association of 100 prominent United States businessmen favoring the Seaway. Fearful of the competition in transportation of the projected seaway were the American Association of Railways, the Railway Brotherhoods and the American Federation of Labor. A tracing of the history of the Seaway legislation through the various Congressional Committees reveals that the votes against the project came from districts where there are major railroad interests. The Great Lakes cities certain to benefit by the ocean shipping to be brought to their ports naturally favored the Seaway. But there can scarcely be found a better display of the play of social forces than the fact that the railroad men in the Chicago Association of Commerce were able to impose the railroad point of view in the association's policy statements, of course, in opposition to the Seaway. The Chamber of Commerce of Toledo, another lake port and railroad center, saw the businessmen's committee report favoring the Seaway tabled until a railroad man became chairman of the transportation committee when the Toledo Chamber's declaration of policy became one of opposition to the Seaway.

The shipping, real estate, mercantile, and other established interests at the Atlantic ports of Boston, New York, Philadelphia, and Baltimore feared the diversion of business from themselves. The private electric-power interests opposed the project as a plan involving government production of hydroelectric power. Such production would also compete

[20] *28 Mich. L. Rev.* (1929), 46, 50.

with coal, and the operators of the mines, as well as the United Mine Workers, opposed the waterway project. Curiously enough one influential group opposed the project because it would be self-liquidating and would entail no drain on the Federal Treasury. These are the Mississippi River Valley flood-control and shipping interests whose projects depend upon Federal expenditures and who wanted no precedent set for costless river improvement. This would handicap somewhat the Rivers and Harbors lobbyists. One curious point given in opposition was the alleged fact that American ocean-going vessels are too broad for the canal while foreign shipping is not.

New England textile workers went on record favoring the Seaway. New England industry is handicapped by the scarcity and high cost of electric power as is also up-state New York. Hydroelectric power from the Seaway would help counteract the competition of southern textile mills for which very reason southern Senators and Representatives were not so favorable to the Seaway. Perhaps the determining factor in carrying the project through the Senate was the about face on the project made by the great steel interests of the Pittsburgh-Youngstown region. Relying on the apparently inexhaustable iron ore resources of the Mesabi Range west of Lake Superior, these steel interests had for years opposed the Seaway. But when World War II brought a drain on these mines foreshadowing their approaching exhaustion the steel interests threw their weight in favor of the Seaway which could make accessible to them the ores of the fabulously rich Labrador mines.

Laws Are Functions of Effective Demand

The competition of social forces pro and con on the St. Lawrence project, as indeed on every hotly contested major policy, reveals Congress as the registrar of the dominant organized pressures. Its "legislative product is some sort of a lagging and imperfect compromise among them. It is generally impossible for any member of Congress to know what he represents other than through the organized forces to which he owes his position. Either he obeys them or he retires to private life." [21] The final vote on any legislative issue records the net result of the process of accommodating conflicting group pressures. It "tends to represent the composition of strength, that is, the balance of power among contending groups at the moment of voting." [22] Laws, then, as Harold Laski puts it, "are the functions of effective demand. They will correspond to the desires of those who know how to make their needs felt at the center of political power." [23]

[21] Harvey Fergusson, op. cit., p. 110.
[22] Earl Latham, The Group Basis of Politics (Ithaca, N.Y., 1952), pp. 35, 36.
[23] From Politics, reprinted in R. C. Snyder and H. H. Wilson (Eds.), Roots of Political Behavior (New York, 1949), p. 87.

Problem of the Legislator in a Single-Interest Constituency.

A legislator is handicapped in exercising his judgment on an issue before him if it is vigorously urged or opposed by a single overwhelming interest to which there is no comparable counterbalancing opposition in his constituency. This is illustrated by the vote on the Harris-Fulbright Bill in 1956 which would have removed the control of the price of gas at the producing well from the Federal Power Commission. Pitted against the bill, outside the producing states, were the mayors of cities and the utility companies distributing gas to consumers in whose interest they couched their arguments against the bill. The five great gas-producing states—Arkansas, Kansas, Louisiana, Oklahoma, and Texas—send 58 men to Congress. But so overwhelming is the prestige and influence of a single interest in these states that their Senators and Representatives, ranging from outstanding liberals to inveterate conservatives, "voted as a monolithic unit: fifty-seven for and none against, with only Speaker Rayburn not voting but supporting the bill from the floor." [24] California also produces gas (more, in fact, than one of the five states above) but in California the diversity of economic interests permits diversity of opinions and the California legislators can and did in this case perform their normal function of mediator seeking the balance of interests that can be translated into policies agreeable to more than one interest.

Pressures Playing upon the Executive

In the American governmental system the executive, whether president of the United States, governor of a state, or mayor of a municipality, is elected by the voters and is consequently responsive to the tides of public opinion as determined by group pressures. It was concerning the chief function of a presidential election that E. P. Herring commented: "The tremendous task of reconciling special interests has been simplified by the absorbing distraction of finding a single man acceptable to the whole nation." After the election of a president it is frequently assumed that he has a mandate from the voters to carry out his stand on pending issues, and a decisive vote does unquestionably strengthen the hand of an executive. In fact, a presidential campaign becomes a competition between candidates to outbid each other for the support of the elements of our multi-group society. A candidate's promises may be: to farmers, the support of prices for their produce; to religious and racial groups, the assurance of their civil rights; to labor, the maintenance of collective bargaining. The strategy of a politically conscious group holding a balance of the voting power may be to appear somewhat coy and to sell its support to the highest bidder it feels it can trust. In any case the candidate's promises are presented by him as plausible policies in the pub-

[24] Richard H. Rovere, "Letter From Washington," *The New Yorker*, Feb. 25, 1956, pp. 122–9.

lic interest, as indeed they are quite likely to be. The most successful candidate is usually the one who makes the most convincing appeal to a combination of groups that constitute a majority of the voters. President Franklin Roosevelt proved to be peculiarly adept at appeals to winning combinations. Once in office the executive is obliged to foster and execute certain legislation. He will be under public pressure to enforce some laws more vigorously than others. He may, for example, prosecute vigorously violators of the anti-trust laws. Or, on the contrary, he may owe his election to influential groups that obligate him to interpret such laws liberally and to deal gently with business.

No executive is motivated solely by the mandate presumed to be given him on the day of his election. There is not a week of his term in office that some of the groups constituting society do not exert pressure upon him. At times the demand is for favors that tax the public treasury so that "the administration often does little more than keep order in the breadline that reaches into the treasury." [25] At its best the play of social forces on the president can strengthen him in establishing and executing wholesome policies in the public interest. Thus the president may synthesize the public will by translating into public policies the agreement of many groups on a domestic or foregin issue.

In their efforts at law enforcement the hands of the president may be palsied by public indifference to numerically insignificant but determined opposition. Public indifference may permit this opposition to pressure the legislature into a reduction of the appropriations required for law enforcement or to weaken an agency assigned a wholesome public function. The latter can be done either by reduction of its personnel or by so changing the statute establishing it that it is deprived of necessary authority. For example, the president cannot vigorously prosecute offenders against the anti-trust laws if the personnel, that is, the number of attorneys, assigned to the Anti-Trust Division of the Department of Justice has been reduced or is inadequate. It is indeed principally through the growing influence of the executive in the United States that there is "any hope of checking the minority forces that turn Congress to their will and make a mockery of representative democracy." [26]

Administration: Its Responsiveness to Interest Groups

While the executive is obligated to see that laws are faithfully executed, the administrators responsible to him supervise the details of their execution. Every executive has under his direction a system of departments, bureaus, divisions, or other agencies each in the charge of an administrator and collectively constituting the administrative system. The administrator is a mediator whose chief function is to preserve harmony

[25] E. P. Herring: *Presidential Leadership* (New York, 1940), p. 22.
[26] E. P. Herring: "Prescription for Democracy." *Annals of the American Academy of Political and Social Science* (1935), 180:141.

between the experts under him, the legislators who created his agency and finance it, and the public whose interests are affected by his agency. Those unfamiliar with the day-to-day work of an administrator might assume that all he need do is keep in mind his oath of office, follow the statute prescribing his duties and the manner of their performance, and execute the law without fear or favor. As a matter of fact, he will do nothing of the kind. He will do what the alert and active interests affected by the functioning of his agency will permit him to do. In the first place, his agency was created because some private interest or set of interests was influential enough to induce the legislature to establish it. The pressures of interests rather than merit determine what agencies will be created. If the interest creating the agency was powerful, it will never relax the vigilance with which it follows the operation of the agency. It will attempt to see that administrators are appointed who are favorable to its point of view, and if unopposed by counter interests may have its way. If sufficiently frustrated an interest's attitude toward a bureau may become: "We got this bureau created, and we can get it reorganized or abolished." [27]

Any important administrative agency, such as the Interstate Commerce Commission, will be matched by a corresponding congressional committee backed by influential economic groups interested in the operation of the agency. The congressional committee can prepare legislation modifying, strengthening, weakening, or even abolishing the agency. The statute which establishes an administrative agency has to be amplified from time to time by administrative regulations issued by the agency and having the effect of law. Almost inevitably the interests affected exert an influence in formulating these rules, and this indeed operates for better understanding and more willing consent to them. Herring has even concluded that "regulation in the past has been effective only when the interest regulated recognized the necessity of the regulation." [28] Consequently, administrative officials have learned the necessary art of swinging the weight of their authority to the side of the strongest among competitive interests exerting pressures upon them. This becomes possible when "conflict among groups each seeking to persuade an agency to adopt its line of policy, will enable the administration to do pretty much as it pleases." [29] It has been said that "a maximum of enforcement with a minimum of resistance" became the fixed policy of the Pure Food Administration. It may be a well-nigh universal principle of administrators.

It need not be assumed that private interests regularly dictate to the agencies that regulate them. A bureau has the best chance to ad-

[27] D. D. McKean, *Party and Pressure Politics* (Boston, 1949), p. 595.
[28] E. P. Herring: *Public Administration and the Public Interest* (New York, 1936), p. 213.
[29] D. D. McKean, *op. cit.*, p. 596.

minister in the public interest when the private interests exerting pressures upon it tend to counterbalance each other. For example, the Pure Food and Drug Administration could perform its duties with higher efficiency if the consumer interest were as well organized and effective as the producer interests. But unless there is public opinion supporting enforcement of a law, the administrator is practically at the mercy of the interest to be regulated. This is true when the aggrieved interest, confronted with vigorous enforcement, can appeal to the legislature. If the interest works through an appropriate legislative committee, the administrator may be influenced by the threat of a legislative investigation, a reduction in the agency's appropriation or personnel, a crippling amendment to the law, or even by a threat to abolish the agency altogether. Consequently it is sometimes said that "the regulated regulate the regulators." No wonder the administrator "selects from the special interests before him a combination to which he gives official sanction. Thus inescapably in practice the concept of the public interest is given substance by its identification with the interest of certain groups." [30]

The Courts Not Immune to Social Forces

A widespread assumption once prevailed that the courts produce abstract justice through a process of pure reason—that judges function in a social vacuum and are immune to the social forces that influence other officials of the government and, as Max Lerner put it, "judicial decisions are babies brought by constitutional storks." However, close inspection reveals that judges are no less human than legislators, executives, and administrators. They too develop patterns of understanding and thought under the influence of the climates of opinion in which they grow up and in which they live as adults. For example, at one time the Supreme Court of the United States consisted mainly of justices who had developed their legal concepts in the Era of *laissez faire*. New govermental regulations of business seemed to them to violate "natural law" as determined by "the dictates of right reason." Consequently in the early decades of the present century they held unconstitutional numerous statutes enacted by Congress and by state legislatures as violations of the Constitution's prohibition of laws depriving any person of life, liberty, or property without due process. The letter of due process as contained in the Constitution remains unchanged today, but a different set of justices who grew up in a different climate of opinion and are products of other social forces reject the inflexible dogmas of *laissez faire* and permit a wide latitude in legislation regulating economic life. Thus in 1937 when the Supreme Court which had struck down in a few years a dozen acts of Congress suddenly stopped that practice it seemed to respond to concepts of a new era. "The practical play of the forces of politics," said the late Associate Justice of the United States Supreme Court, Robert H. Jackson, "has often delayed but never permanently defeated the persist-

[30] E. P. Herring: *Public Administration and the Public Interest,* p. 24.

ent will of a substantial majority." [31] The courts too, in time, respond to the social forces that influence legislator, executive, and administrator.

A Complex Society Essential to a Free State

A constitution indicates what powers are vested in the government but interest groups determine how those powers shall be exercised. No wonder someone has said that the so-called sovereign state might better be described as the registrar of the interest groups. But it matters much whether the interest groups are few or many and how large a portion of the citizens is inert and unorganized. A monolithic, unchecked interest dominating the government inevitably spells despotism no matter what the nominal form of government. Even two dominating social forces in the state almost inevitably break into violence. "Nor can anything surely prevent the rise of dictatorship except a society which is highly organized on a voluntary basis." [32]

The great danger element in any free society is a body of the citizenry unorganized, neglected and handicapped with a feeling of not belonging to the great society that constitutes the state. The worst despotisms spring up, whether of national dictators or state or city bosses, where the unorganized masses are largest and the demagogue has his grand opportunity. But where a great variety of alert organized interests form a complex pattern of interaction, balance is a natural result. The free competition of organized forces in political society restrained by mores and statutes is the *sine qua non* of a free state.

SUMMARY

A democratic government seeks constantly to discover discontent and to reduce it to a minimum by making adjustments that satisfy the demands and protests of the discontented. Knowledge of and insight into this feature of democratic government is essential to intelligent citizenship. The state consists of the citizenry organized as the body politic, achieving the purposes for which the state exists through the set of agencies known as the government.

Awareness of social forces is indispensable to an understanding of the functioning of government. The starting point in acquiring such an awareness is a recognition of the multi-group nature of the modern state. The free competition of these groups, seeking to influence the government, tends to result in the balances and equilibriums that determine consensuses of public opinion, concepts of the public interest, and norms of public policy.

The legislature is the organ through which social forces, largely the competing interest groups, bring their influences to bear in determining

[31] "Maintaining our Freedoms" delivered before the American Bar Association, Aug. 24, 1953.
[32] Harvey Fergusson, *op. cit.,* p. 141.

public policies as expressed in statutes. The fundamental function of the executive is seeing to the execution of these policies to the extent that the social forces playing upon that branch support or impede the enforcement of the law. The chief executive supervises law enforcement through a hierarchy of administrative agencies which, in their turn, are fortified or frustrated in the performance of their duties by the interest groups whose pressures persistently impinge upon them. Even the judiciary, in its function of adjudicating cases and controversies brought before it, is by no means perfectly free from the social forces that, in brief, determine how government functions in all its aspects.

FOUNDATIONS OF AMERICAN GOVERNMENT

PART

I

FOUNDATIONS OF AMERICAN GOVERNMENT

CHAPTER II

COLONIAL AND REVOLUTIONARY GOVERNMENTS

THE GENESIS OF OUR POLITICAL INSTITUTIONS

The Transfer of Political Institutions to America

No MATTER how positively American our political institutions may be, they did not originate as American institutions but instead were brought across the Atlantic mainly by English settlers of the colonial period. Outstanding among English political institutions imported to America were the parish, a political unit for the administration of poor relief, constituting at the same time the ecclesiastical jurisdiction of an Anglican congregation; the township and the county, which were ancient units of local government; boroughs, which were incorporated towns designated as constituencies or districts for the election of members of Parliament; and the institution of electors, which gave to certain individuals the then rare privilege of voting for members of the House of Commons or the councils of local government units. Of course the colonists could not foresee the transformations these institutions would experience under the impact of the New World. Generation by generation the physical, geographical, economic, and social forces of the new environment wrought their changes and converted Europeans into Americans. At the same time the process produced institutions so unique as to be properly distinguished as American.

The Colonial Prototype of the American State

Naturally enough, civil government in the United States did not originate in a deliberate and direct attempt to establish it, but rather as a by-product of the incorporation of profit-seeking ventures. The latter years of Queen Elizabeth's reign had witnessed the chartering of the great trading corporations: the English-Levant Company, the Muscovy Company, and the East Indies Company—whose names indicate their geographical spheres of operation. Patterned after these was the London-Virginia Company which planted the first English settlement in America at Jamestown in 1607. Its charter reveals that its primary purpose was to afford the stockholders an opportunity to exploit the resources of their land grant. But the utter absence of civil government in the American wilderness led to the charter's granting to the London-Virginia Company "full and absolute power and authority to correct, punish, pardon, govern, and rule all such subjects of us . . . as shall . . . inhabit in the precincts and territories . . . of the said colony . . . according to such orders, ordinances, constitution, directions and instructions as by our said council . . . shall be established . . . as near as conveniently may be agreeable to the laws, statutes, government, and policy of this our realm of England." Thus a commercial charter authorized the first government of English-speaking people in America. The settlement of Massachusetts Bay in 1630 closely paralleled the Virginia experience, although there a religious motive complemented the economic one. Soon the economic function of colonial charters everywhere atrophied, leaving only the residuum of civil government. This change was most evident when a charter was revoked and the colony became a royal province. The terms of colonial government were then specifically prescribed in the royal governor's commission, which closely resembled a charter but pertained solely to governmental matters.

The Commercial Charter, the Forerunner of American Constitutions

From the very beginning these commercial charters invested the colonizing corporations with the essential characteristics of self-governing states. Similar to the way American states today are founded on their constitutions, the charter provided the corporation with a fundamental, or superior, law. The colonizing corporation "exercised many functions of a sovereign government: it could make assessments, coin money, regulate trade, dispose of corporate property, collect taxes, manage a treasury, and provide for defense. Thus every essential element long afterward found in the government of the American state appeared in the chartered corporation that started English civilization in America."[1] When, in the 1770's, British authority in America broke down and the colonies became independent states, they adapted their charters to the new status by rewriting, modifying, and transforming them into state constitutions. It was largely a synthesis of these state constitutions which, in 1787, became the Constitution of the United States. Thus the Constitution of the United States may be said to be, in a sense, a lineal descendant of the seventeenth-century commercial charter.

[1] Charles A. and Mary R. Beard: *The Rise of American Civilization* (New York, 1927), Vol. I, p. 37.

Genesis of the Representative Assembly

Slowly and uncertainly there emerged out of colonial political experience the pattern of American government as we know it, with its executive, its bicameral legislature, and its courts. The development of the colonial legislature became the supreme political experience of the American colonists. The very origin of the representative assembly in America is one of the curious accidents of our colonial history. Before the Virginia colony was ten years old, the Puritan members of the London-Virginia Company in England had become involved in a furious controversy with James I. In an effort to effect an alliance with the colonists against the King, the council of the company authorized each "town, hundred, or other particular plantation" in Virginia to elect two burgesses, that is to say, deputies or representatives, to sit and deliberate with the governor and his council in what was called, for the first time in American history, the "General Assembly." So it was not far-sighted political sagacity nor imitation of the British House of Commons, as romantic historians have assumed, but a sharp maneuver of the board of directors of the London-Virginia Corporation to outwit the King that produced the first instance of the representative principle in America. For sixty years these burgesses sat with the governor and his council, exercising legislative, executive, and judicial functions without much attention to the dogma of separated powers. Then in 1680, for some unknown reason, they began meeting as a separate body. So there was in the beginning of the American experience with government no such neatly blue-printed pattern of legislative, executive, and judicial branches functioning independently and as checks on each other which today Americans so often assume to be absolutely essential to sound organization. Whoever has visited the restored colonial capitol at Williamsburg, Virginia, may recall the single room in which governor, council, and burgesses sat together. Here were mingled the elements in embryo that, under the impact of American social forces, were eventually to evolve into the typical colonial executive, upper house, and representative assembly. Massachusetts Bay and indeed all the colonies followed an evolutionary development of these fundamental organs so similar as to suggest that they were shaped by like forces inherent in the American environment and society.

The Assembly Dominant in Colonial Government

No matter how haphazard its origin and growth may have been, the elective branch of the colonial legislatures, such as the houses of burgesses or deputies, eventually became the masters of the thirteen colonial governments. In time every colony had a popularly elected branch whose members felt they had a mandate from their constituents to safeguard taxation and public expenditures. Through this control of the purse they effectively checked the power of the governor even when he was the appointee of the king. The governor was dependent for his salary upon the will of the assembly and he had to bargain for it, quite commonly, by dickering with the legislature when it wished his approval of certain measures. An English administrative commission known as the Lords of Trade and Plantations examined enactments of colonial legislatures and advised the king to allow or disallow them. As the representative of the crown, the governor possessed a preliminary or suspensive veto before the Lords of Trade considered the matter. Thus the colonists became familiar with the executive veto as a governmental device, but they sometimes circumvented it by putting new legislation into effect while waiting for royal approval, and occasionally they nullified the royal veto by persistently re-enacting the vetoed legislation in a slightly altered form until it ran the gauntlet of crown approval.

The Assembly Subordinates the Colonial Governor

The colonial legislatures, by creating special administrative commissions to execute their legislation, frequently took the executive power completely out of the hands of the colonial governor. Sometimes appropriations would be made in such meticulous detail as to leave the governor little discretion in their expenditure. Occasionally the governor was deprived of his appointing power by the legislature's granting of the salary of an office not to the office itself but to a designated individual. This left the governor no choice in making the appointment but to name the person to whom the salary had been assigned. As a consequence of such maneuvers, it could be said of Massachusetts, by 1757, that "almost every act of executive and legislative power, whether it be political, judicial, or military, is ordered and directed by votes and resolves of the General Court (the Legislature), in most cases originating in the House of Representatives."[2] The speaker of the elective branch of the colonial legislature tended to become the rallying point of popular opposition to the governor. The conditioning assemblies received in the colonial setting explains many unique features of American legislatures today.

The Colonial Governor

The office of colonial governor originated in the office of manager or overseer of the incorporated trading companies that made the first settlements. In the seventeenth century the term "governor" was rather less a governmental than a business expression and as such it still survives in such uses as the "governor of the Bank of England" or the "governors of the Federal Reserve System." In Virginia the earliest governors were chosen by the council of the company, which is to say, the board of directors of the enterprise. In this case the primary function of the governor was the production of commodities for the company's profit, and this was sometimes achieved by forced labor in a reign of terror with savage punishments and

---

[2] "The Board of Trade to Governor Pownall." Quoted by Evarts Boutell Greene: *The Provincial Governor in the English Colonies of North America,* Harvard Historical Studies, VIII (New York, 1898), p. 194.

executions under the martial law that the Virginia charter authorized the governor to establish. In the charter colony of Massachusetts, the governor was elected by the "freemen," which term at first included only stockholders in the corporation and later only members of the established church. In the other chartered colonies, Connecticut and Rhode Island, the legislatures elected the governor annually and he was consequently their obsequious agent. In the royal provinces subject to the crown, the governor was an appointee of the king. So lucrative was the patronage of a royal governorship that broken-down court favorites regarded an appointment as governor a means of retrieving their fortunes. This situation intensified the vigor of the colonial assembly's check upon potential executive despotism and fortified its defense of the public interest. The persistent, deep-seated American suspicion that tyranny lurks in the executive is a tradition rooted in colonial experience.

Subordination of the Colonial Governor to the General Assembly

The royal governor was in theory a viceroy of the king. He was commissioned to initiate laws, but the jealousy of the colonial assemblies prevented him from doing so, since they insisted upon initiating legislation. We have seen that now and then the governor was outmaneuvered in the exercise of his veto power. Patronage gave him some leverage in legislation when he had not been deprived of his appointing power by legislative stratagems. At the same time that he was dickering with the colonial assembly in behalf of the interests of the crown, he was being bombarded with further instruction by the home government. Meanwhile his authority was weakened by the fact that the next English ship to arrive might bring directions for his recall. Long before the Revolution, the colonial governor had been reduced almost to begging at the door of the legislature for needed appropriations. When occasionally success did meet his efforts, it was usually because of the personal qualities of leadership he chanced to possess.

The Governor's Council

The colonial governor's council first originated in the council of the corporation of the London-Virginia Company and in the "assistants" of the Massachusetts Bay Company. This was originally the directorate of the trading company and was soon to be transformed into an organ of civil government which, as the progenitor of our state senate, would in turn provide the model for the Senate of the United States. When trading companies metamorphosed into the political societies that constituted the colonies, the council was used by the crown as well as by the autonomous corporate colonies of Connecticut and Rhode Island as a check upon the governor. In the royal province, the council was appointed by the crown upon nomination by the governor; in the corporate colony, by the assembly, subject to the governor's veto; and in the proprietary colony, by the governor himself. The governor's council in practice came to constitute a group of notables selected from the ruling class of the colony. While its functions were primarily executive or administrative, the council was, in most colonies, also the highest court in civil cases. Gradually it evolved into an upper chamber of the legislature whose concurrence was necessary for the enactment of colonial laws. In the Revolutionary period this organ of colonial government made the transition to the state senate, which to this day retains vestiges of the executive, administrative, and even judicial functions once vested in the old colonial governor's council.

THE REVOLUTIONARY STATE GOVERNMENTS

The Transition from Colonies to States

One of the causes of the American Revolution was a belated attempt of the British ministry to reassert and recover the rapidly diminishing power of the home government in the American colonies. As it turned out, this attempt miscarried and served only to accelerate the long and persistent trend of American self-government toward complete independence. With the opening of the hostilities of the American Revolution, the colonies entered a period of uncertain change that was to culminate in their transition into full-fledged states, each claiming the sovereign status of an independent nation. This transformation began with the abdication or flight of the royal governors and other crown officials. The conversion of colonies into states was made easier by the popularly elected assemblies, which now became in fact what they had been approaching in theory: the supreme organ of the sovereign will in each of the thirteen states. Thus the assembly helped maintain the thread of continuity from early colonial governments through the transition of the Revolution down to the governments of our states today.

The Revolutionary State Constitutions

By 1777, state constitutions had been formulated and put into effect in every state except Connecticut and Rhode Island which, as the only remaining corporate colonies at the opening of the Revolution, found their charters satisfactory enough to serve as state constitutions. The eleven state constitutions that had been framed did not so much devise new governmental systems as legalize the changes already brought about by the Revolution. By and large the new governments preceded the constitutions, which converted them from governments that had merely assumed power into legally authorized governments. That is to say, the state constitutions authorized the new state governments to do what they were already doing. The most striking change in the new governments was the altered status of the governor. This official had been tolerated by the colonists as a symbol of external authority. During the controversy preceding the Revolution the very term "governor" had become so opprobrious that four states abandoned its use altogether and substituted instead the new title of "president" to designate their chief executive, and from them the framers of the Constitution of the United States obtained the title for the chief executive of the United States.[3]

The Revolutionary State Governors

In eight states the governor was elected by the legislature whose subservient agent he then inevitably became. In ten states his term of office was only one year, and six southern states restricted his re-election. Every state had an executive or privy council which the governor had to consult on important matters. He lost to the legislature the appointing power and in eleven states he was deprived of the veto power that had been so irksome when exercised by the colonial governor. The latter's power to dissolve the assembly was lost by the state governors. This signified that the governor could no longer appeal to the people for support by ending the term of the members of the legislature and ordering an election to fill the vacancies. No wonder Madison was to declare by 1787 that the governors had become mere "ciphers."

The Revolutionary State Legislatures

The achievement of independence served to make the legislature preeminent among the branches of state government. The Revolutionary state constitutions authorized the legislatures to exercise the sovereign powers they had in fact already assumed. These legislatures now reaped the full advantage of the enormous prestige they had accumulated during the long colonial period as the persistent defenders of the people's interests. Long before the Revolution the legislatures had assumed unchallenged mastery of colonial taxation and appropriation, and now in most states they appointed the governor and other administrative officers, the judiciary, and even many local officials. In no state could the judiciary annul enactments of the legislature, but through impeachment and conviction the removal of every judge in the state was within the power of the legislature.

The Failure of Checks and Balances

In all the states except two the popular branch of the legislature was checked, theoretically at least, by an upper house usually chosen on the aristocratic principle of a higher property qualification for membership in that house and by a higher property qualification for the right to vote for members of the upper house than for members of the lower house. Georgia and Pennsylvania were experimenting with unicameral legislatures. In accordance with prevalent political dogmas the separation of powers was recognized in the state constitutions by prescribing what in fact already existed: legislative, executive, and judicial branches of government. However, this separation of powers proved futile as a check on

[3] Typical of the popular feeling against the very idea of a governor is the resolution voted by a Massachusetts town during the Revolution ". . . that it is our Oppiniun that we do not want any Goviner but the Guviner of the universe and under him a States Gineral to consult with the wrest of the united states for the good of the whole." Quoted in W. M. West: *American History and Government* (Boston, 1913), p. 228n.

the legislature since the precise meanings of "legislative," "judicial," and "executive" had not yet been clarified as they have been today by a century and a half of experience and court opinion. Consequently the Revolutionary state legislatures freely and serenely exercised executive and judicial, in addition to their own appropriate legislative, powers. The assumption was that a legislative power was merely a power exercised by the legislature regardless of the nature of that power. "The legislative department," complained Madison in 1788, "is everywhere expanding its sphere of activity and drawing all its powers into its impetuous vortex."[4]

"The Revolutionary Machine"

The most dynamic instrument in effecting the transition from British to American government was the continent-wide network of self-appointed Revolutionary committees of correspondence. Aggressive local groups of patriots, organized first to agitate against British policies, later busied themselves enforcing resolutions of the Continental Congress, as, for example, the boycott against British imports. These progenitors of our present party committees organized first in town or townships and then collectively constituted themselves as county central committees. County committees chose central provincial or state committees, and the Continental Congress was the national convention of this "Revolutionary Machine." The First Continental Congress met in September, 1774, impelled by a desire to induce the British ministry to abandon its obnoxious policies and thereby restore harmony between Britain and her colonies. The Congress issued a Declaration of Rights and Grievances and formed the "Association" to enforce the boycott through local committees of correspondence. Before adjournment, the First Continental Congress set May, 1775, as the date of a Second Continental Congress.

THE FIRST NATIONAL GOVERNMENT

The Government of the Continental Congress

When the Second Continental Congress convened, the Revolutionary War had already broken out. In no sense had this body convened for the purpose of governing. During the first five weeks it merely passed resolutions consisting of recommendations to the states for their approval. In June, 1775, however, it began performing governmental functions by adopting the Revolutionary army then besieging the British troops penned up in Boston, and by appointing Washington Commander-in-Chief. Though lacking delegated authority, the Continental Congress presently began exercising sovereign governmental powers by raising an army, creating a navy, establishing a postal system, borrowing money, emitting bills of credit, and authorizing captures on land and sea. In time it was to establish diplomatic relations and make treaties with foreign nations. It was, nevertheless, as John Adams put it, "not a legislative assembly, but only a diplo-

[4] *The Federalist*, No. 48.

matic assembly," and in fact did little more than unify the efforts of the states by providing special committees for common action. The Continental Congress, indeed, functioned through a multitude of special and standing executive committees. There was a distinct one for each new activity assumed and they numbered at times more than a hundred. John Adams alone was a member of ninety such committees.[5] No vestige of separated powers or checks and balances ever characterized the organization of the Continental Congress.

Adoption of the Articles of Confederation

The utter lack of specifically delegated authority for the powers the Continental Congress was exercising must have irked the delegates. The states were manifesting dissatisfaction with this unsanctioned exercise of sovereignty. Consequently only a few days after passing the Declaration of Independence, Congress began consideration of what was to become the Articles of Confederation, which had been prepared by a committee. The delays in getting them ratified by all the states were such that not until March, 1781, a few months before the ending of hostilities, did this first written constitution of the United States become valid.

The Provisions of the Articles of Confederation

The Articles of Confederation purported to establish a perpetual union. Provisions were made for working relations between the states by assuring free citizens the rights and privileges of the several states and by providing for their free ingress and egress to and from each state. The Congress was to be composed of not more than seven nor less than two delegates from each state, though each delegation, regardless of size, was to have but one vote. Expenses for the common defense and general welfare were to be paid from a common treasury to be supplied by a system of requisitions from the states. Congress was to have power to make war and peace, enter into treaties, send and receive ambassadors, regulate the matter of prize in captures, grant letters of marque, establish courts for the trial of piracies and felonies on the high seas, and establish a court for adjudicating disputes between states. Many of its clauses, some but slightly paraphrased, were to find their way into the present Constitution of the United States.

Powers of Congress under the Articles of Confederation

Congress was granted sole power to regulate the value of coins struck either by itself or the states, fix standards of weights and measures, regulate Indian affairs, establish post offices, appoint naval and military officers, and regulate land and naval forces. It could borrow money, emit bills of credit, build and equip a navy, and determine the size of the Continental land and naval forces. Only by a vote of nine states could important matters be authorized. Amendments to the Articles required the approval of every state

---

[5] See C. H. Van Tyne: "Continental Congress," *Cyclopedia of American Government* (New York, 1913), Vol. I, pp. 252–3.

legislature. When Congress was not in session "a Committee of the States," consisting of one delegate from each state, was to sit. By the time the Articles went into effect the outline of a permanent administrative organization was taking shape under the headings of four permanent executive departments: a superintendent of finance, a secretary of foreign affairs, a secretary "at war," and a secretary of marine. Here in fact were the progenitors of our present national executive departments whose heads now constitute the president's cabinet.

Transition from an Acting to a Legal Government

Nothing is more significant about the Articles of Confederation than the fact that Congress was vested with scarcely any major power it had not already been exercising for years. Fundamentally what the Articles did was to convert a *de facto* government, which is an unauthorized though actual government, into a *de jure*, or legally authorized, body. Congress now had a mandate to govern from the sovereign peoples of the states, conveyed to it by the signers of the Articles of Confederation, who were authorized by their state legislatures. Two important powers, however, were withheld from Congress. Since the states were then waging a war against the right of Parliament to tax them and to regulate their commerce, the states refused to grant these powers to Congress. These omissions, plus the requirement of unanimous consent for any amendment to the Articles, eventually proved fatal to this fundamental instrument of government.

The Problem of the Framers of the Articles

The paramount problem confronting the framers of the Articles of Confederation was that of the distribution of governmental powers between the states on one side, and the central government, or Congress, on the other. They knew themselves to be limited by circumstances, the chief of which was an almost fanatical popular insistence upon local self-government. This difficulty was intensified by the fact that the Articles had to be framed in the heated atmosphere of a revolution against the central authority of the British government. Here was an ideology so inflexible as to hamper enormously the first attempt to write an American constitution for a central government. The framers of the Articles went as far as they dared, and the assumption that they lacked statesmanship because the Articles eventually proved inadequate is erroneous. They had measured quite accurately the prevalent social forces and did only what was then possible. The Articles of Confederation went beyond anything that had yet been done in a confederacy and probably was the best constitution for such a union that the world had seen thus far.

A Confederation Instead of a Federation

The framers of the Articles knew they could not obtain approval of a federal system such as we have today in which two distinct governments act directly upon individuals. Instead they established a confederation or, as they called it, a "League of Friendship." They provided that: "Each State retains its sovereignty, freedom and independence, and every power, jurisdiction and right, which is not by this confederation expressly delegated to the United States in Congress assembled." Though doubtless necessary in order to obtain unanimous ratification by the states, the painstaking specificity of the recognition of state sovereignty was to have the effect of weakening the government of the Confederation. In practice this proviso defeated the fundamental purpose of the Articles which was to define the distribution of powers between the states and Congress. This specifically reserved sovereignty of the states meant in time that they were to pay no more attention to the policy determinations of Congress than might be voluntarily accorded by a sovereign, that is, one which recognized no political superior. Consequently the Confederation became more and more a distant, shadowy, and impotent authority. As far as the typical American citizen was concerned, the only political authority of consequence was his state government.

THE MOVEMENT FOR THE PRESENT CONSTITUTION

The Popular Party and the Revolutionary Governments

Colonial society shaped the early state governments with their omnipotent state legislatures and their powerless chief executives. It also shaped the Articles of Confederation, which provided for no separate and distinct executive. Throughout the colonial period there had been a privileged ruling class consisting of merchants, landed gentry, clergy of the established churches, lawyers, and colonial officials of the coastal communities. Opposed to these were the popular or democratic elements—the frontiersmen, grain-growing farmers, urban shopkeepers, and mechanics who welcomed the Revolution as an opportunity not only to free themselves from the restraints of parliament but at the same time to snatch from the ruling class in America control of provincial or state governments. They took charge of the committees of correspondence and fortified themselves through state constitutions that assured their control of the state legislatures unchecked by governor, courts, or a powerful central government. The feeble government of the Articles of Confederation was made to order for this popular party. In many states the popular party consisted predominantly of debtors who sought relief through paper money and stay laws and other legislation favorable to their interest.

Elements Dissatisfied with the Confederation

Four years elapsed between the framing of the Articles of Confederation and their going into effect, with the consequence that they were somewhat outmoded before they began to function as a fundamental instrument of government. Moreover, they had been shaped by a military emergency which ended almost as soon as the last state had approved the Articles. Hostile armies in the land had induced at least a semblance of the concurrent action of the states the Articles had been designed to promote, but with the arrival of peace a distressing disintegration began. Gradually the elements dissatisfied with the Articles grew critical of the impotent Confederation whose Congress in the late 1780's almost ceased to function at all. There began to develop among them a demand for amendments to the Articles which would invest Congress with taxing power in order to establish the credit of the Confederation and restore face value to the lamentably depressed Revolutionary War securities. An amendment that would have given Congress power to levy a 5 per cent tariff on imports failed to achieve the ratification of the thirteenth state. Domestic manufacturers, overwhelmed by the dumping of British products, required the protection of a tariff. Commercial interests insisted a central authority was needed to end the paralyzing trade restrictions and tariffs of the thirteen states and to make and enforce commercial treaties. Foreign competition had practically brought to a standstill the employment of our own shipping even in American harbors.

Social Unrest and Shays's Rebellion

Creditors generally longed to see again such a restriction of State issues of legal-tender paper money as parliament and the crown, through the veto, had once exercised against colonial paper money. Such issues were inflating paper prices in more than half the states and had run to such an extreme in Rhode Island that President John Witherspoon of Princeton was led to remark: "For two or three years we constantly saw and were informed of creditors running away from their debtors, and debtors pursuing them in triumph and paying them without mercy." The constitution of Massachusetts as revised in 1780 was so constructed as to over-load the legislature with men who were heavy taxpayers, and they prevented the popular party from enacting any relief for debtors. Inevitably the "hard times" of the 1780's and the consequent widespread foreclosures and sheriff's sales drove the desperate farmers of Massachusetts to the armed movement known as Shays's Rebellion. Only with difficulty was this revolt suppressed by Massachusetts' state militia, financed by private subscriptions of the frightened merchants of Boston after the Confederation proved unable to provide troops for restoring order.

The Movement for Revision of the Articles of Confederation

A fear that unrest such as that manifested by Shays's Rebellion might spread to other states stimulated the movement to strengthen the central government by revision of the Articles of Confederation. As early as 1785 five commissioners representing Virginia and Maryland had met at Mount Vernon to consider problems of navigation on the Potomac. Out of their discussions emerged a plan for a meeting at Annapolis of delegates from all the states to consider "how far a uniform system of commercial regulation may be necessary to their common interests and their permanent harmony." Delegates from only five states arrived at Annapolis and the sole outcome of consequence was a proposal that a convention representing all the states be held at Philadelphia in May, 1787, "to take into considera- tion the situation of the United States, to devise such further provisions as shall appear to them necessary to render the federal government adequate to the exigencies of the Union; and to report such an act for that purpose to the United States in Congress assembled as when agreed upon by them, and afterwards confirmed by the legislatures of every state, will effectively provide for the same."[6]

The Call for the Philadelphia Convention

Following the recommendation of the Annapolis Convention, Congress called upon the states to send delegates to Philadelphia "for the sole and express purpose of revising the Articles of Confederation." Every state responded except Rhode Island, which was in the grip of the paper- money inflationists and quite correctly regarded the movement for the Convention as a deflationary project. In every state the delegates were selected by state legislatures whose representatives grossly under-repre- sented the interior or agrarian regions where the Articles of Confederation were considered quite satisfactory and any movement to revise them was looked upon with more than suspicion.

SUMMARY

It was inevitable that English political institutions, transplanted to the New World, would evolve in the new habitat into something quite differ- ent—in fact into American political institutions. Thus the charters granted by the crown to the trading corporations that established the first settle- ments soon became merely fundamental instruments of civil governments. The governor of the planting corporation donned the garb of the chief executive of the colony. The appointive council created to advise and assist the governor in his administrative and judicial functions came in time to be merely the upper house of the legislature. The lower house, consisting of the popularly elected representatives, through control of taxation and appropriations, gradually subordinated both governor and council.

It was the agitation against the British policies leading to the Ameri- can Revolution that gave emerging democratic forces their great oppor- tunity. Operating through local self appointed committees of correspond- ence knit into county, provincial, and even a continental network, the Revolutionary machine was created. Everywhere the colonists were ready to seize control where British authority collapsed. Almost automatically thirteen colonial governments gave way to thirteen *de facto* state govern- ments soon to be legitimized by written state constitutions.

Meanwhile the second Continental Congress had assumed charge of the collective military and civil concerns of the United States, declared

[6] Henry S. Commager: *Documents of American History* (New York, 1938), Vol. I, pp. 133–4.

them to be independent states, and finally had its power legitimized by the Articles of Confederation. But, with the coming of peace, Congress lost prestige chiefly because of its lack of power to tax and to regulate commerce. Important groups, suffering from the weakness of the central government, managed to get a convention assembled at Philadelphia ostensibly to revise the Articles of Confederation.

CHAPTER III

THE MAKING OF THE CONSTITUTION

THE DELEGATES

The Political Apprenticeship of the Framers

THE assembly that translated the dominant social forces of the 1780's into the Constitution of the United States was one of the most notable in human history. Long experience in colonial self-government and service in the Revolutionary state governments and in the Continental Congress had given its members an incomparable schooling in public affairs. Seven of the fifty-five delegates had been state governors, twenty-eight had sat in the Continental Congress, many had served an apprenticeship in statecraft in the colonial and state legislative assemblies, and all were politically experienced. Though versed in the political philosophy of Harrington, Locke, and Montesquieu, they were by no means formula-bound, but were thoroughly accustomed to the give and take of practical men of affairs. Of course the framers belonged to a ruling class, but no other class of men was then capable of devising a plan that would cement the elements of American society. The framers had developed concepts of the public good that made them conscious of their responsibility to elements of society other than their own. Perhaps never in history has a group of leaders performed their representative functions so well in the public interest. Tested by the wear and tear of time, their product has been pronounced good.

Washington in the Constitutional Convention

Presiding over the deliberations of the delegates was General George Washington, who was even then emerging as one of the first statesmen of his age. Hard times had put him three years in arrears on his taxes and the urge for the restoration of economic stability was naturally strong in this reputedly wealthiest man in America. But eager though he was for a stronger central government, so doubtful was he of the prospects for success of the Philadelphia venture that he hesitated three months before accepting an appointment as delegate. He had even been urged not to attend lest his reputation be damaged by the apprehended failure of the Convention.[1] Indeed, before he had been at Philadelphia a month, he wrote: "I almost despair of seeing a favorable issue to the proceedings of the Convention and do repent therefore having had any agency in the business." Though he contributed but one short speech to the deliberations, so imposing was the prestige of his great name that his absence from the Convention might well have foredoomed it to failure.

The "Father of the Constitution"

Foremost among the framers was thirty-six-year-old James Madison of Virginia, whose constructive contributions earned him the title of "Father of the Constitution." The aristocratic outlook of this heir apparent of a great planting family was somewhat tempered by the inherent democracy of the Virginia Piedmont that had nurtured him. Rare indeed is the analyst of public affairs today who has anything comparable to Madison's skill in interpreting political phenomena in terms of pertinent social forces. None of his contemporaries knew better than he the political experience of the human race from the peoples of antiquity down to his fellow citizens in the thirteen states. One hundred and sixty-one times he rose to speak and throw the searchlight of his knowledge and wisdom on the matter under consideration. With convincing cogency he argued the immediate necessity of a strengthened central government. He reasoned that a radical leader who might be able to stampede a county or state would be baffled by the sheer complexity of interests if he attempted it in "the extended republic of the United States." With a diligence that permanently impaired his health he set down hour after hour the gist of the debates of the Convention, so that to this day Madison's *Notes* constitute the most important source of information on the making of the Constitution.

James Wilson

Second only to Madison as an architect of the Constitution was James Wilson of Pennsylvania. As a native of Scotland he was free from the decentralizing tug of state loyalty and consequently thought in terms of American nationality. He spoke a little oftener than Madison in the Convention, and despite his legal practice for the great merchants of Philadelphia, he stands out as the Convention's chief exponent of popular sovereignty. Thus he advocated the direct election of the president and senators as well as of members of the House of Representatives, whom he would have had elected annually because law receives its binding force

[1] H. C. Hockett: *Constitutional History of the United States, 1776–1826* (New York, 1939), p. 201.

from "the consent of those whose obedience the law requires."[2] Somehow Wilson caught a clearer vision of the United States government that was to be in the future than did any other important delegate.

Gouverneur Morris

Holding the record for loquacity was Gouverneur Morris of Pennsylvania, who spoke oftener than any other delegate. In contrast with Madison and Wilson he was caught more than once in the contradictions of his snap judgments. No one among the delegates manifested more distrust of the masses or was more insistent upon limiting their suffrage. Apparently his arguments had little influence upon the Convention, but his contribution to the making of the Constitution lies in the exquisite phrasing he, as the assigned writer, gave to its final form. He was later to imply that he planted a sly sleeper or two among its clauses, particularly those on the judiciary.

Alexander Hamilton

Even less influential than Morris in the making of the Constitution was Alexander Hamilton of New York. Despite the humble origin of this erstwhile orphan from a West Indies island, his intimate associations with Revolutionary army officers and his marriage into one of the great Hudson Valley families had given Hamilton a pronounced aristocratic outlook. In the Convention he was a chief exponent of the merits of "the rich and well born" while, as he saw it, "the people are turbulent and changing; they seldom judge or determine right." He advocated a senate and an executive with life tenures, and frankly professed an unqualified admiration for the British monarchical system. So extreme were his views that they had practically no influence even upon the conservative framers. Quite correctly one of the delegates, Dr. Johnson, remarked of Hamilton that "the gentleman from New York has been praised by everybody, he has been supported by none." It would be difficult to find a single item in the Constitution marked with Hamilton's influence. Yet his place is among the Fathers of the Constitution, even if his outstanding contributions to the "making of the Constitution" were his arguments for its ratification by the states, preserved in the *Federalist,* and his later success as Washington's Secretary of the Treasury in promoting the financial legislation that harnessed the dominant economic forces of the United States to the new government.

THE SETTING

The Post-Revolutionary Conservative Reaction

By and large the framers of the Constitution had been profoundly affected by the widespread post-Revolutionary disillusionment. Whatever equalitarian inspiration the Declaration of Independence may once have given

[2] James Wilson: *Works* (New York, 1896), Vol. I, p. 88.

those who were to become the Fathers of the Constitution, it had long since been dissipated by the social unrest of the 1780's. Strikingly significant is the fact that only six of the fifty-six signers of the Declaration of Independence sat in the Constitutional Convention. The basic cause of the social unrest was the hard times that had harassed, when it had not ruined, innumerable small farmers at the same time that it left no important interest unembarrassed. Statistical analyses have long since revealed what the framers could not have known, namely, that the trough of the depression had been passed in 1785 and that recovery was in progress in 1787, which meant, as Farrand puts it, that the Constitution was eventually to be "floated on a wave of business prosperity" that gave it a most auspicious launching.

Interests not Represented at Philadelphia

Unquestionably the delegates at Philadelphia constituted a somewhat distorted representation of American interests in 1787. Thirty-five of the thirty-nine signers of the finished Constitution lived adjacent to salt water, and the document was decidely a product of the coastal interests. The grain-growing farmers of the interior, the frontiersmen, and the urban mechanics had no representatives at Philadelphia. Nor was this simply the result of deliberate exclusion. Some representatives of these interests had been appointed as delegates and had rejected the opportunity offered them. Patrick Henry's name was second on the Virginia list of chosen delegates, but he promptly refused to serve as did also Richard Henry Lee, both champions of the vigorous democracy of the western Virginia counties. Another liberal Virginian, Thomas Jefferson, would undoubtedly have been offered membership in the Virginian delegation, but he was abroad as the American minister to France. Samuel Adams, the irrepressible champion of the tumultuous Boston mechanics, would not accept a place in the Massachusetts delegation. So the Constitution was framed without much regard to the ideas of the very elements that had largely shaped the earliest state constitutions and given them their popular character.

THE EVOLVING CONSTITUTION IN THE CONVENTION

The Virginia Plan

It is fascinating to trace in Madison's *Notes* the gradual unfolding of the Constitution. The first stage was the presentation by the Virginia delegates of a set of resolutions known as the Virginia plan; the second, the transformation of these proposals into the twenty-three resolutions of the Committee of the Whole; the third, their integration into the first draft of the Constitution; and the fourth, the final document expressed in Gouverneur Morris's matchless phrasing. The Virginia delegation took the initiative in the framing of the Constitution. Here was a group of remarkable men schooled in responsibility by management of the great tobacco plantations of the Old Dominion. Their delegation was the first to reach Philadelphia and, as they awaited the arrival of tardy delegates, they caucused daily. The outcome of their discussions was fifteen propositions which in due time were presented to the Convention. This Virginia, or large-state plan, became the agenda with which the Constitutional Convention began its discussions. Among the several proposals of the plan was the establishment of distinct legislative, executive, and judicial departments, the first to consist of two houses with powers to legislate in national concerns "to which the separate states are incompetent," with power to veto state laws, to choose the executive, and to employ force when necessary to fulfill its duties. In the light of the call for a convention merely to revise the Articles of Confederation, the Virginia plan was a revolutionary proposal to convert a confederation into a federal union with a national government.

The Resolutions of the Committee of the Whole

Sitting as a Committee of the Whole the Convention debated the fifteen proposals of the Virginia delegation for twenty days, and ended by agreeing upon nineteen resolutions. These still constituted the Virginia plan, but with certain refinements. It was now agreed that the people ought to elect the members of the lower house, and the state legislatures the upper house of Congress. Also, representation should be proportionate to state population in both national houses. This legislature would elect a single executive. It was to have in addition to the legislative powers of the Confederation the power "to legislate in all cases to which the separate states are incompetent" and the astonishing power "to negative all laws passed by the several states contravening national laws." So startling were these new powers that the small-state group took alarm and countered with the New Jersey plan. This proposed merely to fortify the Confederation by giving it powers to tax and to regulate commerce, enforceable through officials of the states. There would be a single house in which the states would be equally represented, and there would be a plural executive. Madison promptly pointed out that this plan was so similar to the Articles of Confederation that it would leave the evils unremedied and the people would be no better off than before. The large-state group was strong enough to effect the rejection of the New Jersey plan, whereupon the Convention returned to the consideration of the nineteen propositions of the Committee of the Whole.

The Connecticut Compromise

In the midst of its deliberations the Convention was brought to a standstill by an ultimatum of the small states that they would withdraw unless representation of the states was made equal in both houses of Congress. The large states had been standing firm on proportionate representation in both houses. The impasse was broken by the "Great Compromise" providing for equal representation in the upper house and proportionate representation in the lower. The origin of this solution is a commentary on the persistent Anglo-Saxon habit of shunning the purely artificial and basing its institutional devices on political experience. Of the eleven states represented in the Convention, five favored the Virginia large-state plan, five favored the New Jersey small-state plan, and Connecticut had a plan of its own: the Compromise. The Connecticut delegates had proposed that the states be represented equally in the Senate and proportionately, according to population, in the House of Representatives. This was the plan finally adopted. For more than a century as a corporate colony, and later as a state, Connecticut had maintained the equality of the towns in the lower house and had chosen the upper house from the body of the people. Here in the long-established practical experience of a state that held the balance of voting power was found the formula for ending a conflict that had threatened to wreck the Convention. Fortunately no one faction in the Convention was strong enough to have its own way, and no leader dominated the delegates.

The Preliminary Draft of the Constitution

By the last week of July the debates of the Convention had resulted in the adoption of twenty-three resolutions. These were then turned over to a Committee of Detail which, during a two-week recess of the Convention, organized and integrated them into a consistent system. Its report turned out to be the preliminary draft of the Constitution of the United States. Particularly interesting are some parts of this draft which do not appear in the Constitution as finally adopted by the Convention. For example, the preamble to the preliminary draft named the states; the draft itself stated that members of the Congress were to be paid by the states, that Congress was to elect the treasurer and the president for a seven-year term, and that navigation acts and the admission of new states were to require a two-thirds vote of both houses of Congress. For the first time the powers of Congress were specified in detail.

THE NATURE OF THE FINISHED CONSTITUTION

The Compromises of the Convention

A misconception has been planted in the American mind by over-emphasis on the three "great" compromises and by the neglect of others. Of course the Connecticut Compromise was of supreme importance since it prevented the breakup of the Convention. Important also was the counting of three out of five slaves as population in apportioning representatives in Congress and in levying direct taxes. The commercial states wanted the African slave trade abolished at once and were irked by the requirement of a two-thirds vote for navigation acts which the planting states had insisted upon including in the preliminary draft of the Constitution. The third "great" compromise was an agreement by which the commercial states were to tolerate the slave trade for twenty years in return for the consent of the planting states to a mere majority vote for the enactment of navigation acts by Congress. The Constitution is indeed a "bundle of compromises" and the ingenuity of the fathers in devising them marks them as statesmen of a high order. Other compromises are hidden in the most unsuspected places. For example, the controversy in the Convention as to whether the Constitution should require the creation of a system of Federal inferior courts instead of simply using state courts for that purpose was resolved by the simple provision that the Congress *may* establish inferior courts. The controversy as to whether or not the Constitution should specifically authorize Congress to assume state debts was ended by the non-committal statement that "all debts . . . shall be as valid against the United States under the Constitution as under the Confederation." The hot contest between the state delegations which insisted that the western territory be kept permanently subordinated in a colonial status and those which wanted admission to statehood for the territory left open as a possibility was ended by merely providing that "new states may be admitted to the Union." Even the Electoral College was clearly recognized by the framers as a compromise in that it was expected to succeed in producing the majority required to elect a president only "once out of twenty times," as Mason put it. It was anticipated that the election would almost always be by the House of Representatives, in which case each state would cast one vote, and that thus the small states would be compensated for the dissatisfaction it was presumed they would feel whenever the Electoral College did succeed in electing a president.[3]

The Constitution Emphatically American

The myth that the fathers modelled the American Constitution on the British instrument dies hard. Scarcely any important speech in the Convention had less effect than that of Alexander Hamilton in which he said: "I believe the British government forms the best model the world ever produced." John Adams, writing when the Constitution had been in operation twenty-five years and referring to the Revolutionary constitutions of New York, Massachusetts, and Maryland, said: "From these three the Constitution of the United States was afterward almost entirely drawn." Concerning the governmental organization of these constitutions he added "that it was not an affected imitation of the English government so much as attachment to their old colonial forms in which there had been three branches—a governor, a council, and a house of representatives."[4] We have seen how the colonial environment evolved the governor out of the business manager of the commercial corporations that planted the earliest colonies, and how it transformed him into a political chief; how the governor's council represented a transformation of the institution of directors into a political body, and how, through a series of accidents, the popularly elected assembly became a separate legislative organ. So positively native to the American soil is the Constitution of the United States that it is surely an American institution if there is any such thing.

[3] See Max Farrand: "The Compromises of the Constitution." *Annual Report of the American Historical Association* (1903), 1:73–84.
[4] John Adams: *Works* (Boston, 1856), Vol. VI, pp. 486–8.

THE PROBLEM OF THE EXECUTIVE

Necessity of an Executive Office

The office of president of the United States was created in response to the imperative press of circumstances created by the legislative powers vested in Congress. There had been nothing like it under the Articles of Confederation, since the government therein prescribed did not operate directly upon persons in private life. Whenever the Confederation policies involved such persons, the executive function was accomplished, if at all, only through the awkward intermediary of the state governments. But no sooner had the Philadelphia Convention decided to abandon the Confederation and create a central government endowed with specific legislative powers operating upon individuals than it came face to face with a new necessity: to create a distinct executive invested with an authority continental in scope.

Creation of the Executive Office

The creation of the executive office turned out to be the most perplexing structural problem facing the framers of the Constitution. Again and again they considered a plural executive and only late in their deliberations did they decide finally upon a single executive. Quite early they agreed that Congress should elect the executive, and they did not abandon this plan until the Convention was near adjournment. Shortly before completing their labors they devised the Electoral College as an instrument for electing the president. This device was adopted in lieu of election by Congress, as Gouverneur Morris explained, to avoid "the danger of intrigue and faction if appointment should be made by the legislature" and to acknowledge "the indispensable necessity of making the Executive independent of the legislature."[5]

The Executive a Counterbalance to Congress

The framers of the Constitution intended the executive to be a counterbalance against a too powerful Congress. Their experience with legislative branches in the states had been unhappy. The "omnipotent" state legislatures had run away with state governments in the face of governors who were, as Madison put it, "mere ciphers." They had enacted legislation inimical to the creditor interests so heavily represented at Philadelphia. An unchecked Federal legislature might prove no less dangerous than the "sovereign" state legislatures were. Moreover, if the Federal authority was to be maintained throughout the Union, the chief executive would have to be endowed with adequate powers of his own instead of being merely the agent of the Congress that elected him. That lesson had been learned from the election of governors by state legislatures.

[5] See Max Farrand: "Compromises of the Constitution." *American Historical Review* 9:662, 663.

The President, a Glorified State Governor

In origin, the president of the United States is a glorified state governor. The delegates at Philadelphia scanned the constitutions of the thirteen states and out of their provisions for the state executives synthesized the office of president of the United States. Four states were even using the title "president" to designate their chief executives. The veto clause for the president was taken almost verbatim from the Constitution of Massachusetts; the president's oath of office from that of Pennsylvania; and the power of pardon was an executive function in almost every state, having come down as a heritage from the colonial governor. In every state the chief executive was commander-in-chief. The prototype of the vice-president of the United States is the deputy or lieutenant-governor. In four states he was even then called the vice-president.

Governor Bowdoin of Massachusetts had captured the attention of the Convention through his success in suppressing Shays's Rebellion. His office carried more than average prestige because in Massachusetts the governor was chosen by popular election instead of by the legislature which was the procedure in eight of the thirteen states. The governor of New York was also popularly elected and even more did that office influence the creation of the presidency since the Federal Constitution incorporated the clauses of the New York Constitution dealing with the governor.[6]

Influence of Washington in Shaping the Presidency

It is impossible to say how much less significant the presidential office might have been had not the delegates sat day after day facing in their presiding officer the man who was, by common consent, destined to be its first incumbent. While the office was by no means created for Washington, the character and prestige of this notable statesman must have unconsciously played a part in shaping it. Thus the personality of a trusted leader became a determinant of the nature of the great office while it was still in the process of creation. We shall see that the dignity and good sense with which he conducted the duties of president strengthened the office with enduring precedents and contributed powerfully to making the presidency what it has become in practice.

THE CREATION OF THE CONGRESS

The State Legislatures Provide the Model for Congress

In creating the Congress of the United States the framers produced a composite of existing state legislatures. Only Pennsylvania had a unicameral legislature. "Senate" was the term used for the upper house in Maryland, Massachusetts, New York, North Carolina, New Hampshire, South

[6] See Alexander Johnson: "What the Federal Constitution Owes to the Several States." *New Princeton Review* (1887).

Carolina, and Virginia; and "house of representatives" was used to designate the lower house in Massachusetts, New Hampshire, South Carolina, and Pennsylvania. The senate was rotated by electing a part of it at intervals in Delaware, New York, Pennsylvania, and Virginia. All the details of the impeachment process were found in the constitutions of Delaware, Massachusetts, New Hampshire, New York, Pennsylvania, South Carolina, and Virginia. The entire fifth section of Article I of the Constitution prescribing the administration of the two houses is found in most of the contemporary state constitutions of that day. "Not creative genius," wrote Alexander Johnson, "but wise and discreet selection, was the proper work of the Convention; and its success was due to the clear perception of antecedent failures and successes, and to the self constraint of its members."[7]

The Contribution of the Articles of Confederation

There is practically nothing in the Constitution not due to the persistent aim of the framers to correct the defects of the Articles of Confederation. "The truth is," wrote Madison in the *Federalist*, "that the great principles of the Constitution proposed by the Convention may be considered less as absolutely new, than as an expansion of principles which are found in the Articles of Confederation. . . . If the new Constitution be examined with accuracy and candor, it will be found that the change [*sic*] which it proposes consist much less in the addition of New Powers to the Union, than in the invigoration of its original powers." The "invigoration" was supplied by providing that Congress have the power necessary and proper to the execution of the "original powers." The number of powers in the Articles of Confederation transferred to the Constitution is striking. Among them are the determining of peace and war, the sending and receiving of ambassadors, the making of treaties, the establishment of rules governing captures on land and water, the granting of letters of marque and reprisal, the regulation of the value of money coined, the fixing of standards of weights and measures, the management of Indians affairs, the establishment and regulation of post offices, and the making of rules for regulating land and naval forces.

RATIFICATION OF THE CONSTITUTION

Ratification by State Conventions

"The ratification of Conventions of nine states shall be sufficient for the establishment of this Constitution, between the states so ratifying" reads the provision for validating the new fundamental instrument. This was certainly a revolutionary departure from the unanimous agreement required for amending the then existing Constitution—the Articles of Confederation. There was plausibility in the argument of the framers that state conventions, invested with authority for that specific purpose by the people be authorized to ratify the Constitution instead of state legislatures.

[7] Ibid.

The latter would scarcely have consented to the self-denial that ratification of the Constitution would have required of them in surrendering the important powers to be delegated to Congress, to say nothing of the restrictions placed upon them by the Constitution's list of powers denied the states. The state legislatures rather weighted the representation in favor of ratification by providing that the delegates to the state ratifying conventions be elected on the same basis as the membership of the lower houses of the legislatures. The districting for this purpose grossly overrepresented the coastal communities, and consequently the interior, where the Constitution was unpopular, was unable to exert its full strength in numbers.

The Opposition to Ratification

The Constitution had been framed in the most carefully guarded secrecy. Its publication instantly created a furor of criticism in the hinterland. Beveridge has succinctly stated the reasons for this opposition: " It [the Constitution] was, to the masses, something new, vague, and awful; something to oppress the poor, the weak, the debtor, the settler; something to strengthen and enrich the already strong and opulent, the merchant, the creditor, the financial interests."[8] The opposition promptly focused attention on the imposing list of powers delegated to Congress. They had not, as they put it, overthrown King George only to enthrone King Congress. Shays's Rebels knew well enough that the Constitution had not been framed for their satisfaction, and twenty of them fought against it as delegates in the Massachusetts ratifying convention. One of them, John Holmes, declared that the Constitution gave Congress the power to "institute judicatories" like "that diabolical institution the Inquisition." "Racks," he cried, "and gibbets may be among the most mild instruments of their [Congress's] discipline."[9] A preacher in the backwoods of North Carolina, campaigning for election as a delegate to the ratifying convention, declared that "the proposed Federal city would be a fortified fortress of despotism. This, my friends, will be walled or fortified. Here an army of 50,000 or perhaps 100,000 men will be finally embodied and will sally forth to enslave the people who will be disarmed."[10] One of the audience who attempted to contradict the speaker was almost mobbed. Here was the phobia that forced the adoption of the Second Amendment to the Constitution: "A well-regulated militia being necessary to the security of a free State, the right of the people to keep and bear arms shall not be infringed."

Small States Rush to Ratify

So satisfactory had been the concessions to the small-state group in the Philadelphia Convention that four of them quite promptly ratified the Constitution. Among these four were Delaware, New Jersey, and Georgia,

[8] Albert J. Beveridge: *Life of John Marshall* (Boston, 1916), Vol. I, p. 37.
[9] Ibid., Vol. I, p. 346.
[10] Ibid., Vol. I, p. 291.

and not only did their conventions ratify unanimously but they were the only ones among the thirteen states to give unanimous approval. Indeed so inclined to hesitate were the large states that when the Constitution had been validated by the votes of nine states, only two of them, Pennsylvania and Massachusetts, were ones that could be designated as large. Virginia, the largest of all the states, was the tenth to ratify. Then, unless New York could be persuaded to join, the Union would be geographically separated. The port of New York City gave that state a transcendent importance. Its customs duties alone practically freed the state from further taxation, and up-state agrarians were dead-set against surrendering this precious advantage to the Federal government.

The Federalist Papers

Winning the ratification of New York was a problem in persuasion to challenge the genius of Alexander Hamilton. He met it by collaborating with James Madison and John Jay in producing a series of essays which, under the title of the *Federalist*, stands to this day in American political history a high-water mark of the discussion of public affairs. The *Federalist* papers sought to take advantage of the prevailing popularity of republican government by showing that the Constitution was analogous to the state constitutions and well adapted to the needs of Americans. They argued the absence of an alternative to the Constitution, and undoubtedly the failure of the opposition to produce a substitute for the proposed fundamental instrument handicapped the opponents and contributed to their failure to prevent ratification.

Demand of the Opposition for a Bill of Rights

Although the opponents of the Constitution failed to defeat its ratification, they did succeed in driving some successful bargains with the proponents of the new instrument of government. The popular party had succeeded in having bills of rights incorporated in the Revolutionary state constitutions, and it was impossible to convince them that a bill of rights was not even more necessary in the Constitution of a central government. In vain did friends of the Constitution insist that, in a government of specified powers, it was illogical to deny to such a government what had never been delegated to it. The difficulty was that, to almost everybody except the powerful coastal interests, potential tyranny inhered in the government prescribed by the Constitution. They would not rest until specific prohibitions of powers not to be exercised by Congress were reduced to writing and added to the Constitution as amendments.

The Gentleman's Agreement to a Bill of Rights

The opposition to the Constitution wrung from the proponents a gentleman's understanding that, as the price of permitting the ratification of the new instrument, there would be proposed in the First Congress a number of amendments specifically denying to Congress interference with what were regarded as the ancient fundamental rights of free peoples. Thus Congress was specifically denied legislative power to restrict freedom of religion, speech, press, and assembly. The security of person and property, due process, and other traditional rights of English-speaking peoples were safeguarded with specific guarantees. Embodied in the first eight amendments these have come to be known as the Federal Bill of Rights.

The Bill of Rights Prevented Formation of an Irreconcilable Element

The satisfaction afforded the inhabitants of the interior counties by the addition of the Bill of Rights to the Constitution seems to have been a factor in preventing the formation of an irreconcilable element in the American population. Concerning the government of the Constitution Woodrow Wilson wrote: "Indeed, after its organization, little more is heard of the party of opposition; they disappeared so entirely that one is inclined to think, in looking at the party history of the time, that they had not only been conquered but convinced as well."

The Genesis of Constitution Worship

Let no one assume that the fathers were confident of the permanence of their handiwork. On the one hand, aristocratically minded Alexander Hamilton privately thought the Constitution so inadequate that it "was good only as a step to something better." On the other hand, the Convention's outstanding democrat, Benjamin Franklin, wanted the Constitution ratified in order to give republican government a fair trial, but more than once in the Convention he expressed the conviction that eventually the American people would turn to monarchy.[11] "The generation that framed the Constitution looked upon the document as very imperfect," wrote A. Lawrence Lowell, "but they clung to it tenaciously as the only defense against national dismemberment and in order to make it popular they praised it beyond their own belief in its merits. This effort to force themselves to admire the Constitution was marvelously successful and resulted in the next generation in a worship of the Constitution of which the framers never dreamed."[12]

SUMMARY

By rare good fortune the state legislatures had selected as delegates to the Constitutional Convention at Philadelphia some of the ablest statesmen of recorded history. Among the outstanding contributors to the framing of the Constitution, James Madison was preeminent not only because of a profound knowledge of political history but, even more, because of a penetrating insight into the mystery of social processes. In contrast with the inspiring idealism of the Declaration of Independence the Constitution represented a conservative reaction. The stark realism

[11] See Madison's *Notes*, June 2, 4.
[12] A. Lawrence Lowell: *Greater European Governments* (Cambridge, Mass., 1925), p. 174n.

of the framers was a consequence of the post-Revolutionary disillusionment of the financial, mercantile, and greater planting interests because of the Confederation Congress's absolute lack of authority to lay taxes and regulate commerce. These were the interests whose representatives as delegates shaped the Constitution after radical leaders had refused to accept appointments as delegates.

Arriving early, the notable galaxy of Virginia delegates drew up a set of proposals that became the initial agenda of the Convention, since known as the Virginia or Large State Plan. In the course of the Convention's deliberations the Virginia Plan was countered by the New Jersey or Small State Plan. In the course of the debates a deadlock between the proponents of the two plans was resolved by "The Great Compromise" derived from the Connecticut Plan whereupon the Convention proceeded smoothly to its close.

The Constitution turned out to be a shrewd synthesis of some of the most practical provisions of state constitutions. The outstanding change from the Articles of Confederation was the delegation to Congress of a list of specific powers to enact laws bearing directly upon individuals and the creation of a chief executive to see to the faithful execution of them.

The failure of the framers to provide a bill of rights proved so provocative of opposition that it was allayed only by the promise to provide a bill of rights by amendments. Whether enough of the states would ratify to validate the Constitution pended for many months, but in the end all thirteen states did ratify. The new government authorized by the Constitution began functioning in the spring of 1789.

CHAPTER IV

THE CONSTITUTION ANALYZED

A DUAL SYSTEM ESTABLISHED

The Federal System

THE FRAMERS, through the Constitution, prescribed a dual system of government to which they assigned the term "Federal." It consists on the one hand of a complete set of national governmental agencies—legislative, executive, and judicial—acting directly upon persons and exercising the powers delegated by the Federal Constitution to the national government. Paralleling this system in each state is another complete set of legislative, executive, and judicial organs acting upon the persons within that state and exercising the reserved powers of the state, that is, powers of the state not delegated to the Federal government or denied to the state by the Constitution. Each of these two systems within its own sphere is presumed to be the master of its own powers. The consequent dualism of this American governmental arrangement is America's peculiar contribution to the science and art of politics. This was perceived by Alexis de Tocqueville who made comprehensive surveys of American institutions in the 1830's. "This Constitution," he wrote, "which may at first sight be confused with the federal constitutions that have preceded it, rests in truth upon a wholly novel theory, which may be considered as a great discovery in modern political science. In all the confederations that preceded the American Constitution of 1789, the states allied for a common object agreed to obey the injunction of a federal government; but, they reserved to themselves the right of ordaining and enforcing the execution of the laws of the Union. The American states which combined in 1789 agreed that the Federal government should not only dictate the laws, but execute its own enactments. In both cases the right is the same, but the exercise of the right is different; and this difference produced the most momentous consequences."[1]

The Distribution of Powers under the Constitution

The Constitution so distributes the powers in the American governmental system that they may be classified under five heads:

First: the specifically delegated powers of the Federal government such, for example, as taxation, regulation of commerce, declaration of war, and regulation of currency. Most of these are found in the list of eighteen clauses of Article I, Section 8, of the Constitution. The framers evidently assumed that these were powers of sufficiently general concern to be exercised by the national government. However one cannot find listed in the Constitution all the powers exercised by Congress. By a liberal interpretation of the expressly granted powers Congress has derived many implied powers and legislates on the basis of them. For example, the first Congress chartered a Bank of the United States thereby exercising a power nowhere listed in the Constitution but derived from the express powers to borrow money, collect taxes, regulate trade, and provide for the common defense as Hamilton reasoned it out at the time and the Supreme Court long afterward accepted it.

Second: the reserved powers of the states, which include the vast body of police powers exercised by American state and local governments. These are sometimes designated "internal police," that is, internal as to each state. By police power is meant the power of government to place restraints on individual freedom and property rights in order to protect the public safety, health, and morals, or to promote education, good order, and public convenience.

Each state has complete legislative, executive, and judicial power over matters relating to its domestic affairs. Herein fall most of the laws that affect American citizens, such, for example, as those concerning ordinary crimes, torts, education, sanitation, and numerous other matters. In contrast with the powers delegated to the Federal government, the reserved powers of the states are not specified. They constitute a continent of unexplored powers the potential extent of which cannot be calculated, and of course an attempted enumeration would prove a futile undertaking. According to circumstances state legislatures will utilize further these reserved powers.

Third: concurrent powers. These are powers common to state and national government and consequently they are not exclusive of the powers named above but overlap them. Outstanding among the concurrent powers are taxation and the power to use coercion in executing other powers. Consequently they are means to the great ends of government, either national or state, rather than ends in themselves. For example, the

---

[1] Alexis de Tocqueville: *Democracy in America,* edited by Phillips Bradley (New York, 1945), Vol. I, p. 157.

maintenance of schools and highways are direct purposes of government while taxation and coercion are less direct in that they are means for attaining the purposes of government. Governments do not exist to tax and to coerce.

Fourth: the powers denied to the national government. These are powers forbidden by the sovereign—the people—through the denial to Congress of the power to pass ex-post-facto laws, bills of attainder, violations of due process, and the numerous forbidden subjects for congressional legislation listed in the first eight amendments to the Constitution.

Fifth: the powers specifically denied to the states. Here again the sovereign has forbidden the states to exercise certain legislative powers by denying the right of state governments to issue bills of credit, to impair obligation of contracts, and to undertake other matters listed in the body of the Constitution and in certain amendments adopted since the Civil War.

THE POPULAR BASIS OF THE CONSTITUTION

The Doctrine of the Social Compact

The generation that saw the birth of the Constitution had strong convictions concerning the nature and basis of political authority and were intolerant of what they conceived to be infractions of it. By and large their political thought followed the pattern of John Locke's exposition as presented in his *Two Treatises of Government* published in 1689 to justify the English Revolution of 1688. This does not signify that the common man in America had read Locke's heavy political disquisitions but rather that, as someone has said: "Most Americans were disciples of Locke even though they had never heard of him." Locke's conception was that, before governments originated, men had lived in a "state of nature," that is, as Locke put it, "a state of perfect freedom to order their actions and dispose of their possessions and persons as they think fit, within the bounds of the law of nature, without asking leave or depending upon the will of any other man." In this state they possessed "natural rights" to life, liberty and property but were under "natural law" which, in the absence of constituted government, the individual ascertained and enforced in person whenever his rights were infringed. The consequent confusion was assumed to have induced men to end this "state of nature" through a "social compact" by means of which they deliberately agreed among themselves to establish a political society—that is to say, the state. Thereupon they proceeded to create a government consisting of a set of organs or agencies to which they delegated limited powers. The principal or sovereign organ, the legislature, was invested with the power to determine the laws of nature while the executive, separated from the legislature, was to enforce what the legislature determined.

Revolutionary State Constitutions Social Compacts

However fantastic and at variance with the historical development of governments Locke's theory of the origin of the state may have been, it nevertheless captured the imagination of Revolutionary Americans because it seemed made to order as an explanation of their political experience. Their popular assemblies had somehow come to be separated from the governor and they did not need Locke to tell them that the legislature was the supreme organ of government, since their assemblies seemed to demonstrate this supremacy. When the Revolution terminated British authority, the patriots assumed that they were thrown back into the "state of nature." They thought of themselves as emerging from this state or condition by re-enacting the drama of the Social Compact in establishing their states. Their state constitutions were to them social compacts reduced to writing and the governments thereby established had only the limited powers the sovereign people of each state saw fit to delegate to them.

Only Republican Government Possible

No matter what kind of government some of the extra-conservative members of the Philadelphia Convention such as Hamilton may have desired to establish by the Constitution, every delegate recognized that none but republican government would be tolerated. All understood monarchy to be utterly out of the question. Madison made this clear in a statement published forty years after the framing of the Constitution in commenting on a fantastic plan in the early 1780's to crown Washington king. "I have always believed," he wrote, "that if General Washington had yielded to a usurping ambition he would have found an insuperable obstacle in the incorruptibility of a sufficient portion of those under his command. I am not less sure that General Washington would have spurned a scepter if within his grasp than I am that it was out of his reach if he had secretly sighed for it."[2]

When is Government Republican in Form?

It would be difficult to improve on Madison's exposition of the phrase "republican in form" as it is used in the Constitution. "It is evident," he wrote in the thirty-ninth number of the *Federalist*, "that no other form would be reconcilable with the genius of the people of America [and] with the fundamental principles of the Revolution. . . . It is sufficient for such a government that the persons administering it be appointed either directly or indirectly by the people." Then Madison proceeded to demonstrate that the Constitution establishes that kind of government. "The House of Representatives like that of at least one branch of all the state legislatures, is elected immediately by the great body of people. The Senate, like the present Congress [that of the Confederation], and the Senate of Maryland derives its appointment indirectly from the people.

[2] Quoted in Charles A. Beard: *The Republic* (New York, 1943), p. 25.

The President is indirectly derived from the choice of the people according to the example of most of the states. Even the judges with all the other officers of the Union will, as in the several states, be the choice, though a remote choice of the people. The duration of the appointments is equally conformable to the republican standard, and to the model of state Constitutions."

Popular Sovereignty and Limited Government

As disciples of Locke the framers based the government of the Constitution upon what they conceived to be the popular sovereignty of the Social Compact. With rare exceptions the delegates at Philadelphia thought of themselves as representing twelve sovereign peoples rather than one. It is impossible to get a clear conception of the distribution of powers between the Federal government and the states without comprehending the general pattern of thought of the framers. To them the states were the original depositories of practically all possible governmental powers whence were drawn for the most part those with which the new Federal government was invested. When the states, through the making of their Constitutions, emerged from the thirteen "states of nature" into which they conceived the Revolution to have thrown them, they were presumed thereby to have made the transformation into thirteen sovereign bodies politic possessing, of course, all the possible governmental powers of independent sovereign nations. The inherent governmental powers of these states then constituted the reservoirs from which were mainly drawn the powers transferred to the new Federal government.[3] It was a corollary of the doctrine of popular sovereignty that the government of the Constitution was limited in its powers to those that had been delegated by the fundamental instrument.

The Delegation of State Powers to the Federal Government

The Constitution specified the powers to be delegated to the Federal government. By their ratification of the Constitution the states effected the transfer of powers derived from them. By and large the Federal government had received by the delegation what the states had lost. But the states still retained all the original powers they had not lost either by delegation to the Federal government or by the Constitution's list of powers denied to the states. The retained or undelegated powers are known as reserved or residual powers of the states. They constitute a vast sphere of power as yet by no means completely explored by state legislatures. The framers of the Constitution assumed that the mere implication of this res-

---

[3] Not every power of the government established by the Constitution could be derived by a transfer of powers from the states. Since the states had unitary instead of federal governments, they could not have provided patterns for the peculiar devices needed by the federation. These had to be invented instead of being transferred through delegation from the states. Illustrative of these new devices are the complicated systems of amendment of the Constitution and of electing the president by means of presidential electors.

ervation to the states of the undelegated powers would be universally satisfactory. But the agrarians of the back country and others protested so
vigorously that what had been only implied had to be set down in the
clear-cut statement of the Tenth Amendment which says: "The powers
not delegated to the United States by the Constitution, nor prohibited by
it to the states, are reserved to the states respectively or to the people."

Powers Denied to the States

The specified list of powers denied to the states by the Constitution was
inserted because of the excesses of state legislatures that had largely
induced the framing of the Constitution. Thus states were not to enter into
any treaty, alliance, or confederation; coin money, emit bills of credit,
make anything but gold or silver legal tender; pass bills of attainder or ex-
post-facto laws or laws impairing the obligation of contract; or grant titles
of nobility. Except with the consent of Congress states were not to lay
imposts and exposts, or tonnage duties, maintain an army or navy in time
of peace, enter into compacts with other states or foreign powers, or make
war unless invaded or in imminent danger of invasion. Amendments have
added to the Constitutional restrictions upon the states. The Thirteenth
Amendment deprived the states of all determinations as to slavery by abolishing it. By the Fourteenth Amendment states were deprived of the determination of citizenship and forbidden to abridge the privileges and
immunities of citizens of the United States; deprive any person of life, liberty, or property without due process of law; or deny to any person the
equal protection of the laws. By the Fifteenth and Nineteenth Amendments respectively, the states were forbidden to limit suffrage on the basis
of race, color, or previous condition of servitude, or of sex.

National versus State Sovereignty

While the Constitution contains no trace of the kind of clause which, in
the Articles of Confederation, specifically declared the states to be sovereign, the idea was so deep-seated that it persisted in some sections for
generations. An opposite pattern of interpretation held that the American
people as a nation constituted the sovereign that created the Constitution.
Heated controversies arose between nationalist and states' rights schools
of constitutional interpretation, one of which culminated in the Civil War.
Chief Justice Marshall, giving the opinion of the Court in the case of
McCulloch v. Maryland, as early as 1819 set forth what was in time to
become the securely established constitutional interpretation of this matter. Referring to what he considered the erroneous arguments of the attorneys representing the State of Maryland, he said: "The powers of the general government, it has been said, are delegated by the States, who alone
are truly sovereign, and must be exercised in subordination to the States
who alone possess supreme dominion. It would be difficult to sustain this

proposition. . . ." From this Constitutional "heresy" Marshall turned to state the now generally accepted judicial pattern of interpretation of the basis of Federal authority. "The government proceeds directly from the people," he continued. "It is ordained and established by the people. . . . The government of the Union then is emphatically and truly a government of the people. In form and substance it emanates from them, its powers are granted by them and are to be exercised directly on them and for their benefit."[4]

THE GREAT ORGANS OF THE FEDERAL GOVERNMENT

The Delegated Powers Mainly Legislative

As disciples of Locke, the framers acted on the assumption that "the legislature is the depository of the Supreme Will of Society," as Roger Sherman expressed it in the Philadelphia Convention.[5] They accordingly assigned to the Congress an imposing list of specific powers, practically *the* powers of the Federal government. These are listed in the famous eighteen clauses of the eighth section of Article I. Outstanding among them are powers of taxing, regulating commerce, declaring war, creating armies and navies, establishing post offices, coining money and regulating its value, and creating inferior courts. These are permissive powers and Congress may use them at its discretion. So completely do the motions of government depend upon the initiative of Congress that it is indeed the depository of the supreme will of American society.

The Congress

The Congress, created and invested with the legislative power of the Constitution, consists of a Senate and a House of Representatives. The former has a membership of two senators from each state, elected for terms of six years, originally by the legislatures of their respective states but now directly by the states' voters. The House of Representatives consists of members elected in even-numbered years for two-year terms by the voters, with representation from each state proportionate to its population as determined by the decennial census directed by the Constitution. No legislation can be valid that has not been approved by both houses preliminary to its submission to the president, whose approval is also necessary unless Congress overcomes his veto by two-thirds majorities in both houses.

Constitutional Restrictions on the Congress

Because the framers had seen the state legislatures of the 1780's run away with state governments, they were fearful that the Congress might do

[4] Wheaton 316 (1819).
[5] *Documents on the Formation of the United States,* edited by C. C. Tansill, 69th Congress, 1st Session, House Document No. 396, p. 396.

likewise with the Federal government. Even the great liberal James Wilson had declared in the Constitutional Convention that state legislatures had come to believe that "the exercise of rights by either the executive or the judiciary is a breach of their prerogative and an outrage to their dignity."[6] So the framers, not content with the mere implication that Congress's powers were limited to the specific ones delegated, introduced the extra precautions of a list of powers denied to Congress. Thus the Congress may enact no bill of attainder, ex-post-facto law, or export duty. It may not favor certain ports over others, or suspend the privilege of the writ of habeas corpus except in time of public danger. Outside the original Constitution, but no less restrictive of the Congress, are the first eight amendments forbidding any Federal legislation that would abridge freedom of religion, the press, speech and assembly, jury trial, due process, and other immemorial rights of English-speaking peoples peculiarly cherished by the generation that had experienced the American Revolution.

Necessity of a Distinct Executive

The so-called "necessary and proper" clause of the Constitution rendered imperative the creation of a distinct though not necessarily separate executive branch. At the end of the list of specific powers of Congress was placed the provision: "Congress shall have power to make all laws which shall be necessary and proper for carrying into execution the foregoing powers and all other powers vested by this Constitution in the Government of the United States, or in any department or officer thereof." Here is the clause that brings into relief the revolutionary change from the Articles of Confederation under which Congress depended upon the states for whatever of its policies required any coercion of private persons. Now Congress was empowered to create whatever agencies it considered "necessary and proper" for carrying into execution the powers of the Federal government. Deciding about the direction of these agencies proved to be a perplexing problem to the framers, but after considering a plural executive they established a single executive styled the President of the United States. It was decided that he be chosen by special electors, consisting of as many in each state as there were senators and representatives in Congress and chosen in whatever manner the respective state legislatures might direct. Custom combined with state legislation has converted this extraordinarily artificial "Electoral College" into a medium for the practically direct election of the president by the American voters. The chief executive takes care that the laws are faithfully executed, signs or vetoes acts of Congress, negotiates treaties, appoints all but certain "inferior officers" by, and with, the advice and consent of the Senate, and serves as commander-in-chief of the Army, Navy and Air Forces.

[6] J. Elliot: *Debates in the Several State Conventions on the Adoption of the Federal Constitution* (2nd ed., Washington, D.C., 1854), Vol. I, p. 503.

Necessity of a National Judiciary

The Constitution prescribed a distinct Federal judiciary. This was inescapable in a dual system of both state and national governments with the bounds of their spheres of power uncertain enough to induce cases and controversies that could not easily be adjudicated by state courts. Conflicts are inevitable over state and national constitutions, state and national statutes, the exercise of the powers of state and national executives and administrators, and the jurisdictions of state and national courts. Even if no controversies arose between the two political branches of our dual system, the cases arising under the Federal Constitution, statutes, and treaties would require a Federal judiciary. The Constitution meets the necessities by vesting the judicial power in a Supreme Court and in such inferior courts as the Congress may from time to time ordain and establish. It assigns to these courts jurisdiction in distinctly Federal cases, in cases involving interstate differences, and in state cases involving conflict with the Federal Constitution, statutes, and treaties.

Limitations of the Judiciary

Such expressions as the "supremacy of the judiciary" or the "sovereignty of the Supreme Court" should be accepted with caution. They would doubtless have astonished the framers, and their publication in 1787–8 might have prevented ratification. They are based on the fact that cases in any jurisdiction—national, state, municipal, county, or township— that involve a question of Federal power may finally be settled by the Supreme Court of the United States. However, we shall see later that the Federal courts are the creatures of Congress, which may alter the size of the Supreme Court and alter or abolish the inferior courts it has created. Congress also has the undoubted constitutional power to give and to take away the entire jurisdiction both original and appellate of all Federal courts below the Supreme Court and could constitutionally deprive the Supreme Court of any of its appellate jurisdiction leaving it only its meager original jurisdiction. Whatever "sovereignty" the judiciary may have is due rather to the high prestige that the conduct and character of its personnel can command rather than to any power specifically assigned it by the Constitution. The "fathers" entertained no illusions of the "supremacy of the judiciary." Hamilton, in the seventy-eighth number of the *Federalist*, pointed to the judiciary's lack of control of the "sword or purse," or of the "wealth or strength of society," which "proves incontestably that the judiciary is beyond comparison the weakest of the three branches of power." This opinion of Hamilton was accepted by the Supreme Court and paraphrased thus in the statement of its opinion in United States v. Lee: " . . . . their power and influence rests solely upon the appeal for the assertion and protection of rights guaranteed by the Constitution and by the laws of the land and on the confidence reposed in the soundness of their decisions and the purity of their motives."[7]

CHECKS AND BALANCES

Separation of Powers

That the three great functions of government—legislative, executive, and judicial—must each be vested in a separate organ or department seemed to most Americans in the 1780's as undebatable as the laws of nature. "If the people are sufficiently enlightened to see all the dangers that surround them," wrote John Adams, "they will always be represented by a distinct personage to manage the whole executive power; a distinct Senate, to be the guardian of property against levelers for the purposes of plunder, to be a repository of the national tradition of public maxims, customs, and manners, and to be controllers in turn of both kings and ministers on one side and representatives of the people on the other when either discover a disposition to do wrong; and a distinct House of Representatives, to be the guardian of the public purse and to protect the people in turn against both kings and nobles."[8]

Separation of Powers Merely Implicit in the Constitution.

The framers knew that an absolute separation of powers was impracticable. When the Constitution was published they even had to defend it against the criticism that the principle was nowhere stated in the Constitution. Separation of powers, however, is to be inferred from the opening sentence of each of the Constitution's first three articles: "All legislative powers herein granted shall be vested in a Congress of the United States, . . . " "The Executive power shall be vested in a President of the United States of America, . . ." "The judicial power of the United States shall be vested in one Supreme Court, and in such inferior courts as the Congress may from time to time ordain and establish." Each of these three branches may exercise their specified powers and whatever other powers are necessary to the performance of these specified powers, but no branch can redelegate its assigned powers. This is equivalent to saying that what the sovereign, the people, has decreed as to the agency that is to exercise a delegated power, neither Congress, the president, nor any other official may shift the power to another agency. The Supreme Court has decided that no one branch may exercise all the powers of another.[9]

Separation of Powers not Complete

While each of the three great departments of the Federal government performs chiefly its appropriate major function, to say simply that the legislature legislates, the executive executes, and the judiciary adjudicates is scarcely even an approximation of the facts. It would be more correct to say

[7] 106 U.S. 196 (1882).

[8] John Adams: *Works* (Boston, 1856), Vol. II, pp. 117–18.

[9] Schechter Poultry Corporation *v.* U.S., 256 U. S. 495 (1935).

that each of the three great departments or branches of the Federal government—the legislative, the executive, and the judicial branches—performs some of the three great functions of government, that is, legislative, executive, and judicial functions. For example, while the Congress in the main legislates, it also performs such judicial functions as determining the qualifications and deciding disputed elections of its members; the House of Representatives presents articles of impeachment, and the Senate sits as a court upon them. Congress tries its own members for misconduct and executes its own judgments on them, and the Senate performs the executive function of confirming the president's nominations. The president, in addition to his peculiarly executive duty "to take care that the laws be faithfully executed," is vested by Congress with the legislative power of making rules, while his department is assigned administrative commissions invested with legislative and judicial powers. While the judiciary in the main adjudicates cases and controversies, it also has the administration of its own branch so completely in its hands that it performs the legislative function of determining its own rules in handling cases and executes its internal affairs through its own officials. Moreover, just to the extent that checks and balances are introduced, the separation of powers is abandoned since the principle generally involves one branch of the government performing some function of another branch. For example, the president's veto is a negative vote—and a powerful one on a piece of legislation.

Separation of Powers Compared with the Union of Powers

Contrasting with the principles of separated powers and its corollary of checks and balances is the principle of the union of powers. This latter principle is illustrated by the structure and functioning of the British ministerial system. The principal ministers are not only heads of the great executive departments but are at the same time parliamentary leaders. On the one hand they must assume the responsibility of appearing in Parliament of which they are members and promoting legislative measures that the Cabinet has selected for passage. Usually the minister has been selected because he had already attained legislative leadership in Parliament and is consequently skilled in parliamentary procedures. In the normal performance of his duties he would, then, from time to time, address Parliament in promoting the measures of his department, and he might be required to answer questions from members of Parliament about matters pertaining to his department and his performance of duties as its administrative head. On the other hand, it is his duty to see that the work of his department is being performed. Collectively the ministry is responsible to Parliament for the satisfactory performance of its dual role, and if the dissatisfaction with either its legislative program or the performance of its executive functions grows to the strength of an adverse vote on an important matter by the House of Commons, the ministry must either resign or appeal to the country through the dissolution of Parliament and the holding of a general election to decide the pending issue. The American cabinet member is responsible to the president for the performance of his administrative duties, and only the president can peremptorily dismiss him. The Constitution forbids his being a member of Congress and an inflexible custom denies him all opportunity to promote, by appearance in Congress, the measures he desires.

Checks and Balances

Americans in the 1780's had not been more impressed by the doctrine of separation of powers than by its corollary of checks and balances as expounded by the French philosopher Montesquieu in his *Spirit of Laws*. They felt as axiomatic truth his statements: "It is the experience of the ages that every man who attains power is prone to abuse it. He goes forward until he finds his limit. If power is not to be abused then it is necessary, in the nature of things, that power must be made a check to power." This seemed to be precisely the experience of Americans with their colonial governors, whom they had checked by their elective assemblies. They would have known this concept even if it had never been publicized by any political philosopher. As early as 1742, half a dozen years before the publication of Montesquieu's masterpiece, the Massachusetts House of Representatives explicitly expressed the doctrine in rejecting Governor Shirley's demand for a permanent salary on the ground that "it would lessen the just weight of the other two branches of the government, which ought ever to be maintained and preserved especially since the governor has so great authority and check upon them."[10]

In accordance with Montesquieu's dictum that "power must be checked with power" the framers wove into the Federal government an intricate system of "checks and balances." This expression signifies that an action by one organ of the government may require for its validation the approval of another organ. Thus the passage of an act by one house of the Congress is futile unless the other also passes it. Even then the further approval of the president is required. However, if he disapproves the measure, his veto is suspensive since by a two-thirds vote of both houses of the Congress it can still become law. Even when Congress and the president agree upon a measure, the courts may still refuse to recognize its validity on the ground that it contravenes the Constitution and is consequently "unconstitutional." But the courts are checked by the fact they must depend for the enforcement of their judgments upon the executive branch, by which their judgments may be ignored, as Jackson is reputed to have ignored one of Marshall's decisions. So absolute is Congress's control of the appellate jurisdiction of the Supreme Court that it can and sometimes does snatch a pending case from the Supreme Court. In the case of all but "inferior officers" the president's power of appointment is checked by the requirement of Senate confirmation of his nominations. The treaties he negotiates require for their validity the "advice and consent" of the Senate. Congress

[10] W. S. Carpenter: "The Separation of Powers in the Eighteenth Century." *American Political Science Review* (1928), 22:37.

holds the power of impeachment over all executive and judicial officers and, through the power of the purse, has practically the power of life and death over the functions of the government.

Checks and Balances Tempered by Mutual Considerations

Checks and balances may seem to operate in a way to stall, oftener than they might check, the functioning of government. Certainly the system does not function like the "hair-trigger" ministerial system. However, when a definite public consensus as to a public policy once develops, the check and balance system does not prevent or long delay the passage and execution of appropriate legislation. This was demonstrated by the promptness with which Congress responded to public demands for passage of the Interstate Commerce Law of 1887 and the Sherman Anti-Trust Law of 1890. Whatever its merits, the Taft-Hartley Labor Act of 1947 was in response to what appeared to be a strong public demand. The check and balance system, functioning mainly in the American states, established manhood suffrage in only a fraction of the time required under the British ministerial system. When a public mandate as to a new policy is clear, bills to carry out the mandate develop in both houses, and differences between them are composed in the Conference Committee consisting of representatives of the two houses. Nor is the presidential veto to be evaluated merely by counting the bills that the president's rejection has kept off the statute book. It is impossible to say how many presidential vetoes Congress has avoided by heeding the president's objections or known desire as to the form of emerging legislation. This is checking without stalling. The president will not often send a nomination to the Senate without ascertaining in advance the chance of its confirmation. Nor is he likely to waste time negotiating a treaty without some idea as to its reception in the Senate.

Checks and Balances Modified by Political Parties

The rise of national parties was unforeseen by the framers of the Constitution, and the functioning of these parties has modified and considerably reduced the possible friction of checks and balances. American major parties on a national scale have grown out of the necessity of nation-wide organization of those influential interests that desire to elect a president. The stake of a presidential election is the control of the presidential office with its appointing power, its veto power in legislation, its direction of administrative agencies, its leadership in legislation, and the enormous prestige of the presidential office. But a party that has elected only the president is checkmated until it has also a majority in Congress. Moreover, the control of only one house is not enough. When a party has a majority of both houses and has elected a president possessing qualities of party leadership, it is possible to integrate the functioning of the executive and legislative branches of the government as Woodrow Wilson and the two Roosevelts did early in their administrations. No matter how non-partisan the judiciary is presumed to be, the Senate in scrutinizing presidential nominees to the Federal bench is not utterly unmindful of the party affiliation of judges. Only by analysis of the check and balance system against the background of political parties can one obtain a realistic interpretation of how it really operates.

The Supreme Law of the Land

Though doubtless the most important part, the Constitution is only the first of three parts of the "Supreme Law" of the land as may be seen in the clause which declares: "This Constitution and the Laws of the United States which shall be made in pursuance thereof, and all Treaties made, or which shall be made under the authority of the United States shall be the Supreme Law of the Land, and the Judges in every state shall be bound thereby, anything in the Constitution or Laws of any state to the contrary notwithstanding." Evidently laws made in pursuance of the Constitution are just as "Supreme" as the Constitution, that is to say, not in any sense less valid than the Constitution. The same may be said of treaties made "under the authority of the United States." That which gives the practically obligatory force of "Supreme Law" to these three parts is the fact that the judges in every state from the justice of peace through the hierarchy of a state's courts up to the justices of its supreme court are obligated by oath to disregard the constitution and statutes of their own state when they find them contravening the "Supreme Law of the Land." State judges who choose to treat lightly this obligation may find their prestige damaged by having their judgments reversed upon appeals to the Federal courts where the Supreme Law is jealously safeguarded and vigorously maintained.

SUMMARY

The Constitution established a dual system with Federal and state governments, each in its own sphere, master of its powers exercised by means of separate and parallel organs of government. Specified delegated powers are vested in the Federal government with unspecified powers left to the states except for certain powers definitely denied to them. The Federal government is republican in form since its officers are chosen either directly or indirectly by the people. The myth of the social compact enabled the framers to conceive of the Constitution as an expression of the sovereign will, and eventually it became an accepted doctrine of constitutional law that the national government is a creature of the American people in a collective sense.

The delegated powers are mainly powers of Congress, but the framers specifically forbade Congress certain powers, and the Bill of Rights of the first eight amendments added to this list of restrictions. The clause empowering Congress to make laws necessary and proper for carrying into execution the Federal powers authorized the creation of executive machinery over which is the chief executive. Now that there are national statutes bearing directly on individuals Congress is authorized to set up a system of Federal courts headed by a Supreme Court.

The prevailing theory and practice in the states in 1787 required a governmental organization of three grand divisions exercising respectively legislative, executive, and judicial powers. The framers, however, modified this separation of powers by checks and balances in order that no single branch might get the upper hand as had happened in many of the states. Finally, citizens and officers of every level of government, national, state, and local, are subject to the Supreme Law of the Land—the Constitution, statutes, and treaties of the United States.

CHAPTER V

THE GROWTH OF THE CONSTITUTION

The Constitution in Its Broadest Sense

WHEN an American uses the term "the Constitution" he usually has in mind the written fundamental instrument of the Federal government, framed at Philadelphia together with its amendments. This is, of course, a perfectly proper use of the word. The student of government must, however, also be familiar with that other meaning of the term "constitution" comprehensive enough in its scope to be applicable to governments of every kind and description, including those governments that have no written constitution whatever. Of this all-inclusive sense Edward M. Sait has written: "A constitution may be defined as the sum of laws and practices which regulate the fundamental concerns of government."[1] A classic comment on this broader meaning of "constitution" is that of the late Judge T. M. Cooley: "We may think we have the Constitution all before us; but for practical purposes the Constitution is that which the government in its several departments and the people in the performance of their duties as citizens recognize and respect as such, and nothing else is. . . ." This, of course, would comprise far more than the Constitution of 1787 and its amendments.

Elements of the Constitution Today

In so far as our Constitution consists of "the sum total of the laws and practices that regulate the fundamental concerns of government," it stands today as the aggregate of five principal elements: *first*, the Constitution framed at Philadelphia in the summer of 1787; *second*, twenty-two amendments to the Constitution; *third*, the statutes enacted by Congress, particularly those dealing with the organization of the government and the

[1] Edward M. Sait: *Government and Politics of France* (Yonkers-on-the-Hudson, 1920), p. 17.

powers assigned to the agencies Congress has created; *fourth*, the monumental decisions of the Supreme Court affecting the powers and operation of the government; *fifth*, the innumerable civic habits and established governmental usages by which Americans from the humblest citizens to the most important public officials achieve the political purposes of the "Great Society" that constitutes the United States of America.

FORMAL AMENDMENT

Unanimous Ratification of Amendments Discarded

The interests that promoted the making of the Constitution had been so frustrated in their purposes by the requirement of the unanimous vote of the states for amendments to the Articles of Confederation that they reduced the requirement for amending the Constitution to only a three-fourths majority. Those who protest today that the framers deliberately introduced too difficult a process of amendment should remember that they were criticized in their day for relaxing the previous requirement of unanimity. In sheer truth the framers had introduced an easier method of amendment than that prevailing under the Articles of Confederation. Yet the process remains, as Marshall put it, "unwieldy and cumbrous." Incidentally we shall see that this cumbrousness has induced a shift to broad judicial interpretation in order to keep the Constitution more nearly abreast of the march of events. Thus, instead of changing the letter of the Constitution by amendment, the Supreme Court accomplishes the same end by discovering in the letter already there the meaning required to carry out the great functions of the Federal government.

The Amending Process

Whenever both houses of the Congress by a two-thirds vote of at least a quorum[2] propose an amendment, it becomes a part of the Constitution when ratified by the legislatures of three-fourths of the states or by conventions of three-fourths of the states. Congress's power of proposing amendments is exclusive of the president's approval despite the fact that President Lincoln inadvertently signed the Thirteenth Amendment. The Supreme Court decided that the requirement in the Constitution of Ohio that the state legislature's ratification be subject to a referendum was invalid since the Constitution of the United States designates the legislature or a state convention for that purpose.[3] Ratification by a state must be forthcoming within a reasonable time after submission of the amendment to the states.[4] A state's approval of an amendment is final and may not later be changed to rejection, but a state may reconsider a rejection of a proposed amendment and change to ratification.[5]

[2] National Prohibition Cases, 253 U.S. 350 (1920).
[3] Hawke v. Smith, 253 U.S. 221 (1920).
[4] Dillon v. Gloss, 256 U.S. 368 (1921).
[5] Coleman et al. v. Miller et al., 71 Pac. (2nd) 518 (Kans. 1937).

Is the Amending Process too Difficult?

If a bottleneck exists in the amending process the bottleneck is Congress, which has submitted to the states only twenty-six of the several thousands of proposed amendments introduced in Congress since the adoption of the Constitution. This may signify that, by the time public opinion has crystallized sufficiently to get two-thirds of both houses of Congress to propose an amendment, the state legislatures are generally ready to ratify it. At any rate only five of the twenty-six amendments submitted to the states have failed to be added to the Constitution, and only one, the so-called "Child Labor Amendment," has failed in the last three-quarters of a century. During the two long periods when no amendments were added to the Constitution—the sixty-one years from 1804 to 1865 and the forty-three years from 1870 to 1913—arguments were advanced that the amending process was too difficult. Early in the present century it was seriously doubted whether the Constitution would ever again be amended. But the adoption of half a dozen amendments in the twenty years from 1913 to 1933 has made it impossible to interest the public in relaxing the process of amendment. This period had just come to a close when Alvin Johnson wrote: "The intolerable rigidity of the American governmental system, the absolute sacredness of private property, and the inviolability of contracts is a myth. There is no insuperable obstacle to the attaining, by regular political means, to any institutional reorganization which a good majority of us really believe to be necessary."[6]

The Amending Power Unlimited

Until the submission to the states of the amendment repealing the Eighteenth, or Prohibition, Amendment, in 1933, only the method of ratification by state legislatures had been employed. The shift to the alternative method of ratification by state conventions whose delegates had been elected for that specific purpose, which the Constitution authorizes Congress to substitute, was undoubtedly due to widespread criticism of the wartime adoption of the Eighteenth Amendment by legislatures without, it was claimed, a proper preliminary test of public opinion and in the absence of millions of voters in the armed services. Now and then some uninformed person is shocked by what he condemns as a radical or unconstitutional proposal to convene a constitutional convention for a general revision of the Constitution. This, however, is specifically authorized by the alternative method of initiating changes set forth in Article V, providing that Congress "on the application of the legislatures of two-thirds of the several states, shall call a convention for proposing amendments." The only prescribed limitation whatever on the amending power is that "no state shall, without its consent, be deprived of its equal suffrage [representation] in the Senate." As the consequence of a strange but futile set of arguments advanced against the "constitutionality" of the Eighteenth Amendment,

[6] Alvin Johnson: "The Coming Revolution." *Yale Review* (1934), 23:649–61.

the Supreme Court in the Prohibition Cases seems to have determined definitely that an amendment cannot be invalidated on the grounds that it is not "germane" to the Constitution, that it tends to destroy the dual form of government, or that it changes the protection of personal liberty.[7] Evidently the American people can use the amending process to do anything they choose with the Constitution and can even abolish it. Any other idea would be repugnant to the concept of the sovereignty of the people inherent in the political ideology of the fathers no less, it is presumed, than in that of the children. Because of this unlimited power to change the Constitution E. S. Corwin has said: "As a law it derives its force and effect from the present generation of American citizens, and should, therefore, be interpreted in the light of present conditions and with a view to meeting present problems."[8]

Inviolability of the People's Undelegated Powers

Since the first ten amendments were a part of the price paid to the opposition in order to get the Constitution accepted, these additions may be regarded as essentially a part of the original Constitution. But even after the ancient rights had been listed in the first eight amendments and Congress had been forbidden to trespass upon them, the opponents were still not satisfied. In order further to reassure them, there was added also the blanket provision of the Ninth Amendment that "the enumeration in the Constitution of certain rights shall not be construed to deny or disparage others retained by the people." This was designed to end once and for all the main argument of those who opposed adding a bill of rights to the Constitution. For example Hamilton had raised the question: "Why should it be said that the liberty of the press shall not be restrained, when no power is given by which restriction can be imposed?" And James Wilson, one of the most active of the framers of the Constitution, had thus expressed the logic of the opposition: "A bill of rights annexed to the Constitution is an enumeration of the powers reserved. If we attempt an enumeration everything that is not enumerated is presumed to be given."[9] The Ninth Amendment put into the Constitution itself a rule of interpretation that disposed of that argument.

Reassurance of the States as to their Reserved Powers

Because of a widespread fear, when ratification of the Constitution was pending, that the "general welfare" provision of Article I, Section 8, Clause 1 might be made the basis of the assumption of powers not named, the Tenth Amendment provided that "the powers not delegated to the United States by the Constitution, nor prohibited by it to the States, are reserved

[7] 253 U.S. 350 (1920); Leser v. Garnett, 258 U.S. 130 (1922); United States v. Sprague, 282 U.S. 716 (1931).
[8] Edward S. Corwin: *The Constitution and What it Means Today* (8th ed.; Princeton, 1946), p. 2.
[9] J. Elliott: *Debates of the Several State Conventions on the Adoption of the Federal Constitution* (2nd ed., Washington, D.C., 1854), Vol. II, p. 436.

to the States respectively or to the people." Thus the states were to be made secure in the exercise of their reserved powers and it was to be presumed that they had the right to exercise these powers. That right can be challenged successfully only by the force of some power delegated to the Federal government by the Constitution. And only through the amending process was the list of powers delegated to the Federal government to be increased."[10] Originally, by popular assumption, this merely guaranteed the security of the states in the possession of their undelegated powers. From time to time, since the era of Chief Justice Marshall and until the 1930's, the Supreme Court proclaimed and applied the strange principle that the powers delegated without qualification by the Constitution were nevertheless limited by the body of powers reserved to the states. Recently, however, the Supreme Court appears to have concluded that this is an untenable rule. At any rate, it is not now being applied.

The States Made Secure Against Suits by Citizens

The Eleventh Amendment originated as the consequence of a judgment given in 1793 by the Supreme Court of the United States against the State of Georgia. Chisholm, as an executor of a citizen of South Carolina, brought suit against Georgia for its confiscation of the estate of a Tory during the Revolution. The case was brought under the provision of the Constitution giving the Federal courts jurisdiction in cases "between a state and citizens of another state." While the ratification of the Constitution was pending, proponents had sought to allay the fears of the opposition by assuring them that this meant only that a state might sue a citizen. Thus John Marshall, the future Chief Justice, speaking in the Virginia Convention gave the typical explanation that it was "not rational to suppose that the sovereign power should be dragged into court. The intent is to enable states to recover claims of [against] individuals residing in other states."[11] Hamilton had reasoned likewise in the eighty-first number of the *Federalist*. Nevertheless, in 1793, the Supreme Court rendered judgment against Georgia and in favor of Chisholm.[12] The Georgia House of Representatives promptly passed a bill "declaratory of certain parts of the retained sovereignty of the state" and subjecting to death without benefit of clergy anyone levying on the property of the state by reason of the authority of any court. Such intense bitterness could never have been aroused merely by the abstract issue of states' rights but was induced by the deep concern of numerous holders of confiscated Tory estates. Since similar suits had been brought in Maryland, New York, Massachusetts, and other states, it was not difficult to obtain ratification of the Eleventh Amendment providing that "the judicial power of the United States shall not be construed to extend to any suit in law or equity, commenced or prosecuted against

[10] See Kansas v. Colorado, 206 U.S. 46 (1907).
[11] J. Elliott: *Debates*, Vol. III, p. 555.
[12] 2 Dallas 419 (1793).

one of the United States by citizens of another State or by citizens of a foreign State." This amendment left unchanged the pertinent passage of the Constitution and simply laid down a rule of interpretation that would prevent further cognizance by Federal courts of suits of citizens against states. The "sovereign"—the American people—had quite properly used the amending process to reverse an interpretation of the Constitution given by the Supreme Court of the United States.

Revision of the Method of Voting for President

A defect in the Constitution led to the tie vote between Thomas Jefferson and Aaron Burr in the Electoral College in 1801. The Constitution had provided that "the electors shall meet in their respective States and vote by ballot for two persons" without designating which ballot was intended for president and which for vice-president. The one obtaining the highest vote was to be president and the second highest vote was to determine who was to be vice-president provided, in each case, that the vote represented a majority. The framers had assumed that the electors would exercise their independent judgment in voting, but the unexpected development of two political parties, the consequent regimentation of the presidential electors in partisan alignments, and the resulting conversion of the Electoral College into a mere registering device for recording the party choice promised a tie vote in practically every subsequent presidential election. The Twelfth Amendment corrected this defect by providing that the presidential electors shall "vote by ballot for President and Vice-President."

The Civil War Amendments

The "Civil War Amendments," as the Thirteenth, Fourteenth, and Fifteenth have been called, were adopted respectively in 1865, 1868, and 1870. By the terms of these three amendments the states lost important items in their reserved police powers and, considered collectively, the adoption of these amendments effected a minor constitutional revolution of a nationalizing tendency. By the Thirteenth Amendment the states surrendered that portion of their police power that had enabled them to legalize the ownership of one person by another. By the Fourteenth Amendment the states surrendered control of the determination of citizenship. They also gave up the possibility of abridging "the privileges and immunities of citizens of the United States," the depriving of "any person of life, liberty, or property without due process of law," and the denying to "any person within its jurisdiction the equal protection of the laws." By the Fifteenth Amendment, the states, hitherto the absolute masters in the determination of the voting privileges of their citizens, lost the right to deny this privilege "on account of race, color, or previous condition of servitude," to which "sex" was added half a century later in the Woman's Suffrage Amendment.

The Income Tax Amendment

In 1894 a flat rate income tax of only 2 per cent on incomes of more than $4,000 was contested with inflexible vigor through the courts, reaching the Supreme Court in 1895. After some astonishing confusion on the part of that tribunal it finally decided that the tax was unconstitutional on the ground that a tax on income derived from property is a direct tax and consequently falls under the Constitution's requirement that it be laid "in proportion to the Census or enumeration."[13] However, as national income came to be more and more concentrated in a few states and localities, as the opinion developed that wealth ought to bear the burden of taxation in more equitable proportion to its ability to bear it, and as the pressure for increased Federal revenues strained increasingly the sources customarily relied upon, the demand developed for the removal of the requirement for apportioning an income tax. Eighteen years after the Court opinion of 1895 came the Sixteenth Amendment providing that "the Congress shall have power to lay and collect taxes on incomes, from whatever source derived, without apportionment among the several states and without regard to any census or enumeration." This Sixteenth Amendment reactivated the amending power after it had lain dormant for forty-three years and many had begun to wonder whether there would ever be another amendment to the Constitution.

Popular Election of United States Senators

Three months after the validating of the Sixteenth Amendment, the Seventeenth was added to the Constitution, both being products of the Progressive Movement of the early years of the twentieth century. Originally the Constitution had provided that the two senators from each state were to be "chosen by the Legislature thereof." But this stipulation left unanswered the question whether the election should be by a joint session or by concurrent votes of the two houses of the state legislature sitting separately. Nor had the procedural problem been settled at the end of the century and a quarter after it had first been raised following the ratification of the Constitution. Prolonged deadlocks of the two houses sometimes prevented elections for years while the legislature's appropriate work was being neglected. The lobbies of sinister interests brought their pressures to bear even when they did not actually dictate the choice of senators. Elements in the Progressive Movement demanded popular election of United States senators, and saw their aim achieved in the Seventeenth Amendment.

The Prohibition Amendment

The Eighteenth Amendment marked the culmination of a prohibition movement which started in local option about the middle of the nineteenth

---

[13] Art. I, Sec. 9, Clause 4; Pollock v. Farmers' Loan and Trust Co., 158 U.S. 601 (1895).

century and increased in tempo until by 1919 only Pennsylvania and New York were without either local option or state-wide prohibition. The Eighteenth Amendment, by forbidding the "manufacture, sale, or transportion of intoxicating liquors . . . for beverage purposes," instantly created an irreconcilable minority that vigorously denied the right of society thus to interfere with what they conceived to be their personal liberty. Loss of revenue because of the outlawed traffic, the difficulty of enforcement evidenced by widespread "bootlegging," and a revival of the drinking habit combined to bring about the repeal of the Eighteenth Amendment in 1933 by the passage of the Twenty-first Amendment.

The "Lame Duck" Amendment

The Constitution and early statutory provisions had set the pace of governmental processes to the tempo of travel by stage coach, sailing vessel, and horseback rider. These were the conditions under which the choosing of the presidential electors had been scheduled for early in November, the casting of the electoral votes the second Monday in January, the counting of the electoral votes before the two houses of the Congress on the second Wednesday in February, and the administering of the oath of office to, and the inauguration of, the president on the fourth of March. The Twentieth Amendment reduced the time of this process from four to two-and-a-half months by setting January 20 as the beginning of the presidential term. Before the adoption of the Twentieth Amendment, members of the House of Representatives were elected early in November of even-numbered years and took the oath of office four months later but, unless the president called Congress into special session, they did not begin their legislative duties until December of the year following, that is, thirteen months after their election and eleven months before the next congressional election. The worst aspect of this plan came to be called the "Lame Duck Session." During the second or "Short Session" of each Congress, lasting the three months from early December to early March, sat many members who had failed to be re-elected in the recent elections—"lame ducks" as they were designated in popular terminology. It seemed absurd that members who had been repudiated by their constituents should continue their legislative duties so long. By moving the date of the first session of a new Congress from the first Monday in December to January 3, the "Lame Duck Session" was not entirely eliminated but its potential length was reduced to one-half of what it had been. Indeed a "Lame Duck Session" now occurs only if the president calls an extra session late in an even-numbered year.

The Democratizing Trend of the Amendments

If those dealing with procedures are omitted, the twenty-two amendments stand out as means by which the influence of the American people has democratized the conservative Constitution of the fathers. Thus the Bill of Rights, consisting of the first eight or ten amendments, was due mainly to the inflexible insistence of the common people of America. They supported the three great Civil War Amendments which finally established national supremacy over the doctrine of states' rights. The same social force decreed in the Fifteenth and Nineteenth Amendments the removal of specific barriers to universal adult suffrage. Later democratic forces insisted upon, and obtained, the popular election of United States senators. Burdened with the consumption taxes consisting of excises and imposts to which the fathers had practically confined Federal taxation, the American people, through the Income Tax Amendment, compelled wealth to bear more equitably the burden of taxation. The people appear to have been no less vigorously behind the repeal than the adoption of the Eighteenth Amendment.

STATUTORY AMPLIFICATION OF THE CONSTITUTION

Statutes as Constitution

If a constitution in its broadest sense is "the sum of laws and practices which regulate the fundamental concerns of government," then there must be essential elements of the Constitution of the United States not to be found in the document framed at Philadelphia and its amendments. For example, the question could be raised whether the provision for determining the line of presidential succession after the vice-presidency is any less a part of the constitution in the sense of a fundamental concern of government because it is provided for in an act of Congress instead of in the Constitution of 1787. Thus it is the nature of the provision, rather than how it is created, that makes the matter "constitution." Filling the interstices of the original Constitution by legislative enactments has been designated statutory amplification. Of course it is a very different kind of legislation from those enactments affecting individuals by "commanding what is right and forbidding what is wrong" as, for example, the statutes defining Federal crimes and prescribing the punishment for them. Likewise congressional legislation regulating commerce, restraint of trade, and labor relations, though important enough, is not so fundamental as the organization and powers of the government.

The First Congress Practically a Constitutional Convention

In a very real sense the First Congress took up the work where the framers had left off and proceeded to complete it. The Constitution was, after all, only a framework, parts of which were slight indeed. Moreover there were strange omissions in the structure, and by no means was it self-executing. Indeed most of the agencies of the new government came into existence only as a creation by Congress after which they proceeded to perform functions only as assigned to them by law. To a remarkable degree the Philadelphia Constitution had merely empowered Congress to organize the Federal government. Sometimes it had merely implied that Congress was to establish certain agencies. Thus it only casually referred to the heads of the executive departments, apparently assuming that such would exist by stating that the president "may require the opinion in writing of the principal officer of each of the executive departments on any subject relating to the duties of their respective offices" and that the Congress may invest the appointment of inferior officers "in the Heads of Departments." Without specific statutory provisions for the executive departments there never would have been any. In creating these departments, the Congress might have followed the prevalent practice of the states and made them directly responsible to itself and specifically removable only with the consent of the Senate. The Constitution does not expressly make the department heads answerable to the president; and the failure of the First Congress to take advantage of its opportunity to do so when the subject was under consideration, and enact statutes denying the president the exclusive power of dismissal was as significant as a constitutional amendment would have been in determining the practice. Thus by congressional decision the president became and is to this day the chief of administration, not because the Constitution inevitably made him such, but because Congress left to him the exercise of the power of dismissal of executive officers. Not until 1926 did the Supreme Court decide that Congress did not, in any case, have the power constitutionally to deprive the president of this dismissal power.[14]

The President's Powers Mainly Statutory

It is the president's duty to "take care that the laws be faithfully executed." Yet he has practically no inherent power to create the administrative agencies required for the performance of this function as chief executive. Statutes provide for almost one hundred per cent of the official personnel and administrative machinery that he supervises. Indeed most of the president's powers consist not of specific duties assigned by the Constitution but of the enormous investments in him of duties created by congressional statutes. Congress might readily have chosen not to do this and thereby have given the character of the Federal government a radically different aspect. Thus dominant social forces of the nation as represented in the Congress have, throughout our history, determined through statutes the direction and nature of our constitutional development. For example, in the post-Civil War period this development was intensely nationalistic. But in the 1920's the dominant interests controlling the national government as represented by President Coolidge openly emphasized the dogma of states' rights, and this dogma influenced legislative trends in those years. The widespread distress due to the depression of the 1930's induced Congress, under the impulse of other group interests, to create through statutes an unprecedentedly vast system of Federal administrative agencies and to invest the president with commensurately enormous powers. A formal constitutional amendment could scarcely have wrought a greater

[14] Myers *v.* U. S., 272 U.S. 52 (1926).

change in our Constitution than did these statutes. Thus the Constitution in its broader sense has been developed by investing the president with statutory powers in the way the framers could not have foreseen.

The Judiciary and Presidential Succession Determined by Statutes

The Constitution authorized, but did not create, the Supreme Court and the inferior Federal courts. The Congress could have stopped with its provisions in respect to the Supreme Court and left the state courts to perform the functions of inferior Federal courts which, as Hamilton pointed out, the Constitution authorized.[15] Congress quite properly, however, exercised its discretion by creating a system of inferior Federal courts, and by determining their procedures, their original and appellate jurisdictions, and their relation to the state courts. Here again the Congress was in a very real sense continuing the making of the Constitution. Likewise in the statute of 1792 providing that, in the case of the removal, death, resignation, or disability of both president and vice-president, the president *pro tem.* of the Senate would succeed, or, if that office was vacant the speaker of the House, Congress was supplying by statutory amplification what might just as well have been a clause in the original Constitution. The original presidential succession act is no longer in force but was superseded in 1886 by a second and in 1947 by a third succession act which is now in force.

CONSTITUTIONAL GROWTH THROUGH COURT DECISIONS

Judicial Interpretation of the Constitution

As cases and controversies come before the Federal courts, these courts are compelled from time to time to determine the extent of the powers which the Constitution has delegated to Congress, the executive, and even the judiciary, as well as the force of the express limitations put on those powers by the Constitution. This signifies that the meaning of the words and phrases of the Constitution must be authoritatively determined. After all, "commerce," "due process," "bills of credit," "direct tax," "freedom of speech," and "treason," are abstractions which, for the purpose of adjudicating cases, must be given a precise and concrete meaning. Thus the Federal courts and pre-eminently the Supreme Court must invest the words of the Constitution with definite meaning.

The Supreme Court Determines What the Constitution Means

"Whatever is enacted by Congress and approved by the Supreme Court," declared the late Howard Lee McBain, "is valid even though to the rest of us it is plain violation of an unmistakable fiat of the fundamental law. There is no limitation imposed upon the national government which Congress, the President, and the Supreme Court, acting in consecutive agreement, may not legally override. In this sense the government as a whole is clearly a government of unlimited powers; for by interpretation it stakes

[15] *The Federalist,* No. 81.

out its own boundaries."[16] This observation brings into relief the fact that the Supreme Court of the United States, as the ultimate authority in determining the powers delegated to its branch of the dual Federal system, sits in judgment upon the powers of its own government. Here is a frank indication of the paramount importance of Supreme Court decisions in the development of our Constitution. This is what induced Woodrow Wilson to denominate the Supreme Court "a kind of Constitutional convention in continuous session." Felix Frankfurter in a pardonable hyperbole declared: "The Supreme Court is the Constitution."

Some Strange Interpretations of the Constitution

Which, it may well be asked, is of greater significance: the specific words of the Constitution or the meaning given those words in cases and controversies brought before the courts? For example, the Sixteenth Amendment authorized the taxation without apportionment according to population among the states of "incomes, from whatever source derived." The Supreme Court decided, nevertheless, that incomes derived from certain sources were exempt.[17] According to the Constitution a fugitive from justice "shall, on demand of the executive authority of the state from which he fled, be delivered up," but the Supreme Court held that this is only a moral obligation and "shall" consequently signifies, in effect, "may."[18] Though the Constitution specifically forbids a state to issue bills of credit, the Supreme Court once held that, through its ownership of all the stock in a state bank, a state might issue paper money, the prohibition of the Constitution to the contrary notwithstanding.[19] Nor should it be concluded that, in any case, the Supreme Court was erratic. These cases merely bring into bold relief the power of the court over the meaning of the Constitution.

Continuous Court Interpretation of Commerce

No finer example can be found of the necessary function of the Supreme Court in continuously revitalizing the Constitution than its interpretation of "commerce." In 1824 "commerce" comprehended navigation. A little later the term came to include railroad transportation. Surveying the broadening interpretations of powers granted to Congress, Chief Justice Waite, in the opinion of the Court on a case given in 1877 extending the meaning of commerce to the telegraph, said: "They extend from the horse with its rider to the stage coach, from the sailing vessel to the steamboat, from the coach and the steamboat to the railroad, and from the railroad to the telegraph as these new agencies are successively brought into use to meet the demands of increasing population and wealth. . . ."[20] In 1885, persons and property were included in the term "commerce"; in 1903, "lottery tickets," in 1910, correspondence schools; in 1914, pipe lines and

[16] Howard Lee McBain: *The Living Constitution* (New York, 1927), p. 38.
[17] Evans v. Gore, 253 U.S. 245 (1920).
[18] Kentucky v. Dennison, 24 Howard 66 (1861).
[19] Briscoe v. Bank of Kentucky, 11 Peters 257 (1837).
[20] Pensacola Telegraph Co. v. Western Union Telegraph Co., 96 U.S. 1 (1877).

oil; in 1926, air transportation. In the 1930's the Supreme Court found the commerce clause sufficiently broad to provide the basis for the Fair Labor Standards Act, involving the setting of minimum wages and maximum hours, and outlawing interstate commerce in goods by "oppressive child labor."

The Power of Judicial Annulment Derived by Judicial Interpretation

The opportunity for constitutional interpretation by the Federal courts comes only when cases are brought before it involving an apparent conflict of statute, treaty, or official act with the Constitution. The Constitution nowhere assigns the judiciary the power to determine whether or not a statute is repugnant to the Constitution, that is to say, is "unconstitutional." Marshall, in the case of Marbury v. Madison,[21] derived the power by a logical process that in itself constitutes a classic example of constitutional development through judicial interpretation. With characteristic cogency he reasoned that whenever a court in deciding a case is confronted with a conflict between a statute and the Constitution, the latter, as a presumably superior law, is to be preferred. The statute, which is consequently invalid or "unconstitutional," is accordingly to be disregarded by the Court. Sixteen years later, in McCulloch v. Maryland,[22] Marshall found the power of Congress to charter the Bank of the United States in the fact that the Bank performed fiscal functions for the government which rendered it "necessary and proper" for the performance of powers specifically delegated to Congress. The State of Maryland consequently might not tax the governmental function of the Bank because thereby one branch of our dual system, the state, might tax to death the other, the Federal.

CUSTOM OR USAGE

Constitutional Growth Through Custom

No matter to what extent amendments, statutes, and judgments of the Supreme Court may amplify the Constitution, established practices still remain to complete the content of the term "constitution" in its broadest sense. Despite the prescriptions of the Philadelphia Constitution, the statutes, and the court decisions, a vast latitude remains in the choice of means to ends in which private citizens and public officials may exercise discretion. In one way or another the work of government must be performed. Improvisations initiated as temporary expedients become permanent practices and then evolve into established customs of an institutional character. Such for example, is the president's cabinet. The written Constitution provides nothing of the kind but it does say that the president "may require the opinion in writing of the principal officer in each of the executive departments upon any subject relating to the duties of their respective offices." President Washington called heads of the executive departments

[21] 1 Cranch 137 (1803).
[22] 4 Wheaton 316 (1819).

together and consulted with them collectively. In time this became a set custom and for over a century it has been so firmly established that a president who now decided to abandon it would probably be denounced as violating the Constitution.[23] The Constitution provides for a speaker of the House of Representatives, but usage has made him also the chief leader of the majority party in the House. According to the Constitution, the representative in Congress must be a resident of the state from which he is elected, but usage has added the almost inflexible rule that he must also live in the district that elects him.

Elements of the British and American Constitutions Compared

It has long been customary to contrast the American with the British constitution on the assumption that the former is written and the latter unwritten. Only in 1789, however, when the government of the Philadelphia Constitution was ready to begin functioning, did we have an exclusively written Federal constitution. Since then we have developed every essential element of the British constitution, although Britain will probably always lack our single, formal, fundamental written instrument. However, to assume that the British constitution is entirely unwritten is to disregard some of its most important elements. The great constitutional "land marks" as Britons call them—Magna Carta, Bill of Rights, and Petition of Right— are as certainly written as our Constitution of 1787. This of course is true also of their statutory law and of their court opinions. These latter are not only "written," but outstanding decisions are no less significant in Britain than here in determining constitutional development, even though British courts never set aside enactments of Parliament.

Only Customs or Usages Compose Unwritten Constitutions

In customs, usages, or, as the British denominate them, the "Conventions of the Constitution," we have the true unwritten constitution. These are the long-established habitual practices with respect to government that have become so firmly knit into the governmental system as to be denominated "constitutional" in the broader sense of the term. Of course these usages may be found described in text books and elsewhere. But these descriptions are not authoritative in the sense of being legally binding on anyone and enforceable in the courts as are the provisions of the written constitutions, statutes, and court judgments. Lawyer though he was, candidate Wendell Willkie was in error when in the campaign of 1940 he argued that Franklin D. Roosevelt would be violating common law by serving a third term. Common law is enforceable in the courts, but the two-term prece-

[23] When, for example, during President Wilson's illness and consequent inability to meet the cabinet, the members held informal conferences under the leadership of Secretary of State Robert Lansing, in order to consider urgent matters, the President denounced such conduct as "unconstitutional" and demanded Lansing's resignation. This term "unconstitutional" revealed the pattern of thought of the former professor of political science and it apparently differed from that of former President Taft, then a professor at Yale Law School, who said that he saw nothing "unconstitutional" about the conduct of Lansing and the cabinet.

dent was sheer custom to which no judicial court in the land would pay the slightest attention. Only the court of public opinion passes judgment on custom, as when it rejected the two-term limit on presidential tenure in 1940.

The Unwritten Prevails over the Written Constitution

Since the unwritten constitution consists of prevailing customs, usages, or practices with respect to fundamental concerns of government, its very existence demonstrates its accepted validity. Consequently, whenever a prevailing usage is contrary to a provision of the written constitution, the latter must at that point be dead letter. In other words, the living reality prevails over the ignored dictum of the written word. For example, the Constitution prescribes that the president "shall appoint by and with the advice and consent of the Senate" all but inferior officers of the United States. But with respect to most of these offices he is so limited by the usage known as "senatorial courtesy" that James T. Young has declared with scarcely any exaggeration: "By the necessity of the case the Senate now nominates while the President gives his consent." Thus usage has practically reversed the provision of the written Constitution. Upon the death of President William Henry Harrison in 1841, Vice-President John Tyler, as recorded in the diary of former President John Quincy Adams, "styled himself President of the United States and not vice-President, acting as President, which would be correct style. But it is a construction which is in direct violation both of the grammar and context of the Constitution which confers upon the vice-President on the decease of the President, not the office but the powers and duties of the office."[24] John Tyler even refused to receive a communication from the Senate addressed to him as acting-president and by his resolute determination firmly established the custom that the vice-president succeeds to the presidency and becomes president when a vacancy occurs in that office. Thus the unwritten overrides the written constitution.

Usage in the Electoral College Nullifies the Intention of the Framers

Usage has nullified the clear intention of the framers in their creation of the Electoral College. Their debates show conclusively their expectation that the electors would exercise unhampered personal discretion in voting for president. However, political parties, which the fathers dreaded and hoped might be avoided, emerged, developed strength, regimented the electors in two-party alignments, and converted the Electoral College into an institution for the automatic registration of the will of the voters who elect the electors. So when, in 1944, the Southern Democrats planned to nominate state electoral tickets pledged not to vote for President Franklin Roosevelt if he were again party candidate, Walter Lippmann denounced their proposed move as "unconstitutional," even though such a resumption of the electors' discretion would have been a return to what the fathers

[24] Entry of April 16, 1841.

had intended. Here is another indication of the growing recognition of the precedence usage takes over paper prescriptions.

Political Parties the Product of Custom

If political parties in the United States were suddenly to cease functioning it is difficult to see how government could continue to operate very long. Without them the probability of any candidate obtaining a majority vote would be small indeed. Imperfect as parties are, they facilitate focusing of attention upon issues as well as candidates. Originally their existence and activities were purely matters of custom and usage. No matter how much political parties have been recognized and regulated by statutes, party activity is still today overwhelmingly determined by civic habits and customs. But for this very reason political parties can be regarded an indispensable element in the American Constitution.

Other Usages

Our written Constitution contains nothing to prevent the heads of the executive departments—that is, the cabinet members—from reporting in person on the floor of Congress. Hamilton, as Secretary of the Treasury, expected to do so, but the House of Representatives apparently did not care to risk the dominating influence of Hamilton's presence and so he was directed to report "in writing." Thus was established a persistent and apparently irrevocable custom of our Constitution. The written Constitution requires that revenue bills originate in the House of Representatives, but the Senate may amend to its heart's content and even nullify this requirement by rejecting every part of a House revenue measure except the preamble and substituting a new revenue bill of its own. On the other hand, strange to say, the Constitution is silent on appropriation bills, but custom has established the inflexible rule that they must originate in the House of Representatives, which usage the Senate respects. Verily the Constitution is "that which the government in its several departments and the people in the performance of their duties as citizens recognize and respect as such and nothing else is."

SUMMARY

When the Constitution of the United States is mentioned most Americans think only of the document signed by the delegates at the Philadelphia Convention in 1787. But this original Constitution was quite promptly amplified by a group of amendments since called the Federal Bill of Rights and to date twenty-two amendments have been made to the original Constitution.

But all this comprises our Constitution only in the narrowest sense of the word. In the truest sense the Constitution of a nation includes also its fundamental principles of government whether written or merely implied in its political institutions and usages. The framers had made the original Constitution brief, and they consequently left to the first and succeeding congresses the amplification of it by outstanding statutes that fill in its interstices.

But sometimes when an individual is "hurt" by the application of a statute he may resort to the courts to ascertain whether the Constitution permits what happened to him. The judgments of the courts in such cases determine by judicial interpretation authoritatively what the Constitution means; in effect this is definitely making constitution.

Finally the customs and usages or civic habits into which Americans almost unconsciously fall in getting the details of these various things done are as significant elements of the Constitution in its broadest sense as if they had been prescribed in the original document, amendments, or by enactments of Congress. Moreover these usages of the Constitution can be more significant than some parts of the written Constitution since items in it can and do become dead letter whereas a usage of a constitution as long as it persists is an indisputable living reality.

CHAPTER VI

FEDERAL-STATE AND INTERSTATE RELATIONS

The Problem of the Relation of Central to Local Government

THE FUNDAMENTAL problem facing the Constitutional Convention of 1787 was the devising of a workable distribution of governmental powers between central and local government. This problem was inherited from the British crown, which had been unconsciously approaching a solution by permitting the colonies an extraordinary degree of self-government with respect to their internal affairs. There is a striking resemblance between the powers of legislation exercised by the colonial legislatures before the Revolution and the powers reserved to the states by the Constitution. In both cases the legislature lays the taxes and appropriates the money for local purposes, borrows money on its credit, regulates its internal trade, enacts its civil and criminal law, and indeed exercises the powers of internal police, that is, the power to legislate in order to promote the safety, health, morals, good order, and general welfare of the colony or the state. Likewise matters of war, peace, and inter-colonial, imperial, and foreign commerce were subjects of parliamentary legislation before the Revolution just as the corresponding matters of American national concern were made delegated powers of Congress by the Constitution.

The British ministry's insistence upon its theoretical "sovereignty" over local matters of legislation provoked the crisis of the American Revolution. This might have been avoided if Parliament had recognized the practical fact that the British Empire was evolving into the Federal system it has since become. A federal system is one in which "those affairs which are of common interest to the federation as a whole and which require uniformity of regulation should be placed under the control of the central government while all matters not of common concern should be left to the care of the local governments." [1] The Revolution brought to Americans the brief era of the "sovereignty" of the thirteen states under the Continental Congress and the Articles of Confederation. But this arrangement created confusion and impelled the Philadelphia Convention to attempt to reconcile the conflict between liberty and authority by devising an avowedly federal system. Acutely aware that they must devise a governmental system suitable for a heterogeneous people, the framers of the Constitution sought tentative adjustments of the conflicting claims of centralization and decentralization. Their product has proved to be a dynamic system continuously responsive to the dominant forces of American society. The balance between state and Federal government is redetermined by each generation of Americans.

Early Prestige of the States Under the Constitution

The Constitution did not instantly give the Federal government anything like its present exalted position. The first generation under the Constitution quite naturally retained a high regard for the states, which indeed were then able to take care of most governmental functions. At first the new Federal government seemed remote and almost foreign to most Americans. The basis of the constitutional theory of the Jeffersonian Republicans who captured control of the Federal government in 1801 was expressed in the Virginia and Kentucky Resolutions with their classic statement of the dogma of states' rights. It must be remembered that Marshall's sturdy nationalistic interpretation of the Constitution did not represent the prevailing ideology of a majority of Americans during his lifetime. Indeed during the long generation that his successor, Chief Justice Taney, presided over the Supreme Court, the reserved powers of the states were more freely exercised than they had been under Marshall's court.

THE CHANGING DISTRIBUTION OF FEDERAL AND STATE POWERS

The Effect of the Civil War

The 1860's mark a turning point in Federal-state relations, for at that time the Federal government began to exercise what had hitherto been regarded as exclusively reserved powers of the states. In the generation preceding the Civil War the growing commercial, financial, and manufacturing interests had been frustrated by the states' rights dogmas of the planting interests which dominated the Federal government. But the requirements of Federal armed forces during the Civil War had given an enormous impetus to the business interests, and they gained the control of Federal policies once held by the planting interests. These new leaders demanded a greater utilization of Federal power in the interest of business. The consequence was an exaltation of Federal at the expense of state power.

[1] J. W. Garner: *Political Science and Government* (New York, 1928), p. 349.

The Grant-in-Aid

One aspect of present Federal-state interrelations is the amount of funds flowing from the Federal to the state treasuries. The grant-in-aid is given by Congress to the states under the power granted in the taxation clause [2] which authorizes the use of Federal funds to provide for the "general welfare." The practice is based on the assumption that some activities conducted by state and local governments are sufficiently matters of "general welfare" to justify support by the Federal government. Furthermore the

TABLE I

Regular Federal Grant Payments to States,
Selected Years, 1930–1950 *
(In Thousands)

	1930	1935	1940	1945	1950
Veterans Services and Benefits ...	$ 575	$ 487	$ 797	$ 1,194	$ 15,277
Social Welfare, Health, and Security	746	1,029	362,771	475,427	1,354,635
Housing and Community Facilities.	....	....	....	....	9,918
Education and General Research ..	10,011	12,622	24,530	24,956	38,613
Agriculture and Agricultural Resources	11,875	12,964	143,123	81,862	106,275
Natural Resources not Primarily Agricultural	1,463	1,547	2,655	7,473	16,456
Transportation and Communication.	77,938	13,453	155,647	33,598	465,086
Labor	....	1,927	3,367	....	207,617
Grand Total, of Regular Grants.	$102,608	$44,029	$639,072	$624,510	$2,213,877

*Source: Council of State Governments: *Book of the States* (Chicago, 1952–53), pp. 46–71.

revenue resources of the Federal government are enormous in comparison with those of the states. Not only are the taxation powers of a state limited to its geographic jurisdiction, but some sources of taxation are so elusive as to be tapped adequately only by the Federal government. Moreover Congress is but responding to public pressures in providing for the expenditure of Federal funds to aid in financing state functions. The Federal government has never adopted a policy of sharing its general revenues with the states except by specific grants usually designated as grants-in-aid. This practice began in 1862 in the Morrill Act which granted large tracts of Federal land to states for establishing colleges of a specified type. There were strings to the gift since it was specified that none of the grant was to be used for constructing buildings, which meant that the state had to spend

[2] *Constitution:* Art. I, Sec. 8, Clause 1.

money in order to take advantage of the grant. In 1890 the Morrill Act was amended to provide these "land grant" colleges with an annual monetary grant which could be withheld in case of their failure to maintain the standards required by Federal law. The "grant-in-aid" then took the form of "matching dollars," that is, in order to obtain the grant, the state had to appropriate for the designated purpose as many dollars as were made available by the Federal government. More recently Congress has sometimes offered two or even more dollars for each dollar provided by the state. Among state functions thereby aided are veterans' services and benefits, social security, welfare and health, housing and community development, education, research, agriculture, conservation, transportation and labor, a total of 54 by 1954.

Expansion of Federal Expenditures for Relief

During the devastating depression of the 1930's the expenditures of Federal funds for relief by both state and Federal agencies attained gigantic proportions. When relief was put on a work basis, the Public Works Administration and the Works Progress Administration supplemented, when they did not supplant, state relief agencies. Youth was aided by the National Youth Administration and the Federal Civilian Conservation Corps. The states largely stood by helpless during this period because few of them were wealthy enough in sources of public credit and taxation to undertake their own relief programs. Consequently during the Great Depression the American people relied for relief chiefly on the Federal government whose prestige thereby increased in comparison with that of the states.

Lack of System in Federal Grants

Originally the grant-in-aid was designed to stimulate the states to undertake a few favored activities. It has, of course, shifted in purpose to become an actual support of the states, so that the Federal government now increasingly bears their burdens. But no consistent pattern for making the grants has ever been devised by Congress. In 1955 the Commission on Intergovernmental Relations created by Congress concluded concerning grants-in-aid: [3] "Because the control is indirect and the execution of the program is given to the States, the impact of a proposed grant on state and local responsibility may not be fully taken into account. The Commission believes that a healthy safeguard here is for the Congress to consult representatives of State governments—those with overall responsibility as well as heads of functional agencies—on the need for and the form of national participation.

"Once a determination has been made that national action is desirable for a given objective, however, the fact that the grant-in-aid involves some diminution of State autonomy is not in itself a compelling

---

[3] The Commission on Intergovernmental Relations. *A Report to the President for Transmissal to the Congress,* June, 1955, p. 131.

argument against its use. Against a direct national program that would give the states no role whatsoever, the grant-in-aid may often be preferred."

Federal Invasion of the Field of Reserved Powers

The Federal grant-in-aid has been criticized as violating the spirit of the Constitution because the Federal government thereby acquires the power to supervise activities and control policies within the spheres of the state's reserved powers. During the first generation under the Constitution there was considerable doubt that the Constitution's delegation to Congress of power to tax and spend "for the general welfare" authorized Congress to spend money for anything outside the fields of the other delegated powers. No less a president than Madison, the "Father of the Constitution," vetoed a bill for internal improvements at Federal expense on the ground that "the power is not expressly given by the Constitution." [4] But the Supreme Court of the United States has not accepted this narrow construction and has left Congress free to decide for itself when a grant is for the general welfare. Though nominally free to accept or reject the proffered grants, the states seem to be practically coerced into acceptance. If they reject the aid tendered, they will, nevertheless, through Federal taxation, be contributing to the Federal treasury funds that go to complying sister states. Sometimes in practice these grants even take from the poorer states and give to the richer ones. Matching dollars may even result in pouring large Federal sums into state treasuries already comparatively well filled.[5]

Through Federal Administrative Agencies

Federal administrative agencies have become increasingly influential in integrating the common activities of the states. The United States Department of Agriculture has been bringing about uniformity in the states' reporting of crop estimates and market statistics, and the Federal office of Agricultural Experiment Stations has cooperated with corresponding state experiment stations to the same end. The Federal Bureau of Public Roads has, through the national associations of state highways officials, promoted a uniform traffic code, uniform numbering of highways, and uniform highway markings. The Federal Food and Drug Administration, operating through conferences with state officials, has promoted uniform administrative handling of problems in this field. Through conferences with state health officers the United States Public Health Service has provided a continuous leadership in its field. The uniform system for reporting vital statistics that now exists can be attributed to the influence of the Federal Census Bureau. The Association of State Government Officials in Industry is a consequence of leadership of the United States Department of Labor.

[4] James D. Richardson: *Messages and Papers of the Presidents* (Washington, D.C., 1903), Vol. I, p. 584.

[5] See Austin F. MacDonald: "Aid to the States: 1940 Model." *American Political Science Review* (1940), 34:498–9.

Partly because of legislation and partly because of liberal interpretation of the duties of Federal officers, kidnapping and racketeering have been reduced. The Interstate Commerce Commission leads in promoting co-operation with the corresponding state agencies through the National Association of Railroad and Utility Commissioners. Without ostentation Federal departments exert a positive influence on the course of legislation in state legislatures. Sometimes this is necessary in order that the states comply with conditions requisite for receiving Federal grants-in-aid and other grants. The Federal Power Commission sought state legislation enabling it to designate state commissions as their agents. Other Federal agencies sought and obtained state legislation for coordinating Federal and corresponding state agencies. The result of Federal administrative influence is to magnify Federal powers and to subordinate even the state powers that are thereby made more efficient.[6]

Through Judicial Interpretation

Though the Federal courts are the universally accepted authorities for discovering the elusive boundary between the powers delegated to the Federal government and those reserved to the states, they were not at once accepted as such by the first generation under the Constitution. Before the Federal government had been functioning a year under the Constitution, Patrick Henry, in a series of resolutions he had put through the Virginia legislature, proclaimed the state legislatures to be the "sentinels" to guard the reserved powers of the states against Federal encroachment. Seven years later the Kentucky Resolutions suggested state nullification of "unconstitutional" Federal statutes as the means of making the sentinel task effective. Under Chief Justice John Marshall's leadership in the judiciary, however, the role of the Federal courts as umpires in controversies over Federal versus state powers was permanently established. The effect of this has been to exalt the Federal government and subordinate the states. As Oliver P. Field said, "despite the fact that the Supreme Court of the United States has been as impartial an umpire in national-state disputes as one of the members of two contending teams could be expected to be . . . the states are members of the federal system, and have had to play against the umpire, as well as against the national government itself. The combination has been too much for them." [7] This was an inevitable consequence of the Supreme Court's tendency to follow the precedents of Marshall's broad construction of the powers of Congress which operated to reduce the scope of the reserved powers of the states.

States Subject to Judicial Action by the Federal Government

The national government not only has the right to bring action against states before the Supreme Court of the United States but has also rather

---

[6] See W. B. Graves: *American State Government* (New York, 1941), pp. 29–37.

[7] Oliver P. Field: "States versus Nation and the Supreme Court." *American Political Science Review* (1934), 28:233.

freely exercised this power.[8] Concerning the proceedings in Federal courts against state railway legislation of a generation ago the late Henry Jones Ford declared: "Offending states were arrested and taken to court almost as promptly as in police action with an ordinary drunk and disorderly case." [9] This, of course, is a one-sided privilege since the states may not bring suit against the national government without its consent. Whenever Federal action appears to trespass upon the constitutional domain of the states and to exceed the constitutional grants to the central government, the states are dependent upon private individuals to assert their claims and contentions in Federal courts.[10] Federal courts may release a party in the custody of state officials, but state courts may not interfere by habeas corpus proceedings with Federal officers or courts. Federal courts freely interfere with state administrative officers by injunction, particularly in the field of utility regulation and taxation. The Supreme Court has repeatedly held that the power of Congress to regulate interstate commerce deprives the states of any power to regulate intra-state commerce that Congress itself requires for making effective its commerce regulations. The maxim still stands that the state is "sovereign" within its sphere, but the Supreme Court of the United States decides finally what that sphere is.[11]

Through Constitutional Amendments

Almost every amendment to the Constitution adopted in the fifty-five years after the Civil War signified a loss of power to the states, and no amendment in a century and a half has increased state power except the repeal of the Eighteenth Amendment, which merely restored a power lost a dozen years earlier. In 1865 the Thirteenth Amendment reduced the states' control of personal relations by prohibiting slavery. By the Fourteenth Amendment the states were deprived of the determination of citizenship, and through "due process," the "privileges and immunities," and the "equal protection of the laws" provisions this amendment gave to the Federal judiciary the opportunity to invalidate considerable state legislation. Through the Fifteenth Amendment the states lost the power to use "race, color, or previous condition of servitude" to limit suffrage. After the Sixteenth Amendment the states no longer had the exclusive right to levy income taxes. By the Seventeenth Amendment the state legislatures lost the power to elect senators. The Eighteenth Amendment deprived the states, for a time, of a portion of their police power by outlawing the manufacture, sale, or transportation of intoxicating liquors for beverage purposes. The Nineteenth Amendment signified that a state could no longer confine the electorate to males.

[8] United States *v.* Texas, 143 U.S. 629 (1892).

[9] Henry Jones Ford: *The Cost of National Government* (New York, 1910), p. 29.

[10] Oliver P. Field: "State versus Nation." *American Political Science Review* (1934), 28:236.

[11] Ibid., p. 244.

Through Treaty Power

The first generation under the Constitution generally considered the reserved powers of the states to be excluded from the scope of the treaty-
making power. This widely held view of that time was expressed by
Thomas Jefferson, who added that the president and Senate ought not to
be allowed to do by way of a treaty what the whole Federal government
lacked the ability to do in any way. Whatever was beyond the power
of Senate, House, and president as to legislation could not be done by
treaty. The scope of the treaty power was thought to be confined to the
specifically delegated powers of Congress. This now outmoded interpretation was once given authoritative promulgation in the early Supreme
Court opinion that whenever an act of Congress would be unconstitutional
as invading the reserved powers of the states, a treaty to the same effect
would be unconstitutional. [12] In striking contrast is the present Supreme Court interpretation that "the treaty-making power of the United
States is not limited by any express provision of the Constitution, and
though it does not extend 'so far as to authorize what the Constitution
forbids' it does extend to all proper subjects of negotiation between our
government and other nations." [13]

Treaty Powers Not Limited by the States' Reserved Powers

In 1921, Seattle enacted an ordinance for the licensing of citizens, but not
aliens, as pawnbrokers. Asakura, a Japanese pawnbroker, claimed the protection of a United States treaty with Japan providing that citizens of either
nation could carry on trade in the other on the same terms as its citizens
and be protected in person and property. In upholding Asakura's claim the
Supreme Court said that the treaty has the "same footing of supremacy as
do the provisions of the Constitution and the laws of the United States.
It operates of itself, without the aid of legislation, state or national; and it
will be applied and given authoritative effect by the courts." [14] In 1913,
Congress enacted a statute to regulate the killing of migratory birds and
thereby prevent their extinction. The habits of these wild fowl carry them
in the course of a year northward and southward across state and international boundaries. Unrestricted hunting would lead to their extinction,
but the states individually could not solve the problem. Yet no delegation
of power could be found in the Constitution authorizing the legislation of
Congress, and the act was consequently held unconstitutional in a Federal
district court. The Supreme Court withheld judgment pending the negotiation of a treaty on the subject.[15] The United States then entered into such
a treaty with Great Britain, and Congress passed appropriate legislation for
its execution. A national game warden, Holland, while enforcing the
Migratory Bird Treaty Act passed by Congress to carry out the treaty, was

[12] Prevost v. Greneau, 19 Howard 7 (1857).
[13] Geoffrey v. Riggs, 133 U.S. 258 (1899); Asakura v. Seattle, 265 U.S. 322 (1924).
[14] Ibid., p. 332.
[15] C. K. Burdick: *The Law of the American Constitution* (New York, 1922), p. 75.

challenged on the ground that the treaty was an invasion of the powers reserved to the states by the Tenth Amendment. The Supreme Court sustained Holland in the performance of his duty, and Justice Oliver Wendell Holmes, speaking for the Court, pointed out that the treaty power is less limited in scope than the law-making power of Congress. "Acts of Congress," Holmes said, "are the supreme law of the land only when made in pursuance of the Constitution while treaties are declared to be so when made under the authority of the United States."[16] Thus the expansion of Federal at the expense of state authority through the treaty power is evident enough when the fact is grasped that the treaty power is a delegated power reducing the states' reserved powers.

LIMITATIONS OF THE FEDERAL CONSTITUTION ON THE STATES

The Prohibition of State Treaties, Alliances, or Confederations

The Constitution declares: "No state shall enter into any treaty, alliance, or confederation." Since the framers intended that these powers of national sovereignty should be exercised exclusively by the Federal government, the prohibitions are absolute. Before forming the abortive union known as the Confederate States of America in 1861, the Southern states enacted ordinances repealing their ratification of the Constitution of the United States. Thus they may have sought to escape the charge of violating the Federal Constitution's prohibition of a state's entering into a confederation. In cases that arose after the Civil War involving the question, the Supreme Court refused to recognize the existence of the Southern confederation as legal.[17]

The War Power Denied to the States

A granting by a state of letters of marque and reprisal as well as the keeping of troops or ships of war in time of peace, or engaging in war unless actually invaded or in such imminent danger as will admit no delay, are all specifically forbidden by the Constitution. The purpose is to insure that such an absolutely sovereign power as arming and making war shall be a monopoly of the Federal government. Early in the American Revolution some states issued letters of marque and reprisal to privateers, that is they authorized private persons to arm vessels and to prey upon British commerce. This prohibition against the states does not apply to the national government, which is specifically empowered to authorize such letters. This now outmoded power authorized the seizure of property in order to redress injuries inflicted by another nation. Although not an act of war the granting of such letters could provoke war and hence could not with safety be a state power. The denial to the states of the power to "keep troops" could not have referred to a state's militia whose existence was clearly recognized

[16] Missouri *v.* Holland, 252 U.S. 416 (1920).
[17] Williams *v.* Bruffy, 96 U.S. 176, 183 (1878).

in the Constitution. The prohibition is against a state maintaining a paid or professional standing army or a navy. During World War I the question was even raised as to whether the states were not exceeding their powers by passing legislation to facilitate the prosecution of the war. The Supreme Court held that a state is free to enact such war legislation as does not conflict with Federal statutes.[18]

Restrictions on the States' Monetary Power

The Constitution absolutely forbids the states to "coin money, emit bills of credit, or make anything but gold or silver a tender in payment of debts." Every part of this prohibition grew out of state monetary practices so harassing to creditors during the period of the Articles of Confederation. In more than half the states, paper money had been issued and made legal tender in the payment of debts. No matter how depreciated in value the paper money might have been in ratio to standard gold and silver money, the creditor was obligated by law to accept it at face value when tendered in payment of debt. The term "bills of credit" was defined by Chief Justice Marshall as including all evidences of indebtedness issued by the state and intended to circulate as money. Even negotiable state bonds issued in such small denominations as to facilitate their circulation from hand to hand were held by Marshall's Court in 1830 to violate the Constitution.[19] However, a few years later, when the State of Kentucky chartered a bank of which the state owned all of the stock, the Supreme Court, now under the chief justiceship of Roger B. Taney, held that its issues of paper money did not violate the Constitution's interdiction of bills of credit since it was not the state as such that issued them.[20] Nor did the Constitution's prohibition prevent banks chartered by the states from issuing paper money recklessly before the Civil War. The matter is now merely of historical interest because the abuse was ended once and for all in 1865 when Congress laid a prohibitive 10 per cent tax on issues of paper money by state banks.

States Forbidden to Grant Any Title of Nobility

This prohibition by the Constitution is absolute. Both Congress and the states are forbidden the practice. The equalitarian tendencies in the colonies had prevented the practice of granting titles of nobility, and the Articles of Confederation included an interdiction of them. The purpose appears to be the preservation of the equality of men before the law. It becomes a corollary of the Constitution's guarantee of a republican form of government to the states. In the thirty-ninth number of the Federalist, Madison expressed the opinion that the most decisive proof that the governments were republican in form is to be found in this "absolute prohibition of titles of nobility." The Constitution's prohibition does not pre-

[18] Gilbert v. Minnesota, 254 U.S. 325 (1920).
[19] Craig v. Missouri, 4 Peters 410 (1830).
[20] Briscoe v. Bank of Kentucky, 11 Peters 257 (1837).

vent a private citizen or even a state officer from accepting a title of nobility or a pension from a foreign state and a state may permit such acceptance. However, most state constitutions forbid even this.

Prohibition of State Taxes that Restrict Commerce

Except with the permission of Congress no state may "lay any imposts or duties on imports or exports, except what may be absolutely necessary for executing its inspection laws." In order to prevent the state from circumventing these prohibitions by laying tonnage duties on vessels in port, that too is forbidden. A tonnage duty is one that is levied on the cubic carrying capacity of a vessel. In these prohibitions two influential interests in the making and ratifying of the Constitution accomplished their purposes. Public creditors were assured that the chief sources of national taxation would be monopolized by Congress, and the commercial interests made sure that the states could not continue, through their taxing power, the chaotic trade restrictions that had prevailed under the Articles of Confederation. The Supreme Court has held that the export and import tax restrictions apply to foreign trade.[21] Taxes levied by a state upon the movement of goods from state to state is an unconstitutional interference with interstate commerce the regulation of which is exclusively a power of Congress.[22]

Implied Constitutional Restrictions on State Power

In addition to the specific prohibitions on the states listed in the Constitution there are others derived by the courts through interpretation. For example, it has been judicially established that the states may not interfere with or burden the agencies and instrumentalities of the Federal government by taxation.[23] They may not tax United States property.[24] Eminent domain may not be used by a state to acquire Federal property if it burdens or obstructs Federal power. A state may not, by taxation or other means, burden the flow of interstate commerce.[25] Habeas corpus proceedings may not be used by a state to interfere with the enforcement of Federal laws.[26] Secession was pronounced unconstitutional by the Supreme Court with the epigrammatic dictum that the nation consists of "an indestructible union composed of indestructible states." [27]

Restrictions Protecting Individuals Against the States

States may not "pass any bill of attainder, ex-post-facto law, or law impairing the obligation of contracts." A bill of attainder has been defined as "a legislative act which inflicts punishment without a judicial trial." [28] The

21 Patapsco Guano Co. *v.* Board of Agriculture, 171 U.S. 345, 350 (1898).
22 Coe *v.* Errol, 116 U.S. 517, 526 (1886).
23 McCulloch *v.* Maryland, 4 Wheaton 316 (1819).
24 Van Brocklin *v.* Tennessee, 117 U.S. 151 (1886).
25 McCarroll *v.* Dixie Lines, 309 U.S. 176 (1940).
26 Ableman *v.* Booth, 21 Howard 506, 185 (1858).
27 Texas *v.* White, 7 Wallace 700 (1869).
28 Cummings *v.* Missouri, 4 Wallace 277 (1867).

ex-post-facto law prohibition applies only to criminal law and is directed against retroactive legislation making an act a crime that was not criminal when done, and against legislation retroactively increasing the penalty of what has already been legally defined as a crime. "Contract" as used in the clause forbidding state impairment of the obligation of contract was given an astonishingly broad interpretation by Marshall in the Dartmouth College Case. Speaking for the Court he held that a charter that had been granted for creating the college by Charles II in the colonial period constituted a contract still binding between the corporation of the college and the State of New Hampshire which the state legislature could not constitutionally change against the will of the college trustees.

Restrictions of the States in Amendments to the Federal Constitution

The Thirteenth Amendment abolishing slavery deprived states absolutely of a very significant police power, that of determining the social relationship of person to person when this relationship consisted of the ownership of one person by another. Nor is this a perfunctory provision of the Constitution today. The Thirteenth Amendment is violated whenever conditions of involuntary servitude obtain. For example, the Amendment is held to prevent an employer from compelling a worker to continue on or complete a contract for personal service. When the worker is unwilling to do so, a statute making the breach of such a contract for personal service a crime is unconstitutional on the ground that such coercion results in involuntary servitude.[29]

The Fourteenth Amendment's prohibition—that a state may not make or enforce any law abridging the privileges and immunities of citizens of the United States—proved disappointing when the Supreme Court of the United States, in the Slaughterhouse Cases, reduced to insignificance its restrictions on the state. The Court pointed out that the amendment protected the privileges and immunities of citizens of the *United States,* not those of citizens of a *state.* Thus the wide range of privileges and immunities deriving from state citizenship were then held to receive no protection whatever from this particular phrase of the Amendment. In the 1920's, however, the Amendment began to take on a new character as a shield protecting the individual against arbitrary state government. The Amendment forbids a state to deprive any person of life, liberty, or property without due process of law. The word "liberty" was gradually given new content through judicial interpretation. In 1931 Chief Justice Hughes expressed the emerging new significance given the amendment by the Supreme Court in this statement: "It is no longer open to doubt that the liberty of the press and of speech is within the liberty safeguarded from invasion by state action." [30] Since then the Supreme Court has added free-

[29] Bailey v. Alabama, 219 U.S. 219 (1911).
[30] Near v. Minnesota, 283 U.S. 697 (1931).

dom of assembly [31] and religious freedom [32] to the liberties protected by the "due process" restriction of the Fourteenth Amendment. The Amendment's prohibition that a state may not deny "to any person within its jurisdiction the equal protection of the laws" is interpreted by the courts to forbid arbitrary or unreasonable state discriminations. For example, excluding Negroes from the lists of citizens liable for jury duty, excluding Negroes from the benefits of a state homestead law, forbidding Negro barbers, through ordinances, to serve white children, and prohibiting a corporation, through statutes, from employing Mongolians, are all denials of the "equal protection of the laws."

OBLIGATIONS OF THE FEDERAL GOVERNMENT TO THE STATES

The Guarantee of a Republican Form of Government

The United States has the constitutional obligation to "guarantee to every State in this Union a Republican Form of Government." The framers evidently took for granted that this would be understood to signify the type of government prevailing in the thirteen states in 1787, in all of which at least one branch of the legislature was elected directly by the people and the other state officers were chosen either directly or indirectly by the people. In the thirty-ninth article of the *Federalist* Madison shows that the Federal government is republican in form because of its resemblance in its several parts to the governments of Maryland, South Carolina, New York, Virginia, and Delaware. In 1912 an Oregon corporation refused to pay a tax laid by means of the initiative and referendum on the ground that this was direct legislation and that Oregon consequently no longer had a government republican in form. The Supreme Court of the United States discreetly concluded that the state still had representative government which might be supplemented with direct legislation.[33] The Supreme Court has, however, consistently refused to settle controversies hinging on whether a particular state government is republican in form on the ground that this is not a judicial but a political question to be settled by the political branches of the government, meaning the executive and legislative branches. Congress can do this through its power to determine the qualifications of its members, whom it may refuse to seat. The president as commander-in-chief has direction of the military force that could displace a state government he deemed not to be republican in form.

Protection Against Invasion and Domestic Violence

Because the burden of the Revolutionary War had fallen with particular weight on a few states, the pledge of the Union to protect each state against invasion seemed necessary to the framers. The guarantee to protect a state

---

[31] De Jonge *v.* Oregon, 299 U.S. 353 (1937).
[32] West Virginia State Board of Education *v.* Barnette, 319 U.S. 624 (1943).
[33] Pacific States Telephone and Telegraph Co. *v.* Oregon, 223 U.S. 118 (1912).

against domestic violence was doubtless caused largely by the failure of the Confederation to come to the aid of Massachusetts when Shays's Rebellion terrorized the state in 1786. The Constitution consequently prescribes that in case of domestic violence the intervention of Federal authority with military force is to be forthcoming upon application of the state legislature or of the executive (when the legislature cannot be convened). President Cleveland ignored this requirement in 1894 when he intervened with Federal troops in the railway strike at Chicago, a strike called in sympathy with the striking Pullman Palace Car Company's employees. Nor was he deterred in the least by the vigorous protests of Governor John P. Altgeld of Illinois who pointed out that state troops were already on duty maintaining order. President Cleveland based his intervention on the ground that the Federal obligation to maintain the postal service and keep free the movement of interstate commerce justified his action. Since the Supreme Court sustained Cleveland's intervention, it provided the precedent for what is now established practice.

Guarantee Against Involuntary Dismemberment of a State

The Constitution gives the assurance that "no new state shall be formed or erected within the jurisdiction of any state; nor any state be formed by the junction of two or more states; or parts of states without the consent of the states concerned as well as of the Congress." There has been a number of practical applications of this provision. Vermont was formed into a state in 1791 out of territory claimed by New York, New Hampshire, and Massachusetts. The states concerned gave their consent and the admission of Vermont to the Union indicated the approval of Congress. Virginia consented to the separation of her western part and to its formation into what became the State of Kentucky in 1792. Until 1820, Maine was a part of the State of Massachusetts, which in that year consented to a separation. After the Civil War had broken out in 1861, the forty western counties of Virginia separated and in 1863 were recognized as the State of West Virginia. The Constitutional requirement of the consent of Virginia, then a member of the Southern Confederacy, was met by the rather specious stratagem of approving the separation by a "rump" legislature of Virginia consisting of members of the legislature of Virginia representing the counties about to constitute the new state.

Guarantee of Equal Representation in the Senate

The Constitution provides that "no state, without its consent, shall be deprived of its equal suffrage [representation] in the Senate." In 1856 the Supreme Court referred to this as a "permanent and unalterable exception to the power of amendment." [34]

Equality of States

This principle, derived by judicial interpretation, has been thus stated by the Supreme Court: "The definition of 'a state' is found in the powers pos-

[34] Dodge v. Woolsey, 18 Howard 331, 338 (1856).

sessed by the original states which adopted the Constitution," and "'this Union' was and is a union of states, equal in power, dignity, and authority, each competent to exert that residuum of sovereignty not delegated to the United States by the Constitution itself."[35] Attempts of Congress to fix permanent special conditions on a new state have consequently proved futile. For example, Congress would not admit Nevada and Nebraska into the Union before they agreed to enfranchise Negroes who did not then have the voting privilege in some other states. Utah was compelled, as a condition of admission, to agree permanently to guarantee religious toleration, to keep the school system free from sectarian control, and to ban polygamous marriages forever. However, as soon as a state is admitted it is instantly as free as other states to order its affairs and exercise fully its reserved powers, since the act of admission is irrevocable, and Congress cannot order continued compliance with pre-admission agreements. Provisions of the Constitution that "all duties, imposts, and excises shall be uniform throughout the United States" and "no preference shall be given by any regulation of commerce or revenue to the ports of one state over those of another" imply the fundamental concept of state equality.

OBLIGATIONS OF THE STATES TO THE FEDERAL GOVERNMENT

Electing Federal Officers

The Constitution lays upon the states the duty of seeing to the election of members of the House of Representatives and of the Senate and the choosing of presidential electors in such manner as the legislatures of the states may direct. Strictly speaking, there is no Federal election. Voting for Federal officers is under state authority and administration. Election officials are state officials and the cost of these elections is borne by the state or by local governments. State legislatures prescribe "the times, places, and manner of holding elections" of senators and representatives, but Congress may alter these and has accordingly set the first Tuesday after the first Monday in November of even numbered years as the time for such elections. Since a state would lose its power in the federal government by failing to perform the duty here assigned by the Constitution, failure to do so is unthinkable.

The States' Part in Amending the Federal Constitution

Thus far every amendment to the Constitution has been submitted to the states after proposal by a two-thirds vote of both houses of Congress. An alternative method of proposing amendments not yet used is by a national convention to be called upon the application of the legislatures of two-thirds of the states. Ratification of a proposed amendment is accomplished either by state legislatures or by state conventions elected for that purpose "as one or the other mode may be proposed by the Congress."

[35] *Coyle v. Oklahoma,* 221 U.S. 559 (1911).

OBLIGATIONS OF THE STATES TO EACH OTHER

The Federal Article of the Constitution

The Fourth Article of the Constitution is sometimes called the "Federal Article" because it defines specifically important relations of the states to each other as well as to the national government. In some ways the states of the Union bear to each other relations comparable to international relations. International law, in fact, provided some of the patterns and precedents for provisions of Article IV of the Constitution, as, for example, the "full faith and credit" provision which is suggestive of the practice by which courts of one nation sometimes recognize and enforce the judgments of another nation's courts. The Articles of Confederation had already dealt with some of the problems of interstate relations, and the Articles were indeed the source of the Constitution's clauses concerning "privileges and immunities," "full faith and credit," and the rendition of fugitives from justice. But the states of the Union are bound together in a federation so that the provisions of Article IV require a national tribunal to adjudicate cases and controversies arising out of the article. Thus the Federal judiciary becomes the organ for applying principles derived from international law to the settlement of interstate relations.

Full Faith and Credit

The Constitution requires that "full faith and credit shall be given in each state to the public acts, records, and judicial proceedings of every other state." The practical value of this provision is that if A in Ohio obtains a court judgment against B who also lives in Ohio and B moves to Pennsylvania before the judgment is executed, A need not produce witnesses before a Pennsylvania court to obtain execution of the judgment. An authenticated copy of the Ohio court's judgment is as valid in Pennsylvania as that judgment was in Ohio, and the Pennsylvania courts are obligated to give "full faith and credit" to the Ohio proceedings. In 1790 Congress enacted appropriate legislation under the constitutional provision that "Congress may . . . prescribe the Manner in which such Records . . . shall be proved . . ." The "full faith and credit" provision requires one state to recognize a divorce granted by another state provided that the latter has jurisdiction over the persons to whom it is granted. The difficulty of determining such jurisdiction is illustrated by a married man who went with the wife of another from North Carolina to Nevada. There they stayed in an auto court long enough to satisfy the Nevada residence requirement, whereupon they obtained divorces, married each other, and returned at once to North Carolina where they were charged with, and convicted of, bigamy. In 1942 the Supreme Court of the United States held that North Carolina was required to recognize or give "full faith and credit" to the divorces obtained in Nevada.[36] But three years later in a

[36] Williams v. North Carolina, 317 U.S. 287 (1942).

startling reversal, the Supreme Court, in effect, sustained the conviction of bigamy by holding that the parties had not established a bona fide domicile in Nevada and that North Carolina was consequently not required to recognize the divorce as valid.[37] The "full faith and credit" obligation covers not only the statutes [38] but also the constitutions of other states.[39] The courts of the United States are bound to give judgments of state courts the same faith and credit that the courts of one state must give the judgments of sister states.[40] Incidentally the "full faith and credit" provision does not obligate the courts of one state to give any greater weight than it otherwise would to the precedents of another state on similar cases.[41]

Privileges and Immunities

"The citizens of each state shall be entitled to all the privileges and immunities of citizens in the several states" was a provision carried over from the Articles of Confederation to the Constitution of the United States. It was designed to prevent the treatment as aliens of citizens of other states. Because of this clause the citizens of one state sojourning in another cannot be singled out and legislated against or otherwise disfavored. Over a century ago the Supreme Court interpreted the "privileges and immunities" of this clause as comprehending "protection of the government; the enjoyment of life and liberty, with the right to acquire and possess property of every kind and to pursue and obtain happiness and safety, subject nevertheless to such restrictions as the government may justly prescribe for the general good of the whole; the right of the citizen to pass through, or to reside in any other state . . . to claim the benefit of the writ of habeas corpus, to institute and maintain actions of any kind in the courts of the state; to take, hold, and dispose of property, either real or personal; and an exemption from higher taxes or impositions than are paid by other citizens of the state, . . . the elective franchise, as regulated and established by the laws or constitution of the state in which it is exercised." [42] Of course the citizen traveling into another state does not carry with him any privilege or immunity peculiar to his own state nor does he gain instantly every privilege of the new state. Such privileges, as voting or fishing, are dependent upon a term of residence. Nor does a corporation, which is an artificial creature of a state, enjoy the privileges and immunities of the clause.[43]

Interstate Rendition

The Constitution provides that a fugitive from justice fleeing from one state and found in another shall, on demand of the executive authority of the state from which he fled, be delivered up to be removed to the state having

[37] Williams *v.* North Carolina, 325 U.S. 226 (1945).
[38] Bradford Electric Light *v.* Clapper, 286 U.S. 145 (1932).
[39] Smithsonian Institution *v.* St. Johns, 214 U.S. 19 (1909).
[40] Cooper *v.* Newell, 173 U.S. 555, 567 (1899).
[41] Wiggins Ferry Co. *v.* Chicago and A. R. Co., 11 Fed. 381 (1882). Affirmed in 108 U.S. 18 (1883).
[42] Corfield *v.* Curyell, 4 Washington U.S. 371, 380 (1823).
[43] Blake *v.* McClung, 172 U.S. 64 (1898).

jurisdiction of the crime. The clause would seem to be conclusive in such matters, but it is not self-executing and there is no express grant of power to Congress to provide for its execution. Nevertheless, in 1793 Congress by statute invested the governors of the states with the duty the Constitution prescribed. In 1861, however, the Supreme Court decided that the duty of a governor to deliver the fugitive to the executive of the state from which he escaped was not mandatory or compulsory but merely moral and hence not subject to mandamus proceedings.[44] Consequently, governors have ever since felt free to refuse requisitions for the rendition of fugitives from justice, often to protect them from what might be persecution but sometimes for reasons bordering on sheer caprice.

Legislation Facilitating Interstate Rendition

The ingenuity with which the American people are circumventing obstructions to the rendition of fugitives from justice is an indication of the political genius of our society. Among the devices invented for this purpose are model uniform state criminal extradition laws already adopted by some forty states. One type of uniform state law gives state police in "fresh pursuit" of a fugitive the right to disregard state lines; another expedites the extradition of material witnesses.[45] Perhaps nothing by the Federal government has done more to strengthen the states' power in this field than the Act of Congress making it an offense against the United States for a person to flee from a state to avoid being prosecuted or called upon to give testimony in certain cases.[46] Congress has also aided the states in this field with legislation based on the commerce clause such as statutes making Federal crimes of the transportation of women across state lines for immoral purposes or taking stolen good, including automobiles, across state lines. By the so-called "Lindbergh Law" taking a kidnapped person across a state line has been made a Federal crime.

INTERSTATE COOPERATION

Interstate Compacts

Only in recent years has the interstate compact come into wide use as a means of collective action of several states on matters that transcend state boundaries. The framers of the Constitution could scarcely have foreseen this development when they forbade states to enter into any agreement or compact with another state except with the consent of Congress. Prior to 1934 this device had been confined principally to the settlement of interstate boundaries and the fair division of the waters of western rivers. However, beginning with the interstate Parole and Probation Compact of 1935, this type of collective state action has been utilized to promote interstate cooperation in such fields as the abatement of water pollution, the conserva-

[44] Kentucky v. Dennison, 24 Howard 66, 107 (1861).
[45] Marc A. Rose: "States Get Together." *Current History* (1938), 48:25–27.
[46] U.S. Code, tit. 18, sec. 408, e.

tion of oil and gas, the development of interstate parks, and the conservation and development of Atlantic marine fisheries. Thirty-seven such compacts were made between 1934 and 1947. The largest is the Crime Compact, providing for interstate supervision of parolees and probationers, which has been agreed to by forty-five states.[47] The Atlantic States Marine Fisheries Commission may be taken as a typical example of the development of an interstate compact. Starting in 1937, it grew out of a series of annual meetings of delegates representing the Atlantic coastal states. By 1940 it had developed into an organization approved by Congress. The Commission was created for "the better utilization of the fisheries, marine, shell and anadromous, of the Atlantic Seaboard by the development of a joint program for the promotion and protection of such fisheries and by the prevention of the physical waste of the fisheries from any cause." The organ of the compact consists of a commission of three members from each of the twelve states. Its purpose is to advise as to legislation that may be enacted by the states in order to carry out the objects of the compact. Interstate compact agencies are still in the early experimental stage and will advance with experience. [48]

Uniform State Laws

While absolute uniformity of state laws would be neither possible nor desirable, uniformity in certain fields is both advantageous and feasible. The movement to bring this about by voluntary acceptance and enactment of model statutes began in 1892 with the organization of the National Conference of Commissioners on Uniform State Laws, which is an affiliate of the American Bar Association. The Conference has drafted and approved nearly a hundred model uniform acts since its organization. In 1940 the Council of State Governments began a program of co-operation with the National Conference with the result that an increasing number of uniform model acts have become state laws. In 1947, for example, eighty such acts were introduced in state legislatures and forty-two were passed. The movement for uniform legislation is only beginning in some fields, but it has already put a model-uniform Negotiable Instruments Law on the statute books of every state. Every state has enacted the Uniform Warehouse Receipts Statute and forty-three states, the Uniform Narcotic Drugs Act. Among the difficulties encountered by the promoters of the uniform state laws are differences in state legal phraseologies, the short tenure of state legislators with a consequent discontinuity of policies, and the problems of capturing the attention of overburdened legislators. Various Federal agencies such as the Department of Justice and the Social Security Board have managed to persuade states to adopt uniform legislation, and in such instances the Federal Supreme Court's interpretations are invaluable in setting standards for the states. The Federal government's grants of

---

[47] Council of State Governments: *Book of the States* (Chicago, 1950–51), p. 48.
[48] Jane P. Clark: "Interstate Compacts and Social Legislation." *Political Science Quarterly* (1935), 50:502–25; (1936), 51:36–61.

financial aid to the states is potent in promoting uniform state legislation.[49] While it is possible to get the states to enact many uniform laws, nothing can be done to obtain uniform interpretation of them by the various state courts, and the Supreme Court has refused to follow the state supreme courts in their decisions on commercial law.[50]

FEDERAL-STATE COOPERATION

Peacetime Federal-State Cooperation

In no less than twenty numbers of the *Federalist* Madison and Hamilton indicated the opinion that the Federal government would make use of state officials to effect its purposes. This proved to be a miscalculation in terms of the immediate future. By 1842 Associate Justice Joseph Story, speaking for the Supreme Court, denied to the states even the power to pass laws to promote the administration of Federal law for the rendition of fugitive slaves.[51] Until comparatively recent years a hard-and-fast separation has obtained between the functioning of the Federal and the state governments. Indeed the statutes and constitutions of some states forbade their officials holding Federal office. The administration of universal military service, when introduced during World War I, gave the first great impetus to the utilization of state machinery by the Federal government. By the 1920's state officials were being appointed at nominal salaries as prohibition officers of the Federal Treasury Department to enforce the National Prohibition Act. Sometimes state officials are designated to aid in the administration of Federal law. For example, state game wardens are deputized as Federal game wardens to aid in the administration of the Migratory Bird Treaty Act. Federal forest officials are generally appointed state deputy fish and game wardens. In order to avoid conflict or duplication, formal contracts of joint activity are sometimes made between Federal and state officials. The same may be accomplished by informal understandings. Arnold Brecht has declared: "The choice before the states is that of participating in the administration of national standards imposed by the federal government or submitting to federal encroachments of those standards." [52]

Wartime Federal-State Cooperation

During World War II, the Federal government relied as never before upon citizen action at the local level. Public school teachers administered the registration for rationing scarce commodities. In response to Federal recommendations, states promptly established the thirty-five-miles-per-

[49] Rodney L. Mott: "Uniform Legislation in the United States." *Annals of the American Academy of Political and Social Sciences* (1940), 207:79–92.

[50] J. A. C. Grant: "The Search for Uniform Law." *American Political Science Review* (1938), 32:1082–98.

[51] 16 Peters 539 (1842).

[52] Jane P. Clark: "Joint Activity Between Federal and State Officials." *Political Science Quarterly* (1936), 51:230.

hour speed limit for motor vehicles to conserve rubber. In order to facilitate motor transportation of war material, the confusion of interstate standards was promptly resolved through the adoption by all the states of uniform maximum size and weight requirements for trucks. In order to ensure adequate financial resources for the Federal government in prosecuting World War II and at the same time not impair the functions of the states, a cooperative fiscal plan prepared by the Tax Committee of the Council of State Governments was adopted by almost every state legislature in session in 1942. The Council was also successful in bringing almost to a standstill the tendency of states to erect trade barriers.

CENTRALIZATION

The Influence of Pressures

The historic alternation of centralizing and decentralizing tendencies in American government has resulted from the tug of war between opposing sets of forces in American society. Corresponding ideological controversies represent little more than rationalizations of these two sets of interests. It must not be forgotten that the Constitution itself was a centralizing instrument produced by a combination of interests whose desires found realization in a strong central government and a dozen years of Federalist party rule. This centralization irked the inland agrarians, and in opposing it they planted the germ of the doctrine of states' rights in American political philosophy. In the course of time the great planting interests, in combating the threatened domination of the Federal government by the growing financial and emerging industrial interests, evolved out of the dogmas of states rights the formula of state nullification of congressional legislation which culminated logically in the secession movement of 1861.

     The forces of finance and industry allied with mixed farming overcame the disruptive forces of secession and achieved the triumph of centralization as a consequence of the Civil War. Centralization was sanctified by the apotheosizing of the concept of the "Union," while the decentralizing dogma of states' rights was bombarded with the emotion-charged propaganda of the dominant interests of the nation in the generation following the Civil War.

The Resurgence of the Doctrine of States' Rights

The revival of the dogma of states' rights by the very interests that had crushed it in the 1860's constitutes one of the ironies of recent political history. When the powers of the national government that had been strengthened by financial and industrial interests came in time to be utilized to check the excesses of these very interests (through regulation of railroad rates, outlawing of monopolistic practices, and financial and stock-market manipulations) these interests made an ideological about-face and revived the ancient slogan of state rights, but without significant results. Two World Wars have had their centralizing effect, but even stronger has been the impact of the gigantic depression of the 1930's on the distribution of power between the Federal and state governments. The unprecedented financial demands for relief purposes promptly exhausted the tax and credit resources of the states and recourse was then had to the vaster resources of the nation. Through grants-in-aid, expansion of the power to regulate commerce, and resort to other powers of Congress, a permanent program of social legislation was established that constituted a revolution in the employment of Federal power.

It is incontrovertible that whenever public opinion or, more realistically, a sufficiently vocal set of interests, is convinced that its desires can best be achieved through employment of Federal power that power will be utilized, dogmas of states' rights to the contrary notwithstanding. The Commission on Intergovernmental Relations in 1955 reached the following conclusions: "Precise divisions of governmental activities need always to be considered in the light of varied and shifting circumstances; they need always to be viewed in the light of principles rooted in our history. Assuming efficient and responsible government at all levels—national, state, and local—we should seek to divide our civic responsibilities so that we leave to private initiative all the functions that citizens can perform privately; use the level of government closest to the community for all public functions it can handle; utilize cooperative intergovernmental arrangements where appropriate to attain economical performance and popular approval; reserve national action for residual participation where State and local governments are not fully adequate, and for the continuing responsibilities that only the National Government can undertake." [53]

SUMMARY

To the first generation under the Constitution the state governments loomed large despite the specific limitations of state power in Article 1, section 10 of the Constitution. The national government then seemed of rather secondary importance. But by the middle of the nineteenth century the national government had become significant indeed. Presently the outcome of the Civil War vindicated Federal authority and exalted enormously the prestige of the national government.

In the midst of the Civil War the policy of Federal grants-in-aid was initiated and, as the practice grew, the states lost some control of their concerns. Moreover, state power has been gradually declining through voluntary cooperation with Federal agencies, through Federal judicial decisions reducing state powers, through the Thirteenth, Fourteenth, Fifteenth, and Nineteenth Amendments to the Constitution, and through exercise of the broad treaty powers of the Federal government.

The Constitution assures each state a republican form of government, equal representation in the Senate, protection against invasion and

[53] *Report to the President*, p. 6.

domestic violence and against involuntary dismemberment. The states, in turn, have the obligations to the Federal government to conduct elections of Federal officers and to participate in amending the Constitution. The states owe full faith and credit to each other's public records, must accord citizens of other states the privileges and immunities of their own citizens, and are morally obligated to return fugitives from justice to the states from which they have fled.

States use the privilege granted by the Constitution of making interstate compacts to solve collectively regional problems. Uniform laws voluntarily enacted by state legislatures supply the lack of congressional power to legislate on certain matters. The cooperation of state and Federal officers in such fields as conservation and the war power solves problems of jurisdiction between Federal and state governments. Dogmas of state rights yield eventually to the pressures of interests determined to use Federal powers to attain their objectives as to public policies.

PART

II

CITIZENSHIP: RIGHTS AND PRIVILEGES

CHAPTER VII

CITIZENSHIP AND CIVIL RIGHTS

What is Citizenship?

Few human relationships are more important than the one signified
by the word "citizen." It is unfortunate that popular usage has er-
roneously made the term synonymous with "voter." A citizen is
simply a member of the great political society that constitutes the state,
and as a consequence of this membership he has obligations to the state.
For most Americans, certainly all native Americans, this membership begins at birth. The designation of native American children as "future citizens" is, of course, incorrect since only unborn children are future citizens
—unless the reference is to aliens not yet naturalized. The term "citizen"
stands in contrast with "alien," that is, one who is not a citizen of the state
or nation in which he resides. The population of a typical national state consists of both citizens and a number of aliens.

How American Citizenship is Determined

The basic American formula for the determination of citizenship comes as
a heritage from England. English Common Law based citizenship on the
place of birth, or *jus soli*. This principle contrasts with the European continental principle of *jus sanguinis* which determines citizenship by parentage. So intensely interested were the American colonists in adding newcomers to their political societies that one of the indictments of King
George III in the Declaration of Independence was that "he has endeavored to prevent the population of these states, for that purpose ob-
structing the laws of naturalization of foreigners, and refusing to pass
others to encourage their migration hither." On the very day the Declaration of Independence was signed Congress passed a resolution that "all persons abiding in any of the United Colonies and deriving protection from

laws of the same owe allegiance to said laws and are members of such colonies." The Articles of Confederation which went into effect in 1781 provided that "the free inhabitants of each of these States . . . shall be entitled to all the privileges and immunities of the free citizens in the several states."

"Citizens" in the Original Constitution

Without attempting to define the term, the framers of the Constitution accepted the existing fact of citizenship—whatever it meant in 1787—and consequently the Constitution only refers to "citizens" in a half dozen clauses. No person was to be a representative in Congress who shall not have "been seven years a citizen of the United States" or "a Senator who shall not have been nine years a citizen of the United States." No person except a natural-born citizen of the United States or a citizen of the United States at the time of the adoption of the Constitution of the United States shall be eligible to the office of President of the United States." State citizenship was just as casually taken for granted in such provisions as that "the judicial power shall extend to all cases between a state and citizens of another state . . . " and "the citizens of each state shall be entitled to all the privileges and immunities of citizens of the several states."

Citizenship Before the Civil War

The accepted basis of citizenship a century ago was succinctly expressed in Joseph Story's classic statement: "Every citizen of a state is *ipso facto* a citizen of the United States." [1] This principle was first given judicial sanction in the Dred Scott decision in 1857 when Chief Justice Taney, speaking for a majority of the Court, said: "Every person, and every class and description of persons who were at the time of the adoption of the Constitution recognized as citizens in the several states, became also citizens of the new political body; but none other." [2] The Court concluded that this absolutely excluded Negroes from United States citizenship and since that interpretation had not been reversed eight years later when the Thirteenth Amendment freed the slaves, the freedmen did not automatically become citizens. The Civil Rights Act of 1866 established their citizenship, but in order to place the matter beyond repeal by a future Congress, the Fourteenth Amendment was adopted.

Citizenship Defined by the Fourteenth Amendment

The opening sentence of the Fourteenth Amendment, adopted in 1868, reversed the Dred Scot decision on citizenship by providing the following: "All persons born or naturalized in the United States, and subject to the

---

[1] Joseph Story: *Commentaries on the Constitution of the United States* (Boston, 1833), sec. 1693.

[2] Dred Scott *v.* Sandford, 19 Howard 393 (1857).

jurisdiction thereof, are citizens of the United States and of the state wherein they reside." As a consequence, United States citizenship is now primary while state citizenship is incidental to residence in a state. The day that a citizen establishes permanent residence in a state he becomes a citizen of that state. Thus it is possible one day to be a citizen of Ohio and the next day a citizen of Indiana. The migrant does not at once acquire all the privileges of citizens of the new state. All the states require a period of residence before the voting privilege may be exercised by a newcomer. The qualifying phrase "subject to the jurisdiction thereof" has the effect of excepting from automatic acquisition of United States citizenship children born to diplomatic representatives living in the United States who, of course, are not subject to its jurisdiction.[3] By the same token a child born at an American embassy abroad is, because of the legal fiction that makes the site of such an embassy American soil, born "in the United States and subject to the jurisdiction thereof," and he is consequently a natural-born citizen of the United States. The Supreme Court of the United States merely applied the plain meaning of the Fourteenth Amendment when it decided that Wong Kim Ark, born of Chinese parents who were subjects of the Emperor of China but permanently domiciled in San Francisco, was a citizen of the United States even though his parents were ineligible for naturalization.[4] In 1943 a California organization, eager to deny citizenship to Japanese born in the United States, sought to have the Wong Kim Ark decision reversed but lost in the circuit court their case which the Supreme Court refused to review.[5] The Supreme Court has held that some territory subject to the jurisdiction of the United States is so uncertainly attached as to be designated "unincorporated territory." Birth within unincorporated territory does not automatically establish American citizenship, but citizenship may be conferred on inhabitants of such territory by act of Congress. Thus Congress conferred United States citizenship upon the inhabitants of the unincorporated territory of Puerto Rico in 1916. The inhabitants of the unincorporated Philippines were never made citizens of the United States since the official assumption always was that the occupation was temporary.

Citizenship Defined by Statute

By an act of June 27, 1952, Congress codified the legislation as to citizens of the United States by birth. With certain qualifications, those persons are citizens of the United States who were: (a) born in the United States and subject to its jurisdiction; (b) born to an Indian, Esquimau, Aleutian, or other aboriginal tribe; (c) born outside the United States and its outlying possessions of parents both of whom are citizens of the United

---

[3] A foreign embassy is deemed, according to international law, to be outside the jurisdiction of the nation in which it is located but within the jurisdiction of the foreign nation that maintains it.

[4] 169 U.S. 649 (1898).

[5] Regan *v.* King, 319 U.S. 753 (1943).

States and one of whom had resided in the United States or its possessions previous to the birth; (d) born outside the United States and its
possessions, if one parent is a citizen of the United States who had resided within the above-described area before the birth; (e) born in an
outlying possession of the United States of parents one of whom is a citizen of the United States who, previous to the birth, resided within
the area mentioned; (f) a child of unknown parentage found in the
United States; (g) born outside the United States and its possessions if
one parent is a citizen who had resided ten years in an outlying possession previous to the birth of the child.

CITIZENSHIP BY NATURALIZATION

Naturalization

From the time of the Revolutionary War to the time when the Constitution
went into effect in 1789 the thirteen states exercised their sovereignty in
establishing state naturalization laws. However, the competition to attract
population by lenient requirements led to much confusion. For example,
an alien who was a resident of a state in which he could not meet the requirements for naturalization could move to another state with less stringent standards and acquire citizenship there. Then he could resume his
former residence and claim the full benefits of that state's citizenship under
the provisions of the Articles of Confederation guaranteeing to the free inhabitants of each state ". . . all privileges and immunities of the free
citizens in the several states."[6] This was the situation that impelled the
framers to assign Congress the power "to establish an *uniform* rule of naturalization." So urgent was this matter that President Washington in his
first annual message to Congress recommended "that the terms on which
foreigners may be admitted to the rights of citizens should be speedily ascertained by a uniform rule of naturalization." [7] Congress promptly enacted
the first Federal naturalization law.

Collective Naturalization

Naturalization may be collective in that groups are involuntarily transformed into American citizens. The treaty-making power was employed to
convert aliens into citizens of the United States when the Louisiana Territory was annexed in 1803, Florida in 1819, the territory acquired from
Mexico in 1848, and Alaska in 1867. When the independent Republic of
Texas was admitted to the Union by a joint resolution of the two houses of
Congress (1845), Texans at once became citizens of the United States. Citizenship was conferred upon Hawaiians collectively by Act of Congress in
1900 and upon Puerto Ricans by the same method in 1916. By a number of

[6] See the *Federalist*, No. 42.
[7] James D. Richardson, editor: *Messages of the Presidents*, Vol. I, p. 66.

statutes enacted since 1887 members of the Indian and other aboriginal tribes were declared to be citizens of the United States if born within the United States.

Naturalization of Individuals

Congress has established by statute a uniform process for the naturalization of aliens as individuals. By the Act of 1790 the naturalization of only "free white persons" was authorized. In 1870, however, under the influence of the sentiment that produced the three Civil War amendments, persons of African nativity and descent also were made eligible for naturalization. The phrase "free white persons" has burdened the courts with the necessity of giving interpretations for a number of cases involving its meaning. As a result the term includes Armenians, Syrians, and Mexicans as eligible for naturalization but excludes Japanese, Burmese, Koreans, native Filipinos, North American Indians and, despite the fact that they are Caucasians, the Asiatic Indians. Orientals have generally been denied naturalization, but an act of Congress in 1943 made the Chinese eligible. "Descendants of races indigenous to the Western Hemisphere" were made eligible for naturalization at the same time.[8]

Statutory Barriers to Naturalization

In addition to the ethnic barriers statutes deny naturalization to anyone who advocates "opposition to all organized government" or who belongs to a group that "believes in the overthrow of the United States or of all forms of law." Also denied naturalization are polygamists, persons unable to speak English, and those who upon the outbreak of war withdrew their declaration of intention to be naturalized and were consequently relieved of military service. Whoever petitions for naturalization must take an oath renouncing and abjuring absolutely allegiance to any foreign power or prince of whom the petitioner had been a subject or citizen, and he must pledge that "he will support and defend the Constitution and laws of the United States against all enemies, foreign and domestic, and bear true faith and allegiance to the same."[9] By the act of June 27, 1952, "the rights of a person to become a naturalized citizen of the United States shall not be denied or abridged because of race or sex or because the person is married."[10] But "any person who advocates or teaches or who is a member of or affiliated with any organization that advocates or teaches opposition to all organized government or who advocates or teaches or who is a member of or affiliated with any organization that advocates or teaches the overthrow by force or violence or other unconstitutional means of the government of the United States" may not be naturalized as a citizen of the United States. These provisions apply to

[8] U.S. Code, tit. 8, sec. 703.
[9] U.S. Code, tit. 8, secs. 705 and 735.
[10] 66 Stat. 163 tit. III, Sec. 311.

any applicant for naturalization who, during the preceding ten years or between application and taking the oath of citizenship, has been within the proscribed classes of this section notwithstanding that at the time the petition is filed he may not be included within such classes.[11]

If it can be shown that the naturalized citizen took his oath of allegiance to the United States with mental reservations or concealed beliefs and affiliations that would disqualify him, his certificate of naturalization may be revoked on the ground of fraud. When President Grant reported that some naturalized citizens were returning to their native country and using their certificates to escape their military obligations there, Congress provided that if, within five years of naturalization such a citizen resumed permanent residence in his native land, his certificate may be revoked on the ground that he never intended to become a citizen of the United States. The naturalized citizen is not eligible to be a representative in Congress until the passing of six years or senator until the end of nine years after naturalization, and he never can become eligible for the presidency. Otherwise he stands "under the Constitution . . . on an equal footing with the native citizen. No less than the native citizen he enjoys the freedom of speech, of the press, of assembly and indeed the whole catalogue of civil rights."[12]

The Process of Naturalizing Individuals

In exercising its power "to establish an uniform rule of naturalization" Congress prescribes the procedure and may and does authorize state courts to administer the function. In doing this state courts become agents of the Federal government. An applicant must demonstrate an understanding of the English language, including an ability to read, write and speak words in ordinary usage in English, unless physically unable to do so, or unless, on December 24th, 1852, he was over 50 years of age and had been living in the United States at least 20 years. An alien 18 years of age or over may file a petition for naturalization. Before doing so, however, he must make preliminary application. Thereafter, he is notified by the Immigration and Naturalization Service when and where to appear with his witnesses for preliminary interrogation, and to file petition for naturalization. The applicant and his witnesses are questioned by an examiner, and if he meets the requirements, the examiner assists him in filing the petition. Generally, the petition must be filed with the clerk of the court in the jurisdiction in which the petitioner resides. After filing of the petition, and after further examination, the petitioner is notified by mail when to appear in a naturalization court for final hearing. If the judge is convinced that the applicant can speak the English language, does not hold views subversive of government, and

[11] *Ibid.*, Sec. 313.
[12] E. S. Corwin: *The Constitution and What It Means Today* (Princeton, 1946), pp. 48–9.

has a reasonable understanding of American government, he orders the administering of the oath and the issuing of the certificate of citizenship. If the petition is granted, the petitioner must renounce allegiance to any foreign state of which he is a citizen or subject, and swear allegiance to the United States. If the Immigration and Naturalization Service recommends that the petition for naturalization be denied, the petitioner may request the court to review the case.

The Trend Toward Administrative Naturalization

It is a curious fact that, with the single exception of Canada, the United States is the only nation that vests naturalization procedure in the courts. In 1926 Congress enacted a statute authorizing judges of the District Courts of the United States to designate examiners or officers of the Bureau of Naturalization to conduct preliminary hearings upon petitions for naturalization and to make findings and recommendations upon them to the Court. In 99 per cent of the cases now heard by these examiners the findings are approved by the courts. Thus the courts appear to be approaching the practice of a routine ratification of the judgments of the commissioners. The next step in this evolution now seems to be naturalization through an administrative process by a designated examiner who issues the certificate as soon as he has determined that the petitioner is qualified for citizenship but with the privilege of review by the courts.[13]

How Citizenship May Be Lost

United States citizenship may be lost by expatriation, which is the act of deliberately giving up one's citizenship and becoming naturalized in another nation. The Supreme Court has held expatriation to be one of the "privileges and immunities of citizens of the United States." There is a widely held but erroneous belief that conviction of treason or other crimes automatically deprives the convict of his citizenship.[14] By the act of June 27, 1952, Congress provided that citizenship may be lost by taking an oath of allegiance to a foreign state; serving in the armed forces of a foreign state without authorization and with consequent acquisition of foreign nationality; assuming public office under the government of a foreign state for which only nationals are eligible; voting in an election of a foreign state; formal renunciation of citizenship before an American foreign service officer abroad; conviction and discharge from the armed services for desertion in time of war; conviction of treason or an attempt

---

[13] See Henry B. Hazard: "The Trend Toward Administrative Naturalization." *American Political Science Review* (1927), 21:342–9; and Marshall E. Dimrock: "Administrative Standards for Improving Naturalization Procedure." *American Political Science Review* (1943), 37:81–90.

[14] This error may be due to the story of Philip Nolan in Edward Everett Hale's *Man Without A Country*. At any rate that was the opinion expressed by one of my classes in American Government when I inquired where they had got the idea that conviction of treason automatically resulted in loss of citizenship.

at forceful overthrow of the United States; formal renunciation of citizenship within the United States in time of war, subject to approval of the Attorney General; fleeing or remaining outside the United States in time of war or proclaimed emergency to evade military training; residing of a naturalized citizen for two to three years in the country of which he formally was a national or for five years in any foreign state.

The citizenship of the naturalized citizen is somewhat less securely held than that of the natural-born citizen since the former may lose his citizenship under the provision of an Act of 1906 which authorizes revocation on the ground that the certificate of naturalization was fraudulently or illegally procured. Thus naturalization has been revoked on the ground that the applicant was a member, during World War I, of the radical labor organization known as the International Workers of the World, or that he was an anarchist, or a communist when the certificate of naturalization was issued and was not therefore "attached to the principles of the Constitution of the United States and well disposed to the good order and happiness of the United States." [15] However the burden of proof rests upon the prosecution and in the early 1940's two district court decisions ordering revocations of citizenship were reversed on the ground that the Government had not discharged the burden of proof. Thus the late Wendell Willkie saved from revocation the citizenship of an alleged Communist, Schneiderman, in a case reviewed by the Supreme Court.[16]

Effect on Citizenship of Marriage to Aliens

No longer does the citizenship of the husband determine the citizenship of the wife when an American citizen marries an alien. It was long the rule that the alien in such a marriage, if she were a woman of a race eligible for citizenship, automatically became an American citizen, while an American woman automatically lost her citizenship when she married an alien. World War I suddenly brought to a focus the paradoxes potential in such regulations. Native German women who had married American citizens were of course citizens of the United States, while American women married to Germans suddenly found themselves legally transformed into enemy aliens. By the Cable Act in 1922 Congress provided first, that an alien woman may be naturalized whether her husband remains an alien or not. (Previously she could not have acquired citizenship except through the naturalization of her husband.) Second, it provided that an alien woman marrying an American citizen does not thereby any longer automatically acquire American citizenship, but may be naturalized by a simplified procedure. Third, it provided that an American woman marrying an alien does not thereby lose her citizenship, and fourth, that an American woman who had already lost her citizenship by

[15] Lawrence Preuss: "Denaturalization on the Ground of Disloyalty." *American Political Science Review* (1942), 36:701–710.

[16] Schneiderman *v.* United States, 320 U.S. 118 (1943).

the operation of the old rule governing marriage to an alien was enabled to recover it by a simplified procedure.

CIVIL LIBERTIES

What Are Civil Liberties?

American traditions of civil liberty grew out of colonial, Revolutionary, and early national political experience. To the fathers these traditions meant freedom of the individual from governmental interference with personal conduct and action. A comprehensive enumeration of them would be impossible, but several of them were written into the body of the Federal Constitution and more of them are found in the amendments, particularly in the first ten which are popularly designated the "Bill of Rights." Freedom of the press, religion, speech, and assembly are typical civil liberties. These liberties are all corollaries of the doctrine of limited governments, that is, governments possessing only the powers delegated by the sovereign people. This doctrine presumes the existence of what one American scholar called a "sphere of anarchy," which signifies an area of human activity in which the government is not to interfere with personal conduct but in which it will exert its authority to prevent any individual from interfering with another's freedom. Our fathers were enabled to clarify their thinking on such matters by use of the now outmoded formula of the social compact as expounded by Locke and set forth in the vibrant phrases of the Declaration of Independence. Thus the fathers conceived civil liberties to be the inherent rights of individuals which were securely possessed by man before governments were instituted and which were never delegated because they were "inalienable." When the Revolutionary state constitutions were constructed on the pattern of the social compact, their framers were not satisfied with the mere implication of the existence of civil liberties but insisted on listing the principal ones in the bills of rights of these constitutions. The framers of the Constitution at Philadelphia included no formal bill of rights, largely because they assumed that in a constitution of specifically delegated powers it was inconsistent to begin enumerating powers not delegated.

The Civil Liberties in the Original Constitution. The Writ of Habeas Corpus

The writ of habeas corpus is a legal process which enables a person held in custody to petition a judge for a hearing to determine the legality of his imprisonment. If the judge concludes that there is insufficient evidence to justify confinement he orders the release of the prisoner. The framers did not specifically guarantee the maintenance of this ancient writ but instead took for granted its universal acceptance among Americans and merely introduced the important safeguard of providing that it "shall not be suspended, unless in case of rebellion or invasion the public safety may require it." [17] Since this provision is found in a list of restrictions of Congress, it has been assumed that only Congress might authorize the suspension. Nevertheless, when the passage of Federal troops through Baltimore to Washington, D. C. was hindered at the opening of the Civil War, President Lincoln authorized General Scott to suspend the writ on the route taken by troops, without consulting Congress which was not then in session. One Merryman, apprehended for interfering with troop movements, sought a writ of habeas corpus from Chief Justice Taney who was unable to have the writ served and had to content himself with a statement condemning Lincoln for what he considered the Executive's usurpation of power that belonged to Congress.[18] When Congress convened it gave Lincoln the somewhat dubious retroactive authority for his suspension of the writ. Since the suspension was confined to a theater of war Lincoln's authority there as commander-in-chief was presumably supreme and the suspension could scarcely have been challenged as unconstitutional. [19]

Bill of Attainder

The Supreme Court has defined this term as a "legislative act, which inflicts punishment without judicial trial." [20] The framers remembered this device as one used by the English Parliament to dispose of political opponents by executions, and it was not unknown to state legislatures during the American Revolution. In 1865 Congress passed the Test Oath Act which, among other things, denied the right to practice in the Federal courts to attorneys who could not take the oath that they had never borne arms against the United States. The Supreme Court found this to be a bill of attainder because it imposed the penalty without judicial trial.[21] In 1943 a sub-committee of the Appropriations Committee of the House of Representatives, after an *ex parte* inquiry into the records, views, and writings of three Federal officials, concluded that they were guilty of "subversive activity" and were "unfit" to continue in government service. In order to force them out of office the House passed a rider to the Urgent Deficiency Appropriation Bill for 1943 providing that no salary or compensation should be paid to the three officials unless the President before November 15, 1943, again appointed them with Senate confirmation. Despite the rejection of this rider five times by the Senate the stubborn insistence of the House forced its acceptance. Three years later the Supreme Court found the rider to be a bill of attainder and consequently unconstitutional. Said the Court: "Section 304 (the rider) thus clearly accomplishes

[17] *Constitution:* Art. 1, Sec. 9, Clause 2.
[18] *Ex parte* Merryman, Fed. Case No. 9487.
[19] See E. S. Corwin: *The Constitution and What It Means Today,* 1946, pp. 68–9.
[20] Cummings *v.* Missouri, 4 Wallace 277 (1867).
[21] *Ex parte* Garland, 4 Wallace 333 (1867).

the punishment of named individuals without a judicial trial. The fact that the punishment inflicted through the instrumentality of an Act specifically cutting off the pay of certain named individuals found guilty of disloyalty makes it no less galling or effective than if it had been done by an Act which designated the conduct as criminal . . . The effect was to inflict punishment without the safeguards of a judicial trial and determined by no previous law or fixed rule. The Constitution declares that that cannot be done by a state or by the United States." [22]

Ex-Post-Facto Law

Both Congress and the state legislatures are forbidden by the Constitution to enact ex-post-facto laws. Interpreted literally the term ought to mean any kind of retroactive legislation, that is, laws making illegal any acts not illegal when committed. This may have been the intended meaning of the framers. However, when the Constitution was made English law did not apply the principle to civil cases. Consequently the Supreme Court, in deciding a case in 1798, set a permanent precedent by confining the ex-post-facto restriction to criminal cases.[23] So an ex-post-facto law is one which penalizes that which was not a crime at the time the act in question was committed or which increases the penalty for a crime that has been committed or alters the rules of evidence or procedure to the disadvantage of the accused. For example, in the Garland case referred to above,[24] the Court held that not only was the act unconstitutional as a bill of attainder but also as an ex-post-facto law since it authorized an eight-man jury whereas twelve had been required when the penalized action had occurred. The chances of acquittal were reduced because an eight-man jury could more easily reach the unanimity required for conviction.

Treason

The American legal conception of treason is that of an offense against the United States or one of the states of the Union and not an offense against an individual. Assassins of presidents, for example, have been prosecuted for murder instead of for treason. The English historian Hallam referred to the trials for treason in the reign of Queen Elizabeth (1558–1603) as "those glaring transgressions of natural as well as positive law that reduced our courts of justice in cases of treason to but little better than caverns of murderers." The framers were familiar with the later English use of the charge of treason as a means of wreaking murderous vengeance on political opponents. They recognized that the difficulty had lain in the loose interpretation of this indefinite term and they consequently decided to give it a precise and limited meaning by confining it to two offenses:

[22] United States *v.* Lovett, 328 U.S. 303 (1946).
[23] Calder *v.* Bull, 3 Dallas 386 (1798).
[24] Supra, p. 114.

"levying war against them [the United States] or adhering to their enemies, giving them aid and comfort." [25] Evidently this means that there can be no treason not connected with actual war or a state of war. Opposition to the enforcement of law by an armed force is not treason unless it is undertaken in order to overthrow the government or to prevent the execution of some governmental power.[26] Protection against persecution by the charge of treason is further assured by the requirement for conviction either on the testimony of two witnesses to the same overt act, or on confession in open court. An "overt act" is one definite enough to be testified to by those who saw it. Aaron Burr escaped conviction because it could not be proved by an "overt act" that he was linked with the conspiracy known to exist, and this proof was required by Chief Justice Marshall who presided at the trial. War is not levied "until the treasonable military force is actually assembled." [27]

THE LIBERTIES OF THE FEDERAL BILL OF RIGHTS

Religious Freedom

At the time of the framing of the Constitution two states had officially established state churches and several other states had just dis-established such churches. These state churches were bitterly denounced by the dissenting denominations because, in addition to other special privileges, the established churches were supported by public taxation with which members of the dissenting denominations were burdened in addition to their voluntary support of their own churches. Dissenters were alarmed by the silence of the new Constitution on this matter because they feared that a national church might be established. Specifically designed to allay this fear is the phrasing of the First Amendment to the Constitution: "Congress shall make no law respecting an establishment of religion, or prohibiting the free exercise thereof." "Establishment of religion" here means an established church. In 1811 Madison, in a rather far-fetched interpretation, vetoed a bill passed by Congress which incorporated a church and also gave certain government lands to a church in one of the territories on the ground that these acts violated the First Amendment.[28]

The prohibitions of the first ten amendments are directed against Congress.[29] This amendment left the states free to establish and maintain state churches as some New England states did for a generation after the adoption of the First Amendment. This amendment also "safeguards the free exercise of the chosen form of religion" [30] of the individual. How-

---

[25] *Constitution:* Art. 3, Sec. 3, Clause 1.
[26] United States v. Vigol, 2 Dallas 346 (1795).
[27] *Ex parte* Bollman, 4 Cr. 75 (1807).
[28] See S. P. Orth and Robert E. Cushman: *American National Government* (New York, 1931), p. 125.
[29] Barron v. Baltimore, 7 Peters 243 (1833).
[30] Cantwell v. Conn., 310 U. S. 296, 303.

ever "the free exercise of religion" cannot be made a defense for socially reprehensible practices such as polygamy or the refusal of a parent to provide medical aid for his children on the ground that his religious beliefs forbid it.[31]

Freedom of Speech and of the Press

The injunction of the First Amendment that Congress shall make no law "abridging the freedom of speech or of the press" seems simple enough, but the courts have been compelled to set up standards of interpretation. For example, the late Justice Oliver Wendell Holmes once observed: "The most stringent protection of free speech would not protect a man in falsely shouting 'fire' in a theater and causing a panic." [32] Free speech does not save a person from liability in damages for slander unless the statement can be proved. Libels, that is published statements, are subject to criminal penalties as well as damages if malice and injury can be shown. Since a criminal libel is a breach of the peace, even the truth of the statement may not constitute a defense. Freedom of the press is not infringed by the outlawing of obscene literature in the interest of public morality.

The issue of freedom of speech and of the press has arisen with respect to Congress's exercise of its power "to make all laws which shall be necessary and proper for carrying into execution" the delegated powers of the Federal government. Thus in 1798 while preparing the country for war, Congress passed the notorious Sedition Act which penalized the "uttering or publishing any false, scandalous, and malignant writing or writings against the government of the United States . . . with intent to defame said government." [33] So indefinite was the language of the statute that Federalist judges pronounced severe sentences upon political opponents for what would pass today for relatively innocent comments on public officials with the consequence that the statute was thoroughly discredited.

Hysteria during World War I induced Congress to supplement the Espionage Act of 1917 with the Sedition Act of 1918 which penalized those who "wilfully utter, print, write, or publish any disloyal, profane, scurrilous, or abusive language about the form of government of the United States or the military or naval forces of the United States or the flag of the United States or the uniform of the army or navy of the United States or any language intended to bring "these into contempt, scorn, contumely, or disrepute." Loose terminology, as in the earlier sedition act, enabled Federal judges to impose stringent prison sentences on persons for advocating heavier taxation instead of bond issues, and for maintaining that conscription was unconstitutional, that the sinking of merchant vessels was legal, that a referendum should have preceded the declaration of war, and that war is contrary to the teachings of Christ. Charles Evans Hughes

[31] People *v.* Pearson, 176 N.Y. 201 (1903).
[32] Schenck *v.* United States, 249 U.S. 47 (1919).
[33] U. S. Statutes at Large, Vol. I, pp. 596–7.

was moved to say in 1920: "We may well wonder in view of the precedents now established whether constitutional government as hitherto maintained in the Republic could survive another great war even victoriously waged."

That no comparable hysteria affecting freedom of speech accompanied World War II may have been due largely to a score of decisions of the Supreme Court clarifying law with respect to freedom of speech and of the press. Conspicuous in this respect was the test formula first stated by Justice Oliver Wendell Holmes in 1919. "The question in every case" said the Justice, "is whether the words used are used in such circumstances and are of such nature as to create a clear and present danger that will bring about the substantive evil that Congress has a right to prevent." [34] Until mid-century the Supreme Court generally applied the "clear and present danger" test in reviewing cases, but in 1951 it upheld the conviction for disorderly conduct of a student soapbox orator addressing only seventy-five people in a side street of Syracuse.

The Right of Assembly and Petition

"Congress shall make no law . . . abridging . . . the right of the people peaceably to assemble and to petition the government for a redress of grievances" concludes the First Amendment. Significant is the adverb "peaceably" since only orderly meetings are exempt from Congressional legislation. This amendment is but another indication of the deep concern over the possibility of Congressional tyranny which existed in the minds of most Americans in the late 1780's. Obviously free government could not exist without freedom to exercise these rights. The Supreme Court has declared: "The right of the people peaceably to assemble for the purpose of petitioning Congress for redress of grievances, or for anything else connected with the powers and duties of the national government is an attribute of national citizenship, and as such under the protection of, and guaranteed by the United States." [35] The right of petition does not insure a corollary guarantee of the consideration of petitions. For example, in the 1830's Congress adopted the "Gag Resolution" which automatically laid on the table antislavery petitions presented to Congress.

The Priority of the Four Freedoms of the First Amendment

Decisions of the Supreme Court during the 1940's indicated that it then considered the four freedoms of the First Amendment "so indispensable to the democratic process and the preservation of the freedom of our people that they occupied a preferred place in our scheme of constitutional values." With respect to most statutes, whether state or Federal, the pre-

[34] Schenck v. United States, 245 U.S. 47 (1919).
[35] United States v. Cruikshank, 92 U.S. 542 (1876).

sumption of the Court was that they were constitutional, and the burden of proof rested with the litigant who challenged their constitutionality. But so vitally important had the Supreme Court come to consider the four freedoms of the First Amendment that the customary presumption of constitutionality would not attach to a statute that appeared to abridge these freedoms.[36] Whether this presumption of the unconstitutionality of legislation restricting these freedoms still stands will be uncertain until new appointees to the Court reveal their position as new cases are decided.

The Right to Bear Arms

The Americans of the 1780's were haunted by the phobia of a standing army. Extreme opponents of the Constitution had pointed to the power of Congress to raise and support armies and one spokesman had seriously predicted that the capital would be a walled city where an "army of 50,000 or perhaps 100,000 men will be finally embodied and will sally forth to enslave the people who will be disarmed." [37] A counterbalance to the army was needed, and to calm the fears of the people the Second Amendment provided: "A well-regulated militia being necessary for a free state, the rights of the people to keep and bear arms shall not be infringed." The key to the interpretation of this amendment is the qualifying term "well-regulated." The right is guaranteed only to those organized in militias.[38] Legislation regulating the carrying of concealed weapons and the possession of sawed-off shot guns does not fall under the interdiction of the amendment.[39]

Unreasonable Search and Seizure

The Fourth Amendment was insisted upon by a generation with fresh and vivid memories of the detested pre-Revolutionary Writs of Assistance that had enabled British officials with roving commissions to range freely in search of unspecified smuggled goods. The Amendment was carefully phrased with every detail designed specifically to prevent this abuse by declaring: "The rights of the people to be secure in their persons, houses, papers and effects against unreasonable searches and seizures, shall not be violated, and no warrants shall issue but upon probable cause, supported by oath or affirmation, and particularly describing the place to be searched, and the persons or things to be seized." Evidence must support the application for the warrant and nothing can be seized but the things specified.[40] "Houses" means dwelling places, not places of business or

---

[36] Justice Rutledge's statement of the opinion of the Court in Thomas *v.* Collins, 323 U.S. 516 (1944).

[37] Albert J. Beveridge: *Life of John Marshall* (Boston, 1916), Vol. I, p. 346.

[38] Presser *v.* Illinois, 116 U.S. 252 (1886).

[39] United States *v.* Nutler, 307 U.S. 174 (1939).

[40] Byers *v.* United States, 273 U.S. 28 (1927).

open fields which may be searched anyway.[41] The latter are no part of the traditionally sacrosanct "man's castle." The amendment applies solely to governmental action and not to the unlawful acts of individuals. Even those accused or suspected of crime are hereby protected against Federal law-enforcement officers. The regulations of the Post Office Department as to inspection of mail must be subordinate to the principle of this amendment.[42] If a search in violation of the Amendment turns up incriminating evidence, the search does not thereby become lawful.[43] The "search and seizure" guarantee has been related to the safeguard against self-incrimination of the Fifth Amendment because, as the Supreme Court has said, "the unreasonable searches and seizures of the Fourth Amendment are almost always made for the purpose of compelling a man to give evidence against himself." [44] Since evidence obtained by the government by unreasonable search and seizure is self-incriminating, "a man's books and papers cannot be made to speak against him."

Freedom From Self-Incrimination

"No one shall be compelled in a criminal case to be a witness against himself" declares the Fifth Amendment and this applies both to the Federal grand jury investigation and the trial before the petit jury. The Supreme Court defines this as meaning that the accused cannot be required to take the stand, that a witness may refuse to answer any question that might be used against him in a future criminal prosecution, and that neither accused nor witness may be required to produce books or papers that might reveal incriminating evidence.[45] The accused may waive immunity and take the stand in his own defense but must then answer all questions asked in cross-examination. Unless he claims his constitutional immunity he will not be considered to have been compelled to testify.[46] Since refusing to testify is a personal privilege it may not be claimed by an agent of a corporation in its behalf or in regard to its books and papers.[47] Thus an officer or agent of a corporation may not refuse to testify on the ground that his testimony might incriminate the corporation. The protection of the Amendment is personal, and testimony may not be refused because it might incriminate a third party.

The Right to Trial by Jury

This cherished right is assured to anyone "held to answer for a capital or otherwise infamous crime." An "otherwise infamous crime" is one penalized by the loss of political privileges or by a sentence of hard

[41] Hester v. United States, 265 U.S. 57 (1924).
[42] Ex parte Jackson, 96 U.S. 727, 733 (1878).
[43] Byard v. United States, 237 U.S. 28, 29 (1927).
[44] Boyd v. United States, 277 U.S. 438 (1928).
[45] Boyd v. United States, 116 U.S. 616 (1886).
[46] United States v. Monca, 317 U.S. 424 (1943).
[47] Hale v. Henkel, 201 U.S. 43 (1906).

labor.[48] Counterfeiting, fraudulent altering of poll books, fraudulent voting, and embezzlement by a national bank president are examples of crimes declared infamous by the Courts. This provision prevents Congress from infringing the right of the accused to a grand jury "presentment" in which the charge is initiated by the grand jury itself or by an "indictment" where the district attorney lays the evidence before the grand jury which leads to the "true bill." The grand jury consists of from twelve to twenty-three persons under instructions of the judge and the immediate guidance of the Federal district attorney, and it decides whether the evidence is sufficient to justify a trial, in which case it decides on the "true bill" or indictment. Thus the grand jury economizes the time of the trial court by sifting out what ought not come to trial at the same time that it presents the accused with specific charges.

More valuable than the grand jury is the petit or trial jury consisting of twelve persons whose verdict must be unanimous in order to convict. The Sixth Amendment requires that the trial be "speedy" and to this end the privilege of the writ of habeas corpus ensures prompt investigation of the charges; that it be "public," that is, in the presence of observers, particularly the friends of the accused; that it be "impartial" which condition is presumed to be obtained through the challenging and rejection of jurors; that it be held in the "district wherein the crime shall have been committed"; and that the accused be informed of the charges against him, "confronted with the witnesses against him," enabled to compel the obtaining of witnesses in his favor and the assistance of counsel in his defense. In brief, Congress is not to tamper with the immemorial traditional rights of an accused person.

Double Jeopardy

To guard against the persecution of an accused person by repeated trials until conviction might be obtained, the Fifth Amendment warns Congress that no "person be subject for the same offense to be twice put in jeopardy of life or limb." "Limb" is an obsolete term reminiscent of the days of drawing and quartering, and "life and limb" has been judicially reinterpreted to signify life and liberty. A person has been "in jeopardy" after indictment as soon as the trial jury has been empaneled and sworn unless the jury finally disagrees or was not legally constituted, in either of which cases there was no trial and hence no jeopardy; nor is there jeopardy if a higher court on appeal by the accused sets aside the verdict.[49] Once acquitted the accused cannot be tried again for the same offense. If the act committed violates both Federal and state laws, trial by both jurisdictions does not violate the double jeopardy clause since there are technically two offenses, one against the state, the other against the Federal statute. The amendment applies only to the Federal law and leaves the state free

[48] *Ex parte* Wilson, 114 U.S. 417 (1885).
[49] See E. S. Corwin: *The Constitution and What It Means Today*, p. 160.

to exercise its jurisdiction in the matter. Even if the act committed violates two Federal statutes and the consequent offenses can be judicially distinguished, trial under both does not violate the double jeopardy prohibition of the Fifth Amendment.

PROTECTION AGAINST STATE RESTRICTIONS
OF CIVIL LIBERTIES

Involuntary Servitude

The abolition of slavery by the Thirteenth Amendment more than three-quarters of a century ago might lead to the erroneous assumption that the amendment is now merely a historical relic. On the contrary it stands today a vital potential threat to certain insidious practices against which the courts maintain a persistent vigilance. Peonage, for example, is a relationship by which a creditor can compel a debtor to work out his obligation or an employer can compel an unwilling employee to complete his labor contract, and the Supreme Court holds these to be in violation of the Thirteenth Amendment.[50] Peonage is commonly interpreted by the Federal courts as the holding to service by physical punishments, of men and women who have contracted to perform certain labor and are unwilling to carry it out. The Supreme Court has held that enjoining an employee against breaking a contract of employment and taking employment elsewhere in violation of that contract would reduce that employee to "involuntary servitude" in violation of the Thirteenth Amendment. Also in violation of this amendment is a statute making a crime of breach of contract for personal service, for this would be reducing the employee to "involuntary sevitude." [51] In 1945 the Department of Justice of the United States prosecuted a case in which a Negro woman and her ten-year-old son had been held in captivity by a Mississippi farmer. They were forced to work by day on the farm and at night were locked in a crude, windowless, chimneyless cabin. After three unsuccessful attempts to escape, their plight was learned by Federal authorities who began the prosecution. In 1947 a Federal court convicted a man and wife of holding a Negro woman in slavery. The Amendment does not deny to a parent the services of a minor child or to a master that of his apprenticed minor.[52] Compulsory military service, compulsory work on the highways as a civic obligation, and compulsory jury service fall outside the interdiction of the Thirteenth Amendment.[53] When Congress considers the enactment of anti-strike legislation it must be circumspect lest its enactments fall victim to the alertness of the Federal courts in guarding against "involuntary servitude."

[50] Peonage Cases, 123 Fed. 671 (1903).
[51] Bailey v. Alabama, 219 U.S. 219 (1911).
[52] Clyatt v. U.S., 197 U.S. 207 (1905).
[53] Butler v. Perry, 240 U.S. 328 (1916).

Privileges and Immunities of Citizens of the United States

"No state shall make any law which shall abridge the privileges and immunities of citizens of the United States" is an injunction of the Fourteenth Amendment. This prohibition pertains, of course, to a statute of a state, that is, of a member of the Union. When the framers of this amendment wrote "privileges and immunities" into the Amendment they almost certainly had in mind "all the ordinary rights of citizens in a free government," [54] especially those specified in the Bill of Rights of the Federal Constitution. However, the Supreme Court promptly decided that these ordinary rights were attributes only of state citizenship. It consequently limited the "privileges and immunities of citizens of the United States" to those due to Federal powers. As a consequence of court opinion this guarantee might be paraphrased: "No state shall make or enforce any law which shall abridge any privilege or immunity conferred by this Constitution, the statutes or treaties of the United States upon any person who is a citizen of the United States." [55] Among the privileges of United States citizenship named in opinions of the Supreme Court are expatriation, protection on the high seas, access to the Federal government, the use of navigable waters of the United States, becoming citizens of states through residence, peaceable assembly and petition of Congress, exemption from race discrimination, voting for members of Congress and presidential electors, the right of a Negro to have his ballot honestly counted in a congressional primary election, and free migration. The list, however, is never complete.[56]

Due Process of Law

This expression occurs in the Fifth Amendment wherein Congress is warned that no person shall "be deprived of life, liberty, or property without due process of law" and in the Fourteenth Amendment where no state is to "deprive any person of life, liberty, or property without due process of law." As to procedure, due process protects the individual against arbitrary governmental action. The opportunity must be given for a fair hearing of interested parties and judicial review both of the interpretation of the law involved and of the pertinent facts. The Court long ago extended the test of due process to the substance of legislation so that statutes have been held unconstitutional on the ground that Congress or a state legislature exercised its powers "unreasonably" (in the judgment of the Court). Since the police powers of the states are reserved, residual, and unspecified, state legislation has felt the heavy weight of due process as applied

[54] E. S. Corwin: *The Constitution and What It Means Today*, p. 181.
[55] D. O. McGourney: *Iowa Law Bulletin* (1918), 4:219–20.
[56] See A. J. Lien: *Privileges and Immunities of Citizens of the United States.* Columbia University Studies in History, Economics and Public Law, Vol. 54 (New York, 1913).

by Federal courts far more than has Congressional legislation with its field defined by constitutionally specified powers.

Four Freedoms Protected by Due Process

"State" in the Fourteenth Amendment includes all state agencies and hence all units of local government—counties, townships, and municipalities— which must all be watchful of restricting the liberties protected by due process. Not only the forms but the very substance of due process must be observed in a judicial trial. Thus a conviction obtained by a threat or a trial dominated by the immediate presence of a mob violates due process as does also a confession obtained under duress or through depriving the accused of counsel. Before World War I a settled principle of judicial interpretation held that only the state constitution protected the four fundamental liberties named in the First Amendment. During the 1920's, however, the Supreme Court began reading new meanings into the "liberty" of the Fourteenth Amendment of which no person could be deprived by a state without "due process of law." "For present purpose," declared the Court in 1924, "we may and do assume that freedom of speech and of the press—which are prohibited by the First Amendment from abridgement by Congress—are among the fundamental personal liberties protected by the due process clause of the Fourteenth Amendment from impairment by the states." [57] In 1934 the Court added freedom of religion [58] and in 1937 freedom of assembly [59] to the liberties protected by "due process" of the Fourteenth Amendment. The Supreme Court of the United States has gone so far in protecting freedom of speech and of the press as to over-rule the action of state judges in citing for contempt news-paper publishers who criticized courts even during pending litigation. This was done on the ground that the criticism in the cases considered constituted no "clear and present danger" to the administration of justice. State statutes outlawing peaceful picketing have been held void as depri-vation of the freedom of speech and of the press in publicizing the issues of a labor dispute.[60] Even the conviction in wartime under the Espionage Act of one Hartzel for distributing circulars opposing World War II and approving German policies was set aside on the ground that his activities did not constitute a "clear and present danger." [61] More valuable still are the lengths to which the Supreme Court has gone in protecting religious freedom as in cases involving the sect known as Jehovah's Witnesses. Thus has been established the right to distribute religious literature on the streets in public places without complying with a municipal ordinance requiring the obtaining of a license for such distribution, the right to accost people on the streets, to play phonograph records, the right to go from

[57] Gitlow v. New York, 268 U.S. 652 (1925).
[58] Hamilton v. California, 293 U.S. 245 (1934).
[59] De Jonge v. Oregon, 299 U.S. 353 (1937).
[60] Carlson v. California, 310 U.S. 106 (1940).
[61] 322 U.S. 680 (1944).

house to house and ring doorbells in the cause, and the right to circulate religious literature in a company-owned town or a Federal Housing Authority project without permission of the owners.[62]

The Clear and Present Danger Formula

By and large the Supreme Court has been inclined to hold constitutional state and Federal legislation aimed at sedition, but it has recently accepted a standard for testing individual cases which was, as we have seen, first given clear statement by Justice Oliver Wendell Holmes. This "clear and present danger" test is applied to state as well as to Federal cases. For example, in 1937 a Negro organizer for the Communist party was convicted of violating a pre-Civil War Georgia statue forbidding "incitement to insurrection by violence." He had held three meetings and the only literature he had distributed urged unemployment and emergency relief which the Supreme Court held created no "clear and present danger" of insurrection and consequently depriving him of the liberty of this activity violated the "liberty" of the "due process" of the Fourteenth Amendment.[63] The Court does not forbid state regulations of the freedom of assembly, petition, speech, and press but it does insist that "any attempt to restrict those liberties must be justified by clear public interest, threatened not doubtfully or remotely, but by clear and present danger." However in upholding the conviction of eleven top-ranking Communist party leaders by a lower court, Chief Justice Vinson reasoned that "overthrow of government by force and violence is certainly a substantial enough interest for the government to limit speech" and the "clear and present danger" doctrine cannot mean that it "must wait until the putsch is about to be executed. It was enough that there was a group ready to make the attempt." [64]

Equal Protection of the Laws

No state may "deny to any person within its jurisdiction the equal protection of the laws." This does not prevent a state from classifying persons for purposes of regulatory legislation but such classifying must be reasonable and not violate recognized principles of government. Race may not be made the basis of distinctions, and requiring white and colored people to travel in separate cars or attend separate schools is now a denial of "equal protection of the laws" even if accommodations provided are not pronouncedly different. Moreover, state authority may not segregate races as to housing. State discrimination between races with respect to ownership and possession of property, the making of contracts, or service

[62] See Hollis W. Barber: "Religious Liberty *v.* Police Power: Jehovah's Witnesses." *American Political Science Review* (1943), 37:226–48; Robert E. Cushman. "Ten Years of the Supreme Court; Civil Liberties." *American Political Science Review* (1948), 42:42–52.
[63] Herndon *v.* Lowry, 301 U.S. 242 (1937).
[64] 341 U.S. 508.

on juries is unconstitutional. As early as 1880 the Supreme Court held that a Negro was entitled to be tried by a jury from which Negroes had not been excluded because of race.[65] In 1954 in one of the most notable decisions in a generation the Supreme Court held that racial segregation in public schools is a denial of "equal protection of the laws." Chief Justice Warren, speaking for a unanimous Court, declared: "Separate educational facilities are inherently unequal." [66] Though time was permitted for compliance with the decision of the Court its judgment was unequivocal.

The Civil Liberties Section of the Department of Justice

In 1939 Attorney General Murphy set up a new unit of the Department of Justice known as the Civil Liberties Section of the Criminal Division of that department. It was established in order to "direct, supervise, and conduct prosecutions of violations of the provisions of the Constitution and Acts of Congress guaranteeing civil rights" and to devote itself to "the aggressive protection of the fundamental rights inherent in free people" and "to pursue a program of vigilant action in the prosecution of infringement of these rights." [67] A stream of petitions daily pours into the Section for aid in protecting civil liberties insofar as they are subject to protection under Federal authority. The petition may represent a protest from New Orleans that labor organizers are being interfered with, that the Ku Klux Klan is riding again in Tennessee, that the Associated Farmers in California are harassing union laborers, or that there is evidence of election frauds in Kansas City. Five hundred such protests may be received in a single month. It is significant that a governmental agency is now available to function positively in a field that hitherto has depended upon chance and circumstance.

    Several handicaps hamper the most efficient functioning of the Civil Liberties Section. Some of the law upon which the protection of civil liberties depends is weak. For example Section 52 of the Criminal Code penalizes deprivation of "rights, privileges, and immunities" secured by the Constitution and laws of the United States, but it is directed only against those deprivations which are "willful" and which occur under "color of any law." The effect of this is to limit prosecutions under this provision exclusively to infringements by public officials. The section may not be used to prosecute outrages against civil liberties perpetrated by private persons. This accounts for the diligent efforts of investigators to discover whether state or local officials are involved. Moreover, the Civil Liberties Section is understaffed, being allotted only a few lawyers, all stationed in Washington, D.C. For investigating reported infringements of civil liberties the Section is dependent upon the overburdened Federal Bureau of Investigation. Prosecutions are handled by Federal district

---

[65] Strader v. West Virginia, 100 U.S. 303 (1880).
[66] 347 U.S. 483 (1954).
[67] Order of the Attorney General, February 3, 1939.

attorneys in the jurisdictions where the alleged crime was committed, but the eagerness for vigorous action is not uniform. The unwillingness of local officials to cooperate in discovering and prosecuting lynchers and other offenders is notorious. Finally, the prestige of the Civil Rights Section suffers from the fact that it is only a section of a division of the Department of Justice and hence is subordinate to a subordinate agency of the Department.[68]

In 1953 Attorney General Herbert Brownell gave special instructions for handling violations of civil rights, directing the attorneys of the Civil Rights Section to give every assistance in the prosecution of violations. But prosecutions cannot start without information as to a violation. The typical civil rights victim is handicapped by poverty or ignorance or both, and may even have a criminal record while his oppressor is almost always a prominent person in his community. "It is fair summary of history," said Justice Frankfurter, "to say that the safeguards of liberty have most frequently been forged in controversies involving not very nice people." [69]

The victim of a civil rights violation may be without benefit of counsel, friendless, poverty stricken and ignorant of his rights. Attorney General Brownell directed the FBI to start investigations without waiting for the complainant to come forth with his lawyer. Investigations in the field are made promptly, sometimes on the basis of very meager information, possibly a news story in the local press. Collaborating with the Civil Rights Section of the Department of Justice is a Civil Rights unit of the FBI composed of trained investigators who are specialists in civil rights. This unit is directed to start promptly upon receiving information without waiting for orders from the Criminal Division of the Justice Department.

SUMMARY

Before the Civil War, state citizenship was held to be fundamental and national citizenship to be derived from it. The Fourteenth Amendment reversed this by making United States citizenship basic, as a consequence of birth or naturalization in the United States, while state citizenship was made incidental to residence of a citizen of the United States in a state. This provision of the Fourteenth Amendment is supplemented with elaborate statutory provisions as to citizenship.

Naturalization may be either collective or individual. The former may be accomplished by treaty or statute. Individual naturalization is prescribed by Congress under its constitutional power "to establish an uniform rule of naturalization." State as well as Federal courts may administer the naturalization procedure which requires, over a period of years, residence in the United States, a declaration of intention, a filing

---

[68] *To Secure These Rights: The Report of the President's Committee on Civil Rights* (New York, 1947).

[69] Dissenting opinion in United States *v.* Rabinowitz, 339 U.S. 56 at 69.

for citizenship, and final papers. Federal courts designate examiners to assist the courts by preliminary examination of applicants for citizenship; this has created a trend toward administrative naturalization.

United States citizenship may be lost by naturalization in a foreign nation, or by accepting duties therein requiring an oath of allegiance to it. Conviction of crime does not automatically deprive a convict of citizenship, but Congress can prescribe loss of the privileges of citizenship as a penalty.

A corollary of the dogma of limited government is the guarantee to individuals of civil liberties written into the Constitution or derived from it by court interpretation. The so-called Federal Bill of Rights restrains Congress from infringements of civil liberties, and the Supreme Court restrains infringements by state legislatures, especially by the application against them of the due process clause of the Fourteenth Amendment.

During the last quarter of a century the Supreme Court of the United States has discovered in the "due process" clause of the Fourteenth Amendment protection of persons against state infringements of four specific freedoms: speech, press, religion and assembly. And for the protection of freedom of speech against both state and federal infringements the Court has devised and applied the formula that the spoken words must constitute a "clear and present danger." Moreover, an agency of the Department of Justice has been created specifically to prosecute violations of civil liberties.

CHAPTER VIII

SUFFRAGE AND THE ELECTORATE

Suffrage

SUFFRAGE signifies the privilege as well as the exercise of voting. In the United States the electorate consists of those citizens who have the suffrage or elective franchise, that is, those who have the qualifications legally prescribed for voters. "Voters" is a narrower term than electorate and includes only those who exercise the privilege of voting. In the city-states of antiquity and of the Renaissance suffrage was considered a function of citizenship. In feudal theory it was a vested privilege of the individual inseparable from his rank in society. In the emerging constitutional regimes of modern times it came to be considered a natural right and consequently a corollary of popular sovereignty. This theory of suffrage as a natural right influenced American thought and stimulated expansion of the electorate. A more scientific contemporary concept was aptly expressed by the late Elihu Root: "If there is one thing settled it is that voting is not a natural right but simply a means of government." This would make the electorate but another major organ of government along with the legislative, executive, and judicial branches and would imply that it ought to be so constituted as best to perform its intended purpose.

Realistically viewed the electorate tends to function in such a way as to protect and promote the purposes of enfranchised groups that are sufficiently conscious of their interests in society. This comes about through the bidding for votes by the candidates who can determine public policies. Disfranchisement, however brought about, can severely penalize a social group at the same time that an enfranchised group may penalize itself by indifference to public policies and to the officials that determine them. It is not sheer caprice that has left the migratory worker with so few legal safeguards, but rather his disfranchisement through residence requirements for voting. Nor is it just a coincidence that loan sharks and the charging of 480 per cent interest are regulated slightly if at all in those states where their victims are disfranchised in one way or another.[1] The voting privilege can be used in a practical way to protect minorities whose group interests may, and often do, coincide with the general public interest.

Suffrage Provisions of the Constitution

When the framers of the Constitution decided that the members of the House of Representatives were the only Federal officers to be elected by the direct vote of the people, they had to determine who would be qualified to vote for these members of Congress. Not only had each member of the Union, as a sovereign state in the 1780's, been determining its own electorate, but some states even had different electorates for choosing the upper and lower houses of their legislatures. The framers prudently decided to accept the existing state electorates by this provision: "The electors in each state shall have the qualifications requisite for electors of the most numerous branch of the state legislature." [2] A century and a quarter later the Seventeenth Amendment, providing for the popular election of senators, prescribed verbatim the same qualifications for voters. Thus the Constitution accepts for these national elections whatever electorate each state has provided, and since no two states have exactly the same qualifications for voting, there are forty-eight different electorates choosing senators and representatives in Congress. The Supreme Court, however, has decided that the right to vote for representatives in Congress is derived not from the states that prescribe the voting qualifications but from the Constitution itself, and, consequently, voting is one of the privileges of American citizenship. This conclusion is deduced from the fact that the Constitution prescribes how this voting qualification is to be determined in Article I, Section 4, Clause 1 of the Constitution. Although this clause empowers the state legislatures to prescribe the time, places, and manner of holding elections for Representatives in Congress, it also provides that Congress may at any time by law alter such regulations.[3]

THE EXPANSION OF SUFFRAGE IN THE UNITED STATES

Early Development of American Suffrage

The English colonists brought to this country the contemporary English conception of a suffrage securely tied to a man's "stake in society," that is, to the ownership of land. But the "freehold" which had been practically unobtainable in England was easily acquired in the New World with its almost unlimited land, and the electorate consequently tended to expand from the very beginning. Nevertheless, it has been estimated that the active colonial electorate ranged from only two to ten per cent of the population. To the founding fathers suffrage was not at all a natural

[1] See *Loan Sharks and Their Victims*, Public Affairs Pamphlet, No. 39. New York, 1940.
[2] *Constitution:* Art. 1, Sec. 2, Clause 1.
[3] *Ex parte* Yarbrough, 110 U.S. 651 (1884).

right. Their favorite philosopher, John Locke, in his exposition of the social compact had listed "life, liberty, and property," but not the right to vote, among the inalienable rights. The fathers saw suffrage as a privilege granted the citizen by the grace of the sovereign, that is, the state.

The Establishment of Universal White Manhood Suffrage

The voting privilege in the colonies had depended upon ownership of property: a certain acreage of land in rural sections, urban real estate, or personal property of a minimum value. The American Revolution did not radically change the electorate, but eight of the thirteen states liberalized somewhat the voting qualification, not by abandoning the property requirement but by reducing it. The Constitution of 1787 accepted, for the election of representatives in Congress, whatever electorate each state had designated for the election of members of the most numerous branch of its legislature. Thus expansion of the electorate was exclusively within the power of the states until they were limited by the adoption of the Fifteenth Amendment in 1870.

During the first half of the nineteenth century the property qualification for voting gradually disappeared. The new trans-Allegheny states revealed a strong tendency to open the elective franchise to all white, adult males. The atmosphere of equality along the frontier contributed to this tendency as did the urge of the Western states to attract immigration and thus promote the growth of population. The example of these newer states had its influence on the seaboard states wrestling as they were with the problem of holding their population. The democratic ferment was at work on the other side of the Atlantic as manifested in the French Revolution of 1830 and the British Reform Bill of 1832 which somewhat expanded the narrow English electorate. The debates in the constitutional conventions of the seaboard states in the 1820's, 1830's, and 1840's revealed heated controversies over the issue of removing suffrage restrictions, but gradually the change came about. There was a tendency to substitute for property ownership a tax-paying requirement and later to abandon even that. The progress toward a broader electorate was such that by 1860 only South Carolina retained a substantial property qualification for voting while six Atlantic coastal states had a tax-paying or alternative qualification that made property ownership unnecessary.[4] Elsewhere throughout the United States universal white manhood suffrage prevailed.

Negro Suffrage

The post-Civil War attempt to establish Negro suffrage by constitutional amendment was a move of the Radical Republicans to counteract the startling gain in Southern representation in Congress and in the Electoral College as a consequence of the abolition of slavery. As long as slavery

---

[4] New Hampshire, Massachusetts, North Carolina, Rhode Island, Pennsylvania, and Georgia.

continued, the Constitution required that three out of every five slaves should be counted in apportioning representatives in Congress. The abolition of slavery created a paradoxical situation for the victors in the Civil War. Now all the former slaves would count as population, and the states formerly of the Confederacy stood to increase their representation in the House and in the Electoral College. It seemed as though the Southern states were to be rewarded instead of penalized for the attempt at secession. The Southerners, however, had no inclination voluntarily to enfranchise the freedmen, knowing they would easily be persuaded to vote with the elements outside the South that then dominated the Federal government.

The Radical Republicans conceived an automatic device for compelling the Southerners to grant the voting privilege to the Negroes. Incorporated in the Fourteenth Amendment was the provision that whenever the right to vote for Federal and state officers "is denied to any of the male inhabitants of such state, being twenty-one years of age, and citizens of the United States, or in any way abridged, except for participation in rebellion, or other crime, the basis of representation therein shall be reduced in the proportion which the number of such male citizens shall bear to the whole number of male citizens twenty-one years of age in such state." This provision failed utterly in its intended purpose. It soon became evident that the Southern states would accept reduced representation rather than enfranchise the Negroes.

The penalty of reduced representation prescribed by the Fourteenth Amendment has never been applied, and this provision remains in the Constitution as a conspicuous example of dead letter. Its enforcement would not be easy. The determination of the exact number of persons disqualified by state action would be difficult, and any plan of reduction would affect Northern states as well. The interests which were elevated to a dominant position by the Civil War and which promoted the penalty, lost interest in the matter when they saw they could achieve their major objectives without Negro suffrage. The question has even been raised as to whether the Fifteenth Amendment's prohibition of the right of a state to deny the franchise on the basis of race, color, or previous condition of servitude may not have repealed the penalty provision of the Fourteenth Amendment, but this question has never been authoritatively answered.

The Fifteenth Amendment

When it became conclusively evident that the Southern states would accept reduced representation in Congress rather than grant suffrage to the Negro, the Fifteenth Amendment was adopted with the idea of settling once and for all the issue of Negro suffrage by providing: "The right of citizens of the United States to vote shall not be denied or abridged by the United States or by any state on account of race, color, or previous condition of servitude." The phrasing of this amendment reveals the pattern of the natural rights theory of suffrage. Yet it does not confer the right of suffrage on the Negro. What it does confer, as expressed in the precise language of the Supreme Court, is "the right of exemption from discrimination in the exercise of the elective franchise on account of race, color, or previous condition of servitude."[5] Indeed, as cases involving the Amendment came before the Supreme Court, it became evident that the Amendment provided far less protection to the Negro than its framers evidently had intended. If a Negro is prevented from voting by a private person through bribery, intimidation, or otherwise, the Fifteenth Amendment is not thereby violated. Its prohibition is against denial of suffrage by the United States or a state, and a Federal statute providing a penalty for violation of the Fifteenth Amendment by a private person has consequently been held invalid by the Supreme Court.[6] The Fifteenth Amendment can be violated only by the legislative, executive, or judicial officers of the Federal or state governments and the latter include county, township, and municipal officials as well as the precinct election boards.

Grandfather Clauses

The "grandfather clause," once a widely used device, but now of only historical interest, was first introduced in Louisiana in 1898 as a method of circumventing the Fifteenth Amendment. Its formula consisted of educational, property, or other prerequisites for voting, sweeping enough to exclude practically all Negroes as well as many whites. The latter, however, were almost completely exempted from the restriction by a provision that these prerequisites were not to apply to lineal descendants of those who were legal voters before 1866, the year in which Negroes were first enfranchised in the South. After the device had been used for nearly two decades, the Supreme Court in 1915 pronounced the grandfather clauses unconstitutional as violations of the Fifteenth Amendment, and consequently they have not been in force for a generation. However, when they were declared unconstitutional, they had already served their purpose of placing on the permanent registration lists the lineal descendants of those persons who had been voters before 1866. The literacy, property, and "understanding" requirements for voting which may be applied so as virtually to deny the Negroes the voting privilege have been held judicially not to violate the Fifteenth Amendment since these forms of restricting the "right to vote" do not exclude anyone from the suffrage "on account of race, color, or previous condition of servitude."[7]

Understanding Clauses

"Understanding" clauses originated as an alternative to a literacy test. When state constitutions introduced the literacy test as an obvious device

[5] United States *v.* Reese, 92 U.S. 214 (1876).
[6] James *v.* Bowman, 150 U.S. 136 (1903).
[7] Williams *v.* Mississippi, 170 U.S. 213 (1898).

for disfranchising most Negroes in Southern states many whites also were disfranchised. However, if a person could not "read" the constitution he might still "understand" a passage read to him. The Mississippi Constitution of 1890, for example, required the voter to be able "to read any section of the state constitution; or be able to understand the same when read to him, or give a reasonable interpretation thereof." County registration boards, exclusively white, which administer the test where understanding clauses are used, may not be as readily satisfied with the explanation of a Negro as of a white, who in any case is not so likely to be challenged. The election official may not even be capable of determining whether the Negro's answer is correct. The device penalizes the Negro for his inadequate opportunity for schooling, but even when he does possess the required "understanding," his admission to the electorate is by no means assured. The purpose of the "understanding" clause is evident enough when colored applicants have been confronted with such perplexing matters as: "Explain *mandamus*"; "Define civil code"; "How should you appeal a case?" "How much revenue did the State Hospital pay the state last year?" In 1920 several colored teachers of Columbia, South Carolina, licensed by the state to teach colored children, were denied the right to register, as being insufficiently educated to read a ballot. Under the circumstances it is not at all surprising that Negroes do not take the literacy and "understanding" tests and that the tests are not commonly administered to whites for whom, of course, they were scarcely intended. No more effective device for circumventing the purpose of the Fifteenth Amendment has ever been devised than the "understanding" test. However when a 1946 amendment to the constitution of Alabama required registrants to be able to "read and write" and also "to understand *and* explain" any article of the Constitution of the United States, the Supreme Court found this to violate the Fifteenth Amendment.[8]

Exclusion of Negroes from Party Primaries

Negroes cannot now constitutionally be excluded by state action from party primaries because the states are forbidden by the Fourteenth Amendment to deny to anyone "the equal protection of the laws." The question of the constitutionality of the exclusion of Negroes from primary elections did not reach the Supreme Court until the 1920's when a Texas statute confined primaries to white voters. Democratic party rule in Texas to the practical exclusion of an opposition party dates from early in the present century, and the 1923 statute excluding Negroes from primaries merely gave legal expression to a long established custom of exclusion by providing that "in no event shall a Negro be eligible to participate in a Democratic party primary election held in the state of Texas, and should a Negro vote in a Democratic primary election officials are herein directed to throw out such ballot and not count same." Since the Republican party has

[8] 336 U.S. 933 (1949).

a negligible strength in Texas, only the primary election is of much consequence. In 1927 the Supreme Court of the United States held the Texas
statute unconstitutional as a denial of "the equal protection of the laws"
guaranteed by the Fourteenth Amendment.[9] The legislature of Texas next
authorized the state executive committee of any party to determine who
may vote in its party primaries and under this authority the State Democratic Committee ruled out Negroes. The Supreme Court of the United
States thereupon over-ruled the action of the committee because the state
had authorized what amounted to the state's denial of "equal protection of
the laws." After the State Democratic Convention of Texas in 1932 confined
party membership to whites, and Negroes were thereby denied the right to
vote in the party primary, the Supreme Court of the United States held
that a Negro who was not permitted to vote in this primary had not been
denied any constitutional right under the Fourteenth Amendment since his
exclusion was not due to any state law or the act of any state official in that
the Democratic party is a private body.[10] Developing trends of Court
opinion in the 1940's, however, rendered this position of the Court untenable so that the current Court rule forbids any state "casting its electoral
process in a form which permitted a private organization (that is a political
party) to practice racial discrimination in an election." [11] It is significant
indeed that the protection of the Negro's right by this court decision was
based upon the Fifteenth Amendment which the Supreme Court step by
step is now interpreting to mean what its framers evidently intended—that
it is a guarantee of the Negro's "right" to vote.

Woman's Suffrage

In 1919 the crusade for woman's suffrage culminated in the adoption of the
Nineteenth Amendment which, patterned after the Fifteenth Amendment,
provided: "The rights of citizens of the United States to vote shall not be
denied or abridged by the United States or by any state on account of sex."
The woman suffrage movement antedated the Civil War in its origin. It
concentrated on the removal of the word "male" from state constitutional
provisions for suffrage, and crusaders in the cause struggled in vain after
the Civil War to have the word "male" kept out of the suffrage clause of the
Fourteenth Amendment. The territorial legislature of Wyoming in 1869
granted woman's suffrage, and twenty years later a convention included it
in the constitution prepared when Wyoming was applying for admission as
a state. Although Congress was inclined to hesitate at such an innovation,
Wyoming was nevertheless admitted as a state with woman's suffrage.
Coincidental with World War I, militant suffragettes employed sensational
publicity to promote adoption of a constitutional amendment for nation-
wide enfranchisement of women. In the election of 1916 they exerted

[9] Nixon *v.* Herndon, 273 U.S. 536 (1927).
[10] Grovey *v.* Townsend, 295 U.S. 45 (1935).
[11] Smith *v.* Allwright, 321 U.S. 649 (1944).

pressure to defeat congressional candidates of the Democratic party which they held responsible, as the party in power, for the failure to obtain the adoption of the Amendment. In 1917 the suffragettes picketed the White House in order to induce President Wilson to promote the Amendment. Arrested and jailed like common criminals they went on hunger strikes whereupon forced feeding resulted in sensational newspaper stories, to the great embarrassment of the Administration. At this point President Wilson took up the cause and, through pressure on Democratic senators, the two-thirds vote required for proposal of the amendment was procured.[12] The Nineteenth Amendment, like the Fifteenth, merely prevented the states and the United States from a specific kind of discrimination. By no means did it "grant" women the voting privilege. Indeed, when the Nineteenth Amendment was adopted, women were already voting in all the Pacific and Rocky Mountain states except New Mexico, as well as in South Dakota, Kansas, Oklahoma, Michigan, and New York. The interference by private persons with women's voting does not fall under prohibition of the Nineteenth Amendment although the refusal of a party organization to permit women to vote in primaries would certainly be unconstitutional under the principle applied by the Supreme Court in the case of Smith *v.* Allwright.

Effect of Woman's Suffrage

Woman's suffrage wrought no miraculous purification of politics such as romantic enthusiasts had predicted. Political machines and bosses still survive. Married women show a tendency to follow their husband's decisions in voting although candidates cannot depend on this. Failure to vote is more frequent among women than among men, and the former are more reluctant than the latter to register their party affiliation where such is required for participation in party primaries. Women seem to hesitate to shift party allegiance more than men do. On the liquor issue they vote drier than men and manifest a somewhat greater interest than men in issues involving the welfare of women and children.[13] Woman's suffrage confronts the politician, from time to time, with the perplexing problem of making effective campaign appeals for the woman's vote. That vote can decide close elections and may have determined the outcome of the presidential contest of 1944. Opinion polls on the eve of that election indicated that 51 per cent of civilian male voters intended to support Dewey and 49 per cent, Roosevelt, while 48 per cent of the women voters were planning to support Dewey and 52 per cent, Roosevelt. Moreover, the absence of millions of male voters in the armed forces gave the women a potential preponderance at the polls.

[12] The long crusade for woman's suffrage included 500 organized efforts with state legislatures, 277 appearances at state party conventions, 30 appeals before national political conventions, and 19 campaigns with Congress. S. P. Breckenridge: "Women in Government." *Recent Social Trends* (New York, 1934), pp. 737–41.

[13] See Edward M. Sait: *American Parties and Elections,* pp. 96, 102.

VOTING QUALIFICATIONS

State Determination of Voting Qualifications

Since the election of United States senators, representatives in Congress, and presidential electors is conducted by state officials and the ballots are cast by state electors, it lies within the reserved powers of the states to determine in detail the qualifications of voters. Each state determines, either by constitution or by statute, the minimum voting age, the period of citizenship, if any, required before the naturalized citizen is entitled to vote, the residence requirement in the state, the county, and the voting district, the property, literacy, tax-paying and other prerequisites, the registration requirements, and the legal procedure for absentee voting. Though the state has a wide range of discretion in determining voting qualifications there are Federal constitutional limitations some of which are explicit but others apparent only through constitutional interpretation by Federal judicial decisions.

Age and Citizenship

The states are free to fix any minimum age they choose as a voting requirement. It is set at twenty-one in every state except Georgia and Kentucky which have made eighteen the minimum age. This reduction was evidently made upon the assumption that if one is old enough for military service he is old enough to vote. Movements to make the same change in many other states failed. Until the 1920's a number of states granted the voting privilege to aliens who had declared their intention of becoming citizens of the United States. At one time or another aliens have voted in twenty-two states that doubtless hoped thereby to attract population.[14] The election of 1928 was the first in which no alien in any state was eligible to vote for any candidate—national, state, or local.

Residence

In two-thirds of the states the minimum length of residence required before the right to vote is established is set at one year. In eleven states it is only six months while four states [15] require two years. However, among these, South Carolina reduces the requirement to six months for "ministers of the gospel." Required residence within the county varies from thirty days to six months in most states, but Alabama, Louisiana, and South Carolina require a year. Fourteen states require thirty days' residence within the precinct, but half a dozen states require as little as ten days. Mississippi requires a full year's residence within the precinct except for "ministers of the gospel" for whom six-month residence is sufficient. The long residence requirements exist mainly in the South and were adopted on

[14] Leon Aylesworth: "The Passing of Alien Suffrage." *American Political Science Review* (1931), 25:114–6.

[15] Alabama, Louisiana, Mississippi, and South Carolina.

the theory that the Negro moved about more than did the white person.

Property Qualifications

In seven states the property qualification for voting is still found in one form or another. In six it is an absolute requirement only for voting on bond issues or special assessments, while in South Carolina the ownership of property is an alternative to literacy. The trend that started over a century ago away from the once universal property tax qualification for voting has now almost run its course. Nowhere is it now a requirement for voting in ordinary elections.

Literacy Test

The literacy test in some form is used in nineteen states. In some southern states [16] the test takes the form of ascertaining whether the would-be voter is able to read or write an article of the state's constitution, but here it is sometimes an alternative to other ways of qualifying. Where it is used outside the South it usually requires the reading of the Constitution and the writing of the voter's name without any alternative qualifications. Since the tests are almost universally administered by registration or election officials the risk of arbitrary rather than judicial discrimination is apparent. The Constitution of New York provides that "no person shall become entitled . . . to vote . . . unless such person is also able, except for physical disability, to read and write English; and suitable laws shall be passed by the Legislature to enforce this provision." Under this constitutional provision the legislature of New York has provided that a certificate of literacy may be issued to all applicants who show that they have completed the fifth grade in the public schools of the state or its equivalent in private schools. This law has the advantage of assigning to public school officials instead of to precinct election boards the certification of the voter's literacy.[17]

The Poll Tax as a Voting Qualification

Strictly speaking a poll tax is merely a per capita or head tax which inherently has nothing to do with voting. It may, however, be made a voting qualification as it is in the five southern states Alabama, Arkansas, Mississippi, Texas, and Virginia. In 1944 the legislature of Georgia, on the recommendation of Governor Arnall, repealed, not the poll tax, but the prerequisite of its payment for voting. Usually the poll tax is one or two dollars due annually but in three states it is cumulative with respect to

[16] V. O. Key, *Politics, Parties and Pressure Groups* (New York, 1952), p. 626.

[17] The tests in New York State are very easy. A typical one consists of a paragraph phrased in simple English. This is used as the basis for a series of extraordinarily easy printed questions on the information in the paragraph. Those who have completed the fifth grade need not take the test. Among those who have taken the test failures have been: in 1923, 21.4 per cent; 1924, 16.1 per cent; 1925, 17.8 per cent; 1926, 19.6 per cent; 1927, 20.66 per cent; 1928, 10.09 per cent; 1929, 10.84 per cent. Finla G. Crawford: "Operation of the Literacy Test for Voters in New York." *American Political Science Review* (1931), 25:342–5. By 1942 the failures were only 7.48 per cent.

voting qualifications so that back poll taxes must be paid. In Alabama, for
example, in order to qualify for voting one must pay all taxes due from the
age of twenty-one, or from the date of taking up residence in the state
until the age of forty-five, after which age the individual who is paid up
is exempt from the poll tax requirement for voting. Veterans of all wars
are exempt from poll taxes in Alabama. To vote in Virginia a person
must have no taxes past due and the tax is cumulative but for only three
years. Since Negroes are disfranchised by the devices mentioned above
as well as by social pressures, the poll tax scarcely affects them and in
practice it operates only against white persons. It was, in fact, introduced
when the Populist Movement of the 1890's, which had aroused the lower
income groups, was sweeping the South and threatening the very existence of the Democratic party in that section.[18] The poll tax as a voting
qualification is found only in one-party states of the "Solid South." One-
party states have a much lower percentage of citizens participating in
elections than those in which two-party contests occur. In the presidential
election of 1944 the states having the poorest record in terms of the percentage of the population voting were: South Carolina, 6; Alabama, 9;
Mississippi, 9; Georgia, 11; Arkansas, 12; Virginia, 14; Louisiana, 15;
Tennessee, 18; and Texas, 18. All of these states with the exception of
Louisiana, were then poll-tax states,[19] but the non-voting would seem to
be due to the single-party condition rather than the poll tax and the
abolition of that tax might have little effect on the percentage of the
population who vote. Since the general election signifies little more than a
ratification of the outcome of the party primary in a one-party state, the
real contest takes place in the primary. In these one-party states several
times as many voters go to the primaries as to the general election.[20]

The Future of the Poll Tax

It is unlikely that poll taxes will persist much longer as voting qualifications in any state. A significant trend is indicated by the fact that the
poll tax was abandoned as a voting qualification by North Carolina in
1920, Louisiana in 1934, Florida in 1937, Georgia in 1945, South Carolina
in 1950, and Tennessee in 1945. This signifies that more than half the
Southern poll-tax states have abolished the tax. The poll tax amounts to
one or two dollars usually payable several months before the Democratic
primary.[21] Since party organizations may and sometimes do pay the poll
tax for selected persons the tax facilitates a vicious and arbitrary manipulation of elections, particularly of primaries, which, as we have seen, are
the only significant elections in poll-tax states. In recent years a movement has been developing to outlaw the poll-tax voting requirements by
Federal statutes. Such a measure repeatedly passed the House but was

[18] J. D. Hicks: *The Populist Revolt* (Minneapolis, 1931), pp. 253–4.
[19] *The Gallup Political Almanac* (Princeton, 1946), pp. 226–7.
[20] See Table 13 in V. O. Key: *Politics, Parties, and Pressure Groups* (2nd ed., New York, 1947), p. 362.
[21] H. A. Bone, *American Politics and the Party System* (New York, 1955), p. 547.

held up in the Senate by threatened or actual filibuster. A case testing the constitutionality of the poll tax may yet reach the Supreme Court of the United States. However, the growing pressure against it in the poll-tax states themselves will probably terminate it rather than a Federal statute, a United States Supreme Court decision, or an amendment to the Federal Constitution.

Disqualifications

In some states conviction of certain crimes such as treason, bigamy, defalcation, perjury, arson, or embezzlement disqualifies citizens from voting. In South Carolina, for example, the list of disqualifications includes burglary, obtaining money or goods under false pretenses, robbery, adultery, housebreaking, receiving stolen goods, breach of trust with fraudulent intent, and certain unnatural crimes. Most states disqualify the insane, idiots, and mental defectives generally. In some states "immoral" persons and the inmates of prisons and other public institutions are denied the suffrage. During the depression of the 1930's there were even suggestions that persons on relief be disfranchised. This was prevented by the nature of our party system which functions largely through the competitive bidding of the candidates of major parties for the support of groups of voters through the candidates's promise to promote policies that will satisfy these groups. Millions of unemployed were, however, automatically disfranchised by the loss of established residence as they migrated from place to place in search of work during the 1930's.

Registration

In order to ascertain officially before election day just who is entitled to vote, registration of voters has been established in every state except Arkansas, where it is prohibited by the state constitution, and in Texas, where the state constitution authorizes it in cities of more than 10,000 but where the legislature has never enacted the necessary statutes to inaugurate it. [22] In states where the two-party system prevails the registration board is usually bi-partisan, but in one-party Southern states the board has been used as a party agency for disfranchising Negroes. Registration may be state-wide, as it is in thirty-one states, or confined to populous communities, as it is, for example, in Ohio where it is required only in cities with a population of 16,000 or more.

When first established, registration was required annually, as it still is in the states of New York and New Jersey. This is both inconvenient for the voter and expensive for the taxpayer, the cost averaging nearly one dollar per voter in New York City. Because of problems peculiar to the South, permanent registration has prevailed in many of the states of that section since early in the present century. Outside the South, in the early 1920's, a trend set in toward permanent instead of periodic registration,

[22] In Arkansas and Texas registration is considered unnecessary since the lists produced by poll-tax administration give the equivalent of registration.

and a permanent type now prevails in thirty-nine states. Under such a system the voter's name and record is set down on a card or loose-leaf form, and when he changes his address within the city he is permitted to transfer his registration without re-registering. Statistical examination has shown that from 5 to 15 per cent more voters are on the rolls under permanent than under periodic registration. Cities with periodic registration have been afflicted with serious election frauds while cities with permanent registration, such as Milwaukee, Omaha, Boston, Minneapolis, and Portland, Oregon have had no scandals for many years. Experience has shown that a sound registration program requires (1) a central office of registration in each city open the year around, (2) loose-leaf or card records, (3) opportunity for the voter to transfer, (4) correction of the lists by constant attention of registrars to death notices and utility installations, (5) attention to transfer and to the failure of the registrant to vote over two-year periods, (6) house-to-house check when necessary, (7) identification of voter at polls by his signature, (8) permanent registration. [23]

NON-VOTING

The Burden of the Long Ballot

Unquestionably American voters are summoned too often to the polls, have too many officers to elect and too many referendum issues to decide, with the consequence that they become surfeited with balloting. In this respect their electoral burden contrasts sharply with that of the British and continental European voters. In a national election the British voter casts his ballot to elect just one member of the House of Commons at average intervals of about four years. He votes annually in electing members of county and borough (municipal) councils but elects no other officials and votes on no referenda. The typical American voter participates in frequent direct primary elections for nominating candidates for numerous national, state, county, township, municipal, school, and other offices. All this is merely preliminary to the regular election in which the candidates nominated at the primary election are again voted on to determine who is to be elected to office. Not long ago the Chicago voter was expected in a single year to register twice, to go to the polls five times and pass judgment on the candidates for fifty offices. In some Illinois counties seventy offices were to be filled at a single election. The number varies from state to state, with twenty to thirty offices to be filled not uncommon. Primary ballots contain even more names. The initiative and referendum add still more to the burden of voting. For example, at a general election in Colorado an average of sixteen issues was submitted to voters who chose thirty public officials at the same election. The effect of the long ballot is made evident in the percentage of the total vote cast for various offices in a California election in 1934. The percentages of the total vote cast for various offices was governor,

[23] Joseph P. Harris: "Registration of Voters," *Encyclopaedia of the Social Sciences*, Vol. XIII, pp. 218–20.

98.6 per cent; lieutenant-governor, 95.2 per cent; secretary of state, 89.4 per cent; controller, 86.5 per cent; state assemblyman, 81.2 per cent. The vote on a referendum involving the sale of liquor was 83.7 per cent while that on another referendum was only 54.5 per cent. [24] Questionnaires sampling voters after a New York election as to whom they had voted for to fill certain specific offices revealed that 73 per cent were unable to recall. The voter tolerates this burden and indeed would resent the reduction of the burden because he assumes that he would lose his share in control of government by shorter ballots and less frequent elections. But the confusing complexity of this maze of primary and regular elections gives to the professional politician and the party machine their opportunity to manipulate elections to the frustration of the democratic purpose. It has been said that the long ballot is the politician's ballot, the short ballot is the people's ballot. Judging by the higher percentage of voting abroad, our long ballot seems to be one of the causes of non-voting in the United States.

The Extent of Non-Voting

Statistical investigations indicate that indifference is the chief cause of failure to vote. Harold F. Gosnell tabulated the reasons given for failure to vote in 3,369 Chicago cases in 1923 and 649 in 1924. These data revealed that one-third of those who failed to register gave as their reason indifference to elections, one-sixth, sickness or absence from the precinct, and one-seventh professed ignorance or timidity concerning elections. [25] It is estimated that more than a third of the electorate habitually fail to participate in presidential elections, and the percentage of non-voters is, of course, considerably higher in off-year congressional, state, and local elections. A greater percentage of men than women vote; the age group 40 to 70 has a greater percentage of voters than does any younger or older age group; whites turn out to vote in greater proportion than Negroes even where there are no racial discriminations of any kind; and voting percentages increase as educational and economic levels rise.

Equalizing the Value of Votes

Considerable non-voting is due in certain areas to a conviction of the futility of casting ballots in general elections. This is true particularly of the so-called one-party states. Voting is heavy where major parties are closely balanced and the voter feels that his ballot is really important and may be decisive. In the presidential election of 1944 Illinois had the best turnout at the polls of all states, with 53 per cent of the population voting. New Hampshire and New York tied for second place with 51 per cent each. Indiana and Nebraska were not far behind with 49 per cent. All of these states have the vigorous competition of a two-party system. [26] The election of the president by the indirect method of the Electoral College induces

[24] V. O. Key: *Politics, Parties, and Pressure Groups*, p. 555.
[25] Charles E. Merriam and Harold F. Gosnell: *The American Party System* (New York, 1940), pp. 410–11.
[26] *Gallup Almanac for 1946*, p. 226.

considerable non-voting. Campaigning for presidential candidates is concentrated in doubtful states where voting is consequently stimulated. In the "sure" states, where the outcome is a foregone conclusion, voting receives little stimulus from campaigning. Proposals to elect the President by direct popular vote arouses no wide-spread interest and might result in an astonishing shift of the power of the electorate. It would certainly reduce the present power of certain ethnic, racial, and religious minorities, concentrated in the metropolitan centers of great pivotal states. Another proposal would divide the presidential electors of each state between parties according to each party's percentage of the popular vote. But the calculations of Professor Ruth Silva indicate that, because of the concentration of Democratic strength in "safe" states, the Democrats could frequently win by a minority of the popular vote while Republicans could never win without a safe popular majority.

Political Effect of a Light or Heavy Vote

Public-opinion polls indicate that the elements constituting the Democratic group-combination have a greater tendency toward non-voting than have those constituting the Republican combination. So well is this understood that predictions as to whether Republicans or Democrats will win a national election have been based on calculations of the percentage of the total electorate that would probably vote in an election. Thus a low percentage might indicate that many Democrats would stay at home and the chance of a Republican victory would thereby be increased. Northern Democratic leaders have consequently been particularly energetic in their efforts to obtain full registration and a heavy turnout at the polls. Republican party leaders can concentrate on getting out the party vote on election day—generally not so much of a problem as that confronting the Democratic organization. But the assumption that a light vote can be depended upon to insure a Republican victory was discredited in 1948 when President Truman was re-elected with only a light vote cast.

Some writers have argued the advantage of maintaining a considerable body of non-voters to constitute an electoral reserve that could be aroused in a crisis and induced to turn out and vote when very important issues pend. "Thus the citizen who is not identified with a party," writes E. P. Herring, "who does not habitually participate in politics, and whose support cannot be counted on by any one group, is the agent that keeps politicians uncertain of power and therefore responsive to the current of opinion. If all men were good citizens in the sense of being participants in all contests they would have to act in practice like declared partisans. This would bring too many political contests to a danger point of intensity." [27]

Stimulating Voting

Concerted efforts to get out the vote have been made by civic and business organizations, newspapers, magazines, ministers of the gospel, and others,

[27] E. P. Herring: *The Politics of Democracy* (New York, 1940), pp. 32–3.

but their efforts have availed little. Even the League of Women Voters succeeds chiefly in reaching only the higher income groups who need less stimulation than others. The most successful efforts to arouse lethargic voters are still generally made by party organizations. The typical precinct committeeman, either in person or through voluntary or paid party workers, is likely to see that the party poll book is checked on election day as registrants vote and that laggard partisans are urged by telephone or personal contact to vote. Abstract interest in good government has never been as potent in politics as the urge of politicians to capture the partonage, power, and prestige implicit in public office—all of which depend upon winning elections. "The very 'wardheeler' with his 'gang,'" wrote Shailer Mathews, "is today, by some strange paradox of American politics, a guarantee that government by the people shall not perish from the earth." [28]

Compulsory Voting

The highest voting records in democracies have been attained in those countries that have adopted compulsory voting. Thus in Belgium, Holland, Czechoslovakia, and Austria 90 per cent or more of the eligible voters have balloted in national elections. The idea of compulsory voting was incorporated in several American colonial statutes, but recent attempts to establish it in the United States have failed. The Kansas City charter of 1889 provided for a poll tax to be levied upon every adult male to be remitted to all persons who voted at a general election. The Supreme Court of Missouri declared the provision to be discriminatory as an invasion of the citizen's sovereign right of suffrage. Compulsory voting was made permissive by the constitutions of North Dakota in 1898 and of Massachusetts in 1918 but in neither case did the legislature enact the necessary legislation to make the policy effective. The voters of Oregon and California have rejected such proposals. The introduction of this system in the United States would revolutionize the primary function of the registration or election board. At present the citizen who seeks to vote must himself establish positively that he is entitled to vote. But under a system of compulsory voting, whenever an elector sought to avoid his legal duty of voting by denying his qualifications, the registration or election board would have to prove that he was a qualified elector. Among the difficulties of administering compulsory voting are the necessity of determining who are the voters to be compelled to vote, of officially notifying them, of determining valid excuses for failure to vote, and of determining the penalty for not voting. Moreover, as long as the ballot is presumed to be secret it is difficult to see just how the voter could be compelled really to vote and not just cast a blank ballot.

[28] Shailer Mathews: *The French Revolution* (New York, 1900), p. 10.

SUMMARY

The only provision as to suffrage in the original Constitution is the stipulation that whoever might vote for the most numerous branch of the state legislature was qualified to vote for a member of the Federal House of Representatives. This left the states then free to determine their own as well as the Federal electorate, and even today, despite the Fifteenth and Nineteenth Amendments, no two states have exactly the same voting qualifications.

When the Constitution went into effect nearly every state limited the electorate to property owners, but this restriction had so largely disappeared by 1850 as to result in practically universal white manhood suffrage. In 1870 the Fifteenth Amendment forbade racial discrimination by the states in prescribing voting qualifications. The design of ensuring Negro suffrage was nevertheless frustrated by social pressures, literacy and understanding tests, along with grandfather clauses (held unconstitutional since 1915), poll taxes, exclusion from primaries, and other specious devices used by some of the states. But the trend of Supreme Court decisions now tends to whittle down the effectiveness of discriminations against Negro suffrage. Woman's suffrage had been growing for decades in the states when it was suddenly made practically universal in 1920 by the Nineteenth Amendment's prohibition against suffrage discrimination based on sex.

The states are still free to set up such voting qualifications as minimum age, period of residence, citizenship, literacy, property and poll tax, and registration requirements. All but two states now require registration either of all voters or merely those residing in populous urban areas. Periodic is gradually giving way to permanent registration.

Non-voting is extraordinarily high in the United States. Apparently the American electorate becomes surfeited with voting because of very frequent elections, both general and primary, long ballots, and numerous referendum issues, both state and local.

PART
III

INSTITUTIONS OF POPULAR CONTROL

CHAPTER IX

PUBLIC OPINION, PRESSURE GROUPS, AND THE PUBLIC INTEREST

MEASURED in round figures there are approximately 100,000,000 eligible voters in the United States, each with the right to his own opinions. Out of this body of opinions must come the direction and guidance for government. Indeed it is from this body of opinions that "the life of a nation must draw its sustenance." [1] But how are the desires of the entire electorate to be made articulate? It is utterly impracticable for a group of this size to meet in a body on the village green and attempt to make opinions known vocally as is still done in a few small cantons in Switzerland where the male voters assemble once a year (the *Landsgemeinde*) to decide public issues by a voice vote. Nor is it practicable for each member of the electorate in the United States to function as an independent political party and register his opinions accordingly. Actually, of course, "people are inclined to believe in company" as the Spanish philosopher, Ortega y Gasset, notes. We may hold to individual opinions but normally we assemble them into larger patterns and associations and we find them identifiable with the opinions and beliefs of others.

Thus we find ourselves in company with those holding common opinions in a variety of ways. It may be through a professional organization, a pressure group, or a political party, but whatever the nature of the organization it may serve as a vehicle for coalescing individual opinions. The importance to government of the process by which individual opinions are merged is great. When persons of similar opinions are brought together by an organization such as a political party or pressure group their opinions may be expressed both in an orderly fashion and far more effectively than if they were acting individually. It is with these processes—the processes by which opinions are formed and travel to influence government that we are here concerned and we may take as our starting point a brief examination of the nature of public opinion.

[1] José Ortega y Gasset: *Concord and Liberty* (New York, 1946), p. 16.

WHAT IS PUBLIC OPINION?

Public opinion, speaking broadly, is a meeting of the minds of a large part of the community on a particular judgment or body of judgments. An essential element of public opinion is that it manifest itself as a conclusion or judgment held in common by a substantial segment of the community. The community, of course, may be the smallest village, a state, an entire country, or the whole world.

Whether public opinion, to qualify as such, must represent only the collective conclusions of the entire community, that is to say a consensus—has been a much-disputed point. In certain cases there are cohesive elements in the outlook of a community that tend to create unanimity of public opinion. Thus universal respect for certain fundamentals of the Constitution or the general observance of law in a community afford examples where public opinion comes close to representing a consensus. Jean Jacques Rousseau, the brilliant eighteenth-century political philosopher, believed in the unanimous concept of public opinion and that it was not divisible. On a constitution a strong case may be made in support of Rousseau's thesis, for to have a government functioning successfully when there is fundamental divergence of popular thought on the constitution is almost unimaginable. [2] Essentially, however, there are probably few if any subjects upon which the opinion of a community is in absolute accord. Even in time of war or serious national crisis we know that it is possible to have a small minority of dissenters. Today, therefore, the tendency is to regard public opinion as divisible.

Public Opinion and Majority Rule

There is some disposition to regard as public opinion only that opinion which represents the majority of the community, but this outlook has serious shortcomings. It is true that for want of a better system of making decisions we have taken over the principle of "majority rule" as the fairest expedient yet devised for carrying on representative government. And it is likewise true that the realization of "majority rule" as a procedural principle of a representative government depends upon the crystallization of public opinion. But it would be a mistake to conclude on this basis that public opinion is simply majority opinion. The opinion of minority groups is also a part of the grand composite we call public opinion, and indeed the end-product which results from the interaction of minority and majority opinion is public opinion.

The divisible character of public opinion becomes more apparent to

[2] Carl J. Friedrich: *Constitutional Government and Democracy* (Boston, 1941), pp. 160–1. The need for broad agreement on fundamental principles of government is a compelling one. "Concord," writes Ortega y Gasset, "that kind of concord which forms the foundation of a stable society, presupposes that the community holds a firm and common, unquestionable, and practically unquestioned, belief as to the exercise of supreme power."—*Concord and Liberty*, p. 19.

us as we examine the processes and workings of representative government. In a democracy there has never been and probably never will be complete unity of public opinion in the political sense. Despite difference, however, democracies have succeeded admirably in subordinating the conflict of opinion to a national purpose. Recently the term bi-partisan foreign policy has become a familiar word as representing an effort to reconcile differences of opinion in both major parties on important questions affecting our foreign policy. Actually, of course, the idea of bi-partisan cooperation is nothing new, for on the home front a large part of our legislation results from the operation of a bi-partisan domestic policy. The highly controversial Taft-Hartley Act which was so strongly opposed by labor organizations was re-passed over a presidential veto—a feat which practically always requires bi-partisan support in Congress. Moreover, even where a legislative program is pushed through Congress largely through the support of one party, the end-product has almost always been sculptured in part by the opinion of the opposition party. Amendments are tacked on, compromises are forced, and in some cases the end-product is barely recognizable as the measure that had originally been introduced. Indeed as Britain's great Prime Minister, Benjamin Disraeli, once summed it up: "The temper of one leader has to be watched, the disposition of a third to be suited; so that a measure is so altered, re-moulded, remodelled, patched, cobbled, painted, veneered, and varnished, that at last no trace is left of the original scope of the scheme . . ." [3] Thus the end-product that comes out of the legislative grist mill really represents an amalgam of all opinion and not simply majority opinion.

Stated briefly, the one compelling area of agreement of public opinion in a democratic society is in the adherence to certain fundamental elements of constitutionalism—that is, belief in government which operates in accordance with well-defined constitutional principles. We must be in general agreement on the rules to be followed no matter what specific policy or program is being advocated for our government. One of the axioms of our constitutional system as it has evolved, for example, is that political decisions are made on the basis of majority rule, but we insist at the same time that the right of the minority to become the majority shall not be impaired. The idea of keeping the channels of communication open to the minority—free speech, freedom of assembly, and a free press —is one of the sacred principles of constitutionalism in the United States, and this constitutes one element of constitutional government upon which public opinion must be in concord.

Outside of the area bounded by principles of constitutionalism, public opinion may be divisible along many lines. Opinion may be divided on immediate economic and social policies in a democracy, and indeed may even divide quite sharply over broad principles of economic organization, as witness the division of opinion in Great Britain on the mild nationaliza-

[3] Quoted in William Monypenny and George E. Buckle: *The Life of Benjamin Disraeli* (New York, 1914), Vol. III, pp. 107–8.

tion program. Public opinion then, may be divided, and while it is an indispensable feature of popular government based upon majority rule, it is an over-simplification to say that public opinion is merely majority opinion. Public opinion makes possible the conduct of government upon a majority rule basis, but it is perfectly clear that public opinion on most issues represents something more than an ascertainable body of opinion which we may readily identify at a given moment as majority opinion.

Analyzing Public Opinion

Besides speculation on the nature of public opinion, an increasing amount of attention has been devoted to the problem of how public opinion works and how it may be influenced. As autocracies and strict monarchies gradually gave way to systems of representative government, where the popular will rather than a select few or a single individual determined governmental policies, it was only natural that men should become deeply concerned with the factors that bring about consensus or a common measure of agreement. In England Edmund Burke, doubtlessly affected by the French Revolution, was early concerned with the means whereby a common belief or conclusion is reached and maintained. In the United States much of the investigation on public-opinion analysis has followed a psychological approach to the subject. Walter Lippmann, who did a great deal to stir up interest in the subject in this country by the publication of *Public Opinion* in 1922, stressed psychological factors as well as the divisions in opinion. There has also been heavy emphasis in the United States upon the study of pressure groups as instruments and molders of public opinion. In close alliance with the investigation of pressure groups, the study of propaganda and the methods of propagating beliefs has been steadily pushed. And finally there has been heavy emphasis in the United States on the testing of public opinion through the development of polling techniques, both with the view of finding out what people believe and why they hold to their beliefs.

That the study of the workings of public opinion is vitally important few would doubt. The role of public opinion in representative government is not to be denied. Nor may we brush aside the fact that the manipulative and skillful use of propaganda in influencing public opinion presents a powerful challenge to democratic government, for the use of propaganda may be aimed at bad as well as good objectives in government. We may well agree with Lord Palmerston that "opinions are stronger than armies," and that "opinions, if they are founded in truth and justice will in the end prevail" but we also know that opinions may sometimes be misguided by the cunning use of propaganda and that in our own time this technique has been used to swing people from the central avenue of truth down the side-streets to the police state.

There has been far too much generalization about public opinion. To many observers it may appear erratic, without settled aims and purposes, or as Sir Robert Peel once described it: "that great compound of folly, weakness, prejudice, wrong feeling, right feeling, obstinacy and newspaper paragraphs which is called public opinion." But the fact remains that it is the energizing force of representative government without which no truly democratic government can exist. "The essence of the State," as Bertrand Russell remarks, "is that it is the repository of the collective force of its citizens." Public opinion constitutes a large part of this collective force and, if a better understanding of it is to be secured, we must know something of the media through which public opinion both influences and is influenced.

THE ROLE OF PRESSURE GROUPS

At the base of our political society lies the diversity of interests which have resulted from various economic and professional specializations. Here also one discovers divisions which stem from religious, racial, and sectional differences. Inevitably, under such circumstances, the lack of homogeneity of interest on all matters affecting society leads to a natural desire for the expression of special interests by various segments of society. These segments are composed of people or groups having common interests who simply desire to press for their own program and policies through individual organizations devised for this purpose. The name commonly ascribed to such organizations in the United States is pressure groups.

The operation of a pressure group and its aim and objectives need not be as generally incompatible with those of society, as many are prone to believe. Pressure groups do, of course, often selfishly pursue a course of action which is not in the best interests of society as a whole. But the work of a pressure group may, as we shall see, be most helpful in legislative matters. Moreover pressure groups, because they tend to fill a vacuum in our political system, render a valuable service by helping to make representative government more responsive to public opinion.

Pressure groups, in effect, might be likened to a kind of government operating within the larger government of society as a whole. The larger pressure groups such as the American Farm Bureau Federation hold conventions to adopt policies. Moreover, they even have their own systems of representation for choosing delegates to meetings where questions of policy will be threshed out. In this way factional differences within pressure groups are adjusted and compromised so that by the time a group is ready to put its case before the legislature of the government its objectives are quite sharply defined. Thus a large part of the conflict of interests is already resolved by the interest groups themselves by the time they carry their cause before the formal machinery of government to secure action. The preliminary settlement of family quarrels among interest groups does much to ease the burden of the legislative branch of government, for it obviously cuts down the volume of dissension with which the latter must deal. It then remains for government to weigh the demands of competing interest groups and transpose them into statutory policies. In essence the vast network of pressure-group organizational machinery in the United States has come not only to be important as a supplement to the functioning of formal institutions of government such as Congress, but it has also been a formidable factor in steering the course of development of our political party system.

Pressure Groups and the Bi-party System

The diversified character of the American economy has, no doubt, helped to create conditions which accelerate the spread of organized pressure groups. Similarly the size of the country with its regional differences and large representations of nationalities and religious cultures has been conducive to the development of interest groups. Whatever the reasons, however, it is an established fact that interest groups were organized very early in this country. [4] The National Association of Cotton Manufacturers, though not the first in the field by any means, was organized in 1854, the National Grange (an organization of farmers) was founded in 1867; and in two decades following the Civil War an abundance of organizations sprang into being such as farmers groups seeking to curb railroad rate abuses or hoping to secure governmental control of grain elevators. Not until the present century, particularly since World War I has the pressure-group movement reached its full stature, but for well over a century interest groups have influenced the architecture of American politics.

The structure of American government with its system of separation of powers, checks and balances, and unitary executive, has been a stabilizing factor in keeping a two-party system in the United States, as most students of government will agree. But the elaborate machinery of organized pressure groups that has developed in this country also deserves a strong share of the credit for preserving the two-party system. In countries such as France where a multi-party system exists, the multiplicity of political parties makes possible more specific commitment to a special interest group than either major party in the United States would be prepared to undertake. Should a major party in the United States commit itself as completely to one special group as some parties do in European countries having a multi-party system, it would doubtlessly alienate other groups from which it derived political support. In multi-party countries, the pressure group is not as important as it is in the United States because the large number of parties makes possible a graduated scale of political choice to the voter. The European voter, in other words, can more readily identify himself with a party that comes closer to representing his specific interest than he can in the United States where the major parties do not narrow down the interest range as sharply. In a sense, a multi-party system which gives a voter more opportunity to identify himself with a party

---

[4] See "The Background of Group Pressures in the United States." *Annals of the American Academy of Political and Social Science* (1935), 179:1–67.

whose policies are closely tuned to his own views has certain advantages. But it also has its penalties. Experience with the multi-party system has demonstrated that its divisive influence may lead to an undesirable instability of government. Where no one party can muster enough support to form a government, the solution must necessarily be coalition government with all the uncertainties the latter entails. The average government in France under the multi-party system between the two World Wars lasted about seven months and in the three years following the liberation of Paris in the summer of 1945 there were thirteen different ministries.

In the United States the proliferation of pressure groups has displaced the need for a multi-party system because the individual special interest organizations work within the major parties to achieve the ends they desire. The presence of interest groups operating within our political parties as well as inside our formal government structure has tended to keep the two-party system intact and has probably helped us to avoid some of the attendant confusion of a multi-party system.

At the same time it should be borne in mind that the two-party system in the United States, although influenced by pressure groups, has in turn had a bearing on the growth of interest group machinery. As Professor Key notes: "In a negative way American political parties stimulate the formation of pressure groups." [5] Our major parties do not, as we noted earlier, commit themselves unequivocally to any special interest group for fear of alienating other constituent elements in the party. Thus pressure groups form an intricate part of the over-all machinery through which the impulses of public opinion make themselves felt in governmental policy.

PRESSURE-GROUP TECHNIQUES

With some appropriateness, the United States is occasionally referred to as a "pressure group" democracy. Scattered throughout the nation are several thousand organizations, each of which hopes to induce those in control of our governmental machinery to adopt policies favorable to its cause. Pressure groups may work at the local level—they may, for example, seek to influence a city council, or they may direct their efforts toward state legislatures. In Washington the representatives of pressure groups are to be found in tremendous force, where special interests seeking favor with Congress range from bolt-and-nut manufacturers to cranberry and peanut-butter producers.

Lobbying

The term "lobbying" is applied to the practice of influencing legislation through persons who are not members of the legislative body. Lobbying may be done by an individual representing a larger group or it may be practiced collectively by a group of persons. The term is derived from

[5] V. O. Key: *Parties, Politics, and Pressure Groups* (New York, 1947), p. 177.

the fact that in the development of the practice it used to be quite common for persons representing interest groups to do some of their persuading in the lobbies adjacent to legislative chambers. Practitioners of lobbying understandably acquired the name "lobbyists." Actually, the real work of lobbying is now done not in the legislative lobby but in places that may be either near the nation's capital or remote from Washington at what might be called the grass roots level.

Nor is modern lobbying today confined to the exercise of influence on legislators and legislative bodies alone. A large portion of the time and effort of lobbyists is directed toward administrators and administrative bodies. Administrative agencies not only make rules and regulations which directly affect pressure groups, but they also make legislative recommendations to Congress which are based upon their experience. Thus some lobbyists urge administrators to change a regulation or to help them secure a statutory change in Congress.

Types of Lobbies

During World War II (1944), it was estimated that there were 12,000 lobbyists in the nation's capital, more than double the number in the profession five years earlier. [6] Roughly speaking, the distribution of the bulk of lobbying activities falls into three main categories: business, labor, and agriculture. Thus about three million factories, stores, and various other businesses in the United States belong to one or more of 11,000 business organizations such as the Chamber of Commerce, and there are 2,800 trade associations actually representing business in Washington. [7] The eighteen million persons belonging to labor organizations are represented by an impressive array of lobbyists and of more than one hundred organizations in the country representing farmers, a large number of the more powerful ones such as the American Farm Bureau Federation maintain continuous lobbying operations in Washington. In addition there are several hundred miscellaneous organizations such as peace groups, research associations, religious associations, and welfare groups, many of whom maintain lobbyists in Washington or at least indulge in lobbying activities at specific times. Finally, a newer lobby perhaps, but certainly not one to be ignored, is that which seeks to look after the interests of various departments and bureaus of the government itself. Each of the Federal departments and many of the specialized agencies of government

[6] *Baltimore Evening Sun*, January 19, 1944. In 1939 the number of lobbyists in Washington was set at 6,000 by one newspaper correspondent. See Kenneth G. Crawford: *The Pressure Boys* (New York, 1939), p. 3.

[7] Interesting accounts of lobbies and lobbying activities may be found in D. C. Blaisdell: *Economic Power and Political Pressure*, Temporary National Economic Committee, Monograph 26 (Washington, D.C., 1941). See also Stuart Chase: *Democracy Under Pressure* (New York, 1945). The operations and organization of a specific pressure group are examined in E. E. Schattschneider: *Politics, Pressures, and the Tariff* (New York, 1935), and an interesting recent article also on a specific pressure group is Alexander F. Crosby: "The Real Estate Lobby." *American Mercury* (1947), 44:287–93.

such as the independent commissions maintain a type of lobbyist "on the hill" (the Capitol) who is expected to advise on legislative matters and work for or against bills which his agency is interested in. Even the White House has its own group of representatives who function outside of Congress in much the same capacity as lobbyists who are hired by private enterprise.

Who Are the Lobbyists?

A large number of persons in the lobbyist profession are lawyers. There are in Washington over 5,000 lawyers—more in proportion to the size of the city than in any other metropolitan center of the world—and the majority of them are engaged in some form of lobbying. Also well represented in the lobby profession is the ex-congressman. Former members of the Senate or House, particularly those who have served many years in either chamber, are often skillful and effective lobbyists because of intimate contacts in the national legislature as well as their wide knowledge of legislative processes. In many cases lobbyists are persons with high technical or professional competence who rank as authorities in their specialty.

It is a matter of common knowledge that the remuneration of some lobbyists is indeed attractive—occasionally running as high as $100,000 a year. To determine the average salary of a lobbyist is difficult even though lobbyists must now register and file statements on their salaries and expenses. For the first quarter of 1948 the Department of Justice reported that 190 lobbyists had received annual salaries totaling well over a million dollars and had received "substantial" expense accounts. [8] This would place the average salary in this group somewhere between $5,000 and $6,000. But many lobbyists do what is termed "piece work," that is, they simply devote their time and energies to a specific task, and once this is completed they are free to turn their efforts elsewhere. The estimate, therefore, that a full-time lobbyist receives about $15,000 annually is probably a reasonable approximation.

Lobbyists in Action

The character and practice of lobbying have undergone a tremendous change in the past fifty years. Gone from Washington is Pendelton's Palace of Fortune—famed as a gathering place for lobbyists who stalked their quarry there in the second half of the last century and known to its frequenters as the Hall of the Bleeding Heart. Gone also from the Washington scene are such colorful personalities as Sam Ward, the generally acclaimed King of the Lobby, whose fabulous parties and gastronomical orgies have now become legendary. Lobbying, in the course of its transformation, has discarded much of the crudity with which it was associated in an earlier day. The cartoon depicting a swollen, greedy figure buy-

[8] *Baltimore Sun,* April 19, 1948.

ing the vote of a cringing congressman with a heavy bag of money may still make blood pound through the veins of an avid reader of the Communist *Daily Worker,* but it is no longer a valid characterization of lobbying.

The problem of the lobbyist is really that of "the engineering of consent," to borrow a phrase from Professors Odegard and Helms. To do this the modern lobbyists cannot simply use one set formula. In the past their predecessors often employed the "buttonhole" technique of persuasion—a form of direct approach which was effective then and still is—but not in all cases. Today the skilled lobbyist may decide that the wisest course is to stir up the grass roots first, at a point far removed from Washington, and await developments. In general there are four or five basic methods of lobbying, each adaptable to several variations. A simple and often most effective method of lobbying is that which depends upon personal friendship. In this case a lobbyist who is respected personally and speaks for a reputable organization may enjoy extraordinary success in getting across what he wants from Congress or an administrative body. The Railroad Brotherhoods and certain farm organizations have often relied upon this technique. Some lobbyists rely heavily upon selective pressure from the grass roots to accomplish their purpose. Thus persons of influence in a congressman's district are instructed to turn the screws on their representative at the proper time either by letter, personal contact, or perhaps by means of a statement expressing the collective views of several prominent people in the community. A related technique is that which concentrates upon bringing a deluge of mail and telegrams from a congressman's constituents urging a stand on specific legislation. The latter method, of course, is somewhat indiscriminate and is a high-pressure technique that relies upon volume of response to bring a congressman around. Occasional checks made by congressmen on this type of lobbying have often revealed that telegrams are sent without the authorization of the persons whose names they bear, and sometimes even without their knowledge. The mail order and telegram variety of lobbying is undoubtedly effective, but it has also probably been overplayed in recent years and may not be quite as dependable as formerly.

The use of the visiting delegation as a means of lobbying is a device not yet wholly abandoned, but most observers agree that its usefulness is limited, and that legislators do not respond well to this type of pressure particularly if the overtones of intimidation and belligerency are present. Most difficult to assess of all types of lobbying is that which is sometimes referred to as "plush-horse" lobbying. The latter is built around social entertainment. Lobbyists are no doubt more skillful than they used to be as well as more discreet in using this technique. Some still maintain luxurious residences or expensive hotel suites where they entertain congressmen and they unquestionably take advantage of this type of fraternization not to talk business, but to ripen their personal contacts. Just how effective these nocturnal frivolities are in having any subsequent bearing on specific legislation is difficult to measure. Obviously they have some, but how much is a matter of conjecture at best.

LOBBYING AND PROPAGANDA

Our discussion of the techniques of lobbying reveals that a large part of this work consists of shaping and influencing the climate of opinion outside of Congress—at the grass roots levels. Thus many lobbyists operate by planting an idea among groups in a certain area or perhaps among people generally throughout the entire nation. A public-utility lobby, for example, may disseminate an idea through a vast number of modern communication devices in the hope of inducing a favorable public attitude. Now the theory behind such a strategy in lobbying is that, if an idea is skillfully planted and cultivated, it will eventually germinate and enable the lobbyist to reap the desired legislative harvest. Our concern with this procedure, of course, lies in the enormous use of the press, radio, and specialized propaganda devices which lobbyists use as mediums for mobilizing favorable opinion.

It is obvious that if widespread public support or sympathy can be obtained for the policies of a special interest group, the task of the lobbyist to nail down a legislative program becomes infinitely less difficult. In recent years the growing recognition that wide public support is a powerful ally in influencing legislation has prompted lobbyists to exploit the communication channels for reaching the public.

A large part of this type of lobbying is carried on under the guise of public-relations work and is charged off as advertising. But radio programs, newspaper advertisements, and television broadcasts seeking to win public favor can be mighty effective instrumentalities of lobbying. And the attractive pamphlets and other printed publications which interest groups cause to be published and distributed are also a form of lobbying, though again often passed off as advertising. Under the Federal Regulation of Lobbying Act, articles or editorials "caused to be published" must be reported, yet experience with this law shows that only about one out of eight lobbyists registers such attempts to lobby in his reports. Much the same result is indicated where lobbyists or lobbying organizations attempt to try their own cases before the bar of public opinion through press advertisements, radio, or pamphlets, on a controversial legislative proposal. Such measures are frequently charged to routine advertising costs and not reported under the Lobbying Act, though they are, of course, a subtle form of lobbying.

Lobbying through the press, radio, pamphlet, and other forms of communication is not inherently bad, but when carried on in various forms of disguise it has certain unwholesome results. Lobbying of this nature, in short, exposes the body public to propaganda, the origins of which individual members of the community may be quite unaware of because of the subtleties employed in putting it across.

What Is Propaganda?

Propaganda, just as pressure-group activity, may serve as a positive force for good in democratic government and should not be adjudged as necessarily pernicious. The term itself has an unfortunate connotation, both because of its intimate association with Fascism, Communism, and the rise of dictatorships, and the ill-founded but widely entertained notion that it always entails a perversion of truth.

The term "propaganda" is an old one. It was used in the name of an agency founded by the Catholic Church late in the sixteenth century whose chief purpose was the propagation of the faith in non-Catholic countries. [9] Thus the history of propaganda concerns the dissemination and transmission of ideas. With the advance of democracy, broader educational facilities, increased literacy, and improved communication channels, along with accelerating demands for social change, the place of propaganda has assumed ever-greater importance.

To understand the workings of propaganda, we may obtain some help from the analysis of Harold Lasswell who defines it as "the management of collective attitudes by the manipulation of significant symbols." [10] Under this interpretation propaganda is simply the tool that is used to influence collective attitudes. Moreover it matters not whether the motivation which impels the use of propaganda is selfish or non-selfish. We have noted that there is a strong tendency to identify propaganda with sly, sleight-of-hand cunning to disseminate falsehoods, but certainly this need not always be the case. The propagandist may propagate the noblest objectives with the general welfare as his motive. And in seeking to manage collective attitudes the propagandist with unselfish aims may even take certain liberties with the truth in presenting his propaganda, or soft-pedal matters that would have a negative effect on his propaganda and highlight only those of positive value. On the other hand the propagandist may be unimpeachably honest. No matter which course is followed, however, he who would attempt to influence collective attitudes by such means is a propagandist. Thus propaganda may be inspired by the noblest or the basest of motives and it may be presented with the most complete regard for truth and honesty or with but slight regard for either.

The Tools of Propaganda

The dissemination of propaganda, irrespective of its nature, is accomplished by means of "significant symbols." We all know that words are a form of symbol and that different words evoke different kinds of response. The reason for this, of course, is that through our training we have learned to respond in certain ways to different words and to different combinations of words. But even within a society enjoying a common language

[9] See Harwood L. Childs: *An Introduction to Public Opinion* (New York, 1940), p. 75.

[10] Harold D. Lasswell: "The Theory of Propaganda." *American Political Science Review* (1927), 21:627.

the same words may not have universal meaning nor convey the same thought. The words "Wall Street" or "malefactors of wealth" will not convey the same meaning to every group nor will they bring about the same response, just as the words "labor racketeers" will not have universal meaning or precipitate uniform reaction when used in different settings. The background, training, education, economic status, and prejudices of a people along with many other factors make them susceptible to various kinds of propagandistic appeals. Thus the careful choice and arrangement of words enhance the success of propaganda in seeking to manage collective attitudes.

In foreign affairs we need only follow the daily newspaper to see for ourselves the intricate effect of words as symbols and their role as tools of propaganda. Even between nations using the same common language, words and phrases may have a different connotation, as thousands of American G.I.'s who were stationed in Great Britain or Australia during World War II can readily testify. And where countries do not speak the same tongue, problems arise in the translation of deliberations by international bodies, when propagandists sometimes take subtle advantage in coloring the translations or giving them different emphasis, thereby managing to sway domestic reception in the desired manner.

Words, of course, are by no means the sole instruments of propaganda. To verbal symbols and catchy slogans must be appended several other possibilities which may be used as facets of propaganda. Propaganda, though we may be reluctant to admit it, does evoke non-rational responses. When the recruitment radio program sponsored by the United States Army Air Forces opens and closes to the strains of a Sousa march, it is not an inadvertent choice. No one would think perhaps of starting such a program with Claude Debussy's "The Afternoon of a Faun," anymore than one would conceive of opening an American Legion or D.A.R. (Daughters of the American Revolution) program with "The Internationale" of the U.S.S.R. Thus the deliberate selection of music may be undertaken by the propagandist with the specific aim of exploiting the psychology of human behavior.

In another vein propaganda may make use of visual symbols. Thus the hammer and sickle, a drawing of Uncle Sam, or an untold number of other familiar figures may be employed as part of a propaganda campaign to secure a negative or positive response.

Wherever propaganda is used its success depends upon its being geared and adapted to work on the known attitudes of a people or a particular group. There are, as we have seen, certain symbols to which various groups within society have been conditioned to respond. Cultural, religious, professional, economic, social, and many other groups habitually respond in certain fashion to particular symbols because they have been so trained and conditioned. The task of the propagandist consists in first learning what these attitudes are, and then selecting symbols accordingly so as to utilize existing attitudes to support the idea favorable to his

purpose. It is often advantageous to the propagandist to present his case
in such a manner that "cultural attitudes will be organized toward it."
Thus during World War II, propagandists in the Soviet Union made
extensive use of posters and other visual imagery showing Russian heroes
far back into Tzarist history to rekindle the flame of patriotism, and they
also played up the works of former literary and musical luminaries such
as Dostoevsky and Tschaikowsky to the same end. And most significant
of all, perhaps, in illustrating the adaptation of propaganda to cultural
heritage and tradition, was the campaign undertaken in the Soviet Union
to bring about a reconciliation of the government and the Orthodox
Church.

In analyzing the use of propaganda there can be little doubt that what
one observer terms "cultural fixations" are indeed important and that
"if a propagandist can identify the opinion he desires to fix with an element
in the tradition of a population, he is likely to succeed." This explains why
propagandists in seeking to strike a responsive chord revert again and
again to established tradition and practice, and as Professor Key observes,
"formulate their program in terms of the accepted values of the group." [11]
Customs and traditions do change, however, and some field-tested symbols
lose their potency or fail to spark any reaction at all. Politicians campaigning on the hustings in American politics who once could rebut programs
with some success by stating that they were the product of theory-minded
professors can no longer rely on this technique of ridicule. The starry-
eyed professor, replete with mortar board and gown who was cartooned
so often as a conjurer of quack reforms appears to have outlived his usefulness as a device of the propagandist. There are always new ones to be
invented, however, and the propagandist must, if he is to succeed, stay
abreast of alterations that occur in thought and tradition—both those that
involve simple shifts and others of a more profound nature. The tremendous movement of people from farms to metropolitan centers, for example,
has created an entirely new situation in the United States, and as Ralph
Turner argues persuasively, it may result in great change of the cultural
habits of a large segment of the population.[12] The use of propaganda,
therefore, calls for the maintenance of a keen sensitivity to each successive
change which affects attitudes; and the propagandist whether possessed
by selfish or non-selfish motives must be alert to these changes if he is to
succeed.

Propaganda Channels and the Public Interest

Propaganda can, as is demonstrably clear, be used to disseminate falsehoods and misrepresentations. That society will in the end be able to
discriminate between patent falsehoods and opinions founded upon truth

[11] V. O. Key: *Politics, Parties, and Pressure Groups*, p. 427.
[12] Ralph Turner: "Culture, Change, and Confusion." *Public Opinion Quarterly*
(1940), 4:579–600. It is interesting to note that from 1940 to January 1, 1947, the
Census Bureau and the Bureau of Agricultural Economics report that 2,996,911 persons have left farms, a loss of 9.8 percent in the total farm population.

is one of the major premises upon which we pin our hopes in democratic government. But we do know that truth and objectivity on the issues facing society are often difficult to obtain for a variety of reasons. Not only may propaganda be skillfully masked and difficult to detect when propagated directly or indirectly by special interest groups, but in the transmission of ideas and reporting of factual information, instrumentalities of a quasi-public character such as newspapers, radio, and the movies may propagandize by deliberately seeking to influence collective attitudes. [13] Daily metropolitan newspapers in the United States have an aggregate circulation of 55,000,000 copies. In many cases these papers are read by more than one reader and when the circulation of weekly or semi-weekly papers is added, the total number of potential readers is indeed impressive. [14] Forthright opinion on an editorial page with due regard for facts, of course, is desirable if we are to maintain the tradition of a free press. But the ownership of newspapers, the dependence of newspapers upon advertising for financial support, and the fact that the facilities of the press are not easily accessible to many groups, raises perplexing problems. One cannot help but have some misgivings today over the fact that the percentage of "one-newspaper towns" has grown, and that there are larger newspaper chains as well as larger organizations of publishers. It is not only the well-known methods of propagandizing in the press with which we need be concerned, such as editorializing in news columns, giving certain items more prominence than others, suggestive headlines, or even the flagrant distortion of the facts. These are matters of serious consequence which we look to the vigilance of public opinion to detect and discount accordingly. But the fact that the control of the press is retained by a relatively small group and that it is a medium affected with a deep public interest—indeed an institution of quasi-public character—suggests that a strong responsibility should attach to publishers for faithful and objective news reporting.[15]

The same arguments for objectivity and truthfulness in a nation's press apply with equal force to radio, the movies, and other instruments of communication through which ideas are transmitted. Thus it is evident that the channels of communication are institutions of vital concern when we are dealing with propaganda. The communication facilities are the means through which the individual members of society are reached and as such are agencies whose conduct is a matter of grave public concern.

Also a question involving communication facilities that is a matter of direct public concern is government reporting itself. Professor E. P. Herring divides government publicity, that is to say public information which the

[13] For a comprehensive treatment of this subject see Ralph D. Casey: *Propaganda, Communication, and Public Opinion* (Princeton, 1946).

[14] See Malcolm M. Willey: "Communication Agencies and the Volume of Propaganda." *The Annals of the American Academy of Political Science* (1935), 179:177–86, 194–200.

[15] On the obligation of the press see Arthur Krock: "The Press and Government." *The Annals* (1935), 182:166. For a critical appraisal of American newspapers see Gerald Johnson: "Great Newspapers, If Any." *Harpers* (1948), 196:538–46.

government distributes itself, into two categories: (1) information whose purpose is to advertise services offered by a particular government agency; and (2) publicity designed not only to solicit support for an agency, but also for the policies with which it is concerned. [16] On an increasing scale government agencies have been disseminating reports covering a great many subjects. The majority of these reports are highly useful to farmers, business men, and other groups. In one year alone, the Department of Agriculture distributed 50,000,000 publications including periodicals. [17] While these reports enjoy a steadfast reputation for accuracy, there has been some criticism particularly since the end of World War II that government agencies are increasingly reluctant to release information concerning the public business—a circumstance that was roundly denounced by the American Society of Newspaper Editors and resulted in the creation of a special inter-departmental committee to study the problem. [18] That the government, of course, exercises a public trust in the matter of disseminating official reports is perfectly obvious, and it hardly need be added that in the performance of its duties under this trust a democratic government bears a heavy responsibility for fairness and objectivity. Indeed as Professor Herring poignantly observes: "We cannot view with equanimity a development which places great powers of persuasion in the administrative branch and brings no countervailing force on the other side." [19]

In our discussions of pressure groups, lobbying, and propaganda we have seen that all three are justified under a democracy, and that furthermore the authority for the existence of all three may be found in a fundamental civil rights guarantee of the Constitution itself—the right of petition. The right of existence for these devices which mold public opinion, therefore, may be clearly upheld under our constitutional system. In the operation of these devices, however, we have already contacted some matters where the techniques employed become questions of vital interest to society. Thus while not denying the right of pressure groups, lobbyists, and propagandists to operate, society has found it expedient and desirable to experiment at least with legislation which prescribes certain conditions as to their mode of operation.

REGULATING PRESSURE GROUP ACTIVITY

Although proceeding at a slow pace, the regulation of pressure-group operations in the United States has made a modest beginning. In a sense

[16] E. P. Herring: "Official Publicity Under the New Deal." *The Annals* (1935), 179:167–75.

[17] See T. Swann Harding: "Genesis of One Government Propaganda Mill." *Public Opinion Quarterly* (1947–8), 11:227–35.

[18] See James E. Warner: "The Ban on Embarrassing Information." *New York Herald Tribune,* October 30, 1947.

[19] E. P. Herring, *The Annals,* 179:172–7. For a trenchant analysis of the problems see also Joseph T. Klapper: "Mass Media and the Engineering of Consent." *American Scholar* (1948), 17:419–29.

the development of pressure-group regulation has been not unlike that which has been applied to political parties. Early in our history, a party was thought of as something comparable to a private club—a sort of voluntary association of voters. In the course of their evolution, however, parties, as we shall note presently, gradually became subject to public regulation. Methods for the nomination of their leaders were prescribed by government, ballots came to be printed by the government instead of by the parties themselves, and many other party activities fell within the purview of government regulation. What happened in short was that party activity came to be identified with a public interest.

Identification of pressure-group activity with the public interest has been slower, but some state and Federal regulation of pressure-group operations has been undertaken nonetheless. Perhaps one of the first congressional attempts to regulate in this field was a statute enacted as a part of the criminal code back in 1852 which provided for heavy fines, imprisonment, forfeiture of public office, and disqualification for holding any future office under the government of the United States, for taking a bribe. Massachusetts enacted the first lobbying law in 1890, and since that date about thirty-five states have passed laws dealing with the subject in varying scope. The chief characteristic of most lobbying legislation thus far is that it attempts to require publicity on lobbying activities. Thus representatives of pressure groups are required to register with a designated government official, file expense accounts, and identify the organization they are representing.

The general lobbying act of the Federal government was passed in 1946—some two years after Franklin Roosevelt had called for lobby regulation in a message to Congress in which he said: "There are the pests who swarm through the lobbies of Congress and the cocktail bars of Washington, representing special groups as opposed to the basic interests of the nation as a whole." The Federal Regulation of Lobbying Act was enacted as a part of the Legislative Reorganization Act of 1946. [20] Up until this time Congress had made only sporadic passes at regulating specific abuses of lobbying activities by legislation, such as that directed against lobbying by public utilities and shipping interests or the measure which curbed the issuance of free railroad passes to legislators. The lobby statute passed in 1946, however, was designed to have general application to all types of lobbying. It requires individuals, organizations, associations, and corporations, as well as other groups seeking to influence legislation to file reports of both their receipts and expenditures. As described by former Senator Robert M. LaFollette, Jr., the lobbying act "was sold to the Seventy-ninth Congress for what it is—an act to reveal the activities of lobbyists, not necessarily to curb or pass judgment thereon, and certainly not to interfere with the rightful access of citizens to their Congress." [21]

[20] See Belle Zeller: "The Federal Regulation of Lobbying Act." *American Political Science Review* (1948), 42:239–71.

[21] Robert M. LaFollette, Jr.: "Some Lobbies are Good." *New York Times Magazine,* May 16, 1948, p. 54.

There appears to be rather common agreement that the idea of turning the cleansing spotlight of publicity on lobbying activities is a sound one. Moreover, a poll taken in 1947 by Elmo Roper indicating the appalling lack of public information on some of our most powerful pressure groups suggests that it might be a healthier thing for democratic government if people were better informed on this subject.

The fact that publicity is required for lobbying activities, of course, does not insure strict compliance, and it is generally agreed that many expenditures to influence legislation go unreported. Nor does the reporting divulge information on how a pressure group determines its legislative program. It does not, for instance, throw any light on whether the lobbyist or lobbyists purporting to act for a group are really representative of the entire group—a factor that should be important to legislators seeking to judge representations made on behalf of the group.

The number of registrants under the Federal Regulation of Lobbying Act has been only a little over four thousand—a figure unquestionably much lower than the actual number engaged in the lobbying profession. The highest individual expenditure reported in 1955 was $32,424, listed by the National Association of Real Estate Boards for the third quarter. Others reporting (for the last quarter of 1955) were various groups representing organized labor, listing $72,416 and topped by the American Federation of Labor with $18,570; farmer groups altogether listed a total of $47,453, with the Farm Bureau Federation alone reporting $27,053; sugar interests listed a total of $47,417, while pipe-line and gas companies reported spending $43,700 with $17,263 reported spent by the pipe-line companies alone. These reports are made to the Clerk of the House of Representatives as the statute requires.

The items for which this money was spent vary greatly. Thus the American Short Line Railroad Association itemized $200 on its report for tickets to the opening baseball game between the Washington Senators and the New York Yankees, while the Independent Bankers Association recorded an expense item for taking twenty-three senators to dinner, and the Aircraft Industries Association of America spent $350 for cocktail parties for the President's Air Policy Commission and the Congressional Air Policy Board. From experience thus far it is obvious that neither all pressure group organizations are registered nor are those reporting giving a full account of their expenditures. The Department of Justice has already prosecuted some individuals for failure to comply with the Lobbying Act and the trend of sentiment generally seems to favor tightening up the publicity requirements for pressure group organizations. [22]

[22] In a telegram to President Truman urging stricter regulation of pressure-group activities, the International Association of Machinists, the largest independent union in the country, stated that at least $12,000,000 had been spent by lobbyists to influence the Eightieth Congress. *New York Times,* November 21, 1948.

TESTING PUBLIC OPINION

The time-honored means of testing public opinion under a system of government in which political decisions are taken in accordance with the wishes of the majority is by an election. Thus pressure groups tugging in different directions, as well as lobbyists and propagandists, must all have their cases tried eventually by the one best known device for sounding public opinion—the free election. Yet elections, although providing the most authoritative way of registering the pulse of public opinion that has been discovered, still leave some questions unanswered. Elections tell us which candidate is to occupy a public office, but for any number of reasons they do not always reveal other factors that are of interest to students of public opinion. An election, as is often the case, may result in a protest against the party in power, the incumbent party being blamed for conditions not altogether within its power to control. Under such circumstances the election does not reveal a positive policy which public opinion may desire—it indicates chiefly a discontent with what has gone before. Another question which elections sometimes leave unanswered is "why" the response is one way or the other? Some of the reasons on the "why" of election results are readily explainable but others are less obvious. Also of interest to students of public opinion and politicians alike is the state of opinion between elections. Just what are the likes and dislikes of the electorate in the period during which there is no election. Obviously the answers to all these questions have long been sought, and they have played an important part in the development of straw polls that seek to sample public opinion.

Public-Opinion Polls

Long before modern polls made their appearance efforts were made to ascertain public attitudes. Politicians were naturally interested in such matters when their own political survival might be at stake, while newspaper writers pursued the subject for a variety of reasons besides their main objective of providing interesting copy for their readers. The sampling of public opinion in this fashion was based upon sifting reports from party leaders and securing information from a number of persons whose judgment about attitudes in a particular locality or special interest group were known to be fairly reliable. While far from scientific such methods often provide an accurate clue to what people are thinking. Thus, Leslie Biffle, Secretary of the Senate in the Eighty-first Congress, after making his own cross-country trek disguised as a poultry dealer with a trailer full of chickens in 1948, accurately divined that the farmers were going to vote for Truman despite a showing of the polls to the contrary. The judgment of the political oracle, however, may sometimes be sadly mistaken and since the middle 1930's interest in the development of scientific polling techniques has rapidly accelerated.

Sampling Methods

An analysis of public opinion through scientific sampling evolved principally from experience in market analysis. A manufacturer with a new product to sell found it expedient to hire people who would go out and test its popularity. In essence the purpose of market analysis was to measure consumer preferences. If a commodity was popular the idea was to find out why; if not, what were the objections to it? To facilitate market analysis, techniques of sampling public attitudes were devised that required only a selective sampling of representative consumer groups. Thus instead of testing all potential buyers, which would be prohibitive because of the expense involved, only a small sampling was made of a representative cross-section of the possible market. And on the basis of the selective sampling the results obtained were used as an index to the attitudes of all the potential buyers. The underlying theory of this technique, of course, is that if the selective sampling of persons interviewed is really representative, the findings will be essentially the same as though the inquiry had been directed to all potential buyers.

The development of methods for sampling public attitudes in market analysis was unquestionably of real value to many business men and manufacturers, and it is notable that in the refinement of the sampling process several men pioneered in this field who are today prominently identified with public-opinion polls that deal chiefly with politics and political issues. From the market-analysis forerunner, two types of political polls have become increasingly popular: the poll on candidates and the poll which attempts to gauge popular sentiment on issues.

A straw poll of a very rough nature was tried by the *New York Herald Tribune* to test the popularity of presidential candidates even before 1900, but it was not until the *Literary Digest* began taking presidential polls in 1916 that popular enthusiasm for the candidate poll began to be reflected. [23] The polls taken by the *Literary Digest* were not based on scientific sampling, but instead several million straw ballots were sent out to persons listed in telephone directories. Although initially the *Literary Digest* had some success with its polls, its prophecy of Alfred Landon's election over Franklin Roosevelt in 1936 when the Republican candidate actually carried only Maine and Vermont, led to its demise as well as the discredit of its methods. At the time the *Literary Digest* presidential straw poll made its grievous error in the 1936 election, the polls of the American Institute of Public Opinion conducted by George Gallup and the *Fortune* poll directed by Elmo Roper were already making modest headway. These polls conducted surveys to sample public opinion on both candidates and issues. In so far as popularity is concerned, the polls on candidates usually arouse more interest. Nonetheless, polls taken on issues probably have greater import for the study of public opinion. An election, as we have

[23] See Charles W. Smith: *Public Opinion in a Democracy* (New York, 1939), pp. 395–6.

seen, provides for a decision on the candidates, but it does not always tell us why one candidate won over another nor does it provide clues to public sentiment on specific issues between elections.

Poll Techniques

Basically, all the modern polls, whether on candidates or issues, operate on the same principle—that of sampling. [24] In this process one of the first steps is to pick sampling areas. The object here is to select areas for sampling that will be representative of the larger region in which they are located. Next, the population within the areas to be sampled is subdivided into a number of representative categories such as race, education, religion, age, economic status, and several others. The underlying assumption of such a breakdown is that a consensus expressed by a small number within each of these categories will accurately reflect the views of a majority of all persons belonging to the same group. A third step involved in a poll is that of conducting interviews in which samples are taken within each of the representative groups mentioned above. Before these interviews can be made, of course, questionnaires must be carefully devised and the interviewers must be given detailed instructions on how to proceed. Finally, the evaluation of the interview findings must be made, and this process, along with the preparation of the questionnaire, involves perhaps the most painstaking effort of the entire procedure.

Poll Problems

That the risk of error in any of the four major steps of poll taking is great hardly needs to be emphasized. Ideally the pollster seeks to construct a miniature model of the electorate which will mirror the sentiment of public opinion generally. In practice the actual samplings are very small. The *Fortune* poll ordinarily interviews only 5,000 persons on a candidate or issue poll, the American Institute of Public Opinion uses from 3,500 to 6,000, and the National Opinion Research Center takes but 2,500 samplings. [25] Dr. Gallup of the American Institute of Public Opinion concludes that if 3,000 people were interviewed each week, less than 1 per cent of the population of this country would be reached annually. On this basis if the average life expectancy is considered as fifty years, a person has one chance in ten of ever being interviewed. All pollsters are agreed, however, that it is the representativeness of the sampling that counts in achieving accuracy and that the smallest selective sampling if carefully obtained may provide the basis for reliable prediction.

In determining the sampling, census figures are used which provide some information about the characteristics of the population, but the problem of the pollster becomes more difficult when he begins to devise

[24] See George Gallup: *A Guide to Public Opinion Polls* (Princeton, 1944).
[25] See Hadley Cantril: "Do Different Polls Get the Same Results." *Public Opinion Quarterly* (1945), 9:61–9.

questionnaires. Questions must be designed which will not offend persons or make them suspicious. Questions which are misleading or are biased will obviously not yield accurate results. Nor will the results of a poll be reliable if the interviewers themselves have not been carefully instructed and indeed carefully selected. In a predominantly colored district, for example, the findings obtained by a colored interviewer may differ from those gathered by a white interviewer. All such factors must be compensated for, in addition to guarding against the possibility of cheating and other practices which would tend to distort the results.

Despite many difficulties both in obtaining accurate samples and in ironing out the obstacles mentioned, the modern public-opinion polls have made rather exceptional progress. In evaluating the polls taken on issues it is not so easy to determine how accurate they have been because elections do not always provide a subsequent check as they do in the case of candidates. Polls on issues are also more subject to error than candidate polls because of the inability of poll experts to frame questions in such a way that they will have no suggestive influence one way or the other on the respondent. In framing questions on issues great care must be exercised to avoid "loaded" questions, that is, to ask questions which either by design or accident are likely to prejudice the response of the person interviewed. [26] Notwithstanding these difficulties polls on issues can be regarded as having made substantial progress if one bears in mind that they are still in an experimental stage. They have been decidedly useful in gauging public sentiment on important legislation.

Poll Limitations

In evaluating and interpreting the results of polls, one admonition should be explicitly followed: public-opinion-poll findings should never be accepted uncritically. Indeed, as Elmo Roper stated in his own post-mortem on the shortcomings of his *Fortune* poll in the 1948 presidential election, persons who follow polls should never again accept "unquestionably" a political prediction based upon a poll. [27] This statement, of course, applies with equal force to both candidate polls and polls on issues.

The poll experts themselves have always endeavored to make clear to their readers that they must be allowed a 4 per cent margin of error in their forecasts. This in itself would be sufficient in a close election to make any prediction extremely hazardous. But the 1948 presidential election—in which the *Fortune* Poll forecast that President Truman would receive 37.5 per cent of the popular vote and Governor Dewey 52.8 per cent whereas Truman actually won 49.5 per cent of the popular vote and Dewey 45.6— demonstrates forcefully that on occasion the polls can be highly mislead-

---

[26] The possibility of error in polls taken on issues is probably greater than on those where the popularity of candidates is taken. See Arthur Kornhauser: "Are Public Opinion Polls Fair to Organized Labor?" *Public Opinion Quarterly* (1946–7), 10:484–500, and Paul Studenski: "How Polls Can Mislead." *Harpers* (1939), 180:80–3.

[27] *Baltimore Sun*, November 26, 1948.

ing. [28] In computing the percentage error of the 1948 presidential election polls some critics marshaled the figures to make the polls appear far more inaccurate than they actually were, but the fact remains—as the poll experts readily admitted—that something had gone drastically awry with their calculations.

Several conjectural observations on why the polls went wrong were offered pending a thorough study of the matter by a group of social scientists whom Gallup and Roper invited to examine their methods and data to determine where mistakes had been made. One possible source of error which seemed to be generally agreed upon was in the rather large percentage of persons polled who were undecided or who expressed no opinion. Between 7 and 8 per cent of those polled by Gallup in mid-October were still undecided. In the final Gallup report these undecided votes were distributed among the presidential candidates in accordance with their prevailing percentages on the assumption that the undecided voters would divide in the same proportion as those with opinions. This assumption obviously might prove a costly one where the undecided vote suddenly swung predominantly to one candidate at the last minute. The latter possibility also suggests another source of difficulty for the poll expert. In the case of an election the last interviews must necessarily be made some time prior to the election itself. The last Gallup interviews in 1948 were concluded by mid-October with the election over two weeks away. Suppose a last minute shift takes place in voter sentiment either because a new issue is injected into the campaign with startling effect or the campaign of one candidate gathers unexpected momentum as many observers were inclined to feel about Mr. Truman's last minute spurt just before November 2, 1948. Here again a shift is possible that the polls are not yet calibrated to measure. Among other sources of error is the stay-at-home vote. No way has yet been devised to foretell accurately which voters will stay at home on election day. Were Republicans overconfident on November 2, 1948, when the polls and experts were in near unanimous agreement that Mr. Dewey would be the next president? Or would the Democratic margin of victory have been even larger except that many Truman supporters stayed at home on the discouraging note that the Democratic standard bearer's cause was hopeless? Such are but a few of the imponderables that call for further refinement of the poll-taking process.

Perhaps a more serious shortcoming of public opinion polls is that they have not yet discovered how to measure the "intensity" of opinion. [29] The degree of intensity with which a person regards an issue or a candidate is a matter of great importance because it may provide the clue on a voter's

[28] The popular vote percentage and poll predictions for President Truman in 1948 were as follows:

President Truman's popular vote	49.5
Crossley Poll	44.8
Gallup (A.I.P.O.) Poll	44.5
Roper (*Fortune*) Poll	37.1

[29] See Edward L. Bernays, "Attitude Polls—Servants or Masters." *Public Opinion Quarterly* (1945–6), 9:2, 268a.

determination to carry through a positive course of action or simply remain passive. A possible illustration of this point is revealed in Roper's analysis of the *Fortune* poll debacle in 1948. Eighty-nine per cent of the pro-Dewey people polled in the *Fortune* survey thought the G.O.P. candidate would be elected, yet only a very small fraction of them rated him as one of the "great men" of the past fifty years. "We should have expected," commented Mr. Roper, "that this combination of overconfidence on the one hand and lack of enthusiasm on the other could well result in a dangerously small turnout." [30] Thus the intensity with which an opinion is held respecting a candidate or an issue, because it is indicative of subsequent action such as voting or not voting, may have a decided bearing on the reliability of a poll.

Polls and the Public Interest

Close on the heels of recent presidential elections have followed proposals for governmental regulation of polls. Some congressmen, miffed because their party's nominee made a poor showing in both the polls and elections, have called for regulation on the ground that polls produce a bandwagon effect. The "bandwagon" theory is that a poll which shows one candidate to be ahead has a tendency to swing voters behind the leading candidate, or in other words to influence voters to climb aboard the "bandwagon." Actually most poll experts deny that a poll produces any appreciable bandwagon effect, and certainly the presidential election of 1948 provided a strong case against the bandwagon theory. [31] But whether polls cause overconfidence by indicating a winner and thereby influence some people not to bother about voting is a question on which there is insufficient evidence thus far to give a categorical answer.

Most of the pro and con verbal jousting over public-opinion polls in the aftermath of elections usually dies down rather quickly, and no proposal to limit the use of polls has received serious consideration. On a somewhat higher level of intellectual debate, however, polls have been attacked from another angle.

Like other communication institutions such as newspapers and the radio, polls are definitely affected with a public interest. Presumably in transmitting their soundings of public opinion—on vital issues as well as candidates—polls are presenting information of serious concern to society. Thus it is imperative that the integrity of those conducting the polls be of a high order. At the moment, friend and critic alike of the polls seem satisfied that the leadership of public opinion polls is in capable hands. This is not to say that all local polls are run either skillfully or without bias, but simply represents an expression of opinion that the leading polls are reputable

---

[30] See *Fortune* (1948), 38:40: "Among those who planned to vote for Dewey, 23 per cent mentioned Roosevelt as one of the great men of the past fifty years, while only 9 per cent registered the same opinion of their 1948 candidate."

[31] Certainly not all of the electorate is familiar with the findings of the polls. In 1946 it was estimated that only 38 per cent of the people knew the results of the Gallup and *Fortune* polls. See Harry Field, Paul Lazarsfeld, Claude Robinson, and Edward Bernays: "The Discussion Goes on." *Public Opinion Quarterly* (1945–6), 9:404.

institutions run by reputable persons who are striving to operate polls honestly. The possibility that polls might fall into unscrupulous hands, however, worries more than a few critics. One check of a poll on candidates, of course, is an election, but on issues no ready check is available. In the latter case heavy reliance must be made upon the integrity and skill of the poll director. The concern, therefore, over keeping the polls only under the direction of persons of unquestioned character and honesty is altogether genuine.

Quite apart from the scepticism over the non-fallible character of polls and their potential misuse by unscrupulous persons are the queries raised by some observers on the social utility of polls. "Is it possible that polls do any disservice to the democratic system?" [32] Assuming the eventual perfection of polling techniques, are polls really beneficial to society or are they harmful in the sense that they gnaw away at the roots of representative government? "Many of us," writes Australia's former Prime Minister, R. G. Menzies, "with sincere respect for the carefulness and accuracy of such poll takers as Dr. Gallup, are anxious about the effect which this new technique will have upon the practice of politics. If it serves to tell the politician of widely entertained errors which he must attack, well and good, but if it merely tells him to beware, because opinion is against him, many good ideas will, I fear, be abandoned. . ." [33] Thus a basic fear raised in this expression of opinion is that elective representatives will become mere puppets of the electorate, ever fearful of exercising independent judgment or seizing the initiative to lead public opinion. The same idea somewhat more forcefully expressed is found in Edmund Burke's classic statement on the function of a representative. A representative, according to Burke, should be in the closest communion with his constituents and should attach great weight to their wishes, but "he betrays" instead of serving them, adds Burke, if he sacrifices his judgment for their opinion.

If legislators depended absolutely on polls as a sort of political seismograph and completely abdicated the leadership corollary of their representative function, the results might well be unhappy for democratic government. Even today, perhaps, there is considerable truth in the charge that some politicians are overly inclined to find out which way the wind is blowing before pursuing a course of action. But polls alone will not bring about the decline of public-opinion leadership by legislators and it is difficult to believe that they will systematically deter all political figures from bucking the popular tide. In their proper sphere, polls can be socially useful. Polls have been used with a good deal of success by the Department of Agriculture in determining attitudes among farmers on the administration of crop allotment programs and other regulatory policies, and they

[32] Both Gallup and Roper in asking that their methods be checked after the 1948 presidential election urged that the committee undertaking the investigation consider the larger question—do polls have a socially useful function? See Elmo Roper: *New York Herald Tribune*, December 2, 1948.

[33] See R. G. Menzies: "Politics, Fine Art and Inexact Science." *New York Times Magazine*, November 28, 1948, p. 74.

have been useful to the Army and the Census Bureau in sampling opinion. Applied to the electorate generally, polls throw light on popular attitudes toward specific issues that are often not revealed by elections. In addition by providing a general sounding board in the gaps between elections, polls afford a current check on public attitudes and thereby make it possible for us to check on the inflated claims of pressure groups as to the popularity or disapproval of a particular issue. That public-opinion polls need to be constantly watched to insure that they will not be used to mislead or misrepresent, is freely admitted by the poll experts themselves. The fact that there are several polls guided by different administrators offers some means of checking their results simply by a comparison of their findings wherever they have undertaken to sample similar issues or election contests. Suggestions have been made by some poll experts that one possible means of checking polls would be through a governmental audit which would check the methods used by those taking polls, give public information on who was sponsoring the polls financially, and also publicize the probable margin of error in the polls. A more extreme proposal is that the government should establish its own poll with the view of determining what the electorate specifically desires. The prospect of governmental regulation of polls, however, is still only in the speculative stage, and as long as reasonable accuracy is a requisite for the survival of polls conducted under private auspices, there is a sturdy incentive for operating them on an honest basis.

PUBLIC OPINION AND THE PUBLIC INTEREST

In evaluating pressure groups, lobbies, propaganda, and straw polls, we must inescapably face the question: Are they in the public interest and are they a reasonably successful means of helping to secure the wishes of the electorate? Judged practically do they serve a useful purpose in transmitting the desires of inarticulate masses into legislative policies? Like political parties as we shall see in the succeeding chapter, pressure groups are extremely important gaskets that help to lock our political structure together and keep it functioning on a satisfactory basis. Not all pressure-group activity, to be sure, is desirable or compatible with the general interest of society. Moreover, one of the chief difficulties with organized pressure groups is that it is not always possible for the public to know how representative the governing body which speaks for the group really is. But the positive need for pressure groups and their importance to the public interest makes their general abolition quite impractical, if not altogether impossible. A great sum of money was spent by pressure groups in trying to lobby through selfish legislation in the Eightieth Congress, but non-selfish programs of pressure groups were also handsomely financed. [34] The Citizens Committee on Displaced Persons spent $385,000 to lobby for the Stratton Bill to admit 400,000 D. P.'s—a measure which could hardly be said to have been inspired by selfish motives. Thus the question of whether

[34] See editorial, "Lobbies and the People." *Chicago Daily News,* October 19, 1948.

pressure-group activity is in the public interest is a matter calling for discrimination with each individual case being decided upon its own merits. To facilitate this discrimination in favor of the public interest, however, the requirement of attendant publicity on all pressure group undertakings, lobbies, propaganda efforts, and straw polls, is surely a prime subject for government regulation.

Public Opinion and Political Parties

The elaborate system of pressure groups with which the United States is interlaced is a tremendous factor in channeling public opinion in such a way that it may have a more effective influence on government. But even the largest pressure groups in this country by no means constitute a majority of the electorate. If we were dependent only upon special-interest groups for the expression of public opinion we might well end up with something vaguely resembling a multi-party system except that there would probably be far more interest groups than there are parties today even where the multi-party system flourishes in its most prolific form. Thus the need for securing a broader instrumentality for merging and reflecting opinions has found expression in the political party. It is the political party through which the widest common measure of political agreement may be obtained and we may turn now to a discussion of the party system in the United States.

SUMMARY

Public opinion is the energizing force of representative government. In a democracy public opinion needs to be united on certain fundamentals, such as majority rule and the right of the minority to become a majority. Except for these fundamentals, publc opinion is likely to divide sharply on a multitude of issues on which such matters as sectional, religious, racial, and economic differences will help to set individual and group attitudes.

Pressure groups seek to bring about political action in conformity with the public opinions for which they serve as spokesmen. These groups fill a vacuum in our political system and substitute for the multi-party system prevailing in other democratic countries.

Business, labor, and agriculture constitute major pressure groups which seek to influence legislation by the diverse techniques of lobbying. Propaganda, one such technique, depends for its success on being geared to the generally accepted attitudes of a people. Despite danger that pressure groups and their techniques will militate against the public interest, the right to organize and to propagandize must be maintained. Disturbing trends are the growth of "one newspaper" communities and the propaganda activities of government agencies, for both of which there is no strong countervailing force.

The regulation of pressure-group activity aims principally at revealing the identity, the sponsors, and the activity of those seeking to influence legislation.

The public opinion polls are affected with a public interest and consequently must be directed by honest and competent agencies. Their desirability is subject to debate. Among their weaknesses, apparent in erroneous predictions of the results of the 1948 election, are inability to measure intensity of opinion and the long interval between the last poll and the date of the election.

CHAPTER X

AMERICAN POLITICAL PARTIES

What Political Parties Are

A POLITICAL party is a group of citizens with political opinions somewhat different from those of the remainder of the community.
This differentiation of opinion is most clear-cut in a minor party
such as the Prohibition party which would abolish the manufacture of, and
traffic in, alcoholic beverages, or the Socialist, which advocates governmental ownership and operation of the means of production. But the
principles of the major parties in the United States are by no means distinct
since each of these parties consists of a combination of groups representing
many and even divergent interests. Nevertheless, major parties, because
of their varying group structures, are distinguished from each other by
somewhat different ideologies. For example, the center of gravity in the
Republican aggregation is, as Charles A. Beard once pointed out and as
the opinion polls persistently reveal, on the side of wealth. Consequently,
Republican party opinion tends toward freeing private enterprise from
governmental regulations, is inclined to bear less heavily upon the wealthy
in levying taxes, and is not enthusiastic over proposals for a broader social
security program. Since the membership of the Democratic party includes
a considerable number of the under-privileged, party policy is inclined to
promote the interests of this consumer-conscious element by governmental
regulations such as anti-monopoly legislation. Quite naturally the outstanding Federal statutes in the interest of labor have been sponsored by
Democratic administrations. The elaborate program of social security of
the Franklin Roosevelt administration tended to serve the peculiar needs
of Democratic voters.

The Necessity of Political Parties

Political parties are institutions that grow out of the sheer necessity of self-
governing peoples to have their public officials nominated and elected,
and to hold them somewhat responsible for their conduct in office. The

emergence and development of political parties are natural consequences of forces implicit in a democratic state. The superficial observer of the political process who concludes that parties are an unnecessary evil and that voters should simply function as good citizens shuts his eyes to certain realities. Functioning at their best, political parties present the voter with alternatives—that is, with opportunities for deciding issues. Ordinarily, however, the issues presented by major political parties are not clear-cut and the voter, in casting his ballot for a particular candidate merely indicates his greater confidence in one candidate than another. The stand of the principal candidate of a party ticket on pending issues may permit an electoral decision on those issues. The party candidate can thus symbolize issues when he does not even go so far as to dramatize them. Voters for the inarticulate Calvin Coolidge felt they were supporting a hands-off policy of the government with respect to business.

THE DEVELOPMENT OF AMERICAN PARTIES

Our Party System Emphatically American

It would be difficult to name an institution more decidedly American than our two-party system. These parties are unquestionably products of the American environment and experience. No doubt the English colonists started with the rich heritage of political concepts and traditions carried hither from the mother country, concepts and traditions which have had their influence to this very day. But if at times the American colonists adopted English party labels such as "Whig" and "Tory" and utilized English dogmas of natural rights, they did so only to rationalize their political experience and clarify their thinking about emerging or accomplished American political facts. An American two-party system almost certainly would have developed without aid of English precedents and ideologies since it is rooted so deep in the soil of the New World. "In every colony," wrote John Adams when the nation was yet very young, "divisions have always prevailed. In New York, Pennsylvania, Massachusetts and all the rest, a court and a country party have always contended." [1] This court party of the colonial period was led by the urban and the rural gentry, respectively, the greater merchants of the towns and cities and the planting aristocrats of the tide-water plantations. The colonial country party, on the other hand, consisted of the lesser folk mainly of the inland counties whose outstanding leader might be the speaker of the elective branch of the colonial legislature. They rallied behind the speaker as he challenged the power of the colonial governor and the court party that supported him. American two-party cleavage antedated the American Revolution.

The Disrepute of Parties in the Early National Period

The founding fathers considered political parties, as they understood them, to be undesirable and fondly hoped to avoid them under the Consti-

[1] John Adams: *Works* (Boston, 1856), X, p. 23.

tution. Vice-President John Adams was only expressing a contemporary attitude when he declared: "There is nothing I dread so much as the division of the Republic into two great parties each under its leader. . . . This, in my humble opinion, is to be feared as the greatest political evil under the Constitution." Adams here expressed the prevailing opinion of the founders, especially of the Federalists, that only those who are competent should govern and that the electorate should be confined to substantial citizens. From the earliest colonial times there had been a governing class, and the common man was expected to submit complacently to its rule. Most of the fathers accepted this as a settled practice, and those who challenged such a regime could never, from the point of view of the governing class, constitute a legitimate political party. The founders saw the citizenry as falling into two classes—good citizens who supported the government and bad ones who obstructed it. This is what they thought to be the inevitable line of cleavage in a two-party system. The only national political parties known to them were the then extraordinarily corrupt personal followings of British political leaders. The most notorious of these consisted of the partisan adherents of King George III known as the "King's Friends," whose odious ministerial policies had provoked the revolt of the colonists.

Yet it was Madison, the "Father of the Constitution," who unconsciously portrayed the pattern of the future major American political party in the fifteenth number of the *Federalist* when he wrote: "In the extended republic of the United States and among the great variety of interests, parties, and sects which it embraces, a coalition of a majority of the whole society could seldom take place on any other principles than those of justice and the general good." Madison reasoned that a single interest might dominate a state and impose its imperious will, but only a nation-wide combination of interests could mobilize the majority necessary to control the national government, and such a combination would have to pursue a moderate or middle course because a radical course would cause the constituent elements to disperse. This search for the middle ground has been necessary in all of our major parties in order to prevent the disintegration of the group combination of which each major party has consisted throughout American history since the 1790's.

The Basis of Major Party Cleavage

On a national scale two major sets of American interests have contended for political power for over a century and a half. On one side are the mercantile, financial, and industrial interests; on the other, the independent agrarians. "This conflict," wrote Arthur W. Macmahon, "was the common feature which related, in an essentially unbroken alignment, political division in the colonies, the split in opinion regarding the adoption of the Constitution, and the cleavage in national politics during the following century." [2] The economic confusion that developed under the Articles of Confederation in the 1780's impelled the mercantile interests, public and

[2] "Political Parties," *Encyclopedia of the Social Sciences,* Vol. XI, p. 597.

private creditors, land speculators, the fishing interests, and the greater planters to promote the establishment of a strong central government. This coastal combination of interests, which assumed the name of Federalists, was opposed by the inland agrarians, designated Anti-Federalists, who had been satisfied with the loose association of states under the Articles of Confederation and who consequently opposed the ratification of the Constitution. However, having lost the contest, the Anti-Federalists accepted the Constitution and the term Anti-Federalist disappeared from the pages of American history.

The Federalist Party

The Federalists, consisting of the combination of interests that had produced the Constitution, controlled the Federal government for a dozen years during the presidencies of George Washington and John Adams. Through the leadership of Alexander Hamilton as Secretary of the Treasury, the Federalist program of policies unfolded. Never has there been a better demonstration of the principle that "politics involves the translation of social pressures into public policies." [3] No important element in the Federalist party failed to obtain satisfaction in one form or another. American ship owners paid tonnage duties of only one-fifth of that charged foreign vessels in American harbors, New England fishermen received a Federal bounty on dried cod fish, public creditors were enabled to redeem securities at par that had once sold for five cents on the dollar, manufacturers enjoyed protective tariffs, Western land speculators had their land freed from the Indian menace by General Wayne's victory at Fallen Timbers, and Jay's Treaty opened lucrative commercial opportunities to the merchant ship owners. The Federalist leaders by and large constituted the governing class of their day. As guardians of the *status quo* they considered themselves the legitimate rulers of the land. They conceived of themselves not as constituting a political party but merely as the promoters of sound government. The opposition, as they saw it, consisted of disgruntled obstructionists to good government. The Federalists, in fact, never organized as a political party and bitterly berated their opponents for presuming to organize. The priceless legacy of the Federalist party to posterity was the firm establishment of the national government prescribed by the Constitution.

The Jeffersonian Republicans

Nearly every item in the Federalist program aroused the indignation of the inland agrarians and even of some coastal planters. They felt that the burdens of this program fell mainly upon them while the specific benefits went almost exclusively to the Federalist interests. According to the strange economic concepts of the planters, practically the only "producers" were conceived to be the agrarians, while all others were "parasites" living on

[3] Peter H. Odegard and E. Allen Helms: *American Politics: A Study in Political Dynamics* (2nd ed., New York, 1947), p. 1.

these "producers." The burden of the Federalist system of taxes seemed to fall mainly upon the "producers" while the benefits accrued to the "para-sites"—merchants, manufacturers, and security holders. The agrarians felt that the Federalist program had divided American society into two classes, "tax payers, and tax consumers" according to their Virginia philosopher John Taylor of Caroline. Here was the ideology that the Federalist program stirred to action, and the opposition to that program rallied under the shrewd leadership of Thomas Jefferson whose following gradually emerged as an organized political party to which he gave the name Republican. It sought, as an opposition party, to reduce the power of the Federalists by insisting upon a strict construction of the Constitution instead of the loose construction that fortified Federal powers. When the Federalists in 1798, in the midst of a nation-wide hysteria over a threatened war with France, enacted the notorious Alien and Sedition laws in order to deport "danger-ous" aliens and suppress criticism of the government, the Republicans de-nounced the legislation as unconstitutional. They set the long-established pattern of state rights in the Virginia and Kentucky Resolutions. These proclaimed the sovereignty of the states which were conceived to be the principals in the compact that formed the Union and as principals could interpret the powers of their agent, Congress, as *they* understood them to be prescribed in the Constitution. The public reaction against the Alien and Sedition Acts brought to a close the Federalist regime, and the Repub-licans gained control of the Federal government with the election of Jefferson in 1801. [4] By and large, Jefferson's election signalized the tri-umph of a following which included some of the greater planters, but consisted mainly of the agrarians and frontiersmen of the interior counties. The Jeffersonian Republican party was, in contrast with the Federalists, heavily weighted with non-English stock—Scotch-Irish and German— with Presbyterians, Methodists, and Baptists, dissenters against the estab-lished state churches, and backwoodsmen—all characterized more or less by a debtor complex.

The Era of One-Party Government

No sooner had the Republicans captured control of the Federal gov-ernment than a majority of them began to lose their fear of governmental power. They became loose constructionists as, for example, in purchasing the Louisiana territory and in the drastic enforcement of the Non-Inter-course and Embargo acts. Meanwhile the Federalists, as the party of the "outs," became strict constructionists, even professing the dogmas of the Virginia and Kentucky Resolutions with their implicit nullification as the party gradually lapsed into oblivion. For a decade or so after the War of 1812 there was something like one-party government under the Repub-licans. Quite naturally in such a situation two factions developed in the Republican party. The "Old Republicans" clung tenaciously to the original

---

[4] The election of Jefferson was by the House of Representatives because of the tie with Aaron Burr in the vote of the Electoral College.

Republican dogma of strict construction as proclaimed in the Virginia and Kentucky Resolutions, while the "Young Republicans" interpreted the Constitution with extraordinary liberality in respect to a Bank of the United States, protective tariffs, and internal improvements at national expense. In 1824, in the absence of competing political parties, the presidential election became a contest between the personal followings of four Republican leaders: John Quincy Adams, Andrew Jackson, William H. Crawford, and Henry Clay. The scattered vote of the Electoral College prevented any candidate from receiving a majority, whereupon the House of Representatives chose John Quincy Adams over his chief competitor, Andrew Jackson. The "New Republicans" had largely supported Adams and the "Old Republicans" had generally backed Jackson. Out of these personal followings the "Adams Men" and the "Jackson Men" evolved respectively what came to be known in the late 1820's as the National Republicans and the Democratic Republicans.

Jacksonian Democracy

The present-day Democratic party dates from the election of Andrew Jackson to the presidency in 1828. This party inherited the less privileged elements of the Jeffersonian Republicans and became pronouncedly the party of the under-dog. Jackson commanded the loyalty of the small planter, the small farmer, and the recently enfranchised and largely immigrant urban masses so that his advent signalized what historians have designated the "Rise of the Common Man." In their interest the party resisted inflation by insisting on "hard money," fought high tariffs, Federally financed internal improvements, land speculation, and corporate monopoly—the latter as represented in the Bank of the United States, whose rechartering Jackson vetoed. As the enemy of governmental paternalism and as the champion of free enterprise Jacksonian Democracy was for two generations pre-eminently the party of laissez faire.

The Whigs

Andrew Jackson's championship of the less privileged aroused the opposition of the well-to-do, who in the 1830's became organized as the Whig party under such leaders as Daniel Webster and Henry Clay. The party concentrated on the condemnation of what it conceived to be the executive usurpations of President Jackson. The backbone of the Whig party consisted of the commercial, financial, and rising industrial interests of the East, the more prosperous Mississippi Valley farmers, and the greater planters of the South who are estimated to have owned upward of two-thirds of the slaves. The Northern Whigs generally favored protective tariffs and internal improvements at Federal expense, neither of which was countenanced by the Southern Whigs. So discordant indeed were the elements of the Whig combination that the party could never produce a real party program but repeatedly sought to capture the presidency by ignoring issues and nominating military heroes. This practice enabled them to elect to the presidency William Henry Harrison in 1840 and Zachary Taylor in 1848. In the main the Whigs sought to prevent the Jacksonian masses from carrying their radical policies too far. The one outstanding positive Whig policy was the preservation of the Union. When the slavery issue became dominant in the 1850's the Whig party's pro- and anti-slavery wings rent that party asunder and caused it to disintegrate suddenly.

Origin of the Present Republican Party

The passage of the Kansas-Nebraska Act in 1854 provoked furious indignation among important elements of the North who resented the repeal of the Missouri Compromise and the consequent opening to slavery of the northern trans-Mississippi territory. This region had been generally presumed by Northerners to be destined for family-sized farms forever free from the competition of slave labor. Candidates for Congress nominated to oppose the measure without reference to party affiliation and known simply as "Anti-Nebraska Men" captured a majority of Congress the year of the passage of the Kansas-Nebraska Act. This aggregation soon evolved into the Republican party and in 1860 elected Abraham Lincoln president on a platform pledging the party to resist the spread of slavery, to enact a free homestead law and protective tariffs, and to construct a Pacific railroad. No sooner had the Civil War begun than many Democratic supporters of the Lincoln Administration combined with Republicans under the designation of the Union Party which re-elected Lincoln in 1864. So disturbed by the Civil War were the old political alignments that not until several years after the war were Republican and Democratic alignments again stabilized. The group compositions of each of these parties then differed considerably from what they had been before the armed conflict.

The Post-Civil War Republican Party

Assuming full credit for Federal victory in the Civil War the Republican party exploited to the limit the slogan "The party that saved the nation must rule it." With general public approval Republican administrations facilitated rapid exploitation of the resources of the national domain so that stock raisers appropriated the prairies; lumber kings the forests; and gold, silver, iron, copper, coal, and later the petroleum barons exploited the mineral sites. At the same time railroad magnates acquired gigantic land grants and industrialists were favored with protective tariffs, all to the satisfaction of laborers who as a consequence obtained jobs. The astonishing success of the Republican party in translating the social pressures of its group interests into appropriate public policies insured it control of the government, with only occasional interruptions, for almost three-quarters of a century. Though inclusive of a portion of almost every social element in the United States the Republican party today is distinctly weighted with upper-income groups, the professions, industrialists, business men, and the more prosperous farmers. Consequently, when the Republicans are in control of the national government there is a perceptible tendency for the dominant elements in the party to translate their desires into such policies as reduced appropriations for the anti-trust division of the Department of Justice and other agencies that regulate business. Business taxes are likely to be reduced on the assumption that this will stimulate production and promote prosperity. Social and welfare legislation tends to be emphasized less and labor can then scarcely expect to gain increased security in collective bargaining. In short the Republican party is pronouncedly production-conscious and conceives the welfare of the nation to be soundly based on business activity.

The Democratic Party

The Civil War experience of the Democratic party had so impaired its prestige that the party did not completely recover from its disadvantage until the 1930's. Then the economic paralysis induced by the Great Depression coinciding with the appearance of an exceptional party leader provided the opportunity. In 1932 the Democratic candidate, Franklin D. Roosevelt, was elected president in what was to be the first of his four successive elections to that office. The policies of the Roosevelt administrations registered the social pressures of the Democratic group combination no less accurately than had Federalist and Republican administrations the interests of their respective combinations. The overwhelming support of the Democratic candidate by labor and the lower-income groups generally was reflected in legislation favorable to labor, in unemployment insurance, and indeed in the entire social security program. The unemployed obtained relief in various forms and on an unprecedented scale. Youth overwhelmingly voted the Democratic ticket, and the National Youth Administration and the Civilian Conservation Corps provided employment for many of them. Six out of ten farmers voted for the Democratic presidential candidate in 1936; the influence of agricultural interests had already been reflected in the Agricultural Adjustment Act, the Farm Mortgage Corporation, and other agencies for the relief of distressed farmers.

The Democratic party has made an about face since its beginning. Jacksonian Democracy originally professed and practiced laissez faire. Since 1896, however, when the party adopted or absorbed the program of the Populists it has been the party of governmental regulation and paternalism in the public interest and incidentally in the interest of the under-privileged who constitute such a significant element of its voting strength. Twice since 1896 the Democratic party has, for the moment, turned its back on such a program only to suffer overwhelming defeats; in 1904 when the Democratic candidate for president, Alton B. Parker, received only 37.6 per cent of the popular vote and in 1924 when John W. Davis received 28.8 per cent.

MINOR PARTIES

The Nature of Minor Parties

American minor parties, unlike major parties, consist either of a single interest or at least of a much less complex group structure than a major party. Minor party platforms can be quite clear-cut and often prove to be in fact pioneers in the raising of new issues. They can proclaim with impunity programs that would prove disruptive to a major party combination. When, in time, issues publicized by minor parties have captured the public imagination they are likely to be appropriated by one or both of the major parties whereupon the issues may soon be translated into established public policies. Thus third parties may prove to be social barometers indicating developing political weather. It may even be possible to forecast somewhat the trend of coming legislation by noting the new issues stressed by minor parties. For example, the Socialist program in 1928 advocated, among other things, old age pensions, unemployment insurance, relief of unemployment by extensive public works, and Federal loans to states and municipalities for public works. Not a trace of such proposals can be found in the major party platforms of that year. Eight years later, however, both Democratic and Republican platforms pledged their respective parties to support these policies, and the Republican platform criticized the social security legislation of the Roosevelt Administration for not extending its benefits to classes still outside its scope. To a remarkable extent major parties obtain their new planks by stealing them from the platforms of minor parties.

Minor Parties Before the Civil War

The Anti-Masons of the 1830's represented a rural mass movement in the northeastern states against the ruling elements of society symbolized by the Masonic lodges to which so many of the well-to-do belonged. In 1832 the Anti-Masons nominated a presidential candidate, William Wirt, who obtained seven out of 286 electoral votes. The party quickly ran its course, however, and clever politicians maneuvered its membership into the emerging Whig party. In the same decade the Equal Rights or Locofoco party evolved out of an earlier urban, Workingmen's, anti-bank party. It demanded legislation in the interest of workers, popular election of local officials, and other policies in the interest of the less privileged, but it concentrated so strongly on opposition to paper money that it converted the Democratic party, which absorbed it, into a hard money party. "Loco focos" was consequently a term applied to Democrats by their opponents for a generation or more. In the late 1830's the Liberty party emerged as a result of the exasperation of certain interests in the North over the domination of the Federal government by the slave-holding interests. Insignificant as it was in numbers, the Liberty party's 15,000 votes in New

York in 1844 threw the electoral vote of the state from Clay to Polk, thereby electing the latter president. However the party had run its course. Its successor appeared in 1848 under the name of the Free Soil Party whose major objective was to exclude slavery from all territories of the United States. Half a dozen years later the exclusion of slavery from the territories became the main plank of the emerging new Republican party as it absorbed the Free Soilers. Thus a major party again incorporated both the program and the personnel of a minor party.

Almost exactly in mid-century the reaction against the flood of immigration, mainly from Ireland, produced a strong anti-alien movement in the form of the American or Know-Nothing party. Since most immigrants joined the Democratic party the American party was anti-Democratic as well as anti-Catholic and anti-alien. Its plan was to disqualify by law all foreign-born citizens from holding public office and to require a long period of residence before they would be permitted to vote. By 1855 it was widely believed that the American party would elect the next president, but when the party split on the slavery issue the Northern wing was absorbed by the emerging Republican party. The latter did not adopt the American party's platform, but on the other hand it has never quite completely freed itself from a nativist tradition and tendency.

Post-Civil War Minor Parties

The post-Civil War depression in farm prices led to the rise of the Greenback party which first arose in the latter 1860's in protest against the deflationary policy then being pursued of retiring the United States notes (Greenbacks) issued during the Civil War. Later the Greenbackers also advocated free coinage of silver to lift farm prices by its inflationary tendency. The Greenbackers quite correctly maintained that the value of money depended upon the relation between the money demand and the money supply and that the latter should be exclusively a function of government, never of a bank. By 1880 their candidate for president received 308,000 votes and their platform contained a number of the planks later to be found in the platforms of their successor, the People's or Populist party.

The Populist party first appeared in 1890 when the debt-ridden farmers of the West and South had grown desperate over the crisis created by eight-cent corn, ten-cent oats, two-cent beef, no market whatsoever for butter and eggs, and a persisting 10 per cent interest on mortgages. By 1892 the Populist platform proposed attacking deflation by providing a per capita circulating medium of fifty dollars obtained by free and unlimited coinage of silver at a ratio with gold of sixteen to one. Also proposed were a graduated income tax, postal savings banks, the return by the railroads of the unused land granted them by the Federal government, governmental ownership of telegraphs and telephones, and a number of planks in the interest of labor. In 1896 the Democratic party adopted the Populist platform as its own and soon absorbed the party membership.

It was indeed the Populist movement that converted the Democratic party from its time-honored advocacy of laissez faire to a program of governmental intervention and regulation.

The Progressive Party

In 1912 the followers of Theodore Roosevelt organized the Progressive party in protest against what they conceived to be the conservative policies of President Taft. This party represented an attempt to institutionalize the progressive movement which had been developing since the disappearance of the Populist party. The Populist program adopted by the Democratic party in 1896 had failed of fulfillment because of the persistent inability of the party to elect a Democratic president and Congress. In spirit, if not in fact, the Progressive party was the heir of the Populist party so far as much of its program was concerned. Like the Populists the Progressives sought by their platform to mobilize the discontented agrarians of the West and South and at the same time appeal to the industrial wage earners. Unlike the Populists the Progressive party sought also the support of big business interests. Although Theodore Roosevelt received more votes than the Republican candidate, President Taft, the split in the Republican party elected to the presidency the Democratic candidate, Woodrow Wilson, under whose leadership the essence of the Populist program began to be translated into Federal statutes such as the moderate Underwood Tariff, governmental regulations as established in the Federal Reserve Banking System, and the Clayton and the Federal Trade Commission Acts.

Minor Parties in the Campaign of 1948

President Truman won the election of 1948 in spite of two minor parties that reduced the voting strength of the Democratic party. In December, 1947, Henry A. Wallace, a former Democratic vice-president, announced that he would be a candidate for the presidency in 1948, pledged to a "positive peace program of abundance and security, not scarcity and war." In July, 1948 his personal following in a national convention adopted the name of the Progressive party and nominated him as its presidential candidate. The new party pledged itself to the seeking of a settlement with Russia and the abandoning of the Marshall plan for the recovery of Western European nations through the use of funds supplied by the United States. The Progressive party entertained hopes of capturing upwards of 5,000,000 votes but only 1,127,641 were received by Wallace on election day, and he did not obtain a single electoral vote. By absorbing the Communist vote the Progressive party relieved Truman completely of the charge of depending upon that element and thereby unintentionally aided the President's candidacy.

President Truman's resolute advocacy of a civil rights program led to a revolt of Southern Democrats who sought in vain to prevent his nomination by the Democratic National Convention. The consequence was a convention held at Birmingham, Alabama, in July, 1948, and the formation of the States' Rights party, popularly known as the Dixiecrats, which nominated Governor J. Strom Thurmond of South Carolina as its presidential candidate. Candidate Thurmond denounced the idea of "white supremacy" and claimed instead that his campaign was based solely on support of the "sovereignty of the states against federal government interference." States' Rights electoral tickets were on the ballots of ten Southern states and the party hoped to capture enough electoral votes to deprive any candidate of a majority in the Electoral College which failure would require the election of the President by the House of Representatives. But Governor Thurmond received only 1,167,870 popular votes and carried only Alabama, Louisiana, Mississippi, and South Carolina with their thirty-eight electoral votes.

WHY THE TWO-PARTY SYSTEM PERSISTS IN THE UNITED STATES

The Effect of Presidential Elections on the Two-Party System

"Considered nationally," wrote Arthur W. Macmahon, "political parties in the United States may be described as loose alliances to win the stakes of power embodied in the presidency." [5] American major political parties exist chiefly in order to capture the prestige, patronage, and control of administration and leadership of legislation in the presidential office. The method of electing a president of the United States so hopelessly handicaps a minor party that none has ever graduated into a major party.[6] The paramount problem of a major party is to accumulate throughout the nation a majority of votes, in order to be capable of electing a presidential candidate. The presidential candidate or his managers must seek to discover the specific appeals to the electorate that will build a combination of supporting interests constituting a majority. Campaign strategy consists largely of calculating the attitude of the labor vote, the white-collar vote, the farmer vote, the woman vote, the church vote, and the vote of all the other groups the politician habitually considers. The historian's comments on the political parties of a century ago are just as pertinent to those of today: "Analysis of the Whig and Democratic parties and their successors reveals a bundle of local, sectional, and class interests. Their cross sections instead of displaying a few simple colors, were a jig-saw puzzle of radicalism and conservatism, nationalism and state rights, personal loyalties and local issues. Party strategy was directed toward accumulating as many bundles as possible; and statesmanship was the art of finding some person or principle common to all the bundles that would

[5] *Encyclopaedia of the Social Sciences*, Vol. XI, p. 596.

[6] The old assumption that the present Republican party began as a minor party appears to be erroneous. The Anti-Nebraska Men with whom the party began in 1854 captured an overwhelming majority of the House of Representatives only six months after the passage of the measure that brought about the Republican party.

make them forget their differences and in union find strength." [7] Considered locally the single-member representative district on the basis of which American legislators are generally elected discourages third party movements. The multi-member district required for systems of proportional representation facilitates the growth of minor parties. But the majorities or pluralities necessary for election as a representative in a congressional or state legislative district compel the candidate to play the same game of group diplomacy to build up a majority on a local scale in his district that the candidate for president must play on a national scale. Indeed the two-party competition for president may consist largely of the synthesis of the local group combinations or local parties into our major national parties.

The Trading of Issues for Votes

In a very real sense the politician, candidate, or party manager is a broker in public policies. In effect the candidate says: "Elect me and, in return for your support at the polls, I will use the powers of my office to promote the policies you desire." We have seen that this is a practice as old as our political parties. Nearly a century ago the consummate politician-statesman William H. Seward said: "A party is, in a sense, a joint-stock association in which those who contribute most direct the action and management of the concern." [8] Of course the terms of the transaction are never boldly stated but remain merely implicit in the political process. Inevitably the promise of candidates to voters must be couched in terms of the public welfare which indeed the policies promised often do promote even when they also serve a special interest. Parties and candidates consequently employ slogans to capture the imagination, slogans such as Mark Hanna's "Full Dinner Pail," Theodore Roosevelt's "Square Deal," Woodrow Wilson's "New Freedom," Herbert Hoover's "New Era," Franklin Roosevelt's "New Deal," and Harry Truman's "Fair Deal." Abstract programs are thus put in packageable form so that the man in the street may respond to the appeal.

Similarity of Party Programs and Platforms

The typical American major party platforms are so lacking in clear-cut statements on current issues that they baffle people not informed about the nature of our parties. In this respect our parties contrast strikingly with the numerous single-interest parties of a continental European nation. These latter each constitute a relatively narrow segment of society and their programs can consequently be quite precise and pointed. American multi-party combinations bent upon the accumulation of nation-wide majorities must make their platform appeals to something approaching the

[7] Samuel Eliot Morison and Henry S. Commager: *The Growth of the American Republic* (New York, 1937), Vol. I, p. 447.

[8] Quoted by Charles A. and Mary R. Beard: *The Rise of American Civilization* (New York, 1927), Vol. II, p. 7. "Most" in this quotation signifies not campaign contributions but rather prestige, influence, and voting strength.

entire sweep of the American electorate. Professors Charles E. Merriam and Harold F. Gosnell have listed in parallel columns and in a simplified form the diverse elements of the Republican and Democratic parties in 1948.[9]

REPUBLICANS	DEMOCRATS
Price control opponents and supporters	Price control supporters and opponents
Tariff advocates and reciprocal trade agreement advocates	Reciprocal trade agreement advocates and opponents
Tax reducers and debt reducers	Debt reducers and tax reducers
Drastic labor curbers and labor defenders	Labor defenders and labor curbers
Farm legislation opponents and supporters	Farm legislation defenders and non-defenders

The conditions represented in the table have persisted throughout American party history, and they confront the platform makers with perplexing problems. The platform committees at our national party conventions come face to face with the pressures of the various interest groups. The American Federation of Labor, the Congress of Industrial Organizations, the National Association of Manufacturers, the American Farm Bureau, the National Association for the Advancement of Colored People, and various other organizations, through their agents, appear before the platform committees of both major parties and urge or oppose the inclusion of certain planks in the platforms. The harassed committeemen working feverishly around the clock, hurriedly calculate party losses or gains while rejecting, including, or crudely compromising proposed planks. Under such circumstances how can major party platforms set forth clear-cut statements of issues? The clash of interests of the groups constituting a major party simply cannot be resolved into a crystal-clear statement. A neat platform might, however, be produced by a bossed convention or dictated by a president being nominated for another term. But corresponding planks in opposing party platforms are by no means identical. Shadings and differences of emphasis frequently reflect certain preponderant interests in one or the other party. Major party platforms are distinguished by issues omitted rather than by those included. For example, a passionate plea for governmental economy need not be looked for in the platform of such a group combination as the Democratic party any more than a demand for sharply graded income taxes is to be expected in a Republican platform. But the real purpose is, after all, not generally understood. The observation of Shailer Mathews is illuminating: "A political platform is not a program. It is rather something upon which the candidate may stand while deciding which way the people at large choose to go."[10] The public quite properly manifests great interest in the views of a presidential candidate but largely ignores the platform on which he is presumed to stand.

[9] Charles E. Merriam and Harold F. Gosnell: *The American Party System* (4th ed.; New York, 1949), p. 56.

[10] Shailer Mathews: *The Validity of American Ideals* (New York, 1922), p. 33.

The Danger of Head-On Collisions Between Major Parties

Some writers and speakers condemn the American party battles as contests over "tweedle dum" and "tweedle dee." They demand an ideological realignment of major parties so that the conservatives may take their place in one party and the progressives in another. But the nature of American society and not logic has set the pattern of American party politics with its two major multi-group combinations. These combinations have forced upon political leaders the persistent search for the common ground on which all the elements of the party can stand together. The so-called cowardice of parties in excluding at times such explosive issues as slavery, religion, and prohibition represents the wisdom of statesmanship. Head-on collisions on burning issues would no doubt prove dramatic, but they also produce social strife and disintegration. The lesson of American party history on this matter stands out in bold relief. From Washington's administration to the 1850's every major party contained both pro-slavery and anti-slavery men. But in 1860 the presidency was captured by a party every member of which was unfriendly to slavery. Civil War promptly followed what was almost the only clear-cut major party alignment on an important issue in American history.

THE COMPOSITION OF MAJOR PARTIES

The Different Social Structures of Our Major Political Parties

No matter how similar major party platforms may be, statistical analysis of party group structure reveals differences between them (See Table II).

The samplings of the public-opinion polls reveal that, vocationally considered, the Republican party is weighted with businessmen while the Democratic party includes a majority of manual laborers. The Democratic party has shown a tendency to attract youth rather than age. Metropolitan centers tend to be overwhelmingly Democratic while the Republicans have generally held at least a narrow edge in the small cities, the towns, villages, and countryside outside of the South. Moreover whenever a trend sets in, social groups tend to change together in the same direction. [11]

The Influence of Status and Ideology on Party Affiliation

The influence of socio-economic status and of ideology on party affiliation has been scientifically investigated. A trained staff of field workers made a systematic study of voter attitudes in the summer of 1944. The area

[11] In the eight states—Maryland, New Jersey, California, Colorado, New York, Oklahoma, Pennsylvania, and Rhode Island—where it was possible to ascertain the party division of the armed forces in the 1944 elections, 59.3 per cent voted Democratic and 40.7 per cent voted Republican. *Gallup Political Almanac for 1946,* p. 207.

TABLE II

*Distribution of Major Party Vote**

| | Per cent of Major Party Vote | | | | | |
| | 1936 | | 1940 | | 1944 | |
	Dem.	Rep.	Dem.	Rep.	Dem.	Rep.
By Occupation						
Professional & Business	48	52	36	64	41	59
White Collar	61	39	48	52	51	49
Manual Workers	74	26	66	34	62	38
All Farmers	59	41	54	46	48	52
By Age						
21–29	68	32	60	40	58	42
30–49	65	35	56	44	53	47
50 and over	56	44	51	49	51	49
By Size of Town						
Over 500,000	71	29	61	39	61	39
10,000 to 500,000	61	39	54	46	54	46
Under 10,000	61	39	52	48	49	51
Farm Residents	59	41	54	46	48	52
By Sections						
New England	54	46	53	47	53	47
Middle Atlantic	60	40	53	47	52	48
East North Central	59	41	51	49	50	50
West North Central	61	39	49	51	48	52
South	76	24	73	27	69	31
Mountain	66	34	56	44	53	47
Pacific	68	32	58	42	56	44

* Source: *Gallup Political Almanac for 1946,* pp. 203–4.

selected was Erie County, Ohio, which, politically considered, seemed to be the typical county in the United States since the percentage of its vote for the major parties had closely coincided with the percentage of the nation-wide popular vote for the major parties' presidential candidates in every election from 1884 to 1940. Interviewers were trained to assess the homes, possessions, appearance, and manner of speech of those interviewed and classify the persons interviewed by economic class, from A, the wealthiest, to E, the poorest. The result indicating also the percentage of the total population in each category was: A, 3 per cent; B, 14 per cent; C, 33 per cent; D, 30 per cent, and E, 20 per cent. The interviewers ascertained that in group A slightly more than seven out of ten persons were Republicans while in group D only three and one-half out of ten were Republicans. They discovered that occupation had little influence on what party the voter supported but that income made a great deal of difference. The most important single determinant of party affiliation was found to be the socio-economic status the voter assigned to himself. It mattered whether he thought of himself as belonging to business, in which case he tended to be a Republican, or to labor, which meant that he was less likely to be a Republican. Highly significant was the power of an ideology in determining party affiliation. Yet strong as it was it could be overpowered by poverty. If the voter thought of himself as affiliated with business and yet was poverty stricken, his economic status tended to overcome the influence of his business affiliation and make him a Democrat. [12]

Geographical Distribution of Major Party Strength

Sectionally considered, the strength of the Democratic party lies preponderantly in the deep South and in the metropolitan centers of the other sections of the country. In 1944 the Republicans cast less than 20 per cent of the major party vote in the cotton planting states of Louisiana, Texas, Alabama, Georgia, Mississippi, and South Carolina. In cities throughout the nation with upward of half a million inhabitants Democratic strength was 61 per cent of the major party vote. In cities of from 10,000 to 500,000 the Democrats had 54 per cent of the major party vote. The geographical area of Republican strength can be seen in maps showing the counties carried by Thomas E. Dewey in 1944. It consists of a vast and irregular zone extending from the rural counties of New England through the St. Lawrence and Great Lakes drainage area and expanding fanlike into the prairies of the upper Mississippi Valley. It includes the more prosperous rural counties containing no large cities and corresponds closely to the area of higher incomes.[13] New England patterns of culture persist throughout this region since it was settled mainly by western migration from that section. If the South is disregarded it can be said that the Republican strength is found in the high-rent wards and suburbs of the great cities, and in the small cities, towns, villages and more prosperous countryside.

Major Party Characteristics Due to Social Composition

Institutions as different in social composition as the Republican and Democratic parties must inevitably reveal distinct differences in social philosophy and public policies. The Republicans as the party of the higher income groups of both the rural and urban areas tend to be production-minded and suspicious of the consumer-conscious urban masses. The elements that compose the Republican party tend toward conservatism and are inclined to be suspicious of new legislation. Denominationally the Republican party tends to be Protestant, and since it consists so largely of descendants of earlier settlers it is inclined to be suspicious of later arrivals as well as of the countries from which they came; the party consequently has long inclined toward isolationism and the stressing of "Americanism." Many Republicans are great-grandchildren of the American or anti-foreign party of the 1850's the northern wing of which the Republican party absorbed and whose tradition it acquired. The Democratic party prevails in the solid South with its Protestant fundamentalism and social conservatism. The balance of power of the Democratic party is held by those who dwell in the crowded wards of the great urban centers outside the South. This

[12] Paul F. Lazarsfeld, Bernard Berleson, and Hazel Gaudet: *The People's Choice: How the Voter Makes Up His Mind in a Presidential Campaign* (New York, 1944), chap. III.

[13] See map showing income distribution in the United States in W. F. Ogburn and M. F. Nimkoff: *Sociology* (Boston, 1940), p. 462.

element is predominantly Catholic, is largely of Irish or more recent immigrant stock, and tends to react politically as consumers. The policies of the New Deal answered the needs of the urban masses and so endeared President Franklin Roosevelt to them that they gave him their overwhelming support in four successive presidential elections. Thus the party politics that once involved so largely the clash of section with section is becoming more and more a competition to establish or retain policies acceptable to property-conscious rural voters as against those desired by the metropolitan masses.

How Republican and Democratic Administrations Differ

So different are the elements constituting the two major parties that a change from one to the other in the control of the government means a distinct shift in the character of legislation and administration. The election of Woodrow Wilson and a Democratic Congress in 1912 was followed by a marked reduction in tariffs and the enactment of the monumental regulative statutes: the Federal Reserve Act, the Clayton Act, and the Federal Trade Act. This meant a somewhat more vigorous policing of business practices than had previously prevailed. No comparable regulative legislation was enacted during the 1920's under Republican control of the government, and the Federal Trade Commission, having acquired a Republican majority, became extraordinarily lenient with respect to enforcement of anti-trust legislation. Upper brackets of income-tax payers received prompt relief. When the Democrats returned to power in the 1930's the interests constituting the party combination managed to enact the most comprehensive regulative legislation in American history, and the urban consumer interests received more satisfaction than ever before. Unquestionably the devastating depression provided the opportunity and the necessity, but it was fitting that the social security program should have been established under the impulse of the Democratic combination. When the Republicans returned to power under Eisenhower, a businessman's Cabinet was appointed and the regulative agencies were gradually filled with appointees less inclined to stringent regulation. Private power was preferred and public power projects like the Tennessee Valley were labeled "creeping socialism." Off-shore oil resources were transferred to states to the satisfaction of oil interests, while safeguarding other natural resources was less vigorous than before. Federal enterprises like the Inland Waterways Corporation were sold. Meanwhile a Hoover Commission recommended transfer of parcel post to the Express company and postal savings to private banks.

WHY POLITICAL PARTIES EXIST
Necessity of Parties and Politicians

Our political parties are by no means the artificial creations of designing conspirators but have evolved rather spontaneously in response to deep-seated social needs. One of the anomalies of American opinion is the rather common conviction that political parties are an evil and scarcely a necessary one at that. This conviction has led to the demand for, and the introduction of, the non-partisan ballot for election to offices which, it is assumed, should be divorced from party pressures. For this purpose the election laws sometimes forbid the ballot indicating in any way any party designation of the candidates for such offices. The assumption is that the voter will then be free from the influence of party affiliation and organization and will consequently simply exercise his untrammeled civic judgment in selecting those officials. In practice, however, so strong is the tendency of the electorate to think in terms of parties that provisions for non-partisan elections are quite commonly circumvented. In Ohio, for example, the non-partisan judicial ballot is "non-partisan" only in name even with respect to the election of members of the Supreme Court of the State. Each party prints its own unofficial ballot which resembles the official one except that the party's own choice of candidates is plainly marked on the unofficial copy. Party workers urge their fellow party members to take this marked ballot along with them into the voting booths to guide them in voting for the party's own candidates on the "non-partisan" ballot. This persistence of party voting in spite of legal provisions to prevent it may indicate that there are, in a democratic state, social forces operating to perpetuate parties that are too strong to be controlled by statutory provisions. Non-partisanship is, of course, widely assumed to be a peculiarly precious civic virtue. If, however, the politicians should decide suddenly to strike or to abdicate, their essential functions would instantly become apparent because of their non-performance. Politicians possess a special knowledge of the details of electoral and governmental processes that the typical busy citizen has neither the time nor inclination to acquire, especially since he knows he can readily obtain such information as long as the politician is available. Politicians see that party tickets are filled and that the voter registers and casts his ballot, and they feel that they are performing a worthy public service. At his best the politician is, as someone has said, a "social coordinator" providing a liaison between the typical private citizen and his government, which the politician frequently humanizes. At his worst he is something else, but this does not change the fact that no one has ever discovered how democratic government can function without him.

Functions of Political Parties

No matter how imperfect political parties may be as media for formulating issues and translating pressures into policies, there is no apparent substitute for them. The paramount problem of the candidate and of the party management is that of finding the elusive areas of agreement among the discordant elements of the typical multi-group party. Lincoln, for example, in the 1850's perceived that the sole principle on which the heterogeneous groups constituting the then young Republican party agreed was that of resistance to the spread of slavery into the territories. He accordingly concentrated attention on this single unifying issue and thus saved the party from disintegration. [14] When functioning at their best political parties provide the voter with an opportunity for deciding on important issues. If elections occur at times when no important questions pend, parties still perform the function of providing candidates to be voted on and in this matter must be circumspect or pay the penalty. In smaller communities the urge of party organizations to provide a complete local ticket is often the only means of obtaining candidates at all for minor offices. There is more drafting of candidates "for the party's sake" than the uninformed would ever imagine. This filling of tickets is a concern of both state and national organizations. The survival of a remnant of the Republican party intrenched during the 1930's in mid-Western county court houses, township halls, and municipal buildings enabled the party to catch its breath and prepare for its recapture of a significant place in the two-party system in the 1940's. Unsatisfactory as campaign literature, speeches, and radio broadcasts may be from an academic point of view, they nevertheless force upon the attention of the electorate the fact of an impending election. The persistent effort of candidates, precinct captains, or committeemen, as well as of voluntary and paid party workers, all urging registration and voting, raises the question what elections would be like if the voter were left solely to an inner urge of civic duty.

PARTY MEMBERSHIP

Party Regulars, Mugwumps, and Independents

A political party consists of an organized group of citizens influenced mainly by the climate of ideas in which they have lived to behave like Democrats, Republicans, Socialists, or whatever the affiliation may be, at least to the extent of usually voting for the candidates of their own party. From 65 to 85 per cent of party members seem to inherit their political affiliation, which indicates that the family environment generally sets the pattern of party ideology and voting habit for the individual. The core of a political party consists of a small group of politically conscious leaders who take the initiative in managing the party. In every major party a large segment of rock-ribbed regulars may boast that they have never scratched a ticket. Next to them are the less partisan members who, even when dissatisfied with the party, are restrained from deserting it by the conviction that it might be reformed from within. A historic example of this was young Theodore Roosevelt who was bitterly disappointed over the nomination of James G. Blaine as the Republican candidate for president in 1884 but refused to follow Republican Mugwumps in supporting the Democratic candidate, Grover Cleveland. The term "Mugwump" is often used to designate party members so loosely affiliated with

[14] See Wilfred E. Binkley: *American Political Parties: Their Natural History* (New York, 1945), pp. 225–6.

their party that they quite readily support the ticket of the other major party. Mugwump is also frequently applied to independents who claim no party affiliation. In 1954 the Institute of Public Opinion found that 20 per cent of the voters classified themselves as Independents, 34 per cent as Republicans, and 46 per cent as Democrats. The Institute calculated that, based on an estimated civilian population of 97 million of voting age, the above percentages might then be translated as follows: Democrats, 44,600,000; Republicans, 33,000,000; Independents, 19,400,000.[15]

The Legal Status of Political Parties

American political parties have acquired a legal status despite the fact that they originated as mere usages in response to civic needs. While seventeen state constitutions incidentally mention the term "political party," nowhere is the existence of a party deliberately authorized. Instead, the courts appear to take political parties for granted as consequences of inherent rights of the people and to take for granted that their existence is safeguarded by freedom of speech, press, assembly, and petition. They are therefore not creatures of law but exist independent of statute, although they are nonetheless subject to law. Parties have no legal personality or legal existence apart from the individuals composing them, and hence are not subject to injunction and cannot appear as legal entities in court. The courts pursue a "hands off" attitude toward them unless a law is violated and will not interfere in the acts and management of a political party to protect a member's purely party right in the organization. [16]

Since an American political party was long considered a merely voluntary association of private persons, the party was presumed to be as free from governmental supervision as a literary society or a sewing circle. Beginning about 1890 with the introduction of the Australian ballot printed at public expense, it became necessary to prescribe a legal method of ascertaining the party's choice of the candidates to be printed on the official ballot. Legal safeguards had to be set up to insure that the party's choice of candidates was determined by its membership. Formerly the nomination of candidates was accomplished by conventions or caucuses for city, county, congressional district, or state. Nominations are now quite generally made through direct party primaries conducted by the regular election boards. Through legislation, political parties which were once merely voluntary associations of private persons have made the transition to legally recognized organs of government. This, however, requires a legal definition of precisely what constitutes a party in order to determine which party candidates are to be printed on the official ballot. Typical of this kind of definition is the provision: "A political party ... shall be any group of voters which at the last preceding general state election, polled for its candidate for governor in the state at least 10 per cent of the entire

---

[15] Gallup Poll, October 23, 1954.
[16] Joseph R. Starr: "The Legal Status of American Political Parties." *American Political Science Review* (1940), 34:439–55, 685–99.

vote cast therein for governor; or which shall have filed with the secretary of state at least ninety days before election a petition signed by qualified voters equal in number to at least fifteen per cent of the total vote for governor at the last preceding election, declaring their intention of organizing a political party . . ." [17] Legislation of this type has made it difficult for minor parties to get on the ballot.

PARTY ORGANIZATION

The Local Party Committee System

Each major party (and sometimes minor parties also) aims to have a party representative in every election unit or precinct where there is party membership of any consequence. These party officials are variously known as precinct committeemen, precinct leaders, or election district captains. Sometimes in addition the precinct has a party committeewoman. These party representatives were once generally chosen by party caucuses but are now almost universally elected for two-year periods at regular party primaries. As a matter of fact, the rank and file of the party often pay little attention to the election of precinct committeemen and as a consequence the party organization has a tendency to be self-perpetuating.[18] The precinct committeeman is presumed to provide local party leadership, promote party harmony, and stimulate political interest among party members. He supervises the preparation of the party poll book for the purpose of getting party members registered and checked as they turn out on election day. The seeker after party patronage, by long established usage, must first obtain the endorsement of his local committeeman, whether it be for a municipal, county, state, or Federal appointment. This specific activity provides the principal dynamic of local politics and tends to strengthen party solidarity. The competent precinct committeemen or captain is a specialist in creating goodwill, ostensibly for the good of the party. His opportunity to perform this function is greatest in the cities, especially in the wards populated by the under-privileged. Here the local party leader busies himself providing bail for persons under arrest, following fire departments, and obtaining temporary living quarters for families whose homes have been burned, staying eviction proceedings, finding jobs for the unemployed, looking after the interests of shopkeepers in difficulty with city administrators, caucusing with fellow political workers, attending weddings, funerals, picnics and church

[17] *The Election Laws of Ohio* (1940), p. 62.

[18] The voter interest in the election of precinct committee men varies widely. An investigation of precinct committeemen in ten rural counties of Illinois revealed that 82.5 per cent of voters going to the polls at a primary election voted for committeemen and that this rose to 90.8 per cent where there were contests for committeemen. A surprisingly large number of committeemen reported that they could get "volunteer" party workers in their precincts and that such workers proved more effective in influencing voters than job holders and paid workers. Leon Weaver: "Some Soundings of the Party System: Rural Precinct Committeemen." *American Political Science Review* (1940), 34:76–84.

carnivals, and making friends everywhere who might accept his suggestions on election day.

The County Committee

The precinct committeemen collectively usually constitute the central committee of the county or sometimes of a city where they may represent and serve a ward instead of a precinct. Often the central committee chooses a smaller and more workable executive committee. Both committees, however, are headed by local or county chairmen who manage campaigns and the distribution of party patronage, and who perform various other duties as party leaders. When citizens speak of the Republican or Democratic organization they usually have in mind county committees. The county chairman is usually a party leader of influence, experience, and ability unless he is only a figurehead acting for the party "boss." His power depends primarily upon his dispensing of patronage in the form of appointive offices and contracts for public works. There are over three thousand counties in the United States with 45,000 officials elected generally on a party ticket together with many other appointed officials available as party patronage. The state and even Federal patronage, in so far as it goes to party men in the county, is generally dispensed through the county chairman and committeemen. Thus the county committee constitutes the backbone of the local political party.

State Committees

Following rather closely the pattern of organization of county committees are the state committees. The unit of representation is the congressional district, county, or state senatorial district. State committees may be elected by direct primary, by state or county conventions, by the candidates for state and legislative offices functioning as a party council, or by the committees of the county or congressional district. In all but five states state committeemen are chosen for periods of two years. The tendency is to give women recognition on the state committees as, for example, in Ohio where a committeeman and a committeewoman are elected bienially at party primaries in each congressional district. These individuals collectively constitute the state central committee. The state chairman is often hand-picked and managed by the real leader, a self-appointed city or state boss, the state governor, or a United States senator. State committees, functioning mainly through the chairmen and their immediate organizations, collect campaign funds, arrange rallies, assign speakers, distribute campaign literature, and manage the other activities designed to influence the electorate to support the state party ticket. When the party is victorious the state committee customarily administers the distribution of party patronage. The state committee is most active in the years of gubernatorial elections and of presidential elections in "pivotal states," that is, states where there is a near balance of political parties. While there is no authority to maintain the relationship, custom has established a close cooperation of the state committees with local and national committees of the party.

The National Committees

Each national committee consists of a committeeman and committeewoman from each state, from the District of Columbia, Alaska, Hawaii, Puerto Rico and, for the Democratic party, from the Virgin Islands and the Canal Zone. But the Republican party includes also the state party chairman of each state that, in the last previous election, was carried by the Republican candidate for President, or elected a Republican Governor or a majority of the State's Republican candidates for both Houses of Congress. The businessman predominates as committeeman in every section but the lower South and the west central states. In these sections his representation on the national committee is shared with the lawyer who, however, is likely to represent the same social and economic ideology as his business client. Banking and insurance exercise a controlling influence through the committeemen representation in all but the two above-mentioned sections.[19] The placing of women on the national committee was merely a gracious gesture when it was begun after the universal enfranchisement of women in 1920. In 1933 a careful investigator observed: "The committeewoman is often a mere shadow of the committeeman, but she is a woman. The door has opened a little." It is not much farther open to women today, and many national committeewomen feel strongly that they play a negligible part.[20]

Several months before the convening of its national party convention the national committee of each major party issues the call for the convention and selects the date and the place of the meeting. It convenes again shortly before the convention in order to examine the credentials of delegates and to decide contests. After the convention it directs the party presidential campaign, collects funds, and publishes and distributes campaign propaganda euphemistically denominated "literature." Because of the unwieldy size of the committee many of these duties are administered by a national chairman selected by the national committee and aided by a staff. Yet the selection of the chairman is little more than the ratification of the choice which the party candidate for president makes in accordance with established party usage.

Congressional Campaign Committees

Each major party has a congressional campaign committee working to maintain as well as to increase its party membership in the House of Representatives. The Republican congressional committee consists of one member from each state having Republican representation in the House. He is selected by the state delegation in the House and ratified by the party

[19] Wallace S. Sayre: "Personnel of Republican and Democratic National Committees." *American Political Science Review* (1932), 26:360–2.

[20] Marguerite J. Fisher and Betty Whitehead: "Women and National Party Organization." *American Political Science Review* (1944), 38:895–903.

conference, as the Republican caucus is designated. The Democratic congressional committee is similarly constituted except that its chairman is empowered to appoint a woman member for each state and also a member from each state without Democratic representation in the House of Representatives. Each committee busies itself supporting the campaign of the congressional candidates of its party. Until recently these committees had no permanent organization and were active only during the congressional campaigns, particularly in the mid-term elections when their work was not overshadowed by that of the national committees. Now, however, as soon as one election ends, congressional committees begin preparing for the next election through a permanent staff maintained at the Washington headquarters. There were no senatorial campaign committees before 1916, but soon after the coming of popular election of senators in 1913 each major party established a senatorial campaign committee to achieve for its party in the upper house what the congressional campaign committees are attempting to do in the lower house. [21]

[21] Politicians undoubtedly overestimate the effectiveness of campaign activities particularly of newspaper support which the electorate largely disregards. It has been estimated that in the presidential campaign of 1936 President Roosevelt had the support of only 42 per cent of the weekly and 37 per cent of the daily party press and yet received 60 per cent of the popular vote; in 1940 he had the support of an estimated 37 per cent of the weekly and 26 per cent of the daily press and received 55 per cent of the popular vote. Of thirty-five presidential contests seventeen appear to have been won by the candidate supported by a minority of the contemporary newspapers. Frank L. Mott: "Newspapers in Presidential Campaigns." *Public Opinion Quarterly* (1944), 8:348–67.

SUMMARY

Competing political parties are a *sine qua non* of representative government, and government in the United States functions through a two-party system. The conflict between the mercantile, financial, and industrial interests on the one hand and the independent agrarians on the other has been the fundamental basis of party alignment throughout American history. As a consequence, Federalists competed with Jeffersonian Republicans, and Jacksonian Democrats with Whigs and later with Republicans. The Anti-Mason, Free Soil, Know Nothing, Greenback, Populist, Progressive, and other third parties have appeared from time to time and forced the major parties to accept part of their program whenever they attracted a heavy vote.

The practically popular election of the President and the consequent necessity of marshalling a group combination constituting a majority is the chief basis of our persisting two-party system. Presidential candidates in effect consequently endeavor to outbid each other in promising the promotion of policies in return for electoral support of interest groups. Since both parties appeal to the same electorate, party platforms tend to be quite similar.

Opinion polls indicate that the Republican party tends to attract the

upper income, the business, professional, and white-collar groups, and
the older voters. Geographically its voting strength is in the metropolitan
suburbs, the lesser cities, towns, villages, and rural sections outside the
South. The Democratic party is strong among manual workers, younger
voters, in crowded urban wards, and among nearly all groups in the
South. Because of the somewhat different group structures of the major
parties a change from one to the other means more or less of a shift as
to policies and their administration.

So persistent is the propensity for political parties that legally established "non-partisan" elections are habitually circumvented. Parties are
indispensable in providing alternatives as to candidates for important
offices and, however imperfectly, as to issues. Thus the electorate can
express its judgment on an administration. Operating at their best, politicians perform a socially integrating function and render an invaluable
service in attending to necessary legal details with which the otherwise
busy citizen is unfamiliar.

CHAPTER XI

NOMINATING PROCEDURES

"The fundamental principle of a republic is individual responsibility. The responsibility is personal at the point in our political system where the citizen comes in direct contact with the system itself. . . . But this ends with the adjournment of the primary or caucus. From that moment the citizen, in a representative democracy, under a caucus, delegate, and convention system, does not again come in direct personal touch with the work of either legislation or administration. How essential, then, if he is to be a factor in government, that he take part, and intelligently too, in this fundamental work. If there be failure here, there is failure throughout. If the minority control in the caucuses, the laws will be made and executed by the agent of the minority, and the first principle of government fails." Speech of Robert M. LaFollette at the University of Chicago on Washington's Birthday, 1897.

B Y FAR the most important function of political parties is that of selecting candidates for public elective office. Political parties do, to be sure, serve the processes of government in several ways other than by nominating candidates. They provide the vehicle for uniting people holding similar views on political principles and policies, they have an educational function in familiarizing the electorate with the issues, and they perform the very practical service of carrying on campaigns. Each of these functions, however, might also be undertaken by pressure groups that desire to influence national policies on their own initiative. But in so far as the nomination of candidates for election to public office is concerned, the political party is sovereign.

That some method of narrowing down the number of candidates from whom the electorate may make a choice is a necessary requisite under our form of government seems fairly obvious. The idea of direct election of public officials without any intervening nominative process is conceivable in an extremely small community or constituency, but the principle can hardly be applied say, in a congressional district, the average size of which runs around 400,000 people. It seems only natural therefore that the number of choices presented to the electorate be sifted down to a few persons, and it is equally logical that the agency to carry out this function be the political party.

In contrast to other democratic countries where nominations are left almost completely in the hands of the party organization and the procedures are not carefully prescribed by government regulation, nominations in the United States are governed by elaborate statutory requirements. Most of the regulations governing nominations are prescribed by the state, not the national government. One of the main reasons for the significance that has been attached to nominations in this country is the unusually large number of elective offices that must be filled. In the case of the Federal government where only a president, vice-president, 435 representatives, and ninety-six senators are chosen the number of elected officials is indeed quite small, but the state and local elective offices total well over 800,000 and they have been extremely important in shaping the course of nominating processes. Another factor contributing to the importance of nominations in this country is the dominance of a single party in large regions—particularly in the South. Under such conditions the nomination becomes tantamount to election underscoring again the desirability of having more than a few select party leaders designate candidates for the elective offices to be filled. In areas where political parties offer very little difference of choice to the electorate on policies, the nominating process is likewise a matter of concern, for it is only through such a procedure that the voters may register a protest against dictatorial rule by the party's elite.

EARLY NOMINATING METHODS

The Caucus

Since the dawn of modern political history the leaders of various movements have staged informal meetings to organize and lay the plans for larger conclaves to be held at a later date. [1] Although such preliminary meetings are often popularly looked upon as a sinister practice, this is not necessarily the case. Where group action is contemplated—as all who have had experience with such matters will confirm—some preparatory work must be undertaken in anticipation of mobilizing a larger effort. As those most interested tend to be the first in the field where political or social action is contemplated, and as small groups are more efficient planning agencies than larger unwieldy bodies, the influence of the smaller units has always had a far-reaching consequence. For describing this device—the planning of political action by an informal meeting of local leaders—the term "caucus" gradually came to be applied. And as used in connection with nominations the caucus simply meant reaching an advance

[1] F. W. Dallinger: *Nominations for Elective Office in the United States* (New York, 1897), p. 3.

agreement on the candidates that the party or group would support in a subsequent election.

One of the earliest descriptions of a caucus in the United States may be found in John Adams's diary. In an entry dated 1763, he describes the caucus held at Tom Dawes garret in Boston as follows: "This day learned that the Caucus Club meets at certain times in the garret of Tom Dawes. He has a large house . . . and the whole club meets in one room. There they smoke tobacco till you cannot see from one end of the garret to the other. There they drink flip, I suppose, and they choose a moderator who puts questions to the vote regularly; and selectmen, assessors, fire-wards, and representatives are regularly chosen before they are chosen in the town." [2]

In its early colonial form, the caucus was chiefly available for the nomination of local officials rather than state-wide or national offices because of travel difficulties. Shortly after the Revolutionary War nominations were made in some states by soliciting the views of political leaders through extensive correspondence and in a few instances nominees were selected by local party chieftains who convened at one of the principal cities of a state for this purpose. Within the span of a very short time, however, the most familiar nominating technique of the post-Revolutionary era became the legislative caucus.

The Legislative Caucus

The idea of having state legislatures make nominations is reported to have started in Rhode Island. This development was favored by the fact that state legislatures were generally composed of local political leaders who had to meet periodically to perform their legislative duties in any event. As state legislatures were also authorized by the Federal Constitution to elect United States senators, their assumption of the nominating function for other officers was not surprising. The actual nominating process consisted of a joint session of party members from both houses—a procedure which soon came to be identified as the legislative caucus. By 1796 the legislative caucus was an established institution among all thirteen states and in 1800 the same mode of making nominations was introduced into Congress where it was known as the congressional caucus.

The Demise of "King Caucus"

For nearly twenty-five years the legislative caucus or "King Caucus" as it came to be called was the device regularly employed to nominate candidates for elective office. Governors, lieutenant governors and other state-wide officers, congressmen, senators, vice-presidents, and presidents were all nominated by legislative caucuses meeting in state or national capitals. Four presidents—Adams, Jefferson, Madison, and Monroe—received their

[2] C. F. Adams, editor: *The Works of John Adams* (Boston, 1850), Vol. II, p. 144.

nominations through the congressional caucus. But the supremacy of "King Caucus" proved to be short-lived.

An early indictment against the legislative caucus among the states highlighted the fact that it was not representative; that is to say, where legislative districts were controlled by the opposition party they went unrepresented in the party legislative caucus. Some attempt was made to remedy this defect by introducing the "mixed caucus," a measure whereby special delegates were chosen to speak for the party members in the legislative districts held by the opposing party. [3] The "mixed caucus" in turn was an intermediate step toward the "mixed convention" where members of the legislature were allowed seats only in case the delegate duly elected in his county or district was not in attendance. The final product of this evolutionary process—which did not proceed uniformly among the states—was of course, the straight convention that was made up of delegates who were all selected on the basis of geographic districts.

While the rule of "King Caucus" gradually gave way to the representative convention in the states, its discard was hastened by the rejection of the congressional caucus for making presidential nominations. Embittered by the congressional caucus of 1824 that showed no warmth for Andrew Jackson, the supporters of "Old Hickory" began a systematic campaign to discredit the congressional caucus and it was never used again for picking presidential candidates. In 1828 the nominations for president were made by "State legislative caucuses, public meetings, and irregular conventions of the people." The national convention for presidential nominations was not to appear for three years (1831), but the congressional caucus was never to rear its head again and the expiration of this device on the national level had a profound effect in bringing about its demise among the states.

THE CONVENTION

Between the Jacksonian period and the end of the nineteenth century the convention system was the dominant nominating method in American politics. [4] In theory at least the convention offered the possibility of democratic participation within the party in selecting the party's nominees for public elective office. The members of political parties in various local units such as the town, city, or county elected delegates to represent them at the state convention where state-wide officials were to be nominated. If the convention was a county convention the delegates were initially selected in local political subdivisions such as the precinct. Where a candidate was to be selected for Congress it was a common practice to hold a district convention which included delegates from all the counties within the congressional district. In all cases where the convention was used the

[3] F. W. Dallinger: *Nominations for Elective Office in U.S.*, p. 20.
[4] For a description of the evolution of the convention system see Henry Jones Ford: *The Rise and Growth of American Politics* (New York, 1898), chap. 16.

principle for its composition was essentially the same. Delegates were selected first at the lowest level of the political hierarchy and these in turn either went directly to the convention or selected delegates to represent them at an intermediate convention. Under this scheme it was felt that representation might flow from the "grass roots" and afford the rank and file of the party membership an opportunity to express themselves. Although the convention has now been largely rejected for nominating state officers, congressmen, and senators, it is still the most popular device for selecting delegates for our national conventions that nominate presidential candidates.

Convention Abuses

As the control of nominations slipped from the hands of the select powers that managed the legislative caucuses to the conventions, whose membership consisted of delegates directly chosen by local assemblies of the party's rank and file, the change was heralded as a progressive reform. Given the ideal condition of a citizenry ever attentive to political affairs, the convention system might have worked admirably as a democratic method of coalescing the wishes of the broad party membership in the matter of selecting candidates for public office. Several factors, however, steadily diminished the prestige of the convention system.

In the first place it was soon evident that conventions were susceptible to control by a few. The conventions may have been more representative and larger bodies than the legislative caucuses, but Hamilton's sage observation made in 1788 that the larger an assembly "the greater is the power of the few in it," had a familiar if forgotten ring of truth for the convention. The apathy of party supporters in many local areas made it comparatively easy for small well-disciplined cliques to gain control on the ground floor, so to speak, of the convention organizational procedure. The struggle for supremacy in political areas where competing groups emerged led to factionalism within the party and this development in turn often meant that rival factions conducted themselves with little regard for the wishes of rank and file membership.

Aiding and abetting the decline of the convention system was the rapid growth of large metropolitan areas and the attendant corruption that followed. As cities expanded the question of control over public utilities, railroads, and other monopolistic enterprises stimulated unscrupulous party leaders to dominate the government officials in these areas in their own selfish interests. [5] Thus they resorted to many feats of political wizardry and roughhouse tactics to accomplish their ends. Unfortunately the broad masses of the party membership were ill prepared to meet the challenge. Already overburdened by the plurality of elective offices that were being established in the post-Jacksonian era upon the somewhat misguided as-

[5] See *Autobiography of William Allen White* (New York, 1946). Also Lincoln Steffens: *The Struggle for Self Government: being an attempt to trace American political corruption to its sources in six states.* (New York, 1906.) See also *The Autobiography of Lincoln Steffens* (New York, 1936).

sumption that a larger number of elective public offices insured greater democracy, the ordinary party member permitted the aides of political schemers to take the initiative by default. Of course the persons who held the reins of political machines connived to discourage broad participation in the convention machinery and it was not pure weariness or disinterest that turned convention control over to the machine organizations. When the official call for local caucuses was issued by the state central committee or appropriate party organ the controlling clique would frequently give only the briefest notice on the time and place of the meeting. In this way persons wishing to oppose the party machine at the local caucuses had insufficient time to mobilize their forces effectively. The machine organization on the other hand knowing of the caucus date in advance could be well primed to carry the meetings.

Among other methods of discouraging attendance at local caucuses political machines often selected such unsavory meeting places that many respectable people stayed away who might otherwise have taken part. Caucuses were scheduled in saloons, livery stables, gaming houses, and in environments deliberately calculated to be offensive to many elements of society. It was not uncommon for caucuses to be packed with crude and coarse representatives of the political machine who were not averse to using physical force if necessary for their side to prevail. Moreover, the local caucuses leading up to the conventions were not the only places where one encountered rough tactics and foul play. At the county, district, or state convention itself, the political faction or machine in control of the temporary organization sometimes refused to seat duly qualified delegates who had been elected by local caucuses. Not only were delegates entitled to seats in conventions denied their rights, but the entire replacement of duly elected delegates by delegates without any legitimate claim to be seated was not unknown. Thus at a notable and riotous convention in Minneapolis early in this century the entire body of assembled delegates that had been duly elected was unseated in favor of a motley crew of vagrants rushed up from the Mississippi river flats for the occasion. In the latter case none of the replacements had any claim whatsoever to being a delegate, but by manipulating the credentials committee— the agency which decides all contests pertaining to the seating of delegates—the victorious political machine completely raided the legitimate convention and won the day by the timely arrival of its "river rat" reinforcements.

In 1866 California took the lead in regulating caucuses and conventions by passing a law which was first optional for parties but later compulsory. [6] Following this date other states fell in line with legislation aimed at moderating some of the worst features of the convention system. Before convention regulation became either general or effective, however, the

[6] E. E. Campbell: "Party Nominations in California (1860–1909)." *Southwestern Social Science Quarterly* (1931), 12:245–57.

system it was meant to improve had yielded to the direct primary. By the end of the nineteenth century the convention not only had developed some shocking abuses measured by ethical standards, but in many areas was also in an advanced stage of degeneration. At a Cook county convention in 1896, before Illinois had adopted the direct primary, there were 723 delegates, of whom 17 had been tried for homicide, 46 had served terms in the penitentiary for homicide or other felonies, 84 were identified as having criminal records, and one-third were saloonkeepers. [7] Several of the other delegates at the same convention were identified as gamblers or operators of houses of prostitution. While the Cook County convention was by no means representative of all communities it had its counterparts in many sections of the country, particularly in the congested urban centers. If most convention members were not tarred by criminal records or shady dealings, there was an uncommon number of officeholders among them. As a means of giving the rank and file party member a voice in the nominating procedure, the convention had failed. Appropriately its obituary might be described by the words of Governor Charles Evans Hughes addressed to the New York Legislature in 1909, when he advocated adoption of the primary: [8] "The ordinary party member who cannot make politics a vocation, feels that he is practically helpless, a victim of a system of indirect, complicated, and pseudo-representative activities which favor control by a few and make party candidates to a great extent the virtual appointees of party managers."

THE DIRECT PRIMARY[9]

In supplanting the convention the direct primary was backed by much the same arguments that were put forward when the convention squeezed out the legislative caucus. The basic idea again was to widen rank and file participation in party nominations and by this means forestall oligarchical control. If only the people could express themselves directly in selecting party nominees, the argument ran, the manipulative tactics under the convention system could be eliminated. And, with the establishment of the primary the democratic impulses could flow direct from the people to the public servants that were eventually elected by this method.

The direct primary had an initial trial in Crawford County, Pennsylvania in 1842, where it was employed by the local organization of the Demo-

[7] See R. M. Easley: "The Sine-qua-non of Caucus Reform." *American Review of Reviews* (1897), 16:322–4.

[8] See address of Governor Charles Evans Hughes to the New York Legislature, January 5, 1910 cited in Charles A. Beard: "The Direct Primary Movement in New York." *Proceedings of the American Political Science Association* (1910), 7:194.

[9] For specialized treatment of the direct primary, see V. O. Key: *Politics, Parties and Pressure Groups* (2nd ed.; New York, 1947), pp. 349–69; Howard R. Penniman: *Sait's American Parties and Elections* (4th ed., New York, 1947), Chap. 18; and Peter H. Odegard and E. Allen Helms: *American Politics: A Study of Political Dynamics* (New York, 1947), chap. 16.

cratic party. [10] Several other counties in the Keystone State soon adopted the practice and in 1868 the local rules of the Republican party abolished the convention for nominating county officers and made provisions for all candidates for county offices to be nominated in a primary. For many years this nominating system was known as the "Crawford County System," and it was not until around the turn of the century that the term "direct primary" was commonly accepted.

After gaining a toehold in the Pennsylvania counties the primary moved westward and southward. [11] Almost everywhere it appeared the primary was under the sponsorship of local party organizations, and it usually started in small areas where reform elements had managed to put the squeeze on machine politicians. The Populists opposed the convention system and were ardent champions of the primary in their crusade against the alliance between vested interest groups and political machines. In South Carolina, under the driving impetus of "Pitchfork" Ben Tillman, the primary received perhaps its first broad test when the convention was replaced in 1891 by a system that brought most public officers, including United States senators, under a primary.

In the development of the primary the South played a significant role that is often overlooked. Here the primary was associated in many areas with the Farmers' Alliance and Populist movement, and it remained entrenched as a popular institution for nominating candidates even after this agrarian reform combination had faded from the political scene. In other sections of the South, once the Democratic party had reasserted its supremacy and put the Populist-Republican coalitions to rout, the adoption or continuance of the primary was assured for an obvious reason. With the political scene completely dominated by one party, conventions would, in effect, elect rather than nominate. Thus it was inevitable that the primary would have to be used if the rank and file voters were to have any hand at all in the choice of their elected public officers.

With the spread of the primary came legislative regulation. Sometimes state legislatures made the direct primary optional, and in other cases mandatory, but no legislature was able to hold it back. The primary spread as rapidly as ink on blotting paper. No matter how exaggerated the claims for the direct primary may have been it took root in the United States like no other reform. Its greatest progress took place after the Progressive movement began to accelerate in the early part of this century. Under Governor Robert M. LaFollette, the Progressives instituted the first mandatory state-

---

[10] See James H. Booser: "Origins of the Direct Primary," *National Municipal Review*, (1935), 24:222–3. In 1903 the Crawford County System was re-baptized the "direct primary" when Wisconsin adopted the first state-wide primary law. The term had been widely used to describe the new nomination system, however, long before it was officially adopted by the Wisconsin Legislature.

[11] For a general account of the development of the direct primary see C. E. Merriam and Louise Overacker: *Primary Elections* (Chicago, 1928); and C. E. Meyer: *Nominating Systems* (New York, 1902).

wide direct primary law in Wisconsin in 1903. [12] By 1915, thirty-eight states had adopted the primary in some form and at the end of 1917 only four states had failed to install the primary for selecting some or all of its officials to be chosen by a state-wide election. Today only three states, New York, Indiana, and Utah are now making use of the convention system for nominating officers selected by a state-wide election, and use of the convention in six states—mainly in the Solid South is optional. The optionality in the South, however, applies chiefly to the Republican party, although there are some exceptions such as Virginia where the convention is optional for all parties.

VARIATIONS IN THE PRIMARY

The Closed Primary

In the great majority of our states, the "closed" primary is now used. The distinguishing feature of this form of primary is that participation is restricted to party members. [13] About one-half of the states record party membership when the voter registers and limit his vote to the party of his choice at registration time. Party membership in turn is defined either by statute or party rule or by a combination of both, and a number of methods have been devised for subsequently checking a voter's partisan allegiance. Among the several methods devised for this purpose are:

(A) *Past allegiance:* The Ohio primary voter, if challenged, must swear that he voted for a majority of the candidates of the party he claims membership in at the last general election.

(B) *Present affiliation:* In South Dakota the challenged voter must declare himself to be "in good faith" a member of the party in question, and "a believer in its principles as declared in the last state and national platforms."

(C) *Future intention:* In Missouri the challenged voter must obligate himself under oath to support the party nominees at the next election.

(D) *Past allegiance and present intention:* In Florida the voter must take an oath declaring present membership and that he "did not vote for any nominee of any other party" at the last election.

(E) *Past allegiance and future intention:* The Indiana voter at a party primary election must have voted for a majority of that party's candidates at the last general election.

(F) *Present affiliation and future intention:* Texas law requires under oath the pledge "I am a Democrat and pledge myself to support the nominees of this primary."

[12] See Robert M. LaFollette: *Autobiography* (Madison, 1913), pp. 292–7. Also A. F. Lovejoy: *LaFollette and the Establishment of the Direct Primary in Wisconsin, 1890–1904* (New Haven, 1941).

[13] For a careful analysis of the closed and open primary differences see Clarence A. Berdahl: "Party Membership in the United States." *American Political Science Review* (1942), 36:16–50, 241–62.

(G) *Past allegiance, present affiliation and future intention:* Maine requires all three of these evidences of party allegiance under oath and New Jersey the same but only if challenged.

The Open Primary

As a nominating method designed to leave the voter completely unfettered in his choice of party at the primary, the "open primary" has been introduced in three states. No public expression of party affiliation is required in the open primary. In Minnesota and Wisconsin the open primary rules require a voter to vote in one party or the other once he has made up his mind about party preference, but in Washington the voter may split his vote between different parties. [14] Under the latter scheme he might vote for a Republican candidate for United States senator in the Republican primary and a Democratic candidate for the House of Representatives in the Democratic primary.

The open primary has been under the fire of "party regularity" champions ever since its adoption. One allegation is that the open primary destroys party "responsibility" by allowing Democrats to masquerade as Republicans in the Republican primary and granting Republicans the same privilege in the Democratic primary. Another contention is that the open primary facilitates party "raids"—a technique whereby the members of one party invade the primary of another in the hope of nominating a mediocre candidate who will be easier to defeat in the general election. Again the experience thus far with the open primary does not warrant any broad generalizations on either party responsibility or party raids. If there has been a decline in party responsibility in some states using the open primary, it is doubtful if the decline has been more perceptible than in other states where the closed primary reigns supreme. There are strong party organizations under the open primary system, as witness Harold Stassen's political organization in Minnesota. Moreover in some regions like the far western states of Oregon and Washington if strong party organizations have not thrived under the open primary the voters themselves have seemed to compensate for this lack by showing a more acute sensitivity to the real issues regardless of differences in party. In a few instances the open primary has probably encouraged abortive attempts at party "raids." And where raids are attempted they are not necessarily aimed at nominating mediocre candidates. Raids have been attempted in the prayerful hope of nominating a more conservative candidate. One of the most striking examples of the latter motivation occured in 1938 when about 200,000 Republican voters in Minnesota invaded the Farmer-Labor party's gubernatorial primary to try to nominate the more conservative-minded Hjalmar Peterson over his radical opponent, Governor Elmer Benson. As a rule party raids are rather difficult to engineer and except for unusual circumstances the normal tendency is for voters to remain in their own party primary even

[14] See C. O. Johnson: "The Washington Blanket Primary." *Pacific Northwest Quarterly* (1942), 33:27–39.

though not compelled to do so under the open primary. The most common reason for a voter to cross party lines at the primary, of course, seems to be for the purpose of nominating a strong candidate whom the voter intends to support in the general election. [15]

Run-Off Primaries

From our discussion of primaries thus far it may be readily understood that the winning candidate may not always be the choice of a majority of those voting in the primary. Let us assume, for example, that four candidates file for the office of United States Senator. If two or three of the candidates are evenly matched the winning candidate is certain to have only a plurality of the votes, not a majority. [16] The winning candidate, in other words, instead of having more than fifty percent of all the votes—a majority—would merely have more votes than his nearest competitor—a plurality. To prevent nominations from being plurality choices several states have adopted the run-off primary. Under this plan if the leading candidate fails to receive a majority of all the votes cast in the primary, a second or run-off primary is held between the highest two candidates. Practically all of the states that use the run-off primary are located in the South. [17] While the idea of the run-off primary seems commendable, particularly for the Southern states where a one-party system prevails, it has no demonstrable advantages elsewhere over plurality nominations. Run-off primaries are expensive and they are also subject to factional machinations which frequently negate any theoretical benefits that might be claimed in their favor.

Cross-filing in the Primary

One of the most curious variations in primary practices among the states is that of cross-filing which permits candidates to seek the nominations of both parties. In most states candidates in party primaries, like voters, must meet certain eligibility requirements before they are permitted to file. A few states, however, notably California where cross-filing is a general practice, allow candidates to file in both primaries. [18] Thus in the 1940 California primary the late Hiram Johnson won the nomination for United States Senator in both the Republican and Democratic parties. The same feat was also accomplished by Governor Earl Warren in the gubernatorial race of 1946. Occasionally the system of cross-filing leads to incongruous results and it has been sharply criticized in recent years. Part of the confusion stems from the fact that under California law unless a candidate wins the nomination of his own party he cannot claim the nomination of the

[15] Professor Pollock in his study of the Michigan direct primary concludes that when voters do jump party lines in the primary they do so to support a strong candidate whom they hope to vote for in the general election. See James K. Pollock: *The Direct Primary in Michigan, 1909–1935* (Ann Arbor, 1943), p. 60.

[16] For treatment of plurality nominations in New Mexico see Paul Beckett and Walter L. McNutt: *The Direct Primary in New Mexico* (Albuquerque, 1947).

[17] The run-off primary states are Alabama, Arkansas, Florida, Georgia, Louisiana, Mississippi, North Carolina, Oklahoma, South Carolina, and Texas.

[18] See Robert W. Binkley, Jr.: *Double Filing in Primary Elections* (Berkeley, 1945).

opposition party. In 1944 the representative of the fifteenth congressional district in California, a Democrat, won the Republican nomination yet could not accept it because he failed to receive a nomination of his own party. At the same primary five other congressmen were elected and exempted from running in the general election because they obtained the nomination of both parties. In a sense the cross-filing system gives the candidates much the same freedom that the open primary gives the voter. There is much more sentiment for the repeal of the cross-filing system than for the repeal of the open primary, however, and an initiated measure was proposed for the ballot in 1952. It was defeated by a narrow margin.[19]

THE PRIMARY ON TRIAL

No student of government today needs to be told that the primary was not the panacea that its champions proclaimed it to be. Almost from its inception the party potentates who had once controlled the convention system exercised great influence over the primary. The more uncritical visionaries who had extolled the virtues of the primary sadly misunderstood the nature of the political process. Even under a primary system an organization may exist within the party; hence the disappearance of the convention did not eclipse political machines. [20] Party organization heads may have found their authority somewhat modified by the changeover from the convention to the primary, and the shift did require different strategies to fit the new political framework, but they took the adjustment in stride. Party machines continued to keep their operatives well organized in the precincts, wards, counties, and state, and in this way they were able to agree in advance upon candidates they would support in the primary. By maintaining discipline within the ranks of the machine organization leaders had little difficulty in dominating the primary. With advance agreement on a list of candidates they favored for nomination the machine leaders had an advantage over the unorganized rank and file of the party. The organization could center its strength on the slate agreed upon prior to the primary, whereas the vote of the party rank and file might be fractionalized among several candidates. In many cases, therefore, the primary appeared to give popular ratification to the choices already agreed upon by the machine organization.

The fact that the political chieftains of a party seem to dictate the primary winners does not mean that a non-machine choice cannot emerge

[19] Robert O. Foote: "The Cross Filing Primary," *Baltimore Evening Sun*, June 13, 1944. In the California primary of June, 1948, the Republican congressional candidates won nine joint or bi-partisan nominations and the Democrats captured three. This meant that in twelve of California's twenty-three congressional districts there would be no contest in the general election unless a third party candidate was on the ballot.

[20] See Henry Jones Ford: "The Direct Primary." *North American Review* (1909), 190:1–14: "The direct primary may take advantage of opportunity from one set of politicians and confer them upon another set, but politicians there will always be so long as there is politics."

as the victor in a primary. Nor does it mean that the choice of an inner core organization within the party is necessarily unacceptable to the rank and file membership. But the frequency with which advance selections by the inner organization do win in the primary underscores the broad influence it has over the primary. Thus we find that the candidates for United States Senator, Representative in Congress, Governor, or other officials, who enter the primary with the official blessings of the party organization, start with an enormous advantage.

A common device to make the wishes of the party organization known to the general membership of the party is the pre-primary indorsing convention. In Colorado, Utah, Rhode Island, and New Mexico, the parties hold indorsing conventions in advance of the primary. As the boost which an indorsing convention gives a candidate is usually enough to put him over in the primary, it can very easily reduce the primary itself to secondary importance.

Since the primary came into general use its opponents have hammered against it with stock arguments, all of which unfortunately have a certain grain of truth, but they have failed to convince a majority of the people that the way of better government is via the convention route. It is true that the primary is more expensive and it is likewise correct that the large number of elective public offices to be filled makes it difficult for the over-burdened voter to cast an intelligent vote. More fundamental, perhaps, is the indictment that the primary is not taken as seriously as one might wish by a large part of the electorate and that this indifference delivers control of the primary into the hands of political bosses. On several charges against the primary, however, the arguments are not convincing and the evidence is too incomplete to pass final judgment.

One finds examples where the party organization has made a clean sweep of the primaries with its candidates over a period of several years. But there are also many instances where the organization legions have been put to rout at the primary by the party's rank and file. The primary does make it more difficult for the political machine to dominate the nominating process. And the record indicates that nominations for public offices carrying great prestige with the electorate such as United States Senator are more difficult for the party organization to control than those for less important offices.

Among the older but still persistent charges hurled against the primary is that it brings more mediocrity into public office than the convention system did. At first blush when one looks around to find the modern counterparts of Clay, Webster, and Calhoun this argument sounds persuasive, but it hardly squares with the facts. Rating the present-day product of the primary system against the man who was elevated to public office by the convention nominating process is like trying to decide whether Jack Dempsey in his prime could have knocked out Joe Louis. The notion that the primary has brought about a decline in party organization and responsibility is also a view that deserves no hard and fast acceptance. In states such as Ohio and Pennsylvania the primary system is characterized by strong party organization and the decisions of the organization are often decisive factors in the primary. Yet in other states, particularly those of the Far West such as Oregon and Washington the party machinery is not as well organized nor does it ordinarily have a significant influence on the primary.

The primary, then, has adjusted to the peculiarities and traditions of the region. In areas where strong political organizations have been the rule, such as Illinois, party organization has held up despite the adoption of the primary, and where party organization is said to have lapsed because of the primary, the reason is probably quite independent of this factor. In weighing the primary one should not be persuaded that the frequent victories of organization candidates are necessarily an indictment against the system. As Charles Evans Hughes noted in 1921: "Why should they not win? If a party is clean, vigorous, and efficient, if it has the confidence of the party members, as such an organization should have, it will be influential in advising candidacies, and those who are presented as candidates with the approval of such an organization will in all probability be men who ought to be selected." The party organization may still operate effectively and maintain its vigor under the primary system. Indeed, as Mr. Hughes says, a presumption that the primary is unsatisfactory because the organization candidates often win is quite illogical. [21]

Today the primary still has many frailties. But no matter how the critics rail against its shortcoming, one incontrovertible truism stands to protect the primary from all assaults and will probably prevent its eclipse. When things get too bad, as Charles Evans Hughes once pointed out, an effective means is needed to turn the rascals out of office. The primary is just such a weapon.

SUMMARY

The nominating process is necessary to narrow down to a manageable number the field of aspirants to political office. This process, once determined solely by party leaders, is now governed by elaborate statutory regulations, a recognition of the fact that parties are not private clubs.

The caucus, which dates back to colonial times, was the common method of selecting candidates for public office in the United States until the Jacksonian era. Nominees of the major parties for national and state-wide offices were usually chosen by a legislative caucus.

The nominating convention, still used for the selection of presidential and vice-presidential nominees, replaced the caucus during the 1830's. It afforded the rank and file of the party greater opportunity to make known their sentiments toward prospective nominees but was often characterized by serious abuses. Conventions often were controlled by

[21] Charles E. Hughes: "The Fate of the Direct Primary." *National Municipal Review* (1921), 10:23–31.

small cliques; the delegates sometimes represented the most unwholesome elements of society.

The first years of the twentieth century brought adoption of the direct primary as the method of nominating candidates for state and local office as well as for the national Congress in almost all states. In most states the closed primary prevails, probably because champions of party regularity believe it strengthens party responsibility and prevents adherents of one party from raiding the rival party's primary. The run-off primary is used in most Southern states, mitigating some undesirable features of a one-party system.

The expense of primary elections, the high percentage of non-voters, and the mediocrity of the candidates selected through primaries are the chief arguments urged by opponents of this method of nomination. The direct primary offers to the voters, however, a readier means of cashiering faithless public servants than does any other method of making nominations.

CHAPTER XII

CONGRESSIONAL PRIMARIES AND ELECTIONS

To RECORD what goes on behind the scenes in a primary campaign, and perhaps even more important, to include the processes that unfold in the pre-primary stage, is not easy within the brief compass of an introductory book on American political institutions. Politics, like many of the professions, is an art the understanding of which is greatly enhanced by intimate association at the operational level. To attend a party caucus, assist in the planning and conduct of a campaign, or to help organize meetings as the candidate takes his stand on the hustings is to know what Frank Kent so appropriately terms "The Great Game of Politics." The entire nominating procedure, as we have already noted, is one of sifting or winnowing the number of candidates who seek the primary nomination. Although in theory any person who meets the customary state requirements on residence and citizenship may enter a primary campaign, usually by paying a filing fee that ranges from fifty to one hundred dollars, the evidence suggests that the elimination process begins very early.

WHO GOES TO CONGRESS

In the normal course of events candidates who carry off nominations are not persons who simply go through the motions of announcing their candidacy and paying the required filing fee. Planning is the keystone of the nominative process. Quite independent of the primary, selective forces are operating within our society to steer some people into the stream of politics. Not all persons, to be sure, who take an active hand in politics will emerge as candidates for public office. Many who willingly serve the party shun the thought of candidacy for public office, while others lack either the qualities or the good fortune to realize ambitions to hold an elective public post. In examining the background of the men and women who eventually reach Congress as representatives and senators two characteristics stand out; first, practically all of them have served their respective party in some capacity prior to their nomination and election to Congress; second, an unusually large number have held down public positions before being elevated to Congress. A study of the Seventy-seventh Congress (1941–1942) revealed that one hundred and fifty-six had formerly served in state legislatures and one hundred and nine as prosecuting attorneys. [1] In addition, several members had also served as governors. In the Eightieth Congress (1947–1948) in the Senate alone there were twenty-eight senators who had formerly been governors. Twenty-one members of the upper chamber had also served in the House before going to the Senate. Besides the many members who had earlier held elective offices such as state legislators, mayors, or city councilmen, seven in the Eightieth Congress had served as county sheriffs. [2] The customary channels therefore, through which a person passes on his way to our national legislature are fairly well defined and it will be readily apparent that the persons serving apprenticeships in political affairs are usually the ones who are rewarded with the party's nomination for representative or senator and subsequent election.

CAMPAIGN STRATEGY

The strategy employed in primary campaigns varies with the circumstances. One technique often employed is to have various organizations urge a likely subject to become a candidate. Thus a labor union local or a business men's association will call upon some person to make the supreme sacrifice and become a candidate for Congress and—after a period of hide and seek during which the prospective candidate remains modestly noncommittal—it is accepted practice to respond to the call of the people with a public declaration of candidacy. In communities where party organizations are strong, the feelers inviting a person to become a candidate may emanate from the party leaders themselves. Elsewhere the party leaders may remain discreetly in the background while prominent civic, professional, business, or labor leaders make the initial advances in urging a potential candidate to run. In Indiana, and also in many other states, the State Editorial Association is a potent body in influencing the selection of senatorial candidates and its more vigorous spokesmen claim

[1] See M. M. McKinney: "The Personnel of the Seventy-seventh Congress." *American Political Science Review* (1946), 36:67–75.

[2] From the standpoint of previous occupations a breakdown of the Eightieth and Eighty-first Congress revealed the following: In the Eightieth Congress there were 248 lawyers in the House and Senate. Thus the legal profession accounted for 59.4 percent of the membership of both houses. After lawyers came businessmen, educators, farmers, and journalists in the order named. The Eighty-first Congress was composed of 301 lawyers, 68 businessmen, 35 politicians, 33 farmers, 31 teachers, 13 bankers, and one actress. In the latter Congress there were 218 war veterans, 80 of whom were veterans of World War II.

that by tradition it has inherited the right to name the Republican candidate for United States Senator. It would be a mistake, of course, to conclude that all nominations are set up very early in the game and that various unorganized groups and party members cannot upset some of the best laid plans by capturing the primary with a candidate of their own. But the evidence is overwhelming that the candidates who receive a well-planned boost from either the party organization or well-disciplined organizations working within the framework of the party are the ones that win the first trial heat on the road to Congress.

Everywhere the choice of candidates is decreed somewhat by the local peculiarities of the region. However unfortunate it is axiomatic that such matters as race, religion, national extraction, and sex, may seriously enhance or impede a candidate's chance of success in winning a nomination or election. A Roman Catholic may easily win a nomination in Boston or Providence, but he would almost certainly be unable to accomplish such a feat in most areas of the South or in other districts where Catholics constitute only a small fraction of the voting population. The state of Utah frequently sends Mormons to the Senate and House of Representatives, and the nationality influence in nominating candidates for Congress may be readily observed in our metropolitan Congressional districts where the great majority of people are of similar national origin. [3]

Should one party faction have dominant control in a congressional district or in a state, the nomination of a candidate for Congress may become a perfunctory matter. The fact that the length of service of the average congressman during the past twenty years seems to be slightly over three terms, suggests some tendency to renominate the incumbent congressman. [4] This trend also appears in the Senate, where renomination and reelection are quite the usual thing. The great majority of representatives and senators however, are regularly faced with opposition in the primary, and they dutifully spend a substantial amount of time mending their political fences in preparation for the primary ordeal.

Occasionally factional fights or other splits in the ranks of the party lead to spirited contests at the primary. In such cases a variety of shenanigans may be tried, some legal, some illegal. The ancient formula of the Hapsburgs—"divide and rule"—is often applied at the primary in the hope of winning the nomination by splitting the vote of the opposition candidate. This is well illustrated by the case of Senator Shipstead of Minnesota, whose contests for renominations were often made simpler by having two or three people file in the primary, all bearing Scandinavian

[3] It is interesting to note that a press poll taken of the Eightieth Congress in January, 1948, revealed that only seven states had congressional delegations composed solely of native-born representatives. Five of these states are located in the South, the other two being Vermont and Utah.

[4] The average senator in the Eightieth Congress had been in office 7.75 years while the average representative had been in office eight years and ten months. In the Senate the average age was fifty-seven, in the House fifty-two.

names such as Olson, Jensen, or Nelson.[5] Where persons are induced to file in a primary for the sake of splitting the vote and thereby increasing or decreasing a candidate's chance of nomination the strategy may work quite smoothly, but occasionally it backfires. A notable case illustrating the latter point centered on the bid of the late Senator George W. Norris of Nebraska for renomination two decades back. Anxious to defeat Senator Norris for the Republican nomination, the Republican National Committee persuaded a little known grocer named George W. Norris to file against him in the primary. The strategy here was not only to split the vote but to deliberately confuse the voter as to the identity of the man he was voting for.[6] The attempt failed, however, and subsequent Senate investigations proved that Senator Norris's opponent had been paid to enter the race.

REGULATING THE PRIMARY

The Federal Constitution, as we have noted, provides that "The times, places, and manner of holding elections for Senators and Representatives shall be prescribed in each state by the legislature thereof..." Yet Congress is not without power to regulate the conduct of Federal elections, for the part of the Constitution just quoted, Article I, Section 4, also declares that the Congress "may at any time by law make or alter such regulations, except as to the places of choosing Senators." Nowhere, however, does the Constitution mention nominative procedures such as primaries or conventions. In consequence, a controversy of long standing has existed over the power of Congress to regulate primaries.

In so far as elections are concerned, Congress has left many questions of election laws governing the choice of senators and representatives up to the individual state. State regulations on elections have, of course, been supplemented and reinforced from time to time by congressional statutes and as noted in the chapter on suffrage there have been many decisions recognizing Federal power over primaries.

Prescribing Primary Procedures

At the outset of our discussion on regulating the primary we observed that the states have a large responsibility for determining the procedures to be used in both primaries and election. Congress as we have seen, has sometimes reinforced state regulatory measures with Federal legislation, and indeed has attempted to reach beyond state regulations on some issues such as the one involving the right to vote in a congressional primary. By far the most primary and election procedures, however, are prescribed by the states themselves.

[5] See Malcolm Moos and E. W. Kenworthy: "Dr. Shipstead Come to Judgment." *Harper's* (1946), 193:21–7.

[6] See George W. Norris: *Fighting Liberal: The Autobiography of George W. Norris* (New York, 1938), chap. XXVIII.

These regulatory prescriptions cover a variety of subjects. Ordinarily they set the time for holding the primary, which in many states is in August and September where nominations are to be made for the general election in November. [7] State regulations also define political parties for purposes of determining a party's eligibility to be on the ballot in primary elections. The usual method of defining a political party for this purpose is to set a percentage of votes that it must have polled at the last general election. Thus in Maine for a party to be on the ballot, it must have polled 1 per cent of the total vote cast for governor at the last general election. In Alabama 20 per cent is required for a party to have a primary at public expense. [8] As it is obvious that a completely new party could never get on the ballot under such a definition, state laws regulating primaries do provide alternatives for nominating candidates. Often the rule is that if a "party" lacks a certain percent of the vote or a specified flat vote it may nominate by convention, petition, or some other means.

In addition to the items mentioned above, the states prescribe a vast number of regulations that seek to govern the primary down to the most minute detail. The form of the ballot is carefully regulated—primaries are no longer the private affairs they were when parties once provided their own ballots. If voting machines are to be used, the states prescribe how they shall be inspected. In many other areas of regulation—determining the rules governing poll judges, prohibiting any electioneering within a specified distance of the polls, setting the rules for marking and tabulating ballots, and even decreeing the suspension of the flow of liquor during the hours the polls are open, the states fill in the details with extensive statutory provisions. In its mature form today, the primary is actually conducted almost like an election, and if one runs over the statutory sections on primaries and elections—which are found side by side in most states—he will find them remarkably similar.

REGULATING ELECTIONS

Corrupt Practices Legislation

All of our forty-eight states have laws commonly referred to as "Corrupt Practices Acts." These laws usually apply to both primary and general elections, and although there is considerable variation among them, they generally attempt to prohibit such practices as bribery, stuffing ballot boxes, and any fraudulent practices designed to alter the results of an honest election. [9] In addition, corrupt practices acts limit the amount of expenditures which may be made in primary and election campaigns,

[7] Some states, however, hold their primaries much earlier. In California and Maine the primaries take place in June and in a few states they occur in March and April.

[8] For a thorough analysis of the legal status of political parties as defined by state statutory regulations, see Joseph R. Starr: "The Legal Status of American Political Parties." *American Political Science Review* (1940), 34:439–55, 685–99.

[9] A summary of state corrupt practices legislation may be found in a study prepared by Harry Best published as Senate Document No. 11, 75th Congress, 1st Session. A more recent work is a mimeographed document, *Corrupt Practices Legislation in the 48 States,* prepared by S. S. Minault and issued by the Council of State Governments.

they forbid contributions by some organizations such as corporations, and they sometimes provide that contributions and expenditures must be publicized. [10]

Federal corrupt practices legislation, began shortly after the close of the Civil War, and gradually expanded in scope to cover both primaries and elections where federal officers are to be chosen.[11] It is unlawful under federal law to solicit contributions from an employee under Federal civil service where such contributions are to be used for political purposes. Federal regulations also forbid corporations to make any political contributions toward the election of senators and representatives, or the election of a president or vice-president. In 1943 the same restrictions were applied to "labor organizations" by the Smith-Connally Act.

Evading Restrictions on Contributions

The actual enforcement of proscriptions forbidding contributions by either corporations or labor organizations has proved exceedingly difficult, and there are a number of ways by which these provisions may be circumvented. [12] In its advertising, for example, a corporation may urge that voters elect candidates who are favorably disposed toward certain governmental policies. The names of candidates for representatives or senators are not directly mentioned, of course, but under the guise of public education or advertising, corporations manage to do some effective missionary work for candidates who are sympathetic to their interests.

Another method by which corporations may indirectly help to elect representatives and senators is through their lobbying activities. Federal legislation forbidding corporations to subsidize candidates does not apply to funds spent for lobbying before Congress. Thus it is possible for part of the large sums that are spent for lobbying in behalf of corporations to trickle into channels where it will prove very beneficial to the election of certain favored candidates.

Contrary to popular impression lobbyists do not spend most of their time working their wiles on congressmen in Washington. Indeed their work may be carried on far afield—at the grass roots—where their efforts are most likely to show results and they often carry on their activities through organizations whose names seem only remotely connected with the real purpose of the lobby. Thus one finds such names on organizations as "People's Committee to Defend Life Insurance and Savings." Behind the facade of a title such as this, an impressive list of supporters may be found, including prominent industrialists, and business and professional men, both large and small. An organization of this kind usually operates unobtrusively but effectively through a skillful executive director. No

[10] The best analysis of the state legislation regulating the use of money in primaries and elections is in Louise Overacker's *Money in Elections*, (New York, 1932) chap. 12.

[11] See E. R. Sikes, *State and Federal Corrupt Practices Legislation* (Durham, 1928).

[12] For a discussion of the problems encountered in attempting to regulate campaign contributions see: V. O. Key: *Politics, Parties, and Pressure Groups* (2nd ed., New York, 1947), pp. 476–88.

elaborate headquarters are maintained, but the person in charge stays in close communication with various political leaders of both parties throughout the country. As their objective these organizations concentrate their fire on congressional elections and seek to lubricate the campaigns of candidates whose policies are in accord with their general aims. In mobilizing their efforts careful score cards are kept on the districts or states where acceptable candidates need help for re-election or where a decision has been taken to unhorse a representative or senator whose policies are not looked upon with favor.

Where no titled organization is employed, corporations may support the elective efforts of representatives or senators in other ways that are also effective. One device is to employ a legal retainer whose actual legal work in representing the corporation consumes but a small fraction of his time, leaving him ample opportunity to indulge in political activities. Steel companies, railroads, public utilities, milling industries, and many other businesses often find it convenient to retain a legal counselor whose chief sideline duty is not to furnish legal advice; whose real duty indeed is to do undercover work for the election of friendly state legislators and members of Congress. Persons who serve corporations in this capacity do not operate by placing corporation's contributions directly at the disposal of friendly candidates for Congress. Their resourcefulness in accomplishing the ends they seek includes a variety of techniques. They may help the candidate line up support by arranging a meeting of prominent people within the district or state, and draw upon their expense account to pay the cost of the meeting. On the other hand, by diligent effort, a corporation's political watchdog may secure voluntary contributions for his candidate from individuals living in the region who have some commercial ties with the corporation he represents, either as buyers or sellers. The upshot of all of these arrangements whereby corporations are able to give substantial indirect financial support to candidates for Congress may be reduced to two simple propositions: first, legislation which would effectively circumscribe these activities is exceedingly difficult, if not well nigh impossible to enforce; second, although the efforts expended for candidates in this fashion may not necessarily involve a direct outlay of money, the real measure of their worth is in the services rendered, and it is not an exaggeration to say that these efforts may be of crucial importance in winning or losing a campaign.

Restricting the Use of Labor Union Funds

The attempt to prohibit labor organizations from making any contribution to a campaign to elect a president, vice-president, senator, or representative offers the same difficulty of enforcement as the legislation which sought to restrict corporations. The real impetus to restrict labor organizations from making contributions to political campaign funds grew out of the 1936 campaign, when the United Mine Workers of America, along with several other labor organizations, contributed a fund of $770,000 to the

Democratic campaign of that year. The Smith-Connally Act of 1943 prohibited "labor organizations" from making contributions for the election of congressmen or the President, but one of the large loopholes in this Act was that the ban it placed on trade union contributions applied to elections and did not cover nominations. In consequence, during the campaign of 1944, the C.I.O. Political Action Committee spent close to a half-million dollars promoting the candidacies of its friends before the national Democratic convention held in July. Although the language of the Smith-Connally Act stated that "contributions" might not be made by unions to political committees or candidates, the unions considered this to be no bar against their making direct "expenditures" on the elections. By this ingenious reasoning they justified union activities in distributing literature, holding political meetings, and in short actively supporting the congressional candidates they deemed to be friends. The Smith-Connally Act expired on June 30, 1947, leaving the question of the right of labor organizations to make contributions to political campaigns still up in the air.

With a number of states passing laws to prohibit unions from contributing to political campaigns, and in the midst of a fairly strong demand that Congress do something by way of tightening regulations generally on unions, Congress passed the Taft-Hartley Act in 1947. An explosive part of the Taft-Hartley Act was Section 304, which prohibited unions from making contributions or expenditures in connection with a Federal election. Again the issue seemed to be one of semantics, the key word in the section being "expenditures." The inclusion of this word, according to union arguments, not only forbade making contributions but it actually prohibited making any expenditures whatsover. Under this interpretation union spokesmen argued that the mere hiring of a hall to discuss politics, buying radio time to broadcast political views, printing or circulating a newspaper with a political opinion, and circulating handbills, were all barred by the one word "expenditures."

Admittedly Section 304 was later considered ambiguous and something of a mistake by men of the Eightieth Congress who drafted this amendment to the Taft-Hartley Act, and the leaders of organized labor were not slow in seizing upon this weakness. The best interests of the union may not always be served by relying upon political parties, politicians or party committees, argued the union philosophizers. It is therefore essential, they insisted, that union organizations be allowed to spend money to propagate their own political views in newspapers, through broadcasts, or other media of public communication, and any legislation which interferes with this right abridges the freedom of speech and press guarantees of the United States Constitution.

Moving for a quick test on the constitutionality of Section 304 of the Taft-Hartley Act, Philip Murray, President of the Congress of Industrial Organizations, used union money to publish his support of a political candidate in *The CIO News* at a special congressional election in Baltimore in June, 1947. Following this incident in which the C.I.O.-endorsed candidate won the election, the Department of Justice obtained a grand jury indictment against Mr. Murray and the C.I.O. The specific charge was illegal campaigning in a congressional by-election. Any doubt over the intention of the government to continue prosecuting violations of Section 304 was confirmed early in 1948 when an American Federation of Labor local in Connecticut was also indicted for buying radio time and advertising space in a newspaper to campaign against the presidential candidacy of Senator Robert A. Taft.

Before the Taft-Hartley Act had been on the statute books a year, Section 304 was declared unconstitutional in a decision rendered by a Federal District Court on March 15, 1948. The ruling of the Federal District Court throwing out the indictment against Philip Murray and the Congress of Industrial Organizations declared that the "plain terms" of the law deprived unions and their members of the constitutional right of free speech, freedom of the press, and assembly. Thus the decision opened the way for labor unions to finance their own campaigns during presidential and congressional election years with union money. The decision did not, however, rule on the question of union "contributions" to a political party or to a committee conducting a political campaign. Furthermore although Section 304 was embodied in a statute designed to deal exclusively with labor-management problems, it actually amends an old law —the Corrupt Practices Act—originally passed in 1907. As Section 304 of the Taft-Hartley Act forbade banks, corporations, and unions alike to make either contributions or expenditures in any Federal election, the court decision left the question of political expenditures by corporations, banks, or unions in a confused state. After a speedy appeal to the Supreme Court, the result of the lower court decision dismissing the suit against Philip Murray and the C.I.O. was affirmed in June, 1948. Like the lower court ruling, the Supreme Court did not pass on the larger question: Can labor unions contribute funds directly to a political campaign? Thus Congress must still act to clear up the dilemma which the provision has created. The weight of public opinion appeared to be behind the judgment against Section 304, but the question of the right of a union to subsidize directly political parties in a campaign is still far from settled and it promises to be a problem of continuing importance in American politics.

Expenditure Ceilings in Congressional Campaigns

Under the Federal Corrupt Practices Act of 1925, unless the law of the individual state provides for a lower figure, the expenditures for a candidate for senator is limited to $10,000 and for representatives to $2,500. To make the law more equitable for candidates living in populous states, however, a person running for senator or representative may elect to take advantage of an alternative rule. The latter provision permits him to spend three cents per vote cast for all candidates for the office which the candidate seeks at the last general election, but the total amount, if the alternative rule is used, may not exceed $25,000 for a senatorial candidate or $5,000 for a person seeking election to the House. [13]

Under the first Hatch Act, candidates for Federal elective office were forbidden to accept contributions from relief workers. The second Hatch Act, passed in 1940, sought to supplement state laws prohibiting the assessment of state and local employees for political purposes. The latter measure prohibits any assessment of state or local employees who are paid either completely or partly out of Federal funds. It also limits the contributions or loans that any individual may make for the nomination or election of Federal officers to $5,000 in any one year for any one committee.

Difficulties in Enforcing Expenditure Limitations

Like the restrictions prohibiting campaign contributions by corporations and labor unions, the limitations placed upon expenditures of candidates for senator or representative are not nearly as meaningful as they appear on the statute books. Expenditures which the candidate makes for "necessary personal, traveling or subsistence expenses or for stationery, postage, writing or printing (other than for use on billboards or in newspapers), for distributing letters, circulars or posters, or for telegraph or telephone service," and several other items are exempted from the limitation. Conceivably a candidate might spend a very large sum on postage or on circulating various campaign propaganda. Moreover it is exceedingly difficult to obtain an accurate check on the sum spent by friends of the candidate in promoting his nomination and election. It is quite apparent, for example, that the services rendered by various lobby groups and pressure groups have an important bearing on the outcome of a nomination or election. Yet one would indeed need psychic powers to see behind the well-screened activities of such groups and accurately measure the monetary worth of their contribution to a campaign. The amounts which candidates claim to have spent, therefore, may often be quite deceptive.

Each senator and representative is required to file an itemized statement of his campaign expenditures with the clerk of the Senate or House following his election. If the expenditures of a senator or representative appear to have exceeded the maximum limit allowed, he may be prosecuted under either Federal or state law or both. As final judge of the qualifications of its members, of course, the Senate or House may simply refuse to seat any person who appears to have violated Federal or state laws limiting expenditures. [14] It is not often, however, that senators or

[13] Actually the amount spent on such campaigns often runs considerably higher than the maximum permitted by law. See for example Richard L. Neuberger: "It Costs too Much to Run." *New York Times Magazine*, April 11, 1948. Mr. Neuberger reports that the minimum cost for seeking the post of United States Senator in Oregon would be at least $40,000.

[14] Vincent M. Barnett, Jr., concludes that partisanship is the exception rather than the rule in deciding contested congressional elections. Out of sixty former contested elections considered by Congress, he found that in thirty-eight cases, the person affiliated with the minority party was seated. "Contested Congressional Elections in Recent Years." *Political Science Quarterly* (1939), 54:187–215.

representatives are denied seats for exceeding the maximum expenditures allowed in a political campaign, nor are congressmen often prosecuted for this offense. At the conclusion of every election, a certain number of charges are bandied back and forth, but after a brief flurry the accusations and denials usually quiet down and nothing further is heard of them. Perhaps, as some writers have suggested, many charges are prematurely dropped because of the popular feeling that the American electorate likes a good loser. Hence a losing candidate is disinclined to injure his chances at a succeeding election by appearing to be a bear with a sore head. But in larger measure, the reason why such charges are usually dropped is because they are very difficult to prove and contesting an election is likely to develop into a costly venture.

CONGRESSIONAL CAMPAIGN COMMITTEES

Although representatives and senators fight out electoral battles in their respective constituencies and states, some effort is made to tie these individual contests to the campaign organization that operates at the national level. Each of the major parties has its own congressional and senatorial committees whose primary concern is to help elect party members to the House or Senate. The congressional and senatorial committees maintain permanent organizations and they keep a careful watch on the areas where they believe the party is in danger of losing a seat or has a close chance of gaining a seat. Thus, in examining the prospects of maintaining Republican control in the Senate in the 1948 general election, Senator Owen Brewster of Maine gave a pessimistic report to his colleagues on the Senatorial Campaign Committee. Of the sixteen Republican senators who were up for re-election that year, only six were classified as definitely safe, three more as probably so, three as fairly uncertain, and four were reported to be in grave danger of defeat. In more practical terms, Senator Brewster's analysis meant that the defeat of three of the sixteen Republicans up for re-elections would bring out an even division between Republicans and Democrats in the Eighty-first Congress, and the defeat of four would give the Democratic Party a clear majority and the opportunity to organize the Senate. [15] Each party, therefore, has an important stake in keeping an overall perspective on congressional elections, and the House and Senate perform this function through their Congressional Campaign Committees.

Of the two committees the senatorial one is smaller, usually having a membership of about a half-a-dozen senators. The congressional committee of both parties is larger—the Republican party attempting to have one member from each state on the committee, or some other representative in states where there is no Republican in the congressional delegation. Congressional committees are most active, of course, during general

[15] Actually Senator Brewster's premonitions proved unusually accurate. The Republicans lost nine seats.

election years, and for financing their work they rely largely upon either the Democratic or Republican National Committee.

CONGRESSIONAL ELECTIONS AND POLITICAL TRENDS

Congressional elections as a barometer of political trends have long been the subject of a lively interest in American politics. Among certain phenomena in congressional elections it has been carefully observed that in the mid-term congressional elections the party out of power almost invariably gains seats in Congress. The notable exception in modern political history where this failed to happen was in 1934, when the Democratic majority in Congress was actually increased over what it had been following the congressional elections of 1932. It is also possible to discern certain political behavior patterns in congressional elections which suggest that a complete cycle occurs about every dozen years, that is, when a party overturn occurs it normally takes from twelve to fourteen years for the party that has been deposed to regain control of Congress. Such cycles, to be sure, do not conform to any immutable law; nonetheless, historical evidence indicates a fairly rhythmic swing of the pendulum of public opinion insofar as congressional elections are concerned. [16] Careful studies of congressional elections suggest that they do reveal portents of a major national political shift just as public opinion polls may indicate a political change-over. These trends reveal themselves only gradually, however, and they must be closely and consistently observed to gain any insight into long range shifts. Finally although there is no doubt that general political trends are reflected in the congressional elections, it is also true that both congressional and presidential election trends run parallel. The real difficulty in studying such trends, of course, lies in projecting the curve and this problem along with the influence of presidential campaigns on congressional elections will be discussed in a later chapter.

THE PAROCHIAL CHARACTER OF CONGRESSIONAL
ELECTIONS

In the mid-term congressional elections particularly, the results are strongly affected by local factors. [17] There is a much smaller turnout of voters at this time than in a presidential election year, and the mid-term congressional elections illustrate very effectively the independence of state and local political leaders on congressional elections even where they are disobeying the president's will in party affairs. State and local leaders have not been an uneven match, as has often been supposed, when they have tussled with presidential leadership on matters of congressional

[16] See V. O. Key: "If the Election Follows the Pattern." *New York Times Magazine*, October 20, 1946.
[17] See Louis Bean: *How to Predict Elections* (New York, 1948), pp. 31–2.

nominations and elections. Whenever a president has attempted to oppose the congressional choice of state and local leaders of his party in a mid-term election, he has usually met with disaster. President Taft, in 1910, tried to spearhead a drive aimed at purging the progressive members of the Republican party who were serving in Congress. This project was a miserable failure. In 1938, when President Roosevelt went ahead with his memorable "purge" over the protests of his political adviser, James A. Farley, he also found it impossible to prevail against the concerted efforts of state and local leaders. Mr. Roosevelt sought to defeat Millard Tydings of Maryland, "Cotton Ed" Smith of South Carolina, Walter F. George of Georgia, and Guy M. Gillette of Iowa. Yet despite the fact that Mr. Roosevelt entered several of the states where these men were campaigning and spoke against them, and notwithstanding vigorous efforts to mobilize the voting power of Federal office holders against the candidates on the purge list, all were re-elected. [18] National leadership, therefore, despite its magnetic qualities has been forced to bow to the authority of state and local organizations in many cases where it has opposed the wishes of the local political organization on the choice of a party candidate.

Why are local, congressional, and senatorial candidates able to buck and prevail against a national leader? The explanation is to be found in a variety of reasons. A partial answer to this question is patronage. On Federal appointments, congressmen under a longstanding tradition enjoy the prerogative of flushing names for appointment to Federal office. Thus the bonds between a congressman and the appointee are usually very strong in any ensuing elective showdown. The tendency of the patronage factor to aid the sitting congressman against any purge attempt by a national leader also manifests itself in another manner. A congressman, it will be recalled, does not simply emerge from nowhere when he becomes a candidate for the House or Senate; more often than not he served his apprenticeship in a local or state public office, where he also had an opportunity to bestow patronage favors. Should a congressman be singled out for attack by a national political leader, the cumulative effects which result from his dispensation of patronage, both at the Federal and the state level, usually stand him in good stead. The political power of the patronage group which a congressman builds gradually multiplies in strength, and the national leader who seeks to marshal support to fight such a combination usually runs up against a stone wall.

Added to the patronage factor, the personal errands which a congressman performs for his constituents are also extremely important in rallying support when a national leader is after his scalp. Like patronage, the good will created because of personal favors tends to pyramid. Ap-

[18] See J. B. Shannon: "Presidential Politics in the South." *Journal of Politics* (1939), 1:295. "It is evident, therefore," writes Professor Shannon, "that a potent if not decisive factor in the primaries was the control of the local party organizations. A sitting senator, especially if he has held office for a long number of years, is well nigh invincible and not even a person as powerful and popular as Franklin Roosevelt can unseat him."

pointments to West Point or Annapolis, helping to straighten out pension allowances, looking after claims against the government, performing a host of other miscellaneous favors, tend to fortify a congressman's position against all aggressors in an election, and national leaders are no exceptions. Finally, a president who seeks to unseat a congressman must reckon with a parochial tendency in American politics which is not easily explained. Whatever it may be called, provincialism, local pride, or simply a resentment against an outside or centralized influence which seeks to dictate the choice to be made at a local election, there is a firmly grounded tradition against it in the orbit of American politics. In 1938 one of the leading newspapers in America, The *Baltimore Sun,* initially planned to give its editorial support to Davy Lewis against the incumbent, Senator Millard Tydings, but when Franklin Roosevelt announced that Senator Tydings was to be purged and issued a statement urging Marylanders to bring about his defeat, the *Sun* backed Tydings. Thus a fissure between the president and congressional candidates of his party over questions of policy has seldom favored a purge at the polls.

NOMINATIONS—THEIR INFLUENCE ON PARTY LEADERSHIP AND PARTY GOVERNMENT

Fundamentally the nominating process is the most important interstitial step to party government. By party government, of course, we mean the control of the government's policies by one party or the other—an acceptance of the principle, in other words, that to have democratic government in a large and complex society political parties are necessary and it is indeed their function to govern. How well political parties do succeed in controlling the government and the forces which mollify strong party government we shall see in the chapters dealing with the presidency and Congress. But here we need first to examine the whole question of national party leadership as it is affected by party nominations. It may be divided into two parts: the influence of congressional nominations and the influence of national party nominations.

In the matter of congressional nominations the extreme localization of political power is very marked. The decision as to who the candidate for the House or Senate will be rests largely with local political authorities. There is no comparable arrangement in the United States to the system found in Great Britain, for example, where a candidate for Parliament must be approved by the national party organization before he can stand for election in a local constituency. The lack of national party control over congressional nominations is well illustrated in the United States by the Republican nominee for Congress in Maryland's Fourth Congressional District in 1948. The man who won the G.O.P. nomination had run for Congress as a Democrat only two years before. Unlike the British we do not have any means of disciplining nominees beforehand by having them passed upon by a body representing the national party organization. Thus the nominees have a sort of grass roots independence and they are not beholden to the national party organization or national party leadership for their election.

Another factor that contributes to our decentralized system of making congressional nominations is the absence of any national platform or of any generally unified party campaigning in the mid-term elections. There is no party platform put forth in congressional mid-term elections nor is there even a leader in the case of the party out of power who can inject some cohesiveness into the campaigns on party policies. Without a national party program the tendency is for each congressional candidate to interpret the party program in terms of his own thinking or in terms of his own constituency. This results in radically different kinds of campaigns among candidates of the same party. In the sure districts or so-called "safe" districts a congressional candidate can conduct his campaign on an entirely different basis from the one he could in a close district. In order to win in a close district it may be necessary for a congressional candidate to take a stand on issues which does not square with the position of candidates in the same party running in sure districts. Republicans running in congressional districts with a heavy labor vote often find it necessary to temporize on the position of their party on some issues if they are to be elected, just as Democrats are compelled to do the same thing when they are not in a sure district. The upshot of all this temporizing and the lack of national party control over congressional nominations is that the party nominees who are subsequently elected to Congress are often party "bedouins." They do not respond well to the program laid down by the national leadership of the party and except for presidential threats to withhold patronage there are few ways of compelling them to go along on party measures.

As national leader of the party the president may resort to expedients other than refusing to honor patronage requests to secure the compliance of a congressman. He may even threaten to work against the congressman's renomination—a technique that often has unhappy results for the president as we have noted. But the fact remains that the highly localized character of our nominating system has a frustrating effect on national party leadership. Instead of producing cohesion at the national level, the nominating system tends to have a divisive effect by reflecting sectional or factional differences rather than national party solidarity. If we seek stronger party leadership at the national level, it is obvious that the powerful influence of the local party organization over nominations will have to yield to a greater degree of national party control. That there are some portents which suggest a change in this direction is revealed by the gradual erosion and breakdown of sectional influence—the rally points that have so often fragmentized a united party front.[19] As yet, however, the machinery for exerting greater national party control over congres-

[19] See V. O. Key: *Politics, Parties, and Pressure Groups*, pp. 167–75.

sional nominations is virtually non-existent and certainly tradition and practice have combined to assert the supremacy of local rather than national control.

At the national level the system employed for nominating the party's presidential candidate is that remarkable device, the national convention. [20] A description of how this institution operates must await a later chapter, but a word should be said here about the relation of the presidential nominating system to national party leadership. In selecting the man of the hour, presidential nominating conventions must also temporize in order to satisfy all factions within the party. There is no escalator of service to the national party organization which is adjudged a qualification for the presidential nomination. A person quite unknown in party circles such as Wendell Willkie may carry off the party's highest honor by a fortuitous combination of circumstances. The party nomination for the presidency does not go to the person who has most faithfully served its national interest. Indeed no way has yet developed by which a person may ascend in the party hierarchy until he is recognized as the titular leader of the party other than to actually receive the presidential nomination. Under such conditions of uncertainty, the presidential nominating system, like that for congressional nominations, is not exactly conducive to a continuous flow of strong party leadership. The nominating method which produces the president is obviously quite different from the system which selects the party's nominees for Congress. Yet both the party's presidential and congressional nominees are expected to supply the necessary teamwork, if elected, to give the country stable and positive leadership in government.

While the emergence of strong party leadership is not consistently encouraged by the flabby arrangements of party organization at the national level in the United States, the presidential convention does, of course, sometimes provide a forceful party leader. Moreover such a leader by custom is given a free hand to mold party policies as he desires during a campaign. But when it comes to working with his party's nominees who reach Congress the president may find himself working at cross-purposes with his own party members in Congress. At the root of this difficulty is the fact that the nominating systems that supply congressmen and presidents are not complementary—they are not so related that they operate to produce strong party government at the national level. To overcome this problem two changes are probably necessary. One is that the method of nominating presidential candidates should be amended in such a way as to secure nominees who clearly have established themselves as national party leaders. The second, and more important, is to develop the congressional nominating system to the point where the influence of the

[20] For a lucid and provocative discussion of the relation of the presidential nominating system to national party leadership, see E. E. Schattschneider: *The Struggle for Party Government* (College Park, Md., 1948), pp. 27–43.

national party leader (the president) over these nominations is commensurate with his broad responsibility for party leadership. Clearly the obstacles to such a change are formidable, and it is obvious that local control over congressional nominations will be surrendered grudgingly and quite likely never as completely as in other countries.

SUMMARY

Biographical data about members of Congress indicate that the vast majority have had prior service in less important political offices. Besides such service, a candidate's race, religion, national extraction, and the degree of organized support he commands are often important factors in determining whether he will be nominated and elected.

The regulation of primary and general elections has been left chiefly to the states, although national law governs some aspects of general elections in which congressmen are chosen, notably the financial aspects. Legal prescriptions on campaign contributions and expenditures have been relatively ineffective. Evasion of such limitations on expenditures is possible because the laws do not in general restrict the spending a candidate's friends may do in his behalf nor do they reach spending that indirectly promotes his candidacy.

The outcome of congressional elections is likely to be determined by a combination of general trends and purely local considerations. The difficulty of separating the two makes prediction of national trends from any given congressional election (particularly an off-year election) hazardous. The unsuccessful purge of recalcitrant Democratic congressmen by President Roosevelt in 1938 underlines the parochial character of contests for congressional seats.

Strong national party leadership is hard to maintain given the fact that service to the party often counts for little in the selection of candidates for national office. In order to make possible such leadership, nominating methods that will provide a national party leader as the presidential nominee and that will enable the national party leadership to influence congressional nominations are needed.

CHAPTER XIII

PRESIDENTIAL NOMINATIONS

THE national convention as a political device for nominating presidents is well over one hundred years old. It grew out of the dissatisfaction with the legislative caucus or "king caucus," as we noted in our chapter on party nominations, and it made its first appearance in 1831. In that year the first national convention was held in Baltimore by the anti-Masonic party. The following year the national convention made its baptismal appearance in the Democratic party when it was used to nominate Andrew Jackson for his second term. Since that time the national convention has not only become the standard device of major political parties for nominating presidents and vice-presidents, but it has also been taken over by minor parties as well.

In seeking a reason for the development of this unique institution it is easy to understand why the behind-the-stage conniving in the days when presidents were nominated by legislative caucus led to popular demand that the president be nominated more openly and that there should be wider participation in this selection. The boisterous political by-product of our constitutional system which has emerged has, of course, been much criticized and ridiculed. One astute foreign observer of American government, M. Ostrogorski, made the comment at the turn of the century that our national conventions were "a colossal travesty of popular institutions." That our national political conventions do have the atmosphere of a carnival or sideshow is hardly disputable. But considering the peculiarities of the American constitutional system with its independent chief executive who does not emerge from the legislature as he would under a cabinet system, the basic reason for the appearance of the institution becomes more understandable. "We may call it," writes Lord Bryce, "an effort of nature to fill the void left in America by the absence of the European or cabinet system, under which an executive is called into being out of the legislature by a majority of the legislature." [1] Stripped of its turbulent overtones then, the national convention has indeed a serious function. That it has many imperfections, both from the standpoint of providing a truly democratic means of nominating a president and from the fact that it has permitted its serious purpose to be engulfed by the most nonsensical kind of folderol is to be regretted. Yet neither of these serious indictments against the national convention detract from the fact that it is a very important political arm of American government, and while all would agree that the convention system leaves much to be desired, its record has been far from one of complete reproach.

CONVENTION PRELIMINARIES AND PRE-CONVENTION CAMPAIGNS

The preliminary arrangements followed by both our major political parties in laying the ground work for presidential conventions is very much the same. [2] In December of the year preceding a presidential election the national committee meets to lay plans for the national conventions to be held the following summer. This committee includes a national committeeman and committeewoman for each state and the Republicans sometimes add the state chairman. The selection of national committeemen and national committeewomen depends upon the laws or customs among the individual states. In some states they are elected at a party primary, in others they may be elected at a state convention, while occasionally they are simply chosen by a caucus of a state's delegates who have been selected to attend the national convention.

The national committee is presided over by a chairman who, in cases where the political party controls the Federal government, is the personal choice of the president. When a political party is out of power, the national chairman may be the choice of the last presidential nominee of the party who is, of course, the titular head of the party until a new presidential nominee is chosen. In the latter case, however, the chairman selected by an unsuccessful presidential nominee is often displaced after a losing campaign and he faces a hard fight to hold his post such as Hugh Scott, Jr., Chairman of the Republican National Committee encountered after Dewey's second defeat for the presidency.

The chief business on the agenda of the national committee at the December meeting prior to a national convention is the selection of the city where the convention is to be held. In accordance with the long

---

[1] James Bryce: *The American Commonwealth* (3rd ed., New York, 1895), Vol. II, p. 221.

[2] For detailed accounts of the presidential nominating system see V. O. Key: *Politics, Parties, and Pressure Groups* (2nd ed., New York, 1947), chap. XIII; Howard R. Penniman: *Sait's American Parties and Elections* (4th ed., New York, 1948), chaps. XIX–XXII, and Peter H. Odegard and E. Allen Helms: *American Politics* (New York, 1947), chap. XVI.

established custom, rivalry is often keen among cities to secure one or both of the major national conventions. As each party sends a little over a thousand delegates with an equal number of alternates and national conventions are known to attract from fifty to a hundred thousand interested spectators from other cities, there is a feeling among many city promotional organizations that a political convention is a good business investment for any metropolitan center. However well founded this theory may be—for there is reason to believe that while a convention stimulates business for hotel proprietors and restaurateurs, it does not help the general prosperity of the community—several cities usually send representatives to lure national political conventions to their communities. The competitive nature of this procedure is illustrated by the fact that it is customary for a city to offer some financial bait in order to attract a national political convention. In 1948, for example, the city of Philadelphia secured both the Republican and Democratic national conventions by offering to pay $250,000 to each party's national committee to help the respective parties pay their expenses. Where does this money come from that cities put up to attract conventions? For the most part, it comes from trade associations, businessmen, and civic promotional organizations who have raised this money for the specific purpose of bringing in conventions to the city.

In reaching a decision on a convention city, the national committee is sometimes influenced by other factors than the amount of money a city is prepared to give. Occasionally, the personal preferences or aversions of contenders for the presidential nomination influence the choice. A leading contender for the nomination might well be anxious to avoid a city that he regarded as being located in a territory hostile or unfavorable to his candidacy. Also, in times of great emergency such as during World War II, common sense and geography dictated that both major political parties hold their conventions in Chicago because of its central location. Since the Civil War, the Democratic party has definitely shown a more nomadic tendency than the Republican party. Twelve of the twenty-four Republican conventions have been held in Chicago, while the Democrats have held their national conclave in Chicago only seven times. With the four exceptions—1892, 1896, 1952, and 1956—the Democrats have never met twice successively in the same city. The more migratory tendency of the Democratic party in holding national conventions is also illustrated by the fact that the Democratic party has gone as far South as Houston, Texas and as far West as San Francisco, California.

The Keynoter

Another important preliminary in arranging for a national convention is the selection of a keynoter. The choice of the person to deliver the keynote address is made by the committee on arrangements for the national convention which is a subcommittee of the national committee. There are two important considerations in making this selection. First, the arrangements committee is anxious to select a person whose oratorical talents are admirably suited to whip up the enthusiasm of the national convention delegates, for, after all, this is one of the primary functions of the keynote address. Second, in settling upon a keynoter, the arrangements committee must exercise some care to choose a person who will not be offensive to any of the leading presidential contenders. A person who is regarded as too friendly to a particular presidential candidate for the nomination might be ruled out on this ground alone, despite his oratorical gifts and pre-eminence among the party's leaders. The person making the keynote address usually serves as the temporary chairman of the national convention. The post is an honor highly coveted in American politics and the national committee finds some difficulty in making a selection for this position. In 1956 the Republican committee chose as temporary chairman and thus the keynote speaker Governor Arthur B. Langlie of Washington. The committee was no doubt motivated in its selection by Governor Langlie's known ability to argue cogently the claims of an incumbent administration for another term at the same time that it would enhance his prestige in his difficult campaign for a seat in the United States Senate. On the other hand the Democrats chose as their temporary chairman Governor Frank Clement of Tennessee, a fiery political evangelist expected to stir the party to extraordinary exertions to recapture the presidency.

The Call

Following the December meeting of the national committees of both major parties, the next important event in the sequence leading up to the national convention is the issuance of the call by the chairman of the national committee. Ordinarily this step takes place in March of the convention year. At this time the national committee chairman sends a letter to each of the three thousand odd county chairmen scattered throughout the United States officially notifying them of the date that the national convention is to convene and giving certain other information such as the apportionment of delegates and the rules to be followed in determining the number of delegates to which the state is entitled. At this point the very practical task of selecting delegates to attend the national convention begins. The methods of accomplishing this end, as we shall see, vary considerably from state to state and not all of them by any means are chosen at the same time. Delegates to the national convention are chosen in New Hampshire as early as March 13, while some states such as New Jersey and South Dakota do not formally choose their delegates until June 5 which in the case of the Republican convention was but a scant three weeks before the national meeting used to convene. The mechanics of selecting delegates we may take up shortly, but before turning to a description of this procedure a few words are in order about the pre-convention campaigns which precede our national conventions as everyone knows, not only by months but indeed sometimes by years.

PRE-CONVENTION CAMPAIGNS

It is sometimes said of American politics that a presidential campaign begins the day after election, which occurs on the first Tuesday after the first Monday in November. This generalization is, of course, a bit broad. Nonetheless it is true that men who aspire to the presidential office frequently get their pre-convention campaigns under way for the nomination far in advance of the actual convention year. [3] Some men set their course for the presidency early in life and manage to follow it with minor deviations until they have won the presidential nomination of one or the other of our major parties and eventually reach the presidential office. From contemporary accounts, it would appear that Franklin Roosevelt early determined to follow such a course of action and kept on his course from the time he first entered the New York State Assembly. It also seems generally agreed that Thomas Dewey acquired the presidential virus at an early age and laid his plans accordingly, and that with the aid of friends and skillful organizers won a second nomination after losing a presidential election, a feat which heretofore had never been accomplished in the history of the party. In many cases those who aspire for the top prize in American politics—the presidency—are dropped out of politics entirely or are shunted off on to a spur track that does not lead to the White House. But those who move up into the strata of American politics where they can be considered as contenders for presidential nominations, one may ordinarily assume, have laid careful plans for this ascendency, and when they have reached the level where there is even faint mention of their names as presidential timber, the major task then is to ripen "possibilities" into presidential nominees.

"Availability"

In the evolution of presidential nominees certain natural and traditional factors operate to enhance or retard one's candidacy. It is, for example, a distinct advantage to hail from New York if you are seeking the presidential nomination. Men who have served as chief executive of New York have been major party candidates for president in fourteen of the twenty-three elections since the Civil War.[4] Moreover as only four men have been elected since the Civil War without carrying the Empire State in a presidential election it is obvious that party leaders anxious to have a winning nominee are not unmindful of the strength of a candidate who has demonstrated that he can be elected governer of New York. Another

[3] For accounts of pre-convention campaigns see James A. Farley: *Behind the Ballots* (New York, 1938); William A. White: *A Puritan in Babylon, The Story of Calvin Coolidge* (New York, 1938); H. L. Mencken, *Making a President* (New York, 1932); and Arthur Link: *Woodrow Wilson: Road to the White House* (Princeton, 1947), Vol. I.
[4] See Warren Moscow: *Politics in the Empire State* (New York, 1948).

state that has furnished an abundance of presidential nominees is Ohio. Since the Civil War, Ohio has contributed nine presidential nominees, and in combination Ohio and New York have contributed twenty-five out of forty-two presidential nominees since the Civil War.

Among "availability" factors other than residence there are few that are easily definable or that one should place much stock in. It seems generally agreed at the present time that a man aspiring to a presidential nomination ought to be a Protestant. Helpful, but not necessarily a "must" for those seeking a presidential nomination is some experience in holding public office. There are exceptions on this point, to be sure, such as Herbert Hoover in 1928, Wendell Willkie in 1940, and Dwight D. Eisenhower in 1952, all of whom captured the Republican presidential nomination without ever having held an elective public office. There has been no other presidential nominee since the turn of the century who has not held some public elective office before his nomination.

Next to residence perhaps the most important element in determining "availability" for the presidential nomination is simply good luck. Fortune, the master political strategist of them all, Machiavelli, once remarked, determines the course of half our lives while the other half we may guide ourselves. Certainly in politics benevolent fortune is a tremendous factor and nowhere is this more apparent than in presidential politics. Had Al Smith, for example, made his real bid for the Democratic presidential nomination in 1932 rather than 1928, what might have been the result? Similarly the fortuitous combination of circumstances in 1940 combined to give amateur Wendell Willkie the Republican presidential nomination over a field of experienced contenders. One of the ingredients of fortune in politics is proper timing which like fortune may also be guided at times yet often operates completely independently of man's judgment. Thus a person coming along at the right moment may sweep the field in winning a presidential nomination while if he had appeared four years earlier or four years later the odds against his chances might have been overwhelming.

Pre-Convention Campaign Strategy

The fact that a man possesses the qualifications which make him available does not provide enough impetus to put him in the running for the presidential nomination. The making of a serious presidential contender requires intensive organization and consummate skill. To build up a candidate and bring him into the home stretch as convention time approaches with enough strength to capture the presidential nomination is an extraordinary operation. For two years prior to the 1932 Democratic convention James A. Farley travelled over 30,000 miles cementing friendships and lining up delegates for Franklin Roosevelt. In a somewhat new version of pre-convention techniques, Harold E. Stassen travelled over 300,000 miles seeking support for himself before the Republican convention of 1948. Much of Mr. Stassen's travel was done in a chartered DC-3 plane equipped with a mimeograph machine for press releases and other accoutrements needed for campaign headquarters, but his traveling equipment also included a large Greyhound bus used to transport himself and his entourage to various presidential primaries held in such states as Wisconsin, Ohio, and Nebraska.

Campaigning to win the delegates chosen by state primaries requires an exhausting expenditure of energy. As they skipped from state to state, Democratic aspirants Stevenson and Kefauver in 1956 or Dewey and Stassen in 1948 sometimes made a dozen or so speeches a day always at heavy expense.[5] Mr. Stassen's friends were reported to have spent over a million dollars in his unsuccessful bid for the nomination. In the Oregon primary alone, an advertising concern estimated the amount of money expended for radio time and other expenses for publicity to be around $100,000 for each of the two candidates (Dewey and Stassen).

Another sample of the amount of money that it takes to conduct a pre-convention campaign is afforded by the Ohio primary in 1948. When Stassen decided to enter the primary in the spring of 1948, Senator Taft who, up to that time, had been the favorite son of Ohio and assured of all of its delegates was forced to leave his Washington duties as majority leader of the Senate to return to his home state to campaign. At the time Mr. Taft commented that the cost of merely printing sample ballots to instruct voters how to vote for Taft delegates cost more than $15,000. [6] This sum was, of course, but a fractional part of the total amount that was spent in the Ohio primary.

Where does this money come from that is sometimes used so lavishly in pre-convention campaigns? The preponderate amount of these contributions comes from a relatively few large contributors. There is no Federal legislation limiting the amount that a candidate may spend during a pre-convention campaign. The total amounts, therefore, may run unusually high and they are exceedingly difficult to estimate with any accuracy. Occasionally some candidates attempt to solicit small contributions from a large number of people. The amount raised through small contributions, however, is usually quite limited. Again in the 1948 pre-convention campaign, the Stassen organization set a ceiling of $1,000 on individual contributions. According to the reports of the Stassen organization the four hundred contributors who gave the largest amounts, ranging from $100 to $1,000, accounted for over $100,000. On the other hand, from two thousand smaller contributors who gave from $1.00 to $100, the total amount raised was around $30,000. [7] It seems highly probable that some contributors gave more than $1,000 although there is no way of actually checking this information. Nonetheless the experience of the candidates competing for

[5] See the *Chicago Daily News*, April 16, 1948, and Alden Hatch: "The Men Around Dewey," *Harper's* (1948), 197:40–1.

[6] See the *New York Times*, May 1, 1948.

[7] See *Minneapolis Star Journal*, November 14, 1947.

the nomination in the 1948 pre-convention campaign as well as the experiences of candidates in other years demonstrate that small contributions provide but a minor part of the total campaign fund.

Political Tactics in Pre-Convention Campaigns

The grooming of a contender for the presidential nomination may be handled in a variety of ways but there are certain general precepts that ordinarily must be followed in a successful pre-convention campaign. It is important that local, county, and state political leaders be cultivated and that they be properly impressed with the candidate's qualifications not only as an able leader but as a person who has what it takes to win a general election. Above all else the local leaders want a winner whom they can look to for patronage and they are sometimes disposed to overlook qualities in a candidate which they deem undesirable if they are satisfied that he is the best bet to capture an election. The strategy of cultivation also requires that a candidate's organizers and friends not overlook the possibility of acquiring second choice votes if local leaders have already decided upon some other leader as their first choice for the presidential nomination. [8] Political currents often change abruptly, particularly in the course of events leading up to a presidential nominating convention. Leading candidates often drop out or are forced out of the race and the tide of events often demands a quick shift of allegiance from one candidate to another. Thus second-choice votes patiently acquired early in the pre-convention campaign often pay heavy dividends at critical moments in the convention balloting.

During the pre-convention stage, it is customary for candidates seeking the presidential nomination to make a number of speeches at well chosen sites. Some of these speeches are made on anniversary dates commemorating patron saints of the party. Thus in the Democratic party a battery of oratorical talent is usually heard on the birth date of Andrew Jackson at various Jackson Day dinners scattered throughout the nation. In the Republican party Lincoln's birthday provides the corresponding opportunity for G.O.P. presidential aspirants to demonstrate their talents. In so far as other speeches are concerned the practice varies both as to number and content. In 1944 Thomas E. Dewey limited himself to a few speeches, insisting that his main function was to serve as the chief executive of New York. He also moved with considerable caution on the stump when referring to many of the more controversial issues of the day. In the same year, however, Wendell Willkie made several exhausting speaking tours to corral the presidential nomination and took a definite stand on most of the issues. Similarly, in 1948, Mr. Dewey again made few public speeches prior to the convention of that year and carefully avoided making any sharp commitments on major political and economic issues until the last stages of the pre-convention campaign, after the press and some of his political opponents had been needling him for more than a year to make

[8] James A. Farley: *Behind the Ballots* (New York, 1939), pp. 97–98.

his opinions known. On the other hand, Senator Taft, while by no means making such an extended speaking tour as Mr. Stassen, did talk in many cities throughout the United States and in contrast to Dewey took a vigorous stand on every issue.

The number of speeches a candidate may make often depends on whether or not he is trying to be deceptive about his real intentions. It is sometimes considered strategic to give the impression that one is not a candidate while at the same time carefully building up an organization to secure the nomination. This was the strategy Dewey used successfully in 1944, and he attempted to use the same strategy in 1948 until shortly before the Wisconsin primary in April when he finally took off his gloves and announced that he was really in the fight to win the nomination. In sharp contrast to this, Stassen publicly announced a full year and six months before the 1948 presidential convention that he was a candidate for the presidential nomination, that he intended to study all the issues, and that he would use all efforts at his command to make his views known to the people.

The usual approach on the matter of revealing the actual intentions of a person being considered as a presidential candidate is not to appear too eager or too reticent. There are several reasons for this somewhat compromising stand. First, there is in the United States some distaste for a candidate who pursues the presidency in a manner described by an English political correspondent that suggests the "humourless calculation of a certified public accountant in pursuit of the Holy Grail." [9] Contrary to English politics where a man may throw his hat into the ring unabashedly, there is considerable sentiment in the United States that a person should not be too solicitous or overanxious in his pursuit of the presidential nomination.

There is also a more compelling reason why candidates while not necessarily disclaiming any intention of seeking the nomination, are reluctant to commit themselves too early in the game. Once the candidate's intentions are well known in advance of the convention, there is some tendency for other competitors to concentrate their attacks upon him and work against him whenever possible. Another disadvantage in declaring one's candidacy too unequivocally early in the pre-convention campaign is that it may upset the timing factor—always a critical matter in making presidential nominations. A candidate whose intentions are known early in the game may shoot his bolt long before the propitious moment and find himself fading into obscurity when the real test comes at convention time. There is an advantage both in having a candidate's name in the race at the pre-convention stage and having solid support under him, but except in unusual years when there is very little opposition, most political field generals prefer not to have their candidate in the front position too long before the convention.

It infrequently happens in American politics that any person who has been prominently mentioned for the presidential nomination has an

[9] See Alistair Cooke in the *Manchester Guardian*, June 17, 1948, p. 12.

244 A GRAMMAR OF AMERICAN POLITICS

overwhelming desire to avoid that honor being bestowed upon him. There have been two notable exceptions to this general rule. The first was the case of General William Tecumseh Sherman, who, after repeated protests against being considered for the Republican nomination in 1884, firmly put an end to all speculation after the convention had assembled in Chicago on June 3, with the following telegram: "I will not accept if nominated and will not serve if elected." In 1948 perhaps an even more dramatic incident was created by the strong desire of political leaders in both major parties to tender General Dwight Eisenhower the presidential nomination. Very early in the pre-convention campaign there were a few unmistakable signs that the General might be interested in the presidential office. In January of 1948, however, in a carefully worded reply to a publisher from New Hampshire who had requested a go-ahead signal for a draft Eisenhower movement, the General tried to remove himself from consideration for at least the Republican presidential nomination. His statement said in part: ... "I am not available for and could not accept nomination to high political office ... It is my conviction that the necessary and wise subordination of the military to civil power will be best sustained, and our people will have greater confidence that it is so sustained, when lifelong professional soldiers, in the absence of some obvious and overriding reasons, abstain from seeking high political office. This truth has a possible inverse application. I would regard it as unalloyed tragedy for our country if ever should come the day when military commanders might be selected with an eye to their future potentialities in the political field rather than exclusively upon judgment as to their military abilities." [10]

Four years later General Eisenhower had changed his mind and permitted his name to be filed in preference primaries. His chief rival in these competitions turned out to be Senator Robert A. Taft. By mid-April Taft was claiming that only he could provide the alternative to the New Deal. Meanwhile his managers were implying that generals were admirably suited to wage war, but inept in the art of statecraft. Eisenhower's managers emphasized the party's need of a winner and the General's indisputable popularity. Early in June Eisenhower returned from his European command, retired from the army, took charge of his own campaign, made his first political speech at Abilene and began receiving party delegations. In May the Taft men, outvoted in the Texas county conventions, nevertheless, through control of the state organization, captured the state's 38 delegates. Thereupon Eisenhower declared, "In this case the rustlers stole the Texas birthright instead of the steers."

The "Texas steal," as the General's supporters denominated it, became eventually a decisive factor in the Convention. Contesting delegates from Georgia and Louisiana, as well as Texas, 68 in all, presented themselves at the Chicago Convention. Senator Taft, in a compromise offer, proposed to divide the Texas delegation equally, to which manager Senator Lodge replied, "General Eisenhower is a no deal man." General

[10] Text in the *New York Herald Tribune,* January 24, 1948.

Eisenhower, enroute from Denver to Chicago by special train, took up the theme at whistle-stops with references to "chicanery," "star chamber methods" and "smoke filled rooms." One of the most sensational turns of the controversy came out of the Conference of Governors at Houston, Texas. A manifesto, signed by 23 of the 25 Republican governors, urged that the contested delegates not be allowed to vote in the Convention until the contests had been settled. This suggested change in the standing rules of the Convention proved to be a severe blow to the hopes of the Taft managers. The proposal of the governors, embraced in the famous Langlie resolution, was adopted by the Convention after an acrimonious debate. The vote presaged the eventual victory of Eisenhower over Taft as the Republican nominee. He was nominated on the first ballot.

Dark Horse Candidates

Throughout the pre-convention campaign right down to the national convention itself there are persistent rumors to quicken the pulse of possible "dark horse" candidates. A romanticized version of the dark horse candidate pictures him as somewhat of a political long-shot who has not received prominent consideration during the pre-convention campaign and who suddenly lunges to the front at the last minute to steal the nomination. Perhaps the most oft-cited example of a dark horse candidate in recent political history is Warren G. Harding who won the Republican presidential nomination in 1920. Harding was scarcely mentioned as presidential timber that year but probably entered the Ohio presidential primary solely for the purpose of gaining prestige in what he expected to be his campaign for re-election to the United States Senate. On the first ballot at the convention he had only 65½ votes, practically all of which came from his own state, Ohio, but in the deadlock that followed between the leading contenders, General Leonard Wood and Governor Frank Lowden, Harding was finally nominated on the tenth ballot. In the Democratic party, John W. Davis, the presidential nominee in 1924, was also regarded as the dark horse and conceded little chance to win the nomination. Davis carried only his own state of West Virginia on the first ballot along with only a smattering of votes scattered among other states. Yet in the historic deadlock which followed between Governor Alfred E. Smith and William McAdoo, Davis was finally named on the one hundred and second ballot.

More recently, Wendell Willkie added to the dark horse legend by his spectacular performance in capturing the Republican presidential nomination in 1940. Although actually listed as a Democrat in the 1940 edition of *Who's Who in America* and almost unknown to the general public and party leaders as late as January, 1940, the Willkie pre-convention campaign rolled along with the speed of a prairie fire and Willkie stalked off with the presidential nomination on the sixth ballot. To the casual observer, the man on the sidelines, the Willkie performance had the general appearance of being inspired by a spontaneous demand of the rank and file of the party that he be made the nominee. It is doubtful, however, if ever a short pre-convention campaign has been planned with more political acumen than that of Willkie in 1940. Through the well directed efforts of the Cowles Brothers, publishers in the mid-west, and Russell Davenport, a former editor of *Fortune Magazine* who resigned to master-mind the Willkie campaign, Willkie's popularity and strength as a political figure rose almost unbelievably within the short span of four months.

The dark horse, therefore, for all of his romantic appeal is not often a riderless horse who suddenly comes out of the dark shadows of political oblivion to win the presidential nomination. The dark horse strategy may be just as shrewd as that of an avowed candidate for the nomination and indeed where it is successful, the ground work has invariably been well planned. Actually the quadrennial speculation about dark horse possibilities is possibly overplayed by political columnists and news writers and is given much more attention than the realities of our political behavior at convention time warrants. In part this may be explained by the fact that the leading contenders in both parties, as convention time nears, may often be persons who do not strike a responsive cord in the hearts of the rank and file or many party leaders. Thus the possibility of the ideal candidate whether known or unknown suddenly emerging to take command of the party, stirs the imagination no matter how remote such an occurrence may be.

Pre-convention Strategy in Renominating a President

Pre-convention campaigns of the party holding power depend upon whether or not the president is seeking renomination. If the president irrevocably takes himself out of consideration for the renomination, this gives the green light to all those who wish to enter the race, and the pre-convention struggle takes on the same appearance as that of the party out of power. Should the chief executive desire a renomination, however, pre-convention arrangements are ordinarily routine, at least in so far as the second nomination is concerned. In accordance with long established custom a president is entitled to a second nomination if he desires it, and with a single exception, this courtesy has been tendered to every president since the Civil War. Even where a president has not been particularly popular, the reasons for his receiving a second nomination if he desires it are obvious. In the first place, he controls the patronage of the party and thereby has great influence over local political leaders who either will be delegates or in turn will control delegates to the national convention. A second factor supporting the renomination of a president who is willing to be a candidate again is the desire of the party in power not to give an impression of a repudiation of its leadership. To discard a president who desired a renomination would lay the party in power open to the charge that it was dissatisfied with its own leadership and attempting to dodge the responsibility for its own record. Where the president is being renominated for a second term, there is occasionally a minor flurry of protest here and there, but since the Civil War except for President Taft of the famous Republican party split in 1912, a second nomination has never been seriously challenged.

The question of a third nomination posed a somewhat different problem because on the rare occasions upon which this issue had been raised the presidents concerned had not given a positive indication of their own desires. Presumably Calvin Coolidge with eight words—"I do not choose to run in 1928"—indicated a personal desire to remove himself from consideration for a second nomination which some of his critics were opposing. It was alleged that if renominated and reelected he would be violating the no third term principle—an argument not completely sound because Coolidge at the time had served only one full term and a fraction of another after he had succeeded to the presidency on the death of President Harding. For a president to admit openly that he desired a third nomination, however, was something no chief executive had ever been willing to do. Several times prior to 1940, Franklin Roosevelt confided to his close advisers that he wished to retire to Hyde Park at the end of his second term. Yet as the threat of a European conflict grew more serious and certain party leaders urged him to run again, Mr. Roosevelt became increasingly discreet about his position on a third nomination. He did nothing to discourage his followers from lining up delegates to assure him the nomination for a third time, and, after some attempts by the more conservative element in the Democratic party to stop the drive for a third nomination—which were almost complete failures—President Roosevelt's renomination became a perfunctory matter. Again in 1944 the same strategy was used with remarkable success, Mr. Roosevelt doing nothing to discourage his followers from engineering another draft, and the nomination being delivered on schedule amid some sharp ripples of protest to be sure, but once more without any formidable opposition.

The pre-convention activities then for those presidents nominated a second or even a third or fourth time follow no fundamentally divergent pattern. The comparative ease with which such feats could be accomplished despite the cross-grained tradition against a third term in American politics firmly suggests that a president who possesses the rare qualifications for inspired leadership of his party occupies indeed a well fortified position. More precarious is the position of the president who does not seek renomination but tries to dictate his successor. This feat was accomplished by Theodore Roosevelt in bringing about the nomination of William Howard Taft—much to his later regret—but few presidents have either tried or had much success in trying to force the nomination of their successors.[11] Particularly opposed to having a president influence the selec-

[11] On occasion a chief executive may have considerable to say about his possible successors. Thus Vice-President Garner in announcing that he would accept a presidential nomination if offered made the brittle remark privately that without the president's support no candidacy was better than "a can of stale beer." Charles Michelson: *The Ghost Talks*, p. 131.

tion of his successor was Woodrow Wilson who wrote to a Democratic party leader in 1916: "It is intolerable that any President should be permitted to determine who should succeed him—himself or another—by patronage or coercion or by any sort of control of the machinery by which delegates to the nominating conventions are chosen . . ." In the case of the vice-presidential nominees it is true that presidential nominees may often write their own ticket. Even on the vice-presidency, however, the party leaders may balk, as witness the difficult time which the Roosevelt forces had in securing the nomination of Henry Wallace over the candidacy of Speaker William Bankhead at Chicago in 1940. And more dramatic was the vice-presidential nomination fight in 1944, when Franklin Roosevelt was forced by party disaffection to retreat from his original position that no one except Henry Wallace would be acceptable as his running mate and to issue a statement that he found both William Douglas and Harry Truman to be acceptable as nominees if the convention so desired.

Our cursory examination of pre-convention campaigns has touched upon only some of the more obvious points, and it is well to bear in mind that a vast variety of circumstances may affect this stage of the presidential nomination race one way or another. Thus, in some years, the presidential nomination may be well settled far in advance of the national convention. This was virtually the case of Alfred Landon in 1936 when, as one of the seven Republican governors in the entire United States, he seemed to tower above other possible choices. But whatever fortune and the combination of circumstances may bring, the pre-convention campaign is a crucial phase of our entire system of nominating presidents and one who would really understand American politics must follow the strategy and techniques employed at this stage with great care.

APPORTIONMENT OF DELEGATES

All delegates chosen to attend the national convention are selected within the states, and the method of their selection is also determined by the states. From the very beginning of national conventions, the number of delegates that a state sends to the national convention has had some relation to its electoral vote. Gradually both parties adopted a general practice allowing each state twice as many delegates as it had electoral votes. Thus, under the rule of thumb generally followed by both parties, each state sends two delegates for each representative and each senator in Congress. This brings the total size of the national convention to somewhat over one thousand delegates. In actual practice the Democratic convention is usually larger than that of the G.O.P., the reason being that some states send twice the number of delegates that they are actually allowed, giving each delegate one-half vote and thereby increasing the actual number of people who are entitled to vote. In 1948 this meant that the Republican convention had 1094 delegates while the Democratic convention had a total of 1234.

Problems of Apportionment

As originally conceived the plan of apportionment which allowed states a quota of delegates proportionate to their electoral vote did not give rise to any serious conflict. Moreover if the relative strength of our major parties had developed so that neither party was almost devoid of support in certain sections of the country, the apportionment of delegates would probably have not presented any special problem. As it happened the Republican party soon found that in seven states of the deep South it was almost wholly without followers—a condition which has persisted down to the present day. In Mississippi, for example, in order for a party to have a place on the ballot it must have polled at least five percent of the vote the last general election. Failing to meet even this minimum requirement the Republican party's presidential candidate of 1944 was placed on the general election ballot of that year only through the magnanimity of state officials.

Despite the paucity of G.O.P. voters in the South, regular Republican organizations exist in this region and the states located therein have always sent delegates to the Republican national convention. When the Republican party is in power, state G.O.P. organizations in the South have control of patronage appointments such as Federal judgeships, district attorneys, Federal marshals, postmasters, and other appointments even though in many states some are without a single representative or senator in the Congress. The organizations, of course, also control the selection of delegates to the national convention—a circumstance which gives a Republican president an independent hand in controlling southern delegates because of his patronage power. Although the inequity of basing southern representation at the national convention upon the same standard as that used in the North had long been protested, it was not until 1912 that Republican apportionment was changed. Following a bad split in the party that year in which Taft's control over the national convention was partly due to the old system of apportioning delegates, a change was made upon recommendation by the Republican National Committee and since 1916, G.O.P. rules on apportionment of delegates have favored states with a heavy Republican vote.

In shaving down Southern strength in the national convention, the most significant change in Republican apportionment policy resulted from the alteration of the G.O.P. formula for determining district delegates. Since the Civil War, it had been Republican practice to allot two delegates for each congressional district and two for each United States senator. Under the rule accepted in 1956, however, a congressional district may have one delegate only if 2,000 Republican votes were cast in the last presidential or subsequent congressional election; if 10,000 are polled, the district is allowed two delegates. In the same year, adoption of another apportionment rule provided that a bonus of three delegates should go to the states voting Republican in the last presidential election or if they subsequently elected a G.O.P. senator. Obviously the matter of arriving at a satisfactory formula for apportioning delegates is far from a simple task. It seems quite well agreed nonetheless that to give Southern states the same number of delegates in the Republican convention as states of comparable population in other sections which delivered G.O.P. majorities on election day, was a practice difficult to defend. Judged in this light the principle of granting some sort of a bonus that rewards a state going Republican by increasing its quota of delegates, affords at least a reasonable compromise.

The Democratic party has not experienced the trouble that the G.O.P. has on apportionment matters as there are few states if any in the union where this party is as completely without support as the Republican party finds itself in certain Southern states. After the two-thirds rule was scrapped in 1936, however, Southerners exerted some pressure to bring about a change in the system of apportionment. Until 1936, the two-thirds rule in the Democratic party required a vote of two-thirds of the entire convention for a presidential nomination rather than a mere majority which the Republican party has always used. As there was a strong feeling in the South that the abolition of the two-thirds rule robbed them of a limited veto power over the presidential nomination, the Democratic National Committee was urged to compensate partially for this change by altering the apportionment scheme so as to reward states that remained in the Democratic column. In 1940, the Democratic party adopted a rule to grant states going Democratic in a presidential election a bonus of two extra delegates. This plan of apportionment was in effect for the first time in 1944 and provided only a limited improvement in the representation of the "Solid South." For the 1948 convention the Democratic bonus for states voting Democratic at the last presidential election was somewhat better, a total of four votes being allowed to each state that had voted for the Democratic presidential candidate in 1944.

Selecting Delegates: The Convention System

With the state apportionment of the delegates to the national convention known, the next vital procedure in the presidential nominating system is the actual designation of delegates. In approximately two-thirds of the states, delegates who will represent the state at the national convention are chosen by state or district conventions. For the remaining one-third of the states, the method of selecting national convention delegates is the presidential primary. In issuing the call during the spring of the convention year, the national committee states that delegates shall be selected by congressional, district, or state conventions and by primary election in accordance with the laws of the particular states.

The two-thirds of our states using the convention method of selecting delegates account for a little over one-half of the total number of national convention delegates. To understand properly the political labyrinth out of which a delegate finally emerges and sets off to the national convention, one should personally follow it from the grass root stage to the election of the delegate. In chronological sequence, the process runs somewhat in this order:

Following the issuance of the call, precinct caucuses are held throughout the entire state where the district convention system is used. The precinct is the lowest political subdivision and it is simply an electoral unit in American politics for the purpose of registration and voting. The holding of precinct caucuses is directed by the county chairman of the political party who in turn has received his instructions directly from the national committee in a communique referred to as the "call." There has been some attempt by the Republican party to prescribe the procedures and rules to be followed in the selection of delegates whereas the Democratic party has in general left the matter up to state law or simply local custom. This distinction is more academic than real, however, and it should be noted that as state legislation has been adopted regulating procedures for selecting delegates to national conventions, local organizations of both parties have conformed with these regulations.

Everywhere the sequence of events and the condition under which the process operates to select national convention delegates may vary. In some areas, the precinct may be well organized by both parties. Under such conditions, a precinct meeting held to select a representative to attend a ward or county meeting might or might not involve a lively controversy. If the precinct is located in an area dominated by a local political boss it is a fairly safe assumption that he will have enough strength on hand to see that one of his own lieutenants is selected to attend either the ward or county convention. On the other hand the neophyte in politics deciding to attend his first precinct caucus may well find that appearing at the designated place he is the only one in attendance. This of course depends completely on the degree of political organization found within the area.

From the precinct caucus the representative selected either attends a ward, city, or county convention. In metropolitan areas the normal move from the precinct caucus is to the ward, a political subdivision in a city, usually composed of a number of precincts. At this meeting much the same process goes on and eventually representatives are selected to attend the city or the county political convention. In some areas, of course, the city and the county are almost identical and this occasionally obviates the necessity of holding two conventions. And, where city, county, and perhaps congressional districts have more or less coterminous borders, it is, of course, possible to eliminate some of the meetings leading up to the district convention itself where delegates to the national convention are ultimately chosen. As the rural areas of the United States have always been well represented in Congress and the county organization is the backbone of the party in suburban regions, the county convention is an extremely important link in the chain of events leading up to the district convention. From the county conventions, of course, go the representatives who will attend the meeting of the congressional district convention which is made up of all the counties lying within the congressional district. Thus at the top of the hierarchy is the congressional district convention which ultimately must select one or two persons to attend the national convention.

One should realize that while this procedure gives the appearance of being long and drawn out, it actually moves very swiftly and the entire business is consummated within a few successive weeks. Mention should also be made of the fact that delegates are occasionally selected by state convention rather than by congressional districts, in which case the sequence of events is practically unchanged. Moreover it is a common practice for a state convention to name four or more delegates not selected by congressional district conventions known as "delegates at large." Those named by the state convention are often important dignitaries such as United States senators, governors, and various professional people such as authors or lawyers or other figures prominent in the party.

When one considers that this system of selecting delegates to the national convention provides at least one-half of the representation which will select the presidential nominee, it is apparent that the number of people who have an actual hand in naming a nominee is indeed very small. Thus it is easy to see how a well disciplined political machine through control of various levels of this all important procedure can manage to have its influence felt all the way to the top. Moreover, with the convention system of selecting delegates spread in full view, it is easy to understand why a mighty mobilization effort is required to build up a candidate for the presidential nomination. The feeblest attempt to acquire delegates pledged to support a candidate requires an outlay of several thousand dollars within one state alone. Advance reconnaissance and publicity work sounding out local leaders must first be undertaken, a headquarters from which to direct the pre-convention campaign is needed, and many additional expenses will be incurred once a decision has been taken to go after delegates in a given state. Great care must be given to the selection of a state campaign manager and unless he happens to be a man of means, he is compensated for his services, often quite handsomely.

Other expenses encountered in securing delegates are perhaps not quite so well known. It is nothing unusual for a delegate who has been selected to attend the national convention to have his expenses paid for this junket out of the funds which have been raised to promote the candidacy of a particular presidential contender. Such expenses may easily run from $500 to $1,000 or higher. The expenses which delegates incur in making sure that they are selected as national convention delegates are also frequently paid from funds raised by friends of a contender for the presidential nomination. This practice, while often abused, is not as bad as it appears. It is quite understandable that a candidate for delegate to the national convention who wishes to support a specific contender for the nomination might desire to attend the convention, yet not be a person who could easily afford to spend several weeks of his time making sure that he was chosen as a delegate. Nor could he then afford to spend over $1,000 to attend the convention. In such a case if the delegate's expenses are paid it is not comparable to buying a vote, since the delegate has determined to support a certain candidate long in advance of any arrangement to pay his expenses. The practice may be abused, however, and delegates have been known to collect funds from the organizations of several contenders for presidential nominations on the pretense of supporting them at the national convention.

The Presidential Primary

Fourteen states use the presidential primary for selecting delegates to the national conventions and in three others it is optional although rarely used. [12] In terms of the total number of votes, these states account for a little less than half the aggregate number of delegates. The rise of the presidential primary began about the same time as the direct primary and the reasons that prompted its appearance were much the same. The same abuses attributed to the state conventions used to nominate state officials, were also charged to the national convention. A presidential primary law was first adopted in Wisconsin in 1905 and around 1916 the idea had reached the height of its popularity. Since the latter date several states have abandoned the presidential primary for reasons which we will soon examine.

As initially conceived the theory of the presidential primary was to give the voters a direct voice in the all important task of selecting a presidential nominee, but as this theory came to be drafted into legislation among the several state legislatures, it was sufficiently cobbled in many instances so that it would be a mistake to speak of some states now known as presidential primary states, as really having a presidential primary system. In all there are five categories of presidential primaries. The largest category among the presidential primary states is the one in which there is a presidential preference vote and direct election of delegates to the national convention who may be pledged. Perhaps the best known states using this system are Ohio, Oregon, and Wisconsin. Under this scheme voters may express their preference for the presidential nomination by voting directly for a delegate or slate of delegates to the national convention who are pledged to a particular candidate. One difficulty with this method is that in some states there is a presidential preference vote combined with the election of delegates while at the same time the voters do not know the delegate's preferences. Obviously this can lead to a great deal of confusion and there is much dissatisfaction with this

[12] See Louise Overacker: *The Presidential Primary* (New York, 1926), for a thorough treatment of this subject. A more recent but brief compilation of state presidential systems may be found in a memorandum on the nomination of delegates to national party conventions by Samuel H. Still of the State Law Section of the Legislative Reference Service of the Library of Congress, released on April 30, 1947.

method. Among the other four methods used in presidential preference primaries a few brief identifying features may be mentioned. In one group are the states where there is a presidential preference vote and direct election of delegates to the national convention but the delegates are not pledged. This system is used in Pennsylvania, Illinois, and West Virginia. It has not, however, proved itself to be very satisfactory. Under the latter system, for example, it is possible to have the presidential preference vote not jibe with the personal preferences of the delegates who are elected to attend the national convention. Thus in 1936, in the Illinois Republican primary, the state-wide preference vote was won by publisher Frank Knox against Senator William E. Borah, yet Borah delegates were elected in thirteen congressional districts. [13]

In a few states there is no presidential preference vote at all but simply direct election of district delegates to the national convention who are not pledged to any one presidential candidate. This system is used in New York. A compromise between the primary and the convention system is used in Maryland where there is a presidential preference vote but where the election of delegates to the national convention is done by state convention, the delegates to which are pledged in accordance with the presidential preference vote in the various communities of the state.

A final group of presidential primary states, in which there has been the least confusion between popular preference and preferences of delegates who are elected, is the group in which there is no separate vote on presidential preference. Under this plan the presidential primary ballot simply lists the candidates for election as delegates along with their preference for president, and the voter designates his preference merely by casting a ballot for the delegate pledged to the candidate for the presidential nomination that he favors. States using this method are California, New Hampshire, and Massachusetts.

In addition to some of the mechanical difficulties already alluded to in our discussion of presidential primaries, there are several criticisms of a more fundamental nature. It is becoming increasingly evident that an inordinate amount of money is being spent in some states having the presidential primary. This was particularly true of the Republican pre-convention campaign in 1948. Several students of politics have pointed out that where the presidential primary is used the candidate with the well-stocked campaign chest has a powerful advantage over other candidates. The thesis of this argument is that to reach the entire voting population of the party requires a greater outlay than where party leaders are the main persons to be contacted, as is true in the convention states. There is no conclusive evidence yet on this point, but there is no doubt that the lavish spending during the presidential primaries in 1956 has given rise to some serious criticism.

[13] See Louise Overacker in E. B. Logan: *The American Political Scene* (New York, 1936), pp. 264–5.

Another factor which has probably obscured a true test of the presidential primary is that the great divergence in laws among the several states has made it almost meaningless as a test of voters preference in many cases. As we have noted, often a delegate is not pledged at all by a preference vote. Of the 496 delegates chosen by presidential primary for the Republican convention in 1948, only 153 from five states were flatly obligated to support the candidate favored by the party voters in their respective states. But even if the delegate is pledged, some difficult problems arise because of the presidential primary. How long should a delegate pledged to support a presidential preference vote be bound? If his candidate obviously has no chance, should he continue to vote for the candidate for whom he is pledged? Statutory directives on this point are not always clear, a few reading, for example, that the delegate shall continue to vote for the candidate to whom he is pledged until all reasonable hope is gone that the candidate can secure the nomination. When, one might ask, does this precise moment occur? Again this is a question upon which reasonable men might differ and it is obviously one which would be very difficult to anticipate by proper legislative action.

An effective test of the presidential primary has often been averted by the fact that many obvious contenders for the presidential nomination are reluctant to enter primaries in certain states because of their desire to avoid offending "favorite sons." The "favorite son" technique is a tested and time tried device in American politics. By having the entire state delegation to the national convention shrouded in the shadow of a "favorite son," party leaders can go into a national convention and wait to see which way the chips will fall before they line up behind one of the major contenders. A vast majority of favorite sons—ordinarily governors or senators—usually have not the slightest chance of receiving the presidential nomination, but they are convenient blinds behind which to hide until the time comes to climb on the bandwagon. As a bargaining device the favorite son technique is a formidable one, but one may easily observe how it frustrates a true test of voter preference on the candidates who are the real contenders for the presidential nomination.

One further difficulty with the presidential primary is that popular preference measured as early as the first state presidential primary on March 5 may shift appreciably by the third week in June when the Republicans convene, or the second week in July when the Democrats ordinarily meet. Wendell Willkie, who was barely heard of early in 1940, and was still being led in the popular polls by Dewey on the eve of the Republican convention was, by the time the convention met, favored by a majority of the general electorate.

In judging the importance of presidential primaries in so far as their influence upon the convention's ultimate choice is concerned, the presidential primary comes off poorly. In 1938 Professor Overacker reached the conclusion that there were only "two cases in which the choice of the convention clearly reflected the choice of the primary" and that in neither of these cases was it clear that the nomination was won because of victories in the primary. In the 1948 Republican primary Harold Stassen made a spectacular showing in several important state primaries yet ran a very poor third in the balloting at the convention. Occasionally a presidential primary may have a certain amount of psychological value in bolstering a sagging candidacy or giving fresh impulse to a slow starting pre-convention campaign. This appeared to be true of the Oregon primary in the spring of 1948 when Governor Dewey after being defeated in both Wisconsin and Nebraska carried on an intensive campaign to keep Oregon's thirteen delegates from going to Stassen. Following Dewey's victory in this primary, things began to look better for his candidacy and steadily worse for Stassen. It is doubtful, however, if even this much-heralded presidential primary had a decisive effect on the outcome of the 1948 convention and certainly when weighed with the accumulated evidence of presidential primaries in other years it in no way changes the general observation that presidential primaries have not been a dominating influence in presidential nominations.

Ever since 1912, when Theodore Roosevelt began beating the drums for it, there has been some sentiment for a nation-wide presidential primary. It had been advocated by Senator LaFollette even before Theodore Roosevelt, it was taken up by President Wilson during his first term, and it was revived again by LaFollette in the 1924 Progressive campaign. The idea has never taken hold seriously, however, and with the more prolific use of the public opinion poll, it may well be that this invention will provide a sort of preference primary that may ultimately have some effect on the convention's choice.

Organizing the Convention

On the designated day after all of the presidential primaries and district conventions have been held to select delegates, the delegates assemble for one of the most dramatic political side-shows to be found in any country. In the matter of sequence, only four times has the Democratic party held its convention before the Republicans—in 1856, 1860, 1888, and 1956. The Democratic presidential nominee was defeated in 1888 and whether from superstition or otherwise the Democratic Convention always afterward followed the Republican Convention until 1956.

The environment of the national convention city defies description. Here in the midst of an unbelievable pandemonium that lasts about ten days from the first preliminaries until adjournment, the delegates must get down to the serious business of selecting presidential and vice-presidential nominees. Blaring bands add to the din of the various candidate's hotel headquarters and many of the stunts are not unlike early fraternity initiation ceremonies on a college campus. At the Stassen headquarters in the 1948 G.O.P. Convention visitors were treated with slabs of a four hundred pound Wisconsin cheese, while in other headquarters organizers were busy handing out small trinkets bearing the name of their candidate. A few weeks later when the Democrats assembled in the same city, they sported a mechanical marvel—a donkey—which snorted live smoke from its nostrils. Everywhere one sees evidence—though artificial—of regional color. There are sombreros, shoe string ties, and both parties usually have one or two full-blooded American Indians as delegates. Perhaps the most colorful Indian in the 1948 conventions was Chief Spotted Crow of South Dakota who not only made all his appearances in full regalia but explained his preference for a taxicab rather than riding in a bus to and from the convention hall with the South Dakota delegation with the simple statement: "Ugh, bus ruffle feathers." Augmenting the two thousand delegates and alternates of both conventions are perhaps 100,000 party well-wishers and visitors from other cities. To handle this influx it was necessary for Philadelphia to make arrangements to bring three thousand taxicabs from neighboring cities for the weeks of the Republican and Democratic conventions. Obviously but a small number of those desiring to see the more exciting phase of the conventions—the balloting—can be accommodated in a convention hall. But the 20,000 fortunate enough to gain admission through a carefully guarded system of distributing tickets through the national committee officers of each state, have full opportunity to observe what Irvin Cobb once called an institution "representing more wasted energy, more futile fruitless endeavor, more useless expenditure of noise, money, and talent than any institution on earth."

In the convention hall, itself, the two thousand delegates and alternates are seated on the floor along with about an equal number of sergeants at arms, honorary sergeants at arms, and various other party potentates who have managed to squeeze their way onto the floor. That the influence of women in politics is steadily increasing is evidenced by the fact that a record total of 113 women were delegates to the 1948 GOP convention and the Democratic convention set an even more impressive record with a total of 192 female delegates. [14] The rostrum is flanked by press boxes, while the broadcasting booths are ordinarily located high above the proceedings of the convention floor. With the advent of television the entire floor is now bathed in a light as intense as a magnesium flare and the heat from these lights added to the smoke, din, and general confusion within the hall is so great that it has never ceased to overwhelm foreign observers witnessing a national convention for the first time.

The opening note of the national convention is intoned by the chairman of the national committee who takes the chair until temporary officers are elected. By custom the national committee presents the temporary slate of officers for the convention which it will be recalled was selected

[14] The Republican convention also had 240 alternate delegates who were women, and the Democratic convention 320.

at their December meeting. Except for unusual cases the convention approves the selection of the national committee. The chief function of the temporary chairman, of course, is to deliver the keynote address which ordinarily provides the first full dress opportunity for whipping up the enthusiasm of the convention delegates. Traditionally the keynote address is a speech heavily loaded with political bear grease in which the virtues of the speaker's party are extolled and that of the opposition excoriated. Occasionally some keynoters have managed to make mild improvements on this formula, but almost invariably the speeches are so studded with clichés and predictions of victory no matter how remote, that they certainly make poor reading once removed from the fever pitched environment of the convention hall.

The Four Great Committees

One of the most important steps early in the convention proceedings is the organization of the four major committees: permanent organization, credentials, resolutions, and rules. Briefly stated, the credentials committee has the function of examining the validity of credentials, hearing appeals where there are contesting delegations for seats at the convention, and making recommendations to the convention. The committee on resolutions has the task of drafting and recommending a platform to the convention while the committee on permanent organization is charged with the duty of recommending a set of permanent officers to the convention. The fourth committee—the rules committee—is responsible for reporting a set of rules to the convention which will govern its procedure. Membership on these committees is composed of one person from each state and territorial delegation, except for the resolutions committee in which case both a man and a woman are designated from each state and territorial delegation.

The Credentials Committee

As the credentials committee is usually the first whose report is considered by the convention, we may examine its work at this point. Like the Congress of the United States the national convention is the judge of the qualifications of its members. As it is perfectly obvious that occasional factional disputes within a state may lead to a situation where two competing groups vie with each other for the state delegation to the national convention, some machinery must be available for handling such a situation.

Initially credentials are passed upon by the national committee which in the case of each party makes a temporary list of the delegates that it deems qualified to sit at the convention. In making up this list the national committee may be called upon to hear cases of contested delegations and make determinations in each case. By party rule the Republican national committee must place on the temporary list all delegates who have been duly certified by the states' public officials as having been selected in accordance with the laws of the states. It is not mandatory that the convention or the credentials committee in hearing an appeal taken from the decision of the national committee in preparing the temporary list, be bound by this rule.

When the credentials committee meets it is often confronted with some spirited and bitter contests. At the root of many disputes between two separate delegations, each claiming legitimacy, is often a disagreement over potential nominees. Thus a decision seating one delegation or another may well mean the loss or gain of a large number of votes for a particular candidate. Less frequently the source of difficulty over contested delegation fights is on issues, and for the most part it is a division which fundamentally involves a difference in loyalties between two contenders for the presidential nomination or a contest between two political leaders for control of the state organization. Some hard feelings may be caused by the decision of the credentials committee and it is greatly to the advantage of a candidate for the nomination to control this committee. In deciding between the so called regular and rump delegations of Texas at the 1944 Democratic convention, the credentials committee recommended seating the "regular" Texas delegation which was opposing the fourth term nomination of Roosevelt and as a conciliatory move, it also recommended that both delegations be seated and each delegate be given a half vote. Following the adoption of this recommendation by the convention, the regular Texas delegation walked out in a huff. In 1948 the contest between the Taft and Dewey forces for the seating of two rival delegations from Georgia was decided at a credentials committee meeting by the margin of one vote in favor of the faction supporting Dewey, thus giving the Dewey forces an early showing of power at the convention while, at the same time, discouraging the followers of Taft.

The Committee on Permanent Organization

The big decision of the committee on permanent organization is the selection of the permanent presiding officer for the convention. As all aspirants to the presidential nomination are naturally desirous that the person who occupies this post be at least impartial to their candidacy, much interest centers on this decision. Customarily the permanent chairman of the convention is expected to be neutral—that is, he is expected not to covet the presidential nomination for himself. The latter qualification, however, is not always observed, for Speaker Joseph Martin, permanent chairman of the Republican convention in 1948, although at no time a serious contender for the nomination in terms of delegate strength, was assuredly a person who hoped that the presidential nomination would come his way.

Although formal designation of the permanent chairman is made by the committee on organization at the time of the convention, the real decision is often made long in advance by the national committee's committee on arrangements. While the permanent chairman is expected to preside with a semblance of fairness, the importance of a "friendly" attitude toward certain candidates must not be underestimated. When the forces behind one particular candidate secure the permanent chairman they have a distinct tactical advantage in matters of recognition and on questions involving a discretionary ruling. Thus it is not at all unusual for a person about to be named as permanent chairman of the convention to meet in preliminary caucus with the leaders backing a particular presidential contender and lay plans for assuring the nomination of their favorite. At such meetings the sequence of the strategy may be mapped out as well as many other matters which would help to bring about a smoothly disciplined victory.

The Rules Committee

The committee on rules has the duty of recommending the rules of procedure under which the convention will operate. Usually this committee simply recommends that the rules of the last convention be adopted, but changes are often recommended on apportionment rules, and in rare instances, the rules committee drafts a change of a more fundamental nature, as happened in 1936 when the committee recommended the abolition of the two-thirds rule in the Democratic party which required that a presidential nominee must receive a two-thirds vote.

The Resolutions Committee

The resolutions committee as already noted is responsible for presenting a draft platform to the convention. Contrary to the sometimes mistaken notion that this committee feverishly prepares the platform during the early sessions of the convention itself, the bulk of this work is done by a small subcommittee working long in advance of the opening convention date. Both American and foreign observers alike speak of the character of our major party political platforms in disparaging overtones. "Its tendency," wrote Lord Bryce, "is neither to define nor to convince, but rather to attract and confuse. It is a mixture of denunciation, declamation, and conciliation." In more abbreviated fashion, shortly before he died, the late Wendell Willkie brushed off party platforms as "fusions of ambiguity." Despite the validity of both of these statements, the major parties quadrennially go through the pretense of having the resolutions committee hold hearings at which various pressure groups may present their views before the final platform is recommended for approval. Some impressions of this procedure may be gained from a description by H. L. Mencken made four days before the national convention assembled in July of 1948: "The only active ganglion in the Democratic nervous system was the Committee on Resolutions in session since Wednesday on the theory that it is drawing up the party platform. That theory, of course, is buncombe

... But ... the committee spent the day going through the motions of listening to advocates of a long string of proposed planks. Advocates consisted of representatives from almost innumerable cells of uplift ranging from the Mothers of America to the National Authority for the Ladies Handbag Industry and from the American League for an Undivided Ireland to the United States Committee for United Nations Genocide Convention." [15]

Where an incumbent president is to be renominated, party platforms usually are constructed according to his own personal wishes. In general it is customary for the convention to accept most of the platform recommendations of the committee on resolutions. But the convention may change or modify the recommendations of the resolutions committee and some notable fights have broken out over the platform. A spirited drive by a minority group of the resolutions committee to throw out the recommendation of the majority favoring continuance of the Eighteenth Amendment was unsuccessful at the Republican convention of 1928. On the other hand Senator Hubert Humphrey's fight to insert a strong civil rights program into the Democratic party platform of 1948 was successful even though it led to the walk-out of the Alabama and Mississippi delegations and subsequently to the formation of a separate party known as the Dixiecrats.

In terms of draftsmanship the Democratic party platforms for the last hundred years seem to be somewhat better written than those of the Republican party, a fact which some students of politics partially attribute to the tactical advantage of the Democrats in holding their convention after the Republicans. The record of both parties on platforms, however, leaves much to be desired and for preciseness and a more clear exposition of aims and purposes one must turn to the party platforms of third and minor parties. In connection with third party and minor party platforms it might also be noted in passing that as the years roll by the major parties often take over planks that have been formulated by these smaller parties in earlier years.

NOMINATIONS

Except for the keynote address and an occasional controversy over the adoption of the platform submitted by the resolutions committee, the early preliminaries of national conventions on the opening two days are often very boring. In the Democratic convention of 1948, for example, there were nineteen different speeches scheduled for the first two days ranging from welcoming addresses to half a dozen eulogies of the party greats of another era. Only after the report of the resolutions committee has been adopted is the deck finally cleared for the real business of the convention, that of nominating the candidates.

[15] *Baltimore Sun,* July 9, 1948.

Candidates are placed in nomination following a roll call of states in alphabetical order. If a state early in the alphabet has no candidate it may simply pass or yield to a state further down the alphabet which has a candidate it intends to support. For every speech placing a different candidate in nomination there are several seconding speeches and adding to the time consumed by this process are wild demonstrations for each candidate that may last from a few minutes to over an hour. The formula for nominating speeches calls for keeping the candidate's identity unknown until the closing words of the address when the speaker finally reveals the name of his candidate to his audience, notwithstanding the fact that they know full well who the candidate is from the very beginning of the speech. A large part of the demonstration which follows a nominating speech is, of course, synthetic. Paid bands, organists, professional noise makers, all combine to build a demonstration into a definite crescendo as the delegates snake around the convention floor carrying their standards aloft. When all nominations and seconding speeches are completed the time arrives for the balloting itself, which begins immediately if the number of nominating speeches and demonstrations has not completely exhausted the delegates.

Balloting

Once more the clerk or secretary of the convention intones in alphabetical order each state and territory of the United States. Beginning with Alabama, the chairman of that state's delegation rises and solemnly announces the vote of his delegation. This vote in the case of the Republican convention and in most states in the Democratic convention may be split among several different candidates. A significant difference between the two conventions, however, is that the Democratic national convention recognizes the unit rule. The so-called unit rule is optional for states wishing to adopt it and when followed it requires that the candidate who is supported by a majority of a state's delegates shall receive the entire vote of the delegation. Thus if a state delegation in the 1956 Democratic Convention at Chicago had 40 delegates with thirty-three favoring Adlai Stevenson and seven Estes Kefauver the unit rule would have given all the forty votes to Stevenson. The unit rule is often used by certain southern states and has been used outside of the South.

While the balloting is proceeding, frantic conferences are going on between the floor leaders of various candidates and the delegations they are attempting to hold in line or entice into their camp. The procedure is also slowed down somewhat by the occasional insistence of a delegate that the entire state delegation be polled individually. This may mean that the individual delegate is not satisfied with the count as relayed by the chairman of the delegation to the secretary of the convention, or it may simply be a stalling device to gain time. It adds much to the discomfort of spectators as well as other delegates, particularly when the delegation to be polled is New York's with over ninety votes.

If at the end of the roll call when all of the votes have been tabulated, no candidate has secured a clear majority, the entire procedure must be repeated until some candidate is nominated. In the great majority of cases, the Republican party has nominated its candidate on the first ballot, but there have been important exceptions. At the 1948 G.O.P. Convention, Dewey was nominated on the third ballot, while more notable were the nominations of Wendell Willkie on the sixth in 1940, Harding on the tenth in 1920, and Garfield on the 36th back in 1880.

The experience of the Democratic party on balloting has been somewhat different because of the two-thirds rule which was not discarded until 1936. Under this rule which required a candidate to receive two-thirds of the total vote before he could be nominated, some historic deadlocks took place at Democratic conventions. Few candidates were able to enter the convention with two-thirds of the vote safely assured. Despite the skillful pre-convention campaigns conducted by Franklin Roosevelt's supporters it took four ballots to nominate Roosevelt in 1932. The bitterest fight within the Democratic party took place in 1924 when 102 ballots were taken before John W. Davis was nominated. With the abolition of the two-thirds rule by the Democratic party, however, it now appears likely that the Democratic party will tend to have more first ballot nominations.

Where a candidate is not nominated on the first ballot, the trading and negotiations between various leaders proceeds at a more furious pace. At such moments—the moments "when success is frankly on the auction block" rumors of "deals" become thicker. Each candidate piously disavows such talk, but his managers who are in the midst of the fighting know differently. "Make no bargains for me," telegraphed Lincoln to his Chicago managers in the 1860 convention. "Hell!" snapped David Davis (later associate justice of the Supreme Court) as he read the message. "We are here and he is not!" [16]

Sometimes a brief recess of the convention is obtained for opportunity to make further arrangements. Such recesses, however, are often opposed where political leaders believe it expedient to force through the nomination before the opposition can coalesce against their leading candidate. Usually the tip-off on an important deal between party leaders is signalled by the switch of the vote in one state. Thus in the course of a second, third, or fourth roll call if a state with a rather large number of delegates shifts its support from one candidate to another it is very likely an indication that the band-wagon rush is on and that other states will quickly scramble aboard. Leaders in all states are anxious not to be left dangling once faint signs appear that the outcome is inevitable, and when the key is turned as it was in 1932 when California's vote shifted from Garner to Roosevelt

[16] Henry L. Stoddard: *Presidential Sweepstakes* (New York, 1948), p. 7.

in the Democratic National Convention other state delegations lose no time in lining up under the winner's pennant.

Nominating the Vice-President

By the time the delegates are ready to turn to the task of nominating a vice-president, their energies are pretty well spent. Starting with the precedent begun by Franklin Roosevelt in 1932 when he flew to Chicago to accept the presidential nomination of the Democratic party, both parties appear to have adopted the practice of having the nominee make an acceptance speech to the convention immediately after he is nominated. This practice seems infinitely preferable to the quaint custom formerly used whereby the candidate made a speech of acceptance a month or so following the convention at a formal notification ceremony.

The nomination of the vice-presidential nominee is conditioned by several factors. [17] First, a successful presidential nominee has a large voice in determining who the vice-presidential running mate will be. Common sense requires that the presidential nominee select a person for the vice-presidential post who is quite popular with party leaders and who will help to heal any wounds that have opened in the fight for the presidential nomination. The vice-presidential nomination may be tendered to an unsuccessful competitor for the presidential prize. This was true in the Democratic convention of 1932 when Jack Garner, then Speaker of the House, was named as Roosevelt's running mate, and it was also true of the Republican convention in 1936 when the runner-up for the presidential nomination, Frank Knox, was named as Alf Landon's running mate.

Heretofore, in choosing the vice-president, strong importance has been attached to geographical considerations. [18] Thus if an Easterner receives the presidential nomination, this theory decrees that a Westerner or a representative of the Midwest must be chosen as his running mate. More recently the theory of geographical balance for the party ticket has been sharply criticized but it still remains as an important factor in deciding upon the presidential running partner.

As the position of the vice-president has been something of a nonentity in American government many highly capable men have shunned the office. Undoubtedly, such men are motivated by the same feeling expressed by John Adams over 150 years ago. "My country," wrote Adams in 1793, "has contrived for me the most insignificant office that ever the invention of man contrived, or his imagination conceived." The fact that there has been a move to make more of the vice-presidential office than

[17] For an account of some of these factors see L. C. Hatch and Earl Shoup: *A History of the Vice-Presidency of the United States* (New York, 1934); Klyde Young and Lamar Middleton: *Heirs Apparent* (New York, 1948); and Peter R. Levin: *Seven by Chance* (New York, 1948).

[18] Some incongruous results occasionally obtain from efforts to "balance the ticket" geographically. See Roy Peel and Thomas C. Donnelly: *The 1928 Campaign* (New York, 1931), p. 34.

a presiding officer of the Senate is encouraging, and it should help to make the post more attractive. [19] At the same time men who are politically ambitious feel the office is somewhat of a crematorium as far as future political ambitions are concerned nor are they persuaded by the "seven by chance" theory—that fate has brought seven vice-presidents to the presidency by succession. "No, thank you," said Daniel Webster in turning down Thurlow Weed's insistent plea that he become "Old Tippecanoe's" (William Henry Harrison's) running mate in 1840. "I do not propose to be buried until I am really dead and in my coffin." [20] But the vice presidency now has a "new look." The National Security Council Act of 1947 gave the Vice President his first statutory duties by making him a member of the Council. President Eisenhower had Vice President Nixon preside over the Council and the Cabinet in his absence. Moreover he assigned Nixon important foreign missions as well as numerous responsibilities at home. It is now inconceivable that the vice presidency will ever revert to its earlier insignificance. Its present high prestige was demonstrated by the hot competition for the nomination in the Democratic Convention of 1956. The battle of ballots between Senators Estes Kefauver and John Kennedy held television viewers breathless to the photo finish that barely gave the nomination to Senator Kefauver.

THE CONVENTION IN RETROSPECT

Has the presidential convention become enmeshed in so many vices that it is no longer a worthy device for designating candidates for the presidency? Many critics think that it has and that it must give way to a more truly representative and dignified method of nominating candidates for the post of chief executive. After studying the preliminaries and actual conventions of both the Republican and Democratic parties, Pulitzer Prize winner James Reston, of the *New York Times,* presented a five count indictment against the convention system. [21] Several of these counts tread familiar ground—that the conventions are not representative because there are few Republicans in the "Solid South" and not many Democrats in Maine or Nebraska and in both instances the convention strength of these areas is disproportionate to their voting strength. Not unfamiliar also are the charges of the same writer that the distribution of delegates at the convention favors the candidates from the large states, particularly New York, and that the convention atmosphere "is not conducive to solemn deliberations either on the qualities of the candidates or the principles of the platform." While all these charges are not without merit, it is a matter of record that the nominating convention when judged on the basis of

[19] See Clinton L. Rossiter: "The Reform of the Vice-Presidency." *Political Science Quarterly* (1948), 68:383–403; and G. Homer Durham: "The Vice Presidency." *Western Political Science Quarterly* (1948), 1:311–15.

[20] Henry L. Stoddard: *Presidential Sweepstakes,* pp. 43–4.

[21] *New York Times Magazine,* July 11, 1948.

the caliber of men it has brought to the presidency has not been disappointing. When lined up alongside the prime ministers of countries using the cabinet system where the chief executive is called out of the legislature, American presidents advanced to office by the system which Lord Bryce described as "an effort of nature to fill the void" compare quite satisfactorily. The final test of the presidential nominating convention is that it works and that it has filled in a tremendous trough in our constitutional system. Professor D. W. Brogan has shrewdly observed that "the Convention system works, works as well, in its own sphere as Congress does in its." Reform can only proceed after carefully drawn experiments have been tried and have proved their worth, and that as in all changes of this nature in a constitutional democracy we may expect such change to follow a leisurely course.

SUMMARY

From the point of view of an aspirant to the presidency, the campaign gets under way long before—perhaps years before—nominations are made. His intensive pre-convention campaigning, however, goes on as the national committee makes arrangements for the nominating convention and the delegates who are to attend it are selected.

Two-thirds of the states select delegates to the national nominating conventions by means of state or district conventions. The presidential primary, used in the remaining states, is often meaningless, since most delegates are not obligated to support the victor in the primary and leading contenders fail sometimes to enter the primaries in certain states.

In an atmosphere that partakes of the circus, the nominating conventions perform their functions of drafting party platforms and choosing their candidates. In procedure the conventions of the two parties do not differ significantly now that the Democrats have abandoned the two-thirds rule; in composition they are unlike only in the fact that Southern states are accorded considerably less representation in the Republican convention than in the Democratic gathering.

To secure the presidential nomination of a major party, a candidate will find it helpful to reside in a large state (preferably New York), to be a white Protestant, to have a background of experience in holding elective office. The presidential nominee will have influence in the selection of his running mate, who is likely to represent a different geographical section from that represented by the head of the ticket.

Though the convention is open to criticism on the ground of inequitable representation of party membership as well as for its shortcomings as a sober deliberative assembly, it has provided candidates who compare well with the political leaders of the parliamentary democracies.

The nomination of the candidate for vice-president occurs in the closing hour of the convention when weary delegates are already scattering and the quality of the candidate nominated for vice-president may consequently suffer, as history reveals. Customarily an attempt is made to balance this nomination with the head of the ticket in respect to region or ideology. Sometimes the vice-presidential nomination is accorded an unsuccessful aspirant for first place on the ticket.

CHAPTER XIV

PRESIDENTIAL ELECTIONS

CONSTITUTIONALLY, the president is named as the head of the executive branch. Yet in electing a president the voters are not merely electing the top executive officer of the Federal government. In a sense they are electing a national legislative representative, for although the president holds no membership in the national legislature—the Congress—he has by custom and practice gradually emerged as a person intimately connected with the formation of legislative policy in the United States. A person voting for a congressman secures local representation, and to the extent that the representative serves the national welfare, the people, taken collectively, might be said to have a national representative. But neither an individual congressman or the Speaker of the House of Representatives is elected by a majority of the voters of the United States; hence, even though they may strive to serve national rather than local interests they are certainly not elected by means of a national referendum. If then any public official may be said to represent the people nationally, it is the president, for he is the only public official whose election depends upon voters in every state of the union.

THE PRESIDENTIAL CAMPAIGN

The quadrennial election of a president is the one occasion upon which the political machinery scattered throughout the United States is temporarily confederated for a supreme effort. At this time the major party labels pull together many discordant elements within each party, and except in unusual cases the factional disputes within the parties are momentarily soft-pedalled. In some instances, of course, dissenting elements within a party have refused to go along. Thus certain disgruntled Democrats protested the nomination of President Truman in 1948 and the civil rights program adopted by the Democratic convention by forming a third party known as the States' Rights Democrats (popularly called Dixiecrats). Other examples of disaffection of political parties during presidential years include the Progressives led by Henry Wallace in 1948, the third party movement led by Senator Robert M. LaFollette in 1924, and the Progressive party—popularly known as the Bull-Moose party—headed by Theodore Roosevelt back in 1912. Despite the fact that the Republican label in North Dakota may stand for something quite different from what it does in Connecticut, just as the Democratic label in New York may indicate a set of beliefs somewhat different from what it would in Mississippi, a presidential election has a remarkable coalescing effect in bringing all elements of the party together behind their standard bearer.

Opening the Campaign

The presidential campaign steadily gathers momentum from the time that the identity of the nominees of both major parties is known right down to general election day. Customarily there is some lull in the presidential campaign between the time the nominees make acceptance speeches and the time when the first major broadsides are issued in early autumn. During this time, the latter part of August, presidential candidates are actively engaged in conferences, knitting the party organizations closer together, briefly vacationing to store up energy for the ordeal that lies ahead, and planning the strategy of the campaign. Early in September the presidential campaigns begin to unfold. For both parties the 1952 campaign opened as usual on Labor Day. After a speech to 2,000 New York mail carriers Eisenhower hurried south for two days of campaigning in Dixie. Skipping up to Philadelphia, he was greeted by 350,000 on his way to his first formal speech in Independence Hall. Friday he conferred with eighty party leaders in Chicago. Stevenson made Labor Day speeches in four Michigan cities. Friday, in Denver, he delivered a televised address to the Volunteers for Stevenson. Meanwhile President Truman, after a Labor Day speech in Milwaukee, delivered "give 'em hell" whistle-stop speeches on the way back to Washington.

It is not customary in American politics for presidential candidates to discuss each other's speeches point by point. Indeed it is often considered sound strategy to ignore the speeches of the presidential rival and treat his candidacy with something of indifference. President Wilson used this strategy against the Republican nominee, Charles Evans Hughes, in 1916, and it was also utilized by Franklin Roosevelt against Republican nominees Willkie and Dewey in 1940 and 1944. Where specific charges have been made in presidential campaigns, the task of answering them is often delegated to some prominent person in the party. For this purpose prominent senators, representatives, governors, and other public officials such as cabinet members are selected, in each case with an eye to choosing a person whose special interest lies somewhat in the subject matter of the problem to be discussed.

Campaign Organization

Behind the oratorical jousting of the presidential candidates lie the organizations which are expected to play a major part in a presidential election. There are two general types of organization in presidential campaigns today: the party organization and the non-party organization. Both are indispensable to the conduct of a winning campaign.

The Party Organization

For this brief—scarcely three months—period of a presidential campaign, the aim of every presidential candidate is to knit the precinct, ward, city, county, congressional district, and state organization into a national unit capable of pressing the campaign into every voting cranny of the nation. It is a Herculean task, of course, and recalcitrant leaders at the local and state levels make the task of integration all the more difficult at times. But the hunger of local political leaders for power and the rewards that go with this power, coupled with the enthusiasm which a presidential campaign always generates among the party faithful, combine to bring some cohesive unity among local, state, and national political organizations.

At the head of this coalition is the party's presidential nominee, who must in the last analysis bear the brunt of the responsibility for securing a well coordinated effort of the party at all levels. The managerial end of the national campaign, however, lies in the hands of the chairman of the national committee, who is hand-picked by the presidential nominee and who must transform local party units scattered throughout the country into a hard-driving organization dedicated to the election of the presidential nominee. Occasionally a national chairman comes to bat with the party organizational line in fairly good shape. Thus the strenuous efforts of certain Democratic leaders to rejuvenate the Democratic party between 1928 and 1932 meant that James A. Farley took over his duties as national chairman in 1932 with a first-class working organization. Hardly a day went by during that campaign, reports the Democratic party's former publicity genius, Charles Michelson, when Jim Farley did not receive a report from each state chairman. Other national chairmen taking over the direction of a campaign have not been so fortunate. In 1936, for example, it is reported that the Republican national chairman started off the campaign without even having a complete list of the Republican county chairmen available to him.

The national headquarters of the party organizations serves as the clearing house for the major campaign activities. It maintains a speaker's bureau, a research division, publicity division, and other subsidiary organizations, each responsible for some specific phase of the campaign. Through the coordinated efforts of these party organs in the national headquarters, and those in state and local areas, hundreds of thousands of pieces of literature, posters, campaign buttons, and other materials are distributed to the voters. In addition the national headquarters arranges for the distribution of press releases to both metropolitan newspapers and country weeklies throughout the United States. Moreover, in arranging for a national broadcast, the national headquarters also sees to it that appropriate foreign language broadcasts are prepared for delivery in cities heavily populated by people of recent European extraction. Finally, leaving no stone unturned, it is customary for the national headquarters of both parties to send fleets of sound trucks, movies, and special exhibits into the regions in geographic areas where they will be most effective.

The regular party organization, extending from the higher echelon at the national committee level down through the lowest precinct, is important not only for the work that it does at the operational stage of the campaign, but, as we shall note in an ensuing chapter, for the role it plays if the party succeeds in taking over the government. Thus the scramble for party leadership among the various states is highly significant, for should the party come to power, state and local leaders will have an important voice when their counsel is solicited on patronage matters.

It is natural, of course, that a presidential nominee should try to throw his weight to the local and state leaders who supported him before he was actually nominated. Very often the strength of local and state leaders and the strong parochialism in American politics prevents a presidential nominee from pushing aside local leaders whom he would like to replace with persons of his own choosing. But with undisputed control of the party during the campaign and through his control over the allocation of money for various state campaigns, the presidential nominee may exert heavy pressure to bring about a change in leadership. Expediency may compel him to go along with local leaders during the campaign. However where local leaders are indifferent toward the campaign because of losing their own candidate for the presidential nomination, they cannot ignore the fact that their future security is in danger. There have been instances where local and state leaders have sulked in their tents during presidential campaigns and have not exerted themselves to support the national ticket. At the same time, the knowledge that there will be a judgment day if the party comes to power and that the president-elect may be severe in dealing with such sabotage is a persuasive factor in discouraging any wavering loyalties among local leaders.

Non-party Campaign Organization

Closely allied with the regular party organization for presidential campaigns are a large number of what might be termed non-party organizations. From the standpoint of effective service the latter may sometimes overshadow the campaign work of the regular party organization. Among these special groups are organizations such as the American Federation of Labor, the Congress of Industrial Organizations, and various associations of businessmen, professional workers, and farmers. Some of these organizations are permanent, others are temporary. Thus in 1940 the Democrats-for-Willkie Clubs illustrated one of the temporary non-party organizations as did the organization known as the Businessmen-for-Roosevelt which was set up during the 1944 campaign. A great many of the non-party organizations are composed of minority groups and while many refrain from taking an official stand on political candidacies, others willingly endorse presidential candidates and urge their membership to vote accordingly. Officially the American Federation of Labor has never endorsed a presidential candidate except in 1924 when it conferred official blessings upon the candidacy of Senator Robert M. LaFollette. In practice, however, the American Federation of Labor, through its leadership and through its publicity has urged its members to take a stand in the presidential race. William Green, the president of the A.F. of L. openly supported Franklin Roosevelt for re-election in 1936, 1940, and 1944, and also called for the election of President Truman in 1948.

A sequel to the A.F. of L. and C.I.O. merger in December, 1955, was its endorsement of the candidacy of Stevenson and Kefauver in the 1956 campaign. Five constituent members of the merger, the International Union of Electrical Workers, the Oil, Chemical, and Atomic Workers International, the United Steel Workers of America, the United Automobile Workers, and the International Association of Machinists at their conventions voted to support the Democratic party's presidential and vice-presidential candidates. The merger's chief organ of political activity was its Committee on Political Education (C.O.P.E.) directed by Jack Kroll, formerly director of the C.I.O. Political Action Committee. C.O.P.E. made a nation-wide drive for voluntary contributions by Union workers for political activity. The goal for C.O.P.E. was one dollar each from at least one-fourth of the 15 million members of the merger with half of each dollar collected to be used by local and state committees for "political Education."

Besides the role played by national labor organizations, certain affiliates also take an active part in presidential campaigns. The powerful Teamsters' Union, under the leadership of Dan Tobin, carried on an active campaign on behalf of President Roosevelt in 1940 and 1944, as did many affiliates of both the A.F. of L. and the C.I.O. Wherever humanly possible, presidential candidates hope for and make overtures to pressure groups and organizations that will endorse their candidacy. Racial, religious, and many other organizations are eagerly looked to for support. Not all endorsements, of course, mean a deliverable vote, and the word of an organization leader by no means signifies that he will be able to deliver the votes even of a majority of his followers. In 1940, John L. Lewis, president of the United Mine Workers, exhorted the miners of the country to follow him into the camp of Wendell Willkie, but the election returns of West Virginia, Kentucky, Illinois, and other coal mining states seemed to indicate that many miners had overwhelmingly elected to ignore their leader's advice. In recent years most of the endorsements from labor organizations have favored the Democratic presidential nominee. After endorsing Stevenson in both his unsuccessful presidential campaigns, labor leadership decided in 1956 to endorse no future presidential candidates but to confine its efforts to the election of friendly congressional candidates.

The work of the non-party organizations parallels that which is done through regular party channels. Broadcasts may be given, literature distributed, special meetings held, and editorials prepared urging the election of one presidential candidate, the only difference being that the work is under different auspices. In recent years, the campaign work of the non-party organizations has come to play a formidable role in American politics, measured both in terms of the budget under which they operate and the results they have been able to achieve. Thus their part in reenforcing the work of the regular party organization is not to be denied.

Presidential Campaign Strategy

The strategy of presidential campaigns is ordinarily based upon a realistic appraisal of the political geography of the country at the time the campaign is launched.[1] In so far as the two major parties are concerned, certain hard political facts have to be considered at the outset of every presidential race. Under normal conditions the Democratic party starts any campaign with approximately 122 "safe" electoral votes. This block of electoral votes is comprised mainly of states in the so-called "Solid South," of which there are eleven, along with several states considered as "border" states, such as Kentucky, West Virginia, Oklahoma, and Missouri. But the "Solid South" is no longer so solid. In 1952 the Republican candidate General Eisenhower carried all but nine of the Southern and Border states and in 1956 all but seven.

During most of its campaigns the Republican party has not been favored with as large a tactical advantage when starting from scratch as the Democratic party has enjoyed. The hard core of Republican strength is found in certain sections of the Middle West and in a few areas of New England, notably Vermont and Maine. Nowhere, however, does the Republican party have the sizeable block of electoral votes upon which the Democratic party may usually depend, and even in the areas which might be classified as leaning strongly Republican, the combined electoral vote of the G.O.P. amounts to only about sixty or seventy electoral votes. This puts the Republicans under a handicap. In view of this circumstance it may be readily appreciated that the Democratic party, start-

[1] Excellent materials on campaign techniques will be found in Frank Kent: *Political Behavior* (New York, 1928); James A. Farley: *Behind the Ballots* (New York, 1938); Charles Michelson: *The Ghost Talks* (New York, 1944); V. O. Key: *Politics, Parties, and Pressure Groups* (2nd ed.; New York, 1947), chap. XIV; Howard R. Penniman: Sait's *American Parties and Elections* (New York, 1948), chap. XXII; and Peter H. Odegard and E. Allen Helms: *American Politics* (New York, 1947), chaps. XVII and XVIII.

ing a presidential campaign with approximately 122 votes—almost half the necessary 266 for election—has quite an advantage.

Perhaps the one outstanding feature of the presidential campaign in which the Democratic party may be said to be at a disadvantage is its relation to the popular vote. In recent years it has become increasingly evident that the Democratic party in order to win a presidential election must poll approximately fifty-two per cent of the popular vote. The Republican on the other hand may win handily with forty-eight per cent of the popular vote. This rather unusual situation—which was first called attention to by the statistician Louis Bean—is to be explained by the restriction of the Democratic party's domination to the South. [2] The Republican vote is negligible in many Southern areas, but the Democratic vote though much larger is still meagre compared with other sections of the country. Thus to offset a low popular vote in the South and out-distance the GOP in the electoral vote, the Democratic party must corral close to fifty-two per cent of the total popular vote. Mathematically, of course, it is not impossible for the Democratic presidential nominee to carry an election with somewhat less than fifty-two per cent. It is not probable, however, and to be on the safe side the Democratic nominee needs to carry this percentage of the popular vote.

The Doubtful States

The tendency to center on doubtful areas and states with huge electoral votes in presidential campaigns has already been mentioned. It is in these areas that key or major addresses are made by presidential candidates and in such areas the vice-presidential nominee along with other party potentates is often sent to stump the state. Large amounts of money are spent to carry doubtful states and to the casual observer they may appear to receive a disproportionate amount of attention.

One element of strategy not neglected in carrying a doubtful state is to entice strong local candidates for public office into the field who will be an asset to the presidential ticket. In New York, Governor Herbert Lehman was assiduously urged to be a candidate for re-election as Chief Executive of the Empire State in 1938 because of his strong popularity and the certain help he would give to the Democratic party in the 1940 presidential election. It is not always possible, of course, either to acquire gubernatorial or senatorial candidates who will strengthen the national ticket, or to remove those from the list who would be a liability to it. [3] But the gravest

[2] See Louis Bean: *Ballot Behavior: A Study of Presidential Elections* (Washington, D.C., 1940). Pp. 40–1.

[3] In the 1948 presidential campaign, Dewey strategists were greatly concerned with the unpopular candidacy of Senator W. Chapman Revercomb of West Virginia and would have liked to replace him with a stronger candidate. Neither Mr. Dewey nor the vice-presidential candidate of the G.O.P., Governor Warren, who made several speeches in the state, uttered one word of endorsement for Senator Revercomb.

consideration is given to this problem by the high command of the presidential campaign.

The Length of Presidential Campaigns

For many years foreign observers and indeed many students of American politics have been critical of the length of presidential campaigns in this country. The nature of our nominating system is responsible in part for this overdrawn electoral contest. Yet even the campaign proper, from the acceptance speeches of the candidates to the general election, probably stretches longer than critics deem advisable.

Originally the size of this country and the slowness of transportation combined to extend the length of presidential campaigns. It was urged that the people be given an opportunity both to see and hear the candidates and to have the issues debated at first hand. [4] With accelerated transportation closing the wide distances between many geographic areas, however, and the development of radio, many protests have been registered against the length of presidential campaigns. Moreover since the recent appearance of television and the certainty that its use will be extended in the ensuing years, the argument has been put forward that the people no longer are in need of personal barn-storming tours by the presidential candidates because they may now view them on a television screen in their own homes.

Responsive to the logic of arguments in favor of shorter presidential campaigns and less grueling ordeals for the candidates, both the Democratic and Republican National Nominating conventions of 1956 were scheduled for August. Those who are cognizant of the need for party organization insist that even under former conditions it was difficult to perfect machinery of party organization within the brief compass then allowed. And besides the contention that a presidential campaign needs sufficient time to be properly organized the point is still strongly pressed that the American people like to see their presidential candidate in person, and that the appearance of presidential candidates, whether in large metropolitan areas or in the most sparsely populated towns, is one aspect of American politics that must not be foregone.

In approaching the length of presidential campaigns from a more unconventional side several questions might be asked. For example, how long does it take for the voters to think over the whole business and come to a decision? There are, as Paul F. Lazarsfeld suggests many voters who know how they will vote in May even before the candidates are nominated. But there are also "June-to-August Voters"; "September-to-November Voters"; and judging by what happened in the 1948 campaign we might add that there appears to be a sizable number of October 15-November 2

[4] Between September 1 and November 2, 1940, Wendell Willkie delivered 540 speeches—66 of which were major addresses carried by national radio networkers. In 1948, President Truman delivered about 300 speeches during September and October.

voters. [5] Had the campaign been shorter in 1948, there is reason to believe that Dewey might have been elected. As yet, too little is known about how long it takes the electorate to size up the issues and candidates, and render its judgment accordingly—thus it is difficult to set a proper limit on the length of campaigns without additional information on this subject.

Are Campaigns Really Effective?

A moot question in American politics which has never been satisfactorily answered is: Does the intensive campaigning and electioneering which is done quadrennially in the presidential race make any change in the final outcome? The output in a campaign we know is tremendous, "but what of the intake?" Furthermore, what is important in affecting the results of a campaign; party allegiance, family, economic status, radio, newspapers, personal influences, or others?

The amount of careful investigation in measuring the effects of different factors in campaigns is limited. Party affiliation as we have already discovered is very important and this in turn we know to be affected by economic status, occupation, family, religion, residence, and many other elements. For the most part, the matter of party affiliation has already been determined long before a campaign gets in motion. During the course of the campaign, however, the politician wants to know how he can reach the voter who belongs to no party or regards his partisanship loosely, and what communication devices will be most effective in winning over this type of voter. The pioneer study, *The People's Choice: How the Voter Makes Up His Mind in a Presidential Campaign,* attempts to break the ground and throw some light on this subject. [6]

"In comparison with formal media of communications," this investigation concludes that "personal relationships are potentially more influential ..." [7] It also arrives at the judgment that people who make up their minds later in the campaign are much more likely to mention personal influences as an explanation of how they reached their final decision. Thus according to this interpretation the voter who does not make up his mind until the later stages of the campaign seems likely to be more influenced by personal associates than campaign speeches or newspapers. Voters who stated they were helped in making up their minds by the radio and newspapers mentioned these institutions about equally, but in so far as the "most important" source of information was concerned the radio had a clear lead over newspapers in the Lazarsfeld study. [8] A large segment of the electorate, however, apparently pays little attention to either the radio or press

[5] See Paul F. Lazarsfeld, Bernard Berelson, and Hazel Gaudet: *The People's Choice: How the Voter Makes Up His Mind in a Presidential Campaign* (New York, 1944), pp. 52–3.
[6] Paul F. Lazarsfeld, Bernard Berelson, and Hazel Gaudet: *The People's Choice.*
[7] Ibid. pp. 150–1.
[8] Ibid. p. 127.

during a presidential campaign. Without more extensive investigation, of course, the several lines of inquiry which were pursued in the Lazarsfeld study must be considered with caution and the evidence as yet is too insufficient to warrant generalizations. But the field of investigation is certainly an interesting one and one which seems assured of receiving increasing attention.

Speaking broadly, what are the general observations that may be made on the influence of campaigns? A skillfully organized campaign, to be sure, may appreciably increase the total vote of a presidential candidate. Yet in some years even the most powerful campaign probably cannot provide sufficient momentum to reverse the trend of a presidential election.

In a close election, effective party organization and campaigning would undoubtedly be enough to swing the scales one way or the other. But close presidential contests are not the usual rule in American politics. It seems abundantly clear that as a presidential election looms up, public opinion has already crystalized to a large extent, either in favor of the incumbent party and its candidate or for the rejection of both. In 1932 the tide against the Republican party had set in long before the presidential race actually commenced, and the campaigning of both major parties probably altered the result very little. Similarly, in 1936, the tempo of social forces and public opinion seemed overwhelmingly in favor of retaining the party in power and its presidential candidate. In voting for a presidential candidate, the American people are not always expressing simply a positive opinion, but indeed are often registering a protest. This was true of the campaign of 1932, and it likewise was a material factor in the campaign of 1948. Under these circumstances it seems probable that a large part of the electorate has already made up its mind by the time the presidential election year starts, thus the campaigning in large part consists of fortifying a trend already under way or stiffening the morale of a party destined to go down to defeat.

In passing general judgment upon the value of presidential campaigns, perhaps the veteran political correspondent of the *New York Times,* Turner Catledge, has offered one of the most pungent analyses. "The party rallies, speeches, and other efforts to make converts," says Mr. Catledge, "do not stampede voters to come over to the party in huge blocks." [9] Those who attend such meetings and faithfully listen to the speeches are, of course, the most ardent rank and file supporters of the party anyway; therefore, campaigning does not recruit new voters among this group. But campaigning does have a highly therapeutic effect on the followers of the party itself. It does, as Mr. Catledge reports, stir up enthusiasm and it reinforces the faith of the hard core of party supporters. In addition to burnishing up their party loyalties and also providing them with new arguments for defending their position, a well-directed campaign creates confidence

[9] See Turner Catledge: "Is Campaigning Worthwhile." *New York Times Magazine,* October 15, 1944.

among the rank and file of the party, which may have an important psychological bearing on public opinion. Thus although the campaigning is unquestionably overdone in presidential races and is doubtless quite insignificant when judged by the amount of effort and money expended, it is not altogether uneffective. Moreover, in the quest for the independent voter—the mythical figure who Walter Lippmann reports represents one out of every five voters—the quality and character of a campaign may be very important. [10] And as the independent vote throws an election one way or the other, it is easy to understand why campaigning may be a highly significant matter in a closely contested campaign.

Campaign Issues

In the midst of the campaign babel surrounding a presidential election the issues are often difficult to define. They are sometimes obscured by the claims and counter-claims of both major party candidates and as in the case of the political party platforms, there is a strong tendency to be evasive. Furthermore the fact that the two major parties have never been too widely divergent in their fundamental philosophies has meant that the issues do not have as clear a line of demarcation as they do in other countries where political cleavages are more sharply delineated. In both the 1940 and 1944 campaigns United States foreign policy was widely heralded as one of the leading issues of the campaign. Yet the presidential candidates of both parties in each instance appeared to espouse a more or less similar course of action. In such a situation the voter must make a choice in accordance with his own conscience as to which party or which presidential candidate has faithfully performed or can in the future be counted upon to fulfill best the promises made in the heat of a campaign. Both Roosevelt and Willkie in 1940 campaigned on promises to keep America out of war, for to have done otherwise might have cost the election. Faced with such a choice, the voter relies on other factors to guide him than the issue being trumpeted the loudest, even though he may rationalize by persuading himself that this was the real issue which determined his vote.

At times the issues may be stated with clarity yet quickly become lost in a sea of statements and contradictions. In opening the 1948 campaign, President Truman high-lighted two issues: the Taft-Hartley law, which he declared punitive and unfair to labor; and the high prices of food and other commodities, the blame for which he attributed to the Republican dominated Eightieth Congress for sweeping away price controls. In answering this charge, however, Republicans quickly pointed out that a majority of Democrats in Congress had joined with Republicans in over-riding the presidential veto of the Taft-Hartley act and they attempted to dodge responsibility for high prices by pointing out that the

[10] Walter Lippmann: *Public Opinion* (New York, 1929), p. 206.

Democrats controlled both the Presidency and the Congress at the time price controls were lifted.

Some presidential campaigns in American politics have been characterized by the vaguest of issues. In 1920, Boies Penrose, ringmaster of Pennsylvania Republican politics for a quarter of a century, issued a statement that the real issue of the 1920 campaign would be "Americanism." When asked by Talcott Williams what the word "Americanism" meant, Penrose replied: "Damned if I know, but you will find it a damned good issue to get votes in an election." In the same election the word "normalcy" was highly popular, and the G.O.P. campaign cry was: "Back to normalcy," again illustrating that what is sometimes passed on to the voters as an issue is not an issue at all, but simply a catchy slogan which parties attempt to dignify as an issue. Thus, in 1944, the Republican theme was: "It's time for a change," while two years later the slogan—"Had enough?" used in the 1946 congressional elections to needle the Democrats on consumer shortages—afforded another leading example of an attempt to inflate a slogan into a campaign issue.

Adding still more to the confusion over issues in presidential campaigns is the fact that the climate of opinion within a party in Congress may be different from that of the presidential nominee. A presidential nominee cannot with impunity repudiate the record of his party in Congress, and although he may soft-peddle certain features of its legislative program which he feels to be distasteful, any marked disparity between the thinking of the presidential nominee and his party's record in Congress leaves him in a somewhat awkward position. The presidential nominee may, to be sure, mold the party platform as he desires, and indeed trespass beyond its limits. But to assure victory he must tred cautiously or he finds himself in diagreement on a leading issue with members of his party in Congress. This does not mean that the presidential nominee need continue a policy of temporizing once elected. But during the campaign itself the caution he must exercise is not conducive to a clarification of the issues.

Beyond the pale of what should be strictly construed as the intellectual issues of a presidential campaign, certain items are sometimes raised that are not really issues at all, but may be comparable in effect to a potent issue. A slip of the tongue by a presidential candidate may give rise to a harmful undercurrent against him, just as an unfortunate statement by one of his supporters may. When presidential candidates Blaine and Cleveland were pitted against each other, there is reasonable ground for believing that the speech of the Reverend Burchard for a group of Protestant clergymen characterizing the Democrats as partisans of "rum, Romanism, and rebellion" was a *faux pas* that cost Blaine the election. The speech carefully exploited by the Democrats was highly obnoxius to Roman Catholic voters in the East, and it seems probable that Blaine, who lost the State of New York by slightly over one thousand votes, might have been elected except for this unfortunate incident. As yet it has not been possible to measure with any great accuracy just how much the question of religion influenced the presidential campaign of 1928. It seems undeniable that the fact that Al Smith, the Democratic presidential candidate, was a Catholic, cost him a lot of votes in the deep South as well as in many regions of the North.

The Democratic candidates Stevenson and Kefauver seized the initiative at the beginning of the 1956 campaign and soon reduced the Eisenhower support from 59 to nearly 55 per cent according to the Gallup poll. The Republican campaigners stressed the prevailing peace and prosperity and relied on Eisenhower's unsurpassed popularity. In an effort to break the spell of the peace issue, Stevenson proposed an international agreement to end H-bomb testing and suggested the possible ending of the draft. The public reaction to these proposals was disappointing. The crisis in the Middle East, due to the attacks of Israel, France, and England on Egypt had the effect of restoring Eisenhower strength to the high percentage of the election.

Campaign Finance

Financing of a presidential campaign has been and remains one of the major headaches of political parties and presidential candidates.[11] With the development of radio, the cost of conducting a presidential campaign has increased enormously. To obtain just one of the major networks for a thirty-minute telecast costs about seventy-five thousand dollars and during the campaign, of course, extensive use is made of television not only by the presidential candidates but by other leading party figures as well. Other large financial items in a campaign budget include special trains carrying the presidential candidates and batteries of newspaper correspondents and local politicians, as well as a long list of items such as campaign literature, the maintenance of local party headquarters, and the support of countless activities that attend a presidential campaign.

An approximation of the total amount spent by both major parties during a presidential campaign would place the figure well over twenty million dollars. Actually this figure probably ranges much higher, for it is not possible to get accurate information on all the sources that are tapped for contributions, and all the monies that are expended in the course of a presidential campaign. With the advent of the New Deal, the Democratic party found it more difficult to raise money from business sources than it had formerly. In recent years, however, the Democratic party has had its own campaign activities heavily re-enforced by the expenditures of labor unions, and this has helped to compensate for the increased difficulty which the party has faced in acquiring funds.

The Republican party, in the main, has been more generously supplied with funds to maintain its presidential campaigns, but it, too, has suffered difficulties in the matter of fund raising, and it often winds up a presidential

---

[11] See Louise Overacker: *Presidential Campaign Funds* (Boston, 1946), and also her *Money in Elections* (New York, 1932). Another helpful reference is J. K. Pollock: *Party Campaign Funds* (New York, 1932).

campaign with a large deficit. [12] The G.O.P. is still able to look to the more well-to-do business men of the country for a large part of its support, although statutory restrictions and much steeper income taxes have probably ended the era of flush campaign contributions when some individuals gave as much as $100,000 or even a quarter of a million towards financing a presidential campaign budget.

Neither of the major parties has had much success in broadening the base of campaign contributions. Several schemes have been tried to solicit small contributions such as a dollar from the rank and file of the party, but most have met with little success. Under the terms of the Hatch Act discussed in a previous chapter, each political committee is limited to $3,000,000 for a presidential campaign. Thus a national committee of a party might spend $3,000,000, and a state committee could do likewise if it could raise that much. Moreover, the $3,000,000 figure does not include money expended by organizations outside of the party, and it is an easy matter to circumvent the Hatch Act in the matter of expenditures by having non-party organizations parallel the campaign work of the party itself. The Hatch Act also limits the amount that an individual may contribute to $5,000. An individual may still, however, give $5,000 to the national committee of the party and also contribute to a non-party organization working for the same purpose. Another method by which the $5,000 contribution limitation may be dodged is by giving $5,000 for each member of the family; thus a wealthy individual desiring to give more than $5,000 might arrange to have each individual member of his family contribute $5,000, though he himself provided it all, and in this way contribute a total amount of perhaps $25,000 or $30,000. The attempt to limit the amount of contributions has not been entirely satisfactory by any means. As it was noted in an earlier chapter of our story, even Senator Hatch himself, author of the Hatch Act, has called for its repeal.

The Press in Presidential Campaigns

Just as the spending of a larger amount of money in a presidential campaign by a political party has not necessarily meant the election of its nominee, so the candidate receiving the greatest newspaper and editorial support has not emerged as the winner in recent years. The press may be very powerful in building up candidates for the presidential nomination, and it certainly has large influence on many questions of political concern. Yet if the results of several recent presidential elections are any index, the power of editorial support in the presidential election seems to be on the wane. In four presidential elections—1936, 1940, 1944, and 1948— the Democratic nominee was opposed in each instance by approximately 70 per cent of the American press. Included in the opposition were most

[12] For an analysis of the size and percentage distribution of cash distributions to the Republican and Democratic national committees in presidential campaigns from 1928 through 1940, see Louise Overacker: "Trends in Party Campaign Funds," in *The Future of Government in the United States,* edited by Leonard D. White (Chicago, 1942), p. 128.

of the largest metropolitan newspapers in the United States as well as countless smaller daily and weekly papers. Notwithstanding this opposition, the Democratic nominees won decisively each time, and their election performances seem to have scotched the notion that the editorial page is all powerful in American presidential elections.

THE PRESIDENTIAL CAMPAIGN AND CONGRESSIONAL ELECTIONS

The influence of the presidential candidate upon congressional elections has evoked a heated debate in this country. Indeed, as Louis Bean observes: "The unanswered theological question of the Middle Ages: 'How many angels can dance on the point of a needle?' has its counterpart in political discussion today: How many congressmen can ride into office on the president's coattail?" [13] The essential idea of the "coattail" theory is that in a presidential election year a sizeable number of congressional candidates are swept into office partly because of the strong momentum generated by the presidential campaign and to a somewhat lesser degree through the prestige of the presidential candidate himself. In substantiation of this theory is the fact that in the mid-term congressional elections the party in power invariably loses congressional seats while in presidential election years the party which captures the chief executive's office usually gains seats in Congress.

Opposed to the "coattail" theory is a school of thought that views the presidential campaign as having little to do with the number of congressmen elected by one party or the other. Thus Professor Ewing, in his study of congressional elections covering a fifty-year-period, concludes that the "coattail theory" is vastly exaggerated. He finds that in several presidential campaigns a larger number of voters cast ballots for congressional candidates than for the presidental nominees, and on the basis of this evidence he opines that the popularity of the presidential candidate and the presidential campaign itself has a very small influence upon congressional elections. [14]

Somewhere between the two extremes—that the presidential campaign and the popularity of the presidential candidate is the controlling factor or that both are of slight significance—lies the truth. Unquestionably the political appeal and charm of a presidential candidate has helped to pull many a congressman safely into port. The popular prestige of

[13] Louis Bean: *How to Predict Elections* (New York, 1948), p. 31.

[14] Cortez A. M. Ewing: *Congressional Elections: 1896–1946* (Norman, Oklahoma, 1947), pp. 25–9. Looking at "coattail riding" in the 1948 general election, Mr. Charles Bartlett of the *Chattanooga Times* found that of the 17 Democratic Senators and 170 Democratic representatives who were elected in the 18 states that Truman carried, only five senators and 24 representatives failed to run ahead of the President in their own districts. See *Chattanooga Times*, March 7, 1949. As Arthur Krock commented later, however, Mr. Bartlett's analysis compared the percentage of victory which each representative chalked up in his own particular district with Truman's percentage of victory for the state as a whole. See *New York Times*, March 15, 1949.

Franklin Roosevelt was pervasive enough to send several of his party's nominees to Congress who might otherwise have been defeated. It may also be noted that in states where the relative strength of the two major parties is quite evenly divided, the winning presidential candidate often carried quite a few of his party's congressional nominees over the hump. There are two important factors, however, that must not be neglected in assessing the influence of presidential candidates upon congressional elections. To begin with, presidential and congressional political trends move along together as we observed earlier. The political tide in this instance is a "duality." [15] Moreover in a presidential election year, the political parties lay out far more money and expend far greater effort to elect their ticket. Thus the combination of both factors is conducive to the election of a House and Senate that will be controlled by the same party as that of the winning presidential candidate.

The actual number of congressmen who ride into office on the coat-tail of a victorious presidential candidate is, of course, a matter of conjecture. It has been estimated that in the presidential elections of 1932, 1936, 1940, and 1944 somewhere between twenty-six and thirty congressmen appear to have ridden into office on President Roosevelt's coattail in each case. In so far as determining the comparative pulling power of one presidential candidate over another, there is not yet sufficient information to make any generalization. Not since 1848 had a President elected by a popular majority failed to carry along a Congress of his own party until 1956. Then, in spite of Eisenhower's reelection by the second greatest popular majority of a presidential election, the opposition obtained a majority of two in the Senate and thirty-seven in the House of Representatives.

The Barometers of Presidential Elections

American voters more so than others appear to have an insatiable desire to know in advance what is going to happen in a national election. [16] Thus early in the campaign the political horizon is eagerly scanned for portents that will reveal a trend for the forthcoming election. For a great many years, the State of Maine, because of its early general election held in September, has been looked to for some indication of how the wind is blowing. Actually, of course, the old saying, "As Maine goes, so goes the nation," is not a reliable portent at all. Eleven counties scattered among eight different states have been on the winning side in presidential elections since 1896, and if it could be predetermined how these counties were going to go they might have some predictive value. But the only way of getting a line on how a state or the nation is leaning is either from com-

[15] For a discussion of this trend see ibid., p. 32, and Louis Bean: *How to Predict Elections*, pp. 31-6.
[16] One can hardly imagine the American electorate showing the unconcern and patience of the British electorate in 1945 while the latter waited three weeks between July 5 and July 25 for the results of the Parliamentary general election to be announced.

petent observers—who are often wrong—or through the various straw polls which have steadily advanced in popularity during the past two decades.

Public opinion polls have come to be carefully observed accompaniments of presidential campaigns. Periodic reports are eagerly followed on these polls of which the two most well established are the *Fortune* poll and the American Institute of Public Opinion poll, commonly referred to as the Gallup poll. With the exception of the 1948 presidential election, both polls have been remarkably successful. [17] The *Fortune* poll attempts only a forecast of the popular vote while the Gallup poll adds to the popular interest by attempting the difficult feat of a state by state prediction.

Criticism of the polls and possible reasons for their failure was discussed in an earlier chapter (chapter IX), and need not be repeated here. In spite of the setback which all polls received in the 1948 presidential election, however, and notwithstanding occasional outbursts against them, there seems every reason to believe that public-opinion polls will continue to be one of the carefully watched sidelights of presidential campaigns.

Major Determinants in a Presidential Election

In the last analysis, the inevitable question that pops up in every presidential campaign is, what really decides the election? Fundamental to the answering of this question are several factors. High on the list is the state of the nation's economy, for certainly the economic conditions of the country have a close bearing on the outcome of presidential elections. As Jim Farley astutely observed, the American people are not usually disposed to turn a president out of office when the economic conditions of the country are prosperous. Another factor that looms large in determining the results of presidential elections is the long-run behavior cycle of American politics. Thus Louis Bean in a remarkable prophecy based upon his analytical study *How To Predict Elections,* stated ten months prior to the 1948 general elections: "The evidence is clear that the year 1947 will go down in our political history as marking the end of the downward trend of the New Deal tide and the beginning of a new one.

". . . numerous signs at the end of 1947 pointed to another presidential term for the Democrats, the fifth in succession since 1928. The popularity of President Truman has risen sharply from the low point to which it had fallen in 1946. Independent voters, whose failure to go to the polls in 1946 helped to restore both houses of Congress to the Republicans, showed at the beginning of 1948 considerably greater preference for the Democrats than for the Republicans."

"There could be no doubt that the Republicans in 1947 had failed to hold the gains made in 1946." [18]

Certainly there is a tendency for parties to oscillate in power, and the trends for or against one party or the other seem to set in with a fair degree

---

[17] The 1940 *Fortune* poll conducted by Elmo Roper forecast the total popular vote for Franklin Roosevelt within one-half of one percent.

[18] Louis Bean: *How to Predict Elections,* pp. 161–3.

of uniformity. Thus the party out of power gradually makes a comeback until it is finally catapulted to power following which its strength ordinarily begins to decline until eventually it is forced out by the other party. The difficulty with the political cycle in American politics lies in accurately plotting the curve, but there is little doubt that this cycle is of great importance for the presidential campaign, and the presidential candidate bucking against a trend that has already set in has scant chance for success.

Two additional hard realities that affect the outcome of a presidential election are the metropolitan vote and the size of the total vote. The steady drift of the American population from rural areas to metropolitan centers has not been without effect on the presidential vote. [19] A traditional stronghold of the Republican party has been the rural vote, but many rural voters who have moved to industrial centers seeking employment have gravitated into the Democratic party. This leakage has weakened the Republican party in states like Michigan, Illinois, and Ohio, where previously the Republican vote in suburban and small towns was ordinarily sufficient to offset any lead that a Democratic presidential candidate might command in the large city vote. [20] In general the Republican party looks to the rural vote to provide its winning margin in a national election. In New York, for example, the Republican presidential candidates usually fail to carry New York City, but they can generally count upon an "up-state" majority of around a half-million votes, and if they can hold down the lead which the Democrats pile up in New York City, they have a fair chance of carrying the state. [21]

Since the 1930's eleven key cities in pivotal states have been tails that could wag the dogs. Republican majorities rolled up in the villages, smaller cities, and countryside have often been nullified by the metropolitan masses, thereby determining the election of Democratic Presidents. Nor was this possibility terminated by Eisenhower's capture of the big city vote in his personal instead of a Republican party victory in 1956.

Closely connected with the metropolitan vote as a strategic factor in presidential elections, is the size of the vote. [22] The latter element as we have seen appears to be particularly significant for the Democratic party. The heavier the vote, the greater the likelihood of a Democratic presidential victory, and this same phenomenon is also observable in the biennial con-

[19] The Census Bureau reported that on election day, 1948, the United States would have about 95,000,000 men and women of voting age. Of this number of potential voters 67,000,000 were registered and 48,000,000 actually voted. In the 1940, 1944, and 1948 presidential elections, the percentages of the potential vote were 59.5, 56.4, and 51.3. On January 1, 1947 there were 27,550,000 persons living on farms, approximately 3,000,000 or 9.8 percent less than the farm population in 1940.

[20] See Wilfred E. Binkley: *American Political Parties* (2d. ed.; New York, 1947), pp. 383–4.

[21] In 1944, despite the half-million vote majority, Mr. Dewey piled up in up-state New York, it was still insufficient to overcome the lead of 770,000 which Franklin Roosevelt obtained in New York City.

[22] ". . . other factors being equal," writes Professor Key, "an increase in participation brings an increase in the Democratic percentage of the total vote in presidential elections."—*Politics, Parties, and Pressure Groups*, p. 594.

gressional elections where the evidence seems to indicate that a light vote is ominous for the Democratic party's fortunes.

Minor Parties in Presidential Elections

Minor parties have not changed the final result of a presidential election in the course of the present century. In the 1912 campaign Theodore Roosevelt captured the largest block of electoral votes (88) ever won by a minor party presidential nominee and in so doing paved the way for Woodrow Wilson's election over William Howard Taft. Senator Robert M. LaFollette, although polling more popular votes (4,826,471) than any third party candidate, carried only thirteen electoral votes (Wisconsin) when he headed the Progressive party ticket in 1924, while the Thurmond-Wright ticket of the States' Rights party won 38 electoral votes with a little over a million popular votes in 1948.

In general not only is the two-party tradition a thoroughly ingrained habit with the American electorate, but many difficulties also exist which stand in the way of a successful minor party movement. The party politicians of both major parties, recognizing the nuisance which splinter movements may cause, have made it increasingly difficult for such groups to get on the ballot. In 1924 the elder LaFollette managed to get on the ballot in all forty-eight states, but in 1936 a third party movement—the Union party—led by Representative Lemke of North Dakota was able to have its electors on the ballot in only thirty-six states. Similar difficulties were encountered by the Dixiecrat party and the Progressive party of Henry Wallace in 1948.

Added to the technical barriers which have made minor party crusades troublesome affairs to engineer are several other factors. A minor party must have both local and regional organizations which must be pulled together at the top by national organization. It must also find financial backing. But to make good on all of these necessities as well as securing cohesive popular support—which it must have if any inroads are to be made on the strength of the major parties—is a formidable task, and thus far minor parties have simply not been able to make the grade.

No minor party has made much of a showing in the presidential lists of recent times. A tremendous amount of publicity attended the appearance of the Progressive and Dixiecrat parties in the 1948 campaign, and while the latter won four states for a total of thirty-eight electoral votes, the combined popular vote of both was a negligible factor in the total presidential vote. Norman Thomas, the Socialist party candidate in every presidential election beginning with 1928 through 1948, polled 837,000 votes in the 1932 election, but since that date his popular vote has usually been around 100,000. Other minor parties such as the Communist, Socialist Labor, and Prohibitionist parties have also usually had presidential nominees, but they have managed to secure only a fraction of the total popular vote. One minor party which has held together for more than a single election that has threatened to have some effect on the outcome of the presidential campaign is the American Labor party of New York. In two presidential elections—1940 and 1944—the American Labor party vote which was thrown to the Democratic nominee was approximately 400,-000—enough to have switched New York's forty-seven electoral votes one way or the other. Speaking broadly, however, minor parties have not made spectacular showings at the ballot box. Conceivably, of course, minor parties could have an invigorating effect on our political system and we cannot rule out the possibility that a minor party might form which would have both strength and permanence, enough perhaps to bring about a major realignment of our political parties.

THE PRESIDENTIAL ELECTION IN RETROSPECT

From the inception of our story of political parties and nominating procedures, we have observed that all forms of party organizations are ultimately given some cohesiveness by our system of nominating and electing a president, and the final emergence of the presidential nominee as the party leader. The security of the lines running between the president and various levels of party organizations are not to be taken for granted. Their strength depends upon the vigor and forceful personality of the president himself. The entire system when reviewed in retrospect, seems to be loosely cemented together at the top, and in appearance, at least, may look very undisciplined. In practice, however, the skillful presidential nominee who ultimately becomes president may keep a live current running through the party organization, reaching from himself as titular leader of the party down through the smallest precinct organization.

That few presidents are able to supply this dynamic form of party leadership is not to be taken as a complete indictment of the system itself, but rather as an indication that brilliant political leadership is exceptional. Clearly a man who emerges as president through the network of our party nominative system has the opportunity to lead and to use the party effectively for backing his legislative program during his tour of service as chief executive. By its very nature our party system leads to a result where leadership by the president is both essential and desirable. One of the first tests for a successful chief executive is to have his party safely in back of him, and while it is to be expected that some fractures will develop between a president and his party, it is axiomatic that once a president loses control of his party, he becomes a sorry figure in the chief executive's office.

In this long campaign drive climaxed by the presidential election, the task of a presidential nominee is not simply to get enough votes to win the election, but also to use the campaign for building effective leadership and responsive party organization that will not melt in the face of the formidable responsibility a president must assume once he is inaugurated. The decisions he makes, therefore, during the heat of the campaign, may

well have an important bearing on the whole future course of his administration. He must be able to decide which of two factions in a state it would
be wisest for him to support, just as he must decide upon which party
leaders he will confide in and what promises he will and will not make.
At the same time, the presidential nominee must also help pull many representatives and senators safely under the wire in their contests for congressional seats. In the latter case the presidential nominee lays the groundwork for favorable treatment and backing from the party organization
which will emerge in the Congress itself, and which it will be most imperative for the president to keep on friendly terms. Thus, if he is a capable
leader, the presidential winner on general election day will have lifted himself into the position of leadership in two brackets of our party organization. On one side he will have inspired the loyalty of the various local,
state, and national party organizations upon which he will depend for
advice on matters of patronage and for keeping the party machinery vitalized for future congressional and presidential contests. At his other side,
the victor in a presidential election has his party delegation in Congress
with which he must work during the ensuing four years. If he has used
his influence wisely he will have greatly tightened his hold on the reins
of party leadership in both instances. When at long last, therefore, the
president-elect takes office on January 20, he should, if he is fortunate, be
in full possession of the party leadership both in the regular party organization outside of the government and of the party organization within the
government, that is, the Congress itself.

FORMALLY ELECTING THE PRESIDENT—THE ELECTORAL
VOTE SYSTEM

Along with the unpaid deficits and heavy or glad hearts in the aftermath
of a presidential campaign, there remains one important piece of unfinished
business—the official election of the president. We may know the results
early on the night of the general election and hordes of the party faithful
may already be reaching out for the offices they hope will soon be theirs,
but under the Constitution the presidential electors must gather in their
respective states to cast their votes and the ballots must be counted in the
presence of a joint session of Congress—all before a president may be declared officially elected.

The Constitution and Presidential Election

Originally the indirect electoral system provided for by the Constitution
called for an Electoral College to be composed of presidential electors
from each state equal in number to the total congressional representation
of the state and selected as the state legislatures might direct. Since the
retirement of President Washington at the end of his second term, however, presidential electors have functioned mainly as figureheads. With
few exceptions, the presidential electors have voted in conformity with the

popular vote of the state. The original conception of the electoral college, therefore, was discarded almost at the inception of American government, yet the institution has survived down to the present day, notwithstanding periodic attacks against it.

The Selection of Presidential Electors

The Federal Constitution leaves the selection of presidential electors in the hands of the states. In an early day, the state legislatures elected presidential electors, but this system gradually yielded to popular election, and the latter method is now the universal rule. In practice, the political party organizations within each state prepare their own list of candidates for the post of presidential elector. This is done by the state central committee in some states and by state convention or direct primary in others. [23] Persons selected as candidates for presidential elector need not necessarily have been active in politics and are often persons of high standing in the community who are named as presidential electors simply as an honor.

Each political party nominates a list of presidential electors equal to the number of representatives and senators to which the state is entitled. Thus, when the voter casts his ballot for president and vice-president on general election day, he does not cast a direct vote for either of these two offices, but instead generally votes for the entire slate of presidential electors nominated by the political party of his choice. [24] In quite a number of states, however, the electors are not on the ballot and only the names of the presidential and vice-presidential candidates appear. Previously, some states selected presidential electors by congressional district and this practice often led to a division of the state's electoral vote between two presidential candidates. But today, all states follow the practice of having each party submit a complete list of presidential elector nominees and the voter votes for the entire list.

HOW THE ELECTORAL COLLEGE OPERATES

A few weeks after the general election the victorious slate of presidential electors assemble (usually at the state capital) to cast formally their vote as electors for president and vice-president. Federal law directs that the time for such meetings shall be the first Monday after the second Wednesday in December following the election. In conformity with the Twelfth Amendment, the electors vote separately for presidential and vice-presidential candidates. In further compliance with requirements prescribed by the same amendment, they arrange to have duplicate lists prepared showing all the candidates receiving support for either office, and after these lists have been signed and sealed, to transmit them to the Secretary

[23] See Ruth C. Silva: "State Law on the Nomination, Election, and Instruction of Presidential Electors." *American Political Science Review* (1948), 42:523–29.

[24] For a description of the forms of ballots used in presidential elections, see S. D. Albright: *The American Ballot* (Washington, D. C., 1942), chap. V.

of State of the United States. Finally, as confirmation of their authority to act, the electors must also forward along with these documents, their own certificates of election bearing the signature of the governor.

Since 1792 the State Department has served as the intermediary between the Federal and state governments in the electoral vote procedure. The duties of the Secretary of State in this connection are to receive from the state authorities two certificates and to transmit them to Congress. Copies of one certificate—the certificate confirming the election of the presidential electors—are forwarded to both the speaker of the House and the president pro tempore of the Senate. [25] The other certificate—the one showing the separate vote of the electors of each state—is transmitted to the president pro tempore of the Senate pending the joint session of Congress to canvass the vote.

Counting the Electoral Vote

Since the adoption of the Twentieth (Lame-Duck) Amendment, the counting of the electoral vote takes place in the presence of a joint session of Congress at high noon on January 6, following the general election, when the new Congress convenes. With the president of the Senate presiding, the certificates sent by the state electoral bodies are opened and the electoral votes tabulated by four tellers—two Democrats and two Republicans (one from each House) who have been previously agreed upon. Theoretically, of course, the president and vice-president are not known until this electoral count has been completed and the persons receiving a majority of the votes for the respective offices have been proclaimed elected. Yet in practice the result of a presidential election may ordinarily be confidently predicted as soon as the popular vote is known because of the certainty that the electoral vote will be cast in accordance with the popular mandate of the state. There are contingencies, however, that may hold the result of a presidential election in abeyance. To be declared elected, a presidential candidate must receive a majority—266—of the electoral votes, otherwise the election goes to the House where the three highest candidates are voted upon, each state having one vote. The latter contingency is not likely except in a three-cornered race where all the candidates are fairly strong. But suppose in a tightly contested campaign between two presidential candidates where the outcome depended upon the electoral vote of one state, two conflicting sets of electoral returns are forwarded from the state in question? Who decides which shall be the valid electoral vote and how is a decision to be reached under such circumstances?

Unfortunately the Constitution is vague on this matter. Until the celebrated Tilden-Hayes contest of 1876, no serious difficulty of this nature was presented. In the latter year two sets of electoral certificates were transmitted to the president of the Senate—one favoring Hayes, the

[25] This certificate also lists all other candidates for electors and the number of votes received by all of them.

G.O.P. nominee, the other supporting the Democratic candidate, Tilden—from three southern states. In addition, one electoral vote from Oregon was also disputed. As the Twelfth Amendment says nothing about whether the president of the Senate should count the electoral votes or who should pass on the validity of the certificates presented to the same officer, the Congress was confronted with a real dilemma, particularly with the Senate under the control of the Republicans and the House Democratic. Without a precedent to guide them and with twenty-one vital electoral votes at stake, Congress sought to meet the crisis (after much jockeying by the Senate to elect Hayes and the House to name Tilden) by setting up an unusual electoral commission composed of five senators, five representatives, and five Supreme Court justices and agreeing to abide by the commission's decision on the certificates in dispute. "The Tilden-Hayes controversy," as constitutional historian Carl Swisher points out, "did not go so far as the verge of civil war, but it was a major controversy in American politics." [26] Not until two days before the time the new president was to be inaugurated was the final decision on the election known. Perhaps the make-up of the commission itself provides the best clue to the intensity of partisan feelings. By a fortuitous combination of circumstances for the Republicans, eight of the fifteen Commission members were either Republicans or stemmed from G.O.P. stock. Thus, whether by design or not, the commission voted to give all twenty-one disputed votes to Hayes, and the latter, though polling a smaller popular vote than Tilden, was proclaimed elected by the close margin of 185 to 184 electoral votes.

The Electoral Count Act of 1887

A little over a decade after the Tilden-Hayes crisis Congress passed the Electoral Count Act of 1887. This Act re-affirmed the principle that presidential electors are state officers, and it sought, in so far as possible, to have the states settle their own controversies involving the validity of electoral vote certificates. If the states are unable to settle such disputes, however, and conflicting certificates are forwarded to the Senate, the law prescribes that the two houses of Congress, each acting independently, shall decide which ones are to be accepted. Should the houses be unable to reach agreement, the Act provides that the electoral returns that have been certified by the governor shall be favored. Finally, if the governor certifies none of the conflicting returns, the state loses its electoral vote in the election.

No contest has yet arisen to test the Electoral Count Act. The law undoubtedly leaves much to be desired, but it must be recognized that it is not easy to draft legislation that will anticipate all conceivable disputes arising out of the electoral college system. As long as the electoral vote system remains, an occasional dispute over the returns, is of course, a possibility. In a great majority of presidential elections, however, there

[26] See Carl B. Swisher: *American Constitutional Development* (Boston, 1943), p. 490.

are no serious breakdowns in the mechanical functioning of the electoral vote system and the counting of the votes is simply a formality. In practice only two presidents have actually been elected by the House of Representatives: Thomas Jefferson in 1801, and John Quincy Adams in 1825. Thus with these two exceptions plus the uproarious Tilden-Hayes election of 1876, the electoral system has operated without serious incident.

Time Limitations in Electing a President

The normal course of events, as we have observed, is for the election of the president to be declared without further ado following the tabulation of the electoral vote in the presence of a joint session of Congress on January 6 following a general election. If, however, no candidate has received a majority of the electoral vote and the House of Representatives has not reached a decision on the election of a new president prior to the date which the Constitution now prescribes for the inauguration of a prsident (January 20), the vice-president-elect "shall act as president until a president shall have qualified."

Regulations Governing the Election of the Vice-President

The vice-president, like the president, must secure a majority of the total vote in the electoral college to be elected. Where none of the vice-presidential candidates receive a majority of electoral votes—an extremely unlikely contingency—the election of the vice-president is thrown into the Senate. Should this be the case, the senators vote as individuals instead of under the rules prescribed for the House when a presidential election is decided by the Lower Chamber, and the senators must elect from the two highest candidates for the vice-presidential office.

RECENT PROBLEMS WITH THE ELECTORAL SYSTEM

Besides the objections that the electoral vote system might result in the election of a president who had run behind in the total popular vote, that it leads to confusion if conflicting electoral returns are transmitted from the states and the election is thrown into the House by the failure of any candidate to secure a majority, one further indictment has been raised against it. In the absence of state regulation compelling it, presidential electors are not legally bound to vote for the presidential or vice-presidential candidates receiving the highest popular vote. It might well be political suicide for a presidential elector to vote for a presidential candidate other than the popular choice whom he was elected to support, but he might still do it though he has a moral obligation to vote for the candidate who was the leading popular choice. Again, the likelihood of the latter happening is scant, but the remote possibility that the electoral vote might not be cast in conformity with the popular vote of a state has caused periodic flurries of excitement in American politics and has likewise prompted several demands that such an occurrence be made impossible.

In so far as individual deflections of presidential electors are concerned there has never been any real problem. But where the party organization succeeds in nominating a list of candidates for presidential electors who are pledged not to vote for a party's presidential nominee despite the popular vote a serious difficulty is presented. Suppose that through a skillful maneuver a well-disciplined party organization nominates a slate of delegates for presidential electors who agree not to vote for presidential candidate A under any circumstances, even though he is the nominee of the party's national convention. Let us further suppose that candidate A is highly popular with the rank and file of the party and that he carries the state in the general election, yet the presidential electors who were elected to support him have no intention of so doing. What may be expected to follow under such conditions?

In practice, tactics of this nature aimed at perverting the verdict of the popular vote have usually been short-circuited before the damage has been done. Such action was threatened by disgruntled anti-Roosevelt Democrats in Mississippi and in Texas in 1944. The plan failed to materialize in either state, although in Texas it was necessary to hold a special convention in September preceding the general election in order to undo what had been done at the May State Democratic convention and replace the list of nominees for presidential electors with one pledged to support Franklin Roosevelt. In the same year, it might also be recorded, that in Mississippi a special session of the legislature had to be called to undo the work of the state convention.

The presidential campaign of 1948 brought the uncertainties and possibilities for manipulation of the electoral vote system into even sharper focus. Early in the year several Southern states, notably Virginia, Alabama, Mississippi, and Louisiana embarked upon a course of action designed to throw the state electoral vote to someone other than Mr. Truman in the event he was the Democratic party's presidential nominee. The plan after appearing to get off to a fast start, gradually bogged down, but not before sounding a pretty clear warning as to how a determined, well-organized political group might go about distorting the popular result of an election by controlling the nomination of presidential electors and stealing the party label.

With the appearance of the States' Rights Democratic party after the split in the Democratic National Convention in July, the way was paved for support of the States' Rights presidential ticket by the Democratic presidential electors pledged not to support Truman. The Democratic electors in South Carolina, Alabama, Mississippi, and Louisiana were pledged to support the States' Rights party before election, thus the voters in these states did know for whom they were voting. But in one state—Alabama—a true test of the popular vote was certainly obscured when the Democrats who supported Truman could not get their slate of presidential electors on the ballot. Elsewhere—in the states where Truman had to appear on the ballot outside the regular Democratic party column—conditions could hardly be called conducive to a fair test of the popular vote. The fact remains that the national organization of the Democratic party had no way to control the local Democratic organizations or to prevent the theft of the party label. Once again the ease with which political leaders in these states were able to impale the ticket of the national party and at the same time take the party label illustrates the looseness of party organization and lack of effective control over local leaders.

PROPOSED CHANGES IN THE ELECTORAL SYSTEM

Spurred on by the shortcomings of the electoral vote system that came to light in the 1948 presidential campaign and the always possible contingency that the present arrangement could bring about the election of a minority president, many critics have been calling for a change in this method of electing a president. President Lincoln was elected without a majority of popular votes, while Presidents Hayes and Benjamin Harrison were elected without even a popular plurality; that is to say they had fewer popular votes than the rivals they defeated. In the 1948 presidential election a shift of only 30,000 votes distributed among three states could have resulted in Governor Dewey's election despite President Truman's plurality of approximately 2,000,000 votes over the Republican nominee.

Among the critics of the electoral college system as it now exists, there are two schools of thought. One regards the Electoral College as a useless appendage and insists that it should be abolished. This group would have the election of the president and vice-president depend solely upon the popular vote. But this plan could require no majority when several candidates were competing, while the present method requires an absolute majority in the Electoral College.

Recently a proposed reform of the Electoral College which would make the electoral vote correspond more accurately with the popular vote has made some headway. This plan, known as the Lodge Amendment, stemmed from a study by the Brookings Institution and was approved by both the Senate and House Judiciary Committees of the Eightieth Congress. [27] In brief the proposed constitutional amendment would retain the electoral vote system, but it would allow the electoral vote of the state to be divided proportionately in accordance with the popular vote. [28] The

[27] A constitutional amendment similar to the proposal advocated by Senator Henry Cabot Lodge of Massachusetts was advocated earlier by the late Senator George W. Norris of Nebraska, but twice failed to secure the necessary two-thirds vote in the Senate in 1934.

[28] In urging the merits of the Lodge Amendment, the Brookings Institution states that the proposed change "preserves the compromise between the large states and small states that permitted the adoption of the Constitution and the formation of a more perfect Union."

proposed change would also make a plurality instead of a majority of electoral votes sufficient for the election of a president. Thus the present requirement of 266 electoral votes would no longer be necessary to win a presidential election. A third difference between the Lodge proposal and present arrangement on the matter of presidential elections is that under the amendment the choice would never be made by the House of Representatives.

Under the Lodge Amendment a presidential candidate who lost out on the popular vote by a slim margin in one state would still divide the electoral vote with his rival on the basis of his relative showing at the ballot box. At present, of course, the electoral vote is often not a fair index of the division of the popular vote. Thus, although Wendell Willkie received 22,304,755 popular votes as against Franklin Roosevelt's 27,243,466 in 1940, he won only eighty-two electoral votes to Roosevelt's 449. Similarly in 1944 Dewey had 22,017,592 votes in the popular column and Roosevelt 25,602,646, yet the electoral votes were: Dewey, 99; Roosevelt, 423. If the plan called for by the Lodge Amendment were applied to the 1944 election, however, the results for the electoral vote would have been Dewey 224, Roosevelt 307. Had the Lodge Amendment been in force in 1948 when President Truman received 303 electoral votes for 23,641,072 popular votes, and Dewey garnered 189 electoral votes for his 21,584,868 popular votes, the modified electoral vote would have been Truman 261.2, Dewey 222.5.

In favor of the Lodge Amendment it has been urged that the plan offers a more equitable method of electing a president and vice-president, and that it would also tend to offset the exaggerated influence of states with a large electoral vote in a presidential campaign. New York, for example, with its forty-five electoral votes has become the "Prussia" of American politics. Neither of the major parties can easily afford to lose its electoral vote; and in their attempts to carry the state, both parties traffic in reckless campaign promises. In other states, such as Pennsylvania, Ohio, Illinois, and California where the electoral vote is also large, the major parties concentrate heavily, knowing full well that defeat in any of these would entail the loss of the entire block of the electoral votes in each state and might well mean disaster when the electoral vote is counted.

Making the electoral vote proportionate to the popular vote would probably have some wholesome effect on our presidential election system. It would encourage both parties to make greater efforts in states where heretofore they had done little if any campaigning because of the certainty that they would lose the entire state electoral vote. In states where the two parties are fairly evenly matched, the proposed constitutional change might also result in improvement as it would tend to have each party still make a formidable bid to capture the state vote. Yet at the same time neither party should feel compelled to make promises to various minority groups that are inconsistent with the general policy aims of the party's program. The Lodge Amendment, in the perhaps overly optimistic appraisal of the

Brookings Institution, "will practically remove the chance that small minority groups can attain and exercise great power over presidents and presidential candidates and political parties because they hold the balance of power in pivotal states. These minority groups would have no power beyond that justified by their number of votes in a presidential election." Undoubtedly minority groups might continue to exercise more influence than their actual size warranted, but it is reasonable to suppose that the Lodge Amendment would tend to reduce their power.

The adoption of the Lodge Amendment would also remove present uncertainties on the casting of electoral votes. It would prevent a recurrence of what happened in 1948, when the Tennessee presidential elector made famous by exercising his own judgment voted against President Truman notwithstanding the fact that Truman carried the state in the popular vote. This particular elector incidentally came from one of two counties in the state with more than 50 per cent negroes. The Lodge Amendment would put an end to any maverick urges which a presidential elector might feel by requiring all presidential electors to vote for the national candidates on the party tickets where their names appeared. Thus a situation such as that which developed in 1948 over the vote of the presidential electors in four states where the States' Rights ticket won would also be averted. In the latter case, it was proposed that the presidential electors—38 in all—cast their votes for Truman and Barkley in order that these states would not lose a bonus of four delegates each at the 1952 Democratic National Convention.

Altogether, the threats to throw the electoral vote contrary to the popular choice have received far more publicity than the chance of their success actually warrants. Moreover, in so far as the results are concerned, the electoral vote system is not nearly so bad as some of its critics have claimed. In almost all instances it has merely officially ratified the popular decision and if it has tended to exaggerate the result of a popular margin of victory, there is something to be said for the argument that it has some psychological value in presenting at least an outward appearance of broader satisfaction with the final result. At the same time the mere fact that the electoral vote system may cause confusion in a presidential election has reinforced the pleas of critics that the electoral procedure be reformed. [29] Certainly according to the opinion of the latter group, electoral procedure should be reformed so as to compel all presidential electors to vote for the popular choice. Even a change of this nature, however, would entail a constitutional amendment, for the selection of presidential electors and their methods of procedure is assigned to the states under the Federal Constitution. Thus, although the electoral vote system is intimately connected with a national election, Federal regulation seems stymied at the moment and could only proceed under a constitutional amendment.

[29] On the reform of the Electoral College see a symposium "Should the Electoral College be abolished?" *Congressional Digest* (1941), 20:67–96; and J. E. Kallenbach: "Recent Proposals to Reform the Electoral College System." *American Political Science Review* (1936), 30:924–9.

THE PRESIDENTIAL INAUGURATION

As the election of the president by the electoral vote system normally occurs without incident, once the president and vice-president have been formally proclaimed by Congress acting in joint session, the one remaining event in ascending to the presidential office is the inauguration, which follows approximately two weeks later. Weather permitting, this event takes place on an open-air platform at the east front of the Capitol, and when climatic conditions are too adverse the ceremony takes place in the Senate chambers. The oath of office is administered by the chief justice, and in accordance with long-established tradition, immediately upon taking the oath of office, the president delivers an inaugural address.

SUMMARY

Presidential campaigns are conducted by party organizations in alliance with heterogeneous non-party organizations which have some stake in the outcome of the election. In recent years labor groups have been prominent among non-party organizations actively campaigning for the election of a party's nominees.

A basic rule of campaign strategy is concentration on doubtful regions; sound tactics dictate the presentation of strong local tickets in such areas. The Democratic Party, normally assured of the electoral votes of the Solid South, enjoys thereby an advantage over Republican opposition, which can regard very few electoral votes as certain.

Campaigns for the presidency are too long and too expensive; they frequently fail to put the issues separating the parties into bold relief. How effective they are in winning votes is an unsettled question. They may influence some undecided voters, and they probably stimulate party followers to greater efforts in behalf of their candidate.

Among important factors affecting the outcome of presidential elections are the nation's economic health at election time and the current phase of the cycle which voting behavior seems to follow. A large turnout at the polls favors the Democratic candidates in a national election.

The electoral college early in our history became a fifth wheel in our political system as electors ceased to vote according to their individual judgment. It has been under attack because its operation can frustrate the will of the majority and because it gives undue influence to a few large states and to strategically placed minority groups. The substitution of a system of election by direct popular vote for the electoral college has many proponents, but it should be remembered that the electoral college has very rarely kept the popular choice out of office; it has only exaggerated the popularity of the victorious candidate.

PART

IV

THE PRESIDENCY

CHAPTER XV

THE OFFICE AND POWERS OF THE PRESIDENT

THE OFFICE

The Uniqueness of the Presidential Office

THOUGH the term "president" is used in other nations there is nothing quite like the American presidency in the organization of any other national government. When the framers of the Constitution gave Congress its list of specific law-making powers the creation of an executive became an imperative necessity. They found the model for the presidency ready at hand in the governorship of the thirteen states. However, the framers proceeded to fortify the great office by the very vagueness of the terms with which they prescribed it in the Constitution. While Congress is limited definitely to "the powers herein delegated," "the Executive powers shall be vested in a President of the United States" who is to "take care that the laws be faithfully executed." Nor has a century and a half of experience sufficed to define precisely the significance or limits of the president's inaugural oath that he "will faithfully execute the office of President of the United States." The framers intended that the president would be the unfettered choice of the group of notables consisting of the presidential electors. Political parties upset this calculation and nothing has affected the nature of the presidential office more than the virtually direct popular election of the presidents which started with Andrew Jackson. This popular election led the late Henry Jones Ford to conclude that "American democracy had revived the oldest institution of the race, the elective kingship." [1] The American presidential system contrasts with the parliamentary

[1] Henry Jones Ford: *The Rise and Growth of American Politics* (New York, 1898), p. 293.

system in which executive power is vested in a group of members or leaders of parliament known collectively as the cabinet or ministry. This group exercises leadership in promoting legislation in parliament and its responsibility to that body is insured by the custom or usage that requires it to resign whenever one of its important proposals is voted down. This contrast with the American system brings into bold relief the uniqueness of the American presidency.

Qualifications for the Presidency

The Constitution established the presidency by the simple statement: "The executive powers shall be vested in a President of the United States." Only a natural-born citizen is eligible for the presidency, but the Constitution exempted from this requirement all who were citizens of the United States at the time of the adoption of the Constitution. This exception was necessary since the generation that made the Constitution was composed of individuals who recently had been natural-born British citizens. The oldest natural-born citizens of the United States, that is, citizens born here since the Declaration of Independence, were still in their early teens when the first presidential election was held. Thirty-five is the minimum age for the president and the incumbent must have been fourteen years a resident of the United States. Evidently this need not be fourteen years immediately preceding inauguration since Herbert Hoover was not challenged for that deficiency.

Re-eligibility

The framers of the Constitution placed no limitation on re-eligibility. Hamilton defended this unlimited re-eligibility in the seventy-second number of the *Federalist*. He argued that the limit of a single term would diminish inducements to good behavior, increase temptations to misconduct, prevent experience in office, deprive the country in emergencies of the services of the best men, and act as a constitutional barrier to stability of administration. "There is an excess of refinement," he observed, "in the idea of disabling the people to continue in office men who had entitled themselves, in their opinion, to approbation and confidence." By universal understanding Washington was to be the first president, and it was hoped he would be available as long as he lived. However, near the end of his second term Washington resolutely declined a third, but with no idea that he was setting a precedent.

The Two-Term Precedent Established

Since no one could foretell whether any later president would repeat Washington's renunciation of a third term it was rather Jefferson, a dozen years later, who established the two-term precedent by his declining a third term. Indefinite re-eligibility, he argued, would make a "nominally elec-

tive" office "in fact for life" and it would "degenerate into an inheritance."
Andrew Jackson also declined a third term, and for a generation following
(1832–64) no president was elected for even a second term. President
Grant was a receptive candidate for a third though non-consecutive term in
1880, but failed to be nominated. Theodore Roosevelt, after making an
apparently irrevocable pledge in 1904 not to accept a third term did, nevertheless, accept nomination and campaign for another, though not a consecutive term, as the candidate of the Progressive Party in 1912.

The Two-Term Tradition Broken

By the 1930's it had long been generally assumed that the anti-third term
precedent was as permanently established as any usage of the American
constitutional system. However, as the campaign of 1940 drew near, the
electorate became deeply concerned over the peril of the United States
because World War II was then raging in Europe. Franklin D. Roosevelt
was nearing the end of his second term. He was renominated, apparently
on the assumption that a change of administration at such a critical time
would be inadvisable. The devastating bombing of London in August 1940
seems to have emphasized the peril to the United States and appears to
have been decisive in the election that gave Roosevelt a third term. Four
years later he was commander-in-chief of the armed forces of a nation in
the midst of its greatest war and was elected for a fourth term.

The Twenty-Second Amendment

Roosevelt's election for a fourth term seemed, at first, to have terminated
decisively the restriction on indefinite presidential tenure. Even before
Roosevelt had completed his second term E. S. Corwin had written: "One
thing is nevertheless fairly certain; if the anti-third-term taboo is once set
aside, it will take a long time for an anti-fourth-term or anti-fifth-term
taboo to develop. In a word, the presidential term will become indefinite—
just what in 1787 it was expected to be!" [2] However reaction against the
executive that had culminated in the impeachment of Johnson after the
Civil War and the frustration of Wilson's plan for American participation
in a world organization after World War I, took the form of a proposed
constitutional amendment to limit presidential re-elections after World
War II. Its adoption in 1951 made it the twenty-second amendment which
provides that no person shall be elected more than twice, and that no person who has held the office of president, or acted as president for more than
two years of a term for which some other person was elected president,
shall be elected president more than once. It was adopted with little
public discussion and in spite of the fact that it would reduce presidential power in an era of international tensions. In 1956 Eisenhower,
the first President to have the potential tenure thus absolutely limited,
thought that the amendment was not "entirely wise."

[2] Edward S. Corwin: *The President: Office and Powers* (New York, 1940), p. 38.

Effect of Limited Re-eligibility

Experience clearly shows that the limitation of re-eligibility distinctly reduces presidential power. A president's party following tends somewhat to withdraw its support of his program and administration once it becomes certain he is not to stand for another election. Despite his firm courage and ability President Hayes impaired his influence by his pre-election pledge not to be a candidate for a second term. Theodore Roosevelt never quite recovered his presidential leadership after his election-night pledge in 1904 not to seek another term. President Wilson before inauguration emphatically repudiated the single-term platform plank on which he had been elected because he believed the president ought not to be hampered by denial of the strength derived from the possibility of re-election. President Coolidge wisely delayed until late in his administration his curious announcement: "I do not choose to run in 1928."

Immunities of the Presidency

The president is not subject to judicial process despite the fact that the Constitution is silent on the matter. This immunity is derived from judicial interpretation based on the principle of the separation of powers. In 1806 President Jefferson refused to comply with Chief Justice Marshall's subpoena for his appearance at the trial of Aaron Burr for treason. The Chief Justice admitted: "In no case of this kind would a court be required to proceed against the President as against an ordinary individual. The objections to such a course are so strong and so obvious that all must acknowledge them." In 1838 the Supreme Court authoritatively settled the matter with the conclusion: "The executive power is vested in the President and as far as his powers are derived from the Constitution he is beyond the reach of any other department." [3] Of course, a president may waive this immunity as did President Grant when he voluntarily appeared to testify in behalf of his private secretary under trial for fraud. But the immunity attaches to the office, not its incumbent, and ceases with his retirement from the presidency.

The Vice-President

The vice-president is elected at the same time as the president and the Electoral College so operates as to assure his being of the same party as the president. He is ex-officio president of the Senate. The Constitution seems to have intended merely that the vice-president "act as President" to fill out the remainder of a term in case of a vacancy, but the inflexible determination with which Vice-President John Tyler assumed the office and title of president when the first vacancy occurred set the precedent that has prevailed for more than a century. Tyler even gave an inaugural address

[3] Kendall v. United States, 12 Peters 524 (1838).

and refused to receive a communication from the Senate addressed to him as "Acting President." President Eisenhower gave new significance to the Vice-presidency by having Vice President Nixon habitually meet with the Cabinet and preside over it in his absence.

Presidential Succession

During Washington's first term as president, Congress provided that in case of the removal, death, resignation, or disability of both president and vice-president, the president pro-tempore of the Senate, and if there was no president of the Senate, then the speaker of the House, was to succeed to the presidency and hold the office only until a special election had chosen a president for a four-year term. It so chanced that there came a time in 1886 when there was neither a speaker of the House nor a president pro tempore of the Senate. Assuming that there would never be a time when all the cabinet positions would be vacant, Congress changed the line of succession to the members of that body beginning with the Secretary of State and following it in the chronological order of the creation of the departments of which they were the heads. This statute specified that the cabinet member "acts as President" by virtue of his cabinet office which he would consequently retain upon assuming the presidential office and thus have been a member of his own cabinet.

The New Presidential Succession Act

In June 1946 President Truman, having recently succeeded President Franklin D. Roosevelt, recommended abandoning the cabinet succession on the ground that no president that had succeeded from the vice-presidency ought to be able to designate his own possible successor. President Truman proposed instead that the succession be first to the speaker of the House and next to the president pro tempore of the Senate. In July 1947, Congress enacted a statute in accordance with this recommendation but provided also for cabinet succession in case of vacancies in the other two offices.

Arguments for the New Succession

It had been argued that succession through the cabinet violated the principle of elective office in the presidency by the routing of the succession through a line of appointive officials. A purpose of the new statute was to correct this by using instead two popularly elected officers. However, eligibility for the speakership of the House is attained only through a seniority slowly acquired by consecutive re-elections from what must, in the nature of the case, be practically a one-party district even in the case of a Republican speaker. A Democratic speaker is almost inevitably a Southerner, typically the choice of an electorate numerically insignificant in comparison with that of congressional districts in other sections. These facts raise

the question as to just how impressive might be the popular mandate of
a speaker who succeeds to the presidency. Presidents pro tempore of the
Senate have been rather less significant than speakers of the House while
a long line of notable secretaries of state have presented a claim for statesmanship scarcely less significant than that of the presidents.

PRESIDENTIAL POWERS

Powers Dependent Upon Legislation

Most of the day-to-day duties performed by the president are due to acts
of Congress. One way to bring this fact into clear relief would be to ascertain what President Washington might have done before Congress enacted
its first statute. Most significant is what he could not have done. He could
not "take care that the laws be faithfully executed" when there were none.
Commander-in-chief was only an empty title until Congress had created
an army and a navy. The power of appointment was latent until Congress
created offices. Washington had to await the congressional creation of the
executive departments before he could appoint what was in time to evolve
into the president's cabinet. Ambassadors, other public ministers and consuls could not be nominated until Congress saw fit to enact the statutes
establishing these offices. Not a judge could be nominated before Congress
had set up the system of courts which the Constitution merely empowered
that body to establish. Even the size of the Supreme Court had to be fixed
by legislation. Pardons and reprieves could not possibly be granted before
statutes had been enacted defining the offenses and establishing courts to
adjudicate cases arising under them. Aside from messages to Congress, the
negotiations of treaties, and the receiving of ambassadors and other public
ministers from foreign countries, President Washington could have performed no official duties before Congress had begun to legislate.

The President Subject to Law

So absolutely subject to law is the president that not even as commander-
in-chief can his orders give legal validity to the action of a subordinate that
is not based on statute or Constitution. Thus when an action of trespass was
brought against a naval officer ordered by President John Adams to capture a foreign vessel mischarged with violating the Non-intercourse Act,
Chief Justice Marshall, speaking for the Supreme Court, held that the President's "instructions cannot change the nature of the transaction, or legalize
an act which without them would have been plain trespass." [4] Likewise
when the heirs of General Robert E. Lee sued to recover the Arlington
estate, confiscated by the United States during the Civil War and held by
an army officer under order of the president, the attorney general was
unable to prevent the ejection of the officer despite his acting under orders

[4] 2 Cranch 170 (1804).

of his commander-in-chief. The Supreme Court rejected the attorney general's argument of "the absolute immunity from judicial inquiry of everyone who asserts authority from the executive branch of the government however clear it may be made that it possessed no such power. . . . No man in this country is so high that he is set above the law." [5]

Are There Inherent Powers in the Presidency?

Presidential powers stem chiefly from the Constitution and statutes, though some are said to inhere in the office itself. Hamilton maintained that some powers not vested by the Constitution or statutes inhere in the office of president. Citing the opening clause of Article II, "The executive power shall be vested in a President of the United States," he argued that "the general doctrine of our Constitution then is that the executive power of the nation is vested in the President, subject only to the exceptions and qualifications which are expressed in the instrument." [6] More than a century later Theodore Roosevelt, in his "stewardship theory of the presidency," practically repeated Hamilton's pattern of intrepretation in his "insistence upon the theory that the executive power was limited only by specific restrictions appearing in the Constitution or imposed by Congress under its constitutional powers. My view was that every executive officer, and above all every executive officer in high position was a steward of the people bound actively and affirmatively to do all he could for the people. . . . I declined to adopt the view that what was imperatively necessary for the Nation could not be done by the President unless he could find some specific authorization to do it. . . ." [7]

Even in its broadest interpretation of executive power the judiciary has never quite countenanced the Hamilton-Roosevelt theory. Yet the Supreme Court has sharply emphasized the broad powers of the president when specific constitutional or statutory directives seem to be lacking. In the language of the Court, his duty is not limited "to the enforcement of acts of Congress or of treaties of the United States according to their express terms," but includes also "the rights, duties and obligations growing out of the Constitution itself, our international relations, and all the protection implied by the nature of the Government under the Constitution." [8]

---

[5] 118 U.S. 356 (1885). The government lost this case because of the constitutional provision that "no attainder of treason shall work corruption of blood, or forfeiture except during the life of the attainted." The legality of the possession of the estate by the government ceased upon the death of General Lee when his heirs claimed their right to recover it.

[6] Alexander Hamilton: *Works*, edited by Henry Cabot Lodge (New York, 1885), Vol. IV, pp. 142–4.

[7] T. Roosevelt: *Autobiography* (New York, 1913), p. 389.

[8] 135 U.S. at 64. Contrary to his earlier views it should be noted that Chief Justice Taft in the Myers case found implied power of the Chief Executive in the very opening sentence of the second article of the Constitution from which Hamilton had derived executive prerogative.

ENFORCEMENT OF LAW

The Meaning of "Law"

"He shall take care that the laws be faithfully executed" is the provision of the Constitution that makes the president the chief executive instead of merely a titular chief. "Laws," of course, is a term signifying statutes, treaties, and ordinances which are rules and regulations made by the president and his subordinates to fill in the details of congressional legislation. Until 1890 the term "laws" was not assumed to include anything else. In that year, however, the attorney general of the United States, under direction of the President but without specific statutory authority, detailed United States Marshall Neagle to act as a body-guard of Associate Justice Field of the United States Supreme Court, whose life had been threatened by a citizen of California. In due time the attack was made and Field's life was saved only by the promptness with which Neagle dispatched Field's enemy. Thereupon Neagle was indicted for murder, under the laws of California, and his defense hinged on finding legal authority for his special assignment—authority for the President's appointment of an agent without statutory authorization. When the case reached the Supreme Court of the United States it was held that, inasmuch as it is the duty of the president "to take care that the laws be faithfully executed," there was vested in the president's office authority for Neagle's assignment. The new doctrine was proclaimed that the president's duty was not confined "to the enforcement of the Acts of Congress or of treaties of the United States according to their express terms" but included "the rights and obligations growing out of the Constitution itself, our international relations and all the protection implied by the nature of the government under the Constitution." [9]

The Administrative Agencies Through Which the Executive Functions

The Constitution does not obligate the president in person to enforce the laws but he shall "take care that the laws be faithfully executed." Congress accordingly creates the agencies to execute the laws, defines their duties and prescribes, frequently in minute detail, the manner in which they are to be performed. Congress appropriates the money for the support of these agencies and continuously investigates their administration both in order to ascertain whether the congressional policy is being executed in the prescribed manner and in order to improve administration by further legislation. The president is presumed to take care that whatever Congress prescribes is faithfully executed through the offices and agencies created. It need not be assumed that the legal theory just described reduces the president to a state of servility to Congress. In practice he has a wide range of discretion to enforce or not to enforce particular laws. If he should become

[9] *In re* Neagle, 135 U.S. 64 (1890).

neglectful of his duty, Congress has only the clumsy if not impossible device of impeachment with which directly to discipline him as an executive. Here are circumstances that give latitude to administration and enormously enhance the president's range of power. It is of importance whether a Coolidge or a Roosevelt occupies the White House.

Factors Determining the Type of Executive a President Will Be

What factors determine the type of chief executive any particular president will be? The answer doubtless lies in the climate of opinion in which a man derived and developed his social philosophy. One man may be obsessed with an obstinate faith in an outmoded economic or social ideology while another is a crusader for the good life by increasing the social services of the government. Even more, however, is the president's executive conduct determined by the immediate pressures that impinge upon his office. Lincoln was peculiarly adept at measuring such forces, and no president utilized them more intelligently. During his first five weeks as president he knew that any attempts to "take care that the laws be faithfully executed," where secession had been proclaimed, would have proved but futile gestures. He bided his time until the firing on Fort Sumter had produced an irresistible public pressure supporting decisive executive action. Pearl Harbor gave President Franklin Roosevelt a similar imperative mandate. In 1863 Lincoln told an importunate friend who was insisting upon a constitutional amendment for the immediate abolition of slavery: "I can see that time coming. Whoever can wait for it will see it, whoever stands in its way will be run over by it." [10] With an engaging frankness Lincoln was to remark near the end of his career: "I claim not to have controlled events but confess plainly that events have controlled me." [11]

Factors That Condition the Executive's Enforcement of Law

Naïve indeed would be the president who resolved to enforce strictly without fear or favor everything he found in the statutes. Just how vigorously could a president enforce the Pure Food and Drug Act if Congress provided too few inspectors to watch the interstate commerce in food and drugs? The interests regulated are ever alert, organized, and determined, while the public is usually indifferent, unorganized, and inert. The president who attempts too vigorous enforcement of a regulative statute will bring the pressures of the affected interests to bear first against the enforcing agency and then upon the congressional bloc supporting their point of view. Nor can the executive ignore potential punitive measures by Congress against an intransigent agency. This action might be the reduction of the appropriations and personnel or even the abolition of the agency. Under such circumstances the aim of a regulative agency becomes, as the Food and Drug Administration once said, "a maximum of compliance with a

[10] E. Hertz: *The Hidden Lincoln* (New York, 1940), p. 298.
[11] Ibid., p. 265.

minimum of resistance." [12] A lethargic public may now and then be stirred to a realization of its interests by an energetic President, but he is too busy to achieve much action of this sort. An executive's hand is no stronger than the social forces that support the policies he undertakes to enforce.

THE PRESIDENT'S POWER OF APPOINTMENT

Presidential Nomination and Senatorial Confirmation

The Constitution provides that the president "shall nominate, and, by and with the advice and consent of the Senate, shall appoint ambassadors, other public ministers and consuls, judges of the Supreme Court and all other officers of the United States whose appointments are not herein otherwise provided for, and which shall be established by law." Since the president cannot be personally acquainted with all potential appointees, he must largely depend upon recommendations, and these come, for the most part, from his own party organization. Those seeking appointment obtain endorsements of their local and state party organizations. Integrated closely with this usage is the custom of "senatorial courtesy" according to which the Senate will not confirm a presidential nomination if the senators of the nominee's state who also belong to the president's party do not approve the nomination. Curiously enough this practice dates from the beginning of government under the Constitution. Washington had been president but a few months when the Senate, without explanation, rejected his nomination of an officer of the port of Savannah. Whether Washington knew it or not, a senator from Georgia had objected to the nomination and thus the practice of "senatorial courtesy" began. [13] A recent notable instance of this usage was the rejection in 1939 of President Franklin D. Roosevelt's nomination of Judge Floyd H. Roberts for a Federal judgeship in Virginia because of the objections of Senators Glass and Byrd of that state. The usage of "senatorial courtesy" leads to a strange inversion of the constitutional provision, thus aptly paraphrased by James T. Young: "By the necessity of the case the Senate now nominates while the President gives his consent." With respect to appointments the Constitution provides: "The President shall have power to fill up all vacancies that may happen during the recess of the Senate, by granting commissions which shall expire at the end of their next session." "Recess" here signifies the period between final adjournment and the next session of the Senate and not temporary adjournments, such as those customary over holidays.

Cabinet Confirmations Not Subject to "Senatorial Courtesy"

The president's freedom in selecting his own cabinet is not limited by senatorial courtesy, and indeed only once since the Civil War has the Senate

[12] See E. P. Herring: *Public Administration and the Public Interest* (New York, 1936), chap. IV.
[13] James Hart: *The American Presidency in Action,* 1789 (New York, 1948), pp. 125-33.

refused to confirm a cabinet nomination. In 1869 President Grant nominated as Secretary of the Treasury Alexander T. Stewart of New York City, the owner of the world's largest dry goods store. Confirmation was in vain because of an old statute disqualifying for that office any one engaged in trade. Nor would the Senate heed Grant's plea for a repeal of the law by which action an importing merchant, perhaps none too friendly to protective tariffs, could be planted in the department that advises the Congress on taxation. In 1925 the Senate refused to confirm President Coolidge's nomination for attorney general, Charles B. Warren, the head of a beet-sugar company that had been charged with violating the anti-trust laws. In this office, among other duties Warren would have been charged with the prosecution of violations of the Anti-trust Acts. No doubt the Senate felt impelled to be circumspect inasmuch as Coolidge had recently been compelled to require the resignation of Attorney General Harry M. Daugherty whose nomination by Harding four years before had been promptly confirmed by a complaisant Senate. This one exception serves to emphasize the general rule that the Senate accepts the president's nominations for Cabinet members.

Another rejection of a cabinet nomination was barely averted in 1945 when President Franklin Roosevelt sent to the Senate the nomination of former Vice-President Henry A. Wallace for Secretary of Commerce. Here is an illustration of the time-honored practice by which presidents use cabinet appointments to build up party or administration support. Thus Lincoln in 1861, according to his private secretaries, sought to "combine the experience of Seward, the integrity of Chase, the popularity of Cameron; to hold the West with Bates, attract New England with Welles, please the Whigs through Smith and convince the Democrats through Blair." [14] Franklin Roosevelt apparently desired Wallace's appointment because of his strong following among the urban masses, the little agrarians, and the tenant farmers without whose support the Democratic party is handicapped in national elections. Wallace was confirmed only after a furious Senate battle, but not before there had been separated from the Commerce Department the Reconstruction Finance Corporation, which handled loans to larger businesses. It was with reluctance that President Truman asked for Wallace's resignation in 1947 following an address by Wallace that challenged the foreign policy of the State Department.

THE PRESIDENT'S POWER OF REMOVAL

Early Assumption that the Senate Does Not Share Removal Power

As to the removal of the officers that the president appoints with the confirmation of the Senate, the Constitution is silent. It might reasonably be assumed that the Senate should share in the removal power as it does in the power of appointment. The matter was long assumed to have been

[14] Carl Sandburg: *The War Years* (New York, 1939), Vol. I, p. 153.

settled in the first session of the First Congress when Madison argued against enacting a statute that would deliberately invest the president with this power of removal which he already had by implication. Such legislation would violate the separation of powers because Congress would be interfering with the constitutional powers of the executive. In any case, reasoned Madison, the framers did not intend to compel the president to retain subordinates he did not trust.

The Post-Civil War Tenure of Office Acts

In the midst of the post-Civil War hysteria Congress passed the Tenure of Office Act requiring senatorial consent for the president's dismissal of his appointees. Congress then felt the pressure of powerful interests obsessed with a phobia that Johnson would pack the public service with officials inimical to their purposes. President Johnson was the resolute champion of homestead rights for the small farmer, the opponent of greedy land speculators and gigantic land grants to railroad promoters, and the critic of high protective tariffs. He even proposed paring down the national debt by partial repudiation. [15] After the failure of the Senate to convict Johnson under impeachment for violation of the Tenure of Office Act and the later failures to limit Presidents Hayes and Cleveland to dismissal of officials only with the consent of the Senate, the Tenure of Office Act was repealed in 1887.

The Myers Case Confirms the President's Removal Powers

In 1926 the Supreme Court of the United States decided the case of one Myers, postmaster of Portland, Oregon, who had been dismissed, by direction of President Wilson, before the expiration of his four-year term of appointment. Chief Justice Taft speaking for the Court held the Tenure of Office Act of 1867 and subsequent legislation of its kind invalid "in so far as it attempted to prevent the President from removing executive officers who had been appointed by him by and with the advice and consent of the Senate." [16] Subsequently for a decade it was generally assumed that the president had unlimited power to dismiss any of his appointees outside the judiciary.

The Humphrey Case Limits the President's Removal Power

A spectacular clash of social philosophies brought to the Supreme Court the case that restored some of the power of Congress to limit the president's power of dismissal. President Wilson had appointed the five members of the Federal Trade Commission established in 1914 to scrutinize business practices for violations of the anti-trust laws. The Commission acquired a new complexion with Coolidge's appointment in 1925 of William E. Humphrey who became the spokesman of the new majority. Humphrey pledged

---

[15] See Louis M. Hacker: *Triumph of American Capitalism* (New York, 1940), p. 375.

[16] Myers v. United States, 272 U.S. 52 (1926).

the Commission to assist business rather than attack it, as he implied the old "socialistic" majority had done. "The effect of Humphrey's appointment," wrote E. P. Herring, "was more far reaching than any decision of the Supreme Court." [17]

Early in his presidency Franklin Roosevelt felt impelled to remove Humphrey as one who was no less disposed to sabotage the regulative legislation of the Roosevelt than of the Wilson administration. The Supreme Court unanimously refused to sustain the removal of Humphrey. Not only had the term of members of the Federal Trade Commission been fixed by statute at seven years but the President's reasons for removal had been limited by that statute to "inefficiency, neglect of duty, or malfeasance in office" with none of which Humphrey had been charged. The Court held that Congress could create quasi-legislative or quasi-judicial agencies free from executive control and might consequently prescribe specifically the sole grounds for removal by the president.[18]

The Appointment and Removal of "Inferior Officers"

The Constitution provides that "the Congress may by law vest the appointment of such inferior officers, as they may think proper, in the President alone, in the courts of law, or in the heads of departments." In the Myers case, mentioned above, the Supreme Court reaffirmed previous decisions that, where Congress has vested the appointment of "inferior officers" in the head of a department, it may attach limitations on the power of removal. Here is a basis of the merit system of the civil service with its limitation on the power of removal of the vast clerical and technical personnel of the executive departments.

MILITARY POWER

Commander-in-Chief

This authority of the president is derived from the provision of the Constitution: "the President shall be Commander-in-Chief of the Army and Navy of the United States, and of the militia of the several states when called into the actual service of the United States." Clearly the president is no less the commander-in-chief in time of peace than in time of war, except in respect to the militia. This provision of the Constitution gives the president at all times authority to direct movements of the land and naval forces placed by law under his command. The unqualified terms of the Constitution's investment of the president with military power allows him a very broad range of discretion. In time of peace he could direct movement of troops that might render hostilities inevitable and leave Congress no choice but to declare a state of war. An example of this was President Polk's movement of troops in 1846 to the Rio Grande and onto disputed

[17] E. P. Herring: *Public Administration and the Public Interest*, p. 254.
[18] Humphrey's Executor *v.* United States, 295 U.S. 602 (1935).

territory, an act which led to the opening of hostilities and the Mexican War. It was Lincoln who pushed to the limit, and even exceeded, the discretionary power of the commander-in-chief in wartime. Without congressional authorization he suspended the privilege of the writ of habeas corpus, increased the army and navy personnel, acquired naval vessels, proclaimed the emancipation of slaves, and put into execution his own plan of reconstruction. Woodrow Wilson and Franklin Roosevelt were more circumspect as war presidents and usually acted only on the basis of appropriate legislation.

Judicial Interpretation of the President's War Power

The Supreme Court has held that the President as commander-in-chief may establish a provisional government outside the United States in conquered or ceded territory and collect duties on imports to support it, and such government continues until Congress establishes civil government for that territory. Since the Court holds that Congress can legalize retroactively any war power of the President that it can authorize him in advance to exercise his war powers appear to be practically unlimited.

Supremacy of Civilian Authority

Despite the broad terms in which the president is vested with military power, the framers of the Constitution took extra precautions against the development of a military dictatorship. This was in the tradition of English constitutional development and moreover reflected the American fear, prevalent during and following the Revolutionary War, of army domination. Thus the Constitution insures that the commander-in-chief will always be a civilian. Moreover he is checked in the exercise of his most important powers by the requirement of preliminary Congressional legislation. Only Congress can declare war. The president is obligated to obtain from Congress authority to "raise and support armies," "to provide and maintain a navy," and "for calling forth the militia to execute the laws of the Union, to suppress insurrections and repel invasions." Thus the commander-in-chief is himself strictly subject to law wherever Congress has the regulatory power, of which the Constitution gives it an abundance.

THE PRESIDENT'S USE OF THE MILITARY IN LAW ENFORCEMENT

The President's Use of Military Force Against Domestic Violence

Shays's Rebellion had induced the delegates of the constitutional convention to hasten to Philadelphia, and undoubtedly such domestic violence as this rebellion induced the framers to assign Congress the power "to provide for calling forth the militia to execute the laws of the Union, suppress insurrection, and repel invasions." This is a power of Congress and without enabling legislation the president would be powerless to use the militia. The new government was not a half dozen years old when Congress passed its first legislation to enable President Washington to assemble 15,000 militiamen and march against the Whiskey Rebels of western Pennsylvania. The statutes of 1794 and 1795 authorized the president's use of the militia in such cases only when "the laws of the United States shall be opposed or the execution thereof obstructed in any state, by combinations too powerful to be suppressed by the ordinary course of judicial proceedings or by powers vested in the marshalls." [19] Two generations later Lincoln interpreted the secession movement in the very phrases of these statutes and summoned the militia under authority of the Statute of 1795 to sustain Federal authority wherever it was challenged.

President Cleveland and the Pullman Strike

President Cleveland set the pattern for an unprecented use of Federal military force in a case of domestic violence. The occasion was the refusal of the American Railway Union in 1894 to handle trains which included Pullman cars in order to support the strike of the Pullman Car Workers. Attorney General Richard Olney, a former railway attorney, exerted himself extraordinarily to create a situation that would induce the President to send Federal troops to Chicago, ostensibly to prevent interference with the mails and interstate commerce, but actually "to break the strike," as an army officer on duty there later boasted. [20] Upon the arrival of Federal troops, the governor of Illinois, John P. Altgeld, protested to the President that the constitutional guarantee to the state of protection against domestic violence was conditioned "on application of the legislature, or of the executive (when the legislature cannot be convened), against domestic violence." Research has long since justified the protestations of the governor that he had been prompt in furnishing sufficient state troops to enforce the processes of United States Courts. Cleveland's conduct is understandable only in the light of the prevalent hysteria of the deepening depression of the 1890's as "rifles clashed and cavalry charged into mobs all over the Mississippi Valley." [21] His drastic action was sustained no less by public opinion than by the later decision of the Supreme Court in a case growing out of the episode. "The entire strength of the nation," concluded the Court, "may be used to enforce in any part of the land the full and free exercise of all national powers and the security of all rights intrusted by the Constitution to its care. The strong arm of the national government may be put forth to brush away all obstructions to the freedom of interstate commerce or the transportation of the mails. If the emergency arises, the army of the nation, and all its militia, are at the service of the nation to compel obedience to its laws." [22] Whatever the merit of the claims of the strikers and the

[19] *U.S. Statutes at Large*, Vol. I, p. 264.
[20] See Charles A. Beard: "Emerging Issues in America." *Current History* (1934), 41:203–9.
[21] W. A. White: *Masques in a Pageant* (New York, 1928), p. 139.
[22] *In re* Debs, 158 U.S. 564 (1895).

arguments of Governor Altgeld, a new precedent had been established greatly expanding the executive power of the president.

POWER OVER FOREIGN RELATIONS

The Medium of Foreign Communications

"The President is the sole organ of the nation in its external relations and its sole representative with foreign nations," declared John Marshall as a member of the House of Representatives in 1799. [23] He is directed, by and with the advice and consent of the Senate, to appoint ambassadors, other public ministers, and consuls. These representatives then become, in effect, his personal agents in the administration of foreign relations. The Constitution authorizes the president to receive ambassadors and other foreign ministers, but by the same authority he may refuse to do so, thereby deciding whether or not a foreign government is to be recognized by the United States. Thus Cleveland refused to recognize the independence of Cuba before the Spanish American War, and McKinley refused to receive representatives of the Boer Republic of South Africa, then at war with England. For years after the establishment of the U.S.S.R., American presidents refused to recognize the Soviet government of Russia on the ground of its repudiation of foreign debts. The president may dismiss foreign diplomatic representatives, thereby severing diplomatic relations with their governments and possibly creating international crises.

Treaty Making

The president has the power, by and with the advice and consent of the Senate, to make treaties, provided that two-thirds of the Senate concur. The negotiation of a treaty may be carried on by the president in person, as Woodrow Wilson did in the case of the Covenant of the League of Nations, but this is exceptional. Often the negotiations are conducted by, or under direction of, the secretary of state. At times special commissioners or personal representatives of the president are appointed for such a purpose. The president may include, in these missions, members of the Foreign Relations Committee of the Senate in the hope of winning the co-operation of the Upper House and its required two-thirds vote. If the treaty requires for its execution an appropriation, the president dare not neglect cultivating good relations with the House of Representatives where all money bills originate.

Executive Agreements

Agreements entered into by the president with foreign governments without senatorial concurrence but having the effect of treaties have become an established practice. The practice started more than a century and a half ago with Congressional authorization to the president to enter into

[23] Quoted by Edward S. Corwin: *The President: Office and Powers*, p. 208.

executive agreements with foreign governments on specified matters, but has long since extended quite beyond such definite authorization. Illustrative of such agreements are the State Department's exchanges of notes in 1899 and 1900 with other nations relative to the "Open Door" in China; the "gentleman's agreement" in 1907 whereby Japanese immigration to the United States was regulated for many years; the protocol ending the Boxer rebellion in 1901; the use of the army and navy in supervising elections in Caribbean countries and, above all, President Theodore Roosevelt's "agreement" with Santo Domingo in 1905 to put its custom houses under United States control after the Senate had refused to ratify a treaty to that effect. Moreover, the Supreme Court has even held executive agreements within range of the president's power to be the law of the land. "Such precedents," says E. S. Corwin, "make it difficult to state any limit to the power of President and Congress, acting jointly, to implement effectively any foreign policy, upon which they agree, no matter how 'the recalcitrant third plus one man' of the Senate may feel about the matter." [24]

PARDONS AND REPRIEVES

Pardon

The president is invested with another duty by the provision of the Constitution, namely, that he "shall have power to grant reprieves and pardons for offenses against the United States except in cases of impeachment." Pardon consists of a release from the legal consequences of a crime or a remission of penalties imposed. It may range from reduction of a fine to full pardon and, strange to say, can be, though it rarely is, granted following indictment but before trial and conviction. In practice, pardon is usually granted on recommendation of the attorney general. The theory of pardon in the American constitutional system was succinctly stated by the late Justice Oliver Wendell Holmes: "A pardon in our day is not a private act of grace from an individual happening to possess power. It is a part of a constitutional scheme. When granted it is a determination of the ultimate authority that the public welfare will be better served by inflicting less than the judgment fixed . . ." [25]

Amnesty

According to the Supreme Court "pardon includes amnesty" which is a collective pardon of a specified classification of persons. Amnesty may be granted by act of Congress or by the president as a corollary of his power of pardon. It has long been used in cases of rebellion and was a principal basis of the presidential power of reconstruction as exercised by Presidents Lincoln and Johnson. On July 4, 1868 President Johnson pardoned most

[24] Edward S. Corwin: *The Constitution and What It Means Today* (9th ed.; Princeton, 1947), p. 102.
[25] Biddle *v.* Perovich, 274 U.S. 480 (1927).

persons who had participated in the secession movement and full pardon was proclaimed on December 25, 1868.

SUMMARY

The presidency of the United States is unique among the national executives of the world and there is a fascinating vagueness as to just what is meant by the Constitution's investing the office with the "executive powers." The Constitution set no limit as to re-eligibility of the President, but custom promptly developed a two-term limit unbroken until President Franklin Roosevelt's re-election to a third term in 1940. In 1951 the Twenty-second Amendment to the Constitution set an inflexible two-term limit.

The President is himself subject to law and outside his war power cannot make legal anything not already otherwise legal. He is to see to the enforcement of law through offices created by Congress, but here he is no stronger than the groups affected by or concerned with law enforcement permit him to be.

The President is invested with the power to appoint, with senatorial confirmation, Federal judges, and all except inferior executive officers. As a consequence of his obligation to see to the enforcement of the laws he has also the power to remove purely executive officers. Congress may limit to specified reasons his power to remove officers whom it has invested with quasi-legislative or quasi-judicial functions.

The President must be a civilian but, aside from Congress's power to appropriate money he may need and to convict upon impeachment, the President's power as commander-in-chief gives him at all times unlimited power to move the armed forces. Only Congress, however, can declare the existence of a state of war. The President has unlimited power to use the army in executing Federal law, and Congress has authorized his using the state militia also for that purpose.

The President is the chief organ of international relations; he negotiates treaties preliminary to submission to the Senate and has broad powers to make executive agreements with foreign nations.

CHAPTER XVI

THE PRESIDENT AND THE CONGRESS

THE PROBLEM OF COORDINATION

The Necessity of Concerted Action

UNQUESTIONABLY the president and Congress have common objectives despite the division of functions between them. It would be naïve to assume that this division is simply a matter of one branch legislating and the other executing, each in serene disregard of the other. This would be indeed a separation of powers—a principle which the Constitution does not mention but merely implies in the provisions: "The legislative power herein delegated shall be vested in a Congress . . ." and "The executive power shall be vested in a President of the United States." Thus the framers provided for legislative and executive departments, invested them with certain powers, contrived some checks for them to use upon each other, and then left them to shift for themselves in discovering how to function together to accomplish the great purposes of government. Nor has upward of a century and a half of groping for workable adjustments yet produced an institutionalized solution of this perplexing problem.

The Quest for Coordination of Congress and the Executive

"The whole art of statesmanship," wrote Woodrow Wilson, "is the art of bringing the several parts of government into effective co-operation for the accomplishment of common objects and daily objects at that." [1] The Federalists understood this from the very beginning, and under the brilliant leadership of President Washington's Secretary of the Treasury, Alexander Hamilton, the national government began with an integrated functioning of the legislative and executive branches. Congress looked to

[1] Woodrow Wilson: *Constitutional Government in the United States* (New York, 1908), p. 54.

Hamilton for leadership, literally asked him to make reports on specific objects on which to base legislation, and the result was Hamilton's program of financial legislation which he put through Congress with consummate skill. This dependence of Congress upon the executive for the preparation of legislative matter for consideration was extremely obnoxious to the opposition, the Jeffersonian Republicans. As soon as Jefferson became president in 1801 they put an end to the Federalist arrangement. In its place, they related the executive to Congress by providing confidential lieutenants of President Jefferson as chairmen of the Congressional committees just being established to formulate legislation, instead of making Congress dependent on heads of the executive departments for that purpose. [2]

Presidential Leadership in Legislation

A quarter of a century later, Andrew Jackson, as a professed "tribune of the people," introduced a radically different conception of the presidency by bringing to bear upon Congress the pressures of his personal following in the electorate, thus establishing a pattern for the presidency that persists to this day. As the nineteenth century was drawing to a close President McKinley, after a long service in the House of Representatives, established and maintained an unobtrusive executive leadership through an engaging cordiality in his dealing with legislators. President Theodore Roosevelt devised an organic connection of the two branches through conferences at the White House with the imperious master of the House of Representatives, Speaker Joseph G. Cannon. President Wilson managed to transform the Federal government into what he conceived to be a quasi-parliamentary system in which he played the role of a prime minister, and his protegé, Franklin Roosevelt, had ways of his own. He might broadcast his "fireside chat" designed to prepare the public for a new policy or to induce the public to put pressure on its representatives. From time to time he would confront Congress with a specific proposal conveyed in a short address or message whereupon a trusted presidential lieutenant in the Senate or House would introduce an appropriate bill prepared in advance for that very project. Certainly no ready formula exists for the needed coordination; as many methods have been attempted as there have been executives aware of the problem and disposed to attempt a solution.

Why There Is No Smooth Coordination

Basically the friction between president and Congress is due neither to the system established by the framers nor to the perversity of executive and legislator. By no means can the friction be attributed solely to the mechanical structure of the government, imperfect though it is. The discord is instead inherent in the heterogeneous nature of American society which produced the American political system and determined the usages by which that system functions from day to day. No governmental pattern

[2] See Wilfred E. Binkley: *President and Congress* (New York, 1947), chaps. II and III.

for the United States, however designed, can make the contrasting sections, competing economic interests, and divergent social forces produce national policies with smooth efficiency and sweet concord. Least of all can a system of checks and balances do this. One set of interests may become intrenched in one branch of the government and another set in another branch. For example, late in the administration of Franklin D. Roosevelt and throughout the first term of President Truman the producing interests of the nation, both industrial and agricultural, dominated Congress through a bloc of Republicans and Southern Democrats that enacted legislation more or less in behalf of these interests. This legislation now and then encountered presidential vetoes in behalf of the consumer-conscious interests whose voting strength as a balance of power had been deciding presidential elections. The resulting deadlocks were sometimes broken by two-thirds votes of the two houses of Congress which overrode the vetoes. By and large, usage has, in the course of time, adapted the major organs of the Federal government awkwardly enough but as best it could to the accomplishing of the great purposes of the republic.

The President as a Mediator

"We can symbolize our national unity in the President, our sections in the Senate, and our localism in the House of Representatives," observed E. P. Herring. [3] A shrewd president imbued with a sense of the great responsibility of his office can make the presidency peculiarly the people's office and so seek out and urge upon Senate and House policies representative of the national interest. Much depends upon current circumstance and opportunity. There is no better illustration than President Woodrow Wilson's use of the culminating force of the Progressive Movement to persuade Congress to reduce the tariff and enact the great regulative statutes of the Federal Reserve Act, the Federal Trade Act, and the Clayton Act. In periods of domestic calm and economic prosperity, with consequent public indifference to national policies, a president may be frustrated in such purposes. But in times of national crisis such as the economic and social paralysis produced by the Great Depression in 1933 a president equipped with the requisite qualities of leadership can utilize an imperious public mandate to bring Senate and House into concerted action with the executive on a program of policies deemed adequate to the occasion. A Pearl Harbor can do as much in enabling a president to set in motion the mobilizing of a nation's resources for defense.

The Presidential Following and Presidential Policies

The president must of necessity discover and promote policies acceptable to his constituency. Theoretically this is the entire nation, but in a peculiar sense he is obligated to his party and his personal following—those considered responsible for his election. Nor is this following a homogeneous aggregation of individuals, but rather a coalition of interest groups. A

[3] E. P. Herring: *Presidential Leadership* (New York, 1940), p. 14.

president without such a combination of strong supporters is practically powerless either as an administrator or as a leader in legislation, as the administrations of Presidents Tyler, Johnson, and Hayes illustrate. A strong president becomes the medium for translating the desires of his supporters into public policies expressed in statutes. In this process we see the dynamics of the president's leadership in legislation. No one has ever devised a system of representative government in which public officials could ignore election returns. Never has the correlation between group support of a presidential candidate and the group benefits dispensed by an administration been more vividly described than they were by a party leader of the Charlestown, Massachusetts ward that voted for President Franklin Roosevelt four to one in 1940. "Probably no section of the country gained more under the New Deal," said the ward leader. "Hundreds got pay raises under the wage-hour law; more hundreds of seasonal workers are having slack months cushioned by unemployment-insurance benefits. The N.Y.A. is helping from 300 to 500 youths; at the worst of the depression thousands held W.P.A. jobs; of 1500 persons past sixty-five in the ward, more than 600 receive old-age assistance; another 600 cases are on direct relief and get aid for dependent children: Charlestown is a food stamp area; the W.P.A. improved the bathing beach, a new low-cost housing project will relieve some of the ward's congestion." [4] Here is the normal functioning of a presidential administration backed by lower-income groups. The election of Dwight D. Eisenhower as a Republican President in 1952 introduced an administration supported by a group combination with influential elements hospitable to business and inclined to cut taxes, balance budgets, and promote free enterprise.

INSTRUMENTALITIES OF THE PRESIDENT'S
LEGISLATIVE LEADERSHIP

The Presidential Message in the Nineteenth Century

Nowhere does the Constitution come closer to suggesting the legislative leadership of the president than in the provision: "He shall, from time to time, give to the Congress information of the state of the Union, and recommend to their consideration such measures as he shall judge necessary and expedient." Here is a provision that might be interpreted as permitting the president to initiate legislation, if not even to prepare bills for the consideration of Congress. Yet so perfunctory was the use of the presidential message to Congress during the first century that in the 1880's James Bryce observed: "The expression of his (the President's) wishes conveyed in a message has not necessarily any more effect on Congress than an article in a prominent party newspaper." [5] President Cleveland,

[4] Wilfred E. Binkley: *American Political Parties Their Natural History* (New York, 1945), pp. 381, 382.

[5] James Bryce: *American Commonwealth* (Commonwealth edition; New York, 1908), Vol. I, p. 230.

however, provoked a violent political eruption by devoting his entire annual message of December, 1887, to a demand for tariff reduction. But so ill-timed was the appeal that the following year it lost his party both the Congress and the presidency and led to the sharp increase in tariff rates of the McKinley Act of 1890. Until a generation ago the presidential messages tended to be products of the scissor and paste method of combining departmental reports in poorly integrated miscellanies that received only the perfunctory attention of Congress. Once when a friendly critic took President Theodore Roosevelt to task for the diffuseness of his exceedingly long messages to Congress, with their miscellaneous topics frequently outside the range of Federal functions, Roosevelt responded with the question: "Are you aware also of the extreme unwisdom of irritating Congress by fixing the details of a bill concerning which they are very sensitive instead of laying down a general policy?" [6]

Woodrow Wilson's Presidential Messages

Woodrow Wilson set the new pattern of the presidential message in 1913. He brought to the presidency this clear-cut new conception of the great office: "The President is at liberty, both in law and conscience, to be as big a man as he can. His capacity will set the limit . . . The Constitution explicity authorizes the President to recommend to Congress such measures as he shall deem necessary and expedient and it is not necessary to the integrity or even the literary theory of the Constitution to insist that recommendations should be merely perfunctory . . . The Constitution bids him speak and times of stress must more and more thrust upon him the attitude of originator of policies." [7] In office President Wilson conceived and executed the idea of giving a dramatic effect to the presidential message by delivering it orally to Congress instead of sending it to be read by Senate and House clerks as had been done since the presidency of Thomas Jefferson. From time to time President Wilson returned to address Congress in brief messages, each precisely promoting one specific measure. Harding and Coolidge, by accepting Wilson's precedent of addressing Congress in person, helped to establish the practice of the occasional oral address instead of the message. Since the time of Coolidge the presidential address has often been broadcast to the nation by radio or television.

The President's Use of Radio and Television

The broadcasting of presidential addresses to Congress has markedly changed their nature because the president is inevitably conscious of the listening nation. Sometimes the appeal is addressed as much to the unseen audience as to senators and representatives. Scarcely veiled is the presidential design of inviting pressure on the public's representatives. Early in his administration President Franklin Roosevelt introduced what he chose to call the "fireside chat," an intimate message broadcast to the

[6] J. B. Bishop: *Theodore Roosevelt and His Times* (New York, 1920), Vol. I, p. 233.
[7] Woodrow Wilson: *Constitutional Government*, pp. 70–3.

American people. During the "Hundred Days" of crisis government in the spring and summer of 1933 the "fireside chat" became the means by which President Roosevelt exerted pressure on intransigent congressmen who dreaded the flood of mail it brought them demanding that they support the president's policies. But President Roosevelt was to discover, when the crisis had passed, what President Coolidge had learned earlier: "a president cannot, with success, constantly appeal to the country. After a while he will get no response." [8] President Truman had to learn that personal qualities and circumstances determine the efficacy of a president's radio appeal to the nation. At the end of a half year as president, Truman's program for domestic legislation was deadlocked in Congress. In a "fireside chat" on January 3, 1946, after listing his "must" legislation, he made an appeal to the "greatest pressure group" in the country, that is to the American people, to urge their views on their congressmen. Telecasting the President's address to Congress began during Truman's second term, and it was continued by President Eisenhower. A new phase of the "fireside chat" appeared with the nation seeing as well as hearing the President promote his program. The climax was reached in 1955 when the public watched a well-staged Eisenhower cabinet meeting.

Presidential Campaigns Waged on Legislative Issues

In the evolution of the relationship of the president to Congress our chief executive has become also our chief legislator. "The prime function of the President is not executive at all. It is legislative," says H. L. McBain. [9] Usage has made the president always the titular, and sometimes the actual, head of his party. He is elected on a party platform which proposes a set of policies he is theoretically pledged to carry out by obtaining from Congress appropriate legislation. When he is a candidate for re-election he points with pride to "his" achieved legislative program. The opposition may fume at what they choose to denounce as his "usurpations," his ineptitude, or his failure to enforce the laws, but the public is more likely to be thinking of the success or failure of the administration's legislative program. This is the normal public expectations and indicates that the purpose of a presidential election is to choose a national leader in legislation.

The Press as an Instrument of Presidential Leadership

By and large the president's power as a leader in legislation is inseparable from the power of publicity. His slightest remark may make news. If he is adept at timing he may perform such feats of legerdemain as did President Theodore Roosevelt, who would let out a blast against "malefactors of great wealth" at just the right moment. The resulting headlines smothered an administrative *faux pas* by relegating it to a minor place in the newspapers. He discovered that he could capture the Monday morning headlines by giving press releases on week-ends when the scarcity of Sunday

[8] Calvin Coolidge: *Autobiography* (New York, 1929), p. 201.
[9] Howard Lee McBain: *The Living Constitution* (New York, 1927), p. 115.

news saved his "publicity" from being crowded off the front page. President Harding, himself a newspaper editor, inaugurated the open presidential press conference, but after a slip on the interpretation of the Disarmament Treaty, he required advance submission of questions in writing, a practice which Coolidge and Hoover continued. President Franklin Roosevelt in his famous news conferences revived and reveled in the informal give-and-take of the free question and captivated the gentlemen of the press. When President Truman at his first press conference coolly faced 348 alert newsmen and answered their barrage of questions with the prompt confidence of an informed man, he too captivated them and benefited immensely by a good press. However, unfortunate slips soon induced Truman to respond to many a question with the laconic "no comment." President Eisenhower found the press conference a trying ordeal at first but with experience gained confidence and benefited by the publicity. Televising the press conference began with President Eisenhower.

Executive Initiative in Legislation

It was a maxim of John Stuart Mill that while a legislature is the best way to get good laws, it is the poorest kind of a body to make them. [10] Mill had in mind what he considered the need for an agency external to the legislature whose function would be the preparation of proposals for the legislature's consideration. Reluctant as Congress is to accept Mill's dictum, it becomes more and more a part of the pattern of the congressional legislative process. We have seen that the Federal government started off with considerable executive initiative in legislation through Hamilton's famous reports to Congress involving his proposals as to legislation, but this proved to be only a temporary practice. Theodore Roosevelt may be said to have initiated the twentieth-century trend toward dynamic presidential leadership in legislation. "A good executive under present conditions of American life," he said, "must take a very active interest in getting the right kind of legislation in addition to performing his executive duties with an eye single to the public welfare." [11] In the fifth year of Theodore Roosevelt's presidency Senator Dolliver of Iowa said: "There are at least five acts of legislation . . . put through both houses of Congress in the last five years practically without change as they came from the office of the Attorney General of the United States." He declared this to have been true also of the Pure Food and Drug Act of the administration. [12] Woodrow Wilson conceived the duties of a president to be substantially those of a prime minister, and in the first years of his presidency, by assuming that role, he took the initiative in legislation and managed the enactment of Federal Reserve Banking, the Clayton, and Federal Trade Commission Acts, and the Underwood Tariff Act.

A thoroughgoing investigation of the origin and enactment of ninety

[10] John Stuart Mill: *Autobiography* (New York, 1873), pp. 264, 265.
[11] Theodore Roosevelt: *An Autobiography* (New York, 1913), p. 292.
[12] *Congressional Record*, April 5 and June 5, 1906.

outstanding Federal statutes of the last three-quarters of a century reveals
that 20 per cent of them can be assigned to the influence of the president
and 30 per cent to the joint influence of president and Congress. It is indicative of the recent increase of presidential leadership in legislation that
almost half of the legislation due to presidential influence has been enacted
since 1932 and falls in the administration of Franklin Roosevelt. Moreover, of the twenty-nine statutes resulting from the joint influence of president and Congress, thirteen were enacted during the presidency of Franklin Roosevelt. Most striking of all is the fact that of the thirty-five acts
in which the influence of Congress was predominant, only two—the Glass-
Stiegel Act of 1933 and the Selective Service Act of 1940—fell within
the incumbency of President Franklin Roosevelt. [13]

Presidential Management of Bills

The president's methods of managing administration measures in Congress
have by no means been standardized but vary with the temper of the
times, the attitude of Congress toward the president, and the aptitudes,
determination, and governmental concepts of the president himself. President Franklin Roosevelt achieved remarkable results through careful advance planning and superior political management of administration measures. He knew from personal experience that legislation is a tedious process
and that committee hearings must be held in order that the groups who
might be affected by the pending legislation might have an opportunity
to be heard. Then the congressmen themselves, particularly the committee
members, must estimate the comparative strength and determination of
the interested groups and make their calculations as to where the balance
of social forces with respect to a pending measure is located and what the
public interests require or will support. President Franklin Roosevelt
paved the way for important measures by having thorough preliminary
studies of relevant data made for him by nationally recognized specialists
in the field of the contemplated legislation. Meanwhile he disseminated
publicity to create a public demand for the projected legislation and to
bring to bear the influence of constituents on their representatives. When
a bill reached a committee answers were ready for the questions that were
raised. President Roosevelt, through conference with congressional leaders, took pains to see that an administration measure would be assigned
to a committee favorable to that particular piece of legislation. Rarely if
ever was one of his measures routed to a committee that, by casual investigation, appeared to be opposed to measures of that kind. [14]

Presidential Patronage as an Instrument of Leadership in Legislation

Patronage due to the power of appointment is a potent if not indispensable
instrument of the president's power in law making. The Constitution for-

[13] Lawrence H. Chamberlain: *The President, Congress, and Legislation* (New
York, 1946), chap. XII.

[14] "Congress's Reasons for Delay in Passing the President's Bills," *United States
News,* January 18, 1946.

bids a congressman from holding an appointive office, but presidents have, from time to time, disposed of anti-administration legislators by promoting them to desirable appointive positions which they accepted after resigning as senators or representatives in Congress. However, the typical use of presidential patronage consists of rewarding a congressman's henchmen with Federal appointments. A classic example of the use of patronage for legislative purpose is that of Lincoln distributing sufficient patronage to congressmen to get Nevada admitted to the Union so that a three-fourths vote of the states could be obtained for the Thirteenth Amendment to abolish slavery. Lincoln was convinced that unless this amendment were ratified the Civil War would continue indefinitely at an enormous cost in lives and money. Believing that the end justified the means, Lincoln sent his personal representative, Charles A. Dana, to interview three doubtful congressmen after giving Dana the assurance: "Whatever promise you make to them I will perform." The patronage that the congressmen asked for was promised, Nevada was admitted to the Union, and the Thirteenth Amendment ratified—all as Lincoln had planned. [15]

The Power of Presidential Patronage at a Change of Parties

When a presidential election brings a different party into power presidential patronage attains a peak of potential power as a lever in legislation. For example, when Democratic Grover Cleveland succeeded Republican President Benjamin Harrison in 1893, the turnover of Federal office holders enabled Cleveland to use patronage to attain his immediate paramount objective, the repeal of the Silver Purchase Act, and thereby check the disastrous drain of gold from the United States Treasury. But presidents like Coolidge, Hoover, or Truman who follow presidents of their own party, lack this advantage. Coming to the presidency after a dozen years of Republican rule, Franklin Roosevelt found practically every office outside the classified service occupied by a Republican. Consequently he had an unusual opportunity to use patronage in promoting his program of emergency and reform legislation. The patronage was further extended by the unprecedented increase of personnel required to administer the new legislation. Democratic congressmen were persistently harassed by local politicians who insisted upon immediate distribution of offices. Roosevelt's strategy was to delay the dispensing of patronage until his legislative program had been translated into statutes. Now and then he whispered to an importunate congressman: "We haven't got to patronage yet." When patronage developed it was dispensed on the basis of answers to the question asked of patronage-seeking congressmen: "How did you vote on the President's Economy bill?" "His (Roosevelt's) control of patronage," wrote E. P. Herring, "was the only means he had of touching individual members of Congress directly. But when he had to marshall Congress behind his program and to persuade congressmen to risk the displeasure of important interests, he needed some means of strengthening his position

[15] C. A. Dana: *Recollections of the Civil War* (New York, 1898), pp. 174 ff.

at home. The dangers, the faults, and the limitations of the methods are obvious. Yet the session indicated that the consummation of a national program is greatly aided by transmuting through patronage the localism of our politics into support of the Chief Executive." [16]

The President as the Synthesizer of the General Will

Out of the mosaic of conflicting blocs and interests, competent presidential leadership must somehow manage to derive policies of the public welfare. This was recognized by Émile Giraud in his observations based on French experience. He perceived that the executive must direct the legislature as the organ with "unity of thought" and "capacity to acquire a view of the whole." [17] Even the phlegmatic Coolidge perceived this and aptly expressed his conception of the president's role: "It is because, in their hours of timidity, the Congress becomes subservient to the importunities of organized minorities that the President comes more and more to stand as the champion of the rights of the whole country." [18] This function of the president calls for shrewd synthesis of the general interests through selection and combination of favorable tendencies and supporting social forces. In this function the president must play the part of a manipulator of Congress as well as a leader. He is the only official with an opportunity for checking the minority pressures that so successfully lobby Congress. This he may do by rallying the public behind him. However, as Harold Laski points out: "The President must pick his issues carefully. They must be wide enough to be generally interesting. They must be of the type that, emotionally can be made pretty rapidly to seem important. They must, if possible, transcend the inherent sectionalism of Congress. And the appeal to the public must not be made too frequently. Just as an excessive use of the radio would dull its influence by making it over-familiar, so the President must not appear as a man who simply cannot 'get on' with Congress." [19]

The Veto Power: Its Original Purpose

The framers invested the president with the veto power as a precaution against Congress becoming as "omnipotent" as state legislatures had been in the 1780's. This was accomplished through the provision that every bill which had passed the two houses of Congress shall be presented to the president who may either sign it or return it with his objections to the house in which it originated. There was a widespread conviction at the time of the framing of the Constitution that the executive branch of a

---

[16] E. P. Herring: "The First Session of the Seventy-Third Congress." *American Political Science Review* (1934), 28:82, 83.

[17] Émile Giraud: *La Crise de la democratie et le réenforcement du pouvoir executif* (Paris, 1938), p. 110. Quoted by Edward S. Corwin: *The President: Office and Powers* (New York, 1940), p. 428.

[18] Calvin Coolidge: "The President Lives Under a Multitude of Eyes." *The American Magazine* (July, 1929), 108:146.

[19] Harold Laski: *The American Presidency: An Interpretation* (New York, 1940), p. 152.

republic could not avoid being inherently weak and was consequently presumed to require a special device for self protection. No doubt Hamilton expressed the consensus of the framers in the following passage from the seventy-third number of the *Federalist:* "The primary inducement to conferring the power in question on the Executive is to enable him to defend himself; the secondary one is to increase the chances in favor of the community against the passage of bad laws, through haste, inadvertence, or design. . . . The superior weight and influence of the legislative body in a free government, and the hazard to the executive in a trial of strength with that body, afford a satisfactory security that the negative will generally be employed with great caution."

Early Use of the Veto Power

President Washington vetoed two bills, one on the grounds of constitutionality, the other on the question of its expediency. John Adams did not veto any, nor did Jefferson, who believed the power should be used only against a bill "unauthorized by the Constitution." Four of Madison's six vetoes were based upon points of constitutionality. With the inauguration of Andrew Jackson there came to the presidency the first incumbent elected by practically universal manhood suffrage. Under him the veto power became, as one of his cabinet members characterized it, "the people's tribunative voice speaking again through their Executive."[20] The reference here is to the Roman tribunes or popular champions who, as the constitutional representatives of the plebeians, had a literal power of veto over Senate legislation they considered inimical to the Roman masses. Since Jackson's following included the underprivileged, he did not hesitate to exercise the veto power in the tribunative sense. Moreover, President Jackson made the veto power what it still is—an instrument of party strategy as, for example, when he asked the head of his cabinet, Van Buren, to find among the pending bills providing for internal improvements at Federal expense, one he could veto with the least harm to the party. Although Jackson's party following included some men who believed that the Federal government should construct rivers, roads, and harbors, a majority of them condemned such activity as paternalism. Van Buren accordingly selected for veto the bill for the short Maysville road located in a congressional district so overwhelmingly Democratic as not to embarrass the Democratic congressman representing that district. Even more was Jackson's veto of the bill to recharter the Bank of the United States an instrument of party warfare in its appeal to every shade of popular prejudice against the "Monster." The message was printed in quantities as a campaign document. When Congress in 1948 passed the Basing Point Bill affecting the pricing of cement, President Truman had to decide whether to sign or veto. The Democratic National Chairman polled the constituent interests of Truman's strength on the basis of which the President decided to veto, thus retaining the good

[20] Levi Woodbury: *Writings* (Boston, 1852), Vol. I, p. 571.

will of the base of his political power, the labor, farming, and small-business interests, instead of strengthening the Dixiecrats by signing.

The Veto Power Since Cleveland

The last two generations have seen an increase in the number and ratio of vetoes to the total number of bills passed. This is attributable to the increase of legislation and its broadening scope as a consequence of the increasing complexity of American society. [21] President Cleveland astonished the nation by vetoing 343 bills, 301 of which were private pension bills which previous presidents had been signing perfunctorily. Even though he sought only to eliminate fraudulent claims, his action incurred the wrath of veterans' organizations. President Franklin Roosevelt, however, far exceeded Cleveland in the number of his vetoes. Even if his last four years are disregarded, an accurate count reveals that he vetoed 505 bills (30 per cent of all the bills vetoed since the establishment of the Federal government). Indeed the vetoes of Cleveland and those of Franklin Roosevelt up to 1941 constitute two-thirds of all presidential vetoes. While Cleveland concentrated his vetoes on private pensions, Franklin Roosevelt swept the entire range of legislation. [22] During World War II President Franklin Roosevelt, for the first time in American history, vetoed a revenue bill which, it had long been assumed, usage decisively exempted from that presidential power. In a message reminiscent of Jackson's Bank veto the President denounced the measure as "not a tax bill, but a tax relief bill providing relief not for the needy but for the greedy." The bill was promptly passed over Roosevelt's veto.

The Veto Today, Still a Tribunative Power

No sooner had World War II ended than the veto, in the hands of President Truman, assumed again its tribunative power as a defense of the interests of organized labor. The coal and railroad strikes of the spring of 1946 created a public demand for legislation restricting strikes, a demand which Congress embodied in the Case Labor Bill. This was vetoed by President Truman, and the proponents of the bill failed to obtain the two-thirds vote of both houses necessary to pass it over the President's veto The congressmen representing the crowded wards of the greater cities for the most part provided the 135 votes sustaining the veto. The election of these congressmen depends largely on the labor vote, in contrast with the 255 who supported the bill and whose constituents dwell largely in suburban, smaller city, town, village, and rural regions. Thus the check and balance system functioned through the presidential veto to safeguard metropolitan organized labor against the combined power of industry, business, and agriculture as represented in Congress. The refusal of Congress to sustain President Truman's veto of the Taft-Hartley Labor Act

[21] Katherine A. Towle: "The Presidential Veto Since 1889." *American Political Science Review* (1937), 31:51–56.

[22] G. C. Robinson: "The Veto Record of Franklin Roosevelt." *American Political Science Review* (1942), 36:75–8.

stimulated labor to seek at the polls at least somewhat more than a one-third representation in Senate and House. [23]

The Veto Power Merely Suspensive

Congress has its constitutional opportunity to reconsider a measure after the president's veto. If, upon such reconsideration, a yea and nay vote of two-thirds of both houses approves the bill it becomes a law without the president's signature. Between 1789 and 1936 there were 750 presidential vetoes (exclusive of pocket vetoes) of which forty-nine, or $6\frac{1}{2}$ per cent, were overridden. Nearly two-thirds of all bills vetoed were private bills mainly providing for special pensions. While 16 per cent of public bills (general legislation) were overridden, only slightly more than one per cent of the vetoes of special bills have been overridden. As to special bills, members of both houses of Congress have from time to time indicated that they take for granted that the president, through his staff and administrative agencies that advise him, is more likely than Congress as a whole to be informed as to what action should be taken. [24]

Effect of the President's Failure to Sign a Bill

The Constitution allows the president ten days in which to consider whether to sign a measure presented to him by Congress. If he holds the bill beyond the ten days while Congress is in session it becomes a law whether he signs it or not. If, however, Congress adjourns either finally or for a short period before the expiration of the ten-day period, the measure fails to become a law by reason of the president's refusal to sign it. This is known as the "pocket veto." This kind of veto is not suspensive but final, and since a flood of bills may be piled on the president's desk at the end of a session the pocket veto may then become extraordinarily significant in the hands of the chief legislator. [25]

No Item Veto: Consequent Riders

The terms of the constitutional provision for the veto power confront the president with the simple alternative of accepting or rejecting a bill in its entirety. A number of state constitutions permit the governor, in what is known as the "item veto," to reject a part of a measure while accepting the remainder of it. The Constitution's limitation of the veto power to all or none has permitted the development of an unfortunate practice by Congress of attaching to appropriation bills irrelevant provisions that the president might veto if presented in a separate bill. The "rider," as such a proviso is called, is attached in the expectation that the president will be compelled to accept it in order to save the main measure, con-

[23] "Labor Holds Its Own Gains" and "The New Strategy of Veto," *United States News*, June 21, 1946, pp. 13, 14.

[24] Clarence A. Berdahl: "The President's Veto of Private Bills." *Political Science Quarterly* (1937), 52:505–31.

[25] The Pocket Veto Cases, 279 U.S. (1929); Wright v. United States, 302 U.S. 583 (1938).

cerning which he has practically no choice in the case of a general or emergency appropriation bill. However, President Hayes did defeat the designs of a hostile Congress by vetoing a number of appropriation bills containing riders designed to repeal certain Reconstruction laws. Despite widespread condemnation of the "rider," the Democratic-Republican bloc used it in the early 1940's to terminate the National Youth Administration and the Home Owners' Loan Corporation. But Congress in 1943 over-reached itself in the notorious "rider" on an appropriation bill providing that "No part of any appropriation . . . of this act . . . shall be used to pay any of the salary or other compensation or for the personal service of Goodwin B. Watson, William E. Dodd, Jr., and Robert Morss Lovett . . ." Three years later the Supreme Court held this rider to be unconstitutional as in violation of the constitutional prohibition of bills of attainder. [26]

The Veto Potentially a Positive Power

The significance of the presidential veto can never be calculated by a mere statistical analysis designed to ascertain what percentage of the whole number of bills has been killed by presidential veto. Much goes on behind the scenes between president and congressional leaders where the potential veto is a factor in determining the conclusions reached. No one can say how much the president's known or suspected disapprobation of this or that provision of a pending bill may induce a congressional committee to recast the measure with a view to avoiding a veto. Now and then there is calculation as to the strength of the majority favoring a measure drafted in a particular way in order to forecast whether the two-thirds majority might be mustered to override a presidential veto. The proponents of the bill may modify the measure with a view to satisfying the two-thirds needed to pass it, or on the other hand they may alter it so as to avoid the veto. The president may now and then forego a possible veto of a particular measure in return for congressional support of some administration measure. Thus the veto by indirection may carry a positive instead of just a negative weight.

Ordinance Making Power of the President

The president has the power to issue rules and regulations that have the effect of laws enforceable in the courts. However, this power does not inhere in the presidency but must be vested in the office by Constitution, treaty, or statute. It is, of course, a fundamental principle of constitutional interpretation that Congress may not redelegate its legislative power, but Congress is no longer quite so inclined, as it once was, to legislate in meticulous detail. There is a growing tendency to enact statutes in broad outline defining the general policy and then authorize the president or his subordinates to "fill in the details of legislation," as the Supreme Court has expressed it. Instances of such ordinances are civil service rules, consular regulations, and income tax and customs regula-

[26] United States v. Lovett, 328 U.S. 303 (1946).

tions. Most acts of Congress with reference to the executive departments authorize the promulgation of necessary rules and regulations which are usually drafted by the department concerned but issued only with the president's approval. The president may derive ordinance making power from treaties, which are also supreme law of the land. Moreover, the president derives directly from the Constitution, by virtue of his being commander-in-chief of the army and navy, the power to promulgate rules and regulations for the guidance of the armed forces. [27]

Growth of Executive Orders

The growth of executive orders calls for a radical modification of the conventional conception of law making. As early as the middle 1930's there were already 115 Federal agencies which, under 964 statutory provisions and 71 executive orders, were issuing ordinances affecting the public. It is impossible to define briefly the limits of executive discretion as to executive orders, but in 1940 the President had the authority to change the weight of the gold dollar, issue up to three billion dollars in currency, regulate farm or work relief, restrict foreign trade and exchange, raise or lower tariffs, suspend the eight-hour day for Federal employees, control the radio, suspend sugar quotas, ban the export of certain raw materials, forbid the transfer of ships to foreign registry, buy military supplies without bids, and seize certain power plants and dams. One explanation of the growing ordinance power of the executive is the increasing recognition that the president is in fact more representative of the people as a whole than is Congress. As Harold W. Stoke writes: "Congress is too often a group of warring partisan representatives of sections, occupations, and classes, unable to find the common denominators of national unity and interest. It is then that we turn hopefully to the president to compose differences and to formulate policies." [28]

The Limits of Congress's Power to Authorize Ordinance Making

As indicated above, the president must keep within the limits set by Constitution, treaty, or statute in his ordinance making, and Congress itself may not redelegate the powers delegated to it by the Constitution. Congress disregarded this principle in its delegation of powers in the National Industrial Recovery Act of 1933. This legislation was intended to raise wages, reduce working hours, eliminate child labor, outlaw cutthroat competition, conserve natural resources, and restore prosperity. All this was to be done by means of codes of fair competition drawn up for each industry by its representatives in close collaboration with government officials. Once adopted and signed by the president these regulations were to have the force of law mandatory upon their respective industries and enforceable by criminal and civil procedures. The Supreme

[27] Harvey Walker: *Law Making in the United States* (New York, 1934), pp. 464–5.
[28] Harold W. Stoke: "Executive Leadership and the Growth of Propaganda." *American Political Science Review* (1941), 35:490–500.

Court eventually held such regulations to be not only beyond the president's power, but beyond even the power of Congress. For example, President Roosevelt had before him the clause of the National Recovery Act of 1933 stating: "The President is authorized to prohibit the transportation in interstate and foreign commerce of petroleum . . . produced or withdrawn from storage in excess of the amount permitted by any state law. . . ." But when President Franklin Roosevelt acted on this apparent authorization by prohibiting such transportation of petroleum, the Supreme Court held the act of the president as well as the provision of the statute to be invalid as an unconstitutional redelegation by Congress of its power to regulate commerce. [29] Likewise the Codes made under the National Recovery Act were held to be unconstitutional redelegations of Congress's legislative power. Congress must define standards and proscribe definite policy under which the ordinance power is to be exercised by the executive.

IMPROVING RELATIONS BETWEEN EXECUTIVE
AND CONGRESS

The Problem of Integrating the Executive and Legislative Departments

The problem of co-ordinating the legislative and executive branches of the Federal government has been aggravated by the fact that usage has intensified a separation that the Constitution only implied. The usage started when the first Congress required Secretary of the Treasury Alexander Hamilton to make his reports in writing instead of orally, which he was ready and eager to do. The consequences of this persistent practice of excluding cabinet members from appearance in Congress are today quite as Joseph Story described them over a century ago: "The Executive is compelled to resort to secret and unseen influences, to private interviews, and private arrangements, to accomplish his own appropriate purposes instead of proposing and sustaining his own duties and measures by a bold and manly appeal to the nation in the face of its representatives." [30] Three-quarters of a century ago James A. Garfield, after a long service in the House of Representatives, declared: "It would be far better for both departments if members of the Cabinet were permitted to sit in Congress and participate in the debates on measures relating to their several departments—but, of course, without a vote. This would tend to secure the ablest men for the chief executive offices; it would bring the policy of the administration into the fullest publicity by giving both parties ample opportunity for criticism and defense." [31]

[29] Panama Refining Co. v. Ryan, 293 U.S. 386 (1935).
[30] Joseph Story: Exposition of the Constitution of the United States (New York, 1840), p. 96.
[31] J. A. Garfield: "A Century of Congress." Atlantic Monthly (1877).

The Cult of Parliamentary Government

Two years after Garfield's recommendation, young Woodrow Wilson proposed giving "the members of the Cabinet seats in Congress, with the privilege of the initiative in legislation." In 1893 he urged that President Cleveland "now assume the role of prime minister with the Cabinet as the agency of coordination to accomplish the popular will." Wilson's fertile imagination read into the Constitution's provision for the president's message to Congress the potentiality of the role of a prime minister. Fate decreed in due time that he should be cast for the part. In office he sought in very truth to be a prime minister. Thus he stressed his function as the leader of his party, addressed Congress in person, and promoted and carried out a program of notable legislation. When he faced possible defeat on the proposed repeal of the exemption of American vessels from payment of Panama Canal tolls he declared: "In case of failure of this matter I shall go to the country after my resignation is tendered." He also considered resignation if the McLenmore Resolution warning Americans against traveling on armed vessels of belligerents were not defeated. His ill-fated appeal for the election of a Democratic Congress in 1918 was again in the pattern of the ministerial system. President Wilson learned eventually that such a system does not conform to American traditions and apparently cannot be institutionalized in the American setting. [32]

Recent Proposals to Adopt a Parliamentary System

Every prolonged deadlock of president and Congress revives discussion of some institutional procedure for breaking the impasse. The Democratic-Republican anti-administration bloc that brought New Deal legislation to a stand-still and plagued President Truman even more than President Roosevelt induced insistent proposals for the adoption of the parliamentary practice of an appeal to the country by a new election. When the congressional elections of 1946 confronted Democratic President Truman with a decisively Republican Congress, Senator Fulbright even proposed that President Truman resign after appointing as Secretary of State a Republican who would then succeed him. Senator Fulbright prepared a proposed constitutional amendment providing that Congress, by concurrent resolu-

[32] Wilfred E. Binkley: *President and Congress,* chap. XI. The following passage from President Wilson's 1918 appeal for the election of a Democratic Congress distinctly implies his conception of the presidency as a premiership: "If you have approved of my leadership and wish me to continue to be your unembarrassed spokesman in affairs at home and abroad, I earnestly beg that you will express yourselves unmistakably to that effect by returning a Democratic majority to both the Senate and the House of Representatives. I am your servant and will accept your judgment without cavil, but my power to administer the great trust assigned me by the Constitution would be seriously impaired should your judgment be adverse, and I must frankly tell you so because so many critical issues depend upon your verdict."—Joseph P. Tumulty, *Woodrow Wilson as I Knew Him* (New York, 1921), p. 331. The American electorate appeared to resent the appeal and a Republican Congress was elected although many other factors doubtless contributed to that event.

tion, or the president by executive order, may order a new election of president and Congress and the terms of incumbents of these offices would end forty days after such elections. The terms of president, senators, and representatives in Congress would be six years unless interrupted by prior election. The purpose of the proposed amendment would be to break a deadlock between president and Congress by an election which, it is presumed, would give the nation an executive and legislature in harmony on the pending issue. There is no certainty, however, that such an election would not give the nation a president of one party and a Congress of another as has happened more than once and could easily have happened in 1916 and 1948. Different parties could even obtain majorities in Senate and House.

The Parliamentary System, A Product of British Society

Those who propose the adoption of a parliamentary system or its adaptation to American government are prone to ignore the historical evolution and even the practical operation of the British system. It was by no manner of means a product of deliberate planning, but was instead a resultant of Britain's peculiar society groping through the centuries for day-to-day adjustments to problems of government. Out of innumerable unplanned episodes and accidents the British parliamentary system emerged and developed. Whenever transplanted to lands outside the British Commonwealth of Nations the system has behaved as an exotic plant and become something quite different from the British model—that is, when it has even survived. This does not signify that the parliamentary system would not work in the United States but rather that its behavior would be unpredictable.

American Government, A Product of American Experience

The American system of separated powers is no less an outgrowth of American society and environment than the British parliamentary system is of another society and environment. Our Federal government is by no means an artificial product of the framers of the Constitution. It, too, is the result of innumerable fortuitous, practical adjustments devised during three and a half centuries of governmental experience in the American environment. Such is the complexity of our society that a resort to a forced settlement of its major issues by the simple majorities implicit in a "hair trigger" parliamentary system might prove socially explosive. One of the keenest of the early American political thinkers perceived the peculiar problem of national government in the United States. If unchecked numerical majorities are always to prevail, then sectional, economic, or other minorities are defenseless. John C. Calhoun saw the remedy as the "concurrent majority" of several interest each capable of vetoing the other. At one time he even proposed two presidents, a northern and a southern, one each with a veto over congressional legislation. In a way, the Federal government functions through a kind of system of concurrent majorities or potential vetoes of

Senate, House, and president. Usually the president exercises his veto as the representative of a set of interests somewhat different from that of the Senate or of the House. Deep-seated conflicts in American society are not likely to be resolved by a simple shift in the mechanism of government. Indeed it is these very conflicts in the society that determine the nature of the government rather than the nature of the government being responsible for the friction. E. P. Herring struck a keynote in his statement: "The concept of checks and balances can never lack meaning in a society of divergent interests." [33] When Americans constitute a more homogeneous people than they now do they may find suggestions of a parliamentary system more acceptable.

The Proposal of a Legislative-Executive Council

The Federal government might well consider the adoption of a Legislative-Executive Council. In the Federal government it might consist of congressional leaders and members of the president's cabinet. It could readily be created by joint resolution of the two houses and an executive order of the president. Its membership probably ought to consist of the vice-president, the speaker, the majority party floor leaders of the two houses, chairmen of major committees, and perhaps designated members of the president's cabinet. Meetings should be held regularly for consideration of the formulation and carrying out of national policy. This council might so function as to be held responsible for setting up the legislative program in consultation with the president. If different parties controlled Senate and House the council would, of course, be bi-partisan. [34] "The penalties for excluding Congress from the national council are high," says Roland Young. "Their exclusion means a continuance of the localisms which are so often a predominant characteristic of congressional behavior. When Congress feels ignored it often retaliates irrationally, by sulking, by refusing to pass needed legislation, and by passing ill-advised legislation. When Congress is nettled, it is well to treat her like a desperate woman and walk the other way."[35]

The Proposal of the Question Hour in Congress

In the British parliamentary system a daily period is set aside when Members of Parliament may put questions to the ministers on matters pertaining to their respective departments. Thus in the most direct manner information as to administration may be solicited. Congress, on the contrary, now obtains its corresponding information by methods characterized by an awkward formality due to the extremes to which congressional custom or usage has, in practice, carried the dogma of the separation of powers. For example, Congress may pass resolutions of inquiry directed to depart-

[33] E. P. Herring: *Presidential Leadership*, p. 14.
[34] George B. Galloway: *Congress at the Cross Roads* (New York, 1946), pp. 120, 211.
[35] Roland Young: *This is Congress* (New York, 1946), p. 257.

ment heads. Hearings may be conducted by congressional committees that consume the time of busy administrators. Too often these investigations are not held jointly by both houses. Departmental information may be obtained by personal interviews or by correspondence of congressmen with administrative officials. Recent presidents have held weekly conferences at the White House with leaders of the Senate and House. The substitution of a question hour, modeled after the British practice, to take the place of the circumlocution of prevailing American practices has been proposed by Representative Kefauver and Senator Fullbright. If the practice is adopted it has been suggested that the questioning should be held frequently before joint sessions of the two houses; that cabinet officers be questioned at intervals in rotation; that time be divided equally between Senate and House and between Republicans and Democrats; that questions and answers be printed in the Congressional Record; that the privilege of postponing answers be given; that questions deal with broad matters of departmental policy, and that questions be addressed to the president and assigned by him to the appropriate executive officer for answering. [36]

SUMMARY

Despite the separation of powers, the functions of President and Congress must somehow be coordinated in order to achieve the ends of government. Washington, Jefferson, Jackson, McKinley, Wilson and the two Roosevelts each in his own way undertook to effect this coordination. As the representative of a nation-wide constituency the President has become a leader in legislation and, as the one best situated to discover the balance of competing social forces, he is the potential synthesizer of national will and policy.

Since Woodrow Wilson the presidential message has had added importance because of its personal delivery before Congress and, more recently, thanks to radio and television, it may be heard and witnessed by the nation. The President's leadership in legislation is indicated by Congress's increasing dependence upon executive initiative and advice in law making. Sometimes a resolute President can manage passage of a bill, even using patronage if necessary to get results.

At first the veto power was used as a defense of executive power and as an executive check on unconstitutional legislation. Since Jackson however, presidents have used the veto to prevent what they considered imprudent legislation. Consequently veto messages are frequently appeals to the nation. Congress often authorizes the President to supplement a statute with rules and regulations known as ordinances or executive orders.

No stable formula has ever been discovered for establishing smooth

[36] George B. Galloway: *Congress at the Crossroads*, pp. 215–19; J. W. Fulbright: "The Legislator." *Vital Speeches*, May 15, 1946.

coordination of the executive and Congress. The framers merely invested the two branches with their separate duties, but the overworked dogma of separated powers and a persisting usage have prevented executive heads from speaking in Congress. Some would give them seats there with the privilege of debating but not of voting. Others would establish an executive-legislative council to give the two branches an organic connection, while others would establish an all-out parliamentary system.

PART

V

*   *

THE FEDERAL ADMINISTRATION

CHAPTER XVII

THE ADMINISTRATION OF NATIONAL AFFAIRS

IN OUR analysis of the texture of American government we have already seen that the term "executive" embraces a wide assortment of functions. Among these functions perhaps none so frequently touches the daily life of the citizens as that of administration. The administrative branch must apply the policies predetermined by Congress and enforce the court orders from the Federal judiciary. From the very size of the administrative branch also we obtain some conception of its importance as one of the component parts of government. In the national legislature there are but 531 law-makers aided by a staff of a few thousand secretaries, clerks, and research assistants. Serving our Federal courts are about 300 judges assisted by a much smaller force of employees than that which aids Congress. The total for the administrative branch, however, hovers around 2,300,000 employees and it is largely their work that carries government into effect.

The propelling drive in the administration of national affairs is provided by the president. By constitutional authority and in practice the chief executive heads the administrative branch. He is, in a word, the "boss" of this vast sprawling division of the Federal government whose activities have such a vital bearing on the everyday life of our community.

ESTABLISHING A STRONG EXECUTIVE

Although there was an ingrained distrust of executive power at the time the Constitution was drafted, fortunately some of this prejudice was diluted by the ideas and forceful character of Alexander Hamilton. One of the principal contributions of the Founding Fathers, therefore, was the establishment of a potent chief executive.

Hamilton's Views on Administration

A paramount need of government as envisaged by Alexander Hamilton was an "energetic Executive" endowed with broad powers to direct the affairs of state with dispatch and efficiency. [1] "We may safely pronounce," he wrote in 1788, "that the true test of a good government is its aptitude and tendency to produce a good administration." [2] Under the Hamilton concept, whatever merit a government might have in theory, if in practice it resulted in poor administration it was a bad government. The quintessence of Hamilton's views on administration may be reduced to three main propositions: First, he believed in national supremacy and he felt that this primary objective could best be achieved through a unified administrative system. Second, he looked to the leadership of the administration to furnish the kind of development and expansion necessary for this branch of government. Finally, and certainly a very radical proposition for his time, he conceived the guidance of public policy and social development to be a responsibility of administration. [3]

THE PRESIDENT AND CABINET

In the structural development of the Federal administrative branch under the president, the cabinet made an early appearance. No provision was made for a cabinet in the Constitution. This institution was formed in the crucible of experience. As Congress created departments to assist the president in executing policy, the chief executive began to have dealings with the heads of these departments. At first, Washington carried on relations with his department heads individually and solicited their advice either in writing or by personal consultation. But as the problems of administration became more formidable the device of a collective meeting of department heads with the president was adopted. Since 1793 the term "cabinet" came to be applied to these joint meetings of the chief executive with his department heads. The cabinet, of course, is simply an advisory body and generally speaking has not had appreciable influence over administration.

In reality, as Lord Bryce has commented, "there is in the government of the United States no such thing as a cabinet in the English sense of the term." The American cabinet member is not ordinarily chosen because of his influence in the legislative branch, and the cabinet in this country does not possess what one British observer describes as "legislative sovereignty." The important ministers in Great Britain always have seats in Parliament; cabinet members in the United States, in contrast, are not members of Congress and the cabinet does not provide legislative leadership.

The extent of the cabinet's influence over policy in both legislative and administrative matters is entirely up to the president. Some presidents have looked to their cabinets for a great deal of guidance, but by and large the cabinet has not been a vigorous policy-making institution. Cabinet

[1] *The Federalist*, No. 70.
[2] *The Federalist*, No. 68.
[3] See Lynton K. Caldwell: *The Administrative Theories of Hamilton and Jefferson* (Chicago, 1944), p. 231. This volumes presents an able discussion of the comparative views of Hamilton and Jefferson on administration.

meetings are held regularly and emergency sessions are not uncommon, yet the tangible contributions of these gatherings to administrative leadership and coordination are negligible.

During cabinet meetings, members are ranked according to precedence—those representing the oldest departments being seated closest to the president. The chief executive observes the same precedence in soliciting their opinions. Votes are sometimes taken, but the consensus of former cabinet members seems to be that at cabinet meetings little is done to reach agreement upon policies of general concern. Furthermore, even when a vote is taken, the president is under no compulsion to be governed by it. This is sometimes illustrated by the oft-quoted story about Lincoln, who wound up a cabinet discussion, during which he had been solidly opposed by all members, with the remark: "Seven nays, one aye, the ayes have it."

Given our presidential form of government the president must rule with a firm hand over his cabinet—a feat which sometimes appears to be a simpler matter for the chief executive than it actually is. Although the president nominates members of his cabinet, various pressures are brought to bear to influence his selections. Once in office all cabinet members have important friends in the party, in Congress, and perhaps among various interest groups in the country. This circumstance accounts for Washington's adage—a president's cabinet members are his worst enemies. Thus cabinet members are not without means of exerting a potent influence of their own should a disagreement on policy occur within the president's official administrative family. For this reason the president must maneuver his cabinet members occasionally, in some cases bestowing certain responsibilities and favors, in other cases gently managing to decrease their influence in the administration. Franklin Roosevelt was exceedingly adept in such matters. When he by-passed his Secretary of State and used his personal adviser Harry Hopkins as a negotiator he did so adroitly, and he often utilized similar procedures on labor problems while Frances Perkins was Secretary of Labor. But in shuffling cabinet members about, the president must move warily to avoid stirring up unwelcome dissension, for a cabinet member who is chafed in the process may give a lot of trouble.

Where difference of opinion between a cabinet member and the president ripens to the point of an open break, the conventional procedure calls for the voluntary submission of the secretary's resignation. But the chief executive may demand a resignation, as President Truman did of Secretary of Commerce Henry Wallace in the summer of 1946 following a much-publicized altercation over foreign policy. The only instance of mass resignation occurred in 1841 when almost the entire cabinet resigned after Vice-President Tyler succeeded William Henry Harrison. In this case, however, the action was a political protest; Harrison's cabinet represented the Clay Whigs while Tyler belonged to the other Whig faction. Perhaps the most dramatic cabinet quarrel was the one we discussed earlier in connection with the president's removal power, in which President Johnson's attempt to dismiss Secretary of War Stanton led to impeachment proceedings against the chief executive. A more recent example of serious disagreement between the cabinet and president took place early in 1946 when Secretary of the Interior Harold L. Ickes, the last member of Franklin Roosevelt's original cabinet, resigned from President Truman's cabinet with the caustic statement that he did not care to "commit perjury for the sake of the party." But dramatic cabinet-president disputes have been relatively few and have done virtually nothing in the long run to strengthen the position of the cabinet in administrative affairs.

A few pregnant suggestions have been advanced for making the cabinet a more potent arm of administration. One view holds that the cabinet could be transformed into a vigorous institution simply by making the proper appointments. "A good cabinet," commented Harold Laski, "ought to be a place where the large outlines of policy can be hammered out in common, where the essential strategy is decided upon, where the President knows that he will hear, both in affirmation and in doubt, even in negation, most of what can be said about the direction he proposes to follow." A cabinet functioning in this spirit could indeed stimulate administrative leadership, but thus far the cabinet has fallen short of such an ideal.

THE PRESIDENT AND THE DEPARTMENTS

With the cabinet as a unit having little influence upon the administration of the departments it is all the more evident that the real propulsion in executive leadership must be supplied by the president himself. Several factors contributed to Hamilton's plan to energize the executive—to strengthen the president's leadership in administration. Basic to this development, of course, was the Constitution which endowed the chief executive with the "capacity of initiative" in matters relating to administration. The president was given the power to nominate important officials; he had the authority to receive diplomatic representatives from foreign countries and the implied power to conduct our foreign relations; he had the responsibility of seeing that the laws of Congress were enforced; and interpreted broadly "he was the legatee of whatever the [Constitutional] Convention, Congress, and later generations would agree to read into the phrase, 'the executive power'." [4] But besides the Constitution, the favorable auspices under which the presidential office developed in the formative years were of no little significance.

Much of the character of the presidential office might turn on the personality and leadership qualities of its first occupant and in this respect the infant Republic was most fortunate. To the chief executive's office George Washington brought a wealth of experience which he combined with a soundness of judgment that won wide respect and confidence. Inspired by the example which Washington set and maintaining an abiding faith in the integrity and ability of this remarkable personality during the critical first

[4] See Leonard D. White: *The Federalists* (New York, 1948), p. 16.

years that he piloted the government of the United States, Congress passed many measures to strengthen the presidential hand in administrative matters. In building up the independence of the executive branch, Congress placed the bulk of administrative authority in the chief executive and they further increased his control over administration by putting him in a position to direct the work of every subordinate officer of the government. Under such conditions, the centralization of administrative control in the presidential office moved off to a brisk start and while in the intervening years Congress has occasionally felt disposed to tamper with the chief executive's directive authority over administration, the course of events has continued to enlarge his leadership in this area.

Establishing the Departments

The architects of the Constitution were not much concerned with the organization of the executive branch other than the office of the president. No specific provisions for separate branches of administration were embodied in the Constitution. The establishment of departments is implied to deal with foreign relations, the military forces, and fiscal affairs, but it was evidently assumed that Congress would provide for additional departments as the need arose. This conclusion is supported by clauses in the Constitution which authorize the president to require opinions in writing from the principal officers "in each of the executive Departments," and empower Congress to delegate to the "heads of Departments" the power to appoint "inferior officers." As a consequence of this arrangement the power either to create new executive departments or abolish old ones is completely in the hands of Congress. However, Congress may authorize the president to make changes such as combining executive agencies and has done so on several occasions.

Until the establishment of the Civil Service Commission in 1883, the policy of Congress was to keep practically all Federal administrative operations under separate departments. From the original three with which the government started in 1789 (State, War and Treasury), the number of departments gradually increased to ten in 1912, but with the reorganization of the War and Navy departments in 1947 as a single department, there were but nine. The creation of the Department of Health, Education and Welfare in 1953 restored the number of ten. The heads of all departments except the post office and justice departments are denominated secretaries.[5]

The Department Heads

A significant factor in our national administrative system is that one of the functions of departmental heads is to carry out, through the permanent

[5] An excellent account of the evolution of departmental growth is given in Lloyd M. Short: *The Development of the National Administrative Organization in the United States* (Baltimore, 1923).

administrative machinery which they direct, the policies of the victorious political party. The secretary of a department is not inert politically; he is, generally speaking, appointed because of his partisanship and he is expected to inject the policies of his party and president into his handling of the administrative affairs of the department he heads. It is desirable, of course, that the policies of the president and his departmental heads set the tone of administrative policy for this is a part of representative government. Nonetheless, the fact that departmental heads are temporary political appointees presents certain problems to administration. The continuity of the permanent administrative machinery of government must continue unbroken—it must not break down quadrennially despite a change in departmental heads and policy. But while the permanent machinery must be able to weather shifts in personnel and policy without having its operating efficiency seriously impaired, it must also be flexible enough to respond to political oscillations. All this is not made easier by the fact that departmental heads are frequently appointed who have little capacity for administrative leadership and who are sometimes incredibly lacking in ability either to influence policy or to give forceful direction to departmental affairs.

Nominations for these posts are made by the president and confirmed by the Senate. With few exceptions the nominations are partisan matters. Herbert Hoover named a Democrat, William D. Mitchell, as his attorney general, and Franklin Roosevelt nominated Republicans Henry L. Stimson and Frank Knox as secretaries of the War and Navy Departments. When a president does reach outside of his own party to nominate a departmental head, the person he selects may be a political maverick who is not on the best of terms with his own party, or he may be designated at a time of serious emergency as a gesture of national political unity. The latter reason had a good deal to do with the appointments of Messrs. Stimson and Knox in 1940 when President Roosevelt was striving to win Republican support for his foreign policies and attempting to create an impression abroad that the United States was not hopelessly torn with internal dissension over the isolationist issue. Most nominations for departmental heads, however, go to persons of the president's political faith, and any chief executive who in selecting his key administrative officials took an intransigent position against this partisan principle would seriously jeopardize his leadership.

It cannot be emphasized too strongly that partisanship in appointing departmental heads is not a sinister evil. Partisanship is essential to the operation of government. If the president is to compose and execute policy it follows that the leading administrative officials who are to assist him should share his views on the fundamental objectives he seeks to accomplish. This does not mean that the president should surround himself with "yes" men as departmental heads, for independence of judgment is highly desirable and may provide stimulating ideas which are most helpful to the president in guiding his administration. But agreement between a president and his departmental heads upon the common objectives in policy is extremely important for sound administration; for this reason partisanship cannot be lightly dismissed in making appointments.

The difficulty in making department-head appointments is not that partisanship cuts down the field from which the president may make nominations, but that in drawing from the field of partisan entrants the best-qualified persons are not always chosen. Long and faithful service to the party is often a criterion for appointment, and liberal contributions to the party's campaign funds are not exactly a handicap, although the latter qualification is probably more common in appointments to ambassadorships. Customarily the office of postmaster general goes to the person who is national chairman of the president's political party, and it is assumed that along with handling the duties of his department he will also function as a sort of potentate on all questions of patronage and do his best to kindle party enthusiasm. Thus in canvassing the field for departmental heads many factors operate to interfere with the selection of the partisan with the most outstanding qualifications. Despite this condition, however, the heads of executive departments are frequently persons with a talent for administrative leadership, and a number have made distinguished records.

ORGANIZING THE DEPARTMENTS

In studying the institutions of government it is often helpful to eject descriptive minutiae momentarily from our minds and ask ourselves an elemental question: What is government trying to accomplish? What are the ends it seeks and what are the alternatives for attaining them? In establishing a national legislature the purpose is to set up a representative body which will transpose the individual desires of the many into a single national policy. In creating an executive branch the purpose is to carry out public policy. How can public policy best be carried out? For one thing, to execute policy someone needs to be in overall command and this direction as we have noted is supplied by the president. But the administrative branch of government in the United States is a gigantic task force. How is it to be organized so that the chief executive may supply competent direction and keep it operating smoothly? The answer to this question, of course, holds one of the most crucial problems for government and leads us to examine the organization of the administrative structures designed to execute public policy in the United States. Of the three most commonly employed—department, government corporation, and independent commission—the erection of a working departmental structure, as we have seen, was first in time, and since the department is the basic unit of our national administrative framework we may begin our investigation of forms of organization with this agency.

The Basis of Departmental Organization

Several alternative methods may be followed in organizing the subordinate administrative units within the departmental structure. Professor Wallace lists four major concepts of organization that are commonly used in the process of departmentalization: (1) function; (2) work processes; (3) clientele; and (4) territory. [6] At first glance the subdivision of departments upon the basis of any one of these four categories would appear to be quite simple. Actually it is not. The functional principle—which is most often used in departmental organization—is usually thought of as an attempt to group subordinate agencies under a department whose work is dedicated to similar or common objectives. In large part the Departments of State, Post Office, Agriculture, Labor, Treasury, and Defense are based upon this principle. In describing the internal organization of departments the limitations of the functional principle are not hard to perceive. Both the Departments of Agriculture and Interior are concerned with the conservation of natural resources, hence in any subdivision of the work of these departments subordinate units in either of them may be concerned with the "solution of the same or similar problems." In the handling of our foreign relations similar overlapping may be observed in certain subordinate units of the State, Commerce, and Agriculture Departments. Thus it is a common occurrence for the subordinate units of different departments to be engaged in work which is the same or closely related despite the general functional principle which is applied in organizing most of the departments.

The organization of a department on a "work processes" basis could be guided either by personnel or equipment. A single department, for example, might be staffed by personnel recruited from one profession. No department in the Federal government is organized wholly on the basis of work processes, but several have been partly subdivided on this principle. Cases in point are the Bureau of Entomology and Plant Quarantine and the Bureau of Agricultural and Industrial Chemistry both located in the Department of Agriculture. A third alternative in organizing a department— the clientele basis—is illustrated by such agencies as the Children's Bureau under the Department of Labor, the Office of Indian Affairs in the Department of Interior, and the Immigration and Naturalization Service located in the Department of Justice. The last of the four suggested alternatives for departmental organization—the territorial basis—is frequently used in the Federal government. The field services found among several departments are organized on a geographic basis and in the State Department such examples might be cited as the Division of Central European Affairs, the Division of Western European Affairs, the Office of Far Eastern Affairs, and the Office of Near Eastern and African Affairs.

The salient fact to be gleaned from this discussion of possible alternatives in organizing the departmental substructure is that each of them may be peculiarly suited to a particular kind of work. Yet subdividing departments according to any one of these methods cannot be expected to produce a result where the subordinate units of one department will be working toward exclusive objectives in which similar agencies of other departments have no interest. The simple truth is that the work of a single

[6] Schuyler Wallace: *Federal Departmentalization* (New York, 1941), p. 91.

department cannot be compartmentalized in so monopolistic a fashion that no other departments will have occasion to trespass upon some phase of it. Often several departments are working on objectives that are similar or vitally linked and no amount of organizational juggling can avert this condition, nor is it desirable to avert it. The execution of policy imposes exacting demands upon the administrative branch of government and as the complexity of our civilization increases and we grow more interdependent the tasks of administration become more interconnected. Thus the solution of a given problem may not rest upon the work of one agency; it may require the attention of several, all of which are converging their efforts toward the solution of a common problem though their approaches may be quite different.

The Pattern of Departmental Organization

In the administrative arrangements of most of the departments the second ranking official is the under-secretary who is the deputy of the departmental head and like his superior is a political appointee. There are no permanent under-secretaries comparable to those serving in the British ministries. Each department also has several assistant secretaries who again are usually political appointees with uncertain tenure. Customarily, the departments are divided and subdivided into subordinate units such as bureaus, divisions, offices, and services. The terms describing these subdivisions are not standardized, however; hence their application tends to be confusing.

The Bureau

Perhaps the most important administrative cog in the department is the bureau. A bureau is essentially an operating unit designed to execute one specific task or a number of related tasks. The Bureau of Census is an example of an agency with a highly specialized responsibility. Each bureau is headed by a chief or a director whose duties compare with those of any executive.

In grasping the significance of the bureau as an instrument for the execution of policy we again need to remind ourselves that government has undertaken huge services and that to run these services the politically responsible department heads must rely upon the sub-chiefs—the bureau heads—to manage problems of considerable magnitude. It is imperative that the chain of management running from the department head be linked to the operating units such as the bureaus, divisions, and offices; and the position of bureau chiefs in this "line of command" is a critical one. [7] Many of the bureau chiefs or directors are permanent officials who entered the government service under the civil service merit system and who in most cases advanced to their positions by promotion. Bureau chiefs are seldom

[7] Arthur W. Macmahon and John D. Millett: *Federal Administrators* (New York, 1939), p. 307.

recruited by examination at that level, the normal course being to reach the post by successive promotions. [8]

Sub-bureau Units

Beneath the bureau, departmental organization is ordinarily subdivided by units known as divisions and these in turn are further fractionalized into sections. Division chiefs have broad administrative responsibilities and politically responsible department heads are heavily dependent upon division chiefs as well as upon bureau chiefs for conducting the various operations of the department.

As observed above, no hard and fast rule is followed in sub-departmental nomenclature and this introduces an element of uncertainty in judging the importance of one departmental sub-division against that of another. This difficulty is well illustrated by use of the titles "bureau" and "office." Both terms are employed to denote significant services within departments, yet there is no clear distinction between a bureau and an office. The fact that the titles are not always interchangeable from department to department, however, is unimportant. What does matter, is that the heads of the sub-units of a department—offices, bureaus, divisions, sections, or whatever they may be called—hold critical positions and constitute the executive corps that keeps the wheels of administrative services turning year in and year out irrespective of changes in the politically responsible departmental heads.

The Field Services

By and large the main work of government is done not in Washington but outside of the nation's capitol where the people who are served reside and where the industries which are regulated and controlled are located. Thus it is necessary for government to maintain extensive field services to carry on its work and it is usual for a bureau to have a home office located in Washington and several field offices scattered throughout the country. [9]

In most cases the headquarters—the home office of a department, bureau or other administrative unit—is policy making. Here the general lines of policy are drawn and then transmitted for the guidance of operating agencies in the field. Any number of examples might be cited to illustrate this division of work. The Bureau of Immigration and Naturalization Service conducts the bulk of its work—admitting and naturalizing immigrants—outside of Washington, the home office functioning as a policy maker and supervisor. A field office is generally an operating agency which may be performing many special functions. The post office of our own city or town is in reality a field office which serves all of us, while the field offices of agencies such as the Bureau of Mines or the Children's Bureau devote their energies to a special subject or a special clientele.

[8] Ibid., p. 318.
[9] See Earl G. Latham: "Executive Management and the Federal Service." *Public Administration Review* (1945), 5:16–27.

Field offices are found most frequently in major metropolitan areas such as Chicago, San Francisco, Atlanta, and New York, but many are located in smaller cities, and those engaged in scientific research are often located in rather remote areas. "Approximately 92 percent of the federal population," writes Professor Latham, "is to be found in the field, not in agency headquarters. Although headquarters organizations have their appointment calendars well-filled, it is the field people of the Federal agencies who meet the general public and impress it with the quality of service rendered or the fairness of the controls exercised. It is in the field also, that the Federal government can acquire a bad reputation for poor performance in both service and regulatory functions." [10] Thus the field services embrace tremendous undertakings. Perhaps too often we tend to visualize only Washington, D.C., as the bulging center for government employees; we need to keep in mind that government also "employs and keeps in the field, lighthouse keepers, forest rangers, county agents, teachers, preachers, clerks, clerks, and more clerks." [11]

THE GOVERNMENT CORPORATION

In addition to the traditional unit of Federal administration, the department with its bureaus, divisions, and field services, another institution markedly different—the government corporation—is used to perform certain types of functions for executing the policy laid down by Congress. The government corporation is a form of organization that has borrowed many characteristics from its counterpart in the business world. In effect, it is "a product of the cross-fertilization of government with business" which was advanced as a specialized form of administrative mechanism to perform functions somewhat out of the usual range of departmental activities. [12] The most important characteristics of the government corporation in its pre-1945 form were freedom from annual appropriation control and the right to use earnings without appropriation by Congress. [13]

As originally conceived, the government corporation was thought of as an institution that would not only be independent of Congress but would also possess some degree of autonomy with regard to the executive branch of the government. Broadly stated, of course, the general idea of the government corporation is that it is an agency engaged in the control and operation of an economic enterprise—but, not all government corporations conduct economic enterprises. Moreover, some economic enterprises are conducted by the Federal government through a non-corporate agency, such as the Post Office.

Except for two early government corporations, the Bank of North

---

[10] Earl G. Latham: *The Federal Field Service* (Chicago, 1947), p. 1.
[11] Ibid., p. 4.
[12] C. Herman Pritchett: "The Paradox of the Government Corporation." *Public Administration Review* (1941), 1:381.
[13] For a careful analysis of the government corporation see John McDiarmid: *Government Corporations and Federal Funds* (Chicago, 1938).

America, chartered by the Continental Congress in 1781, and the Bank of the United States, which received its charter from Congress in 1791, this device was little used until World War I, when several government corporations were set up. These included the Emergency Fleet Corporation and the United States Housing Corporation. With the exception of twelve Federal land banks authorized by Congress in 1916, and twelve Federal intermediate credit banks provided for in 1923, the government corporation did not again come into wide use until the Great Depression was in full swing.

In 1932, confidence in the government corporation as an emergency device was reaffirmed with the establishment of the Reconstruction Finance Corporation, and during the initial years of Franklin Roosevelt's administration this type of government institution made rapid headway. Among the better known agencies that were established during these years were the Tennessee Valley Authority, Home Owners' Loan Corporation, and the Federal Deposit Insurance Corporation. Once again, as a result of the emergency precipitated by World War II, a large number of temporary government corporations sprang into existence. These included the Rubber Reserve Company, Defense Plant Corporation, and Defense Supplies Corporation. The exact number of government corporations is at times somewhat difficult to determine, but the popularity of the institution is revealed in the Report of the President's Committee on Administrative Management. This listed ninety-three that were existing in 1936. In June, 1945, the General Accounting Office recognized some sixty government corporations. [14]

Government corporations are owned by the government and they have authority to borrow money, to buy and sell, and to accumulate profits. Ordinarily they are headed by a board of directors that may perform general executive duties or determine the policies and entrust the administrative management to an executive officer. Certain advantages are claimed for the government corporation as an organization. One is that the establishment of a government corporation stimulates managerial ingenuity and provides incentives that are not to be found in the regular bureaucratic hierarchy of ten executive departments. Greater flexibility is also found in the organization of government corporations because their policies are not so precisely fenced in by congressional statute.

At the moment, a fair evaluation of the government corporation and the determination of its proper relation to the Federal administrative system posits several provocative questions, some of which go to the root of our social thinking on the function of government. Government corporations are, as Professor White notes, "creatures of emergency, war, and depression . . ." [15] But the problems which many of the government cor-

---

[14] Report, *President's Committee on Administrative Management* (Washington, D.C., 1937), p. 305. For an official list see General Accounting Office, *Reference Manual of Government Corporations* (Washington, D.C., 1945), 79th Cong. 1st sess. Doc. No. 86, pp. V, VI.

[15] Leonard D. White: *Introduction to the Study of Public Administration* (New York, 1939), p. 124.

porations were created to cope with have not yet showed signs of fading into complete obscurity. Moreover, the measurable benefits that have flowed from the work of government corporations like the Tennessee Valley Authority have strengthened the likelihood of continued government planning for welfare purposes. It is not the intention of this book to suggest where the lines of demarcation between private and government enterprise should fall. Decisions of this nature—whether the thesis of Professor Hayek's *Road to Serfdom* (that government planning leads to totalitarianism) is correct or should be taken with a grain of salt—must be threshed out elsewhere. But it is not amiss to suggest that the idea of giving some compass to government planning in this country is as old as Alexander Hamilton; and, with the precedents for what economists call a "mixed economy" already well rooted, the probability is slight that long-range government planning will be abandoned. Because in this area the government corporation has found its widest expression, its position within our administrative system raises important questions for the future. The flexibility and freedom that several observers have cited as positive advantages of the government corporation have already been curtailed by recent legislation. Under the Government Corporation Control Act of 1945, the fiscal and financial operations of these agencies were brought within the purview of the Bureau of the Budget and the General Accounting Office, although for the most part they were not placed on the same plane as the ordinary department, being distinguished among other factors by a different budgetary procedure. The same act also forbids the creation of any new corporation without specific authorization from Congress—a measure that choked off the practice of the president sometimes creating a corporation by executive decree. [16] And, from another angle, the freedom of the government corporation to operate its personnel system independently was curtailed by the Ramspeck Act of 1940, which authorizes the president to extend the scope of the Civil Service Act. [17] Both moves, which have brought the corporations under closer financial supervision and pushed their personnel system under the mantle of civil service, have evoked sharp rejoinders from critics who believe that the success of the corporation is dependent upon the absence of irksome bureaucratic controls. [18] Thus, the future of the corporation is far from settled, but its popularity for activities affected with a strong public interest speaks persuasively for its continuance in one form or another, though it will doubtless be gradually moved into closer focus with the entire Federal administration.

[16] Corporations existing when the Act was passed that were originally organized in this fashion had to be dissolved by June 30, 1948.

[17] 54 Stat. 1211, 5 U.S.C.A., par. 631a, November 26, 1940.

[18] For specific recommendations, see Marshall E. Dimock: "These Government Corporations." *Harper's* (1945), 190:569–76.

SUMMARY

In the field of administration the President enjoys broad powers as chief executive and as the agent who appoints the heads of major administrative agencies. The influence of the cabinet on policy and administration is not great although, for political reasons, the President may not ride roughshod over cabinet members in the course he pursues. In general, disagreement between the President and a cabinet member is resolved by the resignation of the latter.

The heads of major departments are usually members of the President's party. That party regularity should be a requirement for appointment to these posts is not objectionable, since President and department heads should agree on basic policy. Fidelity to the party ought not, however, to be considered a substitute for administrative ability.

Most major agencies of the national government are classifiable as departments, government corporations, or independent commissions.

The internal organization of departments may be established according to function, work processes, clientele, or territory. Within most agencies more than one of these principles is followed in determining organization. The overwhelming majority of the national government's employees are in the field service performing operation duties rather than in the "home office" (generally Washington) determining policy and providing central direction.

The government corporation, a form of organization developed chiefly during World War I and the depression years, has the advantages of flexibility and autonomy. Used particularly in governmental enterprises of a business nature, it was granted authority to follow its own personnel policy and to use its own earnings. Legislation enacted during the 1940's curtailed the independence of the government corporation in these respects.

CHAPTER XVIII

THE INDEPENDENT COMMISSIONS

LET me ask you," wrote Justice Frankfurter some years ago in a lively essay on the demands of society upon government, "to bring into sharp focus what it is that a modern state like our own government is actually called upon to do." [1] Surely if we know the nature of the demands made upon the machinery of government, we shall be better able to understand and judge the institutions which have evolved to meet these demands.

Let us take for example the situation posed by the development of radio no less than television. The American people cannot allow everyone in New York City to erect a radio station, for the very obvious reason that if there are more radio stations operating at the same time than there are wave-length frequencies reception would be impossible. Thus government is called upon to devise some means of regulating radio stations to insure reception. But how, actually, is this to be done? Congress has sought to meet the situation by creating the Federal Communications Commission and empowering it "to regulate interstate and foreign commerce in communications by wire and radio, so as to make available, so far as possible to all of the people of the United States a rapid, efficient, nation-wide, and world-wide wire and communications service with adequate facilities at reasonable rates." [2] In prescribing the general policy to be followed by the Federal Communications Commission, Congress provided that the Commission shall license radio stations that will best serve the public interest, and that the agency shall evolve fair and equitable methods of determining which of the competing applicants for a broadcasting license will best serve the public interest. In other words, while indicating the general lines of policy to guide the Federal Communications Commission, Congress has

[1] Felix Frankfurter: *The Public and Its Government* (New Haven, 1930), p. 7.
[2] *Public Act 416*, 73d Congress, June 19, 1934.

left the details of the policy and the bulk of procedures for carrying it into effect to be worked out by the Commission itself. Such delegation of authority has been crucial in shaping our administrative system.

As government has assumed greater positive responsibility for the regulation of industry and social relations in the public interest Congress has, of course, been compelled to delegate authority. It has neither the time nor the specialized knowledge to make detailed rules and regulations on a subject as complicated, say, as the determination of broadcasting licenses or railroad freight rates. This has meant, however, that as new agencies have been created to deal with such problems, delegation of congressional authority has led to a merger of tripartite functions in these agencies that requires our careful attention.

Lying either outside or in some cases within the nine great executive departments are several agencies known as the independent regulatory commissions. The creation of this type of administrative agency marked a new departure in Federal policy that started with the establishment of the Interstate Commerce Commission in 1887. Until this date, Congress had proceeded for almost a quarter of a century on the theory that newly created offices should be placed under one of the executive departments. The leading characteristic of regulatory agencies has been the merger of executive, legislative, and judicial functions—a development that has had far-reaching effect upon our Federal administrative system.

THE TRIPARTITE FUNCTIONS OF THE INDEPENDENT COMMISSIONS

Quasi-legislative Functions

In varying degree, the specialized administrative bodies known as independent regulatory commissions have come to exercise what are termed quasi-legislative and quasi-judicial functions. If the commissions are to fill in the gaps in the general grant of legislative authority empowering them to execute the will of Congress, they must be able to make some rules and regulations. The Interstate Commerce Commission, for example, must work out rules for the hearings it conducts on rate increases or the decisions it reaches on safety-appliance requirements for interstate carriers. This quasi-legislative authority to make rules is sometimes referred to as the "sub-legislative" power. Quasi-legislative rules and regulations have the force of law and the only requirement to which they must conform is that the authority for their issuance must be reasonably clear in the congressional statute delegating such power.

Quasi-judicial Functions

The "quasi-judicial" functions of the independent commissions involve procedures whereby administrative officers using methods analogous to those employed by courts apply a broadly stated legislative policy to specific cases. [3] Thus after holding hearings—conducted under rules which have been specified by the commission concerned—a decision is made somewhat after the manner of a court. To take the problem of radio licensing again as an example, let us assume that the Federal Communications Commission is holding a hearing to decide whether a license shall be issued to operate a broadcasting station in a community. To determine what will best serve the public interest in granting licenses, the Federal Communications Commission must take into account several complex factors. If it is a matter of a license for a community without a station one question that must be considered is does the community need a radio station at all or is it served adequately by the broadcasting facilities of an adjoining community. In another situation quite different problems must be considered. Federal licenses to operate radio stations are granted for a two year period only. Thus the Commission must decide whether to grant a renewal to the old operator, or if there are several applicants for the license, which applicant will best serve the community. Factors involved in reaching such a decision might be which of the several applicants would provide the best-balanced educational and cultural programs or which one would best serve the specialized economic and social interests of the community. A great many different factors, therefore, may be relevant to reaching a decision. In addition to the authority to sub-legislate, then—to make rules and regulations—the independent commissions also have the very important power to apply these rules to specific cases and pass judgment upon their observance—the quasi-judicial function.

Executive Functions

Finally, in common with all administrative agencies, the independent commissions have executive or managerial powers. In this capacity they conduct inspections to see that the rules and regulations they have formulated are followed. Most violations are settled through informal conferences; only those that cannot be disposed of in this manner are adjudicated through quasi-judicial hearings. Two other executive functions that characterize most of the independent commissions are the investigatory power and the authority to draft comprehensive policy plans. The former, which empowers the commissions to summon witnesses, is a highly important adjunct of administrative adjudication (deciding cases), and while the commissions do not have the power to punish for contempt, they may solicit aid from the Federal courts in contempt cases, and the courts may enforce a contempt citation for the commissions. In the planning field, the independent commissions have been authorized to conduct studies and advise Congress from time to time on recommended changes. Often the commissions simply submit suggested statutory changes for Congress to

[3] Robert E. Cushman: *The Independent Regulatory Commissions* (New York, 1944), p. 8.

take under advisement, but on occasion Congress has asked the commissions to conduct extensive investigations as a basis for legislative action as it did when the Interstate Commerce Commission was asked to undertake a study on the consolidation of certain railroad systems, and the Federal Trade Commission was requested to make a study of public utilities.

From this cursory sketch of the tripartite functions exercised by the independent commissions, the significance of the merger of executive, legislative, and judicial powers within a single agency begins to emerge. The independent regulatory commissions are not the only agencies within the Federal administrative system to embody these tripartite functions. But the merger of the powers has been more conspicuous in these agencies than in other Federal administrative bodies. There is reason for departure from the traditional doctrine of separation of powers. Within the past sixty years there have been "wholly new interactions between citizen and government." [4] Government has encountered innumerable difficulties and perplexities that were unheard of among the problems of statecraft a hundred years ago. In 1850 there were 9,000 miles of railroad; today there are over 250,000. On many fronts government is confronted with the problems presented by such industrial developments as the telephone, telegraph, television, oil pipe lines, bus lines, truck lines, and airlines. Moreover, in an effort to guide and regulate economic forces in the public interest with the view of stabilizing our economy and "providing a more equitable distribution of the national wealth," government has taken long strides in the direction of monitoring not only trade, investment, and industry, but the highly complex field of labor-management relations as well. [5] The independent regulatory commission was raised as a possible solution to the problem of developing administrative services competent to meet these challenging demands.

Since the embarkation point in the history of the independent commission—1887—when the Interstate Commerce Commission was created, two basic problems have arisen in connection with this somewhat unique administrative institution. The first concerns the merger of the three functions—executive, legislative, and judicial—in the independent commissions. Many critics have alleged that the merger of these functions violates the doctrine of the separation of powers, one of the premises of our government. The consequence has been a long-standing controversy between those who feel that the exercise of the tripartite functions by the independent commissions is essential if government is to cope with the problems impressed upon it, and those who see a dangerous trend in the exercise of such powers by a single agency and wish to impose strict controls upon the commissions. The second problem is the relation of the independent commissions to the rest of the government. Again we must note that the man-

    [4] Felix Frankfurter: *The Public and Its Government*, p. 27.
    [5] E. P. Herring: *Public Administration and the Public Interest* (New York, 1936), p. 4.

agement of the huge services government has undertaken to operate requires a synthesis of administrative effort. As yet, the work of the independent commissions has not always been articulated with that of the several departments. Both of these problems occasioned by the merger of the tripartite functions and the relation of the commission to the entire administrative system we shall take up presently, but first let us look briefly at the commissions themselves.

THE STRUCTURE OF THE INDEPENDENT COMMISSIONS

The leading independent commissions are: the Interstate Commerce Commission, Federal Trade Commission, Federal Power Commission, Securities and Exchange Commission, Federal Communications Commission, National Labor Relations Board, Board of Governors of the Federal Reserve system, and the United States Maritime Commission. All of these commissions are located outside of the regular Federal departments, hence they are beyond the pale of any departmental supervision. The president has the authority to appoint members of the commissions, but contrary to the general principle that presidential appointees serve at the pleasure of the chief executive, he may (except in two cases), remove them only for causes prescribed by statute. The causes for removal usually include such matters as inefficiency, neglect of duty, or malfeasance in office. In general, Congress has followed a somewhat similar pattern with respect to the personnel of all the independent commissions. Members of these agencies have overlapping terms ranging from five years for the Federal Power Commission to fourteen years for the Board of Governors of the Federal Reserve system. It has also been customary to require the president to select appointees from more than one political party.

Some qualification of the term "independent" is needed in describing the independent commissions. They are not under the supervision of the president or any cabinet officer, but this administrative independence does not put them beyond the control of the president and Congress. Although the president may usually remove only for causes defined by statute, as will be recalled from the Humphrey decision, the members of the Securities and Exchange Commission and the Federal Communications Commission serve at his pleasure. But, more important, the president does have the appointive power, and in selecting personnel he has an excellent opportunity to impress his policies upon the regulatory commissions. A further brake on the independence of the regulatory commission is the requirement of senatorial confirmation for all appointments. And last, but certainly not least in effectiveness, is the congressional check-rein on appropriations. The independent regulatory commission, like any branch of the administration, is dependent upon Congress for its existence, a circumstance that also suggests why the term "independent" should not be interpreted too literally.

THE INDEPENDENT COMMISSIONS VERSUS THE
SEPARATION OF POWERS THEORY

In theory, the three great branches of government—legislative, executive, and judicial—may be compartmentalized, yet in practice we know that this is next to impossible as the demands for society upon government become greater. The independent commission has been saddled with the rule-making task—the quasi-legislative function—because Congress no longer has the time nor the technical knowledge to work out the rules and regulations necessary to achieve the general policy it has decided upon. Thus the independent commission must implement the general policy laid down by Congress by doing some sub-legislating of its own. Similarly, because of the need for a more flexible means than our courts provide of adjudicating certain types of questions—labor-management disputes for example—the independent commission has come to exercise quasi-judicial powers along with quasi-legislative and executive powers. It is obvious that the functions of the independent commissions are not compatible with a strict application of the separation of powers doctrine. As we have noted, the independent commissions are not the only agencies within the Federal administrative system to violate the separation of powers concept of the Founding Fathers. Yet because of the broad powers they exercise over the national economy they have been singled out as the worst offenders.

Criticism of the Independent Commissions

The most strenuous denunciation of the combination of powers in independent commissions has come from the legal profession. In 1933 the American Bar Association appointed a Special Committee on Administrative Law to consider this problem. In the ensuing years the Committee issued several reports dealing with the dangers of a trend which it labelled "administrative absolutism." [6] Most offensive of all to the Bar Association's Committee was the amalgamation of functions in the independent commissions that permitted the tribunals to serve as both prosecutor and judge in the same action. Such a situation in the eyes of the Committee was a perversion of our Anglo-Saxon conception of civil liberty, and it was contrary to the procedure and spirit of our established legal institutions. Part of the revolt against the quasi-judicial and quasi-legislative powers of the independent commissions was symptomatic of the larger struggle that was being waged in the 1930's over policies aimed at more stringent governmental control of the nation's economy. This was true not only of the United States but also of Great Britain, and it is of interest to note that the legal profession in both countries was highly critical of the rapid spread of administrative rule-making and adjudication. Two books par-

[6] See Reports of Special Committee on Administrative Law, in *Annual Reports of the American Bar Association*, Vols. 34–40 (1934–40).

ticularly, *The New Depotism* and *Bureaucracy Triumphant,* by English authors, were relied upon heavily by the Administrative Law Committee in their castigation of procedure before the independent commissions, and a third by an American author, *Our Wonderland of Bureaucracy,* undoubtedly had a part in touching off the controversy. [7]

Besides the general indictment that the independent commissions fused the functions of prosecutor and judge, the Special Committee on Administrative Law attacked the broad powers of the commissions to make rules and regulations, and it took Congress to task for abdicating its legislative responsibilities. But the crux of the attack centered on the unorthodox methods the commissions used in hearings. Because the commissions did not follow the formalized procedure of courts in applying law to concrete cases, the Administrative Law Committee found the quasi-judicial proceedings of these tribunals lacking the essentials of a fair trial. The Committee alleged that the independent commissions often made decisions without what it called a "scintilla" of evidence upon which a decision might properly be based. It also objected vigorously to the trend toward finality in administrative decisions, insisting that each and every decision should be entitled to a full review in one of the regular federal courts.

Suggested Reforms of the A.B.A.'s Special Committee on Administrative Law

At first the Special Committee on Administrative Law toyed with the idea of establishing an administrative appellate court of forty judges composed of the chief justice of the Supreme Court, and members of the Court of Claims Customs Court, Board of Tax Appeals, and Court of Customs and Patent Appeals. Such a court was recommended by the Committee in 1936. If established, it would have provided for the broadest kind of judicial review of decisions of the independent commissions. This measure, which was based on the theory that the judges of the proposed administrative court would develop a special competence to review decisions of particular administrative tribunals, failed to receive the endorsement of the American Bar Association and it was quickly abandoned.

The sequel to the administrative court plan, which emerged from the series of reports by the Special Committee on Administrative Law, was a recommendation for uniformity in the procedures used by all the independent commissions. The recommendation was subsequently embodied in a bill known as the Walter-Logan bill, which also provided for an elaborate system of judicial review of cases decided by administrative tribunals. After passing Congress by a large majority, however, it was vetoed by President Roosevelt, presumably on the advice of his advisers that it would "hamstring" the administrative tribunals and vitiate their

---

[7] See G. H. Hewart: *The New Despotism* (London, 1929); C. K. Allen: *Bureaucracy Triumphant* (London, 1932); and James M. Beck: *Our Wonderland of Bureaucracy* (New York, 1932).

authority as regulatory agencies. Following the failure of the Walter-Logan bill to become law, an Attorney General's Committee on Administrative Procedure was created to study the procedural problems of the independent commissions. This Committee submitted a voluminous report in 1941 emphatically rejecting the view of the American Bar Association's Administrative Law Committee that uniformity of procedure was desirable.

Procedural Differences among the Independent Commissions

In developing rule-making and adjudicatory procedures, the independent commissions—as their critics constantly allege—have not conformed to a strictly uniform pattern. But such variations are not necessarily conducive to arbitrary action, as so often is contended. Moreover, the experience of the independent commissions appears to indicate that some variation in procedure is desirable. The rate-making function of the Interstate Commerce Commission may quite conceivably call for a different procedure than that followed by the National Labor Relations Board in investigating alleged unfair labor practices. The independent commissions have also been criticized for their failure to adopt uniform procedures in conducting hearings and adjudicating cases but here again there are mitigating circumstances. The National Labor Relations Board permits the introduction of hearsay evidence (testimony based on what has been told to the witness by another person) in hearings on unfair labor practices, something which is not permitted in the Federal courts. But while the independent commissions do adopt more flexible procedures than those customarily followed by the Federal courts, their motive in so doing is to get at the truth and adjudicate controversies as equitably as possible. Though it is unquestionably a sound practice for Federal courts to rule out hearsay evidence, yet, in attempting to sift out the facts in a proceeding on unfair labor practices, the admission of hearsay evidence may provide the one clue that will lead to the truth. It would, of course, be unfair to base a decision solely upon hearsay evidence, but when used along with relevant factors that turn up in the course of a hearing it may have an important bearing on the final determination of the case.

No doubt some inconvenience is caused to lawyers accustomed to the uniformity of Federal court procedure, but the practice before the independent commissions has become so technical that the tendency among lawyers today is to specialize in cases falling within the ambit of a particular commission. In short, the fact that the procedures vary before the several regulatory commissions is of no serious consequence so long as those adopted are essentially fair and adequately protect the rights of the affected interests. Admittedly, changes in rules and regulations made from time to time by the independent commissions require persons or parties falling within their jurisdiction to be alert, either to protest through proper procedural channels or to conform. Varying procedures should create no undue hardship unless the independent commissions violate their statutory authority, and in this case an injured party may always seek redress in the Federal courts. Despite the need for a certain degree of flexibility on procedures, however, some conformity with basic standards seems desirable and it was in pursuance of this objective that the Administrative Procedure Act was adopted in 1946.

The Administrative Procedure Act of 1946

At the end of a long sequence of events which started with the creation of the American Bar Association's Special Committee on Administrative Law in 1933, a bill known as the Administrative Procedure Act, designed to introduce certain reforms into the procedural practices of the independent commissions, was finally passed in 1946. [8] In comparison with the drastic Walter-Logan bill which would have put the independent commissions into straight jackets on their procedural practices and secured far more stringent judicial review of their decisions, the Administrative Procedure Act was a watered-down compromise. Broadly stated, it regulates the procedures to be followed by both the independent commissions and other Federal administrative agencies which perform quasi-legislative and quasi-judicial functions, and defines the relations of both to the Federal courts with respect to judicial review of administrative decisions.

On the procedural side, the Administrative Procedure Act stipulates that Federal administrative agencies adequately publicize the methods under which they operate and the procedures to be followed by parties desiring to bring matters to their attention. When a new ruling is contemplated ample notice must be given either through the *Federal Register* or by direct communication to all parties that might be affected. [9] Such notice, moreover, must be accompanied by information showing under what authority the agency is contemplating action. To segregate the functions of prosecutor and judge, the officials who investigate and prepare cases for adjudication are not eligible to take any part in deciding the cases. Among other provisions, the Administrative Procedure Act requires that persons compelled to appear before Federal administrative tribunals shall be entitled to have counsel; that all information relevant to the disposition and settlement of a case be received; and that any interested party be permitted to appear to rebut testimony and to cross-examine witnesses.

Judicial Review of Administrative Decisions

A second general feature of the Administrative Procedure Act provides for broader judicial review of administrative decisions. The question of judicial review of administrative decisions has occasioned a dispute of long stand-

[8] 60 U.S. Statutes at Large 237 (1946). For a good analysis of this Act and its background see Foster H. Sherwood: "The Administrative Procedure Act." *American Political Science Review* (1947), 41:271–81.

[9] The *Federal Register* is a daily compilation of "Federal proclamations, orders, regulations, notices, and other documents - - -" It has been expanded under the Administrative Procedure Act of 1946 to include additional material such as descriptions of the organization of various administrative agencies and the procedures they follow.

ing. It has been commonly agreed that judicial review of administrative decisions on questions of law is desirable, but there is a growing feeling that the courts should not interfere on questions of fact. In other words, judicial review should be limited to issues where the commissions are alleged to have exceeded their statutory authority or where they have been unfair in their quasi-legislative or quasi-judicial work, and to questions of law. While some courts do examine questions of fact under one pretext or another when reviewing decisions of administrative tribunals, in recent years they have been less disposed than they used to be to review the decisions of these agencies. [10] The Administrative Procedure Act, however, has removed some of the uncertainties over the appeal of decisions from administrative tribunals to the courts. It provides that the right of judicial review shall obtain whether or not it is provided for by statute unless it is expressly precluded or unless the administrative tribunal has expressly been granted final authority. In the congressional hearings on the Administrative Procedure Act, the Attorney General's testimony indicated that the Act did not do more than declare the existing law insofar as judicial review was concerned. [11] The intent of Congress on this matter, however, seems clearly in favor of broadening the scope of judicial review and subsequent interpretation of the Act appears to confirm the fact that the measure enhances the opportunity for a court review of administrative decisions.[12] Although the right to appeal would seem to be reinforced by the Act, it does not follow that the courts will be thereby inclined to upset the decisions of administrative tribunals. In hearing appeals the courts are likely to continue the trend of not disturbing a decision unless, of course, it is demonstrably clear that the administrative tribunal acted arbitrarily or exceeded its statutory authority.

Disguised Motives in Attacking the Independent Commissions

While much of the criticism of the independent commissions has been based upon the sincere conviction that there are risks in the exercise of executive, legislative, and judicial powers by a single agency which should not be hazarded by any government, a large part of it has a different motivation. The commission has been blasphemed as the interloper in our constitutional system not simply because of its flexible procedures and its tripartite merger of functions. These objections are often evoked to screen what many of the critics are really quarreling with—not the agencies themselves but the laws they are charged with enforcing. Unable to change them in Congress, some pressure groups sought other means of nullifying the laws they found objectionable. As long as the Federal courts overturned decisions appealed from the administrative tribunals, this expedient afforded one means of circumventing the laws of Congress. As the

[10] See John Dickinson: "Administrative Procedure Act: Scope and Grounds of Broadened Judicial Review." *American Bar Association Journal* (1947), 33:516–17.
[11] 92 *Congressional Record* A3151.
[12] John Dickinson: "Administrative Procedure Act." *American Bar Association Journal* (1947), 33:516–19.

Federal courts inclined toward a more friendly view of administrative decisions, the criticism levelled against the procedure of the independent commissions swelled. Without question, much of the opposition of the legal profession to the growing power of the quasi-judicial tribunals stemmed from a sincere belief that this development was bringing about a perversion of our judicial system and the traditional concept of the separation of powers doctrine. Yet the cumulative record of the interest groups that opposed the regulatory tribunals most vigorously leads to the inescapable deduction that a large part of the quarrel was not over the independent commissions, but over the economic wisdom of the laws Congress gave them to enforce. This is borne out by the fact that the same groups warmly applauded the decisions of the Supreme Court invalidating important New Deal statutory measures designed to secure greater control over the national economy. Instead of turning to Congress—where the tide of public opinion was making it impossible to have such statutes repealed or modified—these interest groups attempted to cripple obnoxious legislation by directing their fire at the independent commissions.

While the struggle over the procedures employed by the independent commissions has not abated, the demonstrated ability of these tribunals to serve the needs of modern administration seems to have established them beyond recall. There are, to be sure, dangers in violating the separation of powers principle. Where broad quasi-judicial and quasi-legislative powers are entrusted to administrative tribunals, prevention of abuse of discretionary power requires not only available mechanical checks but also an alert citizenry and responsible legislators to mobilize these checks when the occasion demands. The possibility that administrative tribunals could act in an "arbitrary and capricious" manner is not to be lightly dismissed. But we need not therefore assume that the administrative tribunals are determined to act in an arrogant and high-handed fashion. Much of the success of the regulatory commissions in coping with the intricate problems in their jurisdiction depends upon the quality of their personnel, as the prestige of the older agencies like the Interstate Commerce Commission indicates. Yet, notwithstanding the presumption accepted by many students of public administration that the helmsmen of the administrative tribunals are motivated only by the noble desire to provide enlightened public service and could not possibly act coutrariwise, a certain amount of vigilance has definite therapeutic value. Unquestionably, irresponsible congressmen too often indulge in diatribes that are unfair to members of the independent commissions as well as to other Federal administrative officials. Congressional attacks are often more than irksome to the personnel of the independent commissions. Some congressmen, animated by political persecution or desire for revenge and relying on congressional immunity to protect them from libel suits, have been downright character assassins, as the attack of Representative Eugene Cox of Georgia against James Fly, former Chairman of the Federal Communications Commission, well illustrates. But the price of representative government and the fundamental desirability of holding administration accountable to the elected representatives of the people is assuredly worth many unfair tirades and even some innocent casualties among the ranks of administrative officialdom.

THE RELATION OF THE INDEPENDENT COMMISSION
TO THE ADMINISTRATIVE SYSTEM

More important to a soundly functioning administrative system than the argument over procedures and judicial review of the independent agencies decisions is the relation of the independent commission to the other institutions of the executive branch—its proper position within the structural framework of the Federal government. Stated succinctly by E. P. Herring: "A larger question remains unanswered. How shall the work of these independent commissions be integrated with the rest of the executive branch? Shall we assume that the general welfare will be realized if each commission interprets to the best of its ability the statutes entrusted to its charge by Congress? Or should the activities of a given commission be joined with related federal activities in the same field and the work of all administrative agencies be integrated through the White House? Here are the riddles that remain unanswered." [13]

In parcelling out regulatory functions, Congress has not been guided by any uniform policy. Consequently some regulatory functions have been given to agencies under one of the nine executive departments. And in some cases regulatory functions originally entrusted to an independent commission have been transferred to one of the departments. The Civil Aeronautics Authority, after a very short life as an independent commission, was placed under the Department of Commerce in 1940, where its functions are now administered by the Civil Aeronautics Board. To many students of government this inconsistency of Congress in allocating some regulatory functions to independent commissions and others to units in the executive departments has been detrimental to a well-integrated Federal administrative system. It has been long suggested, therefore, that steps be taken to pull the independent commissions into the departmental family.

Proposals for Reorganizing the Independent Commissions under the Departments

A proposal for the integration of the independent commissions with the executive departments was submitted in the Report of the President's Committee on Administrative Management in 1937. Taking stock of the dangers it felt were accompanying the growth of a "headless fourth branch of government," this Committee recommended that the independent commission be put into "regular executive departments." If "suitable" depart-

[13] E. P. Herring: *Public Administration and the Public Interest*, p. 109.

ments did not exist, the independent commissions were to remain independent, but it was anticipated that a proper departmental home could be found for most of them. One further recommendation of the President's Committee on Administrative Management that merits attention was the provision for separation of the independent commissions into two sections—a judicial section and an administrative section. The judicial section was to be "in the department for purposes of 'administrative housekeeping,'" but beyond this it was to be completely independent. The administrative section, on the contrary, was to be responsible to the secretary of the department and to the president. The purpose of this division was to keep from executive supervision the section of the independent commissions that handle the judicial and quasi-judicial aspects of regulation—a principle upon which there seems to be general agreement. Although these recommendations were rejected along with several others in the defeat of the administrative reorganization bill of 1937, the issue has been a recurrent one.

Those who have worked for the integration of the independent commissions with the departments have conceded the desirability of independence for the judicial work of these agencies, but they insist that there is a grave need for orienting these tribunals to the regular executive branch of the Federal government. The work of the regulatory tribunals is highly important, and because the president could not easily adjust the policies of these agencies to his general objective for the executive departments, he has often been severely handicapped. If the president is to have the responsibility of carrying into effect the major policies of his administration, it is reasonable that the independent commissions should be keyed to work with the regular executive departments at least on matters of over-all policy. "There are," as one authority on this subject notes, "many points at which commission policies impinge upon the general policies of the President, policies for which the President as the head of the nation is responsible. Commission policies impinge also upon other commission policies. In these areas the President should be given directing authority. . . ." [14]

Part of the way to giving the president such authority was cleared in 1949 when Congress acted favorably on a report of the non-partisan Commission on Organization of the Executive Branch of the Government, headed by former President Herbert Hoover. Declaring that the "numerous agencies of the executive branch must be grouped into departments as nearly as possible by major purposes in order to give a coherent mission to each department," the report of the Hoover Commission recommended that the president be authorized to reorganize the independent commissions under appropriate departments. [15] That such a plan would meet

[14] Robert E. Cushman: *The Independent Regulatory Commissions*, p. 698.

[15] Commission on Organization of the Executive Branch of the Government: *General Management of the Executive Branch* (Washington, 1949), p. 34; *The Hoover Commission Report* (New York, 1949), p. 24.

strong opposition in Congress, however, was quickly apparent. In a House bill granting such authority, introduced early in 1949, certain regulatory commissions were ear-marked for special consideration by a formula whereby reorganization plans that would strip powers from any of three specified regulatory commissions would have to be submitted in a "separate package." The three exceptions were the Board of Governors of the Federal Reserve Board, the Securities and Exchange Commission, and the Interstate Commerce Commissions. It seemed likely that several further exceptions would be made before a bill could finally be agreed upon by both Houses. Thus the final round has not yet been fought over the position of at least some of the regulatory commissions within the executive branch.

Some of the congressional opposition to reorganization of the independent commissions stems from the hard-headed desire to keep the president and the executive branch subservient to Congress. Congressional opposition is aided and abetted by the perfectly natural desire of the personnel of these independent bodies to retain the *status quo*. Among the personnel, of course, there is a substantial segment of opinion supporting the contention of the late Joseph Eastman, distinguished member of the Interstate Commerce Commission, that the "cold neutrality of the Commission ought to be safeguarded." The trend of thought, nonetheless, seems to lean toward a solution that will make the independent commissions a cohesive part of the administrative branch of government without impairing their independence in so far as their quasi-judicial determinations are concerned.

After sixty-five years of experience, the independent commission has become a well-established appendage of the Federal administrative system. The prestige of some of the newer commissions is not firmly grounded, but the fact that the older agencies, like the Interstate Commerce Commission, are highly respected both in government circles and among business men suggests that the neophyte commissions, like the Federal Communications Commission, will enjoy more confidence as they achieve greater maturity. In appraising the work of the commissions it should not be forgotten that they have pioneered the development of administrative law and have been the chief architects of this rapidly growing body of rules and regulations that is binding upon private citizens as well as government officials. Since 1900 the growth of administrative law has been rapid and revolutionary in its implications; hence it is not difficult to understand why a sharp conflict has raged about agencies that have produced a large part of this new body of law. The idea that administrators could make law, apply it, and even pass judgment upon its violation represented quite a radical departure from a constitutional concept that rigidly compartmentalized government into three branches. This administrative development is not an aberration, however; it is simply a more plastic concept, required by modern administration, of the doctrine of the separation of powers. Judged in this light, floundering and false starts were to be expected before the independent commissions came of age as a governmental institution. With the incubation period over, the commissions appear destined to continue their vitally important regulatory work, functioning either as independent units in exceptional cases or as semi-autonomous organizations within the regular executive departments.

SUMMARY

Beginning with the Interstate Commerce Commission in 1887, Congress has created independent regulatory commissions to deal with certain fields in which successful regulation demands flexibility and specialized knowledge. These commissions wield powers that are legislative, judicial, and executive. Their existence poses two basic problems: the wisdom of violating the doctrine of the separation of powers and the proper relationship of these agencies to the rest of the government.

The independence of these bodies is established by granting commission members relatively long terms, staggering the terms of individual members, and restricting the power of the President to remove members.

Much of the criticism of the methods of the independent commissions is motivated by hostility toward government regulation of the areas policed by the commissions. Criticism of the procedures followed has come particularly from the legal profession and has centered on the fusion of the functions of prosecutor and judge in the commissions, the narrow limits to which judicial review of commission decisions was confined, as well as on the broad and vaguely defined powers conferred on the commissions. The Administrative Procedure Act of 1946, enacted in response to such criticism, makes the procedure of administrative tribunals more like that of the courts and defines the relationship of administrative bodies to the judicial branch of government.

Many experts in the field of administration favor fitting the regulatory commissions in appropriate government departments, leaving them independent only in the performance of their quasi-judicial functions.

CHAPTER XIX

FEDERAL PERSONNEL AND THE MERIT SYSTEM

WHETHER or not we approve, we are forced to accept the fact that government is big business and an inescapable part of our national life. The multiplication of services has progressed rapidly in the past quarter century and the addition of new services has been accompanied by a steady increase in personnel. Within thirty years —1928 to 1956—the number of civilian employees in the Federal government jumped from 570,000 to 2,355,192. By January of 1956 the Post Office employees alone accounted for 509,032, approximately one-fourth of the Federal government's payroll.

As in any business enterprise with over two million employees, the personnel policies of government are matters of momentous consequence. Essentially, the personnel problems of large-scale organizations whether private or public are the same. Chief among them are developing policies, methods, procedures, and attractions applicable to the personnel of the organization and securing some degree of uniformity of policies and practices throughout the organization. The government must devise recruitment programs, incentives, promotional policies, compensation scales, separation policies, retirement provisions, and look after many other important details in mobilizing and managing the service which executes its functions. In broad measure, the task of government as outlined in the lofty objectives set by the Hoover Commission is the establishment of a career service which "attracts and holds men and women of the highest intelligence and whose competence is commensurate with the needs of our government."

For a variety of reasons which we shall presently examine, the idea of a carefully regulated personnel program for employees of the government had a hard time gaining traction. That an enterprise as important and as large as government should stumble along without adequate provision for building a sound career service based upon the objectives mentioned above seems incredible, but for a long time it did. The quality of personnel is a basic consideration in the performance of any task. We all know from experiences of one kind or another that two or three competent persons can not only do the work of an incompetent group twice as large but can also do it better. Moreover, competence in employees can even overcome some of the limitations of faulty organization. Selection and retention of capable employees, therefore, is a prime, if not the prime, requisite of administration; for the most efficiently conceived organization of administrative institutions will yield low standards of performance when manned by incompetent employees.

THE EVOLUTION OF THE MERIT SYSTEM IDEA

The idea of a merit system for selecting the officials of the public service probably had its genesis in ancient China. It was certainly a well-established principle in the early Greek city-states, and in Western Europe seems to have found its first expression in Brandenburg-Prussia in the beginning of the seventeenth century. The development of a career service evolved more slowly in France and England. The English system got its start in the second half of the nineteenth century after taking its cue from the personnel policies of the British East India Company which recruited its employees on a competitive basis. But even during the early stages, the growth of a professionalized administrative service was attended by rather marked differences of opinion about what was desirable in the way of qualifications for public servants. In China, emphasis was upon literary skill and certain character traits, while in Germany the predominant stress was initially placed upon law and later on political economy and government. Great Britain—more in line with the traditions of the Greek city-state—used to emphasize training in the classics and humanities when recruiting for positions in the upper brackets of the administrative hierarchy. This group of positions was small proportionately, however, numbering less than 5,000. Since 1910 the tendency to select persons training in the classics and humanities has declined quite sharply. Perhaps because it started somewhat later, but also because of the influence of the general trend in its industries and professions, the United States in its recruitment of government servants tended to favor specialized training with the view of fitting them into a particular niche of the administrative framework. Actually, the contemporary differences between British and American recruitment policies as far as qualifications are concerned are slight. For the great mass of clerical and routine employees both countries use appropriate examinations for measuring specific required skills, such as typing or bookkeeping. Likewise in the upper brackets, recruitment for the professional and technical services in both countries is arranged with the view of reaching out for specialists in a given field. There are certain differences between the two countries on recruitment policies, to be sure, but to avoid perpetuating the mistaken idea that British and American policies are fundamentally divergent because the former stresses training in the classics and humanities in its recruitment program, mention is made here that these differences are slight.

Early Personnel Policies in the United States

In beginning our discussion of the development of employment policies in the United States, we must define at the outset just what it is we are speaking of when we use the term "civil service." Broadly speaking, civil service embraces all services rendered to a state or nation other than those concerned with military, legislative, or judicial affairs. Thus the day that President Washington hired the first employee, the civil service was started in the United States. Civil service is a far more inclusive term than "merit system" or "career system"; for while all government employees are civil servants, by no means all of them are subject to the rules and protection which are commonly applicable to that part of the civil service which operates under the merit or career system. Whether an employee is under the merit system is, of course, a matter of concern to a Federal personnel administrator. All civil servants are paid, hence there are questions of salary scales along with many others even for the non-merit-system employee. In summary we may say that by "civil service" we mean all civilian employees of the government except, of course, those policy-forming officials such as a cabinet member.

At the outset, the evolution of a merit or career system in the United States was conditioned by colonial experience. The British colonial governors were frequently saddled with incompetent administrators who quickly laid the groundwork for a popular mistrust of executive power. One should not be misled into thinking that following the Revolution, American leaders were unmindful of the need for competent and trained government administrators; this was far from the case. George Washington reiterated time and again the need for high qualifications in public office, as did some of his contemporaries. But among the people the anti-executive sentiment was so strong that it prevented establishment of a responsible career service for at least three generations and left a legacy of suspicion that has still not been entirely eradicated.

The Spoils System

For well over a century the spoils system and politics were as closely identified by Americans as Hollywood and the United States are today identified by the foreign observer. Before Washington had filled out his two terms, the Anti-Federalists were already agitating for changes in the government's administrative officialdom. Jefferson was urged to make sweeping changes when he became president, but after making known his disappointment that few Federalist officeholders ever died or resigned, he decided against wholesale dismissals. Andrew Jackson is credited with starting the spoils system, yet Jackson did not discharge any larger proportion of his opponents than Jefferson did. He merely talked more about the practice and elevated it into a doctrine. [1] Recent studies indicate quite clearly that many historical accounts of this period present an exaggerated picture. Perhaps the best estimate is that between a fifth and a tenth of all Federal officeholders were removed during Jackson's two terms, and many of these dismissals were for good reason. [2] What did give rise to a substantial part of the "spoils" legends that have been handed down from the Jackson era was the manner in which the turnover was consummated. Although Jackson was not the uncouth, backwoods oaf popular myths have made him, and was a gentleman who favored horse racing, not bear hunting, his political followers were avid for a new deal. Many officeholders, therefore, were ejected unceremoniously to satiate the desires of Jacksonian partisans who urged that "the barnacles must be scraped clean from the ship of state."

Reasons for the Spoils System

A more basic explanation of the origins of the spoils system lies in the philosophy that animated the desire for rotation in office. For a long time prior to Jackson's appearance in the political arena the seeds of revolt had been germinating against occupancy of public office by an omnipotent elite. [3] The election of Jackson was the signal to remove the governing classes from the controls of government. As justification for the replacement policy a number of cogent reasons were advanced. Jackson believed that political parties were essential to the functioning of a democracy; thus as a starting premise he held that if political parties were necessary it was desirable that they be nourished. The obvious answer to the need for strengthening a party and giving it cohesion was the distribution of public offices, or what is more bluntly called patronage, to the party faithful. As stated by a contemporary of Jackson: "If you wish to keep up the party, you must induce them to believe that it is in their interest. Some few may adhere to the party from mere conscientious conviction of doing right but interest is a powerful stimulus to make them act energetically and efficiently." [4] Jackson believed that political parties need something besides intellectual cement to hold them together.

Jackson believed further that public office should not be considered a "species of property," and that the duties of public office could be made

[1] The credit for coining the maxim, "To the victor belong the spoils," goes to Senator Marcy of New York, but it is interesting to note that the statement was not made until 1832, near the end of Jackson's first term.

[2] E. M. Eriksson: "The Federal Civil Service under President Jackson." *Mississippi Valley Historical Review* (1927), 13:517–40.

[3] For a discriminating analysis of this point see Arthur M. Schlesinger, Jr.: *The Age of Jackson* (Boston, 1946), pp. 46–7.

[4] David Petrikin, a Pennsylvania politician, to Van Buren, November 18, 1836, quoted in Arthur M. Schlesinger, Jr.: *The Age of Jackson*, p. 46.

"so plain and simple that men of intelligence may readily qualify them-selves for their performance." He was convinced, therefore, that once the people voted a political party into power by democratic means, that organization was thereby given a mandate to change officeholders from the presidency down to the lowest Federal subordinate.

Finally, Jackson had what might be termed an uncritical faith in the value of a constant turnover among the public officialdom. No one should hold office for more than a term or two as far as he was concerned. Jackson had a tremendous faith in the ability of the people to cure power complexes and other such maladies that persons might contract while holding public office, hence he believed in turning officeholders back to the people rapidly. Perhaps he had in mind a principle akin to the old adage that water in a stream purifies itself every five hundred feet; but whatever the limitations of this theory may have been, Jackson had an uncompromising belief in the purifying powers of the people.

Despite its corruptive influence on American politics, the spoils system served to make more fluid the relations between the people and their government. In the beginning the spoils system was inspired by the sincere belief that it was a necessary accompaniment of the democratization process, and it is improbable that the eventual consequences of the system could have been foreseen. But while the shortcomings of the principle that "to the victor belongs the spoils" are overwhelmingly against its application if efficient and honest government is to be attained, certain Jacksonian postulates remain valid. Even today it is often asserted that to engineer a sharp change in political policy following a change in administration, the personnel must be in key with the new objectives. Some authorities on public personnel maintain that only the policy-determining officials of the government need to be in strict accord with the declared objectives of a new administration. Yet some sharp dissents have been registered against this view by more politically conscious observers who insist that, to carry out a program effectively, an administration's personnel and its policy aims must be spiritually synchronized. The dissenters hold that policy is not neutralized immediately below the top administrative level but infiltrates the administrative ranks at many levels. Thus they contend that personnel out of sympathy with the economic and social objectives of an administration can weaken the over-all effort to attain these ends. This view is more noticeably adhered to in the United States, as elsewhere, by left-wing political parties. While this attitude is by no means without supporting evidence, it is one more disruptive influence in the long uphill fight to embed permanently the roots of a Federal civil service system.

The Movement for Reform

The steady decline in personnel standards that followed in the wake of Jackson's removal policies did not go unheeded. In 1853 Congress passed a law requiring that all clerks be examined by a board of three examiners before being appointed. [5] This law was not well enforced, however, and its chief importance lies in the fact that it called attention to the serious need of raising the standards for Federal office. By 1879, with the establishment of the National Civil Service Reform League, the reform of Federal personnel policies became a national issue. [6] But it still took a tragedy to force Congress to place a civil service act on the statute books. When President James A. Garfield, about to board a train in Washington in 1881, was fatally shot by a disappointed office seeker, public opinion demanded that something be done to prevent a recurrence. Two years later (1883) Congress reluctantly responded by passing the Pendleton Act that still serves as the Magna Charta of our civil service law.

The Pendleton Act

The Pendleton Act set up an independent commission of three persons to be appointed by the president with the advice and consent of the Senate. Not more than two could belong to the same political party. The Act brought certain groups of employees under what was designated as the classified service, and left other unclassified. The classified employees were under the merit system while the unclassified personnel were not, and the president was given authority to enlarge the classified service from time to time by executive order. Entrance into the classified service was made contingent on competitive examination, and appointments in this service were limited to candidates who had received a passing mark. The Pendleton Act also provided that veteran's preference in both examinations and appointments, granted under an earlier act, should not be discontinued and that employees under the classified service should be free from political assessment and forbidden to participate in politics.

The Pendleton Act has been continuously strengthened. But its greatest extensions have come through executive rather than legislative action, hence the original provision which authorizes the president to expand the number of positions in the classified service is very important. When the merit system made its quite modest appearance in 1883 about 14,000 out of 100,000 positions were brought under the classified service. By 1940 this number had been augmented well beyond the half-million mark. Presidents Franklin Roosevelt and Harry Truman had transferred so many federal jobs to the classified service that when President Eisenhower assumed the office only 170,382 of the 2,306,230 jobs were available for patronage and not protected by the merit system.

[5] Lewis Mayers: *The Federal Service* (New York, 1922), pp. 41–2. For an able treatment of the chronology of civil service history see also United States Civil Service Commission: *A History of the Federal Civil Service, 1789–1939* (Washington, 1939).

[6] A thorough account of the movement for reform is provided in Frank M. Stewart: *The National Civil Service Reform League* (Austin, Texas, 1929).

MANAGING THE MERIT SYSTEM

While the problem of spoils has not yet been entirely solved it has been dwarfed in the past two decades by the more compelling task of establishing adequate procedures for the management of an operating service of more than 2,300,000 employees. Since the end of World War I the grand objective for the steady advance of the merit system has been not the elimination of spoilsmen but the improvement of the procedures and techniques for selecting and holding competent employees to run big government. This shift in emphasis—from concentrating the fight against the spoils system to building soundly conceived personnel practices which strive for excellence in Federal employment—has brought us face to face with the magnitude of governmental personnel administration.

The Civil Service Commission

Like the Bureau of the Budget, whose functions we shall deal with presently, the Civil Service Commission established under the provisions of the Pendleton Act in 1883, is one of the overhead controls in the Federal government. Instead of having its administrative jurisdiction confined to a single organization as is the case with a department or an independent commission, the Civil Service Commission operates as a central agency with broad powers of personnel management running right across most of the sixty-five departments, administrations, agencies, boards, and commissions.

The Commission's activities include drawing up and administering competitive examinations, classifying positions, certifying lists of persons eligible for appointment, formulating rules and regulations covering many phases of routine personnel operations such as vacations and sick leave, investigating complaints against the political activity of employees, and working out promotional policies, efficiency rating plans, and retirement policies. A staff of several divisions and some 4,000 employees assists the Civil Service Commission in looking after these numerous responsibilities.

Although the Civil Service Commission has an enviable record of integrity, it has come under sharp attack for failing to provide positive administrative leadership. In the pioneer era this deficiency was not serious, but as personnel management became increasingly technical, it was recognized that the scope of the merit system had far exceeded its modest beginnings when the main job was to keep the spoilsman at bay. The need for greater initiative and imaginative leadership was emphasized in the highly instructive report of the Commission of Inquiry on Public Service Personnel in 1934, and the report of the President's Committee on Administrative Management struck the same theme in 1937. [7] After an exhaustive study the Committee on Administrative Management recommended that the Civil Service Commission of three be abolished and replaced by a

[7] Report of Commission of Inquiry on Public Service Personnel: *Better Government Personnel* (New York, 1935).

single personnel director who would be immediately responsible to the president. [8] It further recommended that the personnel director be advised by a non-salaried Civil Service Board that would be convened only on call. The purpose of this part-time board was not to advise on the intricacies of personnel administration, but to see that civil service functioned with a minimum of political interference.

Despite the important gains in efficiency and speed that many administrative authorities thought this shift would accomplish, it failed of enactment. The measure was incorporated in the ill-fated administrative reorganization bill of 1937 which was defeated along with the famed Supreme Court "packing bill." The arguments offered in 1937 for these changes in the merit system were confirmed in the later report of the Hoover Commission on Organization of the Executive Branch of the Government. Moreover, although the Office of Director of Personnel was not established because of the defeat of the administrative reorganization bill of 1937, an Office of Liaison for Personnel Management was set up in the Executive Office of the President in 1939. In effect, the Office of Liaison for Personnel Management settles many of the top personnel policy matters that the President's Committee on Administrative Management had in mind for the director of personnel. Actually, since shortly before World War II, the executive work of the Civil Service Commission has been a one-man show. [9] Thus the trend in personnel management has been moving informally in the direction of a single director of personnel.

The Federal Council of Personnel Administration

Also moving toward partial fulfillment of the civil service objectives in the 1937 administrative reorganization bill were two executive orders issued by President Roosevelt in 1938. The first authorized all departments and major agencies not already possessing one to establish a personnel division headed by a director—a measure that did not bring about any profound change in practice because most administrative agencies already had something in the nature of a personnel director. A second and more important executive order created the Federal Council of Personnel Administration. In the management of personnel policies (or anything else in the Federal government, for that matter), it is quite impossible for a top group, or even a single director, to issue directives from a vacuum. By permitting interdepartmental consultation and collaboration the Council helps to mold constructive personnel policies. It has already conducted surveys and studies which have led to important reforms.

[8] President's Committee on Administrative Management: *Report of the Committee with Studies of Administrative Management in the Federal Government* (Washington, 1937).

[9] See Leonard D. White: *Civil Service in Wartime* (Chicago, 1945), p. 242. "So far as the war service is concerned," comments Professor White, "the Commission practically delegated all of its powers to one man, so that in Commissioner Flemming (as far as these war agencies were concerned) we had for the first time a single personnel director for the United States."

The Director of Personnel Recommendation of the Hoover Commission

Once again with the publication of the Hoover Commission's report in 1949, the theme was sounded for a single personnel director to head the Federal civil service. Sweeping alterations were proposed for the Civil Service Commission, some of which we shall examine later, but first let us consider the Office of Personnel recommended in the Hoover report. An Office of Personnel headed by a director of personnel who would also be chairman of the Civil Service Commission, was to be located in the Executive Office of the president. Among his chief duties the director of personnel was to be "principal staff adviser to the President in connection with problems related to the career or merit civilian service of the Federal government. . . . The Director should advise the President on ways and means of identifying exceptional talent within the Federal Civil Service in professional, scientific, and executive positions and of making sure that this talent is being utilized in the most effective possible manner. . . ." [10] He will be in a position to advise the President as to the steps which need to be taken to put the government where it will be looked upon as one of the most progressive employers in the nation. While the benefits from having a single director of personnel might loom larger in a reorganization report than they turn out to be in practice, there is general agreement that some improvement should follow. That operating the personnel enterprise of the government cannot ever be made a simple matter by a shift in the command agency, however, will be quickly apparent when we consider the procedures which any command agency single- or plural-headed must devise and administer.

GENERAL PROCEDURES UNDER THE MERIT SYSTEM

The prime function of a governmental career service is to attract employees of the highest competence and to organize the service in such a way that incentives and opportunities for promotion will be great enough to keep capable men and women in the public service. To accomplish such an objective many procedures have evolved, of which only the more significant will be treated here.

Recruitment

Among the more formidable tasks of personnel management is that of recruiting persons to man the administrative machinery of government. Attracting well-qualified applicants, as well as preparing and administering appropriate examinations to test their fitness, is part of the recruiting process. Everyone who has visited a post-office or some other Federal building has noticed the printed circulars announcing examinations. Not

---

[10] Commission on Organization of the Executive Branch of the Government: *General Management of the Executive Branch* (Washington, 1949), p. 24; *The Hoover Commission Report* (New York, 1949), p. 18.

long ago such notices seemed hardly calculated to attract attention, but in recent years the publicity announcing examinations and giving the particulars about positions in the Federal civil service have lost much of their drabness. As recruitment policies must seek out professional and technical skills as well as those required for routine clerical positions, a variety of techniques are used. Posted notices in Federal buildings and newspaper advertisements are the most common methods of drawing attention to career-service opportunities, but for technical and professional positions, colleges and universities, and technical schools are also widely circularized. For some positions, advertisements are run in trade journals, and special mailing lists are used while some individuals are personally solicited.

The recruitment process is really an early phase of the examining procedure which follows. We have in the recruitment phase a rough winnowing which eliminates the more obvious misfits who are disqualified from taking a competitive examination because of their inability to meet certain requirements. Thus one requirement might be an age limit. In the matter of both age requirements and educational standards, however, the Federal government's policy has come in for sharp criticism. Under present civil service laws no minimum educational qualifications can be required by the Civil Service Commission except for scientific, technical, and professional positions. This policy is apparently in response to the obstinately held notion that every American citizen should be entitled to take an examination, even though it causes needless public expense by admitting to examinations many who are almost certain to fail, and undoubtedly encourages many false hopes. It is also alleged that this policy of giving everyone a chance has pushed age limits "to the point where they fail to serve their most useful purpose,"—a charge that is supported by considerable evidence.

In the past, the Civil Service Commission has been criticized for being too passive about recruitment. Except for certain types of routine positions, the Commission has had a lot of difficulty in attracting good candidates to fill its quotas. In recognition of this need, the Hoover Commission's report dealing with the career service proposed that the president issue an executive order requiring all major departments and agencies to conduct vigorous recruiting programs in the field of high-level administrative, professional, and technical work, as well as in other areas where specialized knowledge is required.

Examinations

In approaching our discussion of examinations it will be advisable for us to recall what the alternatives are in making appointments to the Federal civil service. Many thousands of employees are still selected and appointed on a political basis. These appointments are for positions outside of the classified service—in other words outside of the merit system. They include department heads and other important policy forming officials along with a vast array of minor appointments that many critics urge should be brought under the classified service. None of these employees, of course, is subjected to a competitive examination.

Except for comparatively few positions which are filled through a "non-competitive" or "pass" examination, all appointments to the classified service are based upon a competitive examination. Some examinations are written, others are unwritten, and in some cases both are used. They are prepared by an examining division of the Civil Service Commission, often with outside help from the several departments or from academicians and various specialists. For the great mass of classified positions—the clerical and routine posts—the examinations are written and the candidates are examined in groups. These examinations are given at specified times in some seven hundred cities in the United States either by post-office officials or some designated representative of the Civil Service Commission.

Examinations for technical, scientific, and professional positions are conducted largely by rating the training, experience, education, and other factors that may be relevant to determining an applicant's fitness. Such examinations do not follow the familiar collegiate form; nonetheless, they are competitive.

Appointments

When the results of examinations have been determined, a register of names, sometimes called an eligible list, is prepared of all candidates who scored a passing grade. There are several registers, of course, for varying types of positions. Being on such a register does not carry assurances of appointment. Registers expire at the end of a year unless extended by the Civil Service Commission, and another examination is necessary if no appointment has been secured by the time a register has lapsed.

Appointments from the eligible lists are made as additional employees are needed or as vacancies occur. When employees are needed, the Civil Service Commission supplies the appointing officer—a department head or some other agency head—with three names taken from the top of the appropriate register. The Commission is required to certify the names of the three persons standing highest on the list, and the appointing officer has the option of selecting one of the three. The two who are not appointed resume their places at the top of the register.

The rule of three presumably permits the appointing officer to exercise some discretion with regard to personal qualifications. Prior to 1944 an appointing officer might sometimes select from the register persons whose qualifications were thought to be superior, even though they were not among the highest three. Under the Veterans' Preference Act of 1944, however, the rule that an appointment be made from the ranking three on the eligible list was embodied in the law.

The report of the Hoover Commission on personnel comes out flatly against the "top three rule." In proposing to scrap this measure the Commission recommends that all applicants for civil service posts should be grouped into categories such as "outstanding," "well-qualified," "qualified," and "unqualified." Appointing officers would select first from the top listing in filling vacancies and when this list was exhausted choose from the next. Thus the appointing officer would not be compelled to select from the top three on any listing but would be empowered to select anyone from the entire grouping. As a safeguard against political favoritism the Hoover Commission further recommended that appointing officers be subject to dismissal for misuse of authority. [11]

Veterans' Preference

Since the beginning of the merit system in this country veterans have been given preference in the recruiting of civil servants. All veterans have their scores increased by five points and disabled veterans receive an additional ten points. If a disabled veteran is so physically incapacitated that he is unable to work, his wife is entitled to have ten points added to her examination rating; the same increase is allowed to widows of veterans. In addition, a disabled veteran—or his wife, if he is unable to work—or a veteran's widow, is automatically placed on the top of an eligible list, irrespective of rating as long as the examination has been passed. Exceptions are also made favoring veterans on such matters as age limits and the apportionment provisions of civil service law apportioning classified positions among the several states and territories. Veterans may be certified for appointment even though a state's quota of appointments is already filled.

Many heated controversies have been generated by the question of veterans' preference, but few Congressmen would dare to oppose legislation supporting the principle. The moral case for giving veterans preference in competition for civil service appointments is, needless to say, a strong one. But some criticism against making preference provisions too liberal is also well taken. [12] Adding five or ten points to a veteran's score on an assembled examination, for example, could change a non-passing grade of sixty-five to the passing mark of seventy. The marginal boost of veterans' preference that changes a non-passing grade to a passing mark might not be too serious a matter for one of the lower routine positions in the Federal service. More serious, however, is its effect on the higher administrative positions. "A peculiar consequence of veteran preference," writes John Miller, "is the advantage it gives veterans in original appointment to the more important and responsible, as well as the more remunerative, grades of service. This effect, which has broad implications with regard to efficiency of the service, has been generally overlooked." [13]

Few people would quarrel with the fact that the government owes a

---

[11] A similar statute is now applicable to the Tennessee Valley Authority.

[12] For a dispassionate analysis of this problem see Leonard D. White: *Veterans Preference—A Challenge and an Opportunity.* Civil Service Assembly of the United States and Canada Pamphlet No. 17, 1944.

[13] See John F. Miller: *Problems of the American Public Service* (New York, 1935), p. 283. This is brought about, says Mr. Miller, by "(1) the veterans' natural tendency to make the most of their preference by competing for the best positions and (2) the limited number of appointments to these positions."

tremendous debt to the veterans, but this does not necessarily mean that veterans' preference is the sole method of aiding former members of the armed services. In 1940, 30 per cent of the persons appointed to civil service positions could claim veterans' preference. With the Veterans' Preference Act of 1944 battening down these privileges more securely than ever, the proportion of veterans on the Federal payroll was bound to swell. By October, 1948, the Civil Service Commission reported that 45 per cent of all Federal employees were veterans. As long as this trend does not overstock the civil service with personnel of borderline qualifications veterans' preference seems reasonable but such a possibility is not to be ignored, nor should the greatly diminished opportunities of the non-veteran in the career services be lightly dismissed. The principle that veterans should be considered before non-veterans is retained in the Hoover Commission's report. All disabled veterans who have been graded as "qualified" would be placed in the top listing—"outstanding"—and would have first call on openings. Other veterans would be put immediately behind the disabled group provided they were rated as "outstanding," otherwise they would go to the top of the list in the category their rating justified. In any case an appointing officer would have to show "adequate reasons" for passing over a veteran. The report of the Hoover Commission, therefore, though it would diminish slightly the liberal advantages which veterans have enjoyed heretofore, still makes generous concessions in their favor.

The Routine Functions of Personnel Administration

Among the routine matters of personnel administration are a great variety of procedures and functions the technical details of which need not detain us here. At this point we need only set forth briefly the nature of these functions, and emphasize again that the mastery of techniques that have evolved has as its grand purpose the building of a sound career system adequate to service big-business government.

Classification

One of the major problems of personnel administration is position classification. This involves studying the duties and responsibilities of different types of positions and arriving at some judgment about the training or experience (or both) that are necessary to fill them. Position classification facilitates the examination process in that the requirements for admission to examinations and the tests themselves can be correlated with the duties of the position. In practice, persons on a single register may qualify for a great many different positions; thus in many cases the gearing of an examination to a position is not as close as we might imagine. For some positions with large numbers of employees, such as that of postal clerk, it is, of course, quite important that the examination be closely correlated with the position. The classification of positions is very important in laying a foundation for a more or less rational pay policy. In the days when Congress appropriated pay scales position by position or appropriated without knowing anything about the duties involved in the position, the obvious consequence was that employees in one Federal agency performing the same kind of work as those in another often received quite different pay. Position classification was intended to remove such discrepancies.

Under the Salary Classification Act of 1923, positions in the classified service were to be grouped according to their duties into five broad divisions or "services." The greater part of the classified service outside of the District of Columbia, however, was left unaffected until the passage of the Ramspeck Act in 1940, which authorized the president to begin classification anew. Although far from completion because of the intervention of World War II, the program is being pushed ahead. It calls for first grouping into the five broad services over 2,000 types of positions recognized by the Civil Service Commission and then subdividing each service into grades. The services are: (1) professional and scientific; (2) sub-professional; (3) clerical, administrative, and fiscal; (4) custodial, crafts, and protective; and (5) the clerical-mechanical. Within each of the services there may be several grades ranging from the most menial and routine work to the most responsible. Ideally the salaries for employees doing comparable work in any agency of the government should be based upon a uniform compensation scale. Actually, this has been far from the case. The Hoover Commission found there were five pay policies in the government in 1948 and it stressed the urgent need for the adoption of one pay policy.

Salaries

Along with the problem of fashioning uniform compensative scales, the other great problem of personnel administration with respect to salaries is making them adequate. In the lower brackets the compensation of Federal employees compares favorably with that paid for similar work by private industry. Moving up the ladder, however, the comparison becomes increasingly unfavorable for governmental employees. The discrepancy between the pay of governmental employees earning in the neighborhood of $5,000 a year and above and persons doing comparable work in private industry is particularly marked. Taking stock of this situation, the Hoover Commission noted that since 1939 there have been increases in pay of from 38 to 56 per cent for employees earning less than $5,000 a year, while those making more than this amount have been advanced a maximum of 15 per cent and, in some cases not at all. To forestall loss of some of the government's ablest men to private employment, the Hoover Commission recommended that the pay of employees in the technical, scientific, and executive positions be increased and that the present ceiling of $10,330 for career workers be raised. The Commission also recommended increases in compensation for employees in the middle brackets.

If government is to attract and hold persons with outstanding talent at the higher professional and administrative levels, salaries will have to be edged upward. Today government could hardly be expected to pay its top professional and administrative officials in the career service anything like the salaries garnered by some executives in the business world. Yet if the transfer of government's most capable employees to industry is to be stopped one of the most important questions on the agenda of personnel problems is the liberalization of pay policies. [14]

Promotion and Efficiency Ratings

A supplement to attractive salary scales as a morale builder is the opportunity for advancement. In weighing promotion as an incentive and considering its relation to the merit system, both advance in salary and the time-honored incentive offered by the lure of a more challenging position are important. Undoubtedly many capable persons look upon government service as a confining experience professionally, and take a dim view of the possibilities of a genuine career in the public employ. Promising potential candidates for governmental service too often are deterred from entering by the thought that opportunities for advancement are limited and that meritorious service does not assure promotion to more responsible positions. One of the grave tasks of personnel administration is to discourage this belief and to develop a well-conceived program of promotions. To state the need, however, is a simple matter; to bring about execution is quite another.

How promotions are to be determined posits a delicate problem in any organization, public or private. Under the Pendleton Act no classified officer or employee is to be promoted until he has passed an examination or can be shown to be specially exempted from an examination. By way of reinforcement an executive order of the president also provides that, in so far as practicable, examinations shall be used for promotion in the classified service. Past practice, however, has rather consistently by-passed both directives, although since an executive order of 1938, the Civil Service Commission has been conducting some promotional examinations itself, and the departments and agencies have also administered some promotional examinations for their own employees under the supervision of the Civil Service Commission. One method of trying to determine fitness for promotion is through an efficiency rating—a procedure that has yielded disappointing results where it has been used in the Federal government. Since 1925 efficiency ratings have been used to some extent in the merit system, the general purpose being to use the results of a periodic check-up on the employees either as a basis for determining promotions or as an impetus for self-improvement. There has been a great deal of dissent to the proposition that efficiency ratings serve a useful purpose. The Hoover Commission, in fact, reports to the contrary. [15] It found that efficiency-rating procedures were "undermining supervisor-employee relationships," and that a further disadvantage was the tendency to use adverse efficiency

[14] See H. D. Smith: "Government Must Have Good Men." *New York Times Magazine,* July 14, 1946, p. 9.

[15] Commission on Organization of the Executive Branch of the Government: Personnel Management (Washington, 1949) p. 29; *The Hoover Commission Report* (New York, 1949) p. 126.

ratings as a means of punishment, often to the extent of dismissal, "rather than as a means of developing full potentialities of the employee." In recommending the abolition of efficiency-rating procedures, the Hoover Commission suggested that they be replaced by ability and service records designed to rate each employee's "ability, past performance, progress, and potential usefulness." Such records would not be used as a basis for dismissal or promotion, but for securing greater understanding and confidence between the employee and his superior.

Without question the problem of promotion presents one of the most difficult hurdles to Federal personnel administration. Part of the annual turnover of 500,000 governmental workers is the result of bad morale, and a not insignificant amount of the poor morale may be traced to lack of promotional opportunity. One method of promotion, of course, that should not be overlooked, is the competitive examinations open to everyone, including employees, for positions higher than the employees' incumbent status. This is not promotion in the form with which we usually associate it, but it tends toward the same end. This indirect method of promotion, incidentally, suggests an additional reform in promotional practice that was referred to by the Hoover Commission: promotions across agency lines should be encouraged and job switches, often in the nature of promotions, from one agency to another should be facilitated.

Dismissals

The thought of severance has an unpleasant ring but certainly it is a problem that must be dealt with fairly, yet forcefully, by personnel administration. In introducing our discussion of this topic, we shall digress long enough to mention two items that have some relation to removal—probation and discipline.

New appointees are on probation during the first six months of employment. Ostensibly the purpose is to determine an employee's fitness for the position. If performance is satisfactory, the appointment becomes permanent at the end of the probationary period. On the other hand, if the probationary appointee has failed to measure up to what is expected of him he may be dismissed at the end of six months and the appointing officer need assign no reason for dismissal. Sharp criticism has emerged for failure to make proper use of the probationary period. The basis of the criticism is that a probationary appointee's superior is often too lax in checking the appointee's work, in consequence many unfit persons creep into the Federal service without being challenged before they acquire tenure. Some strides have been taken recently to secure more vigorous use of the probationary period, and the Hoover Commission has also underscored the need for having appointing officers take the procedure more seriously.

After the probationary period, a merit appointee acquires certain tenure rights that makes his removal more difficult; nonetheless, he is still subject to disciplinary and removal procedures. Disciplinary action may be taken against an employee for infraction of the civil service rules. The severity of such action depends upon the nature of the complaint. It may take the form of a simple warning or in serious cases it can lead to suspension without pay.

The most drastic disciplinary action, of course, is dismissal. Contrary to practice under the probationary period, an officer requesting the dismissal of an employee who has acquired tenure must assign his reasons in writing. Regulations on removal state that no person shall be removed for political or religious reasons and that no person shall be removed "except for such cause as will promote the efficiency" of the service. In theory, an officer wishing to remove an employee may do so if there are any grounds at all for such action. That a substantial number of employees are dismissed annually is evidenced by the fact that in 1946 approximately 106,000 government employees were removed. [16] Among the grounds for removal are inefficiency, or more specific charges such as mental unfitness, immorality, intoxication, or unbecoming conduct. Unfortunately, inefficiency is one of the most difficult charges to prove and for this reason many an executive has probably been deterred from pressing for the removal of an incompetent civil servant. At best, the task of discharging an employee is one of the more onerous chores of administration, but when the procedure is encumbered by some of the conditions encountered in dismissing an employee from the Federal career service, it is all the more distasteful.

The process of dismissing an inefficient worker may involve a dreary succession of red tape and delays. Taking a hypothetical case, the Hoover Commission showed that a determined employee may fight a discharge through four boards of review while at the same time retaining the position for several months, merely by following normal separation procedure. In one case cited by the Hoover Commission, an incompetent stenographer had her case reviewed by four boards and compelled the officer requesting removal to present forty-five evidences of tardiness and refusal to do work assigned. The separation procedure in this case dragged out seventeen months before the employee finally quit. Perhaps another factor that has made some administrators timid about removals is that they occasionally cause repercussions from the discharged employee's congressman.

To facilitate the weeding out of incompetent employees, the Hoover Commission recommends the elimination of the three-level appeal procedure that has undoubtedly discouraged supervisory officials from dismissing unsatisfactory employees. A hearing would still be provided but the procedure could not drag out more than thirty days unless the employee succeeded in carrying an appeal to the Civil Service Commission.

The obvious problems in connection with removals, of course, is to strike a happy balance between making dismissals too easy and—equally undesirable—making removals so difficult that mediocre workers or persons whose removal would increase the efficiency of the service cannot be

---

[16] That employees under the merit system are removed for cause more frequently than they are reputed to be is borne out by the evidence. See Barbara Brattin: "The Dismissal Pattern in the Public Service." *Public Personnel Review* (1947), 212–15.

promptly dropped. Actually the danger of abuse of the power to remove is reduced by the fact that the officer securing the dismissal cannot name anyone he pleases to succeed the discharged employee. He must fill the vacancy from names certified to him by the Civil Service Commission taken from an appropriate register. In the opinion of many, therefore, while the back door of the merit system is open, the front door is closed, a circumstance that destroys most of the incentive to remove for political reasons. The mantle of permanent tenure under the merit system is probably still too protective for the welfare of the service, and to achieve the ideal balance between tenure and removal a stiffening of dismissal policies would help.

Training, Transfers, and Retirement

No personnel program would be complete without provision for the improvement of the employees already in the service. For many years the Federal government has encouraged its employees to augment their training by study in technical schools, universities, and other outside training centers. This method is still looked upon with favor, but the great increase in the scope of Federal activity has also led governmental agencies to establish training courses of their own. These courses have been helpful in implementing the unsystematic and somewhat uneven training that employees acquire from their supervisors, and they have also been instrumental in developing more intradepartmental harmony on routine procedural work. In addition, such courses build morale by encouraging an employee to take more pride in competent work and stimulating his desire for promotion and the acquisition of improved skills.

As noted by the Hoover Commission report, transfer across agency lines has not been intelligently encouraged much to the detriment of the career service. Employees have been able to transfer to other agencies under certain conditions, but a transfer may not be made for a position above the grade in which the transferee is serving unless it can be shown that the position in question cannot be practicably filled by promotion. The Hoover Commission recommended that transfer among the departments of personnel capable of advancing further in another agency be encouraged. Moreover, to facilitate such transfers it suggested that training programs be planned with this objective in mind.

No personnel enterprise, private or public, can any longer afford not to develop progressive retirement policies. Even the most liberally paid public servants cannot save enough from their salaries to provide a comfortable pension when they reach retirement age, and certainly those in the lower salary brackets, in company with employees of similar incomes in all walks of life, need pension support when they are no longer able to work. A retirement scheme also permits the orderly retirement of persons at an age beyond which their efficiency may be presumed to decline and in this way aids in keeping up the efficiency of the career system. A retirement system really has three bases: first, it is a humanitarian plan to care for the needs of persons who have devoted a substantial part of their lives to the public service; second, it is a morale builder; and third, it raises the efficiency of the service.

The landmark of the Federal retirement system is the Civil Service Retirement Act of 1920. This Act divides employees covered by its provisions into three groups, each with separate retirement ages. Employees whose work involves heavy manual labor or unusual hazards have a retirement age of sixty-two, while others are set at sixty-five and seventy. The pension allowances have been advanced from time to time and in general they do not compare unfavorably with retirement benefits elsewhere, but the effect of inflation on fixed pension allowances is well known, and in recognition of the importance of liberal retirement programs the Hoover Commission urged that benefits be increased.

PROBLEMS OF UNIONIZATION AND POLITICAL NEUTRALITY

Employee Unions

In line with the general antipathy to unionism during the infancy of labor organizations in this country, moves to organize employees of the Federal government were strongly discouraged. Until 1912, Federal employees were forbidden to present their grievances either to Congress or its committees. [17] But since that date, Federal employees have conducted vigorous campaigns to improve their lot, and there are now several unions with which they are affiliated. [18] The A.F. of L. and the C.I.O. both have Federal employee affiliates, and there is also an independent union of Federal employees known as the National Federation of Federal Employees. In addition employees in the postal service have their own unions, some of which are affiliated with regular labor unions, and skilled laborers in the Federal government's employ usually belong to their own trade union.

There is no longer any question about the right of Federal employees to organize, but the right to strike is not admitted. [19] In recognition of the peculiar position of government employees in this respect, the charters of unions of Federal employees specifically forbid strikes—a principle that the overwhelming segment of public opinion undoubtedly favors. Since the nation-wide railroad strike of May, 1946, public sentiment seems to have crystallized against a repeat performance of any strike of this magni-

[17] In 1912 the Lloyd-LaFollette Act by implication granted to Federal employees the right of affiliation with outside unions.

[18] On the right to organize see David Ziskind: *One Thousand Strikes of Government Employees* (New York, 1940), p. 243. Referring to the National Labor Relations Act which affirms the right of employees in industry to organize, David Ziskind states: "Although the Act expressly exempts public employees, the National Labor Board, acting as arbitrator in a voluntarily submitted charge of discrimination against union men . . . held that the Federal Government was morally obligated to recognize the right of its own employees to organize without coercion, intimidation, or interference from their employer."

[19] On the right to strike see ibid., pp. 232–40.

tude which would paralyze the nation, and it has made people more acutely aware of the unpleasant consequences that a stoppage of essential public services would entail if government employees staged a strike.

In renouncing the strike, Federal employees surrender a weapon that has clearly proved invaluable, in use and as a threat, to organized labor in improving its position. The charge of governmental employees that the public is frequently indifferent to their legitimate complaints is not without foundation. Nor is it always an easy matter for Federal employees to have their economic position and working conditions bettered when confronted by an economy-minded or hostile Congress. [20] For these reasons, it is important that Federal employees be periodically given an opportunity to present their case and have it carefully considered. In this area the employee unions serve a constructive purpose.

Political Neutrality

The idea of making the civil servant politically neutral in the United States is deeply ingrained. Contrary to the policy of some countries such as France, where a governmental employee may not only take part in politics but actually run for public office while holding a civil service job, the established policy in this country seeks to insulate the civil servant from political affairs. To the extent that he is protected from compulsory campaign contributions or party assessments and any other pressure designed to intimidate him, the theory of political neutrality seems well founded. But many queries have been raised about the inadvisability of forcing civil servants to remain on the sidelines in partisan affairs and political campaigns.

There is, unhappily, no easy way of resolving the problem of political neutrality. To give civil servants a completely free hand in partisan activities might encourage the building of a monstrous governmental political machine, and it would certainly increase the drive for self-perpetuation of one political group. Yet, to exclude a million or two governmental employees from political activity posits other distressing alternatives. The task of invigorating the political, social, and economic policies of governmental leaders through a neutralized bureaucracy is a problem that calls for imaginative thought. Indifference or apathy toward given policy objectives can seriously undermine an administration's program, and the evidence is abundant that representative government requires a well-ordered concord between policy-making leaders and the bureaucracy.

Whatever the future of political neutrality problems, the course originally embarked upon has strong support. The Hatch Acts extended prohibitions against political activity for employees in the classified serivce to all unclassified employees except the president, department heads, and certain policy-making officials. And they also made more concrete the long-

[20] For a sympathetic view on the right of government employees to organize and even to use the strike, see Sterling D. Spero: *The Labor Movement in a Government Industry* (New York, 1923).

standing rule forbidding classified employees to take part in political management or political campaigns. As the situation now stands, a Federal employee may vote and discuss politics in private, but beyond these limits he is not permitted to trespass.

Loyalty Tests

The requirement that civil service employees take an oath to support the Constitution of the United States is certainly nothing new, but since World War II strenuous efforts have been made to make this more than a perfunctory matter, and systematically to exclude applicants and to weed out old employees where there is any suspicion of disloyalty. With fifth-column experience fresh in mind and aware of the penetrative powers of certain political groups, President Truman set up a Temporary Commission on Employee Loyalty on November 25, 1947. This Commission was created to study ways of debarring "disloyal or subversive" persons from the Federal payroll, particularly Communists. As a result of the findings of the Commission, President Truman issued an executive order on March 21, 1947, that bars from the entire executive branch any employee who belongs to, aids, or even sympathizes with Communism, Fascism, or any other ideology that advocates the overthrow of the constitutional form of government in the United States. [21]

The standards prescribed for debarring persons from governmental service take into consideration all evidence leading to a conclusion that the person is disloyal—his activities and associations, evidences of sabotage, advocacy of revolution or violence, and evidence that the person was serving another government. Obviously, such standards can be abused and the most careful and sincere intentions can accelerate into a "witch hunt" unless supervised with extreme fairness. The loyalty program became an issue of the 1952 presidential campaign, and soon after inauguration President Eisenhower abolished the Loyalty Review Board by executive order and replaced the loyalty program with a security test as a prerequisite to federal employment. This program was intended to be more stringent than the loyalty program and covered both loyalty and security risks. The new test required that employment of each individual be "clearly consistent with the interests of national security." A special citizens' board of review was created for each disputed removal.

THE MERIT SYSTEM IN PERSPECTIVE

With the three-quarter century mark still some distance away civil service in the United States had definitely emerged from the swaddling clothes stage, and thus far it has muddled through the trial and error phase of personnel administration with reasonable success. There is some disagreement over its considerable shortcomings, and there are a variety of complaints.

[21] Executive Order No. 9835 (March 21, 1947).

One of the liabilities that has caused a certain amount of sniping against the civil service system is that far too much time is consumed in processing a prospective appointee. [22] Administrators complain that they must sometimes wait from six to eight weeks while various civil service officials haggle over procedure. Another perennial complaint of the administrators is that they are constantly plagued and bogged down by the enormous amount of information demanded by the staff of the Civil Service Commission. Some administrators contend that they spend up to one third of their time just in satisfying the Commission. Still another complaint often heard is that the civil service staff has become a somewhat autocratic officialdom, evolving steroryped blueprint procedures upon which it refuses to compromise. The last, of course, is the kind of criticism that is frequently bandied about in an irresponsible fashion; nonetheless it has been too common a complaint not to have some basis in fact.

We should not neglect to look at civil service from time to time in a perspective that will enable us to examine its over-all effect upon our political system. Does it have a corrosive effect upon political party organization and thus emaciate the tools of representative government? If so, how can this process be halted or offset so that a sound career service and a vitalized political system function side by side? The answers to these questions can at best be "shore dimly seen," but they were significant in Jackson's time and they are more so today. In striving for the ideal balance between a career service and a political system, it will be some years before the epitaph of the spoilsman can be chiseled out. There will always be persons who have an over-zealous desire to dispense patronage without regard for vocational qualification, just as there will be some who insist that they "can pick a better postmaster than a Civil Service Commission can." Yet, the spoils system will probably expire, but when it does—like T. S. Eliot's prediction for the world—it will end "not with a bang, but a whimper."

In its relation to administration the real problem of the career service today is to insure that the agencies of government are continuously serviced by men and women of high intelligence and integrity. This calls for vigorous recruitment policies, liberalized pay, and the maintenance of sturdy incentives. The task of keeping the service force of government commensurate in ability with the responsibilities government is required to meet, has not always been duly appreciated by the nation's citizenry—a circumstance that has not made easier the problems of personnel administration. No single element of administration, however, is of more fundamental importance than personnel. Indeed as Arthur S. Flemming, former Civil Service Commissioner, commented at the time the Hoover Commission released its reports on administrative organization, so vital are the

[22] For a hard-hitting article on the liabilities of the civil service system see Floyd W. Reeves: "Civil Service as Usual." *Public Administration Review* (1944), 4:327–40. See also John Fischer: "Let's Go Back to the Spoils System." *Harper's* (1945), 19: 362–76.

recommendations on personnel that if they are not adopted successive reports "will not be worth the paper they are written on."

SUMMARY

It took the assassination of a President to lead the national government to institute a merit system for the recruitment of its employees. The spoils system was accepted and defended until the enactment of the Pendleton Act in 1883 on the ground that rotation in public employment was democratic as well as essential to the maintenance of a vigorous two-party system. Even after 1883 the retreat from the spoils system was slow, for a large percentage of Federal employees were exempt from civil service requirements until very recent years.

The Pendleton Act established the framework of the present civil service system—a bipartisan commission of three members which seeks to maintain adherence to the principle of merit in the personnel policies of government agencies. The work of the Commission includes devising and administering competitive examinations, certifying for appointment, classifying positions, working out policies for promotion, retirement, and for other phases of personnel management. The Hoover Commission recommended that the chairman of the Commission be director of an Office of Personnel to be established and to serve as principal staff adviser to the President in questions of personnel policy.

Recruitment, examination, and appointment are the steps by which personnel are secured for government positions. The preferential treatment of veterans negates the purpose of the competitive examination and the practice of making appointments from the top of the register. The problems of a merit system do not end with the selection of employees. Such matters as position classification, salary scales, promotion and removal policies, in-service training, and retirement must be regulated to provide equitable treatment of government employees and to insure efficiency of administration.

Federal employees in the twentieth century won the right to unionize. They may not strike, however, and may not engage in partisan political activities. By executive order President Truman established the loyalty program for employees in the executive branch in 1947.

Federal personnel policy designed to attract employees of intelligence and integrity to government jobs (and to retain them) is of fundamental importance.

CHAPTER XX

THE PRESIDENTIAL STAFF

AT A PRESS conference a few days after the 1936 presidential election in which the Republican candidate carried only Maine and Vermont, Franklin Roosevelt commented that he felt his opponent had failed to exploit the most vulnerable spot in his first term record—his weakness as an administrator. Although this frank self-indictment was momentarily overshadowed by more compelling issues of New Deal economic reforms, the remark does call attention to one of government's greatest contemporary problems—the problem of gearing administration in such a way that a conscientious executive can competently oversee the agencies responsible to him.

There were, in 1949, sixty-five departments and agencies that reported to the president. Even if this number were reduced two-thirds as recommended by the Hoover Commission, the chief executive would still have to be superhuman to handle unaided "the crushing burden of bringing all the units of the executive branch into harmony, and of fitting them together so that a unified program may be carried out." [1] To facilitate this highly important overhead direction of administration by the president several agencies have gradually developed. Their work is government-wide and their primary purpose is to provide advisory assistance that will aid the president in both determining and carrying out the broad policies of his administration. Essentially the problem is like that of a single person sitting on top of a pyramid; unaided, he cannot possibly get a clear view of everything that is going on at the base or within. Nor is it sufficient that the different unit leaders within the pyramid report individually to the person on top. Such contact is helpful but it needs reinforcement. The person perched on top must have a few trained assistants who can keep a sharp watch on a particular function or group of functions common to all units

[1] Commission on Organization of the Executive Branch of the Government: *General Management of the Executive Branch* (Washington, 1949), p. 11; *The Hoover Commission Report*. (New York, 1949), p. 9.

within the pyramid who can advise him of their findings as well as give suggestions for improvement. Since our mythical figure at the top of the pyramid could hardly watch several operations at once or even penetrate a single operation through some sixty different units his only alternative is to acquire assistants who can keep track of specific operations and advise him accordingly.

In the Federal government, the president is comparable to the person sitting on top of the pyramid. We have already observed the agencies assisting the president that might be referred to as the "functional" arms of the chief executive—the regular departments and such agencies as government corporations and independent commissions. Here we shall be concerned with managerial arms—various agencies that assist the president in directing his administration—sometimes called overhead agencies. One overhead agency was dealt with in the preceding chapter—the Civil Service Commission; in this chapter we open our discussion with another—the Executive Office of the President.

THE EXECUTIVE OFFICE OF THE PRESIDENT

Not until the late 1930's was the first important step taken to develop managerial agencies around the president. "Until the creation of the President's Committee on Administrative Management in 1937," one writer has noted, "the mainspring of all government reorganization was the economy motive." [2] Out of this Committee's labors, however, came a proposal for a central managing agency—a proposal that was carried out by the president under powers granted by the Reorganization Act of 1939. The Office of the President consists of The President's immediate staff, The White House Office; the Bureau of the Budget, which has become the most important organ of executive management; the National Security Council, which threatens to eclipse the President's Cabinet as an advisory group; the Council of Economic Advisers, created to keep the President informed on policies designed to maintain a stable economy; the Office of Defense Mobilization; and the President's Advisory Committee on Government Organization. The Presidency had been implemented.

Under the Reorganization Act of 1939 Congress also authorized the appointment of six administrative assistants to assist the president directly. Clearly the central purpose in establishing the Executive Office was not economy but the development of managerial bodies alongside the president that could help him oversee his administration. The role of these staff services or managerial agencies, as reaffirmed by the Hoover Commission, "is not to assume operating functions or to duplicate the responsibilties of the operating departments. These services should exist only to give the President the greatest possible information on the activities of the Govern-

---

[2] Luther Gulick: "The Executive Office of the President: A Symposium." *Public Administration Review* (1941), 1:139.

ment as a whole, and to enable him to direct the policies of the departments and agencies."

The Bureau of the Budget

Among the managerial agencies included in the Executive Office of the President, the Bureau of the Budget has the most influence over administration, and the director of this staff service has become the most important administrative adviser to the president. The creation of the Bureau of the Budget is comparatively recent. Until 1921, the year in which the Budgeting and Accounting Act was passed, the chief executive was without any systematic means of preparing an annual budget. It is often stated that it took the assassination of President Garfield by a disappointed office seeker to start civil service: similiarly, it took a world war and the first "billion dollar budgets" this country had seen to bring about budgetary reform.

Under the Budget and Accounting Act of 1921, the Bureau of the Budget was created, with a director at its head, and the General Accounting Office was established, headed by the Comptroller General. The Act authorized the Bureau of the Budget to prepare annual budgets and to see that its financial programs are executed in line with the president's policy. The fiscal responsibilities of the Bureau including its work of formulating the budget will be treated elsewhere in this chapter, but the work of the Bureau in administrative planning and research—which was also authorized by the Act of 1921—can be advantageously discussed at this point.[3]

Until 1939, the Bureau of the Budget concerned itself chiefly with reviewing estimates, but since that time, in addition to its fiscal activities, it has steadily developed as an administrative planning agency. The president is empowered to have the Bureau direct management studies for the purpose of recommending improvements to Congress. This work is carried on by the Bureau's Office of Management and Organization. Actually the development of the Bureau as a planning agency is not at all inconsistent with what is perhaps its primary objective—the review of estimates. The review of estimates of department expenses quite naturally leads to an examination of departmental administrative practices and this in turn suggests improvements in management that will help reduce estimates.

The Office of Management and Organization of the Bureau devotes its full time to the study of organization and management with the view of bringing about improvements. It has no authority to compel the adoption of its recommendations. On most intra-departmental matters, the Division's recommendations or suggestions are made directly to operating officials, departmental heads and the like, who accept or reject them on their own motion. The principal types of recommendations that go to the chief executive concern the exercise of his power to organize (when he has congres-

---

[3] A lucid account of this phase of the Bureau of the Budget's work will be found in Fritz Morstein Marx: "The Bureau of the Budget: Its Evolution and Present Role, II." *American Political Science Review* (1945), 39:887–93.

sional authority to do so). Thus the Reorganization Plans, under the Act of 1939 and subsequent acts, went from the Office to the President.

Acting in an advisory capacity, the Office of Management and Organization has become something of a master mechanic for the Federal administrative system. Generally conceded to have one of the ablest staffs in the governmental service, it has influenced changes in management and organization in a great many Federal agencies. To give but a few examples, its recommendations have been adopted for reorganizing the Army services and the State Department, and many of its suggestions have been carried out with respect to the wartime agencies, an area in which the president had wide authority to determine organization—to create, abolish, and consolidate agencies. [4]

The Bureau and Government Reorganization

In a general and sometimes in a specific way, the more urgent administrative reorganization measures were either discussed or suggested in the preceding chapters. There is no need, therefore, for treating the subject extensively at this point; it will serve our purpose to dwell briefly on some of the larger aspects of reorganization.

Reorganization embraces plans for the rearrangement of functions and responsibilities, personnel, the structure of the administrative hierarchy and services, and many other matters. The most comprehensive attacks on the problems of reorganization were made by the President's Committee on Administrative Management in 1937, and more recently by the Commission on Organization of the Executive Branch of the Government whose reports were published in 1949.

While careful reorganization is of immeasurable value and government has been severely handicapped by faulty administrative arrangements, it would be unwise to expect too much from reorganization—to look upon it as a nostrum that will solve all problems of administration. The objective of all tinkering with administrative machinery should be a more skillful mobilization of administrative services for handling government's social responsibilities. The social good rather than economy should be the yardstick to measure reorganization benefits. As Professor Hyneman forcefully asks: "What does the administrative reorganization program, designed to achieve efficiency and economy, offer to the man whose chief concern is for certain other qualities in his government—whose concern is that vision, imagination, and courage predominate in the execution, adaptation, or modification of policy." [5] Furthermore, government reorganization is not something that can be achieved in a single stroke. It is a constant process of piecemeal change to improve administrative services. In this area, obviously, the Bureau of the Budget's Office of Management and

[4] See Leonard D. White: *Introduction to the Study of Public Administration* (3d ed.; New York, 1948), pp. 62–3.

[5] See Charles S. Hyneman: "Administrative Reorganization: An Adventure into Science and Theology." *Journal of Politics* (1939), 1:62–75.

Organization has an important function, a function in which progress is more likely to be modest than revolutionary.

The Legislative and Statistical Divisions of the Bureau

As one of its functions as a staff arm of the president the Bureau of the Budget reviews legislative proposals of the departments. This is done by its Division of Legislative Reference which scrutinizes all proposals for legislation or executive orders submitted by the departments and agencies to see that they conform with presidential policy. A department may take a legislative proposal to Congress after it has been found to be not in accord with presidential policy, but it must indicate that the proposal is at variance with official policy. Another significant phase of the work of the Division of Legislative Reference is ironing out conflicts between contemplated legislative proposals of different departments and agencies.

In still a different area, the Bureau of the Budget serves as a management coordinator through its Statistical Division which clears all governmental statistical operations. Thus the responsibilities for management improvement that the Bureau has taken under its wing cover a wide area. In judging the tendency to broaden the generalship of the Bureau of the Budget over management one point should be clearly understood. The Bureau is not a policy planner as that term is used to describe the social and economic measures which the president has decided upon. Such matters are decided upon by the president after advising with the leaders of his administration in and out of Congress and with such agencies as the Council of Economic Advisers of which we shall speak presently. The chief concern of the Bureau of the Budget is to make Federal administrative machinery operate as smoothly and as efficiently as possible. While the Bureau's responsibility for improving management concentrates on the means and methods of securing more efficient operation, it should not be supposed that this agency is completely neutral on social and economic issues. Through their intimate contact with management at all levels the officials of the Bureau are in a position to form many judgments on general questions of social and economic policy, and they are sometimes able to impregnate departmental officers with recommendations that have little to do with problems of management. Indeed, the suggestions of Bureau officials along these lines may often be embodied in proposals that eventually emerge as official policies from high councils of the president's administration. Thus, in many ways, the Bureau of the Budget has advanced to occupy a unique place in the administrative system—as a coordinator, improver of management, "trouble shooter," and finally an unofficial advisor on problems of long-range social and economic consequence. Clearly, there is no other agency in the Federal service that can boast such unusual distinction. [6]

[6] "The Bureau of the Budget," writes Arthur Krock, "is all-powerful in the executive area under the president and psychologically potent with Congress."—*New York Times*, January 16, 1948.

In the development of the Bureau of the Budget as a managerial over-seer it is not surprising that the director of the Bureau has become the most important administrative adviser to the president. The chief executive can use his Budget Director somewhat like the football coach who, unable to spot the entire action of his team from the bench, sends one of his assistants up to the top of the stadium to telephone reports on specific phases of the play. The assistant may diagnose the line or backfield play, or perhaps he may simply watch one individual, but the information he relays is ex-tremely helpful to the coach. The Director of the Bureau of the Budget serves the president in similar fashion. He is a watchman both in the fields of administrative management and fiscal planning, and while he has no authority to compel adoption of his suggestions, his recommendations are usually accepted by the president who in turn brings about their adoption by an appropriate order. The Office of Budget Review develops general budget policies, prepares economic analyses and reviews, plans and schedules the estimates procedure, and supervises the preparation of the budget.

The Council of Economic Advisers

A postwar addition to the Executive Office of the President that has be-come an important body of staff planners is the Council of Economic Advisers. This agency was created in 1946 and consists of three full-time economic advisers—a chairman and two associate members—whose duties are to keep a trained eye on the nation's economy and recommend eco-nomic policies to the president. The Council of Economic Advisers studies trends in employment, production, and many other aspects of the national economy and prepares an annual report that includes information on the state of the nation's economy as well as recommended measures to keep the economy healthy. It is the duty of the Council to suggest policies that will encourage free competitive enterprise, full employment and produc-tion, and adequate purchasing power.

Here again, in the case of the Council of Economic Advisers, is a clear-cut example of a high-level planning agency that provides the president with machinery for dealing with crucial matters connected with the na-tional economy. The Council is a long-range planning body. Underlying its creation is a philosophy that government must step in to fill the breach when something temporarily gets out of adjustment in the operation of the national economy. [7] Thus the Council is directly concerned, among other things, with the Federal budget—its size, how the money is going to be expended, and its ultimate effect of the nation's economy. When one dollar out of every four or five of the national income goes to support Fed-eral governmental activities, the impact of the Federal budget on the na-tional economy is a matter of leading importance. The relation of the work of the Council of Economic Advisers to the Federal budget will be con-

[7] See Edwin G. Nourse: "Public Administration and Economic Stabilization." *Public Administration Review* (1947), 7:85.

sidered more fully in the chapters on governmental finance and government and the economy.

Other Staff Services in the Executive Office of the President

The National Security Council was created to assess and appraise the objectives, commitments, and risks of the United States in relation to its actual and potential military power, in the interest of national security. During the cold war President Eisenhower considered it so important that he gave it more attention than his cabinet. The Office of Defense Mobilization was established in order to enable one executive office to exercise strong leadership in mobilization efforts currently and for any future national emergency. Its Director directs, controls, and coordinates all mobilization activities of the executive branch of the government. Assisting him are Assistant Directors for manpower, materials, production, stabilization, telecommunications, and plans and readiness. The President's Advisory Committee on Governmental Organization recommends to the President, the Assistant President, and the Director of the Budget changes in organization of the executive branch.

A wartime agency whose experience left a permanent residue of lessons for overhead management was the office of War Mobilization and Reconversion. Created as an overhead agency in 1944 and brought under the Executive Office, its duties embraced both the procurement of materials and the speeding of war production as well as the responsibility for drafting plans for demobilization and reconversion. The O.W.M.R. was a most important experiment in overhead coordination. As the wartime emergency agencies tended to pyramid, it became the only agency that could successfully manage the central planning necessary for the war effort and the transition from war to peace. Perhaps one of the most notable features of the experience with the O.W.M.R. was that its unusually intimate relationship with the president helped to make it a most effective agency. When the war ended and public opinion pressed Congress to prepare for the expected unemployment, it created the Council of Economic Advisers of which the O.W.M.R. was the forerunner.

THE PRESIDENT AND FISCAL PLANNING

Perhaps no single factor adds greater weight to the president's control over administration than his authority as master fiscal planner for the executive departments and various agencies. Although Congress must appropriate the actual funds to finance governmental functions, it is the chief executive who directs the preparation of the budget—a task of enormous magnitude that is borne largely by the Bureau of the Budget.

By means of the budget the president requests Congress to appropriate funds to carry out the activities that have already been authorized by law. The process of budgeting and appropriating thus occurs after questions of governmental policy have been settled by legislation. Beginning in

1948, the budget has included estimates of funds that would be necessary to carry out new legislation proposed by the president. Prior to this date supplemental estimates had to be sent up to Congress to cover activities that were newly authorized, and Congress had no over-all estimate of what the total costs of current and proposed activities would be.

The budget itself reflects the whole program of government. The document has approximately the same dimensions as a Sears Roebuck catalogue and many months of laborious effort go into its annual preparation. Underlying the preparation of the budget is the vital process of program planning for government in which fundamentally there are two issues: (1) What policy, scale of activity, or emphasis of program is to be supported within the limits authorized by law, that is, by Congress? (2) How much money will be required to obtain the personnel, materials, and other equipment necessary to carry out the contemplated policy?

Essentially the process of program planning that underlies the budget begins with a determination of what the department or particular agency proposes to do. Thus the budget review process is directed first to a clarification of the agency's proposed program—the work which the agency contemplates undertaking. Actually, of course, the agency's program will in large measure be a continuation of past practice, but there may be important new projects for which budgetary allowances must be made. A significant feature of the budget review is that the process provides an important means for presidential coordination and direction of administration and it invariably brings about a large measure of interdepartmental coordination.

Once the departmental program is clarified, the second basic element of the budgetary process arises—the question of money. This is a technical matter of translating the program into personnel and material and thence into dollars. If, for example, we propose to double the volume of anti-trust work, how many men, how much travel, communication, and other expense will be involved? In short, what we want to know is how much will the total cost be?

Unfortunately, vivid presentation of the techniques that go into the budgetary process is difficult to achieve, and in consequence the real significance of the budget is not revealed as meaningfully as its importance warrants. A quick glance at the pre-budgetary stage of government, however, as well as a closer look at the processes of budgeting help to bring the full import of the budget into sharper focus.

Origins of the Budgetary System

The executive budget system—so named because it is the president's or chief executive's budget—made a belated entry into our Federal government. In the absence of administrative machinery to aid in the preparation of the budget, Congress attempted to handle the situation by multiplying its committees and having each committee deal with the expenditure of a department or a number of governmental agencies that could be grouped under a subject classification. The procedure under the legislative budget system started with the department or independent agency first making an estimate of its needs for the next fiscal year. This was followed by a hearing before the appropriate congressional committee. Once the committee approved a request and reported its appropriation bill, Congress acted upon each bill individually. Departments that had their requests lowered by their committee could still resort to lobbying techniques at this stage and try to have the original request restored.

At best, the legislative budget was a cumbersome expedient, ill-equipped to service the ever expanding financial operations of government. The heart of the difficulty with the legislative budget was simply that there was no critical administrative review of requests when each department approached Congress directly. Thus there was no over-all financial plan, including a program of expenditures and a program of revenues from existing or proposed tax measures. The system not only militated against the development of centralized financial planning, but it also offered opportunities for congressional log-rolling and wasteful pork-barrel appropriations. Preferential treatment was accorded to some agencies. The administrators of less favored agencies often padded their estimates on the assumption that whatever they asked for would be cut anyway. In almost every respect, the legislative budget system was defective, yet it was not superseded by the executive type of budget until 1921.

The executive budget was first tested in state and local governments in this country, the most notable example being the modern budgetary system introduced in the State of Illinois in 1917. Under the Federal Budget Act of 1921, a Bureau of the Budget was established to aid the president in the preparation of an annual financial program. [8]

Preparing the Budget

Chronologically the Federal budget has three phases but they should not be thought of as unconnected because there is a great deal of cross-consultation throughout the process. [9] It starts with the department, independent commission, government corporation, or some other unit of the government as the case may be. In the second stage, the Bureau of the Budget takes over. In the third stage Congress passes the final judgment.

The cue for starting the budget-making cycle comes from the chief executive in the form of an annual "call for estimates." Following the "call for estimates" a preliminary review of anticipated revenues and expenditures is made by the secretary of the treasury. In the matter of

[8] For an excellent account of the background of this Act see Fritz Morstein Marx: "The Bureau of the Budget: Its Evolution and Present Role: I." *American Political Science Review* (1945), 39:653–84.

[9] For a detailed account of budget-making see Fritz Morstein Marx: "The Bureau of the Budget: II." *American Political Science Review* (1945), 39:871–9; and Robert H. Rawson: "The Formulation of the Federal Budget" in Carl J. Friedrich and Edward S. Mason, editors, *Public Policy* (Cambridge, 1941), pp. 78–135. See also Daniel T. Selko: *The Federal Financial System* (Washington, D.C., 1940), chaps. 23–29.

revenue estimates there is some rivalry between presidential advisers in the Treasury Department and in the Bureau of the Budget. Actually the only one who has clear authority is the president and the guessing about revenues goes on until the last minute.

In the departmental phase of budget-making, estimate forms are provided by the Budget Bureau upon which departmental officials enter their estimated expenditures, the amount they spent for the same items during the year immediately preceding, and several other items. Early in this stage, the bureau chiefs within each department request the heads of the units operating under them to submit an estimate of their needs by a certain date. This process, of course, involves the vital business of program planning. When all estimates have been submitted at this level of the administrative hierarchy, the budget officer of the bureau goes over the estimates, giving administrative officers an opportunity to defend their requests if they have raised their estimates. After this the combined estimates for the bureau are reviewed by the bureau chief. His decision at this stage is final.

When all the bureau estimates have been amassed, the next step is to resolve them into a departmental total. The procedure is similar. This time, however, the bureau chiefs must appear before the departmental budget officer and departmental head to justify the amounts they have requested.

One might think that the process of formulating the budget consists merely of one dreary process after another in an ascending pyramid, and that it is essentially a race between bureaucratic officials to see who can secure the greatest increase in his budget. Administrative officials, of course, are often animated by the desire to garner for their operating units appropriations that would be out of line with their actual needs. But it should be fairly obvious from an analysis of the steps just described that the budget system tends to frustrate such attempts. Moreover, as the budget edges its way slowly toward the final phases—a careful examination of estimates by the Bureau of the Budget and ultimately the final rendezvous with Congress—the questionable items are carefully scrutinized.

Review of Estimates by the Bureau of the Budget

Although we speak of the departmental phase and the Bureau of the Budget phase in the sequence of budget-making, the two are not in fact distinctly separated. All during the early preliminaries persons from the Bureau staff are in constant consultation with departmental personnel and a large amount of joint work and consultation occurs before the formal departmental request gets to the Bureau for review. Moreover, the personnel attached to the Office of Budget Review handle these departmental relations and it is their job to have well in mind most of the underlying facts and situations before the estimate requests actually reach the Bureau.

When the estimate requests reach the Bureau they are referred to appropriate groups within the Bureau that conduct hearings. The budget examiner in charge of the agency budget conducts these hearings and he is flanked by assistants and sometimes individuals from other divisions of the Bureau of the Budget who have a concern in the matter. Bureau chiefs, section heads, and others from the department or agency concerned appear at these meetings much as they do before the appropriation sub-committee hearings in Congress.

From the Bureau of the Budget's examining groups, the revised figures for all governmental departments and agencies are gone over once more, this time by the director and the president. Sometimes the president alters the director's recommendations considerably, but at this stage the process is quite confidential and no one except the chief executive and the director know what will be done. In any case, when the document goes to Congress it is the president's budget.

Congress and the Budget

When the budget is transmitted by the president to the House Committee on Appropriations, much the same procedure must be repeated that we have observed in the earlier phases of budget-making. After a new Congress convenes in January, the House Committee on Appropriations organizes several sub-committees, each of which will hold hearings on the estimates submitted by various categories of Federal agencies. Some of the most serious work in Congress is done by these sub-committees. In practice, they often begin work in December or even as early as October on pieces of the preliminary budget before it goes to Congress. At the sub-committee hearings, departmental officials again are called in both to give them an opportunity to defend their estimates and for questioning. These meetings are in executive session and the general tone is dignified. The work of Congress at this level is mainly earnest and sincere, and it reflects the kind of procedure former Congressman Will Rogers, Jr., had in mind when he commented that it is unfortunate that when people think of Congress they usually visualize the House chamber and the raucous political behavior encountered there. In reality, as Mr. Rogers correctly points out, the real work of Congress is done at the sub-committee level, and there is no sub-committee in Congress to which this generalization may more appropriately be applied than the sub-committees that consider budget estimates.

When the estimates sub-committees have completed their work, the budget is ready for consideration by the full House Appropriations Committee. Before the budget is reported out by the House Appropriations Committee, however, it has also started to run the gauntlet of the Senate Appropriations Committee, which means additional hearings, though not as extensive or thorough as those conducted by the corresponding committee in the House. The Senate committees tend to take a more generous stand on appropriations than the House committees. Finally, after all appropriation bills (usually about ten or a dozen) are reported out by both the Senate and House Appropriations Committees, they come up, one at a time, for debate on the floor in each chamber. Even at this late date, more changes may be made increasing or decreasing the amounts allowed, and if the two houses are unable to agree a conference committee may be required to reach a compromise. The last stage following passage by both houses is the signing by the president, who has no authority to veto separate items and who invariably signs appropriation bills even though he may be displeased with some sections.

Summary of Budget-Making

For the entire cycle of budget-making, many months are consumed. A typical start of the budget-making process in some departments begins around May 1 when the bureaus start to prepare their estimates. This date is fourteen months before the opening of the fiscal year to which the estimates will apply and over two years before the close of that year. By June the bureau estimates must go to the department, and the department must turn in its estimates to the Bureau of the Budget by September 15. This leaves the Bureau of the Budget and the president just a little over three months to complete their work, for the president must submit the budget to Congress early in January. Congress then has until July 1— the official beginning of the Federal fiscal year—to pass the, necessary appropriation bills. Thus, the time span for building the budget is indeed a lengthy one, and it emphasizes again the importance of long-range administrative planning in the Federal system. [10]

Executing the Budget

With the legislative phase of budget-making over, the scene shifts to the task of carrying out the budget. Here again the Budget Bureau has an important part to play. Essential to budget execution is the executive supervision of expenditures. An administrative officer who heads a Federal agency, for example, does not have at his immediate disposal the entire amount that Congress appropriated to his unit. Instead, his agency has an account number in the Treasury Department, where checks will be issued provided the proper requisitions are received. The administrative head, therefore, does not have a lump sum under his control, nor is he completely free to make out requisitions to be drawn on his agency's account. Here he is governed by the rule of the Bureau of the Budget.

Budget Bureau regulations require the heads of administrative agencies to divide their respective appropriations into four quarterly amounts and they are not allowed to draw beyond these quarterly allotments unless authorized to do so by the Bureau. The Budget Bureau also compels each department to set aside a reserve fund for emergencies. This is accomplished by giving each bureau within a department a little less than the

---

[10] See Arthur N. Holcombe: "Overall Financial Planning Through the Bureau of the Budget." *Public Administration Review* (1939), 1:225–30.

amount authorized by Congress. Occasionally bureaus manage to get along without the emergency cuts, and when they do the Budget Bureau may discover one more place where succeeding budgets may be pared.

As a device for fiscal control, the present budget system has wrought far-reaching changes in the operation of the Federal administrative services. The Bureau of the Budget provides the driving force behind the budget system, just as it takes the initiative in coordinating administrative management. But though the Bureau directs the process, the cumulative efforts of the legislative and administrative branches are reflected in the budget's finished form. On the administrative side not only the Budget Bureau, but also the departments and their own bureaus share heavy responsibilities for planning the budget. The budget, therefore, interlaces the work of the legislative and administrative services as well as that of the administrative services themselves.

That the budget system is barely out of the novice stage and requires further refinement is freely admitted. Yet, in a single generation it has achieved a remarkable development. From the vigorous start which was given to the system by the first Budget Bureau Director, Charles G. Dawes, it has gone forward steadily. Several reforms in the administrative services have already been spearheaded by the Bureau of the Budget, and it seems clear that the Bureau will continue to provide leadership on both fiscal and administrative questions.

THE GENERAL ACCOUNTING OFFICE

Like program planning in the preparation of the budget, accounting is an indispensable process in the daily management of government's administrative affairs. Among its important objectives as summarized by the Hoover Commission, "it reveals the status of appropriations, the extent that revenue estimates are realized, the progress of actual expenditures and collections, and comparative operating and other costs." [11] Finally, accounting makes it possible to check the handling of governmental funds thus providing a representative of the legislative branch with the means to check "administrative competence and fidelity."

In the Federal government the legislative "watchdog of the Treasury" is the General Accounting Office headed by the comptroller general. This Office, of course, is in theory responsible to Congress and since the comptroller general is accountable to Congress, not to the chief executive, a discussion of this agency and its work probably seems out of place in a chapter dealing with the presidential staff and managerial agencies. Under the view of the Hoover Commission, however, that accounting is quite properly a primary responsibility of the executive branch and that the accounting duties now assumed by the comptroller general should

[11] Commission on Organization of the Executive Branch of the Government: *Budgeting and Accounting* (Washington, 1949), p. 36; *The Hoover Commission Report* (New York, 1949), p. 50.

henceforth be taken over by a proposed accountant general to head a new accounting service in the Treasury Department, discussion of the comptroller has relevance at this point.

The Comptroller General

Prior to 1921 an independent audit of the expenditures of the administrative services was undertaken by the Comptroller's Office (not to be confused with the office of comptroller general created in 1921) and six auditors from the Treasury Department. Under the Budget and Accounting Act of 1921, however, the Comptroller's Office was abolished and in its place a General Accounting Office was created with the comptroller general at its head.

The comptroller general is appointed by the president with senatorial confirmation for a term of fifteen years. Ostensibly the purpose of the General Accounting Office is to provide Congress "with an independent critic of executive conduct in the use of public funds . . ." [12] The Office was placed beyond the reach of executive influence and was given extensive powers over all Federal expenditures. Among the most significant controls exercised by the comptroller general are the right to approve requisitions for the advance of funds from the Treasury to administrative disbursement officers, the authority to settle all claims against the United States and to recover debts owed to the government, and the power to pass upon the validity of proposed expenditures.

It is the power of the comptroller general to determine the legality of departmental expenditures—exercised either through advance opinions on the validity of proposed actions or through the settlement of accounts covering past expenditures—that has created the real issue over the functions of this officer. The desirability of an independent audit of all governmental expenditures after they have been made is universally conceded by students of public finance, but assumption by the comptroller general of the power to make final interpretation of a statute has drawn sharp criticism. Through the comptroller general's power to countersign warrants, no administrative officer can get funds released for his agency until his requisition has been approved by the former. If the comptroller general challenges a requisition by assuming the power to interpret a statute—in other words to determine the intent of Congress—he may tie up the funds needed by an administrative agency. The assumption of such power is criticized on the ground that it transfers to the comptroller general the power of execution. "The Comptroller General," as Professor Mansfield observes in his illuminating study of this officer, "has practically nothing to do with the *amount* of money that the administrative establishments spend. That is a form of control that is exerted in Congress when appropriation acts are passed." The comptroller general, therefore, does not actually save any money for the government by holding up a requisition because

[12] Harvey C. Mansfield: *The Comptroller General* (New Haven, 1939), p. 2.

"what he does not allow to be spent for one purpose will be spent for another." [13]

During the first term of Franklin Roosevelt's Administration, Comptroller General McCarl's "aggressive" attitude in interpreting statutes led to many clashes with administrative officials, the climax coming over a dispute with the Tennessee Valley Authority and other government corporations when these agencies decided to retain custody of their own funds and accounts. Fortunately the situation has eased considerably since Mr. McCarl's tour of duty ended in 1936; there has been much less friction between the operating departments and the General Accounting Office. Since then better relations have also been established between the General Accounting Office, the Bureau of the Budget, and the Treasury Department—indeed, the cooperation of these three agencies in certain phases of accounting work was cited as "admirable" by the Hoover Commission. [14] Nonetheless the fundamental need for reform of the General Accounting Office has been brought out on frequent occasions.[15]

President Hoover expressed dissatisfaction with the arrangements of the General Accounting Office and as far back as 1932 sought to have the comptroller general's powers reduced. Five years later, the President's Committee on Administrative Management complained of the comptroller general's financial control which it said had tended to become a "judicial rather than an executive process" and it urged several reforms including transference of certain accounting duties to the Department of the Treasury. Substantially the same scheme for shifting the accounting work of the comptroller general to the executive branch was sounded in the Hoover Commission's report on *Budgeting and Accounting* in 1949. The Commission recommended that an accountant general be established in the Treasury Department "with authority to prescribe general accounting methods and enforce accounting procedures." In addition the accountant general would combine accounts of the various Federal agencies into summary accounts of the government and prepare financial reports for the president, Congress, and the public. No change, however, was advocated on the much-disputed power of the comptroller general to interpret statutes. "The Comptroller General," said the Commission, "must obviously continue to check and make certain that laws governing appropriations are being properly interpreted." Thus the real controversial issue over the comptroller general was left largely untouched, but if Congress takes action on the suggestion for transferring the accounting duties to the executive branch it is generally conceded that important improvements will result in the fiscal management of government.

[13] Ibid., p. 3.
[14] Commission on Organization of the Executive Branch of the Government: *Budgeting and Accounting* (Washington, 1949), p. 38; *The Hoover Commission Report* (New York, 1949), p. 51.
[15] See John McDiarmid: "Reorganization of the General Accounting Office." *American Political Science Review* (1937), 31:508–16.

LEADERSHIP AND POLITICS IN MANAGEMENT

Throughout our discussion of administration the importance of presidential leadership has been a recurrent theme but little has been said generally on the significance of the personal or political elements in administrative management. This omission, however, by no means implies an intent to minimize the significance of either. The leadership qualities of a department secretary may well set the tone for the entire organization he heads, and the same may be said of the operating units headed by division or bureau chiefs. Administrative officials may be, and often are, frustrated and fenced in by statutory organizational requirements over which they have little control. Yet the capable ones usually manage to overcome most organizational deficiencies by dint of a capacity for leadership combined with the skills and talents that run with executive ability. "The truly able managers," wrote the late Harold D. Smith, formerly Director of the Budget, "are the ones who—by intuition, by hunch, by observation, by rule of thumb—can see and sense matters that do not yield to purely scientific gauges of management. They can evaluate objectives, they can stimulate the spirit of an organization—all without too much reliance upon the tools of management." [16]

Administration and Politics

The opportunities which administrative officials have for impressing their political views upon the laws they are charged with enforcing and administering may hardly be said to be negligible. "It is clear," wrote V. O. Key, "that the administrative services are not purely inert mechanisms through which the will of the legislature is transmuted into action. These services themselves are an important service in the state and play an important part in the determination of what is to be done in the name of the state." [17] That these conclusions are indeed grounded in fact seems no longer in dispute, though generalizations about the omnipotence of the administrative services in forging legislative policy may often overstate the case. As Professor Key points out, the importance of the administrative services "is not so great as might be inferred from the more extravagant diatribes against the bureaucracy and its assumption of power." Valid as this point may be—that the power of the administrative services is not as sweeping as some editorials and campaign oratory might lead us to believe—the dangers inherent in giving the bureaucracy too much scope on matters of policy are not wholly imaginative.

It is true that the growing complexity of governmental responsibilities has all but erased the separation of powers doctrine and broken down the notion that politics and administration are separable. It is also undeniable

[16] Harold D. Smith: *The Management of Your Government* (New York, 1945), p. 29.

[17] V. O. Key: *Political Parties and Pressure Groups* (New York, 1942), p. 195. See also ibid., pp. 196–7 for further discussion of this problem.

that Congress has suffered a decline in prestige as a consequence of this trend, and this development in turn has accelerated the power and political influence of the administrative services. Some students of government think that this trend is destined to run its course until a conclusion is reached that James Burnham calls the "managerial revolution." According to Professor Burnham, our political, economic, and social institutions ". . . are undergoing a process of rapid transformation." [18] An inevitable consequence of this development is the transference of increasing power to professionally trained administrators who will be the real stewards or "managers" in the social, economic, and political system of the future. Fundamentally the issue is not whether the theory is correct or whether his prophecy will eventually be confirmed; the real issue is how to keep administrative services continuously responsible and accountable to the people they serve.

Mere frontal assaults of oratory will not prevent the administrative services from taking the initiative on matters of policy, nor is such a result desirable so long as Congress is not prepared to provide more vigorous leadership in this area. The assumption of some observers, however, that representative institutions like Congress have calcified and can henceforth play only a secondary role in the initiation of public policy seems dangerously short-sighted. It is desirable and essential that the administrative services continue to fill in large voids in congressional statutes to make laws administrable, but Congress should still chart the main course on policy and the administrative services should always be required to take their major cues from that body. Obviously, the administrative services can be allies of Congress in formulating policy. There can be little objection if the administrative services inspire a major policy that is adopted by Congress. No one, for example, would begrudge the fact that a speech of the president outlining major policies was not drafted and written by the chief executive. In the latter case, it matters not how the policies were formulated once the president expressed them officially as his own. The same is true of policies that have actually gestated among the administrative services before being taken over by Congress. When an elective body like Congress endorses a policy it is accountable for its action to the electorate, and when the record of Congress is before the people it is immaterial whether the policies adopted were initially products of administrative or congressional thought. Congress must still accept the full responsibility for its official deeds.

A further error of assumption by the group of public administrators suddenly turned mortician who claim that Congress is moribund, is the notion that this representative institution is incapable of a renaissance. Instead of working to reaffirm faith in representative institutions, the fraternity of administrative supremacy asserts that Congress is a defunct organization—a circumstance that compels us to turn over the initiation of public policy to the administrative services by default. Momentarily,

[18] James Burnham: *The Managerial Revolution* (New York, 1941), p. 74.

Congress has lost face, partly because of its inability to make a satisfactory adjustment to the increased tempo that the governing of modern society demands, and partly because the vitality of Congress has become sluggish through our inability to divert into politics a larger number of talented leaders. Potential leaders graduate from our universities into governmental administrative posts far more often than into politics. This trend has already left its mark in two ways. First, it has tended to retard constructive legislative action by preventing the fullest use of our leadership resources in congressional chambers. Second, it has accentuated the difference in social outlook between legislators and administrators. The effect of the latter trend has been to increase the friction between our administrative and legislative branches, and the by-product of these clashes is further loss of congressional prestige.

These trends do not warrant the inference that Congress has irretrievably lost the initiative on policy-making to administrative forces. Events during the past quarter of a century have propelled the administrative services into the foreground on policy initiation, but this does not suggest that Congress will or should continue to lag behind in this respect. We are still in a period of transition in which many readjustments remain to be made between representative institutions and administrative services; and democratic government requires that ensuing changes not lead toward the abdication of Congress as policy-maker.

One of the means that will help Congress resume its role as policy-maker is reorganization of its working habits. A start in this direction has already been made by the LaFollette-Monroney Reorganization Act of 1946. Another—and perhaps more fundamental—means is improvement of the standards of its personnel just as we have attempted to raise the quality of persons staffing the administrative services. We must make the conditions of service more attractive and groom leaders for such service. This long-range development, however, can proceed only at a modest pace; meanwhile, efforts should be made concurrently to improve the techniques of administration and to find constructive methods of keeping undesirable features of administrative policy-making at bay.

The undesirable trends—succinctly identified by Charles E. Merriam —bear careful watching, despite attempts from some quarters to dismiss concern about them as alarmist: "Above all, there is the impending danger of the desire for personal self-perpetuation and expansion of power, bureaucratic parochialism of the pettiest type, the sabotage of the ends of office by placing the machinery or the person above the function he is there to serve; or the effort of the administrator to take over the role of policy maker, by various devices, direct or otherwise." [19] A "middle way" which envisages neither the demise of Congress as a vigorous initiator of policy nor a system that reduces the administrative services to fetters should become one of the paramount objectives of this generation. Much

[19] Charles E. Merriam: "Public Administration and Political Theory." *Journal of Social Philosophy* (1940), 5:306.

of the progress toward this end will stem from better proportioned arrangement of administration and improvement of the techniques of management. Basically, however, the lesson for us is reduced to simple terms by the trenchant comment of John M. Gaus: that we must strive "to concentrate our efforts at political improvement at the point of the political agents—the party leaders of administration and legislation—and the recruitment, education, and training of bureaucracy, and at procedures whereby their work and policies may be devised in the light of experience."

SUMMARY

Among other functions the overhead agencies of the national government serve to keep the President informed about, and in control of, the sixty-five agencies that report to him. In 1939 the Executive Office of the President was formed, embracing several major managerial agencies with which the President needs continuous and intimate contact.

The Bureau of the Budget occupies a highly important position in the Executive Office. It has added to its original function of reviewing the estimated expenditures of governmental agencies the duties of central administrative planning, central statistical office, and legislative reference service. Other components of the Executive Office include the Council of Economic Advisers, the National Security Council, and the National Security Resources Board.

The inefficiency of the legislative method of budget-making led to the establishment of the executive budget in 1921. The President, acting through the Bureau of the Budget, screens and modifies the requests of agencies for funds and transmits his revised requests to Congress in his budget message. By a system of quarterly allotments of the funds actually appropriated, the President maintains control over the spending policies of the agencies.

Presidential authority over fiscal matters is restricted by the legislative watch dog of the Treasury, the Comptroller General. He exercises the power to pass on the legality of proposed expenditures, a power which has brought him into collision with the chief executive from time to time.

The scope of authority to be granted to administrators and their relationship to the legislature are major problems in a society that has been touched by something like Burnham's managerial revolution. Congress should be the policy-maker, but, to perform this function satisfactorily, it needs an outlook and procedures equal to the exigencies of the times.

THE NATIONAL LEGISLATURE

CHAPTER XXI

THE STRUCTURE OF CONGRESS

Why Congress Is Bicameral

THE Congress of the United States has two houses primarily because all but one of the thirteen states had that kind of legislature in 1787. Parliament, unpopular then, provided no attractive model. The chief determinant of the framers of the Constitution in making Congress bicameral "was not an affected imitation of the English government," John Adams asserted, "so much as an attachment to their old colonial forms. . . ." Two houses for Congress was accepted as a matter of course by a Convention most of whose members had been accustomed to nothing different for legislative purposes at home in their respective states. The Congress of the Confederation, it should be noted, had not been a law-making body. In the very first week of the deliberations of the Philadelphia Convention that framed the Constitution the resolution "that the national legislature ought to consist of two branches" was agreed to without debate and without dissent of any state except Pennsylvania which then had a one-house legislature.[1] Here are facts that ought to dispel, once and for all, the delusion that the framers devised or adopted two houses for Congress in order to make the "Great Compromise," the provision for proportionate representation of the states in the lower house and equal representation in the upper. The Convention's agreement to make Congress bicameral was seven weeks old when Franklin proposed the famous compromise. The specious explanation that bicameralism was adopted for the purpose of the compromise is, of course, ex-post-facto rationalization.

The Evolution of Congress

Congress has unquestionably evolved quite differently from the expectations of the framers of the Constitution. In the light of their experience

[1] Charles C. Tansill, ed.: *Documents, Illustrative of the Formation of the American States*, 69th Congress, House Document No. 398 (1927), pp. 124–5.

with what Madison called the "omnipotent" state legislatures they had reason to believe that Congress would be the chief organ of the Federal government and consequently, as in the states, destined to overshadow the executive. That the House, composed of the only directly elected representatives of the people in the Federal government, was expected to be more important than the Senate was implied in Madison's choosing to be a representative rather than a senator because he wanted "to improve his reputation as a statesman." No wonder, since the Senate met behind closed doors during the first quarter of a century of its deliberations. Thus was the Senate eclipsed by the House as public attention centered on the latter where the debates took place on the establishment of the Federal government, on the Hamiltonian program, and on the great statutes preceding and following the War of 1812.

Not until the 1830's was public attention diverted from House to Senate as the latter took on the character of the chief forum for discussion of national issues such as those of the Webster-Hayne debate. Meanwhile the presidency, shaped by the commanding personality of Andrew Jackson, had captured the imagination of the American masses both rural and urban with a consequent decline in congressional prestige. In mid-century both Senate and House played very significant parts in shaping the Compromise of 1850, the Kansas-Nebraska Act, and the other legislation constituting the prelude to the Civil War. After the war the House promptly seized the initiative in Reconstruction but a decade later the Senate had established a hegemony in the Federal government over both the House and the executive. It maintained this advantage during the anarchy that characterized the conflict of committees of the House in the 1880's. The House recovered its prestige upon the emergence of exceptional parliamentary leadership in the persons of Speaker Thomas B. Reed (1889–91; 1895–9) and Speaker Joseph G. Cannon (1903–11). The Senate attained another peak of prestige when, after World War I, it frustrated the efforts of President Wilson to obtain ratification of the Covenant of the League of Nations and then succeeded, through a group of its leaders, in getting one of its own members, Warren G. Harding, elected president. Congress as a whole declined in prestige during the long presidency of Franklin Roosevelt, and the Congressional Reorganization Act of 1946 was unquestionably an attempt on its part to recover lost standing in the public esteem.

THE PROBLEM OF APPORTIONMENT

The Apportionment of Representatives in Congress

The proportionate representation of each state in the lower house is due to the Constitution's provision: "Representatives . . . shall be apportioned among the several states which may be included within this union according to their respective numbers." The idea that representation ought to be proportionate to population had grown out of colonial experience. This principle was contrary to contemporary British practice regarding representation in the House of Commons and despite persistent pressures not even a gesture in that direction was made in Britain until forty-five years after the framing of the Constitution of the United States. The fierce resentment of the inhabitants of the interior of the colonies (later to become the coastal states) against the gross over-representation of the population of the tidewater communities in the legislatures planted deep in the minds of the majority of early Americans the conviction that fair representation must be in proportion to numbers. Thus at a time when the issue was not urged vigorously in England the framers wrote into the Constitution a widespread American conviction. Upon Congress rests the obligation of the reapportionment of representation in the lower house in accordance with the successive decennial censuses. This has created problems, chief among which has been the growing size of the House of Representatives. The House began with a total membership of sixty-five apportioned among the states by the Constitution tentatively until a census could be taken. In making each successive reapportionment Congress has been confronted with a choice of alternatives. It could maintain the old ratio of representation to population and assign to growing states additional representatives in proportion to their increase of population; or it could maintain the same total number of representatives in Congress and redistribute them among the several states in accordance with changes in the population in each state since the last apportionment. By the latter method those states that had acquired a larger proportion of the total population of the United States than they had at the last previous apportionment would receive a larger share of the total representation in Congress, and states with a smaller proportion of the population would lose whatever representatives the others gained. If the Constitution's original ratio of representation to population had remained unaltered the House of Representatives would have several thousand members today.

Congress's Experience with the Problem of Reapportionment

For a generation before the Civil War Congress dealt drastically with the problem of apportioning representation and set the successive ratios so that, even with the then galloping growth in the population of the nation, the membership of the House which was 242 in 1830 was only 243 in 1860. Despite the mandatory constitutional injunction to make the reapportionment after each census, none was made from 1850 to 1872. During the following forty years each successive reapportionment was based on a ratio so fixed that no state would suffer a reduction of its representatives and consequently no incumbent congressman would be deprived of his constituency or district. The consequence was that, in slightly more than a generation, the membership of the House of Representatives increased from 293 in 1870 to 435 in 1910. The growing unwieldiness of its membership gave Congress pause. Following the 1920 census it again ignored its constitutional obligation to make a reapportionment.

The Present Formula for Reapportioning Representation

Until recently it was the practice of Congress to fix by statute the quota of representation—that is the number of people a member of the lower house was presumed to represent. Then the population of each state was divided by this quota. Of course the Constitution assures one representative to each state no matter how small its population and Nevada has long had but a minor fraction of the statutory quota. The quotients obtained by the division determined each state's representation, except that many of the statutes apportioning representatives among the states have alloted an extra representative to any state whose quotient contained a major fraction besides its integer. Congress has by legislation now attempted to settle, once and for all, the decennial problem of reapportionment by providing for automatic establishment of a new distribution of representation among the states whenever reapportionment was not accomplished by legislation following a new census. In the future a mathematical formula will be used. Instead of setting a fixed quota and letting the aggregate quotients resulting from its division into the populations of the several states determine the total number of representatives, Congress fixed the total number of representatives in Congress at 435. Then it threw into the lap of the mathematician the matter of devising the technique for apportioning this number in accordance with the constitutional requirement. This is done by first alloting each state the one representative it must have regardless of population. The remaining 387 representatives are distributed among the states in proportion to their respective populations. This can be achieved by a complicated calculation known as the "method of equal proportions," which the typical layman is likely to accept on the basis of a faith in the magic of mathematics. At any rate, the formula is too complicated to be described here. The law now provides that, following each census, the Census Bureau shall prepare for the President a table showing the population of each state and the number of representatives each is entitled to calculated by the formula of "equal proportions." This table is submitted to Congress by the President, and the distribution of representatives indicated goes into effect with the election of the next Congress unless the current Congress legislates otherwise. Congress might bring to life the dead-letter second section of the Fourteenth Amendment, which clearly directs that any state abridging the franchise shall have its representation proportionately reduced; but this is impractical because of statistical difficulties as well as social and political resistance.[2] It remains to be seen whether the admission of new states such as Hawaii and Alaska may not induce Congress to increase the House beyond 435 members.

[2] See Lawrence F. Schmeckebier: *Congressional Apportionment* (Washington, D.C., 1941).

Establishing the Boundaries of Congressional Districts

Once the state's number of representatives is determined it remains for the state legislatures to fix the boundary lines of the congressional districts in accordance with statutory regulations established by Congress. Since the Constitution is silent on the matter some states in the beginning elected their representatives at large on a general ticket just as a state's presidential electors now are elected. Other states elected representatives by districts and some combined the two methods. In 1842 Congress brought about uniformity by establishing the present requirement of election by districts. Congress has also provided that the districts be contiguous in territory and "compact" in form, a requirement which has, however, been given an ultra-liberal interpretation by many a state legislature. For example, some states have resorted to a practice known as "gerrymandering." This means that the party in control of the legislature will so map the congressional districts that the vote of the opposition is concentrated in as few districts as possible while its own party votes are distributed in as many districts as possible with merely safe majorities. Consequently there are such grotesque configurations as the "shoestring district" of Mississippi, an elongated strip running several hundred miles, the Pennsylvania district resembling a "dumb-bell," and the "belt line" and "saddle-back" districts of Illinois. In 1915 Ohioans used the referendum to defeat a gerrymandered redistricting of the state but this merely revived the districting act of 1913 based on the census of 1910. This stood until the legislature redistricted Ohio in 1951. Since 1842 it has been the law that when a state gets an increase in the number of representatives by reapportionment it may elect the additional members at large, that is on a general ticket by vote of the entire state until redistricting.

Urban Under-representation in the House of Representatives

In the typical American state one house of the legislature is likely to have at least one representative for every county or town no matter how little its population. This tends to give the rural areas a disproportionately greater weight than cities in states containing metropolitan centers. In twenty-one states urban population is greater than rural population but in only eleven of these can the majority of the population control the legislature. [3] Thus the idea of Thomas Jefferson is still dominant: "Those who labor in the earth are the chosen people of God" while "the mobs of the great cities add just so much to the support of pure government, as sores do to the strength of the human body." [4] Consequently, state legislatures have a tendency to practice another kind of "gerrymandering" that groups urban voters in populous congressional district at the same time that it leaves rural populations in congressional districts with much smaller populations. This is not so much the result of deliberate distor-

[3] David O. Walter: "Reapportionment and Urban Representation." *Annals of the American Academy of Political and Social Science* (1938), 195:11–20.
[4] Thomas Jefferson: *Notes on the State of Virginia* (1782), p. 302.

tion by legislative action as of delay in remapping districts after a new census. A striking example was Ohio, with redistricting delayed for thirty-nine years during which time population had declined in the northwestern and southeastern counties and become concentrated especially in urbanized northeastern Ohio. The fifth congressional district had declined to only 163,000 while the twenty-second district had accumulated 698,000 inhabitants. Two-thirds of the state's districts had declined below the national average.[5]

Until recently Chicago had three districts each with over 600,000 people, another that fell just short of that number, and one district with a population of 914,053. The distribution of congressional districts in Illinois from 1901 to 1947 was based on the census of 1900 despite urban concentration of population and rural decline. On the basis of the census of 1940 the most populous Chicago district had eight times the population of another Illinois district. In the determination of national policy on matters that concern them city dwellers have found themselves confronted by the rural minority of the nation represented by a powerful majority strength in the lower house of Congress. The significance of this fact becomes strikingly evident in scientific analyses of legislative votes on important measures. The alignments pro and con on many outstanding issues turn out to be contests between urban and non-urban legislators far more than battles between these legislators as Republicans and Democrats. Typical of this was the vote in 1948 on the measure to repeal the excessive tax on oleomargarine colored as butter. For example, Ohio representatives from metropolitan or large city districts voted for the repeal of the tax while all the other Ohio representatives voted against repeal.

ELECTION OF SENATORS AND REPRESENTATIVES

Single-Member Districts Distort Party Strength

Election of representatives from single-member districts by a simple majority or plurality fails signally to represent accurately the proportionate voting strength of political parties. More than three-quarters of a century ago this was recognized by Congressman James A. Garfield who said: "When I was first elected to Congress in the fall of 1862, the State of Ohio had a clear Republican majority of about 25,000; but by the adjustment and distribution of political power in the state, there were fourteen Democratic representatives upon this floor and only five Republicans. In the next Congress there was no great political change in the popular vote of Ohio—a change of only 20,000 but the result was that seventeen Republican members were sent here from Ohio and only two Democrats. Now, no man, whatever his politics, can justly defend a system that may in theory and frequently does in practice, produce such results as these." Ohio still has a vigorous two-party system but several years ago only one of the thirty-five members of the Ohio Senate belonged to the minority party. It would even be theoretically possible for the minority party to

[5] *Official Congressional Directory*, 80th Congress 2nd Session (May, 1946), p. 96.

have a narrow majority in every congressional district of a state except one if the majority party's strength was concentrated in one district.

Proportional Representation

The proportionate strength of all parties both major and minor could be approximately represented by the use of a system of proportional representation. This would require the enlargement of congressional districts so that wherever possible three or more representatives would be elected from each district. It would mean that a party casting one-third of a state's votes for representatives in Congress would elect about one-third of the representatives. There is, however, no public opinion of consequence favoring such an innovation and it would doubtless disturb the normal functioning of the two-party system. It has been argued that the candidate under proportional representation can make his appeal to a narrow group, a minority element whose group consciousness may thereby be intensified. But in the prevailing system of the single-member district a major party candidate must emphasize the common ground that tends to reduce group consciousness and must stress a program of policies attractive to the elements of a multi-group combination which constitutes the typical American major party. Many political scientists believe that the socially integrating tendency of the typical American election appeal under the two-party system is preferable to the disintegrating possibilities of proportional representation. [6] An insuperable obstacle to proportional representation is the ineradicable conviction of the typical American citizen that the one member of Congress elected from his district is his personal representative in the national government.

Congressional Control of Elections

Basically, congressional elections are under the control of the states, and the Constitution prescribes that the "times, places and manner of holding elections for Senators and Representatives, shall be prescribed in each state by the legislature thereof." However, "Congress may at any time by law make or alter such regulations [of state legislatures], except as to the places of choosing senators." Until the adoption of the Seventeenth Amendment providing for the popular election of senators, this clause was the only source of Congress's control of the election of senators and representatives. These constitutional provisions have been the basis of congressional legislation designed to secure fair and honest conduct of the election of members of Congress. Congress may even punish a state election official for violating his duty under a state law governing congressional elections when that law has been adopted as Federal regulation. [7] Congress can, by law, protect the act of voting against personal violence

[6] The outstanding thorough-going study of the functioning of proportional representation and argument against it is F. A. Hermen's *Democracy or Anarchy?* Notre Dame, Ind., 1941.

[7] *In re* Coy, 127 U.S. 731 (1888); *Ex parte* Seibold, 100 U.S. 371 (1880); *Ex parte* Clark, 100 U.S. 399 (1880); United States *v.* Gale, 109 U.S. 65 (1883).

or intimidation and the election itself against corruption and fraud,[8] and in 1941 the Supreme Court decided that this power extends to primary elections.[9] In 1872 Congress required elections to the House, except in Maine, to be held on Tuesday following the first Monday in November of even-numbered years.

Qualifications of Voters for Members of Congress

The Constitution provides that in each state the "electors," that is voters, for representatives in Congress "shall have the qualifications for electors of the most numerous branch of the state legislature." Not only did the electoral qualifications vary among the thirteen states in 1787 but some states had two different sets of voting qualifications for electing members of the two houses of the state legislature. "To have reduced the different qualifications in the different states to one uniform rule," wrote Hamilton in the *Federalist,* "would probably have been as dissatisfactory to some of the states as it would have been difficult to the Convention." The framers hit upon the shrewd expedient of accepting the state electorate for the most numerous branch of the legislature; consequently there are today forty-eight different electorates choosing the members of Congress. Since the Seventeenth Amendment prescribes precisely the same electorate for electing senators as representatives they too are chosen by as many different electorates as there are states. Because the Constitution prescribes these electoral qualifications the Supreme Court has decided that the right to vote for members of Congress is not derived from the constitution and laws of the state in which they are chosen, but has its foundation in the Federal Constitution.[10] Consequently the right to vote for members of Congress is a "privilege and immunity" of citizens of the United States which the Fourteenth Amendment forbids any state to "abridge."[11] Congress has by appropriate legislation provided protection of this privilege.

Election of United States Senators

The Constitution originally provided for the election of senators by the legislatures of their states. This seemed to be in harmony with the "Great Compromise" by which proportionate representation was given the states in the House of Representatives and equal representation in the Senate. The Senate was assumed to be peculiarly representative of the states as such; hence senators would appropriately be chosen by the chief organ of state government, the legislature. As to how the two houses of the state legislatures were to proceed in the election of senators the Constitution was silent and confusion consequently followed. In 1866 Congress, under its constitutional power over elections of members of the two houses, established a precise procedure for state legislatures to follow in electing

[8] *Ex parte* Yarbrough, 110 U.S. 651, 661 (1884).
[9] United States *v.* Classic, 313 U.S. 299 (1941).
[10] Minor *v.* Happersett, 21 Wallace 171 (1875).
[11] *Ex parte* Yarbrough, 110 U.S. 651 (1884).

senators. That this did not solve the problem was made evident by the fact that a generation later legislatures were consuming precious time deadlocked in senatorial elections when they ought to have been engrossed in their appropriate function of legislation. The legislature of Delaware, for example, in 1895 was tied up by the efforts of J. E. Addicks to get himself elected senator and the conflict continued for eight years. Senatorial elections habitually brought to bear upon state legislators the most intense pressures of powerful interests. Railroad lobbies were especially active in these contests. A strong demand for popular election of senators developed as the public became convinced that something should be done to check sinister influences. Proposal of a constitutional amendment for popular election of senators had been introduced in Congress as early as 1826 and President Johnson had recommended such an amendment to Congress in the later 1860's. Finally in 1913 the matter was settled by the adoption of the Seventeenth Amendment which requires election of senators by the voters of each state who are qualified to vote for the most numerous branch of the state legislature.

Contested Elections

The Constitution provides: "Each House shall be the judge of the election returns and qualifications of its members." This is unquestionably a judicial function and consequently it imposes a severe strain on the partisan majority of the chief political organ of the government. The century-old procedure in deciding contested elections as established by Congress requries that within thirty days after the certificate of election to the House of Representatives is filed with the clerk a protest may be filed setting forth the grounds to a counter-claim. Supporting testimony, depositions, and papers of both claimants are submitted to the House Committee on Elections. A member of this Committee in the early 1870's reported that despite the established procedure election cases were determined entirely by party feeling. [12] Apparently there has been an improvement in the judicial character of Congress's judgment or at any rate a decline of partisanship in deciding such election contests. An investigation of congressional election contests settled between 1917 and 1937 inclusive show that nearly two-thirds of the cases were settled in favor of the contestant belonging to the minority party as represented in the House. In that time Democratic Congresses seated nine Democrats and twenty Republicans while Republican Congresses seated thirteen Republicans and eighteen Democrats. There have been proposals to adopt the British practice of settling contested elections in the courts whose decision is then ratified

[12] There is a well-authenticated story about Thaddeus Stevens and the Committee on Elections of which he was a member. He entered the room while a hearing was going on and asked one of his Republican colleagues what was the point in the case. "There is not much point to it," was the answer. "They are both damned scoundrels." "Well," said Stevens, "which is the Republican damned scoundrel? I want to go for the Republican damned scoundrel."—George Frisbie Hoar: *Autobiography*, Vol. I, p. 268. On contested elections see also P. D. Hasbrouck: *Party Government in the House of Representatives*, pp. 39–41.

by a vote of the House of Commons. In 1925 Representative Dallinger introduced a bill to vest in the Court of Appeals of the District of Columbia the power to hear and pass upon all contested elections in the House subject only to final approval by that body, but the bill was defeated. [13]

QUALIFICATIONS OF SENATORS AND REPRESENTATIVES

Age

The Constitution requires a minimum age of twenty-five for eligibility as a member of the House of Representatives and thirty years for the Senate of the United States. The very word "senator" suggests age and maturity and the age requirement is obviously a reasonable one. As an appointee to fill a brief unexpired term, Henry Clay sat as a senator when he was only twenty-nine years old but this may have been tolerated because of the brevity of tenure under the appointment, and at any rate, it is exceptional. While still lacking the required age Clay was elected to the Senate in 1807 whereupon that body decided that, since he took his seat as an elected senator after attaining the age of thirty, it is sufficient if a senator possesses the qualifications of office when he takes his seat. This has become the accepted rule with respect to senators and representatives.

Citizenship

One must have been nine years a citizen of the United States to be eligible for the Senate, and seven years for the House. The Senate itself was only four years old when Albert Gallatin, later to be a notable secretary of the Treasury, was denied a seat after election to the Senate. A native of Geneva he had lived in the United States for thirteen years but had not been a citizen for nine years when he appeared to take his seat in 1793. The Senate has decided that the nine years of citizenship need not be complete at the time of election to the Senate but must be complete at the time of taking a seat in the Senate. When Hiram R. Revels of African descent was elected senator from Mississippi in 1870 the point was raised that the Fourteenth Amendment had conferred citizenship on the Negro only two years before. But the Senate majority then consisted of Republicans who had never accepted the dictum of the Dred Scott decision that Negroes could not be citizens within the meaning of the Constitution, and Revels was seated.

Residence

The Constitution requires that a representative in Congress "be an inhabitant of that state in which he shall be chosen." Evidently the voters of a congressional district might, if they chose to do so, elect as their representative anyone within the bounds of their state. A practically inflex-

[13] Vincent M. Barnett, Jr.: "Contested Congressional Elections in Recent Years." *Political Science Quarterly* (1939), 54:187–215.

ible custom has, however, added the requirement that a representative be an inhabitant of the district that elects him. This contrasts with the British practice of sometimes electing to Parliament a person not residing in the district that elects him. The American requirement of residence within the district became firmly established in colonial times. To this day the conviction persists that the representative is a neighbor representing the neighborhood and commissioned definitely to see that his district gets what is coming to it. In contrast with the British Member of Parliament who functions in a system sealed air tight against his getting special favors for his constituency, the American congressman is assigned so many special errands by his constituents that he has been denominated Uncle Sam's "bell boy." The collective pressures for favors induces the practice of "logrolling," by which, through mutual aid, congressmen satisfy the demands of their districts, particularly for appropriations. Thus the requirement of residence within his district tends to transform the representative into an agent of the district rather than a national legislator. Moreover the requirement is extremely wasteful of one of the nation's most precious resources, political talent. Someone has remarked that the seven ablest statesmen in the United States might live on the same street but only one of them at a time could be a representative in Congress. The British disregard of district residence would enable all seven of such statesmen to be elected by districts throughout Britain.

Officeholding

One of the most significant provisions of the Constitution is that "no person holding any office under the United States, shall be a member of either house during his continuance in office." This contrasts with the British parliamentary system's requirement that the chief officers or ministers hold seats in Parliament. The Constitution's rule against congressmen's holding Federal office insures the formal separation of legislative and executive powers. But it was not so much political theory that induced the framers to include this provision in the Constitution as their abhorrence of the appalling corruption of British politics in their day. Vivid in their memory was the "King's Friends," the British political party consisting of the personal following of George III built up by the Crown's unblushing awards of lucrative offices to Members of Parliament. The King's personal following constituted the parliamentary majority that sustained the ministry whose obnoxious policies were responsible for the Revolutionary War. Usage has carried the separation of powers far beyond the letter of the Constitution by denying cabinet members even the privilege of appearing and speaking in Congress. However, the separation is largely formal and by one means or another legislation and its execution are usually coordinated. Congress itself has decided that "civil office" in the constitutional sense means a position with a tenure of some duration and with substantial compensation and duties. Appointments to positions with transient, occasional, or incidental duties are not considered constitutionally incompatible with service in Congress. For example, the presidential appointment of senators to serve on peace commissions following the Spanish American War did not require the appointees to resign their seats in the Senate. A civil officer may be a candidate for and even be elected to the Senate or House but he must resign from the civil office before taking the oath as a member of either house.

The Judging of Election Qualifications

In the words of the Constitution: "Each house shall be the judge of the elections, returns, and qualifications of its members." The provision might as well have read, "sole judge," since the power is vested in each house without any qualification whatever. Consequently no appeal can be made to the courts, although the courts have decided cases involving such questions as the right of the houses to summon witnesses and compel them to answer questions involving the matter of the qualifications of congressmen. [14] Congress has, then, taken the word "judge" seriously, and it follows at least a semblance of judicial procedure in gathering evidence and judging qualifications. However, a persistent question remains concerning just what is meant by the term "qualifications" as used in the clause. Two divergent views are held by authorities. One is that the Constitution states all the qualifications to be considered by Congress, and that, if a district or state elects someone who meets these requirements, the house to which he has been elected has no choice but to seat him no matter how unfit it may consider him to be. According to this view unfitness is not a valid reason for expulsion by a two-thirds vote. A second view holds that either house may by statute impose additional tests that accord with established usage, including such obvious matters of unfitness as, for example, conviction of a crime. The House of Representatives was acting under the latter interpretation when, in 1900, it refused to seat Brigham H. Roberts who had been elected a representative from Utah. Roberts was charged with the practice of polygamy in violation of law. This action was of course vigorously contested on the ground that the House was adding to the qualifications fixed by the Constitution. In 1928 William S. Vare of Pennsylvania and Frank Smith who had been elected to the Senate from Illinois were both denied seats on the grounds of the vast sums of money spent in their election campaigns. Apparently the precedent has been firmly established that the two houses of Congress will refuse to seat persons possessing the specified qualifications of the Constitution if their election was accomplished by methods considered subversive of public policy even though not in themselves criminal.

Power of the Houses to Expel Members

The Constitution empowers each house to "punish its members for disorderly behavior, and, with the concurrence of two-thirds, expel a member." In contrast with the power dealt with in the preceding paragraph

14 Smith v. Allwright, 321 U.S. 649 (1944).

this provision is concerned with the power of the houses over members who have been seated. The Supreme Court has held that the power to punish members for disorderly behavior "may be, in a proper case, by imprisonment, and it may be for refusal to obey some rule on that subject made by the house for the preservation of order." [15] In 1861 senators who went with their seceding states were expelled from the Senate on the ground of conspiracy against their government. Senator Andrew Johnson, representing the seceded state of Tennessee, retained his seat. Senator Philander C. Knox in 1907 stated what may be accepted as the guiding standard of the two houses in exercising the power of expulsion of members: "The Constitution enables the Senate to protect itself against improper characters by expelling them . . . if they are guilty of crime, offense of immorality, disloyalty or gross impropriety during their service." [16] Respect for the representative principle and the sovereignty of the electorate has impelled both houses and especially the Senate to exercise the power of expulsion with extreme moderation.

Filling Vacancies

The Constitution provides: "When vacancies happen in the representation from any state, the executive authority thereof shall issue writs of election to fill such vacancies." These "special elections" to fill vacancies in the House of Representatives occur at irregular intervals in different sections of the country and are watched with interest by political leaders as indicators of shifts in party electoral strength. Usually the states provide by law for the "time and place" of holding special elections but in the absence of such legislation the governor of a state may fix the time on the basis of the power vested in him by the Constitution of the United States. The filling of vacancies in the Senate has been changed in accordance with the shift from election of senators by state legislatures to direct election by the voters established by Seventeenth Amendment. The Senate is the sole judge of when there is a vacancy; and there has at times been prolonged controversy over whether a vacancy exists. The Seventeenth Amendment provides: "When vacancies happen in the representation of any state in the Senate, the Executive authority of such state shall issue writs of election to fill such vacancies: Provided that the legislature of any state may empower the Executive thereof to make temporary appointments until the people fill the vacancies by election as the legislature may direct."

PRIVILEGES AND IMMUNITIES

Compensation

The Constitution provides that senators and representatives shall receive a compensation for their services, to be ascertained by law and paid out

[15] Kilbourn *v.* Thompson, 103 U.S. 168, 189 (1881).
[16] *Congressional Record*, 59th Congress, 2nd Session, 2935.

of the Treasury of the United States. The first draft of the Constitution provided for the payment of members of both houses by their respective states, and the change to payment by the United States was a distinct improvement. This signified that Congress was to be recognized theoretically as a national legislature rather than an assembly of ambassadors. Since the compensation of members of the two houses is "ascertained by law" they determine their own salaries. For the first quarter of a century the compensation was set at six dollars for each day in attendance. From 1815 to 1817 it was $1,500 but so great was the resentment of the voters at this extravagance that most members who voted for the raise lost their seats in the next election and the salary was then set at eight dollars a day which remained unchanged until 1855 when the annual salary was fixed at $3,000 a year. Raises in 1865, 1907, and 1925 brought congressional salaries to $10,000 a year where it remained until 1947. By the Congressional Reorganization Act of 1946 the salary was raised to $12,500 a year plus an annual tax-free expense account of $2,500. In 1955 Congress raised the salaries of Senators and Representatives to $22,500 without the $2,500 expense account. Upon attaining the age of 62 a former Senator or Representative with at least six years of service becomes eligible for a pension proportionate to his length of service. Thirty years of service would entitle a congressman to an annual pension of $9,375 which, however, is the maximum. In 1789 congressmen were allowed six dollars for each twenty miles of traveling to and from the capital. Since 1865 the allowance has been twenty cents a mile going to and returning from the capital by the nearest route for regular sessions. Before free railroad passes were prohibited in 1906, this was clear gain. Each senator and representative is provided with a large office, completely furnished. He pays nothing for stationery, and his mail goes free. A representative is allowed approximately $25,000 annually and a senator proportionately more to hire clerks. Each senator also has an administrative assistant at $13,500.

The Privilege of Immunity From Arrest

Because legislative duties were considered of paramount importance the framers provided that senators and representatives "shall, in all cases, except treason, felony and breach of the peace, be privileged from arrest during their attendance at the session of their respective houses, and in going to and returning from the same." This provision was lifted from the Articles of Confederation with slight rephrasing that left the meaning intact. Under court interpretation this privilege has proved to be less significant than it would seem at first glance. The exemption does not include immunity from service of judicial process in civil or criminal cases. [17] Indeed the words "treason, felony and breach of peace" are held to include all criminal offenses; [18] from these, of course, the congressman has no priv-

---

[17] Long v. Ansell, 293 U.S. 76 (1934).
[18] Williamson v. United States, 207 U.S. 446 (1908).

ilege of immunity from arrest. "Indeed," writes E. S. Corwin, "since the abolition of imprisonment for debt the immunity has lost most of its significance." [19] For more than a century, then, the privilege has been rather empty. For whatever it may be worth it does, however, apply immediately upon the election of a member before he has been sworn in and, if he is denied a seat, the privilege continues to apply until his return to his home. [20]

Freedom from Prosecution for Legislative Action

In order completely to protect senators and representatives in the exercise of their legislative function the Constitution provides that "for any speech or debate in either house they shall not be questioned in any other place." The source of this provision is the English Bill of Rights of 1689 but so stoutly had the colonial legislatures insisted upon it that the framers must have considered it an American device. The purpose of the provision is to support the rights of the people by enabling their representatives to perform the functions of their office without fear of prosecutions, civil or criminal. [21] The protection is not limited merely to words spoken in debate but extends to written reports, to the act of voting, and to things generally done by members of Congress in relation to the business before it. [22] So broad indeed is the judicial interpretation of this privilege that defamatory words uttered during a speech in the Senate are held to be absolutely privileged despite the allegation that they were not spoken in discharge of a senator's official duties. [23] However, the immunity does not apply when a member of either house quotes or publishes, outside of his house, libelous words spoken there. There are, of course, restraints upon a congressman since he is subject to the rules of his house which may penalize him even to the extent of expulsion. The political effect of his utterances on his constituents also serves to restrain him.

THE PERSONNEL OF CONGRESS

Vocational Composition of Congress

In the thirty-fifth number of the *Federalist* Hamilton predicted that "the representative body, with too few exceptions to have any influence on the spirit of the government, will be composed of land holders, merchants, and men of the learned professions." With a proper allowance for the increased complexity of society this prophecy holds essentially true today although landholders have declined in percentage since the early days of

[19] Edward S. Corwin: *The Constitution and What It Means Today.* Princeton, 1946, p. 16.
[20] Dunton *v.* Holstead, 2 *Pennsylvania Law Journal Rep.*, 450 (Clark) (1840).
[21] Coffin *v.* Coffin, 4 Mass. 1 (1808), approved in Kilbourn *v.* Thompson, 103 U.S. 204 (1881).
[22] Ibid.
[23] Cochran *v.* Couzens, 42 F (2d) 783, certiorari denied 282 U.S. 874 (1930).

the republic. Of the 531 members of the Senate and House in the Seventy-ninth Congress 3.4 per cent were agriculturalists; 13.5 per cent were connected with business; while the "learned professions" claimed 64.6 per cent. The legal profession alone accounted for 57 per cent, and the pattern of thinking of this element has an enormous influence upon their work as legislators. Most of the committee chairmen are lawyers. A natural consequence of the extraordinary overweighting of the membership with lawyers is the marked tendency of Congress to consider public policies legalistically, to look upon the law and the courts as the "touchstone of wisdom." [24] A paradoxical effect of this superabundance of lawyers is that in Congress the judiciary enjoys greater prestige than Congress itself, an attitude probably not to be found in any legislative body outside the United States.

Social Structure of Congress

The median age of members of the House of Representatives has risen from forty-two in the early days of the nation to fifty-two today. For a generation before the Civil War it stood quite steadily near forty-one. The average age of senators in 1944 was fifty-nine. Since the average adult in the United States is forty-three, the age groups under forty-three are quite under-represented by corresponding age groups in Congress. An analysis of the Seventy-Seventh Congress revealed that all the large religious denominations were represented though not in any approximate proportion to their relative strength. The affiliations of representatives and senators were, respectively: Roman Catholic, 20 per cent and 11 per cent; Methodists, 17 per cent and 22 per cent; Presbyterian, 13 per cent and 11 per cent; Episcopalian, 11 per cent and 10 per cent; Lutheran, 4 per cent and 2 per cent. One in every six of the members of the Seventy-Seventh Congress had, at one time or another, been a teacher.[25] If Congress is more conservative than the country at large it should be noted that it is essentially middle class. Only one member of the Seventy-Seventh Congress listed himself as a factory worker, and members of laboring class as such or the so-called "Have Nots" are very scarce in Congress. Much of the conservatism of Congress can be attributed to the fact that metropolitan centers, whence the urge for social amelioration through legislation so largely derives, are grossly under-represented. Not only are the non-urban districts over-represented but they tend to continue the same person in Congress for several terms so that, no matter which major party controls Congress, conservative agrarian representatives become through seniority the chairmen of committees and thereby enormously influence legislation in accordance with the prevailing conservative social philosophies of their districts. One-party districts tend to dominate legislation. Thus the dice are loaded against the metropolitan interests whose

[24] Roland Young: *This Is Congress.* New York, 1946, p. 154.
[25] M. M. McKinney: "The Personnel of the Seventy-Seventh Congress." *American Political Science Review* (1942), 36:67–74.

representatives seldom acquire the seniority that would put them in charge of the committees.

Preparation of a Congressman

Over one-fourth of the Seventy-Seventh Congress had served an apprenticeship in law-making in their state legislatures. One-fifth had been prosecutors or district attorneys and eleven had presided over courts of law. Twenty had been mayors of cities, eighteen had been state governors, and fourteen had been members of state constitutional conventions.[26]

Formal Education—Eighty-second Congress *
(Compiled from Congressional Directory, Eighty-second Congress)

	Senate		House	
	Number	Per Cent	Number	Per Cent
Graduate degree	1	1.04	2	.5
College degree	67	69.8	282	64.2
Some College attendance	13	13.5	62	14.3
Business School	0	0	16	3.6
Secondary School	6	6.3	16	3.6
Public School	3	3.1	18	4.1
No formal schooling	6	6.3	43	9.8

* Includes territorial delegates.

SESSIONS

Regular Sessions of Congress

The Twentieth Amendment provides: "Congress shall assemble at least once in every year, and such meeting shall begin at noon on the 3d day of January, unless they shall by law appoint a different day." This provision remedied a defective schedule of sessions that had prevailed for nearly a century and a half. In 1788 the Congress of the Articles of Confederation had provided that the First Congress under the new Constitution should date from the first Wednesday in March, 1789, which fell on the fourth, and since the Constitution had fixed the term of a representative at two years the life of a Congress thereafter regularly ended and a new one began on March 4 of odd-numbered years. In 1872 Congress set the first Tuesday after the first Monday of even-numbered years as the time for congressional elections. The Constitution had provided for at least one meeting a year to begin on the first Monday in December and since this session continued until Congress chose to adjourn it came to be known as the long session. Obviously, this schedule was set to the tempo of travel by sailing vessel, stage coach, and horseback. Unless the president decided to convene Congress in special session a person elected to Congress in November of an even-numbered year would not begin his legislative duties until December of the following year, thirteen months later. By that time he would be nearing the next election and would be appealing

[26] Ibid., pp. 70, 71.

for re-election before he had begun to learn the difficult art of legislation and before he had any record on which his constituents could base their judgment.

The Lame Duck Session

The very worst feature of the old order before the adoption of the Twentieth Amendment was that a representative defeated in the November election nevertheless resumed his seat a month later in the "short session" which continued until the end of his term. Thus for three months he continued to represent a constituency that had repudiated him at the polls. He was what has been colloquially denominated a "lame duck," that is a defeated candidate for re-election; so numerous were such persons in the "short session" that it came to be known as the "lame duck" session. Sometimes they constituted a majority. Naturally, under the circumstances, the House could be quite unrepresentative of current public opinion. For example, the deflationary Resumption of Specie Payments Act of 1875 was passed by a "lame duck" Congress just before the recently elected inflationary new House would have an opportunity to legislate otherwise or even refuse to enact any current legislation. When the Christmas holidays were subtracted, only about ten weeks remained of the short session, scarcely time for more than passage of the indispensable appropriation bills. The situation invited filibustering by minorities, particularly in the Senate, and powerful interests could thereby prevent legislation objectionable to them. Moreover when the Electoral College failed to elect a president it was always a "lame duck" House of Representatives that elected the president. For example, it was a Federalist House of Representatives that chose between two Republicans, Thomas Jefferson and Aaron Burr, in 1801 and that came near defeating the intention of the electorate. The Twentieth Amendment did not absolutely abolish "lame duck" sessions since the president can still call a special session soon after an election in which defeated congressmen would sit. This possibility is insignificant and the evils of the short session have been quite effectively eliminated.

Special Sessions

The Constitution provides that the president "may, on extraordinary occasion, convene both houses, or either of them, and in case of disagreement between them with respect to the time of adjournment, he may adjourn them to such time as he shall think proper." The president has never had an opportunity to adjourn Congress, and Congress is jealous enough of executive power to prevent, by avoiding disagreement, his ever exercising the power. Presidents are inclined to feel relieved when Congress is not in session and they are consequently reluctant to call extra sessions. Polling by the Institute of Public Opinion indicates that the president's popularity tends to rise when Congress is not in session. There have been more presidents than extra sessions. Again and again a special session has been the starting-point of a chain of misfortunes that have prevented the re-election of the president who called it. Examples are the special sessions called by President Taft in 1909 and 1913 and by President Hoover in 1929. As soon as it is convened in special session the president, by message or address, informs Congress of his purpose in convening it. However he has no control over its agenda and Congress once in session can even ignore the purpose for which it was called. While it has never done this it has more than once wandered far afield of the president's purpose.

The president's power to summon Congress involves the power not to do so. Lincoln, for example, had a free hand in dealing with the emergency created by secession and the fall of Fort Sumter during the eleven weeks until the date he had set for a special session. Four years later President Johnson by not calling a special session in the nine months following Lincoln's assassination gained a free hand in carrying on reconstruction but his action alienated Congress.

Adjournment

This term signifies merely the suspension of a session and has no further effect on legislative business than to suspend consideration of it for the time being. The Constitution prescribes that "neither house, during the session of Congress, shall, without the consent of the other, adjourn for more than three days, nor to any other place than that in which the two houses are sitting." Without this provision either house might stall the operation of the national legislature since the houses function in a manner complementary to each other. Near the close of a regular session the House customarily adjourns for three-day intervals while the more deliberate Senate catches up on legislation. As a session draws near its close, a joint committee of the two houses may confer to agree upon a time of adjournment. Congress could, by adjourning for brief intervals from time to time, practically nullify the president's power to call extra sessions. Indeed, since the Constitution itself requires Congress to assemble once a year on the third day of January, Congress could through repeated adjournments make itself practically a perpetual body for the duration of each Congress.

SUMMARY

The framers of the Constitution modeled Congress on the pattern of the prevailing bicameral state legislature. Each state was permitted two senators but in the House of Representatives each state was to be represented in proportion to its population. The House of Representatives kept increasing after each reapportionment until in 1910 it had 435 members. Congress then attempted to prevent further increase by prescribing an automatic reapportionment of representatives among the states following each census.

Congress has authority to reapportion, but the state legislatures fix the boundaries of the congressional districts. They frequently delay this for many years with the consequence that rapidly growing urban regions are under-represented and sparsely populated rural regions correspondingly over-represented.

The single-member district system tends to give the victorious party in a congressional election more than its proportionate share of the representatives. The Constitution gives Congress considerable control of congressional elections. It not only prescribes the qualifications of senators and representatives but also makes each house of Congress judge of the qualifications of its members. Each house of Congress also settles contested elections of its members and has power to discipline its members even to the extent of expulsion.

Congress does not represent proportionally the elements of American society. For example, a majority of its members are lawyers while less than one-seventh are business men, one-thirtieth are agriculturalists, and laborers as such are scarcely there at all.

CHAPTER XXII

THE ORGANIZATION OF CONGRESS

THE HOUSE OF REPRESENTATIVES

Organizing the House of Representatives

IT IS only a group of representatives-elect that gather in the chamber of the House of Representatives on the third day of January of odd-numbered years. Since the terms of the members who have been re-elected has expired, the group legally consists of 435 private citizens up to the moment when the oath is administered to them as representatives. Inasmuch as nothing done by way of organization by a preceding Congress is binding on a succeeding one a new set of representatives is, at the beginning of a new Congress, without any legal organization whatever. Consequently at the beginning of the Eightieth Congress the House of Representatives organized for the eightieth time. The rules of the last preceding House are no longer valid and general parliamentary law is followed until the previous rules of the House have been revised, reported, and adopted. Sheer usage long decreed that the clerk of the last House should preside while the new House was starting its organization; that duty is now vested in him by statute. He calls the assembly to order and reads the roll of members-elect. The former clerk of the House continues to preside while the speaker is being elected. Although this action takes the form of a deliberate election by the House it amounts, in fact, to nothing more than a ratification by majority party vote of the choice of a speaker already determined by party caucus or conference. The speaker-elect is escorted to the chair by the defeated candidate of the minority party and the oath of office is administered to the speaker by the member of the House with the longest service. Then the speaker administers the oath to the other members in a body, and the House proceeds to elect a clerk, a sergeant-at-arms, a door-keeper, a postmaster and a chaplain, all of which really amounts to a ratification of the slate already decided on by the majority party caucus or conference.

THE SPEAKER

The Background of the Speaker's Power

Despite the formal reduction of the speaker's power a generation ago he remains today the second most powerful national officer. While the title is derived from England the office of Speaker of the House of Representatives contrasts in every essential feature with that of the Speaker of the House of Commons. The latter is an impartial moderator required by usage to exercise a severely judicial impartiality between the minority and the majority of the House of Commons. The Speaker of the House of Representatives, on the contrary, is an unblushing, partisan majority leader invested by usage with the duty of seeing that no opportunity to promote the will of the majority party is neglected. This peculiar characteristic of the American speaker is rooted in colonial experience. The speaker of the colonial assembly provided the rallying point of popular opinion as the champion of the people in countering the power of the colonial governor. This tradition of leadership has persisted unbroken in the legislatures of many states and in the national House of Representatives.

Henry Clay and the Speakership

Henry Clay started the development of the speakership of the national House of Representatives into the leadership of the majority. He came to the office fresh from the speakership of the Kentucky lower house. His imperious mastery of the national House of Representatives was vividly displayed in his subordination of the hitherto incorrigible Representative John Randolph of Virginia, one time floor leader of the Jeffersonian Republicans. In May, 1812, not long after Clay had assumed the office of speaker, Randolph rose to speak against a declaration of war. A member promptly made the point of order that there was no motion before the House. Randolph explained that his remarks were introductory to a motion, whereupon Speaker Clay ruled that the motion must precede the remarks. When Randolph moved that "it is not expedient at this time to resort to war against Great Britain" Clay refused to permit him to speak before the motion was seconded. Randolph appealed to the House which promptly sustained the Speaker. When a seconder was found Randolph was halted by a ruling that the House must vote on the question of considering the motion. [1] Clay was the first speaker to seek control of legislation through standing committees.

The Congressional Revolution of 1890

Second only to Clay in his influence on the development of the speakership was Thomas B. Reed who fortified the powers of the office and used them to resolve a crisis in congressional government. In the late 1880's the House

[1] Homer C. Hockett: *Political and Social Growth of the American People.* New York, 1940, p. 412.

of Representatives had degenerated into a condition of incredible parliamentary anarchy. Filibustering had come to be accepted as inevitable. Democratic Representatives, when their party was slightly in the minority, would raise the point of "no quorum" and then compel adjournment by refusing to answer roll-call. The custom then was not to count a representative as present on such a roll-call unless he answered to his name when read by the clerk. The Fiftieth Congress once remained in continuous session for eight days and nights of filibustering during which there were over one hundred roll-calls on dilatory motions to adjourn and to take a recess and amendments to these motions. In 1890 Speaker Reed decided to end this travesty on legislation. Accordingly, at the end of a roll-call that fell short of a quorum, he directed the clerk to count as present and not voting several Democrats he named. In the face of furious denunciation he stood firm and his ruling was written into a permanent House rule which was eventually sustained by the Supreme Court. [2] Reed completed his control of filibustering by resolutely refusing to recognize any member until satisfied that his purpose was not a dilatory motion. After this "Revolution of 1890," the House never relapsed into the impotence of the 1880's but Reed's imperious methods won him the epithet "Czar Reed."

The Counter-revolution of 1910

In the first decade of the twentieth century, under Speaker Joseph G. Cannon, the office became so much more powerful and dictatorial that his methods resulted in the coinage of a new term, "Cannonism." This dictatorship was achieved through the speaker's power of recognition and even more his power to appoint committees whereby he could make or break members virtually at will. As chairman of the Committee on Rules which he appointed and dominated the speaker could determine what measures the House would consider. Cannon's consistent and arbitrary promotion of conservative or even reactionary legislation in a decade when the Progressive Movement was rising to a climax headed his regime into a crisis. His dictatorship was ended in March, 1910, by a combination of Democrats and insurgent Republicans who succeeded in removing the speaker permanently from the Committee on Rules and in 1911 the speaker was deprived of the power to appoint committees which have ever since been nominally elected by the House. Thus the "czar" was dethroned and the leadership of the House put "in commission."

The Revival of the Speaker's Power

So marked has been the recent revival of the speaker's mastery of the House that today it probably does not fall much short of "Czar" Cannon's dictatorial power in the first decade of this century. The speaker scarcely needs to be chairman of the powerful Rules Committee or to appoint its personnel in order to block a motion for a rule not to his liking. As chieftain of the

[2] United States *v.* Ballin, 144 U.S. 1, 5–6 (1892).

House majority organization he can go far toward regimenting his party. A recalcitrant party member may be reminded by the speaker that the funds of the party's Congressional Committee are available to retire him to private life by financing a rival candidate of his own party at the next nominating primary. Such a threat is of less value to a Democratic Speaker because of the independence of congressmen from one-party districts of the South. He remembers this when shaping his party program. Republicans maintain better floor attendance when crucial issues are at stake. Czar Cannon himself never achieved more perfect party regimentation than the vote of every one of the 236 Republicans present against recommitting the Knutson tax bill in the Eightieth Congress.

Preserving Order

The speaker presides over the House of Representatives and announces the order of business. It is his duty to maintain order and to this end he has authority to suspend all business. He may mention by name an unruly member but only the House can impose punishment or censure upon the offender. In case of extreme disorder the speaker may direct the sergeant-at-arms to restore order. This is presumed to be accomplished by carrying through the aisles the mace, ancient symbol of authority in legislative bodies. The speaker may direct the galleries cleared if visitors are disorderly and his authority extends to the corridors, passages, and rooms in the House wing. Drastic action by the speaker is seldom required since a word of caution usually suffices.

The Power of Recognition

Since 1881 there has been no appeal from the speaker's power of recognition. To a large extent custom guides the speaker in determining who is to be recognized. When a bill is under discussion the speaker recognizes first the member of the committee in charge of the measure, usually the chairman. Committee members enjoy priority in speaking on the measure and usually the speaker is provided with a list of those scheduled by the committee to speak pro and con. However, the speaker is not bound by this list but may exercise his discretion. Customarily when addressed by a member the speaker inquires: "For what purpose does the gentlemen rise?" Unless he is satisfied by the reply the speaker may say: "The gentleman is not recognized for that purpose." Thus he may forestall dilatory tactics or prevent interference with the plans of the majority as they may have been determined by party conference or caucus or by the Committee on Rules. Though the power of the speaker appears to be dictatorial, responsibility must be lodged somewhere if the House is not to lapse into anarchy. By and large the elaborate system of time honored customs hedging about the discretionary power of the speaker saves that office from degenerating into a mere personal dictatorship. Usage sets the pattern of the office.

Deciding Points of Order

Much of the speaker's power in legislation inheres in his duty of deciding points of order as members raise them. No matter how elaborate the rules governing House procedure or how many the recorded rulings that have become precedents, situations arise never before encountered. These may require decisions on points of order. The speaker familiarizes himself with the rules and precedents of the House but the number of precedents is so great that the House supplies the speaker with an expert parliamentarian. Thus fortified he may make his decisions in accordance with the precedents but he is not bound to do so. However he dare not become too arbitrary since his decision may be appealed to the House. Any member may raise a point of order whereupon the question at issue is put to a vote and the speaker is usually sustained. Lively debate may follow the raising of a point of order before it is put to a vote. Sometimes the speaker submits a point of order himself concerning his jurisdiction or asks a member to raise a point so that his judgment may receive House sanction. The speaker's decisions on points of order are entered on the journal of the House and take their place in the long line of precedents.

Routine Duties

Although by the revolution of 1910–11 the speaker lost the power to appoint standing committees he still appoints the select or special committees and the House members of the special joint conference committees. After a measure has passed the two houses in somewhat different forms, it is assigned to a joint conference committee which is expected to compromise differences between Senate and House. Another important power of the speaker inheres in his duty of assigning new bills to what he considers the appropriate committees for their consideration. When a bill is reported from a committee he assigns it to one of the House calendars. The speaker puts questions to a vote and signs bills that have passed the House as well as all warrants and subpoenas issued in the name of the House. In brief he acts for the House in all formal legal matters.

The Speaker as a Party Leader

Though it is not required by the Constitution, the speaker is always a member of the House and also of the majority party. He attains the position of speaker as a consequence of seniority in service in the House combined with aptitude for and experience in party leadership. Joseph G. Cannon had served eight terms in the House before election as speaker; Champ Clark, eight terms; Frederick H. Gillett, twelve terms; and Joseph W. Martin, seven terms. This requirement of prolonged continuous service means that close congressional districts provide no speakers; they are supplied instead by practically one-party districts. Thus every Democratic speaker since the Civil War, with but a single exception, has been from a Southern state. Normally the speaker, through qualities of leadership, first attains the floor leadership of his party, often when it is in the minority in the House, and then succeeds to the speakership when his party obtains a majority in the House.

The Speaker Still Master of the Rules Committee

Depriving speakers of the chairmanship of the Committee on Rules and of the power to appoint its members in 1910–11 has not had the decisive effect that is often assumed. He is still its master and will be as long as, through the power of recognition, he can foil any of its plans that are contrary to his purposes. He can adroitly direct a trusted personal follower to raise a point of order on some technicality and thus forestall incipient insurgency on the part of the Committee. So well understood is all this that it would be considered futile to attempt to pack the Committee on Rules with members not agreeable to the speaker. Consequently the speaker's party selects as members of this Committee only representatives who are acceptable to him. No important business is likely to be considered by the House until the Rules Committee has reported a rule granting that business the right of way. Thus the House is rendered subservient to the Rules Committee which, as we have seen, seldom acts contrary to the speaker's desires. "Prior to 1910," wrote George W. Galloway, "the Speaker controlled the House in collaboration with a coterie of trusted party lieutenants. Since 1910 the leadership has been in commission. The chief difference between the old oligarchy and the new is that the control of the House was formerly open, centralized, and responsible, whereas today it is invisible, dispersed, and irresponsible. Formerly the country could see the wheels go round, but now it cannot. Despite the overthrow of Cannonism, the Speakership thus continues to be the most powerful office in Congress." [3]

PARTY ORGANIZATION IN CONGRESS
Floor Leaders and Whips

The majority and the minority party each, through caucus or conference, selects a floor leader in each house. After the "dethroning" of the speaker in 1910 the burden of the floor leader, particularly of the majority party, became so onerous that he has been relieved of all committee duty. The floor leader is charged with the management of his party on the floor of the House and he performs this function in close cooperation with committee chairmen and the party steering committee. The party caucus or conference may decide party strategy but the floor leader is the tactician for seeing to its execution. This requires leadership, sleepless vigilance, knowledge of the rules, fertility of resource, courage, and cool calculation. It be-

[3] George B. Galloway: *Congress at the Crossroads.* New York, 1946, p. 117.

comes a game of wits between majority and minority floor leaders with the dice loaded in favor of the former through understandings with the speaker and the party leaders. Majority and minority floor leaders confer over the list of party representatives scheduled to speak and arrange the allotment of time and speakers. The majority floor leader may turn over the management of debate on a measure to the chairman of the committee in charge of it. As the pressure of time increases late in a session speeches may be limited to five minutes or even one minute. Since 1900 each floor leader has appointed and has been aided by a whip and a number of assistant whips. The duty of a whip is to canvass his party members on important issues and ascertain for the floor leader how many voters can be depended on in support of party measures or against measures the party is opposing. When an important measure comes to a vote the whips must see that the party members are on hand, and to this end absentees may be gathered from all over Washington. By various acts of persuasion the whips try to hold party members faithful to the party line.

The Steering Committee

This is not an official congressional committee but an extra-legal party committee and each party in each house has one. The name is rather a misnomer since they do little steering. Instead they recommend to their respective party members the order in which bills remaining on the calendar ought to be taken up. Since 1933 the Republican Steering Committee of the House has consisted of the floor leader and one representative from each of seven states. The Democratic Steering Committee of the House includes the floor leader, the chairman of the caucus, the party whip, the ranking party member of the Ways and Means, the Appropriation, and the Rules committees, and one representative from each of fifteen areas into which the United States has been divided for this purpose. The Democratic Steering Committee of the Senate includes seventeen senators, the Democratic floor leader, the Democratic whip and the secretary of the Democratic caucus. There are nine members of the Republican Steering Committee of the Senate among whom are the chairman of the party conference, the floor leader and the party whip. The Republican Steering Committee of the Senate holds weekly meetings while the Senate is in session and discusses party policy, the legislative program, and floor tactics, but no Republican senator feels bound by its recommendations.

The House Rules Committee

By gradual accretion of power this Committee has come to be practically the governing committee of the House. It consists of twelve members, eight from the majority party, four from the minority party. The Rules Committee, of course, merely "reports," that is makes recommendations, to the House. But such is the tradition of party regularity that with rare exceptions the majority party sustains the Rules Committee in its "reports." Over the years, rulings of the speaker favorable to the Rules Committee have built up its power so that its reports have precedence over those of all other committees. Through its power to report special orders or rules it can determine not only what bills the House of Representatives may consider but even the particular form in which it will have the opportunity to consider them. It modifies measures prepared by important committees, even their substance, as a condition of their reaching the floor at all. Through the control of the time alloted to debate it can facilitate or hamper the amending of pending measures and thereby determine whether they can be modified and shaped so as to obtain the vote required for passage. Late in the session the calendars are always crowded and if bills were taken in turn important legislation would not be reached. The power of the Rules Committee has grown largely through its power to take or refuse to take bills off the calendar out of their regular order for consideration. Other committees are at the mercy of the Rules Committee with respect to their size, jurisdiction, and privileges which it can alter almost at will. The autocratic power of the Committee has been the subject of severe criticism and bitter denunciation but those who believe in some semblance of party responsibility in legislation seem disposed to accept as inevitable the dominance of the Committee on Rules of the House of Representatives. [4]

Because in the Eightieth Congress the Rules Committee of the House had been a bottle neck that held up important bills which the House was ready to pass and because of the severe rebuke administered to that Congress in the election of 1948, the Democratic majority in the next Congress took prompt and decisive steps in January, 1949, to curb permanently that power of the Rules Committee. The House rules were so changed that whenever the Rules Committee failed to clear a bill within twenty-one days after it was placed on a House calendar the chairman of the committee that reported the bill could move to bring it before the House for consideration on one of the days when such a motion is in order for that calendar. The new rule directed the speaker of the House to recognize the committee chairman for that purpose. Conceivably, under party discipline such as Speaker Joseph Martin maintained over the Republican majority in the Eightieth Congress, the twenty-one day rule might have been dead letter. Conservatives during the Eighty-first Congress fretted under its restraints. During the next Congress, a Southern Democratic representative moved the repeal of the twenty-one day rule. Republicans joined Southern Democrats in supporting the repeal; consequently the Rules Committee has resumed its practical dictatorship over legislation.

The Caucus or Conference

The congressional caucus or conference is a voluntary and extra-legal association or meeting of the members of each party in either house presumably for the purpose of trying to get concerted action on legislation or other

[4] Ibid., pp. 111–15.

matters. Its primary problem is to compromise differences within the party membership so that the party may come as close as possible to presenting a united front. In practice, however, the caucus functions perfectly only in getting party agreement on its candidates for speaker and the other officers and on its committee nominees. The House caucuses meet a few days before the opening of a new Congress to set up a permanent organization and select these candidates. Since the Senate is a continuous body its caucuses for organizational purposes are held only when vacancies occur or when there is a change of party majority in the upper house. Two factors make it difficult for the caucus of either house to obtain agreement either pro or con on controversial issues: Each major party has a conservative and a liberal wing, and each party reveals sectional as well as urban and rural cleavages. Finally each party is hampered in arriving at common action by the almost universal American conviction that a congressman is an agent of his district, a connection that encourages in congressmen a tendency to become free lances.

The Democratic Caucus Compared with the Republican Conference

In theory at least, the Democratic caucus of the House binds all in attendance to support any measure receiving a two-thirds majority if that also constitutes two-thirds of the Democratic membership in the House. However no Democratic member is to be bound to a caucus action that involves interpretation of the Constitution of the United States or that is contrary to pledges he made to his constituents or contrary to instructions of his nominating authority. Under Speaker Joseph G. Cannon the Republican caucus had declined to insignificance and after he was "dethroned" the party practically abandoned the caucus. The Republicans have substituted for it what they call a conference. In it there is an airing of the views of party members but whatever conclusions are reached are purely advisory. There is, however, despite the weakness of the party conference sufficient party regularity among Republican representatives in the House to sustain the party organization functioning through the speaker, Rules Committee, Steering Committee, floor leader, and party whips.

The Decline of the Caucus

The party caucus reached a peak of power when the Democrats captured the House in 1910 after the dethroning of Speaker Cannon. So dominant did it become that someone described the transition as a shift from "Czar Cannon" to "King Caucus." Since then the caucus has declined until today it is less a means of reaching party consensus on legislation than an instrument for strengthening party leadership by giving it a vote of party confidence. Thus disaffected party members may urge convening a caucus in order to discredit party leadership. This explains why, when Democratic senators asked for a caucus in 1939, Floor Leader Senator Barkley felt a mere meeting would be equivalent to a repudiation of his leadership and threatened to resign whereupon no caucus was called. [5] One cause of the decline of the caucus has been the increasing pressure of duties upon congressmen which leaves less and less time for extra gatherings.

Executive Leadership In Legislation

The president and his cabinet were, of course, excluded from the party caucus, and increasing executive initiative in legislation has been a factor in the decline of the party caucus as a source of legislative action. During the long incumbency of Franklin D. Roosevelt as president the administration came more and more to set the program of legislation and even send prepared bills to the House for introduction. The Republicans denounced this practice but so accustomed had they become to it that in the fall of 1947, when President Truman recommended controls to check inflation, Republican senators and representatives criticized him for not presenting, with his recommendations, a specific program. One Democratic critic of President Truman remarked: "If Roosevelt had made that speech, legislation to cover it, with the last "t" crossed, would have been lying right under his manuscript ready to drop in the hopper." [6]

RULES

Rules of the House of Representatives

The Constitution provides: "Each House may determine the rules of its proceedings." The Supreme Court has held this power to be but little short of absolute. Of course, neither House may ignore constitutional restraints or violate fundamental rights or use a method that does not bear a reasonable relation to the result sought, but otherwise the power is "absolute and beyond the challenge of any other body or tribunal." [7] Constitutional restraints are the rules laid down in the Constitution; for example, each house must keep a journal and publish it, one-fifth of the members present may require a roll-call on a vote and the entering of it on the journal, a majority shall constitute a quorum, and neither house may permanently adjourn without the consent of the other.

Source of the Rules

The rules and precedents of the British House of Commons were the original source of the rules of the House and Senate but these have evolved into American parliamentary law through transformations wrought by the experience of legislative bodies in the New World. Colonial legislatures adapted British rules to their needs and early state legislatures continued to make appropriate modifications of them. Then the Continental Congress

[5] Roland Young: *This Is Congress*. New York, 1946, p. 95.
[6] See Stewart Alsop, Syndicated Column, *Cleveland Plaindealer*, December 7, 1947.
[7] United States *v.* Ballin, 144 U.S. 1, 5 (1892),

adapted the rules of colonial and state legislatures to its purposes. The houses of the First Congress of the United States under the Constitution quite naturally adopted the rules of the Congress under the Articles of Confederation. These rules provided for a simple and regular order of business with unlimited freedom of debate. Political parties had not yet developed and every member was accorded the right to equal attention, a condition that still largely obtains in the Senate. When Jefferson became vice-president and had to preside over the Senate he compiled, with his characteristic thoroughness, a set of rules still known as *Jefferson's Manual*. It, too, was an adaptation of British parliamentary practices to Amercian needs. Though prepared for the Senate it was at once recognized as an authority on parliamentary law and in 1837 the House of Representatives provided that the rules of *Jefferson's Manual* should govern House procedures "in all cases to which they are applicable and in which they are not inconsistent with the standing rules and orders of the House." These "rules and orders" have now quite completely superseded the *Manual*.

Influence of the Party System on House Rules

It was pre-eminently the development of political parties that soon began to set the pattern of the rules of the House of Representatives. Quite early the speaker of the House became the chief organ of majority party control. As new parliamentary situations arose his rulings became precedents tending constantly to facilitate majority control of the House which signified majority party control. Inevitably this led to limitation of the freedom of debate that had prevailed in early sessions of Congress. Filibustering by minorities impelled the House to resort to means of preventing it and for this purpose the "previous question" was adopted as early as 1811. This means that, whenever a motion is made that the previous question be put, debate ends. If a majority of a quorum votes for this motion, no more amendments can be offered and a vote is taken on the pending matter. But filibustering in the House was not brought under control until 1890, when Speaker Reed stopped the dilatory motions by first ascertaining the purpose of any one seeking recognition and refusing it when the purpose was not satisfactory. He also established quorums by having counted present members who were at hand but refused to answer. Both these precedents were soon put into permanent rules of the House.

THE COMMITTEE SYSTEM

A Comparison of the Committee and Ministerial Systems of Law Making

Both houses of Congress depend upon standing or permanent committees for the maturing of bills before they are considered by the houses. This was not the procedure practiced by the earliest Congresses under the Constitution. The only standing committees in the First and Second Congresses were the Committee on Elections and the Committee on Enrolled Bills and the only one in the Senate in the first fifteen years was its Committee on Enrolled Bills. If the initial practice of the House of Representatives had persisted the procedure in the House would now resemble somewhat the British method of law making in which no specialized standing committees participate; bills are not only initiated but also moulded by the ministry in preparation for consideration by the houses. In the beginning the American House of Representatives, instead of establishing standing committees and referring matters of legislation to them, turned to the heads of the executive departments and asked them to report on subjects for legislation. In response to such requests, Secretary of the Treasury Alexander Hamilton made his famous *Report on Public Credit* and *Report on Manufactures* which provided the basis of appropriate legislation. Legislation then took shape in the Committee of the Whole House. Instead of standing committees numerous select or special committees were appointed each for a specific but temporary purpose, a separate one being appointed for each private claim against the government.

The Establishment of the Committee System

The dependence of Congress on department heads proved so transient that the House had seven standing committees at the end of half a dozen years. Extreme distrust of the executive branch and the cabinet induced the Jeffersonian Republicans to set up a system of standing committees for initiating legislation soon after they captured control of the House of Representatives in 1792. By the end of the Third Congress (1793–5) there had been over 350 special committees. In the evolution of the committee system these special committees declined as they tended to be grouped and formed into the developing system of standing committees. When the House was twenty years old it had twelve standing committees and the emerging fields of legislation were clearly indicated by their names, for example: Agriculture, Interstate and Foreign Commerce, Ways and Means, Accounts, Public Lands. The Senate had no similar standing committees until 1816 when it suddenly established them in ten major fields of legislation. By 1946 just before their reduction by the Reorganization Act there were forty-eight standing committees in the House and thirty-three in the Senate.

The Selection of Committee Members

The membership of standing committees is the result of election by the two houses. Actually the process is far more complex than the bare statement implies. Before 1910 the speaker appointed the House committees and he still appoints the special committees including the House members of the joint-conference committees. The nominations of Republican members of the standing committees of the House of Representatives are made by the Republican party Committee on Committees while the Democratic committee nominations are made by the Democratic members of the House

Committee on Ways and Means. These nominations are next ratified by their respective party caucus or conference before being confirmed by a vote of the House of Representatives. Senate committee assignments are determined by the Committee on Committees of each of the major parties in the Senate. Once appointed to a committee a member usually remains on it as long as he continues in the house and desires to remain on the committee. In relations with his party colleagues on the committee he starts at the foot of the class, but if he stays in service he acquires seniority that may make him committee chairman sometime when his party is in power. Of course long service on the same committee develops familiarity, if not expertness, in its field. However, seniority as the sole determinant of the chairmanship of committees is subject to severe criticisms. Roland Young points out that it "flouts established political principles; that of party government; of a legislature responsible to the electoral mandate; and the utilization of the best material for the most important offices. . . . The present method of selecting . . . chairmen does not reflect the election returns in any manner." [8] As long as the speaker appointed committees, members could be and sometimes were demoted and deprived of committee chairmanships on one ground or another. Seniority persists today largely because there is no one person or group responsible for selecting chairmen on the basis of merit as the speaker of the House was before 1911. After twenty years of service in the House the exceptionally able Robert Luce concluded that "on the whole promotion by seniority conduces most to contentment and least endangers morale" and that even an employer ignores seniority at his peril. [9]

However, seniority as a determinant of committee assignment and chairmanship is under an increasing barrage of criticism. The experience of the Eightieth Congress with it was far from happy. An examination of the top seventy-six representatives in the Republican organization in that Congress reveals an average previous tenure of fourteen and a half years. Such a tenure spans the entire epoch of the New Deal despite nearly total eclipse of Republican power. Moreover these seventy-six Republican congressmen, with rare exceptions, represented agrarian districts. Their constituencies were intensely property and production conscious and consequently provided ready allies of business, industrial management, and finance. The election of 1946 brought forty-nine new Republicans to the House from urban-industrial districts with strong labor elements but these new congressmen's lack of seniority relegated them to unimportant committees. Indeed urban districts rather habitually manifest a less stable party tendency, change congressmen more frequently, and thereby fail to attain commanding positions of power in Congress. As a consequence, whenever the president urges upon Congress controversial measures in behalf of urban interests such, for example, as rent or price control or slum

[8] Roland Young: *This Is Congress.* New York, 1946, pp. 108–9.
[9] Robert Luce: *Congress: An Explanation.* Cambridge, Mass., 1926, p. 9.

clearance and housing legislation, he plays the game with Congress against heavily loaded dice. In 1948 the electorate penalized the Eightieth Congress by retiring scores of its members to private life with the consequence that seniority was discredited and a demand arose for abandoning the usage.

Reorganization of the Committee System in 1947

The Reorganization Act of 1946 reduced the number of House committees to nineteen and of Senate committees to fifteen. A principal reason for this drastic reduction was the burden of work imposed upon senators and representatives by the numerous committees. Many representatives had been serving on three committees and each senator was on about six committees while some were on as many as ten. A member's committees might be meeting concurrently and it was possible for the same person to hold membership in committees as divergent in character as Indian Affairs, Invalid Pensions, Labor, Military Affairs, and the Disposal of Useless Executive Papers. The Reorganization Act limited the representative usually to a single committee and the senator to two. Thus committee members have a better opportunity to specialize and familiarize themselves with a particular field of law making. Each committee now has a major function of government, an executive department, or another great agency of government as its special field of legislation and supervision. The reduction of the number of committees by more than one-half required incorporation of the fields of abandoned committees within the new committees. For example, in both the House and the Senate the new Armed Service Committees include the fields of legislation of the former Military and Naval Committees in each house. The new Public Works Committee of the House absorbed the field of the former Flood Control, Public Buildings and Grounds, Rivers and Harbors, and Roads Committees. This committee includes the fields of legislation in which "log-rolling" was practiced by representatives and senators trying to get special favors for their respective constituencies. The new Public Lands Committees of the Senate and the House absorbed the legislative fields of eleven old committees dealing with public lands, irrigation, reclamation, territories, mines, Indians, and insular affairs.

The Organization of Committees

Each standing committee is so constituted that whichever major party has a majority in a house has a majority in every committee. For example, the Ways and Means Committee of the House in the Eightieth Congress consisted of fifteen Republicans and ten Democrats, while the Finance Committee in the then almost evenly balanced Senate had seven Republicans and six Democrats. The most influential member of a standing committee is almost invariably the chairman who is always a member of the majority party in his house. Although the rules of the House of Representatives provide that "at the commencement of each Congress the House shall elect as chairman of each standing committee one of the members thereof," seniority nearly always determines the chairmanship. Reducing the number of committees more than one-half had the effect of leaving the committee chairmanships to still older men than before and a caustic critic observed that "senility was succeeded by super-senility." The names of committee chairmen are frequently used to designate important measures handled by their committees as, for example, the Taft-Hartley Act. The action of a committee on the measures referred to it has a very great influence on the voting of congressmen, and the committee chairmen can and sometimes do exercise arbitrary power in promoting, hindering, or preventing the passage of measures. The Reorganization Act of 1946 authorized, for each Senate and House Committee, ten staff members of whom four at salaries ranging at present as high as $13,500 are to be specialists in the committee's field of legislation. Concerning those chosen by committees of the Eightieth Congress, one who helped work at the reorganization said: "Some of them are personal friends of Congressmen, some are hacks, and some are qualified persons."

Sub-Committees and Special Committees

The drastic reduction of standing committees under the Reorganization Act of 1946 was followed by an astonishing multiplication of sub-committees until there were over a hundred of them in the first session of the Eightieth Congress. The new standing committees found their burden greatly increased by the addition of the functions of the discontinued standing committees. An increase in the number of sub-committees was inevitable but committee members who had once been harassed by the necessity of going from one standing committee to another now found themselves going from sub-committee to sub-committee. The criticism was made that the "simplification" of the Reorganization Act had even complicated the legislative process by adding another stage to the procedure. Before the reorganization the standing committee that prepared a bill brought it directly to the floor but now a sub-committee usually first shapes the measure, perhaps after conducting a hearing, and its product must then be approved by the full standing committee before going to the floor. If the chairman of the standing committee insists upon a detailed study by his committee legislation will be held up.

Under the Reorganization Act, special committees were intended to be temporary sub-committees of standing committees. However, the Eightieth Congress quite promptly established standing independent investigating committees for national defense and small business in the Senate and for supply of newsprint and small business in the House. Incidentally this provided a welcome opportunity for chairmanships for some who had acquired sufficient seniority to have made them chairmen of committees discontinued by the reorganization. Still others of these disappointed members with high seniority rank found some consolation in presiding over important sub-committees.

The Legislative Budget

The Reorganization Act of 1946 provided that the Committee on Ways and Means and the Committee on Appropriations of the House and the Committee on Finance and the Committee on Appropriations of the Senate shall meet jointly at the beginning of each regular session of Congress to adopt an over-all congressional budget for the Federal government for the ensuing fiscal year. This legislative budget must not be confused with the executive budget prepared for the president by the Budget Bureau and submitted to Congress as his recommendation with respect to revenues and expenditures for the ensuing fiscal year. The joint congressional committee was expected to consider the president's budget and then report its own to the houses by February 15 of each year accompanied by a concurrent resolution adopting such budget and fixing the maximum amount to be appropriated for the fiscal year.

The legislative budget has failed in practice. In 1947 the Senate and House majorities were determined to reduce the President's budget but could not agree on the amount of the reduction.[10] In February, 1949, Congress extended to May 1 the date when it must determine its ceiling for appropriations, but this proved ineffectual. In 1950 the legislative budget was ignored and the provision for it may now be considered dead letter despite a strong sentiment in Congress for further trial of a legislative budget.

The Conference Committee

This is a special kind of joint committee of the two houses and one is appointed for each bill that passes the House in one form and the Senate in another. The function of a conference committee is to work the two versions into a form that will be acceptable to majorities in both houses. Usually a conference committee consists of three members of the House of Representatives appointed by the speaker and three members of the Senate appointed by the presiding officer who is usually the vice-president. These appointees are in most cases members of the two committees that reported the measure to their respective houses. In defiance of the rules, conference committees sometimes disregard their obligation merely to reconcile differences and instead rewrite portions of the bill by introducing new matter. In effect this means that, in the final stages of some controversial measures, Congress surrenders its legislative function to this irresponsible committee. Once the conference committee's report reaches the two houses it is likely to be accepted in the form presented by the committee.

[10] Floyd M. Riddick: "The First Session of the Eightieth Congress." *American Political Science Review* (1948), 42:686.

THE SENATE

Organization

Because two-thirds of the senators hold over from one Congress to the next, the Senate of the United States has never been without organization since the spring of 1789. While the House has organized eighty-one times, the Senate has organized but once which accounts for the saying that there has been just one Senate. Of course vacancies in the Senate organization have been filled as they occurred and new Senate offices as they were created. The Constitution provides that the vice-president shall preside over the Senate and in this capacity he is addressed as "Mr. President." The Senate does not elect him and he exercises no such partisan leadership as custom assigns to the speaker of the House but instead presides as an impartial moderator. His decisions are subject to appeal to the house by any senator and frequently he voluntarily submits doubtful questions to the Senate for decision. Parliamentary controversies however are rare in the Senate, and the presiding officer's decisions are usually accepted as the rule of procedure. Some presidents have depended upon the vice-president to keep them informed of the Senate's attitude on important administration measures before it. Since the vice-president is not a member of the Senate he serves on no committee, does not participate in debate, and votes only to break a tie. The Senate elects a president pro tempore who presides in the absence of the vice-president or when that office is vacant. Such leadership as there is in the Senate is exercised by party floor leaders and whips. The Senate elects a secretary who presides when the vice-presidency is vacant until a president pro tempore is elected. He performs duties corresponding to those of the clerk of the House. The Senate also elects a sergeant-at-arms whose chief duty is the preservation of order.

The Rules of the Senate

The Senate has much simpler rules than the House. They are based on *Jefferson's Manual* which was prepared specifically for the Senate and revisions have been few. Though a Senate rule may now and then be altered, by and large the rules are permanent and thus contrast with the House rules which are adopted anew with additions, omissions, and alterations at the beginning of each new Congress. Senators are not nearly so fettered by rules as are members of the House. Indeed the procedure in the Senate is "not unlike that of a board of directors where things are done in an orderly manner, but not according to technicalities." [11] In 1806 the Senate put an end to the "previous question." Debate is consequently unlimited except for the check of the inadequate and very seldom used cloture procedure. The Senate may, however, punish members for disorderly conduct, and censure and suspension have on some rare occasions been imposed upon members

[11] Samuel W. McCall: *The Business of Congress.* New York, 1911, p. 30.

for assaults within the chamber. The rules provide for executive sessions devoted to the consideration of executive matters such as the confirmation of nominations made by the president or the ratification of treaties he has negotiated. Since 1929 executive business has no longer been conducted in secret session.

Assistants to the Senators

In 1947, the Eightieth Congress authorized an administrative assistant for each senator at a salary of $13,500 a year. This is intended to provide some relief from the burden on senators particularly on those from the more populous states. The purpose was not merely to raise the salaries of senator's secretaries. The expectation was that this would provide for each senator a specialist with appropriate training and experience for the position. In the first Congress under the reorganization it was ascertained that 70 per cent of these administrative assistants to the senators were their former secretaries who had been drawing less than $6,000 a year and who admitted they were still doing about the same work as before. Four were sons of senators, one a senator's brother, and one a senator's wife. The fifteen new senators of course, engaged new administrative assistants as did eleven of the old senators. The variety of types selected is revealed by the fact that the twenty-six new assistants included nine lawyers, four newspaper men, a market researcher, a State Department attaché, a political-party official, a member of Congress, a cost accountant, a real-estate man, a farm expert, a honey producer, a senator, a state O.P.A. director, a secretary to a governor, a book salesman, and an office manager.

SUMMARY

The House of Representatives reorganizes after each congressional election. Its principal officer is the Speaker, the choice of the majority party, and he presides as his party's representative rather than as an impartial moderator. The Speaker had evolved into practically a dictator when he was checked by the so-called Congressional Revolution of 1910. Today he has recovered much of his command of the House through his power of recognition by which he can manage the otherwise almost omnipotent Rules Committee.

Party steering committees consider the strategy of handling measures while floor leaders and whips manage debate and round up party members to vote. The House Rules Committee determines what measures are to be considered and under what conditions. The caucus has declined to scarcely more than a gathering to determine party candidates in organizing the houses.

The houses function through standing committees which somewhat resemble miniature legislatures with their membership determined by party caucuses largely in accordance with custom. The Reorganization

Act of 1946 sharply reduced the number of standing committees, but sub-committees then became more numerous.

In contrast with the House, the Senate has been continuously organized since 1789 with the Vice-President (or President pro-tem) presiding as an impartial moderator. As a smaller body than the House, the Senate proceeds deliberately with debate limited only by a practically unused cloture rule. The Reorganization Act of 1946 provided each senator with an administrative assistant.

CHAPTER XXIII

CONGRESS IN ACTION

THE PECULIAR NATURE OF AMERICAN LAW MAKING

Congress, A Unique Legislature

THE Congress of the United States has developed its own legislative methods. British parliamentary practice had been adopted by the American colonial legislatures and reshaped by new circumstances particularly as a consequence of the persistent clash of the popular colonial assembly with the representative of the crown, that is the colonial governor. The Revolution and independence marked the transformation of colonial legislatures into what Madison called the "omnipotent" state legislatures of the 1780's which permitted no initiative in legislation by the "mere ciphers" that the state governors had come to be. Despite this subordination of the early state governors the First Congress of the United States under the Constitution started out as a law-making body mainly dependent upon the executive branch for the initiative in legislation. Instead of establishing specialized standing committees for the several fields of legislation the House of Representatives referred matters to the heads of executive departments and awaited their recommendations. Thus it fell to the first Secretary of the Treasury, Alexander Hamilton, to propose the great financial measures of funding the national debt, assuming the state debts, establishing the Bank of the United States, and the whole legislative program that bears his name. This reliance upon the executive departments, however, was contrary to established American tradition and proved to be but a temporary practice. In a few years the House of Representatives was establishing the specialized standing committees and depending upon them to initiate and shape bills for the consideration of the whole House. This system of standing committees took firm root and became a distinctive feature of law making by Congress. It is the shaping of legislation by standing committees that especially distinguishes the American from the British method of law making.

A Thumbnail Biography of an Act of Congress

Let us assume that a member of the House of Representatives drops his bill into the "hopper," as the basket provided for that purpose is called, and the bill is referred to an appropriate committee according to the rules of the House. [1] As soon as the bill has been printed it is placed on the committee's calendar. Owing to the great number of measures introduced most bills die in committee or are "pigeon-holed" which means that either the Committee deliberately lays them "on the table," or its chairman simply does not bring them up. Measures not thus disposed of are, after consideration and possible amendment by a committee, sooner or later reported to the House either favorably or unfavorably. We may assume that this particular bill in due course is reported by the committee to the House and is there placed on one of the several House calendars or lists of reported bills. A complicated set of rules determines how a measure is taken from a House calendar for consideration by the whole House. Here the measure may be debated, possibly amended, and passed. In the Senate it runs a similar gauntlet of committee consideration, pigeonholing, or report and, on the Senate floor, it is debated and, let us say, passed with or without amendment. If neither house accepts this measure in the form in which it passed the other a joint conference committee consisting of members of the two houses is appointed to compose differences after which we shall assume that it is accepted by both houses, in the form agreed upon and reported by the conference committee. It then goes to the president for his signature or veto.

THE ORIGIN OF ACTS OF CONGRESS

Administrative Initiation of Acts of Congress

Despite the contrast between the congressional and the parliamentary systems, legislation at Washington tends more and more to be initiated by the executive departments. There is where half the bills dropped into the hopper are said to originate. [2] Of course many of the proposals of administrative officials are made in compliance with requests of congres-

---

[1] Of course all except revenue bills may constitutionally originate in either house. The formal steps in legislation in Congress are: (1) introduction of a bill in the House (or Senate as the case may be); (2) reference to a committee; (3) report from committee; (4) placement on a calendar; (5) consideration of bill and committee report in Committee of the Whole; (6) second reading; (7) engrossment and third reading; (8) passage; (9) transmission to Senate by message; (10) consideration by Senate; (11) return from Senate without amendments, or (12) return with amendments; (13) consideration of Senate amendments; (14) settlement of difference by conference committees; (15) enrollment on parchment by the house in which bill originated; (16) examination by Committee on Enrolled Bills; (17) signature of speaker of the House and president of the Senate; (18) transmission to the president; (19) approval and signature of the president, or (20) disapproval and veto by president; (21) action on president's veto; (22) if passed, filing with secretary of state. If the measure originates in the Senate the procedure is similar.

[2] George B. Galloway: *Congress at the Crossroads*, p. 150.

sional committees. Before transmission of these administrative measures to the congressional committees they are routed through the Legislative Reference Division of the Bureau of the Budget to ascertain whether they conform to the president's program. George B. Galloway declares that "much legislation is tailor made in the departments and sent up to the speaker or the appropriate committee chairman for introduction in the House." [3] Many congressional committees regularly refer bills to the department affected and report to the House favorably only if the measure is acceptable to the department. Congress is also somewhat dependent for the initiation of legislation upon the regular and special reports of the numerous administrative agencies and their testimony before committees. Outstanding in this respect are the General Accounting Office, the Federal Trade Commission, the Tariff Commission and the Department of Agriculture.

Presidential Initiative in Legislation

The constitutional basis for presidential initiative in legislation is in the provision that the president "shall from time to time give to the Congress information on the state of the Union and recommend to their consideration such measures as he shall judge necessary and expedient." Many presidents have given this injunction mere perfunctory observance but President Wilson saw in it authority for the role of a prime minister. More and more the annual message of the president on the state of the Union has come to include a multi-point legislative program for the consideration of Congress. Items of this annual message are distributed according to subject matter to appropriate House and Senate committees. Suitable bills covering the points of the message may have already been prepared by the executive departments concerned, ready for introduction by chairmen of committees of both houses. Of course the committee chairmen are not likely to introduce bills to carry out presidential recommendations if the majority is not in favor of the president's recommendations. This is the case whenever the president and the majority in Congress represent opposing political parties or contradictory social philosophies. President Lincoln once incurred the wrath of Congress by accompanying a message to Congress with an appropriate bill and until comparatively recently presidents have been reluctant to venture on such a practice. However it has now come to be expected to such an extent that Republican Senator Homer Ferguson in 1947 criticized President Truman for making a recommendation without accompanying it with an appropriate bill. [4]

---

[3] Ibid., p. 6.

[4] In a round table discussion Senator Ferguson said: "If the President wants to tell the people that he stands for a certain thing, he ought to come out with his proposal. He ought to come to the House and Senate with a message. And he ought to provide a bill if that is exactly what he wants."—"What is your Congress Doing?" *University of Chicago Round Table* No. 483.

Interest Groups as Initiators of Legislation

Many statutes originate as a consequence of the influence of interests upon Congress and are shaped through compromises to conform to the balance among contending groups. Professor Harvey Walker has observed: "It is a commonplace that legislators no longer have time to consult individual constituents unless they represent an organized vote, that is a conscious group. Pressures by these groups upon the legislature produce the resultant forces of legislation." [5] Of course Congress is guided by public opinion but, as Professor John Dickinson put it: "The task of government, and hence of democracy as a form of government, is not to express an imaginary popular will, but to effect adjustments among various special wills and purposes which at any time are pressing for realization." [6] With breath-taking realism the late Justice Oliver Wendell Holmes, a generation before he became a member of the Supreme Court of the United States, observed: "The more powerful interests must be more or less reflected in legislation. . . . If the welfare of the living majority is paramount, it can only be on the ground that the majority have the power in their hands. The fact is that legislation in this country as elsewhere is empirical. It is necessarily made a means by which a body having the power puts burdens disagreeable to them on the shoulders of somebody else." [7]

When one set of interests was predominant the Wagner Labor Relations Law of 1935 was enacted providing far-reaching safeguards to the collective bargaining practices of labor at the same time that it limited management with respect to these practices. A decade later a marked shift in the balance of power between management and labor enabled the former to induce Congress to enact the Taft-Hartley Law releasing management from some restrictions while it distinctly restrained labor. Another example of how active interests can use Congress to shift burdens to other shoulders is the competition between dairy and oleomargarine interests. Over sixty years ago the dairy interests succeeded, with slight opposition, in burdening the infant oleomargarine industry with exacting regulations and numerous taxes the most onerous of which was an excise tax of ten cents a pound on oleomargarine when colored to resemble

---

[5] Harvey Walker: "Who Writes the Laws." *State Government,* Nov., 1939.

[6] John Dickinson: "Democratic Realities and Democratic Dogma." *American Political Science Review* (1930), 24:291.

[7] Oliver Wendell Holmes: "The Gas Stokers' Strike." *American Law Review* (1873), 7:583–4. The occasion of Holmes's commentary was a year's prison sentence given by an English judge to some gas stokers for merely planning to strike. The recently enacted statute under which the judge acted was condemned by some English opinion as class legislation whereupon Holmes observed in the article quoted: "But it is no sufficient condemnation of legislation that it favors one class at the expense of another; for much if not all legislation does that and none the less when the bona fide object is the greatest good to the greatest numbers." Holmes wrote the unsigned article as editor of the *American Law Review.*

butter. The unorganized consumer interest was powerless. But in 1949 it found able allies in powerful interests whose products may be utilized in the manufacture of oleomargarine—the cotton and peanut planters of the South and the soy-bean farmers of the North. Here is a combination that later shifted the burden from oleomargarine according to the principle of legislation given by Holmes. Legislation, then, is the resultant of forces that play upon Congress, and the congressman's chief problem as a law maker is persistent search for the points of equilibrium among social forces. "Laws and decrees," declared R. M. MacIver, "are not the expression of the will of those who issue them. Behind the Senate and the Assembly stand the strong interests and pressure groups." [8]

Other Reasons for the Initiation of Bills

Trivial reasons may account for the initiation of many bills and indeed the "flood of bills" is in some respects illusory. A large portion of the bills introduced by congressmen are private measures instead of public bills. Moreover many bills are duplicates due to the fact that the House rules, in contrast with those of the Senate, do not permit the name of more than one member on a bill. For sheer publicity reasons members may introduce identical copies of the same measures; twenty such bills on tideland oil were introduced in the Eightieth Congress. Then there are the numerous bills introduced upon the request or insistence of constituents and concerning which the congressman has no intention of doing anything.

THE WORK OF THE COMMITTEES

Significance of the Committees

The importance of the work of the standing committees of the two houses is overlooked by those who assume that the action on the floor has very much to do with shaping legislation. Whoever looks down from the gallery upon the scene of confusion, indifference, and small attendance at an ordinary session should be reminded of the fact that laws are taking shape in the committee rooms. The speeches delivered on the floor are frequently of no great significance and may in fact be delivered to attract attention or to impress the constituents of the speaker. Debates do at times contribute to the understanding of pending measures and play an important part in legislation, but this is rather exceptional. The paramount difficulty is that the House of Representatives is far too large and cumbersome to formulate legislation in a collective capacity. Sheer numbers if nothing else would compel the prevailing dependence upon standing committees for this purpose. Congress then, as popularly conceived, scarcely exists; instead the membership is of necessity organized in a system of little congresses—that is, standing committees which get legislation ready for the consideration of the houses. This of course contrasts with the parliamentary system in which the initiation, shaping, and re-

[8] R. M. MacIver: *The Web of Government*. New York, 1947, p. 95.

shaping of bills is done by the ministry instead of by committees of legislators.

Reference to Committees

In the House, the speaker's clerk takes the bills from the hopper and assigns them to the appropriate committees. Usually the reference is easy because the nature of the bill indicates clearly what committee ought to consider it. If the clerk is in doubt the speaker decides. There are, of course, border-line cases where a bill might with equal propriety be assigned to any one of several committees. For example, Speaker Champ Clark once had to decide which committee was to consider a bill to fix the dimensions of an apple barrel. The Committee on Interstate and Foreign Commerce claimed jurisdiction because the barrels were used in interstate commerce. The Committee on Coinage, Weights, and Measures claimed it for obvious reasons. The Agriculture Committee claimed it because apples were raised on farms. After considerable controversy Speaker Clark assigned it to the Committee on Coinage, Weights, and Measures. [9] If party advantage can be obtained by referring a bill to one instead of another committee the speaker decides accordingly, subject to the will of the House which almost invariably sustains him on reference of bills. Since the personnel of a particular committee may be set against a certain measure its life or death may depend upon the speaker's power over reference. Interest groups through their lobbyists try to get the bills they favor referred to friendly committees and the bills they oppose referred to committees they consider likely to pigeon-hole such measures. When the members of congressional committees are being selected lobbyists are busy trying to influence the choices so that committees will be constituted to their advantage. A committee packed with congressmen favorable to its policies is a distinct advantage to an interest group.

In the Senate bills are referred to standing committees in accordance with their subject matter but the senator who introduces a bill may indicate on it the committee to which he desires to have it referred. The presiding officer of the Senate decides to what committee the bill is to go but, unlike the House the Senate feels perfectly free, on appeal of a member from the floor, to take a vote and overrule the presiding officer on reference to a committee. For example, in May, 1948, President pro tempore of the Senate, Arthur Vandenberg quite logically assigned to the Agricultural Committee the bill to repeal the taxes on oleomargarine. But this Committee would probably have pigeon-holed the bill, and the Senate consequently overruled the President pro tempore and voted the reference of the bill to the Finance Committee which was expected to report the measure favorably.

Promptly after reference a bill goes to the printer and as soon as a printed copy is received the committee to which the bill has been referred

---

[9] Clarence Cannon: *Precedents of the House of Representatives*, Washington, D.C., vol. VIII, pp. 2121–3.

puts it on its calendar, that is, the list of bills referred to it. The bill is then available for committee consideration. If it is an important measure it may be referred to a sub-committee appointed by the chairman for study of that particular bill, and hearings may be held on it. Since the reorganization of Congress under the LaFollette-Monroney Act almost all legislation is referred to sub-committees at least for initial consideration and hearings. Government agencies and private interests (through their lobbyists) are constantly at work on committee chairmen, members, and staffs urging the consideration of their particular measures. Committee members are ordinarily told in advance by the chairman what measures will be under consideration at the next committee session. Party leadership through steering committee or caucus advises committee chairmen what bills should be given priority.

THE COMMITTEE'S SOURCES OF INFORMATION

Committee Investigations

As a means of obtaining information, ostensibly for the purpose of performing its functions, Congress makes wide use of the investigating committee. For this purpose a standing committee may be used or more likely a sub-committee of it created for a specific investigation. Personnel of the executive departments and of other Federal administrative agencies may be summoned to appear and answer questions. Officials of private corporations or any citizen may be subpoenaed and questioned by a committee. During the Seventy-eighth Congress, twenty special committees, ten in each house, were investigating such subjects as small business, air accidents, national defense, postwar policies, silver purchases, campaign expenditures, gasoline shortages, un-American activities, executive agencies, and the Federal Communications Commission. The appropriations for these committees aggregated over three-quarters of a million dollars. Sometimes the two houses create a joint committee consisting of members of both houses, such, for example, as the Truman-Mead Committee which investigated production during World War II and became almost a model of its type. Notable also was the joint committee on the Reorganization of Congress known as the LaFollette-Monroney Committee. It was the intention of the Reorganization Act of 1946 to confine investigations to standing committees functioning through sub-committees. However, almost immediately after it went into effect, some special investigating committees were reconstituted or established.

The Purposes of Congressional Investigations

Congressional investigations may be conducted for the purpose of aiding the administration particularly when president and Congress are of the same party. On the other hand, they may be designed to check the conduct of the administration or provide information as a basis for legislation.

Public opinion may be enlightened and influenced by the findings of an investigation. Investigation is a necessary preliminary to impeachment but this device is rarely used. Before judgment is passed upon the qualifications or behavior of members of Congress information may be obtained through investigation by a committee. [10] Congressional investigation is one of the most effective devices for exposing to public scrutiny objectionable private activities and organizations. However, Congress is not restrained by rules of evidence required by the courts for the protection of witnesses and has consequently been criticized for some of the practices of its investigating committees. Grave damage has occasionally been done to some persons by the methods of congressional committees. Representative George Bender of Ohio proposed a set of rules that would protect witnesses by regulating the conduct of investigating committees but Congress has taken no action on the matter.

Investigation for Law-making Purposes

The most important purpose of investigating committees is obtaining information deemed necessary for formulating new legislation or discovering defects in existing legislation with a view to amending it. For example, during the first administration of President Franklin Roosevelt with a Congress overwhelmingly of the President's own party there were fifty-one investigations designed to aid the administration in promoting its legislative program. Often the investigating committee already possesses the information it requires for legislation and uses the hearings to publicize an issue concerning public policy, and thereby influence public opinion for or against a projected measure. The inquiry into lobbying by utilities facilitated passage of the Wheeler-Rayburn Act of 1935 restricting holding companies in the field of privately owned public utilities. Revelations of the lobbying practices of the utilities induced Congress to reverse its earlier stand and include a modified "death sentence" for certain kinds of utility holding companies. The Securities Exchange Acts of 1933 and 1934 were shaped in the light of investigations into stock-exchange practices. [11]

Investigations for Supervising Administration

Through hearings and investigations Congress obtains information on the basis of which it may effectively perform its function of supervising administration. This type of investigation becomes especially prominent and sometimes more than tinged with a partisan objective when administration degenerates as it did in the 1870's and the 1920's. In such circumstances the constitutional basis for congressional investigation derives not from the legislative power of Congress alone but also from its power

[10] M. Nelson McGeary: "Congressional Investigation During Franklin D. Roosevelt's First Term." *American Political Science Review* (1937), 31:680–694.
[11] Ibid.

of the impeachment and trial of officials. Ordinarily, however, the purpose of such investigation is to ascertain the conduct of the executive branch; the use of the investigatory function then becomes a crude means for bridging the gap between legislative and executive powers which, in the congressional type of government, are separated, an important point of contrast with the parliamentary type of government. Congress scrutinizes, studies, and legislates to improve administrative organization and procedures. It can ascertain when the administrator has diverted or even reversed the policy established by statute. Thus arbitrary and autocratic conduct of the administrator can be checked and public grievances redressed. However, this power can be abused. Sometimes a committee investigation seems designed to demonstrate the sovereign power of Congress over administrative agencies due to its constitutional right to grant, increase, reduce, or withhold appropriations. There are two committees on government operations, one in the Senate, the other in the House, which scrutinize and determine how the executive agencies are carrying out the directives of Congress.

Investigations Inform the Public

Sometimes congressional investigations are useful in informing the public on governmental matters that might otherwise be obscure. They may help to satisfy to a degree the observation of President Washington: "In proportion as the structure of government gives force to public opinion it is essential that public opinion should be enlightened." The pressure of public opinion aroused by a congressional investigation may compel the resignation of a public official as it did in the case of Attorney General Harry M. Daugherty in 1924. Thus it may relieve Congress of the necessity of resorting to the clumsy device of impeachment with its devastating diversion of the time of the Senate from its essential legislative function. In short the investigating committee is a means of preventing abuse of power by a bureaucracy out of touch with the public it is designed to serve. "It is," wrote George B. Galloway, "the American method of achieving ministerial responsibility without reducing power. It is one of the checks on a system of checks and balances. It reflects fairly well the mind of the nation from which indirectly it receives power and for which it exercises it." [12]

Investigatory Methods of Congress

Congress obtains information through hearings at which interested persons, including lobbyists, may appear voluntarily. Administrative officials may be summoned, questioned, and required to produce records, subject to the president's power to prevent divulging of information when he deems that contrary to the public interest. Private persons and represen-

---

[12] George B. Galloway: "The Investigative Function of Congress." *American Political Science Review* (1929), 23:65.

tatives of corporations and organizations may be required to appear and answer questions. The courts have sustained Congress in its power to compel private persons, under penalty of citation for contempt of Congress, to answer questions provided the inquiry falls within the prescribed scope of the investigating committee's power as laid down by the resolution creating or empowering the committee and within the fields of power delegated to Congress by the Constitution. Congress can compel the production of papers as well as the answering of questions and in case of refusal may punish for contempt of Congress. The punishment may consist of fine or imprisonment as in the case of Harry F. Sinclair who in 1929 was sentenced to Federal prison for refusing to answer questions put to him by the Senate Committee on Public Lands.

Procedure of a Congressional Committee

Experience indicates that the well-managed investigating committee will plan carefully in advance with the chairman and members working in close cooperation with its staff. To this end preliminary meetings prepare an agenda for each session defining purposes and planning the contribution each witness may make. Failure to develop a systematic procedure has led to some notable fiascos and even boomerangs such as that of the Senate Committee on War Expenditures which, in 1947, produced the rare spectacle of the chief witness maneuvering the Chairman of the Committee himself onto the witness stand and practically putting him on trial with the consequence that the committee suddenly adjourned for an indefinite period. [13] Sometimes a passion for publicity seems to take possession of a committee. With Klieg lights playing upon committeemen and witness, and in a clutter of the apparatus of newsreel men, the proceedings take on a theatrical if not a Hollywood appearance.

Official Reports of Executive Agencies

Congressional committees depend considerably upon information obtained from annual and special reports of administrative agencies. The agencies that present their reports in concise, attractive, and non-technical form, fortified by visual aids, have an advantage in promoting their views in Congress. Sometimes committees assign special investigations to agencies such as the General Accounting Office, the Federal Trade Commission, and the Tariff Commission which more than most Federal agencies are created as agents of Congress.[14] Aware of the importance of maintaining good relations with Congress every executive department and almost every agency maintains a special section to handle congressional inquiries. Many also maintain congressional liaison officers. Congressmen also find useful the United States Information Service under the Office

[13] On recommendations as to hearings, see *Hearings before the Joint Committee on Organization of Congress*, June 29, 1945, pp. 1019–20.
[14] George B. Galloway: *Congress at the Crossroads*, pp. 151, 153.

of Government Reports. Its director testified that during 1945 every senator and 390 representatives had used its facilities.

Information from Private Sources

Congress has available the findings of such research foundations as the Brookings Institution, which has been engaged in conducting examinations in technical matters, and the Twentieth Century Fund. Civic organizations like the League of Women Voters and the National Planning Association also offer their findings. The president's commissions such as the Committee on Economic Security and the Committee on Administrative Management provide Congress with invaluable information and conclusions. Learned societies such as the American Political Science Association, the American Economic Association, and the National Conference of Commissioners on Uniform Law can be depended on for judgments in their respective fields. Contrary to the popular notion the various interest groups through their lobbies often supply Congress with information useful in legislation and sometimes promote in their own behalf policies in which their private objectives happen to coincide with the public interest. "By and large," wrote former Senator Robert M. La Follette, Jr., "lobbying reflects the complexity of our society and government. The bulk of it is a representation of viewpoints and interests which should be and are considered in the legislative process." [15] Indeed Congressman Kefauver declared in 1947 that Congress, even after its reformation under the Reorganization Act, could not function without the lobbyist.

The Legislative Reference Service

The Library of Congress was originally established and still functions primarily as a legislative service for Congress. A division of the Library, designated the Legislative Reference Service, functions exclusively for the legislative branch of the Federal government and provides congressmen with information. The Service has assembled special collections of reference works, statutes, bills, reports, and documents constituting the largest collection of research material of its kind in the world. The Service prepares for members digests and compilations and provides special service on specific topics as required. Congressmen have available every facility in the way of material for speeches, digests of arguments for and against measures, and assistance in organizing committee hearings. Special studies are made on problems of public policy. The Legislative Reorganization Act of 1946 provided for an expansion of the Legislative Reference Service. A staff of eighteen senior specialists, many of whom were outstanding university professors, were appointed to the Advance Research Section. Also on the staff are many recent college graduates who majored in one or another of the social sciences. [16] George Galloway observed the remark-

[15] Robert M. LaFollette, Jr.: "Some Lobbies Are Good." *New York Times Magazine,* May 16, 1948, p. 58.
[16] W. Brooke Graves: "Legislative Reference Service for the Congress of the United States." *American Political Science Review* (1947), 41:289–293.

able fact that some congressmen of considerable length of service had not yet learned of the Legislative Reference Service available to them.

COMMITTEE DELIBERATIONS

Committee Consideration of Bills

During the course of a committee's deliberations a bill may undergo a radical transformation through amendment and recasting. The committee conducts its discussions behind closed doors where it is said partisanship tends to disappear. Secrecy improves the opportunity for compromises, and the pressures of the interests are thus markedly reduced. [17] When the committee has completed the hearings, its study of reports and information from various sources, and has concluded its discussions and deliberations it may vote on whether to report the measure to the house. This report may be either favorable or unfavorable. Whether the bill is reported at all depends on several factors. Sometimes when the measure is an important one the force of public opinion may determine the matter for a committee by compelling the reporting of the bill. There are, of course, congressmen who approach a bill with an open mind but the representative process in America requires a congressman to be responsive to the influence of his constituents usually functioning through organized groups. Whether a bill is reported favorably or unfavorably or pigeonholed often depends on the membership of the committee as well as on the pressures of the constituencies represented by its members. The background of the most influential members and particularly the chairmen are often determinants of the fate of a measure. The associations, education, social philosophies, and even the prejudices of committee members are also important factors. This is why majority party leadership may see to it that important measures are routed to committees that will handle them in conformity with the party line. Thus the known attitude of the committees on an issue rather than the nature of the bill often determines to what committee a measure is referred.

Reporting a Bill

If it is willing to have the house consider a bill referred to it the committee "reports" the measure to the house. It is not easy for the House of Representatives to compel a committee to report a bill it is disposed to pigeon-hole or merely to delay reporting. In the House of Representatives, after a committee has had a bill for thirty days, a petition may be filed to discharge the committee from further consideration of it but this petition requires a minimum of 218 signatures which constitutes a bare majority of the members of the House. If the requisite signatures are obtained the House may either consider the bill at once or place it on the Discharge Calendar. However, the discipline of the House majority is usually sufficient to prevent obtaining the 218 signatures. So rare is a

[17] George B. Galloway: *Congress at the Crossroads.* New York, 1947, p. 180.

successful discharge petition that it created a mild sensation when, in 1948, the House Committee on Agriculture, after having, as it thought, pigeon-holed the bill to repeal the oleomargarine taxes, was by a successful petition discharged from further consideration of the bill. The House quite promptly passed it but it died in the Senate. In this case growing consumer sentiment allied with the pressures of the producers of constituent elements of oleomargarine broke the discipline of the majority party and for a moment upset the practical sovereignty of the committee in determining what bills in its field the House may consider.

In the Senate if a committee fails to report a bill within a reasonable time the rules permit any senator to move that the committee be discharged from further consideration of the bill and if the motion is carried the bill is out of the committee's hands. A senator who reports a bill for his committee may at once request unanimous consent for immediate consideration and if that is granted the bill is usually passed with little or no debate which indicates that it is a non-controversial matter. Whenever unanimous consent for immediate consideration is not obtained a bill goes on one of the Senate calendars.

THE CALENDARS

The Sifting of Bills for Consideration

Gradually each of the two houses of Congress has evolved its own methods for sifting from the many bills introduced the relatively few to be considered and the still fewer to be passed. The committees reduce drastically the volume of potential legislation by reporting to their respective houses only a fraction of the bills referred to them. Even that fraction constitutes many more measures than will be enacted into statutes. Like most legislatures Congress has a habit of proceeding leisurely until the last few weeks of a session when considerable legislation may be jammed through with only cursory consideration. The speed and tempo of Congress is dependent upon the will of the majority leadership which can break a legislative jam at any time. Bills are selected for consideration by a house through a process that is complicated and effective even if somewhat erratic and unpredictable as to definite results. An essential feature of the process is the classification of reported bills in several categories or lists known as calendars. As soon as a bill has been reported to either house its title along with other identifying information is placed at the bottom of one or two of its several calendars. A calendar is simply a chronological listing of reported bills of a certain classification ostensibly subject to consideration by the house. The calendars are printed daily and provide members with a brief but indispensable history of every bill pending before the house. However, bills are not considered in the order in which they appear on the calendars but are taken up for consideration by each house according to an elaborate set of practices and rules that are a heritage of Congress's long experience in law making.

CALENDARS OF THE HOUSE OF REPRESENTATIVES

The Union Calendar

This is the calendar of the Committee of the Whole House on the State of the Union on which are placed all bills, previously considered and reported by committees, for raising revenues, general appropriation bills, and bills of a public character directly or indirectly appropriating money or property. Normally when these measures are taken from the calendar they are considered by the Committee of the Whole House, that is, the entire House of Representatives acting as if it were a committee.

The House Calendar

The House Calendar consists of all bills of a public character not for raising revenue or directly or indirectly appropriating money or property.

The Private Calendar

This is a calendar of the Committee of the Whole House when it considers bills of a private nature. Half or more of all laws enacted by Congress are bills taken from this calendar. The bills on the Private Calendar are not only listed chronologically but they are taken up in the order listed. Generally, individual representatives are concerned only with their own private bills and there are seldom more than fifty representatives present on Private Calendar days, which are the first and third Tuesdays of each month. To prevent raiding the Treasury by private bills each party appoints an unofficial Objectors Committee of three to five who must read every private bill and either remain silent or object when a private bill comes to a vote. These Objectors Committees have a practically absolute veto on private bills, a power they exercise in conformity with their party policy as determined by party leadership.

The Consent Calendar

Minor non-controversial bills already placed on either House or Union Calendars may be placed also on the Consent Calendar and after three legislative days thereon they may be called up on the first and third Mondays of each month. But a single objection against consideration of the measure on the first call prevents its immediate passage.

Discharge Calendar

Whenever a bill, through a petition signed by 218 members of the House, has been taken from the jurisdiction of the committee to which it had been referred it is placed on the Discharge Calendar where it becomes highly privileged for consideration on the second or fourth Mondays of each month.

THE SENATE CALENDARS

Senate Calendars

Unlike the calendars of the House where bills are classified generally with respect to the nature of their subject matter the calendars of the Senate classify them generally with respect to the manner in which they will be taken up for consideration. For example, "General Orders" consists of bills and joint resolutions reported by Senate committees or ordered placed on calendar when received by the Senate; "Subjects on the Table" consists of matters placed there at request for later consideration; the "Executive Calendar" lists business to be disposed of in executive session, which includes treaties and the confirmation of presidential appointees. Executive session here signifies a session dealing with matters in which the Senate shares power with the executive.

THE USE OF THE CALENDARS

Selecting Bills on the Calendars

Long before a session ends the calendars are so crowded that only a fraction of the listed bills could possibly be disposed of by taking them up in order. Consequently Congress has been compelled to devise various ways of selecting for consideration some of the bills listed. For example, in the House on the first and third Mondays of each month the Consent Calendar is called, the rules may be suspended by a two-thirds vote and a bill passed. Fridays are set aside for the Calendar of Private Bills. Wednesdays are set aside for the House Calendar. On Calendar Wednesday, set aside for standing committees, the roll of committees is called in order to bring up for consideration bills and resolutions not otherwise privileged. A committee recognized for this purpose may select one of its bills on the calendar and may even consume the entire day on its measures. An emergency requiring immediate action or merely formal action may be disposed of by a member consulting the speaker and floor leaders in advance and moving unanimous consent for its consideration. On certain days members of the House are privileged to move suspension of the rules in order to consider a bill.

The Rules Committee of the House

The most important agency in determining which among the long lists of bills on the House calendars will be debated and brought to a vote is the Rules Committee. Since there must of necessity be selection from crowded calendars the powerful Rules Committee from time to time accomplishes this purpose by bringing in or proposing a special rule altering or setting aside a general rule. Its achievements may consist of obtaining the passage of "gag rules" limiting debate, prescribing or preventing amendment to specific measures, preventing certain measures from being considered, facilitating consideration of favored legislation, and the introduction of rules advancing certain bills ahead of others on the calendars. Since a majority of this Committee consists of outstanding majority party leaders, party discipline practically compels prompt adoption of any of the Rules Committee's proposals. The refusal of any representative in the House majority party to support the motions made by the Rules Committee may lead to loss of party support for his bills or even use of the party's congressional campaign funds to support a rival candidate against him at the next party nominating primary. This gives the Rules Committee the power to kill practically any pending measure its majority marks for the death sentence. Thus the Rules Committee can determine the agenda of the House as to important bills to be considered and, as an organ of the majority party, it can create a semblance of party government. In its crude and erratic way it does reduce to a workable quantity the volume of bills considered. But so nearly absolute is its power of life and death over important legislation that the House of Representatives has been charged with having abdicated its essential function to this little group, whose personal prejudices can constitute an enormous force in legislation. Seniority due to long continuous service largely determines membership of the Rules Committee. This means that safe or one-party districts notable for conservatism if not reaction provide the representatives who through this committee have almost a power of veto over pending legislation.

DEBATE AND VOTE ON MEASURES

The Committee of the Whole

A bill taken from the calendar is debated in that ancient parliamentary status known as the Committee of the Whole. This is a condition in which either house assumes for the time being that the entire membership present constitutes a committee. In the House the speaker does not preside over this committee but appoints a chairman. One hundred members suffice for a quorum of the Committee of the Whole. Debate during the reading of the bill for amendments is sprightly. It is carried on under the five-minute rule and may not be terminated by voting the previous question. The minority has opportunity to criticize the bill, section by section, as each is taken up. At the close of its deliberations the Committee of the Whole "rises," that is adjourns. When the House has resumed its regular status the chairman of the Committee of the Whole reports to the speaker of the House the action of the Committee on the measure. This report is, of course, merely a recommendation. If the bill is reported favorably, whether with or without amendment, the chairman of the Committee of the Whole moves its final or third reading and passage. Though it is unlikely, the bill may at this stage again be amended, or it may be recommitted with instructions to the standing committee that handled it, or it may be passed.

Methods of Voting

The commonest of the three methods of voting on a bill, resolution, or amendment by the House is by a *viva voce* or voice vote. However, one-fifth of the members on the floor may require a vote by tellers. Two tellers are appointed by the speaker and all the members who vote file between them so rapidly that usually the identity of the "pros" and "cons" cannot be ascertained by the newspaper men. However, on the occasion of an important measure, newspaper men have sometimes, but very rarely, engaged a specialist who has learned to recognize at sight every representative. These he identifies from the gallery one by one as they file between the tellers and, to the embarrassment of members who did not care to have their stand on the issue known, the result is publicized in the newspapers almost as if it had been on a record roll-call. The third method of voting is by "yeas" and "nays," which is required whenever one-fifth of a quorum demands it. This is a tedious and archaic system for a body of 435 members. The clerk first calls a member's name to which the member answers whereupon the clerk calls back again to see that he has heard aright in the echoing chamber. Many are absent when the roll is first called and the roll-call is repeated to give late arrivals an opportunity to vote. When a roll-call is ordered bells ring in corridors, in the congressional office buildings, committee rooms, and restaurants of the Capitol. But members know that they can count on half an hour to go on dictating letters, finishing lunch, making telephone calls, or concluding committee meetings. There was even the case of a representative who was able to rush the nineteen miles from his suburban home in time to beat the speaker's gavel closing a roll-call. It has been estimated that roll-calls in 1943 aggregated the time of twenty-four legislative days in the House and sixteen in the Senate. In a record vote members may arrange what is known as "pairing." This is an agreement between members favoring and opposing a bill that, in the case of the absence of a proponent, an opponent will also be absent or refrain from voting. Where a two-thirds vote is required two proponents have to be paired against an opponent. [18]

The Limitation of Debate

When the House is not sitting as a Committee of the Whole each speaker is limited to one hour except by unanimous consent. This, however, is not sufficient to keep debate within tolerable limits and consequently advance agreements on allotment of time for debate on a measure are usually made between majority and minority leaders. Time limits are sometimes determined by "special orders" introduced by the Rules Committee. The

[18] The clerk of the House supplies each member with a tally of his votes at the end of each session. This tally is so sacrosanct that no other person has access to it without the consent of the member—not even another member of the House. Anyone wishing to get the voting record of a Congressman can get it only by perusing the *Congressional Record* or subscribing to a legislative service which will do the job for him.

time alloted to debate is related to the importance of measures and the amount of controversy over them. Some bills may be given one or two days' time, set in advance, while less important ones may be limited to forty, twenty, or even ten minutes of debate, divided equally between proponents and opponents. Observers have noted the decline of debate over the years. "Fewer and fewer bills have been debated in either house long enough to involve three or more pages [in the *Congressional Record*]," according to Floyd M. Riddick. More than nine hundred bills and resolutions were passed by the House and Senate in the Second Session of the Seventy-eighth Congress and only eighty-six in the House and forty-seven in the Senate stirred any real discussion. [19]

Closure of Debate

At any stage of debate in the House the "previous question" may be moved and, if carried, further amendment is impossible. The speaker may allow each side twenty minutes more after which a vote is taken. This use of the previous question is the closure procedure of the House in ending debate and bringing the matter to vote. In the Senate, debate is almost without limit. Time and again a Senate minority has prevented the enactment of legislation by prolonged filibustering particularly near an end of a session. While a filibuster may be carried on by one senator it is more effective when members of a group arrange among themselves to speak in relays. The most irrelevant and absurd topic may be introduced at such times to prolong the filibuster and wear out the proponents of the bill. In 1917 a closure rule was adopted by the Senate. It required, to begin with, a petition signed by one-sixth of the Senate membership. If, after the expiration of two calendar days following the submission of the petition, it was supported by a two-thirds vote in favor of closing debate on the pending bill, each Senator who chose to speak thereafter might not continue longer than one hour. That the Senate closure was not a very effective device is indicated by the fact that closure motions have been voted down fourteen times in the last quarter of a century. Three closure attempts failed in 1946 alone. [20] Closure was successfully used in ending Senate debate on the Treaty of Versailles in 1919 and on the question of adherence to the World Court in 1926. On March 18, 1949, after a prolonged filibuster against the civil rights program of President Truman, a new closure rule was adopted as a so-called "compromise." It is not to be applied to any debate on a change of rules. With that exception the new rule permits closure of debate at any point in the Senate proceedings by a two-thirds majority vote of the entire Senate. This is generally regarded

[19] George B. Galloway: *Congress at the Crossroad*, p. 196.

[20] It is no simple or easy matter to tell where the dividing line is between debate and a filibuster. Representative Kefauver has said: "There is quite a difference between full debate and delaying tactics, where it is quite well known how everyone is going to vote. No further information is sought or is attempted to be given. That is when we have a filibuster. When the members start reading recipes from cook books and what-not that is really not democracy."—"What is Your Congress Doing." *University of Chicago Round Table* (1947), No. 483, p. 13.

as a weakening of the old rule which required a two-thirds vote of merely a quorum of the Senate.

Legislative Methods of the Senate

A bill that has passed the House and comes to the Senate or one that has originated in the Senate is referred to an appropriate committee. The committee may hold hearings, alter, pigeon-hole, or report the bill to the Senate with a recommendation for or against it. The senator reporting the bill for the committee may ask for unanimous consent for immediate consideration. If he is refused the bill goes on the Senate Calendar of "General Orders" which consists of all bills and joint resolutions reported by Senate committees or ordered placed on the calendar when received by the Senate. On Mondays the Senate follows this calendar unless it is dispensed with by unanimous consent. On all other days at the close of morning business a senator may move to take up any bill on the calendar out of its regular order. The final step in the Senate is the vote on passage which is usually a *viva voce* vote, but a yea and nay vote may be required by the demand of one-fifth of the senators present, as the Constitution provides.

FINAL STEPS IN LEGISLATION

The Conference Committee

Whenever a bill passes the two houses in somewhat different forms and neither house is willing to accept the version of the other a joint conference committee for that particular bill is appointed by the presiding officers of the two houses and assigned the duty of seeking to find a form agreeable to both houses. Conference committees perform this function with almost uniform faithfulness despite the widespread assumption that they often delete matters on which the houses agree and introduce new matter. Only three instances of that kind were found in a case study of fifty-six major bills from 1927 to 1949. However, when one house strikes out all matter after an enacting clause on a bill, the conference committee may write a new bill. The late Senator George W. Norris denominated the conference committee as the third house of Congress and "in very important matters of legislation, the most important branch of our legislature. . . . And for practical purposes, in most cases, it is impossible to defeat the legislation proposed by this conference committee. Every experienced legislator knows that it is the hardest thing in the world to defeat a conference report." [21] The difficulty is that a conference committee's report must be accepted or rejected without amendment by each house.

The President's Approval or Veto

When a measure has passed both houses in identical form it must next be passed upon by the president. If he decides to veto the measure he returns

[21] 73 *Congressional Record*, February 27, 1934, 78:3277; See *The Congressional Conference Committee, Seventieth to Eightieth Congresses* (Urbana, 1951).

it, with a message stating his objections, to the house in which it originated. If both houses pass the measure again and, in this case with two-thirds votes, it becomes law without his signature. If either house fails to muster the two-thirds vote Congress is said to have sustained the president's veto. If the president keeps a bill for ten days without signing it while Congress is in session the bill becomes law without his signature. But failure of the president to sign a measure in the ten days following adjournment kills the measure absolutely with what has been denominated the "pocket veto." So only such ones of the bills dumped on the president's desk at the end of a session as he chooses to sign become law.

SPECIAL SENATE FUNCTIONS

The Treaty-making Power of the Senate

The Constitution in its provision that the president "shall have power by and with the advice and consent of the Senate to make treaties provided two-thirds of the Senate present concur" does not clearly direct that the president negotiate and the senate ratify treaties. Practical considerations however have dictated this long-prevailing division of functions. President Washington was to discover that the Senate would not even consider a proposed treaty while he was present. Since the creation of the Committee on Foreign Relations by the Senate in 1816 presidents have generally kept in touch with the Senate regarding the negotiating of treaties. Secretaries of state who are ordinarily responsible for such projects usually take the Foreign Relations Committee into their confidence. John Hay, one of the ablest in this office, was continually in touch with the Committee but was so frustrated by the requirement of a two-thirds majority for treaty ratification that he once declared the "forefathers in their wisdom had arranged it so that kickers could rule." The Senate is usually represented on treaty-making commissions appointed by the president, particularly commissions to negotiate peace treaties, and at such general international conferences as that which formulated the Constitution of the United Nations.

Senate Procedure on a Proposed Treaty

When the Senate receives a negotiated treaty from the president it is referred to the Committee on Foreign Relations which scrutinizes it section by section. The Committee may ask the president for information on it. When the treaty is reported to the Senate the Committee of the Whole considers and debates it along with changes or reservations that the Committee on Foreign Relations may have recommended. The Committee of the Whole may also propose reservations and reservations may be made even by the Senate in regular sessions which are no longer secret as they once were when treaties were under consideration. The Senate may sabotage a proposed treaty by reservations which compel the president to renegotiate with the other nation or nations or abandon the project. The Covenant of the League of Nations in the Treaty of Versailles illustrates this.

The Senate refused to ratify the Covenant without reservations and Presiden Wilson, who had collaborated in the negotiating of the treaty in the first place, refused to accept the reservations. Evidently a president cannot press the Senate into ratification, as President Wilson discovered in 1919 when he sought to arouse the public in order to influence the Senate to accept the League of Nations.

Criticism of the Method of Making Treaties

A treaty has no greater legal validity than a statute and indeed a new statute may repeal provisions of existing treaties. The Supreme Court holds that treaties may repeal prior statutes just as statutes may repeal prior treaties, the latest always prevailing. Herein lies one of the arguments in favor of validating treaties by the same procedure required for enacting statutes—a simple majority of a quorum of each house. [22] This proposal grew out of the difficulty of obtaining the two-thirds majority in the case of many a meritorious proposal for an international agreement. With understandable exaggeration Secretary of State John Hay once wrote: "A treaty entering the Senate is like a bull going into the arena; no one can say just how or when the final blow will fall—but one thing is certain—it will never leave the arena alive." It is a curious fact that time has hallowed the two-thirds majority requirement which originated by the mere fortuitous circumstance of a deadlock in the Constitutional Convention that required a compromise. It was inserted to satisfy the planting interests which feared that commercial treaties favorable to the trading interests at the expense of agrarians might be enacted by plain majorities. There is evidently no marked sentiment for change and the Senate is not likely to surrender the power given it by the two-thirds majority requirement as long as the proposing of an amendment to make the change requires a two-thirds vote of both houses of Congress.

Impeachment

The Constitution vests in the House of Representatives "the sole power of impeachment" which means bringing charges of misconduct against "civil officers of the United States." The Supreme Court has held that this does not include members of Congress since they are elsewhere in the Constitution forbidden to hold any civil office and consequently cannot be civil officers. The House of Representatives starts impeachment proceedings by passing resolutions consisting of articles of impeachment charging a civil officer with "treason, bribery, or other high crimes and misdemeanors." The House appoints several of its members as a committee of "managers" to prosecute the impeached officer in his trial before

[22] While congressional reorganization was under consideration in the 79th Congress, proposals were made to remove the two-thirds vote in the Senate and substitute a simple majority of both houses. It never received serious consideration. The House has shared in determining foreign policies in the last few years to a greater degree than formerly because of the appropriations necessary to implement many of the treaty agreements and policies.

the Senate which, according to the Constitution, has "the sole power to try all impeachments." This means that the Senate sits as a court in judgment upon the officer who has been impeached. When a president of the United States is on trial under impeachment the Constitution prescribes that the chief justice of the United States shall preside over the Senate instead of the vice-president who might seem to have a personal interest in seeing the presidential office vacated. During the trial of Andrew Johnson congressional leaders insisted that the Senate was not a judicial court, that the senators were not required to confine themselves to the evidence presented but were obligated to respect their constituent's opinion—in short that they were performing a political rather than a judicial function. [23] However, in impeachment trials the Senate has generally followed established court procedure, issuing writs, subpoenaing witnesses, administering oaths, enforcing obedience, and punishing for contempt. Full opportunity is afforded the accused to be heard either in person or by counsel. The vote is taken by yeas and nays on each article of impeachment. The Senate has sat as a Court of Impeachment only twelve times. The most notable of these occasions was the trial of President Andrew Johnson which, after continuing three months, failed by a single vote to attain the two-thirds majority required for conviction.

Inadequacy of Impeachment

Impeachment trial by the Senate is an awkward, time-consuming, and inadequate device. If the House impeaches, the Senate has no choice but to sit in judgment upon the accused. It is practically impossible to keep senators on the floor during an impeachment trial. When the time comes to vote they are unacquainted with the evidence and they hesitate to vote for conviction. This makes it difficult to obtain the two-thirds vote necessary for conviction. Since most impeachments have been of Federal judges, Representative Hatton W. Summers, former Chairman of the House Judiciary Committee, has proposed that special courts be created consisting of circuit judges designated by the Supreme Court of the United States to try all judges of inferior Federal courts accused of misconduct. Upon conviction the judge could appeal his case to the Supreme Court of the United States. Legislation to this end passed the House in 1937 and 1941 but the Senate did not approve it. [24]

Resolutions

Either house of Congress may adopt a *plain resolution* affecting only that house and not submitted to the other house or to the president. This is how each house adopts its rules, calls upon other departments for information, disciplines its members, creates investigating committees, or merely expresses opinion on public issues. A *joint resolution* is one passed by both houses in the same form and submitted to the president for his

[23] See Wilfred E. Binkley: *President and Congress,* New York, 1947, pp. 141 ff.
[24] H. R. 1210, 79th Congress, 1st Session.

approval or veto. Joint resolutions are confusing because they follow the same procedure as statutes and there seems to be little excuse for them. The *concurrent resolution* is passed by both houses and is presumed to be a means of expressing facts, principles, and purposes of the two houses, such as the creation of a joint investigating committee. But usage has taken a strange turn with respect to concurrent resolutions; for a century and a quarter they have not been submitted to the president despite the unequivocal injunction of the Constitution: "Every order, resolution, or vote to which the concurrence of the Senate and House of Representatives may be necessary (except on a question of adjournment) shall be presented to the President of the United States." This usage has led to a subtle approach to infringement of presidential power. For example, in the Reorganization Act of 1939 and in the Lend-Lease Act of 1941, Congress reserved the right to terminate by concurrent resolution the powers granted the president. This, of course, deprived the president of his constitutional power of veto on repeal of legislation. [25]

SUMMARY

Most measures enacted by Congress are conceived outside the houses. More than half the bills introduced originate in the executive departments. Many major statutes of the last generation resulted from presidential initiative, and Congress depends more on the executive than is readily admitted. Energetic interest groups successfully urge many enactments upon Congress.

Every bill introduced is referred to a standing committee, which may pigeonhole it or gather information on it from hearings or from official or private agencies, organizations, or individuals, and report the bill to the house usually considerably altered. Such a reported bill is placed on a calendar from which it may be taken in accordance with house rules for debate in the Committee of the Whole. Debate in the lower house is strictly limited by rules or agreement and may be ended at any time by moving the previous question. A measure passing the two houses in different forms is referred to a joint conference committee which is expected to adjust differences so as to make it acceptable to both houses.

Usage has clarified the ambiguity of the Constitution's provisions for treaty making; the President negotiates the proposed treaty and submits it to the Senate, which may reject or ratify it with or without reservations. The difficulties due to the requirement of the two-thirds majority have led to the proposal that treaties be enacted like statutes by a simple majority vote of both houses.

Impeachment is apparently approaching obsolescence because of its interruption of the increasingly heavy legislative burden of the Senate. All but a few impeachment trials before the Senate have been of federal

[25] Howard White: "The Concurrent Resolution in Congress." *American Political Science Review* (1941), 35:886–9.

judges who might better be tried by a special court to be created by Congress for that purpose.

Three kinds of resolutions are passed by Congress. A plain resolution concerns only the one house that passes it. A concurrent resolution is passed by and concerns both houses. A joint resolution is not only passed by both houses but it also requires the President's signature and also has the effect of a law of general application.

CHAPTER XXIV

THE NATURE OF THE POWERS OF CONGRESS

Congress, the Chief Organ of the National Government

DESPITE their fear of a powerful legislature engendered by the excesses of the Revolutionary state legislatures the framers of the Constitution made Congress the fundamental organ of the Federal government. No one challenged Roger Sherman in the Constitutional Convention when he spoke of the legislature as "the depository of the supreme will of society," for he was only expressing the prevailing opinion on that matter. Colonial developments had given the legislature a commanding position in the thirteen colonial governments and, through its absolute control of public finance in each colony, had reduced the colonial governor to the necessity of begging at its door for needed appropriations. By 1787 legislatures had come to be regarded as peculiarly the people's own organs. To an extraordinary extent Congress is, consequently, the master of the major functions of the Federal government. The Constitution was by no means self-executing, and few indeed are the powers of any branch of the Federal government that are not more or less dependent upon preliminary congressional legislation. Congress determines, authoritatively, what the major public policies will be, creates the agencies for their execution, prescribes the manner of their administration, determines the number and qualifications of the personnel to be employed and its compensation. The manner of the organization of all the Federal courts and the assignment of their jurisdictions, except the original jurisdiction of the Supreme Court, are determined by Congress. Over all this Congress holds the power of life and death through control of the purse since not a dollar in the Federal treasury can be paid out to any official "but in consequence of appropriations made by law." The overwhelming bulk of the long list of powers of the president has been vested in him by acts of Congress, and without them he would be a much less significant official than he is today. Before Congress had begun to legislate in 1789 the only Constitutional function that President Washington could have performed would have been to "receive ambassadors and other public ministers," address Congress, or negotiate a treaty which would, of course, have had no validity without the consent of the Senate. Not only is the article on the legislature given first place in the Constitution but it constitutes more than half of the entire original document.

The Concept of a Government of Limited Powers

The Constitution reveals in its structure evidence that the framers made it under the influence of the idea of the social compact with its dogma of popular sovereignty. This conceived the people to be the original holders of all governmental powers; no government could have legitimate power derived from any other source than the people, and only such powers as the people chose willingly to delegate to it could be legally exercised by any government. Among the causes of the American Revolution was the resolute refusal of the colonists to accept the dictum of English Chief Justice Mansfield that Parliament was limited in power only by the physically impossible—that is, it could not, for example, repeal the law of gravitation. Mansfield was but expounding current English constitutional law, but to the colonists it represented the negation of the idea of limited government. State constitutions then as now granted power to the state legislature in one general expression and not item by item. The Constitution of Ohio, for example, provides: "The Legislative power of the state shall be vested in a general assembly consisting of a Senate and a House of Representatives." But state constitutions limit this wholesale grant of legislative power by bills of rights and other restrictions on the legislature that emphasize the principle of limited government.

The Federal Constitution's Limitation of Legislative Powers

The opening sentence of the body of the Federal Constitution reveals the contrast between its method of granting legislative power and the method of state constitutions. The Federal Constitution declares: "All legislative power *herein* granted shall be vested in a Congress of the United States which shall consist of a Senate and a House of Representatives." Significant indeed is the expression "herein granted" designed to underscore the limited power of Congress but even this did not suffice to allay the fears of the inland agrarians of the 1780's, who would not rest assured until they had got adopted the rather sweeping Tenth Amendment with its proviso: "The powers not delegated to the United States by the Constitution, nor prohibited by it to the States, are reserved to the states respectively or to the people." So far as this reservation is to the states it is, of course, a consequence of the distribution of powers in a Federal system. However, the Supreme Court has held that the "principal purpose" of the Tenth Amendment "was not the distribution of power between the United States and the States, but a reservation to the people of all powers not granted." [1] The Tenth Amendment, then, stands as a monument to the fundamental American constitutional principle of limited government—that is, government confined to delegated powers. The difference between the three types of government represented by the English Parliament, the Congress, and a state legislature can be brought into relief by three pertinent questions. When seeking the limits of legislative power the English Member of Parliament might raise the question: "Is this legislation or regulation within the bounds of the physically possible?" The American congressman might ask: "Has this power been delegated to Congress?" The state legislator's question would be: "Has this power been reserved to the states and not denied to them by the Federal Constitution or by the constitution of my state?"

THE POWERS OF CONGRESS

Classification of the Powers of Congress

Congress has many powers, some of which fall under the head of legislation, but it has others that, in a system of strictly separated powers, would be allocated to judicial or executive branches. Indeed most of a congressman's time is spent on matters that are not legislative in character, and so far as Congress as a whole is concerned the making of laws regulating the conduct of persons consumes but a minor fraction of the time it is in session. The powers of Congress can be classified as: (1) lawmaking, (2) providing for and supervising administration, (3) investigatory, (4) financial, (5) electoral, (6) judicial, (7) constituent, (8) executive, (9) self-management, (10) representative.

Legislative Powers of Congress

Congress's fundamental function is legislation. Legislation has been defined as the "expressly declared will of the sovereign authority. When the sovereign authority declares its will in the form of a law, it is said to legislate; and this function of sovereignty is called legislation." [2] The Constitution assigns this supremely important function to Congress and moreover declares that "laws made in pursuance of the Constitution" are a part of the Supreme Law of the Land. When it is realized that everyone living in the United States and subject to its jurisdiction, from a private person to the Chief Executive, the Congress, and the Supreme Court of the United States is alike subject to law the paramount importance of Congress's fundamental function comes into bold relief. The subjects of legislation assigned Congress by Article I, Section 8 of the Constitution include taxation, borrowing money, regulating commerce, naturalization, bankruptcy, coinage, standards of weights and measures, punishing counterfeiting and offenses against the laws of nations, post-offices, patents and copyrights, creating Federal courts, declaring war, creating an army and navy, super-

[1] Kansas v. Colorado, 206 U.S. 90 (1907).
[2] W. Markley: *Elements of Law* (6th ed.; 1905), chap. II.

vising the training of the state militia, and governing the district where the Federal capital is located.

Congressional Police Power

Congress exercises considerable police power, that is, it legislates so as to regulate the conduct of persons in order "to promote the health, safety, morals, and general welfare" of the American people. The Constitution delegates no police power as such. Yet there is not a feature of the police power as defined above that does not fall within the scope of congressional authority as a consequence of such specifically delegated powers as taxation, regulating commerce, or the postal powers. For example, Congress has forbidden the importation of obscene or indecent literature or pictures, and the use of the mails to defraud. Under its power to regulate interstate commerce it has forbidden transportation of lottery tickets, of women for immoral purposes, of food and drugs deceptively labelled or otherwise failing to comply with statutory requirements, and of diseased meats. The commerce power of Congress is used also for quarantine curbs against human, livestock, and plant diseases. Various kinds of frauds and swindles are outlawed by Congress under this power as well as the denial of interstate commerce for the purpose of violating state law.

The Federal taxing power was used in 1865 to tax to death state bank notes. In 1902 the dairy interests persuaded Congress to place a tax of ten cents a pound on oleomargarine colored as butter. In 1912 a tax of two cents a hundred on matches made by using white phosphorus ended that deadly industrial practice. In 1914 the Narcotic Act dealt illegitimate traffic in that commodity a blow by requiring a nominal license fee of one dollar, later increased to twenty-five dollars. The same year a tax of $300 a pound was laid on the sale of opium. In 1934 a tax of $200 was placed on the sale or transfer of any machine gun, sawed-off shot gun, or gun silencer.

The postal power affords Congress another basis for the exercise of police power. Obscene or indecent writing, pictures, or objects are denied postal privilege. Newspapers and periodicals considered seditious have at times been banned from the mails under statutory authorization. Perpetrators of frauds, swindlers, and dishonest enterprises use the mails under peril of severe penalties. A lesser penalty in these cases is the loss of the mailing privilege itself. Nor does Congress enact such legislation only because the Constitution assigns it the power; almost always it is in response to public influence or social pressures.

Providing for Administration of the Laws

Congress is the source of all Federal administrative power. Public administration has been defined as "the management of men and materials in accomplishing the purposes of the state."[3] Legislation consists mainly in determining what these purposes are. Within the constitutional limits

[3] Leonard D. White: *Public Administration.* New York, 1926, p. 2.

of its powers Congress decides what functions are to be undertaken. Certain fundamental activities are indispensable to the existence of government, for example, public finance, law enforcement, and foreign relations, each represented by an executive department. Other functions have been added as public opinion, operating usually through social pressures, has demanded them. Whenever Congress decides upon a new public function it must determine by law the agencies and the organization to be set up for seeing to the performance of the function. Here Congress exercises a wide discretion; it may establish a department, a bureau, a commission, or some other administrative agency as its judgment determines. But whatever Congress establishes it has to be manned with a personnel for which Congress must provide. Congress must also determine the agency's main rules of procedure and establish them by law. Congress must appropriate funds for operating and maintaining what it has created to execute its purposes. Even then there yet remains the necessity of Congress determining the means for supervising and controlling its created agencies to the end that it may know that the policies established by law are carried out as directed.

Congress as Overseer of Administration

"Legislative oversight of administration is a familiar and well-grounded assumption of responsible government," writes Arthur W. Macmahon. This oversight may be for the purpose of checking dishonesty and waste; or guarding against unsympathetic, overzealous, or harsh administrative conduct; or keeping the administrator acutely aware of the purpose of his agency by applying the layman's attitude of the legislator to the routines of the technician. Here Congress plays its part as the board of directors of the governmental corporation. This it may do through the amendment of statutes thereby correcting evident defects. A special House committee may investigate the extent to which administrative orders are inconsistent with statutes or just arbitrary. It is, however, through the power of the purse that Congress chiefly functions in this field, and the committees on appropriations have been identified as the outstanding instrument of congressional oversight of administration. [4]

The Investigatory Function of Congress

Nearly three hundred congressional investigations have been conducted since the first special congressional committee in Washington's administration investigated the defeat of General Arthur St. Clair by the Indians in 1791. In the course of these investigations Congress may compel witnesses to attend and testify; it may demand the production of papers and

[4] Arthur W. Macmahon: "Congressional Oversight of Administration: The Power of the Purse." *Political Science Quarterly* (1943), 57:161–90; 380–414; Leonard D. White: "Congressional Control of the Public Service." *American Political Science Review* (1945), 39:1–11.

information; and it may punish for contempt in case of refusal to comply with its directions for such purposes. These powers have been sustained by the Supreme Court of the United States in half a hundred cases. Concerning these powers Chief Justice White, speaking for the Court, said: "From the power to legislate given by the Constitution to Congress there was to be implied the right to preserve itself, that is to deal by way of contempt with direct obstruction to legislative duties . . . which include contumacy in refusing to obey orders, to produce documents or give testimony which there was a right to compel." [5] Thus the investigating function is in the first place a means of gathering information on which to base legislation. In the second place it is a device by which Congress may watch, study, correct, and improve administration. It can thereby detect whether a policy established by Congress has been reversed without its sanction or knowledge. Finally the public can be informed by the congressional committee's turning the searchlight on a particular governmental activity. [6]

Financial Function of Congress

The sovereignty of Congress in the field of Federal finance is specified in the constitutional provision: "No money shall be drawn from the Treasury but in consequence of appropriation made by law." The Constitution also provides that all bills for raising revenue shall originate in the House of Representatives, to which usage has added the initiating of appropriation bills. In practice the Senate functions as a court of appeals in financial legislation often mending defects of such measures sent over from the House.

The Electoral Function of Congress

When the presidential electors have cast their ballots in their respective states the Constitution provides that "they shall make distinct lists of all persons voted for as President and of all persons voted for as Vice-President, and of the number of votes for each; which lists they shall sign and certify and transmit sealed to the seat of government of the United States, directed to the President of the Senate; the President of the Senate shall, in the presence of the Senate and House of Representatives, open all the certificates and the votes shall then be counted." This fails to locate precisely the authority for determining a question such as arose in 1876 when several states sent two conflicting certificates each claiming to be the official electoral vote of the state. After a prolonged and inconclusive controversy Congress created and delegated to an electoral commission of fifteen members the duty of determining which certificates were valid. What the majority of the commission did in the case of every disputed

[5] 243 U.S. 577 (1917).
[6] Marshall E. Dimock: *Congressional Investigating Committees,* Johns Hopkins Studies in History and Political Science, XLVII (Baltimore, 1929), pp. 1–182.

vote was to accept the certificate authenticated by the state official authorized by state law to perform that function. To prevent another such dispute Congress in 1887 enacted into law the principle followed by the electoral commission.

Whenever the Electoral College fails to elect a president through the lack of a majority for any candidate, the Constitution provides that the election of the president shall be by the House of Representatives with each state casting one vote. Thomas Jefferson was elected by the House of Representatives in 1801 and John Quincy Adams in 1825. If no candidate for vice-president receives a majority in the Electoral College the Constitution designates the Senate to elect that officer, which it did in 1837 by choosing Richard M. Johnson. The Constitution also vests in Congress the very important power of determining who is to fill the office of president when it becomes vacant and there is no vice-president. In exercising this power Congress enacted Presidential Succession Laws in 1792, 1886, and 1947.

Judicial Powers of Congress

The well-established power of Congress to subpoena witnesses before committees conducting investigations, and to punish intransigent witnesses for contempt are unquestionably judicial powers but the courts have made it clear that these are constitutional powers of Congress only when used to carry out a function of Congress. Congress is performing a judicial function when it determines the qualification of its members. Deciding which of contesting claimants in a disputed election is to be seated partakes of the nature of a judicial function; so also does deciding on the expulsion of or otherwise penalizing its members. Outstanding among the judicial functions of Congress is the power of the House of Representatives to impeach officers of the United States and of the Senate to sit as a court in such cases.

Congress's Part in Amending the Constitution

The Constitution assigns Congress the power of proposing amendments to the Constitution by a two-thirds vote of both houses. This method has been used for initiating every amendment to the Constitution thus far proposed despite the alternate method of proposing amendments by a convention to be called by Congress upon application by the legislatures of two-thirds of the states. That the president's signature is not required on resolutions of the two houses in proposing amendments was decided in 1798 by the Supreme Court when it held that the Eleventh Amendment was validly proposed though the resolution had not been presented to the president. [7] In proposing the Eighteenth Amendment, Congress prescribed a time limit of seven years for its ratification. The Supreme Court held

[7] Hollingsworth v. Virginia, 3 Dallas 378 (1798).

that Congress had not exceeded its power in providing that the amendment would be inoperative unless ratified in seven years. [8]

Executive Powers

The thought and practice of modern nations classify as executive powers the management of a nation's foreign relations and the appointment of higher officers. The Senate shares with the president the exercise of both these powers. The Constitution provides that the President "shall have the power, by and with the advice and consent of the Senate to make treaties, provided that two-thirds of the Senators present concur; and he shall nominate and, by and with the advice and consent of the Senate, shall appoint," all but "inferior" Federal Officers. The Senate has enormously fortified its executive power of confirming nominees through the usage known as "senatorial courtesy." Through this practice senators compel the president to consult in advance the senators of his party from the state in which the Federal office to be filled is located. Thereby individual senators may exercise an absolute veto on the president's choice of an appointee.

Power of Self-Management

No external authority has any control over the internal management of the two houses of Congress. Rules of proceeding, largely inherited from the early state legislatures, are determined by each house with freedom in such determination limited only by specific provisions of the Constitution. Each house has its own police headed by its sergeant-at-arms. The power to punish its members for disorderly conduct may extend to imprisonment.[9] The right to expel members extends to all offenses which, in the judgment of the Senate or House, are inconsistent with the trust and duty of a member. [10]

The Power of Representation

Whatever the framers of the Constitution may have had in mind, congressmen are in truth representatives of their constituents serving as quasi-ambassadors of their states and districts. The unwritten constitution, in this case usage, has supplemented the one framed at Philadelphia, and has determined the functions of representatives and senators in accordance with deep-rooted American traditions. They become the "bell boys" of their constituents, providing for them a liaison with the administrator in department, bureau, or other agency.

Mandatory Powers

Certain powers of Congress are so expressed in the Constitution as to imply that Congress has no choice but to exercise them and they have conse-

[8] Dillon v. Gloss, 256 U.S. 368, 371, 374 (1921).
[9] Kilbourn v. Thompson, 103 U.S. 168, 189 (1881).
[10] *In re* Chapman, 166 U.S. 661, 669 (1897).

quently been designated "mandatory powers." For example, there is the requirement that "representatives shall be apportioned among the several states . . . according to their respective number" to be determined by a decennial census. Congress has always heeded the "shall" with respect to taking the census but it disregarded the injunction to reapportion representatives following the census of 1920. If the legislatures of two-thirds of the states make application for the calling of a convention in order to propose amendments to the Constitution it would be mandatory upon Congress to issue the call. There are no sanctions either executive or judicial to compel Congress to exercise a mandatory constitutional direction if it chooses to ignore it. In such a case only public pressure could compel Congress to perform its obligation.

Discretionary Powers

Nearly all the powers of Congress are discretionary. There is no implied obligation that Congress must exercise these powers. Congress, for example, had the power to regulate interstate commerce for a century before it decided to exercise it in enacting a general statute, the Interstate Commerce Act of 1887. Congress has the power to pass uniform bankruptcy laws. It first exercised this power by passing a bankruptcy law in 1800 which it repealed in 1803; it passed a second bankruptcy law in 1841 and repealed it in 1843; a third such act was passed in 1867 and repealed in 1878; in 1898 Congress enacted the present bankruptcy law. This is certainly the exercise of discretion in using a congressional power. It is, by and large, the pressures that impinge upon Congress that determine how it uses its discretion.

INTERPRETATION OF THE POWERS OF CONGRESS

Loose Construction of Congressional Powers

The final clause of the list of eighteen in Article I, Section 10 of the Constitution, delegating the powers of Congress, authorizes it "to make all laws which shall be necessary and proper for carrying into execution the foregoing powers, and all other powers vested by this Constitution in the government of the United States, or in any department or office thereof." Here is a provision that does not delegate new substantive power to Congress but instead amplifies all the specified powers of Congress even those that are non-legislative. The principle of loose construction of the Constitution is derived from this clause. When in 1791 Congress confronted President Washington with a bill to charter the Bank of the United States, he was undecided whether to sign it. He therefore sought the opinions of his department heads, "in writing" as the Constitution directs. Jefferson, in his opinion, pointed out that no power to charter a bank had been specifically delegated to Congress and it was "not necessary" because the powers of Congress "can be carried into execution without a bank." This was "strict construction" of the Constitution but the validity of Jefferson's reasoning was denied by Hamilton in the opinion he gave Washington. Hamilton argued that "*to be necessary is to be incidental,* and may be denominated the natural means of executing a power," and furthermore, "adherence to the letter of its [Congress's] powers could at once arrest the motions of the government." Nearly a generation later Chief Justice Marshall in the first judicial determination of the constitutionality of the Bank of the United States took a passage from Hamilton's opinion and paraphrased it in the limpid English that stands to this day as the classic statement of the principle of loose construction of the Constitution. "Let the end be legitimate," said Marshall speaking for the Court, "let it be within the scope of the Constitution, and all means which are appropriate, which are plainly adapted to that end, which are not prohibited but consist with the spirit and letter of the Constitution, are constitutional."[11] Jefferson as president discovered in 1803 that the strict construction he had expounded a dozen years earlier proved to be impracticable when he was confronted with the necessity of purchasing the Louisiana territory as a precaution for the defense of the United States. Moreover, an able American scholar concluded that the Embargo Act of Jefferson's administration "carried national authority to logical extremities to which the Federalists would not have dared to go. The Enforcement act, passed to sustain the Embargo, was a greater interference with the ordinary privileges of citizens than would have been necessary in the exercise of war powers."[12] In the main, strict construction has been a slogan of the opposition party, the "outs." It is today little more than a relic in the museum of constitutional history.

Congress Authorized to Provide for Performance of All Federal Functions

The "necessary and proper" clause also authorizes Congress to make all laws that are necessary and proper for carrying into execution all the other or non-legislative functions "vested in the government of the United States or in any department or office thereof." This refers to the executive and judicial branches of the government and is the source of the enormous power Congress possesses over these other great branches. The "necessary and proper" clause authorizes Congress to enact the legislation required to create the inferior courts and absolutely determine all their jurisdiction and to decide how much appellate jurisdiction is to be left to the Supreme Court. Every part of the gigantic administrative machine constituting the executive branch of the government is a consequence of legislation based on the "necessary and proper" clause. The clause also authorizes Congress to legislate in the fields of admiralty and maritime jurisdictions. It is the basis of Congress's power to enact legislation to carry into effect the pro-

[11] McCulloch v. Maryland, 4 Wheaton 316 (1819).
[12] Henry Jones Ford: *The Rise and Growth of American Politics.* New York, 1898, pp. 131–2.

visions of treaties, as illustrated by the statute implementing the Migratory Bird Treaty and upheld by the Supreme Court in Missouri v. Holland. [13] Congress has no delegated statutory power to regulate killing of migratory birds but accomplished that purpose by treaty. Congress has also been granted the "power to enforce by appropriate legislation" the provisions of the Thirteenth, Fourteenth, Fifteenth, Sixteenth, and Nineteenth Amendments. This authorization is contained in the amendments themselves.

Resulting Powers

A resulting power is not traceable to one specific delegation of power in the Constitution but is interpreted to be resultant from several or all of the delegated powers. In his opinion on the constitutionality of chartering the Bank of the United States, Hamilton reasoned that "there is another class of powers which may be properly denominated resulting powers." [14] These he thought might "result from the whole mass of powers of government, and from the nature of political society." Joseph Story accepted this interpretation and expounded it further including thereby the power to sue, to make contracts, to condemn land by eminent domain, and to punish certain crimes. This pattern of exposition was adopted by the Supreme Court in the Legal Tender Cases and so given the added weight of judicial authority. Justice Strong, speaking for the Court, observed: "It is not indispensable to the existence of any power claimed for the federal government that it can be found specified in the words of the Constitution or clearly and directly traceable to some one of the specified powers. Its existence may be deduced fairly from more than one of the substantive powers expressly defined, or from all combined. It is allowable to group together any number of them and infer from them all that the power claimed had been conferred." [15]

Does Congress Possess Inherent Powers?

There are powers presumed to be "inherent in sovereignty" which are authoritatively recognized as belonging to the Federal government such as power to acquire and govern territories, to exclude aliens, and to carry on war. Justice Oliver Wendell Holmes, speaking for the Court, and quoting from an earlier opinion, said: "It is not lightly to be assumed that in matters requiring national action, a power which must belong to and reside in every civilized government is not to be found." [16] The Supreme Court, however, did not accept the doctrine proclaimed by President Theodore Roosevelt in an address delivered at Harrisburg, Pennsylvania in 1905 in which he argued that an "inherent power [rests] in the nation outside the enumerated powers conferred upon it by the Constitution, in all cases where

[13] 252 U.S. 416 (1920).
[14] Alexander Hamilton: *Works* (Henry Cabot Lodge, ed.) (1851), vol. IV, pp. 104–7. 9 vols. New York, 1885.
[15] 12 Wallace 457 (1871).
[16] Missouri v. Holland, 252 U.S. 416 (1920).

the subject involved was beyond the power of the several states." [17] When, in the following year, Roosevelt's Attorney General sought to intervene in a case between two states on the ground that, since a reclamation project overlapped the jurisdictions of the two states, it automatically fell within the sphere of the Federal authority, the Supreme Court denied the claim of Federal jurisdiction. But in 1936 the Supreme Court recognized inherent powers by holding that, with independence, the United States acquired external sovereignty and "it results that the investment of the Federal Government with powers of external sovereignty did not depend upon the affirmative grants of the Constitution." [18]

IMPLIED LIMITATIONS UPON THE POWERS OF CONGRESS

Congress May Not Re-delegate Its Powers

The powers delegated by the Constitution to Congress may not be re-delegated by Congress to any other agency, person, or persons. The principle on which this interpretation is based can be found nowhere in the Constitution. It is a principle of common law and as applied here signifies that the agency which the sovereign, the people, has designated to exercise a power may not shift that power elsewhere. For example, the National Recovery Act in 1933 authorized representatives of an industry acting in cooperation with government officials to draw up codes of fair competition which when signed by the president were to have the force of law. The astonishing feature of all this was that neither the president nor the governmental officials legislated, that is made the codes; they were made by private citizens. Justice Cardozo condemned the act as "delegation run riot." In unmistakable language the Supreme Court declared: "Congress cannot delegate legislative power to the President to exercise an unfettered discretion to make whatever laws he thinks may be needed for the rehabilitation and expansion of trade and industry." [19] In another case involving the National Recovery Act the Supreme Court declared that "the delegation is plainly void because the power sought to be delegated is legislative power yet nowhere in the statute has Congress declared or indicated any policy or standard to guide or limit the President when acting under such delegation." [20]

What Congress May Delegate

It is a recognized principle of constitutional law that Congress may determine a public policy within the scope of its delegated powers and then create an agency to administer the policy according to a formula or stand-

---

[17] Theodore Roosevelt, *Presidential Addresses*, Homeward Bound Edition, 8 vols. New York, 1911, vol. V, p. 754.

[18] Kansas v. Colorado, 206 U.S. 46 (1907); 299 U.S. 304 (1936).

[19] Schechter v. United States, 295 U.S. 495 (1935).

[20] Panama Refining Co. v. Ryan, 293 U.S. 388 (1935).

ard prescribed in the statute creating it. Thus Congress has established the Interstate Commerce Commission and vested in it the power, among other things, to determine rates for common carriers engaged in interstate commerce but the rates must be so calculated as to yield a "fair return" to the carrier on the "value" of his property. The Federal Trade Commission is authorized by statute to "prevent persons, partnerships, or corporations, except banks, and common carriers . . . from using unfair methods of competition in commerce and unfair or deceptive acts or practices in commerce." The unfair methods are specifically described by statutes. The prescription of these formulas by which the agencies administer the statutes saves Congress from unconstitutional delegation of legislative power.

Congress's Powers Limited to its Own Functions

Congress may not constitutionally exercise executive and judicial functions except in so far as they are delegated to it. Nevertheless Congress does assume these functions, not brazenly but in border-line cases. Strict application of the principle of separated powers is, indeed, impossible because the terms "legislative," "executive," and "judicial" are incapable of precise definition. The judgment of a court as to whether a particular act of government falls within one or another of these three fields may be merely a subjective opinion or even a prejudice of the judge called upon to decide the matter. The necessary function of the courts in these questions of congressional jurisdiction is illustrated by the case of District Attorney Kilbourn who made derogatory remarks about a congressional committee and refused to respond to a subpoena to appear before it. The Supreme Court held that the power of inquiry of a house was limited to the subjects over which it "had jurisdiction." Congress might have proceeded against Kilbourn by way of its unquestionable power of impeachment but in its committee investigation of him it was usurping a purely judicial function. [21] When, however, in 1924 the Senate was investigating the Department of Justice and its head, Attorney General Harry M. Daugherty, the Supreme Court sustained the Senate in its subpoena of the Attorney General's brother because the object of the Senate "in ordering the investigation was to aid in legislating." [22] In Myers v. United States the Supreme Court decided in 1926 that the Tenure of Office Acts passed in the 1860's and requiring consent of the Senate for the president's dismissal of executive appointees had been unconstitutional as congressional interference with an exclusively executive power.

Congress May Not Impose Inappropriate Functions on Other Departments

Congress has by statute sometimes assigned to the executive and to the judicial departments what the Supreme Court has held not to be their con-

---

[21] Kilbourn v. Thompson, 103 U.S. 168 (1881).
[22] McGrain v. Daugherty, 272 U.S. 135 (1927).

stitutional functions. During the presidency of Washington, Congress assigned the circuit courts the duty of examining applications for pensions. This led to the statement of Chief Justice Jay and Associate Justice Cushing that neither the legislative nor executive branch may impose upon the courts any but judicial duties. It is believed that Congress may not deny the Supreme Court power to decide whether legislation is unconstitutional except by an extraordinary majority although the Court might voluntarily adopt such a regulation. In 1864 Chief Justice Taney rejected a statutory assignment to the Supreme Court of appeals from judgments of a court of claims. Since payment of the claims would be dependent upon subsequent recommendations of the secretary of the Treasury and on an appropriation by Congress Taney concluded that the Supreme Court's action would be mere recommendation instead of the final judicial determinations which the Constitution assigns to the Court.

Restrictions on Congress Due to the Nature of the Federal System

There are implied restrictions on Congress based on the principle of Constitutional interpretation that neither the Federal nor state governments may exercise their powers in such a manner as to obstruct the operation of the other. For example, Congress may not lay a tax that burdens the instrumentalities of state government or do anything that would cripple state and local governments in the performance of their essential functions. Congress may not exercise its delegated powers in a way to prevent a state's exercise of its police powers, that is the protections of the health, morals, good order, education, and general welfare of the people within the state. Until recently the Supreme Court held that Congress could not use any of its delegated powers in a manner that invaded the reserved powers of the states. But this principle that the reserved powers or undelegated powers of the states constitute a check on the powers of Congress has been abandoned. The Supreme Court's approval of the National Labor Relations Act with its Federal regulation of intra-state manufacturing indicated that it has ceased to use the state's reserved powers to limit Congress's use of its delegated powers. Thus the old assumption that the regulation of intrastate commerce is a reserved power of the states and consequently immune to Federal regulation is now an obsolete constitutional interpretation. "Although activities may be intrastate in character when separately considered, if they have such a close and substantial relation to interstate commerce that their control is essential or appropriate to protect that commerce from burdens and obstructions, Congress cannot be denied the power to exercise that control." [23]

Congress Free from Executive or Judicial Interference

The other two great branches of the Federal government have never manifested a tendency to interfere with Congress. The charge of dictator has

[23] N.L.R.B. v. Jones and Laughlin Steel Corporation, 301 U.S. 1 (1937).

been freely hurled at presidents by partisan opponents since the administration of Andrew Jackson and not even the mild mannered Harding completely escaped the accusations. [24] Such charges ignore the patent fact that most of the specific powers of the president are the results of congressional legislation and what has been enacted can be repealed, as many a President has had well impressed upon him. Presidents who have seemed to dominate Congress have only been the media through whom public pressures were brought to bear upon Congress. Arbitrary executive usurpations of the powers of Congress or interference with its legislative functions are no part of American history. Nor has the judiciary, inherently the weakest branch of the government, ever made the slightest gesture of pressure on Congress. In deciding that an act of Congress is unconstitutional the courts are only performing a long-established judicial function but even this is done only when a legal action in its normal course confronts the court with the question. No matter how flagrantly unconstitutional the judiciary might consider a pending measure before Congress, judges would scrupulously refrain from attempting openly to influence the course of legislation. No mandamus would ever issue from the Supreme Court directing Congress to perform a "mandatory" function such as the decennial reapportionment of representatives in Congress among the states. Time and again the Supreme Court has refused to take cognizance of controversies which it interpreted as political issues and as such to be determined by the political branches of the government, that is Congress and the executive. It must never be forgotten that both the executive and the judiciary are at the disadvantage of being subordinated by the fact that the Congress through the sovereign power of legislation and appropriation can recast the organization of both the other branches of the Federal government.

SUMMARY

The fundamental powers of the national government are legislative powers, and in accordance with the doctrine of limited government they are specified in Article 1, section 8 of the Constitution. As an incident of several of these powers Congress exercises considerable police power. Congress must also provide the machinery for law enforcement and scrutinize its administration. For this purpose it conducts numerous investigations. It levies taxes and appropriates money, witnesses the counting of the electoral votes cast for presidential candidates, decides contested elections of its members, impeaches and tries Federal officers, and proposes constitutional amendments.

Whether the specified powers were to be construed strictly or loosely was settled quite early in favor of the latter by congressional practice and confirmed by judicial decision. Presently resulting powers were being derived from several or all of the specified powers.

By implication it is reasoned that Congress may not redelegate its

[24] See Wilfred E. Binkley: *President and Congress* (New York, 1945), p. 218.

powers, may not exercise the powers of other branches of the government, impose upon another branch inappropriate powers, or infringe upon the reserved powers of the states.

Contrary to a general impression Congress has been free from executive domination. Popular presidents have provided the leadership for translating strong trends of public opinion into national policies and Congress then has no choice but to trail along. Even the judiciary reflects strong trends of public opinion instead of imposing an arbitrary will upon Congress.

PART
VII

THE FEDERAL JUDICIARY

CHAPTER XXV

THE FEDERAL JUDICIARY

The Background of the Federal Judiciary

THE Federal judiciary is a distinctly American institution. No more substantial piece of work was done by the framers of the Constitution than the provision for this branch. Nor need it be assumed that the idea was a collective flash of creative intuition. Without in the least detracting from the credit due the framers it must be said that the judiciary represents the culmination of the adjustments of clashing interests that generations of Americans had already experienced, first as colonists, then as citizens of the thirteen sovereign states and as citizens of the United States under the Articles of Confederation. The chain of pertinent events that preceded the creation of the Supreme Court of the United States was a succession of boundary disputes settled in colonial times by the British crown. During the Revolutionary War the Continental Congress wrestled with these boundary controversies until the Articles of Confederation provided a special Court of Appeals for settling them. The successor to this Court, with vastly broader powers, lives today in the Supreme Court of the United States. Thus again were the competent framers of the Constitution the efficient media through whom historic forces fulfilled their appropriate purposes.

The Necessary Scope of Federal Judicial Powers

The need for an umpire in the dual system of a federation is by no means confined to boundary disputes. There are the inevitable controversies between state and national power as distributed by a written Federal constitution, and the resolving of these controversies is necessarily a judicial function. Far more important is the fact that, since the Federal government prescribed by the Constitution acts directly on individuals, it predicates a system of Federal statutes and, as a consequence, cases to be adjudicated.

While it could have been arranged that state courts exclusively attend to this function in the first instance, the reducing of the various judgments of the courts of the several states to a uniform interpretation would require at least a central Supreme Court. Then there would be questions about the disposition of Federal property and there would be inevitable controversies between citizens of different states involving state laws that only a Federal judiciary, presumably impartial, could appropriately handle. Nor could state courts adjudicate with propriety the rights of foreigners. These are based on international law, that is the "law of nations" as the Constitution puts it, which consists of the regulations laid down by treaties and the international practices established by custom and precedent as revealed in cases adjudicated, and which requires national courts. Likewise inappropriate for state courts would be admiralty and maritime jurisdiction involving maritime contracts, collisions and damages by American vessels on the high seas or on navigable lakes and rivers, and by foreign vessels which later enter American ports.

THE CONSTITUTION'S PROVISIONS FOR A JUDICIARY

Congress's Authority to Organize the Federal Courts

To meet the need of a Federal judiciary the Constitution provided: "The judicial power of the United States shall be vested in one Supreme Court and such inferior courts as Congress may from time to time ordain and establish." The jurisdiction of these courts was to "extend to all cases in law and equity, arising under this Constitution, the laws of the United States, and treaties made, or which shall be made under their authority; to all cases affecting ambassadors, other public ministers and consuls; to all cases of admiralty and maritime jurisdiction; to controversies to which the United States shall be a party; to controversies between two or more states; between a state and citizens of another state; between citizens of different states, between citizens of the same state claiming lands under grants of different states, and between a state, or the citizens thereof, and foreign states, citizens, or subjects." Since the Constitution merely authorized Congress to organize the courts, legislation for that purpose was promptly provided in the Judiciary Act of 1789. This first of the judiciary acts established a Supreme Court consisting of a chief justice and five associate justices and thirteen districts each constituting the jurisdiction of a court presided over by a district judge. This was to be a court of first instance or the starting point of the Federal cases mentioned above except those few cases over which the Constitution had given the Supreme Court original jurisdiction. Eastern,[1] Middle and Southern circuits were established in 1789, each with a court consisting of one district judge and two members of the Supreme Court; consequently there were no circuit judges as such. The circuit courts were to sit on appeals from the district courts. At the same time they also had original jurisdiction concurrent with the district courts. So

[1] New York and the New England states.

CHAPTER XXV: *The Federal Judiciary* 501

far as the Constitution is concerned Congress might have refrained from establishing Federal courts inferior to the Supreme Court and designated the state courts alone for that purpose. Because of state jealousy of the new Federal government many members of Congress in 1789 considered inferior Federal courts not only unnecessary but a positive menace to state power and prestige. They would have vested all original jurisdiction of Federal cases in state courts and provided for appeals of decisions to the Supreme Court of the United States when required in order to protect Federal interests. However, the nationalist influence in Congress was strong enough to get established separate inferior courts at the price of reducing their original jurisdiction to a minimum and leaving the rest of it to the state courts even in Federal cases.

The Limited Original Jurisdiction of the Supreme Court

The Constitution provides that the Supreme Court shall have original jurisdiction in "all cases affecting ambassadors, other public ministers, and consuls, and those in which the state shall be a party." Assuming that this was not intended to be an exclusive list, Congress, in the Judiciary Act of 1789, authorized the Supreme Court to issue "writs of mandamus . . . to any courts appointed, or persons holding office, under the authority of the United States." A writ of mandamus is a court order directing an officer under penalty to perform a purely ministerial or non-discretionary duty. We shall see that this provision was held to be unconstitutional by the Supreme Court early in the chief justiceship of John Marshall on the ground that it was an addition to the original jurisdiction that the Constitution had vested in the Supreme Court.

Appeals from State Courts to the Supreme Court of the United States

It is universally accepted today that cases arising in state courts and involving questions of Federal power may be appealed to the Supreme Court of the United States. However, this was not specifically directed by the Constitution and it consequently was strenuously challenged in the early national period. The twenty-fifth section of the Judiciary Act of 1789 provided that whenever a state supreme court, in a state case involving a question of conflict of a state with Federal power, decides a case in favor of the state's contention, the case might be appealed to and re-examined by the Supreme Court of the United States. Strong opposition, particularly in Virginia, developed later among those who believed that the supreme court of a state must have final jurisdiction in cases of that kind. But for the resolute determination with which Chief Justice Marshall called up such cases for review by the Supreme Court of the United States the provision for their review might have become a dead letter. In 1821, in the case of Cohens v. Virginia, [2] the Supreme Court of the United States under Marshall reviewed on appeal a judgment of the Supreme Court of Virginia.

[2] 6 Wheaton 264 (1821).

502 A GRAMMAR OF AMERICAN POLITICS

Despite the fact that it sustained the judgment of the Virginia court the Supreme Court of the United States brought down a storm of protest upon itself. Virginians violently denounced the appeal as a usurpation of state power for the aggrandizement of the national government. Only the decisions of state supreme courts against the claim of Federal authority were then subject to appeal to the Supreme Court of the United States. But a generation ago reactionary state supreme courts were applying the guarantees of the Federal Constitution, such as "due process," and the "privileges and immunities" provisions of the Fourteenth Amendment so unreasonably against new legislation of their states that Congress in 1914 amended the provision for appeals. Now appeals can be made to the Supreme Court of the United States even when the state supreme court has sustained the claim of Federal authority. Thus it is now possible for the Federal Supreme Court to prevent state courts from arbitrarily using the restrictions of the Federal Constitution on the states to nullify their own state statutes. [3]

THE APPOINTMENT OF FEDERAL JUDGES

Constitutional Provisions for Appointment of Judges

The Constitution provides that Federal judges shall be appointed by the president by and with the advice and consent of the Senate. It might quite naturally be assumed that a tradition of inflexible non-partisanship would develop in selecting judges, particularly members of the Supreme Court and most of all the chief justice. Yet when a president appoints as chief justice someone with a party affiliation different from his own it is headline news. Nothing of this kind happened before the Court was a century and a quarter old. Then President William Howard Taft promoted from associate to chief justice Edward D. White, a conservative Louisiana Democrat not of the dominant wing of his party. The only other exception was the promotion of Republican Associate Justice Harlan F. Stone to the position of chief justice by Democratic President Franklin D. Roosevelt. Stone had manifested a liberal attitude on the constitutionality of important legislation of the Roosevelt administration. While the appointment of judges of the district courts and circuit courts is by no means a matter of party patronage, nevertheless appointment to these positions is cultivated by obtaining the recommendations of county and state committees of the party in control of the presidency. Nor can the president disregard "senatorial courtesy" in this matter. For example, in 1939, the Senate rejected President Franklin D. Roosevelt's nomination of Floyd H. Roberts as Federal district judge of the Virginia judicial district because the two Virginia senators invoked the privilege of "senatorial courtesy." [4] Indeed it can be

[3] Felix Frankfurter and James M. Landis: The Business of the Supreme Court. New York, 1927, pp. 193–8.
[4] The letters of the President and the Senators on this controversy were printed in the United States News, February 13, 1939.

said that in a majority of cases the Senate, or rather two senators, virtually appoint judges, a result certainly never intended by the Constitution.

Scrutiny of the Social Philosophy of Judicial Nominees

Both president and Senate are much less concerned about a judicial nominee's party affiliation or even how strictly judicial he may be than they are about his social philosophy. Classic illustrations of the "standards" in such appointments are revealed in the letters of President Theodore Roosevelt to Senator Henry Cabot Lodge. In 1906 President Roosevelt wrote: ". . . the *nominal* politics of the man has nothing to do with his actions on the bench. His real politics are all important." He would therefore nominate Horace H. Lurton of Tennessee to a seat on the Supreme Court because Lurton was "right on the Negro question . . . right on the power of the federal government . . . right about corporations . . . right about labor even if he was a Democrat." [5] In a similar vein was his comment on nominating Oliver Wendell Holmes to membership in the Supreme Court. "The Supreme Court of the 1860's was good exactly insofar as its membership fairly represented the spirit of Lincoln. . . . This is true at the present day. . . . Now I should like to know that Judge Holmes was in entire sympathy with our views, that is with your views and mine . . . before I would feel justified in appointing him. . . . I should hold myself as guilty of an irreparable wrong to the nation if I should put in his place any man who was not absolutely sane and sound on the great national policies for which we stand in public." [6] Here is a frank statement of what is probably the guiding motivation of most if not all presidents in determining judicial nominations. It is not essentially different from that which guides the Senate in confirming presidential nominations to the Federal courts. Nor is the Senate any less concerned than presidents over the social philosophies of judicial nominees. Not all presidents are as frank as Theodore Roosevelt but it is unlikely that any president ever appoints a judge with a social philosophy known to be very different from his own.

The Impossibility of Packing the Supreme Court

The most exacting scrutiny of the social philosophies of judicial nominees by president and Senate has failed signally to predetermine the trends of judicial decisions. Republican appointees of Jefferson and Madison to the Supreme Court one by one fell under the spell of Federalist Chief Justice Marshall and became loose-construction nationalists. A generation later the early appointees of President Jackson joined Chief Justice Marshall in opposing Jackson's position in the Cherokee Indian Case and Jackson's appointees unanimously opposed his Spanish land claims. The Fugitive Slave Law was unanimously sustained alike by pro- and anti-slavery judges. The

[5] H. C. Lodge: *Selections From the Correspondence of Theodore Roosevelt and Henry Cabot Lodge, 1884–1918.* New York, 1925, vol. II, p. 228.

[6] Ibid., vol. I, pp. 517–19.

military courts established by Lincoln's executive orders and certain provisions of the Legal Tender legislation of his administration were both held unconstitutional by the Supreme Court of which he had appointed a majority of the members. A Republican Supreme Court denied the constitutionality of important acts of the Republican reconstruction legislation. And it was not the new Supreme Court that President Roosevelt appointed but the old Court appointed by his predecessors that made the spectacular about-face of 1937 by suddenly ceasing to declare New Deal statutes unconstitutional and henceforth clearing them as they passed upon them in cases that arose. The outstanding historian of the Supreme Court has concluded that "nothing is more striking in the history of the Court than the manner in which those who expect a judge to follow the views of the President who appointed him have been disappointed." [7]

Appointment and Confirmation of Judicial Nominees

Of 108 presidential nominations for justices of the Supreme Court from the inauguration of President Washington in 1789 to the end of the first term of Franklin D. Roosevelt in 1937, eighty-four were confirmed which constituted 77.7 per cent of the total number nominated. From 1897 to 1937 only one of the twenty nominations made failed of confirmation. The sole nomination to the Supreme Court rejected in this latter period of fifty years was that of John J. Parker, a judge of the district court who had incurred the displeasure of labor by deciding a "yellow dog" [8] contract case in accordance with Supreme Court precedents but contrary to the desires of labor. Moreover Parker was reputed to have made disparaging remarks about the Negro race. Two powerful lobbies consequently pressured senators into rejecting the nomination. It is a significant fact that during the first forty years of the history of the Supreme Court the average age of the justices at the time of their appointment was only forty-seven and a half years but during the forty years ending in 1937 the average age had risen to fifty-seven and a half years. [9] So slight was the prestige of the Supreme Court in the beginning that President Washington had to make eleven appointments during the eight years of his presidency in order to keep the six seats filled. Chief Justice John Jay resigned because of his conviction that the office would never be of much consequence. John Marshall, the fourth chief justice of the United States, assumed his duties before the Supreme Court was quite a dozen years old. It fell to the lot of Presidents Jackson and Taft each to appoint six and Lincoln five members or a majority of the Supreme Court while Franklin D. Roosevelt appointed an almost entirely new court.

[7] Charles Warren: *The Supreme Court of the United States.* 3 vols. Boston, 1922, vol. I, pp. 21–2.

[8] A "yellow dog" contract was one in which an employer required a worker as a condition of employment to submit to automatic discharge if he joined a labor union. It is now generally illegal.

[9] C. A. M. Ewing: *Judges of the Supreme Court, 1789–1937.* Minneapolis, 1938, pp. 14–18, 38, 110, 113.

Tenure of Federal Judges

To secure the independence of the judiciary the Constitution provides that judges "shall hold their offices during good behavior and shall at stated times receive for their services a compensation, which shall not be diminished during their continuance in office." There remains the check of impeachment. Significantly, of the eleven cases of impeachment of Federal officers tried before the Senate of the United States only four resulted in conviction and these involved Federal judges. Those convicted were John Pickering (1804), West H. Humphrey (1862), and Halsted L. Ritter (1936) of the district courts; and Robert W. Archbald (1913) of the short-lived commerce court. However, the effectiveness of impeachment is not to be judged by these three convictions since other judges have resigned to avoid certain impeachment. In 1804 the Jeffersonian Republicans, in control of the House of Representatives, impeached Samuel Chase, a justice of the United States Supreme Court, who had made himself notorious for what practically amounted to Federalist stump speeches from the bench. Failure to convict was due to the refusal of the Northern Republican Senators representing commercial states to vote for conviction and thereby risk the charge of a revolutionary attack on the judiciary. Had Chase been convicted it was generally suspected that Chief Justice Marshall would be the next to be impeached and convicted; thus his judicial career might have terminated in its infancy. In its outcome, as Henry Adams put it, "this impeachment [of Chase] made the Supreme Court impregnable; for the first time the Chief Justice could breathe freely." [10] From this point on, Marshall's remarkable judicial career unfolded. However, since Congress creates the courts it can abolish them. This is precisely what the Jeffersonian Republicans did in 1802 by repealing the new Judiciary Act of 1801 which represented a last-minute reorganization of the judiciary by the retiring Federalists. Among other things the Judiciary Act of 1801 created sixteen new Federal judgeships which President Adams filled with the famous "midnight judges" appointed in the last hours of his presidency. These judges were peremptorily deprived of their offices by the repeal and Congress ignored the constitutional issue of their tenure. Since then, however, Congress has scrupulously respected the constitutional provisions concerning the permanent tenure of judges by providing for their transfer elsewhere whenever a judgeship has been discontinued.

PRESENT ORGANIZATION OF INFERIOR FEDERAL COURTS

The District Courts

Most Federal cases start in one of the ninety-odd district courts that Congress has established. These are the Federal trial courts of first instance for all but a few cases. District courts not only hear most Federal cases within their respective jurisdictions but make final disposition of most of them.

[10] Henry Adams: *John Randolph*. Boston, 1882, p. 152.

Each state has one or more of these district courts each of which has at least one district judge. Each of these courts is provided with a clerk, deputy clerks, assistant United States Attorney, office deputies, referees in bankruptcy, and probation and parole officers. In 1922 Congress authorized the Chief Justice temporarily to transfer district judges whenever they could be spared in their own districts to other districts with crowded dockets. In the beginning the jurisdiction of district courts as to classes of cases was quite limited but it has been gradually broadened by Congress until it now extends to crimes against the United States in admiralty and maritime cases, seizures under Federal law, prize cases, patent and copyright, bankruptcy cases, and suits against consuls and vice-consuls. In most cases the Federal jurisdiction is exclusive despite the fact that the states had long had concurrent jurisdiction in many cases. In the opinion of Charles Warren much power in enforcing Federal criminal law might safely be left to the state courts, thereby relieving the pressure upon Federal courts.[11] Uniformity in construing the Federal law would be assured by the fact that the Supreme Court of the United States would remain the court of last resort. It would seem inappropriate, however, to share with state courts jurisdiction of cases in such peculiarly Federal fields as interstate commerce, postal laws, and others of that kind.

Circuit Courts of Appeal

The circuit courts of appeal were created in 1891 to relieve the overburdened Supreme Court of a great deal of its appellate jurisdiction by making many decrees and judgments of the new circuit courts final. In contrast with the provisions for them in the Judiciary Act of 1789, the circuit courts no longer have any original jurisdiction. There are now ten judicial circuits and the District of Columbia each with a circuit court of appeals. The chief justice is assigned by law to the Court of Appeals of the District of Columbia. The eight associate justices are distributed by assignment among the other ten circuits. Six of them are each assigned to one district; each of the remaining two are assigned to two districts. The attachment is purely nominal since a justice is not required to reside within the circuit to which he is assigned. The requirement of the original judiciary act that justices of the Supreme Court travel on circuit has been repealed and they now only rarely if ever choose to do so. A circuit court must have at least three judges, two of whom are necessary for a quorum.

Circuit courts hear appeals from district courts, territorial courts, and special Federal courts or administrative commissions such, for example, as the Federal Trade Commission and the National Labor Relations Board. The volume of cases once appealable from district courts to the Supreme Court has been drastically reduced and is now confined to only five classes of cases. This former burden of the Supreme Court has been shifted to the circuit courts which now have a vast volume of final jurisdiction. One may now appeal from a circuit court to the Supreme Court when the former has

[11] 38 Harv. L. Rev. 545 (1925).

declared a state statute to be repugnant to the Federal Constitution, a Federal statute, or a treaty. However, the Supreme Court may call up from a circuit court any case it chooses for review. This is done on what is known as a writ of certiorari, a process by which a superior court calls upon an inferior court to deliver up its record of a case. The writ of certiorari is issued not as a matter of right of the parties to a case but only upon the discretion of the superior court. The importance of this writ in the appellate jurisdiction of the Supreme Court can scarcely be exaggerated. It gives that Court the absolute power to call up cases of lower courts and by reviewing them to reduce to unity the conflict and confusion of their judgments. The writ of certiorari accounts for over one-half of the cases heard by the Supreme Court and about half of these involve the government. By means of the writ the Supreme Court also guards civil liberties and maintains the balance of state and Federal powers—in brief, sustains the Federal system.

THE SUPREME COURT

Membership

Congress started the Supreme Court with a membership of six. After various increases and decreases, its present membership of a chief justice and eight associate justices was fixed in 1869. The chief justice receives a salary of $35,000 and the associate justices $35,500 each annually which may not be decreased during a justice's incumbency. A justice may retire at the age of seventy with full pay if he has served ten years as a Federal judge. The officers of the Supreme Court are the clerk, three deputy clerks, the reporter, the marshall, and the librarian who are appointed by the Court to assist in performing its duties. The chief justice is merely the titular officer of the Court presiding at its conferences and assigning each case to a member for the writing of the majority opinion of the Court. If the opinion of the chief justice carries more weight than that of an associate it is to be attributed to his superior ability rather than to his titular position. So remarkable was the personality, intellectual acumen, and influence of Chief Justice Marshall that our sense of propriety takes no offense at calling Marshall's Court. He would probably not have been less influential had he been an associate justice instead of the chief justice. Chief justices have, at times, been quite overshadowed by towering associate justices.

The Prestige of the Supreme Court

Neither the framers of the Constitution nor Congress, through the statutes it enacted prescribing its structure and jurisdiction, made the Supreme Court the imposing institution it is today. Chance and circumstance played their parts in its evolution but above everything else the Supreme Court is the product of the personalities of its outstanding members during its century and a half of development. Its beginnings were unimpressive. As we have seen, President Washington had difficulty getting able men to accept appointment or to remain after once being appointed, and the first

Justice, John Jay, resigned in despair over its future. In the year 1801 when Marshall began his long service as chief justice only ten cases came before the Court.

Marshall's Court

Under the long and competent leadership of Chief Justice Marshall (1801–35) the Court rose to a position of prestige and power. As a soldier at Valley Forge young Captain Marshall had witnessed and experienced the distress of the Continental Army due to the disorganized administration of an inadequate central government and this experience apparently made a profound and permanent impression upon him. He assumed the office of chief justice at the moment when by the election of Jefferson the triumph of the states' rights elements seemed to threaten a perilous reversal of the governmental trends under Federalist administrations and he set about resolutely to prevent a return to the distressing confusion of the period of the Confederation. He accordingly sought constantly to explore the possibilities the Constitution and the Supreme Court afforded for discovering and fortifying national powers. His formal legal education had been slight indeed—half a dozen weeks of desultory listening to Chancellor George Wythe's lectures on jurisprudence at William and Mary College. But his intellect was keen, his insight penetrating, and his grasp of a few fundamental principles, as he understood them, exceptional. Marshall brought to the office of chief justice the experience of a man of affairs—a business man with important clients, a large-scale land speculator, a bank director, and stockholder in many corporations. This was the background that produced the climate of opinion in which his dogmas developed. Thus Marshall was prepared to set the permanent pattern of broad interpretation of the Constitution which has made that instrument the means to the great end of serving perennially the needs of a dynamic national society. No higher tribute was ever paid to the cogency of his reasoning than the complaint of a bitter states' rights opponent against one of Marshall's decisions: "All wrong," wailed John Randolph, "but no one in the United States can tell why or wherein." For a long generation Marshall's tight logic and personal charm captivated his associates on the bench and gave to the Supreme Court an imprint it bears to this day. By and large Marshall's role was that of a statesman rather than a lawyer.

Chief Justices since Marshall

During a second generation, under the leadership of Marshall's able successor, Chief Justice Roger B. Taney, the Supreme Court translated the developing social concepts of Jacksonian Democracy into constitutional law. Because of the Court's tendency under Taney to permit the states freely to exercise their internal police power Taney has sometimes been regarded as a devotee of the dogma of states' rights. But never did Marshall himself state more emphatically "the supremacy conferred on this federal government" than did the aged former Federalist Taney two years before

the opening of the Civil War. "It was felt by the statesmen who framed the Constitution and by the people who adopted it," said Taney, "that it was necessary that many rights of sovereignty which the states then possessed should be ceded to the General Government; and that, in the sphere of action assigned to it, it should be supreme and strong enough to execute its own laws by its own tribunals, without interruption from a state or from state authorities." [12] If the constitutional restrictions on the states were less strictly enforced under Taney the precedents of Marshall with respect to Federal powers were certainly not reversed.

Chief Justice Salmon P. Chase (1864–73) next headed the Court as one of the majority of the Court appointed by Lincoln and, though harassed severely, the Court was never quite subdued by the irrepressible Reconstruction Congress. The chief justiceship of Morrison R. Waite (1874–88) was characterized by a liberalism that ere long gave way to reaction as the national psychology of a people captivated by the gigantic fortunes derived from the exploitation of the nation's resources influenced the Court to sanctify laissez faire and set aside state legislation that sought to control the economic giants. This tendency reached its peak in the 1920's when the Supreme Court declared unconstitutional more state legislation than it had during the preceding half century. Meanwhile congressional legislation was meeting a similar fate and judicial annulment of it reached a climax in the middle 1930's when the Supreme Court held Federal legislation unconstitutional in a dozen decisions within a period of twenty-eight months. But after the overwhelming majority of the re-election of President Franklin Roosevelt in 1936 the pressure of public opinion induced the Supreme Court to make its historic about-face and find constitutional one after another of the monumental statutes that constituted a revolution in Federal social legislation.

The Roosevelt Court

Both because President Franklin Roosevelt's appointments provided an almost completely new personnel for the Supreme Court and because it refrained from challenging the constitutionality of New Deal legislation it came to be called the Roosevelt Court. In the course of a decade this Court revealed several distinguishing characteristics. In the first place it refrained, with a single insignificant exception, from holding acts of Congress unconstitutional, that exception being the stoppage of payment of salaries to three Federal officers by a notorious rider to an appropriation bill which the Court denounced as a bill of attainder. In the second place the Roosevelt Court obliterated that twilight zone in which neither state nor Federal government could legislate because of the so-called "dual federalism" which had maintained that the delegated powers of the Federal government were in some mysterious manner restricted by the powers not delegated to it. By this reversal the Roosevelt Court released Congress from obscure judicial restrictions upon its power to tax and to regulate com-

[12] Ableman v. Booth, 21 Howard 506 (1859).

merce. Third, the Court refrained from the practice of restricting congressional power on the assumption of Congress's unconstitutional delegation of its power. Fourth, the Court stopped exercising its review of the judgments of independent administrative agencies by which it had been itself practically functioning as such an agency. Fifth, it revitalized the Federal system by ending the application of the principle that neither state nor nation could tax the instrumentalities of each other and by ceasing to use the mystic formula of due process to prevent states from experimenting in social and economic legislation.

Method of Deciding Cases

Quite early in its history the Supreme Court developed a systematic method of reaching its decisions. Justice Campbell described the method as it was carried out under Chief Justice Taney before the Civil War and the description is valid for the present as well: "The duties of the Justices of the Supreme Court consist in the hearing of cases; the preparations for the consultations; the consultations in the conference of the judges; the decision of the causes there, and the preparation of the opinion and the judgment of the Court. Their most arduous and responsible duty is in the conference. . . . In these conferences the Chief Justice usually called the case. He stated the pleadings and facts that they presented, the arguments and his conclusion in regard to them, and invited discussion. The discussion was free and open among the Justices till all were satisfied. The question was put, whether the judgment or decree should be reversed, and each Justice, according to his precedence, commencing with the junior judge, was required to give his judgment and his reason for his conclusion. The concurring opinions of the majority decided the case and signified the matter of the opinion to be given. The Chief Justice designated the judge to prepare it." [13] In our day this discussion is conducted at the Saturday conference and the influence of the chief justice essentially lies in managing the conference. Chief Justice Hughes kept things moving briskly, confining discussion to issues, forbidding fruitless argument, and adjourning promptly at four-thirty. His successor Harlan Stone, a veteran dissenter in the tradition of the New England town meeting, found it difficult to end discussion until every justice had had his say. Not even Stone's successor, Chief Justice Frederick M. Vinson, with all his exceptional skill, was quite capable of resolving the clash of the contending factions.[14] But Chief Justice Warren's gracious manner softened dissension among the associate justices, as the unanimous opinion of the Court in the school desegregation cases indicated. They liked his calm in legal argument and his improvement in court operation such as the public address system with microphones at each justice's desk.

[13] Eulogy of Justice John A. Campbell by Justice Benjamin R. Curtis delivered in 1874, 20 Wallace Men. X.
[14] Arthur M. Schlesinger, Jr.: "The Supreme Court," *Fortune* (January, 1947), 73–212.

The Written Opinion

After the members of the Court have given their oral opinion and judgment on the case, in the reverse order of their seniority but with the chief justice always voting last, the writing of the Court's opinion is assigned to one of the majority except when the vote is unanimous. The chief justice bears in mind the special talents and knowledge of individual justices in making these assignments but every justice is kept on the alert by the fact that he does not know until after the vote is taken whether the case is to be assigned to him or to one of his colleagues. Since he may be called upon to write the Court's opinion thereby justifying his own vote he must measure his judgment well before he expresses it in his vote. A justice who constitutes one of the majority on a judgment of the Court but who is not satisfied with the official statement of the majority opinion may publish an independent reason for supporting it in what is known as a "concurring opinion." The minority justices may state their reasons for voting against the majority judgment in what are known as "dissenting opinions." The Supreme Court has a practice of announcing its judgments on important cases at its Monday session and these are usually reported in the Monday evening and Tuesday morning newspapers. Since momentous issues related to gigantic business transactions or matters of the most critical social significance may depend upon the way a Supreme Court decision is to go, extraordinary precautions are taken to prevent advance "leaks."

Criticism of Court Opinions

Despite the high esteem in which it is generally held, the Court has not escaped criticism on the quality of its opinions. One American scholar pointed out that in sixty-one cases from 1860 to 1929 majority court opinions averaged 13.5 pages in length. He concluded "that most, if not all, opinions that are thirteen pages long are the worse for every page beyond seven or eight or even six. No little cause for the confusion among judges on the federal and state courts, the federal and state bars, and the public in general as to what the rules of constitutional law are arises from that fact that the Supreme Court opinions are full of irrelevant matter, and are models of bad judicial writing."[15] On the other hand, the succinct opinions prepared by the late Justice Oliver Wendell Holmes were criticized by some of his colleagues for their brevity. They were "very short and not very helpful" complained Chief Justice Taft and he objected when in one Court opinion Holmes used the undignified phrase "to stop ratholes." [16] This criticism of Holmes was exceptional; his opinions are generally held to be classic examples of cogent reason and clear expression. Nor is it an American tradition that the Supreme Court ought to be free from public

[15] Oliver P. Field: "Unconstitutional Legislation by Congress." *American Political Science Review* (1945), 39:60.

[16] Catherine Drinker Bowen: *Yankee from Olympus* (Armed Services Ed., Boston, 1944), p. 483.

criticism. Jefferson, Madison, Lincoln, and both Roosevelts criticised the Court. The strength of the Court depends upon its ability to weather the storms of public discussion and sometimes be guided by them. Harold E. Stassen found that he had not struck a responsive public chord when, in addressing the Baptist Convention in May, 1947, he said: "I do not consider it to be in keeping with the dignity of the standing of the teachings of my great religious denomination to attack a decision of the Supreme Court after it is made."

Factors Contributing to the Supreme Court's Efficiency

Several features contribute to the generally high quality of the Court's collective judgments. Oral argument instead of oratory is encouraged. Attorneys addressing the Court must be prepared at any moment to give a clarifying answer to a question from the bench. The justices hold frequent long conferences in which every one of them is heard, and the prevailing opinion is ultimately written in the light of the contributions of all at these conferences. Such thoroughness justifies discountenancing the rehearing of cases, which indeed the Court very rarely permits. In addition to these sound procedural practices the Court is sustained by the frank scrutiny it invites, a "sensitiveness to healthy criticism," the long terms of its justices, and its unbroken continuity for more than a century and a half. [17]

The Judiciary Adheres Strictly to Judicial Functions

None of the three great branches of the Federal government adheres more strictly than the judiciary to the principle of the formal separation of powers. President Washington discovered this in 1793 when, upon the advice of his cabinet, he submitted a number of questions to the Supreme Court concerning our treaty rights with France. If the Court had answered these questions President Washington would have obtained what are now known as advisory opinions, such as are authorized by the constitutions of ten states. [18] But the Supreme Court advised Washington that its functions as prescribed by the Constitution are confined to "cases and controversies." As stated by Felix Frankfurter: "The Court can deal only with concrete litigation. Its judgment, upon a constitutional issue can be invoked only when inextricably entangled with a living and ripe law suit. In lawyer's language the Court merely enforces a 'legal right.' " [19]

In 1792 an Act of Congress making Federal judges members of commissions to determine pension claims was rejected by the Court as the vesting of a non-judicial function in the judiciary. More than a century after Washington's administration the overtures of Congress to get the Court's opinion on constitutional questions without a "case or controversy"

[17] See Felix Frankfurter: "The Supreme Court of the United States." *Encyclopedia of the Social Sciences, Vol. XIV*, pp. 474–481.

[18] Alabama, Colorado, Delaware, Florida, Maine, Massachusetts, New Hampshire, North Carolina, Rhode Island, and South Dakota.

[19] Ibid., p. 474.

proved futile. In 1907 an Act of Congress had authorized the instituting of suits in the Court of Claims for the purpose of testing certain acts of Congress. But when a case under this statute was appealed from the Court of Claims to the Supreme Court the latter concluded that "in the legal sense the judgment could not be executed and amounts in fact to no more than an expression of opinion on the validity of the act in question," and hence Congress had sought unconstitutionally to confer upon the judiciary a non-judicial power. [20]

Nor will the Supreme Court settle controversies that, in its opinion, are matters of a purely political nature. On this ground the Court refused to decide which of two contending governments of Rhode Island was the legal one. This was held to be a political or policy problem involving the constitutional guarantee to each state of a government "republican in form" and consequently to be decided by the political branches of the Federal government. This could be done by the president through his control of the military forces or by Congress through its power to determine the qualifications of its members. [21]

JURISDICTION

Original Jurisdiction

The district courts have almost all of the original jurisdiction of the Federal courts today. The circuit courts now have no original jurisdiction and the original jurisdiction of the Supreme Court is confined by the Constitution to "all cases affecting ambassadors, other public ministers and those in which a state shall be a party." Boundary disputes and other differences between states, such as that arising out of Chicago's attempt to divert water from the Great Lakes, invoke, however seldom they occur, the Supreme Court's original jurisdiction. It has been held that the original jurisdiction of the Supreme Court, as prescribed in the Constitution, is exclusive and Congress cannot increase it. For example, the Judiciary Act of 1789 vested in the Supreme Court the issuing of the writ of mandamus to any officer of the United States. Under this provision the Supreme Court was petitioned to issue a writ of mandamus directing Madison as secretary of state to deliver an already prepared and signed commission to one who had been appointed a justice of the peace of the District of Columbia. Chief Justice Marshall, speaking for the Court, refused to exercise the power on the ground that Congress could not add to the original jurisdiction as prescribed by the Constitution; Congress's assignment of the issuing of the writ of mandamus to the Supreme Court was consequently held unconstitutional. [22] However, Congress has been sustained in granting to inferior courts some original jurisdiction concurrent with that of the Supreme Court in the same fields. For example, it has been held that a consul

[20] Muskrat v. United States, 219 U.S. 151 (1911).
[21] Luther v. Borden, 7 Howard 1 (1849).
[22] Marbury v. Madison, 1 Cranch 137 (1803).

may be sued in an inferior court in which Congress has vested the jurisdiction. [23]

Appellate Jurisdiction

In addition to its original jurisdiction the Constitution assigns the Supreme Court in all other Federal cases "appellate jurisdiction both as to law and fact with such exceptions and under such regulations as the Congress shall make." The last dozen words should be noted with care for they give Congress a constitutional control of the Supreme Court that is potentially enormous and, in time of great excitement, has proved to be so in practice. For example, in 1869, despite the fact that the Supreme Court had heard the arguments on an appealed case and was ready to make its judgment, the Radical Republican Reconstruction Congress deprived the Supreme Court of its appellate jurisdiction in cases under the Habeas Corpus Act which was involved in the case then under consideration. Congress, of course, simply exercised its power to make "exceptions" of the Courts' appellate jurisdiction, and the action of Congress compelled the Supreme Court to drop consideration of the case.[24] Only the prevailing post-Civil War hysteria enabled Congress to deal so drastically with the Supreme Court. Public opinion would scarcely tolerate such radical even though constitutional action on the part of Congress in ordinary times. Since the Constitution places no limit to the "exceptions" and "regulations" that Congress may make, that body could constitutionally deprive the Supreme Court of all its appellate jurisdiction leaving it only its meager original jurisdiction. It would then be a Supreme Court only in name. The point is purely academic since Congress is composed so largely of lawyers, who have a high regard for the Court as an institution, and in any case the public would not tolerate trifling with a branch of the government held in such high esteem.

Methods of Getting Cases Reviewed by Higher Courts

There are four ways by which a case may be carried up to the Supreme Court:

1) *Appeal*—a procedure provided for by statute by which a case is sent up to an appellate court for review as to law and facts. Appeal is a matter of the right of the parties to the case where constitutional questions are involved. The consequent retrial is based upon the appellate court's examination of the record of the lower court.

2) *Writ of Error*—a common-law process by which an appellate court brings a case up from a lower court in order to examine the record of a case as to questions of law but not of fact.

3) *Certificate*—a process created by statute empowering a lower court to send up or certify to the Supreme Court a question of law on which it desires an authoritative ruling.

[23] Bors v. Preston, 111 U.S. 252 (1884).
[24] *Ex parte* McCardle, 7 Wallace 506 (1869).

4) *Certiorari*—a form of review resulting from the call of a higher court to a lower court to deliver its record on a stated case. This writ lies absolutely in the discretion of the superior court and, in contrast with appeal, is not a matter of the right of the litigants.

SPECIAL COURTS

Legislative Courts

Legislative courts are established by Congress for special purposes and rest on a basis different from that of the ordinary judicial courts. Article III of the Constitution specifically empowers Congress to establish these latter courts, described earlier in this chapter, and they are consequently sometimes called "constitutional courts." They share in the exercise of the judicial functions and have judges who hold office during good behavior with no power in Congress to provide otherwise. But legislative courts are created by Congress in the exercise of its legislative powers and consequently are called "legislative courts." Their functions are confined to one or more of the powers that are prescribed by Congress independently of Section III. Thus the judges of these legislative courts serve for such terms as Congress may determine, whether a fixed period or during good behavior. [25]

Territorial Courts

Territorial courts are established under Congress's power to make all needful rules and regulations respecting territories of the United States. They have been established in Puerto Rico, Alaska, Hawaii, the Canal Zone, and the Virgin Islands. The typical territorial court performs the same judicial functions as the Federal district courts and in addition adjudicates cases of local territorial jurisdiction. This latter field consists of dealing with cases involving practically the same kinds of laws as are dealt with by state courts.

Courts of the District of Columbia

In addition to its jurisdiction as a Federal court Congress has vested the District Court of the District of Columbia with all the jurisdiction of a state court including probate matters.

United States Court of Claims

This court was created to enable persons having claims against the United States government to obtain satisfaction. The court consists of a chief justice and four associate justices.

United States Court of Customs and Patent Appeals

This is a specialized appellate court consisting of five judges and is designed to facilitate the settlement of disputes in the fields of customs and patents.

[25] Ex parte Bakelite Corporation, 279 U.S. 438 (1929).

United States Customs Courts

This court consists of a presiding judge and eight associates and has sole jurisdiction over actions arising under tariff acts. It holds its sessions in New York City.

SUMMARY

The dual character of a Federal system makes reliance solely on state courts impractical and a Federal judiciary is consequently considered indispensable. The Constitution assigns to the jurisdiction of the Federal courts a long list of categories of cases for which state courts are not considered appropriate. The Supreme Court is given original jurisdiction in a few specified matters and appellate jurisdiction in all other cases except as Congress may make exceptions. State cases involving questions of Federal power may be appealed to the Supreme Court of the United States.

The President appoints Federal judges subject to confirmation by the Senate. Both President and Senate scrutinize closely the social philosophies of nominees for the bench but cannot control their judgments after they are seated. Judges' tenure continues during good behavior, but for violations of this several have been removed by impeachment and conviction.

Congress has established a hierarchy of district and circuit judges and prescribed their jurisdictions. It has also prescribed the personnel and compensation of Supreme Court justices and the appellate jurisdiction left to it.

The rise and decline of the prestige of the Supreme Court is related to its leadership and its decisions in critical cases and controversies. Chief Justices Marshall and Taney made lasting impressions on the Court, and President Franklin D. Roosevelt, because of vacancies that in time occurred in every seat but one, created practically a new Court.

In its efforts to arrive at just decisions the Supreme Court evolved an admirable method of deliberating on cases and reaching collective judgments. The published written opinions give the opportunity for critical public comment, which tends to keep the Court on guard against damaging its high prestige.

CHAPTER XXVI

JUDICIAL REVIEW AND REFORM

JUDICIAL REVIEW

A *Unique Constitutional Development*

BY THE term "judicial review" is meant the power of any court to decide whether a legislative act upon which a case before it is based is repugnant to the Constitution. American judicial review is a peculiar governmental feature among the nations of the world. Thus while the Parliament of Britain is theoretically limited in power only by the physically impossible Congress is limited by what the Supreme Court decides the Constitution means. The British Supreme Court of Appeals, the Law Lords, never challenges the validity of an Act of Parliament. The French are accustomed to consider Parliament's enactment of a statute as having settled, once and for all, the constitutionality of that piece of legislation. They would regard separation of powers as violated if the courts could interfere with the legislature's enactments and veto them by judicial review; consequently that is not permitted. Nor has it been proved that judicial review of Federal statutes is absolutely indispensable in the United States. "Why," asks H. L. McBain, "should it be assumed that Congress, the maker of laws, has any less intelligence concerning the meaning of legal words or has less respect for or willingness to abide by the prescriptions of the fundamental law than have the courts?" [1] Then there is the frank opinion of the late Justice Oliver Wendell Holmes: "I do not think the United States would come to an end if we (the Supreme Court) lost our power to declare an act of Congress void."

Judicial Review of State Legislation and Constitutions

Review of state legislation is a power of the Federal courts that rests securely on the provision of the Constitution: "The Constitution and the

[1] Howard Lee McBain: *The Living Constitution* (New York, 1927), p. 241.

laws of the United States which shall be made in pursuance thereof and all treaties made or which shall be made under the authority of the United States shall be the supreme law of the land; and the judges in every state shall be bound thereby; anything in the Constitution or laws of any state to the contrary notwithstanding." Judicial review of state legislation in so far as it may be repugnant to the "supreme law of the land" is clearly enjoined upon state judges and, by implication, upon Federal judges as cases come before them on appeal. We have seen that, by the first judiciary Act (1789), the Supreme Court of the United States was authorized to re-examine judgments of the highest courts of any state decided in favor of a state act that had been challenged as repugnant to some Federal power. It required the resolute determination of the Supreme Court under Marshall to exercise this authorization of the Constitution and Congress and get cases that had been decided by state supreme courts brought before the Supreme Court of the United States for review. For example, one Cohens had sold in Virginia a ticket of a lottery authorized in the District of Columbia by an Act of Congress. He undertook to operate in Virginia in violation of a state law there forbidding lotteries. After conviction on the Virginia statute by a state court, Cohens got his case before the Supreme Court of the United States on a writ of error. [2] Though the Supreme Court of the United States sustained the conviction Virginians denounced the Supreme Court's action as a "monstrous and unexampled decision" and the "zenith of despotic power" since it set the precedent for the permanent practice of the review of certain judgments of state courts by the Supreme Court of the United States.

Judicial Review of Congressional Statutes

Whatever the framers of the Constitution may have intended concerning judicial review of congressional statutes they made no provision for it in the Constitution. The earliest clear-cut instance of its use by the Supreme Court constitutes a landmark in the history of the judiciary of the United States. We have seen how one Marbury sought to obtain from the Supreme Court a writ of mandamus directing the secretary of state to deliver to Marbury his commission as a justice of the peace of the District of Columbia, to which office President John Adams had appointed him in 1801. The reasoning by which Marshall concluded that the Court could not issue the mandamus set the pattern of judicial review of congressional legislation. Marshall held that mandamus was original jurisdiction and yet it was not to be found in what he held to be the exclusive list of subjects of the original jurisdiction of the Supreme Court prescribed by the Constitution. Here was the Constitution vesting the Court with specific original jurisdiction. There was Congress vesting it, as Marshall argued, with some original jurisdiction not found in the specific list. In such a conflict of instructions what was the Court to do? As Marshall saw it the Court's duty was clear. When a statute applicable to a case conflicts with

[2] Cohens v. Virginia, 6 Wheaton 264 (1821).

a provision of the Constitution applicable to the case the Court must apply the superior law which, under such circumstances, is the Constitution, and disregard the inferior law which is, of course, invalid. Theoretically the Court never declares a law unconstitutional. In adjudicating a case the Court merely, in declaring a right, applies the superior of two conflicting laws, that is the Constitution, instead of the legislative enactment. The latter is held never to have been law owing to the error of Congress in assuming that it had the power to enact that legislation.

Did the Supreme Court Usurp the Power of Judicial Review?

What of the charge, recurring from time to time, that the Supreme Court usurped the power of judicial review since the Constitution nowhere grants the power? The Revolutionary state constitutions had been constructed when state legislatures were at the very peak of their power and, of course, no provision for judicial annulment of their legislation was inserted in any state constitution. For the most part these state constitutions had been the products of the popular pressure of inland agrarian interests, mainly a debtor element among whom the judiciary was anything but popular. Judges gave judgments in favor of creditors, directed foreclosures of mortgages, and, in accordance with prevailing law, ordered the imprisonment of debtors. The Constitution of 1787, on the contrary, had been the product of an opposite set of interests, largely creditors accustomed to rely upon the judiciary for protection of their rights, and that branch consequently was held in high esteem by the framers and proponents of the Constitution. There were matters they dared not baldly insert in the Constitution without imperilling its ratification but they doubtless hoped that implications would eventually be interpreted to supply the thing desired. Judicial review appears to have been one of these. A generation ago Charles A. Beard, after diligent research, ascertained that of the twenty-five members of the Philadelphia Convention who seemed to be most influential in shaping the Constitution, seventeen were on record as having "declared directly or indirectly for judicial control." Only one of the twenty-five is suspected of having been opposed to judicial review but the evidence is too meager to be conclusive. Beard thus states his conclusion about what the framers intended concerning judicial review: "The accepted canons of historical criticism warrant the assumption that, when a legal proposition is before a law-making body [the Constitutional Convention] and a considerable number of the supporters of that proposition definitely assert that it involves certain important and fundamental implications, and it is nevertheless approved by that body without any protests worthy of mention, these implications must be deemed part of that legal proposition when it becomes law. . . ."[3] Whether or not the Supreme Court "usurped" the practice of judicial review is now purely an academic question. So completely has the practice been woven into the

[3] Charles A. Beard: *The Supreme Court and the Constitution.* New York, 1913, pp. 63–4.

warp and woof of our constitutional fabric that the garment could now scarcely endure its elimination.

Self-Restraint of the Supreme Court on Judicial Review

Over a century ago the Supreme Court began taking precautions against imprudent exercise of judicial review. In the early 1830's Marshall's Court was under the stress of the upsurge of popular sovereignty produced by the "rise of the common man" that characterized the new and irrepressible Jacksonian Democracy. In 1834 Chief Justice Marshall announced that the Supreme Court would not, "except in cases of absolute necessity, . . . deliver any judgment in cases where constitutional questions are involved" in which a majority of the whole court did not concur. [4] Moreover the Court assumed that Congress, in enacting a statute had considered the question of its constitutionality and did not consciously pass an unconstitutional act. The burden of proof is therefore, as a rule, on the litigant who argues that the act is unconstitutional. [5] The Court is presumed not to hold a statute unconstitutional unless convinced beyond a reasonable doubt. As early as 1827 Mr. Justice Bushrod Washington, speaking for the Court, observed: "It is but a decent respect to the wisdom, integrity, and patriotism of the legislative body, by which any law is passed to presume in favor of its validity, until its violation of the Constitution is proved beyond a reasonable doubt." [6] Moreover the Supreme Court claims never to hold an act void on the ground that it is unwise legislation, but the frequent use until recently of the utterly undefinable "due process" to set aside legislation has led to the suspicion that the Court has used this elusive legal concept to dispose of what it considers to be simply bad legislation. Likewise, the Court's maxim of never considering the motives of the legislator in voiding legislation is not easy to reconcile with its holding the Child Labor Tax Law unconstitutional on the ground that, while Congress had unquestionably used a power delegated to it, it had used it for a purpose the Court pronounced improper as an invasion of a reserved power of the states. This latter point is, however, merely of historical interest now inasmuch as the Supreme Court seems absolutely to have abandoned the practice of using the reserved powers of the states to check the exercise of the powers delegated to the Federal government.

The "Slot Machine" Theory of Judicial Interpretation

It was long assumed that judicial determination of the constitutionality of a statute was a purely logical process even mechanical in its nature. Put the facts of a case into the Court, pull the lever, and out comes the

[4] Briscoe v. Commonwealth's Bank of Kentucky, 33 U.S. 118, 112 (1834).

[5] One remarkable exception to this rule is to be noted. In recent years the Supreme Court has come to regard freedom of religion, speech, press, petition, and assembly as of such fundamental importance that legislation restricting them is presumed to be unconstitutional and, in a case before the Court, the burden rests upon the prosecution to prove that the statute is constitutional. See Thomas v. Collins, 323 U.S. 516 (1944).

[6] Ogden v. Saunders, 12 Wheaton 213 (1827).

opinion. Dean Roscoe Pound calls this the "jurisprudence of conceptions." These conceptions consisted of "principles of law," "due process," "freedom of contract," and other abstractions which could mean little else than just what the judges conceived them to mean. Thus their task was assumed to be "like fitting together the pieces of a jig-saw puzzle" and when the last piece was in place no one could question its correctness. As late as 1936 the Supreme Court gave expression to this mechanical conception of its function in United States v. Butler: "When an act of Congress is appropriately challenged in the Courts as not conforming to the constitutional mandate, the judicial branch of the government has only one duty—to lay the Article of the Constitution which is invoked beside the statute which is challenged and to decide *whether the latter squares with the former.* All the Court does or can do is to announce its considered judgment upon the question." [7] The words in italics brought down upon the Court a concentrated storm of criticism by authorities in constitutional law.

The Shift to Judicial Recognition of Social Data

Gradually the Court has come to rely less upon fixed concepts of law and more upon social data in making its judgments upon regulative legislation. In 1908 Louis D. Brandeis, in a brief presented to the Supreme Court of the United States defending the Oregon ten-hour law for women, followed his short legal argument with a hundred pages of expert opinion to show the injurious effect of long hours upon the health of women. The Court was impressed and Justice Brewer observed: "When a question of fact is debated and debatable, and the extent to which a constitutional limitation goes is affected by the truth in respect to that fact, a widespread and long-continued belief concerning it is worthy of consideration. We take judicial cognizance of all matters of general knowledge." [8] This was a belated recognition of the truth Oliver Wendell Holmes had proclaimed in the Lowell Lectures of 1880: "The life of the law has not been logic: it has been experience." The Court had indicated that "conceptual jurisprudence," the mechanical or logical theory, no longer reigned supreme. As the years passed, Brandeis confronted the Court in case after case with a mass of social data in order to break the supremacy of "due process" until his method came to be known as the "Brandeis Brief." No longer does the Court so readily declare social legislation unconstitutional on the ground that it deprives a person of "liberty or property without due process of law."

Revision of the Constitution by Judicial Review

Judicial review results in far more acceptance than rejection of statutes on the ground of their constitutionality. By the acceptance of legislation enlarging the definition of congressional powers the Supreme Court has

[7] 297 U.S. 1 (1936). The italics are the author's not the Court's.
[8] Muller v. Oregon, 208 U.S. 412 (1908).

radically changed original conceptions of the meaning of the text of the Constitution of 1787 at the same time that it has rationalized the changes. "Thanks to our rigid Constitution," wrote Edwin Earl Ross, "the powers that enable the federal government to cope with difficulties beyond the ken or foresight of the fathers cannot be granted by the present will of the people. We expect our judges to draw them out of the Constitution as a juggler draws rabbits out of a hat." [9] When it was deemed necessary to regulate collective bargaining on a national scale the power of Congress to regulate interstate commerce was interpreted to include the regulation of intra-state commerce and even other matters that might interfere with the free flow of commerce. Thus the states lost a portion of their hitherto "reserved power." Through the wizardry of Federal expenditures under the "general welfare" clause the states have permitted supervision of some of their reserved powers according to the popular will. Professor Tiedeman observed: "When public opinion . . . requires the written word to be ignored the Court justly obeys the will of the popular mandate at the same time keeping up a show of obedience to the written word by skillful use of legal fictions."

HISTORIC CRISES OF THE SUPREME COURT
The Dred Scott Decision

The crises experienced by the Supreme Court are indicative of the extraordinary degree to which it is dependent upon the reputation and prestige it can maintain. In the Marbury decision (1803) the Supreme Court said to Congress, in effect: "You cannot enlarge our jurisdiction beyond what the Constitution has assigned us." Self-protection was not involved over half a century later when once again the Court ventured to hold an Act of Congress unconstitutional. Dred Scott, a slave, had been taken by a former master from the slave state Missouri into territory believed to have been rendered free by the Missouri Compromise, and he was later taken back to Missouri. Did the slave's living in free territory automatically emancipate him? Since Dred's later master was now Sandford, a citizen of New York, the case could be considered by a Federal court as a controversy "between citizens of different states" provided Dred Scott was a citizen of Missouri. On this basis of diverse citizenship a case was brought in a United States circuit court and later appealed to the Supreme Court of the United States. Here the Court did not stop consideration of the case when it had concluded that it had no jurisdiction because Dred was not a citizen; it proceeded to hold the repealed Missouri Compromise to have been unconstitutional on the ground that Congress could not outlaw slavery in the territories. This decision threw the Court into the hottest of current party politics, since the new Republican party's very reason for existence was the exclusion of slavery from the territories as soon as it could win elections and attain the necessary control of the

[9] Edwin Earl Ross: *Social Psychology* (New York, 1909), p. 280.

government. If the decision stood, the very existence of the Republican party would be futile. The most astute of the Republican leaders, Abraham Lincoln, published the best-reasoned criticism of the Court's decision in what may still be regarded as a standard for judging such controversial Court opinion. Lincoln said: "We do not propose that when Dred Scott has been decided a slave by the Court, we, as a mob, will decide him to be free . . . but we nevertheless do oppose that decision as a political rule, which shall be binding on the voter to vote for no one who thinks it wrong, which shall be binding on the members of Congress or the Presidents to favor no measure that does not actually concur with the principles of the decision. . . . We propose so resisting it as to have it reversed if we can, and a new judicial rule established upon this subject." [10] Because the Court then seemed to be stepping outside its judicial field to decide a question of public policy its prestige declined in the late 1850's to the lowest point in its long history. Curiously enough it soon fell to Lincoln as president to appoint a majority of the Supreme Court as vacancies occurred in the personnel that had rendered the Dred Scott decision. The reversal of the decision, however, came in the Thirteenth Amendment's abolition of slavery and the Fourteenth Amendment's redefinition of national and state citizenship.

The Greenback Cases

Half a dozen years after the close of the Civil War the Supreme Court had regained the prestige lost by the Dred Scott decision when, on an issue of the constitutionality of a Federal statute, it made another false step that impaired the popular confidence in its integrity. By a four to three division the Court held unconstitutional the provision of the Civil War statute making United States notes, popularly known as greenbacks, legal tender in so far as they might be offered in payment of debts contracted before the passage of the Act. Since these notes were not then convertible into standard money they circulated at a depreciated value in terms of gold. On the very day the decision was announced President Grant made appointments to fill two vacancies in the Court with judges who joined the minority and reversed the Court's stand when cases involving the same issue were quite promptly brought up and considered. Even the Chief Justice Salmon P. Chase joined in the ensuing charge that the President had "packed" the Court. The reversal operated to the enormous financial advantage of railroads whose long-term bonds, then falling due, could now be paid in the depreciated currency instead of the gold that the first decision would have required.

The Income Tax Case

Even more serious was the damage sustained by the Court in the Income Tax Case of 1895. The Revenue Act of 1893 had laid a two per cent tax

[10] John G. Nicolay and John Hay, editors, *Complete Works of Abraham Lincoln,* 12 vols. New York, 1905, Vol. I, p. 464.

on incomes over $4,000. In harmony with the precedents of a century the Supreme Court at first held the tax constitutional by a vote of four to four. One justice who had been absent on account of illness believed the tax to be constitutional and was present at a rehearing when one of those who had held that opinion at the first hearing changed his mind, whereupon the tax was held unconstitutional in a five to four vote. Coming in the midst of the universal distress of the harrowing depression of the middle 1890's the Court's shielding of wealth from taxation created a furor somewhat comparable to that following the Dred Scott decision. "Interest in the tax itself," wrote David Rich Dewey, "was lost sight of in the revelation of fickleness and uncertainty in the highest court in the land." Less astutely, but still somewhat as Lincoln in the 1850's had expressed the public dissatisfaction with the Dred Scott decision, William Jennings Bryan in the 1890's became the eloquent spokesman of the opposition to the income tax decision. "They criticize us for our criticism of the Supreme Court," he said. "My friends, we have not criticized; we have simply called attention to what you already know. If you want criticism read the dissenting opinions of the Court. There you will find criticisms. They say we passed an unconstitutional law: we deny it. The income tax was not unconstitutional when it went before the Supreme Court for the first time; it did not become unconstitutional until one of the judges changed his mind, and we cannot be expected to know when a judge will change his mind." [11]

The Court Crisis of the 1930's

One after another outstanding measure of Franklin Roosevelt's administration was held unconstitutional by the Supreme Court. The codes of fair competition prepared under the terms of the National Industrial Recovery Act were held to have been the result of an unconstitutional re-delegation of legislative power. [12] The act abrogating the gold clause in government obligations was held to be a repudiation of the pledge implicit in the power to borrow money.[13] A part of the Home Owners' Loan Act of 1934 was held to be an encroachment on the reserved powers of the states. [14] The processing tax on the Agricultural Act of 1933 was held to be not within the Federal taxing power. [15] The Act providing for readjustment of municipal indebtedness was held invalid as an interference with state sovereignty. [16] The Railroad Retirement Act was held not to be a regulation of commerce. [17] The Frazier-Lemke Act, designed to delay fore-

[11] Henry S. Commager: *Documents of American History*. 2 vols. New York, 1938, Vol. II, p. 176.

[12] Schechter Poultry Corp. v. United States, 295 U.S. 495 (1935).

[13] Perry v. U.S. 330 (1935).

[14] Hopkins Federal Savings and Loan Association v. Cleary, 296 U.S. 315 (1935).

[15] United States v. William M. Butler et. al., Receivers of Hoosac Mills Corp. 297 U.S. 1 (1936).

[16] Ashton v. Cameron County Water Improvement District No. 1, 298 U.S. 513 (1936).

[17] Railroad Retirement Board v. Alton R. R. et. al., 295 U.S. 330 (1935).

closure of mortgages of farmers, was held to be in violation of property rights under the Fifth Amendment. [18] Amendments to the Agricultural Readjustment Act were held not to be within the Federal taxing power. [19] The Bituminous Coal Conservation Act was held not to impose a tax but a penalty not sustained by the commerce clause. [20] Unless the Court could somehow be checked in its setting aside of legislation the apparent will of the electorate as expressed in the overwhelming re-election of Franklin Roosevelt in 1936 would be nullified. Suddenly, in February, 1937, President Roosevelt in a message urged Congress to authorize the appointment of not more than six additional justices of the Supreme Court as aids to those who, having reached the age of seventy and having served ten years on the bench, failed to retire in six months. This "court packing," as its indignant opponents pronounced it, created a furor of condemnation. President Roosevelt failed to get the legislation he asked for, but in the midst of the debate over his proposals the Supreme Court executed its historic reversal. By a series of decisions beginning in 1937, the Supreme Court has held that all of the more important aspects of manufacturing fall within the scope of the power of Congress to regulate interstate commerce. Since that date not a single New Deal statute has been held unconstitutional. [21] The crisis of the 1930's passed and as vacancies occurred President Roosevelt filled them with appointees until all but one of the members of the Supreme Court had been nominated by him.

The Crisis in the Roosevelt Court

Contrary to expectations the new Court, all of whose members but one had been appointed by President Franklin Roosevelt, failed promptly to become an integrated group. Sharp differences found expression in dissenting opinions phrased in scarcely judicial terms which were, as Thomas Reed Powell put it, "often apt to rest more on their own foundations than on the conceived weakness in the majority opinion." So incompatible were the temperaments of some of the justices that in 1946 the conflict burst out in public denunciation through the press. Moreover the differences stood out in relief under statistical analysis. Due to Marshall's qualities of intellect and personal leadership dissenting opinions had been rare under his chief justiceship. As late as 1910–11, 87 per cent of the opinions of the Court had been unanimous. But in the first term after the Court's 1937 reversal of trend as to the constitutionality of statutes, unanimous opinions declined to 63 per cent. By the 1942–3 term for the first time in the long history of the Supreme Court its members disagreed oftener than they agreed in formal opinions. As justice after justice was appointed to fill vacancies until not a single pre-Roosevelt appointee remained in the court, unanimous opinions declined until in the 1946–7 term an all-time

[18] Louisville Joint Stock Land Bank v. Radford, 295 U.S. 55 (1935).
[19] Rickett Rice Mills v. Fontennot, 297 U.S. 110 (1936).
[20] Carter v. Carter Coal Co., 298 U.S. 238 (1936).
[21] O. R. Altman: "First Session of the Seventy Fifth Congress," *American Political Science Review* (1937), 41:1071–1093.

low of only 36 per cent unanimity was reached. The differences between the justices fell into a pattern of opposing ideologies variously designated as those of "conservatives" against "liberals," "right" against "left," or practitioners of "self denial" against "activists" signifying, on the one hand, the justices who leave questions of policy strictly to legislatures against those, on the other hand, who would re-examine the legislative judgment.[22]

The appointment of Earl Warren as Chief Justice brought to the Supreme Court a leadership reminiscent of John Marshall. During the Court's first term under Warren unanimous opinions rose to one-third instead of the one-fifth of the immediately preceding term. Like Marshall, Warren began writing the unanimous opinions, seven in the first term. Outstanding among these was the unanimous opinion in the public school desegregation cases of a court one-third of whose members were natives of the South. Not until a formula had been devised acceptable to all was judgment made and the unanimity was hailed as a stroke of judicial statesmanship. Not long before nine separate opinions, concurring and dissenting, had been filed in adjudicating a single case. The Court promptly brought its burden of cases within workable scope by declining to review cases involving minor issues.

JUDICIAL REFORM

Marshall's Proposal for Checking Judicial Review

President Franklin Roosevelt's proposal for judicial reform was only the most recent occasion when the issue of reforming the courts has been raised since Marshall's Court invalidated a Federal statute and many state statutes. "It should be remarked however," wrote Howard Lee McBain, "that in nearly every instance those who reprobated the power [judicial review] were prompted by their antagonism to the effect of its exercise in this or that particular case." [23] Thus it seems to be largely a question of whose ox has been gored. For example, when Marshall's Court in McCulloch v. Maryland held the Bank of the United States to be constitutional, erstwhile critics of judicial review condemned the Court, not for exercising the power, but for not using it against the constitutionality of the Bank. It is a curious fact that the proposal of a far more drastic check on judicial review than President Roosevelt's "court packing" came from none other than Chief Justice Marshall. His proposal would have amounted to a possible congressional veto upon each instance of the Court's invalidation of Federal legislation. This suggestion was offered in 1806 when the Jeffersonians were determined to reconstitute the Court

[22] See C. Herman Pritchett: "Dissent on the Supreme Court, 1943–44." *American Political Science Review* (1945), 42–54; "The Roosevelt Court: Votes and Values." *American Political Science Review* (1948), 42:53–67. Thomas Reed Powell: "Our High Court Analyzed," *New York Times*, June 18, 1944; Arthur M. Schlesinger, Jr.: "The Supreme Court." *Fortune* (1947), 73–212; Kenneth A. Davis: "Revolution in the Supreme Court," *Atlantic Monthly* (1940), 166:85–96.

[23] Howard Lee McBain: *The Living Constitution,* p. 255.

through impeachment and conviction of Supreme Court justices and the impeachment of Marshall himself seemed imminent. "I think," wrote Marshall, "the modern doctrine of impeachment should yield to an appellate jurisdiction in the legislature. A reversal of those opinions deemed unsound by the legislature would certainly better comport with the mildness of our character than would a removal of the judge who has rendered them unknowing his fault." [24] The Jeffersonian program of impeachment collapsed through the Senate's refusal to convict Associate Justice Samuel Chase, and Marshall, no doubt, gladly forgot his suggestion as the crisis passed and the Court regained its self-confidence.

During the Reconstruction period, we have seen that Congress deprived the Supreme Court of jurisdiction of a case when everything had been done but announcing the Court's judgment. In this same period the House of Representatives passed, by a large majority, a bill that would have required a two-thirds vote of the Supreme Court to hold an Act of Congress unconstitutional but the Senate took no action on the measure. Even if enacted, the Supreme Court would quite probably have disregarded the statute as an unconstitutional invasion of the function of the judicial branch of the Federal government. In states where the extraordinary majority is now required for holding a statute unconstitutional, a minority of the court can sustain the constitutionality of a statute with the curious consequence that this minority then prepares the prevailing opinion while the majority gives the dissenting opinion. In 1912 Theodore Roosevelt startled the bar associations of the nation by proposing the recall, by referendum, of state supreme court decisions that held state statutes unconstitutional. There was no strong favorable popular response to this proposal. Suffice it to say that none of these proposed restrictions have ever been laid permanently on the Supreme Court, and aside from public pressures upon it the only significant restraint upon the Court is its own self-restraint. Indeed the Supreme Court has frankly admitted that its "power and influence rest solely upon the appeal for the assertion and protection of rights guaranteed by the Constitution and by the laws of the land and on the confidence reposed in the soundness of their decisions and the purity of their motives." [25] Here as nowhere else in the government character counts and it is significant that the American people seem to hold the judiciary in higher esteem than either the executive or the legislative branches of the government.

SUMMARY

Judicial review, the practice of a court in deciding a case to base its judgment on the Constitution instead of on a legislative enactment which it considers repugnant to the Constitution, is nowhere specifically directed in the Constitution. Since the judges in every state are bound by the Federal Constitution, statutes, and treaties, "anything in the Consti-

[24] A. J. Beveridge: *Life of John Marshall*, 4 vols. Boston, 1919, Vol. III, p. 177.
[25] United States v. Lee, 106 U.S. 196 (1882).

tution or laws of the state to the contrary notwithstanding" the implication of judicial review of state statutes and constitutions is unmistakable.

Judicial review of acts of Congress is another matter. Researches indicate that the known opinion of the chief framers of the Constitution was in favor of the practice of judicial review. Chief Justice Marshall in Marbury v. Madison set the pattern of constitutional interpretation justifying judicial review of acts of Congress. However, the number of statutes held unconstitutional has been kept within bounds by the avowed self restraint of the Supreme Court in presuming that every statute is constitutional unless the contrary is proved. Moreover the Court's acceptance of social data as pertinent evidence has saved many a statute from being declared unconstitutional.

The historic crises that have, from time to time, impaired the prestige of the Court have all been due to inopportune decisions involving questions of constitutionality: The Dred Scott decision, the Greenback Cases, the Income Tax cases, and the dozen decisions against statutes of Franklin Roosevelt's first administration. Nevertheless, every effort at drastic reform of the Supreme Court has failed because of public opposition or indifference.

PART

VIII

MAJOR FEDERAL FUNCTIONS

CHAPTER XXVII

FEDERAL FINANCE

THE SCOPE OF FEDERAL TAXATION

I T IS an incontestable fact that, in this generation, public finance has become the major economic operation of government in the United States. Only estimates can be made of the total annual expenditures of all our local, state, and national governments but they are probably in excess of one hundred billion dollars. The total taxes of all governments collected in the United States must be nearly ninety billion dollars. The total public debt of all kinds of government in the United States has been estimated to be above three hundred billion dollars, not far behind the aggregate national income—that is, the sum of the incomes of every person in the United States.

This gigantic role of public finance in the economy of the United States is a recent development—easily within a short generation, rather less than a quarter of a century. It began mounting with the big budgets made necessary by the billions spent on "pump-priming" in the 1930's— the public works projects and direct expenditures for relief of the unemployed and of others in dire distress. The greatest single factor, however, in the big budgets was the Second World War, the most expensive by far of all our armed conflicts. Moreover wars are not paid for just by peoples who wage them but, as Benjamin Franklin once observed, "The bill comes later." Monetarily, it comes in hospitalization of veterans and pensions paid to them and their dependents, not to mention the interest and amortization of the war debt. The Korean War piled up more war debt even as it was inflating prices and thereby skyrocketing the current costs of the war. Only less expensive than these "hot" wars has been the persisting "cold" war, with its overloading of a "peace time" budget with many billions appropriated annually for armed forces and fabulous expenditures for the ever-mounting cost of the apparatus of modern war which is growing obsolescent even as it comes off the assembly line.

Then there is the astonishing growth of population. Even if per capita cost of government could, by some miracle, be kept constant, the national budget would nevertheless have mounted 35 per cent in the twenty-five years following the stock market crash of 1929. But per capita costs can never remain constant in a dynamic, multi-group society, many of whose component elements know how to use their pressures persuading their representatives to expand governmental services. Finally, budget dollars spent for consumers' goods today will buy almost exactly half what they would have purchased twenty years earlier. Let it then be noted that present-day budgets are expressed in terms of inflated dollars, and this should be taken into consideration when comparing them with the federal budget of 1930.

Financial Factors in Making the Constitution

The complete absence of any power of Congress to tax under the Articles of Confederation was its outstanding defect as an organ of central government. In 1781 Congress submitted to the states an amendment to the Articles of Confederation that would have given Congress power to levy a 5 per cent duty on imports to be used in paying the interest and principal of the national debt, mainly contracted in prosecuting the Revolutionary War. It was approved by every state but one, but since the Articles required unanimous approval, the amendment failed. A second attempt at a taxation amendment also failed. Securities representing the Confederation's debt then sank, in some cases, to only 5 per cent of face value and complete collapse of the credit of the Confederation seemed imminent.

The threatened collapse of the credit of the United States under the Confederation was a major factor in bringing about the convening of the delegates who framed the Constitution at Philadelphia. It was appropriate that the first of the eighteen powers of Congress should be the grant of the taxing power. Thus it said: "The Congress shall have power to lay and collect taxes, duties, imposts, and excises to pay the debts and provide for the common defense and general welfare of the United States; but all duties, imposts and excises shall be uniform throughout the United States."

The Scope of the Taxing Power

Why, it might be asked, is the comprehensive term "taxes" in Article 1, section 8, clause 1 of the Constitution, followed by three specified kinds of taxes? Evidently because the delegation of taxing power to Congress by this clause "embraces every conceivable power of taxation," [1] at any rate that is what the Supreme Court of the United States decided is the meaning of the clause. Moreover it "reaches every subject." [2] Apparently there is no limit to the per cent Congress may levy and the Constitution

[1] Brushaber v. Union Pacific R. R. 240 U.S. 12 (1916).
[2] Ibid., 1.

contains no formal safeguard against a confiscatory tax. Chief Justice Marshall frankly admitted this in McCulloch *v.* Maryland: "The only security against the abuse of this power is found in the structure of the government itself."[3] However this clause itself imposes an inflexible regulation upon Congress in that "all duties, imposts and excises shall be uniform throughout the United States," and Article 1, section 2, clause 3 requires that "direct taxes shall be apportioned among the several states . . . according to their respective numbers." Moreover no commodity exported from any state may be taxed by Congress.

Judicial Limitations of Taxing Power

Recently, by reversing decisions standing for most of a century, the Supreme Court has removed restrictions to the taxing power of Congress growing out of judicial interpretations. Since 1871 the Supreme Court had, until recently, held steadily that the salary of a state officer might not be taxed by Congress since that would make it possible for Congress, step by step, to destroy the states.[4] But in 1939 the Supreme Court reversed this rule.[5] Also reversed at this time was the judicial ruling that federal judges might not be taxed upon their incomes derived from their salaries. Since 1920 federal judges had been held exempt from the income tax upon their salaries on the ground that this would mean a reduction of their salaries in violation of the Constitution's prohibition of such reduction during their judicial incumbency. In 1939 the Supreme Court declared that the earlier cases were "over-ruled so far as they recognize an implied constitutional immunity from income taxation of the salaries of officers and employees of the national or a state government or their instrumentalities." In more than a dozen cases within the last generation the Supreme Court of the United States has struck from the congressional taxing power most of the shackles built up by nearly a century of judicial restriction.[6]

The Meaning of "Direct" Taxes

When the Constitution required that direct taxes be apportioned among the states according to population, just what manner of tax did that include? The economist means by a direct tax one that cannot be shifted to others such, for example, as a poll tax. From 1796 when the Supreme Court held that a tax on carriages was, in its nature, an excise[7] to the Income Tax Cases in 1895,[8] the Supreme Court apparently assumed that the framers of the Constitution intended that, since direct taxes must be apportioned among the states, the term would include only such taxes

[3] 4 Wheaton, 316.
[4] Collector *v.* Day, 11 Wall. 113 (1871).
[5] Graves *v.* New York ex rel. O'Keefe (1939).
[6] See *The Constitution of the United States: Analysis and Interpretation* (E. S. Corwin, ed.) Washington, 1953, pp. 106, 107.
[7] Hylton *v.* United States, 3 Dallas 171 (1796).
[8] 157 U.S. 429 and 158 U.S. 601 (1905).

as could be apportioned such as land and capitation taxes. A Civil War income tax had successfully run the gauntlet of the Courts without apportionment. But when Congress in 1894 levied an income tax of two per cent on incomes above $4,000, the Supreme Court, after some astonishing wavering, finally held that a tax on income derived from property was a direct tax and must therefore be apportioned. Since apportionment of an income tax would be utterly impracticable, the power of Congress to levy income taxes was ended, except after amending the Constitution. Eighteen years later the Sixteenth Amendment restored the power by providing: "The Congress shall have power to lay and collect taxes on incomes from whatever source derived, without apportionment among the several states, and without regard to any census or enumeration." Even then the Supreme Court decided that "from whatever source derived" did not mean just what it said and that the salaries of federal judges and of state officers were still exempt from a federal income tax no matter what the amendment said.[9] However, as noted above, the Supreme Court has recently removed from tax exemption most incomes by the reversal of earlier decisions.

Regulation by Taxation

Congress' power to tax is not confined to the raising of revenue to be spent for the purposes given in the taxing clause of the Constitution. The taxing power may be employed by Congress for regulative purposes. Most notable of such taxes has been the protective tariff by which customs duties are set with a view to checking imports and sometimes the rate on an article has been set high enough to exclude it absolutely without a dollar of revenue flowing into the Treasury. Congress has taxed sulphur matches out of existence and stopped the circulation of state bank notes by a tax rate on them that the banks could not afford to pay. Oleomargarine, colored to resemble butter, was long made unsalable by a tax of ten cents a pound. Congress has also enacted tax legislation, accompanied by prescribed stringent regulation, under which the sale of certain drugs and firearms has been regulated. In a recent opinion the Supreme Court held: "It is beyond serious question that a tax does not cease to be valid merely because it regulates, discourages, or even definitely deters the activities taxed." [10]

Taxing for the General Welfare

It must always be kept in mind that the "general welfare" provision of the Constitution can never be utilized except by the spending of public money. Indeed this paragraph might well be entitled "spending for the general welfare." Thomas Jefferson's exposition cannot be improved upon: ". . . the laying of taxes is the *power,* and the general welfare the *purpose* for which the power is to be exercised. They (Congress) are

[9] Evans *v.* Gore, 253 U.S. 245 (1920).
[10] Magnano Co. *v.* Hamilton, 292 U.S. 40, 47 (1934).

not to tax *ad libitum for any purpose they please*, but only *to pay the debts or provide for the welfare of the Union*. In like manner, they are not *to do any thing they please* to provide for the general welfare, but only *to lay taxes* for that purpose.[11] The "general welfare" phrase is then a limitation of the taxing power of Congress. Presidents Monroe, Jackson, Tyler, Polk, Grant, Arthur and Cleveland vetoed internal improvement bills on the ground that they provided for *local* rather than the *"general"* welfare but in many such instances Congress has passed the appropriation bill over the President's veto.

Almost from its beginning Congress has acted upon the broad interpretation of the general welfare. It made an appropriation for a subsidy in 1792, and internal improvements at federal expense began in Washington's administration. Since 1914, federal grants-in-aid, that is federal appropriations apportioned among the states, often upon condition that they be matched by the states, dollar for dollar and upon compliance with stipulated conditions, have become common. It is a curious fact that millions of dollars had been appropriated and spent under the "general welfare" provision of the Constitution and over a period of more than a hundred and forty years before the Supreme Court of the United States gave a clear cut decision approving the practice.[12] Now and then a view has been advanced that "provide for the . . . general welfare of the United States" is a sweeping grant of power to Congress to pass whatever laws it considers to be for the general welfare. Obviously this interpretation would make unnecessary the list of delegated powers in section 8 of article one. This has never been an accepted interpretation by any branch of the government.

THE FEDERAL BUDGET
Federal Revenues and Expenditures

Our national government originated at a time when, for historical reasons, the public was extraordinarily sensitive to taxation. The very birth of the government was in the midst of a revolutionary war provoked by the issue of taxation by the English Parliament. The colonists had been insistent that revenue taxes, as contrasted with taxes laid by Parliament to regulate trade, must be laid only by their own elected representatives in the colonial legislature. Quite naturally this idea persisted when the colonies, during the Revolutionary War, became independent states. So persistent was the antipathy to taxes levied by any organ but their own state legislatures that the Articles of Confederation gave Congress no power to tax whatever. Even the grant of plenary power of taxation to Congress by the Constitution was not readily accepted by all citizens. Consequently the first Congress laid only mild customs duties on imports and an excise tax on the stills distilling whiskey. These were consumption

[11] *Writings of Thomas Jefferson* (Library Edition), Vol. III, pp. 147–9.
[12] United States *v.* Butler, 297 U.S. 1 (1936).

taxes, hidden burdens of which the consumers were largely unaware. Even the whiskey excise tax caused a revolt in 1794, reduced by the march of 15,000 militia called into the federal service for that purpose.

The Constitution requires that direct taxes be apportioned among the states according to their respective populations. This made the use of that kind of tax so difficult that, after a mild attempt at its use soon after the adoption of the Constitution and another during the Civil War it was discarded. Up to the Civil War the tariff remained almost the sole source of federal revenue derived from taxes. During the Civil War excise taxes were laid on almost every article of industry and commerce and after the Civil War the excise was continued on liquors and tobacco. For a generation preceding the beginning of the income tax in 1913 excise taxes and the tariff provided 90 per cent of federal revenues.

The income tax on corporations beginning in 1909 and on individual incomes in 1913 revolutionized our system of federal taxation. Shortly thereafter the estate tax also became a permanent part of our federal tax system. Before 1913 we relied on indirect taxes, leaving direct taxes to state and local government. Since then direct taxes have provided most of our revenue, but during the Great Depression when the revenue from income taxes declined sharply, Congress turned to additional indirect or excise taxes which have since provided a substantial percentage of federal revenues. The customs duties have declined to considerably less than one per cent of our total revenues.

Those who have little or no experience with government are inclined to think that balancing the budget is a simple matter of increasing taxes or preferably reducing expenses—cutting out items here and there. Even the party of the outs—the opposition—criticizes public expenditures and extravagance as if they thought the high cost of government were due to the stupidity or mendacity of the majority in control. But when the outs become the ins, they discover that practically every item in the budget is there because history put it there or international tensions and well-organized internal interests are back of them, and Congressmen will reduce or obliterate them only at their own peril—that is at the risk of retirement to private life. Certainly the appropriations for carrying on the government, the legislative, executive, and judicial branches, cannot be spared or reduced. In any case they are but a modest fraction of the budget. A cold war forbids the slashing of appropriations for national defense. Appropriations for care of the veterans are secure as long as the nation's sense of obligation remains, and the veterans constitute the largest bloc in the electorate. Equally secure are the appropriations for the interest on the national debt and for its payment. As long as a prosperous national economy is dependent on the vigor of agriculture, the farmers cannot be set adrift as in the era of raw *laissez faire,* particularly as long as farmers have the ballot and know how to swing the balance of their voting power—as they have demonstrated again and again in the history of American politics. The only question here is how much of the budget is to be devoted to the stabilization of the rural economy. And so it goes with all the other items in the column of public expenses that provide services for citizens who are organized and able to make their influence felt. By and large the items in our national budget are what the social forces of the nation require them to be, and a Man from Mars would have difficulty distinguishing between the budgets of a Republican and a Democratic administration for each is prepared in response to the demands of the same multi-group national society.

National Budgets for 1955, 1956, and 1957
(In millions of dollars)

BUDGET RECEIPTS AND EXPENDITURES

Description	1955	1956	1957
BUDGET RECEIPTS	ACTUAL	ESTIMATE	ESTIMATE
Individual income taxes	$31,650	$33,555	$35,118
Corp. income and excess profits taxes	18,265	20,300	20,300
Excise taxes	9,211	9,894	9,887
Employment taxes	6,220	7,420	7,585
Estate and gift taxes	936	1,025	1,120
Customs	606	690	700
Miscellaneous receipts	2,566	2,505	2,805
Subtotal	69,454	75,389	77,515
Deduct-Transfer to Federal Old Age and Survivors Insurance Trust Fund	5,040	6,475	6,635
Transfer to Railroad Retirement Trust Fund	599	625	660
Refunds of receipts	3,426	3,789	3,920
Net Budget receipts	60,390	64,500	66,300
BUDGET EXPENDITURES			
Major national security	41,124	39,737	40,674
International affairs and finance	2,514	2,497	2,591
Veterans' services and benefits	4,496	4,839	4,934
Labor and welfare	2,554	2,769	2,997
Agriculture and agriculture resources	9,324	8,575	9,070
Natural resources	1,304	1,320	1,297
Commerce and housing	6,139	6,259	6,299
General government	1,204	1,614	1,760
Interest	6,438	6,875	7,066
Reserves for contingencies		100	225
Gross budget expenditures	75,097	74,567	76,914
Deduct applicable receipts *	10,527	10,298	11,049
Net budget expenditures	64,570	64,270	65,865
Budget surplus or deficit	–4,180	230	435

* Receipts of certain government corporations, the postal service, and other revolving funds the receipts of which come primarily from outside the government.

Emergence of the Budget System

Up to a little more than a generation ago the federal budget, if it could be called that, was prepared by the Treasury Department, which was then authorized merely to receive, index, print, and transmit to Congress whatever estimates it had compiled as received from the numerous agencies of the government. In 1911 President Taft had appointed the Committee on Economy and Efficiency to study the problem. It concluded that no improvement was possible without a budget system. But

when President Taft, following the Commission's recommendations, had
the executive departments prepare the necessary estimates, Congress resented "the infringement on their prerogatives" and that ended the matter for the time being.

At the end of World War I a nation that had long been accustomed
to a national debt hovering year after year around a billion dollars was
rather suddenly confronted with a debt of $24 billion. In 1921 Congress
enacted the Budget Act and provided, for its administration, the Bureau
of the Budget, destined to become in time the most important element
of the present Executive Office of the President.[13] By a rare stroke of
good fortune President Harding appointed Charles A. Dawes, a Chicago
banker, the first Director of the Budget. This extraordinary extrovert
made it impossible for the public to ignore the new Bureau of the
Budget. The first assembly of the several hundred personnel of the Bureau and related agencies was treated by Director Dawes to an astonishing theatrical performance. Seated on the stage behind the Director
were the members of President Harding's Cabinet. It must have been a
breath-taking moment when Director Dawes, rushing over in front of
dignified Secretary of State Charles Evans Hughes, shook a menacing
index finger at the Secretary as he shouted, "Mr. Secretary of State, you
must economize" and so on down the line, admonishing Herbert Hoover
and the rest of the Cabinet. Then, rushing into the stage wing, the
Director emerged with a bundle of brooms announcing the bargain price
when purchased in quantity. Next, seizing a single broom, he gave the
retail price paid by a thriftless federal agency which purchased its
brooms one at a time. Such histrionics could not be overlooked by the
ecstatic newsmen, and within twenty-four hours practically every literate
American knew that the United States had a Bureau of the Budget.[14]

Scope of the Budget Bureau's Functions

Budget Director Dawes made economy the keynote of the Budget system—the "paper clip" era, it has been called—and this dominant purpose persisted until 1939 when Harold D. Smith became its director.
The broad objective of the Bureau since then has been the preparation
of expenditures for the carrying out of the President's program of policies. The Budget Bureau thus became the spokesman of the President's
Agency programs as well as of his expenditure plans. The Budget Bureau's Office of Management and Organization assists departments and
agencies in improving organization and methods; its Office of Statistical
Standards curtails the demands of agencies and private parties for statistical reports; through the Council of Economic Advisers the Bureau
views the level of federal expenditures as to its effect on the economy of
the nation as a whole. As Robert Sherwood put it, "The Bureau of

[13] See Harold D. Smith, *The Management of the Government* (1945), Chapter V.
[14] The Budget system is described in Chapter XX, "The Presidential Staff."

the Budget could and must send its agents into every Department of the government . . . to find out for the President himself exactly how the money was being spent, and by whom, and with what results. Thus, the Bureau was actually the President's intelligence service. . . ." [15]

THE BUDGET BUREAU, A PRESIDENTIAL ORGAN

The Bureau an Arm of the President

The first director, General Dawes, had steadily insisted that he acted for the President and required department heads to come to him for conference—not going to them. Once he had to tell a Secretary bluntly that his demand for reduction of estimates was "made by direction of the President." Every President since Harding has given the Budget Bureau strong support. The operations of the Bureau are mainly fiscal, but this function becomes the means of facilitating executive administration of the government. By means of the Legislative Reference Office a co-ordination of the Executive with Congress is achieved. Every recommendation of an executive agency to a congressional committee is routed through this Reference Office to ascertain before it gets to the committee whether it is in accord with the President's policies. Moreover this Office of the Bureau of the Budget assembles the data by which the President decides whether to sign or veto a bill, and it sometimes prepares, by request, his veto message. Executive orders of any agency must have the approval of the Reference Office. Thus it becomes a key agency for the President's over-all chieftainship of administration and national policy

The Scope of Fiscal Management

Fiscal management includes all those governmental operations by means of which funds are made available to the officials and their lawful use ensured. There are the executive agencies which must have the funds, Congress with sole power to grant these funds, the Executive offices which control their expenditure, and finally the auditing offices which determine the legality and propriety of the expenditures. At this point it should be recalled, as has been indicated under taxation, that fiscal functions are inseparable from other policies. A tariff involves regulation of foreign commerce. A federal tax on opium manufactured for smoking is designed to stop its use as a narcotic drug. A social security tax for unemployment payments is so managed as to induce states to establish their own compensation plans. Aside from taxation, appropriations were made in the 1930's for "pump priming" in the expectation that the economic system might be induced to start functioning automatically again. The Walsh-Healey Act sought to secure social reform by requiring minimum standards for labor as a condition of obtaining government contracts. The Marshall Plan endeavored to strengthen our potential allies

[15] Robert Sherwood, *Roosevelt and Hopkins* (1948), Vol. I, pp. 258–9.

among democracies by grants to foreign nations designed to rehabilitate their war-damaged economies. It is practically impossible to divorce public policy from matters of public finance.

The President is in a very real sense the chief finanical officer of the federal government. He is called upon to make some of the highest decisions in fiscal matters. He must decide the top figure of the Budget, whether it is intended to be balanced, to create a surplus, or to be a matter of deficit financing of the government. During the uncertainties of a cold war he is the supreme authority on what percentage of the whole budget is to be allotted to national defense, and then, when army, navy, and air departments cannot resolve their differences as to their respective shares of defense expenditures, the President is a Supreme Court for settling such controversies. He cannot escape responsibility for what per cent of farm parity is to be assured, by attempting to leave it solely to the Secretary of Agriculture. Nor can he delegate absolute responsibility to the Director of the Budget, who is so completely his man that Congress vests in the President alone, without the usual senatorial advice and consent, the power to appoint him. There can be no doubt that the budget system, during the past generation, has greatly increased the President's control as head of the administrative system. At the same time it has enhanced the position of the department heads and increased responsibility and accountability at every level of the administrative pyramid.

The Budget Process a Continuous One

Before the budget system was introduced each agency prepared its estimates in sweet oblivion of and consequent indifference to anyone or anything outside the agency and without any reference to any general administrative policy. Not until these estimates reached the appropriation committees of Congress was there any critical judgment or authority brought to bear upon them. Now the budgetary process is a continuous one going on the year round. Work is in progress on two overlapping federal budgets at the same time. Congress made its appropriations for the 1955 budget (July 1, 1954, to June 30, 1955) before June 30, 1954. The President's budget for that year had been submitted early in January, 1954. The agencies had begun work on it in April or May of 1953 and were at it continuously until December, 1953. But also in April and May, 1953, while working on the plans for 1954–55, the agencies were negotiating with appropriation committees for the fiscal year ahead, that is 1953–54.

The Budget as a Work Program

Now, in contrast with the anarchy of agency estimates in the pre-budget years, each agency is guided by instructions from the Budget Bureau based on the financial program developed and announced by the President. Basic is the revenue expected from existing tax laws with such increases or decreases as the President intends to recommend to Congress, and all this will depend on the emphasis he intends to give to particular policies. For example a cold war threatening to grow hot will call for increased expenditures for defense. Inevitably the over-all budget involves a work program—the President's program of policies. At the same time, each agency's part of the over-all budget is likewise a work program but one that must be coordinated with the grand work plan of the budget as a whole. The documents presenting the Budget are prodigious and when printed exceed the size of mail order catalogues. The Budget for 1955 comprised two volumes of 1302 and 526 pages respectively. The President's budget message explaining the principal features required 104 pages.

The Budget only a Recommendation

It must be borne in mind that the President's Budget is, so far as Congress is concerned, only a recommendation, or rather a comprehensive set of recommendations. Only Congress can give legal validity to it or any part of it. Congress has the constitutional power to raise, lower, or ignore any or all the budget estimates. The President's check on what Congress enacts is only his veto and this cannot be exercised on items of a measure. "The strength of the budget . . . depends upon the political authority of the chief executive, party and factional balance of forces, the weight of outside influences and the inherent soundness of the estimates. The burden of proof, however, is on those who would change the figures proposed by the chief executive and his agencies, and the program set forth is not usually modified to any substantial degree, apart from a few controversial expenditures." [16] Any agency's stiffest battle is said to be with the Bureau of the Budget, not with the congressional appropriations committee.

THE PROBLEM OF A BALANCED BUDGET

Budget Procedure in Congress

The Budget comes to Congress as a comprehensive recommendation of the President with respect to revenues and appropriations. Here it is distributed among the subdivisions, that is the sub-committees of the Appropriations Committee. There are twelve of these sub-committees, each assigned consideration of the appropriations for an executive department or the independent agencies. The sub-committees dealing with affairs of the independent commissions, the Treasury and the Post Office departments start in December before Congress convenes, using advance proofs of the Budget to be delivered to Congress a month later. The other sub-committees begin hearings on estimates for the other departments early in the session, that is in January. At these hearings the department heads

[16] Leonard D. White, *Introduction to the Study of Public Administration,* Fourth edition (1955), p. 252.

appear first, followed by bureau heads, congressmen, and private citizens who want to be heard, and all are heard in secret sessions.

Department officers are cross-examined as to past, current, and expected future expenditures. But the Congressmen, engrossed as they are with numerous other duties, are at a disadvantage here as they quiz the departmental experts skilled in defending their estimates. The committee staff experts are no match for those of the departments. "For the administrators these annual congressional inquisitions are none the less an ordeal and they have a real disciplinary value. But officials soon become adept in the arts of caution, evasion, and concealment. Legislators can disturb but seldom fathom the deeper waters of the federal service." [17] The upshot of the matter is that Congressmen are seldom able to make a penetrating analysis of the Budget and consequently tend to appropriate blindly.

The sub-committee proceeds to consider its appropriate part of the Budget item by item, agreeing upon the appropriation for each with such modifications as it considers proper. Thereupon it reports its conclusions to the full Appropriations Committee, which usually adopts sub-committee recommendations after only a casual discussion. Eventually the appropriation bill is reported to the House and the printed reports of hearings are made available. Since the floor debate on the appropriation bill usually takes place the day it is reported by the main committee, it tends to be pretty futile to challenge items in the face of the vigilant care of the sub-committees. Under the circumstances appropriation bills usually pass with only a few members on the floor and with merely minor changes and amendments. Having passed the House, the appropriation bill runs a quite similar course in the Senate, with any difference between the versions of the two houses being resolved by a joint conference committee of the two houses.

The Concept of a Balanced Budget

The Democratic party came into power in 1933 pledged to a balanced budget only to discover that the burden of relief expenditures, "pump priming," and two wars (World War II and Korean) permitted only three balanced budgets in twenty years. The Republicans returned to power in 1953 expecting to balance the budget soon, only to find that the cold war postponed that hoped-for achievement for three years. Whether the budget can be balanced or not depends upon chance and circumstances and a complex of power forces, national and international, rather than on any cherished dogma. A budget may be too extravagant and suffer from a failure of expected revenues to materialize. Almost as dangerous is a too parsimonious budget that may fail to provide services demanded by citizens, as, for example, when the Republican Eightieth Congress did not provide expected storage for grain and lost both Con-

[17] George Galloway, *Congress at the Cross Roads*, New York, 1946, p. 248.

gress and the presidency in the ensuing election. The greatest risk of all in a cold war is the unpredictability of defense requirement, and an error here could be fatal to a nation.

Pressures for Economy

The major deterrent to spending is the danger of a revolt of the tax payer, and this is pretty unpredictable. The typical Congressman is cautious as to new taxes, especially those that too obviously burden the masses of voters. The second check on expenditure is the Bureau of the Budget, under the discipline that the President may be capable of holding over his administrative personnel. Then there is the professional pride of the career men in the Budget Bureau in submitting budgets free from padding and ill-considered estimates.

Pressures for Spending

Collectively, Congress is economy-minded, but the typical Congressman individually is subject to persistent pressures for spending. In the West he is importuned to get irrigation works, dams, and power installations. The coastal states demand harbor improvements, and inland states the preparing of rivers for navigation. There is the competition for airports, veterans hospitals, and post office buildings. Labor wants appropriations for public housing, the Farm Bureau Federation price supports. The governmental agencies themselves have a vested interest in maintaining and enhancing their respective functions. "Every agency is certain to have a friendly Congressman, preferably influential in his party or chairman of a committee or an appropriation sub-committee. Instances have been known of committee chairmen who have become avowed protagonists of given bureaus or commissions. . . . They can put the right questions [at hearings], give an agency an opportunity to put its best foot forward, and help to protect it against awkward interrogation." [18] A sympathetic committee member can even invite a frustrated bureau chief at a committee hearing to state whether the approved estimates fully meet his needs.

Executive Control of Expenditures

The old concept of an appropriation was that it was not merely the authorization of an expenditure but an imperative order to the executive to see that it was expended. The newer concept is that an appropriation is to be used only if necessary, subject to authorization by the chief executive. This enhances the chief executive's prestige. He cannot legally increase an appropriation, and his tendency is to reduce or postpone expenditures where he can. His interest is in ensuring economy and avoiding deficits. Since 1910 there has been no reversal in the persistent trend of increasing executive control of expenditures. The persistent mounting

[18] Leonard D. White, *op. cit.*, p. 272.

magnitude of public expenditures calls for some extraordinary control to ensure economy, efficiency, elimination of waste and return to the treasury of unexpended appropriations.

Congressional Control of Expenditures

Congressional control includes more than the formal, conventional appropriation. One must often read between the lines to understand a puzzling detail. For example, the Veterans' Administration appropriation of the Seventy-sixth Congress contained a provision, inserted over the protest of the agency's medical staff, "that no part of this appropriation shall be expended for the purchase of oleomargarine or butter substitutes." [19] The pressure of the dairy interest had been successful. But even more important than provisions like this incorporated in statutes is the unrecorded oral understandings reached between the appropriation committees and executive heads.[20] There is, for example, the understanding or "gentlemen's agreement" that lump-sum appropriations will be used in accordance with itemizations in the budget. There are understandings that cotton purchased by the army for distribution in occupied territory should be American grown. These informal gentlemen's agreements enhance the power of committee chairmen and collectively that of Congress itself. They are merely powerful usages that add to the more formal means of Congressional supervision over, even sometimes dictation to, the administrator through the power of the purse.

THE NATIONAL DEBT

Managing the National Debt

The Revolutionary War debt contracted by the Continental Congress was utterly beyond the competence of the government of the Articles of Confederation to manage because of its lack of any power to tax. This very deficiency was, as we have seen, a factor in the movement to obtain the Constitution. The first step in the management of the national debt under the Constitution was the achievement of Secretary of the Treasury Alexander Hamilton in getting Congress to fund this debt and also the debts of the states which Congress assumed. From the beginning the cost of our wars has been the chief factor in creating national debt. Four major wars—the War of 1812, the Civil War, and World Wars I and II—have accounted for the peaks in the national debt.

Every one of our major wars has caused a price inflation due to the increased purchasing power created by the sale of bonds to banking institutions at the same time that production of war material has led to a shortage of consumers' goods. The experience with World War II will illustrate the inflationary process. From July 1, 1941, to June 30, 1946, the

[19] 55 Stat. 545 (March 16, 1939).
[20] Arthur W. Mac Mahon, "Congressional Oversight of Administration: the Power of the Purse," *Political Science Quarterly*, LVIII (1943), pp. 389–400.

federal government raised 383 billion dollars to meet its war and other expenses and to keep a cash balance in the Treasury. Of this amount, 44 per cent was raised by taxation and the Treasury borrowed 56 per cent of which 33 per cent was loaned by the non-banking public, that is by purchasers of government bonds, 6 per cent by the Federal Reserve Banks and about 17 per cent by commercial banks. This concentration of 23 per cent of federal borrowing in the banking system became the basis of excessive bank loans and thereby created purchasing power for consumer goods, which were in shortage because of the war-time concentration of our industrial system on the requirements of the armed forces. A decade after the close of the war the inflationary trend, though slackened, had not yet spent its force.[21]

The national debt is a major problem of public finance, with its solution by no means yet in sight. Alexander Hamilton, in his Report on the Public Credit, referred to a current adage of his day, "A public debt is a public blessing." Today there is an attempt to revive that long discredited adage. Every war in our history before World War II was followed by a prompt effort to reduce the war debt. There are those who consider an annual interest payment of more than six billion dollars a matter of no great concern since the national debt is an internal one and the interest payments merely mean a redistribution of tax payments among tax payers. Conservative economists, however, generally advocate reduction of the national debt in the traditional policy throughout our history.

The great difficulty is the balancing of our federal budget and then accumulating the surplus necessary for payments on the debt. Clearly this should be done in periods of high prosperity and would provide an effective and wholesome check on inflationary tendencies. But no sooner does a surplus appear likely than the game of party politics starts—the competition between the two major parties each to get credit for reducing taxes so as to reap the rewards in the next election. Courage could prove fatal to the party in power. Political leaders, however, may be underestimating the intelligence of the citizens for an opinion poll not so long ago revealed a heavy sentiment in favor of taxation high enough to permit debt reduction.

SUMMARY

Public finance has become the major function of governments in the United States, with budgets totaling, for all levels of government, more than $100 billion annually. Budgets mount with inflation, growth of population, pressing demands for new services, and especially with war-time needs.

A crisis in national finance contributed to the making of the Constitution which consequently granted Congress broad powers of taxation

[21] See *Our National Debt: Its history and its meaning today* by the Committee on Public Debt Policy, New York, 1949, Chapter 3.

with only minor restrictions. Early judicial restrictions of federal taxation were over-ruled in 1939. The Sixteenth Amendment's exempting the income tax from apportionment among the states as to population has enabled Congress to make it the chief source of federal revenue. Taxation is also used for the purpose of regulating certain activities. Because Congress may tax "for general welfare," it makes generous grants-in-aid to the states as well as expending for rivers, harbors, highways, and other improvements.

In 1921 Congress established the Executive Budget with a Bureau which, in 1936, became a means of managing the President's policies at the same time that it constitutes the government's chief fiscal organ. The Bureau shapes the Budget in accordance with the President's whole program of policies and his purpose as to deficit, surplus, or balance. Its preparation is a year-round process with two successive budgets in simultaneous evolution. Every budget is a work program of the President.

The Budget is an elaborate recommendation to which only Congress, through legislation, can give legal force, with such modification as it chooses to make—these are usually minor ones. Appropriation merely authorizes expenditure which the executive is not legally required to carry out.

The peaks of the national debt have coincided with major wars, accompanied, in every case, by inflation. The inflation occurs because the government greatly expands the volume of money and credit to meet its war expenditures, at the same time that output of consumers' goods is being sharply reduced. The traditional policy of prompt post-war reduction of the national debt is challenged today—though still advocated by conservative economists.

CHAPTER XXVIII

FEDERAL CONTROL OF MONEY, BANKING, AND CREDIT

METALLIC MONETARY REGULATIONS

The Persistence of American Monetary Problems

THE extraordinary extent to which human welfare is dependent upon an adequate medium of exchange has been demonstrated by more than three centuries of American experience with money. Quite properly, then, regulation of the media of exchange is universally regarded as a function of national sovereignty. Colonial, state, and national governments in turn have wrestled with American monetary problems. The veto of British crown authority checked one colonial project after another designed to relieve the desperate scarcity of money by means of colonial issues of paper money. Finally by the Currency Act of 1764 Parliament settled the matter once and for all, as it supposed, by outlawing absolutely such colonial issues. Not the least among the cumulative grievances that culminated in independence was the provocation thus produced by the creditor-conscious Parliament upon the currency-starved and debt-ridden colonists. Independence gave free rein to the inflationary urge of the agrarians now entrenched in the strategic seats of power, the state legislatures. Extraordinary issues of legal tender paper money and the consequent economic confusion was one of the important factors that led to the call for the Constitutional Convention of 1787. Nor were promoters of the movement disappointed in the outcome. Clause after clause of the Constitution stamps it as a deflationary document.

Constitutional Restrictions on State Monetary Power

The Constitution provides that no state shall "coin money, emit bills of credit; make anything but gold and silver coin a tender in payment of debts." Money is tender in the payment of debts if a statute requires that it must be accepted by a creditor whenever tendered, that is, offered in payment of an obligation. Legal tender money might be of little or no value, but for the creditor to protest on that ground in a court of law would be futile. "Bills of credit" here signifies paper money or promissory notes based on the credit of the state. In the precise language of the Supreme Court: "To constitute a bill of credit within the meaning of the Constitution it must be issued by the state on the faith of the state and be designed to circulate as money. It must be paper that circulates on the credit of the state; and is so received and used in the ordinary business of life." [1] The Constitution's prohibition of state "bills of credit" has had the intended effect and no states have issued them since the Constitution went into effect. However, the Supreme Court, in the opinion just quoted, held that the paper issues of a bank the entire stock of which was owned by the State of Kentucky did not violate the Constitutional prohibition of state bills of credit because the issues were not acts of the state as such. It should be noted that the prohibition of state issues of bills of credit does not apply to state banks, that is, banks chartered by a state. These banks issued paper money freely until such issues were taxed out of existence by a 10 per cent levy on their paper issues laid by Congress in 1865.

American Experience with a Bimetallic Standard

Having vested Congress with the power "to coin money, regulate the value thereof, and of foreign coin" the framers of the Constitution took pains specifically to prohibit the states from exercising that power. Apparently they assumed that Congress would adopt the bimetallic monetary standard, then almost universal among commercial nations. A standard of value signifies some specified weight of precious metal whose market or exchange value constitutes the standard unit of value in buying and selling, in contracting and paying debts, and in measuring values when they are merely to be estimated. The first act passed under the monetary clause of the Constitution established this unit of value as the dollar with a weight of 24.75 grains of pure gold or 371.25 grains of pure silver exclusive, in both cases, of the alloy used in the coins. Since both metals were used in defining the dollar or the unit of value, it was a bimetallic standard. As can be seen these specified weights represented a ratio of 15 to 1. That is, Congress made fifteen ounces of *coined* silver worth or exchangeable for one ounce of *coined* gold. But gold and silver have a market value independent of what values may have been assigned by the fiat of a statute. This market value depends upon the increase or decrease of the demand for the metals for various purposes balanced against the increase or decrease of the supply of them as old sources of the metals are exhausted or new sources discovered and exploited. No sooner had the first coinage act been put into force than experience revealed that 24.75 grains of gold were worth more than 415.25 grains of silver whereupon gold was not coined and only silver coin circu-

[1] Briscoe v. Bank of Kentucky, 11 Peters 257 (1837).

lated. In 1834 Congress made a futile attempt to correct the coinage ratio by changing it to 16 to 1 but presently gold ceased to circulate. The California gold discoveries in mid-century cheapened gold whereupon silver was too valuable to be used as money and it disappeared from circulation. For eighty years Congress had struggled in vain to keep both gold and silver coin circulating and in 1873 gave it up through legislation that abandoned silver as a basic monetary metal by failing to provide for further dollar coinage of it. Presently silver again became superabundant and the pressures of silver interests and inflationary agrarians induced Congress to stave off the demand for remonetizing silver by coining limited quantities of it and giving a coined silver dollar a face value greater than its bullion value. This value was maintained only by making these silver dollars redeemable in the standard or gold dollar of 23.22 grains. Because silver dollars could be exchanged freely at par for gold dollars they circulated for full face value.

Establishment of the Gold Standard

The Gold Standard Act of 1900 marked the final triumph of the creditor interests in the face of a generation-long counter drive of the inflationary silver interest allied with debt-harassed agrarians, all determined to restore the free and unlimited coinage of silver at the old ratio of 16 to 1 as it had been under the Coinage Act of 1834. The Gold Standard Act established as the "standard unit of value" the gold dollar of 23.22 grains of pure gold and, moreover, provided for a permanent fund of gold coin to be maintained for the redemption of "all forms of money issued by the United States." [2] This meant that all the legal tender notes of the United States, known as greenbacks, would be redeemable in gold coins on demand, and the reserve created for that purpose was set at $150,000,000. For a generation following this legislation all kinds of United States legal tender money was freely exchangeable for gold coin which made the gold dollar the unquestioned standard of exchange and of values.

The Gold Standard Abandoned

In 1933 the United States abandoned the gold standard and substituted for it a system in which legal tender money was no longer freely exchangeable for gold. The depth of the depression of the 1930's had been reached and all the banks of the country were closed. President Franklin Roosevelt, acting under the authority of a sweeping statute enacted by Congress on the fifth day of his presidency, issued an executive order requiring all holders of gold to turn it into the Federal Reserve Banks by May 1, 1933; private possession of this metal was thus outlawed. Another executive order ended the export of gold and thus formally took the United States off the gold standard. By Joint Resolution of June 5, 1933, Congress repudiated all existing private and governmental contractual requirements of payments in gold

[2] Henry S. Commager: *Documents of American History* (New York, 1938), Vol. II, p. 198.

and substituted the provision that such obligations "shall be discharged upon payment, dollar for dollar, in any coin or currency which at the time of payment is legal tender for public and private debts." [3] The agrarians, now dominant in Congress and fortified by the inflationary pressures of depression-harassed producers, authorized the President to reduce the weight of the gold dollar (then 23.22 grains) one-half. Acting under this authority President Roosevelt reduced the weight to 59.06 per cent of its former weight thus giving it a new weight of 13 15/21 grains of pure gold. In due time, as cases arose, the Supreme Court held that all this extraordinary and drastic monetary legislation was merely the exercise of the constitutional power of Congress "to coin money and regulate the value thereof."

The Present Managed, Inconvertible Gold Standard

Nominally at least the United States still has a gold standard since the unit of value is legally defined in terms of gold, and the security of our monetary system rests on the enormous stock of gold at Fort Knox, Kentucky. But the effect of this gold is psychological, as an inspirer of confidence in our monetary system and not, as formerly, through the free exchange of all other forms of legal tender money for gold. It is a managed system because gold no longer functions automatically as a regulator of value through its free exchangeability for other legal tender money. The management of gold is exercised through the president's authority to change the gold content or weight of the dollar, to order the issue of gold certificates based on the increase of the government's stock of gold as a consequence of the devaluation of the dollar, the authority granted the president by Congress to issue United States notes or greenbacks, and his power to purchase silver and issue silver certificates based on such purchases.

Subsidiary Coins

The power of Congress to regulate the value of money is also illustrated by its provisions for coins of a value less than a dollar. Under the bimetallic standard, whenever silver was undervalued at the mint, that is, was worth more as bullion than as coin, it might be melted down at a profit. But if subsidiary silver coins—dimes, quarters, and half dollars—were also melted down their disappearance would be exceedingly inconvenient because of their use in making change and small purchases. Congress consequently made a dollar's worth of these minor silver coins of enough less weight than a silver dollar to delay their disappearance from circulation. The metal in such minor coins as the five-cent and one-cent pieces is of insignificant value and these coins owe their exchange value to the fact that they are freely redeemable in standard dollars. They are, in fact, manufactured by the government and get into circulation by the government's sale of them to private persons at more than the cost of production. Yet to maintain the value stamped on the coin Congress must adjust the supply to

[3] Ibid., Vol. II p. 427.

the demand for them as small change. Nevertheless pennies sometimes become sufficiently over-supplied to sell at a slight discount while at other times they command a small premium. When these minor coins depreciate in value because of an oversupply the government sometimes restores their value by purchasing the redundant supply at face value.

UNITED STATES NOTES

The Establishment of a Federal Currency

The extraordinary expenditures of the Civil War induced Congress to issue United States notes popularly known as greenbacks. They were promissory notes of the United States, theoretically demand notes, but since no provision was then made for their redemption and they consequently were inconvertible paper, they fluctuated in value, falling in 1864 to 39 cents on the dollar in terms of gold. The Civil War issues of these United States notes totalled $450,000,000 and such has been their career that, as a consequence of persistent reissuing, $346,681,016 of them are still in circulation. The Civil War issues of United States notes marked the first time that Congress had invested anything but gold and silver coin with the legal tender quality. The creditor could not reject this paper money, no matter how depreciated, when tendered in payment of a debt if he wanted it paid. Since the Constitution had forbidden the states to make anything but gold or silver a tender in the payment of debts the question was raised whether the framers had not meant to imply that the prohibition held against Congress too. Also involved was the question of the impairment of contracts by enabling debtors to use the depreciated legal tender notes to settle obligations contracted before the initiation of this type of money. Eventually the Supreme Court gave its approval of the unlimited legal tender quality of United States notes. The reasoning by which a majority of the Court reached its conclusion was thus given expression by Justice Gray: "The power as incident to the power of borrowing money and issuing bills or notes of the government for money borrowed, of impressing on these bills or notes the quality of being legal tender for the payment of private debts, was a power universally understood to belong to sovereignty in Europe and America at the time of the framing of the Constitution of the United States." [4] The judgment of the Court settled the matter but the historical evidence did not pass unchallenged. America's most notable contemporary historian declared that the Court's statement was "a stupendous error" and that no such power was understood as belonging to sovereignty in Europe in 1788. [5] The issue of United States notes in the 1860's planted a persistent idea that in the 1870's became the central dogma of the Greenback party. This party was a countermove against powerful creditor interests that were determined to have the greenbacks retired rapidly in exchange for interest-

[4] Julliard v. Greenman, 110 U.S. 421 (1884).
[5] George Bancroft: *The Constitution of the United States Wounded in the House of its Guardians* (1884).

bearing bonds. The Greenback party was shortlived but 77 per cent of the original amount of the Civil War greenbacks still circulate. Moreover, in the depth of the great depression in 1933 Congress authorized the president to issue inconvertible United States notes or greenbacks, not to exceed three billion dollars, for the purpose of paying part of the public debt. Inflationists were again in the saddle.

REGULATION OF BANKING

The First Bank of the United States

The first Federal legislation concerning banking was a statute enacted in 1791 incorporating, for twenty years, a Bank of the United States. This was a private institution with the United States owning one-fifth of the stock and appointing one-fifth of the directors. Its numerous branches distributed throughout the land were the authorized depositories and disbursers of Federal funds. Through its issues of bank notes it provided the country with a sound currency. Secretary of State Thomas Jefferson had considered the Bank unconstitutional on the ground that the Constitution delegated to Congress no power to grant charters and the power was not "necessary" to carry out any delegated power. Secretary of the Treasury Hamilton who had recommended the Bank satisfied Washington's doubts about signing the Bank bill by arguing that the government possessed "resulting powers" derived from "the whole mass of powers of the government." Ultimately the Supreme Court sustained Congress in its chartering the Bank. [6] Not only did the Bank of the United States promptly redeem its own notes upon demand but it presented the notes of state banks to the issuing banks regularly enough to compel them to maintain an adequate specie reserve. This salutary check upon the inflationary tendencies of irresponsible state banks infuriated the agrarians who from the beginning had regarded the Bank of the United States as an unholy alliance of the Federal government with private business. At the expiration of the charter of the first Bank of the United States in 1811 its enemies in Congress prevented rechartering it. A second Bank of the United States on a larger scale was chartered in 1816 but again the agrarians, through the veto of their champion, President Jackson, crushed the "monster" in 1832 thereby planting a permanent American tradition against governmental alliance with private banking.

Unregulated State Banks

The dissolution of the second Bank of the United States left the state banks free to indulge in the most unrestrained issues of bank currency in American history. A bank's issues consist of its circulating promissory notes payable upon demand, presumably in legal tender money which, before the Civil War, consisted only of gold and silver coin. A well-managed bank of issue holds a sufficient reserve of legal tender money but such was the inflationary urge in most communities then that public opinion made it prac-

[6] McCulloch v. Maryland, 4 Wheaton 316 (1819).

tically impossible to compel compliance with this requirement. Paper money was even issued from banks located in inaccessible swamps so that it was practically impossible to present their notes for redemption. For once, a nominating speech gave expression to a sober historical fact when James A. Garfield, speaking of the pre-Civil War currency, said: "The money of the people consisted mainly of the wretched notes of two thousand uncontrolled and irresponsible state banking corporations which were filling the country with a circulation that poisoned rather than sustained the life of business." [7]

National Banks and Their Notes

The chaos of state bank currency was suddenly ended when the Civil War elevated to a dominant position in the government powerful creditor interests. The pressure of these interests for a stable national currency induced Congress in 1863 to enact the National Bank Act. This provided for the chartering, by the Federal government, of National Banks. As a prerequisite for obtaining a charter each bank was required to deposit a specified amount of Federal government bonds on the security of which the bank might receive bank notes for issue in its own name. Since these bonds constituted a guarantee of payment of these bank notes no holder of such notes has ever lost a dollar on them from the failure of a National Bank. A 10 per cent tax levied on state bank notes in 1865 swept the country clean of them.

Inadequacy of the National Bank Currency

Sound as the currency provided by National Banks was, it proved disappointing because of its stubborn inelasticity and its tendency even to contract—that is become scarcer—in a financial crisis. Never was abundant currency or genuine cash more necessary than when a bank, in fear of a financial crisis, restricted its loans and converted what it could into liquid funds. At such a time National Banks used to sell their United States bonds for cash in order to accumulate a liquid reserve as security against runs on the banks. This sale of a bank's government bonds reduced the basis of its currency and thus contracted by that amount the circulation of bank notes in the United States at precisely the moment when the financial crisis required a rapid expansion of the circulating medium. The repercussions on foreign countries of recurring American financial crises led to the designation of the United States as an international nuisance. Finally the Panic of 1907 produced the pressure that soon brought about a remedy and gave the United States an elastic currency.

The Federal Reserve System

The Federal Reserve System of banking was established by Act of Congress in 1913 in order "to furnish an elastic currency, to afford means of redis-

[7] James A. Garfield: *Works.* Edited by B. A. Hinsdale (2 vols. Boston, 1882), Vol. II, pp. 778, 779.

counting commercial paper, to establish a more effective supervision of banking in the United States and for other purposes." [8] When the Federal Reserve System was established, the financial interests of the nation would have preferred one central bank but Congress was then dominated by practically the same set of forces that had destroyed the second Bank of the United States three-quarters of a century earlier and congressmen would tolerate only a decentralized system for controlling banks. The Federal Reserve Act consequently divided the United States into twelve districts each of which contains a Federal Reserve Bank in which all the local affiliated or member banks throughout that district are stockholders. The twelve district Reserve Banks collectively are under the supervision of a board of seven governors appointed by the president with Senate confirmation and so selected as to give fair representation to financial, agricultural, industrial, and commercial interests, and to geographical sections of the country. To accomplish its purpose of providing an elastic currency the Board of Governors may change the requirements concerning reserves to be maintained by member banks. The Board carries on open-market operations which consist of its purchase and sale of obligations of the United States such as government bonds and acceptances, certain other securities, bills of exchange, bankers' acceptances, and other papers eligible for discount by Federal Reserve Banks. Experience has shown that this purchase of securities at one time and their sale at another is one of the most effective methods of controlling the volume of credit. The Board is authorized to alter the discount rate of Federal Reserve Banks to produce an inflationary or a deflationary tendency. It has at times issued orders setting restrictions designed to limit installment buying of consumers' goods.

A Federal Reserve Bank

A Federal Reserve Bank is quite correctly called a banker's bank since it deals directly only with its member banks and not with individuals as such. The entire capital stock of each of the twelve Federal Reserve Banks is owned by the member banks of its district which consist of all the National Banks and such of the state banks as choose to join the Federal Reserve System. Federal Reserve Banks issue Federal Reserve Notes which constitute most of the money now in circulation. When a financial crisis seems imminent, or has arrived, or when a solvent member bank needs to convert some of its assets into cash, its Reserve Bank may "rediscount" its notes, that is, its loans for which the notes were given, drafts, bills of exchange, and bankers' acceptances of short maturities arising out of commercial, industrial, and agricultural transactions, and short-term paper secured by the obligations of the United States such as United States bonds or acceptances. This simply signifies that a Federal Reserve Bank may in effect make loans of cash to member banks on the security of the member bank's loans to individuals and corporations and on other assets. Reserve Banks have adequate funds for this purpose since member banks deposit their reserves in

[8] 38 Stat. 251 (1913); 12 U.S.C. 221 (1913).

their own Federal Reserve Bank. Reserve Banks may also make advances to their member banks on the latter's promissory notes for periods not exceeding ninety days, upon the security of their holdings of direct obligations of the United States or paper eligible for discount or purchase; advances may be made on certain other securities for periods not exceeding fifteen days.

The Reserve Function of Federal Reserve Banks

The term "Reserve" in designating the Federal system of banking is accurately descriptive since these twelve banks serve to concentrate the reserves of all the member banks of the twelve Federal Reserve districts. This constitutes a gigantic fund ready to be shifted as needed in time of financial crisis. The fund is presumed to be available to meet the immediate pressing needs for cash of member banks anywhere in the country and to this end the twelve Federal Reserve Banks may lend to each other. The entire system so functions that the central controlling board can manage it as a whole to serve the pressing needs of any region for liquid funds or cash. The twelve Federal Reserve Banks also serve as clearing houses for the banks of their districts, that is, for the balancing and transferring of funds arising from the exchange between banks as a consequence of the use of checks by individuals and corporations. Finally, like the branches of the first Bank of the United States the twelve Federal Reserve Banks serve as depositories for the receipt and disbursement of monies of the United States government.

Depression Bank Legislation

The widespread failure of banks in the early 1930's and the consequent distress of depositors induced Congress to enact legislation designed to protect the public against some of the disastrous effects of defective banking practices. The system of inspection under the Federal comptroller of the currency was changed so that National Banks are now visited at irregular intervals. Each member bank must now keep a specified proportion of its total deposits in the Federal Reserve Bank of its district. In order to reassure a panic-stricken public that, in the 1930's, had grown timorous about entrusting their money to banks, a Federal Deposit Insurance Corporation was established by Congress. National Banks and state banks affiliated with the Federal Reserve System pay into this corporation a percentage of their total deposits and each one of their depositors is thus insured to the extent of $10,000 against loss of deposits due to bank failure.

Defects of the Federal Reserve System

While the Federal Reserve System has unquestionably provided an elastic currency the high expectations of its founders that it might, through its operation, prevent violent fluctuations of business failed of fulfillment in the first twenty years under the system and proved utterly inadequate in the depression of the 1930's. The system was based on the assumption that continuous business stability might be maintained by providing facilities for converting one kind of money or monetary values into another kind of money or monetary values and especially by the convertibility of money directly or indirectly into gold or whatever had been chosen as standard money. The original Federal Reserve Act provided these facilities but they proved inadequate for the solution of the monetary problems of the modern economic society of the United States, and the theory was in fact abandoned by the depression legislation of the early 1930's. No matter what its statutory powers may be the Federal Reserve Board is subject to the influences and pressures inevitably playing upon an administrative agency. Its quasi-judicial independence does not save it from becoming, in wartime, practically an adjunct of the Treasury Department. It has no choice then but to permit absorption of war bond issues by the banks and to maintain low interest rates to facilitate bond sales despite the inflationary effects of this policy. That the United States now has no agency that is capable of keeping monetary expansion within the bounds of safety by regulating the value of money was demonstrated decisively by the unprecedented price inflation following World War II. Though the Board of Governors of the Federal Reserve System has enormous monetary power it has never been given the responsibility for monetary control. Efforts to check unhealthy economic developments by its published warnings have at times been counteracted by contrary statements of presidents and at other times by the pressures of powerful interests. "Monetary law in the United States," declares a competent authority, "is ambiguous and chaotic, does not contain a suitable principle for the exercise of the monetary power held by the Federal Reserve System, and has caused confusion in the development of Federal Reserve policy." [9] Evidently the Federal Reserve System has not yet attained full development but awaits further improvements in the light of experience.

FEDERAL CREDIT AGENCIES

The Commodity Credit Corporation was created in 1933 for the purpose of making loans to farmers for storing crops in order thereby to stabilize farm prices and markets. Though an agency of the United States government it was, at first, incorporated under the laws of Delaware; in 1948 it was given a permanent federal charter. It is attached to the Department of Agriculture and managed by a board of six directors appointed by the President with confirmation by the Senate, and it functions under the chairmanship of the Secretary of Agriculture. In addition to the board of directors the Corporation has a bi-partisan, five-member advisory board.

The major program of the Corporation is support of the price of corn, wheat, rice, tobacco, cotton, peanuts, wool, mohair, tung nuts, honey, milk and butterfat. The law requires support of the price of these commodities; it permits but does not require support of the prices of other specified products. For this purpose the Corporation is capitalized at $100 million but authorized to borrow up to $10 billion. Commodities acquired under the support program are to be disposed of through sales at home and abroad, transfer to other Government agencies, international barter, and donations for school lunches, relief, and welfare purposes. The Corporation procures agricultural products for administering relief abroad and making cash payments to foreign governments.

For storage purposes the Corporation purchases and maintains granaries and equipment for care and storage of its grain in areas where private facilities are inadequate. It makes loans for construction and expansion of farm storage facilities.

Farm Credit

Paralleling the twelve Federal Reserve Banks are twelve Federal Land Banks established under the Farm Loan Act of 1916. They make long-term 4 per cent loans upon first mortgages on farm lands and issue farm loan bonds secured by these mortgages.

The Farm Credit Administration, established in 1933, provides a co-ordinated system of credit for agriculture by making long-term and short-term credit available to farmers. It provides credit facilities for farmers' cooperative marketing, purchasing, and business service organizations. A Federal Farm Mortgage Corporation makes direct loans to farmers.

The Farmers Home Administration provides credit for types of farmers who cannot get the financing they need elsewhere at rates and on terms they can afford. Credit is supplemented where necessary with advice to borrowers to aid in adopting sound farm and home practices for successful farming. Loans are made through the Farmers Home Administration offices at the county seat. Production and subsistence loans are made to farmers or stockmen, both owners and tenants, on family-type farms, who devote most of their time to and earn most of their income from farming or stock raising and are citizens of the United States. Such loans may be used to buy live stock, equipment, seed, feed, fertilizer, supplies, and other farm necessities.

The Bankhead-Jones Farm Tenant Act of 1937 authorized the Farm Security Administration to make loans at 3 per cent for forty years to a limited number of farm tenants, share croppers, and farm laborers to enable them to buy family-type farms. In 1944 this privilege was extended to veterans of World War II if they were qualified by experience or training for successful agricultural undertakings. The Farm Security Administration was also authorized by the Water Facilities Act to make loans and provide technical services for assisting farmers and ranchers in seventeen Western states in the construction and repair of water facilities such as ponds, wells, pumps, storage tanks, and irrigation ditches.

The Rural Electrification Administration

Through self-liquidating loans this agency provides for financing and constructing electrical facilities to serve rural people who have no central electrical service. The Act of 1944 reduced the interest on such loans to 2 per cent and permitted amortization periods of as much as thirty-five years. Loans may be made for wiring farmsteads and for buying and installing electrical appliances and plumbing, including pressure water systems for home and farm. In 1949 Congress authorized loans for furnishing and improving rural telephone service.

Federal Credit Unions

These are cooperative associations organized under the Federal Credit Union Act, for promoting thrift among their members and creating a source of credit for provident or productive purposes. Credit unions are groups of wage earners, in schools, banks, factories, governmental offices or elsewhere who pool their savings and make loans to each other. The Federal government has met a large part of the cost of promoting these unions.

From the funds of members' savings, installment loans are made to members at rates of interest of not more than one per cent a month on the unpaid balance. The management is vested in the officers elected by the Union and each Union is examined periodically.

Veterans' Loans

Under the Servicemen's Readjustment Act of 1944 veterans of World War II are, subject to statutory limitations, entitled to certain Federal guarantees on loans for the purchase or construction of homes, farms, and business properties. The Federal government's guaranty extends to not over 50 per cent of the loan and may not exceed $2,000 on non-real-estate loans, or $4,000 on real-estate loans. The loans may be made by any Federal Land Bank or by private financial institutions subject to examination and supervision by Federal agencies. Under the Housing Act of 1950 a veteran may receive a direct government loan up to $10,000 if private financing is not available.

Voluntary Home Mortgage Credit

The Housing Act of 1954 authorized the program administered by the National Voluntary Mortgage Credit Extension Committee of which the Federal Housing and Home Finance Administrator is chairman. There are 16 regional committees. Both national and regional committees consist of representatives of private finance institutions, builders, and members of real estate boards and all serve on a voluntary basis. The purpose is to help obtain loans in areas or communities where there is a shortage of local capital available or accessible to minority groups.

SUMMARY

One purpose of the framers of the Constitution was the establishing of a sound medium of exchange. They accordingly forbade the states to coin money, emit bills of credit, or make anything but gold or silver legal tender. Then they authorized Congress to coin money and regulate its value. For a good part of a century Congress endeavored, in vain, by monetary legislation to find and fix a ratio between coined gold and silver that would keep both circulating. In 1900 the freely convertible gold dollar was made the sole standard of monetary value, but a generation later even this was abandoned.

Money in the United States is now based on an inconvertible gold standard. The circulating media now consist of United States notes (greenbacks), Federal Reserve notes, Federal Reserve Bank notes, National Bank notes, silver certificates, silver dollars, and subsidiary and minor coins.

In 1791 the First Bank of the United States was chartered, and a second one, in 1816, each for twenty years. In 1862 Congress authorized the chartering of private National Banks with authority to issue bank notes and then taxed state bank notes out of existence. During the Civil War Congress authorized the issue of $450 million of promissory demand notes, popularly denominated "greenbacks," which have been repeatedly reissued so that $346,681,016 are still circulating. But the failure of the "greenbacks" and the National Bank notes to provide a flexible currency led to the establishment, in 1914, of the system of Federal Reserve Banks with authority to regulate discount rates and to issue a currency adjustable to changing needs. Several Federal lending agencies have been established to make loans for which commercial banks are not adequate.

CHAPTER XXIX

REGULATION OF COMMERCE AND COMMUNICATION

The Constitution a Consequence of the Need for Regulation of Commerce

No single interest contributed more to the demand for the Constitution than commerce. The American shipping that had once flourished under the fostering protection of Britain's Navigation Acts was prostrated by the post-Revolutionary anarchy of state regulations. In the 1780's American vessels lay idle in American harbors unable to meet the competition of foreign shipping that operated in those same harbors. Nor did the coastal and river traffic fare any better under the taxes, tariffs, and trade restrictions of thirteen independent and sovereign states. The Congress of the Confederation was powerless to resolve the commercial confusion since the states that had gone to war against the power of Parliament to regulate colonial commerce permitted no such grant of power to Congress in the Articles of Confederation and refused to permit an amendment for that purpose. It was appropriate, then, that the first of the chain of three events that resulted in the framing of the Constitution—the Alexandria meeting of Maryland and Virginia commissioners—should be concerned with the regulation of commerce, that of the Potomac River. The ultimate fulfillment of this initial impulse found expression in the clause of the Constitution of the United States giving Congress power "to regulate commerce with foreign nations, and among the several states, and with the Indian tribes."

Judicial Interpretation of Commerce

In keeping with his historic role, Chief Justice John Marshall started the Court on the broad interpretation of the term "commerce." Early in the 1800's the State of New York had granted to Robert R. Livingston and Robert Fulton a monopoly of steam navigation in the state's waters, and one Gibbons had obtained a license from them. But when Ogden, who held a Federal coasting license obtained under an Act of Congress based on its power to regulate commerce, invaded the waters of Gibbons's license Gibbons sought to restrain him by court action. When the case reached the Supreme Court of the United States Ogden's attorneys tried to invalidate Gibbons's license by confining the meaning of commerce to mere "traffic" that is "buying and selling, or the interchange of commodities." In deciding the case Marshall rejected this restricted meaning with the statement: "Commerce is undoubtedly traffic, but it is something more; it is intercourse with foreign nations and among the several states" and "all America understands, and has uniformly understood, the word 'commerce' to comprehend navigation." [1]

Under subsequent Court interpretation the meaning of the word "commerce," in the Constitution, has kept step with the necessities of its application to an intensely dynamic economic society. In 1837 "goods" but not "persons" were held to be subjects of commerce[2] but by 1885 commerce included "the transportation of persons and property."[3] In 1877 it was decided that "a company doing an interstate telegraph business . . . is engaged in interstate commerce within the meaning of the Constitution."[4] In 1894 an interstate bridge was held to be a vehicle of interstate commerce.[5] In 1903, "lottery tickets are subjects of traffic and therefore are subjects of commerce,"[6] and in the same year it was held that the driving of sheep from Utah across Wyoming to a point in Nebraska was interstate commerce.[7] By 1910 a correspondence school in one state with students in another was declared to be engaged in interstate commerce. [8] In 1914 conveying oil by pipes across a state line was held to be interstate commerce. [9] Air travel and radio communication, too, have been brought within the meaning of the term "commerce" and thus will it continue to be given new meaning as needed.

In the course of time Court interpretation has given the phrase "to regulate," as used in relation to the commerce clause, the meaning: to foster, to protect, to control, and to restrain, subject to the constitutional rights guaranteed to persons. It also includes the power to prohibit where such prohibition serves to protect the public as, for example, in the exclusion of lottery tickets from interstate commerce.

The Regulation of Commerce with Foreign Nations

The power to regulate foreign commerce was recognized from the beginning as a plenary power of Congress. In the second decade under the Con-

---

[1] Gibbons v. Ogden, 9 Wheaton 1 (1824).
[2] New York v. Miln, 11 Peters 102 (1837).
[3] Gloucester Ferry Company v. Pennsylvania, 114 U.S. 196, 203 (1885).
[4] Pensacola Telegraph Company v. Western Union Telegraph Company, 96 U.S. 1 (1877).
[5] Covington Bridge Company v. Kentucky, 154 U.S. 204 (1894).
[6] Lottery Case, 188 U.S. 321 (1903).
[7] Kelly v. Rhodes, 188 U.S. 1 (1903).
[8] International Textbook Company v. Pigg, 217 U.S. 91 (1910).
[9] The Pipe Line Cases, 234 U.S. 548 (1914).

stitution non-intercourse and embargo laws were enacted and enforced with extraordinary vigor. Congress has also exercised police power over foreign commerce by legislation excluding specific products; for example, by the eighty-year-old statute excluding drugs, medicines, and chemicals not equal in strength to prescribed standards.

THE REGULATION OF RAILROADS
State Regulation of Railroads

When first introduced in the United States the railroads were welcomed with unrestrained enthusiasm by the communities they would serve. The seemingly miraculous access of inland regions to markets induced farmers to grant the right of way while cities raised generous bonuses to induce lines to pass through them. Meanwhile liberal grants of public lands were being made to encourage the construction of lines. However, it was an era of laissez faire and the generous gifts had little effect on railroad builders who felt that "what's mine is mine, and I may manage it as I please." All too common was the attitude expressed by one of the railroad barons in the crisp phrase, "the public be damned." So absolute was their power through arbitrary control of rates, and through service and rebates to favored shippers that the owners could make or ruin an individual, a company, or a community by a shift in the rates on wheat, cattle, or some other product. By distributing free passes to state representatives, by paying their campaign expenses, and by downright bribery, they prevented just taxation of their railroad property and evaded all regulation. By discriminating in freight charges between localities, articles, and individuals, they terrorized merchants, farmers, and communities "until matters reached such a pass, that no man dared engage in any business in which transportation largely entered without first . . . obtaining permission of a railroad manager." [10]

The outrages committed by the railroads eventually provoked an agrarian revolt and the state legislation known as the Granger laws which, among other things, introduced restraint of the railroads. The Supreme Court of the United States dumbfounded the devotees of laissez faire when Chief Justice Morrison R. Waite, in 1876, delivered the opinion of the Court that "property does become clothed with a public interest when used in a manner to make it of public consequence and affect the community at large. When therefore, one devotes his property to a use in which the public has an interest, he, in effect, grants to the public an interest in that use, and must submit to be controlled by the public for the common good, to the extent of the interest he has created. Common carriers exercise a sort of public office and have duties to perform in which the public is interested. . . . Their business is therefore affected with a public interest."

[10] *Report of the U.S. Railway Commission* (1887), Vol. 1, p. 141, quoted by Samuel E. Morison and Henry S. Commager: *The Growth of the Republic,* 2 vols. New York, 1937. Vol. II, p. 115.

Thus in the Granger cases, as they have come to be called, the Supreme Court in a single breath-taking stroke radically modified the scope of laissez faire and laid the foundation for governmental regulation of common carriers. Moreover, the Court, in one of these Granger Cases held that when a railroad "is employed in state as well as interstate commerce, and until Congress acts, the state must be permitted to adopt such rules and regulations as may be necessary for the promotion of the general welfare of the people within its own jurisdiction, even though, in so doing, those without may be indirectly affected." [11] This seemed to clear the way for state railway commissions to regulate, within their respective states, rates of carriers engaged in interstate transportation and this was done for almost a decade after the Supreme Court had given its approval. However, state regulation of rates involving interstate commerce came to a sudden end in 1886 when the Supreme Court of the United States held "that it is not and never has been, the deliberate opinion of a majority of this Court that a statute of a state which attempts to regulate the fares and charges by railroad companies within its limits, for a transportation which constitutes a part of commerce among the states, is a valid law." [12] Thus ended state regulation of the rates of interstate carriers.

The Interstate Commerce Act of 1887

The Wabash decision confronted Congress with a suddenly crystallizing public demand that the gap created by the decision in the Wabash case be filled with Federal legislation. The pressure for Federal regulation had been gathering strength chiefly as a shippers' movement. The demand for national regulation of railroad rates and practices concentrated in the 1870's and early 1880's in the mid-west agrarian regions, as revealed by congressional votes on unsuccessful bills to that end. But as small business men of the East also felt the pinch of railroad discriminations they joined the farmers. Their chief grievance was the discriminations in favor of the big producers. The outcome was the Interstate Commerce Act of 1887. It required that the rates of railroads engaged in interstate and foreign transportation be reasonable, that there be no discrimination in rates or service between persons, corporations, or localities, and it forbade charging more for a short haul than for a long haul whose limits contained that short haul. It also forbade competing railroads to pool business and divide receipts. It required that the rates be reasonable, that they be published, and not advanced without ten-day notice. The Act created for the purpose of administering its provisions an Interstate Commerce Commission consisting of five members appointed by the president with Senate confirmation.

Present Scope of Federal Regulation of Transportation

The scope and powers of the Interstate Commerce Commission have been increased by the Hepburn Act of 1906, the Panama Canal Act of 1912, the

[11] Peik v. Chicago and Northwestern Railway Co., 94 U.S. 164 (1877).

[12] Wabash, St. Louis, and Pacific Railway Co. v. People of the State of Illinois 118 U.S. 557–96 (1886).

Transportation Act of 1920, the Motor Carriers' Act of 1935, and an amendment to the Interstate Commerce Act in 1942. As a consequence of this legislation enacted since 1887 the Commission's jurisdiction now comprises interstate and foreign transportation by express companies, pipe lines (excepting water and gas), sleeping cars, motor carriers, bridges, ferries, car floats and lighters, freight forwarders, and all terminal and transportation facilities used or necessary in the interstate transportation of persons or property.

The Interstate Commerce Commission

The Interstate Commerce Commission now consists of eleven members appointed by the president with Senate confirmation. The Commission selects one of its members as chairman and appoints its secretary, chief counsel, and the directors of its bureaus. It has been given considerable freedom in organizing for the performance of its duties. The Commission is empowered to regulate, in the public interest and within the United States, the transportation by common carriers mentioned above that are engaged in interstate and foreign commerce. The several modes of transportation are to be so regulated as to recognize the inherent advantages of each. Safe, adequate, economical, and efficient service is to be promoted. In addition to the provisions of the original Interstate Commerce Act, fair wages and equitable working conditions are to be maintained by the Commission. The over-all purpose of the Commission's functions is the developing, coordinating, and preserving of a national transportation system by water, highway, rail, and other means adequate to the commercial needs of the United States, to its postal service and to national defense.

Rate Determination

One of the most difficult functions of the Interstate Commerce Commission is calculating rates, fares, and charges of common carriers that are just, reasonable, and non-discriminatory. The Constitution vests in Congress the regulation of interstate and foreign commerce, and the courts will not permit it to re-delegate this power. However, Congress may exercise its regulative function by prescribing a principle of regulation and then delegating to an agency the administering of the regulation in accordance with the principle. Thus in the Transportation Act of 1920 Congress prescribed the rule of rate making by which the Commission was to establish such rates that the carriers as a whole or in each of such regions as the Commission designated would, under efficient management, earn an aggregate annual net income equal to a fair return on the value of the property used in transportation. The Commission was to ascertain the value of the railways and also to determine what would be a fair return. The fundamental purpose was so to protect the investor as to stabilize railroad credit and stimulate a flow of capital into that industry sufficient to ensure the American people an adequate transportation system.

Several factors have hampered the Commission in applying the formula for rate making. The least of these is the fact that the Interstate Commerce Commission's determinations of rates are not necessarily final but are subject to review by the courts which sometimes, though seldom, upset the careful calculations of the Commission by rejecting a specific application of the principles prescribed by the statutes. By and large, the courts have left undisturbed the peculiar function of the Commission and have confined their judgments to protecting the carriers against infringements upon their statutory and constitutional rights. Time and again the fluctuations of the business cycle have rendered obsolete an elaborate system of rates set up by the Commission, and the Great Depression put more than one railroad in the hands of receivers. World War II strained the freight and passenger service to the limit and seemed to initiate an era of railroad prosperity but this was dissipated by the burdens of sharply rising costs that created a postwar crisis for the railroads. Moreover, railroads have been baffled by the inceasing competition of trucks in the transportation of freight and of bus lines in the passenger field as well as by the enormous amount of travel by privately owned automobiles.

Transportation costs are necessarily higher wherever a sparse population or low per capita incomes reduce railroad patronage. The recognition of this condition by the setting of higher ton-mile freight rates and higher passenger rates in such sections has brought down on the Commission the criticism of the West and the South. Indeed the Interstate Commerce Commission encounters the persistent pressures of regions and interests to reduce existing rates or prevent their being raised. This, of course, is inevitable in an agency created and conducted for the purpose of protecting carriers and investors in railroad securities to the end that an essential public service may be maintained.

Pressures on the Interstate Commerce Commission

The functions of the Interstate Commerce Commission are not only quasi-legislative but also quasi-judicial, that is, it must base its judgments on testimony and other evidence. But the law it adjudicates, the rate formula it applies—a "fair return" to the carrier on the "value" of its property—involves two abstractions incapable of scientific determination. And its judgments can spell prosperity or bankruptcy to carriers on one hand or shippers on the other. Consequently, powerful interests bring pressure to bear on the Commission. President Hoover habitually replied to pleas for intercession by him with a form letter in which he pointed out that it would be as improper for him to intercede in a pending rate case as in one before the Supreme Court. Congressmen, however, cannot so easily brush aside such requests from influential constituents. Petitions and memorials from unions, business organizations, farm and live-stock associations, denouncing the Commission, are frequently printed in the *Congressional Record* and widely distributed. The Congressman may threaten the Commission with investigation or with legislation such as the transfer of authority over agricultural rates to the Farm Board, or the Hoch-Smith resolution which ordered the Commission to "consider the conditions prevailing in different industries in adjusting freight rates, specifically those of agriculture." These threats were made in response to the demand of the farmers. When the president's nomination of a new commissioner reaches the Senate it is the signal for a line-up of economic forces. Then the never-ending drive for representation of regions and interests on the Commission is particularly evident. For example, when two nominations were made representing the coal producers of Pennsylvania and the Southern Mine Operators, Senator Reed of Pennsylvania expressed his position with the frank declaration: "I claim, that one-eleventh of the population of the United States live in Pennsylvania and that we are entitled reasonably once in forty years to one-eleventh of the Interstate Commerce Commission." [13]

Federal Power to Regulate Intra-State Transportation

It had long been assumed that the Federal power to regulate interstate commerce left the regulation of intra-state commerce outside of its jurisdiction. But in the second decade of the present century circumstances came about that led to the regulation of some intra-state commerce by the Interstate Commerce Commission. The fundamental purpose of the congressional legislation regulating interstate commerce is that it should be fair and reasonable and prevent discrimination between persons and places. In 1912 the Interstate Commerce Commission found that carriers, under the authority of the Railroad Commission of Texas, were maintaining higher commodity rates from Shreveport, Louisiana, to points in Texas than were in force "from cities in Texas to such points under substantially similar circumstances and conditions" and were thus giving "an unlawful and undue preference and advantage" to the Texas cities. The Interstate Commerce Commission directed the Texas carriers to correct these discriminations against Shreveport which they did by raising the intra-state rates to the level of the interstate rates and then carrying the issue to the courts. In sustaining the Commission the Supreme Court of the United States said: "Whenever the interstate and intrastate transactions of carriers are so related that the government of one involves the control of the other it is Congress, and not the state, that is entitled to prescribe the final and dominant rule. . . . [and Congress] does possess the power to foster and protect interstate commerce, and to take all measures necessary or appropriate to that end, although intrastate transactions of interstate carriers may thereby be controlled." [14]

Acting under the Transportation Act of 1920, which authorized rates designed to ensure carriers of interstate commerce a fair return on the value of their property, the Interstate Commerce Commission directed an advance of 20 per cent in rates on carriers in an area that included Wisconsin.

[13] E. P. Herring: "Special Interests and the Interstate Commerce Commission." *American Political Science Review* 27:738–51, 899–917.

[14] Houston, East and West Texas Railway Company v. United States, 234 U.S. 342 (1914).

Among other things this conflicted with the intra-state rate of two cents a mile for passengers as set by the Wisconsin legislature. The Supreme Court of the United States sustained the Interstate Commerce Commission's rates and thereby reaffirmed "the power of Congress in developing interstate agencies. . . . In such development it can impose any reasonable condition on a state's use of interstate carriers for intra-state commerce it deems necessary or desirable. This is because of the supremacy of national power in this field." [15] It can be said, then, that the power of Congress to regulate interstate commerce includes also power to regulate intra-state commerce to whatever extent it is necessary in order to make the regulation of interstate commerce effective.

The Regulation of Water Transportation

The commerce power of Congress includes the power to protect navigable streams from obstruction and to improve navigation by the construction of dams. Indeed, the term "navigable stream" is no longer narrowly construed as it once was; the Court holds it to include streams made navigable or capable of being made navigable by improvements. By an addition to the Interstate Commerce Act passed in 1940 the Commission is given extensive authority over transportation by water.

The Regulation of Motor Transportation

By 1935 the experience of the states in regulating intra-state motor transportation made it clear that Federal regulation of interstate motor transportation was required in the interest of both the carriers and the public. The Motor Carriers Act of 1935 charged the Interstate Commerce Commission with the regulation of interstate motor carriers. Accordingly, the Commission may establish requirements for continuous and adequate motor transportation of baggage and express, for uniform systems of accounts, records, and reports, for hours of service of employees, and for safety of operation and equipment.

The Regulation of Air Transportation

Regulation of air transportation is gradually taking shape over the same pattern as the regulation of rail and motor transportation. Legislation in 1942 permits air carriers to establish reasonable through service and joint rates with other common carriers. In 1947 it was provided that, in case of through service by air carriers and common carriers subject to the Interstate Commerce Act, the carriers must establish just and reasonable rates, fares, or charges and file them with the Civil Aeronautics Board or the Interstate Commerce Commission.

When an Object of Transportation Becomes Subject to the Interstate Commerce Power

Before an article within a state but intended for transportation in interstate commerce becomes subject to congressional power over interstate

[15] Railroad Commission of Wisconsin v. Chicago, Burlington, and Quincy Railroad Company, 257 U.S. 563 (1922).

commerce it is still subject to the state's taxation and police power, that is, the power to regulate it for the public health, safety, good order, and morals. Consequently it is important in many cases to determine precisely the instant when state power over the article ends and Federal power begins. It has been judicially determined that the article has not passed from state to Federal control when the owner is moving it to the point from which it is to be shipped to another state or country. [16] Federal power begins at the instant the goods to be transported in interstate or foreign commerce are consigned and delivered to the common carrier.

When an Object of Interstate or Foreign Commerce Becomes Subject to State Power

As to foreign commerce it fell to Chief Justice Marshall to express the judgment of the Supreme Court concerning when an import ceased to be an import. It has not ceased to be an import "while remaining the property of the importer, in his warehouse, in the original form, or package in which it was imported." [17] This is the famous "original package doctrine" used to determine when a state's legislative power over imported goods begins. When the original package is broken and the contents commingled with other property within the state the Federal power ceases to apply. The "original package doctrine" was long applied to interstate commerce and an article of interstate commerce was assumed to have ceased to be subject to the Federal power when the package was broken. At the turn of the century cartons of cigarettes (ten packages of twenty cigarettes each) brought into a state in this form in order to evade state taxation were held not to be "original packages." For the purpose of determining state taxation the "original package doctrine" has become obsolete and for determining other state powers it has been seriously questioned. It does not limit the scope of Federal power with respect to interstate commerce.

FEDERAL REGULATION OF COMMUNICATIONS

Regulation of the Telegraph and Telephone

The first Federal regulation of communication by wire was under the Mann-Elkins Act of 1910. It applied only to interstate communication and gave the Interstate Commerce Commission power to ensure that telegraph rates would be just and reasonable, and free from discrimination and unreasonable preferences. In the absence of pressures upon it the Commission did very little beyond requiring uniform systems of accounts for interstate telephone and telegraph communication. But this prepared "the groundwork for effective regulation later."

The Federal Communications Commission

In 1934 Congress passed an act creating the Federal Communications Commission composed of seven members to whom were transferred all

[16] Coe v. Errol, 116 U.S. 517 (1886).
[17] Brown v. Maryland, 12 Wheaton 441 (1827).

the duties, powers, and functions in the communication field formerly exercised by the Interstate Commerce Commission, the Postmaster General, and the Federal Radio Commission. As subsequently amended the purpose of the Act is to regulate interstate and foreign communication by wire and by radio in such a manner as to ensure to the American people a rapid, efficient, nation-wide, and world-wide wire and radio communication service at reasonable charges. The Act specifically provides that persons engaged in radio broadcasting shall not be deemed common carriers. The means of communication that are considered carriers are required to publish and file with the Commission tariffs for all charges.

The operation of radio and television stations can be legally carried on only by persons licensed by the Federal Communications Commission. This Commission has authority to classify radio stations, prescribe the nature of their service, assign frequencies, and make regulations to carry out the Act regulating radio communication. The standard guiding the Commission's granting of licenses is the public interest, convenience, and necessity. Hearings may be held when necessary to determine whether an application meets these legal requirements. The Act specifically provides that the Commission shall have no power of censorship over radio communication. Whenever a legally qualified candidate for public office is permitted use of a broadcasting station, equal opportunity cannot legally be denied any other candidate for that office.

IMMIGRATION

Early Immigration Policies

There is an almost pathetic irony about the Statue of Liberty, erected in New York Harbor more than sixty years ago. On its base is engraved the inscription with its moving reference to the "huddled masses yearning to breathe free" and the injunction to "send these, the homeless tempest tossed to me." This expressed the then traditional conception of the United States as a land of refuge and opportunity for the oppressed of the earth. The superabundance of natural resources in the New World and the scarcity of labor with which to exploit them had led quite naturally to a policy of encouraging immigration in the early days of the nation. Any doubts about the wisdom of unrestricted immigration were usually based upon political rather than economic fears. It is a curious fact that in every generation since the adoption of the Constitution one of the major political parties has been more hospitable than the other to immigrants. The Jeffersonians and later the Jacksonian Democrats welcomed the newcomers to their ranks while Federalists, Whigs, and Republicans in their turn have largely been shunned by the foreign-born citizens. For example, the notorious Alien Law enacted by the Federalists in 1798 required the registration of all aliens in the United States and those who might subsequently arrive and sought to discourage immigration by raising from five to fourteen years the period of residence required before naturalization.

The Volume of Immigration

The United States has admitted more immigrants than any other country, a total of almost 40,000,000 since the adoption of the Constitution. They have come in great tides reaching peaks during periods of prosperity and declining sharply during hard times. In the depth of the Great Depression in 1932 there was the unusual phenomenon of a counter-migration when three times as many migrated out of as entered the United States and indeed for four successive years emigration exceeded immigration. Before 1895 most of our immigrants came from countries of Northern and Western Europe—Great Britain, Ireland, Germany, the Scandinavian countries, France, the Netherlands, and Switzerland; this has come to be known as the "old immigration." But after 1905 a majority of the immigrants have come from Southern and Eastern Europe—largely from Italy, what was once Austria-Hungary, and Russia; this has been called the "new immigration." The striking cultural and economic contrasts between the old and the new immigration finally determined the present immigration policy.

The Development of Restrictive Legislation

Before 1875 immigration was practically unrestricted but in that year convicts and prostitutes were banned. There is no question as to the power of Congress to regulate immigration since the transportation of such persons is foreign commerce. In 1882 "lunatics," mental defectives, and persons liable to become public charges were excluded. In the same year Congress excluded the Chinese and later expanded the ban to include all Orientals. In 1885 the pressure of labor, organized and unorganized, induced Congress to outlaw the entrance of contract laborers, that is, aliens imported under a contract by the terms of which the contractor had a lien on their wages to cover the costs of transportation. In 1892 polygamy and certain diseases were added to the reasons for exclusion. In 1903 anarchists were banned. Immigration policy was developing in a random, hit-and-miss fashion which imposed upon each immigrant certain physical, mental, moral, and economic requirements. If an alien is found undesirable after admission, he may be deported.

The Temporary Quota Act of 1921

The arrival of approximately a million immigrants during each of the ten years prior to World War I and the threatened wholesale postwar inundation by war-stricken Europeans induced a sudden American consensus on limiting immigration. There had developed deep concern that control in the United States might pass to alien cultural groups and that the American tradition might be overwhelmed. Many Americans feared that the saturation point had been reached in the absorption of ethnic groups. The ensuing legislation, the first general restriction of immigration to the

United States, was the Temporary Quota Act of 1921. It reflected the prevailing pattern of American opinion that some European immigrants were more adaptable than others to American ways. The Act authorized the admission of a number of immigrants from each nation equal to 3 per cent of the number of foreign-born persons of such nationality living in the United States as revealed by the Census of 1910. Since there were then more people in the United States from Northern and Western than from Southern and Eastern Europe, the legislation deliberately favored the "old immigration" countries.

The Permanent Immigration Act

The Temporary Quota Act of 1921 was replaced by the permanent Immigration Act of 1924 which, with amendments, is the basic immigration law today. The Act provided that beginning in 1929 the national quotas should be computed on a percentage of a total of 150,000 immigrants a year. This number is apportioned among the eligible countries in proportion to the contribution of each country to the population of the United States as it was in 1920. To determine the quota for any one nationality, it is necessary to ascertain what percentage that nationality had contributed by birth or descent to the population of the United States as it was in 1920 and then multiply 150,000 by that percentage. Since the minimun for each eligible country is 100, the total will aggregate somewhat more than 150,000.

Criticism of Our Immigration Policy

The Act of 1924 restricts the "new immigration" even more severely than did the Act of 1921 and, indeed, permits the entrance of only about 24,-000 Southern and Eastern Europeans as compared with 126,000 Northern and Western Europeans. Thus it restricts where the pressures for immigration are strongest. In practice the immigration legislation fails to achieve its purpose of feeding into the United States a stream of immigration of the same nationality composition as our population. The nations of Western and Northern Europe have a tendency to use only a small part of their quotas. Thus the quota system leaves a wide-open door for those who do not care to migrate hither and a narrow crack for those who are most eager to come to the United States. Moreover there is no restriction on immigration of native Africans or of Latin-Americans and Canadians. Our immigration policy has been criticized on the ground that its standards are negative. After we have excluded a whole category of undesirables from each nation the question remains whether what is left for the quota fits into any pattern of desirables. If we were looking for desirable additions to our population we might, through modern techniques of testing, discover those possessing the skills and talents desirable as well as those with desirable physical qualifications instead of accepting those who did not have certain defects of health. It has been argued that such a system would restrict migration from nations of the newer migration and do it without employing invidious ethnic discrimination.[18]

Recent Immigration Legislation

In 1953 Congress authorized the admission of 214,000 special-quota immigrants during a three-year period. Many of those admitted were displaced persons and orphans, including some who had escaped from Communist-dominated countries. An act of 1954 revised the quotas for Italy, Greece, and the Netherlands, so that previous allocations for refugees can be issued interchangeably for both refugees and close relatives of United States citizens and resident aliens. No refugee or relative of a United States citizen may enter the United States without an assurance of housing, employment, and against becoming a public charge. This requires responsible sponsors of such immigrants.

SUMMARY

The need of some central control of commerce induced the framers to invest Congress with power to regulate commerce among the states and with foreign nations. With each new means of transportation and communication, Congress and the courts have found in the Constitution the necessary meanings of commerce and the power to regulate it.

The confusion of state control of interstate railway transportation led to the Interstate Commerce Act of 1887. It established the Interstate Commerce Commission which, under the original and later acts, establishes rates designed to yield the carriers an income equivalent to a fair return on the property used in transportation. The courts hold that this may require the Commission also to regulate intrastate rates whenever necessary to make interstate regulation effective. Water and motor transportation and wire communication are also subject to the Commission. Air travel is subject to a Civil Aeronautics Board and wireless communication, including radio and television, to the Federal Communications Commission.

The annual immigration to the United States is limited by the permanent Immigration Act of 1924 (with amendments) to approximately 150,000. Each quota nation is permitted a share of the 150,000 equal to whatever percentage that nation had contributed to the total population of the United States in 1920 but no nation is to have a quota of less than 100.

[18] Maurice R. Davie: *A Constructive Immigration Policy* (New Haven, 1923).

CHAPTER XXX

GOVERNMENT AND BUSINESS

PUBLIC ENTERPRISE AND PATERNALISM

I T WAS appropriate indeed that the first English settlement in America —the Jamestown venture—should have been a business enterprise conducted by a chartered commercial corporation with the avowed purpose of earning dividends for the stockholders back home in England. In every colony settlers were to be attracted by a continent fabulously rich in natural resources ready for exploitation. Here were unprecedented opportunities to satisfy the eternal land hunger of the human race. Insofar as our people have developed and possess a philosophy of the economic role of government, it has been arrived at pragmatically, bit by bit, as problems and crises were encountered requiring solutions. As a consequence no other great industrial people is so free from the shackling thralldom of a hard and fast ideological theory as our own people.

Although the consensus of our people is essentially in support of free enterprise, it envisages an economic system by no means divorced from government. Government enterprise is present here in unsuspected forms. An English scholar visiting the United States and hearing of Ohio's state monopoly of the sale of bottled liquor inquired with a curious smile, "Is this your socialized state?" Appearing on a radio program and asked whether he found here a mixed economy—that is both private and public enterprise—he at once remarked on Ohio's half dozen state universities with their tens of thousands of students, something not to be found at all in England. Here was public enterprise on a vast scale. In fact one encounters the naïve rationalization of the unsophisticated Americans who will contend that public education cannot possibly be socialistic since it is an old American institution.

Present Federal Economic Enterprise

The second Hoover Commission made a systematic effort to ascertain the extent of public enterprise in the federal government but was often reduced to the necessity of merely estimating the extent. It reported that the total number of government commercial- and industrial-type facilities within the Department of Defense alone "probably exceeded 2,500" with a capital investment which "probably exceeds $15 billion." Included in these were the manufacture of clothing, paint, ice cream and eye glasses, furniture repair, cement mixing, tree and garden nurseries, coffee roasting, air lines, steamship lines and a railroad. Outside the Defense Department and among the civilian agencies there exists no definitive list of federal economic enterprises. The Commission reported "The total amount of capital invested is unknown, as is the number of their employees, the gross value of their goods and services produced by them annually and the profit or loss resulting from their operation. A few even enjoy a monopoly privilege since, in these cases, private enterprise, in effect, has been excluded from the field." Even this partial list of the Commission confirms the indubitable fact of our mixed economy.

The Constitution an Economic Document

The Constitution of the United States is itself, among other things, an economic document mirroring accurately the framers' conception of the relation of government to private enterprise. Taxation was essential for sound credit, and the assurance was given by the Constitution that whoever held public securities would be paid. Commerce, both foreign and interstate, was to be regulated by statute and treaty to the end that commercial prosperity might be assured. To the same end a sound circulating medium was to be established by a national monopoly of coinage. Authors and inventors were assured the exclusive right to their products. Contracts were to be safeguarded against state legislatures, which were not to pass statutes that would impair their obligation.

Paternalism of Federalists, Whigs, and Republicans

The framers and proponents of the Constitution generally, essentially the Federalist party, were by no means simon-pure devotees of *laissez faire*. The evidence is incontrovertible that they believed in a paternalistic system, one that used the government directly and positively to aid business. Funding the national debt as well as the state debts with gilt edge, six per cent federal securities not only gratified holders of the depreciated Revolutionary War securities, but even provided, as Hamilton prophesied, a liquid circulating medium. The Bank of United States, chartered by Congress, created a sound paper currency. Manufacturers were given a mild protective tariff. American ship owners, crowded out of our harbors by competing foreign vessels, were restored to prosperity by preferential tonnage duties only one fifth as great as those which burdened foreign vessels and they were granted a monopoly of the coast-wise trade. New England fishermen were lifted from the depth of despair by a bounty on every pound of dried cod fish, payable out of the national treasury.

The Whigs, during their brief tenures, in the mid-nineteenth century sought in vain to re-establish the Bank of the United States and maintain high protective tariffs, but, as the spiritual heirs of the Federalist tradition of economic paternalism, they subsidized mail steamers and used the navy and State Department to promote the sale of manufactured goods in the Far East, even breaking into the hermit kingdom of Japan for that purpose. No sooner had the Whigs disintegrated in the 1850's than the Republican party emerged to continue the tradition of fostering prosperity by direct governmental aid. Thus the public domain was given outright to actual settlers or as subsidies to railroads, while the resources of the public lands were made available for a song to stock raisers and exploiters of their lumber and mineral wealth.

Meanwhile the counter policy of pure and unadulterated *laissez faire* was advocated by Jeffersonian Republicans in power (1801–28) and Jacksonian Democracy (1829–61). Cries for aid in harrowing economic depressions were raised in vain until the 1890's when the Populist party, with its elaborate program of governmental regulation in the interest of debt-harassed agrarians, was swallowed up by the Democratic party; since then there has been no party dedicated to the dogmas of unadulterated *laissez faire*. No matter how persistent the protestations to the contrary, the nation is now more or less committed to paternalistic policies. The very survival of both major parties depends on their adherance to governmental aids to various economic interests.

THE DECLINE OF "LAISSEZ FAIRE"

Federal Regulation of Business

Although the movement to make the Constitution had been motivated by eagerness to give the central government the power to regulate interstate commerce, the Constitution had been in operation for a century before the power was exercised in a consequential manner. A hundred years ago the states were regulating such interstate commerce as was passing to or from a state. The Supreme Court was then debating as to whether the power to regulate interstate commerce was concurrent as between state and nation or whether it was exclusively a power of Congress. The business interests of that early day were eager to have it declared exclusively a federal power—under the apparent assumption that the states would thereby be prevented from exercising the power and Congress would probably not use it. "If the states could not regulate, the prospect was there would be no regulation at all." [1] In 1868 the business interests obtained the "due process" clause of the Fourteenth Amendment which enabled the Courts to exercise a powerful restraint upon state regulation of commerce even within the state.

The Sherman Anti-Trust Law

The restraint upon state regulation of commerce led to results disappointing to the emerging gigantic business combinations. In the middle 1880's trusts were increasing in number and size. As Justice Harlan expressed it in a decision in 1911, "All who recall the condition of the country in 1890 will remember that there was everywhere, among the people generally, a feeling of deep unrest." [2] What if the Standard Oil Company would attain a complete monopoly and raise to one dollar a gallon the price of kerosene, then almost universally used for illuminating the home? What if a combination cornered the wheat market and the price of bread rose to a dollar a loaf? That the phobia was fantastic did not matter since error believed is in effect truth. Congress had no choice but to act and it acted promptly.

The Sherman Anti-Trust Act was the first great regulative statute under the commerce power of Congress. The states might use the principles of common law to attack the trust problem within their bounds but only by statute might Congress regulate commerce. What the Sherman Act did was to incorporate in a federal statute some of the common law restraints upon business practices. Thus the Sherman Act declared illegal "every contract, combination in the form of a trust or otherwise, or conspiracy, in restraint of trade or commerce among the several states or with foreign nations." It declared guilty of a misdemeanor "every person who shall monopolize or attempt to monopolize." [3] Heavy fines and prison sentences were prescribed for violations of the statute. The Sherman Act still stands a part of "the Supreme Law of the Land."

The Clayton Act

Early experience with the Sherman Act proved disappointing. In the decision on the first important prosecution, that of the Sugar Trust, the Supreme Court in 1895 held that the act did not apply since the Sugar Trust was engaged in manufacturing which is not commerce. This appeared at first practically to render the law useless. Although in later cases the act recovered its significance and led to some notable convictions, it nevertheless suffered from its very vagueness. By the time the Sherman Act was twenty years old, a number of specific outrageous methods of competition were crying for correction.

The Clayton Act, passed in 1914, specified a number of practices which it forbids under penalties. Local price discrimination by which a

---

[1] Carl B. Swisher, *American Constitutional Development* (Boston, 1943), p. 207.
[2] 221 U.S. 83.
[3] 26 Statutes at Large, pp. 209–10.

gigantic corporation might reduce prices long enough to ruin a local competing small business is declared illegal. "Tying clauses" by which, for example, a retail merchant might handle the cameras of a certain manufacturer only if he sold no film except that manufactured by that camera manufacturer, are declared to be unlawful. Monopolistic holding companies are outlawed, that is, for example, a company obtaining control of enough of the stock of competing companies to create a monopoly. Interlocking directorates are forbidden when the same persons would be directors of competing companies or companies that might compete.

The Federal Trade Commission Act

In order that the enforcement of anti-trust legislation might no longer depend upon the whim of the Attorney General,[4] Congress created an agency specifically to watch business practice with a view to the prosecution of offenders who would not heed warnings. This agency, the Federal Trade Commission, consists of five members appointed by the President with Senate confirmation for seven years. Upon the direction of President or Congress or application of the Attorney General, the commission is empowered to investigate all corporations guilty or alleged to be guilty of violating federal anti-trust laws. The Commission has broad powers to act against unfair competition, make charges against offenders, hold hearings, and issue orders against them to cease and desist from forbidden practices. If such orders are ignored, the Commission may apply to the courts to enforce its order.

Much depends on the party in power and the prevailing climate of opinion as to the kind of members appointed to the Commission as vacancies occur. The businesses to be scrutinized by the Commission are vigilant as to the nominees of the President and exert their influence on the Senate to confirm or reject. The first membership of the Commission appointed by President Wilson was completely dedicated to the carrying out of the purposes of the Commission. But as vacancies occurred, the time came when in 1925 President Coolidge appointed William E. Humphrey, who did not even believe in the purpose of the Commission. Along with two other recent appointees Humphrey's accession reversed the policy of the Commission and even corporations under indictment for violation of anti-trust laws were invited to appear before the Commission and have the matter adjusted. Thus it matters much what the interests affected can do in determining the personnel of the Commission. Nevertheless, "cease and desist" orders continue to be issued and they compel business to be on its guard against too flagrant violations of the anti-trust laws.

[4] Attorney General Richard Olney, whom President Cleveland appointed in 1893, not only did not believe in the Sherman Act but busied himself working for the repeal of a law he was under oath to enforce. Letter of Olney to John G. Carlisle, July 5, 1893, Olney Letter Book, Library of Congress. Quoted by Carl B. Swisher, *op. cit.*, p. 128.

Food, Drug, and Cosmetic Act

The agitation, early in the present century, for federal regulation of food and drugs was climaxed by the publication in 1906 of Upton Sinclair's *The Jungle*, a novel revealing the revolting conditions in the Chicago stockyards and meat-packing establishments. President Theodore Roosevelt took up the issue and Congress was induced to pass the Pure Food and Drug Act; it was revised in 1938 and Cosmetics were added to the matter covered by law. The legislation excludes from interstate commerce adulterated or misbranded foods and drugs. Criminal prosecution with fine and imprisonment is less effective than the provision for forfeiture of the adulterated or misbranded articles upon entry into interstate commerce, which, incidentally, prevents injury to the public when intercepted.

The consumers in whose interest the Food and Drug Law was enacted are always weak and inadequately organized. The wave of indignation that induced passage of the law left no permanent organization in its wake to fortify the arm of the administrators. Appropriations for enforcement are consequently inadequate and the number of field inspectors is pitifully inadequate. It is their function to inspect factories, analyze products, detect adulterated or misbranded goods in stores, institute action and correct abuses. Location of the Pure Food and Drug Administation, formerly in the Agriculture Department, frustrated efforts at enforcement in that area, such as the agency's inability to hold to the rules regarding the use of corn sugar in canning and the regulations as to minimum tolerance of poisonous lead-spray residues on fresh fruit. The bureau has been compelled to attempt "a maximum of compliance with a minimum of resistance." Since 1953 it has been located in the Department of Health, Education and Welfare.

Securities and Exchange Law

The abuses contributing to the Stock Market crash of 1929 and the losses of investors and speculators in securities induced Congress to enact legislation to safeguard the public. The Federal Securities Act of 1934 required the registration of new securities along with detailed information concerning the corporation issuing these securities as well as information about the securities themselves. The Act has been appropriately called a "truth-in-securities law." It is unlawful to use the mails or interstate commerce to send for sale a security unless accompanied by a prospectus containing the information provided at registration. The Securities and Exchange Act of 1934 requires registration of the Exchanges and agents dealing in securities. The Act is designed "to make available currently to the investing public information regarding the corporations whose securities are traded in securities markets," "to prevent the diversion into security transactions of a disproportionate amount of the nation's credit resources, and to eliminate manipulation and other abuses in the security markets." [5]

Securities and Exchange Commission

To administer the laws regulating the sale of securities, Congress created a commission of five members appointed for five-year terms by the President with the advice and consent of the Senate. Because of the nature of its functions the Commission is invested with extraordinarily broad powers to make rules and regulations limited only by the requirement that they be necessary or appropriate in the public interest and for the protection of investors. The Commission is in a position to use its rule-making power to persuade the Exchanges to adopt self-regulating rules of their own. The Commission has the power, after notice and opportunity for hearing, to suspend or withdraw the registration of a security or suspend any officer or member of an exchange. The margin required in purchase of securities may be altered by the Federal Reserve Board with a view to encouraging or discouraging market activity and at one time during World War II it fixed the margin at 100 per cent.

Federal Regulation of Public Utilities

The regulation of utilities began in the states, but as mergers and consolidations transferred management to a few large holding companies, a demand arose in the second and third decades of the present century for federal regulation of certain public utilities. The Federal Power Act of 1920 consequently created the Federal Power Commission and invested it with certain regulatory and licensing functions. For example before issuing a license to a private company for the development of hydroelectric power, the Commission gathers pertinent data on the region, and from these it determines whether the license should be issued. The Act also includes a comprehensive plan for the regulation of electric utilities insofar as the states lack the power to do so and for fortifying the states' power to regulate. The object is to ensure the charging of just, reasonable, non-discriminatory and non-preferential rates and the furnishing of sufficient service in the interstate transmission of electric energy.

A vast system of natural gas pipe lines radiating from Texas, Oklahoma, West Virginia, and Pennsylvania convey gas to communities throughout the nation. The Natural Gas Act provides for regulation of those public utilities engaged in the transportation or sale of natural gas in interstate commerce for resale to ultimate public consumption. If the Commission finds any rate unjust, unreasonable, or unduly discriminatory, it shall fix a fair rate. The Commission is empowered to order a natural gas company to extend or improve its facilities or to establish physical connection with the facilities of any person or municipality engaged in local distribution of its product, and it may not abandon any

[5] *Fifth Annual Report* of the S. E. C., 1939 (1940), p. 35.

of its facilities without approval of the Commission. In 1950 President Truman vetoed a bill that would have exempted from the Federal Commission the regulation of the price at the well of natural gas distributed through interstate pipe lines and left that part of its control to state regulative agencies. In 1956 President Eisenhower vetoed a similar bill.

Regulation of Utility Holding Companies

Following World War I gigantic utility combinations developed. They made possible certain advantages both to the industry and to the public such as engaging expert engineering and construction services and superior managerial talent. However the stock-market crash of 1929 highlighted abuses, and a searching eighteen-month investigation was conducted by the Federal Trade Commission under direction of a resolution of Congress. Evidence was turned up of reorganizations that had led to a write up of capitalization from $148,000,000 to $547,000,000. It was also shown that some companies had paid dividends of 60 per cent and even higher. Holding companies had been pyramided one upon another, enabling a small group to dominate and manipulate the system. Obviously the control of those gigantic combinations, often continental in scope, was beyond the power of state regulation.

As a consequence of the investigation Congress enacted the Public Utility Holding Company Act of 1935 which placed holding companies controlling gas and electric utilities under the jurisdiction of the Securities and Exchange Commission. It requires their registration and forbids such holding companies to use the mails or interstate commerce to sell their securities or those of their subsidiaries when not registered. The law provides for the simplification of holding-company systems and limits operations of each holding company to a single integrated public-utility system. Administration of the law is vested in the Securities and Exchange Commission, and many of the large systems voluntarily submitted their plans of reorganization to the Commission. The Commission has prescribed a uniform system of accounts for these holding companies, designed to render accounting deception difficult and provide investors with information as to what they are purchasing. Moreover this aids state regulatory commissions to perform their function more efficiently.

Regulation of Business by Taxation

With the exception that the Constitution requires that direct taxes must be apportioned according to population of the states and other taxes must be uniform, there is no limitation on the power of Congress to lay and collect taxes. This frequently gives Congress the opportunity to tax in order to regulate instead of to raise revenue. The first notable example was the tax of ten per cent levied in 1865 on the circulation of state bank notes. For half a century Congress levied a prohibitive tax of ten cents a pound on the sale of oleomargarine colored to resemble butter, and it still levies such a tax on persons who manufacture or sell adulterated butter. Congress stopped the manufacture of phosphorus matches by a tax of two cents a hundred. A protective tariff is a device for laying a tax in such a way as to foster an industry. When Congress levies a tariff of 150 per cent on imported straw hats, 140 per cent on "embroidered or embellished leather gloves," 90 per cent on dolls, and 135 per cent on firecrackers, its object is not primarily revenue. When it levies no tariff on bananas and coffee, which are not raised in the United States, the protective principle as it applies to competing imports is evident enough.

Evaluation of the Regulation Policy

It is a far cry indeed since that Inauguration Day in 1801 when Thomas Jefferson proclaimed his ideal of "a wise and frugal government, which shall restrain men from injuring one another, shall leave them otherwise free to regulate their own pursuits of industry and improvement and shall not take from the mouth of labor the bread it has earned. This is the sum of good government, and this is necessary to close the circle of our felicities." [6] Let it be noted that every one of the great regulative statutes above was enacted by Congress under the pressures of public opinion representing, in most cases, a combination of organized interests which succeeded in convincing Congress that the legislation was in the public interest. The laissez-faire philosophy of Jefferson and Jackson, appropriate enough for an agrarian economy, was outmoded by the Industrial Revolution. The states pioneered in regulative legislation, but by 1890 an irresistable combination of pressures upon Congress left the lawmakers no choice but to satisfy it by at least a gesture—than which the Sherman Act at first appeared to be little more. This was but the beginning. The end is by no means in sight.

GOVERNMENT AID TO BUSINESS

Patents

Under the common law of England which was brought over by the English colonists and became fundamental in American law, there was no patent protection for inventions and discoveries. A patent for an invention is a special privilege, a monopoly for a limited period granted by the federal government, after which period it is free to anyone who chooses to take advantage of it. The Constitution granted Congress the power to "promote the progress of science and the useful arts, by securing for a limited time to authors and inventors the exclusive rights to their respective writings and discoveries." Congress has enacted the necessary legislation to give effect to this provision with respect to inventions and has established a patent office to administer it.

The burden of proof rests upon the would-be inventor to convince the Patent Office that he has devised something not already patented.

[6] J. D. Richardson (ed.), *Messages and Papers of the Presidents* (1903), Vol. I, p. 323.

Only an individual can file an application for a patent; this rules out corporations. A patent can be obtained only for the invention or discovery of a machine, art, composition of matter, or manufacture or a new design. Even a new plant can be patented. Evidently a mere new idea cannot be patented such, for example, as a new scientific truth or a new chemical element. Some practical application of an invention must be evident before it is patentable. Moreover to be patented the new contrivance must have utility and a machine cannot be patented unless it can perform its intended function. In case of infringements on a patent the owner may recover damages at law or may proceed in equity to protect his rights and recover not only damages suffered by the infringement but also the profits the defendent has made from the infringement.

Copyrights

In the decade when the Constitution was framed, Noah Webster, the future lexicographer, had obtained copyrights of two of his elementary text books granted by Connecticut, New York, and Massachusetts, but this did not prevent the pirating of these books in other states. It was consequently a gain for authors to have Congress vested with the power of "securing for limited times to authors exclusive right to their respective writings." "Authors" has been given a broad interpretation since Congress includes in the copyright laws the production of musicians, sculptors, painters, and others. "Writing" to be copyrighted may be as little as a page, a paragraph, or even a sentence.

The procedure in obtaining a copyright contrasts with that in obtaining a patent. Before applying for a copyright a book must be printed with the statement in it that it is "Copyright" and the application must be made immediately after publication. No search is made by the Copyright Office to ascertain whether the applicant is entitled to copyright his work. The Copyright Act grants the publisher the exclusive right to print, reprint, publish, copy, and sell the work. The owner of the copyright may proceed by injunction; the one who infringes the copyright is liable not only for damages but also for profits he may have made from the infringements and he may be ordered by the court to destroy the plates involved in the infringement.

Aids to Commerce

One of the services of the federal government is the collection and distribution of information concerning opportunities for American marketing abroad, and the putting of foreign companies in touch with American goods and firms. Consuls collect and distribute information concerning foreign-trade laws, commercial treaties, and other information valuable to business. For these purposes the Bureau of Foreign and Domestic Commerce is maintained; it operates a marketing division, a trade association division, a construction division, an industry division, a transportation division, and an area division and maintains district offices in cities throughout the United States.

Aids Through Collection of Statistics

The Bureau of the Census is probably the world's largest collector of statistics, assembling many that are invaluable to business. The Bureau of Labor Statistics is constantly collecting information on total employment and the total wages paid; and it publishes it in the *Monthly Labor Review*. This Bureau also gathers the necessary data for its index of the cost of living, which is published each month.

The Bureau of Standards

The Bureau of Standards performs a continuous service to business and consumers by devising standard specifications facilitating orders for goods. This signifies a change from hit-and-miss methods to standard, universally understood methods. Waste is reduced by establishing simplified practices and by reduction of the number of sizes of commodities. For example the number of sizes and styles of paving bricks was reduced from 66 to 5, bed blankets from 78 to 12, hot water storage tanks from 120 to 14, and milk bottles from 49 to 9.

Aids Through Experimentation

The Bureau of Standards conducts experiments and tests of great value to industry and commerce. They may be undertaken in response to requests from federal agencies, states, municipalities, or private interests. They may include chemical analyses, tests of heat, power, and electricity or of materials such as rubber, paper, leather, metal, and textiles. For example, by the Bureau's experiments in producing a hard, refined, and cheap sugar from corn, a new industry was developed. When reputable fruit growers were baffled because frozen oranges became dry and pithy by the time they reached the customer, they appealed to the government for assistance in solving the problem.

When the Pure Food and Drug Administration persistently discovered and stopped the shipment of canned blueberries infested with worms, the canners did not know what to do. The government attacked the problem and devised machinery for eliminating the wormy berries, thereby saving an industry while protecting the consumer. Government officials, by conducting classes in the appropriate technique, showed the catsup manufacturers how to make catsup that would keep. When the government was unable to stop the canning of unfit salmon by seizure and condemnation of the product, it sent inspectors into the factories and showed just what types of fish were unfit for canning and by demonstration protected the consumer while aiding industry.[7]

[7] E. Pendleton Herring, *Public Administration and the Public Interest* (1936), p. 235.

Aid to Mining Industry

The Federal Bureau of Mines is the agency maintained to perform a wide range of aids to the mining industry. Coal dust raised into the air by concussion ignites and causes mine explosions; the Bureau discovered the safest explosive and promoted adoption of "permissible explosives" that minimize the possibility of dust explosions. It has encouraged the adoption of safe hand lamps, and it has investigated the cause of falling roofs and introduced means of eradicating that peril. It has conducted studies of nerve diseases. The Bureau maintains mine rescue cars which conduct demonstrations at the mines and are rushed to scenes of disaster to aid in rescue. It studies waste in mining methods and devises more efficient ones not only in the coal industry but also in the oil and gas industry.

Aids to the Fishing Industry

The Fish and Wild Life Service of the Department of the Interior engages in the artificial propagation and distribution of fish in the waters of the United States. By refusing to maintain hatcheries and to stock waters within states that do not enact adequate laws, the Service can exert pressures for compliance in areas beyond the direct authority of a federal agency. The Agency conducts extensive investigations in refrigeration, canning, smoking, drying, and salting of fish, which most commercial fisheries cannot afford to conduct. The Agency's research has resulted in the discovery of uses for many by-products of fish.

Subsidies to Railroads

In 1850 Congress granted 2,700,000 acres of public land to Illinois for the construction of the Illinois Central Railroad, and by 1861 Congress had granted 31,600,842 acres for internal improvements, mostly for railroads.[8] In 1862 Congress chartered two railroad companies to construct a transcontinental railroad from Nebraska to California. Congress gave the railway companies right of way through the public lands with free use of such material as timber, earth, and stone. Moreover the railroads were given ten alternate sections of land on each side of the railroad for each mile constructed; this amounted to 16,800 acres per mile and in 1864 Congress doubled the land grant. Congress also provided for issuance of government bonds in enormous amounts to finance the vast project. Other railroads to the Pacific received similar land grants. It has been estimated that between 1850 and 1871 the federal land grants for railroad construction totaled 158,293,377 acres, an area equal to that of the New England states, New York, and Pennsylvania combined. The

[8] Reginald C. McGrane, *The Economic Development of the American Nation* (1942), p. 271.

federal money grants for construction have been estimated as totaling $407,000,000.[9]

Ship Subsidies

It was fitting that during a Whig administration in 1841 Congress granted a subsidy of $200,000 a year to the Ocean Steamship Company and in 1847 a subsidy to Edward W. Collins, later raised to $858,000, for a line of streamers to operate between New York and Liverpool. In 1858 a Democratic administration practically ended the ship-subsidy policy. [10] The Merchant Marine Act of 1920 created a new Shipping Board authorized to promote and maintain the merchant marine and to sell the government fleet constructed during World War I. To foster the growth of American shipping, $25,000,000 obtained from the sale of the government fleet was set aside to aid in the construction of modern vessels and, to aid further, such enterprise was exempted from the excess profits tax for ten years. The Shipping Board was empowered to maintain the existing government steamship lines and establish new ones when trade warranted it. Because these measures failed to accomplish their purpose, the government turned to heavy mail contract payments which amounted to concealed subsidies. The Merchant Marine Act of 1936 replaced the concealed subsidies with direct subsidies based on the differences between foreign and domestic costs of building and operating competing vessels. [11] It should be noted that national defense requires that the nation must not reach a condition where it would become completely dependent upon foreign shipping.

Subsidies for Silver Mining

In 1873 Congress had passed a monetary act that no longer provided for the coinage of silver dollars. Silver had then ceased to be brought to the mint for coinage because it was scarce enough to be worth more uncoined than coined. But soon there was a greatly increased production of silver and a consequent cheapening of the metal. The silver-mining interests then demanded remonetization and coinage of all silver brought to the mint at the old ratio of sixteen to one with gold. Congress did not quite do this but in 1878 it compromised by authorizing the purchase of from two to four million dollars worth of silver per month to be coined into silver dollars. In effect this artificial demand for silver constituted a subsidy to the extent that it increased the current price of silver above the price that would have prevailed without this extra demand. In 1889 and 1890 Congress admitted six new Western silver-mining states into the Union; their twelve Senators constituted a silver bloc that was able to prevent passage of the McKinley Tariff Act of

[9] *Ibid.*, 328–30.
[10] *Ibid.*, p. 275.
[11] *Ibid.*, pp. 557, 558.

1890 until promised a more generous silver purchasing act than that of 1878. The Sherman Silver Purchasing Act of 1890 required the Secretary of the Treasury to buy each month four and a half million ounces of silver, this time not to be coined but used as the basis of issues of silver certificates to circulate as money. The silver-mining interests were here allied with agrarians seeking means of inflating the low price of farm products. As late as 1934, in the omnibus monetary legislation of that year, the ever-vigilant silver interests, after failing to force the recoinage of silver at the old ratio of 16 to 1, were able to force Congress to require that, in the monetary system, the silver stock should be a quantity equal in value to one fourth that of gold. To that end the Secretary of the Treasury was directed to purchase silver at not less than an artificial price of fifty cents an ounce and to issue silver certificates to the extent of the stock. Thus, during three quarters of a century, silver mining has been subsidized again and again with only slight regard to monetary requirements.

GOVERNMENT OWNERSHIP AND OPERATION

Public Enterprise

When Lincoln expressed his classic formula that private enterprise should do those things that it can do better than the government while the government ought to do those things that it can do better than private enterprise or that cannot be done at all by private enterprise, he was but expressing a consensus generally accepted by our people. Public enterprise has come to be a well-understood term and distinguishes the operation of postal and some transportation, utility, and similar services from those services financed out of general taxation such as education, police, and national defense. Modern public enterprise has tended to center on basic services and industries, many of them natural monopolies, that is on enterprises that in their nature ought not to be competing, such as water supply, transportation or electric power systems that may be owned and operated by municipalities.

The Postal System

So accustomed are we to government ownership and operation of the Post Office that it is difficult to think of it as an "enterprise." There is no doubt that the nation is the sole proprietor and operator of this gigantic enterprise, the largest in the nation either public or private. A graphic chart of the department's organization is plainly that of a vast business enterprise. Quite naturally the Postmaster General is the executive head and has general direction and supervision of its services. He appoints all officers and employees of his department except certain higher officials such as the five assistant postmasters general, a solicitor, a purchasing agent, and a comptroller. The Postmaster General awards and executes contracts and, subject to presidential approval, makes postal agreements with foreign governments. He has authority to establish post offices where he deems expedient and may discontinue them.

Much has been made of the fact that the Post Office operates in the red. But it must be remembered that it cannot be judged in this matter by the criteria for a private profit-motivated enterprise. Public service and not profit is the necessary motive of all governmental agencies. While a private utility will extend its services only to those areas where financial return is adequate, the Post Office has always extended its service to the most remote rural areas that cannot repay the cost of the service. Contributing to the annual deficit is the vast amount of mail carried under the franking privilege, accorded the Vice President, Senators, Representatives, and the numerous administrative agencies. Contributing also to the undue cost of the Post Office department is construction of more elaborate and costly post office buildings than necessary and their location, not with reference to need but often according to the prestige of the individual Congressman and his skill in logrolling. Then there are the subsidies, such as the carriage of periodicals at far less than the cost of the service, and the payment to certain common carriers of an extraordinary compensation involving subsidies concealed from the uninformed. Under the circumstances the wonder is that the deficit is not larger. Withal the Post Office performs its herculean function with rapidity, accuracy, and very few losses of mail and without the distressing difficulties for courts, commissions, and consumers that would be inevitable if it were a private enterprise.

Parcel Post

There are those who assume that parcel post cannot be an economic service if it is provided by a government agency instead of by a private corporation. It is difficult, however, to see how the delivery of a parcel post package by a postal employee is any less an economic act than if it had been delivered by the employee of a private express company impelled by the profit motive. Millions of Americans can remember when such services were rendered at high cost by the express companies, and, while the demand for parcel post was being considered, Senator Platt of New York said he had four reasons for opposing it—the four express companies then operating. Businesses that were alarmed at the advent of parcel post have adjusted to it, and it is doubtful whether the proposal of the second Hoover Commission that this federal service be discontinued and the matter returned to private enterprise will get much public support.

Postal Savings

Here is a downright government banking enterprise established by Congress in response to a strong public demand. For convenience it is attached to the Post Office and thereby the government can offer this service with a minimum of additional cost. When established, it was claimed that instead of competing with private banking it would draw into circulation money hidden in strong boxes, bureau drawers, and elsewhere, and that it would be used by persons averse to depositing in ordinary banks. Not more than $2,500 may be deposited in an account, and amounts deposited may be drawn out in part or all at any time with the accrued 2 per cent interest set by law. Since the postal savings are promptly redeposited in local banks as required by law, there is less competition with private banking than might be assumed. A board of trustees, consisting of the Postmaster General, the Secretary of the Treasury, and the Attorney General administer the system, thereby making it a quasi-governmental corporation.

The Government Printing Office

In 1860, under authority of an Act of Congress, the federal government purchased an existing commercial printing plant. It is now the largest and best-equipped printing plant either public or private in the world. The Government Printing Office executes orders for printing placed by Congress and the agencies of the federal government and distributes the publications. The entire management of the Office, including appointment of all personnel, is vested in the Public Printer who is solely responsible for the management of the Office. Here is a public enterprise so generally accepted as proper that little criticism of it is ever heard. Private enterprise was, of course, depended on prior to 1861 for printing of public requirements of that kind.

The Atomic Energy Commission

The Atomic Energy Commission is engaged in a big business and government business at that. It carries on a thoroughgoing program for government control of production, ownership, and use of fissionable material. It explores and executes the constructive possibilities of using atomic power as a source of energy and in the treatment of disease. It aims to promote world peace, improve the general welfare, raise the standard of living, and strengthen free competition and private enterprise. The Commission is authorized to make arrangements through contracts and loans to carry on its research through private or public means or through its own facilities.

Since ownership and distribution of all fissionable material is vested in the Commission and since, through its licensing power, it controls the transfer, ownership, or export of all source material or ores from which fissionable materials might be refined, we have here a government monopoly conducted by a public enterprise. Moreover the ownership of all the facilities for producing fissionable material is vested in the Commission and the Commission consequently took over all the resources of the United States government devoted to atomic-energy development. The Government-owned plants might be publicly operated or, through contracts, put under private operation, but, in the latter case, the Commission retains supervision and control, which extends to all subcontracting arrangements. Before the Commission licenses for commercial or non-military use of atomic energy, it must report to the President, who transmits its recommendations to Congress. No such license can be issued until a ninety-day period has elapsed while Congress is in session.

The authority is vested in a full time five-member Commission of civilians appointed by the President with the advice and consent of the Senate. The General Manager appointed by the Commission is responsible for the over-all management and administration of the policies established by the Commission.

Government Corporations

Whenever the Federal government undertakes to perform a purely governmental as distinguished from a business or quasi-business function, Congress has created, for that purpose, a department, bureau, commission, or some other conventional governmental agency. But when it undertakes a function in such a field as transportation as in the case of the Panama Railroad, or banking as in the case of the Reconstruction Finance Corporation, and scores of other public enterprises, it has frequently, during the last half century, created a corporation and provided the capital with which to finance the enterprise. In many respects these corporations are organized and function quite like the corporations of private enterprise. The federal corporation ordinarily has a board of directors appointed by the President with Senate confirmation and a single executive to administer the policies determined by the board, while the "stock" belongs to the owner of the enterprise, the federal government. This form of government institution has been adopted under the assumption that its autonomous nature would give it a better opportunity to administer a quasi or actual public enterprise with some of the efficiency that private enterprises have achieved. By 1954 government corporations were operating a wide range of business-type functions such as making or guaranteeing private loans to businessmen, home owners, and foreign governments; insuring private individuals against loss from crop failures and declines in prices; operating power plants, railroads, hotels, barge lines, and harbor facilities; distributing electric power; and purchasing, stock piling and selling commodities.

The Tennessee Valley Authority

The purpose of this gigantic public enterprise is to improve the standard of living of the entire valley. To this end the Corporation is designed to improve navigation, prevent floods, provide for national defense, produce electricity and commercial fertilizer, conserve soil and prevent soil erosion. Private enterprise would be interested only in the production of fertilizer and electricity and would carry the electric current only to such communities as would yield a profit on the extension to them. Private enterprise would not be interested in the social aspects and Congress created the Corporation under the conviction that only as a public enterprise could the numerous purposes be coordinated into the over-all purpose of the development of the valley. Incidentally, an avowed purpose was to provide a yardstick for ascertaining the cost of producing electric power—a project that has produced more controversy than conviction. The policies of the Authority are determined by a Board of three directors appointed by the President with the approval of the Senate, and the General Manager is in charge of administering the policies.

Panama Railroad Company

When the United States purchased the assets of the French Panama Canal Company, it acquired that company's stock in the Panama Railroad and proceeded to purchase the remainder of the stock from private holders. In 1948 the Railroad Company was reincorporated—thus the United States is in the railroad business—and it is a financial success, yielding profits even during the depression. The Corporation also operates a Receiving and Forwarding Agency and harbor and terminal facilities. It operates a steamship line from the Canal to New York and to San Francisco. "It is unquestionably one of the most efficiently conducted steamship services under the American Flag." [12]

Reaction Against the Government Corporation

Government Corporations were used extensively in the first and second world wars for the purpose of supplying war needs and during the Great Depression of the 1930's for various purposes but mainly to provide loans that private financial institutions were unable to provide. The greatest of these corporations was the Reconstruction Finance Corporation, established in 1932, but the Act of 1953 provided for its liquidation. The Inland Waterways Corporation, after operating a system of barges on the Mississippi River and its tributaries for nearly thirty years, was ordered sold to private enterprisers in 1953. The scores of government corporations that remain have been having their independence gradually reduced since the 1930's. In 1935 the Bureau of the Budget was given authority over several government corporations, and by 1942 over all major ones. Next government corporations were prohibited from incurring administrative expenses except in pursuance of annual appropriation. In 1938 their freedom in handling personnel was clipped by bringing that matter under civil service regulations. By 1945 most of them were brought into the grand administrative system

[12] Marshall E. Dimock, *Government Operated Enterprises in the Canal Zone*, p. 81.

by being attached to departments with a view to bringing about a unity of administration policy. Thus autonomy has declined, although it has not been obliterated. As long as the government ventures in public enterprises, the corporation is likely to persist.

SUMMARY

While the nation is committed to a general policy of free enterprise subject, more or less, to government regulation, there is nevertheless considerable public enterprise. The second Hoover Commission was unable to itemize all of it and could only estimate its extent.

From the very beginning the federal government has provided certain aids to business, though checked by Jeffersonian and Jacksonian insistence on laissez-faire policies. Congress did not undertake a nation-wide regulation of business practices until the Sherman Anti-Trust Law of 1890. Its purpose was fortified by the Clayton and Federal Trade Commission Acts in 1914. Consumers were given protection by the Food and Drug Act in 1906, and investors by the Security and Exchange Act in 1934. The Federal Power Act of 1920 provides for regulation of utilities involved in interstate commerce. The Public Utility Holding Act of 1935 is intended to rationalize the structure of holding companies. In addition to direct regulation Congress provides for considerable indirect regulation through the power to tax.

Among aids to business are patents giving inventors a monopoly right for a limited period and copyrights which grant authors a similar monopoly. Commerce is aided through information concerning trade gathered by consuls abroad, through trade statistics, through uniform standards set for certain commodities, through information based on experiments conducted by the Bureau of Standards, through information provided for the mining industry by the Bureau of Mines, and through similar information provided by the Fish and Wild Life Service to the fishing industry.

The chief recipients of federal subsidies have been the railroads, with grants totaling over 150 million acres of land and over $400 million. Large subsidies were made to shipping in the mid-nineteenth century and after World War I. Considerable subsidies have been concealed in contracts for carrying mail. Silver mining is subsidized by the artificially high price of silver and the requirement by law of considerable purchases by the government without regard to monetary needs.

The post office system is the biggest government enterprise, and its parcel post and postal savings branches are economic activities that were initiated during the last half century. The Government Printing Office is a gigantic business. The Atomic Energy Commission operates a big government enterprise.

For conducting semi-autonomous businesses the federal government often resorts to the use of government corporations such as the Reconstruction Finance Corporation. The Tennessee Valley Authority functions through a corporation, as does also the federally owned and operated Panama Railroad.

CHAPTER XXXI

GOVERNMENT AND LABOR

COURT DECISIONS ON LABOR

UNTIL a generation or so ago the attitude of government toward labor presented a perfect example of cultural lag. As late as the early 1920's concepts of the common law that originated before the Industrial Revolution were still being used by the Supreme Court of the United States to curb organized labor. Before 1830 the attitude of government toward combinations of labor had been that of repression. Since this was almost a century before the beginning of federal legislation concerning management-labor relations, the official attitude was that of the state governments. In the absence of state statutes, principles of common law were applied, and these forbade laborers to do collectively what a laborer might do individually. When the Philadelphia journeymen shoemakers in 1806 collectively demanded a higher piece rate, that is, struck for higher pay, their employers got the city officials to prosecute the local union. The judge, applying the prevailing common law principle, held the combination of workingmen to be a criminal conspiracy in restraint of trade, that is, of competition among individual workers. This then became the guiding precedent for state courts throughout the country in similar cases. It amounted to the outlawing of strikes.

In 1842, however, Chief Justice John Shaw of the Massachusetts Supreme Court in *Commonwealth v. Hunt* refused to declare that a strike of Boston shoemakers for a closed shop was unlawful. He rejected the common law doctrine that a combination of workers using economic pressure merely to gain their end constituted *per se* a criminal conspiracy; that is, it required more than such a purpose to make the collective action criminal. Shaw's decision became a landmark in the history of American labor as it started a new trend in court precedents by which unions and strikes were no longer outlawed. Nevertheless, for most of a century, the attitude of the courts was that of grudging tolerance of organized labor and of any action it might take to gain its objectives by means of strikes.

The Supreme Court's Anti-Labor Decisions

Even in the present century labor was long under disadvantage from the interpretation by the Supreme Court of the United States of the meaning of "liberty" in the Fourteenth Amendment's provision that no state shall "deprive any person of life, liberty or property without due process of law." Thus when the State of New York sought to exercise its police power by a statute enacted as a health measure limiting labor in bakeries to sixty hours a week and ten hours a day, the Supreme Court held this to be an infringement of the liberty of workers.[1] In 1907 the United States Supreme Court held unconstitutional (as a violation of the "liberty" protected by the Fourteenth Amendment) a federal statute's outlawing "yellow dog" contracts with employees of interstate railroads.[2] Moreover the courts which hesitated to use the Sherman Anti-Trust Law of 1890 effectively against aggregations of business had so little hesitation in applying it against labor that it was sometimes ironically called the Sherman Anti-Labor Act. Thus in 1902 when the United Hatters, an AFL organization enjoying closed-shop agreements, called a strike against a hat manufacturing company in Danbury, Connecticut, that refused to accept a union demand, and organized a boycott of the company's hats, the Supreme Court of the United States held the United Hatters guilty of violation of the Sherman Act. It awarded the Danbury Hat Company the "triple damage" of the Sherman Act, and the company collected $234,000 damages from the workers. In 1911 the AFL put the Bucks Stove and Range Company on its "We Don't Patronize" list following a strike of the company's workers provoked by the discharge of leaders who demanded shorter hours. When the AFL continued to publicize its list despite a court injunction, the Supreme Court of the United States upheld jail sentences of the Federation's officers, which however were never served.

Federal Legislation to Check the Courts

In an effort to stop the courts from using anti-trust laws against labor, Congress enacted and President Wilson signed an appropriation bill with a provision that none of the money appropriated was to be used to enforce anti-trust laws against labor. Moreover the Clayton Anti-Trust Law enacted in 1914 provided "that the labor of a human being is not a commodity or article of commerce" and that labor organizations shall not "Be held or be construed to be illegal combinations or conspiracies in restraint of trade under the anti-trust laws." Thereupon Samuel

[1] Lochner v. New York, 198 U.S. 45 (1905).
[2] 208 U.S. 172 (1907). "Yellow Dog" contracts required, as a condition of employment, that the employee agree to an automatic discharge if he joined a labor union.

Gompers, the leading labor leader in the United States, hailed the Clayton Act as "Labor's Magna Carta." Nevertheless in 1921, when the Machinist Union of Battle Creek, Michigan, refused to install or work on any newspaper presses made by the Duplex Printing Press Company because the latter refused to meet the terms of its employees, an injunction was obtained against the sympathetic boycott and the Supreme Court of the United States sustained the injunction.[3] In 1925 the Supreme Court held that the United Mineworkers in Arkansas had violated the Sherman Anti-Trust Act in destroying mining property and coal during a clash with guards and strikebreakers following the company's breach of union agreement.[4] And in 1927 when the Stone Cutters Union members refused to work on stone from certain Indiana quarries that had gone on a company-union basis after refusing to renew agreements with the Stone Cutters' Union, an injunction against them was upheld by the Supreme Court. The union was declared guilty of violating the Sherman Anti-Trust Act. Up to the beginning of the 1940's Congress appeared to be utterly unable to prevent laws intended to check monopolistic practices of business from being turned instead against labor by a Court unable to see that the pre-Industrial Revolution dogmas of *laissez faire* were outmoded. In finally reversing its trend, the Supreme Court concluded that the Norris–La Guardia and Clayton Acts together showed that Congress intended to make labor-union activity no longer absolutely subject to injunction and prosecution under the Sherman Anti-Trust Act.

FEDERAL LABOR LEGISLATION

The Beginning of Federal Labor Legislation

In 1888, 1898, and 1913 Congress enacted legislation providing for mediation and voluntary arbitration in labor disputes on railroads in interstate commerce. But in 1916 these devices proved unable to settle the demands of the railway unions for an eight-hour day, with time and a half for overtime. The railroads agreed to arbitrate but the employees refused. With a strike set for Labor Day a crisis was faced by the nation. Congress promptly passed the Adamson Act granting practically what labor was demanding. A case was rushed up to the Supreme Court, which was apparently unable to reach a decision, whereupon the brotherhoods again threatened strike and the railroads granted the demands now that the nation was apparently on the brink of World War I.

New Deal Labor Legislation

In June, 1933, Congress enacted the National Industrial Recovery Act which provided for codes of fair competition and for a public works program. According to the Act each industry formulated its own code

[3] Duplex Printing Press Co. *v.* Deering, 254 U.S. 443 (1921).
[4] Colorado Coal Co. *v.* United Mine Workers 268 U.S. 295 (1925).

but was required to incorporate in it Section 7a. This section provided maximum hours for men and women. Each code was required to state specifically that workers "shall have the right to organize and bargain collectively through representatives of their own choosing . . . free from interference, restraint or coercion of employers or their agents" and that no worker "shall be required as a condition of employment to join any company union or to refrain from joining, organizing, or assisting a labor organization of his own choosing." By implication at least the Act was presumed to have outlawed "yellow dog" contracts, labor spies, and company unions. To administer the Act the National Labor Relations Board was established by executive order of the President. The Board gradually came to interpret Section 7a to mean that the employer had to negotiate in good faith with representatives of the majority of his employees as determined by an election conducted by the Board, but since the Board's authority rested upon executive order instead of statutes, some employers obtained injunctions against the Board's decision.

Depression Legislation

The administration of Franklin Roosevelt broke precedent in its provision for federal relief of unemployment. Over a hundred years earlier President Monroe, in a presidential message during the disastrous depression of the 1820's, had congratulated manufacturers on the "fall in the price of labor, so favorable to the success of domestic manufacturers." President Van Buren had expressed the view that the federal government had no obligation to provide relief during the depression of the 1830's and in his inaugural address of March 4, 1893, President Cleveland had declared, "The lessons of paternalism ought to be unlearned and the better lesson taught that while the people should patriotically and cheerfully support their government, its functions do not include support of the people."

Such an attitude could not be sustained during the Great Depression of the 1930's. The resources of state and local government and of private charity had been exhausted early in the 1930's while unemployment mounted to an estimated total of more than ten million. The first emergency relief agency created was the Civilian Conservation Corps by which 350,000 young men were assembled in camps and set to work reforesting sites and rehabilitating depleted soil. The Federal Emergency Relief Administration, established in 1933, distributed half a billion dollars for direct emergency relief to states and local communities. The National Recovery Act of the same year provided a comprehensive system of public works including highways, parkways, river and harbor improvements, slum clearance, conservation of natural resources and of water power, construction of public buildings, low-cost houses, hospitals, public swimming pools, sewage plants, and other projects. The Public Works Administration organized and coordinated the entire system of public works and 4,000,000 men were promptly set to work on the clearance, construction, and clerical service required for projects deemed socially worth while and at wages adjusted to the scale prevailing in the local communities. Meanwhile the federal government contributed direct relief to drought and flood victims and to farmers cultivating marginal land. A United States Employment Service was set up to coordinate corresponding state services.

In 1935 Congress created the Works Progress Administration and appropriated $4,880,000 to continue and organize better the providing of jobs for the unemployed, to stimulate private business by putting the money into circulation, and to inaugurate and stimulate needed reforms in states indisposed or unable to finance them. Inevitably confusion, waste, and maladministration developed from much of this work which, in the absence of precedents, had to be started from scratch. The pioneering character of the relief projects is indicated by the federal arts, writers, and theater programs supported by federal funds. Thus unemployed writers produced useful state, regional, and city guides, organized state and local archives, indexed newspaper files, and worked on valuable historical and sociological investigations. Artists decorated hundreds of post offices, schools, and other public buildings with murals, generally of high standards of artistry. Unemployed musicians organized symphony orchestras and community singing, while scores of stock companies toured the country presenting old and new plays. Thus precious social values were preserved not only in the human resources conserved but also in the inestimable cultural values not permitted to deteriorate or perish.

The National Labor Relations Act

In May, 1935, the Supreme Court unanimously invalidated the National Industrial Recovery Act on the grounds that it was not a regulation of interstate commerce and therefore unconstitutionally infringed on the reserved powers of the states. This decision struck down Section 7a, preventing further expansion under its protection of trade unions and imperiling the gains already made by labor. Most larger firms were refusing to bargain with unions and also trying to prevent organization of their employees. In a sense the Wagner Act, enacted in 1935, sought to give statutory force to the defunct Section 7a of the NIRA. It thus attempted to protect employee self-organization and to encourage collective bargaining by requiring employers to negotiate with the authorized representatives of their employees. Government intervention was limited to the preliminaries of collective bargaining. Strikes and lockouts even in violation of agreements were no concern of the government. The restrictions were all directed at the employers, who were not to dominate or interfere with the formation or organization of labor, not to encourage or discourage union membership or discriminate in any way against organized labor, not to penalize in any way employees for filing charges or testifying under the act, and not to refuse to bargain, in good faith, collectively with representatives of the employees to be certified by the National Labor Relations Board.

The National Labor Relations Board

The Wagner Act created the National Labor Relations Board to administer the Act by deciding cases and issuing orders against violations of the Act. Thus the government, instead of the union, investigated and prosecuted before a trial examiner and the Board; but the courts had final authority. The Board might order employers to dissolve company unions or to negotiate with a union in good faith under penalty of contempt of court and issue "cease and desist orders." So confident were the legal advisers of employers that, in the light of precedents, the Act was unconstitutional, that employers quite generally ignored the Act. To their astonishment the Supreme Court sustained the Wagner Act as a constitutional regulation of interstate commerce.

Wartime Restrictions of Labor

With strikes ranging from 3,000 to 5,000 annually during World War II, labor fell under severe public criticism as such conduct was viewed as unpatriotic. Under the circumstances their grievances received scant attention. Because the Wagner Act had failed to provide any means for settlement of labor disputes, a National Defense Mediation Board was established by executive order in 1941 before we were at war. After Congress had declared war, President Roosevelt persuaded labor and industry to agree to refrain from strikes and lockouts for the duration of the war and submit labor disputes to the War Labor Board. But the Board suffered severe damage when its CIO members resigned because it had ruled against the Mine Workers' demand for a closed shop in captive mines though the demand was granted later by special arbitration. Nevertheless the War Labor Board succeeded in minimizing lost time from labor disputes. In nearly 40 cases, however, the President felt impelled to seize the property of firms refusing to comply with the Board's "directive orders." The Board's prestige was saved by the fact that its twelve members included an equal representation of labor, industry, and the public. But the restlessness of labor under the wage ceilings compelled the Board to ease tensions by increasing "fringe" benefits.

When the United Mine Workers, in the midst of the war, stopped work, Congress passed, over the President's veto, the War Labor Disputes Act (1943) which marked the turning point after ten years of legislation favorable to labor. This Act required a thirty-day notice after a majority vote of labor by secret ballot before striking; authorized the President to seize labor disrupted plants when necessary to prosecute the war; forbade any person to promote work stoppage of a seized plant; and prohibited union contributions to the election of federal officers. The strike provision was incompatible with labor's no-strike agreement since it provided a formula for legalizing a strike while labor was in honor bound not to strike. In any case the law proved so futile that violations of it were never prosecuted. The law signified the now rising tide against labor.

The Taft-Hartley Law

In the middle thirties the opinion polls had revealed a remarkably strong public sentiment in favor of organized labor. This tended, however, to evaporate under the conduct of labor in its new-found powers assured by the Wagner Act. The battle between the rival AFL and CIO was damaging to the prestige of the Unions. Even, to many impartial observers, the Act seemed one-sided in its restrictions on management while labor seemed to have a free hand. An impression grew that unions were becoming too strong, and that the workers needed to be protected from union power, and employers from having to agree to such things as the closed shop, automatic check off, exactions for services not performed, and union-controlled welfare funds. However the Wagner Act stood for twelve years, until the passage of the Taft-Hartley Law.

The Taft-Hartley Law aimed to balance provisions of the Wagner Act by outlawing certain specific unfair practices of labor as well as unfair practices of employers. Included in the Law were clauses that authorized damage suits against labor for violations of agreements, prohibited contributions or use of union dues for primaries or elections for federal office, required non-Communist affidavits for union officials, and prohibited strikes of employees of the federal government or of federally owned corporations. The Law outlawed the unfair labor practices forbidden employers by the Wagner Act. But now labor was not to coerce workers to join a union, or to coerce an employer to do certain specified things, or to coerce employees to engage in a strike. Technically, the Taft-Hartley Law is a revision of the Wagner Act, which evidently experience had shown needed some changes. Unfortunately labor refused to participate in the revision, and this accounts for some of its defects. When the Law was two years old, its principal sponsor, Senator Taft, submitted a list of 28 changes which he and his Republican colleagues proposed. Organized labor continued to denounce the statute as a "slave labor act" and demanded its absolute repeal, but opinion polls revealed that a substantial per cent of the workers themselves were satisfied with the law.

LABOR STANDARDS LEGISLATION

The Cultural Lag on Labor Legislation

The indubitable facts concerning labor conditions in factories following the Industrial Revolution seem almost incredible today. The cultural lag here was due to the application of the at least tolerable customs, usages, and common law principles that applied to outdoor and domestic labor before that Revolution. There was the Hope Factory in Rhode Island in 1811 with its summertime schedule of over 15 hours a day within the factory; work started at 4:30 in the morning, and there were only two respites of 25 minutes each for a cold breakfast and a cold dinner. More than half the operatives were children, largely and sometimes entirely deprived by continuous employment of opportunity for schooling. Factory conditions were unhealthful, machinery was dangerous, and home living conditions were intolerable in the crowded housing about the factories. Every piece of legislation to correct these primitive industrial conditions was bitterly contested by many employers.

Legislation setting labor standards came later in the United States than in most industrial nations, and it had its feeble and faltering beginnings necessarily in the states. Here the reserved powers of the states included the vast scope of the police power, that is, the power to restrain personal freedom and property rights of persons for the maintenance of public safety, health, and morals or for the promotion of public convenience and prosperity. Here was a state power that ran counter to the once sanctified dogmas of *laissez faire* and the pre-Industrial-Revolution principles of common law governing labor-employer relations. It was long assumed that the states monopolized the police power. Belatedly, legislators discovered that the federal government also had police power as an incident of the power to tax, to regulate interstate and foreign commerce, and to establish post offices.

Early Federal Legislation on Standards

There were four fields of employment in which federal jurisdiction over labor standards was recognized before 1940—the Federal establishment itself, public contracts, the railroads, and the merchant marine. In 1840 the ten-hour day was established in governmental navy yards by executive order of the President. The eight-hour day was adopted for governmental employees and workers on public contracts in 1869, although this requirement was not seriously enforced until 1912. The Adamson Act of 1916, passed under the threat of a nation-wide railroad strike, provided a basic eight-hour day for workers in that industry. Working hours of seamen have been regulated since 1913 by act of Congress. The legislative principle that wages of mechanics and laborers in federal employment should conform to those in private industry has long been recognized; and in 1931 this principle was extended to private contractors on federal public works. The Walsh-Healey Act of 1936 went one step further, and covered all employers supplying the federal government with goods or services. Under the Walsh-Healey Act the secretary of labor periodically certified minimum rates of pay and other standards in each industry and locality. These certifications then became binding upon all who provided government supplies.

Legislation Regulating Labor of Women and Children

States began regulating the labor of women and children as early as the 1840's but regulation was feeble and largely ineffective prior to the advances made between 1907 and 1917. By 1908 the United States Supreme Court upheld the constitutionality of state legislation setting an eight-hour day for women. States had been enacting minimum-wage laws for women for nearly ten years when the Supreme Court of the United States, in 1923, struck down such an act of Congress for the District of Columbia as a denial to the employee and employer of "freedom of contract" which, the Court held, Congress was prevented from denying to any person by the "due process" provision of the Fifth Amendment. Since the Fourteenth Amendment places precisely the same "due process" restriction on states, minimum-wage legislation was delayed for many years in the states also.

Federal Child Labor Legislation

There is no more dismal chapter in the history of our social legislation than that of the prolonged frustrating struggle for federal child-labor legislation. Senator Albert J. Beveridge's futile efforts in 1906–07 to get such federal legislation enacted encountered the economic opposition of those who employed children, the dogmatic charge that it was a socialistic measure, and the constitutional argument that the federal power to regulate commerce did not extend to such manufacturing. When, in 1916, Congress passed a law prohibiting interstate shipment of goods produced by child labor, the Supreme Court of the United States held the act unconstitutional on the grounds, among others, that the goods themselves were harmless and that the commerce clause gave Congress no power to regulate conditions of manufacture. Congress then turned to the taxing power, which had often been used for regulative purposes, and laid a tax on goods knowingly produced by child labor. The Supreme Court of the United States rejected this on the ground that it was a use of the federal taxing power to exercise a power of regulation solely within the regulative power of the states. Thus the Court utilized the now outmoded and rejected principle of constitutional interpretation that a reserved power of the states can cancel a delegated power of the federal government. Congress next proposed an amendment that would grant Congress the power to regulate child labor, but it encountered furious opposition; this did not matter in the long run as the Supreme Court in 1941 reversed itself on Hammer *v.* Dagenhart, by which it had invalidated the first child-labor act of Congress.

Today federal regulation of child labor is provided by the Walsh-Healey Public Contracts Act of 1936 and the Fair Labor Standards Act of 1938. The former prohibits employment of girls under 18 and boys under 16 on government contracts. The latter prohibits employment in interstate commerce of persons under 16 for most jobs, under 18 for hazardous jobs, and under 15 for employment outside of school hours in a limited number of jobs, principally nonagricultural. These prohibitions then applied only to children engaged *in* interstate commerce and not to production *for* interstate commerce. In 1949 amendments corrected this defect by banning both kinds of production by children. Additional restrictions were also enacted in 1949 on employment of children during school hours where the "production is for interstate commerce."

The Fair Labor Standards Act

The Fair Labor Standards Act of 1938 was the first major effort of Congress to regulate wages and hours of workers in interstate commerce or in production of goods for interstate commerce. The original law set the minimum wage at 25 cents an hour but it was raised successively until in 1955 it was set at $1.00 an hour. The Act set maximum hours at 40 per week for those coming under the Act, with one and one-half pay for hours above the maximum. Thus the law does not prevent more than 40 hours work per week but merely imposes a penalty upon the employer for hours beyond the set maximum. Supplementing the Fair Labor Standards Act is the Walsh-Healey Public Contracts Act which requires that "prevailing" hourly rates be paid by all employers with government contracts in excess of $10,000 and a minimum wage is established for each industry.

SOCIAL SECURITY

Workers' Insecurity

Although the problem of economic insecurity is not new, in recent years there have been increasingly insistent demands for protection against interruption of income. The risk of dependency in old age has become more and more serious: families are smaller and more dispersed; the proportion of older persons in the population has increased; interest rates on savings have fallen; and urban patterns of living have replaced rural patterns. As our economy has become more highly mechanized and productive, it has also become more subject to fluctuations. The risk of involuntary unemployment is never far from the forefront of workers' minds. Industrial accidents and diseases take a sizable toll of lives each year and leave many other workers partially or totally disabled. One of the chief risks is that of ordinary illness, nonindustrial in origin, which not only interrupts the flow of income but also frequently requires heavy expenditures for medical care and hospitalization. The problem of dependency among widows, fatherless children, and physically handicapped persons must be added to the list.[5]

Genesis of the Federal Social Security Program

The central idea in a program of social security is that these economic risks should be assumed by society at large rather than by each separate

[5] Lewis Merriam, *Relief and Social Security* (Washington, 1946).

individual. We do not expect a householder to go out and purchase a fire engine when his house catches fire. By the same token we have erected a structure of financial protection to assist the worker and his family in meeting the burden of living costs when income is cut off through no fault of his own. We in the United States were relatively late in deciding that such a structure of protection should be established. Throughout the 1920's we believed that our system of free enterprise provided well-being for all who deserved to enjoy it. During the early 1930's provision for dependency was on an emergency relief basis. (One exception should be noted: industrial accidents and diseases were covered by workmen's compensation laws in most of the states.) Movements such as the Townsend Plan and "Thirty Dollars Every Thursday" began to flourish; demagogues, capitalizing on insecurity and discontent, attracted a large following. Gradually the conviction grew that the prevalent hit-or-miss expedients should be replaced with a systematic, articulated program. Out of this conviction a number of major decisions crystallized in 1935. Responsibility for work relief was assumed by the federal government; direct relief of "unemployables" was turned back to the states; and a long-range program of social insurance and public assistance was established in the Social Security Act.[6]

Old Age Insurance

The distinction between social insurance and public assistance lies in the method of financing. Social insurance benefits are financed out of premiums or "contributions"; as in the case of private life insurance the size and duration of benefits are related more or less directly to the amount of contributions previously paid in. Public assistance is financed out of general government revenues and ordinarily is provided on the basis of need. The Social Security Act provides for both types of benefits for elderly persons. Employers and employees each pay a tax on monthly payrolls of 2 per cent, increasing to 2½ per cent in 1960, 3 per cent in 1965, 3½ per cent in 1970, and 4½ per cent in 1975 and thereafter. Earnings in excess of $4,200 per year are not taxed. Monthly benefits are paid when the worker retires after reaching the age of sixty-five. Benefits are also paid to the retired worker's wife, if she has reached retirement age, and to dependent children under eighteen years of age who are still in school. Widows and children of deceased workers receive survivor's insurance benefits. Monthly payments are computed according to a complicated formula.

Old Age Assistance

The Social Security Act establishes a federal-state assistance program for special groups solely on the basis of their needs. The largest of these groups are aged workers who cannot qualify for old-age survivors insurance. Under the provisions of the federal Social Security Act each

[6] William Withers, *Financing Economic Security in the United States* (New York, 1939), pp. 21–85.

state adopts and administers its own type of public assistance but the state plan must meet requirements set forth in the Act if it is to receive the federal grants for that purpose. The amount of the grant is based on the amount the state expends within certain maximums for public-assistance payments. The federal government also shares half the cost of state administration of old-age assistance. Recipients of aid must be at least 65 years of age. The program of Old Age Assistance has undoubtedly relieved much distress among the aged. Yet the level of assistance was inadequate at the beginning and has in addition fallen behind increasing costs despite the increase of federal contributions to the states.

Unemployment Compensation

The purpose of unemployment compensation is to aid workers in tiding themselves over a period of short-time unemployment. Even during prosperity several million workers must make this change from one job to another every year, to say nothing of those who remain unemployed for longer periods. Prior to the passage of the Social Security Act there had been much debate about whether unemployment compensation should be placed on a state or federal basis. Eventually a system of federal-state cooperation was decided upon. Each state enacts its own unemployment insurance law and administers its own program, with federal grants to pay the cost of state administration. The federal act sets up minimum standards of state administration designed to ensure payments to workers whose previous employment entitles them to such payments under state law and to safeguard the worker's rights when he does not take a job that fails to meet certain labor standards. The United States Employment Service, functioning through the Bureau of Employment Security, operates to shorten the worker's period of unemployment by discovering suitable employment for him. Under the Federal Unemployment Tax Act a federal tax is levied upon employers throughout the country but a credit is allowed them up to 90 per cent of this tax for contributions they pay to state unemployment funds.

The Employment Act of 1946

Before World War II had ended, there developed a deep-seated and widespread concern over the depression and enormous unemployment deemed inevitable following the war, during the period of reconversion of the economic system from production of war material to peacetime demands. During the fall of 1944 *Fortune* conducted a poll on the question "Do you think the federal government should provide jobs for everyone able and willing to work but who cannot get a job in private employment"; slightly more than two thirds of those polled answered in the affirmative. A well-organized movement emerged that did not rest until a bill to this end had been put through Congress.[7] Because the ex-

[7] A fascinating account of this movement and its activities in managing the measure during its tortuous career through Senate and House is found in Stephan K. Bailey's *Congress Makes a Law* (New York: Columbia University Press, 1950).

pected widespread unemployment failed to develop and even labor shortages were increasing while the bill was going through Congress, the promoters saw their original proposed measure considerably watered down by conservatives, and what started out as the Full Employment Act was passed as simply the Employment Act.

The Employment Act constitutes a landmark in the history of our national economic policies. The Declaration of Policy of the Act states: "The Congress hereby declares that it is the continuing policy and responsibility of the Federal Government to use all practical means, consistent with its needs and obligations and other essential conditions of national policy, . . . to promote maximum employment, production and purchasing power." To this end the Act requires the President to submit to Congress near the beginning of each session an Economic Report setting forth "the levels of employment, production and purchasing power obtaining in the United States and such levels needed to carry out the policy . . . [of the Act]; current and foreseeable trends in the levels of employment, production and purchasing power; a review of the economic program of the federal government and a review of economic conditions affecting employment in the United States or any considerable portion thereof during the preceding year and of their effect upon employment, production and purchasing power; and a program for carrying out the policy . . . [of the Act], together with such recommendations for legislation as he may deem necessary or desirable."

To carry out the purposes of the Employment Act, Congress created an Economic Council of three experts appointed by the President with the advice and consent of the Senate and located in the Office of the President. The Act also provides for the creation of a Joint Congressional Committee on the Economic Report of the President which, after the study of the President's recommendations, reports its recommendations to Congress. These Economic Reports have been coming out twice a year but during the prevailing high production and moderate unemployment prevailing since 1946 there has been no test of the efficacy of the Act. A test will no doubt come when a sharp decline in economic activity occurs. It remains to be seen whether Congress will exercise a control of taxation, the Budget, and public expenditures constituting a counter effect to a depression. So far there is no indication that Congress will act in anticipation of a decline and indeed there are specialists who deny that depressions can be foreseen with sufficient certainty to prepare for them in advance. The Act itself was prepared because of a depression that failed to materialize.

SUMMARY

Until about a century ago state courts, applying principles of common law, penalized labor unions as conspiracies in restraint of trade and sentenced strikers to jail. After the adoption of the Fourteenth Amendment the Supreme Court of the United States began holding some state legislation, designed to protect labor's rights, as violations of the "liberty" of the due process provision. After 1890 the Sherman Anti-Trust Law was turned against labor, and efforts of Congress, by provisions of the Clayton Act (1914) to exempt labor from prosecution under anti-trust laws, were persistently frustrated by Supreme Court decisions.

Near the turn of the century Congress began enacting statutes to ensure protection of labor's rights. The first decisive federal action, however, was Section 7a of the Codes authorized by the National Recovery Act of 1933. That section ensured labor's unhampered right to bargain collectively, and it became the basis of the Wagner Act of 1935. In 1938 Congress enacted the Fair Labor Standards Act authorizing the setting of minimum wages and maximum hours for laborers whose product involved interstate commerce.

Labor controversies during World War II led to a turn in public opinion against labor that culminated in the Taft-Hartley Law (1947), designed to balance somewhat the bargaining rights of management with labor. The Supreme Court had been slow to permit Congress to safeguard the employment of women and children. Two child-labor acts were held unconstitutional, and it was not until the Fair Labor Standards Act of 1938, with its specific protection of child labor, was accepted by the Court that Congress had a free hand to legislate in that matter.

The Depression Decade brought also the Federal Social Security program with its old-age insurance, old-age assistance, and unemployment compensation. In 1946 when a gigantic postwar unemployment was generally expected, Congress enacted the Employment Act. It provides the President with a Council of Economic Advisers who study business trends and provide the President with advice on the basis of which he advises Congress as to legislation that might be enacted to maintain a stable economy.

CHAPTER XXXII

AGRICULTURE AND CONSERVATION

EARLY GOVERNMENTAL ACTIVITIES

Government Serves Agriculture in Four Fields

THE activities of the national government in the field of agriculture may be grouped under four general headings: (1) research and education, (2) regulation, (3) service, and (4) economic aids. The United States Department of Agriculture has over 70,000 full-time employees and in the year 1956 had an annual budget of one and a quarter billion dollars with which to carry on these activities. This great development of governmental activity in the interests of farmers began in the first years of our national life. Governmental activities in relation to agriculture have continued to expand primarily because of our national interest in the social and economic welfare of farm people. Society also has been concerned with the conservation of our soil and forestry resources, and a number of governmental activities, beginning as early as 1891, are directed primarily toward these ends. It was primarily our interest in the welfare of consumers, however, which led to pure-food laws and much of the other regulatory work in the field of marketing.

Continental Congress Concerned with Agriculture

The importance of the development of agriculture to the welfare of this new nation, the United States of America, was recognized by the members of the Continental Congress. Congressional action dealing with agriculture dates back to 1776 when John Adams introduced resolutions (which did not pass) to have the Continental Congress encourage agriculture. The failure of Adams' resolutions was no doubt due to the diversity of interests as between different sections of the Union. Agricultural methods were exceedingly wasteful then and indeed for generations later. Methods of tobacco culture were so soil exhausting that Virginia had passed the peak of tobacco production even before the Revolution—this accounts for Washington's persistent and successful efforts to diversify crops at Mount Vernon.

Education and Service Functions Begun in 1839

Twenty years later George Washington, in his last annual message to Congress, asked that a national board of agriculture be created. New varieties of seeds and plants were distributed to enterprising farmers by the Commission of Patents on its own initiative as early as 1836. Not until 1839, however, did the national government actually undertake responsibility for any of the functions it now performs in this field. At this time Congress passed its first appropriation for agriculture, $1,000 to be used "to distribute seeds, conduct agricultural investigations and collect agricultural statistics." Thus, over 110 years ago our Federal government began two of its present functions relative to agriculture, education and service. The collection and distribution of improved seed stocks undertaken in 1839 as a service to agriculture, to improve crop production and thus the welfare of farm people, was continued for some eighty years. By this time state agricultural experiment stations with the cooperation of the Federal government had reached a high level of efficiency in breeding new strains of plants adapted to the farms in their states. The early investigations authorized by this appropriation were the beginning of a great development in research and education relating to agriculture. The research and educational program of our national and state governments is now equalled by few nations in the world and exceeded by none.

The third activity authorized by this initial appropriation, the collection of statistics, has continued to grow until today we have the finest and most complete set of agricultural statistics of any country in the world. From these small beginnings we now gather and use data on so many subjects and in such detail that each year the Department of Agriculture publishes a book of agricultural statistics. By 1954 this book had grown to 586 pages including 787 tables. In addition thousands of printed and mimeographed reports are released each year containing statistical information on specific agricultural subjects including many detailed data for each state in the Union.

Following the small but significant beginnings in 1839, governmental activities in these fields were carried on by the Patent Office for some thirty years. During the Civil War, responding to the demand for an improved status for rural people, the need for more food, and the popular demand for a free land policy, Congress in 1862 passed a number of acts of profound importance to agriculture. Within the space of a few short months legislation was enacted (1) creating a Department of Agriculture (although it was 1889 before the Department had cabinet status), (2) making land grants to states for the establishment and support of colleges of agriculture and mechanic arts, and (3) making 160 acres of government-owned land available as a gift to families who settled on the land and met specified development requirements.

Land Grant Colleges and Experiment Stations

Few activities of the Federal government have had as great an effect on the development of agriculture as the provision for land-grant colleges made in 1862. This initial grant of government lands was followed by additional legislation and grants of funds which resulted in the establishment of an agricultural and engineering college and a state agricultural experiment station in each state. In some states these colleges of agriculture and mechanic arts were made a part of the state university; in others they were established as separate institutions. Several states had established such institutions before this legislation was passed, and the grant of funds made expansion possible. These colleges of agriculture and mechanic arts grew out of the popular demand of the people for education in the occupational fields of the bulk of the nation's citizens. Soon after they started functioning it became apparent that there was little up-to-date subject matter to teach. Teachers and the general public soon came to recognize the need for organized research and experimentation in agriculture.

In 1887 a national charter was granted for Federal-state agricultural experiment stations to be operated a part of the colleges of agriculture and mechanic arts. This gave farmers a research organization comparable to that developed for industry by the large manufacturing corporations. Workers at the experiment stations analyzed the value of mineral fertilizers, measured the productivity of various crop rotations, developed improved strains of seeds, studied the functions of proteins and minerals in live-stock rations, perfected methods of determining the butter-fat content in milk, and conducted other researches and experiments too numerous to mention. Major credit is usually given to this research and educational program for the rapid technological progress by American farmers in the past fifty years. In the early years research and resident instruction at the land-grant colleges were supplemented by off-campus educational programs for farmers. Requests for an expansion of this adult-education program and the desire for increased food production during World War I led to the establishment in 1914 of what is now known as the Federal-state agricultural extension service. This is now a vast educational program cooperatively financed by local, state, and national funds employing one or more county agricultural extension agents and home demonstration agents in most counties in the United States. A state agricultural extension service is now a major part of each agricultural college.

Three years after setting up the Federal-state agricultural extension service, Congress rounded out its support for education in agriculture and home economics by providing grants of funds to high schools for vocational training in these subjects.

The Family Farm and the Homestead Act of 1862

The family farm is today considered one of the great stabilizing institutions in rural life. To a large extent it is a heritage of the aspirations of the families who settled along the northern Atlantic seaboard in early colonial days. But the family farm from time to time has been strengthened by governmental policies. One of the most important of these was the Homestead Act passed in 1862. Under other conditions government-owned land might all have been sold in large units to wealthy individuals. But the tradition of family farm ownership and operation led to strong popular support for donating enough government land for a farm to each family that requested it. Accordingly in 1862 a law was passed granting 160 acres of public land to each family that met minimum development requirements. Although this Act came after most of the better farming areas had been settled, both satisfied a widespread popular demand and started a tradition in favor of governmental policies to strengthen the family farm.

Early Regulatory Activities

Governmental regulation in the field of agriculture began in 1884. The dramatic situation out of which this new area of governmental activity was born has been described as follows: "Another infection [of pleuro-pneumonia] broke out in 1859 in Massachusetts; it had been brought there by four cows from the Netherlands. Port inspectors saw that the animals were sick, but the infection escaped, and within four years it had appeared in 20 towns in Massachusetts. Soon it developed in Connecticut, Delaware, Pennsylvania, Virginia, and the District of Columbia. Alarmed cattlemen demanded joint action by the states, but the states could not get together. It was necessary to invoke federal action. Congress had to pass laws to provide funds and to create an administrative organization, for it was a new type of emergency." [1]

From this small beginning regulatory activities were soon extended to include prevention of interstate movement of insect pests of plants, inspection of articles of food and drugs to prevent adulteration and misbranding, inspection of meat, inspection of dairy products for export. These and other regulatory activities have been designed to control the spread of animal diseases and insect pests, and to prevent the sale to farmers of adulterated or misbranded seeds, insecticides, feeds, fertilizers, and other supplies used in farm production. They also have been designed to prevent the sale of diseased or spoiled meats, dairy products, and other sub-standard farm products which may adversely affect the market for all producers. While much of the present regulatory work of the government was begun before World War I, substantial extensions of regulatory activities have been made in recent years. A general picture of the regulatory activities of the government as they existed following World War II will be presented later.

Early Conservation Efforts

We turn now to another early activity of the government, conservation of forest resources. By the year 1876 Congress became concerned about our

[1] Arthur P. Chew: *The Response of Government to Agriculture* (Washington, D.C., 1939), p. 31.

dwindling forest resources and authorized a study of methods of encouraging timber growing and forest protection. [2] A forestry research and educational unit was formed in the Department of Agriculture several years later. Government sponsorship of forestry research and education was followed by congressional action in 1891 setting aside forestry reserves from the public domain, thus starting our present national forests. In 1911 Congress took another great step and authorized the purchase and retirement from private ownership of lands requiring permanent forest cover to stabilize the flow of navigable streams. Thus as early as 1911 our government had completely reversed its early forest land policy. Instead of getting lands into private ownership as rapidly as possible, Congress recognized its mistake and developed a comprehensive program for repurchasing strategically located forest lands. By 1929 the Forest Service was supervising 160,000,000 acres of national forest. Additional purchases each year brought the total up to 186,000,000 acres by 1954.

Governmental methods of encouraging forestry conservation, developed in these early years, have changed but little. Research and education, the first approach, is still an important part of the program. And reservation or purchase for permanent public ownership continues to be the key to conservation on a steadily increasing acreage. In 1911 a third activity was undertaken, a Federal-state fire protection program to reduce forest fire loss on both public and privately owned forests. A similar program of forest tree nurseries to supply seedlings for reforestation at nominal cost has resulted in considerable reforestation in recent years. At the present time this is the extent of government activity to conserve our forest resources. The National Forest Service has for several years recommended that Congress adopt legislation establishing standards and public controls over timber cutting on private lands in the interests of conservation, but thus far the proposal has not obtained public support.

Reclamation Work of the Government

As early as 1877 Congress passed the Desert Land Act granting title to 640 acres of arid land at $1.25 an acre if the settler met certain requirements regarding irrigating and developing it. Less than nine million acres were settled under this Act and in 1894 and subsequent years grants of arid lands were made by the Federal government to the Western states on condition that they provide for the development of irrigation on them. [3] Throughout this period there was substantial irrigation development by individuals, by partnerships, and by cooperative associations. Usually these irrigation developments were relatively small. By 1902 the demand for direct Federal help in constructing the larger and more expensive irrigation works was irresistible. At this time the first Reclamation Act was passed providing for governmental construction of irrigation works with the costs

[2] Ibid., p. 43.
[3] R. R. Renne: *Land Economics* (New York, 1947), p. 358.

charged to the users of the water. The first Act provided for repayment of construction costs over a ten-year period. This proved to be too short a period, in part because some of the projects were ill-advised, and Congress from time to time has passed legislation extending payment periods and writing off a part of the debts of the reclamation projects. A Water Facilities Act in 1937 extended Federal assistance to farmers in the arid and semi-arid areas. This Act was designed to aid farmers in developing water facilities such as small reservoirs, dams, and wells where large irrigation works are not feasible.

The Federal government had completed irrigation works for four million acres of land by 1949 and had plans for developing irrigation for ten million additional acres as rapidly as Congress appropriated the necessary funds. In addition these plans provided supplemental water for eleven million acres. These accomplishments and plans should be related to the total land now irrigated in the Western states—around seventeen million acres.

Two points should be noted in connection with the reclamation work of the Federal government. First, the Reclamation Bureau itself made the surveys, did the engineering and built the dams and waterways. It did not lend the money to private development and construction companies. Second, it limited to a family-farm unit the amount of government-irrigated land any individual could purchase or hold. This was to prevent speculative profits and to strengthen the family farm. Powerful interest groups in California and elsewhere were attempting to get this last provision eliminated in the postwar reclamation legislation.

THE BEGINNING OF ECONOMIC ASSISTANCE

Farm Leaders Dissatisfied with Rate of Progress

Throughout the early period just discussed American agriculture was shifting from a self-sufficing family occupation to a commercial family-farming enterprise. Machinery was introduced rapidly after the Civil War and in spite of the financial panics at irregular intervals farmers gradually came to depend more and more on markets and market prices in buying supplies and selling farm products. This was also a period of rapid industrial development: the steel industry passed through adolescence; the railroads were built from coast to coast. Farm leaders were dissatisfied with the lack of progress made in rural areas relative to the rapid development in the cities. President Roosevelt appointed a "Country Life Commission" in 1908 to study means of improving rural life. While much of the Commission's report dealt with ways and means of developing rural institutions such as churches and schools, it also reached the conclusion that farmers did not have credit facilities equal to those available to industry. On the recommendation of the Commission a group was sent to Europe to study agricultural credit, especially the cooperative land mortgage credit banks in Germany.

On their return, the members of this group recommended that the government sponsor a national farm-credit cooperative.

Federal Land Banks Established in 1916

Several years later, in 1916, the Federal Farm Loan Act was passed setting up twelve regional land banks with government capital. Borrowing farmers were required to buy stock in the land banks and thus eventually replace the government capital. Credit was to be extended by these banks on long-time amortized farm mortgages. Funds were to be obtained by the sale of mortgage-secured bonds in the private bond market. Government assistance was limited to providing the original capital and a skeleton supervisory staff. This Federal Farm Loan Act, designed to correct the inequalities in availability and cost of credit for farmers as compared with industry, marked the beginning of direct economic aids to farmers. The Land Bank system is cooperative and farmer owned. All the stock of the farm loan associations is owned by their member-borrowers.

As a result of the tightening of credit associated with the fall of prices after World War I live-stock producers asked for governmental intermediate-credit banks. Although the land banks made loans for long periods on real estate security, farmers no longer could obtain private credit for an intermediate period of a few years on their live-stock breeding herds. Legislation in 1923, creating the intermediate credit banks, required them to supply funds through local private banks.

Government Develops Grades and Standards

Commercialization of the family farm both increased the volume of products going to market and increased the farmers' vulnerability to deception and fraud practiced in the markets. This situation led to a great development in governmental grades and standards for farm products and the regulation of trading practices. As early as 1916 three such acts were passed. A Grain Standards Act provided for uniformity in the grading of grain through the establishment of governmental standards of quality and condition. A Cotton Futures Act required the use of certain types of contracts for future trading in cotton. A Federal Warehouse Act required all warehouses storing farm products for shipment in interstate commerce to obtain licenses from the secretary of agriculture. Five years later, in 1921, market regulation was extended to the public stockyards under the Packers and Stockyards Act. At short intervals throughout the 1920's additional market regulatory acts were passed until governmental regulations and standards were extended to all dealings in grain and to most perishable products moving in interstate commerce. Governmental grades and standards and marketing regulations of this period had a common purpose—to provide a more equitable framework for the functioning of free competition. This is in sharp contrast to the market regulations adopted following 1932 to be described later.

Federal Charter of Cooperatives

The sharp fall in prices after World War I led to many conferences to analyze the underlying economic causes and possible remedies. One of the proposed remedies was an expansion of farmer-controlled cooperative marketing associations. Cooperative associations on a fairly large scale date back as far as the 1870's. As early as 1865 Michigan passed a statute dealing specifically with cooperative associations. Following this, from time to time states passed "cooperative laws" dealing more or less adequately with the special problems of cooperative associations. As late as 1921, however, courts had held that cooperative associations were in violation of our anti-trust legislation. Privately owned firms objected to the competition of cooperatives and utilized all available legal weapons to prevent their development. Congress took action to strengthen the cooperative movement and to reduce the crippling legal actions of opposing business firms. The Capper-Volstead Act in 1922 defining a cooperative association, expressed Congress's support of cooperatives and exempted their usual business activities from provisions of the anti-trust legislation. The Act provided that: each member have one vote rather than one vote for each share; gains be distributed according to the patronage; there be no greater volume of business with non-members than with members; patronage refund not to exceed 8 percent; there be no restraint of trade.

The Government Enters the Marketing Field

Until 1929 governmental activities in the field of agriculture were limited to functions which would help farmers themselves to do a better job of producing farm products and selling them at the highest possible competitive prices. But the prices paid in the "freely competitive" market during the 1920's did not satisfy farm leaders. They quoted statistics to show after the war that farm prices had fallen much further than industrial prices. Farmers were in a disadvantageous economic position. Leaders placed most of the blame for the farmers' situation on the fact that unlike industry they could not benefit from protective tariffs. A part of each of the important farm products was exported. Farm prices were set in world, not domestic, markets.

On the basis of this analysis there was widespread demand for legislation "to make the tariff effective for agriculture." This culminated in the so-called McNary-Haugen bills which proposed a governmental board to maintain a fair exchange value on the domestic market for each principal crop. The board would "protect this fair exchange value from world price by a tariff fluctuating with it and with world price. [It would] organize under Federal legislative charter a private corporation to maintain this value by buying carry-over from any such crop from farmers . . . at such value. Such corporation may sell for export exportable surplus at the world price, even if less than the domestic price . . . Purchases and losses by reason of sales to export or of downward fluctuations in such fair exchange value to be financed, viz: From the worst experienced years of price, production, and surplus, determine an empirical formula, which when applied to any year will compute a percentage of price per bushel or per pound, large enough to absorb any probable loss . . . By authority of a Federal statute, collect this percentage as an . . . assessment on each pound or bushel when and as sold by the farmer. . . . Wheat, cotton, corn and oats are tentatively proposed for the operation of this plan." [4] Both in 1927 and 1928 such a measure passed Congress only to be vetoed by the president each time. The farm bloc was unable to pass the measures over the president's veto. By this time agricultural forces were mobilized. While they could not pass a measure over the president's veto they did force the political parties to include measures "to give equality to agriculture" in their 1928 campaign platforms.

Federal Farm Board Created in 1929

Hoover and his associates proposed to help farmers by setting up a Federal Farm Board which would perform two functions: assist in the organization of producers of each commodity into large national cooperatives, and stabilize market prices through loans or direct purchases, utilizing a $500,000,000 revolving fund for such purposes. Soon after his election Congress passed and President Hoover signed such a measure. The passage of the Agricultural Marketing Act establishing the Federal Farm Board Act in 1929 in a real sense marked a new departure in government relative to agriculture. In earlier credit and cooperative marketing legislation the government merely set up machinery whereby farmers could organize and solve their own problems. The government, in the case of the credit measures, furnished the original capital but the lending agencies were to be cooperatively owned or, in the case of intermediate credit, were to be existing credit agencies already dealing directly with farmers. The difference may be one of degree rather than kind but in 1929 for the first time a Federal governmental agency was given funds and a mandate to "operate in the market" to stabilize farm prices.

Federal Farm Board Failed

Our present price support legislation is an outgrowth of experience with this and directly related subsequent legislation. The experience of the Federal Farm Board was most disappointing. At the time of its creation $500,000,000 appeared to be a large fund for stabilization purposes but the Great Depression of the 1930's proved more than a match for the revolving fund. It was all obligated in the first months of the Board's operation

[4] Chester C. Davis: "The Development of Agricultural Policy Since the End of the World War," in *Yearbook of Agriculture* (Washington, D. C., 1940), pp. 302–3.

without effectively stopping the decline in farm prices. Farm Board members became convinced that acreage reductions must accompany government price stabilization measures if they were to be successful in periods of declining demand. The Farm Board and its methods were discredited in the public mind but the groundwork was laid for even more governmental participation in the farm economy. Under the economic pressures of the depression farmers asked for and obtained even more direct governmental aid in spite of the failure of the first attempt.

GROWTH OF GOVERNMENTAL ACTIVITIES SINCE 1932

Governmental Action to Obtain Production Adjustments

The cataclysmic economic events of the Great Depression removed all effective opposition to farm relief proposals. During the presidential campaign of 1932 the Democratic party promised a farm program which would permit farmers to control their acreages and the marketing of farm products and allow local communities to maintain a maximum of local control over governmental policies. After the election the question was not whether there was to be new farm relief legislation, it was what to include in the new legislation. A bill was passed that included authority to adjust production, regulate marketing through voluntary agreements, subsidize exports, and engage in a number of other activities. An Agricultural Adjustment Administration was set up under this new legislation. Largely as a result of the unfortunate experience of the Federal Farm Board the new Agricultural Adjustment Administration decided to enter into contracts with individual farmers to reduce production of the major farm products—corn and hogs, wheat, cotton, tobacco, and rice. Processing taxes were levied on each commodity to accumulate funds to pay farmers for reducing their crop acreages and their hog production.

It is important to note that this new governmental activity at first only involved the voluntary cooperation of farmers. Payments were set high enough to make it profitable for farmers to comply with the acreage reduction goals. Primarily because of these attractive payments but also because of strong local support for the program most producers cooperated on this voluntary basis.

Compulsory Controls Tried for Cotton and Tobacco

Enthusiasm for governmental action to adjust production to declining demands reached such heights among cotton and tobacco growers, however, that they sponsored compulsory control legislation. Under new legislation passed by Congress in 1934 each farmer could market only as much cotton or tobacco as could be grown on his allotted acreage at average yields. Cotton or tobacco offered for sale in excess of this amount was subject to a special tax. This effectively forced full compliance with the allotments and restricted the efforts to increase yields on the allotted acreage.

Adverse Supreme Court Ruling, 1936

Objections to this new agricultural legislation, as might be expected, came from the payers of the processing taxes, not the farmers. By 1936 such a case reached the Supreme Court. "What was involved? A processor objected to the payment of the tax on the ground that it was unconstitutional. In rendering the opinion of the Court, Justice Roberts said that the tax was a mere incident in the regulation of agricultural production. . . .

"The Court found that the tax here and the appropriation of the funds and the directions for their disbursement are but parts of the plan to regulate and control agricultural production which is a purely local purpose, and therefore, unless expressly granted to the Federal government by the Constitution, is a power retained by the states, under the Tenth Amendment. At best it is a scheme for purchasing with Federal funds submission to Federal regulation of a subject reserved to the states. Hence the Act was held unconstitutional." [5]

Agricultural Controls, 1936–38

Farm and public sentiment was overwhelmingly in favor of continuing the farm program in spite of the Supreme Court decision. The question was how to draft legislation which was constitutional. Within a few months the Administration hit upon the idea of expanding a recent Soil Conservation Act to authorize payments to farmers for shifting from the soil-depleting cotton, tobacco, and grain crops, to soil-conserving legumes and grasses. Funds for such payments were authorized from general Treasury appropriations to replace the funds raised by processing taxes. Annual appropriations of around $500,000,000 were made in the early years. The government no longer contracted with individual farmers. Instead it offered them specified payments if they held their listed soil depleting crops within certain limits—usually 15 to 20 per cent below recent acreages—and shifted this land to soil-conserving crops.

Production Controls Under the Interstate Commerce Clause

Excellent crops in 1937 convinced the administration that more effective production controls were needed. By this time lawyers in the Department of Agriculture developed a new legal basis for action. According to George W. Rightmire, "this new art in statute writing to place jurisdiction within the sweep of the 'Commerce' clause, remained unused until the New Deal era had passed through its early legislative experiments. . . .

"In formulating an amended A.A.A. in 1937 and a new act in 1938, the

[5] George W. Rightmire: *Federal Aid and Regulation of Agriculture and Private Industrial Enterprise in the United States* (Columbus, Ohio, 1943), pp. 22–3.

law-makers emphasize the need of reform in conditions which are creating burdens, obstructions and injurious effects upon interstate commerce. The A.A.A. II (1938 Act) completely illustrates the new art of statute writing where interstate commerce is to be involved . . .

"The general policy is declared to be 'to regulate interstate and foreign commerce in cotton, wheat, corn, tobacco and rice to the extent necessary to provide an orderly, adequate and balanced flow of such commodities in interstate and foreign commerce, through storage of reserves, loans, marketing quotas, assisting farmers to obtain, in so far as practicable, parity prices for such commodities, and parity of income, and assisting consumers to obtain an adequate and steady supply . . . at fair prices.'

"Meticulous definitions of terms employed are set out and when 'marketing quotas' are reached we see the peak of the new art of statute writing, which aims at fully advising the courts. In the case of each commodity for which a marketing quota is prescribed, the initial section opens with the statement of the subject: 'Legislative finding of effect upon interstate and foreign commerce and necessity for regulation.' " [6]

This new 1938 Act, relying on authority under the commerce clause, went far toward re-establishing compulsory production and marketing controls. Under the marketing quota provisions whenever reserve supply levels of the important crops reached certain levels producers by a two-thirds majority vote could impose marketing quota restrictions on themselves. These marketing quotas effectively restricted production by placing a high tax on produce offered for sale when grown outside the allotted acreages. The efforts of Congress to make the legislation constitutional were entirely successful, for the cotton, tobacco, wheat, and peanut producers have all voted marketing quotas for themselves at one time or another without the constitutionality of the Act being successfully challenged. Thus we find the government today, under specific conditions spelled out in detail in legislation, permitting farmers to vote compulsory production and marketing controls on themselves while utilizing the government's taxing power as a means of enforcement.

Government Farm Price Supports

Agricultural price supports were the focal point of much public discussion following World War II. By that time they had come to play a dominant role in governmental activities relative to agriculture. As pointed out earlier the Federal Farm Board first attempted to stabilize prices with governmental loans and purchases. In spite of the Farm Board's disastrous experience, non-recourse commodity loans were made a part of the New Deal agricultural program. Farmers who cooperated in the crop acreage adjustment programs were eligible to borrow money on their stored crops, often at rates above existing market levels. If the market price did not rise to the loan level by the end of the loan period, the govern-

[6] Ibid., pp. 24–7.

ment accepted delivery of crops in full repayment of the loan. Hence the title "non-recourse" loans—the government had no recourse to other assets owned by the farmer in case the crop was not worth the face value of the note at maturity date. Early experience of the new Commodity Credit Corporation with these loans was as satisfactory as the Farm Board experience had been unsatisfactory. A combination of factors— rising general price level from the bottom of the depression, two serious droughts in 1934 and 1936 causing temporary shortages, the acreage adjustment programs, and finally, the demands of World War II—all combined to give the Commodity Credit Corporation a substantial profit on its lending operations through the war period. These non-recourse commodity loans were highly popular with farmers. They represented minimum prices or price floors for their products.

With this background of recent favorable experience and a governmental agency at hand to do the job, it was only natural that the Administration should turn to a wider use of government-announced price supports in war food-expansion programs. In the early months of the war Congress enacted legislation requiring the secretary of agriculture to support the price at 90 per cent of parity for the basic farm products and those for which the secretary had requested an increase in production.[7] These price supports were to be continued for two years beyond the first January after the end of the war. Only twenty commodities were covered by the definitions in this legislation but legislation also directed the secretary to support the price of other farm products to the extent of available funds and needs and as a matter of operating policy price supports were extended to more and more commodities until in 1945 the Department of Agriculture announced specific price supports for 166 different commodities. [8] Again the wartime experience was satisfactory; lend-lease and military demands made it relatively easy to carry out any price-supporting operations required. Government guarantees of minimum prices increased in popularity with farmers, and opposition to the government assuming this function declined.

The wartime price supports at 90 per cent of parity for the twenty commodities ended December 31, 1948. In anticipation of this, new legislation was passed in 1948 which redefined the parity formula and set peacetime loan levels for the basic crops in relation to supplies on hand. It also authorized the secretary of agriculture to support prices of other farm products within a range of 60 to 90 per cent of parity by means of loans, purchases, or direct payments, making up the difference between the market prices and announced support levels. The authorized flexible supports of 60 to 90 per cent never went into effect because Congress passed amendments fixing support at 90 per cent. The post-Korean-

[7] Parity was defined as a level which gave a commodity the same purchasing power in terms of products bought by the farm family as it had in 1910–14.

[8] Walter W. Wilcox: *The Farmer in the Second World War* (Ames, Iowa, 1947), p. 246.

War decline in farm prices put a strain on the Commodity Credit Corporation with its accumulated surpluses. Successive Congresses wrestled in vain with the perennial farm problem, but thus far no feasible solution has been devised.

Marketing Agreement Programs

Marketing agreement programs combine voluntary and regulatory control of the marketing of agricultural commodities for the purpose of increasing returns to producers. Authority to undertake marketing agreement programs was included in the 1933 Agricultural Adjustment Act. These agreements have proved helpful in marketing two types of commodities—dairy products in city fluid-milk markets, and specialty crops, particularly fruits, tree nuts, and vegetables.

Under the 1933 legislation the secretary of agriculture was authorized to issue licenses to processors, associations of producers, and others engaged in the handling of farm commodities in interstate or foreign commerce. As later amended, when two-thirds of the growers of a commodity agreed on a marketing program they would petition the secretary to issue an order which would then require recalcitrant minorities to abide by the terms of the agreement.

In the city fluid-milk markets Federal marketing orders prevented excessive competitive price cutting during the period of low prices in the prewar years. In the specialty product field, marketing agreements often took the form of diverting inferior quality fruit from the fresh to the processed market thereby strengthening fresh fruit prices and increasing total returns to growers. Marketing agreements for potatoes have prevented producers from marketing small-size and low-quality potatoes.

Here again Federal authority to control marketing is based on the interstate commerce clause. Court decisions have authorized Federal marketing controls on products processed and consumed within the state where they are grown if they come in competition with similar products moving in interstate commerce. This extends the Federal power of control to all important marketing situations. Marketing agreements have been popular. As a result of the satisfactory experience with them, a definite upward trend in the use of these marketing controls was in evidence in the postwar years.

Expansion of Government-Sponsored Credit Facilities

Developments in the field of farm credit during the 1930's were fully as revolutionary as in government-sponsored marketing controls, production adjustments, and price guarantees. Soon after taking office President Roosevelt recommended new farm credit legislation which greatly enlarged the cooperative credit system and supplemented it with direct government financing. This legislation set up parallel to the land banks a system of banks for cooperatives, and regional production credit banks. The original capital was supplied by the government but the plans called for eventual

cooperative ownership. More than two thousand farmer cooperatives use the credit facilities of the banks for cooperatives. In 1954 the farmer cooperatives borrowed $483,000,000 from these banks.

The year 1933 was a serious one for indebted farm owners. Unable to make their interest and installment payments as they came due in 1931 and 1932, by 1933 many farm owners were about to lose their farms through foreclosure proceedings. Soon after the new farm credit act was passed, President Roosevelt in a radio address invited anyone about to lose his farm through foreclosure proceedings to wire him. Farmers wired him by the hundreds and applied to the local land bank representatives by the thousands. With these extra second mortgage funds to supplement the regular land bank loans, the Federal land banks in effect "bailed out" the private lenders. Farmers refinanced with the land banks by the hundreds of thousands and this governmental action kept many a farm family from losing their farm during those depression years. In a similar but less dramatic manner loans extended by the new production credit banks and the banks for cooperatives financed current production operations which had been suspended when commercial bank credit dried up. General agricultural recovery and the high prices during the war years made possible the retirement of most of this government capital by 1948. By usual business standards the depression operations were highly successful and farmers now have a much more comprehensive cooperative farm credit system.

Another governmental credit development is fully as significant. When in 1933 the Federal government took over from the states responsibility for relief it acquired large relief rolls among rural people as well as in the cities. After a few years of granting relief and operating public-works projects for rural people the Administration decided to make rehabilitation loans to these needy families, repayable over a five-year period. A Resettlement Administration succeeded by the Farm Security Administration was set up in 1935 by executive order to administer these loans and to carry on related activities. One of the unique features of this credit was the provision of farm and home management supervisors to assist the families in their rehabilitation plans. Only families unable to get credit from regular commercial credit institutions were eligible for such loans, which usually were for less than $1,000 and often had to be extended beyond the five-year period. Each family was visited several times a year by the local farm and home management supervisor employed by the government. Loan funds could be spent only on the authority of this supervisor. Destitute families unable to qualify for such loans because of inadequate farming resources continued to receive direct relief grants. In the first five years of operation this agency gave 850,000 farm families a new start.[9]

Popular concern over the increasing trend of farm tenancy led Con-

[9] *Report of the Administrator of the Farm Security Administration, 1940,* (Washington, D.C., 1940) p. 7.

gress in 1937 to pass legislation permitting direct farm purchase loans for a few outstanding tenants each year. These loans could equal the full appraised value of the farm purchased (commercial credit institutions seldom loan over 66 per cent), and were repayable over a forty-year period. Farm supervisors of the Farm Security Administration were designated to supervise these loans. Amounts to be loaned in this manner are specified each year in the annual appropriation for the Department of Agriculture.

In 1946 the Farmers Home Administration was created to provide credit for special types of farmers who cannot get the financing they need elsewhere at reasonable rates and terms. Credit is supplemented, where necessary, by assistance to borrowers in planning and adopting farm and home practices which promote success in farming.

Soil Conservation a Challenge to Government

From the earliest times individuals in our society have been concerned about conserving our natural resources. As noted earlier, we began to reserve publicly owned forest lands as early as 1891. There was another strong conservation movement during Theodore Roosevelt's presidency and at that time we increased our forestry conservation efforts. It was 1933, however, before the government undertook specific programs to conserve our agricultural lands.

Before 1933 soil conservation was discussed as a part of the general problem of getting high crop yields. Soil conservation was an important part of good farm management but was not singled out for special emphasis. A few soil erosion experiment stations were set up in the late 1920's. It was the need for large public works projects in the depression years which first gave erosion control specialists a chance to organize a large government program in this field. Thousands of Civilian Conservation Corps boys [11] were directed by these trained men in erosion control practices.

The new erosion control agency set up under the National Industrial Recovery Act of 1933 publicized both our soil losses and the activities of its C.C.C. boys. This work immediately commanded widespread popular support. In 1935 Congress enacted a special soil conservation statute setting up a separate agency to assist farmers in solving their soil conservation problems. The agency generally known as the Soil Conservation Service or the S.C.S. grew rapidly and by 1940 had a permanent staff of 8,000 workers. These workers would on request make a detailed map of the soil on a farm and work out a complete plan of soil and water con-

[10] For many years the Federal government has appropriated money as needed for drought and flood stricken families. These have been limited to amounts necessary to seed a crop or carry live-stock until the next crop is made. The loans usually are due when the first crop is harvested and have been called feed and seed loans. The new Farmers Home Administration took over the administration of these loans in addition to other responsibilities.

[11] Public employment and training programs for boys from families on public relief.

servation for the farmer. Often these conservation plans required planting the crops on the contour, sodding waterways, and constructing terraces. On request S.C.S. personnel do the technical "lay out" work free of charge for farmers who are willing to undertake these conservation measures. S.C.S. personnel working with Extension Service specialists and others encouraged and assisted farmers in adopting conservation measures during the war, thus minimizing the additional soil losses associated with the great expansion in crop production. In 1947 S.C.S. had a budget of around $45,000,000 which was almost equal to the total Federal-state budgets for all Extension Service educational work.

Other Agencies Concerned with Soil Conservation

In the early postwar years one of the most perplexing administrative problems was how to integrate and coordinate the government's agricultural conservation activities. The change from a strictly acreage adjustment program to one of shifting from soil-depleting to soil-conserving crops has already been mentioned. While it was the adverse decision of the Supreme Court in 1936 which forced this change, popular support for soil conservation work caused Congress to authorize funds for soil conservation practice or soil-building payments. These payments were based on the practices performed and covered a large part of the cost of such practices as applying agricultural limestone, the use of phosphate fertilizers on legumes, and terrace construction. During the war years Congress appropriated as much as $300,000,000 annually for such practices. These annual appropriations were sharply reduced in the immediate postwar years and there was much discussion regarding the need for such payments when farm prices were high. Agreement was general that these practices would be profitable for farmers even though no governmental payments were forthcoming. On the other hand many farmers, without the aid of some payments as an incentive, would neglect needed soil conservation practices. Much public confusion arose out of the fact that this program was administered by the old Agricultural Adjustment Agency staff in the Department of Agriculture quite independently of the technical service program administered by the S.C.S. These agencies maintained separate offices in the states and counties. To add to the confusion the conservation-practice payments were called "The Agricultural Conservation Program" by that agency.

Conservation Education a Separate Program

Educational work on soil conservation is performed by still a different agency, the Federal-state Extension Service. While educational work in this field has expanded in recent years most of the additional governmental resources have gone into the practice-payment and the technical-service program. A fourth governmental approach to conservation of soils on privately owned lands is the flood control legislation, particularly the 1936 and subsequent legislation. Whereas in the 1920's flood control was almost wholly a matter of building levees and flood control dams in major waterways, beginning in the late 1930's, upstream soil management practices were recognized as a key factor in retarding water run-off. Thus watershed flood control programs now emphasize soil conservation practices as one of their primary control measures.

The Soil Bank

By 1955 the Soil Conservation Service under the Soil Erosion Act of 1935 had supervised the organization of 2,618 soil conservation districts covering most of the farm land of the United States. The "soil bank" project was authorized by an act of Congress in 1956. Among other provisions the legislation authorized cut-rate sales and outright giving of some of the government-held farm surpluses to schools and other institutions. At the same time Congress appropriated nearly a billion dollars to purchase pork, beef, and other perishable farm products. Cotton surpluses were to be sold by the government in world markets at prevailing prices there. A farmer desiring to participate in the "soil bank" program applies to his county agricultural committee. If he is eligible, an agreement is made for withdrawal of a part of his farm from cultivation in return for which he is to be paid for the loss of its use. Payment follows inspection (as to compliance) made by the county Agricultural Stabilization and Conservation Committee. Payments are adjusted to encourage producers of basic crops to leave part of their previously allotted acreage idle in order to reduce government surpluses. In the conservation phase the farmer agrees to withdraw some land from cultivation for from 3 to 15 years and plant it to grass or trees. The government may pay up to as much as 80 per cent of the cost of planting plus about $10 per acre. Farmers in need of immediate relief were unenthusiastic about the long-range nature of the conservation program. Whether the "soil bank" policy can reduce surpluses is problematical since farmers might simply cultivate more intensively their remaining land.

INTERGOVERNMENTAL RELATIONS AND AGRICULTURE

Thus far we have centered our attention on the growth and development of the various activities now carried on for agriculture by the Federal government. In this section we shall take an over-all view of these activities as they are carried on today in cooperation with other units of government and with local groups of farmers. We shall also review briefly the relation of government to the conservation of other natural resources.

Governmental Relations in Education and Research

The Federal government now carries on a large research program for agriculture at its Beltsville, Maryland, farms, at regional laboratories in different parts of the United States, and in laboratories located in the nation's capital. In addition Congress each year appropriates funds which are allocated to the state agricultural experiment stations to supplement their state appropriations. Many of these Federal funds must be used for stated lines of research such as the marketing of agricultural products or the discovery of new uses for farm products. Others may be used for research in any field. Research workers in the state agricultural experiment stations and in the United States Department of Agriculture's laboratories cooperate on many of their research projects.

In the field of education Congress appropriates over 35 million dollars annually for the cooperative Extension Service work with the states. The states in turn cooperate with the counties. As a result, the county agricultural extension offices are usually financed by funds from the three sources—the Federal government, the state government, and the county unit (not always the county government). The United States Department of Agriculture has a small staff of Extension Service workers who work with the states but for the most part the leadership and direction of the educational work rests with the state Extension Service directors and their staffs in the forty-eight states. Vocational education funds for the promotion of agriculture are joint federal, state, and local contributions. The federal and state funds are distributed by the state department of education or vocational education board. Funds are distributed within the regulations and according to the plan developed within the state. These vary from state to state.

Government Relations in Farm Credit

Although most of the government's capital in the cooperative farm credit system has been repaid by the banks, existing legislation provides for continuing close supervision by government employees. The majority of the directors of each of the banks are elected by the borrowers, and local associations of borrowers are entirely controlled by their own elected officers. Direct governmental loans made by the Farmers Home Administration are administered by the national, state, and local staff of that agency. Usually a local committee of farmers is appointed to act in an advisory capacity with the local government representative.

Governmental Relations in Regulatory Activities

Regulatory activities can be grouped into two general categories. One group consists of regulations to prevent the movement of diseased animals and insect pests and the misbranding or adulteration of feeds, fertilizers, and similar supplies utilized in farm production. Here again Federal regulation is limited to the movement of interstate commerce. Most states have a body of state legislation in this field, and state departments of agriculture to administer it. Cooperative enforcement procedures are adopted where Federal and state regulations cover the same product. Cases of county regulation are rare. However, some counties acting under state authorization zone their rural lands, preventing unauthorized farming on marginal agricultural lands and restricting other undesirable uses. Counties in northern Wisconsin and Georgia and in a few other states have adopted such regulations. Weed control legislation is another instance where county or even township governments exercise regulatory activities.

The second category of regulatory activities is concerned with the marketing of farm products. Most firms engaged in marketing and processing farm products deal in interstate trade and are directly subject to Federal regulations. The Federal government maintains its inspectors in all the important markets and inspects processing plants to enforce the Federal regulations. In general, state regulations in this field are designed to supplement the Federal regulations by covering situations where the products do not move in interstate trade.

Government Relations in Production and Marketing Controls

Production and marketing controls developed in the 1930's bring the Federal government into direct contact with most farmers in their production and marketing operations. Administrators recognized from the beginning that these programs must have a high degree of local acceptance and support. For this and other reasons they staffed the Agricultural Adjustment Administration very largely with farmers and individuals with direct farm connections. The national administering agency operates through an appointed state committee and farmer-elected county committees, both entirely financed by Federal funds.

Governmental Relations in Conservation

The Federal government cannot exercise regulatory controls over privately owned natural resources such as agricultural land, forests, oil wells and mines. Regulation of the use of private property in the interests of conservation must be exercised by the states. The first conservation activities in most states were concerned with wild-life management.[12] Regulatory acts in this field date back to colonial times. By 1870 most of the New England states had state-wide administrative agencies and other states adopted similar controls at an early date. The Federal government supplements state activities with a Fish and Wild Life Service which regulates the hunting of migratory birds, and exercises other wild-life controls not within the province of a single state. The Federal Fish and Wild Life Service also carried on research, education, and service activities connected with fish and wild-life conservation.

Forest conservation and management ranks second to wild life in state conservation developments. The colonies had legislation encour-

[12] Many of the facts in this section were taken from Clifford J. Hynning: *State Conservation of Resources* (Washington, D.C., 1939).

aging tree planting, restricting tree cutting, prohibiting fires, and establishing preserves. As early as 1885 New York established a commission on forestry and today most states have forestry conservation activities. Most of them, however, date from 1911 when the Federal aid in this field, mentioned earlier, was made available. Public ownership by the states and counties as well as by the Federal government is playing an increasing part in forestry conservation. Other conservation measures include fire control, low cost or free nursery stocks for forestry plantings, disease control, and technical services to growers in selecting and marketing their mature trees.

Conservation of range lands through the establishment of grazing districts began in the late 1920's and the 1930's under state and Federal legislation. In these districts, created under Federal or state law, grazing rights are assigned to live-stock producers in accordance with the carrying capacity of the grazing area. The Federal grazing districts are established on the public domain and grazing on them is limited to the holders of permits. State grazing districts usually cover privately owned lands in the hands of absentee owners and are in effect cooperative associations of live-stock operators leasing these lands.

The first American policy with reference to mineral deposits on public lands was one of reservation and governmental leasing. This policy was abandoned in 1845 and no mineral conservation measures were undertaken until after 1900. Three states—Texas, Michigan, and Minnesota —maintained the policy of mineral reservation on their state lands, and the Federal government and many of the states adopted this policy again after 1900. State control of mineral development on privately owned land has been extremely limited: ". . . even today the most elementary regulations for the conservation of coal are lacking in most states. Greater state control is exercised over oil and gas, starting with crude measures for the prevention of physical waste in the decade 1890–1900 and gradually expanding into 'economic waste' and production control in the principal oil states. The most effective examples of conservational planning of oil (unit operation of pools) are still confined to oil fields on the public lands." [13]

The metallic minerals are substantially unaffected by any mineral conservation program of state governments. Between 1900 and 1912 most of the remaining publicly owned lands known or thought to have valuable oil and mineral deposits were withdrawn from sale (although most of the oil and mineral lands had been sold or given away before then). After much agitation, legislation was passed in 1920 authorizing the leasing of tracts containing coal, phosphate, oil shale, oil, gas, and sodium for private development. This and subsequent legislation sets forth the regulations under which a prospector may now develop his discovery. Royalties are shared between the Federal and state governments.

Conservation of agricultural lands by the Federal and state govern-

[13] Ibid., p. 35.

ments which includes water conservation from the standpoint of reducing run-off has already been reviewed. Another aspect of water conservation should be mentioned briefly. Early in the nineteenth century states engaged in inland waterway development on a large scale. When the panic of 1837 came, eighteen states were in debt for canal construction. By 1880 canal construction by states was largely discredited and the initiative shifted to the Federal government which began the development of navigable streams and flood control activities on the larger rivers.

With the development of industry in the United States, water pollution became an increasing problem. Dams across rivers stopped the normal movement of fish. States early took action to require the building of fishways through or around the dams and to control the pollution of the water. After 1871 the Federal government supplemented state activities in this field. This is still a growing field of regulation in states where industrial expansion continues. Until the Federal government undertook flood control work in the latter part of the nineteenth century, problems of floods and drainage were matters primarily of local concern. States have never engaged in either flood control or drainage activities on any significant scale. Western states have developed a large body of regulations governing the use of water from streams for irrigation and related purposes. These grow out of the shortage of irrigation water relative to the demand for it in these states.

Probably the most significant development in the conservation field in the twentieth century is the undertaking of regional development projects by the Federal government. The two outstanding projects of this type are the Tennessee Valley Authority and the Columbia Basin project. These regional development projects are designed to develop and use in a coordinated manner the water and other natural resources of the area. They represent a new level of achievement in the conservation and use of natural resources.

SUMMARY

In the field of agriculture the national government has engaged in four types of activity: (1) research and education, (2) regulation, (3) services, (4) economic aids. The national government interested itself in this field in earnest during the period of the Civil War although it had rendered some services earlier. In the 1860's it established a Department of Agriculture, made provision for land-grant colleges, and passed a homestead act. Its regulatory activity and its work in the field of conservation and reclamation became of consequence in the present century.

Economic aid to the farmer, begun with the establishment of Federal Land Banks in 1916 to provide an unfailing source of credit, was undertaken on a large scale after 1929. The Federal Farm Board failed in the task of stabilizing farm prices in the face of global depression. It presaged later policy by direct purchase of commodities with government funds for the purpose of bolstering farm prices.

The New Deal program of paying farmers for restricting production was declared unconstitutional in 1936 by a Supreme Court which regarded agricultural production as a local matter beyond the province of the national government. Despite this decision, restriction of production continued, first under the guise of soil conservation, and, after 1938, through marketing quotas imposed by the national government on the strength of the commerce power. The policy of supporting farm prices by non-recourse loans and direct purchase of commodities served further to strengthen the farmer's economic position. During World War II guaranteed prices were a means of stimulating food production.

During the 1930's the Federal Land Banks saved many farm families by providing second mortgage funds, and the Resettlement Administration gave a start to large numbers of farmers.

Federal activities touching agriculture are often carried on in co-operation with state agencies in such particulars as research and education, conservation, and the control of plant and animal diseases.

CHAPTER XXXIII

DEFENSE IN A DEMOCRACY

Democracy is not committed to pacifism by an inherent logic. Government by discussion means that in internal affairs differences will be settled through methods short of violence, but it does not follow that a democratic government is untrue to its tenets if it takes up arms against states that threaten the very assumptions upon which democracy itself is based. All great nations, whatever the political philosophy of their people may be, have to be militarily strong if they are to survive.[1]

ETWEEN 1919 and 1939—the twenty-year crisis—peoples everywhere witnessed probably the most desperate, if somewhat misguided, efforts that have ever been made to achieve world peace. During these critical years the League of Nations was launched, the Kellogg-Briand Pact for outlawing war was signed by some sixty nations, and plans for disarmament were formulated upon three different occasions. In the United States the crusade for peace manifested itself in a great variety of forms—in pacifism, peace strikes, a movement against compulsory military training in land-grant colleges, investigations of munitions makers, and through countless organizations dedicated to the eradication of war. The period could hardly be called a peaceful one, for there were several military conflicts in the Balkans in the twenties, the Japanese invaded Manchuria in 1931, the Italians conquered Ethiopia in 1934, and the Spanish Civil War broke out in 1936.

So long as the peoples of the United States sensed no immediate threat to their own security and were not yet persuaded of the importance of meeting totalitarian threats of aggression by offensive military action if necessary, questions of national defense were regarded with indifference by a large part of our citizenry. Although the annals of its military history contain many brilliant passages, there has been a strong tra-

[1] E. P. Herring: *The Impact of War*.

dition against huge military establishments since the very beginning of our government. That civil authority should be supreme over military authority was a principle embodied in the Constitution itself, and an insistence that this order of precedence be kept unchanged has continued to the present day. In times of crisis, the American public has rallied swiftly to support its government in any military engagement which it has been obliged to undertake. Yet, once these crises were over, public opinion quickly inclined toward a policy of keeping national-defense appropriations at a minimum. In a day when the possibility of a military outbreak cannot be brushed aside, however, the old habit of permitting defenses to slide once the immediate danger has passed seems most short-sighted.

Besides our own immediate security, there is an additional reason for maintaining military establishments. In a negative sense, the armed services are for the defense of this nation against a possible invader; in a positive sense the presence of the well-trained and well-equipped military force is highly useful in upholding our foreign policies. [2] Indeed, as one student of American diplomacy has pointed out: "A basic weakness of American foreign policy is the inability of our people to recognize the intimate relationship between military power and foreign affairs." [3] Thus, despite traditional American hostility toward the professional military, in the turbulent state of world affairs the role of the armed services in both peace and war continues to be a matter of very grave concern for government.

THE CONSTITUTION IN NATIONAL DEFENSE

Nine of the eighteen clauses in the Federal Constitution dealing with the powers of Congress are devoted to questions of military and naval authority. Among the more important powers is the authority to "raise and support armies," to provide and maintain a navy, and to declare war. In addition, Congress also has the power to prescribe rules for the governmental regulation of our land and naval forces. Moreover it has come to exercise broad control over the National Guard, though the Guard is composed of units that are primarily state instrumentalities unless they are drawn into Federal service for putting down insurrections or repelling an invader.

Providing and Maintaining the Army and Navy

The powers to raise and support armies and to provide and maintain a navy give Congress a broad mandate to do everything that the two directives would seem to imply. The size of the Army and Navy, salary scales, and the building of military, naval, and air establishments are all determined by Congress under this constitutional grant of authority.

[2] See Samuel Flagg Bemis: "The Shifting Strategy of American Defense and Diplomacy." *Virginia Quarterly Review* (1948), 24:321–35.
[3] Thomas A. Bailey: *The Man in the Street* (New York, 1948), p. 72.

As a corollary of the powers to provide and maintain an army and navy, Congress has the power to conscript men and women for military service. The constitutionality of military conscription was authoritatively established by the United States Supreme Court during World War I. [4] Peacetime conscription has been assailed by some critics as unwarranted by the Constitution but there no longer appears to be any doubt about the authority of Congress to conscript people for military service whether in time of war or peace.

The Power to Declare War

The Constitution gives Congress alone the power to declare war. A formal declaration, of course, is not essential when nations resort to war; the recent Pearl Harbor attack serves as a grim reminder that wars may break out without any ceremonious notification. Primarily, the declaration of war is to inform neutral countries that a state of war exists and to warn them that they will be expected to observe the rules of neutrality. A declaration of war ordinarily recites the reasons for resorting to arms and it may have psychological value in helping to secure unity at a time of crisis. Frequently a declaration of war is issued after the hostilities have actually begun. This was true in the case of the Spanish American War and more recently in the United States declaration of war on Japan following the Pearl Harbor attack. Besides citing the reasons for taking up arms, it is usually customary in a formal declaration of war to specify the date of the commencement of war and sometimes even the hour and the minute.

Procedurally, Congress declares war by a joint resolution that is passed by both houses and then signed by the president. It is noteworthy, however, that Congress has never yet declared war without being called upon to do so by the president. This does not mean that Congress could not take the initiative nor that Congress would have refused to declare war in the absence of a request by the president. Congress unquestionably could declare war even against the advice of the president, but such an occurrence is hardly likely. In practice, the president has great influence in leading both public opinion and Congress when diplomatic relations become increasingly strained and armed conflict seems inevitable.

Military and Naval Regulations

Under its power to prescribe "rules for the government and regulation of the land and naval forces," Congress has provided for a Uniform Code of Military Justice in 1949 which lays down regulations for the Army, Navy, and Air Force. Some dissatisfaction over the operation of this code, however, still persists.

[4] Selective Draft Law Cases, 245 U.S. 366 (1918).

Congress and the National Guard

Since the inception of the colonial governments, it has been customary for each state to maintain its own volunteer militia which could be called upon to put down an insurrection and to quell any domestic outbreak of violence. As these militia units were in existence when the Federal Constitution was adopted, it was not deemed necessary to provide for them in the Constitution itself. They are referred to, however, in the Second Amendment of the Constitution as bodies "necessary to the security of a free state." Congress has the authority to "provide for arming and disciplining the militia," and also to call up into the Federal service as many units of the National Guard as are necessary to "execute the laws of the union, suppress insurrections, and repel invasions."

Today state militia contingents everywhere are known as the National Guard, and far from being amateur units of citizen volunteers, the Guard is a well-equipped and well-organized arm of our national defense. It is at present linked with the new National Defense Establishment which brings the Army, Navy, and the Air Force under the secretary of defense. Moreover, as a result of a long series of regulatory legislation, the National Guard's training programs have been much improved and the integration of the organization with the Regular Army on matters of training, equipment, and mobilization has steadily been improved. Congress contributes the lion's share of financial aid to the National Guard and in addition provides for auxiliary equipment such as training sites, forts, arsenals, and other military installations.

When the National Guard is not specifically drawn into the Federal service, state authorities maintain control over the appointment of its officers and also retain the right to outline its training program. Since the unification of the armed services under the National Security Act of 1947, however, there have been renewed demands that the training and organization of the National Guard be more securely integrated with that of the Regular Army. In support of these arguments, the point has been made that previously when the National Guard was called into the Federal service there was usually sufficient opportunity between the time when the Guard was called up and the actual outbreak of hostilities properly to integrate the Guard with the regular armed forces. In 1917 several National Guard units had been engaged in active service on the Mexican border prior to their being merged with the Regular Army. Again in 1941, by the time the United States was engaged in war, the National Guard had had more than a year of training, having been called into the Federal service with the declaration of a national emergency in 1940. Since many military experts now believe that a future war may begin with an unexpected blow, it is strongly urged that every military facility be integrated into a cohesive organization in order to repel an invader's attack at a moment's notice.

Attention has also been given to the fact that in our second line of defense—the National Guard and the Organized Reserve Corps—there has been some duplication of effort. The Organized Reserve Corps is an auxiliary force of Regular Army officers who receive periodic training with the armed forces and are held in reserve for any national emergency. As the existence of both the National Guard and Organized Reserve Corps has not only meant a certain amount of duplication of effort, but has also produced a situation of divided authority and varying standards of pay and benefit provisions it has been suggested that the two be combined. In any case the need for bringing the National Guard into closer focus with the Regular Army and reconciling the organization and training programs of both the Guard and the Organized Reserve Corps are subjects that command careful attention in tightening up our all-important second line of defense.

Congress and Mobilization

Wars, as everyone knows, are won not only on the field of battle but to a very large extent behind the lines in the factories, mines, oil fields, and farms. To turn a nation into what Franklin Roosevelt called "an arsenal of democracy" requires vast and carefully directed mobilization of human energy and materials.

Upon Congress falls the responsibility of delegating authority and enacting legislation that will harness for war the human and material resources of the nation. Through conscription acts, appropriations, and other legislation, Congress meets part of this responsibility, but in addition Congress must clothe the president with extensive authority to transform the nation from a peaceful to a wartime basis. This entails authority to tune industry, transportation, commerce, scientific research, and our educational institutions to wartime demands.

To facilitate the wartime mobilization of manpower and industry, Congress usually delegates specified powers to the president which may be exercised either for the duration of the war or for a designated period. In World War II, congressional legislation of this character generally set as the time limit the duration of the war plus six months. In delegating emergency powers to the president, Congress may create the administrative machinery for exercising them or it may simply delegate authority and leave to the president the determination of administrative machinery. Whichever method is used the system of controls subsequently put into effect is administered by the president and his executive subordinates.

Extensive delegation of legislative authority to the president has been looked upon with misgivings by many critics, yet with few exceptions Congress has dispensed broad powers to the executive under wartime conditions. And the courts have not been disposed to challenge legislative grants of authority to the president during wartime. But one should not assume that under the press of wartime conditions Congress is always willing to respond to the chief executive's call for additional authority.

In the fall of 1942, Congress, influenced by the farm bloc, was reluctant to pass legislation giving the president authority to place a ceiling at parity level on the prices of farm commodities. Only when the president told Congress that if he did not have adequate legislation to deal with the subject within a short time, he would act without waiting for supporting legislation, did Congress respond. [5] In threatening this action, Mr. Roosevelt said: "The President has the powers, under the Constitution and under congressional acts, to take measures to avoid a disaster which would interfere with the winning of the war." [6] In this instance, Congress yielded and passed the requested legislation. In 1944, however, when President Roosevelt asked Congress for the authority to conscript labor, his request was turned down. Basically, the authority empowering the chief executive to set up the vast system of controls necessary to the successful prosecution of a war must come from Congress. Nevertheless in wartime Congress has with few exceptions granted the authority required by the chief executive, without interference by the courts, and in most cases where Congress has been hesitant to enact desired legislation, the president has not been completely without means of persuading Congress to act.

The Bill of Rights in Wartime

The Constitution authorizes Congress to impose broad controls over the citizenry and economy of the nation during wartime, but what does it say about the very volatile question of civil liberties? [7] Except for the writ of habeas corpus, which may be suspended in cases of rebellion, invasion, or on such occasions when the "public safety may require it," the Constitution does not discriminate between civil liberties when the nation is at war or peace. It is obvious, however, that military necessity may require limitations on the civil rights which during peacetime are unrestricted. [8] Under the compelling objective of successfully prosecuting the war, civil rights are abridged in ways which would be regarded as intolerable during time of peace. Such measures may result from actions taken by the president under his powers as commander-in-chief of the armed forces, or from authority delegated to the president by Congress. Moreover, Congress may impose restrictions by legislation, prescribing in minute detail the restraints to be placed upon speech, press, freedom of assembly, and other civil liberties. As examples the Espionage Act of 1917, the Sedition Act of 1918, and, more recently, certain sections of the Alien Registration Act of 1940 might be cited.

[5] See Edward S. Corwin: *The President: Office and Powers* (3rd ed., New York, 1948), chap. 5.

[6] See Carl Brent Swisher: *American Constitutional Development* (Boston, 1943), pp. 1009–1010.

[7] For an historical account of civil liberties in wartime see Carl Brent Swisher: "Civil Liberties in Wartime." *Political Science Quarterly* (1940), 55:321–47.

[8] See Robert E. Cushman: "Civil Liberties." *American Political Science Review* (1943), 37:49–56.

In the enforcement of wartime restrictions that trespass upon civil rights occasional injustices inevitably result. An over-zealous prosecutor surrounded by a public opinion more intemperate during wartime than peacetime may cause a person to be punished and maligned unjustly. There were several cases in both world wars although not as many in World War II as in World War I. But the restrictions imposed upon civil liberties in consequence of World War II brought hardships and indignities to many loyal and patriotic citizens in the United States. The physical transplantation of several thousand American citizens of Japanese national extraction from the coastal states of Washington, Oregon, and California to temporary camps located in states of the Rocky Mountain area was highly discommoding to those involved. Not only did this action interfere with the way these peoples lived, but the swiftness of the evacuation ordered meant that families were often required to dispose of businesses, property, and other personal effects at a great sacrifice. Yet no matter how harsh the curtailment of some civil liberties may seem, common sense requires that their unrestrained exercise be temporarily regulated in the interests of the public safety.

One of the more difficult undertakings is handling the matter of free speech during wartime. What is the dividing line between talk that is seditious—speech directed toward disturbing the public order or toward treason—and talk that is simply criticism of governmental policy? In a democracy, it is considered wholesome not to muzzle individual criticism completely even during wartime.[9] But criticism that borders on disloyalty and may be presumed to have an undesirable effect on the unity of the country and the morale of the armed forces cannot be conveniently overlooked when a nation is fighting for its survival. Distinguishing between speech that falls within the confines of criticism and speech that is seditious or treasonable is indeed difficult.

The right to suspend habeas corpus "when in cases of rebellion or invasion the public safety may require it" belongs to Congress. Nonetheless, during the Civil War President Lincoln did not hesitate to suspend the writ when he felt compelled to do so. Speaking broadly, constitutional powers involving civil rights have been dealt with by both Congress and presidents during wartime in light of the more urgent purpose of winning the war. This does not mean that the Constitution is abandoned nor that the fundamental rights guaranteed by the Constitution are completely liquidated when the country is at war. It does mean that in dealing with civil liberties during wartime it is necessary to steer a course which follows a maximum regard for their exercise, while at the same time avoiding the risk of impeding the war effort.

Martial Law

One of the possible consequences of a military conflict (or other form of national emergency) that has a direct bearing upon civil rights is the im-

[9] See Harold Lasswell, *National Security and Individual Freedom* (New York, 1950), and also Louis Smith, *American Democracy and Military Power* (University of Chicago Press, 1951).

position of martial law. Martial law is not to be confused with military law which issues under authority of Congress and applies only to members of the armed forces. Martial law rests upon no definite legal code. It consists of rules and regulations issued daily by the military commander in the area declared to be under martial law. Thus curfews may be ordered, restrictions may be made forbidding assemblies or public meetings, and many other regulations may be imposed that subject civilians temporarily to a tightly controlled daily regimen. The theory of martial law is that during the emergency that justifies it, martial law replaces ordinary law. Special tribunals are set up to handle violations, and for the time being the military commander is the supreme authority.

During time of war a military commander may establish martial law in any area within the zone of military operations or in an area where military activity is probable. While the courts have held that military commanders may not impose martial law (even in wartime) in areas outside of the actual or probable zone of military operations, it was done during the Civil War and there was little that the courts could do about it.

In most of the cases where martial law has been imposed in this country, it has issued under state rather than Federal authority. Where it operates under state authority it is proclaimed by the governor usually when a disaster has taken place or civil disorder is threatened in a particular area as a result of labor-management disputes or some outbreak of violence with which local authorities are unable to cope. In times of great national emergency, of course, the president may proclaim martial law—as Lincoln did during the Civil War.

While martial law is in operation, the writ of habeas corpus is ordinarily suspended. The Constitution is silent on who may suspend this fundamental safeguard of civil liberty. Under the ruling in the celebrated Civil War case, *Ex parte* Milligan, the Supreme Court indicated that Congress alone may suspend the writ, but the accepted opinion today inclines to the view that under special conditions and when acting under congressional authority, the president may.[10] Obviously, in the event of a serious military crisis involving the homeland itself, the opinion in the Milligan case might need to be modified in favor of extending presidential authority to suspend the writ—an argument which today enjoys strong support among many constitutional authorities.

Military Law

Military law is based upon the authority of Congress to prescribe "rules for the government of the land and naval forces." The "Military Laws of the United States" embrace elaborate codes and regulations and each of the services have their own organizations for their enforcement. Military laws define offenses and fix penalties as well as provide for the procedures for trying members of the armed services accused of violations or breach of discipline. Members of the armed services accused of misconduct are

---

[10] *Ex parte* Milligan, 4 Wallace 2 (1866).

tried by a court martial which is a body of officers specially designated to hear cases and render decisions. The charges are brought by a representative of the Judge Advocate General's Office which is comparable to the prosecutor's office in civilian life.

Being subject to military law does not exempt members of the armed services from the processes of a civil court. A crime committed outside a military reservation may be dealt with by civilian authorities or the latter may turn the offender over to military authorities for punishment. Minor offenses that are committed within military reservations are, of course, handled exclusively by military authorities, but a serious capital crime such as murder is apt to be tried in a civil court. Actually most civil crimes are likely to be grave offenses under military law. Disputes between local and military authorities over jurisdiction are not unknown in cases involving state rather than Federal laws, but where a procedure is authorized by Federal law the latter takes precedence and local authorities may not intervene.

THE PRESIDENT AND NATIONAL DEFENSE

The authority of the president over national defense stems from three constitutional sources. Specifically, he is named in the Constitution as the commander-in-chief of the Army and the Navy of the United States and also of the state militia when called into the Federal service. Another source of the president's authority derives from his constitutional status as chief executive. The president has the responsibility of seeing that the laws are faithfully executed and in consequence of this authority and as a corollary inherent in the chief executive's position he exercises important powers over our national-defense system. A third source of authority for the president's defense powers stems from grants of legislative authority delegated by Congress. In the exercise of his powers, it is exceedingly difficult to distinguish which source of authority the president is relying upon or whether, in fact, he is relying upon all three. Moreover, during wartime, and in peacetime when a national emergency may be imminent, the president does not usually indicate the precise authority upon which he is acting when he exercises powers relating to national defense. Taken collectively, the three sources of authority constitute a sturdy base of constitutional power, and as the nation has had strong-minded chief executives during the three largest military conflicts in its history—Lincoln, Wilson, and Franklin Roosevelt—authority for the president has not been found wanting in most instances.

The President as Commander-in-Chief

As commander-in-chief, the president appoints all officers of the armed forces by and with the advice and consent of the Senate. He also has the final word in the actual command of American military forces. The president may, as Theodore Roosevelt did in 1907, order the Navy on a world-wide cruise as part of the "carry a big stick" policy. Conceivably he may go even further by actually committing American armed forces to military engagements when no actual declaration of war has been made by Congress. In 1918, President Wilson ordered an American military expedition under General Knox to Vladivostock, Siberia, and Archangel to join a force of Allied powers fighting Bolshevik troops. At the time, no state of war existed between Russia and the United States and there had been no authorization by Congress for such an invasion. In peacetime, a more recent example may be cited that illustrates the magnitude of the president's power as commander-in-chief. During 1940 and 1941, American war vessels helped convoy war materials across the Atlantic to Great Britain under the orders of the Commander-in-Chief, President Roosevelt. Until late 1941, the United States was not at war, at least formally, and the use of the Navy to aid a belligerent power was a violation of neutrality under international law. Moreover, as submarine warfare in the North Atlantic became more menacing, the President issued orders to naval commanders to open fire on German submarines that threatened the safety of British convoys.

In 1950, another dramatic example of the commitment of American military forces by the President occurred on June 27. On this day President Truman ordered American air and naval forces into action without any prior congressional authorization.

Two further examples also serve to illustrate the strong position of the president as commander-in-chief. Both involve the power of the president to station American troops abroad even though the United States is not at war. In 1941 President Roosevelt sent American troops to Iceland where they were stationed for several years. And ten years later after the great debate in 1949–50 on sending American troops to Europe to fulfill our obligations under the North Atlantic Treaty Organization, President Truman finally won congressional approval for sending six divisions. But he continued to insist that he had the authority to do so anyway, independently of Congress.

Obviously, during time of peace when the president contemplates a bold act in the exercise of his powers as commander-in-chief, he must consider what possible reaction it will have in Congress as well as on public opinion. While the president has complete authority over the use and employment of the armed forces, Congress still holds the purse strings, and a chief executive who acted too rashly in a peacetime commitment of our armed forces might later find Congress reluctant to provide the necessary funds. A serious abuse of the powers of the executive as commander-in-chief might lead to his impeachment. Thus, while the president's powers as commander-in-chief are extremely broad even during peacetime he may hardly exercise them with complete abandon and disregard for Congress and public opinion.

During wartime the president's powers as commander-in-chief are of even greater significance because of the gravity of the major decisions that are involved.[11] The president does not ordinarily plot the military strategy of our land, sea, and air forces. Military and naval experts direct the preparation of strategic plans and the assignment of roles and missions to each of the service branches. Nonetheless, on decisions of extreme importance involving over-all strategy during wartime or peacetime final authority rests with the president. The decision during World War II on whether the invasion of Europe should be attempted through the "soft underbelly" or should proceed by a cross-channel invasion to the Normandy beaches of France was ultimately one which the President himself had to make. The decision to direct our military effort first toward the liberation of Europe rather than toward the Far East likewise devolved upon the President.

DEFENSE ORGANIZATION

For the president to fill successfully his role as commander-in-chief, there are two imperative requirements. First, he must have competent military advice. We cannot expect our presidents to be military experts, nor indeed do we wish it. An adequate defense program, therefore, must assure that the best possible military advice will constantly be available to the president. A second essential for the nation's security program is that the chief executive be fully advised on the ways and means of organizing the nation's industrial and manpower resources in the interests of national defense. Not only does the president need advice on how the industrial and manpower resources of the nation may be integrated into the defense program, it is also desirable that some machinery exist to effect integration. Just as the units of the armed forces need direction, so the vast industries and manpower of the country require skillful coordination for purposes of defense. National defense, it must be emphasized, is not simply a wartime function; it also entails preparedness—readiness for any eventuality. A nation's industrial and manpower resources, of course, need not be organized as rigidly in time of peace as in time of war; nonetheless, careful plans for the immediate conversion of resources, and machinery to carry the plans into effect, should be in readiness against an outbreak of hostilities.

In the matter of furnishing carefully planned military advice to the president as well as providing him with advice on utilizing the nation's economy for defense purposes, the United States groped along until shortly before World War I. Some painful consequences followed the lack of adequate machinery for advising the president on military matters in the War of 1812 and during the Civil War. Out of a study exposing the mistakes made in the Spanish American War came a proposal for the creation of a general staff, the purpose of which was to provide the broad basic policies and plans necessary for the development of the Army as an efficient fighting force. The general staff was established in 1903 under the leader-

[11] For an illuminating account of these problems see E. P. Herring: *The Impact of War* (New York, 1941), chap. 6.

ship of Secretary of War Elihu Root. Under this arrangement a chief of staff was appointed by the president to serve for a period of four years as head of the General Staff and also as adviser on military matters to the president and secretary of war. Thus by the time of World War I some lessons had been mastered on the need for providing the president with a continuous source of military advice.

Defense Organization in World War I

Some six months before the United States became involved in the hostilities of World War I the Council of National Defense was set up and was "charged with the responsibility of investigating industrial resources for war and recommending measures for the mobilization of civilian resources." A few months after war had been declared the War Industries Board was organized to take charge of industrial mobilization.[12] After ineffectual leadership for several months, the War Industries Board finally began to measure up to its enormous task under the able chairmanship of Bernard Baruch. Through the War Industries Board, all orders for war supplies were cleared, priorities were determined, and decisions were made on the mobilization of civilian manpower. The confusion which attended the establishment of authority in the War Industries Board, however, and the length of time consumed in getting started made it all the more apparent that a nation must not be without machinery for industrial mobilization if her defense lines are to be secure.

Defense Organization in World War II

Some of the lessons learned in World War I were put to good use as the nation girded itself for World War II. In May of 1940, over a year and a half before Pearl Harbor, the Office for Emergency Management was established in the Executive Office of the President. This action was taken in accordance with an executive order issued in September, 1939, providing for such an office "in the event of a national emergency, or threat of a national emergency . . ." [13] With the coming of war, fifteen major agencies eventually were placed under the Office for Emergency Management. Speaking broadly, these agencies were vested with wartime powers to control the production and procurement of materials, the mobilization and utilization of the nation's manpower and transportation facilities, censorship, prices and rationing of consumer goods, scientific research, and various other aspects of the nation's economic and social life.[14] While the process of civilian and industrial mobilization in World War II is a complete story in itself that is now being meticulously pieced together by a

---

[12] For an account of industrial mobilization in World War I see Bernard M. Baruch: *American Industry in the War: A Report on the War Industries Board* (Washington, D.C., 1921).

[13] The early period is discussed in J. P. Harris: "The Emergency Defense Organization." *Public Administration Review* (1940), 1:1–24.

[14] For comprehensive treatment of the defense program see War Records Section, Bureau of the Budget: *The United States at War: Development and Administration of the War Program of the Federal Government* (Washington, D.C., 1947).

task force of historians, we may with profit briefly review some of the major agencies of governmental control.

The War Production Board set up in 1942 had general direction over the war procurement and production program. Although there was some sentiment that government should take over all industries whose products were essential to the war effort, this policy was never adopted.[15] The government did build several munitions plants along with some steel and aluminum plants, but these enterprises were operated by private owners under contract to the government. Among its functions the War Production Board determined priorities, authorized the building of critical raw materials stockpiles such as rubber, and curtailed production of consumer goods such as passenger automobiles and a long list of other items.

In charge of civilian mobilization was the War Manpower Commission. Although this agency was never given full powers to order work assignments at its own discretion and to compel workers to work in specific localities or at specific tasks, it did have broad authority to encourage these objectives. To prevent workers from migrating from industry to industry in quest of better salaries or more favorable locations, the War Manpower Commission took steps to "freeze" persons in their jobs and insofar as possible it attempted to keep people at work in positions where they could be the most useful and where there was the most urgent need. Persons disqualified from military service because of physical handicaps were advised to find positions essential to the war effort or face possible draft into the armed services for service in work battalions.

To keep the national economy stable the Office of Economic Stabilization was established in 1942. The director set wage ceilings the primary object of which was economic stabilization but they were also helpful in preventing a heavy labor turnover.

Among the other major defense organizations were the Office of Defense Transportation, the Office of Censorship, the Office of Civilian Defense, the Office of Lend Lease Administration, the Office of Economic Warfare, and the Office of Price Administration. The operation of the railroads was not taken over by the Federal government in World War II as it was in World War I. But the Office of Defense Transportation did exercise broad control over the nation's transportation facilities. It was responsible for utilizing domestic transportation facilities in the best interest of the war effort, and it controlled railroads, motor, pipe-line, and air transport, coastwise and intercoastal shipping, as well as inland waterway facilities. It issued priorities for the shipment of materials and troops and tried in so far as possible to give first call on the transportation lanes to persons and materials most intimately connected with the war effort.

The Office of Censorship, as its name implies, was empowered to censor communications passing between the United States and foreign

[15] See Bureau of Demobilization, Civilian Production Administration: *Industrial Mobilization for War: History of the War Production Board and Predecessor Agencies, 1940–1945*. Vol. 1, Program and Administration (Washington, D.C., 1947).

countries by mail, cable, radio, and other means of communication. The Office of War Information was charged with the responsibility of formulating programs that would facilitate a better understanding of the aims and objectives of the war both at home and abroad. The O.W.I., in short, was a propaganda agency, and it beamed broadcasts throughout the occupied countries that were designed to keep friendly peoples informed on the progress of the war and the policies of this government.

The Office of Civilian Defense was concerned with state and local machinery for caring for the civilian population in case of emergencies and for bringing about full participation in the war effort. The Office of Economic Warfare—later consolidated into the Foreign Economic Administration—had as its responsibility the strengthening of our international economic relations. It was concerned with obtaining strategic raw materials from foreign countries and with the exchange of commodities in a way most beneficial to the prosecution of the war.

An agency that carried out one of the major assignments of the war was the Office of Lend Lease Administration, established in the autumn of 1941 and later consolidated into the Foreign Economic Administration (1943).[16] The Lend Lease Administration was one of the major assignments of the war. It was set up before our entrance into World War II as an administrative agency to handle the supplies that were being exported to stem the advance of totalitarianism. Because of the unhappy experience over the war debts from World War I, it was decided not to repeat earlier mistakes by offering aid as a loan which everyone knew could never be repaid in dollars, but rather to term the assistance "lend lease." Under the Lend Lease Program several billion dollars were expended in the form of credits, military supplies, food, and a vast array of other articles. As it was correctly maintained that no equivalent in human suffering and loss of life could be set as an exchange for supplies, lend lease operated on the theory that the countries receiving lend lease aid were fighting our battles, and that we were giving them the tools to do it, without expecting reimbursement. In many ways, of course, reverse lend lease aid operated to cancel out some lend lease assistance. For example, many of our troops in Great Britain were quartered in British facilities and we also received certain needed materials from our various allies. In general, however, lend lease was never intended to operate on a dollar for dollar basis, and its work progressed on the same assumption that there is no way of balancing human sacrifice and dollars.

To protect the nation's economy from inflation, the Office of Price Administration was established under authority of the Emergency Price Control Act of 1942.[17] The Office of Price Administration rationed consumer commodities such as gasoline, fuel oil, tires, sugar, meat, and other foods, and shoes, along with a rather large list of other articles for which

[16] See Edward R. Stettinius: *Lend Lease: Weapon for Victory* (New York, 1944).
[17] See P. M. Leary: "Rationing and Governmental Organization." *American Political Science Review* (1945), 39:1089–1106.

the demand far exceeded the supply. It was also empowered to set ceilings on prices and on rents. As an institution to further the war effort on the home front, the Office of Price Administration had several vital objectives. By holding down prices, it attempted to avoid the confusion which inevitably follows when the supply of goods is not sufficient to meet the demand. Price controls also tended to assure more equitable distribution of consumer goods for people with fixed incomes, who would have had a far more difficult time had rents and prices been jacked up in a never-ending sequence. By its rationing program, particularly on critical commodities such as tires, gasoline, and fuel oil, the Office of Price Administration helped to insure that the military forces did not suffer for want of supplies because of unnecessary consumption by the civilian population.

Defense Lessons of World War II

The unprecedented military, industrial, and manpower mobilization of World War II was not without effect on subsequent developments in arranging for the nation's defense. Basically, the defense lesson of World War II was simple. There could no longer be any doubt that the security of the nation depended upon the careful coordination of military, industrial, and manpower effort, and that top-level agencies of administrative control were needed to do the directing and planning. It was also recognized that the agencies to conduct such operations should not be thought of as mere wartime organizations but that for security purposes they were sometimes as essential in peace as in war. Rent controls, for example, with some adjustments were still in effect in the 1950's, long after the hostilities of World War II had ceased.

Two areas of conflict were particularly troublesome in World War II —both crucial matters certainly in organizing the nation's defense in time of peace. One was the lack of coordination between the political (diplomatic) operations of the government and the military operations. The second serious problem was the failure to organize and coordinate intelligence activities. In both instances administrative deficiences led to costly errors, and the experience has pointed the way to much needed improvements.

THE NATIONAL SECURITY ORGANIZATION

With the lessons of World War II behind it and the uncertainties and unrest of world politics before it, Congress in 1947 undertook a major overhauling of our defense machinery. The result was the National Security Act. The broad purpose of this law was "to provide a comprehensive program of the future security of the United States." [18] In the long debate which preceded passage of the Act, there were many advocates of a single department of defense that would merge the Army and Navy. The Act did not achieve this end, however, and only after a sulphurous inter-service

[18] 61 U.S. Statutes 495.

battle among the Army, the Navy, and the proponents of a separate air force, was a compromise reached for integrating policies and procedures in the Federal governmental agencies primarily concerned with national security. The administrative structure provided by the National Security Act is called the National Security Organization. Under it are the Department of Defense, the National Security Council, and the Office of Defense Mobilization.

The Department of Defense

The Department of Defense is under the direction of a civilian secretary of defense. It comprises the three service departments—the Department of the Army, the Department of the Navy, and the Department of the Air Force—each under the direction of a civilian secretary. Also under the Department of Defense are the joint chiefs of staff.

The duties of the secretary of defense are to (1) establish general policies and programs for the Department of Defense; (2) exercise general direction, authority, and control over the departments and agencies; (3) take the appropriate steps for the elimination of unnecessary duplication or overlapping in the fields of procurement, supply, transportation, storage, health, and research; (4) formulate and supervise the preparation of budget estimates; and (5) supervise the budget programs of the departments.

The secretary of defense is now served by eleven assistant secretaries who deal with numerous areas of responsibility now assigned to the Department of Defense. Among the most important areas are: manpower, budget, international affairs, supply and logistics, and research and development. All powers not specifically given to the secretary of defense are retained by the respective military departments, a factor that early led to criticism of the National Security Act on the ground that the secretary of defense did not have broad enough control.

This criticism was largely met in 1953 by Presidential Reorganization Plan Number 6, which abolished the Research and Development Board, Munitions Board, Defense Supply Management Agency, and other agencies, and transferred the functions of these agencies to the Office of Secretary of Defense. At the same time provision was made for the establishment of six additional assistant secretaries of defense. Finally, in footing up the all-pervasive nature of the secretary of defense post as it is presently conceived, it should be noted that the secretary now serves as a member of the National Security Council, the Defense Mobilization Board, and the North Atlantic Council.

The joint chiefs of staff comprise the chief of staff of each of the three departments and a chairman; they serve as the principal military advisers to the president, the National Security Council, and the secretary of defense. Individually, of course, the chief of staff of each of the three departments—Army, Navy, and Air Force—advises the secretary of his department on the readiness, composition, and training of the forces under his control, and many other phases of work within his own department.

The joint chiefs of staff, of course, function as the real control tower of the nation's defense program. They prepare strategic plans and provide for the strategic direction of our military forces; establish unified commands in strategic areas; formulate policies for the joint training of military forces; prepare joint logistic plans and assign logistic responsibilities to the different services in accordance with such plans; and provide for the representation of the United States on the Military Staff Committee of the United Nations.

The chairman of the joint chiefs of staff holds a post of sweeping influence. In both the Truman and Eisenhower Administrations, General Bradley and his successor as chairman of the joint chiefs of staff, Admiral Radford, have been commonly considered among the most powerful men in Washington, the president excepted.

The Office of Defense Mobilization is concerned with industrial mobilization and its work is carried out under six suggestive titles—production, materials, stabilization, plans and readiness, manpower, and telecommunications. The Director of the Office of Defense Mobilization directs and coordinates all mobilization activities of the executive branch of the government, and it is his duty to advise the president on the coordination of military, industrial, and civilian mobilization. Clearly this is one of the vital nerve centers in the organization of the nation's national defenses and one designed to meet any emergency.

The National Security Council

The National Security Council is located within the Executive Office of the president and is directly responsible to the president. It is composed of the president, vice-president, secretaries of state, and defense, Director of the Office of Defense Mobilization, and the Director of Foreign Operations Administration. Its supreme task is to correlate defense and foreign policies of the United States. The National Security Council has a permanent staff and executive secretary.

A significant development under the cognizance of the National Security Council was the establishment of the Central Intelligence Agency. This independent body was created to evaluate and interpret the information collected by the several governmental intelligence agencies and it has an important role in the coordination of defense and foreign policy.

An Evaluation of the National Security Organization

As was expected early experience with the operation of the National Security Organization was filled with difficulties. One could hardly expect that the age-old inter-service rivalries between the Army and the Navy would be submerged by depositing the two services within a single defense organization. Nor has the creation of a new department—the Air Force Department—made the task of unification any simpler. The sharp battle between the Air Force and the naval air branch has flared up publicly on several occasions. In theory, under the National Security Act none of the three separate departments may propose military legislation to Congress unless it is first approved by the secretary of defense and the Bureau of the Budget. But it is still possible, of course, for representatives of the different services to by-pass the secretary of defense and carry their pleas for special consideration to individual congressmen.

In a statement tinctured with optimism, the secretary of defense reported at the end of the first year [19] that "unification is not yet a complete success," and that "the predominant overtones of salt spray, wild blue yonder, and rolling caissons are not yet submerged in the three services." Certainly this statement by Secretary Forrestal put the case mildly.

Almost a decade later—in spring, 1956—deep disagreement between service spokesmen for the Army, Air Force, and Navy was still exploding to the surface. And once more the conflict revolved around the divisions of roles and the division of funds between the Army, Air Force, and Navy.

How to reach a sensible predetermination of what each service should do, of course, and how much strength each should have to do with in the event of future military conflict, presents inordinate difficulties. Army spokesmen have frequently asserted that the "use and control of all land-launched missiles is the responsibility of the Army," while the Air Force which today has control over the development and production of long-range and medium-range missiles insists that it be given control over all guided missiles and all anti-aircraft defense. And when the Air Force emphasizes that its "spectacular mobility has outmoded the most modern surface forces," the Army counters by saying that the Air Force already has too many bombers and that with the Soviet Union bent on neutralizing our air power we face subjugation unless "our military structure" is revised and greatly strengthened. And so it goes, with the triangular conflict also heating up periodically from the attacks of both Army and Air Force spokesmen against the development of huge aircraft carriers—long the Navy's special pride.

Obviously these lacerating disagreements involve more than the petty conflict of personalities, though surely such matters are involved. But at the base of the interservice wrangling are deep, earnest beliefs on how the national interest may best be served by the proper organization of the nation's defenses. Unable to compose or hold down these differences, which broke out so angrily in May, 1956, when confidential and private staff papers were "leaked" to the press, the Secretary of Defense and the civilian chiefs of the armed services put a heavy damper on the interservice row. But few doubted that keeping the quarrel quiet would

[19] A sympathetic but useful account of the first year's experience of the National Security Organization is in Robert H. Connery: "Unification of the Armed Forces— The First Year." *American Political Science Review* (1949), 43:38–52.

contain the struggle or that an amicable solution was at hand in the easily foreseeable future.

Yet despite serious ups and downs and a start that looked far from promising, the over-all results from the unification program have been encouraging. Notwithstanding improvements, however, the entire defense effort is still badly decentralized, and it is this circumstance, of course, that poses the real dilemma. For the solution of difficulties attributable to a decentralized condition of the defense program is not simply a matter of administrative technique. Essentially we all want centralization for the greater efficiency it would bring to our national security. But we do not want centralization at the expense of civilian control—a principle stoutly defended and resolutely held in American life and one not likely to yield.

THE ARMED FORCES

As now constituted, the armed forces are organized into three services— the Army, the Navy, and the Air Force. Each of the three services is headed by a civilian secretary who serves under the secretary of defense in the Department of Defense. The ranking military officials in the three services are the chief of staff of the Army, the chief of naval operations of the Navy, and the chief of staff of the Air Force.

The Department of the Army

Under the Department of the Army are the Regular Army, the National Guard, the Organized Reserve Corps, and certain other reserve units. The Organized Reserve Corps is also a formidable auxiliary to the Regular Army. By far the most important element in the O.R.C. is the Reserve Officers' Training Corps. From this group officers are drawn as emergencies arise and like National Guardsmen, reserve officers are among the first to be called in time of need. Training for reserve officers is provided in R.O.T.C. units at various universities and colleges and also in some secondary shcools. Such training is supplemented and encouraged by brief training sessions during summers and by correspondence courses.

Perhaps the most radical innovation in our military forces is the addition of a permanent Women's Army Corps. In 1942 a Women's Auxiliary Corps was authorized by Congress, and so successful was this unit that it was made a part of the Regular Army after a year and renamed the Women's Army Corps. At the recommendation of the Army's Chief of Staff, General Eisenhower, and many others, Congress authorized a small permanent Women's Army Corps in 1948.

The Department of the Navy

At the close of World War II, the United States stood unsurpassed in naval might. The belief that a one-ocean Navy which could be slipped back and forth through the Panama Canal was adequate to maintain our defense was shattered by World War II, and although the Navy has been reduced in strength since the end of hostilities the postwar policy has definitely favored a strong two-ocean Navy.

Linked with the Navy is an air unit and the United States Marine Corps. Originally established in 1798, the Marine Corps has become one of the most noted fighting units in the armed services and tales of its accomplishments in "far away places" are legion in American history. Traditionally, the conception of the Marine Corps has been a compact, highly trained organization that can be dispatched to any trouble spot with remarkable speed. In a word, the Marine Corps is "triphibious" operating on land, sea, and in the air.

Though it operates under the Department of the Treasury in peacetime, mention should be made here of the Coast Guard which becomes associated with the Navy during war. The Coast Guard's peacetime duties consist of effecting rescues at sea, saving property, enforcing customs, counteracting smuggling, enforcing maritime codes, and various other functions. In wartime, the Coast Guard undertakes operations that tie in closely with the Navy's over-all objectives.

Another supplementary aid upon which the Navy relies heavily in time of war is the Merchant Marine. Unlike the Coast Guard the Merchant Marine is not a part of the Navy even during wartime. The Merchant Marine operates under the United States Maritime Commission, but in time of war it becomes a vitally important auxiliary of the Navy and it works intimately with the regular naval forces.

The governing hierarchy of the Navy consists of the secretary who heads the Department, and the top commanding officer under the secretary, the chief of naval operations, who heads the Office of Naval Operations which is the top governing body of the Navy. Like the Army, the Navy also has an important auxiliary, the Naval Reserve, that maintains an active program of training courses and other instructionl work to keep a reserve force of officers and men in readiness for any emergency.

The Department of the Air Force

One of the major changes consummated by the National Security Act of 1947, was the creation of an independent air force. Actually, of course, an independent air force had been in existence all during the war, but the statute put the seal of statutory recognition on reality. All during World War II there was heated argument for and against a separate air force. The proponents of a separate air force cited the successes of the British Royal Air Force as an independent military arm and pointed to the frequent failure of coordination between the air forces of our own Army and Navy. Opponents of the separate air force, on the other hand, could cite some bleak spots in the fighting annals of the R.A.F. where coordination between the independent air arm and the Royal Navy reached a low ebb, and they could advance other formidable arguments against the formation of a separate air force. With the striking power of the air forces conclusively demonstrated in World War II, however, and the likelihood that air power in a war of the future would be the decisive factor, the proponents of a separate air force won the upper hand and Congress set up the Department of the Air Force under the National Military Establishment.

Like the other services, the Department of the Air Force is headed by a civilian secretary. The chief of staff is the ranking officer of the Air Force, and the General Staff—corresponding to Army practice—is the high governing and planning body of the service.

Training Facilities for the Armed Forces

Traditionally, officers for the regular army and naval forces come chiefly from the two service academies: the United States Military Academy at West Point, New York, and the United States Naval Academy at Annapolis, Maryland. Admittance to both is largely through congressional appointment, although the president and the vice-president also have a limited number of appointments. The appointments of the president and vice-president, however, are usually reserved for the sons of Army or Navy officers who because of lack of residence are unable to secure congressional appointments. There are also a limited number of appointments open to enlisted men who meet the qualifications. Each representative and senator has several appointments to West Point and Annapolis— usually around four—which he may elect to fill by competitive examination or by nominating specific candidates. All candidates, of course, must meet the mental and physical requirements before being admitted to either academy, hence it is customary for congressmen to name first, second, and third alternates for each principal candidate they nominate. In 1954 Congress also provided for a permanent air force academy to train officers for the Air Force. Appointments to this academy are made similar to those to Annapolis and West Point and the school is located at Colorado Springs.

In addition to the Military, Naval, and Air Force academies, brief mention should also be made of two other officers' training institutions. The Coast Guard maintains an academy at New London, Connecticut, and the Merchant Marine has an academy at Kings Point, New York. As yet only in the planning stage, is still another officers' training school—a proposed West Point of the Air—which will train officers for the newly created independent Air Force.

On what might be called the post-graduate level, the armed services also maintain several schools for officers. Of those mentioned by the Army, the three most important are: the National War College at Washington, D.C., the Army Industrial College, and the Command and General Staff School at Fort Leavenworth, Kansas. Since World War II, the Command and General Staff School has replaced two famed military schools which attracted students from armies all over the world, the French "École Supérieure de Guerre" and the German "Kriegsakademie," and it is now larger than Great Britain's Camberley. Besides the five hundred United

States officers (representing all three services) enrolled there in 1949, there were over fifty officers representing twenty-six different countries studying some orthodox subjects such as logistics, personnel, and intelligence, and other subjects that seemed a little more unconventional such as "philosophical and scientific concepts of war." Also included in the Army's training program are several schools for officers and enlisted men that specialize in problems of individual branches of the service.

Both of the other services—the Navy and the Air Force—maintain war colleges for the special training of officers and also operate a considerable number of technical schools and training stations for enlisted men. The armed forces also use some of our universities for the special training of officers.

THE DEFENSE DILEMMA

After dropping in the immediate postwar years—World War II—American defense expenditures skyrocketed during the Korean war which broke out in 1950. And now these expenditures average about two-thirds of our national budget. No one, not even the experts, can accurately foretell whether this amount is sufficient or whether it is entirely inadequate to assure the security of this country. As a matter of fact the military experts must certainly think the figure too small, for the preliminary budget estimates submitted by the three departments of the National Military Establishment for 1949 called for a total of thirty billion dollars. Representatives of the military services quite naturally desire large and well-equipped forces; indeed we could hardly expect otherwise. Yet it would be the height of stupidity to spend so much money for munitions and armies that the civilian economy would be dangerously weakened. Since absolute security in a military sense is probably unattainable, it would be extremely unwise to overtax our economy in pursuit of the impossible. Under present conditions large military expenditures appear to be urgent, but prudent judgment demands that they be kept proportionate to what the national economy can stand and that appropriations be spent wisely and effectively.

Interlocked with the problem of determining how large military expenditures should be is the perennial question of what to do about keeping large fighting reserves in readiness for instant action in the event of war. Do we need compulsory military training modelled after the Swiss plan? Or should we rely upon a small well-trained professional army and an organized reserve?

The answers to these questions have never emerged in such convincing fashion as to put an end to the dispute once and for all. In 1947 the President's Advisory Commission on Universal Training unanimously endorsed a plan to provide for a year's military training for every boy of eighteen who was not physically or mentally disqualified. Though this recommendation was urged upon Congress by the Chief Executive, it made little headway, and was finally by-passed in favor of a limited draft law in 1948.

Working against adoption of universal military training is the powerful tradition against large armies and distrust of compulsory peacetime training. The fear that universal military training would tend to "militarize" the outlook of our youth has also been advanced as an argument against such a plan. On the other side, it is said that the choice before us is not whether we like universal military training, but whether we are willing to make the necessary sacrifice to protect our security. Universal training—so runs this argument—is the only answer, and it need not corrode the democratic ideals of American youth if properly executed; on the contrary, it is maintained that it would stimulate more vigorous citizenship.

Whatever the merits of the arguments for universal training, it has consistently proved to be a political issue that many congressmen are anxious to avoid. And with voluntary enlistments increasing late in 1948, so that even the limited induction of draftees could be temporarily relaxed, the universal-training issue seemed dead for the time being. Left unanswered, of course, is the baffling question, has the tremendous advance in scientific warfare rendered obsolete the big Army and Navy? To this the military experts have a ready rejoinder. The same arguments, they point out, were made after World War I, but it took a tremendous military force—including huge ground forces—to turn the tide in World War II. Moreover, say the military experts, falling back upon a more traditional argument, military training aids in building up a nation's manpower physically and in supplying discipline—a discipline that is so essential to the teamwork of successful fighting forces. Perhaps the training quickly becomes outdated, they add, but discipline is something that remains and is a basic factor in the quick mobilization of a nation's manpower when disaster strikes without warning.

Put somewhat differently, much of the real debate in recent years has centered on a question that goes to the heart of modern military strategy. Shall we place our greatest reliance on nuclear weapons or on the more conventional devices of warfare and defense—huge standing armies and the traditional supporting units of large ground, naval, and air forces. The proponents of nuclear strategy with its emphasis upon guided missiles point out that conventional weapons cost more, become quickly outmoded, and are not as effective. Against these arguments, the defenders of conventional weapons insist that a too exclusive reliance upon nuclear strategy gravely limits our flexibility in meeting local outbreaks of violence with weapons suitable for a local war. Thus they maintain that by emphasizing nuclear strategy we prepare only for total war and trust that we can prevent the outbreak of small wars by threatening massive retaliation. But as the Soviet Union and the United States reach a stage of atomic parity, the above reasoning no longer seems valid. For as the USSR begins to catch up with the United States in atomic development, the threat of retaliation with nuclear weapons can be reciprocated by the Soviets.

Until more definitive answers can be given to the many questions relating to national security, and as long as world political conditions remain tense, the nation must grope along uncertainly even though the price for preparedness appears altogether unreasonable when compared with the other costs of government. Military advisers, as the noted strategist Von Clausewitz once commented, will always overestimate their needs in equipment and men. It is their business to see that their country is not vanquished by the superior military might of a conquering nation, and with this responsibility they are not likely to gamble on the short side in matters of men or equipment.

Thus the military expenditures that loom so large in the nation's budget are likely to be with us for some time along with the carping that goes on about them. There is no assurance that preparedness will avert war, yet there is a chance that it might—a possibility that cannot be ignored, particularly when the choice before us hardly favors unilateral disarmament at the moment.

Towering above all other considerations in charting national defense policies is one cardinal principle: the supreme control must remain in civilian hands—a principle vigorously reasserted by the Hoover Commission in its recommendation urging that the authority of the secretary of defense be extended. In the work that lies ahead there can be no doubt about the two most important objectives for national-defense policy. One is getting the three services to work together smoothly within the National Military Establishment; the other is securing finely coordinated teamwork in synchronizing national-defense policy with foreign policy. Our foreign commitments in Europe and in the Far East have had tremendous consequences for the organization of our national defense. The decision to begin the Berlin airlift in June, 1948, called for a careful blending of judgment of the authorities who are responsible for national defense and those whose primary concern is formulating foreign policy. In the same situation, when the question of forcing a land corridor to Berlin was raised, one could hardly conceive of the State Department making a decision without consulting the military authorities, and certainly it would be unthinkable for the military to push ahead without the consent of the persons charting foreign policy.

The problem of national-defense and foreign-policy coordination at the top administrative level is one of the first magnitude. As always, defense is an important stage prop for execution of the nation's foreign policy. The vitality of defense organization gives authority to the nation's commitments; it imparts faith to the nations who are depending upon the commitments and it serves warning to others that the commitments will be upheld by force if necessary. The harmonization of national defense and foreign policies may be expressed through the "speak softly but carry a big stick" idea or in any number of different forms. This idea was underscored in 1907 by sending the United States fleet around the world, and again in 1957 by the around-the-world non-stop flight of three B-52 Stratofortress eight-jet bombers in the record time of 45 hours and 19 minutes.

It is hardly a comforting thought to realize that the day is not yet at hand when huge armaments and military forces can be dispensed with in favor of more constructive projects, particularly in light of the outbreak of the Korean war in June, 1950. The presence of large military installations, secret weapons, big navies, armies, and air forces, breeds suspicion and distrust. There can be little doubt that the sensible long-range objective is to build a world community where national defense and the maintenance of peace is the collective responsibility of the entire community of nations. Speed the day; but meantime—while ideological differences impair progress toward this objective—it need not be assumed that the agencies of national defense may only be used negatively in the quest to build permanent peace. Under civilian control the instrumentalities of national defense can serve constructively in the cause of peace and the avoidance of war—certainly an event not to be hazarded except as a measure of last resort.[20] In terms only of the outlay of the various national treasuries of the world, the Bank of International Settlements placed the cost of World War I at $180,000,000,000 and that of World War II at $680,000,000,000. These sums by themselves are staggering but it must also be kept in mind that they take no account of the "capitalized value of human life." There is, in short, "no mathematics of human agony and misery," and the total bill presented by war is one that presses upon a nation for generations to come in human misery, veterans care, and the halt of progress. More bluntly, as one writer puts it: "The interstellar spaces can be measured in parsecs and light years, but the cost of war still defies the intelligence."

SUMMARY

A great part of the constitutional clauses granting authority to Congress deals with the powers of national defense. The President, by virtue of his authority as commander-in-chief of the armed forces and his general executive authority, likewise has important powers in this field. In time of war, especially modern war, Congress delegates power to the President generously for the purpose of mobilizing the required military and economic force. In such times civil liberties are likely to be curtailed.

Whatever the legal extent of presidential authority in the field of national defense may be, the President in practice enjoys greater freedom of action in time of war than in time of peace. Providing for na-

[20] For an excellent discussion of defense problems, see Neil MacNeil and Harold Metz, *The Hoover Commission, 1953–55* (Washington, D.C., 1956). See also Commission on Organization of the Executive Branch of the Government, *Business Organization of the Defense Department* (Washington, D.C., 1955).

tional defense requires, in time of conflict, a tremendous governmental organization regulating economic activity as well as directing the military effort proper.

The organization of our defense establishment was improved after the war with Spain by the introduction of the Army's general staff. Experience in World War II brought about the unification of the three services in a single Department of Defense in 1947. As might be expected, the passage of a law has not been enough by itself to effect a genuine unification eliminating inter-service antagonisms. Many agree with the Hoover Commission that the powers of the Secretary of Defense over the services are too limited to achieve the unification sought.

The inclusion of the National Security Council and the Office of Defense Mobilization in the Executive Office of the President facilitates planning for defense.

An historic decision was made by the nation when we pooled our defense efforts with that of other powers in the North Atlantic Treaty Organization. Among the matters still awaiting decision are whether universal military training should be put into operation and how our foreign policy and our military policy can be most effectively synchronized.

CHAPTER XXXIV

TERRITORIES AND POSSESSIONS

I N CONTRAST with the territorial possessions of other major powers such as Great Britain or France, those of the United States appear quite small, both in area and population. The total number of people living in American territories and possessions today approximates 3,000,000, now that the Philippine Islands have been given their independence, and the total area covers about 597,000 square miles. With some justification, perhaps, these figures are often cited in substantiation of the claim that the United States has never had any strong imperialistic designs and has not been inclined toward policies leading to the establishment of a vast colonial empire. But it should not be forgotten that the main phase of American territorial expansion moved continental-wise from East to West under the impetus of a series of shrewd, if not sharp, land purchases, and a war with Mexico. As these territorial annexations rolled out like a giant stair-carpet from the original thirteen colonies all the way to the Pacific coast they presented important problems of territorial government and organization. Yet, the United States was blessed by obvious advantages. Its territory was composed of contiguous units, and the frontiers pushed forward so rapidly that despite difficulties arising from the mixture of people representing many nationalities, and the persistence of regionalism, the additional territories soon became an integral part of the amalgam representing continental United States.

GENERAL PROBLEMS IN GOVERNING TERRITORIES

Any introduction to the problems presented by the government of territories and possessions must take into account certain general factors. Out of the world's population of some two billion people, close to 200,000,000, or about one-tenth,[1] live in areas that have not yet achieved full independent status. Naturally endowed with rich mineral deposits or readily adaptable to highly profitable agricultural production, these areas often play important roles in the economy of the country that governs them. They may also have strategic importance for the parent country as sites for harbors, naval coaling stations, or air bases. Thus the rivalry among nations for control of these areas is quite understandable and partly explains why some countries have been reluctant to relinquish voluntarily their authority over territories. Desirable as the idea of autonomy may be, one may not ignore the fact that the conditions among colonial regions differ greatly and that premature severance of territorial ties may actually retard an area's development. Because there are significant differences in the cultural and social development of peoples living in colonial regions and their rate of progress is not uniform, the amount of government control that needs to be imposed in these areas varies. An intelligent governmental policy for the administration of territories, therefore, must take stock of these factors and make allowances for individual differences among them.

A primary problem in the government of territories is the division of powers between the home government and the area to be governed. In the case of a more retarded area obviously the amount of local self-government that the territory is permitted to exercise is quite limited. The island of Guam, for example, was once administered by our Navy without any provision for local self-government. But the naval government of Guam has now been terminated, and Guam's 37,500 inhabitants who have recently obtained full United States citizenship are practicing local self-government under a legislature they elect for themselves (a unicameral body of 21 representatives elected at large). The governor of Guam is appointed by the president and the government is responsible administratively to the Department of Interior. As matters now stand the Guam legislature cannot override the governor's veto, but if a measure is passed over the governor's veto by a two-thirds vote, it goes directly to the president.[2]

As the territories acquire more local autonomy to handle their own affairs, the problem of deciding the scope of their jurisdiction becomes more complex. Thus decisions must be made regarding subjects that territories may regulate by their own laws and these laws in turn must be watched to see that they do not come into conflict with the statutory regulations imposed by the home country. Closely linked with the problem of legislative jurisdiction is that of deciding what powers are to be exercised by the home authorities through their directly appointed agents

---

[1] See W. H. Mallory in *Nationalism and Progress in Free Asia*, edited by Phillip Thayer (Johns Hopkins University Press, 1955), p. 56.
[2] *New York Times*, March 4, 1956.

and what authority is to be delegated to the territory's own units of government. Here the issue is not simply a matter of using local personnel to carry out the policies of the home country; it calls for a careful determining of the authority that is to be entrusted to the territorial government and it also suggests the need for having the agents of the territorial government and those of the home government work together in a harmonious relationship.

Constitutional Authority to Acquire Territory

The immediate constitutional question that bothered some of our early statesmen who faced important decisions on acquiring territory, was whether the Constitution sanctioned such acquisition. Under Article IV, Section 3, the Constitution provides for the admission of new states, and it also gives Congress the right to establish rules and regulations for the governance of territory or other property belonging to the United States. At the time of the Louisiana Purchase, however, it was thought that this section of the Constitution referred only to territory belonging to the United States when the Constitution was adopted. For this reason, and because "of the fear that France might withdraw from the bargain," Thomas Jefferson urged that little be said publicly about the constitutional question pending settlement of the purchase negotiations.[3] The Senate did, of course, ratify the treaty concluded with France for the purchase of the Louisiana Territory, and the House subsequently appropriated the ridiculously low sum of $15,000,000 to pay for it, but it was not until 1819 that the Supreme Court took up the question of the power of this government to acquire and govern territory. In passing upon the issue, Chief Justice Marshall declared that as the Constitution gave the government of the Union absolute powers of making war, "consequently that Government possesses the power of acquiring territory either by conquest or by treaty." [4] Once having acquired territory, therefore, the authority to govern came from the clause of the Constitution empowering Congress "to make all needful rules and regulations respecting territory, or other property belonging to the United States." While this precedent firmly anchored the right of the United States to acquire contiguous territory, it was nearly a century before the Supreme Court tackled the more spectacular issues arising over the right of this nation to acquire and govern territories lying outside the continental limits of the United States.

One further item relating to the means of acquiring territory should be mentioned in passing. Although John Marshall isolated the treaty- and war-making powers as the chief sources of authority for the acquisition of territory, international law also recognizes two other methods—discovery

[3] Carl Brent Swisher: *American Constitutional Development* (Boston, 1943), p. 122.
[4] The American Insurance Co. v. 356 Bales of Cotton, 1 Peters 511 (1828).

and occupation. It was on this basis that jurisdiction was assumed over the Guano Island in 1856. The appropriation of Guano incidentally marked the United States' first acquisition of non-contiguous territory, and was done because of the need for the Island's fertilizer deposits.

Territorial Government in the United States

The leading acquisitions in the territorial expansion of the United States are too well-known to chronicle here. By 1853 the Gadsen Purchase in the Southwest had about completed the contours of this nation's boundaries as we know them today. With each new acquisition, Congress set up a territorial government and awaited the territory's political maturity to qualify it for admission to statehood. Under the Northwest Ordinance of 1787 Congress had carved out a plan which provided for a very rudimentary government to be followed by a full-blown territorial government with an elective legislature as soon as there were "five thousand free male inhabitants of full age in the district." Before this plan could be effected, however, the new Federal Constitution had been adopted and a more comprehensive plan was needed for territorial government. But even when the treaty for the Louisiana Purchase was ratified in 1803, Congress had no well-conceived plan for governing the newly acquired territory. As an emergency expedient, Congress passed an act giving the president broad authority to establish a temporary government, and before adjourning, worked out an extensive measure providing for the establishment of a territorial government.

Obviously the mere addition of contiguous territory raised many problems beyond the basic question of the right of acquisition, problems for which those who concerned themselves with public policy were not completely prepared. For example, when a new territory was acquired, what policy should be followed with respect to import duties? Should goods reaching the United States from the territories be duty free or should they be taxed the same as articles imported from foreign countries? Some persons also objected to the extension of certain constitutional guarantees to the inhabitants of the territories. Thus it was contended by a few that Article III of the Louisiana Purchase Treaty which incorporated the inhabitants of the territory into the United States, and gave them all the rights, advantages, and immunities of citizens of the United States, should not be applied. In resolving all such matters, the fact must not be overlooked that Congress acted knowing that some decision must be taken, and with very little reason to believe that its action would be challenged by any other government tribunal. Fifty years passed after the Marbury v. Madison decision without any Act of Congress being held unconstitutional by the Supreme Court, hence it is quite understandable that in the matter of territory regulation, as in other questions of legislative policy, Congress grew accustomed to having its determinations stand.

Constitutional Issues in the Non-contiguous Territories

The real test of the power of the United States to govern her non-contiguous territories was precipitated by the acquisition of certain insular possessions following the Spanish American War. Alaska, to be sure, was the first non-contiguous territory of any consequence that the United States acquired (by purchase from Russia in 1867), but it presented few problems because of its sparse population. As a result of our treaty with Spain in 1898, however, the islands of Puerto Rico and the Philippines were acquired, and in the same year the Hawaiian Islands were annexed. Thus, the United States possessed an alien colonial empire for the first time. These new additions gave the United States jurisdiction over several million peoples of racial backgrounds different from that of Americans, most of whom were completely unfamiliar with Anglo-Saxon laws and political institutions. The main issue was whether a territory that is annexed to the United States becomes automatically an integral part of the United States. This issue, along with several related questions, was decided by the Supreme Court in May, 1901, in a famous series of judicial decisions known as the Insular Cases.

There were two factors underlying the Insular Cases; one was economic, while the other turned on the more fundamental problem of the applicability of constitutional safeguards of life, liberty, and property to the people of the outlying territories. The economic factor was linked with the general argument over imperialism, and, more specifically, centered on the authority of the United States to impose tariff and customs duties on goods shipped into this country from the territories. It was to the advantage of certain American business and commercial interests to secure the annexation of the territories on a duty-free basis. On the other hand, the opponents of this group—chiefly business competitors— wanted customs duties continued even though ownership of the territories was now vested in the United States. Each side sought to present its case by amassing precedents and various arguments to prove the validity of its contention, one urging that the Constitution requires that duties be uniform and prohibits taxes on exports from any state; the other insisting that the mere acquisition of a territory does not automatically bestow upon it all the blessings of the Constitution. In more popular phrasing, the issue narrowed down to the question: Does the Constitution follow the flag?

A major difficulty in handling this question, as one might expect, is determining how much of the Constitution follows the flag. The initial controversy arose over the collection of tariff duties on goods imported into the United States from Puerto Rico, following the annexation of this island to the United States. On this issue the Supreme Court held that when Puerto Rico was annexed to the United States it ceased to be a foreign territory, and that while it was not made an integral part of the

United States by simply being annexed, duties could not be collected on Puerto Rican imports without further congressional action.[5]

Incorporated and Unincorporated Territories

Soon after Congress followed the above-mentioned decision with legislation that retained some duties upon imports from Puerto Rico and the Philippines, another case was presented to the Supreme Court challenging the tariff laws on the ground that they violated the constitutional requisite that "all duties, imports, and excises, shall be uniform throughout the United States." To the contention that Puerto Rico became an integral part of the United States under the terms of this constitutional provision the Supreme Court gave a negative reply. Apparently taking a cue from the article in the Louisiana Purchase Treaty that declared the "inhabitants of the ceded territory shall be incorporated in the Union of the United States . . ." the Court held that territories might be classified into two categories, incorporated and unincorporated. The test of whether a territory is incorporated or unincorporated depends upon the action or implied intent of Congress, said the Court. Because Congress had not expressly or impliedly indicated an intent that Puerto Rico become an incorporated territory, it was not automatically entitled to equal consideration under our tariff laws, nor would it become so entitled unless Congress acted. Therefore even though a new territory might be annexed, it was not necessarily privileged to enjoy equal treatment under the Constitution and laws of the United States.

More concretely, the decisions in the Insular Cases make it clear that an incorporated territory becomes an integral part of the United States and that it enjoys the full protection of all provisions in the Federal Constitution as well as equality of treatment under the laws and treaties of the United States. The United States now has two incorporated territories—Alaska and Hawaii—but the test of what action does incorporate a territory is still somewhat ambiguous.[6] Citizenship has been extended to inhabitants of both Hawaii and Alaska; however, the conferment of citizenship is an independent act and does not depend upon whether a territory is incorporated or unincorporated. In 1918, for example, Congress conferred American citizenship upon the inhabitants of Puerto Rico, yet the Supreme Court found that this measure did not incorporate Puerto Rico as a territory because other provisions in the same Act suggested a different conclusion.

Besides the economic advantages that accrue to the incorporated

[5] De Lima v. Bidwell, 182 U.S. 1 (1901).

[6] The Hawaiian Islands were incorporated into the United States by the Organic Act for the territory that was enacted in 1900. Alaska, as a result of a Supreme Court decision of 1905, was held to have been incorporated into the United States by the treaty of acquisition and subsequent acts of Congress. See Carl Brent Swisher: *American Constitutional Development*, p. 480.

territories because they are exempted from paying duties on goods exported to the United States, the inhabitants of these areas possess other important privileges which are denied to the nationals of the unincorporated territories. People living in Hawaii, Alaska, or Puerto Rico may travel freely between these territories and continental United States, and they may emigrate to this country permanently without being subject to our immigration laws.[7]

In the non-economic sphere, the distinction between the incorporated and unincorporated territories raised some interesting questions in connection with the Bill of Rights of the Federal Constitution. Do the constitutional provisions guaranteeing a jury trail or a grand-jury indictment apply with equal force in both the incorporated and unincorporated territories? And, if not, to what extent are the civil liberties protected by the first ten amendments of the Constitution applicable in the unincorporated territories? This question the Supreme Court proceeded to answer by distinguishing between the constitutional guarantees of civil liberty that it regarded as fundamental and those that were procedural. The fundamental guarantees were held to follow the flag, while the procedural ones were declared not to be binding upon Congress in governing the unincorporated territories. Thus a jury trial—with which most of the inhabitants living in Puerto Rico or the Philippines under Spanish dominion were completely unfamiliar—was held to be a procedural, rather than a fundamental, guarantee. If Congress desires to substitute a method of judicial trial other than the jury trial in an unincorporated territory, it may do so without violating the Constitution because this is a procedural guarantee, not a fundamental one.

The Supreme Court has not yet been compelled to state which of the several constitutional provisions protecting civil liberties are fundamental. It is generally assumed, however, that the items guaranteeing religious freedom, due process of law, freedom from cruel and unusual punishments, freedom of speech or press, and quite likely, just compensation for property taken by eminent domain, would fall into the fundamental category. In the procedural group, Congress may exercise its discretion in deciding which of the constitutional requirements shall be extended. Should the United States acquire a new territory, Congress might quite conceivably decide that an information indictment might be preferable to the grand-jury indictment in criminal cases. But in any territory, unincorporated or incorporated, the fundamental guarantees of the Constitution apply *in toto*, and in our most important unincorporated territory today—Puerto Rico—the exceptions among the complete list of constitutional guarantees are of minor significance.

[7] The emigration of Puerto Ricans to the United States produced an acute social problem in the City of New York during the summer of 1947. See *New York Times*, July 31, 1947. At that time it was estimated that about 3,000 Puerto Ricans were coming to New York City each month and while most of them were employable the lack of adequate housing created a critical health situation.

THE ORGANIZED TERRITORIAL GOVERNMENTS [8]

Since the Philippines embarked on the first lap of their independence on July 4, 1946, the United States has only five territories that have what might be called organized governments with some measure of legislative autonomy. They are Alaska, Hawaii, Puerto Rico, the Virgin Islands, and Guam. These five territories have similar governmental structures, although the Virgin Islands have a lesser degree of local autonomy. The constitution of each of the territories consists of the basic Acts of Congress that provide for their respective governments. With the exception of Puerto Rico which now elects its own governor, all the territorial governments have a governor, appointed by the president with the Senate's consent, and usually bicameral legislatures.[9] The governor in the incorporated territories serves for a four-year term, but in the unincorporated territories he serves at the pleasure of the president. In the incorporated territories, the governor's veto power may be negated by a two-thirds vote in both branches of the territorial legislature, but this is not true of the unincorporated territories where if a veto is overridden, the governor may submit the law in question to the president of the United States. If the president concurs with the governor's veto, the measure fails of enactment. In practice, the governor's position is frequently awkward. The governor is cast in a dual role, as the representative of the United States and as the executive responsible for enforcing the laws of this country and those enacted by the territory. While his sympathies may lie with the territory on certain matters, he is sometimes constrained to act against his own judgment in the enforcement of legislation, and he not infrequently finds himself caught between the grinders of pressure politics in both the United States and the territory.

Members of territorial legislatures are elected by popular vote, and the voting qualifications are quite liberal. But the authority of these legislative bodies is limited, particularly on indebtedness. In addition to the requirement that the laws of the territorial legislatures be in accord with the Constitution, the territories must keep strictly within the legislative boundaries defined by Congress.

For their judicial systems, the territories have both territorial courts, somewhat comparable to our state courts, and Federal courts. Federal judges are appointed by the president with senatorial confirmation. Representation of the territories in Congress gives Alaska and Hawaii one delegate each, and Puerto Rico one resident commissioner. These three represent the territories and insular possessions in our House of Representatives by taking part in discussions and debate, but are not allowed

---

[8] For a more extended account of the territorial governments see Edwin G. Arnold: "Self-Government in U.S. Territories." *Foreign Affairs* (1947), 25:655-66.

[9] The Virgin Islands are divided into two "municipalities," each of which has a "municipal council."

to vote—a circumstance that has inspired severe criticism among the populace of the territories.

Among the smaller possessions of the United States are places such as the Panama Canal Zone, Samoa, and several other islands located mainly in the Pacific. Because of their strategic importance to our military security their administration has been left nominally in the hands of the president. The actual administration of these areas, however, devolves upon the Army and Navy Departments. In the Panama Canal Zone executive authority is vested in a governor, who is appointed by the president with the Senate's approval. Here, however, the practice has been to select an Army officer as governor, and this in turn has meant that the Department of the Army administers the area. Among the Pacific Islands, several, including Samoa—sometimes referred to as "naval despotisms" —are governed by the Navy. As these scattered areas are small and unable to defend themselves against a powerful aggressor their eventual disposition can be only a matter of conjecture. Pending a more peaceful interlude on the international diplomatic front, the United States will probably continue to weld these areas as firmly as possible into a series of concentric circles that mark our outer military defenses. But it might be noted in passing that while the opportunities for any substantial element of "home rule" or "self-government" have been negligible in these areas, there have been notable improvements in health and education.

The Philippines

The greatest contraction of American territorial possessions took place when the Philippine Commonwealth secured its independence July 4, 1946, under the terms of congressional acts passed in 1933 and 1934. After prolonged debate and several false starts, Congress finally adopted a measure which was acceptable to the Filipinos authorizing their independence approximately ten years after the establishment of the Commonwealth government. The bitterness of this controversy is partly reflected in the fact that after Congress passed the first Independence Act over President Hoover's veto, it was rejected by the Filipinos.[10] In effect, this bill would have granted independence, but at a price that would most certainly have been disastrous for the Philippine economy. Agricultural interests in the United States jockeyed Congress into a position where the Philippines were to be given little advantage under our tariff laws and in this way they hoped to ring down the curtain on Philippine trade with this country. In reality, however, the first Independence Act turned out to be a measure that was disappointing even to its original advocates. "The most that can be said about the independence act," as one investigator reports, "is that it satisfied no one." [11] The disavowal of

[10] In a vigorous veto message, President Hoover said the bill completely failed to discharge our obligation to the American people, the Philippine people, and to the entire world. See Grayson Kirk: *Philippine Independence* (New York, 1936), p. 120.

[11] Ibid., p. 123.

this measure by the Filipinos led to the adoption of another, the Tydings-McDuffie Act, which proved acceptable. Under its terms, elective machinery was organized to select a constitutional convention and, after a constitution was drafted and approved, officers were elected to head the new Philippine government. This government began to function late in 1935 simultaneously with a proclamation by President Roosevelt authorizing the independence of the Philippines.

To graduate the economic hardships that the young Republic would most certainly face, the Philippine Independence Act, as it is now known, did not grant complete independence until July 4, 1946. Moreover, it stipulated favorable concessions on tariffs even following this date, concessions that will be most essential for the trade of the Philippines during her incubation period as a sovereign nation. The present arrangements call for giving Philippine commodities a trade advantage in the American market until 1974. For the first eight years the Republic may export products to the United States duty free on a quota basis; thereafter all commodities become subject to a graduated increase on tariff rates for twenty years at the end of which preferential treatment ceases.

The Japanese occupation of the Philippines during three years of World War II did, of course, seriously impede the progress of this experiment in self-government, but final severance of the tie with the United States went off on schedule nonetheless. In the spring of 1946 the Philippine people elected Manuel Acuna Roxas to the presidency and he was sworn in on July 4, on the one hundred and seventy-first anniversary of the signing of our Declaration of Independence. Thus the Philippine Republic—with its estimated 18,000,000 people and 114,000 square miles—started off as the most important American possession to receive complete autonomy. But with the United States as its chief customer and as the model for many of its political institutions, the association of the two seems destined to continue a course of close collaboration.

For defensive purposes, the Philippines and the United States have strengthened their ties since the Islands secured their independence. In 1947 agreements were concluded providing for the maintenance of naval bases in the Islands, and in 1951 the governments of the United States and the Philippines announced a Treaty of Mutual Defense which provided closer integration of our defense strategy.

Perhaps the most painful experience that the young Philippine government encountered initially was the resistance from the forces of internal subversion. Guerilla bands—the Huks—terrorized many communities, but despite difficulties in putting down these forces, the government made real progress in stabilizing the internal conditions of the country.

On another front the Philippine Government could also report real progress. By early 1957 the Administration of President Ramon Magasaysay could document unusual advances in the fight against disease. Up until 1953 malaria took 100,000 lives annually and caused in excess of 20,-

000,000 attacks of the disease per year. The loss in the labor force, as well as pain suffered, was staggering. But by 1957, preventive medicine had reduced the prevalence of malaria as much as 70 to 80 per cent.

Puerto Rico

Among the remaining territories now owned by the United States the one that presents the most difficult economic and social problems is Puerto Rico. This small island, located at the eastern end of the Greater Antilles in the Caribbean, is only one hundred miles long and approximately thirty-four to forty miles wide. Its population of two million has increased so rapidly that its birth rate is now three times that of the United States. But is mortality rate is nearly twice that of the United States, and the great bulk of its people are living far below standard subsistence levels. Recent estimates show that nearly 90 per cent of the rural, and 40 per cent of the urban population are infected with hookworm, and the death rate from tuberculosis is five times that of the United States.

Coupled with these stark but revealing figures on the living conditions of this island is the ominous fact that Puerto Rico's economy is unable to support this overcrowded population. Moreover, even a most optimistic view of the situation leaves some serious doubts about whether any amount of outside priming can raise the island's domestic economy enough to keep its living standards on a decent level. The main crop of Puerto Rico is sugar, but the sugar supply of the world is already dangerously close to glutting the market. Other crops are produced, such as coffee, tobacco, and bananas, but the island has no mineral resources to speak of and still suffers the usual ills of a one-crop economy.

To top all of these complications, Puerto Rico has been beset with a growing nationalism. Like all colonial regions that begin to experience political growing pains, Puerto Rico yearns for a new deal, and in accepted tradition tends to fix the responsibility for her economic ills upon the country that governs her. The United States is the primary object of many political harangues, and indeed with the utmost frankness many Puerto Rican politicians privately acknowledge the value of a scapegoat and confess that "the wheel that squeaks the loudest gets the most grease." The current idol of Puerto Rican politics is Muñoz Marin, first popularly elected governor (1948), who has succeeded in both acquiring a tremendous following and effecting some land reforms and significant industrialization programs. Muñoz Marin called for independence at first, but now seems to prefer a well-subsidized commonwealth status.

Without question, many of the grievances of Puerto Ricans are well founded. The island has had its share of commercial exploitation, and the $171.29 average yearly wage for the family of a *jibaro* (agricultural worker) suggests an extremely unhealthy economic condition. Until just a few years ago a half-dozen sugar corporations owned 75 per cent of the land fit for sugar raising. This figure has been trimmed recently and a

large part of the acreage fit for sugar production is now owned by the
Puerto Rican Land Authority as a result of a determined move by Muñoz
Marin and his Popular party to nationalize the large land holdings. The
statistics for 1945 showed that four sugar companies owned 69,470 acres,
or about 23 per cent of the land suitable for raising sugar, and of this total 22,940 acres were to be transferred to the Puerto Rican Land Authority during 1946.

While the Popular party program since 1946 seemed mildly radical
with its purchase of corporation lands, dissolution of company villages,
and stoppage of foreclosures, the over-all objectives seem "essentially
conservative." All of these reforms, noted one observer late in 1955, "have
been nurtured within the framework of a social philosophy taking for
granted the perpetuation of a welfare capitalism along American lines." [12]

On the administrative side of governmental policy, the result of
granting Puerto Rico Commonwealth status in 1953 is that it has at present almost complete autonomy in internal matters. But careful note
should be made that almost no power was conceded to Puerto Rico on
external matters—foreign policy and national defense. The government
of the United States, in fact, still has power to conscript in the Island.

However, that the attainment of Commonwealth status by Puerto
Rico significantly alters the relationship between this country and the
United States in the eyes of other nations is commonly acknowledged.
Because of this decision, the United Nations has agreed that the United
States need no longer send information about Puerto Rico as it was formerly obligated to do under Article 73 of the UN Charter. Moreover,
Fernos Isern, speaking on behalf of Puerto Rico, was able to conclude
before the fourth Committee of the United Nations General Assembly
that "the last vestige of colonialism had disappeared in Puerto Rico. . . ."
And the progress of the Puerto Rican Islands in the past decade has
been nothing short of remarkable. In 1957 there were 400 factories;
where in 1940 there were four. Life expectancy in the same period had
been raised from 46 to 68 years, and trade between the United States
and Puerto Rico in the middle 1950's was larger than the per capita trade
between the United States and Brazil.

Serious social and economic problems are still confronting Puerto
Rico in a menacing way, of course. As Muñoz Marin himself puts it,
"population" hangs like a heavy bag of gold around an imaginary swimmer's neck as the swimmer struggles toward a distant shore labeled "industrialization." But nonetheless Puerto Rico no longer fits the answer
Christopher Columbus reputedly gave the Queen of Spain when asked
to describe the island. "It's like that," he said as he tossed a crumpled
piece of paper on the table. Today a far fuller description would be required.

Some complaint has also been lodged against the inadequacy of the

[12] See Gordon K. Lewis's useful article, "Puerto Rico: A Case Study of Change in
an Undeveloped Area," *Journal of Politics* 17 (1955), p. 625.

administrative agency that handles territorial affairs for the United States. Early in Franklin Roosevelt's administration, the executive jurisdiction over the territories was transferred from the War Department to the Department of Interior. The agency under the latter department that now has supervision over Alaska, Hawaii, the Virgin Islands, and a few other scattered possessions is the Division of Territories and Island Possessions. Although definite progress has been made by the Division of Territories during recent years, it has operated under an extremely limited budget. But even conceding the handicaps this supervisory unit has suffered, several critics insist that an agency with more authority and prestige is needed for running the territories. The United States, it is urged, is the only large nation that does not have a ministerial post for colonies, and to govern the territories effectively we need more than the Division of Territories "carrying on routine functions in the bowels of the Interior Department."

Looked at in a full perspective, the problems of governing the territories cannot all be compressed under the jurisdiction of one broad colonial department no matter how great its prestige might be. Like the social and economic problems of the United States, those of the territories become the concern of several governmental agencies. Thus technical and financial assistance has been extended in Puerto Rico by such Federal agencies as the Federal Public Housing Authority, the Farm Security Administration, and the Agricultural Adjustment Administration. The provisions of the National Labor Relations Act are also applicable in some areas, and on matters of labor conciliation, both the Labor Department of the Federal government and the Insular Labor Relations Board have jurisdiction. As the problems call for action by several different Federal departments, so the successful administration of territorial government depends upon the proper coordination of these efforts. A colonial department for the territories with more extensive authority might be of some value, but the more specialized tasks of government are preferably left to the agencies whose experience and training equip them for technical functions. Again, in seeking the coordination of administrative agencies, a balance must be achieved between the home government and that of the territory. Within the United States the same basic problem exists in Federal-state relations where a joint activity is undertaken. In this relationship, the state authorities keep a watchful eye on Federal activities, ever fearful that States' rights are being usurped. Similarly in the relation between the home government and that of the territory, the territorial authorities want whatever jurisdiction they possess to be kept more than a fiction.

Although the shortcomings of our territorial policies have been serious, the positive accomplishments of the United States government in these areas are to be commended. True, millions of dollars have been poured into Puerto Rico without making appreciable improvement in housing and health conditions of the island. But the same is true for the

State of Mississippi. Moreover the question that must always be asked in weighing the territorial policies of a government is what would be the status of the possession if it were either autonomous or under the jurisdiction of some other power. Despite all the flamboyant oratory championing independence for Puerto Rico, it seems probable that much of the talk for immediate independence of this territory refers to a "literary" independence, and that what the Puerto Ricans really want is neither statehood nor independence, but rather a status that will enable the country to enjoy the advantages of both.

Whatever the immediate merits of full autonomy for areas like Puerto Rico, however, there is much to be said for the humanitarian and philanthropic merits of continued colonial rule in extremely backward areas where the tutelage aims not at exploitation but at economic and social improvement, and eventually self-government for these regions. Again, in the larger territories as in the tiny insular possessions like Samoa, the future course of United States' action seems destined to be conditioned by the changing international scene. In the meantime the development of carefully planned "trusteeships" under the auspices of the United Nations offers, perhaps, a hopeful successor to the old mandate system under the League of Nations. But if these areas are eventually going to be able to become an integral part of the economy of the international family of nations, it goes without saying that tariffs and trade barriers will have to be scaled down.

Trusteeships

As a signatory to the United Nations Charter, the United States has pledged itself to be responsible for the 3,000,000 people who live in what the Charter described as "non-self-governing territories." Under Article 73, Chapter XI, of the Charter, administering powers are obligated "to promote to the utmost, within the system of international peace and security . . . the well-being of the inhabitants of these territories." The same article of the Charter also requires administering powers "to develop self-government, to take due account of the political aspirations of the peoples, and to assist them in the progressive development of their free political institutions . . ." Acting in compliance with the trusteeship provisions of the Charter that directs nations with dependencies to submit regular reports on the economic, social, and educational conditions in the territories for which they are responsible, the United States was the first nation to transmit such a report to the secretary general of the United Nations on August 19, 1946.[13] In this report covering Alaska, Hawaii, the Virgin Islands, Puerto Rico, American Samoa, the Panama Canal Zone, and the island possessions of the Pacific, both the accomplishments and shortcomings of our territorial administration were discussed.

One of the most interesting experiments in trusteeship responsibility

[13] U.S. Department of State: *The United States and Non-Self-Governing Territories,* Publication No. 2812 (Washington, 1947), p. 21.

is the administrative program of the United States under the strategic trust agreement for the Pacific Islands. These islands were subjected to the direction of the United States Secretary of the Navy until July 1, 1951, after which administrative responsibility was transferred to the Department of Interior. Initially, the United States has pursued an ambitious program in the islands, striving to build regional governments by perfecting first the governments within the municipalities. The strategy behind this policy is that after regional governments have been built, a government for the entire territory will be more likely to succeed. But such an objective is complicated by the fact that a mere 56,000 people (indigenous inhabitants) live in an area of some 3,000,000 square miles.

The Ryukyu Islands: Problem Child of American Military Administration

Okinawa is the major island of the Ryukyu group (population 1,000,000) which has remained under American military government control since World War II. And while the peace treaty concluded with Japan in 1951 declares that the United States will exercise "immediate control" over the islands but implies that Japan retains "residual sovereignty," the meaning of the latter is far from clear.

There is little doubt that the present policy of the United States suggests an intention to remain custodian of these islands for the foreseeable future, that is for as long as tension exists in the Far East. The Ryukyus, it will be noted, are not trusteeship territories. Instead, our authority has been termed "custodial and temporary."

Recently there has been growing pressure from the Japanese government—motivated by Japanese public opinion—to surrender these islands. But the unsettled condition of world affairs combined with the fact that the United States now has large naval and air bases on these islands may delay our departure from the Ryukyus for some time to come.[14]

THE INCORPORATED TERRITORIES

Hawaii

In the case of our two incorporated territories, Alaska and Hawaii, the interconnections with this country have long precluded the question of divorcement. The main debate of the moment on Alaska and Hawaii is whether their relationship to the United States is sufficiently close to justify statehood.[15] After twenty-seven years of intermittent debate, the House of Representatives passed the Farrington Bill in 1947, providing for the admission of Hawaii as the forty-ninth state, but the measure

[14] For an excellent analysis, see Ralph Braibanti, "The Ryukyu Islands: Pawn of the Pacific," *Amer. Pol. Sci. Rev.*, 48 (1954), pp. 972–8.

[15] Since 1920, twenty-eight statehood bills for Hawaii have been introduced in Congress.

failed to pass the Senate. With a population of 519,000 people, Hawaii, at the time this statehood bill was passed, was larger than any other territory when admitted to the Union, except Oklahoma. The two principal arguments given against Hawaiian statehood were that it was an impractical move because the area was not contiguous with continental United States and that its polyglot population would make its people unassimilable. The first objection has gradually been overcome by the erosion of time and rapid improvement of transportation. Champions of the second argument, pointing out that 32.5 per cent of the Hawaiian Islands inhabitants are Japanese, objected to the "mongrel" composition of the population.[16] Typical of this view was a statement by one congressman that our approval of the statehood for the islands "would put 180,000 Japanese on a political par with those who created this country." Expressing similar sentiments in a letter to the House Committee on Public Lands, the late Nicholas Murray Butler, formerly President of Columbia University, speculated nervously over the prospect of a Japanese United States Senator from Hawaii.[17] To its credit the House Committee rejected such arguments, pointing out that the Japanese of the Hawaiian Islands had loyal records during World War II, and that, of 159,000 persons of Japanese ancestry, all but 35,000 were American citizens. In addition, attention was called to the fact that thus far in Hawaiian local elections there has never been any indications of bloc voting by racial groups. Political sentiments divided quite evenly for a time in the islands—the Democratic candidate for mayor in Honolulu, for example, won election in 1946 by a majority of just 16 votes over his Republican opponent out of 200,000 ballots cast. But in 1956, the Democratic Territorial candidate for Congress easily defeated Republican Territorial delegate, Elizabeth Farrington, and the apparent ascendancy of Democratic party fortunes in the islands along with 116 postwar strikes and work stoppages left Hawaiian statehood fortunes in the 85th Congress very uncertain.

Objections to Hawaiian statehood were voiced by a few labor spokesmen who felt that the addition of two more United States senators from a state that might be classified as agricultural would mean two additional conservative, or anti-labor, votes in the Senate. They charged that a few large sugar and pineapple companies would be able to dominate Hawaiian politics. The contention hardly squares with the political behavior of the islands in their territorial elections, and it might also be noted that labor is well organized, particularly in such groups as the C.I.O.'s Longshoreman's and Warehouseman's Union.[18] Total membership in the C.I.O., for example, grew from 900 in 1943 to 32,000 in 1946 and stood at 22,-000 in 1956.

The chief economic objection to the admission of Hawaii as a state

[16] The latest breakdown of racial extraction groups showed 3 per cent of the population to be Hawaiian, 11 per cent part Hawaiian, 2 per cent Puerto Rican, 6 per cent Chinese, 1.5 per cent Korean, 11 per cent Filipino, and 32.5 per cent Japanese.

[17] See *New York Herald Tribune*, June 9, 1947.

[18] See Blake Clark: *Hawaii: The 49th State* (New York, 1947), pp. 174–82.

appeared to spring from a fear that statehood might have an adverse effect on Hawaiian business. Under territorial status the wholesale importers have been receiving a discount ranging from 5 to 15 per cent on all products coming from the United States. This, apparently, is a general export rate, and it is widely believed that the large importing firms, and most of the small business men, to whom part of this saving is passed on, will lose this advantage after Hawaii becomes a state. As retail prices are far higher in Hawaii than in the United States, however, a satisfactory adjustment should be possible during the transitional period, which would compensate, at least in part, for the former discount advantage.

Favoring statehood for the Islands at this time is an expanding business and trade. Although popularly thought of as a vacation land or playground, the Hawaiian Islands imported from the United States products totalling about $115,000,000 in 1941 and exported commodities to the mainland valued at $101,000,000 in the same year. The Hawaiian Islands at the time the Farrington Bill passed the House were paying more taxes to the Federal government than fourteen of our present states and they were also further advanced in education and some public services than several states.

The Statehood bill proposed in 1947 for Hawaiian admission to the Union followed the usual formula, providing first for a popular election to select delegates for drafting a constitution, and then another election to ratify the instrument. Once ratified, the constitution would go to the president for approval, and a third election would then be held to select Hawaii's new state officials along with two United States senators and two representatives.

In 1951 a constitution was drawn up for Hawaii, but since that time, despite continuing agitation, no affirmative action by Congress has followed. Failure of the Congress to come through with enacting legislation, no doubt, was one reason why delegates to the Alaska Constitutional Convention tried a little different strategy five years later.

Alaska

Running concurrently with the agitation for Hawaii's admission as a state is a similar campaign for Alaska. After eighty years of United States ownership, 60 per cent of the residents of this territory voted for statehood in a plebiscite on October 8, 1946, and this touched off a vigorous plea for the admission of the region as a state. While Alaska is not contiguous with the continental limits of the United States, geographically it can lay claim to closer connections than can the Hawaiian Islands. Alaska is a part of the North American continent and, unlike the Islands, has a homogenous population made up largely of persons who have migrated from the United States.

But Alaska also has social and economic difficulties. Her population is still only around 90,000—30,000 of whom are Indians—a fact which the proponents of Hawaiian statehood emphasized in seeking to prove the superiority over Alaska's of their claim to statehood. Moreover, for a time following World War I, the population of Alaska actually declined and did not pick up again until the 1930's.

The climatic features of the region have constantly been a drawback to large-scale settlement. Economically, Alaska, like other territories, has suffered because of her lopsided economy. Her two main industries are fishing and gold mining. The highly seasonal nature of the former industry has contributed annually to her economic discomfort. Over 12,000 migrant fishermen and cannery workers, and thousands of other laborers who serve seasonal industries, take their earnings to Seattle each autumn, with the result that little of this purchasing power contributes toward the economic well-being of the territory. Careless conservation policies have also endangered this industry. Ernest Gruening in his keynote address to the Alaska Constitutional Convention in November, 1955, reported that the salmon pack had fallen from eight million cases in 1935 to 2,382,131 cases in 1955—the lowest in forty-six years. And the responsibility for this decline he lays to lack of self-government, pointing out that in neighboring British Columbia and Washington State where fisheries are regulated by home rule, and "where fish traps have been abolished, the identical resource has not only been conserved but augmented."

Alaska has not been without its ardent enthusiasts, however, many of whom have recently joined in the crusade for statehood. Spearheaded by its Territorial Governor, Dr. Ernest Gruening, several attacks have been unleased against "absentee ownership," and the campaign for statehood now seems well under way. A salmon industry which produced fish worth $59,000,000 in 1946, an estimated eighty billion feet of virgin spruce and hemlock, along with untold riches in mineral wealth, all give some idea of the economic prize that is at stake in Alaska. As the lines are drawn for the fight to attain statehood, it seems fairly evident that some sturdy opposition will come from business interests that have become acclimated to Federal regulation of the territory, but are dubious, or at least have some reservations, about the consequences of dual sovereignty in the region. On the other hand, a majority of the residents appear to have been persuaded that the advantages to be gained from having two United States senators and one representative in the House with real voting power outweigh any disadvantages the change might entail. Some of the more modern undertakings, like the agricultural settlement in Mantuska Valley and, more recently, the spectacular Alcan Highway, which nevertheless is yet far from a satisfactory engineering project, have undoubtedly contributed some ammunition to the campaign for statehood.

At the moment the strongest ally of Alaskan statehood seems to be the changing international scene.[19] With Alaska separated from Siberia

---

[19] See Governor Ernest Gruening's statement at the New York Herald Tribune Forum, *New York Herald Tribune*, November 19, 1947, and for a full-scale treatment of this region and its problems, see his recent book *The State of Alaska* (New York,

by only a scant seven miles across the Bering Straits, the area takes on a new significance for national defense. Not oblivious to the pressure of military authorities for strengthening this area, Congress may decide that one of the best methods of persuasively reminding other nations where our frontier begins in the North is the admission of Alaska to statehood.[20]

Knocking louder for full statehood, Alaska held a constitutional convention at the University of Alaska in November of 1955, and the constitution drafted by this assembly was submitted to a vote of the people of this territory on April 24, 1956. The constitution won adoption, and at the same time the voters approved a measure known as the "Tennessee-Alaska Plan." The latter was patterned after the example of the Territory of Tennessee some 160 years earlier when its people became impatient because Congress delayed enacting legislation to admit Tennessee as a state. To speed up matters, Tennessee elected senators and representatives and then sent them off to Congress to clamor for admission of their state. The plan carried, and several other states followed the example, including Michigan (1835), California (1849), and Oregon (1857).

In not unexpected results at the first general election held under the new Alaska Constitution on October 9, 1956, the Democratic party elected former Governor Ernest Gruening for the long-term United States senatorship, and William Egan, President of the Alaska Constitutional Convention—also a Democrat—won the short-term senate seat. Another Democrat won the "house" seat, while the over-all results for contests at both state and federal levels gave the Democrats 30 out of 39 offices.

SPECIAL AREAS

In addition to its power to govern territories that lie outside its continental borders, the United States government has responsibility for the management of special areas within this country that are technically not part of the states in which they are geographically located. In this group are such institutions and installations as Federal prisons, veterans' hospitals, national parks, forests, post-offices, dockyards, power sites, military and naval academies, arsenals, and a great variety of others, scattered throughout the country. The jurisdiction of Congress in such places is extensive, and where states are permitted to execute any

---

1956). The day after the Senate defeated the Hawaiian statehood bill, President Truman sent a message to Congress asking that Alaska be speedily brought into the Union as a state. See *New York Times*, May 22, 1948, and in a public address in Denver, September 16, 1950, General Dwight D. Eisenhower said: "Quick admission of Alaska and Hawaii to statehood will show the world that America practices what it preaches."

[20] Military experts requested that $450,000,000 be granted for Alaskan defenses in the 1948 budget, to be used for building hangars, police airfields, and radio stations. See *New York Herald Tribune*, December 2, 1947.

governmental function, it is only with the express consent of Congress. States may have their court officers serve legal processes, and they may now tax private property situated within these areas. But Federal law governs exclusively in certain areas, and all torts or criminal acts committed on the premises are tried in the Federal courts.

Indian Reservations

The two remaining special jurisdictions of the Federal government consist of approximately two hundred Indian reservations located in twenty-one different states, and the nation's capital, the District of Columbia. In a book that deals primarily with problems of American government it seems ironic that the Indians, who once populated this country from the Atlantic to the Pacific and governed it with their chieftains and tribal councils, should receive such brief mention. Yet despite their cultural importance to the nation, the Indian population has dwindled to a very small figure. From an estimated 1,100,000 in 1492, the number dropped to a low of 300,000, and in 1940 the figure was in the neighborhood of 360,000.

The evolution of the present reservation and guardianship policy for American Indians is marked with brutality and failures. In the early stages Congress sought to trade directly with the Indians, and, by channeling trade, it hoped to avoid the abuses of private trading that led to cheating, the sale of intoxicants, and the general shortcomings well known to all students of American history. But the office established to control all Indian trade simply could not enforce such a directive, and the policy finally had to be abandoned. For a long time it was the practice of this government to make treaties with the Indians as a means of protecting their property rights. Treaties were made with tribes in the vain effort to protect both Indians and settlers, but here again the impossibility of enforcing agreements of this nature in frontier communities with weak law enforcement facilities led to the abandonment of the policy. In 1871, Congress passed an act providing that treaties were no longer to be made with Indian tribes, and this marked the beginning of a policy that increasingly brought all Indians, and their property, under Federal control.

Constitutionally, the authority for giving the Federal government control over the Indians is somewhat vague. The only specific mention of the subject provides that Congress shall have the power "to regulate commerce . . . with the Indian tribes." Nonetheless, Congress has brought the Indians together on reservations and provided for the strict supervision of such areas. Gradually the idea has been advanced that Indians are "wards" of the nation, and acting under this assumption all reservation property is held in trust for the Indians by the government. The legal relation of the United States to the Indian tribes is identified by some students of international law as one of "absolute suzerainty." [21]

[21] G. G. Wilson: *International Law* (9th ed.; New York, 1935), pp. 62–3.

A state under suzerainty possesses only such authority as the suzerain confers upon it. In practice this has meant that the United States has made certain concessions to the Indians relative to local self-government and various tribal institutions, but in general the control on all other matters has been stringent.[22]

Indians may not dispose of tribal property except where the government makes individual grants to families who appear to have the competence to manage their own farms or to support themselves. The Office of Indian Affairs, located in the Department of Interior, functions as "trustee" for the Indians and has a large field force, which includes many Indian agents (trained personnel of the Department of Interior) to carry on its activities. This agency arranges the leasing of forests, mineral lands, and other natural resources, and sees to it that the income from these properties is turned over to the members of the tribes that are entitled to receive it. In addition, the Office of Indian Affairs also has charge of health, schools for Indian children, and vocational training programs.

Looking at the status of the American Indian in a perspective beyond the range of the immediate goal of education, agricultural training, and the eradication of disease, it is difficult to assay the proper course of governmental action. For years the policy aimed to prepare the Indian for life within the general social, economic, and political fabric of the United States. To further this end some reservations were divided into separate holdings, and the more advanced Indians were permitted to sell their individual holdings. Perhaps the Indian was not yet ready for such a responsibility, but in any case the plan failed. Many Indians spent the money received for their land or mineral rights as fast as a veteran spends his bonus, and they were soon without any means of support. "To 2,000 Osages, Plains Indians with no experience in money economy," writes John Collier, a renowned authority on Indian Affairs, ". . . in the sixteen years following 1915 there was paid out in cash, by the government, $265,000,000 in royalties from Osage oil. Ninety per cent of this total went 'down the wind' of ruined Osages and corrupted and corrupting whites."[23] Another step aiming at the individualization of the Indian was an Act of 1924, making all Indians born within the territorial limits of the United States American citizens. But after several decades of trying to hasten the adjustment of the red man to modern society the Federal government changed its tactics in 1933. Instead of working to absorb the Indian into the mosaic of American community life, the new policy strives to foster Indian culture and to move Indian civilization to a higher plane. Thus Indian education and vocational training are still being encouraged, but at the same time the Indians are

---

[22] In 1948, a United States District Court ruled that Indians living on Federal reservations could vote. See Thomas C. Donnelly and Charles Judah: "The 1948 Elections in New Mexico." *Western Political Quarterly* (1949), 2:117–18.

[23] John Collier: *The Indians of the Americas* (New York, 1947), p. 244.

encouraged to continue their handicraft with its beautiful ceramics, jewelry, and other products, and to keep alive their cultural heritage.

In the dozen years that the "Indian New Deal" program has been in operation substantial strides have been made in improving the lot of the American Indian. The cattle program particularly has proved a success, but notable improvements have also been made in the fields of conservation, education, and in arts and crafts. Moreover, the death rate has decreased 55 per cent. Notwithstanding this progress, however, some shocking conditions still reveal themselves from time to time. Only recently the vigilance of the Association of American Indian Affairs brought attention to the fact that 61,000 Navahos—about one-sixth of the nation's total Indian population—were on the brink of starvation. Not only were these Indians facing imminent starvation, but they were also threatened by disease and lack of adequate shelter for protection against the rigors of an approaching winter.

The flight of the years makes it increasingly evident that as long as the American Indians continue to be wards of the state, outlays must be forthcoming if the United States is to take the high road of responsibility for this group. In placing the blame for the plight of the Indians much has been made of the hackneyed charge "bureaucratic ineptness," but an open-minded appraisal of the situation will recognize that a larger portion of the responsibility must fall elsewhere. The work of the Bureau of Indian Affairs has been hampered because of the difficulty of recruiting trained personnel who are willing to work among the ioslated regions inhabitated by the Navahos and other Indian tribes and it has had its share of administrative bungling. But more often than not it has been the paucity of funds that has caused Indian policies to deteriorate, and past experience strongly suggests that skimpy appropriations may prove far more wasteful in the long run.

The District of Columbia

The special district within the United States, in which the nerve center of the government itself is encased, is the District of Columbia, an area of approximately sixty-four square miles, lying on the Maryland side of the Potomac. This region was originally ceded by the State of Maryland in 1790 as a site for the nation's capital and is now populated by about 1,500,000 inhabitants. The Constitution gives Congress exclusive authority over this area, and with but few interruptions when mild experiments with local self-government were undertaken, Congress has run the District.

There is no municipal council; the main ordinances and laws of the District are passed by Congress, which has special committees in each house to consider the business of the District in detail. As in the case of the congressional committees on Territorial and Insular Possessions, the committees on the District of Columbia can hardly be thought of as serving the best interest of local government. In 1944 the man who succeeded to the chairmanship of the Senate Committee on the District of Columbia was none other than Theodore G. (The Man) Bilbo. Within a very short time after Mr. Bilbo began his tour of service in this position —which sometimes gives the incumbent the unofficial title of "Mayor" of Washington—the *Washington Post* labelled it "An Adventure in Bigotry," and a large part of the local citizenry was incensed. Yet, as far as taking concrete action for Mr. Bilbo's removal was concerned, little could be done, even against a misfit like Mr. Bilbo.

The District is run by three commissioners, two of whom, appointed by the president and Senate, must be actual residents of the District, and a third, selected by the president from the Army Corps of Engineers. The commission has fairly extensive powers to make appointments, ordinances, and regulations, and to administer the routine services that one expects in a modern metropolitan area, such as fire and police protection, public utilities, health, welfare, safety, and so forth. Until 1920 the cost of maintaining the governmental services of the District was borne equally by the national treasury and the District's taxpayers, but the Federal contribution has been decreased until the local taxpayers now carry all but about one-seventh of the financial load.

In late years the most controversial issue concerns the franchise. The theoretical basis for a politically neutral national capital was probably inspired by the violence of Parisian mobs during the French Revolution, and certainly firm support may be mobilized to back the view that a nation's capital should be under the jurisdiction of the central government. The idea of giving residents of the District representation in the national legislature has many proponents today. Quite a few District residents maintain voting residences in other states, but the vast majority of people living in the District are disfranchised. Of some 583,000 persons of voting age living in the district, only an estimated 100,000 maintain legal residences elsewhere. A moderate view would seem to admit at least the possibility of securing a greater voice in strictly local affairs for the inhabitants of the District. More controversial, perhaps, is the right to vote for a president and congressional representatives. For this, a constitutional amendment would be required, and like the periodic argument over the abolition of the Electoral College, such an issue will probably be warmed over many times before a change is made. In any case the spirited interest of District residents in party primaries for selecting presidential delegates in 1952 and 1956 certainly suggests that voters in the nation's capital are eager to share a hand in national politics.

SUMMARY

Constitutional questions have been encountered with frequency as the United States enlarged its frontier. Whether the Constitution authorized the acquisition of any additional territory troubled Jefferson when Louisiana was purchased. The territorial gains of the Spanish-American War brought the problems of whether import duties might be imposed on goods entering the continental United States from its territories and whether the Bill of Rights and certain other provisions of the Constitution applied in the newly-acquired lands.

These latter questions were resolved by the courts by means of a distinction between incorporated and unincorporated territories. The standards by which one can judge whether a given territory is incorporated or unincorporated are not completely clear, however. The courts also made a distinction between what it designated formal and fundamental parts of the Constitution and held that only the latter were binding in respect to unincorporated territory.

Organized territories enjoy considerable powers of self-direction in local affairs, although their governors are generally appointed by the President. In 1946 the independence of the Philippines was realized, though some military and economic strings still attach them to the United States.

Strong movements to grant statehood to our two incorporated territories, Hawaii and Alaska, have run afoul of stubborn centers of resistance but steady progress has been made, particularly for Alaska.

The peculiar status of the American Indian as a ward of the nation places Indian reservations under complete control of the national government. The responsibility of the nation to its wards was long neglected.

The District of Columbia, governed by a commission under laws passed by Congress, complains that it has no voice in the determination of local or national affairs.

CHAPTER XXXV

THE MANAGEMENT OF FOREIGN AFFAIRS

IN GENERAL, the creation of distinct agencies for the management of foreign affairs coincides with the beginnings of the modern state system, an event which students of international relations usually ascribe to the seventeenth century. That the arm of government which concerned itself with the conduct of foreign relations took a commanding position over other administrative institutions of government, can hardly be surprising. One of the tokens of the coming of age of a neophyte state was diplomatic recognition—an act consummated via diplomatic channels already well-grooved through historical precedent by the time of the American Revolution. Furthermore, since the very inception of intercourse between nations, national security had been firmly manacled to the handling of foreign affairs. Foreign policies, and indeed domestic policies had a direct bearing upon a nation's security within the family of nations, and it is apparent that the persons who had a hand in framing the Federal Constitution were acutely aware of this fact.

CONSTITUTIONAL ARRANGEMENTS FOR HANDLING FOREIGN AFFAIRS

Under the Articles of Confederation (1777–1788) the control of foreign affairs went to Congress by default. The management of foreign relations was one subject over which the Confederacy had definite authority, yet without a central executive the responsibility for the conduct of foreign relations necessarily devolved upon Congress. Congress set up a Committee of Foreign Affairs to maintain connections with American representatives stationed abroad and with friendly governments, but the results of this plan of administering American diplomacy were quite disappointing. Accordingly, it was decided to create a department of foreign affairs with a permanent secretary at its head, and, in 1781, Robert E. Livingstone became the first secretary of foreign affairs. [1]

Presidential Control

Guided by the experience gained under the Articles of Confederation, the framers of the Constitution approached the problem of handling external relations with a clear understanding of the need for firm executive control. But the chief executive was not made omnipotent. Instead, the Constitution stipulated a bilateral formula for the conduct of foreign affairs; the president was given the power to take the initiative but his authority was diminished by the role of the Senate as partner in the matter of ratifying treaties and confirming appointments to important diplomatic posts. [2] Under the Constitution the president has the power to make treaties, "provided two-thirds of the Senators present concur; . . . " [3] He also is empowered to nominate ambassadors, ministers, and consuls and to receive foreign ambassadors and ministers accredited to the United States, but again he must obtain the official approval of the Senate on all nominations he submits.

Notwithstanding constitutional admonitions that would seem to suggest both an ambiguity over the real source of authority in foreign affairs, and an executive who remains more or less constantly hampered, the pattern of presidential leadership in foreign relations has manifested itself distinctly. [4] Possessing the power to negotiate treaties, the president can and does exert positive leadership in this direction. As an auxiliary to this power, he may resort to the executive agreement, which permits him to conclude compacts with foreign governments without ratification by the Senate. In senatorial confirmation of nominations to foreign-service posts, the chief executive has, on rare occasions, suffered a setback, but approval has been the rule rather than the exception.[5] Thus, constitutional directives buttressed by practice and custom have combined to allow the president to stand before alien governments as the official representative of the United States. Official communications from other countries are addressed either to him directly, or to his secretary of state, not to the

[1] Lloyd M. Short: *The Development of National Administrative Organization in the United States* (Baltimore, 1923), pp. 46–7, 55–61.

[2] For a brief useful volume on the many facets of foreign-policy management, see Edgar S. Furniss, Jr. and Richard C. Snyder: *An Introduction to American Foreign Policy* (New York, 1955). More detailed studies of the organizational problems involved in the conduct of American foreign policy are: James L. McCamy, *The Administration of American Foreign Affairs* (New York, 1950) and Arthur Macmahon, *Administration in Foreign Affairs* (University, Ala., 1953).

[3] *Constitution:* Art. II, Sec. 2, Clause 2; Sec. 3.

[4] See James Frederick Green: "The President's Control of Foreign Policy." *Foreign Policy Reports* (1939), 15:10–20; and Harold Laski: *The American Presidency* (New York, 1939), chap. 4.

[5] For an extensive survey of the confirmation of presidential appointments, see Joseph P. Harris, *The Advice and Consent of the Senate* (University of California Press, Berkeley, 1953).

Congress. Moreover the power of the president over recognition is indisputable. Recognition is simply an act by which one state (or more) acknowledges the existence of a new state or of a new government of a state. It may be accomplished in several ways: by treaty, proclamation, or simply through the exchange of accredited diplomatic agents. Finally, the president is the chief architect of American foreign policy. In formulating such policies, the chief executive obviously may be influenced by his advisers, but he is still the government's leading spokesman in the field of foreign affairs. In recent times, the president has been forced to make decisions charged with hazardous consequences. President Roosevelt had to decide whether the United States should aid foreign governments against Germany, Italy, and Japan, while President Truman had to decide whether or not to drop the atomic bomb on Hiroshima, or to intervene in Korea. President Eisenhower was faced with a similar decision in the case of the Indochina crisis. Thus, although the President is surrounded by advisers and technical assistants, he alone must assume the responsibility for such far-reaching decisions.

Authority to Make Treaties

The singular problem in the management of American foreign affairs is the role of the Senate. Ostensibly, the Constitution gives the Senate a partnership with the president in the handling of certain phases of foreign relations. It suggests that the president shall advise with the Senate in the matter of making treaties, and by way of insuring that the president will not exploit the partnership by negotiating a treaty independently, it requires that the Senate concur in the process. By insisting upon a two-thirds ratification vote the Constitution gives the Senate a loaded weapon for attacking treaties. Yet, the two-thirds requirement has not always given the tactical advantage that one might assume, though it has, on occasion, completely stymied presidents.

In appraising the treaty-making power, one may start with the constitutional premise that treaties, along with the Constitution and laws of the United States, "shall be the supreme law of the land; . . ." As no express limitations are found in the Constitution on the content of the matters that may be embodied in treaties, this immediately gives rise to the question whether a treaty may regulate affairs that lie beyond the scope of Federal legislative power. Thus far, the Supreme Court has never held a treaty to be unconstitutional, and although the Court has suggested that a treaty might be invalid if it invaded the rights of states, the precise limitations upon the treaty-making power are not known. But it is certain that the power to conclude treaties is an extensive one. As early as 1817, the Supreme Court held the provisions of a treaty between the United States and France to apply to the inheritance of land in Maryland—a subject which would generally fall under the exclusive jurisdiction of the States. Similarly, when the Japanese government protested that the exclusion of Japanese children from certain public schools in San Francisco violated a treaty between the United States and Japan, the enforcement of this provision by the vigorous stand of Theodore Roosevelt was clearly an interference with state public schools over which the Federal government has little authority.

Perhaps an even broader example of a treaty that infringes upon the reserved rights of the states is the one concluded between the United States and Great Britain to protect the migratory waterfowl of this country and Canada. The regulation of hunting is also assumed to fall within the scope of the states' police power, yet against the protest of the State of Missouri the Supreme Court sustained both the treaty and the Congressional statute passed to enforce it. And, in upholding the treaty, it is significant that Mr. Justice Holmes declared that the "supreme law of the land" clause did not specify that treaties, like statutes, shall be made in pursuance of the Constitution. That he did not regard the treaty power as being without any limitations, however, is evident from his following comment in the same decision: "We do not mean to say that there are no qualifications to the treaty-making power, but they must be ascertained in a different way. It is obvious that there may be matters of the sharpest exigency for the national well-being that an act of Congress could not deal with but that a treaty followed by such an act could, and it is not lightly to be assumed that, in matters requiring national action, 'a power which must belong to and somewhere reside in every civilized government' is not to be found." [6]

The Breadth of Constitutional Authority in Foreign Affairs

In recent times there has been a marked trend toward restricting the treaty power by amending the Constitution. Leaders of this movement, with Senator John Bricker of Ohio as their spokesman, have insisted that treaties have been taken up in recent times which dealt with internal affairs rather than with international relations, thereby trespassing on matters reserved to the states or to the people. And Senator Bricker, in response to complaints that an encroachment on the rights of the states or their people is threatened, proposed an amendment to the Constitution providing: (a) that a treaty could not become effective as internal law unless Congress so provided by legislation; (b) that any legislation passed by Congress for this purpose would have to be valid in the absence of the treaty or would be unconstitutional; and finally (c) that Congress should be specifically given the power to regulate executive and other international agreements.[7]

Opposition to the so-called Bricker Amendment, which attracted nation-wide attention, was led by the president, who strongly resisted any weakening of the powers of the chief executive in the field of

[6] Missouri v. Holland, 252 U.S. 416 (1920).
[7] (S.J. Res. 1. 83rd Congress.)

foreign affairs.[8] After five weeks of debate early in 1954, the Senate, by a margin of one vote, decided against all proposals to curtail the treaty power. But the close vote suggested that the forces behind the movement to restrict the power of the executive in treaty matters were by no means ready to abandon their efforts.

In a long line of decisions, the Supreme Court has held that as a sovereign nation, the United States possesses the same powers with respect to foreign relations that all other sovereign states enjoy. Moreover, these powers are not confined to those specifically delegated by the Constitution; hence Congress—despite the lack of specific constitutional authorization—has been upheld when it passed laws providing for deporting aliens, annexing territory, and setting up courts in foreign countries. The most significant case to state this principle—that the power over foreign affairs is not restricted by the Constitution as is domestic legislative policy—reaffirms the doctrine so broadly that it warrants a brief discussion.

In 1934 Congress passed a joint resolution providing that if the president found that an embargo on the sale of arms and munitions to countries at war (Bolivia and Paraguay) would "contribute to the re-establishment of peace between those countries," he might, after consulting with other American republics, place an embargo by proclamation. The president established the embargo, and subsequently a company violated it by selling machine guns to Bolivia. As a defense, the defendant company contended that the joint resolution did not restrict or guide the president's discretionary power in establishing the embargo, therefore it constituted an unconstitutional delegation of legislative power. It is true that the same argument had prevailed when the Supreme Court held the National Industrial Recovery Act invalid, partly on the ground that the law had not set up precise enough standards to guide the president in exercising his judgment. But does the rule against such delegation in the domestic field apply with equal validity in the sphere of foreign affairs? Apparently not, for the Supreme Court makes it emphatic that the internal and external affairs of the nation are not required to conform to the same principles. Speaking for the majority of the Court, Mr. Justice Sutherland said: "It results that the investment of the Federal government with the powers of external sovereignty did not depend upon the affirmative grants of the Constitution. The powers to declare and wage war, to conclude peace, to make treaties, to maintain diplomatic relations with other sovereignties, if they had never been mentioned in the Constitution, would have vested in the Federal government as necessary concomitants of nationality. . . . As a member of the family of nations, the right and power of the United States in that field are equal to the right and power of the

[8] For an excellent summary of the arguments against the Bricker Amendment, see Henry Steele Commager, "The Perilous Folly of Senator Bricker," *The Reporter* (October 13, 1953), pp. 12–17.

other members of the international family. . . . It is quite apparent that if, in the maintenance of our international relations, embarrassment—perhaps serious embarrassment—is to be avoided and success for our aims achieved, congressional legislation which is to be made effective through negotiation and inquiry within the international field must often accord to the President a degree of discretion and freedom from statutory restriction which would not be admissible were domestic affairs alone involved." [9]

Irrespective of what measures are used for conducting foreign affairs, whether treaty, joint resolution, or the president acting alone, the cumulative evidence makes it apparent that the authority of the government over the entire field is extremely broad. Despite the double standard for judging domestic and foreign policies, however, and the inability to set down even a peripheral boundary for government undertakings in the foreign field, it does not follow that any action would be upheld that seriously impairs or jeopardizes a fundamental safeguard of the Constitution. Certainly the specific restrictions of the Constitution such as the Bill of Rights may not be disregarded in making a treaty.

PROBLEMS OF NEGOTIATIONS

Although the substance of a treaty has frequently given rise to controversy, the most publicized differences of opinion are to be found in the mechanics of negotiating treaties. The Constitution, it will be recalled, contemplates that the president should advise with the Senate on such matters. But just how active a part the Senate is to play in drafting a treaty is far from a settled question. It is generally conceded that the president has the authority to take the initiative in starting negotiations, although the inspiration for the idea of a treaty quite obviously might stem from other sources.

President and Senate in the Treaty Negotiations

A variety of channels are open to the president in negotiating a treaty. He may work through his secretary of state, or one of his diplomatic agents, such as an ambassador or minister, or he may even follow Woodrow Wilson's example and go abroad to take a direct part in the negotiations himself. On the question of consulting the Senate, George Washington began by being extremely solicitous about the Senate's advice. He made several visits to the Senate chamber during his first term to seek its counsel, but following an embarrassing incident when the Senate refused to give immediate consideration to his questions, he stopped making personal visits. [10]

Since then, no president has entered the Senate to seek its aid

[9] United States v. Curtiss-Wright Export Corporation, 299 U.S. 304 (1936).
[10] D. F. Fleming: *The Treaty Veto of the American Senate* (New York, 1930), pp. 16-19.

or counsel in the negotiation of a treaty. But it has become accepted procedure for the president to sound out certain senators on the matter of treaty negotiation, particularly since the tragic experience of Woodrow Wilson with the Treaty of Versailles and the Covenant of the League of Nations.

As the vote of one-third of the Senate is sufficient to reject a treaty, a president is nearly always dependent upon support outside of his own party for ratification, hence he can hardly afford to ignore the Senate even in the preliminary stages of negotiation. Both President Harding and President Hoover had this in mind when they named one Democrat and one Republican to the delegations to the Washington Arms Conference of 1921–2 and the London Naval Conference of 1930. And in recent years with the appearance of the "bipartisan" foreign-policy formula, an unusually close relationship has developed between the president and key members of the Senate in the negotiation of treaties. Franklin Roosevelt named Republican Senator Arthur H. Vandenberg and his Democratic colleague Tom Connolly as delegates to the San Francisco Conference to aid in drafting the United Nations Charter, and President Truman continued this policy by naming the same senators as delegates to the Paris Peace Conference. While such action does not assure subsequent ratification of treaties, it does smooth the way to early reconciliation of differences of opinion and, equally important, it encourages constructive Senate leadership in foreign affairs rather than a policy of negation. As a matter of record, since the end of World War II several proposals for treaties have emanated directly from members of the Senate.

Senate approval of the North Atlantic Treaty Organization in 1949 raised the old issue of the president's ability to involve the nation in war. While the Constitution states that Congress alone has the power to declare war, modern wars are not always declared wars and may come about suddenly and without warning. Under these circumstances only the president, as commander-in-chief, may be able to protect the nation. The problem may be stated as that of speedy action as opposed to constitutional directive.

In the 1949 NATO Treaty, the Senate showed its distrust of presidential power by insisting that the president alone might not interpret American obligations under the treaty and that he might not take any action leading to war without the prior consent of Congress. Thus both legislative treatment of the NATO treaty provisions and the struggle over the Bricker amendment in 1953–54 demonstrate the perennial nature of the conflict over foreign affairs between the executive and the legislature.

In the preliminary stages, treaty negotiations between Washington and foreign capitals are kept confidential. Unfortunately, because of a popular misconception of the term "secret diplomacy" a strong public demand has been manifested in late years for the negotiation of treaties in full view of the public, replete with radio, microphones, klieg lights, and television. The use of "secret diplomacy," as understood to designate the secret and unpublished agreements and commitments between governments so popular in the half-century preceding World War I, was understandably objectionable. But to carry matters to extremes, and insist that all treaty negotiations be threshed out in public, exposed to the emotional tensions of public opinion, seems a dubious principle. Furthermore, in view of the tendency of newspapers to traffic in rumors that disrupt negotiations, there is a strong case to be made for closed negotiation followed by immediate and honest reporting of the agreements concluded.[11]

Once a treaty has been negotiated, the president transmits to the Senate the final draft, together with an explanatory letter. It is then submitted to the Committee on Foreign Relations—one of the most prominent committees in the Senate.[12] As a rule, the Senate goes into executive session when treaties are considered after being reported out by the Committee on Foreign Relations. This simply means that treaties, like nominations, are construed as executive rather than legislative business, even though, once ratified, treaties become law. Formerly, the Senate met in secret executive session when debating the merits of treaties, but because of frequent leaks of the transactions to newspapers, the practice in recent years has been to hold open sessions. Experience in the matter of Senate secrecy does indeed appear to bear out Lord Bryce's comment: "Of course no momentous secret can be long kept, even by the Committee, according to the proverb in the Elder Edda— 'Tell one man thy secret, but not two; if three know, the world knows!'"[13] According to a rule adopted by the Senate in 1929, the Senate—unless it otherwise decides by a majority vote—considers all treaties in open session.[14] The Senate amended its rule on secrecy at the same time, allowing a Senator to make public how he voted in a closed executive session. Previously, a Senator could be expelled for violating the secrecy of a closed session.

Ratification of Treaties

In taking action on a treaty, the Senate may recommend its approval subject to certain amendments or reservations. If this is the case, the president submits the recommended changes to the other countries involved and, if they concur, the concluding steps are taken—formal exchange of ratifications with representatives of the participating foreign

[11] See the article by Drew Middleton, "Open Covenants Unopenly Arrived At," *New York Times,* February 27, 1955, in which the author calls for a return to secret diplomacy and an end to open negotiations that turn diplomats into propagandists; also E. L. Woodward, "The Old and New Diplomacy," *The Yale Review,* 36 (1947), pp. 405–22.

[12] See Eleanor E. Dennison: *The Senate Foreign Relations Committee* (Stanford, 1942).

[13] James Bryce: *The American Commonwealth* (New York, 1922 ed.), Vol. I, p. 108.

[14] George H. Haynes: *The Senate of the United States* (Boston, 1938), Vol. II, p. 670.

countries, and proclamation of the treaty. Should the Senate emasculate the original treaty before returning it to the president, the latter may elect to abandon it completely rather than re-submit the amended measure to the foreign powers concerned. The decision as to whether to reopen negotiations then rests with the president and foreign powers parties to the treaty; the Senate has no way of forcing the issue.

Although in the United States a treaty stands on the same plane as a statute, it is sometimes necessary to pass a law to execute the treaty, or make an appropriation to support it. Congress can, therefore, undermine a treaty by refusing to pass such legislation. According to Anglo-American practice—and in contrast to continental practice—once a treaty has been approved, it generally becomes a part of the law of the land. But there are important exceptions to this general rule. In certain instances the courts have declared that particular treaties are not self-executing and require additional legislation for their implementation. This has been the case, for example, in domestic disputes where certain provisions of the United Nations Charter have been invoked by the litigants. (A recent example would be the disputes arising in California where state laws respecting alienation of property were assailed as being incompatible with the United Nations Charter.)

Usually if the president is able to muster sufficient strength for having a treaty ratified in the Senate, he can secure congressional support for whatever legislation is necessary. But it is not uncommon to find certain senators voting for a treaty and against subsequent legislation imperative for executing the provisions of the treaty. The eighty-nine to two Senate ratification vote on the United Nations Charter in July, 1945, for example, suggested overwhelming support for the new international organization, yet later votes on bills necessary to insure constructive American participation showed the ratification figure to be quite misleading. All of which reminds us of the powerful control Congress holds over foreign affairs by virtue of its authority to make appropriations.

Abrogating Treaties

Just how a treaty may be abrogated in this country has been subject to several interpretations. Clearly, Congress may terminate a treaty by legislation, and there are precedents for abrogation of a treaty by the President acting either on his own authority, or in accordance with a joint resolution of Congress. The denunciation or termination of a treaty by unilateral action, however—unless provision has been made in the treaty for such a contingency—is generally considered a breach of international law.

One further point deserves to be noted in connection with treaties: the question whether the treaty or law prevails in case of a conflict. As both treaties and laws are the "supreme law of the land" this matter has been settled by giving effect to the treaty or law which was made last.

NON-TREATY AGREEMENTS

Joint Resolutions

Recently, there has been a marked tendency in consummating international agreements to by-pass the formal treaty requirements of the Federal Constitution by using several more simple expedients.[15] One such method already mentioned is the joint resolution, which requires only a majority vote in each house and the signature of the president to effect a foreign agreement. World War I was terminated in 1921 by joint resolution as far as the United States was concerned, and both Texas and Hawaii were annexed in this manner. In 1943 the much publicized B_2H_2 proposal, calling for a permanent United Nations Organization, was introduced as a joint resolution, and there have been a number of others in the last few years.[16] The joint resolution may be adopted either by having Congress pass the measure before receiving presidential approval, or by having Congress ratify action already taken by the president.

Two interesting pieces of legislation that illustrate a method of procedure closely related to the joint resolution are the Reciprocal Trade Agreements Act of 1934, and the Lend-Lease Act of 1941. In each instance Congress gave advance statutory authorization for the negotiation of agreements by the president, and the president then used this authority as the basis of effecting the agreements. As a practical method of making agreements with foreign nations, the latter type of executive action has the advantage that, unlike a treaty, the agreement does not have to be subsequently approved by the Senate.

Executive Agreements

The executive agreement may lead to controversy if the president, acting without the aid or consent of the House or the Senate, executes an agreement with foreign powers.[17] The authority of the president to enter into agreements with foreign governments stems from his constitutional powers as "organ of foreign relations and Commander-in-Chief," and it is buttressed by his power to see that the "laws be faithfully executed."[18] The validity of such agreements was at one time seriously challenged. Yet a long chain of precedents culminating in Supreme Court decisions has made it clear that the president, acting alone, may make agreements that are just as legally binding as treaties. The Rush-Bagot Convention of 1817—an agreement between the United

[15] For a concise analysis of these methods see Quincy Wright: "The United States and International Agreements." *International Conciliation* (1945), 411:379–98.

[16] This resolution was introduced by Senators Joseph Ball, Harold Burton, Lister Hill, and Carl Hatch.

[17] See Wallace McClure: *International Executive Agreements; Democratic Procedure under the Constitution of the United States* (New York, 1941).

[18] Edward S. Corwin: *The President: Office and Powers* (3rd ed., New York, 1948), pp. 235–7.

States and Great Britain for the limitation of naval forces on the Great Lakes—is an early example of such action, and more recently the destroyer-naval base transfer of 1940, between the United States and Great Britain, affords a classic modern example of what has sometimes been termed presidential "treaty-making" without the help or consent of either the House or the Senate. In the destroyer-naval-base executive agreement, which provided for the immediate transfer of fifty over-age destroyers to Great Britain in exchange for a ninety-nine year lease of British naval and air bases in the Western Hemisphere, Franklin Roosevelt found it politically expedient to evade the Senate. Had he not done so much valuable time might have been lost in legislative debate, and so divided was the Congress that the measure might not even have carried.

While the probable future course of international events would seem to encourage and justify more use of executive agreements, present trends suggest that Congress, and particularly the Senate, will not always acquiesce to a presidential by-pass without a fight. In the Bermuda Agreement respecting commercial air travel between the United States and Great Britain, negotiated as an executive agreement in 1946, the Senate Commerce Committee protested that Great Britain had driven a "hard bargain," and served warning that it would try to force to a ratification vote all future questions involving foreign commitments. Obviously, this could hardly be done, but the Senate can use its bargaining power in devious ways to discourage use of the executive agreement where its terms might not be acceptable to that body. To keep at a minimum friction between the executive and legislative branches on this subject, the wise course would be to have Congress delineate as carefully as possible the authority which the executive or an executive agency shall have to negotiate agreements, and then see to it that the requisites laid down for negotiation are scrupulously observed. This procedure was followed in the case of the Hull Reciprocal Trade Agreements, and the consensus was that it worked quite satisfactorily.

During the last fifty years more than half of our international agreements have been executive agreements. The executive agreement as a tool for handling international affairs may be abused, but through the observance of proper safeguards such a contingency need not occur. As an instrument for handling intricate problems of foreign affairs and particularly those of a commercial and legal nature, the executive agreement today is well-nigh indispensable. Despite the fluctuating tendency of Congress to be more stringent, the trend toward broader use of the executive agreement is unmistakable; nevertheless, like many other aspects of American politics, its use will vary according to the times and the vigor of presidential leadership.

One unanswered question always causes a certain amount of aches in defining the subject to be embraced by an executive agreement. No clear line has ever been drawn that separates the subject matter regulated by executive agreement and the subject matter to be regulated by formal treaty requirements.

Not readily answerable is still another question: Does an executive agreement made by one administration bind a succeeding administration? An obvious example here is the Yalta agreement, concluded in 1945. To this controversial issue some have argued "no"—that an executive agreement made by an earlier administration is not binding upon its successor. But the Eisenhower Administration did not contend that it was not bound by the Yalta agreement because the Pact was concluded under an earlier administration. Instead, President Eisenhower declared that the agreement was no longer binding upon this country because of persistent violation by the Soviet Union.

The limitations upon presidential leadership in foreign affairs—and they can be severe—will be discussed more fully in the chapter dealing with foreign policy. In this connection it should not be forgotten that, while the Senate appears more prominent in its relation to the management of foreign affairs because of its prerogative in the handling of treaties, the House also has an effective foil. The control of the House over appropriations serves as a continuous reminder to any president that, if he is to effectuate his external aims and policies, he must maintain cordial relations with the House of Representatives. No chief executive can be unmindful of the double-edged legislative threat he faces as he seeks to manage routine diplomatic affairs and articulate a foreign policy with the aid of his Department of State, which serves as the intermediary between the president and other countries.

ADMINISTRATIVE ARRANGEMENTS FOR CONDUCTING FOREIGN AFFAIRS

The Department of State

Following the adoption of the Constitution the first administrative organ established to handle American diplomacy bore the same name as its predecessor under the Articles of Confederation—the Department of Foreign Affairs.[19] This designation proved shortlived, however, and after two months it was changed to the Department of State, a name that is certainly less descriptive than "foreign office" or "ministry of foreign affairs," which are employed by most governments. As the Department of State was the first executive department to be founded (July 27, 1789), it holds the ranking position in the cabinet hierarchy. The secretary of state has been traditionally regarded as the foremost in rank among the departmental heads, a position further acknowledged by the Presidential Succession Act of 1886, which named the secretary of state to succeed the vice-president in the escalator line-up of presidential succession. As

[19] See Graham H. Stuart, *The Department of State* (New York, 1949).

distinguished leaders, the occupants of this much-coveted post have undoubtedly outstripped the officials who have served in any other high appointive position in the Federal government. Included in the list are such names as John Marshall, James Madison, James Monroe, John Quincy Adams, Henry Clay, Daniel Webster, John C. Calhoun, Hamilton Fish, John Hay, Elihu Root, Charles Evans Hughes, and Henry L. Stimson.

The secretary of state is charged with the duty of corresponding with the diplomats and consuls of the United States as well as with the foreign representatives accredited to this country. His other chief functions are to negotiate treaties, formulate policy, and supervise departmental administration. He serves as the nexus between the president and other nations, and is the person to whom foreign powers address their formal notes to the United States government.

As head of the State Department, the secretary of state is a policy maker second in importance only to the president. Moreover, since he represents the president in consultations with Congress and the Senate Foreign Relations Committee, it is a matter of no small importance that he be able to work with Congress if he is to function effectively.

The President and His Secretary of State

The precise relation between the president and his secretary of state in the matter of policy formulation poses what Franklin Roosevelt would have called an "iffy" question.[20] Some presidents have deliberately elected to operate as their own secretaries of state and have pushed their State Department heads into the obscurity of routine diplomacy. Woodrow Wilson, in effect, became his own secretary after William Jennings Bryan was dropped as the pilot of the State Department. During Franklin Roosevelt's several administrations, the focal point of responsibility for leadership in external affairs frequently shifted. At times, President Roosevelt was clearly functioning as his own secretary, on other occasions he gave a free hand to patient Secretary Cordell Hull, and on still other occasions he departed from both practices by giving a free rein to his Undersecretary of State, Sumner Welles. Against such examples, however, are numerous instances of secretaries of state who have exercised a sturdy influence on foreign policy and have sometimes all but eclipsed their chief executive by the sheer force of a vigorous personality. The Hay Open-Door Notes provide a reminder of John Hay's influence in the McKinley Administration, and Charles Evans Hughes and Henry L. Stimson were strong secretaries of state during the Harding, Coolidge, and Hoover eras. But, no matter how this question of personal initiative is resolved or compromised, the problem of integrating policy formation with the diplomatic machinery to execute the policy remains a major undertaking because of the complexity and diversity of subjects under the jurisdiction of the State Department.

[20] See James McGregor Burns, *Roosevelt: The Lion and the Fox* (New York, 1956), p. 383.

ADMINISTRATIVE ORGANIZATION IN THE STATE
DEPARTMENT

Before we examine the machinery of any major power's executive branch for handling foreign affairs, a word of caution is in order about the term "diplomacy." In essence, diplomacy is the "organized system of negotiations between states." Perhaps one of the best-known definitions is that of Sir Ernest Satow, who simply defines it as "the application of intelligence and tact to the conduct of official relations between the Governments of independent States." But, as the word diplomacy is often used to express both the framing of foreign policy and the techniques of executing it, the distinction between the two aspects should be borne in mind when we study the organizational problems of a foreign office. This differentiation has become more important since the advent of the so-called "democratic diplomacy," a development which has tended to make foreign policy more responsive to popular control. Until World War I diplomats in Europe commonly both framed and conducted foreign policy.

In the United States, the distinction between negotiation and policy-making in diplomacy is important because of the unique arrangement that balances foreign policy on a tripod composed of the president, the State Department, and Congress. Not many State Department officials play the dual role of negotiator and policy-maker on matters of high consequence, and those who do must still function as one leg of the tripod. There should be no misunderstanding, however, that negotiation and policy-making, though definitely interrelated, are quite different activities. The two call for different kinds of skills and demand that the State Department organization take cognizance of this difference.

The Growth of the State Department

Throughout the nineteenth century, the Department of State jerked along trailing new subsidiaries as additional responsibilities were undertaken, but never managing to achieve concord of its component parts. As long as our foreign policy vacillated between isolationism and neutrality, and our foreign relations were concerned with a limited number of subjects the State Department, even though an extremely loose-jointed contraption, was able to carry on. The fact that it was the smallest of the ten executive departments until as late as 1941 probably helps to explain why the Department of State could function so long without drastic administrative overhauling, but the impact of World War II underscored the need for extensive revision of its structural organization. The Department's personnel roster of 1,264 in Washington, D.C., early in 1941 increased to well over three times this number by the end of the war. In 1932, the staff of the American Embassy in London—which was then the largest office in the Foreign Service—totalled 32 officers and approximately 60 other employes. By January, 1947, there were 100 officers in our London Embassy, and the total American personnel at the same post had stretched beyond 1,000. Recent years have seen the number of Foreign Service posts expand to some 300. And in 1956 more than 20,000 people were working for the State Department—11,000 Americans and 9,000 aliens (the latter in minor positions abroad).

The Internal Organization of the State Department

The hierarchical ranking of the State Department as a result of several administrative shuffles during World War II keeps the undersecretary of state in his traditional position as the secretary's deputy in all matters, and as acting secretary in the absence of the secretary. Besides the undersecretary, there are deputy undersecretaries for economic affairs, political affairs, and the handling of administrative functions. They are in turn aided by a number of assistant secretaries, each of whom is charged with significant assignments.

The functional structure of the State Department is divided into five areas—the political-geographical, the economic, the informational and cultural, the research and intelligence, and the administrative. Among the most important units are the five regional offices in the political-geographical area, each headed by one of the assistant secretaries. These regional divisions are the Offices of European Affairs; Far Eastern Affairs; Near Eastern, South Asian, and African Affairs; Inter-American Affairs; and International Organization Affairs. The work of these geographic offices is concerned with the over-all formulation of policy toward the countries or agencies lying within their jurisdiction; they also seek to coordinate with the broad aims and objectives of American foreign policy the activities of other State Department offices and those belonging to different Federal agencies. Compared to a living organism, these regional divisions might well be called the main arteries of the State Department. Over the desks of the geographical divisions a constant stream of political reports flow from ambassadors and ministers, as well as from commercial, agricultural, and military attachés.

The Regional Offices

At the helm of the five regional offices are five assistant secretaries, each concerned with formulating and coordinating the policies and activities of the United States government within the confines of the area under his charge. Before any official action would be taken with regard to Turkey, for example, normal procedure would call for consulting the Office of Near Eastern, South Asian, and African Affairs.

The administrative organization lying within the five regional offices leads us quickly to the real nerve centers of our State Department's activities abroad. Here we find what have come to be known as the "country desks" upon which the effectiveness of the entire departmental operations rests. If we take the Office of Near Eastern, South Asian, and African Affairs to illustrate this organization we find that the Office itself is composed of four geographic divisions—the Office of Greek, Turkish, and Iranian Affairs; Office of South Asian Affairs; Office of Near Eastern Affairs; and Office of African Affairs. Besides the geographic divisions, the Office also has a research and analysis division. Each of the divisions is in charge of a chief. In the division of the Near East, we find Greece, Turkey, and Iran, in each of which a "country desk" is established. The official who operates a country desk is known by the State Department as a "desk officer."

By common consent, the "desk officer" is acknowledged as one of the key figures in the far-flung operations of the Department of State. He must keep himself informed about the developing internal politics of the country with which he is concerned as well as about what effect these internal conditions may have on the international situation. The information he obtains is, of course, quickly transmitted to the appropriate officials in the Department and they in turn keep him informed about policies they wish him to pursue. The "desk officer" must have an intimate acquaintance with what our economic, political, and cultural interests are in the country covered by his "desk" and he must also be thoroughly familiar with the work of our diplomatic missions and consular offices within the country. He reads the dispatches and telegrams from our diplomatic and consular officials in that country, and in addition he may read communications affecting the country he is assigned to from other agencies of the United States government or even from American enterprises and American citizens. Another function of the "desk officer" is to keep in contact with the diplomatic mission that the country he is assigned to maintains in Washington. Almost all of the correspondence between that mission and the Department of State passes over the "country desk."

Our observance of the character of the "desk officers" work suggests perhaps the central problem of organization within the Department of State. It is primarily a question of reconciling the specific objectives of the geographical desks with the general policy aims of the so-called functional divisions of the Department. To take a case in point, let us assume that a problem involving commercial air transportation such as use of landing facilities arises in Turkey. In such a situation the "desk officer" should not normally act nor should the Assistant Secretary in charge of Near Eastern and African Affairs make any move without first consulting the Office of Transport and Communications Policy of the State Department. This is a functional agency specializing in problems of this nature and would be looked to for expert advice. To take the reverse of the situation, it would also follow that the Office of Transport and Communications Policy would refrain from taking any action in Turkey on a matter pertaining to aviation without first consulting our Office of Near Eastern, South Asian, and African Affairs in order to satisfy itself that such action was not incompatible with our general established policy in the area.

The problem of reconciling the efforts of the "desk officer" with the functional agencies of the Department of State may and often does carry far beyond the activities of the Department. In our hypothetical aviation problem arising in Turkey, the State Department's Office of Transport and Communications Policy would very likely confer with our Civil Aeronautics authorities before taking action or even making recommendations. The Civil Aeronautics Authority is not an agency within the Department of State; it is a functional body located in our Department of Commerce. Yet to conduct our external affairs successfully it is fairly obvious that the policies of the United States, whatever they may be, must represent the collective effort of all our governmental agencies, not the independent judgments of several uncoordinated governmental bodies.

The Functional Agencies

Besides the geographical divisions there are the functional agencies, such as the Office of Transport and Communications mentioned above, whose purpose is to specialize in a particular activity. These are clustered under one of the five functional areas of the Department. Thus the Office of Special Political Affairs deals with matters centering on the relations with the United Nations and with questions related to international organization. In a different functional category—the economic—are the Office of International Trade, Transport, and Communications, and the Office of Financial and Development Policy. Another unit that might be briefly mentioned to illustrate the enormous scope of State Department operations is the Office of Research and Intelligence, which now serves the geographical divisions and also may carry its analysis of any situation directly to the Secretary of State. All told, there are eighteen separate offices in the Department, and eighty-four divisions. And, capping all of these individual units as a coordinating body, is the secretary's Staff Committee. The Staff Committee's main purpose is to secure a greater perspective over the full swing of departmental activities. It is composed of the undersecretary, the undersecretary for economic affairs, the counselor, the assistant secretaries, the special assistant for research and intelligence, the special assistant for international organization, and the legal adviser. Because the secretary relies heavily upon this advisory body its recommendations are not only important on administrative policies, but are also influential in molding long range foreign policy.

PROBLEMS OF ADMINISTRATIVE REORGANIZATION

That the task of getting this multiplicity of agencies to work in harness is indeed a tremendous one may be readily observed. Already saddled with archaic methods for conducting diplomacy before World War II, the State Department chipped away at the structural contours of its organization several times during the course of the war.[21] In January, 1944, an extensive reorganization was undertaken "to facilitate the conduct of the

[21] Walter H. C. Laves and Francis O. Wilcox: "The Reorganization of the Department of State." *American Political Science Review* (1944), 38:289–301.

foreign relations . . . in war and in peace . . ." and while some highly essential consolidations and regrouping of functions were accomplished, the measurable progress toward a thorough reorganization is still a matter of conjecture. One of the chief criticisms of this reorganization was that the structural reforms did not carry with them changes in personnel. As noted by one critic, there had been no change comparable to it in the last half-century, yet, "the end-result of this architectural metamorphosis boils down to a serried retitling of the same officials. The more it changes, the more it is the same thing." [22] The State Department officials are well aware that their administrative organization needs far more perfecting, and they are continuously experimenting to find better ways of lubricating the machinery for the management of foreign affairs. The smooth functioning of the State Department, however, is beset by a challenging set of conditions.

In the administration of national affairs on the domestic level, it will be recalled that the work of governmental units designed to operate on a functional basis is expected to cut across that of agencies whose plan of organization is geographical. Where our external relations are concerned, however, we have noted that heavy emphasis is placed upon geographical administrative organization. In the international sphere it is the "country desk" that is the vital unit in the administrative framework. Thus the geographical units—the "country desk," the division, and the office are perhaps the most important. But the complexities of international affairs have increased the demand for functionalization.[23] Today the great variety of activity in the intercourse between nations calls for more specialization in the treatment of specific problems. And it follows that the functional units created to handle such matters must cut through the boundaries arranged for geographical organization. However well-suited the geographical divisions may be for handling certain over-all phases of our foreign affairs these units must yield freely to the demands of functionalization.

The problem of administration in international affairs is further complicated by the fact that in addition to the growing number of functional units within the State Department itself, the number of national agencies whose work touches on our external relations is steadily increasing. In particular, the work of the Commerce, Agriculture, Labor, and Justice Departments, and that of the National Defense agency is concerned with our foreign affairs at any number of different points. It is most essential therefore that the foreign activities of the United States government whether they be within the State Department or outside of it be harmonized. Without careful coordination of efforts the obvious results would be duplication, confusion, and an endless conflict in which competing agencies would attempt to substitute one judgment for another.

[22] *Washington Post,* January 17, 1944.
[23] For an astute analysis of this problem see Arthur W. Macmahon: "Function and Area in the Administration of International Affairs," in *New Horizons in Public Administration* (University, Ala., 1945), pp. 117–45.

In short, the real task of the State Department is to pull together the activities affecting our foreign relations by area and function both within and outside of the Department. In coordinating the geographical and functional units, it has been sagely suggested by one observer that the geographical units should "run ahead of events to indicate the frame of policy" that should be followed.[24] The geographical units should take the initiative in political affairs, whereas the functional units should have the major responsibility for the specialized fields. A primary responsibility of the State Department should, of course, be to make certain that the diverse activities of our governmental agencies all fit properly into the pattern of objectives set for our over-all foreign policy.

Clearly recognizing the problems involved in coordinating the nation's foreign policy, the Hoover Commission in 1949 made the following recommendations:

1) Congress should not grant foreign-affairs powers of an executive nature to any officer or agency except the President or an established executive department or agency.

2) Congress should not establish by legislation the precise functions and membership of coordinating and advisory bodies within the executive branch but should leave these flexible.

3) Congress should not make specific grants of foreign-affairs powers and supporting funds below the level of the appropriate department or agency head.

4) The president should make more use of Cabinet-level committees where the issues transcend the responsibility of any single department.

With regard to the State Department itself, the Hoover Commission recommended:

(1) that instead of operating specific programs overseas or at home such as the Voice of America, the State Department should concentrate on defining the objectives of foreign policy and on carrying them out;

2) the Department should continue to discharge its traditional tasks of representation, reporting, and negotiation;

3) the Secretary of State should have a clear and unmistakable line of authority down through all the departmental agencies, including the Foreign Service;

4) the personnel of the State Department and Foreign Service should be merged.

Despite some relief by piecemeal reforms in the State Department's organization, the prospect for quickly smoothing out the wrinkles in handling the administrative phase of our foreign relations does not look too promising. Not only has the character of diplomacy changed from the nineteenth century, when foreign relations were concerned only with sovereigns and foreign offices; the scope of external activities has increased to the point where the State Department must also synchronize its program with the work carried on abroad by the Commerce, Agricul-

[24] Ibid., p. 126.

ture, War, Navy, Labor, and Justice Departments. Such circumstances alone present staggering problems of coordination and integration, but they are made more acute by the fact that the State Department, in company with foreign offices the world over, resolutely clings to tradition in dispatching its affairs.

The mechanics of diplomacy have yielded to change at an unbelievably slow pace, revealing a hide-bound conservatism which prompted the distinguished French diplomatist, Jules Cambon, to remark that no vocation has as many sides, and there is "none which is less shackled by rules and regulations and more governed by tradition. . . ." Even as late as 1945 the reform of foreign offices to speed up the conduct of diplomacy and make it more efficient was doggedly resisted. In Great Britain, where undersecretaries and other important officials had not been allowed to have anyone take phone messages for them even when they were in important conferences, the reliance upon outmoded diplomatic practices evoked the following caustic comment: ". . . because the Foreign Office official believes the Foreign Office is perfect, he grimly defends the present system, and tries to argue that foreign policy does not need newfangled devices such as internal telephones, teleprinters, filing systems, or even secretaries. He and his colleagues can do their jobs, thank you. . . . Anyway, it is very much like life at All Souls, which is all the better for having no bathrooms." [25] In the United States, the Department of State has been conditioned by the same forces that have kept diplomacy in fetters elsewhere, notwithstanding repeated efforts to bring about a break with the past. Several secretaries of state have taken office with the firmest intention of setting off an eruption, but the stoutest hearts have gradually succumbed to the glacier-like pressure exerted by the permanent bureaucracy of the Department. In the words of one harsh critic, other agencies of government "in varying degrees reflect the times, but the faded and moth-eaten tradition of Victorian diplomacy seeps out of every cranny in the antiquated home of the State Department." Much of this attitude has very likely been influenced by the character of the Department's personnel, for until quite recently low salary scales meant that few persons, except those with independent means, could afford a State Department career. Part of the conservative temperament has also been induced by the historical trappings and precedents that have enveloped the practice of diplomacy. Besides the social background of an important segment of its personnel and the confining influence of diplomatic tradition, one further factor has tended to mold State Department practices along conservative lines. In the course of their duties much of the time of State Department representatives is spent representing our commercial interests abroad, and this work has not had an entirely negligible effect upon the permanent bureaucracy. Whatever the cause, however, conservatism is characteristic of the Department, and its significance is of no small importance.

Because much of the work of the State Department is technical, and

[25] *New Statesman and Nation,* August 4, 1945.

because the top positions of the Department shift according to the vicissitudes of politics, a neophyte secretary of state or his immediate deputies are frequently constrained both to seek and follow the advice offered by permanent officials surrounding them. It is natural for an inexperienced political appointee to wish to avoid making a blunder or antagonizing those serving under him, hence he may become increasingly dependent upon the permanent satellites around him. Thus the professional officialdom of the Department of State is in an unusually strategic position to exert steady pressure on matters of foreign policy as well as on administrative organization. This group may influence the instructions that are sent to agents in the field, or it may express its sentiments through the interpretation of a report from an agent residing abroad, but no matter how it operates, it is a potent force within the Department. Moreover, what is true of the State Department in this respect is equally true of the British Foreign Office, the French Quai d'Orsay, and also of the Soviet Union's foreign office, the Minindel, certainly a factor for which due allowance must be made in interpreting the shifting scene of international relations.

THE FOREIGN SERVICE

By far the largest of the units in the State Department is the Foreign Service Office, which maintains posts and personnel among the capitals and important commercial cities of the world.[26] Early in 1947, the United States was operating embassies in thirty-nine countries, and legations in twenty-three. In addition, special missions had been established in three other countries, a personal representative of the president was still accredited to the Vatican, and approximately 250 consular offices were functioning in cities scattered throughout the world.

Diplomatic and Consular Services

Until 1924, the diplomatic and consular services of the United States were separated, but this was changed by the Rogers Act, which formed the basic charter of the American Foreign Service. The diplomatic officers are still considered political representatives while the consular officials— in line with their historic origins—are thought of primarily as commercial agents, but since the passage of the Rogers Act, Foreign Service officers may hold either diplomatic positions, consular positions, or both. The merging of the services has not yet eroded the ancient prejudice of diplomats against the consular service. The idea once expressed in a tome on foreign affairs that "a consul need not be a gentleman" still lurks in the minds of some diplomats, but it seems to be conceded, nonetheless, that the merging of the two services was a worth-while venture from the standpoint of improving both morale and administrative efficiency.

Besides the service merger, the Rogers Act laid the cornerstone for

[26] See *The Foreign Service*, State Department Publication No. 2745 (Washington, 1947).

making the Foreign Service a career service. In 1906, President Theodore Roosevelt brought the consular service under a merit system by executive order and President Taft placed a substantial part of the diplomatic service on a similar basis a few years later, but neither step did much to justify the application of the word "career" to the system. Low salaries were still a deterrent to persons without an independent income, and as the president could change personnel, diplomats and consular officials were at the mercy of political shifts. The Rogers Act, however, put the merit system for the Foreign Service on a statutory basis and must be regarded as a landmark among State Department reforms.[27]

Foreign Service Act of 1946

Since 1924, the Foreign Service has undergone several minor alterations, but a major change was accomplished in 1946 with the passage of the Foreign Service Act. This legislation established five basic categories of Foreign Service personnel: chiefs of mission, Foreign Service officers, Foreign Service reserve officers, Foreign Service staff, and alien clerks and employees. The chiefs of missions, ambassadors, and ministers fall within the first group, while the second—Foreign Service officers—is composed of the professional officers who staff our embassies and consulates abroad. The Foreign Service Reserve officers is a classification used to distinguish the specialists or technicians who serve the Foreign Service for limited periods up to four years. This group also includes the cultural attachés who are attached to some of the more important embassies. The fourth group—Foreign Service staff officers—contains technical and professional personnel who serve in a non-executive capacity with approximately one-half of the staff corps made up of clerical personnel. In the last category—alien clerks and employees—are the persons hired to serve chiefly among our consular posts. Congress does not permit the employment of alien personnel at diplomatic missions for the obvious reason that they might come into contact with confidential political reports and highly classified material. But aliens may be hired at our administrative sections abroad and at consular posts, and both are largely staffed by alien employees.

Along with changes of classification, recent legislation has provided for a long overdue increase in salary scales. Ambassadors and ministers, whose compensation heretofore had been based upon scales established in 1855 were pushed up to levels that provided salaries of $25,000 per annum for the top six or seven posts, and $15,000 for most posts. In the Foreign Service officers category, the salaries now range from $4,450 for a person entering in his early twenties, to $13,500 for a career minister. Reserves, cultural attachés and others are compensated on the same basis as Foreign Service officers, while the Foreign Service staff corps

[27] See Dorothy Fosdick, "A Plea for the Career Diplomat," *New York Times*, March 27, 1955. Here the author, a former State Department official, urges that the chiefs of mission should be drawn mainly from experienced professionals.

salaries have been increased to a scale that allows $720 per annum for a local American messenger boy to $10,000 for the top administrative officers. Normal entrance salaries for general clerical and stenographic personnel abroad are about $2,160. Salaries for alien employees are not standardized and are generally set in accordance with prevailing wage rates in the individual locality.

In furtherance of previously established policy, the Foreign Service Act also provides for more liberal living allowances to supplement the new salary scales. The Moses-Linthicum Act of 1931 granted additional stipends for such items as rent, heat, and increased living costs at posts abroad, and the Foreign Service Act generously increased such allotments. In general, the allowances fall into two classifications: those designed to aid an officer in meeting expenses which he would not ordinarily be expected to incur if he were residing in the United States, and allowances designed to compensate an officer for legitimate expenses incurred in discharging his official obligations. Thus, the first allowance category aims to compensate American officers and employees in the Foreign Service for the increased cost of living abroad as compared with the United States, while the latter is designed primarily to help defray the extraordinary expenses of chiefs of missions who frequently have to live in residences provided by the government that are exceedingly expensive to maintain.[28]

It would be erroneous to conclude that the financial lot of persons in the Foreign Service is utopian; it is far from it. The cost of educating children of Foreign Service employees is a heavy item if parents wish to send them back to the United States. Furthermore, to maintain the standards that are expected of a person of his position, an officer must make heavy outlays. This is particularly true of ambassadors, ministers, and those in the higher echelons of the Foreign Service.[29] A number of officers manage to live on their salaries and allowances quite well—so well, in fact, that many are reluctant to return to Washington and spend a year or two feeling the political pulse of this country, because they lose their allowances while living in the United States. Despite the unquestioned progress that has been made in improving salary standards, the top posts in the Foreign Service must still be cushioned by an independent income, and many officers stationed in other important areas are required to stretch salary and allowance carefully to make ends meet.

In a service which has been so slow to discard political and financial availability as the main determinants for filling the more desirable posts, the development of a well-conceived promotional scheme has been a continuing problem. Much interest therefore centered on the report of a committee headed by Dr. Henry M. Wriston, former president of Brown

[28] Under the Porter Act of 1926, the United States has acquired some residences to house ambassadors and other Foreign Service personnel.

[29] Ambassador Charles G. Dawes reported he spent $75,000 at the Court of St. James, while Ambassador William C. Bullitt is reported to have spent $100,000 a year in Paris.

University, which was submitted to the Secretary of State in June of 1954. This report dealing with conditions affecting the morale of Foreign Service officers strongly censured the traditionalists within the service who seemed intent on preserving the elite character of the corps by deliberately holding down the number of employees, despite the obvious need for expansion. Other matters singled out by the report as factors contributing to the decline in prestige of the Foreign Service were the absence of strong administrative leadership within the Department as well as the presence of a rigid security program.

Major recommendations of the Wriston report were: 1) to integrate the personnel of the Department's staff and the Foreign Service abroad wherever possible; 2) to develop a bold and imaginative program of recruitment. (The report recommended sponsorship of 470 training scholarships to juniors and seniors in American universities, thus enabling the Foreign Service to compete with the military, naval, and air force academies for recruits. Students completing the scholarship programs would be obligated to serve in the Foreign Service for 6 years.) Among the objectives of the proposal were: 1) to encourage better applicants; 2) to increase the prestige of the Service; 3) "to get grass-roots sentiment back of the Service." [30]

Two selection boards are used under the new plan, and their membership consists of four Foreign Service officers and one person not connected with the government.

The retirement age of the Foreign Service has been lowered from sixty-five to sixty—a change that seems to be in harmony with recent trends in personnel policy, and also appears to be particularly sound for a profession that often makes heavy physical demands on its practitioners. Officers who manage to reach Class 1 will not be dismissed (under the new plan, the average career officer will reach Class 1 when he is fifty-two), but will be automatically retired at sixty just the same as officers in the lower classes. As a result of changes in the retirement plan, an officer receives a pension equivalent to 2 per cent of his average salary for the last five years preceding his retirement multiplied by the number of years of service. [31] An officer with twenty years of service may retire at fifty, which leaves him a dignified exit if he fears that a selection board is likely to dismiss him from the Service.

THE FOREIGN SERVICE AS A CAREER

At this juncture it is too early to generalize about the over-all effect of the reorganization changes suggested in recent years. Some encouragement, however, may be deduced from the fact that a little over 60 per

[30] See *The Secretary of State's Public Committee on Personnel, Toward a Strong Public Service*, 1954; and Henry M. Wriston, "Young Men and the Foreign Service," *Foreign Affairs*, 33 (1954), 328–42.

[31] Not to exceed thirty years of service.

cent of our chiefs of missions are men who may be rightfully called career officers, and have attained their present rank either as a result of a merit promotion from the Foreign Service, or the Department, or both. Rigid examinations are now required before the Service may be penetrated at any level—except of course, in the case of several desirable posts at the ambassadorial or ministerial level, which are still bartered across the political counter. Yet, with all its romantic allure and seemingly expansive horizons for service, one should not jump to the conclusion that the Foreign Service can absorb vast numbers of young men and women for service abroad. The number of actual positions open each year is exceedingly small and only a small number of those who pass the examinations, and this is but a small fraction of those who attempt them, eventually secure appointment. Thus far, Harvard, Yale, and Princeton have supplied most of the career officers to the Service, in that order. State Department officials hasten to explain that this circumstance is not caused by any element of social prestige, but rather because of the interest in foreign affairs at these educational institutions. While this explanation is substantially correct, the tie lines between these institutions, along with a few others, and the State Department are well anchored. For example, Georgetown, which supplies the next largest number of graduates among the first ten (the others are California, Stanford, George Washington, Columbia, Dartmouth, and Michigan) has long been noted for feeding its graduates into the Foreign Service corps.

Before taking up a discussion of the Foreign Service office as it functions within the general framework of international diplomacy, a brief comment is in order on the uniqueness of its personnel problems. The Service definitely needs specialists and technicians, but it also desires to strike a proper balance by staffing its posts with men who have had a broad cultural training. This objective has proved particularly vexing in filling the consulate posts where the duties require technical skills, yet the work is so routine that many officers complain that if left in such positions too long they stagnate and thus impair their promotional opportunities. George F. Kennan states it well for the man of breadth when he says that what is important in "ninety-nine cases out of one hundred is the totality of the man himself: his character, his judgment, his insight, his knowledge of the world, his integrity, his adaptability, his capacity for human sympathy and understanding. With these things, all specialties (and who would challenge the need for specialties) will flower and bear fruit; without them no specialty will really help." [32]

Another personnel difficulty centers on a matter that ordinarily would be unimportant: in the Foreign Service, the role of an officer's wife or

---

[32] See "The Future of Our Professional Diplomacy," *Foreign Affairs*, 33 (1955), p. 572. In this article Kennan takes exception to several features of the Wriston report and singles out for particular criticism the failure of the Wriston Committee to face up to the problem of the security system, which he says has been "the greatest single factor in the collapse of Foreign Service morale."

family often poses a chronic problem. The Foreign Service does not maintain a file on "wives" as is sometimes uncharitably alleged, but its personnel administrators do not hesitate to admit that wives take up an inordinate amount of space in the personnel files. Here, the problem is not simply the pressure brought to bear by an officer for a change in posts because of his wife's or family's health; it can be more serious. Where a profession revolves to a considerable extent around social amenities, it is not a happy situation where the wife of Officer A cannot get along with Mrs. Y., or someone else in the diplomatic colony. Nor is it helpful if Mrs. Y. has a strong dislike for "Lower Slobovians," or specific nationalities, and sets up a constant clamor for a change. Clearly, the wife of a Foreign Service officer may have an important influence upon her husband's career, and it is equally certain that these family considerations give rise to personnel problems unique in the Federal government.

The forces of the Foreign Service are now distributed throughout the 300 embassies, legations, and consulates that the United States maintains. Among the diplomatic missions, the embassy ranks highest, and wherever the government sends an ambassador the mission is known as an embassy. Where the American representative is a minister, the mission is called a legation, and the full title of the minister is Envoy Extraordinary or Minister Plenipotentiary. Quite frequently a Foreign Service officer may hold the personal rank of minister without being credited as Minister Plenipotentiary. A consul general, for example, may be a minister in rank, and yet not be accredited as a Minister Plenipotentiary. Among foreign capitals, the consulate is a part of the mission staff. In other cities, the consular office may be either a consulate general, or a consulate. These offices in turn are headed by a consul general, a consul, or in very small offices, by a vice-consul.

The Consular Service

The consular service demands a substantial degree of technical competence from its agents. To certify properly the invoices of goods and thereby seek to prevent violations of customs regulations a consul must be well acquainted with United States tariff laws. He also has important responsibilities in connection with the American Merchant Marine. All masters of American vessels must deposit papers with the local United States consul when docking in a foreign port, and must secure the return of the papers before clearing port. Consuls have some jurisdiction over disputes arising between masters, officers, and seamen, and in addition they attempt to care for American seamen who need relief in foreign ports.

Many of the consul's duties are of a quasi-legal character. Thus he frequently administers oaths, certifies official documents, and occasionally administers the estate of an American citizen who dies abroad. In China, under the terms of the celebrated Cushing Treaty between the United States and that country in 1844, American consuls exercise rather broad legal jurisdiction over American citizens. Because of the peculiarities of Chinese law, the Cushing Treaty permitted United States consuls to try and punish American citizens who committed crimes in China. Since 1906, consular officials shared this jurisdiction with the United States Court for China but in 1944 by mutual agreement of the two countries, the United States gave up this unusual arrangement to which China had graciously consented for a full century.

Besides the lengthy list of miscellaneous functions undertaken by consular officials, they have traditionally been expected to keep track of trade opportunities that would further American business and commerce. Consuls are customarily granted certain immunities by the receiving governments, but unless specifically provided for, they do not enjoy the broad immunities accorded diplomatic agents. Unlike diplomatic officers, consuls are not accredited to governments but are simply instructed to perform specified duties, with the permission of the receiving state.

Diplomatic Customs and Practice

In accordance with accepted custom, the diplomatic representatives of the State Department take the titles and ceremonial ranking decided upon by the Congress of Vienna in 1815, and the Congress of Aix-la-Chapelle in 1818. The diplomats thus fall into four classes: ambassadors, envoys or ministers plenipotentiary, ministers resident or charges d'affaires, and take precedence over each other in that order. For the first century, the United States did not send any ambassadors abroad, electing instead to have the country represented by diplomatic agents in the other classes. But in 1893, Congress passed an act stipulating that a representative of the United States should hold the same rank as that of a foreign representative serving in this country. In practice this has meant that the United States usually reciprocates when a foreign nation sends an ambassador, although this is, of course, subject to the wishes of Congress. Until shortly before World War II, it was customary to send about 18 ambassadors abroad, but this number was augmented in the years following World War II. In June of 1956 the United States was represented abroad by 74 embassies, 4 legations, 2 missions, 62 consulates-general, 96 consulates and 30 consular agencies.

The general practices in diplomacy with regard to such questions as letters of credentials, immunities, and other conditions surrounding the profession have become well standardized by custom and international law, and the United States adheres closely to these conventions. Before sending a diplomatic agent abroad, an attempt is usually made to see if the proposed diplomat will be acceptable to the receiving state. The president generally tries to select a person who will be acceptable to the receiving state, but the latter is not compelled to accept an appointee who is a *persona non grata*, nor must it give a reason for refusing to receive him. All diplomatic representatives of the United States above the fourth class (charges d'affaires) receive, before starting out on a mission, a letter of credence from the president which is signed by the secretary of state and addressed to the head of the foreign state.

During his service abroad, the diplomat enjoys the broadest exemptions from the criminal and civil jurisdiction of the state to which he is accredited. Technically, the country where he is serving cannot try him for any criminal offense, nor can he be sued for any civil injury that he might have committed while serving his government. The immunities which the diplomat enjoys also extend to his family and the diplomatic suite which includes all persons whose work is necessary for the satisfactory functioning of the mission. In actual practice, it need hardly be mentioned that the successful diplomat rarely places himself in an awk-ward position that would give him the option of falling back on his immunities, and the same is true of members of the diplomatic suite. The head of a mission, moreover, can voluntarily turn over a member of his staff to the local authorities when an offense has been committed, and American diplomats, anxious to secure observance of local law and keep foreign relations on a cordial basis, have not hesitated to exercise this prerogative. As further insurance against the possibility of an abuse of diplomatic immunity, the State Department issues to all persons starting out on a mission specific instructions that their own real or personal property is subject to local jurisdiction—a warning that is also quite unnecessary for the diplomat who well knows that his professional career requires exemplary conduct in both his personal and official affairs.

Should a diplomatic agent prove to be no longer acceptable during the course of a mission, he may be dismissed by the receiving country or a demand may be made that he be recalled. During the presidential campaign of 1888, the British Minister, Lord Sackville, made an unfortunate comment on the impending election in a letter which subsequently came to public attention. The United States government cabled a demand for his recall. When this request was not immediately granted, he was dismissed and given his passport, establishing a precedent that the British Ambassador to this country in 1940, Lord Halifax, was perhaps not unmindful of when queried about the relative merits of presidential candidates Roosevelt and Willkie. "Make me an American citizen," he added quickly, "and I'll tell you how I would cast my vote."

American diplomats are assiduously instructed to refrain from taking an active part in the politics of the country to which they are accredited and they are quite effectively muzzled under threat of stern disciplinary measures if they write articles or make speeches on political subjects that have not first been cleared through proper channels in the State Department. Although the United States has probably been involved in more than its share of recalls, these are the exception rather than the rule. As far as our own diplomats are concerned, there have, it is true, been instances of subtle suggestion whereby foreign powers have made it known that they would like to have an American diplomatist recalled and replaced with a more acceptable successor. The waning popularity of the former American Ambassador to the Soviet Union, William C. Bullitt, was undoubtedly a factor which led to his replacement by Joseph E. Davies. In the vast majority of cases where a diplomat falls into gradual disfavor, however, the situation is handled without a sharp rupture of cordial relations. Again, the fact that an American diplomat is recalled does not necessarily mean that such action has been requested or that his mission has been terminated. Diplomats are frequently recalled for the purpose of giving them further instructions or gathering their advice. And they may be recalled by way of a protest against the domestic practices of the foreign country where they are serving, as was the case when President Roosevelt recalled Ambassador Dodd from Nazi Germany in November, 1938, to express disapproval of the outbreak of the Jewish pogroms.

Life in the diplomatic corps, as one might readily surmise, subjects a person to a rigid discipline. Professionally, the diplomats serving in the Foreign Service might be said to represent this nation's radar equipment. Among the foremost of their duties is that of training a keen eye on all political developments and faithfully reporting these events to Washington. They are also negotiators both in executing current agreements and in maintaining a lookout for future agreements that might prove beneficial to this country; and finally they have protective responsibilities for the safeguarding of personal and property rights of Americans residing or travelling abroad.

In the course of his tour of service, the diplomat must measure up to exacting and trying social demands. He must quickly learn to tune himself to the wave-length frequencies of foreign people, if he is to win their confidence and be able to understand them. In consequence, he must strive to adjust to their customs and manners as far as possible. At the same time, the diplomat must also function within the confines of strictly prescribed codes of etiquette in the diplomatic colony and of the inflexible business procedures decreed by the State Department. And, as in the Army, rank in diplomacy is not a matter to be taken lightly. Here again, the rule followed by the State Department is the one laid down by the Congress of Vienna, under which diplomats of the same class—that is, ambassadors, envoys, ministers, or charges d'affaires—rank according to the precedence of the date giving official notification of their arrival.

But if the American Foreign Service officer chafes under the many diplomatic niceties, he is likely to become exacerbated over the regulations prescribing the methods he must use in making out reports and covering a great variety of other matters in minute detail. He must, for example, never say "I believe," or "I suggest," in writing a report, but is always required to use the third person. Much of the diplomat's time is consumed by extremely trivial matters, which are made to sound all the more so because of the stilted, if not pontifical, methods that govern their disposition. The following cablegram signed by the undersecretary of state (probably drafted by a subordinate and signed for the undersecretary) well illustrates this point:

AMEMBASSY   RESTRICTED

HABANA, (CUBA)   APRIL 3, 1946

Reference Embassy's airgram No. 218, February 18 regarding sprinkling by a group of distinguished ladies, on the Pan American tree, of certified waters from the rivers or lakes of the Sister Republics.

The Department concurs with the Embassy's approval of this project. A container of genuine Potomac River water from the capital of the United States is being sent air express.

It is suggested that if the container suffers damage in transit and the liquid therein be dissipated, that water be secured from a source in the Embassy which may be considered United States soil. It is believed that the Embassy can supply an appropriate container into which the specimen can be transferred prior to the activities of the lady who will represent the United States.

ACHESON

Again, to correct any false notions concerning the glamour of the Foreign Service it is worth noting a comment of an officer, whose six-word summary of the work involved is not an exaggeration. A surprising amount of the work done by our three hundred embassies, legations, and consulates, he describes as "undramatic drudgery performed in unrewarded anonymity." Not all of the duties, of course, are as unimaginative or unchallenging as this characterization would imply, but there is much sterile routine from which even the high functionaries of the Service do not escape.

For personal accounts of the more trying aspects of a diplomat's profession, the memoirs or autobiographies of some of our ambassadors provide rich quarries of information. The activities that a diplomat must suffer through are as incredible as they are multitudinous, yet they are a part of the task of securing a better understanding between two peoples and they contribute to what Walter Hines Page, Ambassador to the Court of St. James, called the "warp and woof of our international friendliness." That qualities of temperament are inseparably linked with the success or failure of a diplomat, few would deny, though they are by no means reducible to packageable form. The United States has produced some remarkably able diplomats like James Russell Lowell and John G. Winant, both of whom differed greatly in training and personality. Oliver Wendell Holmes's reference to the "enchantments" and "alluring arts" by which "our truthful James led captive British hearts," have been quite simply set down as "his gift for friendship and his beguiling talent for after-dinner oratory." Upon his arrival at the Court of St. James, Lowell was advised by Lord Coleridge, perhaps the most talented speaker in Great

Britain, that he would receive a wearisome number of invitations to speak. "Select your anecdote beforehand," counselled Coleridge, "and when called upon, lead up to your anecdote, tell it, go gently away from it and your speech is made." Lowell heeded this advice with the result that his popularity with the British people has probably never been equalled by an American representative. That sharp wit and clever tongue are effective catalysts in winning over a people is also borne out by the career of Sir Gerald Campbell, one of the most successful British diplomatists to serve in the United States, who began his mission after landing in Philadelphia on July 4, 1920, with the remark that "it was nice to see everyone enjoying taxation with representation."

On the other hand, quite a few American diplomats have given highly creditable performances without any oratorical skill whatsoever. Public speaking admittedly was not the forte of Ambassador Winant, yet he won the warm affection of the British people and established an enviable record as an able diplomat. As a tool of the trade, of course, skill in public speaking will continue to serve the diplomat in good stead, but the lack of it may be compensated for by other abilities just as surely as much of the personal charm and elegance of the nineteenth-century diplomat has been superseded by other qualities.

THE CHANGING NATURE OF DIPLOMACY

Within the general framework of international diplomacy there have been important changes that have affected the working habits of the American diplomat. Radical changes in communication have whittled down his opportunities for making personal decisions that were justified in the days when it took six weeks or more to wait for proper instructions. To state that the diplomat today is merely a "clerk at the end of a telegraph or telephone wire" is an over-simplification though technical advances have unquestionably bound the diplomat to the policy-making authorities in the home office in so far as instructions are concerned. But the contention that there is a radical distinction between the old diplomacy and the new has probably been overworked. The diplomatic representatives of the United States are still agents of a sovereign government and are committed to serving the interests of that government. Diplomatic practices, or perhaps what might be called the rules of the game, have been refined, but diplomacy still has the essential marks of a domestic political struggle diffused to global proportions. Indeed, Lord Grey's remark on this subject a quarter of a century ago is unfortunately pertinent to post–World War II diplomacy: "Representatives of governments call each other Excellency, and so forth, but the game they play is essentially the same as if they were called Tom, Dick, or Harry."

On the optimistic side, however, the upward swing of a progressive diplomacy that seeks to orient the diplomatic practices of an individual state with the larger and more compelling interest of a community of nations deserves to be emphasized. In the course of its evolution, diplomacy has progressed "from the narrow conception of exclusive tribal rights to the wider conception of inclusive common interests," and the United States, after failing to help nourish this trend by joining the League of Nations, has now nailed its standard firmly to the Charter of the United Nations. Under the impetus of being a leading participant in the United Nations, American diplomacy takes on a new significance. Its task is not only to recast its operations to fit within the larger framework of the United Nations organization, but also to harmonize them with the many important subsidiaries of the parent organization in coping with problems that transcend national boundaries. In such a setting, it does not seem too much to hope that the evolutionary trend in the management of foreign affairs will continue toward a world federation without destroying the individuality of its component members.

SUMMARY

Though both President and Congress share in the control of foreign affairs, the President occupies the position of preeminence by virtue of the power of recognition, of making executive agreements, and of initiation of policy in this field. In making treaties the president must secure ratification by two-thirds of the Senate, but this restraint can be circumvented in part by the use of a joint resolution or an executive agreement.

Authority of the national government in the area of foreign relations is extensive. Here the courts permit Congress to delegate power to the executive in broader terms than would be permissible if the power was to be exercised in domestic matters. Under the treaty power the national government may invade the field of reserved powers conferred on the states.

Negotiation and the ratification of a treaty must be so conducted by the president as to avoid alienating his political opposition since the vote required for ratification can be mustered only with some bi-partisan support in the Senate.

The State Department has long sought a form of organization that will harmonize its functional agencies with its area "desks" and that will coordinate its activity with that of other government agencies which impinge on our foreign relations.

Strides have been taken since the passage of the Rogers Act of 1924 to make the Foreign Service a career service. Improved pay and allowances, and the adoption of an enlightened promotion and retirement plan in recent years help toward inducing able men to make the Foreign Service their life's work. The talents required for success in this field are diverse and unusual. Hence the personnel problem of this branch of service is unique.

In an intensely dynamic world diplomacy is undergoing a marked change. Rapid communication keeps the diplomat in close contact with the home office. It is a far cry from the concept of exclusive tribal rights held by primitive man to the current emerging concept of common world interests and the institutions to implement their realization in functioning world policies.

CHAPTER XXXVI

FOREIGN POLICY AND THE AMERICAN GOVERN-
MENT IN ITS INTERNATIONAL SETTING: I

There are critical moments in the life of every nation which call for the straightest, the plainest and the most courageous thinking of which we are capable. We confront such a moment now. It is not only desperately important to America. It is important to the world. . . .

The thing . . . we need to do, Mr. President . . . is to frankly face the postwar alternatives which are available. . . .

There are two ways to do it. One way is by exclusive individual action in which each of us tries to look out for himself. The other is by joint action in which we undertake to look out for each other.

The first is the old way which has twice taken us to Europe's interminable battlefields within a quarter of a century. The second way is the new way in which our present fraternity of war becomes a new fraternity of peace. I do not believe that either we or our Allies can have it both ways. They serve to cancel out each other. We cannot tolerate unilateral privilege in a multilateral peace. . . .[1]

AMONG the nations not bent upon territorial conquest or world aggression in furtherance of a revolutionary ideal there are three fundamental motives in charting foreign policy—security, the desire for favorable trade, and the humanitarian quest for a peaceful world in which the cultural and material interchange of people and ideas will remain fluid. It takes no fine discernment to observe that the first of these objectives may rest upon the third or vice versa, and that perhaps to enjoy any of these goals for more than a brief period a nation must strive to secure all three. National policies aimed at security which fail to take into account the stake of all nations in keeping peace may only postpone and increase the magnitude of eventual conflict. Similarly, unsound and narrowly conceived trade policies designed to undercut the economic health of other nations may start an infection that will sooner or later destroy security and peace.

To live—that is, to provide employment and food for her people—

[1] Speech of the Hon. Arthur H. Vandenberg delivered in the United States Senate, January 10, 1945.

Switzerland must import 75 per cent of the raw materials that are processed into watches, precision instruments, and other articles for which
she is noted, and she has to import about 50 per cent of her required
foodstuffs. A larger nation that is today in much the same situation as
Switzerland is Great Britain, whose survival depends upon her ability to
import the materials she needs and to vastly step up the sale of her
exports. The realization that a country must not only export but must
also import goods if the sources of economic conflict among nations are
to be removed has, by slow stages, made definite inroads. The reasonable-
ness of this proposition should be fairly evident. Inequities in the distribution of natural resources among different nations require some countries to import raw materials. And in order to pay for the raw materials,
they must be able to sell in the export market articles manufactured
from them.

The residents of many countries have often been painfully aware of
the conditions imposed upon them by their geographic position both in
terms of military and economic security. But the inhabitants of the United
States have for many years been able to side-step this worry because of
(1) the unusual fertility of their soil, (2) the abundance of their resources, and (3) the strategic security afforded by their remoteness
from other nations. Although the individual citizen may not always have
been conscious of it, each of these geographic factors has also influenced
the evolution of American foreign policy. In an earlier period the geography of the United States encouraged withdrawal policies and fostered
a general attitude of indifference toward international affairs. More recently, however, the change in pace of communication, linked with the
disastrous effects of two world wars and the emergence of America as the
world's foremost Power, has wrought a significant alteration in our conception of the United States' role in the international community. The
fabulous Yankee Clipper of the 1850's with its top speed of eighteen
knots has given way to the modern jet-propelled airliner with a cruising
speed of four hundred miles per hour—and modern warfare with its
radioactive missiles leaves no cranny of the earth's surface impregnable
to attack. Thus the aims of our foreign policy may no longer be based
upon the assumption that our geographic setting makes us invulnerable
in terms of military security.[2] Nor may the course of foreign policy be
mapped with the comfortable assurance that strategic materials are inexhaustible, for it is already ominously apparent that our mineral reserve
has been tapped to dangerously low levels in some instances.[3]

[2] See Nicholas J. Spykman: *America's Strategy in World Politics* (New York, 1942),
pp. 446–8.

[3] See The President's Materials Policy Commission Report, *Resources for Freedom*
(Washington, 1952). The Commission's central conclusion bears repeating: "There
is no such thing as a purely domestic policy toward materials that all the world must
have; there are only world policies that have domestic aspects." By the early 1950's
the United States was importing in substantial quantity over seventy materials essential to the defense effort. In providing for the stockpiling of these materials vital
to national defense, the Congress has classified them as "strategic and critical."

In the course of its evolution American foreign policy has not always favored political abstention. At times our diplomacy has made bold advances in expanding our foreign relations, just as it has carried us in the opposite direction on other occasions. Speaking broadly, the problems of American foreign policy divide into two groups, those that may be thought of as primarily political and those that may be regarded as economic. In dealing with both of these facets of our foreign policy, it is well to recall that initially the United States concerned itself specifically with one nation at a time in working out its foreign policies. The idea of involvement in larger commitments where we shared responsibility for enforcement with a group of nations was slow in evolving.[4] Like the industrial revolution, acceptance of our international responsibility for helping to insure a peaceful and prosperous world was not consummated in a single moment; it was a gradual process that spanned the better part of a century and a half. In the course of that period—which saw many false starts toward international collaboration—American foreign policy took on certain doctrines and characteristics, some of which have long since outlived their usefulness. Others, however, have remained as vital anchorage points, and continue to be invoked as the architects of American foreign policy cope with the international problems of the hour.[5]

SHIFTING CURRENTS IN AMERICAN FOREIGN POLICY: POLITICAL TRENDS [6]

The Origins

"The American foreign policy," wrote De Tocqueville in 1832, "is reduced by its very nature to await the chances of the future history of the nation, and for the present it consists more in abstaining from interference than in exerting its activity."[7] Almost from its inception the United States government proclaimed its intention to refrain from participating in the struggle for power that marked the political relations of the European states.[8] The origins of the political isolationist doctrine are

---

[4] The successive contributions of the United States toward the objectives of international organization are brought out in a unique study by Malbone W. Graham: *American Diplomacy in the International Community* (Baltimore, 1948).

[5] An illuminating and brilliantly conceived book of readings on the problems of American foreign policy is Lawrence H. Chamberlain and Richard S. Snyder: *American Foreign Policy* (New York, 1955). In connection with this chapter see particularly chaps. 11–18, 24, and 25. See also Richard C. Snyder and Edgar S. Furniss, Jr.: *American Foreign Policy* (New York, 1954), chaps. 1 and 2.

[6] The most complete account of American diplomacy will be found in Samuel Flagg Bemis: *A Diplomatic History of the United States* (New York, 1950). See also Thomas A. Bailey: *A Diplomatic History of the American People* (New York, 1950). And for a brief, though excellent, history of the main historical currents in American foreign policy, see Dexter Perkins: *The Evolution of American Foreign Policy* (New York, 1948).

[7] Alexis de Tocqueville: *Democracy in America* (New York, 1900), Vol. I, p. 237.

[8] An extensive and carefully selected book of significant documents in United States diplomatic history is R. J. Bartlett, editor: *The Record of American Diplomacy: Documents and Readings in the History of American Foreign Relations* (New York, 1947).

generally attributed to Washington, who warned his fellow countrymen that the best rule for this country in regard to foreign nations was "in extending our commercial relations," and in maintaining "as little political connection as possible." [9] The outbreak of the French Revolution, and of the wars that were to occupy the European Powers for two decades, provided an early test of the policy whose purpose was to abstain, whenever possible, from interfering in the affairs of Europe. Although not unmindful of the debt this country owed to France for assistance during the Revolutionary War, the United States declined to come to the aid of France in her conflict with Great Britain at the close of the eighteenth century, and this policy was set forth by Washington's Proclamation of Neutrality in 1793. Another early occupant of the presidency who took a critical attitude toward entangling alliances with European powers was Thomas Jefferson. He was ever fearful that the United States by soliciting favors from other countries might be called upon itself to reciprocate and thus become involved in the conflicts of the European continent. Jefferson's fears were strongly shared by many of the leaders of the new Republic who insisted that America must use the opportunity provided her by the struggle in Europe to secure the foundations of the infant state. As matters turned out, the government managed to avoid being drawn into the Napoleonic Wars, and it was not a participant in the Congress of Vienna, which formulated the peace treaties at the end of these wars. At the same time, the result of prolonged European conflict had been used to full advantage by the United States to secure her position through further territorial expansion and the conclusion of favorable treaties with Great Britain and France.

Closely allied with the policy of refraining from taking any part in European affairs was the desire to ward off any threat of further European expansion in the Western Hemisphere. In pursuit of this latter goal President Monroe, in his annual message to Congress in 1823, laid down the principles of what has come to be known as the Monroe Doctrine. In the immediate sense the Doctrine was aimed at European Powers helping Spain to recover control of her lost provinces in the Western Hemisphere and also at Russia in her attempt to expand the frontiers of her colonies on the West Coast. The Doctrine reaffirmed the intention of the United States to remain outside of European affairs but warned that any attempt on the part of the European Powers "to extend their system to any nation of this hemisphere" would be regarded as "dangerous to

[9] But it is worthwhile to note that at another point in his farewell address in 1796 Washington declared: "It is our true policy to steer clear of permanent alliances with any portion of the foreign world, so far, I mean, as we are now at liberty to do it; for let me not be understood as capable of patronizing infidelity to existing engagements." And Walter Lippman has well observed that "These are not the words of a man with a dogmatic prejudice against all alliances as such: these are the words of a man cautiously measuring the necessity and wisdom of extending an alliance." *U.S. Foreign Policy: Shield of the Republic* (Boston, 1943). At the time Washington was under strong pressure to extend the alliance made with France in 1778 and to enter the European war on the side of France against England.

our peace and safety." [10] The Doctrine enunciated further that any moves on the part of the European Powers which sought to control or interfere with the newly created Latin American republics would be considered "manifestation of an unfriendly disposition toward the United States." [11]

Although the Declaration of President Monroe was supported by Great Britain and the Latin American Republics, it nevertheless was undertaken by the United States acting alone. The Doctrine contained no promise that this country would refrain from further territorial expansion in North America, and, in fact, was never interpreted as having this effect. Nor did it mean that the United States was prepared to conclude definite treaties with the Latin American states whereby a threat to the independence and territorial integrity of the latter would require America to come to the assistance of the threatened state. Indeed, such a treaty was to be concluded only in the years following the second World War. Even so, the Declaration represented one of the most significant milestones in the history of American foreign policy. It served to round out the outlines of a policy that was to prevail throughout the nineteenth century, and whose momentum was to carry the boundaries of the United States to the Pacific Ocean and to open up the seemingly inexhaustible resources of a virgin continent.

It is only with the advantage of hindsight that we are able to see that American security during the nineteenth century rested upon a number of fortunate circumstances. The relative geographic isolation of this country from Europe must undoubtedly rank among the most favorable of these circumstances. Almost of equal importance, however, was the fact that the nineteenth century represented the era of *Pax Britannica,* and that British interests were only infrequently inimical to the interests of this country. For many decades the principal guarantee of the Monroe Doctrine was provided by the unchallenged naval supremacy of Great Britain. This importance of Great Britain in the equation of American security was to become apparent only after the decline of British power in the twentieth century. Finally, note must be taken of the fact that the nineteenth century was itself one of the most peaceful periods—if not the most peaceful period—in the turbulent history of the modern state system.

Enough has been said to indicate that the character and spirit of traditional American foreign policy were largely the reflection of the unique quality of the American experience during the nineteenth century. This experience was, above all, one of expanding over and developing a continent. In consequence, most Americans knew little and cared even less about foreign affairs. Preoccupied with internal concerns

[10] J. D. Richardson, editor: *Messages and Papers of the Presidents* (Washington, 1896–99), Vol. II, p. 209.

[11] For general histories of the Monroe Doctrine and American policy toward Latin America, see Dexter Perkins, *Hands Off! A History of the Monroe Doctrine* (Boston, 1941) and Samuel Flagg Bemis, *The Latin American Policy of the United States* (New York, 1943).

and enjoying the blessing of momentary security, Americans could afford themselves the luxury of viewing with disdain the seemingly endless intrigue and struggle for power that went on in the old world. Gradually the conviction grew that this sordid struggle for power which marked European diplomacy was somehow due to the innate defects characterizing European society as a whole, whereas the freedom America enjoyed from power politics was a fitting reward that a just Providence had granted to a virtuous people.[12] America's mission was conceived as one which, though standing apart from the European struggle, could set a lofty moral example for other states to follow. Hence the foreign policy pronouncements of American statesmen contained almost from the start of this nation's history an unusually high moral content. However hypocritical and gratuitous they frequently appeared to others, they formed a sincere expression of the American outlook toward world affairs. In essence, this outlook was one which insisted that the conduct of state relations should be governed largely by rules operative within a democratic society. To the peoples of Europe, looking as they did upon war and power diplomacy as the inevitable concomitants of the state system, this attitude could not but appear naive. To Americans it merely represented the logical projection of their domestic experience—a domestic experience buttressed by a singular security from attack—onto the international plane. However intractable the "realities" of international politics might appear to others less fortunate, Americans viewed the obstacles to be overcome in shaping a democratic society of states where reason and moderation would prevail, as no more difficult than the obstacles they had already overcome in building American society.

America Becomes a World Power

The last decade of the nineteenth century provides one of the great watersheds in the evolution of American foreign policy. By general agreement the Spanish-American War of 1898 marks the end of what the American historian Charles Beard has termed the period of "American Continentalism." It is not our purpose here to inquire into the origins of this war and the causes that led America to abandon, at least in part, a policy that had been pursued for a century.[13] The significant point is that the Spanish-American War signaled the emergence of the United

[12] See on this general theme, Reinhold Niebuhr: *The Irony of American History* (New York, 1952).

[13] The character of the Spanish rule in Cuba and the wretched condition of the native population had long been of concern to the United States, not for the reason that American security interests were at stake but because of the sympathy that the unhappy plight of the Cuban people aroused in Americans. In consequence, each insurgent movement in the island elicited American support. In the final analysis, however, the more profound causes of the Spanish-American War are intangible. What can be said is simply that during this period the American people manifested a willingness to look outward beyond their borders and to undertake a war that was to lead to commitments heretofore regarded as alien to the American tradition. And see Julius W. Pratt: *Expansionists of 1898* (Baltimore, 1937).

States as a world power with interests and commitments outside the Western hemisphere. As a result of that conflict the United States acquired the Philippines. Whatever judgment is finally placed upon the wisdom or folly of that acquisition, its result was to commit America to the defense of islands located seven thousand miles from her shores. Even more, the acquisition of the Philippines almost of necessity required the United States to increase its naval power in the Pacific and to play a more active role in Far Eastern affairs generally. Thus in 1900 the United States proclaimed the so-called "Open Door" policy with respect to China, and sought by this policy to obtain the assurance of other states that the territorial integrity of China would be preserved and that the principle of equality in commerce and trading would be observed within the Chinese Empire.[14]

The increased tempo of American foreign policy during the decade and a half prior to World War I was equally noticeable elsewhere. Additional foreign commitments resulting from the Spanish-American War required not only a larger navy but a fleet that could be easily transferred between the two oceans as occasion demanded. The pressure for a canal grew stronger and in the early years of the century work was begun on the project in Panama. At the same time, America's strategic interest in the Caribbean became more marked and a number of naval bases were established in the area. Actually by the time of the outbreak of war in 1914 the Caribbean had been converted into what resembled an American lake. One of the unfortunate by-products of this period, however, was the increased intervention by the United States in the domestic affairs of the Central American states. The charge that these states had been virtually turned into American protectorates by 1914 is an exaggeration, though one not far from the actual fact. During this period America's relations with Latin America sank to a very low state, and the rising cry in Latin America of imperialism had a ring of truth that could not be denied.

In the end, however, the United States could not pursue for long a policy of imperialism, whether in this hemisphere or in the Pacific. The entire weight and purpose of American tradition were in firm opposition to a policy that led either to domination over other peoples or to the

[14] In two notes addressed to Great Britain, Russia, Germany, France, and Japan—dated September 6, 1899, and November 17, 1899—the American Secretary of State John Hay proposed recognition of the principle of non-discrimination in trade and the protection of vested interests in China. In a later circular of July 3, 1900, Hay declared that the policy of the United States was "to seek a solution which may bring about permanent safety and peace to China, preserve Chinese territorial and administrative entity, protect all rights guaranteed to friendly powers by treaty and international law, and safeguard for the world the principle of equal and impartial trade with all parts of the Chinese Empire." The immediate significance of these notes ought not to be exaggerated. At the time, the United States had no intention to take practical measures to insure the territorial integrity of China. Nevertheless, in the years that followed, the policy of the "Open Door" did gradually attain a central position in American Far Eastern policy. See, generally, A. Whitney Griswold: *The Far Eastern Policy of the United States* (New York, 1938).

interference in their internal affairs. Retention of the Philippines was approved by the Senate only by the narrowest of margins and after one of the most bitter and soul-searching debates in the history of that body. In large measure, the debate in the Senate also went on throughout the country generally. Proponents made use of a number of arguments, ranging from manifest destiny and the white man's burden to considerations of economic advantage. Probably the weightiest argument was simply that America had taken control of the islands and that if we abandoned them they would fall victim to one of the other great Powers. Opponents insisted that the acquisition of foreign territory by conquest and the governing of people whose consent had neither been asked for nor given was contrary to the whole of the American experience. Though losing over the immediate issue of annexation, history has clearly vindicated the latter argument. And in the period of less than a half century that America retained the Philippines the feeling that their possession represented a denial of the American tradition never lost its force.

In similar manner, American intervention in the domestic affairs of the Central American states was never regarded as consonant with the American tradition in foreign policy. The doctrine that affirmed the right of each nation to determine its own form of government and to handle its domestic affairs without foreign interference had long been a central tenet of that tradition.[15] Of course it is easy enough to point out departures from that principle by this country, even in the years immediately following the declaration of the Monroe Doctrine.[16] In the first two decades of this century such departures became much more numerous. Recognition of Latin American governments was occasionally withheld if they failed to meet American specifications. And on a number of occasions United States forces were landed in Central American states in order to restore order and protect American investments.

In the wake of these policing ventures and other measures, the conviction grew apace that although the United States regarded the Monroe Doctrine as an instrument of foreign policy designed to keep European Powers out of the Western Hemisphere, it did not interpret the Doctrine to require any corollary obligation to exclude American intervention. Nor can there be any real doubt about the validity of the charge that the "Colossus of the North" did abuse its power during this particular period. Still, it would be misleading to identify this form of "imperialism" with what is normally associated with that term. "As we look back upon it," writes Dexter Perkins, "we can see that the democratic tradition of the American people gave it a peculiar and distinctive flavor. It was the optimistic faith of the Americans that the peoples over whom they assumed control could be prepared for self-government. The idea of an

[15] See John Bassett Moore: *Principles of American Diplomacy* (2nd ed.; New York, 1918), p. viii.

[16] Thus, American recognition of Haiti by the United States in 1826 was withheld because the government of Haiti was considered unstable and discriminated against American trade.

enduring domination ran counter to their deepest instincts and to their national habits." [17] Essentially, despite its rather presumptuous attitude of moral superiority displayed toward peoples south of the border, the United States could never escape the feeling of unease which resulted from this short-lived policy, and by the 1920's America was placed squarely on the moral defensive. With the advent of the 1930's a new corner was turned in the history of our relations with Latin America which was to provide the opportunity for developing relationships based on mutuality and trust.

World War I and Its Aftermath

When the first general European war since 1815 broke out in August, 1914, the international position of the United States no longer resembled the American position of mid-nineteenth century. By 1914 the nature of the peace that had been enforced for almost a century by Great Britain was under serious threat. In the West a strong Germany was challenging both the balance of power on the European continent and the supremacy of British naval power in the Atlantic. And in the East, Japan had emerged as a world power. Meanwhile the United States itself had emerged as a world power with commitments that extended over a third of the globe.

Only a few perceptive observers had diagnosed the subtle, yet significant, changes that had occurred in the world power structure during the period immediately prior to World War I; they had forecast that the United States would sooner or later be confronted with the task of taking over a substantial part of the burden that had been borne for so long by Great Britain. Already the rise of American naval power since the Spanish-American War had served, at least in some small measure, to fulfill this very function. In brief, the enlarged scope of American commitments, the expanding character of America's other interests as a world power, and the gradual decline of British power appeared to point to the conclusion that the United States could no longer afford to pursue a policy suited to an era that had irrevocably passed.

By 1914, therefore, the time was ripe for a reappraisal of United States foreign policy in the light of the changes that had occurred in the world power structure as well as in America's new position in that structure. At best, such reappraisal necessarily would have been a difficult and painful one since it would have involved challenging the validity of one of the central tenets of that policy—that the affairs of Europe did not form a legitimate part of the American national interest. But the vast majority of Americans were unprepared to undertake this reappraisal and unwilling to reinterpret what had long appeared to form an integral part of America's national interest. And with the outbreak of war President Wilson proclaimed the nation's strict neutrality. Again it was gen-

[17] Dexter Perkins, *The Evolution of American Foreign Policy*, p. 77.

erally assumed that America would be able—as she had been able in the past—to refrain from participating in the conflict and to continue to enjoy much of the trading opportunities with the belligerents that were normally afforded in time of peace.

The development of the neutrality principle owed much to the early history of the United States. Essentially, the institution of neutrality, as developed in the nineteenth and early twentieth centuries, signified the status of a state that refrained from participating in hostilities and that behaved in a strictly impartial manner toward the belligerents. The belligerents, in turn, were obliged to abstain from committing any hostile measures in neutral territory or waters and to respect the neutral's right to maintain an uninterrupted trade—contraband excepted—with the belligerents. In retrospect, however, it is abundantly clear that the institution of neutrality can flourish only under certain conditions. These conditions are that wars will be limited in the number of active participants, that they will be conducted with restraint, and that they will be waged for limited purposes. During the nineteenth century these conditions were largely present. In the twentieth century, however, wars have tended increasingly to become total in scope, method, and purpose. In consequence, the status of neutrality has become increasingly difficult for states to maintain. Belligerents, fighting for their very existence, have not been overly sensitive to the demands of neutrals. The United States, influenced by its experience in a preceding era, had to learn this lesson the hard way in the course of two World Wars.[18] Both World Wars clearly demonstrated that under the modern conception of warfare any trade between a neutral and a belligerent is likely to strengthen the belligerent's position, and for this reason nations at war have utilized every effort to seal off—by any means—trade between neutrals and enemy countries.[19] The neutral is thus placed in a position in which it must either abandon traditional neutral rights or insist upon belligerent observance of these rights at the risk of being finally drawn into the hostilities.

During the years 1914–17 the United States sought vainly to pursue a policy of neutrality toward the European conflict, although the belligerents made clear almost from the start of hostilities that they were not

[18] "The United States as a champion of neutral rights," comments Professor Bemis, "found that the defense of these rights led not to neutrality but to war, when violations touched American lives rather than American property. Reflective opinion slowly began to ask whether legal rights, the defense of which spells war rather than neutrality, were after all the best kind of rights." *Diplomatic History of The United States*, p. 666.

[19] "Even before World War I the list of goods that were considered contraband in time of war had become far more extensive than it was during the nineteenth century. In the course of the two World Wars the list of materials considered contraband by belligerents expanded to such an extent that it embraced practically all articles which would normally flow between countries in the course of trade. Thus, during World War II, the most elaborate precautions were taken by Great Britain and the United States to prevent products received via neutral channels in Portugal, Switzerland, and Sweden from being transferred to the German Reich." See Malcolm Moos: "Swiss Neutrality." *The Yale Review* (1943), 33:121–34.

prepared to accord this country the rights at sea which neutrals had formerly enjoyed. In the end United States intervention on the side of the Allies was brought about over the issue of neutral rights and the German policy of unrestricted submarine warfare.[20] Nevertheless, the entrance of America into World War I did not mean that this country was yet prepared to abandon permanently its traditional policy of isolation from the affairs of Europe. Despite the argument of a few that American intervention was made necessary by the threat of a German victory —which would not only upset the balance of power in Europe but which would threaten American security directly by cutting her lines of communication in the Atlantic [21]—the great majority of the American people believed that the purpose of intervention was to vindicate the rule of law among nations. And later, after the United States had been at war for some time, the struggle was placed upon a still broader basis. The interpretation grew in the popular mind that the war was one of democracy against the principle of autocracy. With the defeat of the latter the democracies were to be made safe by the establishment of a League of Nations whose purpose would be to preserve the peace and to insure the sanctity of international law.[22]

As events turned out the experience of World War I failed to turn the United States away from a policy of isolation. And the high note of idealism struck in the later stages of the war dissolved quickly into disillusionment on the morrow of victory. The reasons for this abrupt shift are not difficult to trace.

The average American failed to see any real connection between the security of his nation and entrance into the war. On the contrary, he believed that American participation, though not called for by reason of security interests, formed a response to principles that had little if any tangible connection with our immediate self-interest. In the absence of a more realistic appraisal of the war, and of America's new position in the international society, it could hardly be expected that Americans would readily abandon a policy that had apparently been so successful for a century. If America was to participate in the League of Nations, it had to be demonstrated how such participation would serve to promote her interests. This, President Wilson, despite sustained effort, failed to do. Furthermore, negotiation over the peace settlement eventually revealed the numerous bargains belligerents had struck during the war and focussed attention upon the inevitable insistence of states to secure their own interests whatever the result. In consequence, American public opinion re-

[20] See Alice M. Morrissey: *The American Defense of Neutral Rights* (Cambridge, Mass., 1939) and Edward H. Buehrig: *Woodrow Wilson and The Balance of Power* (Bloomington, 1955).

[21] Over the years, the most prominent exponent of this thesis has been Walter Lippmann. See, in particular, Lippmann's *U.S. Foreign Policy: Shield of the Republic*, pp. 33–9.

[22] For a perceptive analysis of the debate preceding, accompanying, and following American intervention in World War I, see Robert E. Osgood: *Ideals and Self-Interest in America's Foreign Relations* (Chicago, 1953).

acted by giving its support to a policy of withdrawal from any active participation either in the affairs of Europe or in the League of Nations.

At this point it serves our purpose to sketch briefly the broad outlines of American foreign policy during the inter-war period—the twenty years' peace. In the Western Hemisphere, America's relations with Latin America continued to decline in the 1920's only to be sharply reversed in the following decade. Then in a gesture calculated to remove past grievances and lay continuing fears at rest, Secretary of State Cordell Hull signed a non-intervention agreement at Montevideo in 1933 which inspired warm approval throughout Latin America. And by action taken at the Buenos Aires Peace Conference in 1936 the Monroe Doctrine was presumably internationalized, each individual country in the Western Hemisphere assuming responsibility for keeping the Doctrine intact.

As events of world diplomacy unfolded prior to World War II, it became increasingly clear that while the Latin American republics retained an understandable fear of American intervention they were increasingly restive over the possibility of becoming pawns of some European aggressor. Thus the assurance of the United States not to intervene in Latin American affairs made the Monroe Doctrine more palatable to our southern neighbors and helped inspire a reciprocal gesture from the countries of Latin America—affirmation of solidarity with the United States in halting potential aggressors. The extent of this newly formed solidarity was put to successful test when war finally did break out in Europe in 1939. Almost immediately the United States sought, and was able to achieve, a substantial measure of harmony in the neutrality policies followed by the American states. Later, when the United States became a belligerent, the Latin American states—with few exceptions—declared their support of the principles and policies of the United Nations. In 1945 at Chapultepec the solidarity principle laid down almost a decade earlier at Buenos Aires was reinforced by a further pledge of hemispheric solidarity and the mutual undertaking to take common action against any power threatening the security of the Western Hemisphere.

In the Far East, Japanese power had continued to grow during the period accompanying and immediately following World War I. Japanese aspirations to reduce China to a position of "political tutelage" had not diminished; if anything, they had been sharpened. Apprehension over Japanese power and the possible consequences of Japanese policy led the United States to call the Washington Conference of 1922. In the field of armaments the Conference agreed that the United States and Great Britain were to retain a parity in naval strength, while Japan was limited to a ratio of three fifths the naval power accorded the United States. At the same time, the agreement on arms limitation was made possible only on condition that the United States would not fortify Guam and the Philippines. Japan was given control, as a mandate power, of the strategic Marianas and Carolines islands. Finally, the Pacific powers agreed to incorporate the principles of the Open Door, guaranteeing the territorial and administrative integrity of China, into a multilateral convention which took the title of the Nine-Power Treaty.

At the time of its conclusion the Washington Conference of 1922 was widely viewed as a striking achievement of American Far Eastern policy. The level of naval armaments were presumably scaled down, legitimate Japanese aspirations were believed to have been satisfied, and the security of China was thought to have been accomplished. Unhappily, none of these anticipated consequences were ever realized. Despite agreement, Japanese naval power steadily increased until it caught up with and exceeded that of America. The islands placed under Japanese mandate were turned into strategic bases, while America refrained from further fortification of her insular possessions. And in 1931 the Nine-Power Treaty became meaningless with the Japanese invasion of Manchuria.

The course of events in the Far East during this period provide a striking example of the state to which American policy had been reduced. The root of the difficulty was not so much the absence of reasonably well-defined interests in that area. Nor was it to be found in an inability to discern the scope of American commitments. If in Europe it could be said that the United States refused to acknowledge any well-defined interest, and hence made no commitment, in the Far East this was hardly the case. For at the Washington Conference we actually increased the scope of our commitments by virtue of the Nine-Power Treaty. Obligated to defend the Philippines and to guarantee Chinese territorial integrity, the United States nevertheless proceeded to liquidate its power in the Pacific on the justification that the agreements made at Washington in 1922 constituted sufficient safeguard for American interests. Thus the quicksand upon which that alleged security system rested was revealed in less than a decade. With the Japanese attack upon China in 1931 the serious threat to American interests became apparent. Equally apparent, however, was the inability of American power in the Pacific to deter that threat, and to make good on its commitments, short of immediate rearmament.

Yet, the United States, while unwilling to rearm, was equally unwilling to acknowledge the legitimacy of Japanese expansion into China. Instead, America chose to answer the Japanese challenge by proclaiming the "Stimson Doctrine," and thereby refusing to recognize the validity of any change in the territorial or administrative integrity of China brought about by violation of treaties to which both China and Japan were contracting parties.[23] But Japan was not to be deterred by doc-

---

[23] The "Stimson Doctrine" derives its name from the then Secretary of State, Henry Stimson. The Doctrine was initially set forth in a note (January 7, 1932) sent by Stimson to Japan and China, and which read in part: "The American Government deems it to be its duty to notify both the Imperial Japanese Government and the Government of the Chinese Republic that it cannot admit the legality of any situation *de facto* nor does it intend to recognize any treaty or agreement entered into between those governments . . . which may impair the treaty rights of the United States or its citizens in China, including those which relate to the sovereignty, the independence,

trines, however noble in conception, that were not backed up by physical power. And in the end Japanese expansion in the Far East could be stopped only at the cost of war.

On December 7, 1941, America was to learn that lesson, though not without first paying a tragic price. It was also to learn that the interests of a state can be preserved only through a willingness to maintain sufficient power, and that the making of commitments without the power to back them up violated a fundamental rule of any viable foreign policy.

In Europe the principal objective was to resist being drawn once again into a position that might require active American intervention. Hence, when during the middle 1930's the outbreak of war in Europe seemed imminent, the reaction of the United States was to enact neutrality legislation that—in both intent and in effect—amounted to an almost complete renunciation of neutral rights. The proponents of this legislation argued, simply enough, that since the United States had gone to war in 1917 over the issue of neutral rights, America could only maintain a status of non-participation in future hostilities by the renunciation of these rights. The argument seemed difficult to refute, if only for the reason that the opponents of the neutrality legislation themselves frequently shared the same interpretation of the earlier American intervention. Still further, it was no easy task to demonstrate that the logic of the American position, and the changing requirements of American security in an age of rapid advance in technology, would ultimately dictate a radically different course of action. From the time of his famous "quarantine the aggressors" speech in 1937 President Roosevelt was undoubtedly aware of the possible danger to American security posed by the combined strength of Germany and Italy, and as time went on his opposition to the neutrality legislation increased. Yet Roosevelt was reluctant to press the issue too rapidly, presumably out of fear that public opinion would not support him. But once war broke out in 1939 the pressure of events alone proved decisive.

With the fall of France and the low countries in the late spring of 1940, American policy began to shift markedly toward giving aid to the states opposing the forces of Fascism. In September, 1940, the President

or the territorial and administrative integrity of the Republic of China, or to the international policy relative to China, commonly known as the open-door policy . . ." In later years the "Stimson Doctrine" came to have a more general application to territorial changes that had been brought about in violation of international treaty or agreement. The Doctrine belongs to the same category of measures as does the General Treaty For The Renunciation of War (Kellogg-Briand Pact) concluded in 1928. Largely a product of American thought, the Kellogg-Briand Pact obligated the contracting parties to renounce war as an "instrument of national policy" and to undertake to settle their disputes by peaceful means. The criticism of these measures is not so much that they were excessively "idealistic," but that they rested upon nothing other than the good faith of states. Nor is it unfair to point out that the United States viewed these pacts and pronouncements as a "soft option" for the much more difficult—though essential—task of insuring international peace and security through the undertaking of concrete obligations and the assumption of definite responsibilities.

concluded the "Destroyer-base" executive agreement with Great Britain, under which the United States turned over fifty over-age destroyers to England in return for the lease of British naval and air bases in the Atlantic. And in March, 1941, Congress enacted the "Act to Promote the Defense of the United States" (Lend-Lease Act), which authorized the production and disposal of articles to "the government of any country whose defense the President deems vital to the defense of the United States." By the late summer of 1941 American naval vessels were escorting convoys to Great Britain with orders to attack German submarines on sight. Thus from a policy in which traditional neutral rights were renounced in favor of a self-imposed isolation, the United States rapidly moved to a policy of discrimination and to an open abandonment of neutral duties which finds new parallels in the modern history of neutrality.[24]

The reaction that followed open American intervention in World War II was altogether different from our earlier experience. Both the directness and immediacy of the threat to American security in the early 1940's were too apparent to allow for widespread misinterpretation. Moreover, the further decline in influence and power of Great Britain and France, and the complete defeat of Germany and Italy, only served to magnify the primary position of the United States in the world power structure. Nor was there any indication as the war drew to an end that America would withdraw once again from Europe and refuse to participate in an international collective security system. The old policy, in short, was dead. What remained in question—and, admittedly, it was a very large question—was the form and characteristics the new policy would assume—a story to which we now turn.

The Broadening Pattern of American Foreign Relations [25]

The task of redefining the character and purposes of American foreign policy began even before the entrance of the United States into hostilities. Through the Atlantic Charter, concluded by Great Britain and the United States in August, 1941, the signatories pledged themselves to promote a world in which the various peoples would enjoy an ever greater measure of freedom from fear and want, a world in which each people would be free to choose the form of government under which it would live, and, finally, a world in which territorial changes would occur only with the freely expressed wishes of the peoples concerned. These aims

[24] For a detailed history of the events of the period 1937–41, see William L. Langer and S. Everett Gleason: *The World Crisis and American Foreign Policy* (Vol. I, *The Challenge to Isolation, 1937–40;* Vol. II, *The Undeclared War, 1940–41*) (New York, 1952–53).

[25] For general surveys of American foreign policy since World War II, see William G. Carleton: *The Revolution in American Foreign Policy, 1945–1954* (New York, 1954) and W. Reitzel, M. A. Kaplan, and C. G. Coblenz: *United States Foreign Policy, 1945–1955* (Washington, 1956). A detailed yearly review and analysis of United States foreign policy may be found in the studies undertaken by the Council On Foreign Relations under the title *The United States in World Affairs.*

were repeated in the Declaration by the United Nations on January 1, 1942. And at the Moscow Conference in 1943 the United States, Great Britain, and the Soviet Union expressed their determination to establish an international security organization whose purpose would be to realize the principles laid down in the Atlantic Charter. Thus the stage was set for that remarkable evolution that was to occur in American foreign policy, an evolution whose essential feature—despite occasional and serious lapses—has been a steady abandonment of a policy of isolation and unilateral action and the growing acceptance of responsibilities requiring mutuality and a continuous effort toward international cooperation.

The changing character of American foreign policy was forcefully demonstrated through the initiative and leadership shown by the United States in pushing plans for creation of an international security organization. In the fall of 1944 the preliminary spadework for the new organization was undertaken at Dumbarton Oaks. By June of 1945, with the war against Japan still in progress, the Charter of the United Nations had been completed and signed by fifty-one signatories. The principal purpose of the United Nations was declared to be the maintenance of international peace and security, and to that end the Organization was empowered in Article 1 of its Charter "to take effective collective measures for the prevention and removal of threats to the peace, and for the suppression of acts of aggression or other breaches of the peace." [26] Members of the Organization were obliged to "settle their international disputes by peaceful means in such a manner that international peace and security, and justice, are not endangered" (Art. 2, para. 3). And they were further obligated "to refrain in their international relations from the threat or use of force against the territorial integrity or political independence of any State, or in any other manner inconsistent with the Purposes of the United Nations" (Art. 2, para. 4).

The principal organs of the United Nations are: a General Assembly, a Security Council, an Economic and Social Council, a Trusteeship Council, an International Court of Justice, and a Secretariat. Each of these organs has been assigned important functions. But the hard core of the collective security system established by the written Charter was concentrated in one organ, the Security Council, made up of eleven members and including as permanent members the United States, Great Britain, France, the Soviet Union, and China. In conferring upon the Security Council primary responsibility for the maintenance of international peace and security, the member states agreed that in carrying out

[26] On the United Nations generally, see L. M. Goodrich and E. Hambro: *The United Nations Charter: Commentary and Documents* (Boston, 1949). Other purposes of the United Nations were declared to be the development of friendly relations among nations "based on the respect for the principle of equal rights and self-determination of peoples," and the achievement of "international cooperation in solving international problems of an economic, social, cultural, or humanitarian character, and in promoting and encouraging respect for human rights and for fundamental freedoms for all without distinction as to race, sex, language, or religion."

its functions the Council would act on their behalf. Not only was the Security Council granted authority to make binding decisions on the existence of a threat to, or breach of, the peace, it was also given authority to decide what action, including the use of armed force, should be taken to maintain or restore international peace and security. Finally, provision was made for the armed forces of the member states to be placed at the disposal of the Council.

The distinctive feature of the system established by the Charter of the United Nations was the extraordinary authority and power concentrated in the Security Council. The General Assembly, composed of all the member states in the Organization, could discuss and examine the widest range of issues. But the Assembly could only make nonbinding recommendations to members. The International Court of Justice could render decisions in disputes arising between members, but only on the condition that the disputants voluntarily submitted to the Court's jurisdiction. And even if, after having submitted a dispute, the Court clearly found against one of the parties, the principal means of enforcing the Court's decision rested with an appropriate decision by the Security Council. In looking back upon the scheme originally envisaged[27] by the framers of the Charter, it is well to recall that the Charter was very largely a great power product. One of the central ideas that went into its drafting was the conviction that since the guarantee of peace and security would inevitably be the major responsibility of the great powers, an effective collective security system would have to recognize this fact and confer upon the major powers the necessary authority to discharge their responsibility. Equally important, however, was the idea that an essential condition for any action on the part of the Security Council must be the political unanimity of the great powers having permanent seats in that body. Hence the Charter required that any decision of the Security Council on a substantive matter could be made only by an affirmative vote of seven members including the concurring votes of the five permanent members.

In the period immediately following the termination of hostilities (1945–46) the United States gave every indication that it intended to make the United Nations the principal channel through which foreign policy would be directed. Only as a temporary arrangement for working out problems of the postwar settlement, and particularly the disposition of the enemy states, did the United States contemplate continuing its wartime meetings with the other major powers at the heads of government and foreign minister levels. Furthermore, it was assumed that the existence of the United Nations would itself provide the necessary broad framework of security and confidence within which the problems of the postwar settlement could more readily be resolved. But once this settlement had been accomplished the necessity for major power collaboration

[27] On the later developments in the United Nations, and the shift in practice from the Security Council to the General Assembly, see pp. 749–50.

outside the United Nations would disappear and the international organization would henceforth become the principal forum for international action.

Unfortunately, Americans did not fully appreciate the kind of world that emerged from World War II and the extent as well as the gravity of the crisis confronting them. The reliance initially placed in the United Nations could find a justification only if that organization proved able to function effectively. In turn, this would necessarily depend upon the continued possibility of political unanimity among the major powers, for the breakdown of great-power agreement would not only result in the paralysis of the Security Council but in the absence of that postwar settlement without which the United Nations might never have a permanent foundation for its effective operation.

During the war years the presence of a common—and dangerous—foe temporarily operated to submerge deep-rooted differences between the Soviet Union and the West and to produce at least the façade of unity. Nevertheless, the expediency of wartime collaboration could not overcome the fact that the nature and characteristics of the Soviet state were basically incompatible with the political traditions of the West. Prior to the war this incompatibility had been an important factor in preventing any real cooperation between Russia and the Western democracies in making common cause against the forces of fascism. And there was no real reason to believe that these differences could now be easily glossed over or that they were somehow irrelevant in essaying the chances of future agreement—and this despite the surge of optimism over the Soviet Union in the West during the war years. Nor was there any substantial reason for believing that the character of the Soviet state would—or could—permit anything but a dynamic and expansionist foreign policy, particularly if the Soviet Union were surrounded by weak states. Even apart from the peculiar nature of the Soviet regime an analysis of traditional Russian foreign policy might itself have provided sufficient reason for anxiety over the postwar situation.

With the defeat of the enemy states the differences that had characterized Soviet-Western relations during the interwar period not only reappeared, but reappeared in a very aggravated and menacing form. While before the war there were six or seven major powers enjoying an approximate equality, now there were two "super-powers"—the United States and the Soviet Union—standing in a class by themselves. Germany and Japan were decisively defeated and could no longer act as a kind of buffer between Russia and the West. The continent of Europe appeared as one vast social and political vacuum, weakened terribly by war; an edifice that might topple over at any time. Great Britain, economically reduced by the war, clearly could not play her former role or even maintain the commitments that were left to her. Throughout Asia and the Middle East the subject peoples were in revolt, not only against their colonial masters but against poverty and deprivation. These revolutionary movements displayed a fervent nationalism and a strong sense of collectivism as well. Admittedly, the latter characteristic alarmed Americans, who found it hard to comprehend why any people would wish for a system other than that which had proven so successful for them. But what alarmed Americans even more was that the situation extending throughout Europe and Asia was one made to order for the Soviet Union, should that state desire to pursue a policy of imperialism. And there was an abundance of evidence that the Soviets would pursue just such a policy unless prevented from doing so by a determined show of force from the West, accompanied by a policy designed to stabilize and strengthen those unsettled areas extending around the vast perimeter of the Soviet Union.

Nevertheless, it was with considerable reluctance and misgiving that the United States gradually came to admit the breakdown of wartime unity and the reality of Soviet-American rivalry. For some time the feeling persisted widely in this country that Soviet policy in the eastern European states was designed only to insure the security of the Soviet Union's western boundaries and that it was not aimed at dominating these states. The West conceded that Russia had a legitimate security interest in this area but no right to deny the eastern European states national self-determination and the holding of free elections. Despite the Russian claim that only the remnants of fascist groups were being repressed and that free elections were being held, it was apparent that the Soviets were rapidly moving to a position where they would be able, with the assistance of local communist parties, to reduce Eastern Europe to a position of complete subservience. Elsewhere the same picture of Soviet intransigence and repression appeared. In Germany the Control Council made up of the four occupant Powers, and established at the Potsdam Meeting of the heads of state in 1945, was never able to operate effectively. Almost from the start the Soviet zone of occupation in the east was closed off to the Western powers. In Germany the Soviets vigorously pursued a policy of enforced reparations, carried out largely through the shipment of industrial equipment to Russia, while accusing the West of encouraging the return of fascism. Finally, the continued presence of the Red Army in Austria, Czechoslovakia, the Balkan states, Manchuria, and Korea only served to emphasize the danger of further penetration of Soviet power in Europe and Asia. And in the West at least, the activity of local communist movements appeared almost directly proportional to their proximity to the Red Army. But in both Europe and Asia it was equally clear that the strength of communist movements depended upon a condition of economic and social instability.

Broadly stated, then, these were the principal characteristics of the postwar world: an essentially bi-polar power structure, economic and political instability left in the wake of the war, the rise of nationalist liberation movements in Asia and the Middle East, and—most important—the growing menace of Soviet imperialism throughout Eurasia. The dramatic developments that have marked American foreign policy during the years since 1947 must be viewed in the context of, and as a response to, the situation described above. Rather than attempt to provide a detailed description of these developments, it is possible here only to indicate in broad outline what may well be considered as the "second revolution" in American foreign policy.[28]

The Truman Doctrine

Early in the spring of 1947 the British Government quietly advised the United States that British troops stationed in Greece could no longer cope with the growing civil war in that country. Communist forces, aided by Albania, Bulgaria, and Yugoslavia, were rapidly gaining in strength, and Great Britain decided to withdraw its forces. Unless economic and military aid to the elected government in Greece was forthcoming from the United States in the immediate future, a communist victory appeared quite probable. Furthermore, during the preceding year the Soviet Union had directed demands to Turkey concerning a revision of the Montreaux Convention governing the Turkish Straits. Considered as a whole, these events indicated the clear possibility of the extension of Soviet influence, and even control, in the strategic area of the eastern Mediterranean.

It was in response to this situation that President Truman sent a message to Congress on March 12, 1947, requesting $400 million for economic and military aid to Greece and Turkey.[29] The message proposed to send civilian and military missions to these countries to supervise the aid and to assist in training the Greek and Turkish armies. In making his request, the President stated that the aid was to be given as part of a broader policy of the United States "to support free peoples who are resisting attempted subjugation by armed minorities or by outside pressures." However, emphasis was placed upon the intention to render assistance primarily of an economic and financial character "which is essential to economic stability and orderly political processes." No attempt was made to hide the fact that the new policy—immediately dubbed the Truman Doctrine—constituted the initial application on the part of American policy makers of a basic decision to contain the advance of Soviet power wherever possible. Thus the implications of a bi-polar world in which the United States must expect to encounter what appeared to be the unremitting hostility of the Soviet Union, and devise a strategy offering the possibility of containing

[28] From the point of view adopted here, the initial revolution in American foreign policy extends over the period 1940–47. It is characterized by abandonment of the traditional policy of isolation and unilateral action and the acceptance of a policy of international cooperation, though marked as yet by a reluctance to undertake specific peacetime commitments aside from the general commitments resulting from membership in the United Nations. The period 1947–52 is characterized by the emergence of the United States as the leader of a vast coalition, deeply committed to a network of security pacts, and undertaking to extend economic and military assistance to more than two score states.

[29] For text of message see U.S. Department of State *Bulletin* (March 23, 1947), 16:536.

Soviet expansion, were presented to the American public and to the world at large.[30]

Although generally supported by public opinion, the new policy was looked upon with considerable misgiving by many. The loudest criticism was that the Truman proposal constituted a long step toward a return to the practices of power politics and an abandonment of the principle that major policy measures should be taken through United Nations channels. In short, the proposal was viewed as a deliberate attempt to by-pass the world organization. The Truman Administration sought to counter this charge by contending that the nature of the crisis required immediate attention and that the United Nations was not in a position to extend the kind of help that was required. But not all critics were satisfied by what they regarded as a rather belated profession of continued faith in the United Nations. Yet it was perfectly obvious that in the two years of its operation the United Nations had not been able to live up to advance expectations because of Soviet recalcitrance in the Security Council. If the attempt were made to initiate action through that body, the chances were almost certain to be that no action at all would be taken. In consequence, the Truman Doctrine, while certainly not presaging the abandonment of the United Nations, did mean that the United States was in the process of altering the significance it had heretofore attached to the world organization. In the future, policy could no longer be wholly subordinated to the aim of achieving a global security system through the United Nations. Instead, the strategy of containing communism implied the building up of a coalition whose nucleus would be the United States. In this task the United Nations would have to occupy a subordinate position and, if need be, would itself have to be utilized as an instrument in the achievement of a coalition of states capable of countering the threat of Soviet imperialism.

The European Recovery Program

The assistance provided to Greece and Turkey proved to be the forerunner of a much more comprehensive proposal directed toward shoring up a badly sagging Western European economy—a condition whose continu-

[30] It now appears that the policy of containing the Soviet Union was decided upon some months earlier, at least in broad outline. A detailed exposition of the premises upon which this policy rested appeared in July, 1947, in the journal *Foreign Affairs*. See X: "The Sources of Soviet Conduct," *Foreign Affairs* (1947), 25:566–82. The author has since been identified as George F. Kennan. In essence, Mr. Kennan argued that communist doctrine, and the nature of the Soviet regime, required the United States to develop a consistent, long-term policy that would seek to contain Soviet power by a skillful application of counter-force "at a series of constantly shifting geographical and political points, corresponding to the shifts and manoeuvres of Soviet policy." Such a policy, if successful, would not only have a frustrating effect upon the Soviet ruling group but would aggravate the points of weakness existing within that state. In time, these internal divisive forces plus steady external pressures would lead to the "break-up or the gradual mellowing" of Soviet power. For an effective criticism of the policy of containment and of the assumptions of that policy, see Walter Lippman: *The Cold War* (New York, 1947).

ance was an important factor in preventing a return of political stability in Europe. At the heart of Europe's economic difficulties was the simple fact that in the aftermath of destructive war European production was insufficient to meet basic demands. Europe had formerly been a great exporter, but her exports now declined markedly in relation to a continued high level of imports. In addition, the multilateral trading pattern that had existed prior to the war was replaced by a trading pattern much less favorable to the European economy. The specific form the crisis assumed was a growing imbalance of payments, principally with the United States.

The measures taken in 1945–46 to assist in European economic recovery were largely of a sporadic character and without any overall plan. But the lend-lease program was stopped in 1945 and the United Nations Relief and Reconstruction Administration in 1946. Meanwhile the steady rise in American prices resulting from the abandoning of wartime controls only served to widen the dollar gap. Nor could the economic institutions established at Bretton Woods—the International Monetary Fund and the International Bank for Reconstruction and Development—be expected to provide the answer. Private loans in sufficient quantity were out of the question, and governmental loans would merely increase European dependence on America. The only feasible solution seemed to be the granting of large credits by the United States to enable Europe to acquire the necessary materials in order to increase its productive capacity. With such an increase in agricultural and industrial production, a corresponding increase might occur in exports. Finally, given time, both intra-European trade and the international trading pattern as a whole might become more normal with increased European exports.

It was against this background that Secretary of State George C. Marshall in a commencement address at Harvard University on June 5, 1947, proposed that if the European countries would draw up a common plan for their economic recovery, the United States would respond with help and encouragement.[31] Instead of proceeding on a unilateral basis and offering a blueprint for the reconstruction of Europe, Secretary Marshall called first for a meeting of European nations to determine their own needs. Following such a conference the United States would consider these needs and the means it could offer for their fulfillment.

Some awkward moments followed the announcement of the Marshall Plan, because of the Soviet Union's opposition to the proposal. Not only did the Soviet Union denounce the plan; it became readily apparent that the leaders in the Kremlin would use all their influence to keep countries within the Soviet sphere from participating. Despite strong opposition from the Soviet Union, a conference of sixteen western European nations was held in the summer of 1947, and the recommendations resulting from

[31] The broad framework for the European Recovery Program—or Marshall Plan, as it was frequently called—may be found in the State Department publication entitled "The Development of the Foreign Reconstruction Policy of the United States," published in May, 1947.

this meeting were transmitted to the American Secretary of State. In the United States several governmental groups were established to consider the role America could play in European economic recovery. The Europeans proposed a plan that would require American aid of approximately $22,000,000,000 over a four-year period. Included in the plan, which was a country by country survey as well as a survey of the needs of the entire area, was the promise to work toward a much greater degree of economic cooperation. To promote this goal the participating countries immediately created the Organization for European Economic Cooperation (OEEC) to initiate and administer measures of economic cooperation, to review the program of economic aid in the various countries, to examine the steps taken by each country in furthering the common goal of greater economic cooperation, and, finally, to represent the participating countries by assisting the United States in the initial distribution of funds.

In June, 1948, the Economic Cooperation Act came into existence as the product of this joint effort. The Act provided for the establishment of a new agency to administer the plan, the Economic Cooperation Administration (ECA), with headquarters in Washington. Congressional opposition to having the European Recovery Program administered by the State Department resulted in the creation of a special agency to administer the program, with a director appointed by the President and confirmed by the Senate. In the debate that preceded Congressional approval it was made clear that the United States Congress was not prepared to write a blank check for European recovery. Secretary Marshall cut the sum requested to $17,000,000,000 as the total for the four years, and after prolonged debate in the House and Senate the Marshall Plan emerged with an appropriation of $6,300,000,000 for the first fifteen months.

The detailed technical operation of the European Recovery Program cannot be recounted here, even in brief outline. Europeans were dissatisfied with various aspects of the act and the manner by which it was administered. Objection was taken to the cut in the amount proposed, to the fact that the plan was used to dispose of domestic agricultural surpluses, to the requirement that the recipients assist in stockpiling strategic materials for the United States and refrain from trading in strategic materials with the Soviet bloc, to the allegedly preferential status given West Germany in the program, and to several other features. In the United States it was a different story. Charges were heard that the European Recovery Program would be used to further programs of nationalization or socialization in the countries of Western Europe. And in the heat of congressional debate one group took the position that American money should not be used "to shore up socialism in Britain" or, for that matter, to prop up the sagging economy of any European country whose political program called for further nationalization of industry. Wisely Congress did not place a restriction upon the use of funds in countries where programs of nationalization of industry were being carried out. But by its insistence that the administering agency be quite apart from the jurisdiction of the Department of State, Congress indicated concern over the manner and purpose for which expenditures were to be made. Nevertheless in the opinion of a large number of qualified observers one of the significant effects of the European Recovery Program is that it allowed for the first time the American capitalist system to have a pronounced impact upon Europe.

Despite reservations and criticisms on both sides, the Marshall Plan clearly achieved a substantial part of the purpose for which it was devised. By late 1949 and early 1950 the productivity of Europe had increased appreciably and the dollar gap had been narrowed. In terms of the national income of the participating states the amount of aid provided seemed quite small. Yet the results of the aid could not be measured simply in terms of the percentage of national income they provided, for in many instances the aid was concentrated upon critical areas which had become bottlenecks in the economy. No doubt it is true that the strides taken toward European recovery in the late forties were due to a number of other factors as well. Yet, all in all, the European Recovery Program must be given considerable weight in the final reckoning.

Elsewhere, note must also be taken of the fact that the Marshall Plan provided an added stimulus to the movement speeding the integration of Western Europe. In the course of original discussions on the plan for European recovery this aspect had not received any marked emphasis. The creation of the Organization for European Economic Cooperation was initially viewed as a means for the promotion of economic cooperation and not as a step toward the ultimate economic or political unification of Europe. But in 1949 the United States Congress in amending the Economic Cooperation Act declared that it was the "policy of the people of the United States to encourage the unification of Europe." And in the same year Paul G. Hoffman, the ECA Administrator, declared that an American purpose was to move ahead toward nothing less than an integration of the economies of Western European states. This idea proved immensely attractive to Americans who immediately thought of the benefits they received from a single market of over 150,000,000 consumers. In Western Europe the creation of a permanent, freely trading area comprising 270,-000,000 consumers would result—so it was assumed—in similar benefits. Actually, so much did the concept of European integration impress American thinking that by 1950 the opinion was widely voiced that American aid should be made conditional upon the measures taken by Europeans to integrate their economic systems.

Europeans did not remain unresponsive to this challenge. Nor were they unaware of the fact that economic integration probably constituted the most hopeful solution of Europe's recurring economic crises. The Organization for European Economic Cooperation began to consider plans that would point toward an ever greater measure of intra-European cooperation. In May, 1949, the Council of Europe was established with its seat in Strasbourg. Composed of three organs—a Committee of Ministers, a

Consultative Assembly, and a Secretariat—this fifteen-nation body has as its purpose the task of working for greater cooperation on the economic, political, and cultural levels. In practice, the Committee of Ministers—representing the foreign ministers of each state—has been a conservative force balanced against the more forward-looking Consultative Assembly, where representation is based upon population, though representatives are generally drawn from the domestic parties of the member states. But decisions by the Consultative Assembly, where voting frequently cuts across national lines, are without effect unless approved by the Committee of Ministers. One of the most substantial steps that has been taken to date in the direction of economic integration is the European Coal and Steel Community (the so-called Schuman Plan), which seeks to create a common market for the participating states in coal, iron, and steel. Brought into effect in July, 1952, the Schuman Plan includes France, West German, Italy, Belgium, the Netherlands and Luxemburg. Any mature judgments on the plan are not yet possible, but to date the results have been very encouraging.

An even more impressive step toward the economic union of Europe seemed to be well under way in early 1957. Meeting at Paris in February 1957, the heads of governments of France, West Germany, Italy, Belgium, the Netherlands and Luxemburg agreed on the basic provisions of two treaties which, if finally approved, could have the most far-reaching consequences. One would commit the nations involved to pool nuclear resources under a European Atomic Energy Commission. The other would provide for the gradual introduction—during a period ranging from twelve to seventeen years—of a single or common market without tariffs or other trade barriers, and would apply as well to the overseas territories of the six European states. Finally, serious consideration was given to the British proposal of a free trade zone in Europe which would include the above-mentioned six nations, Great Britain, and other European countries professing a desire to join it.

It is obvious, of course, that any movement toward economic integration in Europe cannot be usefully considered apart from parallel steps in the direction of political unification. For recent experience appears to have clearly revealed that the roots of the problems involved in the unification of Europe are political problems and require political decisions. Invariably, it has been discovered that far reaching plans for economic integration cannot be seriously contemplated in a political vacuum. The task of constructing a greater measure of European unity must therefore be viewed largely in the light of concurrent developments in the vital areas of security and defense.

The Forging of a Security System for the Non-Soviet World.

In principle there are three choices open to states in the perennial quest for security: they may seek security through a policy of isolation and unilateral action, they may attempt to find security through the conclusion of specific agreements with a limited number of states which share common interests, and, finally, they may try to obtain security through a system embracing all—or potentially all—states of the world. During the years preceding World War II the United States chose the first of these alternatives. In the years 1940–47 the third alternative became the foundation of a new policy. In the late forties and early fifties American policy makers turned to the second alternative as a means of devising a policy to counter the menace of an expanding Soviet empire. Within a five-year period (1948–53) the United States developed a complex pattern of security extending throughout every continent of the world. Mutual defense treaties—whether taking a multilateral or bilateral character—were concluded with almost forty states comprising the non-Soviet world. In certain instances the United States has given encouragement and support to regional arrangements though not itself becoming a party to the agreements.

The nature of the commitments undertaken by the United States in these agreements vary considerably. In some there is an obligation to extend both economic and military assistance to a state if it is attacked. In others the nature of the obligation is more loosely defined. But whatever the precise nature of the commitment, the significance lies in the decision to regard the security of the United States as being intimately related to the security of areas covering a large part of the globe. And this decision has given rise to what must certainly be regarded as the most signal development in postwar American foreign policy.

If American participation in the United Nations marked a clear break with the tradition of isolation and withdrawal, it did not simply suggest American willingness to accept direct responsibility for insuring the security of specific areas outside the Western Hemisphere. For often the international system established by the Charter of the United Nations was looked upon as removing the necessity for future American involvement in what appeared to many as a covert return to the outmoded—and odious—system of alliances. In a word, the common expectation was that America could jump from isolation to participation in a truly international system. Interestingly, this attitude implied a continued aversion to any kind of participation in the methods of "power politics." And it is largely for this reason that American acceptance of the necessity to act, and to act resolutely, in a world where considerations of power could be ignored only at the greatest peril came as a painful surprise. What is remarkable, however, is the rapidity with which Americans did become aware of and accept the existence of a situation whose complexity and seeming intractability would require measures leading to an involvement in "power politics" that would not have appeared possible even in 1945!

Prior to 1949 the only mutual defense agreement entered into by the United States was confined to the Western Hemisphere. In September, 1947, the Inter-American Treaty of Reciprocal Assistance (Rio Pact) was concluded. By this treaty the principle of hemispheric solidarity was given institutional form in the creation of a regional arrangement that included the United States and nineteen Latin American states as members. Under the Rio Pact the region to which the security system applies embraces the whole of the Western Hemisphere and extends from the North Pole to the South Pole. Hence, although Canada and Greenland are not parties to the Inter-American regional arrangement, they are included within the zone of security established by the arrangement. The Rio Pact obligates the parties to settle their disputes by peaceful means and stipulates that if an armed attack should occur against any "American state," whether the aggressor is a non-American or an American power, all other members are obliged to assist the state so attacked. And upon request of the state or states directly attacked each one of the contracting parties may determine the immediate measures that it will take in fulfillment of its obligation. In addition, the Rio Pact provides that by a two-thirds vote of the member states represented in the Organ of Consultation, decisions may be taken imposing diplomatic, economic, and military sanctions against the aggressor. But there is an important difference between a decision of the Organ of Consultation requesting the use of armed force, and decisions on other measures. While the latter are binding upon all the contracting parties, no state is required to use armed force without its consent.

The Rio Pact proved to be the precursor of a still more comprehensive organization of American states. At the Bogotá Conference in 1948 the Organization of American States (OAS) was given a formal basis, and official headquarters of the Organization were established in Washington, D.C. In effect, the Bogotá Conference sought to overhaul and integrate, as well as place on a permanent basis, a system that had developed without plan for over a half century. The Bogotá Pact provided that a supreme organ, the Inter-American Conference, should hold meetings every five years, with such meetings to be supplemented by more frequent gatherings of the Organ of Consultation established by the Rio Pact. The former Pan-American Union gave place to a secretariat that is in turn directed by a special Council. In addition, the Bogotá Pact created an Inter-American Economic and Social Council, an Inter-American Council of Jurists, and an Inter-American Cultural Council.[32]

In undertaking to place regional security in the Western Hemisphere on a permanent basis, the United States both reaffirmed and further clarified traditional policy. Yet a clear departure from tradition would come only with acceptance of a responsibility to assist in the defense and security of areas outside the Western Hemisphere, and particularly in Europe. In June, 1948, however, the Senate pointed the way to such an extension of America's international commitments by passing a resolution introduced by Senator Vandenberg that encouraged the President to foster the "pro-

[32] See, generally, A. P. Whitaker: "Development of American Regionalism," *International Conciliation* (1951) and C. G. Fenwick: "The Inter-American Regional System: Fifty Years of Progress," *American Journal of International Law* (1956), 50:18–31.

gressive development of regional and other collective arrangements for individual and collective self-defense in accordance with the purposes, principles, and provisions of the Charter" of the United Nations. The Vandenberg Resolution went on to endorse association of the United States "with such regional and other collective arrangements as are based on continuous and effective self-help and mutual aid, and as affect its national security." In the month following the passage of the Vandenberg Resolution negotiations began between the United States and the signatories of the Brussels Pact [33] (and Canada) over conclusion of a security pact for the North Atlantic Area. Significantly, the result of these negotiations was the North Atlantic Treaty, signed in April, 1949, and ratified by the Senate in July of that year, though only after long debate and several attempts to restrict the scope of the commitments laid down in the treaty.

Officially, the North Atlantic Pact has been described as a "collective self-defense arrangement among countries of the North Atlantic area. . . . aimed at coordinating the exercise of the rights of self-defense specifically recognized in Article 51 of the United Nations Charter." [34] But whatever the official characterization given the Pact, in substance it was designed to build as closely knit alliance against what appeared in 1948 and 1949 as an ever increasing danger of Soviet armed penetration into Western Europe. The key provisions of the North Atlantic Treaty lie in Articles 3 and 5. The former obligates the parties to maintain and develop "by means of continuous and effective self-help and mutual aid" their individual and collective capacity to resist armed attack. Under Article 5, the parties agree that an armed attack against one of them "shall be considered an attack against them all." Consequently, "if such an armed attack occurs, each of them in exercise of the right of individual or collective self-defense recognized by Article 51 of the Charter of the United Nations, will assist the Party or Parties so attacked by taking forthwith, individually and in concert with other Parties, such action as it deems necessary, including the use of armed force, to restore and maintain the security of the North Atlantic area."

The final form taken by Article 5 was strongly influenced by the Senate's insistence that the right to declare war was vested in Congress, and hence there could be no blanket commitment that legally obligated the

---

[33] Under the Brussels Pact (signed March 17, 1948) a fifty-year military alliance was established which was composed of five European nations—Great Britain, France, Belgium, the Netherlands, and Luxemburg. In addition to the Brussels Pact members and Canada, original signatories of the North Atlantic Pact included Denmark, Iceland, Norway, Italy, and Portugal. Since 1949 Greece, Turkey, and the German Federal Republic have been included.

[34] *The North Atlantic Pact,* Department of State Publication 3462 (1949). A distinction was therefore drawn between the Rio Pact and the North Atlantic Pact, the former assuming the character of a "regional" arrangement and governed by Articles 52–4 of the United Nations Charter; the latter being presented as a "collective self-defense arrangement," in implementation of the right of individual or collective self-defense against an armed attack provided for under Article 51 of the Charter. In fact, the principal purpose of both regional and so-called collective defense arrangements is largely identical.

United States to go to war. Indeed, both the Chairman of the Senate Foreign Relations Committee and the ranking minority member emphatically rejected the idea that the Pact involved even a "moral commitment" for the United States to go to war should any of the European signatories be made the object of an armed attack. Congress, it was argued, must judge whether or not to take military action against an aggressor in each case. Hence the obligation contained in Article 5 to assist a party to the Pact that has been made the victim of an armed attack arises only after the state furnishing assistance has decided that an armed attack has actually occurred. Even then there is no strict obligation to assist the attacked state by furnishing military forces; whether or not such forces are furnished is made dependent upon the individual judgment of each party to the treaty.[35]

Notwithstanding this temporization, the decisive fact remains, that in ratifying the North Atlantic Treaty the United States clearly entered into a military coalition, and thereby squarely abandoned a 160-year-old tradition against alliances with European powers. In the period that has elapsed since the conclusion of the North Atlantic Treaty the parties have engaged in the ardous task of constructing a defense system possessing sufficient unity and strength to deter any potential aggressor. To further this goal the Congress passed the Mutual Defense Assistance Act, in October, 1949, with the proviso that the defense funds made available by the Act could be made available to the NATO states only when these states had agreed upon an integrated defense plan that was approved by the President. And with the outbreak of hostilities in Korea the seeming reluctance of the European states to shift their energies from economic reconstruction to defense preparation was broken down. So also was the apparent reluctance of Congress to move from a program emphasizing economic assistance to one whose emphasis was directed principally toward military assistance and security. By 1952 long strides had been taken toward the development of an integrated defense plan for the whole of western and southeastern Europe, and the military assistance program for Europe had become a going concern.[36]

[35] Controversy in the Senate over the precise scope of the obligation contained in the North Atlantic Treaty was accompanied by numerous attempts to enter reservations to the Treaty. These reservations took the form of restrictions upon executive action, e.g., the stationing of American troops in Europe, the furnishing of nuclear weapons and information, etc. Although defeated, the debate and voting over the proposed amendments indicated a strong residue of sentiment against too broad a commitment to the European states.

[36] See, generally, the following works for a review and analysis of NATO's problems and progress during this period: Royal Institute of International Affairs: *Atlantic Alliance* (New York, 1952) and Lord Ismay: *NATO, The First Five Years, 1949–1954* (1954). A brief word concerning the organizational structure established by NATO is in order. According to the Treaty, the North Atlantic Council is empowered to establish such subsidiary bodies as it may deem necessary to carry out its functions. The Council itself is composed of top cabinet officers from each NATO country plus a permanent representative from each country. The Defense Committee established by the Council is composed of the chiefs of staff from each country and is charged with the task of recommending measures for the implementation of Articles 3 and 5 of the

The development of new relationships with Western Europe has not always followed the smooth path of agreement, nor is it likely to do so in the future. Moreover the Korean War, while providing the impetus for a more concentrated effort upon rearmament and a common defense system, also introduced strains within the Atlantic Alliance. In the attempt to bring about a more rapid build up of NATO strength, the United States proposed a limited rearmament of West Germany and her inclusion into NATO. Not unexpectedly, resistance from France was immediately forthcoming. As a compromise, the idea of a European Defense Community (EDC) was conceived, which was to include France, Germany, Italy, Belgium, the Netherlands, and Luxemburg. Signed in May, 1952, along with the Peace Contract with the Federal Republic of Germany, the EDC agreement provided that the contracting states replace their national forces by European defense forces which would have been placed at the disposal of the defense community represented in the form of a six-member Council of Ministers, a Commissariat made up of nine members and acting as an executive organ, and, finally, an Assembly. Although recruitment of the defense forces was to be left to the individual countries, national units comprising from 13,000 to 15,000 men would be combined into multinational army corps. An integrated command and general staff was provided for which, in turn, would have been subordinate to the supreme NATO command. A common system of training, equipment, and organization was also made part of the agreement. Most important, a unified defense budget was contemplated.

After a period of over two years the European Defense Community finally foundered in the fall of 1954 on the rock of traditional French fears of Germany, and British as well as American reluctance to provide what France regarded as essential safeguards against a resurgent Germany. Although EDC was intimately tied to NATO, with the result that an attack upon EDC would have been regarded as an attack upon NATO and vice versa, this did not prove sufficient to allay French fears. Nor did the fact that Great Britain was closely associated with—though not a member of—EDC, and had promised, as had the United States, that forces would remain stationed in Western Europe in numbers and equipment sufficient to provide for the area's defense. What France demanded of the United States was a definite military commitment for the future, and this the United States was unwilling to give. As for Great Britain, France intimated that only British membership in EDC would

Treaty. Below the Defense Committee is the Standing Group, a permanent full-time executive agency of the Military Committee, and made up of special representatives of the British, French, and American chiefs of staff. Finally, there is a Secretary General who heads an international staff with its headquarters in Paris. The actual military organization of NATO is headed by a Supreme Allied Commander, Europe, with headquarters outside Paris. Under the Supreme Allied Commander are the regional commands of central, northern, southern, southeastern Europe and the Mediterranean. In addition, there is a Supreme Allied Commander, Atlantic, for the combined naval forces of NATO. The first Supreme Allied Commander for the NATO forces in Europe was General Dwight D. Eisenhower.

suffice. Great Britain, invoking her ties and responsibilities to the Commonwealth countries and reticent to weaken in any way her close bonds with the United States, refused direct participation in EDC. In the end French failure to ratify EDC led the United States to conclude that any further effort toward a more integrated European defense system must come from the European states themselves and not as a result of American insistence. To mend the situation created by the defeat of EDC, a nine-power meeting of Western European states was held in September–October of 1954 and resulted in the London and Paris Agreements. West Germany was finally restored to full sovereignty. In addition, an epoch-making undertaking by Great Britain to assign land and air forces to the defense of Western Europe on a permanent basis in time of peace, and a strong reaffirmation (though nothing more definite) by the United States of its commitment to NATO, overcame French resistance to the rearmament of Germany and the inclusion of that state into NATO. At the same time French insistence on the control of West German rearmament through a European organization in which Great Britain would be a member, was resolved by amending and strengthening the provisions of the Brussels Pact and the Western European Union.[37] Both organizations were expanded to include West Germany and Italy. The Western European Union was given authority to control, through a Council, the force levels and armaments of the member states, though Great Britain was exempted from the control system. West Germany assumed the obligation not to manufacture in its territory any atomic, chemical, or biological weapons, as well as various other types of weapons. The Bonn Republic further undertook to refrain in the future from any action inconsistent with the defensive character of NATO and the Western European Union, and particularly to refrain from having recourse to force either to achieve the reunification of Germany or the modification of West Germany's present boundaries.[38]

Thus by the beginning of 1955 the character of the defense structure Western Europe would possess, and the crucial problems of fitting West Germany into that defense structure, were resolved—at least for the present. Though a complex mechanism that fell short of that supranational organization originally hoped for by America, it was by no means an unimpressive edifice. Seldom had a group of independent states

[37] Originally the Western European Union had been created by the Brussels Treaty powers in 1948. For the following six years it had been completely overshadowed by NATO until it was suddenly revived, though for quite different reasons, in 1954. It is an ironic commentary on the character of international politics that both the Brussels Treaty and the Western European Union initially had as their purpose the function of providing for security against Germany. Thus from an anti-German arrangement in 1948 the Brussels Treaty (and its stepchild the Western European Union) was converted into an alliance with the German Federal Republic in 1954.

[38] The implications of the defense structure resulting from the London and Paris Agreements are perceptively examined by a study group of the Royal Institute of International Affairs: *Britain in Western Europe: WEU and the Atlantic Alliance* (New York, 1956).

worked to create as close an alliance in time of peace. Perhaps the real weakness of NATO is to be found more in the political than in the military aspect. Ultimately the strength of the alliance must rest upon the ability of the member states to achieve, through constant consultation and the ironing out of differences, a common understanding and basic unity in their major political interests—both in Europe and elsewhere. Indeed, the Korean War, though strengthening NATO by creating a sense of urgency over European defense, also demonstrated how disparity of policy between the United States and its European allies in an area far removed from Europe may nevertheless create strains in the Atlantic Alliance. More recently, the lesson that the strength of NATO depends very largely upon agreement over world—and not merely European—policy, has been driven home with particular force. In the fall of 1956 the absence of a common policy in the Near East led to a serious rift between the United States, Great Britain, and France over the proper methods to employ in coping with a rising tide of Arab nationalism and the serious threat of Soviet penetration into an area long denied it.[39] The broader implication of this divergence of policy between America and her closest allies will be considered later in our story.

In the Far East the development of a viable security system has proven far more difficult than in Europe, and primarily for the reason that in the Pacific-Asian area there is a much smaller mutuality of interest

---

[39] The intimate relationship between the security of the NATO states and the prevention of Soviet penetration into the Middle East is evident. In a broad sense the latter area constitutes the right flank of NATO, and its occupation by Soviet forces would seriously endanger the entire strategic position upon which NATO is based. For this reason the United States, together with Britain and France, sought, from 1952 on, to develop a viable defense pattern in the Middle East, only to encounter Arab hostility toward entering into any arrangement including Great Britain and France. In 1955 a defensive pact was finally concluded at Baghdad which comprised Great Britain, Turkey, Iran, Iraq, and Pakistan. Though promising support, the United States declined to accede to the Baghdad Pact. In the immediate wake of British-French intervention in Egypt in November, 1956, the Pact suffered a further loss in effectiveness.

As a consequence, early in January 1957, the Eisenhower Administration indicated that it considered the most advisable policy to be one of unilateral warning to the Soviet Union that any overt aggression against a Middle Eastern state might well be met by armed resistance on the part of the United States. In a special message to Congress the President requested that authority be granted him to employ armed force to defend the Middle East against overt armed aggression by any Communist-controlled country and to use $200,000,000 of previously appropriated funds in an emergency program to bolster the military and economic strength of the Middle Eastern countries. The request precipitated a debate of major proportions in the Senate, but on March 5, 1957, the so-called Eisenhower Middle East Doctrine was finally given senatorial approval. In part, opposition to the Administration's plan stemmed from the President's request for "authority" to use American armed forces, and as a consequence the term was deleted by the Senate. In part, however, opposition to the request registered a growing reluctance to continue support of economic aid programs, a reluctance which was aggravated in this instance by the Administration's insistence that the President be given almost complete discretion in the spending of the funds. From a broader perspective, the President's request signaled the decision of American policy makers to step into still another area threatening to become a military and political vacuum as a result of British and French withdrawal.

among non-communist states than in Europe. Furthermore, the problem of devising an effective defense system in so large an area is greatly complicated by the fact that in Asia the United States must bear part of the brunt of anticolonial sentiment. Nor is the nature of the communist threat the same in Asia as it is in Europe. Despite the existence of large communist parties in a number of Western European countries, the principal threat to Europe has taken the form of Soviet military power rather than of internal subversion. In Asia (and the Middle East) the greatest danger stems more often from the communist attempt to obtain control of genuine indigenous revolutionary movements.

Despite these difficulties, which have operated to prevent the formulation of a clear and uniform policy, the United States has concluded a number of security agreements with countries in the Asian-Pacific region. Bilateral security pacts have been entered into with Japan, the Philippines, South Korea, and the Republic of China (Formosa). In September, 1951, the United States entered into a collective defense arrangement with Australia and New Zealand (ANZUS Pact), whereby the parties agreed that in case of an armed attack in the Pacific area on any of the parties each shall "act to meet the common danger in accordance with its constitutional processes." The obligation to render assistance is thus far less explicit in the ANZUS Pact than in the NATO agreement. Attention must also be drawn to the Southeast Asia Treaty Organization, which resulted from the Manila Conference of September, 1954. Including as members the United States, Great Britain, France, Australia, New Zealand, the Philippines, Thailand, and Pakistan, the purpose of SEATO is to provide for the collective defense of the Southeast Asian area. Unlike other agreements of a broadly similar type there is a provision in the SEATO Pact stipulating that if any party to the pact believes that the area of the treaty is threatened by subversion and "indirect aggression," the parties shall meet and agree upon measures to meet the danger.

In becoming a member of SEATO the United States made a reservation to the effect that only an armed attack emanating from a communist state would constitute a danger sufficient to provide automatic action on America's part. In the event danger of armed action arose from other quarters the United States undertook only to consult with other treaty partners concerning the measures to be taken. Finally, it should be remarked that the SEATO Pact has been hampered from the start by the refusal of India, Indonesia, and Burma either to participate in, or even to manifest a cooperative attitude toward, the Southeast Asian agreement. SEATO has, in contrast to NATO, no joint forces or international military command. If military action is to be taken in the future, it must come from those states able and willing to make individual contributions, and it is a significant fact in any analysis of SEATO's possible effectiveness that only the non-Southeast Asian powers possess adequate forces to counter a serious threat to the area.

In Asia, therefore, there is no system of security really comparable to the security system developed in the west. Nor is this surprising in view of the complex and frequently contradictory interests that necessarily condition American policy in this area. While in Europe there has been a clearly defined threat in response to which the European states have been able to plan common defense policy, in Asia the assessment of the danger posed by the Soviet Union and Communist China has been far from uniform. In many quarters the conviction persists that the remnants of colonialism, still identified almost exclusively with Western Europe, remains a greater danger to Asian freedom than does communist expansion. To the degree that the United States remains identified with Western Europe, it must bear at least a part of the burden that would otherwise fall upon the former colonial powers.

Means of Implementation: The Mutual Security Program

The development of an effective security system embracing a large number of states is, of course, a difficult undertaking requiring continuous effort and an ability to adapt policy to the most varying conditions. In the course of devising means to counter the threat of communist expansion, American policy makers have come to realize that just as aggression may assume many forms, so the achievement of security is a many-sided task, dependent upon time and place as well as a variety of factors unique to a particular situation. It is therefore misleading to argue that security may best be achieved by pursuing any one method, regardless of the specific conditions that characterize a given situation. In 1947 the chief threat to the security of Western Europe appeared to stem from economic instability and the danger that this situation might lead to the subversion of free government. At that moment, the European Recovery Program represented an appropriate means for combating this danger. Later the nature of the security threat to Western Europe assumed a different form, that of a direct military assault by Soviet forces. In response to this changing situation the United States began to shift its emphasis to the provision of military assistance, and to this end the Congress enacted the Mutual Defense Assistance Act of 1949. Elsewhere, as for example in Asia, the problem of devising the proper means by which to implement the basic goal of security against Soviet penetration has appeared almost impossible to resolve in a clear and definitive manner, and policy makers have had to proceed along lines necessarily tentative in character and subject to frequent change.

The basic instrument for implementing the system of security briefly described in the preceding section has been the mutual security program.[40] Through this program the United States has extended mili-

[40] Since 1951 the mutual security program has operated within the broad framework established in the Mutual Security Act of that year, although amendments to the 1951 Act have been made in annual mutual security acts subsequently passed by the Congress. Section 2 of the 1951 Act stated that: "The Congress declares it to be the purpose of this Act to maintain the security and to promote the foreign policy of

tary, economic, and technical assistance to most of the countries of the free world. The type of assistance rendered to a particular state has been tailored to both the position and needs of the recipient as well as to the security interests of the United States. To many states military assistance in the form of equipment and matériel and, occasionally, military training, has been given. By the conclusion of mutual defense agreements this military assistance is integrated to the greatest possible extent with the defense plans of the United States. In certain instances, however, these states do not possess the economic strength to maintain forces that they would be willing, without this assistance, to place in the field. In order to assist the latter in maintaining the burden of these forces the United States has undertaken a form of economic assistance which is known as "defense support."

Under the mutual security program provision is also made for rendering economic aid and technical assistance to certain countries that do not have military assistance agreements with the United States, and particularly to those less developed countries that do not possess sufficient resources—whether in the form of food, farm and industrial equipment, technical expertise, etc.—to develop and improve their standards of living. In affording economic and technical assistance to such underdeveloped countries, the United States has not pretended to be motivated simply by disinterested and humanitarian aims. Recognition has been given the fact that these programs represent in large measure the use of American resources for the more effective pursuit of American security interests. At the same time, American security interests are well served if states receiving economic and technical assistance are thereby placed in a position to maintain their independence and strengthen free institutions.[41]

Despite a considerable measure of success the mutual security program has been the object of increasing doubt in recent years. To a relatively small minority the whole concept of foreign assistance—whether assuming an economic, technical, or military character—is objectionable. Although it would appear that this group is motivated principally by traditional isolationist sentiment, it is nevertheless able to formulate its position in other, and seemingly more cogent, terms. For example it is

---

the United States by authorizing military, economic and technical assistance to friendly countries to strengthen the mutual security and individual and collective defenses of the free world, to develop their resources in the interest of their security and independence and the national interest of the United States and to facilitate the effective participation of those countries in the United Nations system for collective security." All other foreign assistance programs were deemed to share this basic purpose.

[41] On the development of American assistance programs, see W. A. Brown and R. Opie: *American Foreign Assistance* (Washington, 1953). An examination of American foreign economic policy in the light of relevant strategic, political, and psychological factors may be found in a report of a study group, headed by W. Y. Elliott, sponsored by the Woodrow Wilson Foundation and the National Planning Association: *The Political Economy of American Foreign Policy, Its Concepts, Strategy, and Limits* (New York, 1955).

argued that foreign assistance programs have resulted in a drain upon American resources which has not been compensated for by a proportionate increase in American security. The point is also raised that assistance furnished to states on the periphery of the Soviet Union may turn into a positive liability in the event they fall under Soviet domination.

Arguments for the foreign assistance programs have emphasized chiefly the ultimate dependence of American security and well-being upon the retention of allies—or at least friendly states—in both Europe and Asia. However powerful America might be, its power—and hence its security—could be brought to bear upon potential enemies only through cooperation with other states possessing manpower as well as important material resources, and affording bases in highly strategic areas. Continued American access to such areas and denial of access of the Soviet Union has been deemed essential for American security. And although some risk is necessarily involved in extending aid and assistance to states located in the shadow of Soviet power, this risk has been held to be more than warranted in view of the stakes involved. Finally, supporting arguments for foreign assistance programs has placed much emphasis upon the idea that economic and technical assistance is justified quite apart from the problem of security against Soviet expansion. The maintenance of a healthy and expanding economy requires the United States not only to insure continued access to necessary raw materials but to work toward the goal of a healthy and expanding international economy.

While the latter position has generally prevailed, and continues to enjoy acceptance, a number of basic problems remain. Undoubtedly there is an upper limit on the amount of foreign assistance America can reasonably afford. But where this line is to be drawn is a matter of continuing controversy. Equally controverted is the proper degree of emphasis foreign assistance programs should place upon security considerations, which in turn require concentration upon military assistance and economic aid in direct support of that assistance. Obviously the type of program that is to be undertaken must depend upon the nature of the situation to which it must apply. And this requires continuous change and adaptation to current estimates of Soviet intentions as well as to the conditions obtaining within the territories of the recipients. Flexibility in the administration of foreign assistance is therefore of critical importance, and both the Truman and Eisenhower administrations have urged the Congress to enact legislation permitting the executive greater discretion. Yet to date, the Congress has shown a pronounced reluctance to admit the validity of this argument.

FOREIGN POLICY: TODAY AND TOMORROW

In the brief decade following announcement of the Truman Doctrine and the policy of containment, the United States has had to assume international responsibilities that find no parallel in modern history. If mistakes have been made—which no one seriously doubts—there is at least some justification for them, considering the scope and complexity of the problems that have confronted us since 1947. Nor should it be forgotten that America did not enjoy the luxury of a long apprenticeship before being thrust into the position of world leadership. By way of contrast, the leadership of Great Britain during the nineteenth century was preceded by more than two centuries of intense training in the subtle art of diplomacy. Besides, the era of *Pax Britannica* was relatively peaceful as compared with the turbulent world of the mid-twentieth century. Small wonder, then, that the United States, emerging suddenly from a position of comparative isolation to a position where the slightest shift in its policy is immediately felt throughout the world, has been able to play its new role only with some awkward gestures and more than occasional fumbling. The burden of "coming of age" is never an easy one to assume. Nor have Americans yet succeeded in overcoming many of the traits that have traditionally characterized their outlook toward foreign affairs—traits that formed a response to conditions which have long since disappeared. Thus, there remains what Denis Brogan has aptly termed "the illusion of American omnipotence," that is, the belief that in foreign affairs—as in domestic affairs—America can accomplish practically anything it sets out to do. However inspiring in providing the impetus to act, this belief has frequently led to frustration and disillusion when confronted with the hard realities of international politics. The complexity and magnitude of international problems do not readily lend themselves to the easy generalizations and short-cut solutions in which Americans are all too apt to indulge.

In the years immediately following World War II the United Nations was looked upon as providing just such a short-cut solution to the achievement of international security and cooperation. With the emergence of Soviet-American rivalry, and the consequent paralysis of the Security Council, faith in the United Nations declined markedly. Acceptance of the implications of a bi-polar world soon led not only to the pursuit of security through channels other than the United Nations but to the forging of a policy which viewed the United Nations as a negligible factor in world politics. In short, the pendulum swung from an unfounded overoptimism in the United Nations to an almost equally unfounded pessimism. Both extremes of opinion have neglected to appraise the limited, though not insignificant, functions the United Nations is able to serve in moderating state rivalry and restraining those powers intent upon resorting to the use of force in order to resolve international disputes. Although the Security Council has not been able to operate as originally intended, the General Assembly has gained steadily in prestige and power, to a point where it has become in practice the primary organ of the United Nations. In the fall of 1950 the necessity of filling at least a part of the gap left by the paralysis of the Security Council led to the adoption by the General Assembly of the resolution "Uniting

For Peace." By the terms of this resolution the General Assembly is enabled, in the event of Security Council inaction, to determine the existence of a threat to or breach of the peace and to make recommendations to the member states for collective measures, including the use of armed force. In addition, the Assembly may—under this resolution—recommend that members maintain national armed forces available to respond to the recommendations of the General Assembly. Admittedly, such recommendations of the General Assembly carry no legally binding force. But Assembly resolutions supported by the great majority of the member states carry a moral force that has not been lightly treated by the states of the international society. And while it would be useless to deny that the United Nations still represents only a relatively weak institutional expression of the ideal of world community, experience has shown that no state can openly flout the clear intent of the purposes and principles of the Charter, as applied by the General Assembly in the form of recommendations, without incurring substantial liabilities. The Soviet Union and her satellites have shown themselves to be quite aware of these liabilities, and the care they have shown to avoid—wherever possible—the stigma attached to a condemnatory resolution of the General Assembly is a testimony to the role the United Nations is yet able to play in world politics.

Whereas the United Nations appeared in 1945 as a short-cut solution of difficult problems, the concept of a bi-polar world, marked by intense Soviet-American rivalry, emerged after 1948 as an easy generalization of a global situation. The consequences of this bi-polarity appeared equally easy to discern. States situated between the United States and the Soviet Union were confronted with the choice of joining either the one side or the other. The possibility of independent action was largely dismissed. The task of the United States was judged to be that of constructing in Europe and in Asia a grand alliance of those states willing to resist Soviet imperialism. And although in the initial stages of the strategy of containment the main emphasis was concentrated upon providing economic assistance to build up situations of strength, as time went on the importance of subordinating economic assistance more directly to immediate political and security purposes gained in strength. In the years following the outbreak of hostilities in Korea the trend toward the primacy of military assistance and the use of economic resources to obtain the direct ends of security grew even more pronounced.

There is, of course, much to be said for the concept of bi-polarity as formulated in 1947–48, although even then it represented an over-simplification of a more complex reality. In the aftermath of war the utter defeat of Germany and Japan, the exhaustion of Europe, and the temporary power vacuums existing in subject areas where the colonial powers were either pulling out or engaged in combating revolutionary movements combined to emphasize the unique positions held by the United States and the Soviet Union. This picture began to change, however, with the recovery of Western Europe, the emergence of the former enemy states, and the creation of new states in the former colonial areas. By late 1956 and early 1957 these latter developments had proceeded far enough to cast serious doubt upon any policy resting upon the basic assumption of a rigidly bi-polar world. In the Soviet bloc the so-called policy of "liberalization" in the satellite states, initiated in the years following the death of Stalin, had resulted in serious unrest and even open rebellion against Moscow. Indeed, throughout the Soviet empire there were numerous indications that the Soviet rulers would experience increasing difficulty in maintaining their absolute hold over subject peoples. In the non-Soviet world there were parallel indications of an increasing unrest among states that in the late 1940's and early 1950's had either closely allied themselves with the United States or at least acquiesced to the implications of a bi-polar world.

In Europe this unrest could be attributed largely to the continued partition of Germany and the dissatisfaction felt by Great Britain and France over United States policy outside Europe—particularly in the Middle East. The failure of western policy to achieve the unification of Germany appeared to be pushing the Bonn Government into an increasingly independent position. However, the most serious breach in the North Atlantic Alliance occurred in November, 1956, when Great Britain and France resorted to the use of force against Egypt for the ostensible purpose of safeguarding the Suez Canal from what seemed to be an impending Israeli-Egyptian conflict. In back of this dramatic event was the conviction of Great Britain and France that the regime of President Nasser in Egypt, and the continued occurrence of armed reprisals between Israel and Egypt, represented a vital threat to their interests in that area. Egyptian seizure of the Suez Canal in July, 1956, only served to confirm that conviction. Finally, the refusal of the United States to respond to the seizure by supporting the firmest measures on the part of Great Britain and France eventually led the latter states to armed action. In supporting the General Assembly's resolution condemning the British and French action in Egypt, and in bringing strong pressure to bear upon Great Britain and France to abandon the action, the United States revealed the extent of the rift that had been opened with her closest allies. The logic of these events appeared to result in creating a still stronger incentive among the western European states to draw closer together and to attempt a greater degree of independence in their relations with America.

The extent to which this break-up of the bi-polar world had gone by the fall of 1956 was further illustrated in the voting over important resolutions in the United Nations General Assembly. Whereas in the early 1950's the United States had been able to take a leading position in that body, and to put through resolutions largely favorable to the anti-Soviet coalition, by 1956 it had become increasingly clear that the initiative was passing to the so-called neutralist bloc, whose nucleus was made up by the Asian and African states. These states had never been counted in the western fold. Now they were in a position, however, to take a still more independent—even an aggressive—position both within the United Nations and without. And there were few knowledgeable prophets who would hazard any forecast other than that the majority of Asian and African states would continue to pursue policies that would offer strong resistance against being drawn into alliance with either the Soviet Union or the United States.

In view of the foregoing, there is a strong probability that the immediate future will see a number of far-reaching changes made in the world political structure that has prevailed since the initiation of Soviet-American rivalry. The emerging situation will require a revision of many of the assumptions which have guided American policy makers during the past decade. But there appears little reason to believe that the main currents of American foreign policy, though perhaps requiring substantial reinterpretation to fit changing conditions, will be markedly altered in this process.

CHAPTER XXXVII

FOREIGN POLICY AND THE AMERICAN GOVERN-MENT IN ITS INTERNATIONAL SETTING: II

SHIFTING CURRENTS IN AMERICAN FOREIGN POLICY: ECONOMIC TRENDS

ALTHOUGH the United States has been much criticized in the past for its policy of nurturing home industries and agriculture by raising high tariff barriers, one wholesome trend that emerged early in our history was that the United States was against discriminatory policies in our trade relations with other nations. Both Hamilton and Jefferson favored the principle that whatever commercial and trading privileges the United States accorded to one country should also be granted to other countries engaged in friendly trade with the United States. This principle is found in our first commercial treaty with France in 1778. In its preamble the treaty called for "the most perfect equality and reciprocity" as one of the basic tenets of Franco-American commercial relations. While tending to bestow no special favors among the countries with whom it traded, however, the United States hewed to a definitely protectionist line during the greater part of the nineteenth century and into the contemporary period.

Protectionism

The early decision to protect infant industries and agriculture was easily defended. The plan was not inspired by any diabolical plot to destroy the trade of other nations or seriously to impair the livelihood of nations depending upon an export trade. As initially conceived, protectionism was simply an expedient to nourish home industries and agricultural production in order that the United States might continue to enjoy an independence which continued to be precarious well into the first quarter of the nineteenth century. The need for fostering home industry was convincingly phrased by Alexander Hamilton in his celebrated report *On the Subject of Manufactures*. Since during the colonial period America had generally been regarded by Great Britain as a source of raw materials rather than as a competing industrial outpost, the need for stimulating the development of industry was self-evident.

From 1816 to the present day, the United States has leaned toward a protectionist policy for domestic manufactures. There seemed little reason to doubt that the policy of protectionism at an earlier date tended to further strengthen the position of neophyte industry in the United States. Following the Civil War, however, the policy of subordinating foreign trade interests in order to bolster "infant industries" began to have some noticeably negative effects. Even the vast West was not entirely consuming all American manufactured products and some surpluses remained which required foreign markets. As long as the United States imported more than it exported, protective tariffs did not too seriously impinge upon the foreign trade. But when this country gradually began to find itself saddled with surpluses of manufactured products, our restrictive tariff policies, which tended to discourage imports, interfered with the exchange of foreign imports for our own manufactured products. Several efforts were made to keep our foreign trade from being seriously damaged, such as the McKinley Tariff Law of 1890 which authorized reciprocity treaties with some foreign countries. At no time, however, could it be said that the United States abandoned protectionism.

After some attempt to lower tariff barriers shortly before World War I, a more determined protectionist policy was resumed in the 1920's—a policy which continued until the adoption of the Reciprocal Trade Agreements Act of 1934. In 1916, Congress authorized the creation of a tariff commission, and the Fordney-McCumber Act of 1922 provided for flexible tariff rates which the Commission was authorized to recommend to the president after studying foreign and domestic market conditions. Under this scheme Congress provided a yardstick to guide the Commission by setting the range within which the Commission might adjust tariff rates. In theory, the purpose of this arrangement was to compensate for the higher cost of American manufacturing. It authorized the president upon being advised by the Tariff Commission, to change tariff rates for the purpose of equalizing differences between domestic and foreign manufacturing costs. For almost two decades after the establishment of the Tariff Commission, however, the United States continued a policy of protectionism notwithstanding the fact that upon occasion— such as at the International Economic Conference held at Geneva in 1927 —this country took a stand favoring the reduction of tariff barriers.

The Reciprocal Trade Agreements

In 1934 the United States softened its high-tariff policy by the adoption of the Reciprocal Trade Agreements Act, which was urged upon Congress by Secretary of State Cordell Hull. Under this law Congress gave the president advance authority to negotiate mutually beneficial trade agreements with foreign countries. An underlying assumption of the law was that it would be used to negotiate agreements that would facilitate the exchange of goods produced in large quantities by one of the two contracting parties. Thus tariff reductions on products not produced in abundant quantities in the United States were not usually granted in the trade agreements that followed the adoption of the Reciprocal Trade Act.

The Hull reciprocal trade program was hailed in many quarters as an outstanding contribution to the improvement of world trade and international economic relations. In essence, the program was based on the simple truth that trade between nations, like all trade, is not a unilateral proposition. If the United States is to sell its products abroad it must also buy from foreign countries. Moreover, as a creditor nation—and the United States is at present the chief creditor nation—it cannot expect to have its foreign loans repaid unless it is willing to accept payment in goods.

During the first ten years of operation, twenty-eight reciprocal trade agreements were made with foreign nations. The Hull program was extended during the war, but in the spring of 1948, with the Reciprocal Trade Agreements Act due to expire on June 12 of that year, a long-contained revolt broke out in Congress. In an attack spearheaded by the farm bloc, the House passed the Gearhartt Bill limiting the extension of the Reciprocal Trade Agreements Act to a single year instead of setting three years for the extension of the law as it had always done previously. Indeed, since the end of the war, each renewal of the Reciprocal Trade Agreements Act has been accompanied by bitter controversy and progressively greater limitations upon the powers of the president to take action for lower tariffs and increased trade.

World War II and Its Aftermath

In marked contrast to the period immediately following World War I, the government and people of the United States considered themselves substantially committed to participation in international affairs after World War II. The policy of withdrawal in both economic and political spheres which had followed World War I was not seriously entertained twenty-five years later. In the immediate postwar period the United States undertook, in cooperation with other states, to repair the devastation of war and to expedite the return to peacetime relationships. The basis of American foreign economic policy was the restoration of the convertibility of national currencies, nondiscriminatory commercial and payments policies, and the elimination of prewar "beggar-my-neighbor" economic policies. Behind these moves was the hope that such a policy would gradually lead to the best possible use of resources and a steady and widespread improvement in standards of living throughout the world.

Early attempts at international cooperation, sponsored largely by the United States, were the International Monetary Fund, the International

Bank for Reconstruction and Development, the General Agreement on Tariffs and Trade, and the proposed International Trade Organization. By its adherence to the International Monetary Fund—the purposes of which were determined by the United Nations Monetary and Financial Conference at Bretton Woods, New Hampshire (July, 1944), the United States indicated its willingness to promote currency stabilization on a world-wide basis. Membership in the Fund also committed the United States to pursue policies to "hasten the removal of artificial barriers to international payments." This objective sought to prevent countries from trying to work out an artificial balance of trade by lopping off their sales or purchases abroad. The problem is, of course, intimately connected with the maintenance of a stable currency. If large fluctuations in money values are likely to occur, the trade between nations tends to move toward barter, which results in awkward two-sided trading. And when barter arrangements do not balance out, countries resort to the methods mentioned above to restore an artificial balance. Currency stabilization is one of the chief means of overcoming this dilemma. It stimulates trade by facilitating the handling of foreign credits, and paves the road for a flexible multilateral system of trade in which country A might sell to B any claims on C that A did not desire to collect himself. Unfortunately, in the decade since its establishment, the International Monetary Fund has not been able to bring about the desired international exchange-rate stability.

Further evidence of the broader scope of our economic foreign policy in the early postwar period is suggested by the membership of the United States in the International Bank for Reconstruction and Development. For many years the United States had made extensive financial loans to other countries for various purposes, including national defense, economic reconstruction, and the stabilization of a sagging currency. Most of this financing, however, had been carried on independently. But in becoming a member of the International Bank (created in 1945), the United States moved again to the cadence of the trend toward greater international economic collaboration. The Bank is a world-wide effort to guide the flow of international investment. It seeks to direct capital investment for the purpose of rebuilding the devastated areas of Europe and also to increase production in the retarded regions of the world. The Bank may lend funds either directly from its capital funds or from funds that it borrows. Although the United States contributed heavily to its capital stock ($3,175,000,000), the Bank has proved incapable of financing the total burden of reconstruction. The greater part of this burden has instead been supplied by the Economic Recovery, Mutual Assistance and Foreign Operations Administrations of the United States. The International Bank, like the International Monetary Fund, represents a constructive development in the direction of international cooperation and a marked departure from earlier economic policies of isolation.

A substantial effort was also made to gain acceptance of an International Trade Organization (ITO) that would lead to a gradual relaxation of trade barriers, including tariffs, and the elimination of discriminatory trade practices. But so many countries, including the United States, failed to ratify the charter of the proposed ITO that the agency did not come into existence. A second major effort directed toward the liberation of trade practices was the General Agreement on Tariffs and Trade (GATT), signed in Geneva in 1947 by twenty-three participating states. More than 120 sets of negotiations were completed, covering 45,000 items, affecting two-thirds of the import trade of the participating countries and about half of overall world imports representing a total value in excess of 10 billion. At successive conferences of the participants in GATT there were noticeable retreats from earlier tariff concessions, symptomatic of an increasing protectionist trend, especially on the part of the United States. Although negotiations continue from year to year among the member countries, the outcome of these negotiations has been a disappointment to those who had hoped for more constructive modifications in the trade politics of countries involved.

Much of American economic policy in the war and immediate post-war years aimed at reparation of war damage in European countries and at rebuilding the foundations of international trade, and it was characterized by piecemeal policy decisions that were essentially short-run in their outlook. The creation of the United Nations Relief and Rehabilitation Administration (UNRRA) in 1943, for example,—largely the result of American policy makers—was terminated only three years after its establishment. From the outset the task of UNRRA was envisaged as a purely temporary one, and there was no expectation that it would undertake the enormous job of a long-term reconstruction. Thus the agency was concerned with making available food, clothing, medical facilities, seed for planting, and other materials to people in areas liberated from Axis control, in the immediate postwar period. Although the administration of UNRRA was confused and not highly efficient, the agency rendered important service at a critical period. With the termination of the agency in 1946, arrangements were made for the transfer of its more important functions to other organizations under the general supervision of the United Nations, such as the World Health Organization, the International Refugee Organization, and the International Children's Emergency Fund.

A second short-run policy decision was made in 1945, when the United States agreed to lend Great Britain $3.75 billion to aid in her reconstruction and to assist in restoring the international convertibility of the British pound. More interesting than the Anglo-American Loan itself was a pamphlet issued by the Department of State at the time of the signing, outlining the basic aims of American economic foreign policy. The pamphlet, entitled *Proposals for Expansion of World Trade and Employment*,[1] clearly set forth the existing restrictions on international

[1] Dept. of State Pub. 2411, Commercial Policy Series 79.

trade and suggested appropriate measures for releasing trade from some of these restrictions. Among the major impediments to free trade among nations it listed limitations imposed by governments, limitations imposed by private combines and cartels, the fear of disorder in the markets for certain primary commodities, and the irregularity or fear of irregularity in production and employment. In order to counteract the tendency toward contraction of trade that resulted from these impediments, the *Proposals* urged reduction of tariffs, the gradual elimination of embargoes, quotas, or other restrictions, the abolition of discriminations through exchange techniques, and the avoidance of subsidies wherever possible. As we have seen, the *Proposals* ran directly counter to American domestic interests in the agricultural and shipping realm, and were subsequently modified by the prior claims of these groups. Agricultural policies in the postwar period, despite the early statement of freer trade expressed in the 1945 *Proposals*, have embraced import quotas, export subsidies, and even embargoes as part of the price support program, while shipping policies have relied heavily on operating subsidies and cargo preferences.[2]

Economic Policy in a Period of Cold War

Although United States financial assistance to foreign countries in the immediate postwar period was motivated largely by economic or humanitarian objectives, the objectives became political as well as economic in 1947, with the loans to Greece and Turkey. Two short years after the end of the war, confronted with an economic-political crisis in Great Britain and Western Europe and with noncooperative and expansionist Soviet policies, the United States began to use its economic resources for foreign policy objectives that had strong security overtones. The tendency to fit economic policy into the overall foreign policy designed to contain communism is demonstrated by the Marshall Plan, the Mutual Security Program, and the Foreign Operations Program. The changes in emphasis of United States foreign-aid policy directly paralleled the rift between East and West, for as relations between the United States and the Soviet Union grew worse, major stress shifted from economic aid for economic objectives to economic aid for political objectives, and thence to military aid.

The United States technical assistance program, popularly known as the Point Four Program from its introduction as the fourth item in the 1949 inaugural address of President Truman, came into being by the passage of the Foreign Assistance Act of 1950. Point Four aimed to reduce the appeal of communism by improving production and raising living standards. However, this time the area concerned was not Europe, but underdeveloped countries throughout the world. Using the services of technical experts in many fields, the plan sought to increase knowledge

[2] Gordon Gray: *Report to the President on Foreign Economic Policies* (Washington, 1950).

in the fundamentals of industrial and agricultural development in these countries. Adoption of modern and efficient techniques, in turn, was to encourage foreign investment, increased productivity, and eventually a higher level of world trade.[3] Proponents of Point Four stressed the positive, long-range approach to international cooperation provided by the plan. Financed partly by the United States and partly by recipient countries, Point Four has been one of the least expensive devices of foreign policy in the Cold War. Expenditures have been estimated at not more than $125 million a year, in striking contrast to the $40 billion a year of the defense budget.[4]

Present Trends and Problems in United States Economic Problems

American economic policy in the present day may be considered under three major categories: (1) domestic economic policy; (2) trade and monetary policy; and (3) investment and aid policy. A stable domestic economy is a primary requisite to the conduct of sound foreign economic relations. As we have seen elsewhere, the federal government, through such measures as the Employment Act of 1946, has assumed responsibility for the maintenance of high levels of employment and productivity, and for built-in protections against the possibility of future depression. With a relatively secure domestic economic position, the United States can feel capable of pursuing a dynamic program in matters of both foreign trade and aid.

In the area of trade and monetary policy the United States has generally attempted to follow a policy of liberalized foreign trade through the Reciprocal Trade Agreements and GATT. Although critics point out that "peril point" and "escape clauses" as well as subsidies to American shipping detract from the overall pattern of freer international trade, the United States has made important steps in this direction. As one high State Department official has pointed out, "The decade since World War II has seen much headway in removing the obstacles to trade among the free nations. Doubtless much more remains to be done and further progress will have its difficulties. But [recent] efforts have produced important results."[5]

Not all matters pertaining to the economic aspects of American for-

[3] For an examination of the problem of economic development in underdeveloped countries, which are the primary targets of communism, see Eugene Staley: *The Future of Underdeveloped Countries* (New York: Harper and Bros., for the Council on Foreign Relations, 1954). Also see Edward S. Mason: *Promoting Economic Development: The United States and Southern Asia* (Claremont College, 1955).

[4] For recent expressions of the opinion that only through increased economic aid and technical assistance can the United States effectively meet the challenge of the Soviet Union in foreign affairs, see Chester Bowles: "The Crisis That Faces Us Will Not Wait," *New York Times*, November 27, 1955, and Barbara Ward: "Needed, Point I Plus a Renewed Point IV," *New York Times*, April 11, 1954.

[5] Robert R. Bowie: "United States Foreign Economic Policy," *Department of State Bulletin* (1956), 35:139. See Clarence B. Randall: *A Foreign Economic Policy for the United States* (Chicago, 1954), for a cogent argument in favor of lowering present tariffs on certain commodities.

eign policy have been confined to questions of trade and tariff. The investment of American capital in foreign countries has posed many problems. Such investments sometimes must be safeguarded, and in the past occasional threats to American investments when foreign countries undertook expropriation measures have raised extremely delicate questions. Should the United States government intercede to protect American investments about to be expropriated? Mutual respect for contractual obligations is, of course, to the advantage of the international community and today American capital is sorely needed in many parts of the world, particularly for the economic development of backward regions. But today also, there is a growing feeling against the idea of government intervention to protect American investments abroad. Moreover, in line with this attitude there is also increasing support for the idea that the foreign investments and the rewards derived from foreign investments are proper subjects of a trust whose regulation should be shared by the international community. Like areas of activity within the domestic jurisdiction of a nation which are said to be affected with a public interest, foreign investments raise questions of concern for the international community of nation. The return on the investments, the elimination of restrictive devices such as international monopolies or cartels, and many other problems which may result from foreign investment of capital are being more and more regarded as subjects calling for international regulation—a trend to which American foreign relations are gradually being oriented on many fronts.

While private investment abroad is still a substantial figure, averaging about $1.5 billion a year, it should be noted that approximately 80 per cent of this amount goes to Canada, Latin America, and Western Europe. Many countries in Asia and Africa which are in greater need of capital investment for their development are considered bad risks by American investors and are therefore by-passed in favor of countries with more stable governments, or countries with greater protection from foreign aggression. Public agencies such as the United States government and the specialized agencies of the United Nations have therefore stepped in to fill the breach left by private investment. In the past decade, for example, nonmilitary grants from the United States to Asia, Africa, and Latin America have amounted to $7.7 billion, indicating a trend toward increasing public, rather than private, investment in certain areas.

Since 1947 the United States has placed great emphasis on loans and grants, and to a lesser degree on technical assistance, as a means to obtain certain political objectives. Whether we should or will be capable of continuing such a program over the long run is highly uncertain. The alternative of "trade not aid" has been suggested, but those favoring this point may be underestimating the problem of economic nationalism at home and abroad. Actually, the question of the type and scope of future American economic policy is one of the most crucial of our time. Initially foreign aid to war-torn countries in Europe was an essential and useful measure, but it is doubtful that indefinite continuation of such assistance is a sound basis upon which to build mutual respect and confidence. There is always a tendency on the part of the donor to consider this type of aid as little more than charity and to attach strings to assistance, thereby inviting the charge of interference in the domestic affairs of the recipient. The technical assistance program, on the other hand, seems to prophesy more favorable future results, for it represents a gradual approach to the solution of change in underdeveloped areas. But while gradualism was successful in presiding over the nineteenth-century metamorphosis of agricultural communities into industrial metropolises, it is by no means certain that it will be equally successful in the twentieth century. The demands of underdeveloped countries in our day are frequently strident and call for immediate progress that may not be supplied soon enough by the slow-moving methods of technical assistance.

A further problem concerns the relation of the United States to countries dependent on her trade for their continued prosperity. Since the war, such countries as Great Britain, France, Belgium, the Netherlands, Switzerland, and Japan have been unable to earn enough dollars to buy the food and raw materials necessary for their basic requirements. These dollar deficits have been assumed by the United States through loans and grants yet such a policy is at best a temporary one. And in the near future these countries must find export markets, either in the United States through tariff reduction (which is hampered by domestic interests) or in other countries. The possibility that the Soviet Union may offer the next best alternative to many of these countries is obviously a matter of grave concern for American policy makers. For a large increase in trade with the Soviet Union, accompanied by a decrease in trade with the United States leading to susceptibility to Communist pressures, is certainly not desirable from the point of view of the international political objectives of the United States. To avoid such a situation, the United States might reduce tariffs on light manufactured goods and agricultural products, and increase total imports in relation to exports. One effect of such changes, of course, might be the temporary decline in national income and the obliteration of less efficient national industries. But drastic as they may seem, these changes could be cushioned by appropriate government measures. Whether or not the American public and the interest groups concerned will react favorably to such suggestions, however, is quite another matter, and bears heavily on those charged with the responsibility for the future development of international economic policy.

THE FRAMING OF FOREIGN POLICY IN TRANSITION

Committed at last to international responsibility and pressed on all sides to shoulder the consequences and problems such a position entails, the people of the United States are finding that the framing of foreign policy presents one of the greatest challenges to their government. The governmental arrangements for handling external relations noted in Chapter

XXXV have both furthered and hindered the framing of foreign policy. Fortunately, the Constitution and practice under it have given the president broad powers to initiate policy. Despite his supremacy in this field, however, the president must still look to Congress for support of his policies and in case of treaties, of course, must have the concurrence of two-thirds of the Senate.[6] Not only is the president's task of framing policy made difficult by the possibility that legislative support may not be forthcoming, but it is further complicated by the fact that more than one agency assists in the formation of policy. The president does not formulate policy with the aid of the State Department alone; he is helped by a great many other departments and agencies. There is, moreover, an increasing tendency for departments and agencies to formulate policies which conflict with those of the State Department. Some conception of this problem is given by the foreign affairs sub-committee report of the Hoover Commission on Organization of the Executive Branch of the Government which states that in 1948 there were thirty-three interdepartmental committees and 142 interdepartmental subcommittees dealing with foreign affairs in Washington.

Some of the interdepartmental disputes over foreign policy have been brought into sharp public focus such as the one in 1947–48 between the State Department and the Defense Department over our foreign policy toward Germany on industrial reconstruction.[7] Many interdepartmental disputes on foreign policy, however, go unnoticed in the public eye and

[6] Recent notable studies on the problems involved in the framing of foreign policy that result from the familiar division of powers between executive and legislative branches are: William Y. Elliott: *United States Foreign Policy: Its Organization and Control* (New York, 1952); and Daniel S. Cheever and H. Field Haviland, Jr.: *American Foreign Policy and the Separation of Powers* (Cambridge, Mass., 1952).

[7] In more recent years the State and Defense Departments have come into conflict on a growing number of important policy issues. Actually the emerging importance of the Defense Department in the shaping of foreign policy has been a principal factor in the relative decline in prestige of the Department of State. Another element in this decline, however, has been the tendency of Congress to create new agencies to deal with such significant problems as foreign assistance programs and American information projects abroad. By and large the latter trend has resulted from the rather widespread conviction that the traditional techniques of diplomacy—and hence the regular diplomatists—are unsuited to the development of novel techniques required for an era of "cold war." But it is also true that the removal of certain important areas of foreign policy from State Department control has stemmed from the lack of confidence in this Department shared both by Congress and a sizable segement of the American public in the late 1940's and early 1950's. This lack of confidence, originally brought on by a rapidly deteriorating international situation, was immensely aggravated by the accusations of Senator McCarthy that the State Department had become corrupted by Communists and fellow travelers. So serious did the situation become that when the Eisenhower Administration came to power in 1952, the State Department seemed almost incapable of even carrying on the denuded responsibilities left to it. Since 1954, however, the situation has improved, and by 1957 all indications suggested that the State Department was on its way toward again assuming its primary role in foreign policymaking. One indication of this revival was the liquidation of the Foreign Operations Administration, the independent agency having jurisdiction over foreign economic assistance, and the creation of an International Cooperation Administration within the Department of State directly under the control of the Secretary of State.

apparently some important ones fail to receive the attention of the president. Since the president alone has the ultimate responsibility for the conduct of the nation's foreign policy, the task of formulating foreign policies and coordinating the operation of foreign programs with one another or with domestic policies, must be directed by the chief executive. But to direct such work skillfully the president needs able assistants and an administrative organization that will facilitate coordination. Consequently, if the president is to meet the complexities of world affairs and prevent the agencies formulating foreign policies from working at cross purposes, it has been suggested that he be given more help from an executive secretariat organized to assist and watch the work of all departments and agencies touching on foreign affairs. One way of attacking the problem, then, would be to organize the cabinet into a series of high-level committees which by working closely with a small executive secretariat might resolve many of the inconsistencies that derive from improper coordination of the numerous agencies involved in framing foreign policy. Some progress along this line of approach has already been realized by the formation of important interdepartmental committees at the cabinet level, such as the National Security Council and the National Advisory Council on International Monetary and Financial Problems. Admittedly the accomplishment of such an objective is far from simple, and the problem, like so many other governmental problems, does not yield readily to reorganizational experiment. Yet it is one of the most urgent of all problems of American government, and its solution has a tremendous bearing on the quality of American leadership in world affairs.

Public Opinion and the Framing of Foreign Policy

Contributing to the complexity of framing foreign policy is the increased demand for popular control over foreign policy decisions. To insist that the course of foreign policy be responsive to public opinion is a wholesome idea, but there remains the vital problem of seeing that the public is properly informed if it is to exercise critical judgment—a feat which cannot be easily accomplished on short notice, yet decisions must often be made quickly.[8] At the moment when a decisive step is called for and those who are informed are ready to take it, public opinion may not be prepared to take the step. Thus while popular control is desirable, it makes the fram-

[8] Public opinion polls have disclosed that about 30 per cent of our electorate is unaware of almost any given event in American foreign affairs, approximately 45 per cent may be aware of important events but cannot be considered well-informed, and only about 25 per cent consistently reveal a knowledge of foreign problems: See Martin Kriesberg: "Dark Areas of Ignorance," in Lester Markel, et al.: *Public Opinion and Foreign Policy* (New York, 1949). These figures correspond favorably with the conclusions of other students. Even so, however, they have reference only to "important questions" of foreign policy, and may therefore tell us very little about the opinions of those who do manifest some knowledge of foreign affairs. Thus even though a substantial part of the electorate may hold definite ideas, the people in this group are frequently at cross purposes with each other, and the same person who insisted upon a clear-cut victory in the Korean hostilities was often opposed to undertaking the risks such a policy would necessarily imply.

ing and execution of foreign policies far more difficult than under the old scheme of diplomacy where decisions were made without waiting on public opinion.[9] This difficulty was experienced in the adoption of the Marshall Plan. Once the plan had been formulated after months of preparation and announced by the Secretary of State it was warmly acclaimed by the governmental leaders of several Western European states. But the better part of a year went by before the measure was adopted by Congress. All during this period attempts were made to mobilize favorable public opinion in this country in the hope that public opinion would impress upon Congress the urgent need for action. The delay in obtaining congressional approval proved a serious handicap for those charged with the responsibility for guiding our foreign policy. Promise of American aid under the Marshall Plan was a potent factor in the Anti-Communist stand of political leaders in Western Europe, but when the promised help was not forthcoming, the situation in some countries threatened to get out of hand. So serious was the situation thought to be in Italy, that in the weeks immediately before the parliamentary elections on April 18, 1948, the American ambassador made several speeches at Italian ports as a commemorative gesture when ships arrived bringing United States aid. Thus the time lag in handling foreign policy—the time between the announcement of a policy and the date when it actually takes effect is a matter of serious concern. Taking a decision to operate a foreign policy on one time belt when in reality it may be slowed down to another by an unresponsive public opinion and delay-minded Congress makes it difficult to meet the challenges of present-day diplomacy. Moreover, the fact that an original foreign policy set by the president and his advisers may be drastically remodeled by Congress wraps American foreign policy with an element of uncertainty—a handicap not incurred under a cabinet system where the government leaders ordinarily count upon Parliamentary support.

Among other problems of public opinion affecting foreign policy statecraft in the United States is one which Charles Evans Hughes forcefully called attention to in 1922, shortly after he took up his duties as Sec-

[9] For a formidable indictment of the role played by public opinion in foreign affairs since the first World War, see Walter Lippmann: *Essays in the Public Philosophy* (New York, 1955). Lippmann believes that experience demonstrates that "the prevailing public opinion has been destructively wrong at the critical junctures." The errors of public opinion argues Lippmann, "have a common characteristic. The movement of opinion is slower than the movement of events. Because of that, the cycle of subjective sentiments on war and peace is usually out of gear with the cycle of objective developments." And this can hardly be otherwise, says Lippmann, given the normal apathy and indifference of public opinion toward foreign policy, its inability to follow foreign affairs through their successive phases of development, and its distortion of the events it does seek to understand. In this setting Lippmann concludes, solution of the difficulty can only come through the "revitalization" of the executive—a revitalization that would serve to give the executive greater independence from both the legislature and shifting opinions of the electorate.

For a spirited rejoinder to Lippmann's views, see particularly: Henry M. Wriston: *Diplomacy in a Democracy* (New York, 1956). Also on this general problem see; Gabriel Almond: *The American People and Foreign Policy* (New York, 1950); and Max Beloff: *Foreign Policy and the Democratic Process* (Baltimore, 1955).

retary of State: ". . . the difficulty of maintaining a true perspective and a distinctively American opinion in the field of foreign affairs is greatly increased by the natural and persistent efforts of numerous groups to bend American policy to the interest of particular peoples to whom they are attached by ties of kinship and sentiment. The conflicts of opinion and interest in the old world are reproduced on our own soil. Then there are the various sorts of propaganda by which organized minorities and special interests seek to maintain a pervasive influence." [10] The difficulties of which Hughes spoke are abundantly illustrated in American politics.[11] Congressmen are threatened with trouble at the next election if they fail to vote in accordance with the wishes of minority groups seeking specific objectives in foreign policies, and presidential candidates are likewise badgered.[12] Under such conditions it is difficult indeed to maintain a clear-minded foreign policy. The heterogeneous character of our population is one of our strongest assets, yet it presents obstacles to the framing of foreign policy. Religious differences as well as the mixed nationality background of our citizenry still put many obstacles in the way of making foreign policy.

Improvement of foreign relations and of the leadership which the United States now exercises in the international community may proceed along many lines. There is a pressing need for helping all citizens better to understand the problems of foreign affairs. "Today," as Professor Whitehead notes, "the world is passing into a new stage of existence. New knowledge and new technologies have altered the proportions of things." In our own generation the facilities of communication have expanded several times faster than the general ability to judge the significance of events in foreign affairs. An informed citizenry can greatly expedite the handling of foreign policy, and our duty in this connection is clear.

Through another approach, solving the problems of foreign policy in the United States has also made modest progress—the bipartisan method. A substantial amount of misunderstanding persists over the meaning of the term "bipartisan" foreign policy. "If," as one editor puts it, "the expression merely means that foreign policy may be an exception to the rule of parliamentary government whereby a majority 'yes' almost automatically meets a minority 'no' then the words carry some freight." By and large the idea behind the bipartisan treatment of foreign-policy questions is that a certain area of agreement on the broad objectives of American foreign policy is desirable to give continuity to our policies. But we should not expect too much from the "bipartisan" formula nor should we

[10] Charles E. Hughes: "Some Observations on the Conduct of our Foreign Relations." *American Journal of International Law* (1922), 16:367.

[11] For a lively discussion of propagandist and pressure group activity in influencing foreign policy, see Thomas A. Bailey: *The Man in the Street* (New York, 1948), chap. 25.

[12] See John W. Masland: "Pressure Groups and American Foreign Policy Preceding Pearl Harbor." *Public Opinion Quarterly* (1942), 6:115–22; and Harold H. Sprout: "Pressure Group and Foreign Policies." *Annals of the American Academy of Political and Social Science* (1935), 179:114–23.

feel that it has broken down beyond repair when a conflict arises. The term "bipartisan foreign policy" is a misnomer. It does not and was never intended to signify an unbreachable agreement to achieve certain objectives in a prescribed manner. Actually a more meaningful name to describe the cooperative approach in dealing with foreign policy would be "nonpartisan," for it is inevitable that on the means to be followed in carrying out foreign policies many divisions will occur that are not prevented by the "bipartisan" formula. A "nonpartisan" rather than strictly partisan approach, however, is most desirable for coping with major foreign-policy problems.

What the prospects are for American foreign policy statecraft is befogged by many uncertainties. Little by little some of the instruments we have forged, and which we have not been able to operate efficiently in the bi-polar climate of post World War II, have lost their force. Many of our former hopes for an age when power would be tamed and the international community would live in a cozy confidence of permanent peace have dissolved in disillusionment. But despite disappointments and faltering footsteps, American diplomacy has taken on new and unbelievably heavy burdens with results that have not been inconsiderable in a strangely divided world. And wherever the course of the future lies, few will deny that the political ideals and all the value clusters the West holds dear may well depend upon the ability of the United States to speak with clear mind and act with resolute will in the critical years before us. For hopefully, as Edmund Burke said long ago, "As yet we work in the light."

SUPPLEMENTARY READING

CHAPTER I

Beard, Charles A.: *The Economic Basis of Politics.* New York, 1922.
Bentley, A. F.: *The Process of Government.* Chicago, 1908.
Blaisdell, D. C.: *Economic Power and Political Pressure.* Temporary National Economic Committee, Monograph 26. Washington, D.C., 1941. New York, 1942.
——: *Government Under Pressure.* Public Affairs Pamphlet, No. 67.
Calhoun, John C.: *Works.* Edited by R. K. Cralle. Vol. I. New York, 1853.
Chase, Stuart: *Democracy Under Pressure.* New York, 1945.
Childs, H. L.: *Labor and Capital in National Politics.* New York, 1930.
Childs, H. L.: "Pressure Groups and Propaganda," in *The American Political Scene.* Edited by E. B. Logan. New York, 1936.
Crawford, Kenneth G.: *The Pressure Boys.* New York, 1939.
Ebersole, Eugene Luke: *Church Lobbying in the Nation's Capital.* New York, 1951.
Eulau, Heinz, ed.: *Political Behavior.* New York, 1956.
Giddings, Franklin H.: *Studies in the Theory of Human Society.* New York, 1922. Chapter 11.
Herring, E. P.: *Group Representation Before Congress.* New York, 1929.
——: *Presidential Leadership.* New York, 1940.
——: *Public Administration and the Public Interest.* New York, 1936.
Holcombe, Arthur N.: *The Middle Class in American Politics.* Cambridge, Mass., 1940.
Key, V. O.: *Politics, Parties and Pressure Groups.* Third edition. New York, 1952.
Latham, Earl: *The Group Basis of Politics: a Study of Basing Point Legislation.* New York, 1952.
MacIver, R. M.: *The Web of Government.* New York, 1946.
Mathews, Shailer: *The Validity of American Ideals.* New York, 1922.
Mosher, W. E., (ed.). *Introduction to Responsible Citizenship.* New York, 1941.
Munro, William Bennett: *The Invisible Government.* New York, 1928.
Riggs, Fred W.: *Pressures on Congress.* New York, 1950.
Schattschneider, E. E.: *Politics, Pressures, and the Tariff.* New York, 1935.
Schriftgiesser, Karl: *The Lobbyists.* New York, 1951.
Truman, David: *The Governmental Process.* New York, 1951.
Wilson, M. L.: *Democracy Has Roots.* New York, 1939.
Zeller, Belle: *Pressure Politics in New York.* New York, 1937.

PERIODICALS

Cantwell, Frank V.: "Public Opinion and the Legislative Process." *American Political Science Review* (1946), 40:924–35.
Borneman, Ernest: "The Public Opinion Myth." *Harpers* (1947), 195:3–40.
Dickinson, John: "Democratic Realities and Democratic Dogmas." *American Political Science Review* (1930), 24:283–309.
Dillion, Mary Earhart: "Pressure Groups." *American Political Science Review* (1942), 36:471–81.
Herring, E. P.: "The Balance of Social Forces in the Administration of the Pure Food and Drug Act." *Social Forces* (1935), 13:358–66.
——: "Prescription for Democracy." *Annals of the American Academy of Political and Social Science* (1935), 180:138–48.
LaFollette, Robert M., Jr.: "Some Lobbies are Good." *New York Times Magazine,* May 16, 1948.
Wiltse, C. M.: "The Representative Function of Bureaucracy." *American Political Science Review* (1941), 35:510–16.

CHAPTER II

Adams, H. B.: *Maryland Influences in Founding a National Commonwealth.* New York, 1927.

Andrews, Charles M.: *Colonial Self-Government, 1652–1689.* American Nation, V. New York, 1905.

Beard, Charles A. and Mary R.: *The Rise of American Civilization.* 2 vols. New York, 1927.

Channing, Edward: *History of the United States.* 6 vols. New York, 1905–1925. Vol. III, *On Revolutionary States,* Chapter 14.

Commager, Henry S.: *Documents of American History.* New York, 1950.

Cushing, H. A.: *History of the Transition from Provincial to Commonwealth Government in Massachusetts.* New York, 1896.

Dealy, J. Q.: *Growth of American State Constitutions.* New York, 1915.

Dickerson, O. M.: *American Colonial Government 1696–1765: A Study of the Board of Trade in its Relation to the American Colonies.* New York, 1912.

Fiske, John: *The Critical Period of American History, 1783–1789.* Boston, 1888.

Frothingham, Richard: *The Rise of the Republic of the United States.* Boston, 1910.

Greene, Evarts Boutell: *The Provincial Governor in the English Colonies of North America.* Harvard Historical Studies, VII. New York, 1898.

Hockett, H. C.: *Constitutional History of the United States, 1776–1826.* New York, 1939.

Holcombe, A. N.: *State Governments in the United States.* New York, 1926. Chapters 2–3.

McIlwain, C. H.: *The American Revolution: A Constitutional Interpretation.* New York, 1923.

McLaughlin, A. C.: *Constitutional History of the United States.* New York, 1935.

——: *Foundations of American Constitutionalism.* New York, 1932.

Nevins, Allan: *The American States During and After the Revolution 1775–1789.* New York, 1927.

Rossiter, Clinton: *Seedtime of the Republic.* New York, 1956.

Van Tyne, C. H.: *The American Revolution.* New York, 1905.

PERIODICALS

Corwin, Edward S.: "The Progress of Constitutional Theory between the Declaration of Independence and the Meeting of the Philadelphia Convention." *American Historical Review* (1925), 30:511–36.

Farrand, Max: "Compromises of the Constitution." *Annual Reports of the American Historical Association* (1903), 1:73–84.

McLaughlin, A. C.: "The Background of American Federalism." *American Political Science Review* (1918), 12:215–40.

Morey, W. C.: "The First State Constitutions." *Annals of the American Academy of Political and Social Science* (1893), 4:201–32.

CHAPTER III

Bancroft, George: *History of the Formation of the Constitution of the United States of America.* 2 vols. New York, 1882.

Beard, Charles A.: *An Economic Interpretation of the Constitution.* New York, 1913.

——: *The Republic.* New York, 1943.

Beck, James M.: *The Constitution of the United States.* New York, 1924.

Beveridge, Albert J.: *Life of John Marshall.* 4 vols. Boston, 1916.

Brandt, Irving: *James Madison, Father of the Constitution.* New York, 1950.

Crosskey, W. W.: *Politics and the Constitution in the History of the United States.* 2 vols. Chicago, 1953.

Elliott, Edward: *Biographical Story of the Constitution.* New York, 1910.

Elliott, J.: *Debates of the Several State Conventions on the Adoption of the Federal Constitution.* 5 vols., 2nd edition. 1854.

Erikson, E. M. and Rowe, D. M.: *American Constitutional History.* New York, 1933.

Farrand, Max: *The Fathers of the Constitution.* New Haven, 1921.

———: *The Making of the Constitution*. New York, 1913.

———: *The Records of the Federal Convention of 1787*. 3 vols. New Haven, 1911.

Fisher, Sydney G.: *The Evolution of the Constitution*. Philadelphia, 1900.

Ford, Paul Leicester, editor: *Essays on the Constitution, 1787–1788*. Brooklyn, 1892.

Hendrick, B. J.: *The Bulwark of the Republic*. Boston, 1947.

Kelly, Alfred H. and Harbison, Winfred A.: *The American Constitution: Its Origin and Development*. New York, 1948.

Libby, O. G.: *The Geographical Distribution of the Vote of the Thirteen States on the Federal Constitution, 1787–1788*. New York, 1894.

Mussati, James: *The Constitution of the United States: Its Origins, Principles, and Problems*. Princeton, 1956.

McLaughlin, A. C.: *The Confederation and the Constitution, 1783–1789*. American Nation, X. New York, 1905.

———: *A Constitutional History of the United States*. New York, 1935.

Meigs, W. M.: *The Growth of the Constitution in the Federal Convention of 1787*. Philadelphia, 1900.

Rodell, Fred: *Fifty-Five Men: the Story of the Constitution*. New York, 1936.

Schlesinger, Arthur M.: *New Viewpoints in American History*. New York, 1922. Chapter 8.

Schachner, Nathan: *The Founding Fathers*. New York, 1954.

Stephens, Frank Fletcher: *The Transitional Period: 1788–1789 in the Government of the United States*. Social Science Series, The University of Missouri Studies, II, No. 4. Columbia, 1909.

Stevens, C. E.: *Sources of the Constitution of the United States*. New York, 1894.

Swisher, Carl Brent: *American Constitutional Development*. Boston, 1954.

Tansill, C. C., editor: *Documents Illustrative of the Formation of the United States*. 69th Congress, 1st Session, House Document No. 396.

Thatch, Charles C., Jr.: *The Creation of the Presidency*. Johns Hopkins Studies in History and Political Science, Series XL, No. 4. Baltimore, 1922.

Warren, Charles: *The Making of the Constitution*. Boston, 1928.

PERIODICALS

Alexander, L. H.: "James Wilson, Patriot, and the Wilson Doctrine," *North American Review* (1906), 183.

Farrand, Max: "The Compromises of the Constitution." *Annual Report of the American Historical Association* (1903), 1:73–84.

Johnson, Alexander: "What the Federal Constitution Owes to the Several States." *New Princeton Review* (1887).

Robinson, J. H.: "The Original and Derived Features of the Constitution." *Annals of the American Academy of Political and Social Sciences* (1890), 1:202–43.

CHAPTER IV

Beard, Charles A.: *The Republic*. New York, 1943.

———: *The Supreme Court and the Constitution*. New York, 1912.

Burdick, C. K.: *The Law of the American Constitution*. New York, 1922.

Corwin, Edward S., ed.: *The Constitution of the United States of America: Analysis and Interpretation*. Annotation of cases decided by the Supreme Court of the United States to June 30, 1952. Government Printing Office, Washington, 1953.

———: *The Constitution and What It Means Today*. 11th edition. Princeton, 1954.

Elliott, J.: *Debates in the Several State Conventions on the Adoption of the Federal Constitution*. 5 vols. 2nd edition. Washington, 1854.

The Federalist.

McBain, Howard Lee: *The Living Constitution*. New York, 1927.

Munro, William Bennett: *The Constitution of the United States*. New York, 1930.

Norton, Thomas J.: *The Constitution of the United States: Its Sources and Its Application*. Boston, 1922.

Rickard, J. A.: *Our National Constitution: Origin, Development, and Meaning*. Harrisburg, 1956.

Story, Joseph: *Commentaries on the Constitution*. 2 vols. 5th edition. Boston, 1891.

Swisher, Carl Brent: *The Growth of Constitutional Power in the United States.* Revised edition. Chicago, 1954.
Tocqueville, Alexis de: *Democracy in America.* 2 vols. Edited by Phillips Bradley. New York, 1945.
Willoughby, W. W.: *The American Constitutional System.* New York, 1904.
Wilson, Woodrow: *Constitutional Government in the United States.* New York, 1908.

PERIODICALS

Anderson, William: "The Intention of the Framers; A Note on Constitutional Interpretation." *American Political Science Review* (1955), 49:340–52.

CHAPTER V

Ames, H. V.: "The Proposed Amendments to the Constitution of the United States during the First Century of its History." *Annual Report of the American Historical Association for 1896.* Vol. II. Washington, D.C.
Beard, Charles A.: *The Republic.* New York, 1943.
Cahn, Edmond, ed.: *Supreme Court and Supreme Law.* Bloomington, 1955.
Gerald, Edward J.: *The Press and the Constitution, 1931–1947.* Minneapolis, 1948.
Horwill, Herbert W.: *The Usages of the American Constitution.* Oxford University Press, 1925.
Jackson, Robert H.: *Full Faith and Credit: The Lawyer's Clause of the Constitution.* New York, 1945.
Kelly, Alfred H. and Harbison, Winfred A.: *The American Constitution: Its Origin and Development.* New York, 1948.
MacDonald, W.: *A New Constitution for a New America.* New York, 1921.
Mathews, John M.: *Legislative and Judicial History of the Fifteenth Amendment.* New York, 1909.
Mott, Rodney L.: *Due Process of Law.* Indianapolis, 1926.
Munro, W. B.: *The Makers of the Unwritten Constitution.* New York, 1930.
Pierson, C. W.: *Our Changing Constitution.* New York, 1922.
Proposed Amendments to the Constitution. 70th Congress, 2nd Session. House Document No. 551.
Rodick, Burleigh Cushing: *American Constitutional Custom.* New York, 1953.
Swisher, Carl B.: *American Constitutional Development.* Boston, 1954.

PERIODICALS

Ames, H. V.: "The Amending Provision of the Federal Constitution in Practice." *Proceedings of the American Philosophical Society* (1924), 63:62–75.
Benson, George C. A.: "State Rights and Home Rule." *State Government* (1940).
Brown, Everett S.: "The Ratification of the Twenty-first Amendment." *American Political Science Review* (1935), 29:1005–17.
Dodd, W. F.: "Amending the Federal Constitution." *Yale Law Journal* (1921), 30:321.
Munroe, Smith: "The Development of American Constitutional Law." American Academy of Political Science, *Proceedings* (1912–13), 3:52–69.
Powell, T. R.: "Logic and Rhetoric of Constitutional Law." *Journal of Philosophy, Psychology, and Scientific Methods* (1918), 15:645–58.
Smith, T. V.: "State Rights and the Rights of the States." *State Government* (1940).
Tanger, J.: "Amending Procedure of the Federal Constitution." *American Political Science Review* (1916), 10:689–99.

CHAPTER VI

Anderson, William: *The Nation and the States.* New York, 1955.
Clark, Jane P.: *The Rise of a New Federalism.* New York, 1938.
Council of State Governments: *Book of the States.* Chicago, biennially.
Council of State Governments: *Grants-in-Aid and Other Federal Expenditures Within the States.* Chicago, 1947.
Fite, Emerson D.: *Government by Cooperation.* New York, 1932.

Graves, W. Brooke: *Uniform State Action.* Chapel Hill, N.C., 1934.
Key, V. O., Jr.: *The Administration of Federal Grants to the States.* Chicago, 1937.
Macmahon, Arthur W., ed.: *Federalism, Mature and Emergent.* Garden City, 1955.
Report to the President for Transmissal to the Congress: *The Commission on Inter-governmental Relations.* Washington, 1955.
Thursby, Vincent V.: *Interstate Cooperation.* Washington, 1953.
Zimmerman, F. L. and Wendell, M.: *Interstate Compacts since 1925.* Chicago, 1951.

PERIODICALS

Clark, Jane P.: "Interstate Compacts and Social Legislation." *Political Science Quarterly* (1935), 50:502–25; (1936), 51:36–61.
———: "Joint Activity Between Federal and State Officials." *Political Science Quarterly* (1936), 51:230–69.
Field, Oliver P.: "States versus Nation and the Supreme Court." *American Political Science Review* (1934), 28:233–45.
Frankfurter, Felix: "The Compact Clause of the Constitution—A Study in Interstate Adjustments." *Yale Law Journal* (1925), 34:685–758.
Grant, J. A. C.: "The Search for Uniform Law." *American Political Science Review* (1938), 32:1082–98.
Harris, Joseph P.: "The Future of Federal Grants-in-Aid." *Annals of the American Academy of Political and Social Science* (1940), 207:14–26.
———: "Should Grants-in-Aid Have a Policy?" *State Government* (1940), 13:106–8.
Holcombe, A. N.: "The States as Agents of the Nation." *Southwestern Political Science Quarterly* (1921), 1:307–27.
MacDonald, Austin F.: "Aid to the States: 1940 Model." *American Political Science Review* (1940), 34:498–9.
Morley, Felix: "The Roots of Democracy." *State Government* (1939), 2:23–5.
Mott, Rodney L.: "Uniform Legislation in the United States." *Annals of the American Academy of Political and Social Science* (1940), 207:79–92.
Rose, Marc A.: "States Get Together." *Current History* (1938), 48:25–27.

CHAPTER VII

Bachrach, Peter: *Problems in Freedom.* Harrisburg, 1953.
Beard, Charles A.: *The Republic.* New York, 1943.
Cushman, Robert E.: *Civil Liberties in the United States: A Guide to Current Problems and Experience.* Ithaca, 1956.
Chafee, Zechariah, Jr.: *Free Speech in the United States.* Cambridge, Mass., 1955.
———: *Freedom of Speech.* New York, 1920.
Commager, Henry Steel: *Freedom, Loyalty, Dissent.* New York, 1953.
Gelhorn, Walter: *Individual Freedom and Governmental Restraints.* Baton Rouge, 1956.
———: *The State and Subversion.* Ithaca, 1952.
Getty, Luella: *The Law of Citizenship in the United States.* Chicago, 1934.
Griswold, Erwin N.: *The Fifth Amendment Today.* Cambridge, 1955.
Hays, Arthur Garfield: *Let Freedom Ring.* Revised edition. New York, 1937.
Hocking, William Ernest: *Freedom of the Press: A Framework of Principle.* Chicago, 1947.
Howell, R.: *The Privileges and Immunities of State Citizenship.* Baltimore, 1918.
Ickes, Harold L.: *Freedom of the Press Today.* New York, 1941.
Konvitz, Milton R.: *The Constitution and Civil Rights.* New York, 1947.
Lien, A. J.: *Privileges and Immunities of Citizens of the United States.* New York, 1913.
Mason, Alpheus T.: *Security through Freedom.* Ithaca, 1956.
Nelson, Bernard H.: *The Fourteenth Amendment and the Negro Since 1920.* Washington, 1946.
Orth, S. P. and Cushman, Robert E.: *American National Government.* New York, 1931.
Parsons, Wilfrid: *The First Freedom: Considerations on Church and State in the United States.* New York, 1948.
Pritchett, C. Herman: *Civil Liberties and the Vinson Court.* Chicago, 1954.

Thomas, Norman: *The Test of Freedom.* New York, 1954.
To Secure These Rights: The Report of the President's Committee on Civil Rights. New York, 1947.

PERIODICALS

Barber, Hollis W.: "Religious Liberty *v.* Police Power." *American Political Science Review* (1947), 41:226–47.
Cushman, Robert E.: "Ten Years of the Supreme Court, 1937–1947, Civil Liberties." *American Political Science Review* (1948), 42:42–52.
Harris, Robert J.: "Ten Years of the Supreme Court, 1937–1947, Civil Liberties." *American Political Science Review* (1948), 42:32–42.
Hazard, Henry B.: "The Trend Toward Administrative Naturalization." *American Political Science Review* (1927), 21:342–9.
Heller, Francis J.: "A Turning Point for Religious Freedom." *Virginia Law Review,* 29:440–59.
Preuss, Lawrence: "Decentralization on the Ground of Disloyalty." *American Political Science Review* (1942), 36:701–710.

CHAPTER VIII

Breckenridge, S. P.: "Women in Government." *Recent Social Trends.* New York.
Bernard, Bertram: *Election Laws of the Forty-eight States.* New York, 1950.
Buchanan, Lamont: *Ballots for Americans.* New York, 1956.
Hicks, J. D.: *The Populist Revolt.* Minneapolis, 1931.
Key, V. O., Jr.: *Politics, Parties, and Pressure Groups.* 3rd edition. New York, 1952.
——: *Southern Politics.* New York, 1949.
McKinley, A. E.: *The Suffrage Franchise in the Thirteen English Colonies in America.* Philadelphia, 1905.
Magnum, C. S., Jr.: *The Legal Status of the Negro.* Chapel Hill, N.C., 1940.
Miller, George Frederick: *Absentee Voters and Suffrage Laws.* Washington, D.C., 1948.
Moon, Henry Lee: *Balance of Power: The Negro Vote.* 2nd edition. New York, 1948.
Porter, Kirk H.: *A History of Suffrage in the United States.* Chicago, 1918.

PERIODICALS

Aylesworth, Leon: "The Passing of Alien Suffrage." *American Political Science Review* (1931), 25:114–6.
Boudin, L. B.: "State Poll Taxes and the Federal Constitution." *Virginia Law Review* (1941), 28:1–25.
Bromage, A. W.: "Literacy and the Electorate." *American Political Science Review* (1930), 24:946–62.
Burdette, F. L.: "Lowering the Voting Age in Georgia." *South Atlantic Quarterly* (1945), 44:300–7.
Crawford, Finla G.: "Operation of the Literacy Test for Voters in New York." *American Political Science Review* (1931), 25:342–5.
Overacker, Louise: "The Negro's Struggle for Participation in Primary Elections." *Journal of Negro History* (1945), 30:54–61.
Weeks, S. B.: "The History of Negro Suffrage in the South." *Political Science Quarterly* (1894), 9:671–703.
Wilson, Francis G.: "The Pragmatic Electorate." *American Political Science Review* (1930), 24:16–37.

CHAPTER IX

Albig, William: *Public Opinion.* New York, 1939.
Cantril, Hadley: *Gauging Public Opinion.* Princeton, 1944.
Childs, Harwood L.: *An Introduction to Public Opinion.* New York, 1947.
Crawford, Kenneth G.: *The Pressure Boys.* New York, 1939.
Detzer, Dorothy: *Appointment on the Hill.* New York, 1948.

Doob, Leonard W.: *Propaganda: Its Psychology and Technique.* New York, 1948.
Ernst, Morris L.: *The First Freedom.* New York, 1946.
The Federalist, No. 10.
Gallup, George: *A Guide to Public Opinion Polls.* Princeton, 1944.
Gallup, George and Rae, Saul F.: *The Pulse of Democracy.* New York, 1940.
Graves, W. Brooke: *Readings in Public Opinion.* New York, 1928.
Herring, E. Pendleton: *Group Representation Before Congress.* Baltimore, 1929.
Key, V. O.: *Politics, Parties, and Pressure Groups.* 3rd edition. New York, 1952. Chapters 2–7, 18.
Lasswell, Harold D.: *Democracy through Public Opinion.* Menasha, Wisconsin, 1941.
Lazarsfeld, Paul F.: *Radio and the Printed Page.* New York, 1940.
Lippmann, Walter: *Public Opinion.* New York, 1922.
McCamy, J. L.: *Government Publicity.* Chicago, 1939.
Ortega y Gasset, José: *Concord and Liberty.* New York, 1946.
Rogers, Lindsay: *The Pollsters.* New York, 1949.
Siepmann, Charles A.: *Radio's Second Chance.* Boston, 1946.
Temporary National Economic Committee: *Economic Power and Political Pressure.* Monograph No. 26. Washington, 1941.
David B. Truman: *The Governmental Process.* New York, 1951.
Waples, Douglas (ed.): *Print, Radio, and Film in a Democracy.* Chicago, 1942.
Zeller, Belle: *Pressure Politics in New York.* New York, 1937.

PERIODICALS

Childs, Harwood L. (ed.): "Pressure Groups and Propaganda." *Annals of the American Academy of Political and Social Science* (1935), 179:1–67.
Committee on Analysis of Pre-Election Polls and Forecasts of the Social Science Research Council: "Report on the Analysis of the Pre-Election Polls and Forecasts." *Public Opinion Quarterly* (1949), 12:599–622.
Connelly, Gordon M. and Cantril, Hadley: "The Questions the Polls Ask." *Public Opinion Quarterly* (1945), 9:51–69.
"Public Opinion Polls: Dr. Jekyll or Mr. Hyde?" *Public Opinion Quarterly* (1940), 4:212–84.
Tannenbaum, Frank: "The Balance of Power in Society." *Political Science Quarterly* (1946), 51:481–504.
Woodward, Julian L.: "Public Opinion Polls as an Aid to Democracy." *Political Science Quarterly* (1946), 61:238–46.

CHAPTER X

Anderson, Dewey and Davidson, Percy E.: *Ballots and the Democratic Class Struggle.* Stanford University, 1943.
Bean, Louis H.: *Ballot Behavior.* New York, 1940.
——: *How to Predict Elections.* New York, 1948.
Beard, Charles A.: *The American Party Battle.* New York, 1928.
——: *Economic Origins of Jeffersonian Democracy.* New York, 1915.
Binkley, Wilfred E.: *American Political Parties: Their Natural History.* New York, 1945.
Campbell, Agnes and Cooper, Homer C.: *Group Differences in Attitudes and Votes.* Institute for Social Research. Ann Arbor, 1956.
Ford, Henry Jones: *The Rise and Growth of American Politics.* New York, 1898.
Forthal, Sonya: *Cogwheels of Democracy: A Study of the Precinct Captain.* New York, 1946.
Goodman, William: *The Two-party System in the United States.* Princeton, 1956.
Hesseltine, William B.: *The Rise and Fall of Third Parties.* Washington, D.C., 1948.
Holcombe, A. N.: *The Middle Class in American Politics.* New York, 1940.
——: *The New Party Politics.* New York, 1933.
——: *The Political Parties of Today.* New York, 1924.
Key, V. O.: *Politics, Parties and Pressure Groups.* 3rd edition. New York, 1952.
Lazarsfeld, Paul F., Berteson, Bernard, and Gaudet, Hazel: *The People's Choice: How the Voter Makes Up his Mind in a Presidential Campaign.* New York, 1944.

Kirkpatrick, Evron M.: *Elections, U.S.A.* New York, 1956.
Merriam, C. E. and Gosnell, H. F.: *The American Party System.* 3rd edition. New York, 1940.
Moon, Henry L.: *Balance of Power: The Negro Vote.* 2nd edition. New York, 1948.
Moos, Malcolm: *The Republicans.* New York, 1956.
Odegard, Peter H. and Helms, E. Allen: *American Politics: A Study in Political Dynamics.* 2nd edition. New York, 1947.
Paullin, C. O.: *Atlas of Historical Geography of the United States.* Washington, D.C., 1932.
Porter, Kirk H.: *National Party Platforms.* New York, 1924.
Scammon, Richard M.: *America Votes.* New York, 1956.
Schattschneider, E. E.: *Party Government.* New York, 1942.
——: *Politics, Pressures, and the Tariff.* New York, 1935.
——: *The Struggle for Party Government.* College Park, Md., 1948.

PERIODICALS

Ranney, Austin and Kendall, Willmore: "The American Party Systems." *American Political Science Review* (1954), 48: 477–85.
Fisher, Marguerite J. and Whitehead, Betty: "Women and National Party Organization." *American Political Science Review* (1944), 38:895–903.
Sayre, Wallace S.: "Personnel of Republican and Democratic National Committees." *American Political Science Review* (1932), 26:360–2.
Starr, Joseph R.: "The Legal Status of American Political Parties." *American Political Science Review* (1940), 34:439–55, 685–99.
Weaver, Leon: "Some Soundings of the Party System: Rural Precinct Committeemen." *American Political Science Review* (1940), 76–84.

CHAPTER XI

Binkley, Robert W., Jr.: *Double Filing in Primary Elections.* Berkeley, 1945.
Brogan, D. W.: *Government of the People.* New York, 1933, Chapter 4.
Dallinger, F. W.: *Nominations for Elective Office in the United States.* New York, 1897.
Ford, Henry J.: *The Rise and Growth of American Politics.* New York, 1898. Chapter 16.
Key, V. O.: *Politics, Parties and Pressure Groups.* 3rd edition, New York, 1952, pp. 207–498.
Lovejoy, A. F.: *LaFollette and the Establishment of the Direct Primary in Wisconsin, 1890–1904.* New Haven, 1941.
Martin, Boyd A.: *The Direct Primary in Idaho.* Stanford, 1947.
Merriam, Charles E. and Gosnell, Harold F.: *The American Party System.* 4th edition. New York, 1949. Chapter 14.
Meyer, C. E.: *Nominating Systems.* New York, 1902.
Odegard, Peter H. and Helms, E. Allen: *American Politics: A Study of Political Dynamics.* New York, 1947. Chapter 16.
Ostrogorski, M.: *Democracy and the Organization of Political Parties.* 2 volumes, New York, 1903.
Penniman, Howard R.: *Sait's American Parties and Elections.* 5th edition. New York, 1952. Chapter 18.
Pollock, James K.: *The Direct Primary in Michigan.* Ann Arbor, 1943.
Schattschneider, E. E.: *The Struggle for Party Government.* College Park, Maryland, 1948.
Steffens, Lincoln: *The Struggle for Self Government.* New York, 1906.
——: *The Autobiography of Lincoln Steffens.* New York, 1936.
Whittridge, F. W.: *Caucus System.* New York, 1883.

PERIODICALS

Berdahl, C. A.: "Party Membership in the United States." *American Political Science Review* (1942), 36:16–50, 241–62.
Booser, James H.: "Origins of the Direct Primary." *National Municipal Review* (1935), 24:222–3.

Campbell, E. E.: "Party Nominations in California (1860–1909)." *Southwestern Social Science Quarterly* (1931), 12:245–57.

Easley, R. M.: "The Sine-qua-non of Caucus Reform." *American Review of Reviews* (1897), 16:322–4.

Hughes, Charles E.: "The Fate of the Direct Primary." *National Municipal Review* (1921), 10:23–31.

Johnson, C. O.: "The Washington Blanket Primary." *Pacific Northwest Quarterly* (1942), 33:27–39.

CHAPTER XII

Albright, Spencer D.: *The American Ballot.* Washington, 1942.

——: *Ballot Analysis and Ballot Changes since 1930.* Chicago, 1940.

Bean, Louis H.: *Ballot Behavior: A Study of Presidential Elections.* Washington, 1940.

——: *How to Predict Elections.* New York, 1948.

Carlson, Oliver and Blake, Aldrich: *How to Get into Politics.* New York, 1946.

Ewing, Cortez A. M.: *Congressional Elections: 1896–1944.* Norman, 1947.

Gosnell, Harold F.: *Democracy: The Threshold to Freedom.* New York, 1948.

Harris, Joseph P.: *Election Administration in the United States.* Washington, 1934.

——: *Registration of Voters in the United States.* Washington, 1929.

Herring, E. P.: *The Politics of Democracy.* New York, 1940, Chapters 9–11.

Kent, Frank: *The Great Game of Politics.* New York, 1923.

Key, V. O.: *Politics, Parties, and Pressure Groups.* 3rd edition. New York, 1952. Chapters 16–19.

Merriam, C. E. and Gosnell, H. F.: *Non-Voting: Causes and Methods of Control.* Chicago, 1924.

Merriam, C. E. and Overacker, L.: *Primary Elections.* Chicago, 1928.

Minault, S. S.: *Corrupt Practices Legislation in the 48 States.* Chicago, 1942.

Norris, George W.: *Fighting Liberal, the Autobiography of George W. Norris.* New York, 1945.

Odegard, P. H. and Helms, E. A.: *American Politics.* 2nd edition. New York, 1947. Chapters 16–23.

Overacker, Louise: *Money in Elections.* New York, 1932.

Penniman, Howard R.: *Sait's American Parties and Elections.* 5th edition. New York, 1952. Chapters 2–4, 13, 18–19, 24.

Pollock, James K.: *Party Campaign Funds.* New York, 1926.

Sikes, Earl R.: *State and Federal Corrupt Practices Legislation.* Durham, 1928.

Turner, Julius: *Party and Constituency: Pressures on Congress.* Baltimore, 1951.

PERIODICALS

Barnett, Vincent M., Jr.: "Contested Congressional Elections in Recent Years." *Political Science Quarterly* (1939), 54:187–215.

Key, V. O.: "If the Election Follows the Pattern." *New York Times Magazine,* October 20, 1946.

Moos, Malcolm and Kenworthy, E. W.: "Dr. Shipstead Come to Judgment." *Harper's* (1946), 193:21–27.

Neuberger, Richard L.: "It Costs too Much to Run." *New York Times Magazine,* April 11, 1948.

Starr, Joseph R.: "The Legal Status of American Political Parties." *American Political Science Review* (1940), 34:439–455, 686–699.

CHAPTER XIII

Brogan, Denis W.: *Politics in America.* New York, 1954.

David, Paul T., Moos, Malcolm, and Goldman, Ralph M.: *Presidential Nominating Politics in 1952.* 5 vols. Baltimore, 1954.

Farley, James A.: *Behind the Ballots.* New York, 1938. Chapter 2.

Hatch, L. C. and Shoup, Earl: *A History of the Vice-Presidency of the United States.* New York, 1934.

Herring, Pendleton: *The Politics of Democracy.* New York, 1940. Chapter 16.

Key, V. O.: *Politics, Parties, and Pressure Groups.* New York, 1952. Chapter 13.

Levin, Peter R.: *Seven by Chance.* New York, 1948.

Link, Arthur: *Woodrow Wilson: Road to the White House.* Princeton, 1947, vol. 1.

Logan, E. B.: *The American Political Scene.* New York, 1936, Chapter 5.

Mencken, H. L.: *Making a President.* New York, 1932.

Michelson, Charles: *The Ghost Talks.* New York, 1944. Chapters 1–2.

Moscow, Warren: *Politics in the Empire State.* New York, 1948.

Odegard, Peter H. and Helms, E. A.: *American Politics.* New York, 1947. Chapter 16.

Overacker, Louise: *The Presidential Primary.* New York, 1926.

Peel, Roy and Donnelly, Thomas C.: *The 1928 Campaign; an Analysis.* New York, 1931. Chapters 1–2.

Peel, Roy and Donnelly, Thomas C.: *The 1932 Campaign; an Analysis.* New York, 1935. Chapters 2–3.

Penniman, Howard R.: *Sait's American Parties and Elections.* 5th edition. New York, 1952. Chapters 20–21.

Porter, K. H.: *National Party Platforms.* New York, 1924.

Schattschneider, E. E.: *The Struggle for Party Government.* College Park, Maryland, 1948.

Stoddard, Henry L.: *Presidential Sweepstakes.* New York, 1948.

White, William A.: *A Puritan in Babylon, The Story of Calvin Coolidge.* New York, 1938.

Young, Klyde and Middleton, Lamar: *Heirs Apparent.* New York, 1948.

Official Report of the Proceedings of the Democratic National Convention. (Issued after each convention.)

Official Report of the Proceedings of the Republican National Convention. (Issued after each convention.)

PERIODICALS

Becker, C.: "The Unit Rule in National Nominating Conventions." *American Historical Review* (1899), 5:64–82.

Hatch, Alden: "The Men Around Dewey." *Harper's* (1948), 197:38–46.

Ross, Earle D.: "The National Spare Tire." *North American Review* (1935), 239:275–279.

Rossiter, Clinton L.: "The Reform of the Vice-Presidency." *Political Science Quarterly* (1948), 63:383–403.

Shannon, J. B.: "Presidential Politics in the South." *The Journal of Politics* (1948), 10:464–489.

CHAPTER XIV

Agar, Herbert: *The People's Choice.* New York, 1933.

——: *The Price of Union.* Boston, 1950.

Bean, Louis H.: *Ballot Behavior; A Study of Presidential Elections.* Washington, 1940.

——: *How to Predict Elections.* New York, 1948.

Beman, L. T.: *The Abolishment of the Electoral College.* New York, 1926.

Burnham, W. Dean: *Presidential Ballots, 1836–92.* New York, 1955.

Corwin, Edward S.: *The President: Office and Powers.* 3rd edition. New York, 1948. Chapter 2.

Ewing, C. A. M.: *Presidential Elections.* Norman, 1940.

Farley, James A.: *Behind the Ballots.* New York, 1938. Chapters 3 and 5.

Herring, E. P.: *The Politics of Democracy.* New York, 1940. Chapters 17–19.

Kent, Frank: *Political Behavior.* New York, 1928.

Key, V. O.: *Politics, Parties, and Pressure Groups.* New York, 1952. Chapter 14.

Lazarsfeld, P. F., Berelson, B., and Gaudet, H.: *The People's Choice: How the Voter Makes Up His Mind in a Presidential Campaign.* New York, 1945.

Lubell, Samuel: *The Future of American Politics.* New York, 1952.

——: *The Revolt of the Moderates.* New York, 1956.

Michelson, Charles: *The Ghost Talks.* New York, 1944. Chapters 3–5.

Odegard, Peter H. and Helms, E. Allen: *American Politics.* New York, 1947. Chapters 17 and 18.
Overacker, Louise: *Presidential Campaign Funds.* Boston, 1946.
——: "Trends in Party Campaign Funds." *The Future of Government in the United States.* Edited by Leonard D. White. Chicago, 1942. Chapter 7.
Penniman, Howard R.: *Sait's American Parties and Elections.* 5th edition. New York, 1952. Chapters 22–24.
Pollock, James K.: *Party Campaign Funds.* New York, 1932.
Robinson, E. E.: *The Presidential Vote, 1896–1932.* Stanford, 1934.
——: *They Voted for Roosevelt.* Stanford, 1947.
Ross, J. F. S.: *Elections and Electors.* New York, 1956.
Stanwood, Edward: *A History of the Presidency from 1788 to 1916.* 2 volumes, revised edition by Charles Knowles Bolton. Boston, 1928.
Stein, Charles W.: *The Third Term Tradition; Its Rise and Collapse in American Politics.* New York, 1936.

PERIODICALS

"Should the Electoral College be Abolished?" (Symposium) *Congressional Digest* (1941), 20:67–96.
Catledge, Turner: "Is Campaigning Worth-while?" *New York Times Magazine,* October 15, 1944.
Kallenbach, J. E.: "Recent Proposals to Reform the Electoral College System." *American Political Science Review* (1936), 30:924–929.

CHAPTER XV

Agar, Herbert: *The People's Choice.* Boston, 1933.
Berdahl, Clarence A.: *The War Powers of the Executive in the United States.* Urbana, 1921.
Calvert, Thomas H.: *The Constitution and the Courts.* Long Island, 1924.
Cleveland, Grover: *Presidential Problems.* New York, 1904.
Corwin, Edward S.: *The President: Office and Powers.* 2nd edition. New York, 1940.
——: *The Removal Power of the President.* Princeton, 1927.
Corwin, E. S. and Koenig, L. W.: *The Presidency Today.* Chicago, 1956.
Hart, James: *The American Presidency in Action, 1789.* New York, 1948.
——: *The Ordinance Making Power of the President.* Baltimore, 1925.
——: *Tenure of Office Under the Constitution.* Baltimore, 1930.
Hatch, L. E. and Shoup, E. L.: *History of the Vice-Presidency.* New York, 1934.
Hyman, Sidney: *The American President.* New York, 1954.
Lorant, Stefan: *The Presidency.* New York, 1952.
Milton, George Fort: *The Use of Presidential Power, 1789–1943.* Boston, 1944.
Patterson, C. Perry: *Presidential Government in the United States: The Unwritten Constitution.* Chapel Hill, N.C., 1947.
Pollard, James E.: *The Presidents and the Press.* New York, 1947.
Rossiter, Clinton: *The American Presidency.* New York, 1956.
Silva, Ruth: *Presidential Succession.* Ann Arbor, 1951.
Smith, Merriman: *A President Is Many Men.* New York, 1948.
Stein, C. W.: *The Third Term Tradition: Its Rise and Collapse.* New York, 1943.
Sturm, A. L.: *Presidential Power and National Emergencies.* New York, 1941.
Taft, William Howard: *Our Chief Magistrate and His Powers.* New York, 1916.
Young, Klyde and Middleton, Sanvar: *Heirs Apparent: The Vice Presidents of the United States.* New York, 1948.

PERIODICALS

Borchard, Edwin M.: "Treaties and Executive Agreements." *American Political Science Review* (1946), 40:729–39.
Brown, Everett S.: "The Term of Office of the President." *American Political Science Review* (1947), 41:447–52.
Fowler, D. G.: "Congressional Dictation of Local Appointments." *Journal of Politics* (1946).

Kallenbach, Joseph E.: "The New Presidential Succession Act." *American Political Science Review* (1947), 41:931–41.

Rossiter, Clinton L.: "The American President." *Yale Review* (1948), 37:619–37.

———: "The Reform of the Vice Presidency." *Political Science Quarterly* (1948), 63: 383–403.

Rankin, R. S.: "The Presidential Succession in the United States." *Journal of Politics* (1946).

Schlesinger, A. M.: "Third Term Issue." *American Mercury* (1947), 64:407–12.

Waldo, C. D. and Pincus, William: ",The Statutory Obligations of the President: Executive Necessity and Administrative Burdens." *Public Administration Review* (1946), 4:339–47.

CHAPTER XVI

Binkley, Wilfred E.: *President and Congress*. New York, 1947.

Beard, Charles A.: *The Republic*. New York, 1943.

Black, H. C.: *The Relation of the Executive Power to Legislation*. Princeton, 1919.

Chamberlain, Lawrence H.: *The President, Congress, and Legislation*. New York, 1946.

Griffith, E. S.: *Congress: Its Contemporary Role*. New York, 1956.

Galloway, George B.: *Congress at the Crossroads*. New York, 1946.

Hyman, Sidney: *The American President*. New York, 1953.

Kefauver, Estes and Levin, Jack: *A Twentieth-Century Congress*. New York, 1947.

Koenig, L. W.: *The President and the Crisis*. New York, 1944.

Moos, Malcolm: *Politics, Presidents, and Coattails*. Baltimore, 1952.

Rossiter, Clinton: *The American Presidency*. New York, 1956.

Roosevelt, Theodore: *An Autobiography*. New York, 1913.

Story, Joseph: *An Exposition of the Constitution of the United States*. New York, 1840.

Thatch, Charles C., Jr.: *The Creation of the Presidency*. Johns Hopkins Studies in History and Political Science, Series XL, No. 4. Baltimore, 1922.

PERIODICALS

Armstrong, W. P.: "The President and Congress: Unsolved Problems of Leadership and Power." *American Bar Association Journal* (1947), 33:417–20.

Berdahl, Clarence A.: "The President's Veto of Private Bills." *Political Science Quarterly* (1937), 52:505–31.

Garfield, James A.: "A Century of Congress." *Atlantic Monthly* (1877).

Herring, E. P.: "Executive-Legislative Responsibilities." *American Political Science Review* (1944), 38:1153–65.

Kefauver, E.: "The Need for Better Executive-Legislative Teamwork in the National Government." *American Political Science Review* (1944), 38:317–25.

Robinson, G. C.: "The Veto Record of Franklin Roosevelt." *American Political Science Review* (1942), 36:75–78.

Rowe, James, Jr.: "Cooperation or Conflict—the President's Relationships with an Opposition Congress." *Georgetown Law Journal* (1947), 36:1–15.

Sapp, C. R.: "Executive Assistance in the Legislative Process." *Public Administration Review* (1945).

Stoke, Harold W.: "Executive Leadership and the Growth of Propaganda." *American Political Science Review* (1941), 35:490–500.

Towle, Katherine A.: "The Presidential Veto Since 1889." *American Political Science Review* (1937), 31:51–56.

CHAPTER XVII

Barnard, Chester I.: *The Functions of the Executive*. Cambridge, Mass., 1938. Chapter 17.

Commission on Organization of the Executive Branch of the Government: *Reports*. Washington, D.C., 1949.

Corwin, Edward S.: *The President: Office and Powers*. 3rd edition. New York, 1948.

Gaus, John Merriam, White, Leonard D., and Dimock, Marshall E.: *The Frontiers of Public Administration*. Chicago, 1936.
Gulick, Luther and Urwick, L.: *Papers on the Science of Administration*. New York, 1937.
Hyneman, Charles: *Bureaucracy in a Democracy*. New York, 1950.
Laski, Harold J.: *The American Presidency: An Interpretation*. New York, 1940.
Latham, Earl G.: *The Federal Field Service*. Chicago, 1947.
Macmahon, Arthur W. and Millett, John D.: *Federal Administrators*. New York, 1939.
McDiarmid, John: *Government Corporations and Federal Funds*. Chicago, 1938.
Millett, John D.: *Management in the Public Service*. New York, 1954.
Pfiffner, John M.: *Public Administration*. Revised edition. New York, 1946.
Pritchett, C. H.: *The Tennessee Valley Authority*. Chapel Hill, N.C., 1943.
Short, Lloyd M.: *The Development of the National Administrative Organization in the United States*. Baltimore, 1923.
Taft, William H.: *Our Chief Magistrate and His Powers*. New York, 1926.
Van Dorn, Harold: *Government-Owned Corporations*. New York, 1926.
Wilson, Woodrow: *Study of Public Administration*. Washington, 1954.
White, Leonard D.: *Introduction to the Study of Public Administration*. Fourth edition. New York, 1952.

PERIODICALS

Lilienthal, D. E. and Marquis, R. H.: "The Conduct of Business Enterprises by the Federal Government." *Harvard Law Review* (1941), 54:545–601.
Person, H. S.: "Research and Planning as Functions of Administration and Management." *Public Administration Review* (1940), 1:65–73.
Pritchett, C. H.: "The Government Corporation Control Act of 1945." *American Political Science Review* (1946), 40:495–509.
——: "The Paradox of the Government Corporation." *Public Administration Review* (1941), 1:381–9.
Wilson, Woodrow: "The Study of Administration." *Political Science Quarterly* (1941), 56:481–506.

CHAPTER XVIII

Blachly, F. F. and Oatman, M. E.: *Federal Regulatory Action and Control*. Washington, D.C., 1940.
Blaisdell, Thomas C.: *The Federal Trade Commission*. New York, 1932.
Cushman, Robert E.: *The Independent Regulatory Commissions*. New York, 1944.
Herring, E. P.: *Public Administration and the Public Interest*. New York, 1936.
——: *Federal Commissioners*. Cambridge, Mass., 1936.
Landis, James M.: *The Administrative Process*. New Haven, 1938.

PERIODICALS

Dickinson, John: "Administrative Procedure Act: Scope and Grounds of Broadened Judicial Review." *American Bar Association Journal* (1947), 33:434–7, 513–19.
Sherwood, Foster H.: "The Federal Administrative Procedure Act." *American Political Science Review* (1947), 41:271–81.
Swisher, Carl Brent: "Joseph B. Eastman—Public Servant." *Public Administration Review* (1945), 5:34–54.

CHAPTER XIX

Commission of Inquiry on Public Service Personnel: *Better Government Personnel*. New York, 1935.
Commission on Organization of the Executive Branch of the Government: *Personnel Management*. Washington, D.C., 1949.
Carpenter, W. S.: *The Unfinished Business of Civil Service*. Princeton, 1952.
Dubin, Robert: *Human Relations in Administration*. New York, 1951.

Mosher, W. E. and Kingsley, J. D.: *Public Personnel Administration.* Revised edition. New York, 1941.
President's Committee on Administrative Management: *Report of the Committee with Studies of Administrative Management in the Federal Government.* Washington, D.C., 1937.
Spero, Sterling D.: *Government as Employer.* New York, 1948.
Torpey, William G.: *Public Personnel Management.* Princeton, 1953.
———: *Public Personnel Administration.* New York, 1953.
United States Civil Service Commission: *A History of the Federal Civil Service,* 1789–1939. Washington, D.C., 1939.
White, Leonard D.: *Civil Service in Wartime.* Chicago, 1945.
Ziskind, David: *One Thousand Strikes of Government Employees.* New York, 1940.

PERIODICALS

Brattin, Barbara: "The Dismissal Pattern in the Public Service." *Public Personnel Review* (1947), 8:122–15.
Reeves, Floyd W.: "Civil Service as Usual." *Public Administration Review* (1944), 4:327–40.

CHAPTER XX

Appleby, Paul: *Big Democracy.* New York, 1945.
Burnham, James: *The Managerial Revolution.* New York, 1941.
Christensen, A. N. and Kirkpatrick, E. M.: *Running the Country.* New York, 1947. Chapters 17–18.
Commission on Organization of the Executive Branch of the Government: *Budgeting and Accounting.* Washington, D.C., 1949.
———: *General Management of the Executive Branch.* Washington, D.C., 1949.
Dimock, Marshall E.: *The Executive in Action.* New York, 1945. Chapter 11.
———: *Modern Politics and Administration.* New York, 1947.
Friedrich, Carl J. and Cole, Taylor: *Responsible Bureaucracy.* Cambridge, Mass., 1932.
Key, V. O.: "Politics and Administration" in Leonard D. White, editor: *The Future of Government in the United States.* Chicago, 1942.
Kingsley, J. Donald: *Representative Bureaucracy.* Yellow Springs, Ohio, 1944.
Macmahon, Arthur W. and Millet, John D.: *Federal Administrators.* New York, 1939.
Mansfield, Harvey C.: *The Comptroller General.* New Haven, 1939.
Morstein Marx, Fritz, editor: *Elements of Public Administration.* New York, 1946.
Pfiffner, John M.: *Public Administration.* Revised edition. New York, 1946. Chapters 23–5.
President's Committee on Administrative Management: *Report with Special Studies.* Washington, D.C., 1937.
Rawson, Robert H.: "The Formulation of the Federal Budget" in Carl J. Friedrich and Edward S. Mason, editors: *Public Policy.* Cambridge, Mass., 1941.
Smith, Harold D.: *The Management of Your Government.* New York, 1945.
White, Leonard D.: *Introduction to the Study of Public Administration.* Third edition, New York, 1948. Chapters 6–7, 13, 18–21.
White, Leonard D. and others: *New Horizons in Public Administration.* University, Ala., 1945.

PERIODICALS

Brownlow, Louis and others: "The Executive Office of the President: A Symposium." *Public Administration Review* (1941), 1:101–40.
Holcombe, Arthur N.: "Overall Financial Planning Through the Bureau of the Budget." *Public Administration Review* (1939), 1:225–30.
Macmahon, Arthur W.: "Congressional Oversight of Administration: The Power of the Purse." *Political Science Quarterly* (1943), 58:161–90.
McDiarmid, John: "Reorganization of the General Accounting Office." *American Political Science Review* (1937), 31:508–16.
Pearson, Norman A.: "A General Administrative Staff to the President." *Public Administration Review* (1944), 4:127–47.

CHAPTER XXI

Beard, Charles A.: *The Republic.* New York, 1943.
Corwin, Edward S.: *The Constitution and What It Means Today.* Princeton, 1946.
Flynn, J. T.: *Meet Your Congress.* New York, 1944.
Galloway, George B.: *Congress at the Crossroads.* New York, 1946.
Haynes, G. H.: *The Senate of the United States: Its History and Practice.* 2 vols. Boston, 1938.
Huntington, E. V.: *Methods of Apportionment in Congress.* 76th Congress, 3rd Session, Senate Document No. 304 (1940).
Kefauver, Estes and Levin, Jack: *Twentieth Century Congress.* New York, 1947.
Luce, Robert: *Congress: an Explanation.* Cambridge, Massachusetts, 1926.
———: *Legislative Problems.* Boston, 1935.
McCall, Samuel W.: *The Business of Congress.* New York, 1911.
Rogers, Lindsay: *The American Senate.* New York, 1926.
Schmeckebier, L. F.: *Congressional Apportionment.* Washington, D.C., 1941.
Torrey, V.: *You and Your Congress.* New York, 1944.
Willoughby, W. F.: *Principles of Legislative Organization and Administration.* New York, 1934.
Wilson, Woodrow: *Constitutional Government in the United States.* New York, 1908.

PERIODICALS

Barnett, Vincent M., Jr.: "Contested Congressional Elections in Recent Years." *Political Science Quarterly* (1939), 54:187–215.
McKinney, M. N.: "The Personnel of the Seventy-fifth Congress." *American Political Science Review* (1942), 36:67–74.
Sauer, C. O.: "Geography and the Gerrymander." *American Political Science Review* (1918), 12:403–26.
"A Study of the Structure and Methods of Congress." *Congressional Digest*, August–September, 1945.
Walters, David O.: "Reapportionment and Urban Representation." *Annals of the American Academy of Political and Social Science* (1938), 195:11–20.
Wooddy, C. H.: "Is the Senate Unrepresentative?" *Political Science Quarterly* (1926), 41:219–39.

CHAPTER XXII

Beard, Charles A.: *The Republic.* New York, 1943.
Black, H. C.: *The Relation of the Executive Power to Legislation.* Princeton, 1919.
Brown, George Rothwell: *The Leadership of Congress.* Indianapolis, 1922.
Cannon, Clarence: *Procedures in the House of Representatives.* 4th edition. Washington, D.C., 1944.
Chamberlain, J. P.: *Legislative Processes: National and State.* New York, 1936.
Chamberlain, Lawrence H.: *The President, Congress, and Legislation.* New York, 1946.
Dimock, M. E.: *Congressional Investigating Committees.* John Hopkins University Studies in History and Political Science. Vol. 57. Baltimore, 1929.
Finletter, Thomas K.: *Can Representative Government Do the Job?* New York, 1945.
Hasbrouck, P. D.: *Party Government in the House of Representatives.* New York, 1927.
Herring, E. P.: *Presidential Leadership.* New York, 1940.
Huntington, E. V.: *Methods of Apportionment in Congress,* 76th Congress, 3rd Session, Senate Document No. 304 (1940).
Laski, Harold: *The American Presidency: An Interpretation.* New York, 1940.
Legislative Reorganization Act of 1946. Public Law 601, 79th Congress.
McBain, H. L.: *The Living Constitution.* New York, 1927.
McCown, A. C.: *The Congressional Conference Committee.* New York, 1927.
Story, Joseph: *An Exposition of the Constitution of the United States.* New York, 1840.

Willoughby, W. F.: *Principles of Legislative Organization and Administration.* Washington, 1934.

PERIODICALS

Coyl, David C.: "Reorganizing Congress." *Virginia Quarterly Review,* Winter, 1948.
Graves, W. Brooke: "Legislative Reference Service for the Congress of the United States." *American Political Science Review* (1947), 41:289–93.
Kefauver, E.: "The Need for Better Executive-Legislative Teamwork in the National Government." *American Political Science Review* (1944), 38:317–25.
Rogers, Lindsay: "The Staffing of Congress." *Political Science Quarterly* (1941), 56:1–22.
White, Howard: "The Concurrent Resolution in Congress." *American Political Science Review* (1941), 35:886–9.

CHAPTER XXIII

Bailey, S. K. and Samuel, H. D.: *Congress at Work.* New York, 1952.
Beard, Charles A.: *The Republic.* New York, 1943.
Burdette, Franklin L.: *Filibustering in the Senate.* Princeton, 1940.
Chamberlain, J. P.: *Legislative Process: National and State.* New York, 1936.
Crandall, Samuel B.: *Treaties, Their Making and Enforcement.* Washington, 1916.
Dimock, M. E.: *Congressional Investigating Committees.* Johns Hopkins University Studies in History and Political Science. Baltimore, 1929. Vol. 57.
Eberling, E. J.: *Congressional Investigations.* New York, 1928.
Fleming, D. F.: *The Treaty Veto of the American Senate.* New York, 1930.
Galloway, George B.: *The Legislative Process in Congress.* New York, 1953.
Griffith, E. S.: *Congress: Its Contemporary Role.* 2nd edition. New York, 1956.
Gross, Bertram M.: *The Legislative Struggle.* New York, 1953.
Luce, Robert: *Legislative Procedure.* Boston, 1922.
McGeary, M. N.: *The Development of Congressional Investigative Power.* New York, 1940.
Munro, William Bennett: *The Invisible Government.* New York, 1928.
Redfield, W. C.: *With Congress and Cabinet.* Garden City, 1924.
Steiner, Gilbert: *The Congressional Conference Committee.* Urbana, 1951.

PERIODICALS

Armstrong, W. P.: "The President and Congress: Unsolved Problems of Leadership and Powers." *American Bar Association Journal,* May, 1947.
Beard, Charles A.: "In Defense of Congress." *American Mercury* (1942), 53:647–55.
Cantwell, Frank V.: "Public Opinion and the Legislative Process." *American Political Science Review* (1946), 40:924–35.
Huitt, Ralph: "The Congressional Committee: a Case Study." *American Political Science Review* (1954), 48: 340–65.
McGeary, M. Nelson: "Congressional Investigations During Franklin D. Roosevelt's First Term." *American Political Science Review* (1937), 31:680 ff.
Macmahon, A. W.: "Congressional Oversight of Administration: The Power of the Purse." *Political Science Quarterly,* 55:161–90; 380–414.
Sapp, C. R.: "Executive Assistance in the Legislative Process." *Public Administration Review,* Winter, 1946.
Waldo, C. D. and Pincus, William: "The Statutory Obligations of the President: Executive Necessity and Administrative Burden." *Public Administration Review,* Autumn, 1946.
White, L. D.: "Congressional Control of the Public Service." *American Political Science Review* (1945), 39:1–11.

CHAPTER XXIV

Beard, Charles A.: *The Republic.* New York, 1943.
Burdick, C. K.: *The Law of the American Constitution.* New York, 1922.
Corwin, Edward S., ed.: *The Constitution of the United States of America: Analysis*

and Interpretation. Annotation of cases decided by the Supreme Court of the United States to June 30, 1952. Government Printing Office, Washington, 1953.
——: *The Constitution and What It Means Today*. Princeton, 1954.
——: *The Commerce Power versus States Rights*. Princeton, 1936.
Dimock, M. E.: *Congressional Investigating Committees*. Johns Hopkins Studies in History and Political Science. Baltimore, 1929.
Eberling, E. J.: *Congressional Investigations*. New York, 1928.
The Federalist.
Lawson, J. F.: *The General Welfare Clause: A Study of the Power of Congress Under the Constitution*. Second Printing. Washington, 1934.
Mathews, J. M.: *The American Constitutional System*. 2nd edition. New York, 1929.
Norton, Thomas J.: *The Constitution of the United States: Its Sources and Its Application*. Boston, 1922.
Story, Joseph: *Commentaries on the Constitution*. 2 vols. 5th edition. Boston, 1891.
Willoughby, W. W.: *The American Constitutional System*. New York, 1904.
Wilmerding, Lucius: *The Spending Power: A History of the Efforts of Congress to Control Expenditures*. New Haven, 1943.
Wilson, Woodrow: *Constitutional Government in the United States*. New York, 1908.

PERIODICALS

Galloway, George B.: "The Investigative Function of Congress." *American Political Science Review* (1929), 21:47–70.
Macmahon, A. W.: "Congressional Oversight of Administration: The Power of the Purse." *Political Science Quarterly* (1943), 58:161–90; 380–414.

CHAPTER XXV

Alfange, Dean: *The Supreme Court and the National Will*. New York, 1937.
Bates, E. S.: *The Story of the Supreme Court*. New York, 1936.
Baldwin, S. E.: *The American Judiciary*. New York, 1905.
Beard, Charles A.: *The Republic*. New York, 1943.
Beveridge, A. J.: *John Marshall*. 4 vols. New York, 1916.
Cohn, Edmond, ed.: *Supreme Court and Supreme Law*. Bloomington, Indiana, 1954.
Cahill, Fred V.: *Judicial Legislation*. New York, 1952.
Carpenter, W. S.: *Judicial Tenure in the United States*. New Haven, 1918.
Corwin, Edward S.: *The Twillight of the Supreme Court*. New Haven, 1934.
Ewing, Cortez A. M.: *The Judges of the Supreme Court, 1789–1937*. Minneapolis, 1938.
Frankfurter, Felix and Landis, James M.: *The Business of the Supreme Court*. New York, 1927.
Haines, C. H.: *The Role of the Supreme Court in American Government and Politics, 1789–1835*. Berkeley, California, 1944.
Horn, Robert A.: *Groups and the Constitution: the Role of Voluntary Groups in Democratic Society*. Stanford, 1956.
Hughes, Charles Evans: *The Supreme Court of the United States: Its Foundation, Methods and Achievements*. Garden City, 1938.
Levy, Beryl Harold: *Our Constitution: Tool or Testament?* New York, 1941.
McBain, Howard Lee: *The Living Constitution*. New York, 1927.
Rowe, Gilbert P.: *Our Judicial Oligarchy*. New York, 1912.
Swisher, C. B.: *Roger B. Taney*. New York, 1935.
Twiss, Benjamin R.: *Lawyers and the Constitution: How Laissez-Faire Came to the Supreme Court*. Princeton, 1942.
Umbreit, H. B.: *Our Eleven Chief Justices*. New York, 1938.
Warren, Charles: *The Supreme Court in the United States History*, 3 vols. Boston, 1926.
Williams, J. S.: *The Supreme Court Speaks*. University of Texas Press, 1956.

PERIODICALS

Dodd, W. F.: "United States Supreme Court." *American Political Science Review* (1947), 41:1–11.

Field, Oliver P.: "States versus Nation and the Supreme Court." *American Political Science Review* (1934), 28:233–45.
Mitchell, W. D.: "Appointment of Federal Judges." *American Bar Association Journal* (1931), 17:569–74.

CHAPTER XXVI

Beard, Charles A.: *The Supreme Court and the Constitution.* New York, 1912.
Boudin, L. B.: *Government by Judiciary.* 2 vols. New York, 1932.
Brant, I.: *Storm Over the Constitution.* Indianapolis, 1936.
Carr, R. H.: *Democracy and the Supreme Court.* Oklahoma City, 1936.
Corwin, Edward S.: *Court Over Constitution: A Study of Judicial Review as an Instrument of Popular Government.* Princeton, 1938.
Curtis, Charles P., Jr.: *Lions Under the Throne.* Boston, 1947.
Daugherty, J. Hampden: *The Power of the Federal Judiciary Over Legislation.* New York, 1912.
Davis, Horace A.: *The Judicial Review.* New York, 1913.
Haines, C. G.: *The American Doctrine of Judicial Supremacy.* New York, 1914.
Jackson, Robert H.: *The Struggle for Judicial Supremacy.* New York, 1940.
McCune, Wesley: *The Nine Young Men.* New York, 1947.
Pritchett, C. Herman: *The Roosevelt Court: A Study in Judicial Politics and Values, 1937–1947.* New York, 1948.
Swisher, Carl Brent: *American Constitutional Development.* Boston, 1954.
Warren, Charles: *The Supreme Court in United States History,* 3 vols. New York, 1926.

PERIODICALS

Ballantine, A. A.: "The Supreme Court: Principles and Personalities." *American Bar Association Journal,* March, 113–15.
Cantwell, Frank V.: "Public Opinion and the Legislative Process." *American Political Science Review* (1946), 40:924–35. An analysis of the Debate on the Roosevelt Court Reorganization Bill.
Commager, Henry S.: "Judicial Review and Democracy." *Virginia Quarterly Review,* Summer (1943).
Cushman, Robert E.: "Ten Years of the Supreme Court." *American Political Science Review,* February (1948), 42:42–52.
Davis, Kenneth C.: "Revolution in the Supreme Court." *Atlantic Monthly* (1940), 166:85–96.
Field, Oliver P.: "Unconstitutional Legislation by Congress." *American Political Science Review* (1945), 39:54–61.
Harris, Robert J.: "The Decline of Judicial Review." *Journal of Politics,* February (1948).
Jaffe, Louis L.: "The Supreme Court Today." *Atlantic* (1944), 174:76–80.
Powell, Thomas Reed: "Our High Court Analyzed." *New York Times,* June 18, 1944.
Pritchett, C. H.: "Dissent in the Supreme Court." *American Political Science Review* (1945), 39:42–54.
——: "Ten Years of the Supreme Court, 1937–1947: The Roosevelt Court: Votes and Values." *American Political Science Review* (1948), 42:53–67.
Rutner, Sidney: "Was the Supreme Court Packed by President Grant?" *Political Science Quarterly,* 50:343–58.
Schlesinger, Arthur M., Jr.: "The Supreme Court." *Fortune,* January (1947), 73–212.

CHAPTER XXVII

Abbott, C. C.: *The Federal Debt.* New York, 1953.
Ashen, Melvin and Wormuth, Francis D.: *Private Enterprise and Public Policy.* New York, 1954.
Blough, Roy: *The Federal Taxing Process.* New York, 1952.
Fainsod, Merle and Gordon, Lincoln: *Government and the American Economy.* 2nd edition, New York, 1949.

Groves, Harold M.: *Financing Government*. Revised edition. New York, 1954.
——: *Production, Jobs, and Taxes*. New York, 1944.
Hansen, Alvin H.: *Monetary Theory and Fiscal Policy*. New York, 1949.
——: *Fiscal Policy and Business Cycles*. New York, 1941.
——: *Economic Policy and Full Employment*. New York, 1947.
——, and Perloff, Harvey S.: *State and Local Finance in the National Economy*. New York, 1944.
Harris, Seymour: *The National Debt and the New Economics*. New York, 1947.
Lerner, Abba P.: *The Economics of Control*. New York, 1944.
Murad, Anatol: *Private Credit and Public Debt*. Washington, 1954.
Nathan, Robert R.: *National Income, 1929–36*. U.S. Department of Commerce. Washington, 1937.
U.S. Treasury Department: *Annual Reports*. Washington.

PERIODICALS

Lerner, Abba P.: "Functional Finance and the Federal Debt." *Social Research* (1943), 10:38–51.
Morstein Marx, Fritz (ed.): "Formulating the Federal Government's Economic Program: A Symposium." *American Political Science Review* (1948), 42:272–336.
——: "The Bureau of the Budget: Its Evolution and Present Role, II." *American Political Science Review* (1945), 39:869–898.

CHAPTER XXVIII

Burgess, W. R.: *Reserve Banks and the Money Market*. Revised edition. New York, 1936.
Cole, G. D. H.: *What Everyone Wants to Know About Money*. New York, 1933.
Dewey, D. R.: *Financial History of the United States*. 12th edition. New York, 1934.
Donaldson, J.: *The Dollar, A Study of the "New" National and International Monetary System*. New York, 1937.
Harris, S. E.: *Twenty Years of Federal Reserve Policy*. Cambridge, Massachusetts, 1934.
Helderman, L. C.: *National and State Banks—A Study of Their Origin*, Boston, 1931.
Kemmerer, E. W.: *The ABC of the Federal Reserve System*. 11th edition. Princeton, 1938.
National Industrial Conference Board: *The New Monetary System of the United States*. New York, 1934.
Noyes, A. D.: *Forty Years of American Finance*. New York, 1909.
Westerfield, Ray B.: *Money, Credit and Banking*. New York, 1938.
White, Horace: *Money and Banking*. Boston, 1935.

PERIODICALS

Carson, W. J.: "The Federal Reserve System in Transition." *Annals of the American Academy of Political and Social Science* (1934), 171:83–93.
French, D. M.: "The Contest for a National System of Home Mortgage Finance." *American Political Science Review* (1941), 35:53–59.
Greer, G.: "This Business of Monetary Control." *Harper's Magazine* (1935), 171:169–80.
Hart, S. K.: "Government Agencies of Credit." *Annals of the American Academy of Political and Social Science* (1938), 196:162–75.
Warburton, Clark: "Monetary Control Under the Federal Reserve Act." *Political Science Quarterly* (1946), 61:505–34.

CHAPTER XXIX

Bauer, Irston R.: *Transforming Public Utility Regulation*. New York, 1950.
Buck, Solon J.: *The Granger Movement*. Cambridge, Massachusetts, 1913.

Daggett, Stuart: *Principles of Inland Transportation.* Revised edition. New York, 1934.

Davie, Maurice R.: *A Constructive Immigration Policy.* New Haven, 1923.

——: *World Immigration.* New York, 1936.

Haney, L. H.: *Congressional History of Railways in the United States.* 2 vols. Madison, 1910.

Hansen, Marcus L.: *The Immigrant in American History.* Cambridge, Massachusetts, 1940.

Johnson, E. R.: *Government Regulation of Transportation.* New York, 1938.

Johnson, E. R., Huebner, G. G. and Henry, A. K.: *Transportation by Water.* New York, 1935.

Locklin, D. Phillips: *Economics of Transportation.* New York, 1935.

Mosher, W. E. and Crawford, F. G.: *Public Utility Regulation.* New York, 1933.

Moulton, H. G.: *The American Transportation Problem.* Washington, 1933.

Regulation of Transportation Agencies. 73rd Congress, 2nd Session, Senate Document No. 152 (1934).

Sharfman, I. L.: *The Interstate Commerce Commission.* 5 vols. New York, 1936.

Wagner, W. H.: *A Legislative History of the Motor Carriers Act.* New York, 1935.

Ziegler, Benjamin M., ed.: *Immigration: an American Dilemma.* Boston, 1953.

Wilson, G. L., Herring, J. M., and Eutsler, R. B.: *Public Utility Regulation.* New York, 1938.

PERIODICALS

Herring, E. P.: "Special Interests and the Interstate Commerce Commission." *American Political Science Review* (1933), 27:738–51; 899–917.

Lane, H. F.: "I.C.C. Begins Motor Carrier Regulation." *Railway Age* (1936), 100:24–5.

CHAPTERS XXX and XXXI

Berle, Adolph A. and Means, Gardiner C.: *The Modern Corporation and Private Property.* 2nd edition. New York, 1940.

Bloom, Gordon F. and Northrup, Herbert R.: *The Economics of Labor Relations.* New York, 1954.

Citizens Committee for the Hoover Report: *Digest and Analyses of the Nineteen Hoover Commission Reports.* New York, 1955.

Dahl, R. A. and Lindblom, C. E: *Politics, Economics, and Welfare.* New York, 1953.

Fine, Sidney: *Laissez Faire and the General Welfare State.* Ann Arbor, 1956.

Fainsod, Merle and Gordon, Lincoln: *Government and the American Economy.* 2nd edition. New York, 1949.

Hansen, Alvin H.: *Economic Policy and Full Employment.* New York, 1947.

Harris, Seymour E.: *The New Economics: Keynes' Influence on Theory and Public Policy.* New York, 1947.

Keynes, John Maynard: *The General Theory of Employment, Interest, and Money.* New York, 1936.

Larkin, John D.: *Trade Agreements; A Study in Democratic Methods.* New York, 1940.

Leek, J. H.: *Government and Labor in the United States.* New York, 1954.

Lewis, Arthur W.: *Principles of Economic Planning.* Washington, 1950.

Merriam, Lewis: *Relief and Social Security.* Washington, 1946.

Maxwell, James A.: *The Fiscal Impact of Federalism in the United States.* Cambridge, 1946.

Nathan, Robert P.: *Mobilizing for Abundance.* New York, 1944.

Redford, Emmette: *The Administration of National Economic Control.* New York, 1952.

Rohlfing, Charles C. *et al.*: *Business and Government.* 5th edition. New York, 1949.

Steiner, George A.: *Government Role in Economic Life.* New York, 1953.

The Commission on Organization of the Executive Branch of the Government: *Department of Labor.* Washington, 1949. *The Hoover Commission Report.* New York, 1949, pp. 319–22.

The Commission on Organization of the Executive Branch of the Government: *Medical Activities.* Washington, 1949. *The Hoover Commission Report.* New York, 1949, pp. 333–55.

The Commission on Organization of the Executive Branch of the Government: *Social Security and Education—Indian Affairs.* Washington, 1949. *The Hoover Commission Report.* New York, 1949, pp. 441–60.

Werne, Benjamin: *The Law of Labor Relations.* New York, 1951.

Wootton, Barbara: *Freedom Under Planning.* Chapel Hill, 1945.

Wells, Henry A.: *Monopoly and Social Control.* Washington, 1952.

PERIODICALS

Carter, Isabel G. (ed.): "Appraising the Social Security Program." *The Annals* (1939), 202:1–99.

Morstein Marx, Fritz (ed.): "Maintaining High Level Production and Employment: A Symposium." *American Political Science Review* (1945), 39:1119–79.

Morstein Marx, Fritz (ed.): "Formulating the Federal Government's Economic Program: A Symposium." *American Political Science Review* (1948), 42:272–336.

CHAPTER XXXII

Chew, Arthur P.: *The Response of Government to Agriculture.* Washington, D.C., 1939.

Davis, Chester C.: "The Development of Agricultural Policy Since the End of the World War." *Yearbook of Agriculture, 1940.* Washington, D.C., 1940.

Edwards, Everett E.: "American Agriculture the First 300 Years." *Yearbook of Agriculture, 1940.* Washington, D.C., 1940. Pp. 171–276.

Gulick, Luther H.: *American Forest Policy.* New York, 1951.

Gaus, J, M. and Wolcott, L. O.: *Public Administration and the United States Department of Agriculture.* Chicago, 1940.

Harding, T. Swann: *Two Blades of Grass: A History of Scientific Development in the United States Department of Agriculture.* Norman, Oklahoma, 1947.

McCune, Wesley: *Who's Behind our Farm Policy?* New York, 1956.

Nourse, E. G., Davis, J. S. and Black, J. D.: *Three Years of the Agriculture Adjustment Administration.* Washington, D.C., 1937.

Peffer, Louise: *The Closing of the Public Domain.* Palo Alto, 1951.

Rightmire, George W.: *Federal Aid and Regulation of Agriculture and Private Industrial Enterprise in the United States.* Columbus, 1943.

True, Calres Alfred: *A History of Agricultural Experimentation in the United States, 1607–1925.* United States Department of Agriculture Miscellaneous Publication No. 251. Washington, D.C., 1937.

Wilcox, Walter W.: *The Farmer in the Second World War.* Ames, Iowa, 1947.

CHAPTER XXXIII

Baruch, Bernard M.: *American Industry in the War: A Report on the War Industries Board.* Washington, D.C., 1921.

Beard, Charles A.: *The Navy: Defense or Portent?* New York, 1932.

Berdahl, Clarence A.: *War Powers of the Executive in the United States.* Urbana, Ill., 1920.

Brodie, Bernard: *A Guide to Naval Strategy.* 3rd edition. Princeton, 1944.

Chase, Stuart: *Where's the Money Coming From?* New York, 1943.

Corwin, Edward S.: *The President: Office and Powers.* 3rd edition. New York, 1948. Chapter 5.

Davis, Elmer and Price, Byron: *War Information and Censorship.* Washington, D.C., 1943.

Finletter, Thomas K.: *Power and Policy.* New York, 1954.

Fitzpatrick, Edward A.: *Universal Military Training.* New York, 1945.

Herring, E. P.: *The Impact of War.* New York, 1941.

Laswell, Harold: *National Security and Individual Freedom.* New York, 1950.

NacNeil, Neil and Metz, Harold: *The Hoover Report, 1953–55.* Washington, D.C., 1956.
Mahan, A. T.: *The Interest of America in Sea Power, Present and Future.* Boston, 1898.
President's Advisory Commission on Universal Training: *A Program for National Security.* Washington, D.C., 1947.
Smith, Louis: *American Democracy and Military Power.* University of Chicago Press, 1951.
Sprout, Harold H. and Margaret, editors: *Foundations of National Power.* Princeton, 1945.
Stettinius, E. R.: *Lend-Lease: Weapon for Victory.* New York, 1944.
Tobin, H. J. and Bidwell, P. W.: *Mobilizing Civilian America.* New York, 1940.

PERIODICALS

Bemis, Samuel F.: "The Shifting Strategy of American Defense and Diplomacy." *Virginia Quarterly Review* (1948), 24:321–35.
Brodie, Bernard: "Nuclear Weapons: Strategic or Tactical?" *Foreign Affairs* (1954), 32:217–29.
——: "Unlimited Weapons and Limited War." *The Reporter* (1954), 11:16–21.
——: "How War Became Absurd." *Harpers* (1955), 211:33–37.
Connery, Robert H.: "Unification of the Armed Forces—The First Year." *American Political Science Review* (1949), 43:38–52.
Cushman, Robert E.: "Civil Liberties." *American Political Science Review* (1943), 37:49–56.
Fairman, Charles: "The Law of Martial Rule and the National Emergency." *Harvard Law Review* (1942), 55:1253–1302.
Harris, J. P.: "The Emergency Defense Organization." *Public Administration Review* (1940), 1:1–24.
Kissinger, Henry A.: "Military Policy and Defense of the Grey Areas." *Foreign Affairs* (1955), 33:416–28.
Leary, P. M.: "Rationing and Governmental Organization." *American Political Science Review* (1945), 39:1089–1106.
Price, Byron: "Governmental Censorship in Wartime." *American Political Science Review* (1942), 36:837–49.
Swisher, Carl Brent: "Civil Liberties in Wartime." *Political Science Quarterly* (1940), 55:321–47.
——: "The Control of War Preparations in the United States." *American Political Science Review* (1940), 34:1085–1103.

CHAPTER XXXIV

Brown, Wenzel: *Dynamite on Our Doorstep.* New York, 1948.
Clark, Blake: *Hawaii, The 49th State.* New York, 1947.
Collier, John: *The Indians of the Americas.* New York, 1947.
Evans, L. H.: *The Virgin Islands: From Naval Base to New Deal.* Ann Arbor, Mich., 1945.
George, W. H. and Bachman, P. S.: *The Government of Hawaii: Federal, Territorial and County.* Fourth edition. Honolulu, 1934.
Gruening, Ernest: *The State of Alaska.* New York, 1954.
Haas, W. H., editor: *The American Empire: A Study of the Outlying Territories of the United States.* Chicago, 1940.
Hayden, J. Ralston: *The Philippines: A Study in National Development.* New York, 1942.
Hilscher, Herbert H.: *Alaska Now.* New York, 1948.
Kinney, J. P.: *A Continent Lost—A Civilization Won.* Baltimore, 1937.
Kirk, Grayson L.: *Philippine Independence.* New York, 1936.
Littler, Robert M. C.: *The Government of Hawaii: A Study in Territorial Administration.* Stanford, Calif., 1929.
Mathews, J. M.: *The American Constitutional System.* 2nd edition. New York, 1940. Chapter 20.
Padelford, Norman J.: *The Panama Canal in Peace and War.* New York, 1942.

Roosevelt, T.: *Colonial Policies of the United States.* New York, 1937.

Schmeckebier, L. F.: *The District of Columbia.* Baltimore, 1928.

Spicer, George W.: "The Constitutional Status and Government of Alaska." *Johns Hopkins University Studies in Historical and Political Science* (1927), 45:450–567.

Swisher, Carl Brent: *American Constitutional Development.* Boston, 1954. Chapter 21.

Thayer, Philip, Editor: *Nationalism and Progress in Free Asia.* Johns Hopkins University Press, Baltimore, 1956.

Tugwell, Rexford G.: *Stricken Land: The Story of Puerto Rico.* New York, 1947.

U.S. Department of State: *The United States and Non-Self-Governing Territories.* U.S.–U.N. Information Series, No. 18, Publication No. 2812. Washington, D.C., 1947.

White, T.: *Puerto and Its People.* New York, 1938.

Willoughby, W. W.: *Constitutional Law of the United States.* 2nd edition, New York, 1929. Vol. I, Chapters 23–32.

PERIODICALS

"The Question of Granting Statehood to Hawaii and Alaska." *Congressional Digest* (1947), 26:257–8.

Arnold, Edwin G.: "Self-Government in U.S. Territories." *Foreign Affairs* (1947), 25:655–66.

Braibanti, Ralph: "The Ryukyu Islands: Pawn of the Pacific." *American Political Science Review* (1954), 48:972–98.

Lewis, Gordon K.: "Puerto Rico: A Case of Change in an Underdeveloped Area." *Journal of Politics* (1955), 17:614–50.

Rutherford, G. W.: "Reorganization of the Government of the District of Columbia." *American Political Science Review* (1939), 33:653–5.

CHAPTER XXXV

Bailey, Thomas A.: *A Diplomatic History of the American People.* New York, 1944.

Bartlett, Ruhl J.: *The Record of American Diplomacy: Documents and Readings in the History of American Foreign Relations.* New York, 1947.

Bendiner, R.: *The Riddle of the State Department.* New York, 1942.

Burns, James McGregor: *Roosevelt: The Lion and the Fox.* New York, 1956.

Chamberlain, Lawrence H. and Snyder, Richard C.: *American Foreign Policy.* New York, 1948.

Childs, J. Rives: *American Foreign Service.* New York, 1948.

Colegrove, Kenneth: *The American Senate and World Peace.* New York, 1944.

Corwin, Edward S.: *The Constitution and World Organization.* Princeton, 1944.

——: *The President: Office and Powers.* 3rd edition. New York, 1948.

——: *The President's Control of Foreign Relations.* Princeton, 1917.

Dangerfield, R. J.: *In Defense of the Senate.* Norman, Okla., 1933.

Dennison, E. E.: *The Senate Foreign Relations Committee.* Stanford, Calif., 1942.

Dodd, W. E. and Martha: *Ambassador Dodd's Diary.* New York, 1941.

Fleming, D. F.: *The Treaty Veto of the American Senate.* New York, 1930.

Harris, Joseph P.: *The Advice and Consent of the Senate.* Berkeley, 1953.

Hulen, B. D.: *Inside the Department of State.* New York, 1936.

Kirk, Grayson L.: *The Study of International Relations in American Colleges and Universities.* New York, 1947.

Macmahon, Arthur W.: "Function and Area in the Administration of International Affairs" in *New Horizons in Public Administration.* University, Ala., 1945. Chapter 6.

Mathews, John M.: *American Foreign Relations: Conduct and Policies.* Second edition. New York, 1938.

McCamy, James L.: *The Administration of American Foreign Affairs.* New York, 1950.

McClure, Wallace: *International Executive Agreements: Democratic Procedure under the Constitution of the United States.* New York, 1941.
Perkins, Dexter: *The Evolution of American Foreign Policy.* New York, 1951.
Stuart, Graham H.: *American Diplomatic and Consular Practice.* New York, 1936.
U.S. Department of State: *Foreign Service of the U.S.: General Information and Pertinent Laws and Regulations.* Washington, D.C., 1947, No. 2745.
Westphal, A. C. F.: *The House Committee on Foreign Affairs.* New York, 1942.
Williams, B. H.: *American Diplomacy, Policies, and Practice.* New York, 1936.
Wright, Quincy: *The Control of American Foreign Relations.* New York, 1922.

PERIODICALS

Cohen, Benjamin V.: "The Evolving Role of Congress in Foreign Affairs." *Congressional Record* (1948), 94:A3973–A3975.
Green, J. F.: "The President's Control of Foreign Policy." *Foreign Policy Reports* (1939), 15:10–20.
Henderson, Loy W.: "Foreign Policies: Their Formulation and Enforcement." *Department of State Bulletin* (1946), 15:590–6.
Kennan, George F.: "The Future of Our Professional Diplomacy," *Foreign Affairs* (1955), 33:566–86.
Laves, Walter H. C. and Wilcox, Francis O; "The Reorganization of the State Department." *American Political Science Review* (1944), 38:289–301.
Woodward, E. L.: "The Old and New Diplomacy," *The Yale Review* (1947), 36:405–22.
Wright, Quincy: "The United States and International Agreements." *International Conciliation* (1945), 411:379–98.
Wriston, Henry M.: "Young Men and the Foreign Service." *Foreign Affairs* (1954), 33:28–42.

CHAPTERS XXXVI and XXXVII

Bailey, Thomas A.: *The Man in the Street.* New York, 1948.
Barlett, Ruhl J.: *The Record of American Diplomacy; Documents and Readings in the History of American Foreign Relations.* New York, 1947.
Bemis, Samuel Flagg: *A Diplomatic History of the United States.* New York, 1942.
Borchard, Edward: *American Foreign Policy.* Indianapolis, 1946.
Brookings Institution: *Major Problems of United States Foreign Policy.* Washington, D.C., 1947, 1948, 1949.
Brown, W. A. and Opie, R.: *American Foreign Assistance.* Washington, 1953.
Buehrig, Edward: *Woodrow Wilson and the Balance of Power.* Bloomington, 1955.
Carleton, William G.: *The Revolution in American Foreign Policy, 1945–1954.* New York, 1954.
Chamberlain, Lawrence H. and Snyder, Richard S.: *American Foreign Policy.* New York, 1955.
Cook, Thomas I. and Moos, Malcolm: *Power Through Purpose: The Realism of Idealism as a Basis for Foreign Policy.* Baltimore, 1954.
Eagleton, Clyde: *International Government.* Revised edition. New York, 1948. Chapters 12–14.
Goodrich, Leland M. and Hambro, Edward: *Charter of the United Nations: Commentary and Documents.* Boston, 1946.
Graham, Malbone W.: *American Diplomacy in the International Community.* Baltimore, 1948.
Grassmuck, George L.: *Sectional Biases in Congress on Foreign Policy.* Baltimore, 1950.
Langer, William L. and Gleason, S. Everett: *The World Crisis and American Foreign Policy.* (Vol. I, *The Challenge to Isolation, 1937–40;* Vol. II, *The Undeclared War, 1940–41.*) New York, 1952–53.
Latane, John H.: *A History of American Foreign Policy.* Revised edition by David W. Wainhouse. New York, 1934.
Lewis, Cleona: *The United States and Foreign Investment Problems.* Washington, D.C., 1948.
London, Kurt: *How Foreign Policy Is Made.* New York, 1949.

Lord Ismay: *NATO, The First Five Years, 1949–1954.* New York, 1954.
MacMahon, J. L.: *Recent Changes in the Recognition Policy of the United States.* Washington, D.C., 1933.
Mathews, John M.: *American Foreign Relations: Conduct and Policies.* Revised edition. New York, 1938.
Moore, John Bassett: *Principles of American Diplomacy.* 2nd edition. New York, 1918.
Morgenthau, Hans J.: *Politics Among Nations.* New York, 1948. Pp. 379–83.
Niebuhr, Reinhold: *The Irony of American History.* New York, 1954.
Osgood, Robert E.: *Ideals and Self-Interest in America's Foreign Relations.* Chicago, 1953.
Perkins, Dexter: *The Evolution of American Foreign Policy.* New York, 1951.
———: *Hands Off: A History of the Monroe Doctrine.* Boston, 1941.
Potter, Pitman B.: *International Organization.* 5th edition. New York, 1948. Pp. 258–75.
Reitzel, W., Kaplan, M. A. and Coblenz, C. G.: *United States Foreign Policy, 1945–1955.* Washington, 1956.
Royal Institute of International Affairs: *Atlantic Alliance.* New York, 1952.
Schuman, Frederick L.: *International Politics.* Fourth edition, New York, 1948. Pp. 326–53.
Spykman, Nicholas J.: *America's Strategy in World Politics.* New York, 1912.
U.S. Department of State: *Peace and War: United States Foreign Policy, 1931–1941.* Washington, D.C., 1943.
Woodrow Wilson Foundation and National Planning Association: *The Political Economy of American Foreign Policy, Its Concepts, Strategy, and Limits.* New York, 1955.

PERIODICALS

Bolles, Blair: "Bipartisanship in American Foreign Policy." *Foreign Policy Reports* (1949), 224:190–9.
Briggs, Herbert W.: "The Problems of World Government." *American Journal of International Law* (1947), 41:108–12.
Diebold, William: "East West Trade and the Marshall Plan." *Foreign Affairs* (1948), 26:709–22.
Fenwick, C. G.: "The Inter-American Regional System: Fifty Years of Progress." *American Journal of International Law* (1956), 50:18–31.
Fox, William T. R.: "Collective Enforcement of Peace and Security." *American Political Science Review* (1945), 39:970–81.
Henderson, Loy W.: "Foreign Policies: Their Formulation and Enforcement." *The Department of State Bulletin* (1946), 15:590–6.
Hughes, Charles E.: "Some Observations on the Conduct of Our Foreign Relations." *American Journal of International Law* (1922), 16:365–74.
Kennan, George F.: "The Sources of Soviet Conduct." *Foreign Affairs* (1947), 25:566–82.
Laves, Walter H. C. and Wilcox, Francis O.: "Foreign Affairs and Interdepartmental Coordination." *American Political Science Review* (1944), 38:913–30.
Masland, John W.: "Pressure Groups and American Foreign Policy Preceding Pearl Harbor." *Public Opinion Quarterly* (1942), 6:115–22.
May, Stacy: "Measuring the Marshall Plan." *Foreign Affairs* (1948), 26:457–69.
Padelford, Norman J.: "The Use of the Veto." *International Organization* (1948), 2:227–46.
Sharp, Walter: "The Specialist Agencies of the UN: Progress Report II." *International Organization* (1948), 2:247–67.
Sprout, Harold H.: "Pressure Groups and Foreign Policies." *Annals of the American Academy of Political and Social Science* (1935), 179:114–23.
Weyl, Nathaniel and Wasserman, Max J.: "The International Bank." *American Economic Review* (1947), 37:92–106.
Whitaker, A. P.: "Development of American Regionalism." *International Conciliation* (1951).
Wilcox, Clair: "The American Trade Program." *Department of State Bulletin* (1947), 16:288–93.

APPENDIX

THE CONSTITUTION
OF THE UNITED STATES OF AMERICA

WE THE PEOPLE of the United States, in Order to form a more perfect Union, establish Justice, insure domestic Tranquility, provide
for the common defence, promote the general Welfare, and secure
the Blessings of Liberty to ourselves and our Posterity, do ordain and establish
this CONSTITUTION for the United States of America.

ARTICLE I.

SECTION 1. All legislative Powers herein granted shall be vested in a
Congress of the United States, which shall consist of a Senate and House of
Representatives.

SECTION 2. The House of Representatives shall be composed of Members
chosen every second Year by the People of the several States, and the Electors
in each State shall have the Qualifications requisite for Electors of the most
numerous Branch of the State Legislature.

No Person shall be a Representative who shall not have attained to the Age
of twenty-five Years, and been seven Years a Citizen of the United States, and
who shall not, when elected, be an Inhabitant of that State in which he shall be
chosen.

[Representatives and direct Taxes [2] shall be apportioned among the several
States which may be included within this Union, according to their respective
Numbers, which shall be determined by adding to the whole Number of free
Persons, including those bound to Service for a Term of Years, and excluding
Indians not taxed, three fifths of all other Persons.[3]] The actual Enumeration
shall be made within three Years after the first Meeting of the Congress of the
United States, and within every subsequent Term of ten Years, in such Manner
as they shall by Law direct. The Number of Representatives shall not exceed
one for every thirty Thousand, but each State shall have at Least one Repre-

---

1 This version of the Constitution is that published by the Office of Education, United States
Department of the Interior, 1935, and follows the original document in spelling and capitalization.

2 Modified as to income taxes by the 16th Amendment.

3 Replaced by the 14th Amendment.

sentative; and until such enumeration shall be made, the State of New Hampshire shall be entitled to chuse three, Massachusetts eight, Rhode-Island and Providence Plantations one, Connecticut five, New-York six, New Jersey four, Pennsylvania eight, Delaware one, Maryland six, Virginia ten, North Carolina five, South Carolina five, and Georgia three.

When vacancies happen in the Representation from any State, the Executive Authority thereof shall issue Writs of Election to fill such Vacancies.

The House of Representatives shall chuse their Speaker and other Officers; and shall have the sole Power of Impeachment.

SECTION 3. [The Senate of the United States shall be composed of two Senators from each State, chosen by the Legislature thereof, for six Years; and each Senator shall have one Vote.] [4]

Immediately after they shall be assembled in Consequence of the first Election, they shall be divided as equally as may be into three Classes. The Seats of the Senators of the first Class shall be vacated at the Expiration of the second Year, of the second Class at the Expiration of the fourth Year, and of the third Class at the Expiration of the sixth Year, so that one-third may be chosen every second Year; [and if Vacancies happen by Resignation, or otherwise, during the Recess of the Legislature of any State, the Executive thereof may make temporary Appointments until the next Meeting of the Legislature, which shall then fill such Vacancies.] [5]

No Person shall be a Senator who shall not have attained to the Age of thirty Years, and been nine Years a Citizen of the United States, and who shall not, when elected, be an Inhabitant of that State for which he shall be chosen.

The Vice President of the United States shall be President of the Senate, but shall have no vote, unless they be equally divided.

The Senate shall chuse their other Officers, and also a President pro tempore, in the absence of the Vice President, or when he shall exercise the Office of President of the United States.

The Senate shall have the sole Power to try all Impeachments. When sitting for that purpose, they shall be on Oath or Affirmation. When the President of the United States is tried, the Chief Justice shall preside: And no person shall be convicted without the Concurrence of two thirds of the Members present.

Judgment in Cases of Impeachment shall not extend further than to removal from Office, and disqualification to hold and enjoy any Office of honor, Trust, or Profit under the United States: but the Party convicted shall nevertheless be liable and subject to Indictment, Trial, Judgment, and Punishment, according to Law.

SECTION 4. The Times, Places and Manner of holding Elections for Senators and Representatives, shall be prescribed in each State by the Legislature thereof; but the Congress may at any time by Law make or alter such Regulations, except as to the Places of Chusing Senators.

[The Congress shall assemble at least once in every Year, and such Meeting shall be on the first Monday in December, unless they shall by Law appoint a different Day.] [6]

SECTION 5. Each House shall be the Judge of the Elections, Returns and Qualifications of its own Members, and a Majority of each shall constitute a Quorum to do Business; but a smaller number may adjourn from day to day,

[4] Superseded by Seventeenth Amendment.
[5] Modified by Seventeenth Amendment.
[6] Superseded by Twentieth Amendment.

and may be authorized to compel the Attendance of absent Members, in such Manner, and under such Penalties, as each House may provide.

Each House may determine the Rules of its Proceedings, punish its Members for disorderly Behavior, and, with the Concurrence of two thirds, expel a Member.

Each House shall keep a Journal of its Proceedings, and from time to time publish the same, excepting such Parts as may in their Judgment require Secrecy; and the Yeas and Nays of the Members of either House on any question shall, at the Desire of one fifth of those Present, be entered on the Journal.

Neither House, during the Session of Congress, shall, without the Consent of the other, adjourn for more than three days, nor to any other Place than that in which the two Houses shall be sitting.

SECTION 6. The Senators and Representatives shall receive a Compensation for their Services, to be ascertained by Law, and paid out of the Treasury of the United States. They shall in all Cases, except Treason, Felony, and Breach of the Peace, be privileged from Arrest during their Attendance at the Session of their respective Houses, and in going to and returning from the same; and for any Speech or Debate in either House, they shall not be questioned in any other Place.

No Senator or Representative shall, during the Time for which he was elected, be appointed to any civil Office under the Authority of the United States, which shall have been created, or the Emoluments whereof shall have been increased, during such time; and no Person holding any Office under the United States shall be a Member of either House during his continuance in Office.

SECTION 7. All Bills for raising Revenue shall originate in the House of Representatives; but the Senate may propose or concur with Amendments as on other bills.

Every Bill which shall have passed the House of Representatives and the Senate, shall, before it become a Law, be presented to the President of the United States; If he approve he shall sign it, but if not he shall return it, with his Objections, to that House in which it shall have originated, who shall enter the Objections at large on their Journal, and proceed to reconsider it. If after such Reconsideration two thirds of that House shall agree to pass the bill, it shall be sent, together with the objections, to the other House, by which it shall likewise be reconsidered, and if approved by two thirds of that House, it shall become a Law. But in all such Cases the Votes of both Houses shall be determined by Yeas and Nays, and the Names of the Persons voting for and against the Bill shall be entered on the Journal of each House respectively. If any Bill shall not be returned by the President within ten Days (Sundays excepted) after it shall have been presented to him, the Same shall be a Law, in like Manner as if he had signed it, unless the Congress by their Adjournment prevent its Return, in which Case it shall not be a Law.

Every Order, Resolution, or Vote to which the Concurrence of the Senate and House of Representatives may be necessary (except on a question of Adjournment) shall be presented to the President of the United States; and before the Same shall take Effect, shall be approved by him, or being disapproved by him, shall be repassed by two thirds of the Senate and House of Representatives, according to the Rules and Limitations prescribed in the Case of a Bill.

SECTION 8. The Congress shall have Power To lay and collect Taxes,

Duties, Imposts and Excises, to pay the Debts and provide for the common Defence and general Welfare of the United States; but all Duties, Imposts and Excises shall be uniform throughout the United States;

To borrow money on the credit of the United States;

To regulate Commerce with foreign Nations, and among the several States, and with the Indian Tribes;

To establish an uniform Rule of Naturalization, and uniform Laws on the subject of Bankruptcies throughout the United States;

To coin Money, regulate the Value thereof, and of foreign Coin, and fix the Standard of Weights and Measures;

To provide for the Punishment of counterfeiting the Securities and current Coin of the United States;

To establish Post Offices and post Roads;

To promote the Progress of Science and useful Arts, by securing for limited Times to Authors and Inventors the exclusive Right to their respective Writings and Discoveries;

To constitute Tribunals inferior to the Supreme Court;

To define and punish Piracies and Felonies committed on the high Seas, and Offenses against the Law of Nations;

To declare War, grant Letters of Marque and Reprisal, and make Rules concerning Captures on Land and Water;

To raise and support Armies, but no Appropriation of Money to that Use shall be for a longer Term than two Years;

To provide and maintain a Navy;

To make Rules for the Government and Regulation of the land and naval Forces;

To provide for calling forth the Militia to execute the Laws of the Union, suppress Insurrections and repel Invasions;

To provide for organizing, arming, and disciplining the Militia, and for governing such Part of them as may be employed in the Service of the United States, reserving to the States respectively, the Appointment of the Officers, and the Authority of training the Militia according to the discipline prescribed by Congress;

To exercise exclusive Legislation in all Cases whatsoever, over such District (not exceeding ten Miles square) as may, by Cession of particular States, and the acceptance of Congress, become the Seat of the Government of the United States, and to exercise like Authority over all Places purchased by the Consent of the Legislature of the State in which the Same shall be, for the Erection of Forts, Magazines, Arsenals, dock-Yards, and other needful Buildings;—And

To make all Laws which shall be necessary and proper for carrying into Execution the foregoing Powers, and all other Powers vested by this Constitution in the Government of the United States, or in any Department or Officer thereof.

SECTION 9.   The Migration or Importation of such Persons as any of the States now existing shall think proper to admit, shall not be prohibited by the Congress prior to the Year one thousand eight hundred and eight, but a tax or duty may be imposed on such Importation, not exceeding ten dollars for each Person.

The privilege of the Writ of Habeas Corpus shall not be suspended, unless when in Cases of Rebellion or Invasion the public Safety may require it.

No Bill of Attainder or ex post facto Law shall be passed.

No capitation, or other direct, Tax shall be laid unless in Proportion to the Census or Enumeration herein before directed to be taken.

No Tax or Duty shall be laid on Articles exported from any State.

No Preference shall be given by any Regulation of Commerce or Revenue to the Ports of one State over those of another: nor shall Vessels bound to, or from, one State, be obliged to enter, clear, or pay Duties in another.

No Money shall be drawn from the Treasury, but in Consequence of Appropriations made by Law; and a regular Statement and Account of the Receipts and Expenditures of all public Money shall be published from time to time.

No Title of Nobility shall be granted by the United States: And no Person holding any Office of Profit or Trust under them, shall, without the Consent of the Congress, accept of any present, Emolument, Office, or Title, of any kind whatever, from any King, Prince, or foreign State.

SECTION 10.   No State shall enter into any Treaty, Alliance, or Confederation; grant Letters of Marque and Reprisal; coin Money; emit Bills of Credit; make any Thing but gold and silver Coin a Tender in Payment of Debts; pass any Bill of Attainder, ex post facto Law, or Law impairing the Obligation of Contracts, or grant any Title of Nobility.

No State shall, without the Consent of the Congress, lay any Imposts or Duties on Imports or Exports, except what may be absolutely necessary for executing its inspection Laws: and the net Produce of all Duties and Imposts, laid by any State on Imports or Exports, shall be for the Use of the Treasury of the United States; and all such Laws shall be subject to the Revision and Control of the Congress.

No State shall, without the Consent of Congress, lay any duty of Tonnage, keep Troops, or Ships of War in time of Peace, enter into any Agreement or Compact with another State, or with a foreign Power, or engage in War, unless actually invaded, or in such imminent Danger as will not admit of delay.

ARTICLE II.

SECTION 1.   The executive Power shall be vested in a President of the United States of America. He shall hold his Office during the Term of four years, and, together with the Vice-President, chosen for the same Term, be elected, as follows:

Each State shall appoint, in such Manner as the Legislature thereof may direct, a Number of Electors, equal to the whole Number of Senators and Representatives to which the State may be entitled in the Congress: but no Senator or Representative, or Person holding an Office of Trust or Profit under the United States, shall be appointed an Elector.

[The Electors shall meet in their respective States, and vote by Ballot for two persons, of whom one at least shall not be an Inhabitant of the same State with themselves. And they shall make a List of all the Persons voted for, and of the Number of Votes for each; which List they shall sign and certify, and transmit sealed to the Seat of the Government of the United States, directed to the President of the Senate. The President of the Senate shall, in the Presence of the Senate and House of Representatives, open all the Certificates, and the Votes shall then be counted. The Person having the greatest Number of Votes shall be the President, if such Number be a Majority of the whole Number of

Electors appointed; and if there be more than one who have such Majority, and have an equal Number of Votes, then the House of Representatives shall immediately chuse by Ballot one of them for President; and if no Person have a Majority, then from the five highest on the List the said House shall in like Manner chuse the President. But in chusing the President, the Votes shall be taken by States, the Representation from each State having one Vote; a quorum for this Purpose shall consist of a Member or Members from two-thirds of the States, and a Majority of all the States shall be necessary to a Choice. In every Case, after the Choice of the President, the Person having the greatest Number of Votes of the Electors shall be the Vice President. But if there should remain two or more who have equal votes, the Senate shall chuse from them by Ballot the Vice-President.] [7]

The Congress may determine the Time of chusing the Electors, and the Day on which they shall give their Votes; which Day shall be the same throughout the United States.

No person except a natural-born Citizen, or a Citizen of the United States, at the time of the Adoption of this Constitution, shall be eligible to the Office of President; neither shall any Person be eligible to that Office who shall not have attained to the Age of thirty-five years, and been fourteen Years a Resident within the United States.

In Case of the Removal of the President from Office, or of his Death, Resignation, or Inability to discharge the Powers and Duties of the said Office, the same shall devolve on the Vice President, and the Congress may by Law provide for the Case of Removal, Death, Resignation, or Inability, both of the President and Vice President, declaring what Officer shall then act as President, and such Officer shall act accordingly, until the disability be removed, or a President shall be elected.

The President shall, at stated Times, receive for his Services a Compensation, which shall neither be increased nor diminished during the Period for which he shall have been elected, and he shall not receive within that Period any other Emolument from the United States, or any of them.

Before he enter on the execution of his Office, he shall take the following Oath or Affirmation:—"I do solemnly swear (or affirm) that I will faithfully execute the Office of President of the United States, and will, to the best of my Ability, preserve, protect, and defend the Constitution of the United States."

SECTION 2. The President shall be Commander in Chief of the Army and Navy of the United States, and of the Militia of the several States, when called into the actual Service of the United States; he may require the Opinion, in writing, of the principal Officer in each of the executive Departments, upon any subject relating to the Duties of their respective Offices, and he shall have Power to Grant Reprieves and Pardons for Offenses against the United States, except in Cases of Impeachment.

He shall have Power, by and with the Advice and Consent of the Senate, to make Treaties, provided two-thirds of the Senators present concur; and he shall nominate, and by and with the Advice and Consent of the Senate, shall appoint Ambassadors, other public Ministers and Consuls, Judges of the supreme Court, and all other Officers of the United States, whose Appointments are not herein otherwise provided for, and which shall be established by Law: but the Congress may by Law vest the Appointment of such inferior Officers, as they

---

[7] Superseded by Twelfth Amendment, which, in turn, is modified by the Twentieth Amendment.

think proper, in the President alone, in the Courts of Law, or in the Heads of Departments.

The President shall have Power to fill up all Vacancies that may happen during the Recess of the Senate, by granting Commissions which shall expire at the End of their next Session.

SECTION 3.   He shall from time to time give to the Congress Information of the State of the Union, and recommend to their Consideration such Measures as he shall judge necessary and expedient; he may, on extraordinary occasions, convene both Houses, or either of them, and in Case of Disagreement between them, with respect to the Time of Adjournment, he may adjourn them to such Time as he shall think proper; he shall receive Ambassadors and other public Ministers; he shall take Care that the Laws be faithfully executed, and shall Commission all the Officers of the United States.

SECTION 4.   The President, Vice President and all civil Officers of the United States, shall be removed from Office on Impeachment for, and Conviction of, Treason, Bribery, or other high Crimes and Misdemeanors.

ARTICLE III.

SECTION 1.   The judicial Power of the United States, shall be vested in one supreme Court, and in such inferior Courts as the Congress may from time to time ordain and establish.   The Judges, both of the supreme and inferior Courts, shall hold their Offices during good Behaviour, and shall, at stated Times, receive for their Services, a Compensation, which shall not be diminished during their Continuance in Office.

SECTION 2.   The judicial Power shall extend to all Cases, in Law and Equity, arising under this Constitution, the Laws of the United States, and Treaties made, or which shall be made, under their Authority;—to all Cases affecting ambassadors, other public ministers and consuls;—to all cases of admiralty and maritime Jurisdiction;—to Controversies to which the United States shall be a Party;—to Controversies between two or more States;—between a State and Citizens of another State; [8]—between Citizens of different States,—between Citizens of the same State claiming Lands under Grants of different States, and between a State, or the Citizens thereof, and foreign States, Citizens or Subjects.

In all Cases affecting Ambassadors, other public Ministers and Consuls, and those in which a State shall be Party, the supreme Court shall have original Jurisdiction.   In all the other Cases before mentioned, the supreme Court shall have appellate Jurisdiction, both as to Law and Fact, with such Exceptions, and under such Regulations as the Congress shall make.

The trial of all Crimes, except in Cases of Impeachment, shall be by Jury; and such Trial shall be held in the State where the said Crimes shall have been committed; but when not committed within any State, the Trial shall be at such Place or Places as the Congress may by Law have directed.

SECTION 3.   Treason against the United States, shall consist only in levying War against them, or in adhering to their Enemies, giving them Aid and Comfort.   No Person shall be convicted of Treason unless on the Testimony of two Witnesses to the same overt Act, or on Confession in open Court.

The Congress shall have power to declare the Punishment of Treason, but no Attainder of Treason shall work Corruption of Blood, or Forfeiture except during the Life of the Person attainted.

[8] Restricted by the 11th Amendment.

ARTICLE IV.

SECTION 1.   Full Faith and Credit shall be given in each State to the public Acts, Records, and judicial Proceedings of every other State. And the Congress may by general Laws prescribe the Manner in which such Acts, Records and Proceedings shall be proved, and the Effect thereof.

SECTION 2.   The Citizens of each State shall be entitled to all Privileges and Immunities of Citizens in the several States.

A Person charged in any State with Treason, Felony, or other Crime, who shall flee from Justice, and be found in another State, shall on demand of the executive Authority of the State from which he fled, be delivered up, to be removed to the State having Jurisdiction of the crime.

No Person held to Service or Labour in one State, under the Laws thereof, escaping into another, shall, in Consequence of any Law or Regulation therein, be discharged from such Service or Labour, but shall be delivered up on Claim of the Party to whom such Service or Labour may be due.

SECTION 3.   New States may be admitted by the Congress into this Union; but no new State shall be formed or erected within the Jurisdiction of any other State; nor any State be formed by the Junction of two or more States, or parts of States, without the Consent of the Legislatures of the States concerned as well as of the Congress.

The Congress shall have Power to dispose of and make all needful Rules and Regulations respecting the Territory or other Property belonging to the United States; and nothing in this Constitution shall be so construed as to Prejudice any Claims of the United States, or of any particular State.

SECTION 4.   The United States shall guarantee to every State in this Union a Republican Form of Government, and shall protect each of them against Invasion; and on Application of the Legislature, or of the Executive (when the Legislature cannot be convened) against domestic Violence.

ARTICLE V.

The Congress, whenever two-thirds of both Houses shall deem it necessary, shall propose Amendments to this Constitution, or, on the Application of the Legislatures of two-thirds of the several States, shall call a Convention for proposing Amendments, which, in either Case, shall be valid to all Intents and Purposes, as part of this Constitution, when ratified by the Legislatures of three-fourths of the several States, or by Conventions in three-fourths thereof, as the one or the other Mode of Ratification may be proposed by the Congress; Provided that no Amendment which may be made prior to the Year One thousand eight hundred and eight shall in any Manner affect the first and fourth Clauses in the Ninth Section of the first Article; and that no State, without its Consent, shall be deprived of its equal Suffrage in the Senate.

ARTICLE VI.

All Debts contracted and Engagements entered into, before the Adoption of this Constitution, shall be as valid against the United States under this Constitution, as under the Confederation.

This Constitution, and the Laws of the United States which shall be made in Pursuance thereof; and all Treaties made, or which shall be made, under the Authority of the United States, shall be the supreme Law of the Land; and the

Judges in every State shall be bound thereby, any Thing in the Constitution or Laws of any State to the Contrary notwithstanding.

The Senators and Representatives before mentioned, and the Members of the several State Legislatures, and all executive and judicial Officers, both of the United States and of the several States, shall be bound by Oath or Affirmation to support this Constitution; but no religious Test shall ever be required as a qualification to any Office or public Trust under the United States.

ARTICLE VII.

The Ratification of the Conventions of nine States shall be sufficient for the Establishment of this Constitution between the States so ratifying the same.

Done in Convention by the Unanimous Consent of the States present the Seventeenth Day of September in the Year of our Lord one thousand seven hundred and Eighty seven, and of the Independence of the United States of America the Twelfth. In Witness whereof We have hereunto subscribed our Names.

[Signatures of members of the convention.]

ARTICLES IN ADDITION TO, AND AMENDMENT OF, THE CONSTITUTION OF THE UNITED STATES OF AMERICA, PROPOSED BY CONGRESS, AND RATIFIED BY THE LEGISLATURES OF THE SEVERAL STATES, PURSUANT TO THE FIFTH ARTICLE OF THE ORIGINAL CONSTITUTION [9]

[ARTICLE I.] [10]

Congress shall make no law respecting an establishment of religion, or prohibiting the free exercise thereof; or abridging the freedom of speech, or of the press; or the right of the people peaceably to assemble, and to petition the Government for a redress of grievances.

[ARTICLE II.]

A well regulated Militia, being necessary to the security of a free State, the right of the people to keep and bear Arms shall not be infringed.

[ARTICLE III.]

No Soldier shall, in time of peace, be quartered in any house, without the consent of the Owner, nor in time of war, but in a manner to be prescribed by law.

[ARTICLE IV.]

The right of the people to be secure in their persons, houses, papers, and effects, against unreasonable searches and seizures, shall not be violated, and no Warrants shall issue, but upon probable cause, supported by Oath or affirmation, and particularly describing the place to be searched, and the persons or things to be seized.

[ARTICLE V.]

No person shall be held to answer for a capital or otherwise infamous crime, unless on a presentment or indictment of a Grand Jury, except in cases

9 This heading appears only in the joint resolution submitting the first ten amendments.
10 In the original manuscripts the first twelve amendments have no numbers.

arising in the land or naval forces, or in the Militia, when in actual service in time of War or public danger; nor shall any person be subject for the same offence to be twice put in jeopardy of life or limb; nor shall be compelled in any criminal case to be a witness against himself, nor be deprived of life, liberty, or property, without due process of law; nor shall private property be taken for public use, without just compensation.

[ARTICLE VI.]

In all criminal prosecutions, the accused shall enjoy the right to a speedy and public trial, by an impartial jury of the State and district wherein the crime shall have been committed, which district shall have been previously ascertained by law, and to be informed of the nature and cause of the accusation; to be confronted with the witnesses against him; to have compulsory process for obtaining witnesses in his favor, and to have the Assistance of Counsel for his defence.

[ARTICLE VII.]

In suits at common law, where the value in controversy shall exceed twenty dollars, the right of trial by jury shall be preserved, and no fact tried by a jury, shall be otherwise reexamined in any Court of the United States, than according to the rules of the common law.

[ARTICLE VIII.]

Excessive bail shall not be required, nor excessive fines imposed, nor cruel and unusual punishments inflicted.

[ARTICLE IX.]

The enumeration in the Constitution, of certain rights, shall not be construed to deny or disparage others retained by the people.

[ARTICLE X.]

The powers not delegated to the United States by the Constitution, nor prohibited by it to the States, are reserved to the States respectively, or to the people.

[Amendments I-X, in force 1791.]

ARTICLE XI.[11]

The Judicial power of the United States shall not be construed to extend to any suit in law or equity, commenced or prosecuted against one of the United States by Citizens of another State, or by Citizens or Subjects of any Foreign State.

ARTICLE XII.[12]

The Electors shall meet in their respective States and vote by ballot for President and Vice-President, one of whom, at least, shall not be an inhabitant of the same State with themselves; they shall name in their ballots the person voted for as President, and in distinct ballots the person voted for as Vice-President, and they shall make distinct lists of all persons voted for as President, and of all persons voted for as Vice-President, and of the number of votes for each, which

11 Adopted in 1798.
12 Adopted in 1804.

lists they shall sign and certify, and transmit sealed to the seat of the government of the United States, directed to the President of the Senate;—The President of the Senate shall, in the presence of the Senate and House of Representatives, open all the certificates and the votes shall then be counted;—The person having the greatest number of votes for President, shall be the President, if such number be a majority of the whole number of Electors appointed; and if no person have such majority, then from the persons having the highest numbers not exceeding three on the list of those voted for as President, the House of Representatives shall choose immediately, by ballot, the President. But in choosing the President, the votes shall be taken by states, the representation from each state having one vote; a quorum for this purpose shall consist of a member or members from two-thirds of the states, and a majority of all the states shall be necessary to a choice. And if the House of Representatives shall not choose a President whenever the right of choice shall devolve upon them, before the fourth day of March next following, then the Vice-President shall act as President, as in the case of the death or other constitutional disability of the President.—The person having the greatest number of votes as Vice-President, shall be the Vice-President, if such number be a majority of the whole number of Electors appointed, and if no person have a majority, then from the two highest numbers on the list, the Senate shall choose the Vice-President; a quorum for the purpose shall consist of two-thirds of the whole number of Senators, and a majority of the whole number shall be necessary to a choice. But no person constitutionally ineligible to the office of President shall be eligible to that of Vice-President of the United States.

ARTICLE XIII.[13]

SECTION 1. Neither slavery nor involuntary servitude, except as a punishment for crime whereof the party shall have been duly convicted, shall exist within the United States, or any place subject to their jurisdiction.

SECTION 2. Congress shall have power to enforce this article by appropriate legislation.

ARTICLE XIV.[14]

SECTION 1. All persons born or naturalized in the United States, and subject to the jurisdiction thereof, are citizens of the United States and of the State wherein they reside. No State shall make or enforce any law which shall abridge the privileges or immunities of citizens of the United States; nor shall any State deprive any person of life, liberty, or property, without due process of law; nor deny to any person within its jurisdiction the equal protection of the laws.

SECTION 2. Representatives shall be apportioned among the several States according to their respective numbers, counting the whole number of persons in each State, excluding Indians not taxed. But when the right to vote at any election for the choice of electors for President and Vice-President of the United States, Representatives in Congress, the Executive and Judicial officers of a State, or the members of the Legislature thereof, is denied to any of the male inhabitants of such State, being twenty-one years of age, and citizens of the United States, or in any way abridged, except for participation in rebellion, or other crime, the basis of representation therein shall be reduced in the proportion which the number of such male citizens shall bear to the whole number of male citizens twenty-one years of age in such State.

13 Adopted in 1865.
14 Adopted in 1868, proclaimed July 28, 1868.

SECTION 3.   No person shall be a Senator or Representative in Congress, or elector of President and Vice-President, or hold any office, civil or military, under the United States, or under any State, who, having previously taken an oath, as a member of Congress, or as an officer of the United States, or as a member of any State legislature, or as an executive or judicial officer of any State, to support the Constitution of the United States, shall have engaged in insurrection or rebellion against the same, or given aid or comfort to the enemies thereof. But Congress may by a vote of two-thirds of each House, remove such disability.

SECTION 4.   The validity of the public debt of the United States, authorized by law, including debts incurred for payment of pensions and bounties for services in suppressing insurrection or rebellion, shall not be questioned. But neither the United States nor any State shall assume or pay any debt or obligation incurred in aid of insurrection or rebellion against the United States, or any claim for the loss or emancipation of any slave; but all such debts, obligations, and claims shall be held illegal and void.

SECTION 5.   The Congress shall have the power to enforce, by appropriate legislation, the provisions of this article.

ARTICLE XV.[15]

SECTION 1.   The right of citizens of the United States to vote shall not be denied or abridged by the United States or by any State on account of race, color, or previous condition of servitude—

SECTION 2.   The Congress shall have power to enforce this article by appropriate legislation.

ARTICLE XVI.[16]

The Congress shall have power to lay and collect taxes on incomes, from whatever source derived, without apportionment among the several States, and without regard to any census or enumeration.

ARTICLE XVII.[17]

The Senate of the United States shall be composed of two Senators from each State, elected by the people thereof, for six years; and each Senator shall have one vote. The electors in each State shall have the qualifications requisite for electors of the most numerous branch of the State legislatures.

When vacancies happen in the representation of any State in the Senate, the executive authority of such State shall issue writs of election to fill such vacancies: *Provided,* That the legislature of any State may empower the executive thereof to make temporary appointments until the people fill the vacancies by election as the legislature may direct.

This amendment shall not be so construed as to affect the election or term of any Senator chosen before it becomes valid as part of the Constitution.

ARTICLE XVIII.[18]

SECTION 1.   After one year from the ratification of this article the manufacture, sale, or transportation of intoxicating liquors within, the importation

---

[15] Proclaimed March 30, 1870.

[16] Passed July, 1909; proclaimed February 25, 1913.

[17] Passed May, 1912, in lieu of Article I, Section 3, Clause I, of the Constitution and so much of clause 2 of the same Section as relates to the filling of vacancies; proclaimed May 31, 1913.

[18] Passed December 3, 1917; proclaimed January 29, 1919. Repealed by the Twenty-first Amendment.

thereof into, or the exportation thereof from the United States and all territory subject to the jurisdiction thereof for beverage purposes is hereby prohibited.

SECTION 2.   The Congress and the several States shall have concurrent power to enforce this article by appropriate legislation.

SECTION 3.   This article shall be inoperative unless it shall have been ratified as an amendment to the Constitution by the legislatures of the several States, as provided in the Constitution, within seven years from the date of the submission hereof to the States by the Congress.

ARTICLE XIX.[19]

The right of citizens of the United States to vote shall not be denied or abridged by the United States or by any State on account of sex.

Congress shall have power to enforce this article by appropriate legislation.

ARTICLE XX.[20]

SECTION 1.   The terms of the President and Vice-President shall end at noon on the 20th day of January, and the terms of Senators and Representatives at noon on the 3d day of January, of the years in which such terms would have ended if this article had not been ratified; and the terms of their successors shall then begin.

SECTION 2.   The Congress shall assemble at least once in every year, and such meeting shall begin at noon on the 3d day of January, unless they shall by law appoint a different day.

SECTION 3.   If, at the time fixed for the beginning of the term of the President, the President elect shall have died, the Vice-President elect shall become President. If a President shall not have been chosen before the time fixed for the beginning of his term, or if the President elect shall have failed to qualify, then the Vice-President elect shall act as President until a President shall have qualified; and the Congress may by law provide for the case wherein neither a President elect nor a Vice-President elect shall have qualified, declaring who shall then act as President, or the manner in which one who is to act shall be selected, and such person shall act accordingly until a President or Vice-President shall have qualified.

SECTION 4.   The Congress may by law provide for the case of the death of any of the persons from whom the House of Representatives may choose a President whenever the right of choice shall have devolved upon them, and for the case of the death of any of the persons from whom the Senate may choose a Vice-President whenever the right of choice shall have devolved upon them.

SECTION 5.   Sections 1 and 2 shall take effect on the 15th day of October following the ratification of this article.

SECTION 6.   This article shall be inoperative unless it shall have been ratified as an amendment to the Constitution by the legislatures of three-fourths of the several States within seven years from the date of its submission.

ARTICLE XXI.[21]

SECTION 1.   The eighteenth article of amendment to the Constitution of the United States is hereby repealed.

[19] Adopted in 1920.
[20] Adopted in 1933.
[21] Adopted in 1933.

SECTION 2. The transportation or importation into any State, Territory, or possession of the United States for delivery or use therein of intoxicating liquors, in violation of the laws thereof, is hereby prohibited.

SECTION 3. This article shall be inoperative unless it shall have been ratified as an amendment to the Constitution by conventions in the several States, as provided in the Constitution, within seven years from the date of the submission hereof to the States by the Congress.

ARTICLE XXII.[22]

No person shall be elected to the office of the President more than twice, and no person who has held the office of President, or acted as President, for more than two years of a term to which some other person was elected President shall be elected to the office of the President more than once.

But this Article shall not apply to any person holding the office of President when this Article was proposed by the Congress, and shall not prevent any person who may be holding the office of President, or acting as President, during the term within which this Article becomes operative from holding the office of President or acting as President during the remainder of such term.

[22] Adopted in 1951.

INDEX

cies, 374; spoils system, 374–6; reasons for spoils system, 375–6; movement for reform, 376–7; Pendleton Act of 1883, 377; establishment of Civil Service Commission, 378–9; Federal Council of Personnel Administration, 379; Hoover Commission recommendations, 380; recruitment procedures, 380–1; examinations, 381–2; appointments, 382–3; veterans' preference, 383–4; classification, 384–5; salaries, 385–6; promotion and efficiency ratings, 386–7; dismissals, 387–9; training, transfers, and retirement, 389–90; and right to strike, 390–1; employee unions, 390–1; political neutrality of employees, 391–2; loyalty and security requirements, 392; appraisal of, 392–3; Foreign Service career system, 700–10

Civil War Amendments, 67

Civilian Conservation Corps, 596, 622

Clark, Jane P., 97n, 98n

Clayton Act of 1914, 576–7, 594, 595; citation as labor's "Magna Carta," 595

"Clear and present danger" formula, 118, 125

Clement, Frank, keynoter, 238

Cleveland, Grover, 596

"Closed" primaries, 211–12

Closed shop, under Taft-Hartley Act, 599

Clyatt v. United States (1905), 122n

Coast Guard, 649

Coblenz, C. G., 727n

Coleman et al. v. Miller et al. (1937), 63n

Collective bargaining: basis of industrial relations, 596, 597; under National Labor Relations Act, 597

Collector v. Day (1871), 533n

Colonies, the: charters, 20; genesis of representative assembly, 21; transition into states, 24

Colorado Coal Co. v. United Mine Workers (1925), 595n

Commager, Henry S., 189n, 684n

Commerce, aids to, 582–3

Commerce: regulation of, 560; judicial definition of, 560; regulation of railroads, 562; Interstate Commerce Act, 563; Interstate Commerce Commission, 564, 569; regulation of air transportation, 567; regulation of motor transportation, 567; regulation of water transportation, 567; regulation of communication, 568; Federal Communications Commission, 568–9; regulation of immigration, 569–71

Commission of Inquiry on Public Service Personnel, 378n

Commission on Government Operations, 194, 574, 587

Commission on Intergovernmental Relations: on grants-in-aid, 82–3; on division of governmental responsibilities, 100

Commission on Organization of the Executive Branch of the Government: on independent commissions, 369; on merit system, 372; on Civil Service Commission, 379; on civil service "rule of three," 382–3; on appointments in civil service, 384; on dismissals in civil service positions, 387–8; on transfers in civil service system, 389; on coordinating administration, 395; and General Accounting Office, 407; on national defense, 654n; on conduct of foreign affairs, 698, 762

Committee on Permanent Organization, national convention, 259–60

Committee on Political Education (COPE), AF of L-CIO, in campaigns, 272

Committees (of Congress): work of, 460; reference of bills to, 461; investigations by, 462; investigatory methods of, 464–5; procedures, 465; information from executive agencies, 465; information from private sources, 466; reporting a bill, 467–8; Committee of the Whole, 471; conference committee, 474

Committees of correspondence (Revolutionary), 26

Commodity Credit Corporation, 556–7, 619–20

Commonwealth v. Hunt (1842), 593

Comptroller General of the United States, 397, 408–9

Compulsory military training, arguments for and against, 651–2

Congress: delegated powers, 53; restrictions on, 53–4; lobbying, 155–9, 174–5; previous occupation of congressmen, 218–19; members' average length of service, 219; and election laws, 221–2; trend in congressional elections, 229; presidential leadership, 320; effect of veto power, 328–32; integration with executive branch of Federal government, 334; proposal of parliamentary system, 335; proposal of Legislative-Executive Council, 337; proposal of question hour, 337; and increased administration policy-making, 411–13; why bicameral, 417; evolution of, 417–18; apportionment of representatives, 418–19; present formula for reapportionment, 420; mapping congressional districts, 421; urban under-representa-

A NOTE ON THE TYPE IN WHICH THIS BOOK IS PRINTED

The text of this book is set in Caledonia, a Linotype face designed by W. A. Dwiggins (1880-1956), who was responsible for so much that is good in contemporary book design. Though much of his early work was in advertising and he was the author of the standard volume, Layout in Advertising, Mr. Dwiggins later devoted his prolific talents to book and type design and worked with great distinction in both fields. In addition to his designs for Caledonia, he created the Metro, Electra, and Eldorado series of type faces, as well as a number of experimental cuttings that have never been issued commercially.

Caledonia belongs to the family of printing types called "modern face" by printers—a term used to mark the change in style of type-letters that occurred at the end of the eighteenth century. It is best evidenced in the type-shapes designed by Baskerville, Martin, Bodoni, and Bell....

This book was composed, printed, and bound by Kingsport Press, Inc., Kingsport, Tenn. The paper was manufactured by P. H. Glatfelter Co., Spring Grove, Pa.

A NOTE ON THE TYPE IN WHICH
THIS BOOK IS PRINTED

The text of this book is set in Caledonia, a Linotype face designed by W. A. Dwiggins (1880–1956), who was responsible for so much that is good in contemporary book design. Though much of his early work was in advertising and he was the author of the standard volume, Layout in Advertising, *Mr. Dwiggins later devoted his prolific talents to book and type design and worked with great distinction in both fields. In addition to his designs for Caledonia, he created the Metro, Electra, and Eldorado series of type faces, as well as a number of experimental cuttings that have never been issued commercially.*

Caledonia belongs to the family of printing types called "modern face" by printers—a term used to mark the change in style of type-letters that occurred at the end of the eighteenth century. It is best evidenced in the lettershapes designed by Baskerville, Martin, Bodoni, and the Didots.

This book was composed, printed, and bound by Kingsport Press, Inc., Kingsport, Tenn. The paper was manufactured by P. H. Glatfelter Co., Spring Grove, Pa.